1985

THE ENGLISH POETS
GENERAL EDITOR: CHRISTOPHER RICKS

Also available in this series

Jonathan Swift

The Complete Poems

EDITED BY PAT ROGERS

NEW HAVEN AND LONDON
YALE UNIVERSITY PRESS

First published 1983 in the United Kingdom in a paperback edition
by Penguin Books Limited in the series Penguin English Poets.
First published 1983 in the United States of America by Yale University Press.

Introduction and Notes copyright © 1983 by Pat Rogers

Printed in Great Britain

Library of Congress Cataloging in Publication Data

Swift, Jonathan, 1667–1745.
　　Jonathan Swift, the complete poems.

　　(The English poets; 14)
　　I. Rogers, Pat.　II. Title.
PR3721.R63 1983　　821'.5　　82-13547
ISBN 0-300-02966-7
ISBN 0-300-02967-5 (pbk.)

10 9 8 7 6 5 4 3 2 1

*This edition of Swift's Poems
is dedicated to*
CLAUDE RAWSON

Contents

Introduction

HISTORICAL SURVEY

During his own lifetime Swift's verse appeared in a confused, intermittent, and largely haphazard fashion. The publishing history presents a bewildering array of mystifying devices – piracy, pseudo-piracy, clandestine issues, anonymous and pseudonymous works, misattributions and misreadings. Over the course of the next two centuries the undergrowth became even thicker, as more and more spurious items and unauthorized editions sprouted in the fertile soil of conjecture. Luckily, much tidier bibliographical habits have set in recently. More of Swift's manuscripts have become available, and Sir Harold Williams's monumental work on the *Poems* (1937; rev. edn, 1958) has brought something like order to the former chaos. However, a well-charted jungle (if such a thing exists) is still a jungle. Although I have had the advantage of the photo-reconnaissance and aerial-survey techniques of modern scholarship, I must acknowledge that the textual thickets remain hard going, and that some tangles have proved impenetrable. This edition, then, cannot claim to be final or definitive. It rests firmly on the achievements of Williams, together with those of other scholars including Herbert Davis, George P. Mayhew, Frank H. Ellis, David Foxon, and David Woolley. It is, nevertheless, based on independent collation of the texts and the exercise, for good or ill, of independent editorial judgement.

Out of the 280 poems included in this collection, just over fifty appeared while Swift was alive. There were also some sixty miscellanies containing one or more of Swift's poems between 1692 and 1744, the year before his death. The separately published poems enjoyed something like four or five editions each, on average: popular items such as *Cadenus and Vanessa* ran to many more. There are degrees of inauthenticity in this group of texts, but few have any serious bibliographical claim; they belong commonly to the ephemeral wing of literature – ballads, broadsides, pamphlets, and poster-like sheets with effigies. There is little likelihood that Swift paid much attention to the nuances of such a text, even in those cases (by no means all) where he knew of its appearance. None the less, this is not a ground for editorial licence. Where no more reliable edition exists, we must find the best text we can, however murky and uncertain its origin.

Three collections of Swift's work rise above this standard, together with a handful of separate publications. The first is *Miscellanies in Prose and Verse*, issued in February 1711, perhaps in some sense as a response to the pirated sub-collection put out by Edmund Curll in April 1710. However, we know that Swift had jotted down 'subjects for a volume' as far back as October 1708, including many items which duly appeared in the *Miscellanies*.[1] In general, it is fair to say that Swift took more care with this edition than he was willing to admit. It has been said that he 'silently rewrote his literary history to his advantage' in compiling the selection,[2] and while this does not mean that he necessarily took great pains with the text itself, there is independent evidence that he revised some items meticulously. The imprint on the title-page is that of John Morphew, a bookseller whose name appears on most of the celebrated Tory pamphlets around this date. In fact Morphew was a distributor and front-man, closer to a wholesaler than a bookseller in the modern sense. The effective publisher through whom Swift operated was Benjamin Tooke, who owned the copyright of many of the early works.

The second authentic collection comprises the five volumes which make up the first series of Pope-Swift *Miscellanies* (1727–35). There are complications here, too: the fifth volume is of little independent value, since it mostly derives from Faulkner's Dublin edition (of which more in a moment). The first two volumes appeared in June 1727; another, misleadingly titled 'the last', followed in March 1728; and the so-called 'third' in October 1732. From the point of view of Swift's poetry the 'last' volume is the most important one, since it includes all the thirteen poems collected by Tooke/Morphew in 1711 with the addition of twenty more, including most of the birthday poems to Stella. The 'third' volume of 1732 also contained many items by Swift, but they were selected by Pope – only one of a number of dissatisfactions which Swift had with the volume. As regards textual authority, 1728 has a limited claim and 1732 a very small one: but a copy of the set with Swift's own corrections fortunately survives in the Rothschild collection, now at Trinity College, Cambridge. Moreover, the collected *Miscellanies* do settle various questions of attribution and dating.

1. *Ehrenpreis*, II, 768–9: see also pp. 422–4. (For cue-titles used in the notes, see p. 598 below.)

2. C.P. Daw, introductory note to facsimile reprint of the *Miscellanies* (Menston, 1972), p. [iii]. Daw supplies a useful background to the publication of the volume.

By far the most important collection, however, is the set of Swift's *Works* issued in Dublin by George Faulkner. Four volumes appeared between November 1734 and January 1735; the second volume is entirely devoted to poetry, and there is also a late supplement in the fourth volume. Over the next few decades the Faulkner edition was gradually augmented, with important addenda to the verse in 1746. Nevertheless, it is the '1735' edition (generally so called, as here) which represents the central core of Swift's work, and embodies his most careful restatement of his own poetic history. As issued to the public, it contains almost a hundred items in verse, including nearly everything previously collected or acknowledged. It is overwhelmingly the most reliable collection, and indeed was considered so even before recent evidence emerged to confirm its standing. We now know that Pope told Spence, not long after the Faulkner set had appeared, that it was 'under [Swift's] own eye'.[3] Furthermore, an uncancelled copy of the second volume has turned up in the English Faculty Library, Oxford, and its contents have been fully set out by Margaret Weedon.[4] Aside from minor changes, the cancels show that five poems, potentially explosive on personal or political grounds, were taken right out, and nine new poems inserted of a more inoffensive (and frankly duller) kind. All the changes involved in the cancellation process are of some literary interest: but the most striking general deduction to be drawn relates to the detailed supervision Swift gave to this volume at proof-stage.

Nothing else of comparable moment occurred within Swift's lifetime, although the Pope-Swift *Miscellanies* continued to expand, and for the best part of a generation biographic controversies held the centre of the stage. It was not until 1754–5 that a London trade edition was instituted, under the supervision of John Hawkesworth, a friend of Dr Johnson and fellow-contributor to the *Gentleman's Magazine*. Henceforth the London and Dublin editions rivalled one another, and by degrees expanded the canon with varying reliability. The Hawkesworth set was the basis for the *Works* (1784) edited by Thomas Sheridan, son of a close friend of Swift and in turn father of the dramatist Richard Brinsley Sheridan. A further, and better, recension was that of John Nichols in 1801. This phase of endeavour was brought to an end in 1814 by a set of nineteen volumes issued by Walter Scott, then known as a poet and diligent compiler in the years before *Waverley*. (There was a second edition with new material in 1824.) With understandable

3. Joseph Spence, *Observations, Anecdotes, and Characters of Books and Men*, ed. J.M. Osborn (Oxford, 1966), I, 55.

4. M. Weedon, 'An Uncancelled Copy of the First Collected Edition of Swift's Poems', *The Library*, XXII (1967), 44–56.

crossness, Nichols observed that Scott, 'by abridging my tedious annotations, (turning lead to gold)... presented to the booksellers of Edinburgh an edition somewhat similar to mine...'.[5] Scott certainly made heavy raids on his predecessors, but like everything to which he put his hand, the Swift set is marked by taste and intelligence.

None of these editions carry high textual authority, but they need to be consulted for new attributions and information. From the time of Scott onwards, scarcely a single collection merits any sort of attention for over a century. The Aldine edition (1833–4) is pleasant to look at; the *Poems* issued by W.E. Browning (1910) do not match up to the contemporary *Prose Works* by Temple Scott or the *Correspondence* by Elrington Ball. The posthumously published 'essay', *Swift's Verse*, by Ball (1929) helped to prepare the way for Williams's magnificent *Poems* of 1937. This collection, in its revised form, is definitive in most important respects. Williams determined the canon much more strictly, he went back to the early editions (indeed, generally the earliest) for his text, and he annotated the poems discreetly. All subsequent work on the subject has its origin in this edition.

The year 1937 also saw the first edition of Herman Teerink's bibliography of Swift. This appeared in a revised form, edited by Arthur H. Scouten, in 1963, and is rightly regarded as the standard reference tool. All references here are to the second edition.

Apart from the revision of Williams's *Poems*, two post-war editions have appeared. Joseph Horrell produced an attractive two volumes for the Muses' Library, with light but interesting annotation. Horrell accepted the canon as outlined by Williams with very few exceptions, but he made something of an innovation by arranging the poems in groups according to theme and subject. This almost Wordsworthian practice is by no means indefensible, but I have preferred a chronological scheme even though our knowledge of the order in which the poems were composed is something less than total. Horrell followed wherever possible the 1737 or 1746 Faulkner readings, apparently for reasons of typographic and orthographic consistency. Finally, Herbert Davis edited the Oxford Standard Authors *Poetical Works* (posthumously published, 1967). The uncancelled copy of Faulkner's 1735 volume was discovered in time to permit an editorial note by David Woolley and some adjustment to the text. Davis had in any case inclined to give the 1735 volume high authority. His work was confessedly based on Williams, though it placed the poems in a stricter chronological scheme; textually, he was readier to 'correct' early separate printings by

5. John Nichols, *Minor Lives*, ed. E L. Hart (Cambridge, Mass., 1971), p. xxxi.

reference to subsequent collections, especially that of 1735. He continued to do this in a conservative fashion, and in such instances his basic copy-text was clearly still the early printing. As with other O.S.A. volumes, the text is not annotated. It might be added that a short selection of the poems, with a text based on Williams, and helpful brief notes, was prepared by James Reeves for the Poetry Bookshelf series also in 1967.

THIS EDITION

The Penguin text differs from all those discussed in that it is a modern-spelling edition. As well as orthography, typographic conventions regarding the use of italics, capitals, and so on, have been brought into line with modern usage. So far as possible, punctuation has been left unamended, except where it is confusing or distracting. The use of hyphens and apostrophes has, for example, been normalized.

There is not much evidence of keen interest on Swift's part in matters of presentation. He will annotate a volume of his poems with a marginal note 'enuff' for 'enough', to indicate pronunciation. But he did not punctuate with the care of his friend Pope, and most of his extant manuscripts are largely unpointed. Though Faulkner's 1735 text is certainly the most authentic, as regards the words on the page, there is no reason to believe that Swift took any more trouble with the accidentals in this case. Most Faulkner editions are sensibly punctuated, and I have made their style the basis of the Penguin text even in cases where an earlier separate printing exists – for the broadside printers had their own conventions (notably, ultra-heavy use of italics) which bear no relation to any known practice of Swift's. There is scarcely any value in following such typographic oddities in a literal fashion; they relate to modes of emphasis no longer within reach. For instance, italics were sometimes needed because the older habits of capitalization obscured a point easily made today; they were often used, even by Faulkner, where quotation marks would be automatic in the twentieth century. I have not hesitated to introduce roman type in such cases.

A number of particular rules have been followed. Proper nouns are modernized where no issue of accent or pronunciation is involved: thus 'Henly' becomes 'Henley' and 'Sommers' is replaced by 'Somers'. However, this does not extend to a form like 'Vanbrug', and I have retained forms like 'Sheelah' which preserve a desirably 'Irish' quality. Foreign quotations are left in their original form. Citations from older

English sources in the notes are modernized according to exactly the same principles as the main text (this includes Swift's own prose works and correspondence); this applies to both spelling and typography. The main problem in the text itself concerns the decision to capitalize abstract nouns which may or may not be regarded as personifications. As a matter of policy, I have used capitals only where a clear personifying agency is evident, e.g. through the presence of a personal pronoun or an active verb. There are still cases where a measure of doubt exists, often involving words such as 'fate', 'fortune', 'death' or 'heaven'. The rule adopted is to prefer lower-case where uncertainty remains. I have also regularly eliminated capitals for 'muse' or 'muses'.

The title of each poem has been chosen in accordance with the same guidelines as operate for the text. This means that a number of poems appear in slightly unfamiliar guise: the work generally known as *The Journal* appears as *The Part of a Summer*, whilst *The Day of Judgement* becomes *On the Day of Judgement* and *The Progress of Love* becomes *Phyllis*. There is a risk of seeming affectation here, but that is outweighed by the advantages of consistency and a closer approximation to Swift's presumed intentions.

One small difficulty which arises from normalization makes itself felt in Swift's punning poems, e.g. *A Quibbling Elegy on the Worshipful Judge Boat* or *A Serious Poem upon William Wood*. Here the ambiguity allowed by the typographic conventions of Swift's day is lost when we reduce 'Boat' to 'boat', or 'Wood' to 'wood'. There is in fact no way of preserving the easy transition from proper to common noun which the Augustan satirists exploited so fully – unless, that is, we preserve their general habits of capitalization.

The logic of these procedures goes back essentially to the initial decision to offer, according to the usual practice of this series in the case of post-Renaissance authors, a modern-spelling edition. If we print 'partridge' for the common noun 'Partrige' in the text, it becomes awkward and inconsistent to retain the proper noun '*Patrige*' in that form. The Penguin text is intended to provide the reader with the kind of signals he or she would have received as a contemporary of Swift's. It is not meant to turn Swift into an honorary twentieth-century poet, even if that were possible. The aim is rather to supply a simple, uncluttered, and *substantially* authentic version of the poems, avoiding both intrusive modernization and mindless perpetuation of unintelligible archaisms in presentation.

It might be thought that a modern-spelling edition can afford to be less punctilious about the choice of a copy-text. In fact the reverse is the case: as the accidentals of eighteenth-century printing are lost, so the need to find the right substantive text increases, if we are to get in reading any sense of contact with Swift himself. I have attempted as far as I could to make a full collation of all early readings, whether printed or manuscript, which might plausibly produce the best critical text, though I have allotted contemporary transcripts by any outsider less weight than Williams did. ('Outsider' here means simply a person outside Swift's immediate circle – the transcripts by Stella and by Ford are, of course, excluded.) Having chosen the copy-text, I have adopted readings from other sources with caution but without extreme puritanical inhibition. Where a blank or abbreviated form can be supplied from another text, I have printed the name or word in full: 'D—n' for 'Dean' is a common and easy case. Elsewhere dubious editions occasionally prove helpfully explicit where the copy-text is reticent. The best single version of *Verses on the Death of Dr Swift* needs supplementation at many points if that poem is to become thoroughly intelligible.

The policy of this edition has been to base the text on Faulkner's 1735 volume wherever practicable. The dictates of a modern-spelling edition have tilted the balance in what would always be a narrow decision. The 1735 text is not just a polished and well-printed version of the poems; it is outstandingly intelligent from a literary standpoint. In particular, its pointing of rhetorical devices like parallelism and antithesis shows consistent understanding of the words on the page – where earlier printings frequently blur the symmetry. It may be taken as certain that Faulkner, rather than Swift, was responsible for this tidiness: but that does not affect the issue. (As already stated, Swift's own manuscripts are virtually unpunctuated for the most part.) I have therefore tended to follow Faulkner in the matter of accidentals, even where Swift's holograph is available. The collections of 1711 and 1727–32 have been given a much lower priority in establishing a copy-text, but, where the 1735 volume seemed defective for any reason, they have been adopted. Early printings, which can be consulted in Williams, have in this edition been relegated to a subsidiary place vis-à-vis the collections; but they naturally take on primary significance for more than half the poems, where the item was uncollected in Swift's lifetime.

The discovery of the uncancelled 1735 volume causes some difficulty. In the Oxford Standard Authors *Poetical Works*, it was stated: 'The substantive variants now supplied by the leaves in their original state have been incorporated in the text of this edition, in the belief that they provide, quite strikingly, evidence of Swift's primary intentions in

1734.' My own policy has been rather different. Where a change from the uncancelled to the cancelled state seems to have been dictated by a kind of auto-censorship, arising from a fear of suppression, I have followed the original reading. This happens in several places with the verses *To Mr Gay*. (Naturally, where the poem was dropped entirely in the cancelled volume, the uncancelled state becomes the 1735 reading.) Nevertheless, in one or two instances the variant found in the cancelled state appears to represent something like second thoughts on Swift's part, and here I have been ready to follow the later version. To oversimplify a little, political changes indicate the uncancelled text is to be followed; literary changes, the cancelled.

The term 'broadside' is used in a generic sense to indicate a category of printed material, rather than in the strictest bibliographical sense. It is applied to any single-sheet production, whether printed on one side or on both sides, regardless of the dimensions. Most, but not quite all, of Swift's 'broadside' ballads appeared in folio half-sheets, with the recto blank. Many are cropped and they are, in the majority of cases, badly printed. Even where they were published with Swift's authority (e.g. *The Fable of Midas*, issued through agents Swift knew well) I have been more ready than previous editors to base my text on a later collection. That Swift was on good terms with John Barber, who certainly printed some of these items, does not prove that he took much care with the text. In fact, such 'authorized' editions may be no more reliable, as far as particular readings go, than the pirated sort, when Curll or Roberts obtained a copy by some illicit means.

Williams and Davis both print as separate poems the autograph draft and later printed version of three items, the most important of which is *Baucis and Philemon*. I have taken the view that the printed poem represents Swift's considered text, and have used this version in the body of the edition. Swift's drafts are printed in Appendix 3, with the spelling unmodernized. On the other hand *The Life and Genuine Character of Dr Swift* and the *Verses on the Death of Dr Swift* are unquestionably different poems (however the former came into being), and not alternative drafts: both are included in the main Penguin text.

Footnotes supplied by Swift, Faulkner or some trustworthy third person are retained, but they have been moved to the back to take their place in the explanatory Notes.

Another departure from the practice of most previous editors, including Williams and Davis, is that verses by others (Delany, Sheridan, Orrery) are excluded as a matter of policy. These were the occasion of answers or continuations by Swift, but in the great majority of cases

Swift's poem is intelligible by itself. Information concerning the non-Swiftian verses is given in the Notes.

Poems are printed in chronological order of composition, in so far as this can be established. In something like ten per cent of cases my dating differs from that of Williams, but not to any great extent generally. Faulkner's 1735 edition, paramount in other respects, is an unreliable guide in this particular, and I have jettisoned its suggested dates almost as freely as my predecessors. Items which cannot be given even a vague dating are grouped together at the end.

For discussion of the canon, see Appendix 4. I have inevitably found few occasions to dissent from Williams's judgement. Like Davis, I have excluded the *Ode to King William*: I have dropped altogether *The Birth of Manly Virtue*, whose credentials seem to me exceedingly slender. I have retained with some hesitation *Apollo's Edict*, which Swift probably looked over if he did not compose it throughout. New attributions include Swift's ballad on the Westminster election in 1710, which has been described by George P. Mayhew and Frank H. Ellis. One or two of the doubtful items have been moved into the main chronological sequence (notably *A Town Eclogue*, in which Swift must have had a hand). Others among the former 'dubious' attributions have been removed altogether, e.g. *Blue-skin's Ballad*. Without much enthusiasm I (like Horrell) have accepted as authentic *A Description of Mother Ludwell's Cave*, although I had rather it were not. Finally, unlike Davis, I have retained most of the 'trifles' which seem to be allotted to Swift with some certainty. Only the riddles which appeared in the 1735 edition are included. No poem which can be confidently attributed to Swift, however slight, has been omitted. Both Latin and the strange 'Anglo-Latin' developed by Swift and Sheridan are printed as well as the English poems.

The annotation lays much heavier stress than that of Williams on points of linguistic usage – meaning, pronunciation, punning effects, and so on. The progress of scholarship has enabled me to supply fuller details in many parts of the commentary. Through no virtue of my own, I am the first editor to inherit the revised Teerink/Scouten bibliography, and to have Foxon's superb *Catalogue* of verse available; likewise to have the two volumes of Ehrenpreis's definitive biography (still in progress), the completed *Prose Works*, and the excellent Cornell concordance. Historical inquiries have advanced in such a way as to permit fuller exploration of political issues (Plumb's biography of Walpole has opened up many new points in the text), whilst the 'History of Parliament' volumes edited by Romney Sedgwick enable an editor to provide information which was not previously available on many figures. For convenience, all personal details regarding Swift's contemporaries have been grouped in the Biographical Dictionary (pp. 907–42), which can perhaps claim to be the easiest reference guide to Swift's personal contacts and relationships. A cross-reference to the Dictionary is always supplied in the notes, keyed to the appropriate line. In such areas, if this edition does not make a substantial advance on its predecessors, it can only be through massive incompetence on the part of the editor.

However, it is in the more inward features of Swift's writing that the commentary attempts to break new ground. Williams confined his annotations of literary allusion to direct quotation (and even here it has been possible to supply many more examples). I have sought to bring out a wider range of echo, parody, and reminiscence. Scores of biblical, classical, and modern references are supplied for the first time. Parallels with Swift's closest associates, Pope, Gay, and Prior, have been extensively observed, whilst cross-reference to his own poems and prose works has been made considerably fuller. In some cases this has interesting literary implications. For example, the thirty-odd parallels with *Polite Conversation* discovered show in a new light Swift's fondness for mimicking speech-patterns. His use of proverbs is far more wide-ranging than has been realized, and in some poems (e.g. *The Fable of the Bitches* and *Upon the Horrid Plot*) furnishes the basic imaginative structure of the poem. Similarly, his exploitation of puns, archaisms, wrenched accents, comic rhymes, and the like, which has been discussed by recent commentators but ignored by previous editors, now finds documentation in the notes. The increasing use of 'Irish' rhymes in his later verse is one feature which emerges. Equally I have tried to point out what might be termed Swift's 'generic transfers', where words appropriate to a pastoral register, say, are employed in a formally inappropriate context such as the lampoon or night-piece. Finally, an attempt has been made to set particular linguistic, metrical, or phonetic effects in a literary context, so that a reader today can judge their rhetorical point and not merely their historical justification. The verbal texture of Swift's poetry is more dense and richly fraught than was once supposed; it is the job of a modern editor to keep up with our new critical awareness, and to give concrete evidence of these poetic resources actually in play. The commentary to poems such as *Pethox the Great* will illustrate the variety of verbal manoeuvre.

Since the commentary gathers together a fuller (though assuredly not complete) listing of Swift's literary echoes, a better understanding of his habits of allusion may now be possible. The notes show that his borrowings derive chiefly from Latin rather than Greek sources, and the three most common sources are Virgil, Ovid, and Horace. Indeed, the two poems of the ancient world which bit most deeply into his consciousness were plainly, on this evidence, the *Aeneid* and the *Metamorphoses*. Among earlier English poets, the key texts include *Paradise Lost; Hudibras*; the works of Cowley; and certain areas of Dryden, notably the translations, the odes, and the panegyrical poems. As for contemporary poetry, the obvious echoes are those of Prior's *Alma*; Gay's *Trivia* and *Fables*; and the major works of Pope, above all, *The Rape of the Lock*. Swift's elective affinities as a poet emerge quite clearly: though his allusions indicate a catholic range of reading in prose and verse (Pliny, Vida, Donne, Ambrose Philips – to choose names at random), the writers who lay close to the heart of his poetic practice were a select few. Biblical references are fairly evenly divided between the Old and the New Testament; there are many references to the prophetic books and to the Pauline epistles.

Acknowledgements

I am grateful to the institutions which have permitted me to consult books and manuscripts in their care, and in some cases to base the Penguin text on these materials. These are the British Library; the Public Record Office; the Victoria and Albert Museum; the University of London Library; the Bodleian Library; the English Faculty Library, Oxford; Cambridge University Library; the Library of Trinity College, Cambridge; the John Rylands Library; the Library of Trinity College, Dublin; Archbishop Marsh's Library, Dublin; the National Library of Ireland; the National Library of Scotland; the Henry E. Huntington Library and Art Gallery; Harvard College Library; the Pierpont Morgan Library; University of Texas Library.

Equally I am indebted to individuals who have permitted use to be made of their private holdings of Swift materials: the Marquis of Bath; the Duke of Bedford; Lord Rothschild.

The making of this edition has occupied, in part or whole, some 2,000 working days. There must be a degree of error proportionate to this labour; and I should be grateful to be informed of slips noticed by users of the book.

My principal obligation is to the General Editor of this series, Professor Christopher Ricks, for his patience when he did not have the typescript and for his helpful and detailed criticism when this finally emerged. He has saved me from innumerable obscurities and inelegancies, and has improved the commentary in all sorts of ways.

Table of Dates

22 October: Installed as prebend of St Patrick's Cathedral, Dublin.

1701   April: Berkeley, dismissed as Lord Justice, returns to England; Swift goes with him.

August: Esther Johnson emigrates to Dublin; Swift follows with the new Lord Lieutenant a month later.

October: Publication of *Contests and Dissentions*.

1702   16 February: D.D., Trinity College, Dublin.

1704   10 May: At the end of another period in England, publishes *A Tale of a Tub*. Intermittent visits to England in following years.

1707–9   Back in England as emissary of the Irish clergy. In contact with Addison, Steele, and other literary men.

1708   *Bickerstaff Papers*.

1709   Inception of the *Tatler* by Steele (runs 271 numbers to 1711); Swift contributes several items.

1710   March: Sacheverell trial foreshadows the fall of Whig ministry; Godolphin ultimately forced out of office (8 August) and Tories, led by Harley and Bolingbroke, replace him.

24 April: Death of Swift's mother.

September: Swift comes to England and begins *Journal to Stella*. Allies himself to the Tory ministry and begins to write on its behalf (thirty-three numbers of the *Examiner* from 2 November to 14 June 1711).

1711   27 February: Publication of first authorized collection, *Miscellanies in Prose and Verse*.

27 November: First edition of the hugely successful pamphlet attacking Marlborough, *The Conduct of the Allies*.

1712   Met Arbuthnot in this year, if not earlier. Friendship with Addison and (especially) Steele cooling fast, for political reasons.

1713   13 June: Installed as Dean of St Patrick's in the course of a rapid visit to Ireland.

Probable first meeting of Swift and Pope, who shortly after help to form the Scriblerus group with Gay, Arbuthnot, and Parnell. Swift enjoys close relations with the leading Tory ministers.

1714   1 August: Death of Queen Anne, in the midst of ministerial crisis which sees fall of the Tories; Swift leaves almost immediately for Dublin (arriving 24 August) and thereafter takes up permanent residence in Ireland.

November: Esther Vanhomrigh ('Vanessa'), who had made Swift's acquaintance in London, moves to Ireland and settles in Celbridge.

1720   April or May: Publication of *A Proposal for the Universal Use of Irish Manufacture*, later declared seditious on account of its criticism of English economic policy towards Ireland.

1721   Working on *Gulliver's Travels*.

1723   June: Death of Vanessa. Atterbury affair comes to a head.

1724–5 Publication of *The Drapier's Letters* (first letter in March).

1726   March–August: Visits England, spends much time in company with Pope, and prepares for publication of *Gulliver's Travels* (28 October).

1727   April–September: Final visit to England, again staying with Pope at Twickenham. The joint *Miscellanies* begin to appear (24 June).

1728   28 January: Death of Stella.

        7 March: The 'last' (wrongly so called) volume of *Miscellanies*, containing many poems by Swift.

1729   October: Publication of *A Modest Proposal*.

1731   November: Probable composition of *Verses on the Death of Dr Swift*, initially published in garbled version in 1739 and then in an authoritative form the same year.

1732   October: Another volume of Pope-Swift *Miscellanies*.

        4 December: Death of Gay.

1734–5 Publication of four volumes of collected works in Dublin, issued by George Faulkner under the supervision of Swift; reprinted and augmented in subsequent years.

1735   27 February: Death of Arbuthnot.

1738   Spring: Publication of *Polite Conversation*.

1742   August: Found 'of unsound mind and memory', and guardians appointed to manage his affairs; his condition was caused by the intensified effects of Ménière's disease.

1744   30 May: Death of Pope.

1745   19 October: Death of Swift; buried in St Patrick's alongside Stella; bequeathed money to found hospital for the insane.

Map Showing Places in Ireland Associated with Swift and His Friends

Further Reading

EDITIONS

The only early editions listed are those with some claim to authority, as explained in the Introduction (pp. 15–19). The complicated later history of the Faulkner, Hawkesworth, and other trade editions can be followed in Teerink's bibliography: see especially charts on pp. 47, 60, 77, 104, and 119. The numerous unauthorized collections are among those listed by Williams in his edition of the *Poems*, I, lii–lxi.

[J. Swift], *Miscellanies in Prose and Verse*, London (J. Morphew), 1711; 2nd edn 1714 (dated 1713). Facsimile reprint, ed. C.P. Daw, Menston, 1972.

[J. Swift, A. Pope *et al.*], *Miscellanies*, London (B. Motte, L. Gilliver, C. Davis), 5 vols., 1727–35.

The Works of J.S., D.D., D.S.P.D., Dublin (G. Faulkner), 4 vols., 1734–5 (dated 1735). There are editions in octavo and in duodecimo.

J. Hawkesworth (ed.), *The Work of Jonathan Swift, D.D.*, London, 6 vols., 1754–5. Like Faulkner's edition, this underwent periodic revision and amplification, by W. Bowyer, Deane Swift, J. Nichols, *et al.*

Walter Scott (ed.), *The Works of Jonathan Swift, D.D.*, Edinburgh, 19 vols., 1814; rev. edn, 1824.

W.E. Browning (ed.), *The Poems of Jonathan Swift, D.D.*, London, 2 vols., 1910.

Harold Williams (ed.), *The Poems of Jonathan Swift*, Oxford, 3 vols., 1937; 2nd edn, 1958. The standard edition.

Joseph Horrell (ed.), *Collected Poems of Jonathan Swift*, London, 2 vols., 1958.

Herbert Davis (ed.), *Swift: Poetical Works*, London, 1967.

A.C. Guthkelch and D. Nichol Smith (eds.), *A Tale of a Tub*, Oxford, 1920; 2nd edn, 1958.

Herbert Davis (ed.), *The Prose Works of Jonathan Swift*, Oxford, 14 vols., 1939–68.

Harold Williams (ed.), *Journal to Stella*, Oxford, 2 vols., 1948; reprinted 1975.

Harold Williams (ed.), *The Correspondence of Jonathan Swift*, Oxford, 5 vols., 1963–5.

REFERENCE

Donald M. Berwick, *The Reputation of Jonathan Swift*, 1781–1822, Philadelphia, 1941.

Claire Lamont, 'A Checklist of Critical and Biographical Writings on Jonathan Swift, 1945–65', *Fair Liberty was All His Cry*, ed. A. Norman Jeffares, London, 1967.

Louis A. Landa and J.E. Tobin, *Jonathan Swift: List of Critical Studies Published from 1895 to 1945*, New York, 1945.

The Rothschild Library, Cambridge, 2 vols., 1954. Describes extensive Swift holdings, now in the Library of Trinity College, Cambridge.

Michael Shinagel, *A Concordance to the Poems of Jonathan Swift*, Ithaca, 1972.

James J. Stathis, *A Bibliography of Swift Studies 1945–1965*, Nashville, 1967.

H. Teerink, *A Bibliography of the Writings of Jonathan Swift*, 2nd rev. edn by A.H. Scouten, Philadelphia, 1963.

Milton Voigt, *Swift and the Twentieth Century*, Detroit, 1964.

Margaret Weedon, 'An Uncancelled Copy of the First Collected Edition of Swift's Poems', *The Library*, XXII (1967), 44–56.

Harold Williams (ed.), *Dean Swift's Library*, Cambridge, 1932.

BIOGRAPHY AND CRITICISM

F. Elrington Ball, *Swift's Verse*, London, 1929; reprinted New York, 1970.

F.W. Bateson, 'Swift's "Description of the Morning"', *English Poetry: A Critical Introduction*, pp. 175–80, London, 1950.

Herbert Davis, *Jonathan Swift: Essays on His Satire*, New York, 1964. Contains 'Swift's View of Poetry' and 'Alecto's Whip'.

Nigel Dennis, *Jonathan Swift: A Short Character*, London, 1965.

Denis Donoghue, *Jonathan Swift: A Critical Introduction*, Cambridge, 1969.

Denis Donoghue (ed.), *Jonathan Swift: A Critical Anthology*, Harmondsworth, 1971.

Irvin Ehrenpreis, *The Personality of Jonathan Swift*, London, 1958.

Irvin Ehrenpreis, *Swift: The Man, His Works, and the Age*, London, 1962– (2 vols. of 3 projected so far published, covering years to 1714).

Oliver W. Ferguson, *Jonathan Swift and Ireland*, Urbana, 1962.

John Irwin Fischer, *On Swift's Poetry*, Gainesville, Florida, 1978.

Nora Crow Jaffe, *The Poet Swift*, Hanover, New Hampshire, 1977.

Maurice Johnson, *The Sin of Wit: Jonathan Swift as a Poet*, Syracuse, 1950.

Louis A. Landa, *Swift and the Church of Ireland*, Oxford, 1954.

George P. Mayhew, *Rage or Raillery: The Swift Manuscripts at the Huntington Library*, San Marino, 1967.

C.T. Probyn (ed.), *The Art of Jonathan Swift*, London, 1978.

Ricardo Quintana, *The Mind and Art of Jonathan Swift*, London, 1936.

Ricardo Quintana, *Swift: An Introduction*, London, 1955.

C.J. Rawson (ed.), *Focus: Swift*, London, 1971. Contains 'The Poetry of Age' by D.W. Jefferson.

Peter J. Schakel, *The Poetry of Jonathan Swift*, Madison, Wisconsin, 1978.

Brian Vickers (ed.), *The World of Jonathan Swift*, Oxford, 1968. Contains 'Swift: The Poetry of "Reaction"' by Geoffrey Hill and 'Swift's Fallen City' by Roger Savage.

Kathleen Williams (ed.), *Swift: The Critical Heritage*, London, 1970.

Almost the whole of the Spring 1978 issue of *Papers on Language & Literature*, XIV, was given over to eight essays on Swift's poetry.

A Note on Rhythm and Rhyme

Swift's metric is a straightforward one for the most part. His favourite octosyllabic couplets seldom involve marked wrenching of the accent; the familiar elision of syllables in words such as 'every' or 'reverence' is not indicated in the text.[1] Nor is the elision of the definite article; in fact, more often than not Swift requires us to pronounce 'the' in full even where it precedes a vowel. However, the common eighteenth-century forms 'on't' and 'in't' (for 'on it', 'in it') are printed in the contracted form. Words stressed in an unexpected way ('recórd' as a noun; 'siníster') are given an accent in the text and, where appropriate, a gloss in the notes. A note is also supplied to words where the syllables fall differently from today; as with 'really', an unambiguously trisyllabic form in Swift. In words which have exhibited some vacillation historically regarding pronunciation or stress (such as 'coadjutor'), Swift's preference is indicated.

Among what may appear to be irregular or bad rhymes, some (but by no means all) can be explained by reference to the habits of pronunciation prevalent in Swift's day: for example, 'spirit'/'merit' (see note to *Twelve Articles* 23–4). Swift's increasing readiness to rhyme words like 'Dean' and 'gain' reflects an older pronunciation losing ground in his own day, in England at least; it seems to go with a certain pervasive 'Irishness' of idiom, and has been characterized as an 'Irish' rhyme in the notes. Distorted pronunciations required for rhyming purposes are rare except in the multiple-rhyme 'crambos' and other trifles: in cases such as *An Answer to the Ballyspellin Ballad* 81 a note is supplied.

Swift's preference for the octosyllabic couplet can be firmly documented from this edition. Among the 280 English poems 135, or almost 49 per cent, are in this measure. A further seven, including *To a Lady* and *A Character, Panegyric, and Description of the Legion Club*, are

---

1. Accordingly, the elision of the past participle form '-ed' (as in 'pleased') is assumed in appropriate cases. It should be noted that Swift commonly uses the monosyllabic word 'learned' (that is, 'learn'd'), where the meaning is that of the modern 'learnéd'. See for example *On Censure* 28.

based on a seven-syllable couplet with the first foot truncated. Octosyllabics were not used in the first phase of Swift's career, when he produced his odes and 'heroic' verse; but thereafter they are always the commonest metre employed. In successive decades from 1700 to 1740 octosyllabic poems constitute respectively 46, 48, 54, and 45 per cent of the total. The next most frequent form is the couplet in a triple rhythm, usually an eleven-syllable line stressed $-- \cdot\cdot -- \cdot\cdot -- \cdot\cdot --$. A good example is furnished by *The Grand Question Debated*. Swift showed a particular fondness for this form in the last stages of his career: twenty-five of the thirty-three occurrences are found after 1720. Next comes the heroic couplet, with thirty-one instances; then the quatrain with an alternating rhyme, used in twenty-two poems (however, only two such poems figure in the last decade of Swift's career). Other metrical forms include six-line stanzas (five examples), the pindaric ode (four, all early), the exaggerated long lines of *Mrs Harris's Petition* (four), and verses to existing airs such as 'Packington's Pound' (four). A variety of miscellaneous forms make up the total; a notable case is the fourteen-syllable line used in *An Excellent New Song upon His Grace Our Good Lord Archbishop of Dublin*, though in reality this is a ballad stanza (eight- and six-syllable lines alternating) concealed by the typography.

Despite some uncertainties of dating and even attribution, the figures compiled from this edition have some suggestive interest. A major turning-point in Swift's career was his return to Ireland in 1714: by that time he had composed just under fifty of his surviving poems, that is, 18 per cent. However, because of the presence of longer poems such as the odes and *Cadenus and Vanessa*, these poems constitute 25 per cent of the lines he ever wrote. These earlier poems average ninety-five lines per poem, as against sixty-six overall. The shape of Swift's career can be better seen if we set out the totals for each individual decade, as shown in Table 1.

TABLE 1

Years of Composition	Number of Poems	Total Number of Lines	Average Number of Lines per Poem	Lines as a Proportion of Total
−1699	11	1587	144	8.6%
1700–1709	13	809	62	4.4%
1710–1719	44	3078	70	16.7%
1720–1729	137	7269	53	39.4%
1730–	70	5679	81	30.3%

The same data can be processed according to Swift's own age, rather than the external calendar. The results are shown in Table 2.

TABLE 2

Swift's Age	Number of Poems	Total Number of Lines	Average Number of Lines per Poem	Lines as a Proportion of Total
−30	7	1393	199	7.6%
31–40	10	469	47	2.5%
41–50	33	2793	85	15.1%
51–60	126	5653	45	30.7%
61–	99	8114	82	43.5%

In fact Swift's last datable poem was written as he came up to the age of seventy. The scale of his activity in his last productive decade is immediately apparent. His fifties produced 46 per cent of his poems, but only 31 per cent of the line-count; his sixties yielded 36 per cent of the poems, and 43 per cent of the bulk of his verse. This is occasioned by a large number of long poems written in this phase. Nine of Swift's twelve longest poems were written in his sixties, as emerges from the following list:

Cadenus and Vanessa	897	To a Lady	286
On Poetry: a Rhapsody	548	Directions for a Birthday	
Verses on the Death of		Song	282
Dr Swift	488	Mad Mullinix and Timothy	272
A Panegyric on the Dean	346	Ode to Dr William Sancroft	264
Strephon and Chloe	314	A Character, Panegyric,	
Ode to the Athenian		and Description of the Legion	
Society	307	Club	242
The Journal of a Modern			
Lady	293		

In all, 19.3 per cent of Swift's poems contain 100 lines or more; by coincidence, precisely double this number (38.7 per cent) contain fifty lines or more. Eighteen poems contain more than 200 lines, including the twelve poems listed above. However, the proportion of poems over 100 lines in length rises to 29 per cent after Swift's sixtieth birthday.

It can be seen that Swift wrote very nearly three quarters of his extant poetry (in terms of bulk) after the age of fifty, and rather more than four fifths of his separate poems. For these calculations, the Latin

and Anglo-Latin verses have been omitted, as have the composite
Scriblerian verses; however, of the seven undatable items, five, totalling
109 lines, have been included, but the last two English poems in this
edition, that is, *The Elephant* (thirty-four lines) and *Aye and No:
A Fable* (forty-one), were excluded from the calculation. The riddles
have been entered as separate poems. The count ignores variant
lines recorded only in the notes, as well as draft versions printed in
Appendix 3.

The Poems

Ode to the King

ON HIS IRISH EXPEDITION
AND THE SUCCESS OF HIS ARMS IN GENERAL

I

Sure there's some wondrous joy in doing good;
Immortal joy, that suffers no allay from fears,
   Nor dreads the tyranny of years,
By none but its possessors to be understood:
     Else where's the gain in being great?
   Kings would indeed be victims of the state;
   What can the poet's humble praise?
   What can the poet's humble bays?
   (We poets oft our bays allow,
10   Translated to the hero's brow)
   Add to the victor's happiness?
   What do the sceptre, crown and ball,
Rattles for infant royalty to play withal,
   But serve t' adorn the baby dress
   Of one poor coronation day,
     To make the pageant gay:
   A three hours' scene of empty pride,
   And then the toys are thrown aside.

II

   But the delight of doing good
20   Is fixed like fate among the stars,
     And deified in verse;
   'Tis the best gem in royalty,
   The great distinguisher of blood,
   Parent of valour and of fame,
   Which makes a godhead of a name,
And is contemporary to eternity.
   This made the ancient Romans to afford
   To *valour* and to *virtue* the same word:
To show the paths of both must be together trod,
30   Before the hero can commence a god.

III

    These are the ways
By which our happy prince carves out his bays;

Thus he has fixed his name
First, in the mighty list of Fame,
And thus he did the airy goddess court,
He sought her out in fight,
And like a bold romantic knight
Rescued her from the giant's fort:
The tyrant Death lay crouching down,
40   Waiting for orders at his feet,
Spoiled of his leaden crown;
He trampled on this haughty Bajazet,
Made him his footstool in the war,
And a grim slave to wait on his triumphal car.

IV

And now I in the spirit see
(The spirit of exalted poetry)
I see the fatal fight begin;
And, lo! where a destroying angel stands,
(By all but heaven and me unseen,)
50 With lightning in his eyes, and thunder in his hands;
'In vain', said he, 'does utmost Thule boast
No poisonous beast will in her breed,
Or no infectious weed,
When she sends forth such a malignant birth,
When man himself's the vermin of her earth;
When Treason there in person seems to stand,
And Rebel is the growth and manufacture of the land.'
He spake, and a dark cloud flung o'er his light,
And hid him from poetic sight,
60 And (I believe) began himself the fight,
For straight I saw the field maintained,
And what I used to laugh at in romance,
And thought too great even for the effects of chance,
The battle almost by great William's single valour gained;
The angel (doubtless) kept the eternal gate,
And stood twixt him and every fate;
And all those flying deaths that aimed him from the field,
(The impartial deaths which come
Like love, wrapped up in fire;
70 And like that too, make every breast their home)
Broke on his everlasting shield.

V

The giddy British populace,
 That tyrant guard on Peace,
 Who watch her like a prey,
 And keep her for a sacrifice,
 And must be sung, like Argus, into ease
Before this milk-white heifer can be stole away,
 Our prince has charmed its many hundred eyes;
  Has lulled the monster in a deep
80 And (I hope) an eternal sleep,
 And has at last redeemed the mighty prize.
The Scots themselves, that discontented brood,
Who always loudest for religion brawl,
 (As those do still wh'have none at all)
Who claim so many titles to be Jews,
(But, surely such whom God did never for his people choose)
 Still murmuring in their wilderness for food,
  Who pine us like a chronical disease;
 And one would think 'twere past omnipotence to please;
90 Your presence all their native stubbornness controls,
 And for a while unbends their contradicting souls:
  As in old fabulous hell,
When some patrician god would visit the immortal gaol,
  The very brightness of his face
 Suspended every horror of the place,
 The giants under Etna ceased to groan,
 And Sisyphus lay sleeping on his stone.
Thus has our prince completed every victory,
  And glad Ïerne now may see
100 Her sister isles are conquered too as well as she.

VI

How vainly (sir) did your fond enemy try
Upon a rubbish heap of broken laws
  To climb at victory
  Without the footing of a cause;
His laurel now must only be a cypress wreath,
 And his best victory a noble death;
His scrap of life is but a heap of miseries,
  The remnant of a falling snuff,
  Which hardly wants another puff,

110   And needs must *stink* whene'er it dies;
          Whilst at your victorious light
              All lesser ones expire,
          Consume, and perish from our sight,
          Just as the sun puts out a fire;
          And every foolish fly that dares to aim
              To buzz about the mighty flame;
          The wretched insects singe their wings, and fall,
              And humbly at the bottom crawl.

          VII
          That restless tyrant, who of late
120   Is grown so impudently great,
              That tennis-ball of fate;
          This gilded meteor which flies
          As if it meant to touch the skies;
              For all its boasted height,
              For all its plagiary light,
              Took its first growth and birth
          From the worst excrements of earth;
          Stay but a little while and down again 'twill come,
          And end as it began, in vapour, stink, and scum.
130   Or has he like some fearful star appeared?
          Long dreaded for his bloody tail and fiery beard,
              Transcending nature's ordinary laws,
              Sent by just heaven to threaten earth
              With war, and pestilence, and dearth,
          Of which it is at once the prophet and the cause.
              Howe'er it be, the pride of France
              Has finished its short race of chance,
              And all her boasted influences are
              Wrapped in the vortex of the British star;
140   Her tyrant too an unexpected wound shall feel
              In the last wretched remnant of his days;
          Our prince has hit him, like Achilles, in the heel,
              The poisonous darts has made him reel,
              Giddy he grows, and down is hurled,
          And as a mortal to his vile disease,
          Falls sick in the posteriors of the world.

Ode to the Athenian Society

I

As when the deluge first began to fall,
    That mighty ebb never to flow again,
(When this huge body's moisture was so great
It quite o'ercame the vital heat,)
That mountain which was highest first of all
Appeared, above the universal main,
To bless the primitive sailor's weary sight,
And 'twas perhaps Parnassus, if in height
    It be as great as 'tis in fame,
10   And nigh to heaven as is its name.
So after the inundation of a war
When Learning's little household did embark
With her world's fruitful system in her sacred ark,
    At the first ebb of noise and fears,
    Philosophy's exalted head appears;
And the dove-muse, will now no longer stay
But plumes her silver wings and flies away,
    And now a laurel wreath she brings from far,
    To crown the happy conqueror,
20   To show the flood begins to cease,
    And brings the dear reward of victory and peace.

II

The eager muse took wing upon the waves' decline,
    When war her cloudy aspect just withdrew,
    When the bright sun of peace began to shine,
And for a while in heavenly contemplation sat
    On the high top of peaceful Ararat;
And plucked a laurel branch (for laurel was the first that grew,
The first of plants after the thunder, storm and rain)
    And thence with joyful, nimble wing
30   Flew dutifully back again,
    And made an humble chaplet for the King.
    And the dove-muse is fled once more,
(Glad of the victory, yet frighted at the war)
    And now discovers from afar
    A peaceful and a flourishing shore:
    No sooner does she land

On the delightful strand,
When straight she sees the country all around,
Where fatal Neptune ruled e'rewhile,
40   Scattered with flowery vales, with fruitful gardens crowned,
And many a pleasant wood,
As if the universal Nile
Had rather watered it, than drowned:
It seems some floating piece of paradise,
Preserved by wonder from the flood,
Long wandering through the deep, as we are told
Famed Delos did of old,
And the transported muse imagined it
To be a fitter birthplace for the god of wit;
50   Or the much-talked oracular grove
When with amazing joy she hears,
An unknown music all around,
Charming her greedy ears
With many a heavenly song
Of nature and art, of deep philosophy and love,
Whilst angels tune the voice, and God inspires the tongue.
In vain she catches at the empty sound,
In vain pursues the music with her longing eye,
And courts the wandering echoes as they fly.

III
60   Pardon *Ye great unknown*, and far-exalted men,
The wild excursions of a youthful pen;
Forgive a young and (almost) virgin-muse,
Whom blind and eager curiosity
(Yet curiosity, they say,
Is in her sex a crime needs no excuse)
Has forced to grope her uncouth way
After a mighty light that leads her wandering eye;
No wonder then she quits the narrow path of sense
For a dear ramble through impertinence,
70   Impertinence, the scurvy of mankind,
And all we fools, who are the greater part of it,
Though we be of two different factions still,
Both the good-natured and the ill,
Yet wheresoe'er you look you'll always find
We join like flies, and wasps, in buzzing about wit.

In me, who am of the first sect of these,
All merit that transcends the humble rules
    Of my own dazzled, scanty sense
Begets a kinder folly and impertinence
80   Of admiration and of praise:
And our good brethren of the surly sect
        Must e'en all herd with us their kindred fools,
    For though possessed of present vogue, they've made
Railing a rule of wit, and obloquy a trade,
Yet the same want of brains produces each effect;
    And you whom Pluto's helm does wisely shroud
        From us the blind and thoughtless crowd,
    Like the famed hero in his mother's cloud,
Who both our follies and impertinences see,
90   Do laugh perhaps at theirs, and pity mine and me.

IV
            But censure's to be understood
            The authentic mark of the elect,
The public stamp heaven sets on all that's great and good,
    Our shallow search and judgement to direct.
            The war methinks has made
    Our wit and learning, narrow as our trade;
    Instead of boldly sailing far to buy
    A stock of wisdom and philosophy,
            We fondly stay at home in fear
100   Of every censuring privateer,
    Forcing a wretched trade by beating down the sale,
            And selling basely by retail,
        The wits, I mean the atheists of the age,
Who fain would rule the pulpit, as they do the stage,
    Wondrous reformers of philosophy,
            Of morals and divinity,
By the new modish system of reducing all to sense,
    Against all logic and concluding laws,
            Do own the effects of Providence,
110   And yet deny the cause.

V
This hopeful sect, now it begins to see
How little, very little do prevail

Their first and chiefest force
To censure, to cry down, and rail,
Not knowing what, or where, or who, you be,
Will quickly take another course
And by their never-failing ways
Of solving all appearances they please,
We soon shall see them to their ancient methods fall,
120   And straight deny you to be men, or anything at all;
I laugh at the grave answer they will make,
Which they have always ready, general and cheap;
'Tis but to say, that what we daily meet,
And by a fond mistake
Perhaps imagine to be wondrous wit
And think, alas, to be by mortals writ,
Is but a crowd of atoms jostling in a heap,
Which from eternal seeds begun,
Jostling some thousand years till ripened by the sun,
130   They're now, just now, as naturally born,
As from the womb of earth a field of corn.

VI

But as for poor contented me,
Who must my weakness and my ignorance confess,
That I believe in much, I ne'er can hope to see;
Methinks I'm satisfied to guess
That this new, noble, and delightful scene
Is wonderfully moved by some exalted men,
Who have well studied in the world's disease,
(That epidemic error and depravity
140   Or in our judgement or our eye)
That what *surprises* us can only please:
We often search contentedly the whole world round,
To make some great discovery,
And scorn it when 'tis found.
Just so the mighty Nile has suffered in its fame,
Because 'tis said, (and perhaps only said)
We've found a little inconsiderable head
That feeds the huge unequal stream.
Consider human folly, and you'll quickly own,
150   That all the praises it can give,
By which some fondly boast they shall for ever live,
Won't pay the impertinence of being known;

Else why should the famed Lydian king,
Whom all the charms of an usurped wife and state,
With all that power unfelt, courts mankind to be great,
Did with new, unexperienced glories wait,
Still wear, still doat on his invisible ring.

VII

Were I to form a regular thought of fame,
Which is perhaps as hard t'imagine right
160   As to paint Echo to the sight:
I would not draw the idea from an empty name;
Because, alas when we all die
Careless and ignorant posterity,
Although they praise the learning and the wit,
And though the title seems to show
The name and man, by whom the book was writ,
Yet how shall they be brought to know
Whether that very name was he, or you, or I?
Less should I daub it o'er with transitory praise,
170   And water-colours of these days,
These days! where even the extravagance of poetry
Is at a loss for figures to express
Men's folly, whimsies, and inconstancy,
And by a faint description makes them less.
Then tell us what is fame? where shall we search for it?
Look where exalted virtue and religion sit
Enthroned with heavenly wit,
Look where you see
The greatest scorn of learned vanity,
180   (And then how much a nothing is mankind!
Whose reason is weighed down by popular air,
Who by that, vainly talks of baffling death,
And hopes to lengthen life by a transfusion of breath,
Which yet whoe'er examines right will find
To be an art as vain, as bottling up of wind:)
And when you find out these, believe true fame is there.
Far above all reward, yet to which all is due,
And this ye great unknown, is only known in you.

VIII

The juggling sea-god when by chance trepanned
190   By some instructed querist sleeping on the sand,

Impatient of all answers, straight became
A stealing brook, and strove to creep away
   Into his native sea,
Vexed at their follies, murmured in his stream;
But disappointed of his fond desire
Would vanish in a pyramid of fire.
This surly, slippery god, when he designed
   To furnish his escapes,
Ne'er borrowed more variety of shapes
200   Than you to please and satisfy mankind,
And seem (almost) transformed to water, flame, and air,
   So well you answer all phenomenas there;
Though madmen and the wits, philosophers and fools,
With all that factious or enthusiastic dotards dream,
And all the incoherent jargon of the schools,
   Though all the fumes of fear, hope, love, and shame,
Contrive to shock your minds, with many a senseless doubt,
Doubts, where the Delphic god would grope in ignorance and
   night,
   The god of learning and of light
210   Would want a god himself to help him out.

IX

Philosophy, as it before us lies,
Seems to have borrowed some ungrateful taste
Of doubts, impertinence, and niceties,
   From every age through which it passed,
But always with a stronger relish of the last.
   This beauteous queen by heaven designed
   To be the great original
For man to dress and polish his uncourtly mind,
In what mock-habits have they put her, since the Fall!
220   More oft in fools' and madmen's hands than sages'
   She seems a medley of all ages,
With a huge fardingale to swell her fustian stuff,
   A new commode, a topknot, and a ruff,
   Her face patched o'er with modern pedantry,
     With a long sweeping train
Of comments and disputes, ridiculous and vain,
   All of old cut with a new dye,
   How soon have you restored her charms!

And rid her of her lumber and her books,
230   Dressed her again genteel and neat,
            And rather tight than great,
How fond we are to court her to our arms!
How much of heaven is in her naked looks.

        x
Thus the deluding muse oft blinds me to her ways,
        And even my very thoughts transfers
        And changes all to beauty, and the praise
            Of that proud tyrant sex of hers.
            The rebel muse, alas, takes part
            But with my own rebellious heart,
240   And you with fatal and immortal wit conspire
                To fan the unhappy fire:
            Cruel unknown! what is it you intend!
Ah, could you! could you hope a poet for your friend!
        Rather forgive what my first transport said,
May all the blood, which shall by woman's scorn be shed
        Lie on you, and on your children's head,
For you (ah, did I think I e'er should live to see
        The fatal time when that could be)
        Have even increased their pride and cruelty.
250   Woman seems now above all vanity grown,
            Still boasting of her great unknown;
Platonic champions, gained without one female wile,
            Or the vast *charges of a smile*;
        Which 'tis a shame to see how much of late
        You've taught the covetous wretches to o'errate,
And which they've now the conscience to weigh
        In the same balance with our tears,
        And with such scanty wages pay
        The bondage and the slavery of years.
260   Let the vain sex dream on, their empire comes from us,
        And had they common generosity
            They would not use us thus.
        Well – though you've raised her to this high degree,
            Ourselves are raised as well as she,
        And spite of all that they or you can do,
        'Tis pride and happiness enough to me
Still to be of the same exalted sex with you.

XI

Alas, how fleeting, and how vain,
Is even the nobler man, our learning and our wit,
270   I sigh whene'er I think of it
As at the closing an unhappy scene
Of some great king and conqueror's death,
When the sad, melancholy muse
Stays but to catch his utmost breath,
I grieve, this noble work so happily begun,
So quickly, and so wonderfully carried on,
Must fall at last to interest, folly, and abuse.
There is a noontide in our lives
Which still the sooner it arrives,
280   Although we boast our winter sun looks bright,
And foolishly are glad to see it at its height
Yet so much sooner comes the long and gloomy night.
No conquest ever yet begun
And by one mighty hero carried to its height
E'er flourished under a successor or a son;
It lost some mighty pieces through all hands it passed
And vanished to an empty title in the last.
For when the animating mind is fled,
(Which nature never can retain,
290   Nor e'er call back again)
The body, though gigantic, lies all cold and dead.

XII

And thus undoubtedly 'twill fare,
With what unhappy men shall dare,
To be successors to these great unknown,
On Learning's high-established throne.
Censure, and Pedantry, and Pride,
Numberless nations, stretching far and wide,
Shall (I foresee it) soon with Gothic swarms come forth
From Ignorance's universal north,
300 And with blind rage break all this peaceful government;
Yet shall these traces of your wit remain
Like a just map to tell the vast extent
Of conquest in your short and happy reign;
And to all future mankind show
How strange a paradox is true,

That men, who lived and died without a name,
Are the chief heroes in the sacred list of fame.

Ode to the Honourable Sir William Temple

I

Virtue, the greatest of all monarchies,
    Till its first emperor rebellious man
Deposed from off his seat
It fell, and broke with its own weight
Into small states and principalities,
    By many a petty lord possessed,
But ne'er since seated in one single breast.
        'Tis you who must this land subdue,
        The mighty conquest's left for you,
10   The conquest and discovery too:
        Search out this Utopian ground,
        Virtue's *Terra incognita*,
        Where none ever led the way,
Nor ever since but in descriptions found,
    Like the philosopher's stone,
With rules to search it, yet obtained by none.

II

    We have too long been led astray,
Too long have our misguided souls been taught
    With rules from musty morals brought,
20   'Tis you must put us in the way;
    Let us (for shame) no more be fed
    With antique relics of the dead,
    The gleanings of philosophy,
    Philosophy! the lumber of the schools,
    The roguery of alchemy,
        And we bubbled fools
Spend all our present stock in hopes of golden rules.

III

But what does our proud ignorance learning call,
    We oddly Plato's paradox make good,
30 Our knowledge is but mere remembrance all,

Remembrance is our treasure and our food;
Nature's fair table-book our tender souls
We scrawl all o'er with old and empty rules,
　　Stale memorandums of the schools;
　　　For learning's mighty treasures look
　　　　In that deep grave a book,
　　Think she there does all her treasures hide,
And that her troubled ghost still haunts there since she died;
　　Confine her walks to colleges and schools,
40　　　　Her priests, her train and followers show
　　　　As if they all were spectres too,
　　　They purchase knowledge at the expense
　　　Of common breeding, common sense,
　　　And at once grow scholars and fools;
　　　Affect ill-mannered pedantry,
　　Rudeness, ill-nature, incivility,
　　　And sick with dregs of knowledge grown,
　　　Which greedily they swallow down,
　　Still cast it up and nauseate company.

　　IV
50　Cursed be the wretch, nay doubly cursed,
　　　　(If it may lawful be
　　　To curse our greatest enemy)
　　Who learnt himself that heresy first
　　　(Which since has seized on all the rest)
　　That knowledge forfeits all humanity;
　　Taught us, like Spaniards, to be proud and poor,
　　　　And fling our scraps before our door,
　　Thrice happy you have 'scaped this general pest;
　　Those mighty epithets, learned, good, and great,
60　Which we ne'er joined before, but in romances meet,
　　　We find in you at last united grown.
　　　　You cannot be compared to one,
　　　I must, like him that painted Venus' face,
　　　Borrow from everyone a grace;
　　Virgil and Epicurus will not do,
　　　Their courting a retreat like you,
　　Unless I put in Caesar's learning too,
　　　　Your happy frame at once controls
　　　　This great triumvirate of souls.

V

70 Let not old Rome boast Fabius' fate,
    He saved his country by delays,
        But you by peace,
    You bought it at a cheaper rate;
Nor has it left the usual bloody scar,
    To show it cost its price in war,
War! that mad game, the world so loves to play,
    And for it does so dearly pay;
For though with loss or victory awhile
    Fortune the gamesters does beguile,
80 Yet at the last the box sweeps all away.

VI

    Only the laurel got by peace
        No thunder e'er can blast,
        The artillery of the skies
        Shoots to the earth and dies;
Forever green and flourishing 'twill last,
Nor dipped in blood, nor widow's tears, nor orphan's cries:
    About the head crowned with these bays,
    Like lambent fire the lightning plays;
Nor its triumphal cavalcade to grace
90   Make up its solemn train with death;
It melts the sword, yet keeps it in its sheath.

VII

The wily shafts of state, those juggler's tricks
Which we call deep design and politics
(As in a theatre the ignorant fry,
    Because the cords escape their eye
    Wonder to see the motions fly)
    Methinks, when you expose the scene,
    Down the ill-organed engines fall;
Off fly the vizards and discover all,
100   How plain I see through the deceit!
    How shallow! and how gross the cheat!
    Look where the pulley's tied above!
    Great God! (said I) what have I seen!
        On what poor engines move
The thoughts of monarchs, and designs of states,

What petty motives rule their fates!
How the mouse makes the mighty mountain shake!
The mighty mountain labours with its birth,
   Away the frighted peasants fly,
110   Scared at the unheard-of prodigy,
Expect some great gigantic son of earth;
      Lo, it appears!
   See, how they tremble! how they quake!
Out starts the little beast, and mocks their idle fears.

VIII

   Then tell (dear favourite muse)
What serpent's that which still resorts,
Still lurks in palaces and courts,
    Take thy unwonted flight,
    And on the terrace light.
120   See where she lies!
    See how she rears her head,
   And rolls about her dreadful eyes,
To drive all virtue out, or look it dead!
'Twas sure this basilisk sent Temple thence,
And though as some ('tis said) for their defence
   Have worn a casement o'er their skin,
    So he wore his within,
Made up of virtue and transparent innocence:
   And though he oft renewed the fight,
130 And almost got priority of sight,
   He ne'er could overcome her quite,
   (In pieces cut, the viper still did reunite)
   Till at last tired with loss of time and ease,
Resolved to give himself, as well as country peace.

IX

Sing (beloved muse) the pleasures of retreat,
   And in some untouched virgin strain
Show the delights thy sister Nature yields,
Sing of thy vales, sing of thy woods, sing of thy fields;
    Go publish o'er the plain
140   How mighty a proselyte you gain!
How noble a reprisal on the great!
    How is the muse luxuriant grown,
     Whene'er she takes this flight

She soars clear out of sight,
These are the paradises of her own;
(The Pegasus, like an unruly horse
      Though ne'er so gently led
To the loved pasture where he used to feed,
Runs violently o'er his usual course.)

150   Wake from thy wanton dreams,
           Come from thy dear-loved streams,
       The crooked paths of wandering Thames.
          Fain the nymph would stay,
          Oft she looks back in vain,
      Oft 'gainst her fountain does complain,
And softly steals in many windings down,
As loath to see the hated court and town,
       And murmurs as she glides away.

x
In this new happy scene

160   Are nobler subjects for your learned pen;
         Here we expect from you
More than your predecessor, Adam, knew;
Whatever moves our wonder or our sport,
Whatever serves for innocent emblems of the court;
      How that which we a kernel see,
Whose well-compacted forms escape the light,
      Unpierced by the blunt rays of sight,
      Shall e'er long grow into a tree,
Whence takes it its increase, and whence its birth

170 Or from the sun, or from the air, or from the earth,
       Where all the fruitful atoms lie,
       How some go downwards to the root,
     Some more ambitiously upwards fly,
And form the leaves, the branches, and the fruit,
You strove to cultivate a barren court in vain,
Your garden's better worth your noble pain,
Hence mankind fell, and here must rise again.

XI
Shall I believe a spirit so divine
    Was cast in the same mould with mine?

180 Why then does Nature so unjustly share
Among her elder sons the whole estate

And all her jewels and her plate?
Poor we cadets of heaven, not worth her care,
Take up at best with lumber and the leavings of a fate:
    Some she binds prentice to the spade,
    Some to the drudgery of a trade,
Some she does to Egyptian bondage draw,
Bids us make bricks, yet sends us to look out for straw;
    Some she condemns for life to try
190 To dig the leaden mines of deep philosophy:
Me she has to the muse's galleys tied,
In vain I strive to cross this spacious main,
    In vain I tug and pull the oar,
    And when I almost reach the shore
Straight the muse turns the helm, and I launch out again;
        And yet to feed my pride,
Whene'er I mourn, stops my complaining breath,
With promise of a mad reversion after death.

XII

Then (sir) accept this worthless verse,
200   The tribute of an humble muse,
'Tis all the portion of my niggard stars;
Nature the hidden spark did at my birth infuse,
And kindled first with indolence and ease,
    And since too oft debauched by praise,
'Tis now grown an incurable disease:
In vain to quench this foolish fire I try
    In wisdom and philosophy;
    In vain all wholesome herbs I sow,
        Where nought but weeds will grow.
210 Whate'er I plant (like corn on barren earth)
        By an equivocal birth
    Seeds and runs up to poetry.

Ode to Dr William Sancroft

LATE LORD ARCHBISHOP OF CANTERBURY

I

Truth is eternal, and the son of heaven,
    Bright effluence of the immortal ray,

Chief cherub, and chief lamp of that high sacred seven,
Which guard the throne by night, and are its light by day:
First of God's darling attributes,
Thou daily seest Him face to face,
Nor does thy essence fixed depend on giddy circumstance
Of time or place,
Two foolish guides in every sublunary dance:
10   How shall we find thee then in dark disputes?
How shall we search thee in a battle gained,
Or a weak argument by force maintained?
In dagger-contests, and the artillery of words,
(For swords are madmen's tongues, and tongues are madmen's
swords)
Contrived to tire all patience out,
And not to satisfy the doubt:

II

But where is even thy image on our earth?
For of the person much I fear,
Since heaven will claim its residence as well as birth,
20   And God Himself has said, He shall not find it here.
For this inferior world is but heaven's dusky shade,
By dark reverted rays from its reflection made;
Whence the weak shapes wild and imperfect pass,
Like sunbeams shot at too far distance from a glass;
Which all the mimic forms express,
Though in strange uncouth postures, and uncomely dress;
So when Cartesian artists try
To solve appearances of sight
In its reception to the eye,
30   And catch the living landscape through a scanty light,
The figures all inverted show,
And colours of a faded hue;
Here a pale shape with upward footstep treads,
And men seem walking on their heads;
There whole herds suspended lie
Ready to tumble down into the sky;
Such are the ways ill-guided mortals go
To judge of things above by things below.
Disjointing shapes as in the fairy-land of dreams,
40   Or images that sink in streams;
No wonder, then, we talk amiss

Of truth, and what, or where it is:
Say muse, for thou, if any, know'st
Since the bright essence fled, where haunts the reverend ghost?

III

If all that our weak knowledge titles virtue, be
(High truth) the best resemblance of exalted Thee,
     If a mind fixed to combat fate
With those two powerful swords, Submission and Humility,
          Sounds truly good, or truly great;
50   Ill may I live, if the good SANCROFT in his holy rest,
          In the divinity of retreat,
     Be not the brightest pattern earth can show
          Of heaven-born truth below:
     But foolish man still judges what is best
          In his own balance, false and light,
          Following opinion, dark, and blind,
          That vagrant leader of the mind,
Till Honesty and Conscience are clear out of sight.

IV

And some, to be large ciphers in a state,
60   Pleased with an empty swelling to be counted great;
Make their minds travel o'er infinity of space,
          Rapt through the wide expanse of thought,
          And oft in contradiction's vortex caught,
To keep that worthless clod, the body, in one place:
Errors like this did old astronomers misguide,
Led blindly on by gross philosophy and pride,
          Who, like hard masters, taught the sun
          Through many a needless sphere to run,
Many an eccentric and unthrifty motion make,
70   And thousand incoherent journeys take,
          Whilst all the advantage by it got,
     Was but to light earth's inconsiderable spot.
The herd beneath, who see the weathercock of state
          Hung loosely on the church's pinnacle,
Believe it firm, because perhaps the day is mild and still;
But when they find it turn with the first blast of fate,
          By gazing upwards giddy grow,
          And think the church itself does so;
          Thus fools, for being strong and numerous grown,

80   Suppose the truth, like all the world, their own;
And holy SANCROFT's motion quite irregular appears,
        Because 'tis opposite to theirs.

        V

In vain then would the muse the multitude advise,
    Whose peevish knowledge thus perversely lies
        In gathering follies from the wise;
    Rather put on thy anger and thy spite,
        And some kind power for once dispense
    Through the dark mass, the dawn of so much sense,
To make them understand, and feel me when I write;
90   The muse and I no more revenge desire,
Each line shall stab, shall blast, like daggers and like fire;
    Ah, Britain, land of angels! which of all thy sins,
        (Say, hapless isle, although
        It is a bloody list we know)
    Has given thee up a dwelling-place to fiends?
        Sin and the plague ever abound
In governments too easy, and too fruitful ground;
        Evils which a too gentle king,
        Too flourishing a spring,
100   And too warm summers bring:
    Our British soil is over-rank, and breeds
Among the noblest flowers a thousand poisonous weeds,
    And every stinking weed so lofty grows,
    As if 'twould overshade the royal rose,
    The royal rose the glory of our morn,
        But, ah, too much without a thorn.

    VI

Forgive (original mildness) this ill-governed zeal,
    'Tis all the angry slighted muse can do
    In the pollution of these days;
110   No province now is left her but to rail,
And poetry has lost the art to praise,
    Alas, the occasions are so few:
        None e'er but you,
        And your almighty master, knew
    With heavenly peace of mind to bear
(Free from our tyrant-passions, anger, scorn, or fear)
    The giddy turns of popular rage,

And all the contradictions of a poisoned age;
    The Son of God pronounced by the same breath
120   Which straight pronounced his death;
And though I should but ill be understood
In wholly equalling our sin and theirs,
And measuring by the scanty thread of wit
What we call holy, and great, and just, and good,
(Methods in talk whereof our pride and ignorance makes us use)
    And which our wild ambition foolishly compares
        With endless and with infinite;
    Yet pardon, native Albion, when I say
Among thy stubborn sons there haunts that spirit of Jews,
130   That those forsaken wretches who today
        Revile His great ambassador,
    Seem to discover what they would have done
    (Were his humanity on earth once more)
To his undoubted master, heaven's almighty son.

VII
But zeal is weak and ignorant, though wondrous proud,
    Though very turbulent and very loud;
    The crazy composition shows,
Like that fantastic medley in the idol's toes,
    Made up of iron mixed with clay,
140   This, crumbles into dust,
    That, moulders into rust,
    Or melts by the first shower away.
Nothing is fixed that mortals see or know,
Unless, perhaps, some stars above be so;
    And those, alas, do show
Like all transcendent excellence below;
    In both, false mediums cheat our sight,
And far exalted objects lessen by their height:
    Thus, primitive SANCROFT moves too high
150   To be observed by vulgar eye,
    And rolls the silent year
    On his own secret regular sphere,
And sheds, though all unseen, his sacred influence here.

VIII
Kind star, still mayst thou shed thy sacred influence here,
    Or from thy private peaceful orb appear;

For, sure, we want some guide from heaven to show
The way which every wandering fool below
    Pretends so perfectly to know;
    And which for aught I see, and much I fear,
160   The world has wholly missed;
    I mean, the way which leads to Christ:
Mistaken idiots! see how giddily they run,
    Led blindly on by avarice and pride,
       What mighty numbers follow them;
       Each fond of erring with his guide:
Some whom ambition drives, seek heaven's high son
    In Caesar's court, or in Jerusalem;
       Others, ignorantly wise,
Among proud doctors and disputing pharisees:
170 What could the sages gain but unbelieving scorn;
    Their faith was so uncourtly when they said
That heaven's high son was in a village born;
       That the world's saviour had been
       In a vile manger laid,
    And fostered in a wretched inn.

IX

Necessity, thou tyrant conscience of the great,
Say, why the church is still led blindfold by the state?
    Why should the first be ruined and laid waste,
    To mend the dilapidations in the last?
180 And yet the world, whose eyes are on our mighty prince,
    Thinks heaven has cancelled all our sins,
And that his subjects share his happy influence;
Follow the model close, for so I'm sure they should,
But wicked kings draw more examples than the good;
    And divine SANCROFT, weary with the weight
Of a declining church, by faction her worse foe oppressed,
       Finding the mitre almost grown
       A load as heavy as the crown,
    Wisely retreated to his heavenly rest.

X

190   Ah, may no unkind earthquake of the state,
       Nor hurricano from the crown,
Disturb the present mitre, as that fearful storm of late,
    Which in its dusky march along the plain,

Swept up whole churches as it list,
Wrapped in a whirlwind and a mist;
Like that prophetic tempest in the virgin reign,
And swallowed them at last, or flung them down.
Such were the storms good SANCROFT long has borne;
The mitre, which his sacred head has worn,
200   Was, like his master's crown, enwreathed with thorn.
Death's sting is swallowed up in victory at last,
The bitter cup is from him passed:
Fortune in both extremes,
Though blasts from contrariety of winds,
Yet to firm heavenly minds,
Is but one thing under two different names;
And even the sharpest eye that has the prospect seen,
Confesses ignorance to judge between;
And must, to human reasoning opposite, conclude
210   To point out which is moderation, which is fortitude.

XI

Thus SANCROFT, in the exaltation of retreat,
Shows lustre that was shaded in his seat;
Short glimmerings of the prelate glorified;
Which the disguise of greatness only served to hide;
Why should the sun, alas, be proud
To lodge behind a golden cloud;
Though fringed with evening gold the cloud appears so gay,
'Tis but a low-born vapour kindled by a ray;
At length 'tis over-blown and past,
220   Puffed by the people's spiteful blast,
The dazzling glory dims their prostituted sight,
No deflowered eye can face the naked light:
Yet does this high perfection well proceed
From strength of its own native seed,
This wilderness the world, like that poetic wood of old,
Bears one, and but one branch of gold,
Where the blessed spirit lodges like the dove,
And which (to heavenly soil transplanted) will improve,
To be, as 'twas below, the brightest plant above;
230   For, whate'er theologic levellers dream,
There are degrees above I know
As well as here below,

(The goddess muse herself has told me so)
Where high patrician souls dressed heavenly gay,
Sit clad in lawn of purer woven day,
There some high spiritual throne to SANCROFT shall be given,
    In the metropolis of heaven;
Chief of the mitred saints, and from arch-prelate here,
    Translated to arch-angel there.

XII

240   Since, happy saint, since it has been of late
      Either our blindness or our fate,
      To lose the providence of thy cares,
    Pity a miserable church's tears,
    That begs the powerful blessing of thy prayers.
    Some angel say, what were the nation's crimes,
    That sent these wild reformers to our times;
      Say what their senseless malice meant,
      To tear Religion's lovely face;
    Strip her of every ornament and grace,
250 In striving to wash off the imaginary paint:
    Religion now does on her deathbed lie,
Heartsick of a high fever and consuming atrophy;
How the physicians swarm to show their mortal skill,
And by their college-arts methodically kill:
Reformers and physicians differ but in name,
    One end in both, and the design the same;
    Cordials are in their talk, whilst all they mean
    Is but the patient's death, and gain –
    Check in thy satire, angry muse,
260   Or a more worthy subject choose:
Let not the outcasts of this outcast age
Provoke the honour of my muse's rage,
    Nor be thy mighty spirit raised,
    Since heaven and Cato both are pleased –

To Mr Congreve

Thrice, with a prophet's voice and prophet's power,
The muse was called in a poetic hour,
And insolently thrice, the slighted maid

Dared to suspend her unregarded aid;
Then with that grief we form in spirits divine,
Pleads for her own neglect, and thus reproaches mine:

'Once highly honoured! False is the pretence
You make to truth, retreat, and innocence;
Who, to pollute my shades, bringst with thee down
10   The most ungenerous vices of the town;
Ne'er sprang a youth from out this isle before
I once esteemed, and loved, and favoured more,
Nor ever maid endured such court-like scorn,
So much in mode, so very city-born;
'Tis with a foul design the muse you send,
Like a cast mistress to your wicked friend;
But find some new address, some fresh deceit,
Nor practise such an antiquated cheat;
These are the beaten methods of the stews,
20   Stale forms of course, all mean deceivers use,
Who barbarously think to 'scape reproach,
By prostituting her they first debauch.'

Thus did the muse severe unkindly blame
This offering long designed to Congreve's fame;
First chid the zeal as unpoetic fire,
Which soon her merit forced her to inspire;
Then call this verse, that speaks her largest aid,
The greatest compliment she ever made,
And wisely judge, no power beneath divine
30   Could leap the bounds which part your world and mine;
For, youth, believe, to you unseen, is fixed
A mighty gulf unpassable betwixt.

Nor tax the goddess of a mean design
To praise your parts by publishing of mine;
That be my thought when some large bulky writ
Shows in the front the ambition of my wit;
There to surmount what bears me up, and sing
Like the victorious wren perched on the eagle's wing;
This could I do, and proudly o'er him tower,
40   Were my desires but heightened to my power.

Godlike the force of my young Congreve's bays,
Softening the muse's thunder into praise;

Sent to assist an old unvanquished pride
That looks with scorn on half mankind beside;
A pride that well suspends poor mortals' fate,
Gets between them and my resentment's weight,
Stands in the gap 'twixt me and wretched men,
T' avert the impending judgements of my pen.

Thus I look down with mercy on the age,
50 By hopes my Congreve will reform the stage;
For never did poetic mine before
Produce a richer vein or cleaner ore;
The bullion stamped in your refining mind
Serves by retail to furnish half mankind.
With indignation I behold your wit
Forced on me, cracked, and clipped, and counterfeit,
By vile pretenders, who a stock maintain
From broken scraps and filings of your brain.
Through native dross your share is hardly known,
60 And by short views mistook for all your own;
So small the gain from those your wit do reap,
Who blend it into folly's larger heap,
Like the sun's scattered beams which pass,
When some rough hand breaks the assembling glass.

Yet want your critics no just cause to rail,
Since knaves are ne'er obliged for what they steal.
These pad on wit's high road, and suits maintain
With those they rob, by what their trade does gain.
Thus censure seems that fiery froth which breeds
70 O'er the sun's face, and from his heat proceeds,
Crusts o'er the day, shadowing its parent beam
As ancient nature's modern masters dream;
This bids some curious praters here below
Call Titan sick, because their sight is so;
And well, methinks, does this allusion fit
To scribblers, and the god of light and wit;
Those who by wild delusions entertain
A lust of rhyming for a poet's vein,
Raise envy's clouds to leave themselves in night,
80 But can no more obscure my Congreve's light
Than swarms of gnats, that wanton in a ray
Which gave them birth, can rob the world of day.

What northern hive poured out these foes to wit?
Whence came these Goths to overrun the pit?
How would you blush the shameful birth to hear
Of those you so ignobly stoop to fear;
For, ill to them, long have I travelled since
Round all the circles of impertinence,
Searched in the nest where every worm did lie
90 Before it grew a city butterfly;
I'm sure I found them other kind of things
Than those with backs of silk and golden wings;
A search, no doubt, as curious and as wise
As virtuosos' in detecting flies;
For, could you think? the fiercest foes you dread,
And court in prologues, all are country-bred;
Bred in my scene, and for the poet's sins
Adjourned from tops and grammar to the inns;
Those beds of dung, where schoolboys sprout up beaux
100 Far sooner than the nobler mushroom grows:
These are the lords of the poetic schools,
Who preach the saucy pedantry of rules;
Those powers the critics, who may boast the odds
O'er Nile, with all its wilderness of gods;
Nor could the nations kneel to viler shapes,
Which worshipped cats, and sacrificed to apes;
And can you think the wise forbear to laugh
At the warm zeal that breeds this golden calf?

Haply you judge these lines severely writ
110 Against the proud usurpers of the pit;
Stay while I tell my story, short, and true;
To draw conclusions shall be left to you;
Nor need I ramble far to force a rule,
But lay the scene just here at Farnham school.

Last year, a lad hence by his parents sent
With other cattle to the city went;
Where having cast his coat, and well pursued
The methods most in fashion to be lewd,
Returned a finished spark this summer down,
120 Stocked with the freshest gibberish of the town;
A jargon formed from the lost language, wit,
Confounded in that Babel of the pit;

Formed by diseased conceptions, weak, and wild,
Sick lust of souls, and an abortive child;
Born between whores and fops, by lewd compacts,
Before the play, or else between the acts:
Nor wonder, if from such polluted minds
Should spring such short and transitory kinds,
Or crazy rules to make us wits by rote
130 Last just as long as every cuckoo's note:
What bungling, rusty tools are used by fate!
'Twas in an evil hour to urge my hate,
My hate, whose lash just heaven has long decreed
Shall on a day make sin and folly bleed;
When man's ill genius to my presence sent
This wretch, to rouse my wrath, for ruin meant;
Who in his idiom vile, with Gray's Inn grace,
Squandered his noisy talents to my face;
Named every player on his fingers' ends,
140 Swore all the wits were his peculiar friends;
Talked with that saucy and familiar ease
Of Wycherley, and you, and Mr Bays;
Said, how a late report your friends had vexed,
Who heard you meant to write heroics next;
For, tragedy, he knew, would lose you quite,
And told you so at Will's but t'other night.

Thus are the lives of fools a sort of dreams,
Rendering shades, things, and substances of names;
Such high companions may delusion keep,
150 Lords are a footboy's cronies in his sleep.
As a fresh miss, by fancy, face, and gown,
Rendered the topping beauty of the town,
Draws every rhyming, prating, dressing sot,
To boast of favours that he never got;
Of which, whoe'er lacks confidence to prate,
Brings his good parts and breeding in debate;
And not the meanest coxcomb you can find,
But thanks his stars, that Phyllis has been kind;
Thus prostitute my Congreve's name is grown
160 To every lewd pretender of the town.
Troth I could pity you; but this is it,
You find, to be a fashionable wit;
These are the slaves whom reputation chains,

Whose maintenance requires no help from brains.
For, should the vilest scribbler to the pit,
Whom sin and want e'er furnished out a wit;
Whose name must not within my lines be shown,
Lest here it live, when perished with his own;
Should such a wretch usurp my Congreve's place,
170 And choose out wits who ne'er have seen his face;
I'll bet my life but the dull cheat would pass,
Nor need the lion's skin conceal the ass;
Yes, that beau's look, that voice, those critic ears,
Must needs be right, so well resembling theirs.

Perish the muse's hour, thus vainly spent
In satire, to my Congreve's praises meant;
In how ill season her resentments rule,
What's that to her if mankind be a fool?
Happy beyond a private muse's fate,
180 In pleasing all that's good among the great,
Where though her eldest sisters crowding throng,
She still is welcome with her innocent song;
Whom were my Congreve blessed to see and know,
What poor regards would merit all below!
How proudly would he haste the joy to meet,
And drop his laurel at Apollo's feet.

Here by a mountain's side, a reverend cave
Gives murmuring passage to a lasting wave;
'Tis the world's watery hour-glass streaming fast,
190 Time is no more when the utmost drop is past;
Here, on a better day, some druid dwelt,
And the young muse's early favour felt;
Druid, a name she does with pride repeat,
Confessing Albion once her darling seat;
Far in this primitive cell might we pursue
Our predecessors' footsteps, still in view;
Here would we sing – But, ah! you think I dream,
And the bad world may well believe the same;
Yes; you are all malicious standers-by,
200 While two fond lovers prate, the muse and I.

Since thus I wander from my first intent,
Nor am that grave advisor which I meant;

Take this short lesson from the god of bays,
And let my friend apply it as he please:

Beat not the dirty paths where vulgar feet have trod,
   But give the vigorous fancy room.
For when like stupid alchemists you try
     To fix this nimble god,
     This volatile mercury,
210 The subtle spirit all flies up in fume;
     Nor shall the bubbled virtuoso find
More than a fade insipid mixture left behind.

Whilst thus I write, vast shoals of critics come,
And on my verse pronounce their saucy doom;
The muse, like some bright country virgin, shows,
Fallen by mishap among a knot of beaux;
They, in their lewd and fashionable prate,
Rally her dress, her language, and her gait;
Spend their base coin before the bashful maid,
220 Current like copper, and as often paid:
She, who on shady banks has joyed to sleep
Near better animals, her father's sheep;
Shamed and amazed, beholds the chattering throng,
To think what cattle she has got among;
But with the odious smell and sight annoyed,
In haste she does the offensive herd avoid.

'Tis time to bid my friend a long farewell,
The muse retreats far in yon crystal cell;
Faint inspiration sickens as she flies,
230 Like distant echo spent, the spirit dies.

In this descending sheet you'll haply find
Some short refreshment for your weary mind,
Naught it contains is common or unclean,
And once drawn up, is ne'er let down again.

A Description of Mother Ludwell's Cave

Hae latebrae dulces, et si mihi credis, amoenae.

Let others with Parnassus swell their theme,
Drink inspiration from the Aonian stream:
Let them draw Phoebus down to patch a line,
Invoke, that hackney fry, the tuneful nine:
I that of Ludwell sing, to Ludwell run,
Herself my muse, her spring my Helicon.
The neighbouring park its friendly aid allows;
Perfumed with thyme, o'erspread with shady boughs;
Its leafy canopies new thoughts instil,
10 And Crooksberry supplies the cloven hill.
Pomona does Minerva's stores dispense,
And Flora sheds her balmy influence;
All things conspire to press my modest muse,
The morning herbs adorned with pearly dews,
The meadows interlaced with silver floods,
The frizzled thickets, and the taller woods.
The whispering zephyrs my more silent tongue
Correct, and Philomela chirps a song.
Is there a bird of all the blooming year,
20 That has not sung his early matins here?
That has not sipped the fairy matron's spring,
Or hovered o'er her cave with wishful wing?
An awful fabric built by nature's hand
Does raise our wonder, our respect command.
Three lucky trees to wilder art unknown
Seem on the front a growing triple crown.
At first the arched room is high and wide,
The naked walls with mossy hangings hid;
The ceiling sandy: as you forward press
30 The roof is still declining into less;
Despair to reach the end – a little arch
Narrow and low forbids your utmost search.
So to her lover the chaste, beauteous lass
Without a blush vouchsafes to show her face,
Her neck of ivory, her snowy breast,
These shown, she modestly conceals the rest.
A shallow brook, that restless underground

Struggled with earth, here a moist passage found.
Down through a stony vein the waters roll
40   O'erflowing the capacious iron bowl:
Oh! happy bowl, that gladness can infuse,
And yet was never stained with heady juice.
Here thirsty souls carouse with innocence,
Nor owe their pleasure to their loss of sense.
Here a smooth floor had many a figure shown,
Had virgin footsteps made impression,
That soft and swift Camilla-like advance,
While even movements seem to fly a dance.
No quilted couch, the sick man's daily bed,
50   No seats to lull asleep diseases made,
Are seen; but such as healthy persons please
Of wood or stone, such as the wearied ease.
O might I still enjoy this peaceful gloom!
The truest entrance to Elysium.
Who would to the Cumaean den repair?
A better Sibyl, wiser power is here.
Methinks I see him from his palace come,
And with his presence grace the baleful room:
Consider, Ludwell, what to him you owe,
60   Who does for you the noisy court forego;
Nay he a rich and gaudy silence leaves,
You share the honour, sweet Moor Park receives.
You with your wrinkles admiration move,
That with its beauty better merits love.
Here's careless Nature in her ancient dress,
There's she more modish, and consults the glass.
Here she's an old, but yet a pleasant dame;
There she'll a fair, not painted virgin seem.
Here the rich metal hath through no fire passed,
70   There, though refined, by no alloy debased.
Thus nature is preserved in every part,
Sometimes adorned, but ne'er debauched by art.
When scattered locks, that dangle on the brow,
Into more decent hairy circles grow,
After inquiry made, though no man love
The curling iron, all the comb approve.

Occasioned by Sir William Temple's Late Illness and Recovery

Strange to conceive, how the same objects strike
At distant hours the mind with forms so like!
Whether in time, deduction's broken chain
Meets, and salutes her sister link again;
Or hunted fancy, by a circling flight,
Comes back with joy to his own seat at night;
Or whether dead imagination's ghost
Oft hovers where alive it haunted most;
Or if thought's rolling globe her circle run,
10   Turns up old objects to the soul her sun;
Or loves the muse to walk with conscious pride
O'er the glad scene whence first she rose a bride.

   Be what it will; late near yon whispering stream,
Where her own Temple was her darling theme;
There first the visionary sound was heard,
When to poetic view the muse appeared.
Such seemed her eyes, as when an evening ray
Gives glad farewell to a tempestuous day;
Weak is the beam to dry up nature's tears,
20   Still every tree the pendent sorrow wears;
Such are the smiles where drops of crystal show,
Approaching joy at strife with parting woe.

   As when to scare the ungrateful or the proud
Tempests long frown, and thunder threatens loud,
Till the blessed sun to give kind dawn of grace
Darts weeping beams across heaven's watery face;
When soon the peaceful bow unstringed is shown,
A sign God's dart is shot, and wrath o'erblown;
Such to unhallowed sight the muse divine
30   Might seem, when first she raised her eyes to mine.

   'What mortal change does in thy face appear,
Lost youth,' she cried, 'since first I met thee here!
With how undecent clouds are overcast
Thy looks, when every cause of grief is past!

Unworthy the glad tidings which I bring,
Listen while the muse thus teaches thee to sing.

As parent earth, burst by imprisoned winds,
Scatters strange agues o'er men's sickly minds,
And shakes the atheist's knees; such ghastly fear
40   Late I beheld on every face appear;
Mild Dorothea, peaceful, wise, and great,
Trembling beheld the doubtful hand of fate;
Mild Dorothea, whom we both have long
Not dared to injure with our lowly song;
Sprung from a better world, and chosen then
The best companion for the best of men:
As some fair pile, yet spared by zeal and rage,
Lives pious witness of a better age;
So men may see what once was womankind,
50   In the fair shrine of Dorothea's mind.

You that would grief describe, come here and trace
Its watery footsteps in Dorinda's face;
Grief from Dorinda's face does ne'er depart
Further than its own palace in her heart:
Ah, since our fears are fled, this insolent expel,
At least confine the tyrant to his cell.
And if so black the cloud, that heaven's bright queen
Shrouds her still beams; how should the stars be seen?
Thus, when Dorinda wept, joy every face forsook,
60   And grief hung sables on each menial look;
The humble tribe mourned for the quickening soul,
That furnished spirit and motion through the whole;
So would earth's face turn pale, and life decay,
Should heaven suspend to act but for a day;
So nature's crazed convulsions make us dread
That time is sick, or the world's mind is dead. –
Take, youth, these thoughts, large matter to employ
The fancy furnished by returning joy;
And to mistaken men these truths rehearse,
70   Who dare revile the integrity of verse:
Ah favourite youth, how happy is thy lot! –
But I'm deceived, or thou regard'st me not;

Speak, for I wait thy answer, and expect
Thy just submission for this bold neglect.'

Unknown the forms we the high priesthood use
At the divine appearance of the muse,
Which to divulge might shake profane belief,
And tell the irreligion of my grief;
Grief that excused the tribute of my knees,
80   And shaped my passion in such words as these.

Malignant goddess! bane to my repose,
Thou universal cause of all my woes;
Say, whence it comes that thou art grown of late
A poor amusement for my scorn and hate;
The malice thou inspirest I never fail
On thee to wreak the tribute when I rail;
Fools' commonplace thou art, their weak ensconcing fort,
The appeal of dullness in the last resort:
Heaven with a parent's eye regarding earth,
90   Deals out to man the planet of his birth;
But sees thy meteor blaze about me shine,
And, passing o'er, mistakes thee still for mine:
Ah, should I tell a secret yet unknown,
That thou ne'er hadst a being of thy own,
But a wild form dependent on the brain,
Scattering loose features o'er the optic vein;
Troubling the crystal fountain of the sight,
Which darts on poets' eyes a trembling light;
Kindled while reason sleeps, but quickly flies,
100   Like antic shapes in dreams, from waking eyes:
In sum, a glittering voice, a painted name,
A walking vapour, like thy sister Fame.
But if thou be'st what thy mad votaries prate,
A female power, loose-governed thoughts create;
Why near the dregs of youth perversely wilt thou stay,
So highly courted by the brisk and gay?
Wert thou right woman, thou shouldst scorn to look
On an abandoned wretch by hopes forsook;
Forsook by hopes, ill fortune's last relief,
110   Assigned for life to unremitting grief;
For, let heaven's wrath enlarge these weary days,
If hope e'er dawns the smallest of its rays,
Time o'er the happy takes so swift a flight,

And treads so soft, so easy, and so light,
That we the wretched, creeping far behind,
Can scarce the impression of his footsteps find;
Smooth as that airy nymph so subtly borne
With inoffensive feet o'er standing corn;
Which bowed by evening breeze with bending stalks,
120 Salutes the weary traveller as he walks;
But o'er the afflicted with a heavy pace
Sweeps the broad scythe, and tramples on his face.
Down falls the summer's pride, and sadly shows
Nature's bare visage furrowed as he mows;
See muse, what havoc in these looks appear,
These are the tyrant's trophies of a year;
Since hope his last and greatest foe is fled,
Despair and he lodge ever in its stead;
March o'er the ruined plain with motion slow,
130 Still scattering desolation where they go.
To thee I owe that fatal bent of mind,
Still to unhappy restless thoughts inclined;
To thee, what oft I vainly strive to hide,
That scorn of fools, by fools mistook for pride;
From thee whatever virtue takes its rise,
Grows a misfortune, or becomes a vice;
Such were thy rules to be poetically great,
'Stoop not to interest, flattery, or deceit;
Nor with hired thoughts be thy devotion paid;
140 Learn to disdain their mercenary aid;
Be this thy sure defence, thy brazen wall,
Know no base action, at no guilt turn pale;
And since unhappy distance thus denies
To expose thy soul, clad in this poor disguise;
Since thy few ill-presented graces seem
To breed contempt where thou hast hoped esteem.' –

Madness like this no fancy ever seized,
Still to be cheated, never to be pleased;
Since one false beam of joy in sickly minds
150 Is all the poor content delusion finds. –
There thy enchantment broke, and from this hour
I here renounce thy visionary power;
And since thy essence on my breath depends,
Thus with a puff the whole delusion ends.

On the Burning of Whitehall in 1698

This pile was raised by Wolsey's impious hands,
Built with the church's patrimonial lands.
Here bloody Henry kept his cruel court,
Hence sprung the martyrdoms of every sort.
Weak Edward here, and Mary the bigot,
Did both their holy innovations plot.
A fiercer Tudor filled the churchman's seat
In all her father's attributes complete.
Dudley's lewd life doth the white mansion stain
10 And a slain guest obscures a glorious reign.
Then northern James dishonoured every room
With filth and palliardism brought from home.
Next the French consort dignified the stews,
Employing males to their first proper use.
A bold usurper next did domineer,
Whirled hence by the angry demons of the air.
When sauntering Charles returned, a fulsome crew
Of parasites, buffoons, he with him drew;
Nay worse than these fill the polluted hall,
20 Bawds, pimps and pandars the detested squall
Of riots, fancied rapes, the devil and all.
This pious prince here too did breathe his last,
His certain death on different persons cast.
His wise successor brought a motley throng,
Despising right, strongly protecting wrong,
To these assistant herds of preaching cowls
And troops of noisy senseless fools.
Guerdon for this: he heard the dread command,
'Embark and leave your native land –'
30 He gone, the rank infection still remains,
Which to repel requires eternal pains.
No force to cleanse it can a river draw,
Nor Hercules could do it, nor great Nassau.
Most greedy financiers, and lavish too,
Swarm in, in spite of all that prince could do,
Projectors, peculates the palace hold,
Patriots exchanging liberty for gold,
Monsters unknown to this blessed land of old.
Heaven takes the cure in hand, celestial ire
40 Applies the oft-tried remedy of fire;
The purging flames were better far employed,

Than when old Sodom was, or Troynovant destroyed.
The nest obscene of every pampered vice,
Sinks down of this infernal paradise,
Down come the lofty roofs, the cedar burns,
The blended metal to a torrent turns.
The carvings crackle and the marbles rive,
The paintings shrink, vainly the Henrys strive,
Propped by great Holbein's pencil, down they fall,
50   The fiery deluge sweeps and swallows all.

But mark how providence with watchful care,
Did Inigo's famed building spare,
That theatre produced an action truly great,
On which eternal acclamations wait,
Of kings deposed, most faithful annals tell,
And slaughtered monarchs would a volume swell.
Our happy chronicle can show alone
On this day tyrants executed – one.

Verses Wrote in a Lady's Ivory Table-Book

Peruse my leaves through every part,
And think thou seest my owner's heart;
Scrawled o'er with trifles thus; and quite
As hard, as senseless, and as light:
Exposed to every coxcomb's eyes,
But hid with caution from the wise.
Here may you read, 'Dear charming saint',
Beneath 'A new receipt for paint.'
Here, in beau-spelling, 'tru tel death.'
10   There, in her own, 'far an el breath.'
Here, 'lovely nymph pronounce my doom.'
There, 'a safe way to use perfume.'
Here, a page filled with billet-doux;
On t'other side, 'laid out for shoes.
(Madam, I die without your Grace.)
Item, for half a yard of lace.'
Who that had wit would place it here,
For every peeping fop to jeer?
In power of spittle and a clout,
20   Whene'er he please, to blot it out;
And then to heighten the disgrace,
Clap his own nonsense in the place.

Whoe'er expects to hold his part
In such a book, and such a heart,
If he be wealthy, and a fool,
Is in all points the fittest tool;
Of whom it may be justly said,
He's a *gold* pencil tipped with *lead*.

The Problem

Did ever problem thus perplex,
Or more employ the female sex?
So sweet a passion, who would think,
Jove ever formed to make a stink?
The ladies vow and swear they'll try,
Whether it be a truth or lie.

   Love's fire, it seems, like inward heat,
Works in my Lord by stool and sweat:
Which brings a stink from every pore,
10 And from behind, and from before:
Yet, what is wonderful to tell it,
None but the favourite nymph can smell it.
But now to solve the natural cause
By sober philosophic laws:
Whether all passions when in férment,
Work out, as anger does in vermin?
So, when a weasel you torment,
You find his passion by his scent.
We read of kings, who in a fright,
20 Though on a throne, would fall to shite.
Beside all this deep scholars know,
That the mainstring of Cupid's bow,
Once on a time, was an ass's gut,
Now to a nobler office put,
By favour or desert preferred
From giving passage to a turd.
But still, though fixed among the stars,
Doth sympathize with human arse.
Thus, when you feel an hard-bound breech,
30 Conclude Love's bow-string at full stretch,
Till the kind looseness comes, and then
Conclude the bow relaxed again.

And now the ladies all are bent
To try the great experiment;
Ambitious of a regent's heart,
Spread all their charms to catch a fart!
Watching the first unsavoury wind,
Some ply before and some behind.
My Lord, on fire amidst the dames,
40 Farts like a laurel in the flames.
The fair approach the speaking part,
To try the back way to his heart.
For, as when we a gun discharge,
Although the bore be ne'er so large,
Before the flame from muzzle burst,
Just at the breech it flashes first:
So from my Lord his passion broke,
He farted first, and then he spoke.

The ladies vanish in the smother,
50 To cónfer notes with one another:
And now they all agree to name
Whom each one thought the happy dame.
Quoth Neal, 'Whate'er the rest may think,
I'm sure 'twas I that smelt the stink.'
'You smelt the stink! By God, you lie,'
Quoth Ross, 'for I'll be sworn 'twas I.'
'Ladies,' quoth Levens, 'pray forbear,
Let's not fall out, we all had share;
And, by the most I can discover,
60 My Lord's an universal lover.'

The Discovery

When wise Lord Berkeley first came here,
    We Irish folks expected wonders,
Nor thought to find so great a peer
    E'er a week passed committing blunders:

Till on a day cut out by fate,
    When folks came thick to make their court,
Out slipped a mystery of state
    To give the town and country sport.

Now enter Bushe with new state-airs,
10   His Lordship's premier ministre,
And who in all profound affairs
    Is held as needful as his clyster.

With head reclining on his shoulder,
    He deals and hears mysterious chat,
While every ignorant beholder
    Asks of his neighbour, 'Who is that?'

With this he put up to my Lord,
    The courtiers kept their distance due,
He twitched his sleeve, and stole a word,
20   Then to a corner both withdrew.

Imagine now my lord and Bushe
    Whispering in junto most profound,
Like good King Phiz and good King Ush,
    While all the rest stood gaping round.

At length, a spark not too well bred,
    Of forward face, and ear acute,
Advanced on tiptoe, leaned his head
    To overhear the grand dispute.

To learn what northern kings design,
30   Or from Whitehall some new express,
Papists disarmed, or fall of coin,
    For sure (thought he) it can't be less.

'My Lord', said Bushe, 'a friend and I
    Disguised in two old threadbare coats
Ere morning's dawn stole out to spy
    How markets went for hay and oats.'

With that he draws two handfuls out,
    The one was oats, the other hay,
Puts this to's Excellency's snout,
40   And begs he would the other weigh.

My Lord seems pleased, but still directs
    By all means to bring down the rates,
Then with a congee circumflex
    Bushe, smiling round on all, retreats.

Our listener stood a while confused,
  But gathering spirits wisely ran for't,
Enraged to see the world abused
  By two such whispering Kings of Brentford.

Mrs Harris's Petition

To their Excellencies the Lords Justices of Ireland.
The humble petition of Frances Harris,
Who must starve, and die a maid if it miscarries.

Humbly showeth

That I went to warm myself in Lady Betty's chamber, because I
    was cold,
And I had in a purse seven pound, four shillings and sixpence
    (besides farthings) in money and gold;
So because I had been buying things for my Lady last night,
I was resolved to tell my money, to see if it was right.
Now you must know, because my trunk has a very bad lock,
Therefore all the money I have (which, God knows, is a very small
    stock)
I keep in my pocket tied about my middle, next my smock.
So, when I went to put up my purse, as God would have it, my
    smock was unripped;
And, instead of putting it into my pocket, down it slipped:
10 Then the bell rung, and I went down to put my Lady to bed;
And, God knows, I thought my money was as safe as my
    maidenhead.
So, when I came up again, I found my pocket feel very light,
But when I searched, and missed my purse, Lord! I thought I
    should have sunk outright:
Lord! Madam, says Mary, how d'ye do? Indeed, said I, never
    worse;
But pray, Mary, can you tell what I have done with my purse?
Lord help me, said Mary, I never stirred out of this place!
Nay, said I, I had it in Lady Betty's chamber, that's a plain case.
So Mary got me to bed, and covered me up warm,
However, she stole away my garters, that I might do myself no
    harm.

20   So I tumbled and tossed all night, as you may very well think;
But hardly ever set my eyes together, or slept a wink.
So I was a-dreamed, methought, that we went and searched the
folks round;
And in a corner of Mrs Duke's box, tied in a rag, the money was
found.
So next morning we told Whittle, and he fell a-swearing;
Then my Dame Wadgar came, and she, you know, is thick of
hearing:
Dame, said I, as loud as I could bawl, do you know what a loss I
have had?
Nay, said she, my Lord Collway's folks are all very sad,
For my Lord Dromedary comes a Tuesday without fail;
Pugh, said I, but that's not the business that I ail.

30   Says Cary, says he, I have been a servant this five and twenty
years, come spring,
And in all the places I lived, I never heard of such a thing.
Yes, says the steward, I remember when I was at my Lady
Shrewsbury's,
Such a thing as this happened, just about the time of gooseberries.
So I went to the party suspected, and I found her full of grief;
(Now you must know, of all things in the world, I hate a thief.)
However, I was resolved to bring the discourse slily about,
Mrs Dukes, said I, here's an ugly accident has happened out;
'Tis not that I value the money three skips of a louse;
But the thing I stand upon, is the credit of the house;

40   'Tis true, seven pound, four shillings, and six pence, makes a great
hole in my wages;
Besides, as they say, service is no inheritance in these ages.
Now, Mrs Dukes, you know, and everybody understands,
That though 'tis hard to judge, yet money can't go without hands.
The Devil take me, said she (blessing herself), if ever I saw't!
So she roared like a Bedlam, as though I had called her all to
naught;
So you know, what could I say to her any more:
I e'en left her, and came away as wise as I was before.
Well: but then they would have had me gone to the cunning-man;
No, said I, 'tis the same thing, the chaplain will be here anon.

50   So the chaplain came in. Now the servants say he is my sweetheart,
Because he's always in my chamber, and I always take his part;
So, as the Devil would have it, before I was aware, out I
blundered,

Parson, said I, can you cast a nativity, when a body's plundered?
(Now you must know, he hates to be called 'Parson' like the devil.)
Truly, says he, Mrs Nab, it might become you to be more civil:
If your money be gone, as a learned divine says, d'ye see,
You are no text for my handling, so take that from me;
I was never taken for a conjuror before, I'd have you to know.
Lord, said I, don't be angry, I am sure I never thought you so;
60   You know, I honour the cloth, I design to be a parson's wife,
I never took one in your coat for a conjuror in all my life.
With that, he twisted his girdle at me like a rope, as who should
     say,
Now you may go hang yourself for me, and so went away.
Well; I thought I should have swooned: Lord, said I, what shall I
     do?
I have lost my money; and I shall lose my true-love too.
So, my Lord called me; Harry, said my Lord, don't cry,
I'll give something towards thy loss; and says my Lady, so will I.
Oh but, said I, what if after all, the chaplain won't come to?
For that, he said (an't please your Excellencies) I must petition
     you.

70   The premises tenderly considered, I desire your Excellencies'
     protection,
And that I may have a share in next Sunday's collection:
And over and above, that I may have your Excellencies' letter,
With an order for the chaplain aforesaid; or instead of him, a
     better.
And then your poor petitioner, both night and day,
Or the chaplain (for 'tis his trade) as in duty bound, shall ever
     pray.

A Ballad on the Game of Traffic

My Lord to find out who must deal
   Delivers cards about,
But the first knave does seldom fail
   To find the Doctor out.

But then his Honour cried, 'Gadzooks!'
   And seemed to knit his brow;
For on a knave he never looks
   But h'thinks upon Jack Howe.

My Lady though she is no player
10   Some bungling partner takes,
And wedged in corner of a chair
    Takes snuff, and holds the stakes.

Dame Floyd looks out in grave suspense
    For pair-royals and sequents;
But wisely cautious of her pence,
    The castle seldom frequents.

Quoth Herries, fairly putting cases,
    'I'd won it on my word,
If I had but a pair of aces,
20   And could pick up a third.'

But Weston has a new-cast gown
    On Sundays to be fine in,
And if she can but win a crown,
    'Twill just new dye the lining.

With these is Parson Swift,
    Not knowing how to spend his time,
Does make a wretched shift,
    To deafen 'em with puns and rhyme.

A Ballad to the Tune of the Cutpurse

I

Once on a time, as old stories rehearse,
    A friar would needs show his talent in Latin;
But was sorely put to't in the midst of a verse,
    Because he could find no word to come pat in.
        Then all in the place
        He left a void space,
And so went to bed in a desperate case.
When behold the next morning, a wonderful riddle,
He found it was strangely filled up in the middle.

10 CHO[RUS]
Let censuring critics then think what they list on't,
Who would not write verses with such an assistant.

II

This put me the friar into an amazement;
  For he wisely considered it must be a sprite,
That came through the keyhole, or in at the casement,
  And it needs must be one that could both read and write:
      Yet he did not know
      If it were friend or foe,
  Or whether it came from above or below.
How'er, it was civil in angel or elf,
20 For he ne'er could have filled it so well of himself.

  CHO.   Let censuring *etc.*

III

Even so Master Doctor had puzzled his brains
  In making a ballad, but was at a stand,
He had mixed little wit with a great deal of pains;
  When he found a new help from invisible hand.
      Then good Dr Swift
      Pay thanks for the gift,
  For you freely must own you were at a dead lift;
And though some malicious young spirit did do't,
30 You may know by the *hand*, it had no cloven *foot*.

  CHO.   Let censuring *etc.*

The Description of a Salamander

OUT OF PLINY'S NAT. HIST. LIB.10 C.67 AND LIB.29 C.4

As mastiff dogs in modern phrase are
Called Pompey, Scipio, and Caesar;
As pies and daws are often styled
With Christian nicknames like a child;
As we say '*Monsieur*' to an ape
Without offence to human shape:
So men have got from bird and brute
Names that would best their natures suit:
The lion, eagle, fox and boar
10 Were heroes' titles heretofore,
Bestowed as hieroglyphics fit

To show their valour, strength or wit.
For what is understood by fame
Besides the getting of a name?
But e'er since men invented guns,
A different way their fancy runs:
To paint a hero, we inquire
For something that will conquer fire.
Would you describe Turenne or Trump,
20   Think of a bucket or a pump.
Are these too low? Then find out grander,
Call my Lord Cutts a salamander.
'Tis well: but since we live among
Detractors with an evil tongue,
Who may object against the term,
Pliny shall prove what we affirm:
Pliny shall prove, and we'll apply,
And I'll be judged by standers-by.

First then, our author has defined
30   This reptile, of the serpent kind,
With gaudy coat, and shining train,
But loathsome spots his body stain:
Out from some hole obscure he flies
When rains descend, and tempests rise,
Till the sun clears the air; and then
Crawls back, neglected, to his den.

So when the war has raised a storm
I've seen a snake in human form,
All stained with infamy and vice,
40   Leap from the dunghill in a trice;
Burnish and make a gaudy show,
Become a general, peer and beau,
Till peace hath made the sky serene,
Then shrink into its hole again.

All this we grant – why, then look yonder,
Sure that must be a salamander!

Farther we are by Pliny told,
This serpent is extremely cold;
So cold, that put it in the fire,
50   'Twill make the very flames expire:

Besides, it spews a filthy froth,
(Whether through rage, or lust, or both)
Of matter purulent and white,
Which happening on the skin to light,
And there corrupting to a wound,
Spreads leprosy and baldness round.

So have I seen a battered beau
By age and claps grown cold as snow,
Whose breath or touch, where'er he came,
60   Blew out love's torch, or chilled the flame:
And should some nymph who ne'er was cruel,
Like Carleton cheap, or famed Du Ruel,
Receive the filth which he ejects;
She soon would find the same effects,
Her tainted carcass to pursue,
As from the salamander's spew:
A dismal shedding of her locks
And, if no leprosy, a pox.

Then I'll appeal to each bystander,
70   If this be not a salamander?

The History of Vanbrug's House

When Mother Clud had rose from play,
And called to take the cards away;
Van saw, but seemed not to regard,
How Miss picked every painted card;
And busy both with hand and eye,
Soon reared a house two storeys high;
Van's genius, without thought or lecture,
Is hugely turned to architecture:
He saw the edifice, and smiled,
10   Vowed it was pretty for a child:
It was so perfect in its kind,
He kept the model in his mind.

But when he found the boys at play,
And saw them dabbling in the clay;
He stood behind a stall to lurk,
And mark the progress of their work:

With true delight observed 'em all
Raking up mud to build a wall;
The plan he much admired, and took
20   The model in his table-book;
Thought himself now exactly skilled,
And so resolved a house to build;
A real house, with rooms and stairs,
Five times at least as big as theirs,
Taller than Miss's by two yards;
Not a sham thing of clay or cards.
And so he did; for in a while
He built up such a monstrous pile,
That no two chairmen could be found
30   Able to lift it from the ground;
Still at Whitehall it stands in view,
Just in the place where it first grew:
There all the little schoolboys run
Envying to see themselves outdone.

From such deep rudiments as these
Van is become by due degrees
For building famed, and justly reckoned
At court, Vitruvius the second.
No wonder, since wise authors show,
40   That best foundations must be low.
And now the Duke has wisely taken him
To be his architect at Blenheim.

But raillery for once apart,
If this rule holds in every art,
Or if his Grace were no more skilled in
The art of battering walls than building;
We might expect to see next year
A mousetrap-man chief engineer.

Verses Said to be Written on the Union

The Queen has lately lost a part
Of her entirely English heart,
For want of which by way of botch,
She pieced it up again with Scotch.

Blessed revolution, which creates
Divided hearts, united states.
See how the double nation lies;
Like a rich coat with skirts of frieze:
As if a man in making posies
10 Should bundle thistles up with roses.
Whoever yet a union saw
Of kingdoms, without faith or law.
Henceforward let no statesman dare,
A kingdom to a ship compare;
Lest he should call our commonweal,
A vessel with a double keel:
Which just like ours, new rigged and manned,
And got about a league from land,
By change of wind to leeward side
20 The pilot knew not how to guide.
So tossing faction will o'erwhelm
Our crazy double-bottomed realm.

An Elegy on the Supposed Death of Mr Partridge, the Almanac Maker

Well, 'tis as Bickerstaff had guessed,
Though we all took it for a jest:
Partridge is dead, nay more, he died
E'er he could prove the good squire lied.
Strange, an astrologer should die,
Without one wonder in the sky;
Not one of all his crony stars,
To pay their duty at his hearse?
No meteor, no eclipse appeared?
10 No comet with a flaming beard?
The sun has rose, and gone to bed,
Just as if Partridge were not dead:
Nor hid himself behind the moon,
To make a dreadful night at noon:
He at fit periods walks through Aries,
Howe'er our earthly motion varies,
And twice a year he'll cut the Equator,
As if there had been no such matter.

Some wits have wondered what analogy
20   There is 'twixt cobbling and astrology;
How Partridge made his optics rise,
From a shoe-sole to reach the skies.
A list the cobblers' temples ties,
To keep the hair out of their eyes;
From whence 'tis plain the diadem
That princes wear, derives from them;
And therefore crowns are nowadays
Adorned with golden stars and rays;
Which plainly shows the near alliance
30   Betwixt cobbling and the planets' science.

Besides, that slow-paced sign Boötes,
As 'tis miscalled, we know not who 'tis;
But Partridge ended all disputes,
He knew his trade, and called it boots.

The hornéd moon, which heretofore
Upon their shoes the Romans wore,
Whose wideness kept their toes from corns,
And whence we claim our shoeing-horns,
Shows how the art of cobbling bears
40   A near resemblance to the spheres.

A scrap of parchment hung by geometry
(A great refinement in barometry)
Can like the stars foretell the weather;
And what is parchment else but leather?
Which an astrologer might use,
Either for almanacs or shoes.

Thus Partridge, by his wit and parts,
At once did practise both these arts:
And as the boding owl, or rather
50   The bat, because her wings are leather,
Steals from her private cell by night,
And flies about the candle-light;
So learned Partridge could as well
Creep in the dark from leathern cell,
And in his fancy fly as far,
To peep upon a twinkling star.

Besides, he could confound the spheres,
And set the planets by the ears:
To show his skill, he Mars would join
60 To Venus in aspéct malign;
Then call in Mercury for aid,
And cure the wounds that Venus made.

Great scholars have in Lucian read,
When Philip King of Greece was dead,
His soul and spirit did divide,
And each part took a different side;
One rose a star, the other fell
Beneath, and mended shoes in hell.

Thus Partridge still shines in each art,
70 The cobbling and stargazing part;
And is installed as good a star
As any of the Caesars are.

Triumphant star! Some pity show
On cobblers militant below,
Whom roguish boys in stormy nights
Torment, by pissing out their lights;
Or through a chink convey their smoke,
Enclosed artificers to choke.

Thou, high exalted in thy sphere,
80 Mayst follow still thy calling there.
To thee the Bull will lend his hide,
By Phoebus newly tanned and dried.
For thee they Argo's hulk will tax,
And scrape her pitchy sides for wax.
Then Ariadne kindly lends
Her braided hair to make thee ends.
The point of Sagittarius' dart,
Turns to an awl, by heavenly art:
And Vulcan, wheedled by his wife,
90 Will forge for thee a paring-knife.
For want of room by Virgo's side,
She'll strain a point, and sit astride,
To take thee kindly in between,
And then the signs will be thirteen.

THE EPITAPH

Here, five foot deep, lies on his back
A cobbler, star-monger, and quack;
Who to the stars in pure good will,
Does to his best look upward still.
Weep all you customers that use
His pills, his almanacs, or shoes:
And you that did your fortunes seek,
Step to his grave but once a week,
This earth, which bears his body's print,
You'll find has so much virtue in't,
That I durst pawn my ears, 'twill tell
Whate'er concerns you full as well,
In physic, stolen goods, or love,
As he himself could, when above.

100

Vanbrug's House

BUILT FROM THE RUINS OF WHITEHALL THAT WAS BURNT

In times of old, when time was young,
And poets their own verses sung,
A verse could draw a stone or beam,
That now would overload a team;
Lead 'em a dance of many a mile,
Then rear 'em to a goodly pile.
Each number had its different power;
Heroic strains could build a tower;
Sonnets, or elegies to Chloris,
Might raise a house about two storeys;
A lyric ode would slate; a catch
Would tile; an epigram would thatch.

10

But, to their own, or landlord's cost,
Now poets feel this art is lost;
Not one of all our tuneful throng
Can raise a lodging for a song.
For Jove considered well the case;
Observed they grew a numerous race,
And should they build as fast as write,
'Twould ruin undertakers quite.

20

This evil, therefore to prevent,
He wisely changed their element:
On earth, the god of wealth was made
Sole patron of the building trade,
Leaving the wits the spacious air,
With licence to build castles there:
And 'tis conceived their old pretence
To lodge in garrets, comes from thence.

Premising thus in modern way
30 The better half we have to say;
Sing muse, the house of poet Van
In higher strains then we began.

Van (for 'tis fit the reader know it)
Is both a herald and a poet;
No wonder then, if nicely skilled
In both capacities to build.
As herald, he can in a day
Repair a house gone to decay;
Or by achievement, arms, device,
40 Erect a new one in a trice.
And as a poet, he has skill
To build in speculation still.
'Great Jove!' he cried, 'the art restore
To build by verse as heretofore;
And make my muse the architect;
What palaces shall we erect!
No longer shall forsaken Thames
Lament his old Whitehall in flames:
A pile shall from its ashes rise
50 Fit to invade, or prop the skies.'

Jove smiled, and like a gentle god,
Consenting with his usual nod,
Told Van he knew his talent best,
And left the choice to his own breast.
So Van resolved to write a farce;
But well perceiving wit was scarce,
With cunning that defect supplies;
Takes a French play as lawful prize;
Steals thence his plot, and every joke,
60 Not once suspecting Jove would smoke;

And (like a wag) sat down to write,
Would whisper to himself, 'A bite.'
Then from this motley mingled style
Proceeded to erect his pile.
So men of old, to gain renown, did
Build Babel with their tongues confounded.
Jove saw the cheat, but thought it best
To turn the matter to a jest:
Down from Olympus top he slides,
70   Laughing as if he'd burst his sides:
'Ay,' thought the god, 'are these your tricks?
Why then, old plays deserve old bricks,
And since you're sparing of your stuff,
Your building shall be small enough.'
He spake, and grudging lent his aid;
The experienced bricks that knew their trade
(As being bricks at second hand)
Now move, and now in order stand.

The building, as the poet writ,
80   Rose in proportion to his wit:
And first the prologue built a wall
So wide as to encompass all.
The scene, a wood, produced no more
Than a few scrubby trees before.
The plot as yet lay deep, and so
A cellar next was dug below:
But this a work so hard was found,
Two acts it cost him underground.
Two other acts we may presume
90   Were spent in building each a room:
Thus far advanced, he made a shift
To raise a roof with act the fift.
The epilogue behind, did frame
A place not decent here to name.

Now poets from all quarters ran
To see the house of brother Van:
Looked high and low, walked often round,
But no such house was to be found:
One asks the waterman hard by,
100 'Where may the poet's palace lie?'

Another, of the Thames inquires,
If he has seen its gilded spires?
At length they in the rubbish spy
A thing resembling a goose-pie:
Thither in haste the poets throng,
And gaze in silent wonder long;
Till one in raptures thus began
To praise the pile, and builder Van.

'Thrice happy poet, who may trail
110 Thy house about thee, like a snail;
Or harnessed to a nag, at ease,
Take journeys in it like a chaise;
Or in a boat, whene'er thou wilt
Canst make it serve thee for a tilt.
Capacious house! 'tis owned by all,
Thou'rt well contrived, though thou art small;
For every wit in Britain's isle
May lodge within thy spacious pile.
Like Bacchus thou, as poets feign,
120 Thy mother burnt, art born again;
Born like a Phoenix from the flame,
But neither bulk nor shape the same:
As animals of largest size
Corrupt to maggots, worms and flies.
A type of modern wit and style,
The rubbish of an ancient pile.
So chemists boast, they have a power
From the dead ashes of a flower
Some faint resemblance to produce;
130 But not the virtue, taste, or juice.
So modern rhymers wisely blast
The poetry of ages past,
Which after they have overthrown,
They from its ruins build their own.'

On Mrs Biddy Floyd

When Cupid did his grandsire Jove entreat,
To form some beauty by a new receipt;
Jove sent and found far in a country scene,

Truth, innocence, good nature, look serene:
From which ingredients, first the dexterous boy
Picked the demure, the awkward, and the coy:
The Graces from the court did next provide
Breeding, and wit, and air, and decent pride.
These Venus cleansed from every spurious grain
10 Of nice, coquette, affected, pert and vain.
Jove mixed up all, and his best clay employed;
Then called the happy composition Floyd.

Apollo Outwitted

TO THE HONOURABLE MRS FINCH (SINCE COUNTESS
OF WINCHILSEA), UNDER THE NAME OF ARDELIA

Phoebus now shortening every shade,
    Up to the Northern Tropic came,
And thence beheld a lovely maid
    Attending on a royal dame.

The god laid down his feeble rays,
    Then lighted from his glittering coach;
But fenced his head with his own bays
    Before he durst the nymph approach.

Under those sacred leaves, secure
10   From common lightning of the skies,
He fondly thought he might endure
    The flashes of Ardelia's eyes.

The nymph, who oft had read in books,
    Of that bright god whom bards invoke,
Soon knew Apollo by his looks,
    And guessed his business ere he spoke.

He in the old celestial cant,
    Confessed his flame, and swore by Styx,
Whate'er she would desire, to grant;
20   But wise Ardelia knew his tricks.

Ovid had warned her to beware
    Of strolling gods, whose usual trade is,

Under pretence of taking air,
    To pick up sublunary ladies.

Howe'er, she gave no flat denial,
    As having malice in her heart;
And was resolved upon a trial,
    To cheat the god in his own art.

'Hear my request,' the virgin said,
30   'Let which I please of all the nine
Attend whene'er I want their aid,
    Obey my call, and only mine.'

By vow obliged, by passion led,
    The god could not refuse her prayer;
He waved his wreath thrice o'er her head,
    Thrice muttered something to the air.

And now he thought to seize his due,
    But she the charm already tried,
Thalia heard the call and flew
40   To wait at bright Ardelia's side.

On sight of this celestial prude,
    Apollo thought it vain to stay,
Nor in her presence durst be rude,
    But made his leg and went away.

He hoped to find some lucky hour,
    When on their queen the muses wait;
But Pallas owns Ardelia's power,
    For vows divine are kept by fate.

Then full of rage Apollo spoke,
50   'Deceitful nymph, I see thy art;
And though I can't my gift revoke,
    I'll disappoint its nobler part.

'Let stubborn pride possess thee long,
    And be thou negligent of fame,
With every muse to grace thy song,
    Mayst thou despise a poet's name.

'Of modest poets thou be first,
    To silent shades repeat thy verse,

Till Fame and Echo almost burst,
60   Yet hardly dare one line rehearse.

'And last, my vengeance to complete,
    May you descend to take renown,
Prevailed on by the thing you hate,
    A Whig, and one that wears a gown.'

Baucis and Philemon

IMITATED FROM THE EIGHTH BOOK OF OVID

In ancient times, as story tells,
The saints would often leave their cells,
And stroll about, but hide their quality,
To try good people's hospitality.

    It happened on a winter night,
(As authors of the legend write)
Two brother hermits, saints by trade,
Taking their tour in masquerade,
Disguised in tattered habits, went
10 To a small village down in Kent;
Where, in the stroller's canting strain,
They begged from door to door in vain;
Tried every tone might pity win,
But not a soul would let them in.

    Our wandering saints in woeful state,
Treated at this ungodly rate,
Having through all the village passed,
To a small cottage came at last;
Where dwelt a good old honest yeoman,
20 Called in the neighbourhood, Philemon.
Who kindly did the saints invite
In his poor hut to pass the night;
And then the hospitable sire
Bid Goody Baucis mend the fire;
While he from out the chimney took
A flitch of bacon off the hook;
And freely from the fattest side,
Cut out large slices to be fried:

Then stepped aside to fetch 'em drink,
30   Filled a large jug up to the brink;
And saw it fairly twice go round;
Yet (what was wonderful) they found
'Twas still replenished to the top,
As if they ne'er had touched a drop.
The good old couple was amazed,
And often on each other gazed:
For both were frighted to the heart,
And just began to cry, 'What art!'
Then softly turned aside to view,
40   Whether the lights were burning blue.
The gentle pilgrims soon aware on't,
Told them their calling, and their errand:
'Good folks, you need not be afraid,
We are but saints,' the hermits said;
'No hurt shall come to you, or yours;
But, for that pack of churlish boors,
Not fit to live on Christian ground,
They and their houses shall be drowned:
Whilst you shall see your cottage rise,
50   And grow a church before your eyes.'

They scarce had spoke; when fair and soft
The roof began to mount aloft;
Aloft rose every beam and rafter;
The heavy wall climbed slowly after.

The chimney widened, and grew higher,
Became a steeple with a spire.

The kettle to the top was hoist,
And there stood fastened to a joist:
But with the upside down, to show
60   Its inclination for below;
In vain; for some superior force
Applied at bottom, stops its course,
Doomed ever in suspense to dwell,
'Tis now no kettle, but a bell.

A wooden jack, which had almost
Lost, by disuse, the art to roast,
A sudden alteration feels,

Increased by new intestine wheels:
And what exalts the wonder more,
70   The number made the motion slower,
The flier, which though't had leaden feet,
Turned round so quick you scarce could see't;
Now slackened by some secret power,
Can hardly move an inch an hour.
The jack and chimney, near allied,
Had never left each other's side;
The chimney to a steeple grown,
The jack would not be left alone;
But up against the steeple reared,
80   Became a clock, and still adhered:
And still its love to household cares
By a shrill voice at noon declares,
Warning the cook-maid not to burn
That roast meat which it cannot turn.

The groaning chair was seen to crawl,
Like an huge snail half up the wall;
There stuck aloft, in public view;
And with small change, a pulpit grew.

The porringers, that in a row
90   Hung high, and made a glittering show,
To a less noble substance changed,
Were now but leathern buckets, ranged.

The ballads pasted on the wall,
Of Joan of France, and English Moll,
Fair Rosamund, and Robin Hood,
'The little children in the wood':
Now seemed to look abundance better,
Improved in picture, size, and letter;
And high in order placed describe
100   The heraldry of every tribe.

A bedstead of the antique mode,
Compact of timber many a load;
Such as our grandsires wont to use,
Was metamorphosed into pews;
Which still their ancient nature keep,
By lodging folks disposed to sleep.

The cottage by such feats as these,
Grown to a church by just degrees;
The hermits then desire their host
110   To ask for what he fancied most.
Philemon having paused a while,
Returned 'em thanks in homely style;
Then said, 'My house is grown so fine,
Methinks I still would call it mine:
I'm old, and fain would live at ease,
Make me the parson, if you please.'

He spoke, and presently he feels
His grazier's coat fall down his heels;
He sees, yet hardly can believe,
120   About each arm a pudding-sleeve:
His waistcoat to a cassock grew,
And both assumed a sable hue;
But being old, continued just
As threadbare, and as full of dust.
His talk was now of tithes and dues:
Could smoke his pipe, and read the news;
Knew how to preach old sermons next,
Vamped in the preface and the text;
At christening well could act his part,
130   And had the service all by heart:
Wished women might have children fast,
And thought whose sow had farrowed last:
Against dissenters would repine,
And stood up firm for right divine:
Found his head filled with many a system,
But classic authors – he ne'er missed 'em.

Thus having furbished up a parson,
Dame Baucis next they played their farce on:
Instead of homespun coifs were seen
140   Good pinners edged with colbertine:
Her petticoat transformed apace,
Became black satin, flounced with lace.
Plain Goody would no longer down;
'Twas Madam, in her grogram gown.
Philemon was in great surprise,
And hardly could believe his eyes;

Amazed to see her look so prim:
And she admired as much at him.

Thus, happy in their change of life,
150 Were several years the man and wife:
When on a day, which proved their last,
Discoursing o'er old stories past,
They went by chance, amidst their talk,
To the churchyard, to fetch a walk;
When Baucis hastily cried out,
'My dear, I see your forehead sprout!'
'Sprout,' quoth the man, 'what's this you tell us?
I hope you don't believe me jealous:
But yet, methinks, I feel it true;
160 And really yours is budding too –
Nay – now I cannot stir my foot:
It feels as if 'twere taking root.'

Description would but tire my muse:
In short, they both were turned to yews.

Old Goodman Dobson, of the Green,
Remembers he the trees has seen;
He'll talk of them from noon to night,
And goes with folks to show the sight;
On Sundays, after evening prayer,
170 He gathers all the parish there:
Points out the place of either yew;
Here Baucis, there Philemon grew:
Till once, a parson of our town,
To mend his barn, cut Baucis down;
At which, 'tis hard to be believed,
How much the other tree was grieved:
Grew scrubby, died a-top, was stunted:
So, the next parson stubbed and burnt it.

'In Pity to the Emptying Town'

In pity to the emptying town
   Some god May Fair invented,
When nature would invite us down,
   To be by art prevented.

What a corrupted taste is ours
    When milkmaids in mock-state
Instead of garlands made of flowers
    Adorn their pails with plate.

So are the joys which nature yields
10   Inverted in May Fair;
In painted cloth we look for fields,
    And step in booths for air.

Here a dog dancing on his hams
    And puppets moved by wire
Do far exceed your frisking lambs
    Or song of feathered quire.

Howe'er such verse as yours, I grant
    Would be but too inviting
Were fair Ardelia not my aunt,
20   Or were it Worsley's writing.

Then pray think this a lucky hit,
    Nor ne'er expect another,
For honest Harry is no wit,
    Though he's a younger brother.

A Description of the Morning

Now hardly here and there a hackney coach
Appearing, showed the ruddy morn's approach.
Now Betty from her master's bed has flown,
And softly stole to discompose her own.
The slipshod prentice from his master's door
Had pared the dirt, and sprinkled round the floor.
Now Moll had whirled her mop with dexterous airs,
Prepared to scrub the entry and the stairs.
The youth with broomy stumps began to trace
10   The kennel-edge, where wheels had worn the place.
The smallcoal man was heard with cadence deep;
Till drowned in shriller notes of chimney-sweep.
Duns at his Lordship's gate began to meet;
And Brickdust Moll had screamed through half a street.
The turnkey now his flock returning sees,
Duly let out a-nights to steal for fees.

The watchful bailiffs take their silent stands;
And schoolboys lag with satchels in their hands.

On the Little House by the Churchyard of Castleknock

Whoever pleaseth to inquire,
Why yonder steeple wants a spire,
The grey old fellow poet Joe
The philosophic cause will show.

Once, on a time a Western blast,
At least twelve inches overcast,
Reckoning roof, weathercock and all,
Which came with a prodigious fall;
And tumbling topsyturvy round
10 Light with its bottom on the ground.

For by the laws of gravitation,
It fell into its proper station.

This is the little strutting pile,
You see just by the churchyard stile;
The walls in tumbling gave a knock;
And thus the steeple got a shock;
From whence the neighbouring farmer calls
The steeple 'Knock', the vicar 'Walls'.

The vicar once a week creeps in,
20 Sits with his knees up to his chin;
Here cons his notes, and takes a whet,
Till a small ragged flock is met.

A traveller, who by did pass,
Observed the roof behind the grass;
On tiptoe stood and reared his snout,
And saw the parson creeping out;
Was much surprised to see a crow
Venture to build his nest so low.

A schoolboy ran unto't and thought,
30 The crib was down, the blackbird caught.
A third, who lost his way by night,

Was forced, for safety, to alight,
And stepping o'er the fabric roof,
His horse had like to spoil his hoof.

Warburton took it in his noddle,
This building was designed a model,
Or of a pigeon-house, or oven,
To bake one loaf, and keep one dove in.

Then Mrs Johnson gave her verdict,
40   And everyone was pleased, that heard it:
'All that you make this stir about,
Is but a still which wants a spout.'
The Reverend Dr Raymond guessed,
More probably than all the rest;
He said, but that it wanted room,
It might have been a pigmy's tomb.

The Doctor's family came by,
And little Miss began to cry;
Give me that house in my own hand;
50   Then Madam bid the chariot stand,
Called to the clerk in manner mild,
'Pray reach that thing here to the child,
That thing, I mean, among the kale,
And here's to buy a pot of ale.'

The clerk said to her in a heat,
'What? sell my master's country seat?
Where he comes every week from town;
He would not sell it for a crown.'
'Poh! Fellow keep not such a pother,
60   In half an hour thou'lt make another.'

Says Nancy, 'I can make for Miss,
A finer house ten times than this,
The Dean will give me willow sticks,
And Joe my apron full of bricks.'

The Virtues of Sid Hamet the Magician's Rod

The rod was but a harmless wand,
While Moses held it in his hand;

But soon as e'er he laid it down,
'Twas a devouring serpent grown.

Our great magician, Hamet Sid,
Reverses what the prophet did:
His rod was honest English wood,
That senseless in a corner stood,
Till metamorphosed by his grasp,
10   It grew an all-devouring asp;
Would hiss and sting, and roll, and twist,
By the mere virtue of his fist:
But when he laid it down, as quick
Resumed the figure of a stick.

So to her midnight feasts the hag
Rides on a broomstick for a nag,
That raised by magic of her breech,
O'er land and sea conveys the witch:
But with the morning dawn resumes
20   The peaceful state of common brooms.

They tell us something strange and odd,
About a certain magic rod,
That bending down its top divines
Whene'er the soil has golden mines:
Where there are none, it stands erect,
Scorning to show the least respect.
As ready was the wand of Sid
To bend where golden mines were hid;
In Scottish hills found precious ore,
30   Where none e'er looked for it before:
And by a gentle bow divined
How well a cully's purse was lined:
To a forlorn and broken rake,
Stood without motion, like a stake.

The rod of Hermes was renowned
For charms above and under ground;
To sleep could mortal eyelids fix,
And drive departed souls to Styx.
That rod was just a type of Sid's,
40   Which o'er a British senate's lids

Could scatter opium full as well,
And drive as many souls to hell.

Sid's rod was slender, white, and tall,
Which oft he used to fish withal:
A *place* was fastened to the hook,
And many a score of gudgeons took;
Yet, still so happy was his fate,
He caught his fish, and saved his bait.

Sid's brethren of the conjuring tribe
50 A circle with their rod describe,
Which proves a magical redoubt,
To keep mischievous spirits out:
Sid's rod was of a larger stride,
And made a circle thrice as wide;
Where spirits thronged with hideous din,
And he stood there to take them in.
But, when the enchanted rod was broke,
They vanished in a stinking smoke.

Achilles' sceptre was of wood,
60 Like Sid's, but nothing near so good:
Though down from ancestors divine,
Transmitted to the hero's line,
Thence, through a long descent of kings,
Came an heirloom, as Homer sings,
Though this description looks so big,
That sceptre was a sapless twig;
Which, from the fatal day when first
It left the forest where 'twas nursed,
As Homer tells us o'er and o'er,
70 Nor leaf, nor fruit, nor blossom bore.
Sid's sceptre, full of juice, did shoot
In golden boughs, and golden fruit;
And he, the dragon never sleeping,
Guarded each fair Hesperian pippin.
No hobbyhorse, with gorgeous top,
The dearest in Charles Mather's shop,
Or glittering tinsel of May Fair,
Could with this rod of Sid's compare.

Dear Sid, then why wert thou so mad
80   To break thy rod like naughty lad?
You should have kissed it in your distress,
And then returned it to your mistress;
Or made it a Newmarket switch,
And not a rod for thy own breech.
But since old Sid has broken this,
His next may be a rod in piss.

A Dialogue between Captain Tom and Sir Henry Dutton Colt

Come, fair muse of Grub Street, the dialogue write,
Betwixt Captain Tom and a goodly old knight.
Quoth ancient Sir Harry, 'My dear Captain Thomas,
Sure you and your subjects will not depart from us.
Then hold hat and heart, and right hand every man up,
And bawl out old Colt, and brave General Stanhope.
Let the General's merits and mine be maintained:
Turn off the old brewer, and be not cross-grained.
In a protestant country, why are you for crosses?
10   And brewers will poison you all with molosses.
Besides, are not all the damned Jacobite brewers,
Still brewing of mischief, and so may be yours?
And papists are brewers, with faggots to burn us;
But if you love brewing, you may have a Furnese.
Then Stanhope shall send you each laurel he crops;
And laurels are sometimes as bitter as hops.'

When comely Sir Harry had thus shot his bolt,
Then replied Captain Tom, 'God-a-mercy, old Colt,
You had better have been at your spade and your club,
20   Than take up our time with a tale of a tub.
You shall be discarded, I say't to your face;
We'll all play the game, and not bate you an ace.
Then let me advise you no longer to stay;
But pack up and shuffle, and cut it away.
And though you have wit, youth, beauty, and parts,
While we keep our clubs, you shall ne'er win our hearts.
Brave Stanhope for fighting will have his reward,

And the Queen, when she pleases, can make him a lord.
But we are true friends of the church and Sacheverell;
30 And vote for a manager surely we never will!
Besides, we have found too much heat in some rulers,
And will give them a brewer, because they want coolers.
If Christians love crosses, why should they be blamed?
You shall see us bear ours, and not be ashamed.
But we know what you aim at; you all would engross,
And not leave the church or the nation a cross.'

When the Captain had finished, away went old Numps;
He had got a bad game, and could not turn up trumps.
His eggs they are addled, and dough was his cake;
40 So fairly he left them to brew as they bake.

A Description of a City Shower

Careful observers may foretell the hour
(By sure prognostics) when to dread a shower.
While rain depends, the pensive cat gives o'er
Her frolics, and pursues her tail no more.
Returning home at night you find the sink
Strike your offended sense with double stink.
If you be wise, then go not far to dine,
You spend in coach-hire more than save in wine.
A coming shower your shooting corns presage,
10 Old aches throb, your hollow tooth will rage:
Sauntering in coffee-house is Dulman seen;
He damns the climate, and complains of spleen.

Meanwhile the south, rising with dabbled wings,
A sable cloud athwart the welkin flings;
That swilled more liquor than it could contain,
And like a drunkard gives it up again.
Brisk Susan whips her linen from the rope,
While the first drizzling shower is born aslope:
Such is that sprinkling which some careless quean
20 Flirts on you from her mop, but not so clean:
You fly, invoke the gods; then turning, stop
To rail; she singing, still whirls on her mop.
Nor yet the dust had shunned the unequal strife,

But aided by the wind, fought still for life;
And wafted with its foe by violent gust,
'Twas doubtful which was rain, and which was dust.
Ah! where must needy poet seek for aid,
When dust and rain at once his coat invade?
Sole coat, where dust cemented by the rain
30   Erects the nap, and leaves a cloudy stain.

    Now in contiguous drops the flood comes down,
Threatening with deluge this devoted town.
To shops in crowds the daggled females fly,
Pretend to cheapen goods, but nothing buy.
The templar spruce, while every spout's abroach,
Stays till 'tis fair, yet seems to call a coach.
The tucked-up seamstress walks with hasty strides,
While streams run down her oiled umbrella's sides.
Here various kinds by various fortunes led,
40   Commence acquaintance underneath a shed.
Triumphant Tories, and desponding Whigs,
Forget their feuds, and join to save their wigs.
Boxed in a chair the beau impatient sits,
While spouts run clattering o'er the roof by fits;
And ever and anon with frightful din
The leather sounds; he trembles from within.
So when Troy chairmen bore the wooden steed,
Pregnant with Greeks, impatient to be freed;
(Those bully Greeks, who, as the moderns do,
50   Instead of paying chairmen, run them through)
Laocoon struck the outside with his spear,
And each imprisoned hero quaked for fear.

    Now from all parts the swelling kennels flow,
And bear their trophies with them as they go:
Filths of all hues and odours, seem to tell
What streets they sailed from, by the sight and smell.
They, as each torrent drives with rapid force
From Smithfield, or St Pulchre's shape their course;
And in huge confluent join at Snow Hill ridge,
60   Fall from the conduit prone to Holborn Bridge.
Sweepings from butchers' stalls, dung, guts, and blood,
Drowned puppies, stinking sprats, all drenched in mud,
Dead cats and turnip-tops come tumbling down the flood.

To Mr Harley's Surgeon

On Britain Europe's safety lies,
And Britain's lost if Harley dies:
Harley depends upon your skill,
Think what you save or what you kill.

A Town Eclogue

CORYDON   Now the keen rigour of the winter's o'er,
No hail descends, and frosts can pinch no more,
Whilst other girls confess the genial spring,
And laugh aloud, or amorous ditties sing,
Secure from cold their lovely necks display,
And throw each useless chafing-dish away,
Why sits my Phyllis discontented here,
Nor feels the turn of the revolving year?
Why on that brow dwells sorrow and dismay,
10   Where loves were wont to sport, and smiles to play?

PHYLLIS   Ah Corydon! Survey the 'Change around,
Through all the 'Change no wretch like me is found:
Alas! the day, when I, poor heedless maid,
Was to your rooms in Lincoln's Inn betrayed,
Then how you swore, how many vows you made?
Ye listening zephyrs, that o'erheard his love,
Waft the soft accents to the gods above.
Alas! the day; for oh eternal shame!
I sold you handkerchiefs, and lost my fame.

20   CORYDON   When I forget the favour you bestowed,
Red herrings shall be spawned in Tyburn Road,
Fleet Street transformed become a flowery green,
And mass be sung where operas are seen.
The wealthy cit, and the St James's beau,
Shall change their quarters, and their joys forego;
Stockjobbing this to Jonathan's shall come,
At the Groom Porter's that play off his plum.

PHYLLIS   But what to me does all that love avail,
If whilst I doze at home o'er porter's ale,
30   Each night with wine and wenches you regale?

My livelong hours in anxious cares are past,
And raging hunger lays my beauty waste.
On templars spruce in vain I glances throw,
And with shrill voice invite them as they go.
Exposed in vain my glossy ribbons shine,
And unregarded wave upon the twine.
The week flies round, and when my profit's known,
I hardly clear enough to change a crown.

CORYDON   Hard fate of virtue thus to be distressed,
40   Thou fairest of thy trade, and far the best!
As fruitmen's stalls the summer market grace,
And ruddy peaches them; as first in place
Plum-cake is seen o'er smaller pastryware,
And ice on that; so Phyllis does appear
In playhouse and in park, above the rest
Of belles mechanic, elegantly dressed.

PHYLLIS   And yet Crepundia, that conceited fair,
Amidst her toys, affects a saucy air,
And views me hourly with a scornful eye.

50   CORYDON   She might as well with bright Cleora vie.

PHYLLIS   With this large petticoat I strive in vain
To hide my folly past, and coming pain;
'Tis now no secret; she, and fifty more,
Observe the symptoms I had once before.
A second babe at Wapping must be placed,
When I scarce bear the charges of the last.

CORYDON   What I could raise I sent; a pound of plums,
Five shillings, and a coral for his gums:
Tomorrow I intend him something more.

60   PHYLLIS   I sent a frock and pair of shoes before.

CORYDON   However, you shall home with me tonight,
Forget your cares, and revel in delight.
I have in store a pint or two of wine,
Some cracknels, and the remnant of a chine.
And now on either side, and all around,
The weighty shop-boards fall, and bars resound;

Each ready seamstress slips her pattens on,
And ties her hood, preparing to be gone.

Lines from *A Famous Prediction of Merlin*

Seven and Ten addyd to nyne,
Of Fraunce hir woe thys is the sygne,
Tamys rivere twys y-frozen,
Walk sans wtynge shoes ne hosen.
Then comyth foorthe, Ich understonde,
From Toune of Stoffe to fattyñ Londe
An herdie Chiftan, woe the morne
To Fraunce, that evere he was borne.
Than shall the Fyshe beweyle his Bosse;
10 Nor shall grin Berris make up the Losse.
Yonge Symnele shall agayne miscarrye:
And Norways pryd agayne shall marreye.
And from the Tree where Blosums fele,
Ripe fruit shall come, and all is wele.
Reaums shall daunce honde in honde,
And it shall be merye in olde Inglonde.
Then olde Inglonde shall be noe more,
And no Man shall be sorie therefore.
Geryon shall have three Hedes agayne
20 Till Hapsburge makyth them but twayne.

An Excellent New Song

BEING THE INTENDED SPEECH OF A FAMOUS ORATOR
AGAINST PEACE

An orator dismal of Nottinghamshire,
Who has forty years let out his conscience to hire,
Out of zeal for his country, and want of a place,
Is come up, *vi & armis*, to break the Queen's peace.
He has vamped up an old speech, and the court to their sorrow,
Shall hear him harangue against Prior tomorrow.
When once he begins, he never will flinch,

But repeats the same note a whole day, like a finch.
I have heard all the speech repeated by Hoppy,
10   And, mistakes to prevent, I have obtained a copy.

THE SPEECH

Whereas, notwithstanding, I am in great pain,
To hear we are making a peace without Spain;
But, most noble senators, 'tis a great shame
There should be a peace, while I'm not in game.
The Duke showed me all his fine house; and the Duchess
From her closet brought out a full purse in her clutches:
I talked of a peace, and they both gave a start,
His Grace swore by God, and her Grace let a fart:
My long old-fashioned pocket was presently crammed;
20   And sooner than vote for a peace I'll be damned.
But some will cry, 'Turncoat!', and rip up old stories,
How I always pretended to be for the Tories:
I answer; the Tories were in my good graces,
Till all my relations were put into places.
But still I'm in principle ever the same,
And will quit my best friends, while I'm not in game.

When I and some others subscribed our names
To a plot for expelling my master King James;
I withdrew my subscription by help of a blot,
30   And so might discover, or gain by the plot:
I had my advantage, and stood at defiance,
For Daniel was got from the den of the lions:
I came in without danger; and was I to blame?
For rather than hang, I would be not in game.

I swore to the Queen that the Prince of Hanover
During her sacred life, should never come over:
I made use of a trope; that 'an heir to invite,
Was like keeping her monument always in sight.'
But when I thought proper, I altered my note;
40   And in her own hearing I boldly did vote,
That her Majesty stood in great need of a tutor,
And must have an old, or a young coadjutor:
For why; I would fain have put all in a flame,
Because, for some reasons, I was not in game.

Now my new benefactors have brought me about,
And I'll vote against peace, with Spain, or without:
Though the court gives my nephews, and brothers, and cousins,
And all my whole family, places by dozens;
Yet since I know where a full purse may be found,
50 And hardly pay eighteen pence tax in the pound:
Since the Tories have thus disappointed my hopes,
And will neither regard my figures nor tropes;
I'll speech against peace while Dismal's my name,
And be a true Whig, while I am not in game.

The Windsor Prophecy

When a holy black *Suede*, the Son of *Bob*,
With a *Saint* at his Chin, and a *Seal* in his Fob;
Shall not see one New Years-day in that Year,
Then let old *Englond* make good Chear:
Windsor and *Bristow* then shall be
Joyned together in the Low-Countree.
Then shall the tall black *Daventry Bird*
Speak against Peace right many a Word;
And some shall admire his conyng Witt,
10 For many good *Groats* his Tongue shall slitt:
But spight of the *Harpy* that *crawls on all four*,
There shall be Peace, pardie, and War no more.
But *Englond* must cry alack and well a day,
If the *Stick* be taken from the *dead Sea*.
And dear *Englond*, if ought I understond,
Beware of *Carrots* from *Northumberland*.
Carrots sown *Thyn* a deep root may get,
If so be they are in *Sommer* set:
Their *Conyngs mark* thou, for I have been told,
20 They *Assassine* when young, and *Poison* when old.
Root out these *Carrots*, O Thou, whose *Name*
Is backwards and forwards always the same;
And keep close to Thee always that *Name*,
Which backwards and forwards is allmost the same.
And *Englond* wouldst thou be happy still,
Bury those *Carrots* under a *Hill*.

Corinna

This day (the year I dare not tell)
    Apollo played the midwife's part;
Into the world Corinna fell,
    And he endowed her with his art.

But Cupid with a satyr comes;
    Both softly to the cradle creep:
Both stroke her hands, and rub her gums,
    While the poor child lay fast asleep.

Then Cupid thus: 'This little maid
10   Of love shall always speak and write;'
'And I pronounce', the satyr said,
    'The world shall feel her scratch and bite.'

Her talent she displayed betimes;
    For in a few revolving moons,
She seemed to laugh and squall in rhymes,
    And all her gestures were lampoons.

At six years old, the subtle jade
    Stole to the pantry-door, and found
The butler with my Lady's maid;
20   And you may swear the tale went round.

She made a song, how little Miss
    Was kissed and slobbered by a lad:
And how, when Master went to piss,
    Miss came, and peeped at all he had.

At twelve, a poet, and coquette;
    Marries for love, half whore, half wife;
Cuckolds, elopes, and runs in debt;
    Turns authoress, and is Curll's for life.

Her commonplace book all gallant is,
30   Of scandal now a cornucopia;
She pours it out in an *Atlantis*,
    Or *Memoirs of the New Utopia*.

Atlas

Atlas, we read in ancient song,
Was so exceeding tall and strong,
He bore the skies upon his back,
Just as a pedlar does his pack;
But, as a pedlar overpressed,
Unloads upon a stall to rest;
Or when he can no longer stand,
Desires a friend to lend a hand;
So Atlas, lest the ponderous spheres
10 Should sink and fall about his ears,
Got Hercules to bear the pile,
That he might sit and rest awhile.
Yet Hercules was not so strong,
Nor could have borne it half so long.

Great statesmen are in this condition;
And Atlas is a politician;
A premier minister of state;
Alcides, one of second rate.
Suppose then Atlas ne'er so wise,
20 Yet when the weight of kingdom lies
Too long upon his single shoulders,
Sink down he must, or find upholders.

A Fable of the Widow and Her Cat

I
A widow kept a favourite cat,
   At first a gentle creature;
But when he was grown sleek and fat,
With many a mouse, and many a rat,
   He soon disclosed his nature.

II
The fox and he were friends of old,
   Nor could they now be parted;

They nightly slunk to rob the fold,
Devoured the lambs, the fleeces sold,
10   And Puss grew lion-hearted.

III

He scratched her maid, he stole the cream,
    He tore her best laced pinner;
Nor Chanticleer upon the beam,
Nor chick, nor duckling 'scapes, when Grim
    Invites the fox to dinner.

IV

The dame full wisely did decree,
    For fear he should dispatch more,
That the false wretch should worried be:
But in a saucy manner he
20   Thus speeched it like a Lechmere.

V

'Must I, against all right and law,
    Like pole-cat vile be treated?
I! who so long with tooth and claw
Have kept domestic mice in awe,
    And foreign foes defeated!

VI

'Your golden pippins, and your pies,
    How oft have I defended?
'Tis true, the pinner which you prize
I tore in frolic; to your eyes
30   I never harm intended.

VII

'I am a cat of honour –' 'Stay,'
    Quoth she, 'no longer parley;
Whate'er you did in battle slay,
By law of arms became your prey,
    I hope you won it fairly.

VIII

'Of this, we'll grant you stand acquit,
    But not of your outrages:
Tell me, perfidious! was it fit

To make my cream a *perquisite*,
40   And steal to mend your wages?

IX
'So flagrant is thy insolence,
   So vile thy breach of trust is;
That longer with thee to dispense,
Were want of power, or want of sense:
   Here, Towser! – Do him justice.'

The Fable of Midas

Midas, we are in story told,
Turned everything he touched to gold:
He chipped his bread; the pieces round
Glittered like spangles on the ground:
A codling e'er it went his lip in,
Would straight become a golden pippin:
He called for drink, you saw him sup
Potable gold in golden cup.
His empty paunch that he might fill,
10 He sucked his victuals through a quill;
Untouched it passed between his grinders,
Or't had been happy for gold-finders.
He cocked his hat, you would have said
Mambrino's helm adorned his head.
Whene'er he chanced his hands to lay,
On magazines of corn or hay,
Gold ready coined appeared, instead
Of paltry provender and bread:
Hence we are by wise farmers told,
20 Old hay is equal to old gold;
And hence a critic deep maintains,
We learned to weigh our gold by grains.

    This fool had got a lucky hit,
And people fancied he had wit:
Two gods their skill in music tried,
And both chose Midas to decide;
He against Phoebus' harp decreed,

And gave it for Pan's oaten reed:
The god of wit to show his grudge,
30 Clapped asses' ears upon the judge,
A goodly pair, erect and wide,
Which he could neither gild nor hide.

And now the virtue of his hands,
Was lost among Pactolus sands,
Against whose torrent while he swims,
The golden scurf peels off his limbs:
Fame spreads the news, and people travel
From far, to gather golden gravel;
Midas, exposed to all their jeers,
40 Had lost his art, and kept his ears.

This tale inclines the gentle reader,
To think upon a certain leader,
To whom from Midas down, descends
That virtue in the fingers' ends:
What else by perquisites are meant,
By pensions, bribes, and three per cent?
By places and commissions sold,
And turning dung itself to gold?
By starving in the midst of store,
50 As t'other Midas did before?

None e'er did modern Midas choose,
Subject or patron of his muse,
But found him thus their merit scan,
That Phoebus must give place to Pan:
He values not the poet's praise,
Nor will exchange his plums for bays:
To Pan alone, rich misers call,
And there's the jest, for Pan is *all*:
Here English wits will be to seek,
60 Howe'er, 'tis all one in the Greek.

Besides, it plainly now appears,
Our Midas too has asses' ears;
Where every fool in his mouth applies,
And whispers in a thousand lies;
Such gross delusions could not pass,
Through any ears but of an ass.

> But gold defiles with frequent touch,
> There's nothing fouls the hands so much:
> And scholars give it for the cause,
> 70   Of British Midas' dirty paws;
> Which while the senate strove to scour,
> They washed away the chemic power.
> While he his utmost strength applied,
> To swim against this popular tide,
> The golden spoils flew off apace;
> Here fell a pension, there a place:
> The torrent, merciless, imbibes
> Commissions, perquisites, and bribes;
> By their own weight sunk to the bottom;
> 80   Much good may do 'em that have caught 'em.
> And Midas now neglected stands,
> With asses' ears, and dirty hands.

Toland's Invitation to Dismal to Dine with the Calves' Head Club

IMITATED FROM HORACE, EPISTLE 5, LIBER 1

> If, dearest 'Dismal', you for once can dine
> Upon a single dish, and tavern wine,
> Toland to you this invitation sends,
> To eat the Calves' Head with your trusty friends.
> Suspend a while your vain ambitious hopes,
> Leave hunting after bribes, forget your tropes:
> Tomorrow we our mystic feast prepare,
> Where thou, our latest proselyte, shalt share:
> When we, by proper signs and symbols tell,
> 10   How, by brave hands, the royal traitor fell;
> The meat shall represent the tyrant's head,
> The wine, his blood, our predecessors shed:
> Whilst an alluding hymn some artist sings,
> We toast confusion to the race of kings:
> At monarchy we nobly show our spite,
> And talk what fools call treason all the night.

> Who, by disgraces or ill fortune sunk,
> Feels not his soul enlivened when he's drunk?

Wine can clear up Godolphin's cloudy face,
20 And fill Jack Smith with hopes to keep his place;
By force of wine even Scarborough is brave,
Hal grows more pert, and Somers not so grave:
Wine can give Portland wit, and Cleveland sense,
Montagu learning, Bolton eloquence;
Cholmondley, when drunk, can never lose his wand,
And Lincoln then imagines he has land.

My province is, to see that all be right,
Glasses and linen clean, and pewter bright;
From our mysterious club to keep out spies,
30 And Tories (dressed like waiters) in disguise.
You shall be coupled as you best approve,
Seated at table next the men you love.
Sunderland, Orford, Boyle and Richmond's Grace
Will come; and Hampden shall have Walpole's place.
Wharton, unless prevented by a whore,
Will hardly fail, and there is room for more:
But I love elbow-room whene'er I drink,
And honest Harry is too apt to stink.

Let no pretence of business make you stay,
40 Yet take one word of counsel by the way:
If Guernsey calls, send word you're gone abroad;
He'll tease you with King Charles and Bishop Laud,
Or make you fast, and carry you to prayers:
But if he will break in, and walk upstairs,
Steal by the back-door out, and leave him there;
Then order Squash to call a hackney chair.

         January 29.

Peace and Dunkirk

BEING AN EXCELLENT NEW SONG UPON THE SURRENDER
OF DUNKIRK TO GENERAL HILL

To the tune of 'The king shall enjoy his own again'

I

Spite of Dutch friends and English foes,
 Poor Britain shall have peace at last;
Holland got towns, and we got blows,

But Dunkirk's ours, we'll hold it fast:
    We have got it in a string,
    And the Whigs may all go swing,
For among good friends, I love to be plain;
    All their false deluded hopes,
    Will, or ought to end in ropes;
10 But the Queen shall enjoy her own again.

II

Sunderland's run out of his wits,
    And Dismal double-dismal looks;
Wharton can only swear by fits,
    And strutting Hal is off the hooks;
        Old Godolphin full of spleen,
        Made false moves, and lost his Queen;
Harry looked fierce, and shook his ragged mane:
        But a prince of high renown,
        Swore he'd rather lose a crown,
20 Than the Queen shall enjoy her own again.

III

Our merchant ships may cut the line,
    And not be snapped by privateers,
And commoners who love good wine,
    Will drink it now as well as peers:
        Landed men shall have their rent,
        Yet our stocks rise cent per cent,
The Dutch from hence shall no more millions drain;
        We'll bring on us no more debts,
        Nor with bankrupts fill gazettes,
30 And the Queen shall enjoy her own again.

IV

The towns we took ne'er did us good,
    What signified the French to beat?
We spent our money and our blood,
    To make the Dutchmen proud and great:
        But the Lord of Oxford swears,
        Dunkirk never shall be theirs,
The Dutch-hearted Whigs may rail and complain;
        But true Englishmen will fill
        A good health to General Hill,
40 For the Queen now enjoys her own again.

Lines from *Dunkirk to be Let*

Old Lewis thus the terms of peace to burnish,
Has lately let out Dunkirk ready furnished;
But whether 'tis by lease, or copyhold,
Or tenure *in capite*, we've not been told:
But this we hope, if yet he pulls his horns in,
He'll be obliged to give his tenants warning.

To Lord Harley, since Earl of Oxford, on His Marriage

Among the numbers who employ
Their tongues and pens to give you joy,
Dear Harley, generous youth, admit
What friendship dictates more than wit.

    Forgive me, when I fondly thought
(By frequent observation taught)
A spirit so informed as yours
Could never prosper in amours.
The god of wit, and light, and arts,
With all acquired and natural parts,
Whose harp could savage beasts enchant,
Was an unfortunate gallant.
Had Bacchus after Daphne reeled,
The nymph had soon been brought to yield;
Or, had embroidered Mars pursued,
The nymph would ne'er have been a prude.
Ten thousand footsteps, full in view,
Mark out the way where Daphne flew.
For such is all the sex's flight,
They fly from learning, wit, and light:
They fly, and none can overtake
But some gay coxcomb, or a rake.

    How then, dear Harley, could I guess
That you should meet, in love, success?
For, if those ancient tales be true,
Phoebus was as beautiful as you:

Yet Daphne never slacked her pace,
For wit and learning spoilt his face.
And, since the same resemblance held
30   In gifts, wherein you both excelled,
I fancied every nymph would run
From you, as from Latona's son.

Then where, said I, shall Harley find
A virgin of superior mind,
With wit and virtue to discover,
And pay the merit of her lover?

This character shall Cavendish claim,
Born to retrieve her sex's fame.
The chief among that glittering crowd,
40   Of titles, birth, and fortune proud,
(As fools are insolent and vain)
Madly aspired to wear her chain:
But Pallas, guardian of the maid,
Descending to her charge's aid,
Held out Medusa's snaky locks,
Which stupefied them all to stocks.
The nymph, with indignation, viewed
The dull, the noisy, and the lewd:
For Pallas, with celestial light,
50   Had purified her mortal sight;
Showed her the virtues all combined,
Fresh blooming, in young Harley's mind.

Terrestrial nymphs, by formal arts,
Display their various nets for hearts:
Their looks are all by method set,
When to be prude, and when coquette;
Yet, wanting skill and power to choose,
Their only pride is to refuse.
But, when a goddess would bestow
60   Her love on some bright youth below,
Round all the earth she casts her eyes;
And then, descending from the skies,
Makes choice of him she fancies best,
And bids the ravished youth be blessed.

Thus the bright empress of the morn
Chose, for her spouse, a mortal born:
The goddess made advances first,
Else what aspiring hero durst?
Though, like a virgin of fifteen,
70 She blushes when by mortals seen;
Still blushes, and with speed retires,
When Sol pursues her with his fires.

Diana thus, heaven's chastest queen,
Struck with Endymion's graceful mien,
Down from her silver chariot came,
And to the shepherd owed her flame.

Thus Cavendish, as Aurora bright,
And chaster than the Queen of Night,
Descended from her sphere to find
80 A mortal of superior kind.

Cadenus and Vanessa

The shepherds and the nymphs were seen
Pleading before the Cyprian queen.
The counsel for the fair began,
Accusing that false creature, man:
The brief with weighty crimes was charged,
On which the pleader much enlarged;
That 'Cupid now has lost his art,
Or blunts the point of every dart;
His altar now no longer smokes,
10 His mother's aid no youth invokes:
This tempts freethinkers to refine,
And brings in doubt their power divine.
Now love is dwindled to intrigue,
And marriage grown a money-league.
Which crimes aforesaid' (with her leave)
'Were' (as he humbly did conceive)
'Against our sovereign lady's peace,
Against the statute in that case,
Against her dignity and crown.'
20 Then prayed an answer, and sat down.

    The nymphs with scorn beheld their foes:
When the defendant's counsel rose;
And, what no lawyer ever lacked,
With impudence owned all the fact:
But, what the gentlest heart would vex,
Laid all the fault on t'other sex.
That 'Modern love is no such thing
As what those ancient poets sing;
A fire celestial, chaste, refined,
30   Conceived and kindled in the mind.
Which having found an equal flame,
Unites, and both become the same,
In different breasts together burn,
Together both to ashes turn.
But women now feel no such fire;
And only know the gross desire:
Their passions move in lower spheres,
Where'er caprice or folly steers:
A dog, a parrot, or an ape,
40   Or some worse brute in human shape,
Engross the fancies of the fair,
The few soft moments they can spare,
From visits to receive and pay;
From scandal, politics, and play,
From fans and flounces, and brocades,
From equipage and park-parades;
From all the thousand female toys,
From every trifle that employs
The out or inside of their heads,
50   Between their toilets and their beds.

    'In a dull stream, which moving slow
You hardly see the current flow;
If a small breeze obstructs the course,
It whirls about for want of force,
And in its narrow circle gathers
Nothing but chaff, and straws, and feathers:
The current of a female mind
Stops thus, and turns with every wind;
Thus whirling round, together draws
60   Fools, fops, and rakes, for chaff and straws.

Hence we conclude, no women's hearts
Are won by virtue, wit, and parts;
Nor are the men of sense to blame,
For breasts incapable of flame;
The fault must on the nymphs be placed,
Grown so corrupted in their taste.'

The pleader having spoke his best,
Had witness ready to attest,
Who fairly could on oath depose,
70   When questions on the fact arose,
That every article was true;
'Nor further those deponents knew':
Therefore he humbly would insist,
The bill might be with costs dismissed.

The cause appeared of so much weight,
That Venus, from her judgement-seat,
Desired them not to talk so loud,
Else she must interpose a cloud:
For if the heavenly folks should know
80   These pleadings in the courts below,
That mortals here disdain to love;
She ne'er could show her face above.
For gods, their betters, are too wise
To value that which men despise:
'And then,' said she, 'my son and I
Must stroll in air 'twixt land and sky;
Or else, shut out from heaven and earth,
Fly to the sea, my place of birth;
There live with daggled mermaids pent,
90   And keep on fish perpetual Lent.'

But since the case appeared so nice,
She thought it best to take advice.
The muses, by their king's permission,
Though foes to love, attend the session;
And on the right hand took their places
In order; on the left, the Graces:
To whom she might her doubts propose
On all emergencies that rose.
The muses oft were seen to frown;

100 The Graces half ashamed looked down;
And 'twas observed, there were but few
Of either sex, among the crew,
Whom she or her assessors knew.
The goddess soon began to see
Things were not ripe for a decree:
And said, she must consult her books,
The lovers' *Fleta*'s, Bractons, Cokes.
First to a dapper clerk she beckoned,
To turn to Ovid, book the second;
110 She then referred them to a place
In Virgil (*vide* Dido's case):
As for Tibullus's reports,
They never passed for laws in courts;
For Cowley's briefs, and pleas of Waller,
Still their authority was smaller.

There was on both sides much to say:
She'd hear the cause another day;
And so she did, and then a third:
She heard it – there she kept her word;
120 But with rejoinders and replies,
Long bills and answers, stuffed with lies;
Demur, imparlance, and essoign,
The parties ne'er could issue join:
For sixteen years the cause was spun,
And then stood where it first begun.

Now, gentle Clio, sing or say,
What Venus meant by this delay.
The goddess much perplexed in mind,
To see her empire thus declined,
130 When first this grand debate arose
Above her wisdom to compose,
Conceived a project in her head,
To work her ends; which if it sped,
Would show the merits of the cause,
Far better than consulting laws.

In a glad hour Lucina's aid
Produced on earth a wondrous maid,
On whom the Queen of Love was bent

To try a new experiment:
140   She threw her law-books on the shelf,
And thus debated with herself.

'Since men allege, they ne'er can find
Those beauties in a female mind,
Which raise a flame that will endure
For ever, uncorrupt and pure;
If 'tis with reason they complain,
This infant shall restore my reign.
I'll search where every virtue dwells,
From courts inclusive, down to cells,
150   What preachers talk, or sages write,
These I will gather and unite,
And represent them to mankind
Collected in the infant's mind.'

This said, she plucks in heaven's high bowers
A sprig of amaranthine flowers,
In nectar thrice infuses bays,
Three times refined in Titan's rays:
Then calls the Graces to her aid,
And sprinkles thrice the new-born maid:
160   From whence the tender skin assumes
A sweetness above all perfumes;
From whence a cleanliness remains,
Incapable of outward stains;
From whence that decency of mind,
So lovely in the female kind;
Where not one careless thought intrudes,
Less modest than the speech of prudes;
Where never blush was called in aid;
That spurious virtue in a maid;
170   A virtue but at second hand;
They blush because they understand.

The Graces next would act their part,
And showed but little of their art;
Their work was half already done,
The child with native beauty shone;
The outward form no help required:
Each breathing on her thrice, inspired

That gentle, soft, engaging air,
Which, in old times, adorned the fair;
180 And said, 'Vanessa be the name,
By which thou shalt be known to fame:
Vanessa, by the gods enrolled:
Her name on earth – shall not be told.'

But still the work was not complete;
When Venus thought on a deceit:
Drawn by her doves, away she flies,
And finds out Pallas in the skies:
'Dear Pallas, I have been this morn
To see a lovely infant born:
190 A boy in yonder isle below,
So like my own, without his bow:
By beauty could your heart be won,
You'd swear it is Apollo's son;
But it shall ne'er be said, a child
So hopeful, has by me been spoiled;
I have enough besides to spare,
And give him wholly to your care.'

Wisdom's above suspecting wiles:
The Queen of Learning gravely smiles;
200 Down from Olympus comes with joy,
Mistakes Vanessa for a boy;
Then sows within her tender mind
Seeds long unknown to womankind,
For manly bosoms chiefly fit,
The seeds of knowledge, judgement, wit.
Her soul was suddenly endued
With justice, truth and fortitude;
With honour, which no breath can stain,
Which malice must attack in vain;
210 With open heart and bounteous hand:
But Pallas here was at a stand;
She knew in our degenerate days
Bare virtue could not live on praise,
That meat must be with money bought;
She therefore, upon second thought,
Infused, yet as it were by stealth,

Some small regard for state and wealth:
Of which, as she grew up, there stayed
A tincture in the prudent maid:
220   She managed her estate with care,
Yet liked three footmen to her chair.
But lest he should neglect his studies
Like a young heir, the thrifty goddess
(For fear young master should be spoiled)
Would use him like a younger child;
And, after long computing, found
'Twould come to just five thousand pound.

The Queen of Love was pleased, and proud,
To see Vanessa thus endowed;
230   She doubted not but such a dame
Through every breast would dart a flame;
That every rich and lordly swain
With pride would drag about her chain;
That scholars would foresake their books
To study bright Vanessa's looks:
As she advanced, that womankind
Would by her model form their mind,
And all their conduct would be tried
By her, as an unerring guide.
240   Offending daughters oft would hear
Vanessa's praise rung in their ear:
Miss Betty, when she does a fault,
Lets fall a knife, or spills the salt,
Will thus be by her mother chid,
' 'Tis what Vanessa never did.'
'Thus by the nymphs and swains adored,
My power shall be again restored,
And happy lovers bless my reign –'
So Venus hoped, but hoped in vain.

250   For when in time the martial maid
Found out the trick that Venus played,
She shakes her helm, she knits her brows,
And fired with indignation vows,
Tomorrow, ere the setting sun,
She'd all undo, that she had done.

But in the poets we may find,
A wholesome law, time out of mind,
Had been confirmed by fate's decree;
That gods, of whatsoe'er degree,
260 Resume not what themselves have given,
Or any brother god in heaven:
Which keeps the peace among the gods,
Or they must always be at odds.
And Pallas, if she broke the laws,
Must yield her foe the stronger cause;
A shame to one so much adored
For wisdom, at Jove's council-board.
Besides, she feared, the Queen of Love
Would meet with better friends above.
270 And though she must with grief reflect,
To see a mortal virgin decked
With graces, hitherto unknown
To female breasts, except her own;
Yet she would act as best became
A goddess of unspotted fame:
She knew, by augury divine,
Venus would fail in her design:
She studied well the point, and found
Her foe's conclusions were not sound,
280 From premises erroneous brought,
And therefore the deductions naught;
And must have contrary effects
To what her treacherous foe expects.

In proper season Pallas meets
The Queen of Love, whom thus she greets
(For gods, we are by Homer told,
Can in celestial language scold),
'Perfidious goddess! but in vain
You formed this project in your brain,
290 A project for thy talents fit,
With much deceit and little wit;
Thou hast, as thou shalt quickly see,
Deceived thyself, instead of me;
For how can heavenly wisdom prove
An instrument to earthly love?

Knowst thou not yet that men commence
Thy votaries, for want of sense?
Nor shall Vanessa be the theme
To manage thy abortive scheme;
300   She'll prove the greatest of thy foes:
And yet I scorn to interpose,
But using neither skill, nor force,
Leave all things to their natural course.'

The goddess thus pronounced her doom:
When, lo! Vanessa in her bloom,
Advanced like Atalanta's star
But rarely seen, and seen from far:
In a new world with caution stepped,
Watched all the company she kept,
310   Well knowing from the books she read
What dangerous paths young virgins tread;
Would seldom at the park appear,
Nor saw the playhouse twice a year;
Yet not incurious, was inclined
To know the converse of mankind.

First issued from perfumers' shops
A crowd of fashionable fops;
They asked her, how she liked the play,
Then told the tattle of the day,
320   A duel fought last night at two;
About a Lady – you know who;
Mentioned a new Italian, come
Either from Muscovy or Rome;
Gave hints of who and who's together;
Then fell to talking of the weather:
'Last night was so extremely fine,
The ladies walked till after nine.'
Then in soft voice and speech absurd,
With nonsense every second word,
330   With fustian from exploded plays,
They celebrate her beauty's praise,
Run o'er their cant of stupid lies,
And tell the murders of her eyes.

With silent scorn Vanessa sat,
Scarce listening to their idle chat;

Further than sometimes by a frown,
When they grew pert, to pull them down.
At last she spitefully was bent
To try their wisdom's full extent;
340 And said, she valued nothing less
Than titles, figure, shape, and dress;
That, merit should be chiefly placed
In judgement, knowledge, wit, and taste;
And these, she offered to dispute,
Alone distinguished man from brute:
That, present times have no pretence
To virtue, in the noblest sense,
By Greeks and Romans understood,
To perish for our country's good.
350 She named the ancient heroes round,
Explained for what they were renowned;
Then spoke with censure, or applause,
Of foreign customs, rites, and laws;
Through nature, and through art she ranged,
And gracefully her subjects changed:
In vain: her hearers had no share
In all she spoke, except to stare.
Their judgement was upon the whole,
'That lady is the dullest soul' –
360 Then tipped their forehead in a jeer,
As who should say – 'she wants it here;
She may be handsome, young and rich,
But none will burn her for a witch.'

A party next of glittering dames,
From round the purlieus of St James,
Came early, out of pure good will,
To catch the girl in dishabille.
Their clamour lighting from their chairs,
Grew louder, all the way upstairs;
370 At entrance loudest, where they found
The room with volumes littered round.
Vanessa held Montaigne, and read,
Whilst Mrs Susan combed her head:
They called for tea and chocolate,
And fell into their usual chat,
Discoursing with important face,

On ribbons, fans, and gloves and lace;
Showed patterns just from India brought,
And gravely asked her what she thought,
380 Whether the red or green were best,
And what they cost? Vanessa guessed,
As came into her fancy first,
Named half the rates, and liked the worst.
To scandal next – 'What awkward thing
Was that, last Sunday in the Ring?'
– 'I'm sorry Mopsa breaks so fast;
I said her face would never last.'
'Corinna with that youthful air,
Is thirty, and a bit to spare.
390 Her fondness for a certain earl
Began when I was but a girl.'
'Phyllis, who but a month ago
Was married to the Tunbridge beau,
I saw coquetting t'other night
In public with that odious knight.'

    They rallied next Vanessa's dress;
'That gown was made for old Queen Bess.'
'Dear madam, let me set your head:
Don't you intend to put on red?'
400 'A petticoat without a hoop!
Sure, you are not ashamed to stoop;
With handsome garters at your knees,
No matter what a fellow sees.'

    Filled with disdain, with rage inflamed,
Both of her self and sex ashamed,
The nymph stood silent out of spite,
Nor would vouchsafe to set them right.
Away the fair detractors went,
And gave, by turns, their censures vent.
410 'She's not so handsome, in my eyes:
For wit, I wonder where it lies.'
'She's fair and clean, and that's the most;
But why proclaim her for a toast?'
'A babyface, no life, no airs,
But what she learnt at country fairs;

Scarce knows what difference is between
Rich Flanders lace, and colbertine.'
'I'll undertake my little Nancy
In flounces has a better fancy.'
420 'With all her wit, I would not ask
Her judgement, how to buy a mask.'
'We begged her but to patch her face,
She never hit one proper place;
Which every girl at five years old
Can do as soon as she is told.'
'I own, that out-of-fashion stuff
Becomes the creature well enough.'
'The girl might pass, if we could get her
To know the world a little better.'
430 (*To know the world*, a modern phrase,
For visits, ombre, balls and plays.)

Thus, to the world's perpetual shame,
The Queen of Beauty lost her aim.
Too late with grief she understood,
Pallas had done more harm than good;
For great examples are but vain,
Where ignorance begets disdain.
Both sexes armed with guilt and spite,
Against Vanessa's power unite;
440 To copy her, few nymphs aspired;
Her virtues fewer swains admired:
So stars beyond a certain height
Give mortals neither heat nor light.

Yet some of either sex, endowed
With gifts superior to the crowd,
With virtue, knowledge, taste and wit,
She condescended to admit:
With pleasing arts she could reduce
Men's talents to their proper use;
450 And with address each genius held
To that wherein it most excelled;
Thus making other wisdom known,
Could please them, and improve her own.
A modest youth said something new,

She placed it in the strongest view.
All humble worth she strove to raise;
Would not be praised, yet loved to praise.
The learned met with free approach,
Although they came not in a coach.
460 Some clergy too she would allow,
Nor quarrelled at their awkward bow.
But this was for Cadenus' sake;
A gownman of a different make;
Whom Pallas, once Vanessa's tutor,
Had fixed on for her coadjutor.

But Cupid, full of michief, longs
To vindicate his mother's wrongs.
On Pallas all attempts are vain;
One way he knows to give her pain:
470 Vows, on Vanessa's heart to take
Due vengeance, for her patron's sake.
Those early seeds by Venus sown,
In spite of Pallas, now were grown;
And Cupid hoped they would improve
By time, and ripen into love.
The boy made use of all his craft,
In vain discharging many a shaft,
Pointed at colonels, lords, and beaux;
Cadenus warded off the blows:
480 For placing still some book betwixt,
The darts were in the cover fixed,
Or often blunted and recoiled,
On Plutarch's *Morals* struck, were spoiled.

The Queen of Wisdom could foresee,
But not prevent the fates' decree;
And human caution tries in vain
To break that adamantine chain.
Vanessa, though by Pallas taught,
By love invulnerable thought,
490 Searching in books for wisdom's aid,
Was, in the very search, betrayed.

Cupid, though all his darts were lost,
Yet still resolved to spare no cost;

He could not answer to his fame
The triumphs of that stubborn dame;
A nymph so hard to be subdued,
Who neither was coquette nor prude.
'I find,' says he, 'she wants a doctor,
Both to adore her and instruct her;
500 I'll give her what she most admires,
Among those venerable sires.
Cadenus is a subject fit,
Grown old in politics and wit;
Caressed by ministers of state,
Of half mankind the dread and hate.
Whate'er vexations love attend,
She need no rivals apprehend.
Her sex, with universal voice,
Must laugh at her capricious choice.'

510 Cadenus many things had writ;
Vanessa much esteemed his wit;
And called for his poetic works;
Meantime the boy in secret lurks,
And while the book was in her hand,
The urchin from his private stand
Took aim, and shot with all his strength
A dart of such prodigious length,
It pierced the feeble volume through,
And deep transfixed her bosom too.
520 Some lines more moving than the rest,
Stuck to the point that pierced her breast;
And born directly to the heart,
With pains unknown increased her smart.

Vanessa, not in years a score,
Dreams of a gown of forty-four;
Imaginary charms can find,
In eyes with reading almost blind;
Cadenus now no more appears
Declined in health, advanced in years.
530 She fancies music in his tongue,
Nor further looks, but thinks him young.
What mariner is not afraid,

To venture in a ship decayed?
What planter will attempt to yoke
A sapling with a fallen oak?
As years increase, she brighter shines,
Cadenus with each day declines,
And he must fall a prey to time,
While she continues in her prime.

540   Cadenus, common forms apart,
In every scene had kept his heart;
Had sighed and languished, vowed and writ,
For pastime, or to show his wit;
But time, and books, and state affairs,
Had spoiled his fashionable airs;
He now could praise, esteem, approve,
But understood not what was love:
His conduct might have made him styled
A father, and the nymph his child.

550   That innocent delight he took
To see the virgin mind her book,
Was but the master's secret joy
In school to hear the finest boy.
Her knowledge with her fancy grew;
She hourly pressed for something new:
Ideas came into her mind
So fast, his lessons lagged behind:
She reasoned, without plodding long,
Nor ever gave her judgement wrong.

560   But now a sudden change was wrought,
She minds no longer what he taught.
She wished her tutor were her lover;
Resolved she would her flame discover:
And when Cadenus would expound
Some notion subtle or profound,
The nymph would gently press his hand,
As if she seemed to understand;
Or dextrously dissembling chance,
Would sigh, and steal a secret glance.

570   Cadenus was amazed to find
Such marks of a distracted mind;
For though she seemed to listen more

To all he spoke, than e'er before;
He found her thoughts would absent range,
Yet guessed not whence could spring the change.
And first he modestly conjectures
His pupil might be tired with lectures;
Which helped to mortify his pride,
Yet gave him not the heart to chide;
580 But in a mild dejected strain,
At last he ventured to complain:
Said, she should be no longer teased;
Might have her freedom when she pleased:
Was now convinced he acted wrong,
To hide her from the world so long;
And in dull studies to engage,
One of her tender sex and age.
That every nymph with envy owned,
How she might shine in the *grand monde*,
590 And every shepherd was undone
To see her cloistered like a nun.
This was a visionary scheme,
He waked, and found it but a dream;
A project far above his skill,
For nature must be nature still.
If he was bolder than became
A scholar to a courtly dame,
She might excuse a man of letters;
Thus tutors often treat their betters.
600 And since his talk offensive grew,
He came to take his last adieu.

Vanessa, filled with just disdain,
Would still her dignity maintain,
Instructed from her early years
To scorn the art of female tears.

Had he employed his time so long,
To teach her what was right or wrong,
Yet could such notions entertain,
That all his lectures were in vain?
610 She owned the wandering of her thoughts,
But he must answer for her faults.

She well remembered to her cost,
That all his lessons were not lost.
Two maxims she could still produce,
And sad experience taught their use:
That virtue, pleased by being shown,
Knows nothing which it dare not own;
Can make us without fear disclose
Our inmost secrets to our foes:
620 That common forms were not designed
Directors to a noble mind.
'Now,' said the nymph, 'to let you see
My actions with your rules agree,
That I can vulgar forms despise,
And have no secrets to disguise:
I knew by what you said and writ,
How dangerous things were men of wit,
You cautioned me against their charms,
But never gave me equal arms:
630 Your lessons found the weakest part,
Aimed at the head, but reached the heart.'

Cadenus felt within him rise
Shame, disappointment, guilt, surprise.
He knew not how to reconcile
Such language, with her usual style:
And yet her words were so expressed
He could not hope she spoke in jest.
His thoughts had wholly been confined
To form and cultivate her mind.
He hardly knew, till he was told,
640 Whether the nymph were young or old;
Had met her in a public place,
Without distinguishing her face.
Much less could his declining age
Vanessa's earliest thoughts engage.
And if her youth indifference met,
His person must contempt beget.
Or grant her passion be sincere,
How shall his innocence be clear?
650 Appearances were all so strong,
The world must think him in the wrong;

Would say, he made a treacherous use
Of wit, to flatter and seduce:
The town would swear he had betrayed,
By magic spells, the harmless maid;
And every beau would have his jokes,
That scholars were like other folks:
That when platonic flights were over,
The tutor turned a mortal lover.
660   So tender of the young and fair?
It showed a true paternal care –
'Five thousand guineas in her purse:
The doctor might have fancied worse . . .'

Hardly at length he silence broke,
And faltered every word he spoke;
Interpreting her complaisance,
Just as a man *sans consequence*.
She rallied well, he always knew,
Her manner now was something new;
670   And what she spoke was in an air,
As serious as a tragic player.
But those who aim at ridicule
Should fix upon some certain rule,
Which fairly hints they are in jest,
Else he must enter his protest:
For, let a man be ne'er so wise,
He may be caught with sober lies;
A science, which he never taught,
And, to be free, was dearly bought:
680   For, take it in its proper light,
'Tis just what coxcombs call, a 'bite'.

But not to dwell on things minute;
Vanessa finished the dispute,
Brought weighty arguments to prove
That reason was her guide in love.
She thought he had himself described,
His doctrines when she first imbibed;
What he had planted, now was grown;
His virtues she might call her own;
690   As he approves, as he dislikes,

Love or contempt, her fancy strikes.
Self-love, in nature rooted fast,
Attends us first, and leaves us last:
Why she likes him, admire not at her,
She loves herself, and that's the matter.
How was her tutor wont to praise
The geniuses of ancient days!
(Those authors he so oft had named
For learning, wit, and wisdom famed);
700 Was struck with love, esteem and awe,
For persons whom he never saw.
Suppose Cadenus flourished then,
He must adore such godlike men.
If one short volume could comprise
All that was witty, learned, and wise,
How would it be esteemed, and read,
Although the writer long were dead?
If such an author were alive,
How would all for his friendship strive;
710 And come in crowds to see his face:
And this she takes to be her case:
Cadenus answers every end,
The book, the author, and the friend.
The utmost her desires will reach,
Is but to learn what he can teach;
His converse is a system, fit
Alone to fill up all her wit;
While every passion of her mind
In him is centred and confined.

720 Love can with speech inspire a mute,
And taught Vanessa to dispute.
This topic, never touched before,
Displayed her eloquence the more:
Her knowledge, with such pains acquired,
By this new passion grew inspired:
Through this she made all objects pass,
Which gave a tincture o'er the mass:
As rivers, though they bend and twine,
Still to the sea their course incline:
730 Or, as philosophers, who find

Some favourite system to their mind,
In every point to make it fit,
Will force all nature to submit.

Cadenus, who could ne'er suspect
His lessons would have such effect,
Or be so artfully applied,
Insensibly came on her side;
It was an unforeseen event,
Things took a turn he never meant.

740 Whoe'er excels in what we prize,
Appears a hero to our eyes;
Each girl when pleased with what is taught,
Will have the teacher in her thought:
When Miss delights in her spinnet,
A fiddler may a fortune get;
A blockhead with melodious voice
In boarding schools can have his choice;
And oft the dancing-master's art
Climbs from the toe to touch the heart.

750 In learning let a nymph delight,
The pedant gets a mistress by't.
Cadenus, to his grief and shame,
Could scarce oppose Vanessa's flame;
But though her arguments were strong,
At least could hardly wish them wrong.
Howe'er it came, he could not tell,
But sure she never talked so well.
His pride began to interpose,
Preferred before a crowd of beaux:

760 So bright a nymph to come unsought,
Such wonder by his merit wrought:
'Tis merit must with her prevail,
He never knew her judgement fail;
She noted all she ever read,
And had a most discerning head.

'Tis an old maxim in the schools,
That vanity's the food of fools;
Yet now and then your men of wit
Will condescend to take a bit.

770   So when Cadenus could not hide,
     He chose to justify his pride;
     Construing the passion she had shown,
     Much to her praise, more to his own.
     Nature in him had merit placed,
     In her, a most judicious taste.
     Love, hitherto a transient guest,
     Ne'er held possession of his breast;
     So, long attending at the gate,
     Disdained to enter in so late.
780   Love, why do we one passion call?
     When 'tis a compound of them all;
     Where hot and cold, where sharp and sweet,
     In all their equipages meet;
     Where pleasures mixed with pains appear,
     Sorrow with joy, and hope with fear;
     Wherein his dignity and age
     Forbid Cadenus to engage.
     But friendship in its greatest height,
     A constant, rational delight,
790   On virtue's basis fixed to last,
     When love's allurements long are past;
     Which gently warms, but cannot burn;
     He gladly offers in return:
     His want of passion will redeem,
     With gratitude, respect, esteem:
     With that devotion we bestow,
     When goddesses appear below.

      While thus Cadenus entertains
     Vanessa in exalted strains,
800   The nymph in sober words entreats
     A truce with all sublime conceits.
     For why such raptures, flights, and fancies,
     To her, who durst not read romances;
     In lofty style to make replies,
     Which he had taught her to despise.
     But when her tutor will affect
     Devotion, duty, and respect,
     He fairly abdicates his throne,
     The government is now her own;

810   He has a forfeiture incurred:
     She vows to take him at his word,
     And hopes he will not think it strange
     If both should now their stations change.
     The nymph will have her turn, to be
     The tutor; and the pupil, he:
     Though she already can discern,
     Her scholar is not apt to learn;
     Or wants capacity to reach
     The science she designs to teach:
820   Wherein his genius was below
     The skill of every common beau;
     Who, though he cannot spell, is wise
     Enough to read a lady's eyes;
     And will each accidental glance
     Interpret for a kind advance.

     But what success Vanessa met,
     Is to the world a secret yet:
     Whether the nymph, to please her swain,
     Talks in a high romantic strain;
830   Or whether he at last descends
     To like with less seraphic ends;
     Or, to compound the business, whether
     They temper love and books together;
     Must never to mankind be told,
     Nor shall the conscious muse unfold.

     Meantime the mournful Queen of Love
     Led but a weary life above.
     She ventures now to leave the skies,
     Grown by Vanessa's conduct wise:
840   For though by one perverse event
     Pallas had crossed her first intent;
     Though her design was not obtained,
     Yet had she much experience gained;
     And, by the project vainly tried,
     Could better now the cause decide.

     She gave due notice, that both parties,
     Coram Regina prox' die Martis,
     Should at their peril without fail,

'Come and appear, and save their bail.'
850   All met, and silence thrice proclaimed,
One lawyer to each side was named.
The judge discovered in her face
Resentments for her late disgrace;
And, full of anger, shame and grief,
Directed them to mind their brief;
Nor spend their time to show their reading;
She'd have a summary proceeding.
She gathered, under every head,
The sum of what each lawyer said;
860   Gave her own reasons last; and then
Decreed the cause against the men.

But in a weighty cause like this,
To show she did not judge amiss,
Which evil tongues might else report,
She made a speech in open court;
Wherein she grievously complains,
'How she was cheated by the swains:
On whose petition (humbly showing
That women were not worth the wooing;
870   And that unless the sex would mend,
The race of lovers soon must end)
She was at Lord knows what expense
To form a nymph of wit and sense;
A model for her sex designed,
Who never could one lover find.
She saw her favour was misplaced;
The fellows had a wretched taste;
She needs must tell them to their face,
They were a stupid, senseless race:
880   And were she to begin again,
She'd study to reform the men;
Or add some grain of folly more
To women than they had before,
To put them on an equal foot;
And this, or nothing else, would do't.
This might their mutual fancy strike,
Since every being loves its like.

'But now, repenting what was done,
She left all business to her son:

890　She puts the world in his possession,
　　　And let him use it at discretion.'

　　　The crier was ordered to dismiss
　　　The court, so made his last 'Oyez!'
　　　The goddess would no longer wait;
　　　But rising from her chair of state,
　　　Left all below at six and seven,
　　　Harnessed her doves, and flew to heaven.

Horace, Epistle VII, Book I: Imitated and Addressed to the Earl of Oxford

　　　Harley, the nation's great support,
　　　Returning home one day from court
　　　(His mind with public cares possessed,
　　　All Europe's business in his breast)
　　　Observed a parson near Whitehall,
　　　Cheapening old authors on a stall.
　　　The priest was pretty well in case,
　　　And showed some humour in his face;
　　　Looked with an easy, careless mien,
10　A perfect stranger to the spleen;
　　　Of size that might a pulpit fill,
　　　But more inclining to sit still.
　　　My Lord, who (if a man may say't)
　　　Loves mischief better than his meat,
　　　Was now disposed to crack a jest;
　　　And bid friend Lewis go in quest
　　　(This Lewis is an arrant shaver,
　　　And very much in Harley's favour);
　　　In quest, who might this parson be,
20　What was his name, of what degree:
　　　If possible, to learn his story,
　　　And whether he were Whig or Tory?

　　　Lewis his patron's humour knows;
　　　Away upon his errand goes;
　　　And quickly did the matter sift,
　　　Found out that it was Dr Swift:
　　　A clergyman of special note,

For shunning those of his own coat;
Which made his brethen of the gown,
30   Take care betimes to run him down:
No libertine, nor over-nice,
Addicted to no sort of vice;
Went where he pleased, said what he thought;
Not rich, but owed no man a groat.
In state opinions *à la mode*,
He hated Wharton like a toad;
Had given the faction many a wound,
And libelled all the Junta round;
Kept company with men of wit,
40   Who often fathered what he writ;
His works were hawked in every street,
But seldom rose above a sheet:
Of late indeed the paper-stamp
Did very much his genius cramp;
And since he could not spend his fire,
He now intended to retire.

Said Harley, 'I desire to know
From his own mouth, if this be so?
Step to the Doctor straight, and say,
50   I'd have him dine with me today.'
Swift seemed to wonder what he meant,
Nor would believe my Lord had sent;
So never offered once to stir,
But coldly said, 'Your servant, sir.'
'Does he refuse me?', Harley cried.
'He does, with insolence and pride.'

Some few days after, Harley spies
The Doctor fastened by the eyes,
At Charing Cross, among the rout,
60   Where painted monsters dangle out.
He pulled the string, and stopped his coach,
Beckoning the Doctor to approach.

Swift, who could neither fly nor hide,
Came sneaking to the chariot-side,
And offered many a lame excuse:
He never meant the least abuse –

'My Lord – the honour you designed –
Extremely proud – but I had dined –
I'm sure I never should neglect –
70   No man alive has more respect...'
'Well, I shall think of that no more,
If you'll be sure to come at four.'

The Doctor now obeys the summons,
Likes both his company and commons;
Displays his talent, sits till ten;
Next day invited, comes again:
Soon grows domestic, seldom fails
Either at morning, or at meals;
Comes early, and departeth late:
80   In short, the gudgeon took the bait.
My Lord would carry on the jest,
And down to Windsor takes his guest.
Swift much admires the place and air,
And longs to be a canon there;
In summer, round the park to ride,
In winter – never to reside.
'A canon! that's a place too mean:
No, Doctor, you shall be a dean;
Two dozen canons round your stall,
90   And you the tyrant o'er them all:
You need but cross the Irish seas,
To live in plenty, power and ease.'
Poor Swift departs, and, what is worse,
With borrowed money in his purse;
Travels at least a hundred leagues,
And suffers numberless fatigues.

Suppose him, now, a dean complete,
Demurely lolling in his seat;
The silver virge, with decent pride,
100   Stuck underneath his cushion-side:
Suppose him gone through all vexations,
Patents, instalments, abjurations,
First-fruits and tenths, and chapter-treats,
Dues, payments, fees, demands and – cheats
(The wicked laity's contriving,

To hinder clergymen from thriving),
Now all the Doctor's money's spent,
His tenants wrong him in his rent;
The farmers, spitefully combined,
110   Force him to take his tithes in kind;
And Parvisol discounts arrears,
By bills for taxes and repairs.

Poor Swift, with all his losses vexed,
Not knowing where to turn him next,
Above a thousand pounds in debt;
Takes horse, and in a mighty fret,
Rides day and night at such a rate,
He soon arrives at Harley's gate;
But was so dirty, pale, and thin,
120   Old Read would hardly let him in.

Said Harley, 'Welcome, reverend Dean!
What makes your worship look so lean?
Why sure you won't appear in town,
In that old wig and rusty gown?
I doubt your heart is set on pelf
So much, that you neglect yourself.
What! I suppose now stocks are high,
You've some good purchase in your eye;
Or is your money out at use?' –
130   'Truce, good my Lord, I beg a truce!'
(The Doctor in a passion cried),
'Your raillery is misapplied:
Experience I have dearly bought,
You know I am not worth a groat:
But it's a folly to contest,
When you resolve to have your jest;
And since you now have done your worst,
Pray leave me where you found me first.'

The First Ode of the Second Book of Horace Paraphrased and Addressed to Richard Steele, Esq.

Dick, thou'rt resolved, as I am told,
Some strange arcana to unfold,

And with the help of Buckley's pen
To vamp the 'good old cause' again:
Which thou (such Burnet's shrewd advice is)
Must furbish up and nickname 'Crisis'.
Thou pompously wilt let us know
What all the world knew long ago,
(E'er since Sir William Gore was mayor,
10   And Harley filled the Commons' chair)
That we a German prince must own
When Anne for heaven resigns her throne.
But more than that, thou'lt keep a rout
With – who is *in* – and who is *out*,
Thou'lt rail devoutly at the peace,
And all its secret causes trace,
The bucket-play 'twixt Whigs and Tories,
Their ups and downs, with fifty stories
Of tricks, the Lord of Oxford knows,
20   And errors of our plenipo's.
Thou'lt tell of leagues among the great
Portending ruin to our state,
And of that dreadful *coup d'éclat*,
Which has afforded thee much chat,
The Queen forsooth (despotic!) gave
Twelve coronets, without thy leave!
A breach of liberty, 'tis owned,
For which no heads have yet atoned!
Believe me, what thou'st undertaken
30   May bring in jeopardy thy bacon;
For madmen, children, wits and fools
Should never meddle with edged tools.
But since thou'rt got into the fire,
And canst not easily retire,
Thou must no longer deal in farce,
Nor pump to cobble wicked verse;
Until thou shalt have eased thy conscience,
Of spleen, of politics and nonsense,
And when thou'st bid adieu to cares,
40   And settled Europe's grand affairs,
'Twill then, perhaps, be worth thy while
For Drury Lane to shape thy style:
'To make a pair of jolly fellows,

The son and father, join to tell us,
How sons may safely disobey,
And fathers never should say nay,
By which wise conduct they grow friends
At last – and so the story ends.'

When first I knew thee, Dick, thou wert
50 Renowned for skill in Faustus' art,
Which made thy closet much frequented
By buxom lasses – some repented
Their luckless choice of husbands – others,
Impatient to be like their mothers,
Received from thee profound directions
How best to settle their affections;
Thus thou, a friend to the distressed,
Didst in thy calling do thy best.

But now the senate (if things hit
60 And thou at Stockbridge wert not bit)
Must feel thy eloquence and fire,
Approve thy schemes, thy wit admire,
Thee with immortal honours crown,
Whilst patriot-like thou'lt strut and frown.

What, though by enemies 'tis said,
The laurel, which adorns thy head,
Must one day come in competition,
By virtue of some sly petition:
Yet mum for that, hope still the best,
70 Nor let such cares disturb thy rest.

Methinks I hear thee loud as trumpet,
As bagpipe shrill, or oyster-strumpet,
Methinks I see thee, spruce and fine,
With coat embroidered richly shine,
And dazzle all the idol faces
As through the Hall thy worship paces:
(Though this I speak but at a venture,
Supposing thou hast tick with Hunter)
Methinks I see a blackguard rout
80 Attend thy coach, and hear them shout
In approbation of thy tongue,
Which (in their style) is 'purely hung'.
Now, now you carry all before ye,

Nor dares one Jacobite or Tory
Pretend to answer one syl-lable,
Except the matchless hero Abel.
What though her Highness and her spouse
In Antwerp keep a frugal house,
Yet not forgetful of a friend,
90   They'll soon enable thee to spend,
If to Macartney thou wilt toast,
And to his pious patron's ghost.
Now manfully thou'lt run a tilt
'On popes, for all the blood they've spilt,
For massacres, and racks, and flames,
For lands enriched by crimson streams,
For inquisitions taught by Spain,
Of which the Christian world complain.'

Dick, we agree – all's true, thou'st said,
100   As that my muse is yet a maid.
But, if I may with freedom talk,
All this is foreign to thy walk:
Thy genius has perhaps a knack
At trudging in a beaten track,
But is for state affairs as fit,
As mine for politics and wit.
Then let us both in time grow wise,
Nor higher than our talents rise;
To some snug cellar let's repair
110   From duns and debts, and drown our care;
Now quaff of honest ale a quart,
Now venture at a pint of port,
With which inspired we'll club each night
Some tender sonnet to indite,
And with Tom D'Urfey, Philips, Dennis,
Immortalize our Dolls and Jennies.

Scriblerian Verses

I

The Doctor and Dean, Pope, Parnell and Gay
In manner submissive most humbly do pray,
That your Lordship would once let your cares all alone

And climb the dark stairs to your friends who have none:
To your friends who at least have no cares but to please you
To a good honest Junta that never will tease you.

From the Doctor's chamber,
past eight.

2

Let not the Whigs our Tory club rebuke;
Give us our Earl, the devil take their Duke.
Quaedam quae attinent ad Scriblerum,
Want your assistance now to clear 'em.
    One day it will be no disgrace,
    In 'Scribler' to have had a place.
Come then, my Lord, and take your part in
The important *History of Martin.*

3

My Lord, foresake your politic utopians,
To sup, like Jove, with blameless Ethiopians.
                  Pope.

In other words, you with the staff,
Leave John of Bucks, come here and laugh.
                  Dean.

For frolic mirth give o'er affairs of state,
Tonight be happy, be tomorrow great.
                  Parnell.

Give clans your money, us your smile,
Your scorn to Townshend and Argyll.
                  Doctor.

Leave courts, and hie to simple swains,
10 Who feed no flock upon no plains.
                  Gay.

4

    A pox of all senders
    For any pretenders
Who tell us these troublesome stories,
    In their dull humdrum key

Of '*arma virumque*
Hannoniae qui primus ab oris . . .'

A fig too for Hanmer
Who prates like his *grande mère*,
And all his old friends would rebuke
10   In spite of the carle
Give us but our Earl,
And the devil may take their Duke.

Then come and take part in
The *Memoirs of Martin*,
Lay by your white staff and grey habit,
For trust us, friend Mortimer,
Should you live years forty more
Haec olim meminisse juvabit.

By order of the club
A. Pope
J. Gay
J. Swift
J. Arbuthnot
T. Parnel

The Faggot

WRITTEN IN THE YEAR 1713, WHEN THE QUEEN'S MINISTERS
WERE QUARRELLING AMONG THEMSELVES

Observe the dying father speak:
'Try, lads, can you this bundle break;'
Then, bids the youngest of the six,
Take up a well-bound heap of sticks.
They thought it was an old man's maggot;
And strove by turns to break the faggot:
In vain – the complicated wands
Were much too strong for all their hands.
'See,' said the sire, 'how soon 'tis done':
10   Then, took and broke them one by one.
So strong you'll be, in friendship tied;
So quickly broke if you divide.

Keep close then, boys, and never quarrel.
Here ends the fable and the moral.

The tale may be applied in few words
To treasurers, controllers, stewards,
And others, who in solemn sort
Appear with slender wands at court:
Not firmly joined to keep their ground,
20   But lashing one another round:
While, wise men think they ought to fight
With quarter-staffs instead of white;
Or constable with staff of peace,
Should come and make the clattering cease;
Which now disturbs the Queen and court,
And gives the Whigs and rabble sport.

In history, we never found
The consul's fasces were unbound;
Those Romans were too wise to think on't,
30   Except to lash some grand delinquent.
How would they blush to hear it said,
The praetor broke the consul's head;
Or, consul in his purple gown,
Came up, and knocked the praetor down.

Come, courtiers: every man his stick:
Lord Treasurer, for once be quick:
And, that they may the closer cling,
Take your blue ribbon for a string.
Come, trimming Harcourt; bring your mace;
40   And squeeze it in, or quit your place:
Dispatch; or else that rascal Northey
Will undertake to do it for thee:
And, be assured, the court will find him
Prepared to leap o'er sticks, or bind 'em.

To make the bundle strong and safe,
Great Ormonde lend thy general's staff:
And, if the crozier could be crammed in,
A fig for Lechmere, King, and Hampden.
You'll then defy the strongest Whig,
50   With both his hands to bend a twig;

Though with united strength they all pull,
From Somers down to Craggs and Walpole.

The Author upon Himself

By an old red-pate, murdering hag pursued,
A crazy prelate, and a royal prude.
By dull divines, who look with envious eyes,
On every genius that attempts to rise;
And pausing o'er a pipe, with doubtful nod,
Give hints, that poets ne'er believe in God.
So, clowns on scholars as on wizards look,
And take a folio for a conjuring book.

    Swift had the sin of wit, no venial crime;
10 Nay, 'twas affirmed, he sometimes dealt in rhyme:
Humour, and mirth, had place in all he writ:
He reconciled divinity and wit.
He moved, and bowed, and talked with too much grace;
Nor showed the parson in his gait or face;
Despised luxurious wines, and costly meat;
Yet, still was at the tables of the great.
Frequented lords; saw those that saw the Queen;
At Child's or Truby's never once had been;
Where town and country vicars flock in tribes,
20 Secured by numbers from the laymen's gibes;
And deal in vices of the graver sort,
Tobacco, censure, coffee, pride, and port.

    But, after sage monitions from his friends,
His talents to employ for nobler ends;
To better judgements willing to submit,
He turns to politics his dangerous wit.

    And now, the public interest to support,
By Harley Swift invited comes to court.
In favour grows with ministers of state;
30 Admitted private, when superiors wait:
And, Harley, not ashamed his choice to own,
Takes him to Windsor in his coach, alone.

At Windsor Swift no sooner can appear,
But, St John comes and whispers in his ear;
The waiters stand in ranks; the yeomen cry,
'Make room', as if a duke were passing by.

Now Finch alarms the Lords; he hears for certain,
This dangerous priest is got behind the curtain:
Finch, famed for tedious elocution, proves
40   That Swift oils many a spring which Harley moves.
Walpole and Aislabie, to clear the doubt,
Inform the Commons, that the secret's out:
'A certain Doctor is observed of late,
To haunt a certain minister of state:
From whence, with half an eye we may discover,
The peace is made, and Perkin must come over.'
York is from Lambeth sent, to show the Queen
A dangerous treatise writ against the spleen;
Which by the style, the matter, and the drift,
50   'Tis thought could be the work of none but Swift.
Poor York! The harmless tool of others' hate;
He sues for pardon, and repents too late.

Now Madam Königsmark her vengeance vows
On Swift's reproaches for her murdered spouse:
From her red locks her mouth with venom fills;
And thence into the royal ear instils.
The Queen incensed, his services forgot,
Leaves him a victim to the vengeful Scot;
Now, through the realm a proclamation spread,
60   To fix a price on his devoted head.
While innocent, he scorns ignoble flight;
His watchful friends preserve him by a sleight.

By Harley's favour once again he shines;
Is now caressed by candidate divines;
Who change opinions with the changing scene:
Lord! how they were mistaken in the Dean!
Now, Delaware again familiar grows;
And in Swift's ear thrusts half his powdered nose.
The Scottish nation, whom he durst offend,
70   Again apply that Swift would be their friend.

By faction tired, with grief he waits a while,
His great contending friends to reconcile.
Performs what friendship, justice, truth require:
What could he more, but decently retire?

In Sickness

WRITTEN SOON AFTER THE AUTHOR'S COMING TO LIVE
IN IRELAND, UPON THE QUEEN'S DEATH, OCTOBER 1714

'Tis true – then why should I repine,
To see my life so fast decline?
But, why obscurely here alone?
Where I am neither loved nor known.
My state of health none care to learn;
My life is here no soul's concern.
And, those with whom I now converse,
Without a tear will tend my hearse.
Removed from kind Arbuthnot's aid,
10 Who knows his art but not his trade;
Preferring his regard for me
Before his credit or his fee.
Some formal visits, looks, and words,
What mere humanity affords,
I meet perhaps from three or four,
From whom I once expected more;
Which those who tend the sick for pay
Can act as decently as they.
But, no obliging, tender friend
20 To help at my approaching end,
My life is now a burden grown
To others, e'er it be my own.

Ye formal weepers for the sick,
In your last offices be quick:
And spare my absent friends the grief
To hear, yet give me no relief;
Expired today, entombed tomorrow,
When known, will save a double sorrow.

The Fable of the Bitches

WROTE IN THE YEAR 1715, ON AN ATTEMPT TO REPEAL
THE TEST ACT

A bitch that was full pregnant grown,
By all the dogs and curs in town;
Finding her ripened time was come,
Her litter teeming from her womb,
Went here and there, and everywhere,
To find an easy place to lay her.

At length to Music's house she came,
And begged like one both blind and lame;
'My only friend, my dear,' said she,
10   'You see 'tis mere necessity,
Hath sent me to your house to whelp,
I'll die, if you deny your help.'

With fawning whine, and rueful tone,
With artful sigh and feignèd groan,
With couchant cringe, and flattering tale,
Smooth Bawty did so far prevail;
That Music gave her leave to litter,
But mark what followed – faith, she bit her.

Whole baskets full of bits and scraps,
20   And broth enough to fill her paps,
For well she knew her numerous brood,
For want of milk, would suck her blood.

But when she thought her pains were done,
And now 'twas high time to be gone;
In civil terms, 'My friend,' says she,
'My house you've had on courtesy;
And now I earnestly desire,
That you would with your cubs retire:
For should you stay but one week longer,
30   I shall be starved with cold and hunger.'

The guest replied, 'My friend, your leave,
I must a little longer crave;
Stay till my tender cubs can find

Their way – for now you see they're blind;
But when we've gathered strength, I swear,
We'll to our barn again repair.'

The time passed on, and Music came,
Her kennel once again to claim;
But Bawty, lost to shame and honour,
40   Set her cubs at once upon her;
Made her retire, and quit her right,
And loudly cried 'A bite, a bite.'

THE MORAL

Thus did the Grecian wooden horse,
Conceal a fatal armed force;
No sooner brought within the walls,
But Ilium's lost, and Priam falls.

Horace, Lib. 2, Sat. 6

PART OF IT IMITATED

I often wished that I had clear
For life, six hundred pounds a year,
A handsome house to lodge a friend,
A river at my garden's end,
A terrace walk, and half a rood
Of land, set out to plant a wood.

Well: now I have all this and more,
I ask not to increase my store;
And should be perfectly content,
10   Could I but live on this side Trent;
Nor cross the Channel twice a year,
To spend six months with statesmen here.

I must by all means come to town,
'Tis for the service of the crown.
'Lewis; the Dean will be of use,
Send for him up, take no excuse.'
The toil, the danger of the seas;
Great ministers ne'er think of these;

Or let it cost five hundred pound,
20   No matter where the money's found;
It is but so much more in debt,
And that they ne'er considered yet.

'Good Mr Dean, go change your gown,
Let my Lord know you're come to town.'
I hurry me in haste away,
Not thinking it is levee day;
And find his honour in a pound,
Hemmed by a triple circle round,
Chequered with ribbons blue and green,
30   How should I thrust myself between?
Some wag observes me thus perplexed,
And smiling, whispers to the next,
'I thought the Dean had been too proud,
To jostle here among a crowd.'
Another in a surly fit,
Tells me I have more zeal than wit,
'So eager to express your love,
You ne'er consider whom you shove,
But rudely press before a duke.'
40   I own, I'm pleased with this rebuke,
And take it kindly meant to show
What I desire the world should know.

I get a whisper, and withdraw,
When twenty fools I never saw
Come with petitions fairly penned,
Desiring I would stand their friend.

This, humbly offers me his case:
That, begs my interest for a place.
A hundred other men's affairs
50   Like bees are humming in my ears.
'Tomorrow my appeal comes on,
Without your help the cause is gone –'
'The Duke expects my Lord and you,
About some great affair, at two –'
'Put my Lord Bolingbroke in mind,
To get my warrant quickly signed:
Consider, 'tis my first request.'

Be satisfied. I'll do my best –
Then presently he falls to tease:
60   'You may for certain, if you please;
I doubt not, if his Lordship knew –
And Mr Dean, one word from you –'

'Tis (let me see) three years and more
(October next, it will be four)
Since Harley bid me first attend,
And chose me for an humble friend;
Would take me in his coach to chat,
And question me of this and that;
As 'What's o-clock?' and 'How's the wind?'
70   Whose chariot's that we left behind?'
Or gravely try to read the lines
Writ underneath the country signs;
Or, 'Have you nothing new today
From Pope, from Parnell or from Gay?'
Such tattle often entertains
My Lord and me as far as Staines:
As once a week we travel down
To Windsor and again to town;
Where all that passes, *inter nos*,
80   Might be proclaimed at Charing Cross.

Yet some I know with envy swell,
Because they see me used so well:
'How think you of our friend the Dean?
I wonder what some people mean;
My Lord and he are grown so great,
Always together, *tête à tête*:
What, they admire him for his jokes –
See but the fortune of some folks!'

There flies about a strange report
90   Of some express arrived at court;
I'm stopped by all the fools I meet,
And catechized in every street.
'You, Mr Dean, frequent the great;
Inform us, will the Emperor treat?
Or do the prints and papers lie?'
Faith, Sir, you know as much as I.

'Ah Doctor, how you love to jest!
'Tis now no secret' – I protest
'Tis one to me. 'Then, tell us, pray
100   When are the troops to have their pay?'
And though I solemnly declare
I know no more than my Lord Mayor,
They stand amazed, and think me grown
The closest mortal ever known.

Thus in a sea of folly tossed,
My choicest hours of life are lost;
Yet always wishing to retreat;
Oh, could I see my country seat!
There leaning near a gentle brook,
110   Sleep, or peruse some ancient book;
And there in sweet oblivion drown
Those cares that haunt a court and town.

To the Earl of Oxford, Late Lord Treasurer

SENT TO HIM WHEN HE WAS IN THE TOWER, BEFORE HIS TRIAL

OUT OF HORACE

How blessed is he, who for his country dies;
Since death pursues the coward as he flies.
The youth, in vain, would fly from Fate's attack,
With trembling knees, and terror at his back;
Though fear should lend him pinions like the wind,
Yet swifter Fate will seize him from behind.

Virtue repulsed, yet knows not to repine;
But shall with unattainted honour shine;
Nor stoops to take the Staff, nor lays it down,
10   Just as the rabble please to smile or frown.

Virtue, to crown her favourites, loves to try
Some new unbeaten passage to the sky;
Where Jove a seat among the gods will give
To those who die, for meriting to live.

Next, faithful silence hath a sure reward:
Within our breast be every secret barred:

He who betrays his friend, shall never be
Under one roof, or in one ship with me.
For, who with traitors would his safety trust,
20 Lest with the wicked, heaven involve the just?
And, though the villain 'scape a while, he feels
Slow vengeance, like a bloodhound at his heels.

Dean Swift's Answer to the Reverend Dr Sheridan

Sir,
In reading your letter alone in my hackney,
Your damnable riddle, my poor brains did rack nigh.
And when with much labour the matter I cracked,
I found you mistaken in matter of fact.

A woman's no sieve (for with that you begin)
Because she lets out more, than e'er she takes in.
And that she's a riddle, can never be right,
For a riddle is dark, but a woman is *light*.
But grant her a sieve, I can say something archer,
10 Pray what is a man? he's a fine-linen searcher.

Now tell me a thing that wants interpretation,
What name for a maid, was the first man's damnation?
If your worship will please to explain me this rebus,
I swear from henceforward you shall be my Phoebus.

From my hackney-coach,
September 11, 1718.
Past 12 at noon.

The Dean of St Patrick's to Thomas Sheridan

I cannot but think that we live in a bad age,
O tempora, o mores! as 'tis in the adage.
My foot was but just set out from my cathedral,
When into my hands comes a letter from the droll.
I can't pray in quiet for you and your verses, –
But now let us hear what the muse from your car says.

Hum – excellent good – your anger was stirred:
Well, punners and rhymers must have the last word.
But let me advise you, when next I hear from you,
10   To leave off this passion which does not become you:
For we who debate on a subject important,
Must argue with calmness, or else will come short on't.
For myself, I protest, I care not a fiddle
For a riddle and sieve, or a sieve and a riddle:
And think of the sex as you please, I'd as lief
You call them a riddle, as call them a sieve.
Yet still you are out (though to vex you I'm loth),
For I'll prove it impossible they can be both.
A schoolboy knows this, for it plainly appears
20   That a sieve dissolves riddles by help of the shears;
For you can't but have heard of a trick among wizards,
To break open riddles with shears or with scissors.

Think again of the sieve, and I'll hold you a wager,
You dare not to question my minor or major.
A sieve keeps half in, and therefore, no doubt,
Like a woman it keeps in less than it lets out.
Why sure, Mr Poet, your head got a jar
By riding this morning too long in your car:
And I wish your few friends, when they next see your car go,
30   For the sake of your senses would lay an embargo.

You threaten the stocks: I say you are scurrilous,
And you durst not talk thus if I saw you at our alehouse.
But as for your threats, you may do what you can,
I despise any poet that truckled to Dan.
But keep a good tongue, or you'll find, to your smart,
From rhyming in cars you may swing in a cart.

You found out my rebus with very much modesty;
But thanks to the lady: I'm sure she's too good to ye;
Till she lent you her help, you were in a fine twitter:
40   You hit it, you say – you're a delicate hitter.
How could you forget so ungratefully a lass?
And if you be my Phoebus, pray who was your Pallas?

As for your new rebus, or riddle, or crux,
I will either explain, or repay it by trucks;

Though your lords, and your dogs, and your catches, methinks,
Are harder than ever were put by the Sphinx.

And thus I am fully revenged for your late tricks,
Which is at present all from

Dean of St Patrick's.

From my closet,
September 12, 1718,
just 12 at noon.

A Left-Handed Letter to Dr Sheridan

Sir,
Delany reports it, and he has a shrewd tongue,
That we both act the part of the clown and the cow-dung;
We lie cramming ourselves, and are ready to burst,
Yet still are no wiser than we were at first.
Pudet haec opprobria, I freely must tell ye,
Et diu potuisse, et non potuisse refelli.
Though Delany advised you to plague me no longer,
You reply and rejoin like Hoadly of Bangor.
I must now, at one sitting, pay off my old score:
10 How many to answer? One, two, three, four.
But because the three former are long ago past,
I shall, for method sake, begin with the last.
You treat me like a boy that knocks down his foe,
Who, ere t'other gets up, demands the riding blow.
Yet I know a young rogue, that thrown flat on the field,
Would, as he lay under, cry out, 'Sirrah, yield':
So, the French, when our generals soundly did pay 'em,
Went triumphant to church, and sang stoutly *Te deum*:
So the famous Tom Leigh, when quite run aground,
20 Comes off by out-laughing the company round.
In every vile pamphlet you'll read the same fancies,
Having thus overthrown all our further advances.
My offers of peace you ill understood.
Friend Sheridan, when will you know your own good?
'Twas to teach you in modester language your duty;
For, were you a dog, I could not be rude t'ye.

As a good quiet soul, who no mischief intends
To a quarrelsome fellow, cries, 'Let us be friends.'
But we like Antaeus and Hercules fight,
30   The oftener you fall, the oftener you write;
And I'll use you as he did that overgrown clown,
I'll first take you up, and then take you down:
And, 'tis your own case, for you never can wound
The worst dunce in your school, till he's heaved from the ground.

The Dean to Thomas Sheridan

Sir,
When I saw you today, as I went with Lord Anglesey,
Lord! said I, who's that person? how awkwardly dangles he!
When whip you trot up, without minding your betters,
To the very coach side, and threaten your letters.

Is the poison and dagger you boast in your jaws, trow?
Are you still in your cart with *convitia ex plaustro*?
But to scold is your trade, which I soon should be foiled in,
For scolding is just *quasi diceres* – school-din:
And I think I may say, you could many shillings get,
10   Were you dressed like a bawd, and sold oysters at Billingsgate.
But coach it or cart it, I'd have you know, sirrah,
I'll write, though I am forced to write in a wheelbarrow:
Nay, hector and swagger, you'll still find me staunch,
And you and your cart shall give me *carte blanche*.
Since you write in a cart, keep it *tecta et sarta*,
'Tis all you have for 't; 'tis your best Magna Carta;
And I love you so well, as I told you long ago,
That I'll never give my vote for *Delenda Cart-ago*.

Now you write from your cellar – I still find out your art,
20   You rhyme, as folks fence, in *tierce* and *carte*.
Your ink is your poison, your pen is what not;
Your ink is your drink, your pen is your pot.
To my goddess Melpomene, pride of her sex,
I gave, as you beg, your most humble respects:
The rest of your compliment I dare not tell her,
For she never descends so low as the cellar;

But before you can put yourself under her banners,
She declares from her throne you must learn better manners.

If once in your cellar my Phoebus should shine,
30 I'll tell you I'd not give a fig for your wine;
So I'll leave him behind, for I certainly know it,
What he ripens above ground, he sours below it.

But why should we fight thus, my partner so dear,
With three hundred and sixty-five poems a year?
Let's quarrel no longer, since Dan and George Rochfort
Will laugh in their sleeves: I can tell you they watch for 't.
Then George will rejoice, and Dan will sing high day:
Hoc Ithacus velit, et magni mercentur Atridae.

Jon: Swift.

Written, signed, and sealed, five minutes
and eleven seconds after the receipt of
yours, allowing seven seconds for sealing
and superscribing, from my bedside, just
eleven minutes after eleven, September
15th 1718.

To Thomas Sheridan

Dear Tom, I'm surprised that your verse did not jingle;
But your rhyme was not double, 'cause your sight was but single.
For, as Helsham observes, there's nothing can chime,
Or fit more exact than one eye and one rhyme.
If you had not took physic, I'd pay off your bacon,
But now I'll write short, for fear you're short taken.
Besides, Dick forbid me, and called me a fool;
For he says, short as 'tis, it will give you a stool.

In libris bellis, tu parum parcis ocellis,
10 Dum nimium scribis, vel talpâ caecior ibis,
Aut ad vina redis, nam sic tua lumina laedis:
Sed tibi coenanti sunt collyria tanti?
Nunquid eges visu, dum comples omnia risu?

Heu! Sheridan caecus, heu eris nunc cercopithecus.

Nunc bene nasutus mittet tibi carmina tutus:
Nunc ope Burgundi, malus Helsham ridet abunde,
Nec Phoebi fili versum quis mittere Ryly.

Quid tibi cum libris? relavet tua lumina Tybris
Mixtus Saturno; penso sed parcè diurno
20   Observes hoc tu, nec scriptis utere noctu.
Nonnulli mingunt et palpebras sibi tingunt.
Quidam purgantes, libros in stercore nantes
Linquunt; sic vinces videndo, mi bone, lynces.
Culum oculum tergis, dum scripta hoc flumine mergis;
Tunc oculi et nates, ni fallor, agent tibi grates.
Vim fuge Decani, nec sit tibi cura Delani:
Heu tibi si scribant, aut si tibi fercula libant,
Pone loco mortis, rapis fera pocula fortis.
Haec tibi pauca dedi, sed consule Betty Mi Lady,
30   Huic te des solae, nec egebis pharmacopolae.

Haec somnians cecini,
J^n Swift.

October 23rd 1718.

Sheridan, a Goose

Tom, for a goose you keep but base quills,
They're fit for nothing else but pasquils.
I've often heard it from the wise,
That inflammations in the eyes
Will quickly fall upon the tongue,
And thence, as famed John Bunyan sung,
From out the pen will presently
On paper dribble daintily.
Suppose I called you goose, it is hard
10   One word should stick thus in your gizzard.
You're my goose, and no other man's;
And you know all my geese are swans:
Only one scurvy thing I find,
Swans sing when dying, geese when blind.
But now I smoke where lies the slander, –
I called you goose instead of gander;

For that, dear Tom, ne'er fret and vex,
I'm sure you cackle like the sex.
I know the gander always goes
20 With a quill stuck across his nose.
So your eternal pen is still,
Or in your claw, or in your bill.
But whether you can tread or hatch,
I've something else to do than watch.
As for you're writing I am dead,
I leave it for the second head.

Deanery House
October 27th 1718.

Mary the Cook-Maid's Letter to Dr Sheridan

Well; if ever I saw such another man since my mother bound my
head,
You a gentleman! marry come up, I wonder where you were bred?
I am sure such words does not become a man of your cloth,
I would not give such language to a dog, faith and troth.
Yes; you called my master a knave; fie Mr Sheridan, 'tis a shame
For a parson, who should know better things, to come out with
such a name.
Knave in your teeth, Mr Sheridan, 'tis both a shame and a sin,
And the Dean my master is an honester man than you and all your
kin:
He has more goodness in his little finger, than you have in your
whole body,
10 My master is a parsonable man, and not a spindle-shanked
hoddy-doddy.
And now whereby I find you would fain make an excuse,
Because my master one day, in anger, called you goose.
Which, and I am sure I have been his servant four years since
October,
And he never called me worse than 'sweetheart', drunk or sober:
Not that I know his Reverence was ever concerned to my
knowledge,
Though you and your come-rogues keep him out so late in your
wicked college.

You say you will eat grass on his grave: a Christian eat grass!
Whereby you now confess yourself to be a goose or an ass:
But that's as much as to say, that my master should die before ye;
20 Well, well, that's as God pleases, and I don't believe that's a true
    story,
And so say I told you so, and you may go tell my master; what care
    I?
And I don't care who knows it, 'tis all one to Mary.
Everybody knows, that I love to tell truth, and shame the devil;
I am but a poor servant, but I think gentlefolks should be civil.
Besides, you found fault with our victuals one day that you was
    here,
I remember it was upon a Tuesday, of all days in the year.
And Saunders the man says, you are always jesting and mocking,
'Mary' said he, (one day, as I was mending my master's stocking,)
'My master is so fond of that minister that keeps the school;
30 I thought my master a wise man, but that man makes him a fool.'
'Saunders' said I, 'I would rather than a quart of ale,
He would come into our kitchen, and I would pin a dishclout to
    his tail.'
And now I must go, and get Saunders to direct this letter,
For I write but a sad scrawl, but sister Marget she writes better.
Well, but I must run and make the bed before my master comes
    from prayers,
And see now, it strikes ten, and I hear him coming upstairs:
Whereof I could say more to your verses, if I could write written
    hand,
And so I remain in a civil way, your servant to command,
                                      MARY.

A Letter to the Reverend Dr Sheridan

WRITTEN IN THE YEAR 1718

Whate'er your predecessors taught us,
I have a great esteem for Plautus;
And think your boys may gather there-hence
More wit and humour than from Terence.
But as to comic Aristophanes,
The rogue's too bawdy and too prophane is.

I went in vain to look for Eupolis,
Down in the Strand just where the new pole is,
For I can tell you one thing, that I can,
10   You will not find it in the Vatican.
He and Cratinus used, as Horace says,
To take his greatest grandees for asses.
Poets, in those days, used to venture high,
But these are lost full many a century.

    Thus you may see, dear friend, *ex pede* hence
My judgement of the old comedians.

    Proceed to tragics, first Euripides
(An author, where I sometimes dip a-days)
Is rightly censured by the Stagirite,
20   Who says, his numbers do not fadge a-right.
A friend of mine, that author despises
So much, he swears the very best piece is,
For aught he knows, as bad as Thespis's.
And that a woman, in those tragedies
Commonly speaking, but a sad jade is.
At least, I'm well assured, that no folk lays
The weight on him, they do on Sophocles.
But above all I prefer Aeschylus,
Whose moving touches, when they please, kill us.

30   And now I find my muse but ill able
To hold out longer in trisyllable.
I chose these rhymes out, for their difficulty.
Will you return as hard ones, if I call t'ye?

To Mr Delany

To you, whose virtues I must own
With shame, I have too lately known;
To you, by art and nature taught
To be the man I long have sought,
Had not ill fate, perverse and blind,
Placed you in life too far behind;
Or what I should repine at more,
Placed me in life too far before;

To you the muse this verse bestows,
10 Which might as well have been in prose;
No thought, no fancy, no sublime,
But simple topics told in rhyme.

Three gifts for conversation fit
Are humour, raillery and wit:
The last, as boundless as the wind,
Is well conceived though not defined;
For, sure, by wit is only meant
Applying what we first invent:
What humour is, not all the tribe
20 Of logic-mongers can describe;
Here, only nature acts her part,
Unhelped by practice, books, or art.
For wit and humour differ quite,
That gives surprise, and this delight:
Humour is odd, grotesque, and wild,
Only by affectation spoiled,
'Tis never by invention got,
Men have it when they know it not.

Our conversation to refine
30 True humour must with wit combine;
From both, we learn to rally well;
Wherein French writers most excel:
Voiture in various lights displays
That irony which turns to praise;
His genius first found out the rule
For an obliging ridicule:
He flatters with peculiar air
The brave, the witty, and the fair;
And fools would fancy he intends
40 A satire where he most commends.

But as a poor pretending beau
Because he fain would make a show,
Nor can afford to buy gold lace,
Takes up with copper in the place;
So, the pert dunces of mankind
Whene'er they would be thought refined,

Because the difference lies abstruse
'Twixt raillery and gross abuse,
To show their parts, will scold and rail,
50 Like porters o'er a pot of ale.

Such is that clan of boisterous bears
Always together by the ears;
Shrewd fellows, and arch wags, a tribe
That meet for nothing but to gibe;
Who first run one another down,
And then fall foul on all the town;
Skilled in the horse-laugh and dry rub,
And called by excellence, 'the Club':
I mean your Butler, Dawson, Carr,
60 All special friends, and always jar.

The mettled and the vicious steed
Do not more differ in their breed,
Nay, Voiture is as like Tom Leigh,
As rudeness is to repartee.

If what you said, I wish unspoke,
'Twill not suffice, it was a joke.
Reproach not though in jest a friend
For those defects he cannot mend;
His lineage, calling, shape or sense
70 If named with scorn, gives just offence.

What use in life, to make men fret?
Part in worse humour than they met?
Thus all society is lost,
Men laugh at one another's cost;
And half the company is teased
That came together to be pleased:
For all buffoons have most in view
To please themselves by vexing you.

When jests are carried on too far,
80 And the loud laugh proclaims the war;
You keep your countenance for shame
Yet still you think your friend to blame.
And though men cry, they love a jest,

'Tis but when others stand the test,
For would you have their meaning known?
They love a jest – when 'tis their own.

You wonder now to see me write
So gravely, where the subject's light.
Some part of what I here design
90　Regards a friend of yours and mine,
Who full of humour, fire and wit,
Not always judges what is fit;
But loves to take prodigious rounds,
And sometimes walks beyond his bounds.
You must, although the point be nice,
Venture to give him some advice.
Few hints from you will set him right,
And teach him how to be polite.
Let him, like you, observe with care
100　Whom to be hard on, whom to spare:
Nor indiscreetly to suppose
All subjects like Dan Jackson's nose.
To study the obliging jest,
By reading those who teach it best.
For prose, I recommend Voiture's,
For verse, (I speak my judgement) yours:
He'll find the secret out from thence
To rhyme all day without offence;
And I no more shall then accuse
110　The flirts of his ill-mannered muse.

If he be guilty, you must mend him,
If he be innocent, defend him.

On Dan Jackson's Picture

Whilst you three merry poets traffic
To give us a description graphic
Of Dan's large nose, in modern Sapphic,

I spend my time in making sermons,
Or writing libels on the Germans,
Or murmuring at Whigs' preferments.

But when I would find rhyme for Rochfort,
And look in English, French, and Scotch for 't,
At last I'm fairly forced to botch for 't.

10 Bid Lady Betty recollect her,
And tell who was it could direct her
To draw the face of such a spectre.

I must confess that as to me, sirs,
Though I never saw her hold the scissors,
I now could safely swear it is hers.

'Tis true no nose could come in better,
'Tis a vast subject stuffed with matter,
Which all may handle, none may flatter.

Take courage, Dan, this plainly shows,
20 That not the wisest mortal knows
What fortune may befall his nose.

Show me the brightest Irish toast,
Who from her lover e'er could boast,
Above a song or two at most:

For thee three poets are drudging all,
To praise the cheeks, chin, nose, the bridge and all,
Both of the picture and original.

Thy nose's length and fame extend
So far, dear Dan, that every friend
30 Tries who shall have it by the end.

And future poets, as they rise,
Shall read with envy and surprise,
Thy nose outshining Celia's eyes.

Dan Jackson's Reply

WRITTEN BY THE DEAN IN THE NAME OF DAN JACKSON

Wearied with saying grace and prayer,
I hastened down to country air,
To read your answer, and prepare
        Reply to 't.

But your fair lines so grossly flatter,
Pray do they praise me or bespatter?
I much suspect you mean the latter,
      Ah sly-boot!

It must be so; what else, alas,
10 Can mean my culling of a face,
And all that stuff of toilet, glass,
      And box-comb?

But be 't as 'twill, this you must grant,
That you're a daub, whilst I but paint,
Then which of us two is the quaint-
      er coxcomb?

I value not your jokes of noose,
Your gibes and all your foul abuse,
More than the dirt beneath my shoes,
20   Nor fear it.

Yet one thing vexes me, I own,
Thou sorry scarecrow of skin and bone,
To be called lean by a skeleton,
      Who'd bear it?

'Tis true indeed, to curry friends,
You seem to praise to make amends,
And yet before your stanza ends
      You flout me

'Bout latent charms beneath my clothes;
30 For everyone that knows me, knows
That I have nothing like my nose
      About me.

I pass now where you fleer and laugh
'Cause I call Dan my better half,
Oh, there you think you have me safe!
      But hold sir,

Is not a penny often found
To be much greater than a pound?
By your good leave, my most profound
40   And bold sir,

Dan's noble metal, Sherry base;
So Dan's the better, though the less,
An ounce of gold's worth ten of brass,
   Dull pedant.

As to your spelling, let me see,
If S H E makes *sher*, and R I makes *ry*,
Good spelling, master, your crany
   Has lead on't.

Another Reply by the Dean

IN DAN JACKSON'S NAME

Three days for an answer I have waited,
I thought an ace you'd ne'er have bated,
And art thou forced to yield, ill-fated
   Poetaster?

Henceforth acknowledge, that a nose
Of thy dimension's fit for prose,
But everyone that knows Dan, knows
   Thy master.

Blush for ill spelling, for ill lines,
10 And fly with hurry to Ramines;
Thy fame, thy genius now declines,
   Proud boaster.

I hear with some concern you roar,
And flying think to quit the score,
By clapping billets on your door
   And posts, sir.

Thy ruin, Tom, I never meant,
I'm grieved to hear your banishment,
But pleased to find you do relent
20   And cry on.

I mauled you when you looked so bluff,
But now I'll secret keep your stuff;
For know, prostration is enough
   To the lion.

Sheridan's Submission

WRITTEN BY THE DEAN

Cedo jam, miserae cognoscens proemia rixae,
Si rixa est, ubi tu pulsas, ego vapulo tantum.

Poor Sherry, inglorious,
To Dan the victorious,
Presents, as 'tis fitting,
Petition and greeting.

To you victorious and brave,
Your now subdued and suppliant slave
   Most humbly sues for pardon.
Who when I fought still cut me down,
And when I, vanquished, fled the town,
10   Pursued and laid me hard on.

Now lowly crouched, I cry 'Peccavi',
And prostrate, supplicate *pour ma vie.*
   Your mercy I rely on.
For you, my conqueror and my king,
In pardoning, as in punishing,
   Will show yourself a lion.

Alas, sir I had no design,
But was unwarily drawn in;
   For spite I ne'er had any.
20   'Twas the damned squire with the hard name,
The de'il too that owed me a shame,
   The devil and Delany.

They tempted me to attack your highness,
And then, with wonted wile and slyness,
   They left me in the lurch.
Unhappy wretch! for now, I ween,
I've nothing left to vent my spleen
   But ferula and birch;

And they, alas, yield small relief,
30   Seem rather to renew my grief,
   My wounds bleed all anew:
For every stroke goes to my heart,

And at each lash I feel the smart
Of lash laid on by you.

The Author's Manner of Living

On rainy days alone I dine,
Upon a chick, and pint of wine.
On rainy days, I dine alone,
And pick my chicken to the bone:
But this my servants much enrages,
No scraps remain to save board-wages.
In weather fine I nothing spend,
But often sponge upon a friend:
Yet where he's not so rich as I;
10   I pay my club, and so God b' y' –

Stella's Birthday

WRITTEN IN THE YEAR 1718 [/9]

Stella this day is thirty-four,
(We shan't dispute a year or more:)
However Stella, be not troubled,
Although thy size and years are doubled,
Since first I saw thee at sixteen,
The brightest virgin on the green.
So little is thy form declined;
Made up so largely in thy mind.

     Oh, would it please the gods to *split*
10   Thy beauty, size, and years, and wit,
No age could furnish out a pair
Of nymphs so graceful, wise and fair:
With half the lustre of your eyes,
With half your wit, your years, and size:
And then before it grew too late,
How should I beg of gentle fate,
(That either nymph might have her swain,)
To split my worship too in twain.

A Quiet Life and a Good Name

TO A FRIEND, WHO MARRIED A SHREW

Nell scolded in so loud a din,
That Will durst hardly venture in:
He marked the conjugal dispute;
Nell roared incessant, Dick sat mute:
But, when he saw his friend appear
Cried bravely, 'Patience, good my dear.'
At sight of Will she bawled no more,
But hurried out, and clapped the door.

'Why Dick! the devil's in thy Nell,'
10   Quoth Will; 'thy house is worse than hell:
Why, what a peal the jade has rung!
Damn her, why don't you slit her tongue?
For nothing else will make it cease.'
'Dear Will, I suffer this for peace;
I never quarrel with my wife,
I bear it for a quiet life.
Scripture you know exhorts us to it;
Bids us to *seek peace and ensue it.*'

Will went again to visit Dick
20   And entering in the very nick,
He saw virago Nell belabour,
With Dick's own staff, his peaceful neighbour;
Poor Will, who needs must interpose,
Received a brace or two of blows.

But now, to make my story short,
Will drew out Dick to take a quart,
'Why Dick, thy wife has devilish whims:
Od's-buds, why don't you break her limbs?
If she were mine, and had such tricks,
30   I'd teach her how to handle sticks:
Zounds, I would ship her to Jamaica
And truck the carrion for tobacca;
I'd send her far enough away –'
'Dear Will; but what would people say?
Lord! I should get so ill a name,
The neighbours round would cry out shame.'

Dick suffered for his peace and credit;
But who believed him when he said it?
Can he who makes himself a slave,
40 Consult his peace, or credit save?
Dick found it by his ill success,
His quiet small, his credit less.
She served him at the usual rate;
She stunned, and then she broke his pate.
And what he thought the hardest case,
The parish jeered him to his face:
Those men who wore the breeches least,
Called him a cuckold, fool and beast.
At home, he was pursued with noise;
50 Abroad, was pestered by the boys.
Within, his wife would break his bones,
Without, they pelted him with stones:
The prentices procured a riding
To act his patience and her chiding.

False patience, and mistaken pride!
There are ten thousand Dicks beside;
Slaves to their quiet and good name,
Are used like Dick, and bear the blame.

Phyllis

OR, THE PROGRESS OF LOVE

Desponding Phyllis was endued
With every talent of a prude:
She trembled when a man drew near;
Salute her, and she turned her ear:
If o'er against her you were placed
She durst not look above your waist:
She'd rather take you to her bed,
Than let you see her dress her head;
In church you heard her, through the crowd
10 Repeat the absolution loud;
In church, secure behind her fan
She durst behold that monster, man:
There practised how to place her head,

And bit her lips to make them red;
Or on the mat devoutly kneeling
Would lift her eyes up to the ceiling,
And heave her bosom, unaware,
For neighbouring beaux to see it bare.

At length a lucky lover came,
20 And found admittance to the dame.
Suppose all parties now agreed,
The writings drawn, the lawyer fee'd,
The vicar and the ring bespoke:
Guess, how could such a match be broke?
See then what mortals place their bliss in!
Next morn betimes the bride was missing.
The mother screamed, the father chid;
Where can this idle wretch be hid?
No news of Phyl! The bridegroom came,
30 And thought his bride had skulked for shame,
Because her father used to say
The girl had such a bashful way.

Now John, the butler, must be sent
To learn the road that Phyllis went;
The groom was wished to saddle Crop;
For John must neither light nor stop;
But find her whereso'er she fled,
And bring her back, alive or dead.

See here again the devil to do;
40 For truly John was missing too.
The horse and pillion both were gone!
Phyllis, it seems, was fled with John.

Old Madam, who went up to find
What papers Phyl had left behind,
A letter on the toilet sees,
To my much honoured father, – these:
('Tis always done, romances tell us,
When daughters run away with fellows)
Filled with the choicest commonplaces,
50 By others used in the like cases;
'That, long ago a fortune-teller

Exactly said what now befell her;
And in a glass had made her see
A serving-man of low degree.
It was her fate, must be forgiven,
For marriages were made in heaven:
His pardon begged, but to be plain,
She'd do't if 'twere to do again.
Thank God, 'twas neither shame nor sin;
60 For John was come of honest kin.
Love never thinks of rich and poor,
She'd beg with John from door to door:
Forgive her, if it be a crime,
She'll never do't another time.
She ne'er before in all her life
Once disobeyed him, maid nor wife.
One argument she summed up all in,
The thing was done and past recalling:
And therefore hoped she should recover
70 His favour, when his passion's over.
She valued not what others thought her,
And was – his most obedient daughter.'

Fair maidens all attend the muse
Who now the wandering pair pursues.
Away they rode in homely sort,
Their journey long, their money short;
The loving couple well bemired;
The horse and both the riders tired:
Their victuals bad, their lodging worse;
80 Phyl cried, and John began to curse;
Phyl wished, that she had strained a limb,
When first she ventured out with him:
John wished, that he had broke a leg
When first for her he quitted Peg.

But what adventures more befell 'em,
The muse hath now no time to tell 'em.
How Johnny wheedled, threatened, fawned,
Till Phyllis all her trinkets pawned:
How oft she broke her marriage vows
90 In kindness to maintain her spouse,

Till swains unwholesome spoiled the trade;
For now the surgeon must be paid,
To whom those perquisites are gone,
In Christian justice due to John.

When food and raiment now grew scarce,
Fate put a period to the farce,
And with exact poetic justice;
For John is landlord, Phyllis hostess:
They keep, at Staines, the Old Blue Boar,
100   Are cat and dog, and rogue and whore.

The Progress of Beauty

When first Diana leaves her bed,
Vapours and steams her looks disgrace,
A frowzy dirty coloured red
Sits on her cloudy wrinkled face;

But, by degrees, when mounted high,
Her artificial face appears
Down from her window in the sky,
Her spots are gone, her visage clears.

'Twixt earthly females and the moon,
10   All parallels exactly run;
If Celia should appear too soon,
Alas, the nymph would be undone!

To see her from her pillow rise
All reeking in a cloudy steam,
Cracked lips, foul teeth, and gummy eyes;
Poor Strephon, how would he blaspheme!

The soot or powder which was wont
To make her hair look black as jet,
Falls from her tresses on her front
20   A mingled mass of dirt and sweat.

Three colours, black, and red, and white,
So graceful in their proper place,
Remove them to a different light.
They form a frightful hideous face.

For instance, when the lily skips
Into the precincts of the rose,
And takes possession of the lips,
Leaving the purple to the nose.

So, Celia went entire to bed,
30 All her complexions safe and sound;
But when she rose, white, black, and red,
Though still in sight, had changed their ground.

The black, which would not be confined,
A more inferior station seeks,
Leaving the fiery red behind,
And mingles in her muddy cheeks.

The paint by perspiration cracks,
And falls in rivulets of sweat,
On either side you see the tracks,
40 While at her chin the confluents met.

A skilful housewife thus her thumb
With spittle while she spins, anoints,
And thus the brown meanders come
In trickling streams betwixt her joints.

But Celia can with ease reduce,
By help of pencil, paint and brush,
Each colour to its place and use,
And teach her cheeks again to blush.

She knows her early self no more:
50 But filled with admiration stands,
As other painters oft adore
The workmanship of their own hands.

Thus, after four important hours
Celia's the wonder of her sex;
Say, which among the heavenly powers
Could cause such marvellous effects?

Venus, indulgent to her kind,
Gave women all their hearts could wish
When first she taught them where to find
60 White lead and Lusitanian dish.

Love with white lead cements his wings,
White lead was sent us to repair
Two brightest, brittlest, earthly things,
A lady's face, and china-ware.

She ventures now to lift the sash,
The window is her proper sphere:
Ah, lovely nymph! be not too rash,
Nor let the beaux approach too near.

Take pattern by your sister star,
70   Delude at once, and bless our sight,
When you are seen, be seen from far,
And chiefly choose to shine by night.

In the Pall Mall when passing by,
Keep up the glasses of your chair,
Then each transported fop will cry,
'God damn me Jack, she's wondrous fair.'

But, art no longer can prevail
When the materials all are gone,
The best mechanic hand must fail,
80   When nothing's left to work upon.

Matter, as wise logicians say,
Cannot without a form subsist;
And form, say I, as well as they,
Must fail, if matter brings no grist.

And this is fair Diana's case;
For all astrologers maintain,
Each night a bit drops off her face,
While mortals say she's in her wane.

While Partridge wisely shows the cause
90   Efficient of the moon's decay,
That Cancer with his poisonous claws,
Attacks her in the Milky Way:

But Gadbury, in art profound,
From her pale cheeks pretends to show,
That swain Endymion is not sound,
Or else, that Mercury's her foe.

But, let the cause be what it will,
In half a month she looks so thin,
That Flamsteed can, with all his skill
100 See but her forehead and her chin.

Yet, as she wastes, she grows discreet,
Till midnight never shows her head:
So rotting Celia strolls the street,
When sober folks are all abed.

For sure if this be Luna's fate,
Poor Celia, but of mortal race,
In vain expects a longer date
To the materials of her face.

When Mercury her tresses mows
110 To think of black lead combs is vain,
No painting can restore a nose,
Nor will her teeth return again.

Two balls of glass may serve for eyes,
White lead can plaster up a cleft,
But these alas, are poor supplies
If neither cheeks, nor lips be left.

Ye powers, who over love preside,
Since mortal beauties drop so soon,
If you would have us well supplied,
120 Send us new nymphs with each new moon.

The Progress of Poetry

The farmer's goose, who in the stubble,
Has fed without restraint, or trouble;
Grown fat with corn and sitting still,
Can scarce get o'er the barn-door sill:
And hardly waddles forth, to cool
Her belly in the neighbouring pool:
Nor loudly cackles at the door;
For cackling shows the goose is poor.

But when she must be turned to graze,
10   And round the barren common strays,
Hard exercise, and harder fare,
Soon make my dame grow lank and spare:
Her body light, she tries her wings,
And scorns the ground, and upward springs,
While all the parish, as she flies,
Hear sounds harmonious from the skies.

Such is the poet, fresh in pay,
(The third night's profits of his play;)
His morning-draughts till noon can swill,
20   Among his brethren of the quill:
With good roast beef his belly full,
Grown lazy, foggy, fat, and dull:
Deep sunk in plenty, and delight,
What poet e'er could take his flight?
Or stuffed with phlegm up to the throat,
What poet e'er could sing a note?
Nor Pegasus could bear the load,
Along the high celestial road;
The steed, oppressed, would break his girth,
30   To raise the lumber from the earth.

But, view him in another scene,
When all his drink is Hippocrene;
His money spent, his patrons fail,
His credit out for cheese and ale;
His two-year's coat so smooth and bare,
Through every thread it lets in air;
With hungry meals his body pined,
His guts and belly full of wind;
And, like a jockey in a race,
40   His flesh brought down to flying case:
Now his exalted spirit loathes
Incumbrances of food and clothes;
And up he rises like a vapour,
Supported high on wings of paper;
He singing flies, and flying sings,
While from below all Grub Street rings.

From Dr Swift to Dr Sheridan

Dec. 14, 1719, 9 at night

SIR

It is impossible to know by your letter whether the wine is to be bottled tomorrow, or no.

If it be, or be not, why did you not in plain English tell us so?

For my part, it was by mere chance I came back to sit with the ladies this night.

And, if they had not told me there was a letter from you, and your man Alexander had not gone, and come back from the Deanery, and the boy here had not been sent to let Alexander know I was here, I should have missed the letter outright.

Truly I don't know who's bound to be sending for corks to stop your bottles, with a vengeance.

Make a page of your own age, and send your man Alexander to buy corks, for Saunders already hath got above ten jaunts.

Mrs Dingley and Mrs Johnson say, truly they don't care for your wife's company, although they like your wine; but they had rather have it at their own house, to drink in quiet.

However, they own it is very civil in Mr Sheridan, to make the offer; and they cannot deny it.

I wish Alexander safe at St Catherine's tonight, with all my heart and soul, upon my word and honour.

But I think it base in you to send a poor fellow out so late at this time of year, when one would not turn out a dog that one valued; I appeal to your friend Mr Conna.

I would present my humble service to my Lady Mountcashel: but, truly, I thought she would have made advances to have been acquainted with me, as she pretended.

But now I can write no more, for you see plainly my paper is ended.

P.S. I wish when you prated,
       Your letter you'd dated,
       Much plague it created,
       I scolded and rated;
       My soul it much grated,
       For your man, I long waited.
       I think you are fated,
       Like a bear to be baited:

Your man is belated,
The case, I have stated,
And me you have cheated.
My stable's unslated,
Come back t'us well freighted;
I remember my late-head
And wish you translated,
        For teasing me.

2 P.S.   Mrs Dingley
30   Desires me singly
Her service to present you,
Hopes that will content you;
But Johnson Madam
Is grown a sad dame,
For want of your converse,
And cannot send one verse.

3 P.S.   You keep such a twattling
With you and your bottling,
But I see the sum total,
40   We shall ne'er have one bottle;
The long and the short,
We shall not have a quart.
I wish you would sign't,
That we may have a pint.
For all your colloguing,
I'd be glad of a knogging:
But I doubt 'tis a sham,
You won't give us a dram.
'Tis of shine, a mouth moon-full,
50   You won't part with a spoon-full,
And I must be nimble,
If I can fill my thimble,
You see I won't stop,
Till I come to a drop;
But I doubt the oraculum
Is a poor supernaculum;
Though perhaps you may tell it
For a grace, if we smell it.
            STELLA.

Dr Swift's Answer to Dr Sheridan

The verses you sent on the bottling your wine
Were in everyone's judgement exceedingly fine,
And I must confess as a dean and divine,
I think you inspired by the muses all nine.
I nicely examined them every line,
And the worst of them all like a barn-door did shine.
Oh, that Jove would give me such a talent as thine!
With Delany or Dan I would scorn to combine;
I know they have many a wicked design,
10   And give Satan his due, Dan begins to refine.
However I wish, honest comrade of mine,
You would really on Thursday leave St Catherine,
Where I hear you are crammed every day like a swine.
But the loss of your cough will be the best sign;
With me you'll no more have a stomach to dine,
Nor after your victuals lie sleeping supine;
So I wish you were toothless like Lord Massereene.
But were you as wicked as lewd Aretine
I wish you would tell me which way you incline.
20   If when you return, your road you don't line,
On Thursday I'll pay my respects at your shrine,
Wherever you bend, wherever you twine,
In square or in opposite circle, or trine,
Your beef will on Thursday be salter than brine.
I hope you have swilled with new milk from the kine
As much as the Liffey's outdone by the Rhine:
And Dan shall be with us with nose aquiline.
If you do not come back we shall weep out our eyn,
Or may your gown never be good Lutherine.
30   The beef you have got, which I hear is a chine,
But if too many come your madam will whine;
And then you may kiss the low end of her spine.
But enough of this poetry Alexandrine:
I hope you will not think this a pasquine.

The Dean's Answer to 'Upon Stealing a Crown'

So about twelve at night, the punk
Steals from the cully when he's drunk;

Nor is contented with a treat,
Without her privilege to cheat.
Nor can I the least difference find,
But that you left no clap behind.
But jest apart, restore, you capon ye,
My twelve thirteens and sixpence halfpenny.
To eat my meat, and drink my Medlicot,
10 And then to give me such a deadly cut –
But 'tis observed, that men in gowns
Are most inclined to plunder *crowns*.
Could you but *change* a crown as easy
As you can steal one, how 'twould please ye!
I thought the lady at St Catherine's
Knew how to set you better patterns;
For this I will not dine with Agmondisham,
And for his victuals let a ragman dish 'em.

Swift to Sheridan

Poor Tom, wilt thou never accept a defiance,
Though I dare you to more than quadruple alliance?
You're so retrograde, sure you were born under Cancer:
Must I make myself hoarse with demanding an answer?
If this be your practice, mean scrub, I assure ye,
And swear by each Fate, and your new friends, each Fury,
I'll drive you to Cavan, from Cavan to Dundalk;
I'll tear all your rules, and demolish your pun talk:
Nay, further, the moment you're free from your scalding,
10 I'll chew you to bullets, and puff you to Baldwin.

To Stella, Visiting Me in My Sickness

Pallas, observing Stella's wit
Shine more than for her sex was fit;
And that her beauty, soon or late,
Might breed confusion in the state,
In high concern for human kind,
Fixed *honour* in her infant mind.

But, (not in wranglings to engage
With such a stupid vicious age,)
If *honour* I would here define,
10   It answers *faith* in things divine.
As natural life the body warms,
And, scholars teach, the soul informs;
So honour animates the whole,
And is the spirit of the soul.

Those numerous virtues which the tribe
Of tedious moralists describe,
And by such various titles call;
True honour comprehends them all.
Let melancholy rule supreme,
20   Choler preside, or blood, or phlegm,
It makes no difference in the case,
Nor is complexion honour's place.

But, lest we should for honour take
The drunken quarrels of a rake;
Or think it seated in a scar,
Or on a proud triumphal car,
Or in the payment of a debt
We lose with sharpers at piquet;
Or, when a whore in her vocation,
30   Keeps punctual to an assignation;
Or that on which his lordship swears,
When vulgar knaves would lose their ears:
Let Stella's fair example preach
A lesson she alone can teach.

In points of honour to be tried,
All passions must be laid aside:
Ask no advice, but think alone,
Suppose the question not your own:
How shall I act? is not the case,
40   But how would Brutus in my place?
In such a cause would Cato bleed?
And how would Socrates proceed?

Drive all objections from your mind,
Else you relapse to human kind:

Ambition, avarice, and lust,
And factious rage, and breach of trust;
And flattery tipped with nauseous fleer,
And guilty shame, and servile fear,
Envy, and cruelty, and pride,
50 Will in your tainted heart preside.

Heroes and heroines of old,
By honour only were enrolled
Among their brethren of the skies,
To which (though late) shall Stella rise.
Ten thousand oaths upon recórd,
Are not so sacred as her word:
The world shall in its atoms end,
E'er Stella can deceive a friend.
By *honour* seated in her breast,
60 She still determines what is best:
What indignation in her mind
Against enslavers of mankind!
Base kings and ministers of state,
Eternal objects of her hate.

She thinks that nature ne'er designed
Courage to man alone confined:
Can cowardice her sex adorn,
Which most exposes ours to scorn?
She wonders where the charm appears
70 In Florimel's affected fears:
For Stella never learned the art,
At proper times to scream and start;
Nor calls up all the house at night,
And swears she saw a thing in white:
Doll never flies to cut her lace,
Or throw cold water in her face,
Because she heard a sudden drum,
Or found an earwig in a plum.

Her hearers are amazed from whence
80 Proceeds that fund of wit and sense;
Which though her modesty would shroud,
Breaks like the sun behind a cloud,
While gracefulness its art conceals,
And yet through every motion steals.

Say, Stella, was Prometheus blind,
And forming you, mistook your kind?
No: 'twas for you alone he stole
The fire that forms a manly soul;
Then to complete it every way,
90 He moulded it with female clay:
To that you owe the nobler flame,
To this, the beauty of your frame.

How would ingratitude delight?
And how would censure glut her spite?
If I should Stella's kindness hide
In silence, or forget with pride.
When on my sickly couch I lay,
Impatient both of night and day,
Lamenting in unmanly strains,
100 Called every power to ease my pains:
Then Stella ran to my relief
With cheerful face, and inward grief;
And, though by heaven's severe decree
She suffers hourly more than me,
No cruel master could require
From slaves employed for daily hire,
What Stella, by her friendship warmed,
With vigour and delight performed:
My sinking spirits now supplies
110 With cordials in her hands, and eyes:
Now, with a soft and silent tread,
Unheard she moves about my bed.
I see her taste each nauseous draught,
And so obligingly am caught:
I bless the hand from whence they came,
Nor dare distort my face for shame.

Best pattern of true friends, beware;
You pay too dearly for your care,
If, while your tenderness secures
120 My life, it must endanger yours.
For such a fool was never found,
Who pulled a palace to the ground,
Only to have the ruins made
Materials for an house decayed.

To Stella, Who Collected
and Transcribed His Poems

As when a lofty pile is raised,
We never hear the workmen praised,
Who bring the lime, or place the stones;
But all admire Inigo Jones:
So if this pile of scattered rhymes
Should be approved in after-times,
If it both pleases and endures,
The merit and the praise are yours.

    Thou, Stella, wert no longer young,
10 When first for thee my harp I strung:
Without one word of Cupid's darts,
Of killing eyes, or bleeding hearts:
With friendship and esteem possessed,
I ne'er admitted love a guest.

    In all the habitudes of life,
The friend, the mistress, and the wife,
Variety we still pursue,
In pleasure seek for something new:
Or else, comparing with the rest,
20 Take comfort, that our own is best:
(The best we value by the worst,
As tradesmen show their trash at first:)
But his pursuits are at an end,
Whom Stella chooses for a friend.

    A poet, starving in a garret,
Conning old topics like a parrot,
Invokes his mistress and his muse,
And stays at home for want of shoes:
Should but his muse descending drop
30 A slice of bread, and mutton-chop,
Or kindly when his credit's out,
Surprise him with a pint of stout,
Or patch his broken stocking soles,
Or send him in a peck of coals;
Exalted in his mighty mind
He flies, and leaves the stars behind;

Counts all his labours amply paid,
Adores her for her timely aid.

Or should a porter make inquiries
40 For Chloe, Sylvia, Phyllis, Iris;
Be told the lodging, lane, and sign,
The bowers that hold those nymphs divine;
Fair Chloe would perhaps be found
With footmen tippling underground;
The charming Sylvia beating flax,
Her shoulders marked with bloody tracks;
Bright Phyllis mending ragged smocks,
And radiant Iris in the pox.

These are the goddesses enrolled
50 In Curll's collections, new and old,
Whose scoundrel fathers would not know 'em,
If they should meet 'em in a poem.

True poets can depress and raise;
Are lords of infamy and praise:
They are not scurrilous in satire,
Nor will in panegyric flatter.
Unjustly poets we asperse;
Truth shines the brighter, clad in verse;
And all the fictions they pursue,
60 Do but insinuate what is true.

Now, should my praises owe their truth
To beauty, dress, or paint, or youth,
What Stoics call *without our power*,
They could not be insured an hour:
'Twere grafting on an annual stock,
That must our expectation mock,
And making one luxuriant shoot,
Die the next year for want of root:
Before I could my verses bring,
70 Perhaps you're quite another thing.

So Maevius, when he drained his skull
To celebrate some suburb trull;
His similes in order set,
And every crambo he could get;

Had gone through all the commonplaces
Worn out by wits who rhyme on faces;
Before he could his poem close,
The lovely nymph had lost her nose.

Your virtues safely I commend,
80 They on no accidents depend:
Let malice look with all her eyes,
She dare not say the poet lies.

Stella, when you these lines transcribe,
Lest you should take them for a bribe;
Resolved to mortify your pride,
I'll here expose your weaker side.

Your spirits kindle to a flame,
Moved with the lightest touch of blame;
And when a friend in kindness tries
90 To show you where your error lies,
Conviction does but more incense;
Perverseness is your whole defence:
Truth, judgement, wit, give place to spite,
Regardless both of wrong and right.
Your virtues, all suspended, wait
Till time hath opened reason's gate:
And what is worse, your passion bends
Its force against your nearest friends;
Which manners, decency, and pride,
100 Have taught you from the world to hide:
In vain; for see, your friend hath brought
To public light your *only* fault;
And yet a fault we often find
Mixed in a noble generous mind;
And may compare to Etna's fire,
Which, though with trembling, all admire;
The heat that makes the summit glow,
Enriching all the vales below.
Those who in warmer climes complain,
110 From Phoebus' rays they suffer pain;
Must own, that pain is largely paid
By generous wines beneath a shade.

Yet when I find your passions rise,
And anger sparkling in your eyes,
I grieve those spirits should be spent,
For nobler ends by nature meant.
One passion, with a different turn,
Makes wit inflame, or anger burn;
So the sun's heat, by different powers,
120   Ripens the grape, the liquor sours.
Thus Ajax, when with rage possessed,
By Pallas breathed into his breast,
His valour would no more employ;
Which might alone have conquered Troy;
But blinded by resentment, seeks
For vengeance on his friends the Greeks.

You think this turbulence of blood
From stágnating preserves the flood;
Which thus fermenting, by degrees
130   Exalts the spirits, sinks the lees.

Stella, for once you reason wrong;
For should this ferment last too long,
By time subsiding, you may find
Nothing but acid left behind.
From passion you may then be freed,
When peevishness and spleen succeed.

Say Stella, when you copy next,
Will you keep strictly to the text?
Dare you let these reproaches stand,
140   And to your failing set your hand?
Or if these lines your anger fire,
Shall they in baser flames expire?
Whene'er they burn, if burn they must,
They'll prove my accusation just.

Upon the South Sea Project

Ye wise philosophers! explain,
    What magic makes our money rise,

When dropped into the Southern Main;
    Or do these jugglers cheat our eyes?

Put in your money fairly told;
    Presto begone – 'tis here again:
Ladies and gentlemen, behold,
    Here's every piece as big as ten.

Thus in a basin drop a shilling,
10   Then fill the vessel to the brim;
You shall observe, as you are filling,
    The ponderous metal seems to swim.

It rises both in bulk and height,
    Behold it swelling like a sop!
The liquid medium cheats your sight,
    Behold it mounted to the top!

'In stock three hundred thousand pounds;
    I have in view a lord's estate;
My manors all contiguous round;
20   A coach and six, and served in plate!'

Thus the deluded bankrupt raves,
    Puts all upon a desperate bet;
Then plunges in the Southern waves,
    Dipped over head and ears – in debt.

So, by a calenture misled,
    The mariner with rapture sees
On the smooth ocean's azure bed
    Enamelled fields, and verdant trees.

With eager haste he longs to rove
30   In that fantastic scene, and thinks
It must be some enchanted grove;
    And *in* he leaps, and *down* he sinks.

Five hundred chariots just bespoke,
    Are sunk in these devouring waves,
The horses drowned, the harness broke,
    And here the owners find their graves.

Like Pharaoh, by directors led,
    They with their spoils went safe before;

His chariots tumbling out the dead,
40   Lay shattered on the Red Sea shore.

Raised up on Hope's aspiring plumes,
    The young adventurer o'er the deep
An eagle's flight and state assumes,
    And scorns the middle way to keep.

On paper wings he takes his flight,
    With wax the father bound them fast;
The wax is melted by the height,
    And down the towering boy is cast.

A moralist might here explain
50   The rashness of the Cretan youth;
Describe his fall into the main,
    And from a fable form a truth.

His wings are his paternal rent,
    He melts his wax at every flame;
His credit sunk, his money spent,
    In Southern Seas he leaves his name.

Inform us, you that best can tell,
    Why in yon dangerous gulf profound,
Where hundreds, and where thousands fell,
60   Fools chiefly float, the wise are drowned?

So have I seen from Severn's brink
    A flock of geese jump down together,
Swim where the bird of Jove would sink,
    And swimming never wet a feather.

But I affirm, 'tis false in fact,
    Directors better know their tools,
We see the nation's credit cracked,
    Each knave hath made a thousand fools.

One fool may from another win,
70   And then get off with money stored;
But if a sharper once comes in,
    He throws at all, and sweeps the board.

As fishes on each other prey
    The great ones swallowing up the small;

So fares it in the Southern Sea;
    But, whale directors eat up all.

When stock is high, they come between,
    Making by second hand their offers,
Then cunningly retire unseen,
80   With each a million in his coffers.

So when upon a moonshine night
    An ass was drinking at a stream;
A cloud arose, and stopped the light,
    By intercepting every beam;

The day of judgement will be soon,
    (Cries out a sage among the crowd;)
An ass hath swallowed up the moon,
    The moon lay safe behind the cloud.

Each poor subscriber to the Sea,
90   Sinks down at once, and there he lies;
Directors fall as well as they,
    Their fall is but a trick to rise.

So fishes rising from the main
    Can soar with moistened wings on high;
The moisture dried, they sink again,
    And dip their fins again to fly.

Undone at play, the female troops
    Come here their losses to retrieve;
Ride o'er the waves in spacious hoops,
100   Like Lapland witches in a sieve.

Thus Venus to the sea descends
    As poets feign; but where's the moral?
It shows the Queen of Love intends
    To search the deep for pearl and coral.

The sea is richer than the land,
    I heard it from my grannam's mouth,
Which now I clearly understand,
    For by the sea she meant the South.

Thus by directors we are told,
110   Pray gentlemen, believe your eyes,

Our ocean's covered o'er with gold,
  Look round, and see how thick it lies!

We, gentlemen, are your assisters,
  We'll come and hold you by the chin,
Alas! all is not gold that glisters;
  Ten thousand sunk by leaping in.

Oh! would those patriots be so kind,
  Here in the deep to wash their hands,
Then, like Pactolus, we should find
120 The sea indeed had golden sands.

A shilling in the Bath you fling,
  The silver takes a nobler hue,
By magic virtue in the spring,
  And seems a guinea to your view.

But as a guinea will not pass
  At market for a farthing more
Shown through a multiplying glass,
  Than what it always did before.

So cast it in the Southern Seas,
130 And view it through a jobber's bill;
Put on what spectacles you please,
  Your guinea's but a guinea still.

One night a fool into a brook
  Thus from a hillock looking down,
The golden stars for guineas took,
  And silver Cynthia for a crown.

The point he could no longer doubt,
  He ran, he leapt into the flood;
There sprawled awhile, and scarce got out,
140 All covered o'er with slime and mud.

Upon the water cast thy bread
  And after many days thou'lt find it;
But gold upon this ocean spread
  Shall sink, and leave no mark behind it.

There is a gulf where thousands fell,
  Here all the bold adventurers came,

A narrow sound, though deep as hell,
    'Change Alley is the dreadful name.

Nine times a day it ebbs and flows,
150   Yet he that on the surface lies,
Without a pilot seldom knows
    The time it falls, or when 'twill rise.

Subscribers here by thousands float,
    And jostle one another down;
Each paddling in his leaky boat,
    And here they fish for gold and drown:

Now buried in the depth below,
    Now mounted up to heaven again,
They reel and stagger to and fro,
160   *At their wits' end, like drunken men.*

Meantime, secure on Garr'way cliffs,
    A savage race by shipwrecks fed,
Lie waiting for the foundered skiffs,
    And strip the bodies of the dead.

But these, you say, are factious lies
    From some malicious Tory's brain,
For, where directors get a prize,
    The Swiss and Dutch whole millions drain.

Thus, when by rooks a lord is plied,
170   Some cully often wins a bet,
By venturing on the cheating side,
    Though not into the secret let.

While some build castles in the air,
    Directors build 'em in the seas;
Subscribers plainly see 'em there,
    For fools will see as wise men please.

Thus oft by mariners are shown,
    Unless the men of Kent are liars,
Earl Godwin's castles overthrown,
180   And palace roofs, and steeple spires.

Mark where the sly directors creep,
    Nor to the shore approach too nigh!

The monsters nestle in the deep,
    To seize you in your passing by.

Then, like the dogs of Nile, be wise,
    Who taught by instinct how to shun
The crocodile that lurking lies,
    Run as they drink, and drink and run.

Antaeus could by magic charms
190   Recover strength whene'er he fell,
Alcides held him in his arms,
    And sent him up in air to hell.

Directors thrown into the sea
    Recover strength and vigour there,
But may be tamed another way,
    Suspended for a while in air.

Directors! for 'tis you I warn,
    By long experience we have found
What planet ruled when you were born;
200   We see you never can be drowned.

Beware, nor over-bulky grow,
    Nor come within your cully's reach,
For if the sea should sink so low
    To leave you dry upon the beach;

You'll owe your ruin to your bulk:
    Your foes already waiting stand,
To tear you like a foundered hulk
    While you lie helpless on the sand.

Thus when a whale hath lost the tide,
210   The coasters crowd to seize the spoil;
The monster into parts divide,
    And strip the bones, and melt the oil.

Oh, may some Western tempest sweep
    These locusts whom our fruits have fed,
That plague, directors, to the deep,
    Driven from the South Sea to the Red.

May He, whom nature's laws obey,
    Who lifts the poor, and sinks the proud,

Quiet the raging of the sea,
220   And still the madness of the crowd.

But never shall our isle have rest
    Till those devouring swine run down,
(The devil's leaving the possessed,)
    And headlong in the waters drown.

The nation then too late will find
    Computing all their cost and trouble,
Directors' promises but wind,
    South Sea at best a mighty *bubble*.

Apparent rari nantes in Gurgite vasto,
Arma virum, tabulaeque, et Troia gaza per undas.

                                            VIRG.

An Elegy on the Much Lamented Death of Mr Demar, the Famous Rich Usurer

WHO DIED THE SIXTH OF JULY, 1720

Know all men by these presents, Death the tamer
By mortgage hath secured the corpse of Demar;
Nor can four hundred thousand sterling pound
Redeem him from his prison underground.
His heirs might well, of all his wealth possessed,
Bestow to bury him one iron chest.
Pluto the god of wealth, will joy to know
His faithful steward, in the shades below.
He walked the streets, and wore a threadbare cloak;
10   He dined and supped at charge of other folk;
And by his looks, had he held out his palms,
He might be thought an object fit for alms.
So to the poor if he refused his pelf,
He used 'em full as kindly as himself.

    Where'er he went he never saw his betters;
Lords, knights and squires were all his humble debtors;
And under hand and seal, the Irish nation
Were forced to own to him their obligation.

He that could once have half a kingdom bought,
20 In half a minute is not worth a groat;
His coffers from the coffin could not save,
Nor all his *interest* keep him from the grave.
A golden monument would not be right,
Because we wish the earth upon him light.

Oh London Tavern! thou hast lost a friend:
Though in thy walls he ne'er did farthing spend,
He touched the pence when others touched the pot;
The hand that signed the mortgage paid the shot.

Old as he was, no vulgar known disease
30 On him could ever boast a power to seize;
But as his gold he weighed, grim Death in spite,
Cast in his dart which made three moidores light;
And as he saw his darling money fail,
Blew his last breath to sink the lighter scale.

He who so long was current 'twould be strange
If he should now be cried down since his change.

The sexton shall green sods on thee bestow.
Alas the sexton is thy banker now!
A dismal banker must that banker be,
40 Who gives no bills, but of mortality.

THE EPITAPH

Beneath this verdant hillock lies
Demar the wealthy, and the wise.
His heirs that he might safely rest,
Have put his carcass in a chest:
The very chest, in which, they say,
His other self, his money, lay.
And if his heirs continue kind,
To that dear self he left behind,
I dare believe, that four in five
50 Will think his better self alive.

Lines from Cadenus to Vanessa

Nymph, would you learn the only art
To keep a worthy lover's heart?
First, to adorn your person well,
In utmost cleanliness excel,
And though you must the fashions take,
Observe them but for fashion's sake.

The strongest reason will submit
To virtue, honour, sense, and wit.
To such a nymph the wise and good
10 Cannot be faithless if they would:
For vices all have different ends,
But virtue still to virtue tends.
And when your lover is not true,
'Tis virtue fails in him or you:
And either he deserves disdain,
Or you without a cause complain.
But here Vanessa cannot err,
Nor are these rules applied to her:
For who could such a nymph forsake
20 Except a blockhead or a rake,
Or how could she her heart bestow
Except where wit and virtue grow.

*

A fig for partridges and quails –
Ye dainties, I know nothing of ye,
But on the highest mount in Wales
Would choose in peace to drink my coffee.

'Dorinda Dreams of Dress Abed'

Dorinda dreams of dress abed,
    'Tis all her thought and art,
Her lace hath got within her head,
    Her stays stick to her heart.

An Excellent New Song on a Seditious Pamphlet

TO THE TUNE OF PACKINGTON'S POUND

The author having writ a treatise, advising the people of Ireland to wear their own manufactures; that infamous wretch Whitshed prosecuted Waters the printer with so much violence and injustice, that he kept the jury nine hours, and sent them away eleven times, till out of mere weariness they were forced to give a special verdict.

I

Brocado's, and damasks, and tabbies, and gauzes,
    Are by Robert Ballentine lately brought over;
With forty things more: now hear what the law says,
    Whoe'er will not wear them, is not the King's lover.
        Though a printer and Dean
        Seditiously mean
    Our true Irish hearts from old England to wean;
We'll buy English silks for our wives and our daughters,
In spite of his Deanship and journeyman Waters.

II

10 In England the dead in woollen are clad,
    The Dean and his printer then let us cry fie on;
To be clothed like a carcass would make a Teague mad,
    Since a living dog better is than a dead lion,
        Our wives they grow sullen
        At wearing of woollen,
    And all we poor shopkeepers must our horns pull in.
Then we'll buy English silks, &c.

III

Whoever our trading with England would hinder,
    To *inflame* both the nations do plainly conspire;
20 Because Irish linen will soon turn to tinder;
    And wool it is greasy, and quickly takes fire.
        Therefore I assure ye,
        Our noble Grand Jury,
    When they saw the Dean's book they were in a great fury:
They would buy English silks for their wives, &c.

IV

This wicked rogue Waters, who always is sinning,
    And before *Corum Nobus* so oft has been called,

Henceforward shall print neither pamphlets nor linen,
 And, if swearing can do't, shall be swingingly mauled:
30   And as for the Dean,
         You know whom I mean,
 If the printer will peach him, he'll scarce come off clean.
Then we'll buy English silks for our wives and our daughters,
In spite of his Deanship and journeyman Waters.

Part of the Ninth Ode
of the Fourth Book of Horace

ADDRESSED TO DOCTOR WILLIAM KING,
LATE LORD ARCHBISHOP OF DUBLIN

Paulum sepultae, &c.

Virtue concealed within our breast
Is inactivity at best:
But, never shall the muse endure
To let your virtues lie obscure,
Or suffer envy to conceal
Your labours for the public weal.
Within your breast all wisdom lies,
Either to govern or advise;
Your steady soul preserves her frame
10   In good and evil times the same.
Pale Avarice and lurking Fraud
Stand in your sacred presence awed;
Your hand alone from gold abstains,
Which drags the slavish world in chains.

    Him for an happy man I own,
Whose fortune is not overgrown;
And, happy he, who wisely knows
To use the gifts, that heaven bestows;
Or, if it please the powers divine,
20   Can suffer want, and not repine.
The man, who infamy to shun,
Into the arms of death would run,
That man is ready to defend
With life his country, or his friend.

The Run upon the Bankers

The bold encroachers on the deep,
    Gain by degrees huge tracts of land,
Till Neptune with one general sweep
    Turns all again to barren strand.

The multitude's capricious pranks
    Are said to represent the seas;
Breaking the bankers and the banks,
    Resume their own whene'er they please.

Money, the life-blood of the nation,
10   Corrupts and stágnates in the veins,
Unless a proper circulation
    Its motion and its heat maintains.

Because 'tis lordly not to pay,
    Quakers and aldermen, in state,
Like peers have levees every day
    Of duns attending at their gate.

We want our money on the nail;
    The banker's ruined if he pays;
They seem to act an ancient tale,
20   The birds are met to strip the jays.

Riches, the wisest monarch sings,
    Make pinions for themselves to fly:
They fly like bats, on parchment wings,
    And geese their silver plumes supply.

No money left for squandering heirs!
    Bills turn the lenders into debtors,
The wish of Nero now is theirs,
    That they had never known their letters.

Conceive the works of midnight hags,
30   Tormenting fools behind their backs;
Thus bankers o'er their bills and bags
    Sit squeezing images of wax.

Conceive the whole enchantment broke,
    The witches left in open air,

With power no more than other folk,
   Exposed with all their magic ware.

So powerful are a banker's bills
   Where creditors demand their due;
They break up counter, doors, and tills,
40   And leave the empty chests in view.

Thus when an earthquake lets in light
   Upon the god of gold and hell,
Unable to endure the sight,
   He hides within his darkest cell.

As when a conjuror takes a lease
   From Satan for a term of years,
The tenant's in a dismal case
   Whene'er the bloody bond appears.

A baited banker thus desponds,
50   From his own hand foresees his fall,
They have his soul who have his bonds,
   'Tis like the writing on the wall.

How will that caitiff wretch be scared
   When first he finds himself awake
At the last trumpet, unprepared,
   And all his grand account to make?

For in that universal call
   Few bankers will to heaven be mounters:
They'll cry, 'ye shops upon us fall,
60   Conceal and cover us, ye counters.'

When other hands the scales shall hold,
   And they in men and angels' sight
Produced with all their bills and gold,
   Weighed in the balance, and found light.

Mr Jason Hassard, a Woollen Draper in Dublin

[WHO] PUT UP THE SIGN OF THE GOLDEN FLEECE,
AND DESIRED A MOTTO IN VERSE

Jason, the valiant prince of Greece,
From Colchos brought the golden fleece:

We comb the wool, refine the stuff,
For modern Jasons that's enough.
Oh! could we tame yon watchful dragon,
Old Jason would have less to brag on.

The Description of an Irish Feast

TRANSLATED ALMOST LITERALLY OUT OF THE ORIGINAL IRISH

O'Rourk's noble fare
    Will ne'er be forgot,
By those who were there,
    And those who were not.
His revels to keep,
    We sup and we dine,
On seven score sheep,
    Fat bullock and swine.
Usquebaugh to our feast
10   In pails was brought up,
An hundred at least,
    And a madder our cup.
O there is the sport,
    We rise with the light,
In disorderly sort,
    From snoring all night.
O how was I tricked,
    My pipe it was broke,
My pocket was picked,
20   I lost my new cloak.
I'm rifled, quoth Nell,
    Of mantle and kercher,
Why then fare them well,
    The de'il take the searcher.
Come, harper, strike up,
    But first by your favour,
Boy, give us a cup;
    Ay, this has some savour:
O'Rourk's jolly boys
30   Ne'er dreamt of the matter,
Till roused by the noise,
    And musical clatter,
They bounce from their nest,

No longer will tarry,
They rise ready dressed,
  Without one *Ave Mary*.
They dance in a round,
  Cutting capers and ramping,
A mercy the ground
40   Did not burst with their stamping,
The floor is all wet
  With leaps and with jumps,
While the water and sweat,
  Splishsplash in their pumps.
Bless you late and early,
  Laughlin O' Enagin,
By my hand you dance rarely,
  Margery Grinagin.
Bring straw for our bed,
50   Shake it down to the feet,
Then over us spread,
  The winnowing sheet.
To show, I don't flinch,
  Fill the bowl up again,
Then give us a pinch
  Of your sneezing, a Yean.
Good Lord, what a sight,
  After all their good cheer,
For people to fight
60   In the midst of their beer:
They rise from their feast,
  And hot are their brains,
A cubit at least
  The length of their skenes.
What stabs and what cuts,
  What clattering of sticks,
What strokes on the guts,
  What bastings and kicks!
With cudgels of oak,
70   Well hardened in flame,
An hundred heads broke,
  An hundred struck lame.
You churl, I'll maintain

My father built Lusk,
The castle of Slane,
  And Carrickdrumrusk:
The Earl of Kildare,
  And Moynalta, his brother,
As great as they are,
80 I was nursed by their mother.
Ask that of old Madam,
  She'll tell you who's who,
As far up as Adam,
  She knows it is true,
Come down with that beam,
  If cudgels are scarce,
A blow on the wame,
  Or a kick on the arse.

Stella's Birthday

WRITTEN IN THE YEAR 1720–21

All travellers at first incline
Where'er they see the fairest sign;
And if they find the chamber neat,
And like the liquor, and the meat,
Will call again, and recommend
The Angel Inn to every friend:
What though the painting grows decayed,
The house will never lose its trade;
Nay, though the treacherous tapster Thomas
10 Hangs a new angel two doors from us,
As fine as dauber's hands can make it,
In hopes that strangers may mistake it;
We think it both a shame and sin
To quit the true old Angel Inn.

    Now, this is Stella's case in fact,
An angel's face, a little cracked;
(Could poets, or could painters fix
How angels look at thirty-six:)
This drew us in at first, to find

20   In such a form an angel's mind:
And every virtue now supplies
The fainting rays of Stella's eyes.
See, at her levee crowding swains,
Whom Stella freely entertains
With breeding, humour, wit, and sense;
And puts them to so small expense:
Their mind so plentifully fills,
And makes such reasonable bills;
So little gets for what she gives,
30   We really wonder how she lives!
And had her stock been less, no doubt
She must have long ago run out.

      Then who can think we'll quit the place
When Doll hangs out her newer face;
Nailed to her window full in sight
All Christian people to invite;
Or stop and light at Chloe's head
With scraps and leavings to be fed.

      Then Chloe, still go on to prate
Of thirty-six, and thirty-eight;
Pursue your trade of scandal-picking,
40   Your hints that Stella is no chicken;
Your innuendos, when you tell us
That Stella loves to talk with fellows:
But let me warn you to believe
A truth, for which your soul should grieve;
That, should you live to see the day
When Stella's locks must all be grey;
When age must print a furrowed trace
On every feature of her face;
Though you and all your senseless tribe,
50   Could art, or time, or nature bribe,
To make you look like beauty's queen,
And hold forever at fifteen:
No bloom of youth can ever blind
The cracks and wrinkles of your mind,
All men of sense will pass your door,
And crowd to Stella's at fourscore.

The Answer to Vanessa's Rebus

The nymph who wrote this in an amorous fit,
I cannot but envy the pride of her wit.
Which thus she will venture profusely to throw,
On so mean a design, and a subject so low.
For mean's her design, and her subject as mean,
The first but a rebus, the last but a Dean.
A Dean's but a person, and what is a rebus?
A thing never known to the muses or Phoebus:
The corruption of verse, for when all is done,
10   It is but a paraphrase made on a pun;
But a genius like hers no subject can stifle,
It shows and discovers itself through a trifle.
By reading this trifle I quickly began
To find her a great wit, but the Dean a small man.
Rich ladies will furnish their garrets with stuff,
Which others for manteaus would think fine enough;
So the wit that is lavishly thrown away here,
Might furnish a second-rate poet a year:
Thus much for the verse, we proceed to the next,
20   Where the nymph has entirely forsaken her text:
Her fine panegyrics are quite out of season,
And what she describes to be merit is treason:
The changes which faction has made in the state,
Have put the Dean's politics quite out of date:
Now no one regards what he utters with freedom,
And should he write pamphlets, no great man would read 'em:
And should want or desert stand in need of his aid,
This racer would prove but a dull foundered jade.

Apollo to the Dean

Right trusty, and so forth, – We let you to know,
We are very ill used by you mortals below.
For, first, I have often by chemists been told,
Though I know nothing on't, it is I that makes gold,
Which when you have got, you so carefully hide it,
That since I was born, I hardly have spied it.

Then, it must be allowed, whenever I shine,
I forward the grass, and I ripen the vine;
To me the good fellows apply for relief,
10   Without whom they could get neither claret, nor beef;
Yet their wine and their victuals, these curmudgeon lubbards,
Lock up from my sight in cellars and cupboards.
That I have an ill eye, they wickedly think,
And taint all their meat, and sour all their drink.
But thirdly and lastly, it must be allowed,
I alone can inspire the poetical crowd;
This is gratefully owned by each boy in the college,
Whom if I inspire, it is not to my knowledge;
This every pretender to rhyme will admit,
20   Without troubling his head about judgement or wit:
These gentlemen use me with kindness and freedom,
And as for their works, when I please I may read 'em;
They lie open on purpose on counters and stalls,
And the titles I view, when I shine on the walls.
But a comrade of yours, that traitor Delany,
Whom I, for your sake, love better than any;
And of my mere motion, and special good grace,
Intended in time to succeed in your place;
On Tuesday the tenth, seditiously came,
30   With a certain false traitress, one Stella by name,
To the Deanery house, and on the north glass,
Where for fear of the cold, I never can pass;
Then and there, *vi et armis*, with a certain utensil,
Of value five shillings, in English a pencil,
Did maliciously, falsely, and traitorously write,
Whilst Stella aforesaid stood by with the light;
My sister has lately deposed upon oath,
That she stopped in her course to look at them both;
That Stella was helping, abetting and aiding,
40   And still as he writ, stood smiling and reading;
That her eyes were as bright as myself at noonday;
But her graceful black locks were all mingled with grey.
And by the description I certainly know,
'Tis the nymph that I courted some ten years ago;
Who, when I with the best of my talents endued,
On her promise of yielding; she acted the prude.
That some verses were writ with felonious intent,

Direct to the North, where never I went;
That the letters appeared reversed through the pane,
50   But in Stella's bright eyes they were placed right again;
Wherein she distinctly could read every line,
And presently guessed the fancy was mine.
Now you see why his verses so seldom are shown,
The reason is plain, they are none of his own;
And observe while you live, that no man is shy
To discover the goods he came honestly by:
If I light on a thought, he will certainly steal it,
And when he has got it, find ways to conceal it;
Of all the fine things he keeps in the dark,
60   There's scarce one in ten, but what has my mark;
And let them be seen by the world if he dare,
I'll make it appear, they are all stolen ware.
But as for the poem he writ on your sash,
I think I have now got him under my lash;
My sister transcribed it last night to his sorrow,
And the public shall see't, if I live till tomorrow;
Through the zodiac around, it shall quickly be spread,
In all parts of the globe, where your language is read.
He knows very well I ne'er gave a refusal,
70   When he asked for my aid in the forms that are usual:
But the secret is this. I did lately intend
To write a few verses on you as my friend;
I studied a fortnight, before I could find,
As I rode in my chariot, a thought to my mind;
And resolved the next winter, for that is my time,
When the days are at shortest, to get it in rhyme;
Till then it was locked in my box at Parnassus;
When the subtle companion, in hopes to surpass us,
Conveys out my paper of hints by a trick,
80   (For I think in my conscience he dines with old Nick;)
And from my own stock provided with topics,
He gets to a window beyond both the tropics;
There out of my sight, just against the North zone,
Writes down my conceits, and then calls them his own:
And you like a cully, the bubble can swallow;
Now who but Delany that writes like Apollo?
High treason by statute. But here you object,
He only stole hints, but the verse is correct.

Though the thought be Apollo's, 'tis finely expressed.
90 So a thief steals my horse, and has him well dressed.
Now, whereas the said criminal seems past repentance,
We Phoebus think fit to proceed to the sentence;
Since Delany has dared, like Prometheus his sire,
To climb to our region, and thence to steal fire;
We order a vulture, in shape of the spleen,
To prey on his liver, but not to be seen.
And we order our subjects of every degree,
To believe all his verses were written by me:
And, under the pain of our highest displeasure,
100 To call nothing his, but the rhyme and the measure.
And lastly, for Stella, just out of her prime,
I am too much revenged already by time.
In return to her scorn, I sent her diseases,
But will now be her friend, whenever she pleases.
And the gifts I bestowed her, will find her a lover,
Though she lives to be grey as a badger all over.

An Epilogue to a Play for the Benefit of the Weavers in Ireland

Who dares affirm this is no pious age,
When Charity begins to tread the stage?
When actors who at best are hardly savers,
Will give a night of benefit to weavers?
Stay, – let me see, how finely will it sound!
Imprimis, From his Grace an hundred pound.
Peers, clergy, gentry, all are benefactors;
And then comes in the *Item* of the actors.
Item, the actors, freely gave a day, –
10 The poet had no more who made the play.

But whence this wondrous charity in players?
They learnt it not at sermons, or at prayers:
Under the rose, since here are none but friends,
(To own the truth) we have some private ends.
Since waiting women, like exacting jades,
Hold up the prices of their old brocades;

We'll dress in manufactures, made at home;
Equip our kings, and generals at the Comb.
We'll rig in Meath Street Egypt's haughty queen,
20 And Antony shall court her in ratteen.
In blue shalloon, shall Hannibal be clad,
And Scipio trail an Irish purple plaid.
In drugget dressed, of thirteen pence a yard,
See Philip's son amidst his Persian guard;
And proud Roxana fired with jealous rage,
With fifty yards of crape, shall sweep the stage.
In short, our kings and princesses within,
Are all resolved the project to begin;
And you, our subjects, when you here resort,
30 Must imitate the fashion of the court.

O! could I see this audience clad in stuff,
Though money's scarce we should have trade enough;
But chintz, brocades, and lace take all away,
And scarce a crown is left to see a play:
Perhaps you wonder whence this friendship springs,
Between the weavers and us playhouse kings:
But wit and weaving has the same beginning,
Pallas first taught us poetry and spinning;
And next observe how this alliance fits,
40 For weavers now are just as poor as wits:
Their brother quill-men, workers for the stage,
For sorry stuff, can get a crown a page;
But weavers will be kinder to the players,
And sell for twenty pence a yard of theirs,
And to your knowledge there is often less in
The poet's wit, than in the player's dressing.

Apollo's Edict

Ireland is now our royal care,
We lately fixed our Viceroy there:
How near was she to be undone,
Till pious love inspired her son?
What cannot our Viceregent do,
As poet and as patriot too?

Let his success our subjects sway ⎫
Our inspirations to obey, ⎬
And follow where he leads the way: ⎭
10   Then study to correct your taste,
Nor beaten paths be longer traced.

No simile shall be begun,
With rising or with setting sun:
And let the secret head of Nile
Be ever banished from your isle.

When wretched lovers live on air,
I beg you'll the chameleon spare.
And when you'd make a hero grander,
Forget he's like a salamander.
20   No son of mine shall dare to say, ⎫
Aurora ushered in the day, ⎬
Or ever name the Milky Way. ⎭

You all agree, I make no doubt,
Elijah's mantle's worn out.

The bird of Jove shall toil no more,
To teach the humble wren to soar.

Your tragic heroes shall not rant,
Nor shepherds use poetic cant:
Simplicity alone can grace,
30   The manners of the rural race,
Theocritus and Philips be,
Your guides to true simplicity.

When Damon's soul shall take its flight, ⎫
Though poets have the second sight, ⎬
They shall not see a trail of light: ⎭
Nor shall the vapour upwards rise,
Nor a new star adorn the skies:
For who can hope to place one there,
As glorious as Belinda's hair?
40   Yet if his name you'd eternize
And must exalt him to the skies:
Without a star this may be done,
So Tickell mourned his Addison.

If Anna's happy reign you praise,
Pray not a word of halcyon days.
Nor let my votaries show their skill

In aping lines from *Cooper's Hill*;
For know I cannot bear to hear,
The mimicry of 'deep yet clear'.
50   Whene'er my Viceroy is addressed,
Against the phoenix I protest.
When poets soar in youthful strains,
No Phaeton to hold the reins.
When you describe a lovely girl,
No lips of coral, teeth of pearl.
Cupid shall ne'er mistake another
However beauteous for his mother:
Nor shall his darts at random fly
From magazine in Celia's eye.
60   With women compounds I am cloyed,
Which only pleased in Biddy Floyd:
For foreign aid what need they roam,
Whom fate has amply blessed at home?
Unerring heaven, with bounteous hand,
Has formed a model for your land;
Whom Jove endowed with every grace,
The glory of the Granard race;
Now destined, by the powers divine,
The blessing of another line:
70   Then would you paint a matchless dame,
Whom you consign to endless fame?
Invoke not Cytherea's aid,
Nor borrow from the blue-eyed maid,
Nor need you on the Graces call,
Take qualities from Donegal.

George Nim-Dan-Dean, Esq. to Mr Sheridan

ON HIS VERSES, WRITTEN JULY 15, 1721,
AT TEN IN THE MORNING

Dear Sheridan, a loving pair
Of Gaulstown lads (for so they are)
Beside a brace of grave divines,
Adore the smoothness of thy lines:
Smooth as our basin's gentle flood,

'Ere George had robbed it of its mud.
Smoother than Pegasus' old shoe,
'Ere Vulcan comes to make him new.
Compared with which (and that's enough)
10   A smoothing iron, itself is rough.

Nor praise we less that circumcision,
By modern poets, called *elision*;
Which in its proper station placed,
Makes thy verse smooth, and makes them last.
Thus a wise tailor is not pinching,
But turns at every seam, an inch in.
Or, else be sure, your broadcloth breeches,
Will ne'er be smooth, nor hold the stitches.
Thy verse like bricks, defy the weather,
20   When smoothed by rubbing them together:
Thy words so closely wedged, and short are,
Like walls, more lasting without mortar:
By leaving out the needless vowels,
You save the charge of lime and trowels.
One letter still another locks;
Each grooved, and dovetailed, like a box.
Thy muse is tucked up, and succinct;
In chains, thy syllables are linked.
Thy words together tied in small hanks,
30   Close, as the Macedonian phalanx:
Or, like the *umbo* of the Romans,
Which fiercest foes, could break by no means.
The critic to his cost will find,
How firmly these indentures bind.
So in the kindred painter's art,
The shortening is the nicest part.

Philologers of future ages,
How will they pore upon thy pages?
Nor will they dare to break the joints,
40   But help thee to be read with points.
Or else, to show their learned labour, you
May backwards be perused, like Hebrew.
Wherein they need not lose a bit,
Or, of thy harmony, or wit.

To make a work completely fine,
Number, and weight, and measure join.
Then all must grant, your lines are weighty,
Where thirty weigh, as much as eighty.
All must allow, your numbers more,
50   Where forty lines, exceed fourscore.
Nor can we think your measure short,
Where less than forty, fill a quart.
With Alexandrian in the close.
Long, long, long, long, like Dan's long nose.

George Nim-Dan-Dean's Invitation to Mr Thomas Sheridan

Gaulstown, August 2nd, 1721.

Dear Tom, this verse, which however the beginning may appear,
     yet in the *end's good metre*,
Is sent to desire that, when your August vacation comes, your
     friends you'd meet here.
For why should you stay in that filthy hole, I mean the *city so
     smoky*,
When you have not one friend left in town, or at least not one
     that's *witty, to joke w'ye?*
For, as for honest John, though I'm not sure on't, yet I'll be
     hanged, less he
Be gone down the county of Wexford with that great peer the
     Lord *Anglesey.*
Oh! but I forgot, perhaps, by this time, you may have one come to
     town, but I don't know whether he be friend or *foe, Delany*;
But, however, if he be come, bring him down, and you shall go
     back in a fortnight, for I know, there's *no delaying ye.*
Oh! I forgot too, I believe there may be one more, I mean that
     great fat joker, *friend Helsham, he*
10   That wrote the prologue, and if you stay with him, depend on't, in
     the *end, he'll sham ye.*
Bring down Long Shanks Jim too, but now I think on't, he's not
     come yet from *Courtown, I fancy*;
For I heard, a month ago, that he was down there a-*courting sly
     Nancy.*

However, bring down yourself, and you bring down all; for, to say
　　it *we may venture*,
In thee Delany's spleen, John's mirth, Helsham's jokes, and the
　　soft soul of amorous *Jemmy centre*.

POSTSCRIPT

I had forgot to desire you to bring down what I say you have,
　　and you'll believe me as sure as a *gun, and own it*;
I mean, what no other mortal in the universe can boast of,
　　your own spirit of *pun, and own wit*.
And now I hope you'll excuse this rhyming, which I must say is
　　(though written somewhat at *large) trim and clean*;
And so I conclude, with humble respects as usual, your most
　　dutiful and obedient

George Nim-Dan-Dean.

To Mr Sheridan, upon His Verses Written in Circles

It never was known that circular letters,
By humble companions were sent to their betters:
And, as to the subject, our judgement mehercle
Is this, that you argue like fools in a circle.
But now for your verses; we tell you, *imprimis*,
The segment so large 'twixt your reason and rhyme is,
That we walk all about, like a horse in a pound,
And, before we find either, our noddles turn round.
Sufficient it were, one would think, in your mad rant,
10　To give us your measure of lines by quadrant.
But we took our dividers, and found your damned metre,
In each single verse, took up a diameter.
But how, Mr Sheridan, came you to venture
George, Dan, Dean and Nim to place in the centre?
'Twill appear, to your cost, you are fairly trepanned,
For the cord of your circle is now in their hand;
The cord, or the radius, it matters not whether,
By which your jade Pegasus fixed in a tether,
As his betters are used, shall be lashed round the ring,
20　Three fellows with whips, and the Dean holds the string.

Will Hancock declares you are out of your compass,
To encroach on his art by writing of bombas';
And has taken just now a firm resolution
To answer your style without circumlocution.

Lady Betty presents you her service most humble,
And is not afraid your worship will grumble,
That she makes of your verses a hoop for Miss Tam,
Which is all at present; and so I remain –

The Part of a Summer

AT THE HOUSE OF GEORGE ROCHFORT, ESQ.

Thalia, tell in sober lays,
How George, Nim, Dan, Dean, pass their days.

   Begin, my muse, first from our bowers,
We sally forth at different hours;
At seven, the Dean in night-gown dressed,
Goes round the house to wake the rest:
At nine, grave Nim and George facetious,
Go to the Dean to read Lucretius.
At ten, my Lady comes and hectors,
10 And kisses George, and ends our lectures;
And when she has him by the neck fast,
Hauls him, and scolds us down to breakfast.
We squander there an hour or more;
And then all hands, boys, to the oar;
All, heteroclite Dan except,
Who never time nor order kept,
But by peculiar whimsies drawn,
Peeps in the pond to look for spawn;
O'ersees the work, or 'Dragon' rows,
20 Or mars a text, or mends his hose;
Or – but proceed we in our journal –
At two, or after, we return all.
From the four elements assembling,
Warned by the bell, all folks come trembling,
From airy garrets some descend,
Some from the lake's remotest end.

My Lord and Dean, the fire foresake;
Dan leaves the earthly spade and rake:
The loiterers quake, no corner hides them,
30   And Lady Betty soundly chides them.
Now water's brought, and dinner's done,
With Church and King, the lady's gone;
(Not reckoning half an hour we pass
In talking o'er a moderate glass.)
Dan, growing drowsy, like a thief
Steals off to doze away his beef;
And this must pass for reading Hammond –
While George and Dean, go to backgammon.
George, Nim and Dean set out at four,
40   And then again, boys, to the oar.
But when the sun goes to the deep
(Not to disturb him in his sleep,
Or make a rumbling o'er his head,
His candle out, and he abed)
We watch his motions to the minute,
And leave the flood when he goes in it:
Now stinted in the shortening day,
We go to prayers, and then to play:
Till supper comes, and after that,
50   We sit an hour to drink and chat.
'Tis late – the old and younger pairs,
By Adam lighted walk upstairs.
The weary Dean goes to his chamber,
And Nim and Dan to garret clamber.
So when this circle we have run,
The curtain falls, and all is done.

I might have mentioned several facts,
Like episodes between the acts;
And tell who loses, and who wins,
60   Who gets a cold, who breaks his shins.
How Dan caught *nothing* in his net,
And how the boat was overset,
For brevity I have retrenched,
How in the lake the Dean was drenched:
It would be an explóit to brag on,
How valiant George rowed o'er the 'Dragon';
How steady in the storm he sat,

And saved his oar, but lost his hat.
How Nim (no hunter e'er could match him,)
70 Still brings us hares, when he can catch them:
How skilfully Dan mends his nets,
How fortune fails him when he sets:
Or how the Dean delights to vex
The ladies, and lampoon the sex.
Or how our neighbour lifts his nose,
To tell what every schoolboy knows:
And, with his finger on his thumb,
Explaining, strikes opposers dumb;
Or how his wife, that female pedant,
80 (But now there need no more be said on't,)
Shows all her secrets of housekeeping,
For candles how she trucks her dripping;
Was forced to send three miles for yeast
To brew her ale, and raise her paste:
Tells everything that you can think of,
How she cured Tommy of the chin-cough;
What gave her brats and pigs the measles,
And how her doves were killed by weasels:
How Jowler howled, and what a fright
90 She had with dreams the other night.

But now, since I have gone so far on,
A word or two of Lord Chief Baron;
And tell how little weight he sets
On all Whig papers and gazettes:
But for the politics of Pue,
Thinks every syllable is true;
And since he owns the King of Sweden
Is dead at last without evading;
Now all his hopes are in the Czar;
100 'Why, Muscovy is not so far;
Down the Black Sea, and up the straits,
And in a month he's at your gates:
Perhaps from what the packet brings,
By Christmas we shall see strange things.'

Why should I tell of ponds and drains,
What carps we met with for our pains:
Of sparrows tamed, and nuts innumerable,

To choke the girls, and to consume a rabble?
But you, who are a scholar, know
110 How transient all things are below:
How prone to change is human life;
Last night arrived Clem and his wife –
This grand event hath broke our measures;
Their reign began with cruel seizures:
The Dean must with his quilt supply,
The bed in which these tyrants lie:
Nim lost his wig-block, Dan his jordan;
(My Lady says she can't afford one)
George is half scared out of his wits,
120 For Clem gets all the tiny bits.
Henceforth expect a different survey;
This house will soon turn topsyturvy;
They talk of further alterations,
Which causes many speculations.

A Quibbling Elegy on the Worshipful Judge Boat

To mournful ditties, Clio, change thy note,
Since cruel fate hath sunk our Justice Boat;
Why should he sink where nothing seemed to press?
His lading little, and his ballast less.
Tossed in the waves of this tempestuous world,
At length, his anchor fixed, and canvas furled,
To Lazy Hill retiring from his court,
At his Ring's End he founders in the port.
With water filled he could no longer float,
10 The common death of many a stronger boat.

A post so filled, on nature's laws entrenches;
Benches on boats are placed, not Boats on benches.
And yet our boat, how shall I reconcile it?
Was both a boat, and in one sense a pilot.
With every wind he sailed, and well could tack:
Had many pendants, but abhorred a jack.
He's gone, although his friends began to hope
That he might yet be lifted by a rope.

Behold the awful bench, on which he sat,
20 He was as hard, and ponderous wood as that:
Yet, when his sand was out, we find at last,
That, death has overset him with a blast.
Our Boat is now sailed to the Stygian ferry,
There to supply old Charon's leaky wherry:
Charon in him will ferry souls to hell;
A trade, our Boat has practised here so well.
And, Cerberus hath ready in his paws,
Both pitch and brimstone to fill up his flaws;
Yet, spite of death and fate, I here maintain
30 We may place Boat in his old post again.
The way is thus; and well deserves your thanks:
Take the three strongest of his broken planks,
Fix them on high, conspicuous to be seen,
Formed like the triple tree near Stephen's Green;
And when we view it thus, with thief at end on't,
We'll cry; look, here's our Boat, and there's the pendant.

THE EPITAPH

Here lies Judge Boat within a coffin.
Pray gentlefolks forbear your scoffing.
A boat a judge! yes, where's the blunder?
40 A wooden judge is no such wonder.
And in his robes, you must agree,
No boat was better decked than he.
'Tis needless to describe him fuller.
In short, he was an able sculler.

The Bank Thrown Down

TO AN EXCELLENT NEW TUNE

Pray, what is this Bank of which the town rings?
The banks of a river I know are good things,
But a pox o' those banks that choke up the springs.
 Some mischief is brewing, the project smells rank,
 To shut out the river by raising the bank.

The dams and the weirs must all be your own,
You get all the fish, and others get none.
We look for a salmon, you leave us a stone.
    But thanks to the House, the projectors look blank,
10   And thanks to the members that kicked down the Bank.

This Bank is to make us a new paper mill,
This paper, they say, by the help of a quill,
The whole nation's pocket with money will fill.
    But we doubt that our purses will quickly grow lank,
    If nothing but paper comes out of this bank.

'Tis happy to see the whole kingdom in rags,
For rags will make paper, and pa-ba-ba-brags,
This paper will soon make us richer than Craggs.
    From a bo-bo-bo-boy he pursues his old hank,
20   And now he runs mad for a ba-ba-ba-bank.

Oh! then but to see how the beggars will vapour,
For beggars have rags and rags will make paper.
And paper makes money, and what can be cheaper?
    Methinks I now see them so jovial and crank,
    And riding on horseback to hell and the Bank.

But the cobbler was angry, and swore he had rather
As they did in old times, make money of leather,
For then he could coin and could cobble together;
    And then he could pay for the liquor he drank
30   With the scrap of a sole, and a fig for a bank.

By a parliament man when the farmer was told,
That paper would quickly be dearer than gold,
He wondered for how much an inch would be sold:
    Then plodding, he thought on a whimsical prank
    To turn to small money a bill on the Bank.

For nicely computing the price by retail,
He found he could purchase two tankards of ale,
With a scrap of bank paper the breadth of his nail;
    But the tapster well cudgelled him both side and flank,
40   And made him to curse the poor innocent Bank.

The ghost of old Demar, who left not his betters,
When it heard of a Bank, appeared to his debtors,

And lent them for money the backs of his letters:
>His debtors they wondered to find him so frank,
>For old Nick gave the papers the mark of the Bank.

In a Chancery bill your attorney engages,
For so many sixpences, so many pages,
But sixpence a letter is monstrous high wages:
>Those that dropped in the South Sea discovered this plank,
50 >By which they might swimmingly land on a Bank.

But the squire he was cunning and found what they meant,
That a pack of sly knaves should get fifty per cent,
While his tenants in paper must pay him his rent:
>So for their quack bills he knows whom to thank,
>For those are but quacks, who mount on a Bank.

To Stella on Her Birthday

WRITTEN AD 1721–2

While, Stella, to your lasting praise
The muse her annual tribute pays,
While I assign myself a task
Which you expect, but scorn to ask;
If I perform this task with pain
Let me of partial fate complain;
You, every year the debt enlarge,
I grow less equal to the charge:
In you, each virtue brighter shines,
10 But my poetic vein declines.
My harp will soon in vain be strung,
And all your virtues left unsung:
For, none among the upstart race
Of poets dare assume my place;
Your worth will be to them unknown,
They must have Stellas of their own;
And thus, my stock of wit decayed;
I dying leave the debt unpaid,
Unless Delany as my heir,
20 Will answer for the whole arrear.

A Satirical Elegy on the Death
of a Late Famous General

His Grace! impossible! what, dead!
Of old age too, and in his bed!
And could that Mighty Warrior fall?
And so inglorious, after all!
Well, since he's gone, no matter how,
The last loud trump must wake him now:
And, trust me, as the noise grows stronger,
He'd wish to sleep a little longer.
And could he be indeed so old
As by the newspapers we're told?
Threescore, I think, is pretty high;
'Twas time in conscience he should die.
This world he cumbered long enough;
He burnt his candle to the snuff;
And that's the reason, some folks think,
He left behind *so great a stink*.
Behold his funeral appears,
Nor widow's sighs, nor orphan's tears,
Wont at such times each heart to pierce,
Attend the progress of his hearse.
But what of that, his friends may say,
He had those honours in his day.
True to his profit and his pride,
He made them weep before he died.

Come hither, all ye empty things,
Ye bubbles raised by breath of kings;
Who float upon the tide of state,
Come hither, and behold your fate.
Let pride be taught by this rebuke,
How very mean a thing's a Duke;
From all his ill-got honours flung,
Turned to that dirt from whence he sprung.

The Progress of Marriage

Aetatis suae fifty-two
A rich divine began to woo

A handsome young imperious girl
Nearly related to an Earl.
Her parents and her friends consent,
The couple to the temple went:
They first invite the Cyprian queen,
'Twas answered, she would not be seen.
The Graces next, and all the Muses
10 Were bid in form, but sent excuses:
Juno attended at the porch
With farthing candle for a torch,
While Mistress Iris held her train,
The faded bow distilling rain.
Then Hebe came and took her place
But showed no more than half her face.

Whate'er these dire forebodings meant,
In mirth the wedding-day was spent.
The wedding-day, you take me right,
20 I promise nothing for the night:
The bridegroom dressed, to make a figure,
Assumes an artificial vigour;
A flourished nightcap on, to grace
His ruddy, wrinkled, smirking face,
Like the faint red upon a pippin
Half withered by a winter's keeping.

And, thus set out this happy pair,
The swain is rich, the nymph is fair;
But, which I gladly would forget,
30 The swain is old, the nymph coquette.
Both from the goal together start;
Scarce run a step before they part;
No common ligament that binds
The various textures of their minds,
Their thoughts, and actions, hopes, and fears,
Less corresponding than their years.
Her spouse desires his coffee soon,
She rises to her tea at noon.
While he goes out to cheapen books,
40 She at the glass consults her looks;
While Betty's buzzing at her ear,
Lord, what a dress these parsons wear,
So odd a choice, how could she make,

Wished him a colonel for her sake.
Then on her fingers' ends she counts
Exact to what his age amounts,
The Dean, she heard her uncle say,
Is sixty, if he be a day;
His ruddy cheeks are no disguise;
50   You see the crow's feet round his eyes.

At one she rambles to the shops
To cheapen tea, and talk with fops.
Or calls a council of her maids
And tradesmen, to compare brocades.
Her weighty morning business o'er
Sits down to dinner just at four;
Minds nothing that is done or said,
Her evening work so fills her head;
The Dean, who used to dine at one,
60   Is mawkish, and his stomach gone;
In threadbare gown, would scarce a louse hold,
Looks like the chaplain of the household,
Beholds her from the chaplain's place
In French brocades and Flanders lace;
He wonders what employs her brain;
But never asks, or asks in vain;
His mind is full of other cares,
And in the sneaking parson's airs
Computes, that half a parish dues
70   Will hardly find his wife in shoes.

Canst thou imagine, dull divine,
'Twill gain her love to make her fine?
Hath she no other wants beside?
You raise desire as well as pride,
Enticing coxcombs to adore,
And teach her to despise thee more.

If in her coach she'll condescend
To place him at the hinder end
Her hoop is hoist above his nose,
80   His odious gown would soil her clothes,
And drops him at the church, to pray
While she drives on to see the play.

He like an orderly divine
Comes home a quarter after nine,
And meets her hasting to the ball,
Her chairmen push him from the wall:
He enters in, and walks upstairs,
And calls the family to prayers,
Then goes alone to take his rest
90   In bed, where he can spare her best.
At five the footmen make a din,
Her ladyship is just come in,
The masquerade began at two,
She stole away with much ado,
And shall be chid this afternoon
For leaving company so soon;
She'll say, and she may truly say't,
She can't abide to stay out late.

But now, though scarce a twelve month married,
100   His lady has twelve times miscarried,
The cause, alas, is quickly guessed,
The town has whispered round the jest:
Think on some remedy in time,
You find his Reverence past his prime,
Already dwindled to a lathe;
No other way but try the Bath.

For Venus rising from the ocean
Infused a strong prolific potion,
That mixed with Achelous' spring,
110   The 'hornéd flood', as poets sing:
Who with an English beauty smitten
Ran underground from Greece to Britain,
The genial virtue with him brought,
And gave the nymph a plenteous draught;
Then fled, and left his horn behind
For husbands past their youth to find;
The nymph who still with passion burned,
Was to a boiling fountain turned,
Where childless wives crowd every morn
120   To drink in Achelous' horn.
And here the father often gains
That title by another's pains.

Hither, though much against his grain,
The Dean has carried Lady Jane.
He for a while would not consent,
But vowed his money all was spent;
His money spent! a clownish reason!
And must my Lady slip her season?
The doctor with a double fee
130 Was bribed to make the Dean agree.

Here, all diversions of the place
Are proper in my Lady's case:
With which she patiently complies,
Merely because her friends advise;
His money and her time employs
In music, raffling-rooms, and toys,
Or in the Cross Bath, seeks an heir
Since others oft have found one there;
Where if the Dean by chance appears
140 It shames his cassock and his years.
He keeps his distance in the gallery
Till banished by some coxcomb's raillery;
For, it would his character expose
To bathe among the belles and beaux.

So have I seen within a pen
Young ducklings, fostered by a hen;
But when let out, they run and muddle
As instinct leads them, in a puddle;
The sober hen not born to swim
150 With mournful note clucks round the brim.

The Dean with all his best endeavour
Gets not an heir, but gets a fever;
A victim to the last essays
Of vigour in declining days.
He dies, and leaves his mourning mate
(What could he less?) his whole estate.

The widow goes through all the forms;
New lovers now will come in swarms.
Oh, may I see her soon dispensing
160 Her favours to some broken ensign!
Him let her marry for his face,

And only coat of tarnished lace;
To turn her naked out of doors,
And spend her jointure on his whores:
But for a parting present leave her
A rooted pox to last forever.

Upon the Horrid Plot Discovered by Harlequin the Bishop of Rochester's French Dog

IN A DIALOGUE BETWEEN A WHIG AND A TORY

I asked a Whig the other night,
How came this wicked plot to light:
He answered, that a dog of late
Informed a minister of state.
Said I, from thence I nothing know;
For, are not all informers so?
A villain, who his friend betrays,
We style him by no other phrase;
And so a perjured dog denotes
10 Porter, and Prendergast, and Oates.
And forty others I could name –

WHIG   But you must know this dog was lame.

TORY   A weighty argument indeed;
Your evidence was lame. Proceed:
Come, help your lame dog o'er the stile.

WHIG   Sir, you mistake me all this while:
I mean a dog, without a joke,
Can howl, and bark, but never spoke.

TORY   I'm still to seek which dog you mean;
20 Whether cur Plunket, or whelp Skean,
An English or an Irish hound;
Or t'other puppy that was drowned,
Or Mason that abandoned bitch:
Then pray be free, and tell me which:
For, every stander-by was marking

That all the noise they made was barking:
You pay them well; the dogs have got
Their dog's-heads in a porridge-pot:
And 'twas but just; for, wise men say,
30   That, 'every dog must have his day'.
Dog Walpole laid a quart of nog on't,
He'd either make a hog or dog on't,
And looked since he has got his wish,
As if he had thrown down a dish.
Yet, this I dare foretell you from it,
He'll soon return to his own vomit.

WHIG   Besides, this horrid plot was found
By Neno after he was drowned.

TORY   Why then the proverb is not right,
40   Since you can teach dead dogs to bite.

WHIG   I proved my proposition full:
But, Jacobites are strangely dull.
Now, let me tell you plainly, sir,
Our witness is a real cur,
A dog of spirit for his years,
Has twice two legs, two hanging ears;
His name is Harlequin, I wot,
And that's a name in every plot:
Resolved to save the British nation,
50   Though French by birth and education:
His correspondence plainly dated,
Was all deciphered, and translated.
His answers were exceeding pretty
Before the secret wise committee;
Confessed as plain as he could bark;
Then with his fore-foot set his mark.

TORY   Then all this while I have been bubbled;
I thought it was a dog in doublet:
The matter now no longer sticks;
60   For statesmen never want dog-tricks.
But, since it was a real cur,
And not a dog in metaphor,

I'll give you joy of the report,
That he's to have a place at court.

WHIG Yes, and a place he will grow rich in;
A turnspit in the royal kitchen.
Sir, to be plain, I tell you what;
We had occasion for a plot;
And when we found the dog begin it,
70 We guessed the Bishop's foot was in it.

TORY I own it was a dangerous project;
And you have proved it by dog-logic.
Sure such intelligence between
A dog and bishop ne'er was seen,
Till you began to change the breed;
Your bishops all are dogs indeed.

The Storm

MINERVA'S PETITION

Pallas, a goddess chaste and wise,
Descending lately from the skies,
To Neptune went, and begged in form
He'd give his orders for a storm;
A storm, to drown that rascal Hort,
And she would kindly thank him for't.
A wretch! whom English rogues to spite her,
Had lately honoured with a mitre.

The god, who favoured her request,
10 Assured her he would do his best:
But Venus had been there before
Pleaded the Bishop loved a whore,
And had enlarged her empire wide,
He owned no deity beside.
At sea, or land, if e'er you found him,
Without a mistress, hang or drown him.
Since Burnet's death, the bishops' bench,
Till Hort arrived ne'er kept a wench;
If Hort must sink, she grieves to tell it,

20   She'll not have left one single prelate:
     For to say truth, she did intend him,
     Elect of Cyprus *in commendam*.
     And since her birth the ocean gave her,
     She could not doubt her uncle's favour.

     Then Proteus urged the same request,
     But half in earnest, half in jest;
     Said he, – 'Great sovereign of the main,
     To drown him all attempts are vain,
     Hort can assume more forms than I,
30   A rake, a bully, pimp, or spy.
     Can creep, or run, can fly or swim,
     All motions are alike to him:
     Turn him adrift, and you shall find
     He knows to sail with every wind;
     Or, throw him overboard, he'll ride
     As well against, as with the tide,
     But, Pallas, you've applied too late,
     For 'tis decreed by Jove and fate,
     That Ireland must be soon destroyed,
40   And who but Hort can be employed?
     You need not then have been so pert,
     In sending Bolton to Clonfert.
     I found you did it by your grinning;
     Your business is to mind your spinning.
     But how you came to interpose,
     In making bishops, no one knows.
     And if you must have your petition,
     There's Berkeley in the same condition;
     Look, there he stands, and 'tis but just
50   If one must drown, the other must;
     But, if you'll leave us Bishop Judas,
     We'll give you Berkeley for Bermudas.
     Now, if 'twill gratify your spite,
     To put him in a plaguy fright,
     Although 'tis hardly worth the cost,
     You soon shall see him soundly tossed.
     You'll find him swear, blaspheme, and damn,
     And every moment take a dram,
     His ghostly visage with an air

60 Of reprobation and despair:
    Or, else some hiding hole he seeks,
    For fear the rest should say he squeaks;
    Or as Fitzpatrick did before,
    Resolve to perish with his whore;
    Or, else he raves, and roars, and swears,
    And, but for shame, would say his prayers.
    Or, would you see his spirits sink,
    Relaxing downwards in a stink?
    If such a sight as this can please ye,
70 Good Madam Pallas, pray be easy,
    To Neptune speak, and he'll consent;
    But he'll come back the knave he went.'

    The goddess, who conceived an hope,
    That Hort was destined to a rope,
    Believed it best to condescend
    To spare a foe, to save a friend:
    But fearing Berkeley might be scared
    She left him virtue for a guard.

Billet to the Company of Players

The enclosed prologue is formed upon the story of the Secretary's
not suffering you to act, unless you would pay him £300 *per
annum*, upon which you got a licence from the Lord Mayor to act
as strollers.

    The prologue supposes that, upon your being forbidden to act, a
company of country-strollers came and hired the playhouse, and
your clothes, etc. to act in.

THE PROLOGUE

Our set of strollers, wandering up and down,
Hearing the house was empty, came to town;
And, with a licence from our good Lord Mayor,
Went to one Griffith, formerly a player:
Him we persuaded with a moderate bribe,
To speak to Elrington, and all the tribe,
To let our company supply their places,
And hire us out their scenes, and clothes, and faces.

Is not the truth the truth? Look full on me;
10   I am not Elrington, nor Griffith he.
When we perform, look sharp among our crew,
There's not a creature here you ever knew.
The former folks were servants to the king,
We, humble strollers, always on the wing.
Now, for my part, I think upon the whole,
Rather than starve, a man would better stroll.

Stay, let me see – three hundred pounds a year,
For leave to act in town? 'Tis plaguy dear.
Now, here's a warrant; gallants, please to mark,
20   For three thirteens and sixpence to the clerk.
Three hundred pounds! Were I the price to fix,
The public should bestow the actors six.
A score of guineas, given underhand,
For a good word or so, we understand.
To help an honest lad that's out of place,
May cost a crown or so; a common case:
And, in a crew, 'tis no injustice thought
To ship a rogue, and pay him not a groat.
But, in the chronicles of former ages,
30   Who ever heard of servants paying wages?

I pity Elrington with all my heart;
Would he were here this night to act my part.
I told him what it was to be a stroller,
How free we acted, and had no controller:
In every town we wait on Mr Mayor,
First get a licence, then produce our ware:
We sound a trumpet, or we beat a drum;
Huzza! the schoolboys roar, the players are come!
And then we cry, to spur the bumpkins on,
40   Gallants, by Tuesday next we must be gone.
I told him, in the smoothest way I could,
All this and more, yet it would do no good.
But Elrington, tears falling from his cheeks,
He that has shone with Betterton and Weeks,
To whom our country has been always dear,
Who chose to leave his dearest pledges here,
Owns all your favours; here intends to stay,
And, as a stroller, act in every play

And the whole crew this resolution takes,
50 To live and die all strollers for your sakes;
Not frighted with an ignominious name,
For your displeasure is their only shame.

A pox on Elrington's majestic tone!
Now to a word of business in our own.

Gallants, next Thursday night will be our last,
Then, without fail, we pack up for Belfast.
Lose not your time, nor our diversion miss,
The next we act shall be as good as this.

To Charles Ford, Esq. on His Birthday

Come, be content, since out it must,
For, Stella has betrayed her trust,
And, whispering, charged me not to say
That Mr Ford was born today:
Or if at last, I needs must blab it,
According to my usual habit,
She bid me with a serious face
Be sure conceal the time and place,
And not my compliment to spoil
10 By calling this your native soil;
Or vex the ladies, when they knew
That you are turning forty-two.
But if these topics should appear
Strong arguments to keep you here,
We think, though you judge hardly of it,
Good manners must give place to profit.

The nymphs with whom you first began
Are each become a harridan;
And Montagu so far decayed,
20 That now her lovers must be paid;
And every belle that since arose
Has her cotemporary beaux.
Your former comrades, once so bright,
With whom you toasted half the night,
Of rheumatism and pox complain,

And bid adieu to dear champagne:
Your great protectors, once in power,
Are now in exile, or the Tower,
Your foes, triumphant o'er the laws,
30 Who hate your person, and your cause,
If once they get you on the spot
You must be guilty of the plot,
For, true or false, they'll ne'er inquire,
But use you ten times worse than Prior.

In London! what would you do there?
Can you, my friend, with patience bear,
Nay, would it not your passion raise,
Worse than a pun, or Irish phrase,
To see a scoundrel strut and hector,
40 A foot-boy to some rogue director?
To look on vice triumphant round,
And virtue trampled on the ground:
Observe where bloody Townshend stands
With informations in his hands,
Hear him blaspheme, and swear, and rail,
Threatening the pillory and gaol.
If this you think a pleasing scene
To London straight return again,
Where you have told us from experience,
50 Are swarms of bugs and Hanoverians.

I thought my very spleen would burst
When fortune drove me hither first;
Was full as hard to please as you,
Nor persons' names, nor places knew;
But now I act as other folk,
Like prisoners when their gall is broke.

If you have London still at heart,
We'll make a small one here by art:
The difference is not much between
60 St James's Park and Stephen's Green;
And, Dawson Street will serve as well
To lead you hither, as Pall Mall,
(Without your passing through the palace
To choke your sight, and raise your malice).

The Deanery house may well be matched
(Under correction) with the Thatched,
Nor shall I, when you hither come,
Demand a crown a quart for stum.
Then, for a middle-agéd charmer,
70 Stella may vie with your Mountharmar:
She's now as handsome every bit,
And has a thousand times her wit.
The Dean and Sheridan, I hope,
Will half supply a Gay and Pope,
Corbet, though yet I know his worth not,
No doubt, will prove a good Arbuthnot:
I throw into the bargain, Jim:
In London can you equal him?
What think you of my favourite clan,
80 Robin and Jack, and Jack and Dan?
Fellows of modest worth and parts,
With cheerful looks, and honest hearts.

    Can you on Dublin look with scorn?
Yet here were you and Ormonde born.
Oh, were but you and I so wise
To look with Robin Grattan's eyes:
Robin adores that spot of earth,
That literal spot which gave him birth,
And swears, Cushogue is to his taste,
90 As fine as Hampton Court at least.

    When to your friends you would enhance
The praise of Italy or France,
For grandeur, elegance and wit,
We gladly hear you, and submit:
But then, to come and keep a clutter
For this, or that side of a gutter,
To live in this or t'other isle,
We cannot think it worth your while.
For, take it kindly, or amiss,
100 The difference but amounts to this,
We bury, on our side the channel
In linen, and on yours, in flannel.
You, for the news are ne'er to seek,

While we perhaps must wait a week:
You, happy folks, are sure to meet
A hundred whores in every street,
While we may search all Dublin o'er
And hardly hear of half a score.

You see, my arguments are strong;
110   I wonder you held out so long,
But since you are convinced at last
We'll pardon you for what is past.

So – let us now for whisk prepare;
Twelve pence a corner, if you dare.

Stella's Birthday (1723)

A GREAT BOTTLE OF WINE, LONG BURIED, BEING THAT DAY DUG UP

Resolved my annual verse to pay,
By duty bound, on Stella's day;
Furnished with papers, pen, and ink,
I gravely sat me down to think:
I bit my nails, and scratched my head,
But found my wit and fancy fled:
Or, if with more than usual pain,
A thought came slowly from my brain,
It cost me Lord knows how much time
10   To shape it into sense and rhyme:
And, what was yet a greater curse,
Long-thinking made my fancy worse.

Forsaken by the inspiring nine,
I waited at Apollo's shrine;
I told him what the world would say
If Stella were unsung today;
How I should hide my head for shame,
When both the Jacks and Robin came;
How Ford would frown, how Jim would leer;
20   How Sheridan the rogue would sneer:
And swear it does not always follow,

That '*Semel'n anno ridet Apollo.*'
I have assured them twenty times,
That Phoebus helped me in my rhymes;
Phoebus inspired me from above,
And he and I were hand in glove.
But finding me so dull and dry since,
They'll call it all poetic licence:
And when I brag of aid divine,
30   Think Eusden's right as good as mine.

    Nor do I ask for Stella's sake;
'Tis my own credit lies at stake
And Stella will be sung, while I
Can only be a stander-by.

    Apollo, having thought a little,
Returned this answer to a tittle.

    'Though you should live like old Methusalem,
I furnish hints, and you should use all 'em,
You yearly sing as she grows old,
40   You'd leave her virtues half untold.
But to say truth, such dullness reigns
Through the whole set of Irish deans;
I'm daily stunned with such a medley,
Dean White, Dean Daniel, and Dean Smedley;
That, let what dean soever come,
My orders are, I'm not at home;
And if your voice had not been loud,
You must have passed among the crowd.

    'But now, your danger to prevent,
50   You must apply to Mrs Brent,
For she, as priestess, knows the rites
Wherein the god of Earth delights.
First, nine ways looking, let her stand
With an old poker in her hand;
Let her describe a circle round
In Saunders' cellar on the ground:
A spade let prudent Archy hold,
And with discretion dig the mould:
Let Stella look with watchful eye,
60   Rebecca, Ford, and Grattans by.

'Behold the bottle, where it lies
With neck elated towards the skies!
The god of winds and god of fire
Did to its wondrous birth conspire;
And Bacchus, for the poet's use,
Poured in a strong inspiring juice:
See! as you raise it from its tomb,
It drags behind a spacious womb,
And in the spacious womb contains
70   A sovereign medicine for the brains.

'You'll find it soon if fate consents;
If not, a thousand Mrs Brents,
Ten thousand Archies armed with spades,
May dig in vain to Pluto's shades.

'From thence a plenteous draught infuse,
And boldly then invoke the muse:
(But first let Robert, on his knees,
With caution drain it from the lees)
The muse will at your call appear,
80   With Stella's praise to crown the year.'

The First of April

A POEM INSCRIBED TO MRS E.C.

This morn the god of wit and joke,
Thus to his choir of muses spoke;

'Go, sisters nine, into that cabin,
Where most true sons of Phoebus ha' bin.
Each take a child into her care,
There's one for each and one to spare:
Though there's a boy whom a lord chooses,
Who is as good as all the muses;
And beauteous Bess a different case is,
10   For she belongs to all the Graces;
Divide the rest, but then take care,
Ye don't fall out about the heir.'

They dropped low curtseys, one and all,
And took their progress towards Loughgall.

Apollo laughed till he was sick,
That he had served the prudes a trick.

    'With due submission to the god,'
Thalia said, ''tis somewhat odd,
That we should march on this occasion,
20 And not leave one for invocation.
Poets till they grow hoarse may bawl,
And not a muse will hear their call:
Besides, to me this seems a bubble,
'Tis all to save their mother trouble;
I'll warrant she's some flaunting dame,
Regardless of her house and fame;
When we come there we'll stand unseen,
T' observe her management within.'

    They peeped, and saw a lady there
30 Pinning on coifs and combing hair;
Softening with songs to son or daughter,
The persecution of cold water.
Still pleased with the good-natured noise,
And harmless frolics of her boys;
Equal to all in care and love,
Which all deserve and all improve.
To kitchen, parlour, nursery flies,
And seems all feet, and hands, and eyes.
No thought of hers does ever roam,
40 But for her squire when he's from home;
And scarce a day, can spare a minute
From husband, children, wheel, or spinet.
The muses when they saw her care,
Wondered the God had sent them there.
And said, 'His Worship might ha' told us,
This house don't want, nor will it hold us.
We govern here! where she presides
With virtue, prudence, wit besides;
A wife as good as heart could wish one,
50 What need we open our commission,
There's no occasion here for us,
Can *we* do more than what *she* does?'

    Thalia now began to smoke,
That all this business was a joke.

'Sisters,' said she, 'my life I'll lay,
Ye have forgot this month and day. –
'Tis a fair trick, by ancient rules –
The god has made us April fools.'

Stella at Woodpark

A HOUSE OF CHARLES FORD ESQ. EIGHT MILES FROM DUBLIN

Cuicunque nocere volebat
Vestimenta dabat pretiosa.

Don Carlos in a merry spite,
Did Stella to his house invite:
He entertained her half a year
With generous wines and costly cheer.
Don Carlos made her chief director,
That she might o'er the servants hector.
In half a week the dame grows nice,
Got all things at the highest price.
Now at the table-head she sits,
10   Presented with the nicest bits:
She looked on partridges with scorn,
Except they tasted of the corn:
A haunch of venison made her sweat,
Unless it had the right *fumette.*
Don Carlos earnestly would beg,
'Dear madam, try this pigeon's leg';
Was happy when he could prevail
To make her only touch a quail.
Through candle-light she viewed the wine,
20   To see that every glass was fine.
At last grown prouder than the devil,
With feeding high, and treatment civil,
Don Carlos now began to find
His malice work as he designed:
The winter sky began to frown,
Poor Stella must pack off to town.
From purling streams and fountains bubbling,
To Liffey's stinking tide in Dublin:

From wholesome exercise and air
30 To sossing in an easy chair;
From stomach sharp and hearty feeding,
To piddle like a lady breeding:
From ruling there the household singly,
To be directed here by Dingley:
From every day a lordly banquet,
To half a joint, and God be thank it:
From every meal Pontac in plenty,
To half a pint one day in twenty.
From Ford attending at her call,
40 To visits of Archdeacon Wall.
From Ford, who thinks of nothing mean,
To the poor doings of the Dean.
From growing richer with good cheer,
To running out by starving here.

But now arrives the dismal day:
She must return to Ormond Quay:
The coachman stopped, she looked, and swore
The rascal had mistook the door:
At coming in you saw her stoop;
50 The entry brushed against her hoop:
Each moment rising in her airs,
She cursed the narrow winding stairs:
Began a thousand faults to spy;
The ceiling hardly six foot high;
The smutty wainscot full of cracks,
And half the chairs with broken backs:
Her quarter's out at Lady Day,
She vows she will no longer stay,
In lodgings, like a poor *grisette*,
60 While there are houses to be let.

Howe'er, to keep her spirits up,
She sent for company to sup;
When all the while you might remark,
She strove in vain to ape Woodpark.
Two bottles called for, (half her store;
The cupboard could contain but four;)
A supper worthy of her self,
Five nothings in five plates of Delf.

Thus, for a week the farce went on;
70 When all her country-savings gone,
She fell into her former scene.
Small beer, a herring, and the Dean.

Thus far in jest. Though now I fear
You think my jesting too severe:
But poets when a hint is new
Regard not whether false or true:
Yet raillery gives no offence,
Where truth has not the least pretence;
Nor can be more securely placed
80 Than on a nymph of Stella's taste.
I must confess, your wine and victual
I was too hard upon *a little*;
Your table neat, your linen fine;
And, though in miniature, you shine.
Yet, when you sigh to leave Woodpark,
The scene, the welcome, and the spark,
To languish in this odious town,
And pull your haughty stomach down;
We think you quite mistake the case;
90 The virtue lies not in the place:
For though my raillery were true,
A cottage is Woodpark with you.

Pethox the Great

From Venus born, thy beauty shows;
But who thy father, no man knows;
Nor can the skilful herald trace
The founder of thy ancient race.
Whether thy temper, full of fire,
Discovers Vulcan for thy sire;
The god who made Scamander boil,
And round his margin singed the soil;
(From whence philosophers agree,
10 An equal power descends to thee.)
Whether from dreadful Mars you claim
The high descent from whence you came,

And, as a proof, show numerous scars
By fierce encounters made in wars;
(Those honourable wounds you bore
From head to foot, and *all before*;)
And still the bloody field frequent,
Familiar in each leader's tent.
Or whether, as the learn'd contend,
20   You from your neighbouring Gaul descend;
Or from Parthenope the proud,
Where numberless thy votaries crowd:
Whether thy great forefathers came
From realms that bear Vesputio's name:
For so conjectors would obtrude,
And from thy painted skin conclude.
Whether, as Epicurus shows
The world from jostling seeds arose;
Which mingling with prolific strife
30   In chaos, kindled into life;
So your production was the same,
And from the contending atoms came.

Thy fair indulgent mother crowned
Thy head with sparkling rubies round;
Beneath thy decent steps, the road
Is all with precious jewels strewed.
The bird of Pallas knows his post,
Thee to attend where'er thou goest.

Byzantians boast, that on the clod
40   Where once their sultan's horse hath trod,
Grows neither grass, nor shrub, nor tree;
The same thy subjects boast of thee.

The greatest lord, when you appear,
Will deign your livery to wear,
In all thy various colours seen,
Of red, and yellow, blue, and green.

With half a word, when you require,
The man of business must retire.

The haughty minister of state
50   With trembling must thy leisure wait;

And while his fate is in thy hands,
The business of the nation stands.

Thou darest the greatest prince attack,
Canst hourly set him on the rack,
And, as an instance of thy power,
Enclose him in a wooden tower,
With pungent pains on every side:
So Regulus in torments died.

From thee our youth all virtues learn,
60 Dangers with prudence to discern;
And well thy scholars are endued
With temperance and with fortitude;
With patience, which all ills supports,
And secrecy, the art of courts.

The glittering beau could hardly tell,
Without your aid, to read or spell;
But, having long conversed with you,
Knows how to scrawl a billet-doux.

With what delight, methinks, I trace
70 Thy blood in every noble race!
In whom thy features, shape, and mien,
Are to the life distinctly seen.

The Britons, once a savage kind,
By you, were brightened and refined:
Descendants of the barbarous Huns,
With limbs robust, and voice that stuns;
But you have moulded them afresh,
Removed the tough superfluous flesh,
Taught them to modulate their tongues,
80 And speak without the help of lungs.

Proteus on you bestowed the boon
To change your visage like the moon;
You sometimes half a face produce,
Keep t'other half for private use.

How famed thy conduct in the fight,
With Hermes, son of Pleias bright:
Outnumbered, half encompassed round,
You strove for every inch of ground;

Then, by a soldierly retreat,
90 Retired to your imperial seat.
The victor, when your steps he traced,
Found all the realms before him waste;
You, o'er the high triumphal arch
Pontific, made your glorious march;
The wondrous arch behind you fell,
And left a chasm profound as hell:
You, in your Capitol secured,
A siege as long as Troy endured.

Three Epigrams

1

As Thomas was cudgelled one day by his wife,
He took to the street, and fled for his life:
Tom's three dearest friends came by in the squabble,
And saved him at once from the shrew and the rabble;
Then ventured to give him some sober advice –
But Tom is a person of honour so nice,
Too wise to take counsel, too proud to take warning,
That he sent to all three a challenge next morning:
Three duels he fought, thrice ventured his life;
10 Went home, and was cudgelled again by his wife.

2

Joan cudgels Ned, yet Ned's a bully:
Will cudgels Bess, yet Will's a cully.
Die Ned and Bess; give Will to Joan,
She dares not say, her life's her own.
Die Joan and Will; give Bess to Ned,
And every day she combs his head.

3

When Margery chastises Ned
She calls it combing of his head,
A kinder wife was never born,
She combs his head, and finds him horn.

A Portrait from the Life

Come sit by my side, while this picture I draw:
In chattering a magpie, in pride a jackdaw;
A temper the devil himself could not bridle,
Impertinent mixture of busy and idle.
As rude as a bear, no mule half so crabbed;
She swills like a sow, and she breeds like a rabbit:
A housewife in bed, at table a slattern;
For all an example, for no one a pattern.
Now tell me, friend Thomas, Ford, Grattan, and merry Dan,
10 Has this any likeness to good Madam Sheridan?

A New Year's Gift for Bec

Returning Janus now prepares,
For Bec, a new supply of cares,
Sent in a bag to Doctor Swift,
Who thus displays the New Year's gift.

First, this large parcel brings you tidings
Of our good Dean's eternal chidings;
Of Nelly's pertness, Robin's leasings,
And Sheridan's perpetual teasings.
This box is crammed on every side
10 With Stella's magisterial pride.
Behold a cage with sparrows filled,
First to be fondled, then be killed.
Now to this hamper I invite you,
With six imagined cares to fright you.
Here in this bundle Janus sends
Concerns by thousands for your friends:
And here's a pair of leathern pokes,
To hold your cares for other folks.
Here from this barrel you may broach
20 A peck of troubles for a coach.
This ball of wax your ears will darken,
Still to be curious, never hearken.
Lest you the town may have less trouble in,
Bring all your Quilca cares to Dublin,

For which he sends this empty sack;
And so take all upon your back.

Dingley and Brent

A SONG TO THE TUNE OF 'YE COMMONS AND PEERS'

Dingley and Brent
Wherever they went,
Ne'er minded a word that was spoken;
Whatever was said,
They ne'er troubled their head,
But laughed at their own silly joking.

Should Solomon wise
In majesty rise,
And show them his wit and his learning;
They never would hear,
But turn the deaf ear,
As a matter they had no concern in.

You tell a good jest,
And please all the rest,
Comes Dingley, and asks you, 'What was it?'
And curious to know,
Away she will go
To seek an old rag in a closet.

To Stella

WRITTEN ON THE DAY OF HER BIRTH,
BUT NOT ON THE SUBJECT, WHEN I WAS SICK IN BED

Tormented with incessant pains,
Can I devise poetic strains?
Time was, when I could yearly pay
My verse on Stella's native day:
But now, unable grown to write,
I grieve she ever saw the light.
Ungrateful; since to her I owe

That I these pains can undergo.
She tends me, like a humble slave;
10   And, when indecently I rave,
When out my brutish passions break,
With gall in every word I speak,
She, with soft speech, my anguish cheers,
Or melts my passion down with tears:
Although 'tis easy to descry
She wants assistance more than I;
Yet seems to feel my pains alone,
And is a Stoic in her own.
When, among scholars, can we find
20   So soft, and yet so firm a mind?
All accidents of life conspire
To raise up Stella's virtue higher;
Or else, to introduce the rest
Which had been latent in her breast.
Her firmness who could e'er have known,
Had she not evils of her own?
Her kindness who could ever guess,
Had not her friends been in distress?
Whatever base returns you find
30   From me, dear Stella, still be kind;
In your own heart you'll reap the fruit,
Though I continue still a brute.
But when I once am out of pain,
I promise to be good again:
Meantime your other juster friends
Shall for my follies make amends:
So may we long continue thus,
Admiring you, you pitying us.

His Grace's Answer to Jonathan

Dear Smed, I read thy brilliant lines
Where wit in all its glory shines;
Where compliments with all their pride
Are by thy numbers dignified.
I hope to make you yet as clean,
As that same, *viz.* St Patrick's Dean.

I'll give thee 'surplice, virge and stall,'
And maybe something else withal.
And were you not so good a writer
10   I should present you with a mitre.
Write worse then, if you can – be wise –
Believe me 'tis the way to rise.
Talk not of 'making of thy nest,'
Ah never 'lay thy head to rest!'
That head so well by wisdom fraught!
That writes without the toil of thought.
While others wrack their busy brains,
You are not in the least at pains.
Down to your deanery repair
20   And build a castle in the air.
I'm sure a man of your fine sense
Can do it with a small expense.
There your dear spouse and you together
May breathe your bellies full of ether.
When Lady Luna is your neighbour
She'll help your wife when she's in labour.
Well skilled in midwife artifices;
For she herself oft falls in pieces.
There you shall see a raree-show
30   Will make you scorn this world below.
When you behold the Milky Way
As white as snow, as bright as day;
The glittering constellations roll,
About the grinding Arctic pole;
The lovely tingling in your ears,
Wrought by the music of the spheres –
Your spouse shall there no longer hector,
You need not fear a curtain lecture.
Nor shall she think that she is 'un-done'
40   For quitting her beloved London.
When she's exalted in the skies,
She'll never think of mutton pies.
When you're advanced above Dean, *viz.*
You'll never think of Goody Griz.
But ever ever live at ease,
And strive, and strive, 'your wife to please.'
In her you'll centre all your joys,

And get ten thousand girls and boys.
Ten thousand girls and boys you'll get
50 And they like stars shall rise and set.
While you and spouse transformed shall soon
Be a new sun, and a new moon.
Nor shall you strive your horns to hide,
For then your horns will be your pride.

On Dreams

AN IMITATION OF PETRONIUS

Somnia quae mentes ludunt volitantibus umbris, etc.

Those dreams that on the silent night intrude,
And with false flitting shades our minds delude,
Jove never sends us downwards from the skies,
Nor can they from infernal mansions rise;
But all are mere productions of the brain,
And fools consult interpreters in vain.

For, when in bed we rest our weary limbs,
The mind, unburdened, sports in various whims,
The busy head with mimic arts runs o'er
10 The scenes and actions of the day before.

The drowsy tyrant, by his minions led,
To regal rage devotes some patriot's head.
With equal terrors, not with equal guilt,
The murderer dreams of all the blood he spilt.

The soldier smiling hears the widow's cries,
And stabs the son before the mother's eyes.
With like remorse his brother of the trade,
The butcher, feels the lamb beneath his blade.

The statesman rakes the town to find a plot,
20 And dreams of forfeitures by treason got.
Nor less Tom Turdman of true statesman mould,
Collects the city filth in search of gold.

Orphans around his bed the lawyer sees,
And takes the plaintiff's and defendant's fees.

His fellow pickpurse, watching for a job,
Fancies his fingers in the cully's fob.

The kind physician grants the husband's prayers,
Or gives relief to long-expecting heirs.
The sleeping hangman ties the fatal noose,
30   Nor unsuccessful waits for dead men's shoes.

The grave divine with knotty points perplexed,
As if he were awake, nods o'er his text:
While the sly mountebank attends his trade,
Harangues the rabble, and is better paid.

The hireling senator of modern days,
Bedaubs the guilty great with nauseous praise:
And Dick the scavenger with equal grace,
Flirts from his cart the mud in Walpole's face.

The Answer to Dr Delany

The wise pretend to make it clear,
'Tis no great loss to lose an ear;
Why are we then so fond of two?
When by experience one will do.

'Tis true, they say, cut off the head,
And there's an end; the man is dead;
Because, among all human race,
None e'er was known to have a brace.
But confidently they maintain,
10   That, where we find the members twain,
The loss of one is no such trouble,
Since t'other will in strength be double;
The limb surviving, you may swear,
Becomes his brother's lawful heir:
Thus, for a trial, let me beg of
Your reverence, but to cut one leg off,
And you shall find by this device,
The t'other will be stronger twice;
For, every day you shall be gaining
20   New vigour to the leg remaining.

So, when an eye hath lost its brother,
You see the better with the other:
Cut off your hand, and you may do
With t'other hand the work of two:
Because, the soul her power contracts,
And on the brother limb *reacts*.

But, yet the point is not so clear in
Another case; the sense of hearing:
For though the place of either ear,
30 Be distant as one head can bear;
Yet Galen most acutely shows you,
(Consult his book *De Partium Usu*)
That from each ear, as he observes,
There creep two auditory nerves,
(Not to be seen without a glass)
Which near the *os petrosum* pass;
Thence to the neck; and moving through there;
One goes to this, and one to t'other ear.
Which made my grand-dame always stuff her ears,
40 Both right and left, as fellow sufferers.
You see my learning; but to shorten it,
When my left ear was deaf a fortnight,
To t'other ear I felt it coming on,
And thus I solve this hard phenomenon.

'Tis true, a glass will bring supplies
To weak, or old, or clouded eyes.
Your arms, though both your eyes were lost,
Would guard your nose against a post.
Without your legs, two legs of wood
50 Are stronger, and almost as good.
And, as for hands, there have been those,
Who, wanting both, have used their toes.
But no contrivance yet appears,
To furnish artificial ears.

A Serious Poem upon William Wood

BRAZIER, TINKER, HARDWARE-MAN, COINER,
COUNTERFEITER, FOUNDER AND ESQUIRE

When foes are o'ercome, we preserve them from slaughter,
To be hewers of wood and drawers of water,
Now, although to draw water is not very good,
Yet we all should rejoice to be hewers of wood.
I own it hath often provoked me to mutter,
That, a rogue so obscure should make such a clutter,
But ancient philosophers wisely remark,
That old rotten wood will shine in the dark.
The heathens, we read, had gods made of wood,
10 Who could do them no harm, if they did them no good:
But this idol Wood may do us great evil,
Their gods were of wood, but our Wood is the devil:
To cut down fine wood is a very bad thing,
And yet we all know much gold it will bring,
Then if cutting down Wood brings money good store,
Our money to keep, let us cut down one more.

    Now hear an old tale. There anciently stood
(I forget in what church) an image of wood;
Concerning this image there went a prediction,
20 It would burn a whole forest; nor was it a fiction;
'Twas cut into faggots, and put to the flame,
To burn an old friar, one Forest by name.
My tale is a wise one if well understood,
Find you but the friar, and I'll find the Wood.

    I hear among scholars there is a great doubt
From what kind of tree this Wood was hewn out.
Teague made a good pun by a brogue in his speech,
And said: 'By my shoul he's the son of a beech':
Some call him a thorn, the curse of a nation,
30 As thorns were designed to be from the creation.
Some think him cut out from the poisonous yew,
Beneath whose ill shade no plant ever grew.
Some say he's a birch, a thought very odd,
For none but a dunce would come under his rod.
But I'll tell you the secret, and pray do not blab,

He is an old stump cut out of a crab,
And England has put this crab to hard use,
To cudgel our bones, and for drink give us verjuice;
And therefore his witnesses justly may boast
40   That none are more properly knights of the post.

But here Mr Wood complains that we mock,
Though he may be a blockhead, he is no real block.
He can eat, drink and sleep; now and then for a friend
He'll not be too proud an old kettle to mend;
He can lie like a courtier, and think it no scorn,
When gold's to be got, to forswear and suborn.
He can rap his own raps, and has the true sapience
To turn a good penny to twenty bad ha'pence.
Then in spite of your sophistry, honest Will Wood
50   Is a man of this world all true flesh and blood;
So you are but in jest, and you will not I hope
Unman the poor knave for the sake of a trope.
'Tis a metaphor known to every plain thinker,
Just as when we say, the devil's a tinker,
Which cannot in literal sense be made good,
Unless by the devil we mean Mr Wood.

But some will object, that the devil oft spoke
In heathenish times from the trunk of an oak:
And, since we must grant, there never were known
60   More heathenish times than those of our own;
Perhaps you will say, 'tis the devil that puts
The words in Wood's mouth, or speaks from his guts:
And then your old argument still will return:
Howe'er let us try him and see how he'll burn.
You'll pardon me sir, your cunning I smoke,
But Wood I assure you is no heart of oak;
And instead of the devil, this son of perdition
Hath joined with himself two hags in commission.

I ne'er could endure my talent to smother,
70   I told you one tale, I will tell you another.
A joiner to fasten a saint in a niche,
Bored a large auger-hole in the image's breech;
But finding the statue to make no complaint,

He would ne'er be convinced it was a true saint:
When the true Wood arrives, as he soon will no doubt,
(For that's but a sham Wood they carry about)
What stuff he is made on you quickly may find,
If you make the same trial, and bore him behind;
I'll hold you a groat, when you wimble his bum,
80   He'll bellow as loud as a de'il in a drum:
From me I declare you shall have no denial,
And there can be no harm in making a trial;
And when to the joy of your hearts he has roared,
You may show him about for a new groaning board.

    Now ask me a question. How came it to pass
Wood got so much copper? He got it by brass;
This Brass was a dragon (observe what I tell ye)
This dragon had gotten two sows in its belly;
I know you will say, this is all heathen Greek;
90   I own it, and therefore I leave you to seek.

    I often have seen two plays very good,
Called, *Love in a Tub*, and *Love in a Wood*.
These comedies twain friend Wood will contrive
On the scene of this land very soon to revive.
First, *Love in a Tub*: 'squire Wood has in store
Strong tubs for his raps, two thousand and more;
These raps he will honestly dig out with shovels,
And sell them for gold, or he can't show his love else.
Wood swears he will do it for Ireland's good,
100   Then can you deny it is *Love in a Wood*?
However, if critics find fault with the phrase,
I hope you will own it is *Love in a Maze*;
For when to express a friend's love we are willing,
We never say more than, your love is a million;
But with honest Wood's love there is no contending,
'Tis fifty round millions of love, and a mending.
Then in his first love why should he be crossed?
I hope he will find that no love is lost.

    Hear one story more, and then I will stop.
110   I dreamt Wood was told he should die by a drop:
So methought, he resolved no liquor to taste,

For fear the first drop might as well be his last:
But dreams are like oracles, hard to explain 'em,
For it proved that he died of a drop at Kilmainham:
I waked with delight, and not without hope,
Very soon to see Wood drop down from a rope.
How he and how we at each other should grin!
'Tis kindness to hold a friend up by the chin;
But soft, says the herald, I cannot agree;
120 For metal on metal is false heraldry:
Why that may be true, yet Wood upon wood,
I'll maintain with my life, is heraldry good.

An Epigram on Wood's Brass Money

Carteret was welcomed to the shore
First with the brazen cannon's roar.
To meet him next, the soldier comes,
With brazen trumps and brazen drums.
Approaching near the town, he hears
The brazen bells salute his ears:
But when Wood's brass began to sound,
Guns, trumpets, drums, and bells were drowned.

A Poetical Epistle to Dr Sheridan

Some ancient authors wisely write,
That he who drinks will wake at night,
Will never fail to lose his rest,
And feel a straitness in his chest;
A straitness in a double sense,
A straitness both of breath and pence:
Physicians say, it is but reasonable,
He that comes home at hour unseasonable,
(Besides a fall and broken shins,
10 Those smaller judgements for his sins;)
If, when he goes to bed, he meets
A teasing wife between the sheets,
'Tis six to five he'll never sleep,
But rave and toss till morning-peep.

Yet harmless Betty must be blamed
Because you feel your lungs inflamed;
But if you would not get a fever,
You never must one moment leave her.
This comes of all your drunken tricks,
20 Your Parry's and your brace of Dicks;
Your hunting Helsham in his laboratory
Too, was the time you saw that drab lae a pery.
But like the prelate who lies yonder-a
And always cries he is like Cassandra;
I always told you, Mr Sheridan,
If once this company were rid on,
Frequented honest folk, and very few,
You'd live till all your friends were weary of you.
But if rack punch you still would swallow,
30 I then forewarned you what would follow.
Are the Deanery sober hours?
Be witness for me all ye powers.
The cloth is laid at eight, and then
We sit till half an hour past ten;
One bottle well might serve for three
If Mrs Robinson drank like me.
Ask how I fret when she has beckoned
To Robert to bring up a second;
I hate to have it in my sight,
40 And drink my share in perfect spite.
If Robin brings the ladies word,
The coach is come, I 'scape a third;
If not, why then I fall a-talking
How sweet a night it is for walking;
For in all conscience, were my treasure able,
I'd think a quart a piece unreasonable;
It strikes eleven – get out of doors –
This is my constant farewell.

                              Yours,
                              J.S.

October 18th 1724, nine in the morning.

To His Grace the Archbishop of Dublin

Serus in caelum redeas diuque
Laetus intersis populo – Hor.

'Great, good and just' was once applied
To one who for his country died;
To one who lives in its defence,
We speak it in a happier sense.
O may the fates thy life prolong!
Our country then can dread no wrong:
In thy great care we place our trust,
Because thou'rt great, and good, and just.
Thy breast unshaken can oppose
10 Our private and our public foes,
The latent wiles, and tricks of state,
Your wisdom can with ease defeat.
When power in all its pomp appears,
It falls before thy reverend years,
And willingly resigns its place
To something nobler in thy face.
When once the fierce pursuing Gaul
Had drawn his sword for Marius' fall,
The godlike hero with one frown
20 Struck all his rage and malice down;
Then how can we dread William Wood,
If by thy presence he's withstood?
Where wisdom stands to keep the field,
In vain he brings his brazen shield.
Though like the Sibyl's priest he comes,
With furious din of brazen drums,
The force of thy superior voice
Shall strike him dumb, and quell their noise.

An Excellent New Song upon His Grace Our Good Lord Archbishop of Dublin

BY HONEST JO, ONE OF HIS GRACE'S FARMERS IN FINGAL

I sing not of the Drapier's praise, nor yet of William Wood;
But I sing of a famous lord, who seeks his country's good.

Lord William's Grace of Dublin town, 'tis he that first appears,
Whose wisdom and whose piety, do far exceed his years.
In every council and debate he stands for what is right;
And still the truth he will maintain, whate'er he loses by't.
And though some think him in the wrong, yet still there comes a
    season
When everyone turns round about, and owns His Grace had
    reason.
His firmness to the public good, as one that knows it swore,
10 Has lost His Grace for ten years past ten thousand pounds and
    more:
Then come the poor and strip him so, they leave him not a cross,
For he regards ten thousand pounds no more than Woods's dross.
To beg his favour is the way new favours still to win,
He makes no more to give ten pounds than I to give a pin.
Why, there's my landlord now the squire, who all in money
    wallows,
He would not give a groat to save his father from the gallows.
'A bishop', says the noble squire, 'I hate the very name,
To have two thousand pounds a year, O 'tis a burning shame!
Two thousand pounds a year, good lord! and I to have but five.'
20 And under him no tenant yet was ever known to thrive.
Now from his lordship's Grace I hold a little piece of ground,
And all the rent I pay is scarce five shillings in the pound.
Then master steward takes my rent, and tells me, 'Honest Jo,
Come you must take a cup of sack or two before you go.'
He bids me then to hold my tongue, and up the money locks,
For fear my lord should send it all into the poor man's box.
And once I was so bold to beg that I might see His Grace,
Good lord! I wondered how I dared to look him in the face.
Then down I went upon my knees, his blessing to obtain,
30 He gave it me, and ever since I find I thrive amain.
Then said my lord, 'I'm very glad to see thee honest friend,
I know the times are something hard, but hope they soon will
    mend,
Pray never press yourself for rent, but pay me when you can,
I find you bear a good report, and are an honest man.'
Then said his lordship with a smile, 'I must have lawful cash,
I hope you will not pay my rent in that same Woods's trash.'
'God bless your Grace,' I then replied, 'I'd see him hanging higher,
Before I touched his filthy dross, than is Clondalkin spire.'
To every farmer twice a week all round about the yoke,

40   Our parsons read the Drapier's books, and make us honest folk.
      And then I went to pay the squire and in the way I found,
      His bailie driving all my cows into the parish pound.
      'Why sirrah,' said the noble squire, 'how dare you see my face,
      Your rent is due almost a week beside the days of grace.'
      And yet the land I from him hold is set so on the rack,
      That only for the bishop's lease 'twould quickly break my back.
      Then God preserve his lordship's Grace, and make him live as long
      As did Methusalem of old, and so I end my song.

Prometheus

ON WOOD THE PATENTEE'S IRISH HALFPENCE

As, when the squire and tinker, Wood,
Gravely consulting Ireland's good,
Together mingled in a mass
Smith's dust, and copper, lead and brass;
The mixture thus by chemic art,
United close in every part,
In fillets rolled, or cut in pieces,
Appeared like one continuous species,
And by the forming engine struck,
10   On all the same *impression* stuck.

So, to confound this hated coin,
All parties and religions join;
Whigs, Tories, trimmers, Hanoverians,
Quakers, conformists, presbyterians,
Scotch, Irish, English, French unite
With equal interest, equal spite,
Together mingled in a lump,
Do all in one opinion jump;
And everyone begins to find
20   The same impression on his *mind*.

A strange event! whom gold incites,
To blood and quarrels, brass unites:
So goldsmiths say, the coarsest stuff
Will serve for solder well enough;
So, by the kettle's loud alarm,

The bees are gathered to a swarm:
So by the brazen trumpet's bluster,
Troops of all tongues and nations muster:
And so the harp of Ireland brings,
30   Whole crowds about its brazen strings.

There is a chain let down from Jove,
But fastened to his throne above;
So strong, that from the lower end,
They say, all human things depend:
This chain, as ancient poets hold,
When Jove was young, was made of gold.
Prometheus once this chain purloined,
Dissolved, and into money coined;
Then whips me on a chain of brass,
40   (Venus was bribed to let it pass.)

Now while this brazen chain prevailed,
Jove saw that all devotion failed;
No temple to his godship raised;
No sacrifice on altars blazed;
In short, such dire confusions followed,
Earth must have been in chaos swallowed.
Jove stood amazed, but looking round,
With much ado the cheat he found;
'Twas plain he could no longer hold
50   The world in any chain but gold;
And to the god of wealth his brother,
Sent Mercury to get another.

Prometheus on a rock was laid,
Tied with the chain himself had made;
On icy Caucasus to shiver,
While vultures eat his growing liver.

Ye powers of Grub Street, make me able,
Discreetly to apply this fable.
Say, who is to be understood
60   By that old thief Prometheus? Wood.
For Jove, it is not hard to guess him,
I mean His Majesty, God bless him.
This thief and blacksmith was so bold,

He strove to steal that chain of gold,
Which links the subject to the king:
And change it for a brazen string.
But sure, if nothing else must pass
Between the King and us but brass,
Although the chain will never crack,
70 Yet our devotion may grow slack.

But Jove will soon convert I hope,
This brazen chain into a rope;
With which Prometheus shall be tied,
And high in air for ever ride;
Where, if we find his liver grows,
For want of vultures, we have crows.

Whitshed's Motto on His Coach

Libertas & natale solum
Liberty and my native country.

Libertas & natale solum;
Fine words; I wonder where you stole 'em.
Could nothing but thy chief reproach,
Serve for a motto on thy coach?
But let me now the words translate:
Natale solum: my estate:
My dear estate, how well I love it;
My tenants, if you doubt, will prove it:
They swear I am so kind and good,
10 I hug them till I squeeze their blood.

Libertas bears a large import;
First; how to swagger in a court;
And, secondly, to show my fury
Against an uncomplying jury:
And, thirdly, 'tis a new invention
To favour Wood and keep my pension:
And, fourthly; 'tis to play an odd trick,
Get the Great Seal, and turn out Brodrick.
And, fifthly; you know whom I mean,
20 To humble that vexatious Dean.

And, sixthly; for my soul to barter it
For fifty times its worth, to Carteret.

Now, since your motto thus you construe,
I must confess you've spoken once true.
Libertas & natale solum;
You had good reason when you stole 'em.

Verses on the Upright Judge

WHO CONDEMNED THE DRAPIER'S PRINTER

The church I hate, and have good reason:
For, there my grandsire cut his weasand:
He cut his weasand at the altar;
I keep my gullet for the halter.

*

In church your grandsire cut his throat;
To do the job too long he tarried,
He should have had my hearty vote,
To cut his throat before he married.

*

THE JUDGE SPEAKS

I'm not the grandson of that ass Quin;
Nor can you prove it, Mr Pasquin.
My grand-dame had gallants by twenties,
And bore my mother by a prentice.
This, when my grandsire knew, they tell us he
In Christ Church cut his throat for jealousy.
And, since the alderman was mad you say,
Then, I must be so too, *ex traduce.*

Verses Left in a Window of Dublin Castle

My very good lord, 'tis a very hard task,
For a man to wait here, who has nothing to ask.

A Letter from Dean Swift to Dean Smedley

Quid de quoque viro, cui dicas sepe caveto

Dear Dean, if e'er again you write,
Beware of subjects you call *trite*,
For satire's now so common grown
That every s—th and type in town
Have teased, by calling to their aid
The Graces and the other maid,
That, faith, I think there scarce is room
For you or I to crave a boon;
But, yet, you'll find by what will follow,
10 That I'm befriended by Apollo,
And that by all I e'er did hear
Minerva ne'er an oath did swear
Unless by you she was entreated
When first of Griz, you Grafton rated;
But as to *ditto'd through the town*,
You never did, for 'twould not down.

My country's saved, as you have shown,
And skin's yet whole, I needs must own,
But if by chance I should deny it
20 I'm sure old Jour – you'd not stand by it;
And if you should, we'd ne'er have end on't,
Both church and state, being still dependent.
The weather's fair, nay that is true,
But what is it to me or you?
Or if 'tis true, great Phoebus smiles
On this, as upon other isles,
I know no reason at this time
We should them quote, unless for rhyme.
In gold, perhaps, my friend you wallow
30 And Woods's ditto pills do swallow,
Being positive there is no priest
So bent on gains, *juro* by Christ,
As you dear Smedley are, being sure
The coin's current and the metal pure.
If Wood's coin should 'mongst us pass
Though now I'm poor I then might pass
As well as you, for a Midas:

Then as to war's alarms I pray
What is't that you or I've to say,
40　(Who ought for peace and plenty pray.)
Science and art you say at stand are,
How can that be, when you at hand are,
I can't conjecture, for dear Dean,
You hate to see aught that seems clean
Since Cindercola first you courted
And with the youthful damsel sported.
Helsham does truly wit command
And surely writes with sleight of hand;
For Sherry's quibbles and thy skill
50　They are as once, and *idem* still.
Since I'm Apollo styled by you,
Whene'er I 'gin, you should pursue
And boldly force the wingéd quill
Unto the utmost bounds of skill,
And never turn upon thy master
Who saved thee from a great disaster.
What's meant by *chapon* I can't guess
And making some for idiots pass
Unless i' the answer of his Grace,
60　Which if right taken, and but good luck hold
By the horned sun, he sure meant cuckold,
Not saying, lest I go too far,
That you an Actaeon was, or are.

Now let's no more caress thy French,
Nor Cindercola, charming wench!
Lest my mob's mouth, being seldom quiet
Should them ordain for Lenten diet;
Snarlerus next, I'm sure has need
Of prayers, that he might well succeed,
70　And bravely Precox might oppose
Cum multis aliis (all his foes)
When they're to pull him by the nose,
And by the order of his betters
Have him confined in iron fetters;
Now you've done right, *no knight attempting*
To oppose the Dean, yourself exempting
Because no – but, black-gowned foe,
As when time serves, you more shall know.

Stella's Birthday (1725)

As, when a beauteous nymph decays,
We say, she's past her dancing days;
So, poets lose their feet by time,
And can no longer dance in rhyme.
Your annual bard had rather chose
To celebrate your birth in prose;
Yet, merry folks, who want by chance
A pair to make a country dance,
Call the old housekeeper, and get her
10 To fill a place, for want of better;
While Sheridan is off the hooks,
And friend Delany at his books,
That Stella may avoid disgrace,
Once more the Dean supplies their place.

Beauty and wit, too sad a truth,
Have always been confined to youth;
The god of wit, and beauty's queen,
He twenty-one, and she fifteen:
No poet ever sweetly sung,
20 Unless he were like Phoebus, young;
Nor ever nymph inspired to rhyme,
Unless, like Venus, in her prime.
At fifty-six, if this be true,
Am I a poet fit for you?
Or at the age of forty-three,
Are you a subject fit for me?
Adieu bright wit, and radiant eyes;
You must be grave, and I be wise.
Our fate in vain we would oppose,
30 But I'll be still your friend in prose:
Esteem and friendship to express,
Will not require poetic dress;
And if the muse deny her aid
To have them *sung*, they may be *said*.

But, Stella say, what evil tongue
Reports you are no longer young?
That Time sits with his scythe to mow
Where erst sat Cupid with his bow;

That half your locks are turned to grey;
40 I'll ne'er believe a word they say.
'Tis true, but let it not be known,
My eyes are somewhat dimmish grown;
For nature, always in the right,
To your decays adapts my sight,
And wrinkles undistinguished pass,
For I'm ashamed to use a glass;
And till I see them with these eyes,
Whoever says you have them, lies.

No length of time can make you quit
50 Honour and virtue, sense and wit,
Thus you may still be young to me,
While I can better *hear* than *see*;
Oh, ne'er may fortune show her spite,
To make me *deaf*, and mend my *sight*.

Verses on the Revival of the Order of the Bath

Quoth King Robin, our ribbons I see are too few,
Of St Andrew's the green, and St George's the blue.
I must have another of colour more gay,
That will make all my subjects with pride to obey.
Though the Exchequer be drained by prodigal donors
Our king ne'er exhausted his fountain of honours.
Men of more wit than money, our pensions will fit,
And this will suit men of more money than wit.
Thus my subjects with pleasure will obey my commands,
10 Though as empty as Yonge and as saucy as Sandys;
And he who will leap over a stick for the king
Is qualified best for a dog in a string.

Wood, an Insect

By long observation I have understood,
That three little vermin are kin to Will Wood:
The first is an insect they call a wood-louse,
That folds up itself in itself for a house:

As round as a ball, without head, without tail,
Enclosed cap-a-pee in a strong coat of mail.
And thus William Wood to my fancy appears
In fillets of brass rolled up to his ears:
And, over these fillets he wisely has thrown,
10 To keep out of danger, a doublet of stone.

The louse of the wood for a medicine is used,
Or swallowed alive, or skilfully bruised.
And, let but our mother Hibernia contrive
To swallow Will Wood either bruised or alive.
She need be no more with the jaundice possessed;
Or sick of obstructions, and pains in her chest.

The third is an insect we call a woodworm,
That lies in old wood like a hare in her form;
With teeth or with claws it will bite or will scratch,
20 And chambermaids christen this worm a death-watch:
Because like a watch it always cries 'Click':
Then woe be to those in the house who are sick:
For, sure as a gun they will give up the ghost
If the maggot cries 'Click' when it scratches the post.
But a kettle of scalding hot water injected,
Infallibly cures the timber affected;
The omen is broke, the danger is over;
The maggot will die, and the sick will recover.
Such a worm was Will Wood when he scratched at the door
30 Of a governing statesman, or favourite whore:
The death of our nation it seemed to foretell,
And the sound of his brass we took for our knell.
But now, since the Drapier hath heartily mauled him,
I think the best thing we can do is to scald him.
For which operation there's nothing more proper
Than the liquor he deals in, his own melted copper;
Unless, like the Dutch, you rather would boil
This coiner of raps in a cauldron of oil.
Then choose which you please, and let each bring a faggot,
40 For our fear's at an end with the death of the maggot.

On Wood the Ironmonger

Salmoneus, as the Grecian tale is,
Was a mad coppersmith of Elis:
Up at his forge by morning-peep,
No creature in the lane could sleep.
Among a crew of roistering fellows
Would sit whole evenings at the ale-house:
His wife and children wanted bread,
While he went always drunk to bed.
This vapouring scab must needs devise
10   To ape the thunder of the skies;
With brass two fiery steeds he shod,
To make a clattering as they trod.
Of polished brass, his flaming car,
Like lightning dazzled from afar:
And up he mounts into the box,
And he must thunder, with a pox.
Then, furious he begins his march;
Drives rattling o'er a brazen arch:
With squibs and crackers armed, to throw
20   Among the trembling crowds below.
All ran to prayers, both priests and laity,
To pacify this angry deity;
When Jove, in pity to the town,
With real thunder knocked him down.
Then what a huge delight were all in,
To see the wicked varlet sprawling;
They searched his pockets on the place,
And found his copper all was base;
They laughed at such an Irish blunder,
30   To take the noise of brass for thunder!

The moral of this tale is proper,
Applied to Wood's adulterate copper;
Which, as he scattered, we like dolts,
Mistook at first for thunderbolts;
Before the Drapier shot a letter,
(Not Jove himself could do it better)
Which lighting on the impostor's crown,
Like real thunder knocked him down.

A Simile

ON OUR WANT OF SILVER, AND THE ONLY WAY TO REMEDY IT

As when of old, some sorceress threw
O'er the moon's face a sable hue,
To drive unseen her magic chair,
At midnight, through the darkened air;
Wise people, who believed with reason,
That this eclipse was out of season,
Affirmed the moon was sick, and fell
To cure her by a counter-spell:
Ten thousand cymbals now begin
10   To rend the skies with brazen din;
The cymbals' rattling sounds dispel
The cloud, and drive the hag to hell:
The moon, delivered from her pain,
Displays her silver face again.
(Note here, that in the chemic style,
The moon is silver all this while.)

   So, (if my simile you minded,
Which, I confess, is too long-winded)
When late a feminine magician,
20   Joined with a brazen politician,
Exposed, to blind the nation's eyes,
A parchment of prodigious size;
Concealed beneath that ample screen,
There was no silver to be seen.
But, to this parchment let the Draper
Oppose his counter-charm of paper,
And ring Wood's copper in our ears
So loud, till all the nation hears;
That sound will make the parchment shrivel,
30   And drive the conjurors to the devil:
And when the sky is grown serene,
Our silver will appear again.

On Wisdom's Defeat in a Learned Debate

Quid est sapientia? semper idem velle atque idem nolle.

Minerva has vowed since the bishops do slight her,
Should the reverend peers, by chance e'er invite her,
She's resolved never more to be known by the mitre.

The temporal lords, who voted against her,
She frankly forgives, as not having incensed her,
For securing their pensions is best proof of their sense, sir.

At first putting the question, their lordships were for 't,
And his Grace's wise motion did bravely support,
Till positive orders was whispered from court.

10   So this they allege in their justification,
They vote for their bread in undoing the nation,
And the first law of nature is self-preservation.

Rose Common,
Shameless woman.

Horace, Book I, Ode XIV

O navis, referent, &c.

PARAPHRASED AND INSCRIBED TO IRELAND

THE INSCRIPTION

Poor floating isle, tossed on ill fortune's waves,
Ordained by fate to be the land of slaves:
Shall moving Delos now deep-rooted stand,
Thou, fixed of old, be now the moving land?
Although the metaphor be worn and stale
Betwixt a state, and vessel under sail;
Let me suppose thee for a ship awhile,
And thus address thee in the sailor style.

Unhappy ship, thou art returned in vain:
New waves shall drive thee to the deep again.
Look to thyself, and be no more the sport

Of giddy winds, but make some friendly port.
Lost are thy oars that used thy course to guide,
Like faithful counsellors on either side.
Thy mast, which like some aged patriot stood
The single pillar for his country's good,
To lead thee, as a staff directs the blind,
10   Behold, it cracks by yon rough eastern wind.
Your cables burst, and you must quickly feel
The waves impetuous entering at your keel.
Thus, commonwealths receive a foreign yoke,
When the strong cords of union once are broke.
Torn by a sudden tempest is your sail,
Expanded to invite a milder gale.

As when some writer in a public cause,
His pen to save a sinking nation draws,
While all is calm, his arguments prevail,
20   The people's voice expands his paper sail;
Till power, discharging all her stormy bags,
Flutters the feeble pamphlet into rags.
The nation scared, the author doomed to death,
Who fondly put his trust in popular breath.

A larger sacrifice in vain you vow;
There's not a power above will help you now:
A nation thus, who oft heaven's call neglects,
In vain from injured heaven relief expects.

'Twill not avail, when thy strong sides are broke,
30   That thy descent is from the British oak:
Or when your name and family will boast,
From fleets triumphant o'er the Gallic coast.
Such was Ierne's claim, as just as thine,
Her sons descended from the British line;
Her matchless sons, whose valour still remains
On French records for twenty long campaigns;
Yet from an empress, now a captive grown,
She saved Britannia's right, and lost her own.

In ships decayed no mariner confides,
40   Lured by the gilded stern, and painted sides.
So, at a ball, unthinking fools delight
In the gay trappings of a birthday night:

They on the gold brocades and satins raved,
And quite forgot their country was enslaved.

Dear vessel, still be to thy steerage just,
Nor change thy course with every sudden gust:
Like supple patriots of the modern sort,
Who turn with every gale that blows from court.

Weary and seasick when in thee confined,
50   Now, for thy safety, cares distract my mind.
As those who long have stood the storms of state,
Retire, yet still bemoan their country's fate.
Beware, and when you hear the surges roar,
Avoid the rocks on Britain's angry shore:
They lie, alas! too easy to be found,
For thee alone they lie the island round.

A Copy of Verses upon Two Celebrated Modern Poets

Behold those monarch oaks that rise
With lofty branches to the skies,
Have large proportioned roots that grow
With equal longitude below:
Two bards that now in fashion reign,
Most aptly this device explain:
If this to clouds and stars will venture,
That creeps as far to reach the centre;
Or more to show the thing I mean,
10   Have you not o'er a sawpit seen
A skilled mechanic that has stood
High on a length of prostrate wood,
Who hired a subterraneous friend,
To take his iron by the end;
But which excelled was never found,
The man above, or underground.

The moral is so plain to hit,
That had I been the god of wit,
Then in a sawpit and wet weather,
20   Should Young and Philips drudge together.

An Apology to the Lady Carteret

ON HER INVITING DEAN SWIFT TO DINNER

He came accordingly, but her Ladyship being abroad, went away.
At her return, she inquired for him; and not hearing of him, sent the
next day to invite him again. When he came, he went to make an
apology, for his going away, but my Lady would accept of none but
in verse.

A lady, wise as well as fair,
Whose conscience always was her care,
Thoughtful upon a point of moment:
Would have the text as well as comment;
So hearing of a grave divine,
She sent to bid him come and dine.
But you must know he was not quite
So grave, as to be unpolite;
Thought humane learning would not lessen
10   The dignity of his profession;
And if you had heard the man discourse,
Or preach, you'd like him scarce the worse.
He long had bid the court farewell,
Retreating silent to his cell;
Suspected for the love he bore
To one who swayed some time before;
Which made it more surprising how
He should be sent for thither now.

The message told, he gapes – and stares,
20   And scarce believes his eyes, or ears;
Could not conceive what it should mean,
And fain would hear it told again;
But then the squire so trim and nice,
'Twere rude to make him tell it twice;
So bowed, was thankful for the honour;
And would not fail to wait upon her.
His beaver brushed, his shoes, and gown,
Away he trudges into town;
Passes the Lower Castle Yard,
30   And now advances to the guard,
He trembles at the thoughts of state;

For, conscious of his sheepish gait,
His spirits of a sudden failed him,
He stopped, and could not tell what ailed him.

What was the message I received;
Why certainly the Captain raved?
To dine with her! and come at three!
Impossible! it can't be me.
Or maybe I mistook the word;
40   My Lady – it must be my Lord.

My Lord's abroad; my Lady too;
What must the unhappy Doctor do?
'Is Captain Cracherode here, pray?' – 'No.'
'Nay then, 'tis time for me to go.'
Am I awake, or do I dream?
I'm sure he called me by my name;
Named me as plain as he could speak:
And yet there must be some mistake.
Why what a jest should I have been,
50   Had now my Lady been within.
What could I've said? I'm mighty glad
She went abroad – she'd thought me mad.
The hour of dining now is past;
Well then, I'll e'en go home, and fast;
And since I scaped being made a scoff,
I think I'm very fairly off.
My Lady now returning home
Calls, 'Cracherode, is the Doctor come?'
He had not heard of him – 'Pray see,
60   'Tis now a quarter after three.'
The Captain walks about, and searches
Through all the rooms, and courts, and arches;
Examines all the servants round,
In vain – no Doctor's to be found.
My Lady could not choose but wonder:
'Captain, I fear you've made some blunder;
But pray, tomorrow go at ten,
I'll try his manners once again;
If rudeness be the effect of knowledge,
70   My son shall never see a college.'

The Captain was a man of reading,
And much good sense, as well as breeding:
Who, loath to blame, or to incense,
Said little in his own defence:
Next day another message brought;
The Doctor, frightened at his fault,
Is dressed, and stealing through the crowd,
Now pale as death, then blushed and bowed;
Panting – and faltering – hummed and ha'd,
80   'Her Ladyship was gone abroad;
The Captain too – he did not know
Whether he ought to stay or go.'
Begged she'd forgive him; in conclusion,
My Lady, pitying his confusion,
Called her good nature to relieve him;
Told him, she thought she might believe him;
And would not only grant his suit,
But visit him, and eat some fruit;
Provided, at a proper time,
90   He told the real truth in rhyme.
'Twas to no purpose to oppose,
She'd hear of no excuse in prose.
The Doctor stood not to debate,
Glad to compound at any rate;
So, bowing, seemingly complied;
Though if he durst, he had denied.
But first resolved, to show his taste
Was too refined to give a feast,
He'd treat with nothing that was rare,
100   But winding walks and purer air;
Would entertain without expense,
Or pride, or vain magnificence;
For well he knew, to such a guest,
The plainest meals must be the best:
To stomachs clogged with costly fare,
Simplicity alone is rare;
Whilst high, and nice, and curious meats,
Are really but vulgar treats:
Instead of spoils of Persian looms,
110   The costly boast of regal rooms,

Thought it more courtly and discreet,
To scatter roses at her feet;
Roses of richest dye, that shone
With native lustre like her own;
Beauty that needs no aid of art,
Through every sense to reach the heart.
The gracious dame, though well she knew
All this was much beneath her due,
Liked everything – at least thought fit
120   To praise it, *par manière d'acquit*;
But yet, though seeming pleased, can't bear
The scorching sun, or chilling air;
Frighted alike at both extremes,
If he displays, or hides his beams;
Though seeming pleased at all she sees,
Starts at the rustling of the trees;
Can scarcely speak for want of breath,
In half a walk fatigued to death.
The Doctor takes his hint from hence,
130   To vindicate his late offence:
'Madam, the mighty power of use
Now strangely pleads in my excuse:
If you, unused, have scarcely strength
To move this walk's untoward length,
If startled at a scene so rude,
Through long disuse of solitude;
If long confined to fires and screens,
You dread the waving of these greens;
If you, who long have breathed the fumes
140   Of city fogs and crowded rooms,
Do now solicitously shun
The cooler air, and dazzling sun;
If his majestic eye you flee,
Learn hence to excuse and pity me.
Consider what it is to bear
The powdered courtier's witty sneer;
To see the important men of dress,
Scoffing my college awkwardness.
To be the strutting cornet's sport,
150   To run the gauntlet of the court;

Winning my way by slow approaches,
Through crowds of coxcombs and of coaches;
From the first fierce cockaded sentry,
Quite through the tribe of waiting gentry;
To pass to many crowded stages,
And stand the staring of your pages;
And after all, to crown my spleen,
Be told – "You are not to be seen";
Or, if you are, be forced to bear
160   The awe of your majestic air?
And can I then be faulty found
In dreading this vexatious round?
Can it be strange if I eschew
A scene so glorious and so new?
Or is he criminal that flies
The living lustre of your eyes?'

A Receipt to Restore Stella's Youth

The Scottish hinds, too poor to house
In frosty nights their starving cows,
While not a blade of grass, or hay,
Appears from Michaelmas to May;
Must let their cattle range in vain
For food, along the barren plain;
Meagre and lank with fasting grown,
And nothing left but skin and bone;
Exposed to want, and wind, and weather,
10   They just keep life and soul together,
Till summer showers and evening dew,
Again the verdant glebe renew;
And as the vegetables rise,
The famished cow her wants supplies;
Without an ounce of last year's flesh,
Whate'er she gains is young and fresh;
Grows plump and round, and full of mettle,
As rising from Medea's kettle;
With youth and beauty to enchant
20   Europa's counterfeit gallant.

Why, Stella, should you knit your brow,
If I compare you to the cow?
'Tis just the case: for you have fasted
So long till all your flesh is wasted,
And must against the warmer days
Be sent to Quilca down to graze;
Where mirth, and exercise, and air,
Will soon your appetite repair.
The nutriment will from within
30   Round all your body, plump your skin;
Will agitate the lazy flood,
And fill your veins with sprightly blood:
Nor flesh nor blood will be the same,
Nor aught of Stella, but the name;
For, what was ever understood
By human kind, but flesh and blood?
And if your flesh and blood be new,
You'll be no more your former *you*;
But for a blooming nymph will pass,
40   Just fifteen, coming summer's grass:
Your jetty locks with garlands crowned,
While all the squires from nine miles round,
Attended by a brace of curs,
With jockey-boots, and silver spurs;
No less than justices o' quorum,
Their cowboys bearing cloaks before 'em,
Shall leave deciding broken pates,
To kiss your steps at Quilca gates;
But, lest you should my skill disgrace,
50   Come back before you're out of case;
For if to Michaelmas you stay,
The new-born flesh will melt away;
The squires in scorn will fly the house
For better game, and look for grouse:
But here, before the frost can mar it,
We'll make it firm with beef and claret.

To Quilca

A COUNTRY HOUSE IN NO GOOD REPAIR,
WHERE THE SUPPOSED AUTHOR, AND SOME OF HIS FRIENDS,
SPENT A SUMMER IN THE YEAR 1725

Let me my properties explain,
A rotten cabin, dropping rain;
Chimneys with scorn rejecting smoke;
Stools, tables, chairs, and bedsteads, broke:
Here elements have lost their uses,
Air ripens not, nor earth produces:
In vain we make poor Sheelah toil,
Fire will not roast, nor waters boil.
Through all the valleys, hills, and plains,
10   The goddess Want in triumph reigns;
And her chief officers of state,
Sloth, Dirt, and Theft around her wait.

Verses from Quilca

1

Eat like a Turk,
    Sleep like a dormouse;
Be last at work,
    At victuals foremost.

2

THE BLESSINGS OF A COUNTRY LIFE

Far from our debtors,
No Dublin letters,
Not seen by our betters.

3

THE PLAGUES OF A COUNTRY LIFE

A companion without news,
A great want of shoes;
Eat lean meat, or choose;
A church without pews,

Our horses astray,
No straw, oats or hay;
December in May,
Our boys run away,
All servants at play.

Lines to Pope

The heathen doth believe in Christ
    And doth all Christians hate;
For never was informer he
    Nor minister of state.

Riddles

I

In youth exalted high in air,
Or bathing in the waters fair;
Nature to form me took delight,
And clad my body all in white:
My person tall, and slender waist,
On either side with fringes graced;
Till me that tyrant man espied,
And dragged me from my mother's side:
No wonder now I look so thin;
10   The tyrant stripped me to the skin:
My skin he flayed, my hair he cropped;
At head and foot my body lopped:
And then, with heart more hard than stone,
He picked my marrow from the bone.
To vex me more, he took a freak,
To slit my tongue, and make me speak:
But, that which wonderful appears,
I speak to eyes and not to ears.
He oft employs me in disguise,
20   And makes me tell a thousand lies:
To me he chiefly gives in trust
To please his malice, or his lust.

From me no secret he can hide;
I see his vanity and pride:
And my delight is to expose
His follies to his greatest foes.

All languages I can command,
Yet not a word I understand.
Without my aid, the best divine
30   In learning would not know a line:
The lawyer must forget his pleading,
The scholar could not show his reading.
Nay; man, my master, is my slave:
I give command to kill or save.
Can grant ten thousand pounds a year,
And make a beggar's brat a peer.

But, while I thus my life relate,
I only hasten on my fate.
My tongue is black, my mouth is furred,
40   I hardly now can force a word.
I die unpitied and forgot;
And on some dunghill left to rot.

2

All-ruling tyrant of the earth,
To vilest slaves I owe my birth.
How is the greatest monarch blessed,
When in my gaudy livery dressed!
No haughty nymph has power to run
From me; or my embraces shun.
Stabbed to the heart, condemned to flame,
My constancy is still the same.
The favourite messenger of Jove,
10   And Lemnian god consulting strove,
To make me glorious to the sight
Of mortals, and the gods' delight.
Soon would their altar's flame expire,
If I refused to lend them fire.

3

By fate exalted high in place;
Lo, here I stand with double face;

Superior none on earth I find;
But see below me all mankind.
Yet, as it oft attends the great,
I almost sink with my own weight;
At every motion undertook,
The vulgar all consult my look.
I sometimes give advice in writing,
10 But never of my own inditing.

I am a courtier in my way;
For those who raised me, I betray;
And some give out, that I entice
To lust and luxury, and dice:
Who punishments on me inflict,
Because they find their pockets picked.

By riding post I lose my health;
And only to get others wealth.

4

Because I am by nature blind,
I wisely choose to walk behind;
However, to avoid disgrace,
I let no creature see my face.
My words are few, but spoke with sense:
And yet my speaking gives offence:
Or, if to whisper I presume,
The company will fly the room.
By all the world I am oppressed,
10 And my oppression gives them rest.

Through me, though sore against my will,
Instructors every art instil.
By thousands I am sold and bought,
Who neither get, nor lose a groat;
For none, alas, by me can gain,
But those who give me greatest pain.
Shall man presume to be my master,
Who's but my caterer and taster?
Yet, though I always have my will,
20 I'm but a mere depender still:
An humble hanger-on at best;
Of whom all people make a jest.

In me, detractors seek to find
Two vices of a different kind:
I'm too profuse some censurers cry,
And all I get, I let it fly:
While others give me many a curse,
Because too close I hold my purse.
But this I know, in either case
30   They dare not charge me to my face:
'Tis true, indeed, sometimes I save,
Sometimes run out of all I have;
But when the year is at an end,
Computing what I get and spend,
My goings out, and comings in,
I cannot find I lose or win,
And therefore, all that know me, say
I justly keep the middle way.
I'm always by my betters led;
40   I last get up, am first abed;
Though, if I rise before my time,
The learned in sciences sublime,
Consult the stars, and thence foretell
Good luck to those with whom I dwell.

5

The joy of man, the pride of brutes,
Domestic subject for disputes,
Of plenty thou the emblem fair,
Adorned by nymphs with all their care:
I saw thee raised to high renown,
Supporting half the British crown;
And often have I seen thee grace
The chaste Diana's infant face;
And whensoe'er you please to shine,
10   Less useful is her light than thine;
The numerous fingers know their way,
And oft in Celia's tresses play.

To place thee in another view,
I'll show the world strange things and true;
What lords and dames of high degree,
May justly claim their birth from thee;
The soul of man with spleen you vex;

Of spleen you cure the female sex.
Thee, for a gift, the courtier sends
20   With pleasure to his special friends:
He gives; and with a generous pride,
Contrives all means the gift to hide:
Nor oft can the receiver know
Whether he has the gift or no.
On airy wings you take your flight,
And fly unseen both day and night;
Conceal your form with various tricks,
And few know how and where you fix.
Yet, some who ne'er bestowed thee, boast
30   That they to others give thee most:
Meantime, the wise a question start,
If thou a real being art;
Or, but a creature of the brain,
That gives imaginary pain:
But the sly giver better knows thee;
Who feels true joys when he bestows thee.

6

Though I, alas! a prisoner be,
My trade is, prisoners to set free.
No slave his lord's commands obeys,
With such insinuating ways.
My genius piercing, sharp and bright,
Wherein the men of wit delight.
The clergy keep me for their ease,
And turn and wind me as they please.
A new and wondrous art I show
10   Of raising spirits from below;
In scarlet some, and some in white;
They rise, walk round, yet never fright.
In at each mouth the spirits pass,
Distinctly seen as through a glass:
O'er head and body make a rout,
And drive at last all secrets out:
And still, the more I show my art,
The more they open every heart.

A greater chemist none, than I,
20   Who from materials hard and dry,

Have taught men to extract with skill,
More precious juice than from a still.

Although I'm often out of case,
I'm not ashamed to show my face,
Though at the tables of the great,
I near the sideboard take my seat;
Yet, the plain squire, when dinner's done,
Is never pleased till I make one;
He kindly bids me near him stand;
30   And often takes me by the hand.

I twice a day a-hunting go;
Nor ever fail to seize my foe;
And, when I have him by the pole,
I drag him upwards from his hole.
Though some are of so stubborn kind,
I'm forced to leave a limb behind.

I hourly wait some fatal end;
For, I can break, but scorn to bend.

7
THE GULF OF ALL HUMAN POSSESSIONS

Come hither and behold the fruits,
Vain man, of all thy vain pursuits.
Take wise advice, and look behind,
Bring all past actions to thy mind.
Here may you see, as in a glass,
How soon all human pleasures pass.
How will it mortify thy pride,
To turn the true impartial side!
How will your eyes contain their tears,
10   When all the sad reverse appears!

This cave within its womb confines
The last result of all designs:
Here lie deposited the spoils
Of busy mortals' endless toils:
Here, with an easy search we find
The foul corruptions of mankind.
The wretched purchase here behold
Of traitors who their country sold.

The gulf insatiable imbibes
20 The lawyer's fees, the statesman's bribes.
Here, in their proper shape and mien,
Fraud, perjury, and guilt are seen.

Necessity, the tyrant's law,
All human race must hither draw:
All prompted by the same desire,
The vigorous youth, and aged sire:
Behold, the coward, and the brave,
The haughty prince, the humble slave,
Physician, lawyer, and divine,
30 All make oblations at this shrine.
Some enter boldly, some by stealth,
And leave behind their fruitless wealth.
For, while the bashful sylvan maid,
As half ashamed, and half afraid,
Approaching, finds it hard to part
With that which dwelt so near her heart;
The courtly dame, unmoved by fear,
Profusely pours her offerings here.

A treasure here of learning lurks,
40 Huge heaps of never-dying works;
Labours of many an ancient sage,
And millions of the present age.

In at this gulf all offerings pass,
And lie an undistinguished mass.
Deucalion, to restore mankind
Was bid to throw the stones behind;
So, those who here their gifts convey,
Are forced to look another way;
For, few, a chosen few, must know
50 The mysteries that lie below.

Sad charnel-house! a dismal dome,
For which all mortals leave their home;
The young, the beautiful, and brave,
Here buried in one common grave;
Where each supply of dead, renews
Unwholesome damps, offensive dews:
And lo! the writing on the walls

Points out where each new victim falls;
The food of worms, and beasts obscene,
60   Who round the vault luxuriant reign.

See where those mangled corpses lie;
Condemned by female hands to die;
A comely dame once clad in white,
Lies there consigned to endless night;
By cruel hands her blood was spilt,
And yet her wealth was all her guilt.

And here six virgins in a tomb,
All beauteous offerings of one womb,
Oft in the train of Venus seen,
70   As fair and lovely as their queen:
In royal garments each was dressed,
Each with a gold and purple vest;
I saw them of their garments stripped,
Their throats were cut, their bellies ripped,
Twice were they buried, twice were born,
Twice from their sepulchres were torn;
But, now dismembered here are cast,
And find a resting place at last.

Here, oft the curious traveller finds,
80   The combat of opposing winds:
And seeks to learn the secret cause,
Which alien seems from nature's laws;
Why at this cave's tremendous mouth,
He feels at once both north and south:
Whether the winds in caverns pent
Through clefts oppugnant force a vent;
Or, whether opening all his stores,
Fierce Aeolus in tempests roars.

Yet from this mingled mass of things,
90   In time a new creation springs.
These crude materials once shall rise,
To fill the earth, and air, and skies:
In various forms appear again
Of vegetables, brutes, and men.
So Jove pronounced among the gods,
Olympus trembling as he nods.

8

LOUISA TO STREPHON

Ah, Strephon, how can you despise
Her, who without thy pity, dies?
To Strephon I have still been true,
And of as noble blood as you;
Fair issue of the genial bed,
A virgin in thy bosom bred;
Embraced thee closer than a wife;
When thee I leave, I leave my life.
Why should the shepherd take amiss
10   That oft I wake thee with a kiss?
Yet you of every kiss complain;
Ah, is not love a pleasing pain?
A pain which every happy night
You cure with ease and with delight;
With pleasure, as the poet sings,
Too great for mortals less than kings.

Chloe, when on thy breast I lie,
Observes me with revengeful eye:
If Chloe o'er thy heart prevails,
20   She'll tear me with her desperate nails;
And with relentless hands destroy
The tender pledges of our joy.
Nor have I bred a spurious race;
They all were born from thy embrace.

Consider, Strephon, what you do;
For, should I die for love of you,
I'll haunt thy dreams, a bloodless ghost;
And all my kin, a numerous host,
Who down direct our lineage bring
30   From victors o'er the Memphian king;
Renowned in sieges and campaigns,
Who never fled the bloody plains,
Who in tempestuous seas can sport,
And scorn the pleasures of a court;
From whom great Sylla found his doom;
Who scourged to death that scourge of Rome,
Shall on thee take a vengeance dire;

Thou, like Alcides, shall expire,
When his envenomed shirt he wore,
40   And skin and flesh in pieces tore.
Nor less that shirt, my rival's gift,
Cut from the piece that made her shift,
Shall in thy dearest blood be dyed,
And make thee tear thy tainted hide.

9
Deprived of root, and branch, and rind,
Yet flowers I bear of every kind;
And such is my prolific power,
They bloom in less than half an hour;
Yet standers-by may plainly see
They get no nourishment from me.
My head, with giddiness, goes round;
And yet I firmly stand my ground:
All over naked I am seen,
10   And painted like an Indian queen.
No couple-beggar in the land
E'er joined such numbers hand in hand;
I join them fairly with a ring;
Nor can our parson blame the thing:
And though no marriage words are spoke,
They part not till the ring is broke.
Yet hypocrite fanatics cry,
I'm but an idol raised on high;
And once a weaver in our town,
20   A damned Cromwellian, knocked me down.
I lay a prisoner twenty years;
And then the jovial cavaliers
To their old posts restored all three,
I mean the church, the king, and me.

The Answer to Delany's Riddle

With half an eye
Your riddle I spy.
I observe your wicket
Hemmed in by a thicket,

And whatever passes
Is strained through glasses.
You say it is quiet,
I flatly deny it:
It wanders about,
10   Without stirring out,
No passion so weak
But gives it a tweak;
Love, joy, and devotion
Set it always in motion.
And as for the tragic
Effects of its magic,
Which you say it can kill,
Or revive at its will,
The dead are all sound
20   And revive above ground,
After all you have writ,
It cannot be wit.
Which plainly does follow,
Since it flies from Apollo.
Its cowardice such,
It cries at a touch,
'Tis a perfect milksop,
Grows drunk with a drop.
Another great fault,
30   It cannot bear salt;
And a hair can disarm
It of every charm.

Upon Four Dismal Stories in the Doctor's Letter

RELATING TO FOUR OF MY FRIENDS

Here four of you got mischances to plague you,
Friend Congreve a fever, friend Howard an ague,
Friend Pope overturned by driving too fast away,
And Robin at sea had like to be castaway:
But alas, the poor Dean neither shudders nor burns,
No sea overwhelms him, no coach overturns;
Though his claret is bad, and he foots it on stones,
Yet he gets home at night with health and whole bones.

On the Collar of Mrs Dingley's Lap-Dog

Pray steal me not, I'm Mrs Dingley's,
Whose heart in this four-footed thing lies.

Bec's Birthday

This day, dear Bec, is thy nativity,
Had Fate a luckier one, she'd give it ye:
She chose a thread of greatest length
And doubly twisted it for strength;
Nor will be able with her shears
To cut it off these forty years.
Then, who says care will kill a cat?
Rebecca shows they're out in that.
For she, though overrun with care,
10　Continues healthy, fat, and fair.

　　As, if the gout should seize the head,
Doctors pronounce the patient dead;
But, if they can, by all their arts,
Eject it to the extremest parts,
They give the sick man joy, and praise
The gout that will prolong his days:
Rebecca thus I gladly greet,
Who drives her cares to hands and feet:
For, though philosophers maintain
20　The limbs are guided by the brain,
Quite contrary Rebecca's led,
Her hands and feet conduct her head,
By arbitrary power convey her
She ne'er considers why, or where:
Her hands may meddle, feet may wander,
Her head is but a mere bystander:
And all her bustling but supplies
The part of wholesome exercise:
Thus, nature hath resolved to pay her
30　The cat's nine lives and eke the care.

　　Long may she live, and help her friends
Whene'er it suits her private ends;
Domestic business never mind

Till coffee has her stomach lined;
But, when her breakfast gives her courage,
Then, think on Stella's chicken porridge;
I mean when Tiger has been served,
Or else poor Stella may be starved.

    May Bec have many an evening nap
40 With Tiger slabbering in her lap;
But always take a special care
She does not overset the chair;
Still be she curious, never hearken
To any speech but Tiger's barking.

    And, when she's in another scene,
Stella long dead, but first the Dean,
May fortune and her coffee get her
Companions that will please her better;
Whole afternoons will sit beside her,
50 Nor for neglects or blunders chide her;
A goodly set as can be found
Of hearty gossips prating round;
Fresh from a wedding, or a christening,
To teach her ears the art of listening,
And please her more to hear them tattle
Than the Dean storm, or Stella rattle.

    Late be her death, one gentle nod,
When Hermes, waiting with his rod,
Shall to Elysian fields invite her,
60 Where there will be no cares to fright her.

Stella's Birthday (1727)

This day, whate'er the fates decree,
Shall still be kept with joy by me:
This day then, let us not be told,
That you are sick, and I grown old,
Nor think on our approaching ills,
And talk of spectacles and pills.
Tomorrow will be time enough
To hear such mortifying stuff.

Yet, since from reason may be brought
10 A better and more pleasing thought,
Which can in spite of all decays,
Support a few remaining days:
From not the gravest of divines,
Accept for once some serious lines.

Although we now can form no more
Long schemes of life, as heretofore;
Yet you, while time is running fast,
Can look with joy on what is past.

Were future happiness and pain,
20 A mere contrivance of the brain,
As atheists argue, to entice,
And fit their proselytes for vice;
(The only comfort they propose,
To have companions in their woes.)
Grant this the case, yet sure 'tis hard,
That virtue, styled its own reward,
And by all sages understood
To be the chief of human good,
Should acting, die, nor leave behind
30 Some lasting pleasure in the mind;
Which by remembrance will assuage,
Grief, sickness, poverty, and age;
And strongly shoot a radiant dart,
To shine through life's declining part.

Say, Stella, feel you no content,
Reflecting on a life well spent?
Your skilful hand employed to save
Despairing wretches from the grave;
And then supporting with your store,
40 Those whom you dragged from death before:
(So Providence on mortals waits,
Preserving what it first creates)
Your generous boldness to defend
An innocent and absent friend;
That courage which can make you just,
To merit humbled in the dust:
The detestation you express
For vice in all its glittering dress:

That patience under torturing pain,
50 Where stubborn Stoics would complain.

Shall these, like empty shadows pass,
Or forms reflected from a glass?
Or mere chimeras in the mind,
That fly and leave no marks behind?
Does not the body thrive and grow
By food of twenty years ago?
And, had it not been still supplied,
It must a thousand times have died.
Then, who with reason can maintain,
60 That no effects of food remain?
And, is not virtue in mankind
The nutriment that feeds the mind?
Upheld by each good action past,
And still continued by the last:
Then, who with reason can pretend,
That all effects of virtue end?

Believe me Stella, when you show
That true contempt for things below,
Nor prize your life for other ends
70 Than merely to oblige your friends;
Your former actions claim their part,
And join to fortify your heart.
For virtue in her daily race,
Like Janus, bears a double face;
Looks back with joy where she has gone,
And therefore goes with courage on.
She at your sickly couch will wait,
And guide you to a better state.

O then, whatever heaven intends,
80 Take pity on your pitying friends;
Nor let your ills affect your mind,
To fancy they can be unkind.
Me, surely me, you ought to spare,
Who gladly would your sufferings share;
Or give my scrap of life to you,
And think it far beneath your due;
You, to whose care so oft I owe,
That I'm alive to tell you so.

Clever Tom Clinch Going to be Hanged

As clever Tom Clinch, while the rabble was bawling,
Rode stately through Holborn, to die in his calling;
He stopped at the George for a bottle of sack,
And promised to pay for it when he came back.
His waistcoat and stockings, and breeches were white,
His cap had a new cherry ribbon to tie't.
The maids to the doors and the balconies ran,
And said, lackaday, he's a proper young man.
But, as from the windows the ladies he spied,
10 Like a beau in the box, he bowed low on each side;
And when his last speech the hawkers did cry,
He swore from his cart, it was all a damned lie.
The hangman for pardon fell down on his knee;
Tom gave him a kick in the guts for his fee.
Then said, 'I must speak to the people a little,
But I'll see you all damned before I will whittle.
My honest friend Wild, may he long hold his place,
He lengthened my life with a whole year of grace.
Take courage, dear comrades, and be not afraid,
20 Nor slip this occasion to follow your trade.
My conscience is clear, and my spirits are calm,
And thus I go off without prayer-book or psalm.'
Then follow the practice of clever Tom Clinch,
Who hung like a hero, and never would flinch.

On Seeing Verses Written upon Windows in Inns

I

The sage, who said he should be proud
    Of windows in his breast;
Because he ne'er one thought allowed
    That might not be confessed;
His window scrawled by every rake,
    His breast again would cover;
And fairly bid the devil take
    The diamond and the lover.

2

By Satan taught, all conjurors know
Your mistress in a glass to show,
    And you can do as much:
In this the devil and you agree;
None e'er made verses worse than he,
    And thine I swear are such.

3

That love is the devil, I'll prove when required:
    These rhymers abundantly show it:
They swear that they all by love are inspired,
    And the devil's a damnable poet.

4

The church and clergy here, no doubt,
    Are very near akin;
Both, weatherbeaten are without;
    And empty both within.

On Reading Dr Young's Satires

CALLED 'THE UNIVERSAL PASSION',
BY WHICH HE MEANS PRIDE

If there be truth in what you sing;
Such godlike virtues in the King:
A minister so filled with zeal,
And wisdom for the common weal:
If he who in the chair presides,
So steadily the senate guides:
If others, whom you make your theme,
Are seconds in this glorious scheme:
If every peer whom you commend,
10   To worth and learning be a friend:
If this be truth, as you attest,
What land was ever half so blessed?
No falsehood now among the great,
And tradesmen now no longer cheat;

Now, on the bench fair Justice shines,
Her scale to neither side inclines.
Now Pride and Cruelty are flown,
And Mercy here exalts her throne;
For such is good example's power,
20   It does its office every hour,
Where governors àre good and wise;
Or else the truest maxim lies:
For, so we find, all ancient sages
Decree, that *ad exemplum regis*,
Through all the realm his virtues run,
Ripening and kindling like the sun.
If this be true, then how much more,
When you have named at least a score
Of courtiers, each in their degree
30   If possible, as good as he.

   Or, take it in a different view,
I ask, if what you say be true,
If you affirm, the present age
Deserves your satire's keenest rage:
If that same *Universal Passion*
With every vice hath filled the nation;
If virtue dares not venture down,
But just a step below the crown:
If clergymen, to show their wit,
40   Prize classics more than holy writ:
If bankrupts, when they are undone,
Into the senate house can run,
And sell their votes at such a rate,
As will retrieve a lost estate:
If law be such a partial whore,
To spare the rich, and plague the poor;
If these be of all crimes the worst;
What land was ever half so cursed?

Advice to the Grub Street Verse-Writers

Ye poets ragged and forlorn,
  Down from your garrets haste,

Ye rhymers, dead as soon as born,
  Nor yet consigned to paste;

I know a trick to make you thrive;
  O, 'tis a quaint device:
Your still-born poets shall revive,
  And scorn to wrap up spice.

Get all your verses printed fair,
10   Then let them well be dried;
And Curll must have a special care
  To leave the margin wide.

Lend these to paper-sparing Pope;
  And, when he sits to write,
No letter with an envelope
  Could give him more delight.

When Pope has filled the margin round,
  Why, then recall your loan;
Sell them to Curll for fifty pound,
20   And swear they are your own.

To the Earl of Peterborough

Mordanto fills the trump of fame,
The Christian world his deeds proclaim,
And prints are crowded with his name.

  In journeys he outrides the post,
Sits up till midnight with his host,
Talks politics, and gives the toast.

  Knows every prince in Europe's face,
Flies like a squib from place to place,
And travels not, but runs a race.

10   From Paris Gazette à la main,
This day arrived without his train,
Mordanto in a week from Spain.

  A messenger comes all a-reek,
Mordanto at Madrid to seek:
He left the town above a week.

Next day the post-boy winds his horn,
And rides through Dover in the morn:
Mordanto's landed from Leghorn.

Mordanto gallops on alone,
20   The roads are with his followers strewn,
This breaks a girth, and that a bone.

His body active as his mind,
Returning sound in limb and wind,
Except some leather lost behind.

A skeleton in outward figure,
His meagre corpse, though full of vigour,
Would halt behind him, were it bigger.

So wonderful his expedition,
When you have not the least suspicion,
30   He's with you like an apparition.

Shines in all climates like a star;
In senates bold, and fierce in war,
A land commander, and a tar.

Heroic actions early bred in,
Ne'er to be matched in modern reading,
But by his namesake Charles of Sweden.

Dr Swift to Mr Pope

WHILE HE WAS WRITING THE 'DUNCIAD'

Pope has the talent well to speak,
    But not to reach the ear;
His loudest voice is low and weak,
    The Dean too deaf to hear.

Awhile they on each other look,
    Then different studies choose;
The Dean sits plodding on a book,
    Pope walks, and courts the muse.

Now backs of letters, though designed
10   For those, who more will need 'em,

Are filled with hints, and interlined,
    Himself can hardly read 'em.

Each atom by some other struck,
    All turns and motions tries;
Till in a lump together stuck,
    Behold a poem rise!

Yet to the Dean his share allot;
    He claims it by a canon;
That, *without which a thing is not*
20   Is, *causa sine qua non.*

Thus, Pope in vain you boast your wit;
    For, had our deaf divine
Been for your conversation fit,
    You had not writ a line.

Of Sherlock thus, for preaching famed,
    The sexton reasoned well,
And justly half the merit claimed
    Because he rang the bell.

A Pastoral Dialogue between Richmond Lodge and Marble Hill

WRITTEN JUNE 1727, JUST AFTER THE NEWS
OF THE KING'S DEATH

In spite of Pope, in spite of Gay,
And all that he or they can say;
Sing on I must, and sing I will
Of Richmond Lodge, and Marble Hill.

Last Friday night, as neighbours use,
This couple met to talk of news.
For by old proverbs it appears,
That walls have tongues, and hedges, ears.

MARBLE HILL
Quoth Marble Hill, right well I ween,
10   Your mistress now is grown a queen;

You'll find it soon by woeful proof,
She'll come no more beneath your roof.

RICHMOND LODGE

The kingly prophet well evinces,
That we should put no trust in princes;
My royal master promised me
To raise me to a high degree:
But now he's grown a king, God wot,
I fear I shall be soon forgot.
You see, when folks have got their ends,
20   How quickly they neglect their friends;
Yet I may say 'twixt me and you,
Pray God they now may find as true.

MARBLE HILL

My house was built but for a show,
My Lady's empty pockets know;
And now she will not have a shilling
To raise the stairs, or build the ceiling;
For, all the courtly madams round,
Now pay four shillings in the pound.
'Tis come to what I always thought;
30   My dame is hardly worth a groat.
Had you and I been courtiers born,
We should not thus have lain forlorn;
For, those we dexterous courtiers call,
Can *rise* upon their master's *fall*.
But we, unlucky and unwise,
Must *fall*, because our masters *rise*.

RICHMOND LODGE

My master scarce a fortnight since,
Was grown as wealthy as a prince;
But now it will be no such thing,
40   For he'll be poor as any king:
And, by his crown will nothing get;
But, like a king, to run in debt.

MARBLE HILL

No more the Dean, that grave divine,
Shall keep the key of my (no) wine;

My ice-house rob as heretofore,
And steal my artichokes no more;
Poor Patty Blount no more be seen
Bedraggled in my walks so green;
Plump Johnny Gay will now elope;
50   And here no more will dangle Pope.

RICHMOND LODGE

Here wont the Dean when he's to seek,
To sponge a breakfast once a week;
To cry the bread was stale, and mutter
Complaints against the royal butter.
But, now I fear it will be said,
No butter sticks upon his bread.
We soon shall find him full of spleen,
For want of tattling to the Queen;
Stunning her royal ears with talking,
60   His Reverence and her Highness walking:
Whilst Lady Charlotte, like a stroller,
Sits mounted on the garden roller.
A goodly sight to see her ride,
With ancient Mirmont at her side.
In velvet cap his head lies warm;
His hat for show, beneath his arm.

MARBLE HILL

Some South Sea broker from the city,
Will purchase me, the more's the pity,
Lay all my fine plantations waste,
70   To fit them to his vulgar taste;
Changed for the worse in every part,
My master Pope will break his heart.

RICHMOND LODGE

In my own Thames may I be drownded,
If e'er I stoop beneath a crowned head:
Except her Majesty prevails
To place me with the Prince of Wales.
And then I shall be free from fears,
For, he'll be prince these fifty years.
I then will turn a courtier too,
80   And serve the times as others do.

Plain loyalty not built on hope,
I leave to your contriver, Pope:
None loves his king and country better,
Yet none was ever less their debtor.

MARBLE HILL
Then, let him come and take a nap,
In summer, on my verdant lap:
Prefer our villas where the Thames is,
To Kensington, or hot St James's;
Nor shall I dull in silence sit;
90   For, 'tis to me he owes his wit;
My groves, my echoes, and my birds,
Have taught him his poetic words.
We gardens, and you wildernesses,
Assist all poets in distresses,
Him twice a week I here expect,
To rattle Moody for neglect;
An idle rogue, who spends his quarterage
In tippling at the Dog and Partridge;
And I can hardly get him down
100   Three times a week to brush my gown.

RICHMOND LODGE
I pity you, dear Marble Hill;
But hope to see you flourish still.
All happiness – and so adieu.

MARBLE HILL
Kind Richmond Lodge; the same to you.

Desire and Possession

'Tis strange, what different thoughts inspire
In man, *possession*, and *desire*;
Think what they wish so great a blessing,
So disappointed when possessing.

A moralist profoundly sage,
I know not in what book or page,

Or, whether o'er a pot of ale,
Related thus the following tale.

Possession, and Desire, his brother,
10   But still at variance with each other,
Were seen contending in a race;
And kept at first an equal pace:
'Tis said, their course continued long;
For, this was active, that was strong:
Till Envy, Slander, Sloth, and Doubt,
Misled them many a league about.
Seduced by some deceiving light,
They take the wrong way for the right.
Through slippery by-roads dark and deep,
20   They often climb, and oftener creep.

Desire, the swifter of the two,
Along the plain like lightning flew:
Till entering on a broad highway,
Where Power and Titles scattered lay,
He strove to pick up all he found,
And by excursions lost his ground:
No sooner got, than with disdain,
He threw them on the ground again;
And hasted forward to pursue
30   Fresh objects fairer to his view;
In hope to spring some nobler game:
But all he took was just the same:
Too scornful now to stop his pace,
He spurned them in his rival's face.

Possession kept the beaten road;
And gathered all his brother strewed;
But overcharged, and out of wind,
Though strong in limbs, he lagged behind.

Desire had now the goal in sight:
40   It was a tower of monstrous height,
Where on the summit Fortune stands:
A crown and sceptre in her hands;
Beneath, a chasm as deep as hell,
Where many a bold adventurer fell.
Desire, in rapture gazed awhile,

And saw the treacherous goddess smile;
But, as he climbed to grasp the crown,
She knocked him with her sceptre down.
He tumbled in the gulf profound;
50   There doomed to whirl an endless round.

Possession's load was grown so great,
He sunk beneath the cumbrous weight:
And, as he now expiring lay,
Flocks every ominous bird of prey;
The raven, vulture, owl, and kite,
At once upon his carcass light;
And strip his hide, and pick his bones,
Regardless of his dying groans.

On Censure

Ye wise, instruct me to endure
An evil, which admits no cure:
Or, how this evil can be born,
Which breeds at once both hate and scorn.
Bare innocence is no support,
When you are tried in scandal's court.
Stand high in honour, wealth, or wit;
All others who inferior sit,
Conceive themselves in conscience bound
10   To join, and drag you to the ground.
Your altitude offends the eyes,
Of those who want the power to rise.
The world, a willing stander-by,
Inclines to aid a specious lie:
Alas; they would not do you wrong;
But, all appearances are strong.

Yet, whence proceeds this weight we lay
On what detracting people say?
For, let mankind discharge their tongues
20   In venom, till they burst their lungs,
Their utmost malice cannot make
Your head, or tooth, or finger ache;
Nor spoil your shape, distort your face,

Or put one feature out of place;
Nor, will you find your fortune sink,
By what they speak, or what they think.
Nor can ten hundred thousand lies,
Make you less virtuous, learned, or wise.

The most effectual way to balk
30   Their malice is – to let them talk.

The Dog and the Thief

Quoth the thief to the dog; 'let me into your door,
    And I'll give you these delicate bits:'
Quoth the dog, 'I should then be more villain than you're,
    And besides must be out of my wits:

'Your delicate bits will not serve me a meal,
    But my master each day gives me bread;
You'll fly when you get what you come here to steal,
    And I must be hanged in your stead.'

The stockjobber thus, from Change Alley goes down,
10   And tips you the freeman a wink;
'Let me have but your vote to serve for the town,
    And here is a guinea to drink.'

Said the freeman, 'your guinea tonight would be spent,
    Your offers of bribery cease;
I'll vote for my landlord to whom I pay rent,
    Or else I may forfeit my lease.'

From London they come, silly people to chouse,
    Their lands and their faces unknown;
Who'd vote a rogue into the parliament-house,
20   That would turn a man out of his own?

The Furniture of a Woman's Mind

A set of phrases learned by rote;
A passion for a scarlet coat;
When at a play to laugh, or cry,

But cannot tell the reason why:
Never to hold her tongue a minute;
While all she prates has nothing in it.
Whole hours can with a coxcomb sit,
And take his nonsense all for wit:
Her learning mounts to read a song,
10   But, half the words pronouncing wrong;
Has every repartee in store,
She spoke ten thousand times before.
Can ready compliments supply
On all occasions, cut and dry.
Such hatred to a parson's gown,
The sight will put her in a swoon.
For conversation well endued;
She calls it witty to be rude;
And, placing raillery in railing,
20   Will tell aloud your greatest failing;
Nor makes a scruple to expose
Your bandy leg, or crooked nose.
Can, at her morning tea, run o'er
The scandal of the day before.
Improving hourly in her skill,
To cheat and wrangle at quadrille.

In choosing lace a critic nice,
Knows to a groat the lowest price;
Can in her female clubs dispute
30   What lining best the silk will suit;
What colours each complexion match:
And where with art to place a patch.
If chance a mouse creeps in her sight,
Can finely counterfeit a fright;
So, sweetly screams if it comes near her,
She ravishes all hearts to hear her.
Can dexterously her husband tease,
By taking fits whene'er she please:
By frequent practice learns the trick
40   At proper seasons to be sick:
Thinks nothing gives one airs so pretty;
At once creating love and pity.
If Molly happens to be careless,

And but neglects to warm her hair-lace,
She gets a cold as sure as death;
And vows she scarce can fetch her breath.
Admires how modest women can
Be so *robustious* like a man.

    In party, furious to her power;
50 A bitter Whig, or Tory sour;
Her arguments directly tend
Against the side she would defend:
Will prove herself a Tory plain,
From principles the Whigs maintain;
And, to defend the Whiggish cause,
Her topics from the Tories draws.

    O yes! If any man can find
More virtues in a woman's mind,
Let them be sent to Mrs Harding;
60 She'll pay the charges to a farthing:
Take notice, she has my commission
To add them in the next edition;
They may outsell a better thing;
So halloo boys! God save the King.

The Power of Time

If neither brass, nor marble can withstand
The mortal force of Time's destructive hand:
If mountains sink to vales, if cities die,
And lessening rivers mourn their fountains dry:
When my old cassock, says a Welsh divine,
Is out at elbows, why should I repine?

Holyhead. September 25, 1727

Lo here I sit at Holyhead
With muddy ale and mouldy bread:
All Christian victuals stink of fish,
I'm where my enemies would wish.

Convict of lies is every sign,
The inn has not one drop of wine.
I'm fastened both by wind and tide,
I see the ship at anchor ride.
The captain swears the sea's too rough,
10   He has not passengers enough.
And thus the Dean is forced to stay,
Till others come to help the pay.
In Dublin they'd be glad to see
A packet though it brings in me.
They cannot say the winds are cross;
Your politicians at a loss
For want of matter swears and frets,
Are forced to read the old gazettes.
I never was in haste before
20   To reach that slavish hateful shore:
Before, I always found the wind
To me was most malicious kind,
But now the danger of a friend
On whom my hopes and fears depend,
Absent from whom all climes are cursed,
With whom I'm happy in the worst,
With rage impatient makes me wait
A passage to the land I hate.
Else, rather on this bleaky shore
30   Where loudest winds incessant roar,
Where neither herb nor tree will thrive,
Where nature hardly seems alive,
I'd go in freedom to my grave,
Than rule yon isle and be a slave.

Ireland

Remove me from this land of slaves,
Where all are fools, and all are knaves;
Where every knave and fool is bought,
Yet kindly sells himself for naught;
Where Whig and Tory fiercely fight
Who's in the wrong, who in the right;
And when their country lies at stake
They only fight for fighting's sake,

While English sharpers take the pay,
10   And then stand by to see fair play;
Meantime the Whig is always winner
And for his courage gets a dinner.
His Excellency too perhaps
Spits in his mouth and strokes his chaps.
The humble whelp gives every vote:
To put the question strains his throat.
His Excellency's condescension
Will serve instead of place or pension,
When to the window he's trepanned,
20   When my Lord shakes him by the hand,
Or in the presence of beholders,
His arms upon the booby's shoulders,
You quickly see the gudgeon bite.
He tells his brother fools at night
How well the Governor's inclined,
So just, so gentle and so kind:
'He heard I kept a pack of hounds,
And longed to hunt upon my grounds;
He said our ladies were so fair,
30   The court had nothing to compare;
But that indeed which pleased me most,
He called my Doll a perfect toast.
He whispered public things at last,
Asked me how our elections passed.
Some augmentation, sir, you know
Would make at least a handsome show.
New kings a compliment expect;
I shall not offer to direct –
There are some prating fools in town,
40   But, sir, we must support the crown.
Our letters say a Jesuit boasts
Of some invasion on your coasts;
The King is ready, when you will,
To pass another popery bill;
And for dissenters he intends
To use them as his truest friends:
I think they justly ought to share
In all employments we can spare.
Next for encouragement of spinning,
50   A duty might be laid on linen;

An act for laying down the plough,
England will send you corn enough.
Another act that absentees
For licences shall pay no fees.
If England's friendship you would keep,
Feed nothing in your lands but sheep;
But make an act secure and full
To hang up all who smuggle wool.
And then he kindly gives me hints
60   That all our wives should go in chintz.
Tomorrow I shall tell you more,
For I'm to dine with him at four.'

This was the speech, and here's the jest:
His arguments convinced the rest.
Away he runs with zealous hotness
Exceeding all the fools of Totnes,
To move that all the nation round
Should pay a guinea in the pound:
Yet should this blockhead beg a place
70   Either from Excellence or Grace,
'Tis pre-engaged and in his room
Townshend's cast page or Walpole's groom.

'When Mrs Welch's Chimney Smokes'

When Mrs Welch's chimney smokes,
'Tis a sign she'll keep her folks;
But when of smoke the room is clear,
It is a sign we shan't stay here.

On Lord Carteret's Arms

GIVEN, AS THE CUSTOM IS, AT EVERY INN
WHERE THE LORD LIEUTENANT DINES OR LIES,
WITH ALL THE TITLES IN A LONG PARCHMENT

'Tis forty to one
When Carteret is gone,
These praises we blot out;

The truth will be got out;
And then we'll be smart on
His Lordship as Wharton.
Or Shrewsbury's Duke
With many rebuke.
Or Bolton the wise
10 With his Spanish flies.
Or Grafton the deep,
Either drunk or asleep.
These titles and arms
Will then lose their charms,
If somebody's grace
Should come in his place,
And thus it goes round:
We praise and confound.
They can do no good,
20 Nor would if they could,
To injure the nation
Is recommendation,
And why should they save her,
By losing their favour?
Poor kingdom, thou wouldst be that governor's debtor,
Who kindly would leave thee no worse nor no better.

On the Five Ladies at Sot's Hole, with the Doctor at Their Head

THE LADIES TREATED THE DOCTOR

SENT AS FROM AN OFFICER IN THE ARMY

Fair ladies, number five,
    Who in your merry freaks,
With little Tom contrive
    To feast on ales and steaks.
While he sits by a-grinning,
    To see you safe in Sot's Hole,
Set up with greasy linen,
    And neither mugs nor pots whole.
Alas! I never thought

10 A priest would please your palate;
  Besides, I'll hold a groat,
   He'll put you in a ballad:
 Where I shall see your faces
  On paper daubed so foul,
 They'll be no more like Graces,
  Than Venus like an owl.
 And we shall take you rather
  To be a midnight pack
 Of witches met together,
20 With Beelzebub in black.
 It fills my heart with woe,
  To think such ladies fine,
 Should be reduced so low,
  To treat a dull divine:
 Be by a parson cheated!
  Had you been cunning stagers,
 You might yourselves be treated
  By captains and by majors.
 See how corruption grows,
30 While mothers, daughters, aunts,
 Instead of powdered beaux,
  From pulpits choose gallants.
 If we who wear our wigs
  With fantail and with snake,
 Are bubbled thus by prigs;
  Zounds, who would be a rake?
 Had I a heart to fight,
  I'd knock the Doctor down;
 Or could I read and write,
40 Egad I'd wear a gown.
 Then leave him to his birch;
  And at the Rose on Sunday,
 The parson safe at church,
  I'll treat you with Burgundy.

The Beau's Reply to the Five Ladies' Answer

 Why, how now dapper black,
  I smell your gown and cassock,

As strong upon your back
  As Tisdall smells of a sock.

To write such scurvy stuff!
  Fine ladies never do't;
I know you well enough,
  And eke your cloven foot.

Fine ladies when they write,
10 Nor scold, or keep a splutter.
Their verses give delight,
  Are soft and sweet as butter.

But Satan never saw
  Such haggard lines as these;
They stick athwart my maw
  As bad as Suffolk cheese.

An Elegy on Dicky and Dolly

Under this stone lie Dicky and Dolly,
Doll dying first, Dick grew melancholy,
For Dick without Doll thought living a folly.

Dick lost in Doll a wife tender and dear,
But Dick lost by Doll, twelve hundred a year,
A loss that Dick thought, no mortal could bear.

Dick sighed for his Doll and his mournful arms crossed,
Thought much of his Doll, and the jointure he lost;
The first vexed him much, but the other vexed most.

10 Thus loaded with grief, Dick sighed and he cried,
To live without both full three days he tried:
And liked neither loss, and so quietly died.

One bed while alive held both Doll and Dick,
One coach oft carried them when they were quick,
One grave now contains them both *haec et hic*.

Dick left a pattern few will copy after,
Then, reader, pray shed some tears of salt water,
For so sad a tale is no subject of laughter.

Meath smiles for the jointure, though gotten so late;
20 The son laughs that got the hard-gotten estate,
And Cuffe grins for getting the Alicant plate.

Here quiet they lie, in hopes to rise one day,
Both solemnly put, in this hole on a Sunday,
And here rest, *sic transit gloria mundi*.

Mad Mullinix and Timothy

M. I own 'tis not my bread and butter,
But prithee Tim, why all this clutter?
Why ever in these raging fits,
Damning to hell the Jacobits?
When, if you search the kingdom round,
There's hardly twenty to be found;
No, not among the priests and friars.

   T. 'Twixt you and me God damns the liars.

   M. The Tories are gone every man over
10 To our illustrious house of Hanover.
From all their conduct this is plain,
And then – *T*.   God damn the liars again.
Did not an earl but lately vote
To bring in (I could cut his throat)
Our whole account of public debts?

   M. Lord how this frothy coxcomb frets! [*aside*]

   T. Did not an able statesman bishop
This dangerous horrid motion dish up?
As Popish craft? Did he not rail on't?
20 Show fire and faggot in the tail on't?
Proving the earl a grand offender,
And in a plot for the Pretender?
Whose fleet, in all our friends' opinion,
Was then embarking at Avignon.

   M. These brangling jars of Whig and Tory,
Are stale, and worn as Troy-town story.
The wrong 'tis certain you were both in,

And now you found you fought for nothing.
Your faction, when their game was new,
30 Might want such noisy fools as you;
But you when all the show is past
Resolve to stand it out the last;
Like Martin Marall, gaping on,
Not minding when the song was done.
When all the bees are gone to settle,
You clutter still your brazen kettle.
The leaders who you listed under,
Have dropped their arms, and seized the plunder.
And when the war is past you come
40 To rattle in their ears your drum.
And, as that hateful hideous Grecian
Thersites (he was your relation)
Was more abhorred, and scorned by those
With whom he served, than by his foes,
So thou art grown the detestation
Of all thy party through the nation.
Thy peevish, and perpetual teasing,
With plots; and Jacobites and treason;
Thy busy never-meaning face;
50 Thy screwed-up front; thy state grimace;
Thy formal nods; important sneers;
Thy whisperings foisted in all ears;
(Which are, whatever you may think,
But nonsense wrapped up in a stink)
Have made thy presence in a true sense
To thy own side so damned a nuisance,
That when they have you in their eye,
As if the devil drove, they fly.

    T.   My good friend Mullinix forbear.
60 I vow to God you're too severe.
If it could ever yet be known
I took advice except my own,
It should be yours. But damn my blood
I must pursue the public good.
The faction, (is it not notorious?)
Keck at the memory of *glorious*.
'Tis true, nor need I to be told,

My quondam friends are grown so cold,
That scarce a creature can be found,
70   To prance with me his statue round.
The public safety I foresee,
Henceforth depends alone on me.
And while this vital breath I blow,
Or from above, or from below,
I'll sputter, swagger, curse and rail,
The Tories' terror, scourge and flail.

    M.   Tim, you mistake the matter quite,
The Tories! you are their delight.
And should you act a different part,
80   Be grave and wise, 'twould break their heart.
Why, Tim, you have a taste I know,
And often see a puppet-show.
Observe, the audience is in pain,
While Punch is hid behind the scene,
But when they hear his rusty voice,
With what impatience they rejoice.
And then they value not two straws,
How Solomon decides the cause,
Which the true mother, which Pretender,
90   Nor listen to the witch of Endor;
Should Faustus, with the devil behind him,
Enter the stage they never mind him;
If Punch, to spur their fancy, shows
In at the door his monstrous nose,
Then sudden draws it back again,
O what a pleasure mixed with pain!
You every moment think an age,
Till he appears upon the stage.
And first his bum you see him clap,
100 Upon the Queen of Sheba's lap.
The Duke of Lorraine drew his sword,
Punch roaring ran, and running roared.
Reviles all people in his jargon,
And sells the King of Spain a bargain.
St George himself he plays the wag on,
And mounts astride upon the dragon.
He gets a thousand thumps and kicks

Yet cannot leave his roguish tricks;
In every action thrusts his nose
110   The reason why no mortal knows.
In doleful scenes, that break our heart,
Punch comes, like you, and lets a fart.
There's not a puppet made of wood,
But what would hang him if they could.
While teasing all, by all he's teased,
How well are the spectators pleased!
Who in the motion have no share;
But purely come to hear, and stare;
Have no concern for Sabra's sake,
120   Which gets the better, saint, or snake.
Provided Punch (for there's the jest)
Be soundly mauled, and plagues the rest.

Thus Tim, philosophers suppose,
The world consists of puppet-shows;
Where petulant, conceited fellows
Perform the part of Pulcinellos;
So at this booth, which we call Dublin,
Tim thou'rt the Punch to stir up trouble in;
You wriggle, fidge, and make a rout,
130   Put all your brother-puppets out,
Run on in one perpetual round,
To tease, perplex, disturb, confound,
Intrude with monkey grin, and clatter
To interrupt all serious matter,
Are grown the nuisance of your clan,
Who hate and scorn you, to a man;
But then the lookers-on, the Tories
You still divert with merry stories;
They would consent, that all the crew
140   Were hanged, before they'd part with you.

But tell me, Tim, upon the spot,
By all this coil what has thou got?
If Tories must have all the sport,
I feel you'll be disgraced at court.

T.   Got? Damn my blood I frank my letters,
Walk by my place, before my betters,

And simple as I now stand here,
Expect in time, to be a peer.
Got? Damn me, why I got my will!
150 Ne'er hold my peace, and ne'er stand still.
I fart with twenty ladies by;
They call me beast, and what care I?
I bravely call the Tories Jacks,
And sons of whores – behind their backs.
But could you bring me once to think,
That when I strut, and stare, and stink,
Revile and slander, fume and storm,
Betray, make oath, impeach, inform,
With such a constant, loyal zeal,
160 To serve myself and common weal,
And fret the Tories' souls to death,
I did but lose my precious breath,
And when I damn my soul to plague 'em,
Am, as you tell me, but their May-game,
Consume my vitals! they shall know,
I am not to be treated so,
I'd rather hang myself by half,
Than give those rascals cause to laugh.

But how, my friend, can I endure
170 Once so renowned to live obscure?
No little boys and girls to cry
'There's nimble Tim a-passing by.'
No more my dear delightful way tread
Of keeping up a party hatred.
Will none the Tory dogs pursue,
When through the streets I cry 'halloo'?
Must all my damme's, bloods and wounds
Pass only now for empty sounds?
Shall Tory rascals be elected,
180 Although I swear them disaffected?
And when I roar 'a plot, a plot',
Will our own party mind me not?
So qualified to swear and lie,
Will they not trust me for a spy?
Dear Mullinix, your good advice
I beg, you see the case is nice,

O were I equal in renown,
Like thee, to please this thankless town!
Or blessed with such engaging parts,
190 To win the truant schoolboys' hearts!
Thy virtues meet their just reward,
Attended by the sable guard,
Charmed by thy voice the prentice drops
The snowball destined at thy chops;
Thy graceful steps, and colonel's air,
Allure the cinder-picking fair.

    M.   No more – in mark of true affection
I take thee under my protection.
Thy parts are good, 'tis not denied,
200 I wish they had been well applied.
But now observe my counsel, *viz*.
Adapt your habit to your phiz.
You must no longer thus equip ye
As Horace says, ' *Optat ephippia*.'
(There's Latin too that you may see
How I improved by Dr Lee).
I have a coat at home, that you may try,
'Tis just like this, which hangs by geometry.
My hat has much the nicer air,
210 Your block will fit it to a hair.
That wig, I would not for the world
Have it so formal, and so curled,
'Twill be so oily, and so sleek,
When I have lain in it a week!
You'll find it well prepared to take
The figure of toupee or snake.
Thus dressed alike from top to toe,
That which is which, 'tis hard to know.
When first in public we appear,
220 I'll lead the van, keep you the rear.
Be careful, as you walk behind,
Use all the talents of your mind.
Be studious well to imitate
My portly motion, mien, and gate.
Mark my address, and learn my style,
When to look scornful, when to smile,

Nor sputter out your oaths so fast,
But keep your swearing to the last.
Then at our leisure we'll be witty,
230   And in the streets divert the city,
The ladies from the windows gaping:
The children all our motions aping.
Your conversation to refine,
I'll take you to some friends of mine;
Choice spirits, who employ their parts,
To mend the world by useful arts.
Some cleansing hollow tubes, to spy
Direct the zenith of the sky;
Some have the city in their care,
240   From noxious steams to purge the air;
Some teach us in these dangerous days,
How to walk upright in our ways;
Some whose reforming hands engage,
To lash the lewdness of the age;
Some for the public service go,
Perpetual envoys to and fro;
Whose able heads support the weight,
Of twenty ministers of state.
We scorn, for want of talk, to jabber
250   Of parties o'er our bonnyclabber.
Nor are we studious to enquire,
Who votes for manners, who for hire.
Our care is to improve the mind,
With what concerns all humankind,
The various scenes of mortal life,
Who beats her husband, who his wife;
Or how the bully at a stroke
Knocked down the boy, the lantern broke;
One tells the rise of cheese, and oatmeal,
260   Another when he got a hot meal;
One gives advice in proverbs old,
Instructs us how to tame a scold;
Or how by almanacs 'tis clear,
That herrings will be cheap this year.

    T.   Dear Mullinix, I now lament
My precious time, so long misspent,
By nature meant for nobler ends,

O, introduce me to your friends!
For whom, by birth, I was designed,
270 Till politics debased my mind.
I give myself entire to you,
God damn the Whigs and Tories too.

Tim and the Fables

My meaning will be best unravelled,
When I premise, that Tim has travelled.

In Lucas's by chance there lay
The *Fables* writ by Mr Gay.
Tim set the volume on a table,
Read over here and there a fable,
And found, as he the pages twirled,
'The monkey, who had seen the world'.
(For Tonson had, to help the sale,
10 Prefixed a cut to every tale.)
The monkey was completely dressed,
The beau in all his airs expressed.
Tim with surprise and pleasure staring,
Ran to the glass, and then comparing
His own sweet figure with the print,
Distinguished every feature in't;
The twist, the squeeze, the rump, the fidge an' all,
Just as they looked in the original.
'By God,' says Tim (and let a fart)
20 'This graver understood his art.
'Tis a true copy, I'll say that for't,
I well remember when I sat for't.
My very face, at first I knew it,
Just in this dress the painter drew it.'
Tim, with his likeness deeply smitten,
Would read what underneath was written,
The merry tale with moral grave.
He now began to storm and rave;
'The cursed villain! now I see
30 This was a libel meant at me;
These scribblers grow so bold of late,
Against us ministers of state!

Such Jacobites as he deserve –
Damme, I say, they ought to starve.'
Dear Tim, no more such angry speeches,
Unbutton and let down your breeches,
Tear out the tale, and wipe your arse,
I know you love to act a farce.

Tom Mullinex and Dick

Tom and Dick had equal fame,
    And both had equal knowledge;
Tom could write and spell his name,
    But Dick had seen a college.

Dick a coxcomb, Tom was mad,
    And both alike diverting,
Tom was held the merrier lad,
    But Dick the best at farting.

Dick would cock his nose in scorn,
10   But Tom was kind and loving;
Tom a footboy bred and born,
    But Dick was from an oven.

Dick could neatly dance a jig,
    But Tom was best at borees;
Tom would pray for every Whig,
    And Dick curse all the Tories.

Dick would make a woeful noise,
    And scold at an election;
Tom huzza'd the blackguard boys,
20   And held them in subjection.

Tom could move with lordly grace,
    Dick nimbly skip the gutter;
Tom could talk with solemn face,
    But Dick could better sputter.

Dick was come to high renown
    Since he commenced physician;
Tom was held by all the town
    The deeper politician.

Tom had the genteeler swing,
30   His hat could nicely put on;
Dick knew better how to swing
    His cane upon a button.

Dick for repartee was fit,
    And Tom for deep discerning;
Dick was thought the brighter wit,
    But Tom had better learning.

Dick with zealous no's and aye's,
    Could roar as loud as Stentor;
In the House 'tis all he says;
40   But Tom is eloquenter.

Dick, a Maggot

As when rooting in a bin,
All powdered o'er from tail to chin;
A lively maggot sallies out,
You know him by his hazel snout:
So, when the grandson of his grandsire,
Forth issues wriggling Dick Drawcansir,
With powdered rump, and back and side,
You cannot blanch his tawny hide;
For 'tis beyond the power of meal,
10   The gypsy visage to conceal:
For, as he shakes his wainscot chops,
Down every mealy atom drops
And leaves the Tartar phiz, in show
Like a fresh turd just dropped on snow.

Clad All in Brown

IMITATED FROM COWLEY

TO DICK

Foulest brute that stinks below,
    Why in this brown dost thou appear?
For, wouldst thou make a fouler show,

Thou must go naked all the year.
Fresh from the mud a wallowing sow
Would then be not so brown as thou.

'Tis not the coat that looks so dun,
  His hide emits a foulness out,
Not one jot better looks the sun
10   Seen from behind a dirty clout:
So turds within a glass enclose,
The glass will seem as brown as those.

Thou now one heap of foulness art,
  All outward and within is foul;
Condenséd filth in every part,
  Thy body's clothéd like thy soul.
Thy soul, which through thy hide of buff,
Scarce glimmers, like a dying snuff.

Old carted bawds such garments wear,
20   When pelted all with dirt they shine;
Such their *exalted* bodies are,
  As shrivelled and as black as thine.
If thou wert in a cart, I fear
Thou wouldst be pelted worse than they're.

Yet when we see thee thus arrayed,
  The neighbours think it is but just
That thou shouldst take an honest trade,
  And weekly carry out our dust.
Of cleanly houses who will doubt,
30 When Dick cries, 'Dust to carry out'?

Dick's Variety

Dull uniformity in fools
I hate, who gape and sneer by rules.
You, Mullinex, and slobbering Carr
Who every day and hour the same are;
That vulgar talent I despise
Of pissing in the rabble's eyes.
And when I listen to the noise,

Of idiots roaring to the boys,
To better judgements still submitting,
10 I own I see but little wit in:
Such pastimes, when our taste is nice,
Can please at most but once or twice.

But then, consider Dick, you'll find
His genius of superior kind;
He never muddles in the dirt,
Nor scours the streets without a shirt;
Though Dick, I dare presume to say,
Could do such feats as well as they.
Dick I could venture everywhere,
20 Let the boys pelt him if they dare;
He'd have them tried at the assizes,
For priests and Jesuits in disguises;
Swear they were with the Swedes at Bender,
And listing troops for the Pretender.

But Dick can fart, and dance and frisk,
No other monkey half so brisk;
Now has the Speaker by the ears,
Next moment in the house of peers,
Now scolding at my Lady Eustace,
30 Or thrashing Babby in her new stays.
Presto, begone! with t'other hop
He's powdering in a barber's shop;
Now at the antechamber thrusting
His nose to get the circle just in,
And damns his blood that in the rear
He sees one single Tory there:
Then, woe be to my Lord Lieutenant,
Again he'll tell him, and again on't.

My Lady's Lamentation
and Complaint against the Dean

Sure never did man see
A wretch like poor Nancy,
So teased day and night

By a dean and a knight;
To punish my sins,
Sir Arthur begins,
And gives me a wipe
With Skinny and Snipe:
His malice is plain,
10 Hallooing the Dean.
The Dean never stops,
When he opens his chops;
I'm quite overrun
With rebus and pun.

Before he came here
To sponge for good cheer,
I sat with delight,
From morning till night,
With two bony thumbs
20 Could rub my own gums,
Or scratching my nose,
And joggling my toes;
But at present, forsooth,
I must not rub a tooth:
When my elbows he sees
Held up by my knees,
My arms, like two props,
Supporting my chops,
And just as I handle 'em
30 Moving all like a pendulum;
He trips up my props,
And down my chin drops,
From my head to my heels,
Like a clock without wheels;
I sink in the spleen,
An useless machine.

If he had his will,
I should never sit still:
He comes with his whims,
40 I must move my limbs;
I cannot be sweet
Without using my feet;
To lengthen my breath

He tires me to death.
By the worst of all squires,
Through bog and through briars,
Where a cow would be startled,
I'm in spite of my heart led:
And, say what I will,
50   Hauled up every hill;
Till, daggled and tattered,
My spirits quite shattered,
I return home at night,
And fast out of spite:
For I'd rather be dead,
Than it e'er should be said
I was better for him
In stomach or limb.

    But, now to my diet,
60   No eating in quiet,
He's still finding fault,
Too sour or too salt:
The wing of a chick
I hardly can pick,
But trash without measure
I swallow with pleasure.

    Next, for his diversion,
He rails at my person:
What court-breeding this is?
70   He takes me to pieces.
From shoulder to flank
I'm lean and am lank;
My nose, long and thin,
Grows down to my chin;
My chin will not stay,
But meets it halfway;
My fingers, prolix,
Are ten crooked sticks:
He swears my elbóws
80   Are two iron crows,
Or sharp pointed rocks,
And wear out my smocks:
To scape them, Sir Arthur

Is forced to lie farther,
Or his sides they would gore
Like the tusks of a boar.

Now, changing the scene,
But still to the Dean;
He loves to be bitter at
90   A lady illiterate;
If he sees her but once,
He'll swear she's a dunce;
Can tell by her looks
A hater of books:
Through each line of her face
Her folly can trace;
Which spoils every feature
Bestowed her by nature,
But sense gives a grace
100   To the homeliest face:
Wise books and reflection
Will mend the complexion.
(A civil divine!
I suppose meaning mine.)
No lady who wants them
Can ever be handsome.

I guess well enough
What he means by this stuff:
He haws and he hums,
110   At last out it comes.

'What, madam? No walking,
No reading, nor talking?
You're now in your prime,
Make use of your time.
Consider, before
You come to threescore,
How the hussies will fleer
Where'er you appear:
That silly old puss
120   Would fain be like us,
What a figure she made
In her tarnished brocade!'

And then he grows mild;
'Come, be a good child:
If you are inclined
To polish your mind,
Be adored by the men
Till threescore and ten,
And kill with the spleen
130   The jades of sixteen,
I'll show you the way:
Read six hours a day.
The wits will frequent ye,
And think you but twenty.'

Thus was I drawn in,
Forgive me my sin.
At breakfast he'll ask
An account of my task.
Put a word out of joint,
140   Or miss but a point,
He rages and frets,
His manners forgets;
And, as I am serious,
Is very imperious.
No book for delight
Must come in my sight;
But, instead of new plays,
Dull Bacon's *Essays*,
And pore every day on
150   That nasty *Pantheon*.
If I be not a drudge,
Let all the world judge.
'Twere better be blind,
Than thus be confined.

But, while in an ill tone,
I murder poor Milton,
The Dean, you will swear,
Is at study or prayer.
He's all the day sauntering,
160   With labourers bantering,
Among his colleagues,

A parcel of Teagues,
(Whom he brings in among us
And bribes with mundungus.)
Hail fellow, well met,
All dirty and wet:
Find out, if you can,
Who's master, who's man;
Who makes the best figure,
170   The Dean or the digger;
And which is the best
At cracking a jest.
How proudly he talks
Of zigzags and walks;
And all the day raves
Of cradles and caves;
And boasts of his feats,
His grottos and seats;
Shows all the gewgaws,
180   And gapes for applause!
A fine occupation
For one of his station!
A hole where a rabbit
Would scorn to inhabit,
Dug out in an hour,
He calls it a bower.

But, oh, how we laugh,
To see a wild calf
Come, driven by heat,
190   And foul the green seat;
Or run helterskelter
To his arbour for shelter,
Where all goes to ruin
The Dean has been doing.
The girls of the village
Come flocking for pillage,
Pull down the fine briars,
And thorns, to make fires;
But yet are so kind
200   To leave something behind:
No more need be said on't,
I smell when I tread on't.

Dear friend, Dr Jenney,
If I could but win ye,
Or Walmsley or Whaley,
To come hither daily,
Since fortune, my foe,
Will needs have it so,
That I'm, by her frowns,
210   Condemned to black gowns;
No squire to be found
The neighbourhood round,
(For, under the rose,
I would rather choose those:)
If your wives will permit ye,
Come here out of pity,
To ease a poor lady,
And beg her a play-day.
So you may be seen
220   No more in the spleen:
May Walmsley give wine,
Like a hearty divine;
May Whaley disgrace
Dull Daniel's whey-face;
And may your three spouses
Let you lie at friends' houses.

On Cutting Down the Old Thorn at Market Hill

At Market Hill, as well appears
   By chronicle of ancient date
There stood for many a hundred years,
   A spacious thorn before the gate.

Hither came every village maid
   And on the boughs her garland hung,
And here, beneath the spreading shade,
   Secure from satyrs sat and sung.

Sir Archibald, that valorous knight,
10   Then lord of all the fruitful plain,
Would come to listen with delight,
   For he was fond of rural strain.

(Sir Archibald whose favourite name
   Shall stand for ages on recórd,
By Scottish bards of highest fame,
   Wise Hawthornden and Stirling's lord.)

But time with iron teeth I ween
   Has cankered all its branches round;
No fruit or blossom to be seen,
20   Its head reclining towards the ground.

This aged, sickly, sapless thorn
   Which must alas no longer stand;
Behold! the cruel Dean in scorn
   Cuts down with sacrilegious hand.

Dame Nature, when she saw the blow,
   Astonished gave a dreadful shriek;
And Mother Tellus trembled so
   She scarce recovered in a week.

The sylvan powers with fear perplexed
30   In prudence and compassion sent
(For none could tell whose turn was next)
   Sad omens of the dire event.

The magpie, lighting on the stock,
   Stood chattering with incessant din;
And with her beak gave many a knock
   To rouse and warn the nymph within.

The owl foresaw in pensive mood
   The ruin of her ancient seat;
And fled in haste with all her brood,
40   To seek a more secure retreat.

Last trotted forth the gentle swine
   To ease her itch against the stump,
And dismally was heard to whine
   All as she scrubbed her measly rump.

The nymph who dwells in every tree,
   (If all be true that poets chant)
Condemned by Fate's supreme decree,
   Must die with her expiring plant.

Thus, when the gentle Spina found
50   The thorn committed to her care,
Receive its last and deadly wound,
      She fled and vanished into air.

But from the root a dismal groan
      First issuing, struck the murderer's ears;
And in a shrill revengeful tone,
      The prophecy he trembling hears.

'Thou chief contriver of my fall,
      Relentless Dean! to mischief born,
My kindred oft thine hide shall gall;
60   Thy gown and cassock oft be torn.

'And thy confederate dame, who brags
      That she condemned me to the fire,
Shall rent her petticoats to rags,
      And wound her legs with every briar.

'Nor thou, Lord Arthur, shalt escape:
      To thee I often called in vain,
Against that assassin in crape,
      Yet thou couldst tamely see me slain.

'Nor, when I felt the dreadful blow,
70   Or chid the Dean, or pinched thy spouse:
Since you could see me treated so,
      An old retainer in your house,

'May that fell Dean, by whose command
      Was formed this Machiavellian plot,
Not leave a thistle on thy land;
      Then who will own thee for a Scot?

'Pigs and fanatics, cows, and Teagues
      Through all thy empire I foresee,
To tear thy hedges join in leagues,
80   Sworn to revenge my thorn and me.

'And thou, the wretch ordained by Fate,
      Neal Gahagan, Hibernian clown,
With hatchet blunter than thy pate
      To hack my hallowed timber down;

'When thou, suspended high in air,
  Diest on a more ignoble tree,
(For thou shalt steal thy landlord's mare)
  Then bloody caitiff think on me.'

An Answer to the Ballyspellin Ballad

Dare you dispute,
You saucy brute,
And think there's no refelling
Your scurvy lays,
And senseless praise
You give to Ballyspellin.

Howe'er you bounce,
I here pronounce
You medicine is repelling,
10 Your water's mud,
And sours the blood
When drunk at Ballyspellin.

Those pocky drabs
To cure their scabs
You thither are compelling,
Will back be sent
Worse than they went
From nasty Ballyspellin.

Llewellyn! why,
20 As well may I
Name honest Doctor Pelling;
So hard sometimes
You tug for rhymes
To bring in Ballyspellin.

No subject fit
To try your wit
When you went colonelling,
But dull intrigues
'Twixt jades and teagues
30 That met at Ballyspellin.

Our lasses fair
Say what you dare,
Who sowens make with shelling;
At Market Hill
More beaux can kill
Than yours at Ballyspellin.

Would I was whipped
When Sheelah stripped
To wash herself our well in;
40 A bum so white
Ne'er came in sight
At paltry Ballyspellin.

Your mawkins there
Smocks hempen wear;
For Holland, not an ell in;
No, not a rag,
Whate'er you brag,
Is found at Ballyspellin.

But Tom will prate
50 At any rate,
All other nymphs expelling;
Because he gets
A few grisettes
At lousy Ballyspellin.

There's bonny Jane
In yonder lane,
Just o'er against the Bell Inn;
Where can you meet
A lass so sweet
60 Round all your Ballyspellin?

We have a girl
Deserves an earl,
She came from Enniskillen;
So fair, so young,
No such among
The belles of Ballyspellin.

How would you stare
To see her there,

The foggy mists dispelling,
70 That cloud the brows
Of every blowze
Who lives at Ballyspellin.

Now, as I live,
I would not give
A stiver or a skilling
To touse and kiss
The fairest miss
That leaks at Ballyspellin.

Whoe'er will raise
80 Such lies as these
Deserves a good cudgelling;
Who falsely boasts
Of belles and toasts
At dirty Ballyspellin.

My rhymes are gone
To all but one,
Which is, our trees are felling;
As proper quite
As those you write
90 To force in Ballyspellin.

The Answer to 'Paulus'

PAULUS, BY MR LINDSAY

A slave to crowds, scorched with the summer's heats,
In court the wretched lawyer toils, and sweats:
While smiling nature, in her best attire,
Doth soothe each sense, and joy and love inspire.
Can he who knows, that real good should please,
Barter for gold his liberty and ease?
Thus Paulus preached: when entering at the door,
Upon his board a client pours the ore:
He grasps the shining gift, pores o'er the cause,
10 Forgets the sun, and dozes on the laws.

THE ANSWER, BY DR SWIFT

Lindsay mistakes the matter quite,
And honest Paulus judges right.
Then, why these quarrels to the sun,
Without whose aid you're all undone?
Did Paulus e'er complain of sweat?
Did Paulus e'er the sun forget?
The influence of whose golden beams
Soon licks up all unsavoury steams;
The sun, you say, his face has kissed:
10   It has; but then it greased his fist.
True lawyers, for the wisest ends,
Have always been Apollo's friends;
Not for his superficial powers
Of ripening fruits, and gilding flowers;
Not for inspiring poets' brains
With pennyless and starveling strains;
Not for his boasted healing art;
Not for his skill to shoot the dart;
Nor yet, because he sweetly fiddles;
20   Nor for his prophecies in riddles:
But for a more substantial cause:
Apollo's patron of the laws;
Whom Paulus ever must adore,
As parent of the golden ore,
By Phoebus (an incestuous birth)
Begot upon his grandam Earth;
By Phoebus first produced to light:
By Vulcan formed so round and bright:
Then offered at the throne of justice,
30   By clients to her priests and trustees.
Nor when we see Astraea stand
With equal balance in her hand,
Must we suppose she has in view,
How to give every man his due:
Her scales you only see her hold
To weigh her priests', the lawyers', gold.
Now, should I own your case was grievous,
Poor sweaty Paulus, who'd believe us?

'Tis very true, and none denies,
40 At least, that such complaints are wise:
'Tis wise, no doubt, as clients fat ye more,
To cry, like statesmen, *quanta patimur!*
But, since the truth must needs be stretched
To prove, that lawyers are so wretched;
This paradox I'll undertake
For Paulus' and for Lindsay's sake
By topics, which though I abomine 'em,
May serve, as arguments *ad hominem.*
Yet I disdain to offer those,
50 Made use of by detracting foes.

I own, the curses of mankind
Sit light upon a lawyer's mind:
The clamours of ten thousand tongues
Break not his rest, nor hurt his lungs:
I own his conscience always free,
(Provided he has got a fee.)
Secure of constant peace within,
He knows no guilt, who knows no sin.

Yet well they merit to be pitied,
60 By clients always overwitted.
And, though the gospel seems to say,
What heavy burdens lawyers lay
Upon the shoulders of their neighbour,
Nor lend a finger to the labour,
Always for saving their own bacon:
No doubt the text is here mistaken:
The copy's false, and sense is racked:
To prove it I appeal to fact;
And thus by demonstration show,
70 What burdens lawyers undergo.

With early clients at his door,
Though he were drunk the night before,
And crop-sick with unclubbed-for wine,
The wretch must be at court by nine:
Half sunk beneath his brief and bag,
As ridden by a midnight hag:
Then, from the bar, harangues the bench

In English vile, and viler French,
And Latin, vilest of the three:
80   And all for ten poor moidores' fee!
Of paper how he is profuse,
With periods long, in terms abstruse!
What pains he takes to be prolix!
A thousand words to stand for six!
Of common sense without a word in!
And is this not a grievous burden?

The lawyer is a common drudge,
To fight our cause before the judge:
And, what is yet a greater curse,
90   Condemned to bear his client's purse;
While he, at ease, secure and light,
Walks boldly home at dead of night;
When term is ended, leaves the town,
Trots to his country mansion down;
And, disencumbered of his load,
No danger dreads upon the road;
Despises rapparees, and rides
Safe through the Newry mountain sides.

Lindsay, 'tis you have set me on
100   To state the question *pro* and *con*:
My satire may offend, 'tis true:
However, it concerns not you.
I own, there may in every clan
Perhaps be found one honest man:
Yet link them close; in this they jump,
To be but rascals in the lump.
Imagine Lindsay at the bar:
He's just the same, his brethren are;
Well taught by practice to imbibe
110   The fundamentals of his tribe;
And, in his client's just defence,
Must deviate oft from common sense,
And make his ignorance discerned,
To get the name of council learned;
(As *lucus* comes *a non lucendo*)
And wisely do as other men do.
But, shift him to a better scene,

Got from his crew of rogues in grain;
Surrounded with companions fit
120 To taste his humour, and his wit;
You'd swear, he never took a fee,
Nor knew in law his A B C.

'Tis hard, where dullness overrules,
To keep good sense in crowds of fools;
And we admire the man, who saves
His honesty in crowds of knaves;
Nor yields up virtue, at discretion,
To villains of his own profession.
Lindsay, you know, what pains you take
130 In both, yet hardly save your stake.
And will you venture both anew?
To sit among that scoundrel crew,
That pack of mimic legislators,
Abandoned, stupid, slavish praters!
For, as the rabble daub, and rifle
The fool, who scrambles for a trifle;
Who for his pains is cuffed, and kicked,
Drawn through the dirt, his pockets picked;
You must expect the like disgrace,
140 Scrambling with rogues to get a place:
Must lose the honour, you have gained,
Your numerous virtues foully stained;
Disclaim forever all pretence
To common honesty and sense;
And join in friendship, with a strict tie,
To Marshall, Conolly, and Dick Tighe.

Lady Acheson Weary of the Dean

The Dean would visit Market Hill,
    Our invitation was but slight;
I said, 'Why let him, if he will,'
    And so I bid Sir Arthur write.

His manners would not let him wait,
    Lest we should think ourselves neglected,
And so we saw him at our gate
    Three days before he was expected.

After a week, a month, a quarter,
10   And day succeeding after day,
Says not a word of his departure,
    Though not a soul would have him stay.

I've said enough to make him blush,
    Methinks, or else the devil's in't,
But he cares not for it a rush,
    Nor for my life will take the hint.

But you, my life, may let him know,
    In civil language, if he stays,
How deep and foul the roads may grow,
20   And that he may command the chaise.

Or you may say, 'My wife intends,
    Though I should be exceeding proud,
This winter to invite some friends,
    And, sir, I know you hate a crowd.'

Or, 'Mr Dean, I should with joy
    Beg you would here continue still,
But we must go to Aghnacloy,
    Or Mr Moore will take it ill.'

The house accounts are daily rising,
30   So much his stay does swell the bills;
My dearest life, it is surprising
    How much he eats, how much he swills.

His brace of puppies how they stuff,
    And they must have three meals a day,
Yet never think they get enough;
    His horses too eat all our hay.

Oh! if I could, how I would maul
    His tallow face and wainscot paws,
His beetle brows and eyes of wall,
40   And make him soon give up the cause.

Must I be every moment chid
    With skinny, boney, snip and lean,
Oh! that I could but once be rid
    Of that insulting tyrant Dean.

On a Very Old Glass

The following lines were written upon a very old glass
of Sir Arthur Acheson's:

> Frail glass, thou mortal art, as well as I,
> Though none can tell, which of us first shall die.

Answered extempore by Dr Swift:

> We both are mortal; but thou, frailer creature,
> Mayst die like me by chance; but not by nature.

To Janus

ON NEW YEAR'S DAY

Two-faced Janus, god of Time,
Be my Phoebus while I rhyme.
To oblige your crony Swift,
Bring our dame a New Year's gift:
She has got but half a face;
Janus, since thou hast a brace,
To my Lady once be kind;
Give her half thy face behind.

 God of Time, if you be wise,
Look not with your future eyes:
What imports thy forward sight?
Well, if you could lose it quite.
Can you take delight in viewing
This poor isle's approaching ruin?
When thy retrospection vast
Sees the glorious ages past.

 Happy nation were we blind,
Or, had only eyes behind. –

 'Drown your morals,' Madam cries;
'I'll have none but forward eyes:
Prudes decayed about may tack,
Strain their necks with looking back:
Give me Time when coming on:

Who regards him when he's gone?
By the Dean though gravely told,
New Years help to make me old;
Yet I find, a New Year's lace
Burnishes an old year's face.
Give me velvet and quadrille,
30 I'll have youth and beauty still.'

The Journal of a Modern Lady

It was a most unfriendly part
In you, who ought to know my heart,
Are well acquainted with my zeal
For all the female commonweal:
How could it come into your mind,
To pitch on me, of all mankind,
Against the sex to write a satire,
And brand me for a woman-hater?
On me, who think them all so fair,
10 They rival Venus to a hair;
Their virtues never ceased to sing,
Since first I learnt to tune a string.
Methinks I hear the ladies cry,
Will he his character belie?
Must never our misfortunes end?
And have we lost our only friend?
Ah lovely nymphs, remove your fears,
No more let fall those precious tears.
Sooner shall . . .&c.

[*Here several verses are omitted.*]

20 The hound be hunted by the hare,
Than I turn rebel to the fair.

'Twas you engaged me first to write,
Then gave the subject out of spite:
The 'Journal of a Modern Dame'
Is by my promise what you claim:
My word is passed, I must submit;
And yet perhaps you may be bit.
I but transcribe, for not a line
Of all the satire shall be mine.

30 Compelled by you to tag in rhymes
The common slanders of the times,
Of modern times; the guilt is yours,
And me my innocence secures.

Unwilling muse begin thy lay,
The annals of a female day.

By nature turned to play the Rakewell,
(As we shall show you in the sequel)
The modern dame is waked by noon,
Some authors say, not quite so soon;
40 Because, though sore against her will,
She sat all night up at quadrille.
She stretches, gapes, unglues her eyes,
And asks if it be time to rise;
Of headache, and the spleen complains;
And then to cool her heated brains,
(Her nightgown and her slippers brought her,)
Takes a large dram of citron-water.
Then to her glass; and 'Betty, pray
Don't I look frightfully today?
50 But was it not confounded hard?
Well, if I ever touch a card:
Four matadors, and lose codille!
Depend upon't, I never will.
But run to Tom, and bid him fix
The ladies here tonight by six.'
'Madam, the goldsmith waits below,
He says, his business is to know
If you'll redeem the silver cup
He keeps in pawn?' – 'Why, show him up.'
60 'Your dressing-plate, he'll be content
To take, for interest *cent percent*.
And, Madam, there's my Lady Spade
Hath sent this letter by her maid.'
'Well, I remember when she won;
And hath she sent so soon to dun?
Here, carry down those ten pistoles
My husband left to pay the coals:
I thank my stars they all are light;
And I may have revenge tonight.'

70   Now, loitering o'er her tea and cream,
    She enters on her usual theme;
    Her last night's ill success repeats,
    Calls Lady Spade a hundred cheats:
    She slipped Spadillo in her breast,
    Then thought to turn it to a jest.
    There's Mrs Cut and she combine,
    And to each other give the sign.
    Through every game pursues her tale,
    Like hunters o'er their evening ale.

80   Now to another scene give place,
    Enter the folks with silks and lace:
    Fresh matter for a world of chat,
    Right Indian this, right Mechlin that.
    'Observe this pattern; there's a stuff!
    I can have customers enough.
    Dear madam, you are grown so hard,
    This lace is worth twelve pounds a yard:
    Madam, if there be truth in man,
    I never sold so cheap a fan.'

90   This business of importance o'er,
    And madam almost dressed by four;
    The footman, in his usual phrase,
    Comes up with, 'Madam, dinner stays';
    She answers in her usual style,
    'The cook must keep it back awhile;
    I never can have time to dress,
    No woman breathing takes up less;
    I'm hurried so, it makes me sick,
    I wish the dinner at Old Nick.'

100 At table now she acts her part,
    Has all the dinner-cant by heart:
    'I thought we were to dine alone,
    My dear, for sure if I had known
    This company would come today –
    But really 'tis my spouse's way;
    He's so unkind, he never sends
    To tell, when he invites his friends:
    I wish you may but have enough.'
    And while with all this paltry stuff,

110 She sits tormenting every guest,
Nor gives her tongue one moment's rest,
In phrases battered, stale, and trite,
Which *modern* ladies call polite;
You see the booby husband sit
In admiration at her wit!

But let me now awhile survey
Our madam o'er her evening tea;
Surrounded with her noisy clans
Of prudes, coquettes, and harridans;
120 When frighted at the clamorous crew,
Away the god of Silence flew,
And fair Discretion left the place,
And Modesty with blushing face:
Now enters overweening Pride,
And Scandal ever gaping wide,
Hypocrisy with frown severe,
Scurrility with gibing air;
Rude Laughter seeming like to burst;
And Malice always judging worst;
130 And Vanity with pocket-glass;
And Impudence with front of brass;
And studied Affectation came,
Each limb, and feature out of frame;
While Ignorance with brain of lead,
Flew hovering o'er each female head.

Why should I ask of thee, my muse,
An hundred tongues, as poets use,
When, to give every dame her due,
An hundred thousand were too few!
140 Or how should I, alas! relate,
The sum of all their senseless prate,
Their innuendos, hints, and slanders,
Their meanings lewd, and *double entendres*.
Now comes the general scandal-charge,
What some invent, the rest enlarge;
And, 'Madam, if it be a lie,
You have the tale as cheap as I:
I must conceal my author's name,
But now 'tis known to common fame.'

150 Say, foolish females, bold and blind,
  Say, by what fatal turn of mind,
  Are you on vices most severe
  Wherein yourselves have greatest share?
  Thus every fool herself deludes;
  The prude condemns the absent prudes;
  Mopsa, who stinks her spouse to death,
  Accuses Chloe's tainted breath;
  Hircina rank with sweat, presumes
  To censure Phyllis for perfumes;
160 While crooked Cynthia sneering says,
  That Florimel wears iron stays:
  Chloe of every coxcomb jealous,
  Admires how girls can talk with fellows,
  And full of indignation frets
  That women could be such coquettes:
  Iris, for scandal most notorious,
  Cries, 'Lord, the world is so censorious!'
  And Rufa with her combs of lead,
  Whispers that Sappho's hair is red:
170 Aura, whose tongue you hear a mile hence,
  Talks half a day in praise of silence;
  And Sylvia full of inward guilt,
  Calls Amoret an arrant jilt.

  Now voices over voices rise,
  While each to be the loudest vies;
  They contradict, affirm, dispute,
  No single tongue one moment mute;
  All mad to speak, and none to hearken,
  They set the very lap-dog barking;
180 Their chattering makes a louder din
  Than fishwives o'er a cup of gin:
  Not schoolboys at a barring-out,
  Raised ever such incessant rout:
  The jumbling particles of matter
  In chaos made not such a clatter:
  Far less the rabble roar and rail,
  When drunk with sour election ale.

  Nor do they trust their tongue alone,
  But speak a language of their own;

190   Can read a nod, a shrug, a look,
    Far better than a printed book;
    Convey a libel in a frown,
    And wink a reputation down;
    Or by the tossing of the fan,
    Describe the lady and the man.

    But see, the female club disbands,
    Each twenty visits on her hands.
    Now all alone poor madam sits,
    In vapours and hysteric fits:
200   'And was not Tom this morning sent?
    I'll lay my life he never went:
    Past six, and not a living soul!
    I might by this have won a vole.'
    A dreadful interval of spleen!
    How shall we pass the time between?
    'Here Betty, let me take my drops,
    And feel my pulse, I know it stops:
    This head of mine, Lord, how it swims!
    And such a pain in all my limbs!'
210   'Dear madam, try to take a nap –'
    But now they hear the footman's rap:
    'Go run, and light the ladies up:
    It must be one before we sup.'

    The table, cards and counters set,
    And all the gamester ladies met,
    Her spleen and fits recovered quite,
    Our madam can sit up all night;
    'Whoever comes I'm not within –
    Quadrille's the word, and so begin.'

220   How can the muse her aid impart,
    Unskilled in all the terms of art?
    Or in harmonious numbers put
    The deal, the shuffle, and the cut?
    The superstitious whims relate,
    That fill a female gamester's pate?
    What agony of soul she feels
    To see a knave's inverted heels:
    She draws up card by card, to find

Good fortune peeping from behind;
230 With panting heart, and earnest eyes,
In hope to see Spadillo rise;
In vain, alas! her hope is fed;
She draws an ace, and sees it red.
In ready counters never pays,
But pawns her snuff-box, rings, and keys.
Ever with some new fancy struck,
Tries twenty charms to mend her luck.
'This morning when the parson came,
I said I should not win a game.
240 This odious chair how came I stuck in't,
I think I never had good luck in't.
I'm so uneasy in my stays;
Your fan, a moment, if you please.
Stand further, girl, or get you gone,
I always lose when you look on.'
'Lord, madam, you have lost codille,
I never saw you play so ill.'
'Nay, madam, give me leave to say,
'Twas you that threw the game away;
250 When Lady Tricksy played a four,
You took it with a matador;
I saw you touch your wedding-ring
Before my Lady called a king.
You spoke a word began with H,
And I know whom you meant to teach,
Because you held the king of hearts:
Fie, madam, leave these little arts.'
'That's not so bad as one that rubs
Her chair to call the king of clubs,
260 And makes her partner understand
A matador is in her hand.'
'Madam, you have no cause to flounce,
I swear I saw you thrice renounce.'
'And truly, Madam, I know when
Instead of five you scored me ten.
Spadillo here has got a mark,
A child may know it in the dark:
I guess the hand, it seldom fails,
I wish some folk would pare their nails.'

270   While thus they rail, and scold, and storm,
It passes but for common form;
And conscious that they all speak true,
They give each other but their due;
It never interrupts the game,
Or makes 'em sensible of shame.

The time too precious now to waste,
And supper gobbled up in haste,
Again afresh to cards they run,
As if they had but just begun.
280 But I shall not again repeat
How oft they squabble, snarl and cheat.
At last they hear the watchman knock,
'A frosty morn – past four o'clock.'
The chairmen are not to be found,
'Come, let us play another round.'

Now, all in haste they huddle on
Their hoods and cloaks, and get them gone:
But first, the winner must invite
The company tomorrow night.

290   Unlucky madam, left in tears,
(Who now again quadrille forswears,)
With empty purse, and aching head,
Steals to her sleeping spouse to bed.

On Paddy's Character of 'The Intelligencer'

As a thorn-bush, or oaken bough,
Stuck in an Irish cabin's brow,
Above the door, at country fair,
Betokens entertainment there,
So, bays on poet's brows have been
Set, for a sign of wit within.
And as ill neighbours in the night,
Pull down an alehouse bush, for spite,
The laurel so, by poets worn,
10 Is by the teeth of envy torn,
Envy, a canker-worm which tears

Those sacred leaves that lightning spares.
And now t' exemplify this moral,
Tom having earned a twig of laurel,
(Which measured on his head, was found
Not long enough to reach half round,
But like a girl's cockade, was tied
A trophy, on his temple side)
Paddy repined to see him wear
20 This badge of honour in his hair,
And thinking this cockade of wit
Would his own temples better fit,
Forming his muse by Smedley's model,
Lets drive at Tom's devoted noddle,
Pelts him by turns with verse and prose,
Hums, like a hornet at his nose;
At length presumes to vent his satire on
The Dean, Tom's honoured friend and patron.
The eagle in the tale, ye know,
30 Teased by a buzzing wasp, below,
Took wing to Jove, and hoped to rest
Securely, in the Thunderer's breast;
In vain; even there to spoil his nod
The spiteful insect stung the god.

Dean Smedley Gone to Seek His Fortune

Per varios casus, per tot discrimina rerum
Virgil, *Aeneid* I, 204

The very reverend Dean Smedley,
Of dullness, pride, conceit, a medley,
Was equally allowed to shine,
As poet, scholar and divine.
With godliness could well dispense,
Would be a rake, but wanted sense.
Would strictly after truth inquire
Because he dreaded to come nigher.
For liberty no champion bolder,
10 He hated bailiffs at his shoulder.
To half the world a standing jest,

A perfect nuisance to the rest.
From many (and we may believe him)
Had the best wishes they could give him.
To all mankind a constant friend,
Provided they had cash to lend.
One thing he did before he went hence,
He left us a laconic sentence,
By cutting of his phrase, and trimming,
20   To prove that bishops were old women.
Poor Envy durst not show her phiz,
She was so terrified at his.
He waded without any shame,
Through thick and thin, to get a name.
Tried every sharping trick for bread,
And after all he seldom sped.
When fortune favoured, he was nice,
He never once would cog the dice,
But if she turned against his play,
30   He knew to stop *à quatre trois*.
Now sound in mind, and sound in corpus,
(Says he) though swelled like any porpoise,
He hies from hence at forty-four,
(But by his leave he sinks a score,)
To the East Indies, there to cheat,
Till he can purchase an estate;
Where after he has filled his chest,
He'll mount his tub, and preach his best,
And plainly prove by dint of text,
40   This world is his, and theirs the next.

Lest that the reader should not know,
The bank where last he set his toe,
'Twas Greenwich. There he took a ship,
And gave his creditors the slip.
But lest chronology should vary,
Upon the ides of February,
In seventeen hundred eight and twenty,
To Fort St George a pedlar went he.
Ye fates, when all he gets is spent,
50   Return him beggar as he went.

Verses Occasioned by the Sudden Drying Up of St Patrick's Well near Trinity College, Dublin

By holy zeal inspired, and led by fame,
To thee, once favourite isle, with joy I came;
What time the Goth, the Vandal, and the Hun,
Had my own native Italy o'errun.
Ierne, to the world's remotest parts,
Renowned for valour, policy and arts.

    Hither from Colchus, with the fleecy ore,
Jason arrived two thousand years before.
Thee, happy island, Pallas called her own,
10 When haughty Britain was a land unknown.
From thee, with pride, the Caledonians trace
The glorious founder of their kingly race:
Thy martial sons, whom now they dare despise,
Did once their land subdue and civilize:
Their dress, their language, and the Scottish name,
Confess the soil from whence the victors came.
Well may they boast that ancient blood, which runs
Within their veins, who are thy younger sons,
A conquest and a colony from thee,
20 The mother-kingdom left her children free;
From thee no mark of slavery they felt,
Not so with thee thy base invaders dealt;
Invited here to vengeful Morough's aid,
Those whom they could not conquer, they betrayed.
Britain, by thee we fell, ungrateful isle!
Not by thy valour, but superior guile:
Britain, with shame confess, this land of mine
First taught thee human knowledge and divine;
My prelates and my students, sent from hence,
30 Made your sons converts both to God and sense:
Not like the pastors of thy ravenous breed,
Who come to fleece the flocks, and not to feed.

    Wretched Ierne! with what grief I see
The fatal changes time hath made in thee.
The Christian rites I introduced in vain:
Lo! Infidelity returned again.

Freedom and Virtue in thy sons I found,
Who now in Vice and Slavery are drowned.

By faith and prayer, this crozier in my hand,
40 I drove the venomed serpent from thy land;
The shepherd in his bower might sleep or sing,
Nor dread the adder's tooth, nor scorpion's sting.

With omens oft I strove to warn thy swains,
Omens, the types of thy impending chains.
I sent the magpie from the British soil,
With restless beak thy blooming fruit to spoil,
To din thine ears with unharmonious clack,
And haunt thy holy walls in white and black.
What else are those thou seest in bishop's gear
50 Who crop the nurseries of learning here?
Aspiring, greedy, full of senseless prate,
Devour the church, and chatter to the state.

As you grew more degenerate and base,
I sent you millions of the croaking race;
Emblems of insects vile, who spread their spawn
Through all thy land, in armour, fur and lawn.
A nauseous brood, that fills your senate walls,
And in the chambers of your Viceroy crawls.

See, where the new-devouring vermin runs,
60 Sent in my anger from the land of Huns;
With harpy claws it undermines the ground,
And sudden spreads a numerous offspring round;
The amphibious tyrant, with his ravenous band,
Drains all thy lakes of fish, of fruits thy land.

Where is the sacred well, that bore my name?
Fled to the fountain back, from whence it came!
Fair Freedom's emblem once, which smoothly flows,
And blessings equally on all bestows.
Here, from the neighbouring nursery of arts,
70 The students drinking, raised their wit and parts;
Here, for an age and more, improved their vein,
Their Phoebus I, my spring their Hippocrene.
Discouraged youths, now all their hopes must fail,
Condemned to country cottages and ale;

To foreign prelates make a slavish court,
And by their sweat procure a mean support;
Or, for the classics read the attorney's guide;
Collect excise, or wait upon the tide.

O! had I been apostle to the Swiss,
80 Or hardy Scot, or any land but this;
Combined in arms, they had their foes defied,
And kept their liberty, or bravely died.
Thou still with tyrants in succession cursed,
The last invaders trampling on the first:
Nor fondly hope for some reverse of fate,
Virtue herself would now return too late.
Not half thy course of misery is run,
Thy greatest evils yet are scarce begun.
Soon shall thy sons, the time is just at hand,
90 Be all made captives in their native land;
When, for the use of no Hibernian born,
Shall rise one blade of grass, one ear of corn;
When shells and leather shall for money pass,
Nor thy oppressing lords afford thee brass.
But all turn leasers to that mongrel breed,
Who from thee sprung, yet on thy vitals feed;
Who to yon ravenous isle thy treasures bear,
And waste in luxury thy harvests there;
For pride and ignorance a proverb grown,
100 The jest of wits, and to the courts unknown.

I scorn thy spurious and degenerate line,
And from this hour my patronage resign.

To Dean Swift

BY SIR ARTHUR ACHESON

Good cause have I to sing and vapour,
For I am landlord to the Drapier:
He, that of every ear's the charmer,
Now condescends to be my farmer,
And grace my villa with his strains;
Lives such a bard on British plains?

No; not in all the British court;
For none but witlings there resort,
Whose names and works (though dead) are made
10   Immortal by the *Dunciad*;
And sure, as monument of brass,
Their fame to future times shall pass,
How, with a weakly warbling tongue,
Of brazen knight they vainly sung:
A subject for their genius fit;
He dares defy both sense and wit.
What dares he not? He can, we know it,
A laureate make that is no poet;
A judge, without the least pretence
20   To common law, or common sense;
A bishop that is no divine;
And coxcombs in red ribbons shine:
Nay, he can make what's greater far,
A middle state 'twixt peace and war;
And say, there shall, for years together,
Be peace and war, and both, and neither.
Happy, O Market Hill! at least,
That court and courtiers have no taste:
You never else had known the Dean,
30   But, as of old, obscurely lain;
All things gone on the same dull track,
And Drapier's Hill been still Drumlack:
But now your name with Penshurst vies,
And winged with fame shall reach the skies.

Drapier's Hill

We give the world to understand,
Our thriving Dean has purchased land;
A purchase which will bring him clear,
Above his rent four pounds a year;
Provided, to improve the ground,
He will but add two hundred pound,
And from his endless hoarded store,
To build a house five hundred more.
Sir Arthur too shall have his will,
10   And call the mansion Drapier's Hill;

That when the nation long enslaved,
Forgets by whom it once was saved;
When none the Drapier's praise shall sing;
His signs aloft no longer swing;
His medals and his prints forgotten,
And all his handkerchiefs are rotten;
His famous *Letters* made waste paper;
This hill may keep the name of Drapier:
In spite of envy flourish still,
20 And Drapier's vie with Cooper's Hill.

Robin and Harry

Robin, to beggars, with a curse
Throws the last shilling in his purse,
And when the coachman comes for pay,
The rogue must call another day.

Grave Harry, when the poor are pressing
Gives them a penny, and God's blessing;
But, always careful of the main,
With twopence left, walks home in rain.

Robin from noon to night will prate,
10 Runs out in tongue, as in estate;
And e'er a twelvemonth and a day
Will not have one new thing to say.
Much talking is not Harry's vice,
He need not tell a story twice,
And, if he always be so thrifty,
His fund may last to five and fifty.

It so fell out, that cautious Harry
As soldiers use, for love must marry,
And with his dame the ocean crossed,
20 All for love, or the world well lost.
Repairs a cabin gone to ruin,
Just big enough to shelter two in;
And, in his house, if anybody come,
Will make them welcome to his modicum:
Where goody Julia milks the cows,
And boils potatoes for her spouse,

Or darns his hose, or mends his breeches,
While Harry's fencing up his ditches.

Robin, who ne'er his mind could fix
30   To live without a coach and six,
To patch his broken fortunes, found
A mistress worth five thousand pound;
Swears, he could get her in an hour
If Gaffer Harry would endow her;
And sell, to pacify his wrath,
A birthright for a mess of broth.

Young Harry, as all Europe knows,
Was long the quintessence of beaux;
But, when espoused, he ran the fate
40   That must attend the married state;
From gold brocade, and shining armour,
Was metamorphosed to a farmer;
His grazier's coat with dirt besmeared,
Nor, twice a week will shave his beard.

Old Robin, all his youth a sloven,
At fifty-two, when he grew loving,
Clad in a coat of paduasoy,
A flaxen wig, and waistcoat gay,
Powdered from shoulder down to flank,
50   In courtly style addresses Frank;
Twice ten years older than his wife,
Is doomed to be a beau for life;
Supplying those defects by dress
Which I must leave the world to guess.

The Grand Question Debated

WHETHER HAMILTON'S BAWN SHOULD BE TURNED
INTO A BARRACKS OR A MALTHOUSE

PREFACE

The author of the following poem, is said to be Dr J.S.D.S.P.D.
who writ it, as well as several other copies of verses of the

like kind, by way of amusement, in the family of an honourable
gentleman in the North of Ireland, where he spent a summer
about two or three years ago.

A certain very great person, then in that kingdom, having
heard much of this poem, obtained a copy from the gentleman,
or, as some say, the lady, in whose house it was written, from
whence, I know not by what accident, several other copies were
transcribed, full of errors. As I have a great respect for the
supposed author, I have procured a true copy of the poem, the
publication whereof can do him less injury than printing any
of those incorrect ones which run about in manuscript, and would
infallibly be soon in the press, if not thus prevented.

Some expressions being peculiar to Ireland, I have prevailed
on a gentleman of that kingdom to explain them, and I have put
the several explanations in their proper places.

Thus spoke to my Lady, the knight full of care;
'Let me have your advice in a weighty affair.
This Hamilton's Bawn, while it sticks on my hand,
I lose by the house what I get by the land;
But how to dispose of it to the best bidder,
For a barrack or malthouse, we must now consider.

'First, let me suppose I make it a malthouse:
Here I have computed the profit will fall t'us.
There's nine hundred pounds for labour and grain,
10 I increase it to twelve, so three hundred remain:
A handsome addition for wine and good cheer,
Three dishes a day, and three hogsheads a year.
With a dozen large vessels my vault shall be stored,
No little scrub joint shall come on my board:
And you and the Dean no more shall combine,
To stint me at night to one bottle of wine;
Nor shall I for his humour, permit you to purloin
A stone and a quarter of beef from my sirloin.
If I make it a barrack, the crown is my tenant.
20 My dear, I have pondered again and again on't:
In poundage and drawbacks, I lose half my rent,
Whatever they give me I must be content,
Or join with the court in every debate,
And rather than that, I would lose my estate.'

Thus ended the knight: thus began his meek wife:
'It *must*, and it *shall* be a barrack, my life.
I'm grown a mere Mopus; no company comes;
But a rabble of tenants, and rusty dull rums;
With parsons, what lady can keep herself clean?
30 I'm all over daubed when I sit by the Dean.
But, if you will give us a barrack, my dear,
The Captain, I'm sure, will always come here;
I then shall not value his Deanship a straw,
For the Captain, I warrant, will keep him in awe;
Or should he pretend to be brisk and alert,
Will tell him that chaplains should not be so pert;
That men of his coat should be minding their prayers,
And not among ladies to give themselves airs.'

Thus argued my Lady, but argued in vain;
40 The knight his opinion resolved to maintain.

But Hannah, who listened to all that was passed,
And could not endure so vulgar a taste,
As soon as her Ladyship called to be dressed,
Cried, 'Madam, why surely my master's possessed;
Sir Arthur the malster! how fine will it sound?
I'd rather the Bawn were sunk underground.
But madam, I guessed there would never come good,
When I saw him so often with Darby and Wood.
And now my dream's out; for I was a-dreamed
50 That I saw a huge rat: O dear, how I screamed!
And after, methought, I had lost my new shoes;
And, Molly, she said, I should hear some ill news.

'Dear madam, had you but the spirit to tease,
You might have a barrack whenever you please:
And, madam, I always believed you so stout,
That for twenty denials you would not give out.
If I had a husband like him, I purtest,
Till he gave me my will, I would give him no rest:
And rather than come in the same pair of sheets
60 With such a cross man, I would lie in the streets.
But, madam, I beg you contrive and invent,
And worry him out, till he gives his consent.

'Dear madam, whene'er of a barrack I think,
An I were to be hanged, I can't sleep a wink:
For, if a new crotchet comes into my brain,
I can't get it out, though I'd never so fain.
I fancy already a barrack contrived
At Hamilton's Bawn, and the troop is arrived.
Of this, to be sure, Sir Arthur has warning,
70 And waits on the Captain betimes the next morning.

'Now, see when they meet, how their honours behave;
"Noble Captain, your servant" – "Sir Arthur, your slave";
"You honour me much" – "The honour is mine" –
"'Twas a sad rainy night" – "But the morning is fine" –
"Pray, how does my Lady?" – "My wife's at your service."
"I think I have seen her picture by Jervas."
"Good morrow, good Captain" – "I'll wait on you down" –
"You shan't stir a foot" – "You'll think me a clown" –
"For all the world, Captain, not half an inch farther" –
80 "You must be obeyed – your servant, Sir Arthur;
My humble respects to my Lady unknown" –
"I hope you will use my house as your own."'

'Go, bring me my smock, and leave off your prate,
Thou hast certainly gotten a cup in thy pate.'
'Pray, madam, be quiet; what was it I said?
You had like to have put it quite out of my head.

'Next day, to be sure, the Captain will come,
At the head of his troop, with trumpet and drum:
Now, madam, observe, how he marches in state:
90 The man with the kettle-drum enters the gate;
Dub, dub, adub, dub. The trumpeters follow,
Tantara, tantara, while all the boys holler.
See, now comes the Captain all daubed in gold lace:
O lor'! the sweet gentleman! look in his face;
And see how he rides like a lord of the land,
With the fine flaming sword that he holds in his hand;
And his horse, the dear *creter*, it prances and rears,
With ribbons in knots, at its tail and its ears:
At last comes the troop, by the word of command
100 Drawn up in our court; when the Captain cries, "Stand."

Your Ladyship lifts up the sash to be seen,
(For sure, I had dizened you out like a Queen;)
The Captain, to show he is proud of the favour,
Looks up to your window, and cocks up his beaver.
(His beaver is cocked; pray, madam, mark that,
For, a Captain of Horse never takes off his hat;
Because he has never a hand that is idle;
For, the right holds the sword, and the left holds the bridle,)
Then flourishes thrice his sword in the air,
110   As a compliment due to a lady so fair;
How I tremble to think of the blood it hath spilt!
Then he lowers down the point, and kisses the hilt.
Your Ladyship smiles, and thus you begin;
"Pray, Captain, be pleased to light, and walk in:"
The Captain salutes you with congee profound;
And your Ladyship curchies half way to the ground.

   '"Kit, run to your master, and bid him come to us.
I'm sure he'll be proud of the honour you do us;
And, Captain, you'll do us the favour to stay,
120   And take a short dinner here with us today:
You're heartily welcome: but as for good cheer,
You come in the very worst time of the year;
If I had expected so worthy a guest –"
"Lord! madam! your Ladyship sure is in jest;
You banter me, madam, the kingdom must grant –"
"You officers, Captain, are so complaisant."'

   'Hist, huzzy, I think I hear somebody coming –'
'No, madam; 'tis only Sir Arthur a-humming.

   'To shorten my tale, (for I hate a long story,)
130   The Captain at dinner appears in his glory;
The Dean and the Doctor have humbled their pride,
For the Captain's entreated to sit by your side;
And, because he's their betters, you carve for him first,
The parsons, for envy, are ready to burst:
The servants amazed, are scarce ever able,
To keep off their eyes, as they wait at the table;
And, Molly and I have thrust in our nose,
To peep at the Captain, in all his fine clothes:
Dear madam, be sure he's a fine-spoken man,
140   Do but hear on the clergy how glib his tongue ran;

"And madam," says he, "if such dinners you give,
You'll never want parsons as long as you live;
I ne'er knew a parson without a good nose,
But the devil's as welcome wherever he goes:
God damn me, they bid us reform and repent,
But, zounds, by their looks, they never keep Lent:
Mister Curate, for all your grave looks, I'm afraid,
You cast a sheep's eye on her ladyship's maid;
I wish she would lend you her pretty white hand,
150   In mending your cassock, and smoothing your band:"
(For the Dean was so shabby and looked like a ninny,
That the Captain supposed he was curate to Jenny.)
"Whenever you see a cassock and gown,
A hundred to one, but it covers a clown;
Observe how a parson comes into a room,
God damn me, he hobbles as bad as my groom;
A *scholard*, when just from his college broke loose,
Can hardly tell how to cry boo to a goose;
Your Noveds, and Blutraks, and Omurs and stuff,
160   By God they don't signify this pinch of snuff.
To give a young gentleman right education,
The army's the only good school in this nation;
My schoolmaster called me a dunce and a fool,
But at cuffs I was always the cock of the school;
I never could take to my book for the blood o' me,
And the puppy confessed, he expected no good o' me.
He caught me one morning coquetting his wife,
But he mauled me, I ne'er was so mauled in my life;
So I took to the road, and what's very odd,
170   The first man I robbed was a parson, by God.
Now madam, you'll think it a strange thing to say,
But, the sight of a book makes me sick to this day."

'Never since I was born did I hear so much wit,
And, madam, I laughed till I thought I should split.
So, then you looked scornful, and sniffed at the Dean,
As, who should say, "Now, am I skinny and lean?"
But he durst not so much as once open his lips,
And, the Doctor was plaguily down in the hyps.'

Thus merciless Hannah ran on in her talk,
180   Till she heard the Dean call, 'Will your Ladyship walk?'
Her Ladyship answers, 'I'm just coming down;'

Then, turning to Hannah, and forcing a frown,
Although it was plain, in her heart she was glad,
Cried, 'Huzzy, why sure the wench is gone mad:
How could these chimeras get into your brains? –
Come hither, and take this old gown for your pains.
But the Dean, if this secret should come to his ears,
Will never have done with his gibes and his jeers:
For your life, not a word of the matter, I charge ye:
190 Give me but a barrack, a fig for the clergy.'

A Pastoral Dialogue

A nymph and swain, Sheelah and Dermot hight,
Who wont to weed the court of Gosford knight,
While each with stubbed knife removed the roots
That raised between the stones their daily shoots;
As at their work they sat in counterview,
With mutual beauty smit, their passion grew.
Sing, heavenly muse, in sweetly flowing strain,
The soft endearments of the nymph and swain.

DERMOT
My love to Sheelah is more firmly fixed
10 Than strongest weeds that grow these stones betwixt:
My spud these nettles from the stones can part,
No knife so keen to weed thee from my heart.

SHEELAH
My love for gentle Dermot faster grows
Than yon tall dock that rises to thy nose.
Cut down the dock, 'twill sprout again: but O!
Love rooted out, again will never grow.

DERMOT
No more that briar thy tender leg shall rake:
(I spare the thistle for Sir Arthur's sake.)
Sharp are the stones, take thou this rushy mat;
20 The hardest bum will bruise with sitting squat.

SHEELAH

Thy breeches torn behind, stand gaping wide;
This petticoat shall save thy dear backside;
Nor need I blush, although you feel it wet;
Dermot, I vow, 'tis nothing else but sweat.

DERMOT

At an old stubborn root I chanced to tug,
When the Dean threw me this tobacco plug:
A longer ha'porth never did I see;
This, dearest Sheelah, thou shalt share with me.

SHEELAH

In at the pantry door this morn I slipped,
30   And from the shelf a charming crust I whipped:
Dennis was out, and I got hither safe;
And thou, my dear, shalt have the bigger half.

DERMOT

When you saw Tady at long-bullets play,
You sat and loused him all the sunshine day.
How could you, Sheelah, listen to his tales,
Or crack such lice as his betwixt your nails?

SHEELAH

When you with Oonagh stood behind a ditch,
I peeped, and saw you kiss the dirty bitch.
Dermot, how could you touch those nasty sluts!
40   I almost wish this spud were in your guts.

DERMOT

If Oonagh once I kissed, forbear to chide:
Her aunt's my gossip by my father's side:
But, if I ever touch her lips again,
May I be doomed for life to weed in rain.

SHEELAH

Dermot, I swear, though Tady's locks could hold
Ten thousand lice, and every louse was gold,

Him on my lap you never more should see;
Or may I lose my weeding-knife – and thee.

DERMOT

O, could I earn for thee, my lovely lass,
50   A pair of brogues to bear thee dry to mass!
But see where Norah with the sowens comes –
Then let us rise, and rest our weary bums.

Directions for a Birthday Song

To form a just and finished piece,
Take twenty gods of Rome or Greece,
Whose godships are in chief request,
And fit your present subject best.
And should it be your hero's case
To have both male and female race,
Your business must be to provide
A score of goddesses beside.

Some call their monarchs sons of Saturn,
10   For which they bring a modern pattern,
Because they might have heard of one,
Who often longed to eat his son:
But this I think will not go down,
For here the father kept his crown.

Why then appoint him son of Jove,
Who met his mother in a grove;
To this we freely shall consent,
Well knowing what the poets meant:
And in their sense, 'twixt me and you,
20   It may be literally true.

Next, as the laws of song require,
He must be greater than his sire:
For Jove, as every schoolboy knows,
Was able Saturn to depose;
And sure no Christian poet breathing
Should be more scrupulous than a heathen.

Or if to blasphemy it tends,
That's but a trifle among friends.

Your hero now another Mars is,
30 Makes mighty armies turn their arses.
Behold his glittering falchion mow
Whole squadrons with a single blow:
While Victory, with wings outspread,
Flies like an eagle o'er his head;
His milk-white steed upon its haunches,
Or pawing into dead men's paunches.
As Overton has drawn his sire
Still seen o'er many an alehouse fire.
Then from his arm hoarse thunder rolls
40 As loud as fifty mustard bowls;
For thunder still his arm supplies,
And lightning always in his eyes:
They both are cheap enough in conscience,
And serve to echo rattling nonsense;
The rumbling words march fierce along,
Made trebly dreadful in your song.

Sweet poet, hired for birthday rhymes,
To sing of wars choose peaceful times.
What though for fifteen years and more
50 Janus hath locked his temple door?
Though not a coffee-house we read in
Hath mentioned arms this side of Sweden;
Nor *London Journal*'s, nor *Post-Men*,
Though fond of warlike lies as most men;
Thou still with battles stuff thy head full
For must a hero not be dreadful?

Dismissing Mars, it next must follow
Your conqueror is become Apollo:
That he's Apollo, is as plain as
60 That Robin Walpole is Maecenas:
But that he struts, and that he squints,
You'd know him by Apollo's prints.
Old Phoebus is but half as bright,
For yours can shine both day and night,

The first perhaps may once an age
Inspire you with poetic rage;
Your Phoebus royal, every day
Not only can inspire but pay.

Then make this new Apollo sit
70   Sole patron, judge, and god of wit.
'How from his altitude he stoops
To raise up Virtue when she droops,
On Learning how his bounty flows,
And with what Justice he bestows.
Fair Isis, and ye banks of Cam,
Be witness if I tell a flam:
What prodigies in arts we drain
From both your streams in George's reign!
As from the flowery bed of Nile –'
80   But here's enough to show your style.

Broad innuendos, such as this,
If well applied, can hardly miss:
For when you bring your song in print,
He'll get it read, and take the hint,
(It must be read before 'tis warbled,
The paper gilt, and cover marbled)
And will be so much more your debtor
Because he never knows a letter.
And as he hears his wit and sense,
90   To which he never made pretence,
Set out in hyperbolic strains,
A guinea shall reward your pains.
For patrons never pay so well,
As when they scarce have learned to spell.

Next call him Neptune with his trident,
He rules the sea, you see him ride in't;
And if provoked, he soundly firks his
Rebellious waves with rods like Xerxes.
He would have seized the Spanish plate,
100   Had not the fleet gone out too late,
And in their very ports besiege,
But that he would not disoblige,
And made the rascals pay him dearly,
For those affronts they give him yearly.

'Tis not denied that when we write,
Our ink is black, our paper white;
And when we scrawl our paper o'er,
We blacken what was white before.
I think this practice only fit
110 For dealers in satiric wit:
But you some white-lead ink must get,
And write on paper black as jet:
Your interest lies to learn the knack
Of whitening what before was black.

Thus your encomiums, to be strong,
Must be applied directly wrong:
A tyrant for his mercy praise,
And crown a royal dunce with bays:
A squinting monkey load with charms;
120 And paint a coward fierce in arms.
Is he to avarice inclined?
Extol him for his generous mind:
And when we starve for want of corn,
Come out with Amalthea's horn.
For all experience this evinces
The only art of pleasing princes;
For princes love you should descant
On virtues which they know they want.

One compliment I had forgot,
130 But songsters must omit it not.
(I freely grant the thought is old)
Why then, your hero must be told,
In him such virtues lie inherent,
To qualify him God's vicegerent,
That with no title to inherit,
He must have been a king by merit.
Yet be the fancy old or new,
'Tis partly false, and partly true,
And take it right, it means no more
140 Than George and William claimed before.

Should some obscure inferior fellow
As Julius, or the youth of Pella,
When all your list of gods is out,
Presume to show his mortal snout,

And as a deity intrude,
Because he had the world subdued:
Oh! let him not debase your thoughts,
Or name him, but to tell his faults.

Of gods I only quote the best,
150 But you may hook in all the rest.

Now birthday bard, with joy proceed
To praise your empress, and her breed.
First, of the first, to vouch your lies,
Bring all the females of the skies:
The Graces and their mistress Venus
Must venture down to entertain us.
With bended knees when they adore her
What dowdies they appear before her!
Nor shall we think you talk at random,
160 For Venus might be her great grandam.
Six thousand years hath lived the goddess,
Your heroine hardly fifty odd is.
Besides you songsters oft have shown,
That she hath graces of her own:
Three graces by Lucina brought her,
Just three; and every grace a daughter.
How many a king his heart and crown
Shall at their snowy feet lay down:
In royal robes they come by dozens
170 To court their English-German cousins,
Besides a pair of princely babies,
That five years hence will both be Hebes.

Now see her seated on her throne
With genuine lustre all her own.
Poor Cynthia never shone so bright,
Her splendour is but borrowed light;
And only with her brother linked
Can shine, without him is extinct.
But Carolina shines the clearer
180 With neither spouse nor brother near her,
And darts her beams o'er both our isles,
Though George is gone a thousand miles.
Thus Berecynthia takes her place,
Attended by her heavenly race,

And sees a son in every god
Unawed by Jove's all-shaking nod.

Now sing his little Highness Freddy,
Who struts like any king already.
With so much beauty, show me any maid
190 That could refuse this charming Ganymede,
Where majesty with sweetness vies,
And like his father early wise.
Then cut him out a world of work,
To conquer Spain, and quell the Turk.
Foretell his empire crowned with bays,
And golden times, and halcyon days,
But swear his line shall rule the nation
For ever – till the conflagration.

But now it comes into my mind,
200 We left a little Duke behind;
A Cupid in his face and size,
And only wants to want his eyes.
Make some provision for the yonker,
Find him a kingdom out to conquer;
Prepare a fleet to waft him o'er,
Make Gulliver his commodore,
Into whose pocket valiant Willy put,
Will soon subdue the realm of Lilliput.

A skilful critic justly blames
210 Hard, tough, cramp, guttural, harsh, stiff names.
The sense can never be too jejune,
But smooth your words to fit the tune,
Hanover may do well enough,
But George, and Brunswick are too rough.
Hesse Darmstadt makes too rough a sound,
And Guelph the strongest ear will wound.
In vain are all attempts from Germany
To find out proper words for harmony:
And yet I must except the Rhine,
220 Because it clinks to Caroline.
Hail Queen of Britain, queen of rhymes,
Be sung ten hundred thousand times.
Too happy were the poetic crew,
If their own happiness they knew.

Three syllables did never meet
So soft, so sliding, and so sweet.
Nine other tuneful words like that
Would prove even Homer's numbers flat.
Behold three beauteous vowels stand
230   With bridegroom liquids hand in hand,
In concord here forever fixed,
No jarring consonants betwixt.

May Caroline continue long,
Forever fair and young – in song.
What though the royal carcass must
Squeezed in a coffin turn to dust;
Those elements her name compose,
Like atoms are exempt from blows.

Though Caroline may fill your gaps
240   Yet still you must consult the maps,
Find rivers with harmonious names,
Sabrina, Medway, and the Thames.
Britannia long will wear like steel
But Albion's cliffs are out at heel,
And patience can endure no more
To hear the Belgic lion roar.
Give up the phrase of haughty Gaul,
But proud Iberia soundly maul,
Restore the ships by Philip taken,
250   And make him crouch to save his bacon.

Nassau, who got the name of glorious
Because he never was victorious,
A hanger-on has always been,
For old acquaintance bring him in.

For Walpole you might lend a line,
But much I fear he's in decline;
And if you chance to come too late
When he goes out, you share his fate,
And bear the new successor's frown;
260   Or whom you once sung up, sing down.

Reject with scorn that stupid notion
To praise your hero for devotion:

Nor entertain a thought so odd,
That princes should believe in God:
But follow the securest rule,
And turn it all to ridicule:
'Tis grown the choicest wit at court,
And gives the maids of honour sport.
For since they talked with Doctor Clarke,
270 They now can venture in the dark.
That sound divine the truth has spoke all
And pawned his word hell is not local.
This will not give him half the trouble
Of bargains sold, or meanings double.

Supposing now your song is done,
To Minheer Handel next you run,
Who artfully will pare and prune
Your words to some Italian tune.
Then print it in the largest letter,
280 With capitals, the more the better.

Present it boldly on your knee,
And take a guinea for a fee.

On Burning a Dull Poem

An ass's hoof alone can hold
That poisonous juice which kills by cold.
Methought, when I this poem read,
No vessel but an ass's head,
Such frigid fustian could contain;
I mean the head without the brain.
The cold conceits, the chilling thoughts,
Went down like stupefying draughts:
I found my head began to swim,
10   A numbness crept through every limb:
In haste, with imprecations dire,
I threw the volume in the fire:
When, who could think, though cold as ice,
It burnt to ashes in a trice.

How could I more enhance its fame?
Though born in snow, it died in flame.

The Revolution at Market Hill

From distant regions, Fortune sends
An odd triumvirate of friends;
Where Phoebus pays a scanty stipend,
Where never yet a codling ripened:
Hither the frantic goddess draws
Three sufferers in a ruined cause.
By faction banished here unite,
A Dean, a Spaniard, and a knight.
Unite; but on conditions cruel;
10   The Dean and Spaniard find it too well;
Condemned to live in service hard;
On either side his Honour's guard:
The Dean, to guard his honour's back,
Must build a castle at Drumlack:
The Spaniard, sore against his will,
Must raise a fort at Market Hill.
And thus, the pair of humble gentry,
At North and South are posted sentry;
While in his lordly castle fixed,
20   The knight triumphant reigns betwixt:
And, what the wretches most resent,
To be his slaves must pay him rent;
Attend him daily as their chief,
Decant his wine, and carve his beef.

   O Fortune, 'tis a scandal for thee
To smile on those who are least worthy.
Weigh but the merits of the three,
His slaves have ten times more than he.

   Proud baronet of Nova Scotia,
30   The Dean and Spaniard must reproach ye;
Of *their* two fames the world enough rings;
Where are *thy* services and sufferings?
What, if for nothing once you kissed,
Against the grain, a monarch's fist?
What, if among the courtly tribe,
You lost a place, and saved a bribe?
And, then in surly mode came here

To fifteen hundred pounds a year,
And fierce against the Whigs harangued?
40 You never ventured to be hanged.
How dare you treat your betters thus?
Are you to be compared to us?

   Come Spaniard, let us from our farms
Call forth our cottagers to arms;
Our forces let us both unite,
Attack the foe at left and right;
From Market Hill's exalted head,
Full northward, let your troops be led:
While I from Drapier's Mount descend,
50 And to the south my squadrons bend:
New River Walk with friendly shade,
Shall keep my host in ambuscade;
While you, from where the basin stands,
Shall scale the ramparts with your bands.
Nor need we doubt the fort to win;
I hold intelligence within.
True, Lady Anne no danger fears,
Brave as the Upton fan she wears:
Then, lest upon our first attack
60 Her valiant arm should force us back,
And we of all our hopes deprived;
I have a stratagem contrived;
By these embroidered high heel shoes,
She shall be caught as in a noose:
So well contrived her toes to pinch,
She'll not have power to stir an inch;
These gaudy shoes must Hannah place
Direct before her lady's face.
The shoes put on; our faithful portress
70 Admits us in, to storm the fortress;
While tortured madam bound remains,
Like Montezume in golden chains:
Or, like a cat with walnuts shod,
Stumbling at every step she trod.
Sly hunters thus, in Borneo's isle,
To catch a monkey by a wile;
The mimic animal amuse;

They place before him gloves and shoes;
Which when the brute puts awkward on,
80 All his agility is gone;
In vain to frisk or climb he tries;
The huntsmen seize the grinning prize.

But, let us on our first assault
Secure the larder, and the vault.
The valiant Dennis you must fix on,
And, I'll engage with Peggy Dixon:
Then if we once can seize the key,
And chest, that keeps my Lady's tea,
They must surrender at discretion:
90 And soon as we have got possession,
We'll act as *other* conquerors do;
Divide the realm between us two.
Then, (let me see) we'll make the knight
Our clerk, for he can read and write;
But, must not think, I tell him that,
Like Lorimer, to wear his hat.
Yet, when we dine without a friend,
We'll place him at the lower end.
Madam, whose skill does all in dress lie,
100 May serve to wait on Mrs Leslie:
But, lest it might not be so proper,
That her own maid should overtop her;
To mortify the *creature* more,
We'll take her heels five inches lower.

For Hannah; when we have no need of her,
'Twill be our interest to get rid of her:
And when we execute our plot,
'Tis best to hang her on the spot;
As all your politicians wise
110 Dispatch the rogues by whom they rise.

A Dialogue between an Eminent Lawyer and Dr Swift, Dean of St Patrick's

BEING AN ALLUSION TO THE FIRST SATIRE
OF THE SECOND BOOK OF HORACE

Sunt quibus in satyra, &c.

[SWIFT]   Since there are people who complain
There's too much satire in my vein,
That I am often found exceeding
The rules of raillery and breeding,
With too much freedom treat my betters,
Not sparing even men of letters,
You, who are skilled in lawyer's lore,
What's your advice? shall I give o'er,
Nor ever fools or knaves expose
10   Either in verse or humorous prose,
And, to avoid all future ill,
In my scrutoire lock up my quill?

[FRIEND]   Since you are pleased to condescend
To ask the judgement of a friend,
Your case considered, I must think
You should withdraw from pen and ink,
Forbear your poetry and jokes,
And live like other Christian folks;
Or if the muses must inspire
20   Your fancy with their pleasing fire,
Take subjects safer for your wit
Than those on which you lately writ,
Commend the times, your thoughts correct
And follow the prevailing sect,
Assert that Hyde in writing story
Shows all the malice of a Tory,
While Burnet in his deathless page
Discovers freedom without rage;
To Woolston recommend our youth
30   For learning, probity, and truth,
That noble genius, who unbinds
The chains which fetter free-born minds,

Redeems us from the slavish fears
Which lasted near two thousand years,
He can alone the priesthood humble,
Make gilded spires and altars tumble.

[SWIFT]   Must I commend against my conscience
Such stupid blasphemy and nonsense?
To such a subject tune my lyre
40   And sing like one of Milton's choir,
Where devils to a vale retreat
And call the laws of wisdom fate,
Lament upon their hapless fall
That force free virtue should enthral?
Or, shall the charms of wealth and power
Make me pollute the muses' bower?

[FRIEND]   As from the tripod of Apollo
Hear from my desk the words that follow;
Some by philosophers misled,
50   Must honour you alive and dead,
And such as know what Greece has writ
Must taste your irony and wit,
While most that are or would be great,
Must dread your pen, your person hate,
And you on Drapier's Hill must lie,
And there without a mitre die.

An Epistle upon an Epistle

FROM A CERTAIN DOCTOR TO A CERTAIN GREAT LORD:
BEING A CHRISTMAS BOX FOR DR DELANY

– *Palatinae Cultor facunde Minervae,*
Ingenio frueris qui propriore Dei.
Nam tibi nascentes DOMINI cognoscere Curas,
Et secreta DUCIS Pectora nosse licet.
Martial, *Lib. 5, Ep. 5.*

As Jove will not attend on less,
When things of more importance press:
You can't, grave sir, believe it hard,
That you, a low Hibernian bard,

Should cool your heels awhile, and wait
Unanswered at your patron's gate;
And would my Lord vouchsafe to grant
This one, poor, humble boon I want,
Free leave to play his secretary,
10 As Falstaff acted old King Harry:
I'd tell of yours in rhyme and print:
Folks shrug, and cry, 'There's nothing in't.'
And after several readings over,
It shines most in the marble cover.

How could so fine a taste dispense
With mean degrees of wit and sense?
Nor will my Lord so far beguile
The wise and learnèd of our isle;
To make it pass upon the nation,
20 By dint of his sole approbation.
The task is arduous, patrons find,
To warp the sense of all mankind:
Who think your muse must first aspire;
E'er he advance the Doctor higher.

You've cause to say he 'meant you well':
That you 'are thankful', who 'can tell'?
For still you're short (which grieves your spirit)
Of his intent, you mean, your merit.

Ah! *Quanto rectius, tu adepte,*
30 *Qui nil moliris tam inepte?*
Smedley, thou Jonathan of Clogher,
'When thou thy humble lays dost offer
To Grafton's Grace, with grateful heart;
Thy thanks and verse, devoid of art:
Content with what his bounty gave,
No larger income dost thou crave.'

But you must have cascades, and all
Ierna's lake, for your canal,
Your vistos, barges, and (a pox on
40 All pride) our Speaker for your coxon:
It's pity that he can't bestow you
Twelve commoners in caps to row you.
Thus Edgar proud, in days of yore,

Held monarchs labouring at the oar;
And as he passed, so swelled the Dee
Enraged, as Erne would do at thee.

How different is this from Smedley?
(His name is up, he may in bed lie)
'Who only asks some pretty cure,
50 In wholesome soil and aether pure;
The garden stored with artless flowers,
In either angle shady bowers:
No gay parterre with costly green,
Must in the ambient hedge be seen;
But freely Nature takes her course,
Nor fears from him ungrateful force:
No shears to check her sprouting vigour,
Or shape the yews to antic figure.'

But you forsooth, your *all* must squander
60 On that poor spot, called Delville, yonder:
And when you've been at vast expenses
In whims, parterres, canals and fences:
Your assets fail, and cash is wanting
For farther buildings, farther planting.
No wonder when you raise and level,
Think this wall low, and that wall bevel.
Here a convenient box you found,
Which you demolished to the ground:
Then built, then took up with your arbour,
70 And set the house to Rupert Barber.
You sprung an arch, which in a scurvy
Humour, you tumbled topsyturvy.
You change a circle to a square,
Then to a circle, as you were:
Who can imagine whence the fund is,
That you *quadrata* change *rotundis*?

To Fame a temple you erect,
A Flora does the dome protect;
Mount, walks, on high; and in a hollow
80 You place the muses and Apollo;
There shining midst his train, to grace
Your whimsical poetic place.

These stories were, of old, designed
As fables: but you have refined
The poets' mythologic dreams,
To real muses, gods, and streams.
Who would not swear, when you contrive thus,
That you're Don Quixote *Redivivus?*

Beneath a dry canal there lies,
90 Which only winter's rain supplies.
Oh! couldst thou, by some magic spell,
Hither convey St Patrick's Well;
Here may it reassume its stream,
And take a greater Patrick's name.

If your expenses rise so high;
What income can your wants supply?
Yet still you fancy you inherit
A fund of each superior merit,
That you can't fail of more provision,
100 All by my Lady's kind decision.
For the more livings you can fish up,
You think you'll sooner be a bishop:
That could not be my Lord's intent,
Nor can it answer in the event.
Most think what has been heaped on you,
To other sort of folk was due:
Rewards too great for your flimflams,
Epistles, riddles, epigrams.

Though now your depth must not be sounded,
110 The time was, when you had compounded
For less than Charly Grattan's school:
Five hundred pound a year's no fool.

Take this advice then from your friend,
To your ambition put an end.
Be frugal, Pat: pay what you owe,
Before you 'build and you bestow'.
Be modest: nor address your betters
With begging, vain, familiar letters.

A passage may be found, I've heard,
120 In some old Greek or Latin bard,

Which says, would crows in silence eat
Their offals, or their better meat,
Their generous feeders not provoking
By loud and unharmonious croaking:
They might, unhurt by envy's claws,
Live on, and stuff, to boot, their maws.

A Libel on the Reverend Dr Delany and His Excellency John, Lord Carteret

TO DR DELANY, OCCASIONED BY HIS EPISTLE
TO HIS EXCELLENCY JOHN, LORD CARTERET

Deluded mortals, whom the great
Choose for companions *tête à tête*,
Who at their dinners, *en famille*,
Get leave to sit whene'er you will;
Then, boasting tell us where you dined,
And, how his Lordship was so kind;
How many pleasant things he spoke,
And, how you laughed at every joke:
Swear, he's a most facetious man,
10   That you and he are cup and can.
You travel with a heavy load,
And quite mistake preferment's road.

Suppose my Lord and you alone;
Hint the least interest of your own;
His visage drops, he knits his brow,
He cannot talk of business now:
Or, mention but a vacant post,
He'll turn it off with, 'Name your toast.'
Nor could the nicest artist paint,
20   A countenance with more constraint.

For, as their appetites to quench,
Lords keep a pimp to bring a wench;
So, men of wit are but a kind
Of pandars to a vicious mind;
Who proper objects must provide
To gratify their lust of pride,

When wearied with intrigues of state,
They find an idle hour to prate.
Then, should you dare to ask a place,
30 You forfeit all your patron's grace,
And disappoint the sole design,
For which he summoned you to dine.

Thus, Congreve spent, in writing plays,
And one poor office, half his days;
While Montagu, who claimed the station
To be Maecenas of the nation,
For poets open table kept,
But ne'er considered where they slept;
Himself as rich as fifty Jews,
40 Was easy, though they wanted shoes;
And, crazy Congreve scarce could spare
A shilling to discharge his chair,
Till prudence taught him to appeal
From Paean's fire to party zeal;
Not owing to his happy vein
The fortunes of his latter scene,
Took proper principles to thrive;
And so might every dunce alive.

Thus, Steele who owned what others writ,
50 And flourished by imputed wit,
From perils of a hundred gaols,
Withdrew to starve, and die in Wales.

Thus Gay, the hare with many friends,
Twice seven long years the court attends,
Who, under tales conveying truth,
To virtue formed a princely youth,
Who paid his courtship with the crowd,
As far as modest pride allowed,
Rejects a servile usher's place,
60 And leaves St James's in disgrace.

Thus Addison by lords caressed,
Was left in foreign lands distressed,
Forgot at home, became for hire,
A travelling tutor to a squire.
But, wisely left the muses' hill;

To business shaped the poet's quill,
Let all his barren laurels fade;
Took up himself the courtier's trade:
And grown a minister of state,
70   Saw poets at his levee wait.

Hail! happy Pope, whose generous mind,
Detesting all the statesman kind!
Contemning courts, at courts unseen,
Refused the visits of a queen;
A soul with every virtue fraught
By sages, priests, or poets taught:
Whose filial piety excels
Whatever Grecian story tells:
A genius for all stations fit,
80   Whose meanest talent is his wit:
His heart too great, though fortune little,
To lick a rascal statesman's spittle;
Appealing to the nation's taste,
Above the reach of want is placed:
By Homer dead was taught to thrive,
Which Homer never could alive:
And, sits aloft on Pindus' head,
Despising slaves that cringe for bread.

True politicians only pay
90   For solid work, but not for play;
Nor ever choose to work with tools
Forged up in colleges and schools.
Consider how much more is due
To all their journeymen, than you.
At table you can Horace quote;
They at a pinch can bribe a vote:
You show your skill in Grecian story,
But, they can manage Whig and Tory:
You, as a critic, are so curious
100   To find a verse in Virgil spurious;
But, they can smoke the deep designs,
When Bolingbroke with Pulteney dines.

Besides; your patron may upbraid ye,
That you have got a place already.

An office for your talents fit,
To flatter, carve, and show your wit;
To snuff the lights, and stir the fire,
And get a dinner for your hire.
What claim have you to place, or pension?
110   He overpays in condescension.

But, reverend Doctor, you, we know,
Could never condescend so low;
The Viceroy, whom you now attend,
Would, if he durst, be more your friend;
Nor will *in you* those gifts despise,
By which himself was taught to rise:
When he has virtue to retire,
He'll grieve he did not raise you higher,
And place you in a better station,
120   Although it might have *pleased* the nation.

This may be true – submitting still
To Walpole's more than royal will.
And what condition can be worse?
He comes to drain a beggar's purse:
He comes to tie our chains on faster,
And show us, England is our master:
Caressing knaves and dunces wooing,
To make them work their own undoing.
What has he else to bait his traps,
130   Or bring his vermin in, but scraps?
The offals of a church distressed,
A hungry vicarage at best;
Or, some remote inferior post,
With forty pounds a year at most.

But, here again you interpose;
Your favourite Lord is none of those,
Who owe their virtue to their stations,
And characters to dedications:
For, keep him in, or turn him out,
140   His learning none will call in doubt:
His learning, though a poet said it,
Before a play, would lose no credit:
Nor Pope would dare deny him wit,

Although to praise it Philips writ.
I own, he hates an action base,
His virtues battling with his place;
Nor wants a nice discerning spirit,
Betwixt a true and spurious merit:
Can sometimes drop a voter's claim,
150   And give up party to his fame.
I do the most that friendship can;
·I hate the Viceroy, love the man.

But, you, who till your fortune's made
Must be a *sweetener* by your trade,
Should swear he never meant us ill;
We suffer sore against his will;
That, if we could but see his heart,
He would have chose a milder part;
We rather should lament his case
160   Who must obey, or lose his place.

Since this reflection slipped your pen,
Insert it when you write again:
And, to illustrate it, produce
This simile for his excuse.

'So, to destroy a guilty land,
An angel sent by heaven's command,
While he obeys almighty will,
Perhaps, may feel compassion still;
And wish the task had been assigned
170   To spirits of less gentle kind.'

But I, in politics grown old,
Whose thoughts are of a different mould,
Who, from my soul, sincerely hate
Both kings and ministers of state:
Who look on courts with stricter eyes,
To see the seeds of vice arise,
Can lend you an allusion fitter,
Though flattering knaves may call it bitter:
Which, if you durst but give it place,
180   Would show you many a statesman's face.
Fresh from the tripod of Apollo,
I had it in the words that follow.

(Take notice, to avoid offence
I here except his Excellence.)

So, to effect his monarch's ends,
From hell a Viceroy devil ascends,
His budget with corruptions crammed,
The contributions of the damned;
Which with unsparing hand, he strews
190   Through courts and senates as he goes;
And then at Belzebub's Black Hall,
Complains his budget was too small.

Your simile may better shine
In verse; but there is truth in mine.
For, no imaginable things
Can differ more than God and kings.
And statesmen, by ten thousand odds
Are angels, just as kings are gods.

On the Irish Club

Ye paltry underlings of state,
Ye senators, who love to prate;
Ye rascals of inferior note,
Who, for a dinner, sell a vote;
Ye pack of pensionary peers,
Whose fingers itch for poets' ears;
Ye bishops far removed from saints;
Why all this rage? Why these complaints?
Why against printers all this noise?
10   This summoning of blackguard boys?
Why so sagacious in your guesses?
Your *effs* and *tees*, and *arrs*, and *esses*?
Take my advice; to make you safe,
I know a shorter way by half.
The point is plain: remove the cause;
Defend your liberties and laws.
Be sometimes to your country true,
Have once the public good in view:
Bravely despise champagne at court,
20   And choose to dine at home with port:

Let prelates, by their good behaviour,
Convince us they believe a saviour;
Nor sell what they so dearly bought,
This country, now their own, for naught.
Ne'er did a true satiric muse
Virtue or innocence abuse;
And 'tis against poetic rules
To rail at men by nature fools:
But * * * * * * * * * * * * *
* * * * * * * * * * * * * *

A Panegyric on the Reverend Dean Swift

IN ANSWER TO THE LIBEL ON DR DELANY
AND A CERTAIN GREAT LORD

Could all we little folks that wait,
And dance attendance on the great,
Obtain such privilege as you,
To rail, and go unpunished too;
To treat our betters like our slaves,
And all mankind as fools, or knaves;
The pleasure of so large a grant
Would much compensate all we want.
Mitres, and glebes could scarce do more
10　To scratch our endless itch of power.
For next to being great ourselves
It is to think all great ones elves,
And when we can't be *tête à tête*
Their fellows, turn their dread and hate.
How amply then does power provide
For you to gratify your pride?
Where'er the wind of favour sits,
It still your constitution hits.
If fair, it brings you safe to port,
20　And when 'tis foul, affords you sport.
A deanery you got, while in,
And now you're out, enjoy your grin.

But hark'ee, is it truly so,
(And you of all mankind should know)

That men of wit can be no more
Than pimps to wickedness in power?
Then pray, dear Doctor, condescend
To teach the science to your friend.
For long inured to musty rules,
30 And idle morals in the schools
My highest progress in the mystery
Is of short sessions a long history;
Lampoons on Whigs, when in disgrace;
Or vile submissions, when in place;
Poems addressed to great men's whores;
Or other lapdog cures for sores.
But formed more perfect gamester, you
The deepest tricks of courtiers knew.
Your Horace not content to quote,
40 You at a pinch could forge a plot;
The fatal box itself displayed,
Where Whigs their cursed trains had laid;
Nor ceased the faction to pursue,
Till you had got them in a screw.
Oh, wondrous box! my lyre unstrung
Shall be, when thou art left unsung;
More precious far than even the gift
Of our metropolis to Swift;
The gift (good heavens preserve't from thieves)
50 Of Lord Mayor, aldermen and shrieves,
Where, if the curious list to read 'em,
They'll find his life, and acts, and freedom,
And the great name engraved most fairly,
Of him that Ireland saved, and Harley;
With quaint inscription, which contains, ⎫
Laid out with no less art than pains, ⎬
Most of his virtues, all *my* brains. ⎭

No wonder you should think it little
To 'lick a rascal statesman's spittle',
60 Who have, to show your great devotion,
Oft swallowed down a stronger potion,
A composition more absurd,
Bob's spittle mixed with Harry's turd.
Oh, couldst thou teach us how to zest

Such draughts as this, and then digest,
Then we might also have in time
More beneficial ways than rhyme;
Refuse our patron's call to dine;
'Pish' at his cookery, damn his wine;
70 Assume a dignitary's airs,
And go to church, and say our prayers.

Rightly you show, that wit alone
Advances few, enriches none,
And 'tis as true, or story lies,
Men seldom by their good deeds rise:
From whence the consequence is plain,
You never had commenced a Dean,
Unless you other ways had trod
Than those of wit, or trust in God.
80 'Twas therefore cruel hard, by Jove,
Your industry no better throve,
Nor could achieve the promised lawn,
Though Robin's honour was in pawn;
Because it chanced, an old grave Don
Believed in God, and you in none.
Be this however your relief,
Whene'er your pride recalls your grief,
That all the loss your purse sustained
By that rebuff your virtue gained.
90 For must you not have often lied,
And grieved your righteous soul beside,
The Almighty's orders to perform,
Not to direct a plague, or storm,
But 'gainst the dictates of your mind,
To bless, as now you curse mankind?

You tell me, till my fortune's made,
I must take up the sweetening trade.
I own, the counsel were not wrong,
Did Congreve's wit inspire my song:
100 Or could my muse exert the rage
Of Addison's immortal page,
When rapt in heavenly airs, he sings
The acts of gods, and godlike kings.

But formed by you, how should their model
E'er enter any mortal's noddle?
Our thoughts, to hit your nicer taste,
Must in a different mould be cast;
The language Billingsgate excel,
The sentiments resemble hell.

110   Thus, should I give your humour place,
And draw like you my patron's face;
To pay him honour due, in course
I must compare him to a horse;
Then show, how statesmen oft are stung
By gnats, and draw the nation's dung,
The stinking load of all the crimes,
And nastiness of modern times,
Not only what themselves have shit,
For that were not unjust a bit,
120   But all the filth both spiss, and sparse
Of every rogue that wears an arse.

To add more dignity and light
To an allusion so polite,
The devil ready stands, my Swift,
To help our fancy at a lift;
Yet envy not, that I repeat
The damnable, the dear conceit.

'So when poor Irish rapparee,
Is sentenced to the fatal tree,
130   Or naughty boy escapes from school,
Or pretty miss has played the fool,
And cracked her tender maidenhead
With lying on too hard a bed;
Their loads they all on Satan lay:
The devil did the deed, not they!'

The simile would better jump,
Were you but placed on Satan's rump;
For if bestrode by you, old Nick
Himself could scarce forbear to kick,
140   And curse his wicked burden more
Than all the sins he ever bore.

Is this the art, good Doctor, say,
The true, the genuine sweetening lay?
Then must it truly be confessed;
Our ministers are void of taste,
When such adepts as you, and I
So long unbishopricked lie by,
While dunces of the coarsest clay,
That only know to preach and pray,
150   Devour the church's tiddest bits,
The perquisites of pimps and wits.
And leave us naught but guts and garbage,
Or dirty offals cooked with herbage.

No less than reasons of such weight,
Could make you so sincerely hate
Both kings and ministers of state.
For once there was a time, God wot,
Before our friends were gone to pot,
When Jonathan was great at court,
160   The ruined party made his sport,
Despised the beast with many heads,
And damned the mob, which now he leads.
But things are strangely changed since then,
And kings are now no more than men;
From whence 'tis plain, they quite have lost
God's image, which was once their boast.
For Gulliver divinely shows,
That humankind are all Yahoos.
Both envy then and malice must
170   Allow your hatred strictly just;
Since you alone of all the race,
Disclaim the human name, and face,
And with your virtues pant to wear
(May heaven indulgent hear your prayer!)
The proof of your high origin,
The horse's countenance divine.
While Grattan, Sheridan, and I,
Who after you adoring fly,
An humbler prospect only wait,
180   To be your asses' colts of state,
The angels of your awful nods,
Resembling you as angels gods.

To Dr Delany,
on the Libels Writ against Him

— Tanti tibi non sit opaci
Omnis arena Tagi.
Juv.

As some raw youth in country bred,
To arms by thirst of honour led,
When at a skirmish first he hears
The bullets whistling round his ears,
Will duck his head, aside will start,
And feel a trembling at his heart:
Till, scaping oft without a wound,
Lessens the terror of the sound:
Fly bullets now as thick as hops,
10 He runs into the cannon's chops.
An author thus who pants for fame
Begins the world with fear and shame,
When first in print, you see him dread
Each pot-gun levelled at his head:
The lead yon critic's quill contains,
Is destined to *beat out his brains*.
As if he heard loud thunders roll,
Cries, Lord have mercy on his soul;
Concluding, that another shot
20 Will strike him dead upon the spot:
But, when with squibbing, flashing, popping,
He cannot see one creature dropping:
That, missing fire, or missing aim,
His life is safe, I mean his fame,
The danger past, takes heart of grace,
And looks a critic in the face.

Though splendour gives the fairest mark
To poisoned arrows from the dark,
Yet, 'in yourself when smooth and round',
30 They glance aside without a wound.

'Tis said, the gods tried all their art,
How, pain they might from pleasure part:
But, little could their strength avail,
Both still are fastened by the tail.

Thus, fame and censure with a tether
By fate are always linked together.

Why will you aim to be preferred
In wit before the common herd?
And yet, grow mortified and vexed
40 To pay the penalty annexed.

'Tis eminence makes envy rise,
As fairest fruits attract the flies.
Should stupid libels grieve your mind,
You soon a remedy may find;
Lie down obscure like other folks
Below the lash of snarlers' jokes.
Their faction is five hundred odds,
For every coxcomb lends them rods;
Can sneer as learnedly as they,
50 Like females o'er their morning tea.

You say, the muse will not contain,
And write you must, or break a vein:
Then, if you find the terms too hard,
No longer my advice regard:
But raise your fancy on the wing;
The Irish senate's praises sing:
How jealous of the nation's freedom,
And, for corruptions, how they weed 'em.
How each the public good pursues,
60 How far their hearts from private views,
Make all true patriots up to shoe-boys
Huzza their brethren at the Blue Boys'.
Thus grown a member of the club,
No longer dread the rage of Grub.

How oft am I for rhyme to seek?
To dress a thought, may toil a week;
And then, how thankful to the town,
If all my pains will earn a crown.
Whilst, every critic can devour
70 My work and me in half an hour.
Would men of genius cease to write,
The rogues must die for want and spite;

Must die for want of food and raiment,
If scandal did not find them payment.
How cheerfully the hawkers cry
A satire, and the gentry buy!
While my hard-laboured poem pines
Unsold upon the printer's lines.

A genius in the reverend gown,
80　Must ever keep its owner down:
'Tis an unnatural conjunction,
And spoils the credit of the function.
Round all your brethren cast your eyes,
Point out the surest men to rise,
That club of candidates in black,
The least deserving of the pack;
Aspiring, factious, fierce and loud;
With grace and learning unendowed,
Can turn their hands to every job,
90　The fittest tools to work for Bob:
Will sooner coin a thousand lies
Than suffer men of parts to rise:
They crowd about preferment's gate,
And press you down with all their weight.
For, as of old, mathematicians
Were by the vulgar thought magicians;
So academic dull ale-drinkers
Pronounce all men of wit, free-thinkers.

Wit, as the chief of virtue's friends,
100　Disdains to serve ignoble ends.
Observe what loads of stupid rhymes
Oppress us in corrupted times:
What pamphlets in a court's defence
Show reason, grammar, truth, or sense?
For, though the muse delights in fiction,
She ne'er inspires against conviction.
Then keep your virtue still unmixed,
And let not faction come betwixt.
By party-steps no grandeur climb at,
110　Though it would make you England's primate:
First learn the science to be dull,

You then may soon your conscience lull;
If not, however seated high,
Your genius in your face will fly.

When Jove was, from his teeming head,
Of wit's fair goddess brought to bed,
There followed at his lying-in
For afterbirth, a sooterkin;
Which, as the nurse pursued to kill,
120   Attained by flight the muses' hill;
There in the soil began to root,
And littered at Parnassus' foot.
From hence the critic-vermin sprung,
With harpy claws, and poisonous tongue,
Who fatten on poetic scraps;
Too cunning to be caught in traps.
Dame Nature, as the learned show,
Provides each animal its foe:
Hounds hunt the hare, the wily fox
130   Devours your geese, the wolf your flocks:
Thus, envy pleads a natural claim
To persecute the muses' fame;
On poets in all times abusive,
From Homer down to Pope inclusive.

Yet, what avails it to complain?
You try to take revenge in vain.
A rat your utmost rage defies
That safe behind the wainscoat lies.
Say, did you ever know by sight
140   In cheese an individual mite?
Show me the same numeric flea,
That bit your neck but yesterday:
You then may boldly go in quest
To find the Grub Street poet's nest.
What sponging-house in dread of gaol
Receives them while they wait for bail?
What alley are they nestled in,
To flourish o'er a cup of gin?
Find the last garret where they lay;
150   Or cellar, where they starve today:

Suppose you had them all trepanned
With each a libel in his hand:
What punishment would you inflict?
Or call 'em rogues, or get them kicked:
These they have often tried before;
You but oblige 'em so much more:
Themselves would be the first to tell,
To make their trash the better sell.

You have been libelled – let us know
160 What fool officious told you so.
Will you regard the hawker's cries
Who in his titles always lies?
Whate'er the noisy scoundrel says
It might be something in your praise:
And praise bestowed in Grub Street rhymes,
Would vex one more a thousand times.
Till critics blame, and judges praise,
The poet cannot claim his bays;
On me, when dunces are satiric,
170 I take it for a panegyric.
'Hated by fools, and fools to hate',
Be that my motto, and my fate.

To a Friend Who had been Much Abused in Many Inveterate Libels

The greatest monarch may be stabbed by night,
And fortune help the murderer in his flight;
The vilest ruffian may commit a rape,
Yet safe from injured innocence escape:
And calumny, by working underground,
Can, unrevenged, the greatest merit wound.

What's to be done? shall wit and learning choose,
To live obscure, and have no fame to lose?
By censure frighted out of honour's road,
10 Nor dare to use the gifts by heaven bestowed;
Or fearless enter in through virtue's gate,
And buy distinction at the dearest rate?

An Answer to Dr Delany's Fable
of the Pheasant and the Lark

In ancient times the wise were able,
In proper terms to write a fable:
Their tales would always justly suit
The characters of every brute:
The ass was dull, the lion brave,
The stag was swift, the fox a knave:
The daw a thief, the ape a droll,
The hound would scent, the wolf would prowl:
A pigeon would, if shown by Aesop,
10 Fly from the hawk, or pick his pease up.
Far otherwise a great divine,
Has learnt his fables to refine;
He jumbles men and birds together,
As if they all were of a feather:
You see him first the peacock bring,
Against all rules to be a king:
That in his tail he wore his eyes,
By which he grew both rich and wise.
Now pray observe the Doctor's choice,
20 A peacock chose for flight and voice:
Did ever mortal see a peacock
Attempt a flight above a haycock?
And for his singing, Doctor, you know,
Himself complained of it to Juno.
He squalls in such a hellish noise
It frightens all the village boys.
This peacock kept a standing force,
In regiments of foot and horse;
Had statesmen too of every kind,
30 Who waited on his eyes behind.
(And this was thought the highest post;
For, rule the rump, you rule the roast.)
The Doctor names but one at present,
And he of all birds was a pheasant.
This pheasant was a man of wit,
Could read all books were ever writ;
And when among companions privy,

Could quote you Cicero and Livy.
Birds, as he says, and I allow,
40 Were scholars then, as we are now;
Could read all volumes up to folios,
And feed on fricassees and olios.
This pheasant by the peacock's will,
Was viceroy of a neighbouring hill:
And as he wandered in his park,
He chanced to spy a clergy lark;
Was taken with his person outward,
So prettily he picked a cow-turd:
Then in a net the pheasant caught him,
50 And in his palace fed and taught him.
The moral of this tale is pleasant,
Himself the lark, my Lord the pheasant:
A lark he is, and such a lark
As never came from Noah's ark:
And though he had no other notion,
But building, planning, and devotion;
Though 'tis a maxim you must know,
Who does no ill, can have no foe,
Yet how shall I express in words,
60 The strange stupidity of birds.
The lark was hated in the wood,
Because he did his brethren good.
At last the nightingale comes in,
To hold the Doctor by the chin:
We all can find out whom he means,
The worst of disaffected deans:
Whose wit at best was next to none,
And now that little next is gone.
Against the court is always blabbing,
70 And calls the senate-house a cabin;
So dull, that but for spleen and spite,
We ne'er should know that he could write:
Who thinks the nation always erred,
Because himself is not preferred;
His heart is through his libel seen,
Nor could his malice spare the Queen;
Who, had she known his vile behaviour,

Would ne'er have shown him so much favour;
A noble lord hath told his pranks,
80   And well deserves the nation's thanks.
O! would the senate deign to show
Resentment on this public foe;
Our nightingale might fit a cage,
There let him starve, and vent his rage.
Or would they but in fetters bind,
This enemy of humankind.
Harmonious Coffey, show thy zeal,
Thou champion for the common weal:
Nor on a theme like this repine,
90   For once to wet thy pen divine:
Bestow that libeller a lash,
Who daily sends seditious trash:
Who dares revile the nation's wisdom,
But in the praise of virtue is dumb:
That scribbler lash, who neither knows,
The turn of verse, nor style of prose;
Whose malice, for the worst of ends,
Would have us lose our English friends.
Who never had one public thought,
100 Nor ever gave the poor a groat.
One clincher more, and I have done,
I end my labours with a pun.
Jove send, this nightingale may fall,
Who spends his day and *night in gall*.
So nightingale and lark adieu,
I see the greatest owls in you,
That ever screeched or ever *flew*.

Traulus

THE FIRST PART
IN A DIALOGUE BETWEEN TOM AND ROBIN

TOM   Say, Robin, what can Traulus mean
By bellowing thus against the Dean?
Why does he call him paltry scribbler,
Papist, and Jacobite, and libeller?
Yet cannot prove a single fact.

ROBIN   Forgive him, Tom, his head is cracked.

TOM   What mischief can the Dean have done him,
That Traulus calls for vengeance on him?
Why must he sputter, spawl and slaver it
10   In vain, against the people's favourite?
Revile that nation-saving paper
Which gave the Dean the name of Drapier?

ROBIN   Why Tom, I think the case is plain,
Party and spleen have turned his brain.

TOM   Such friendship never man professed,
The Dean was never so caressed:
For Traulus long his rancour nursed,
Till, God knows why, at last it burst.
That clumsy outside of a porter,
20   How could it thus conceal a courtier?

ROBIN   I own appearances are bad;
But still insist the man is mad.

TOM   Yet many a wretch in Bedlam knows,
How to distinguish friends from foes;
And though perhaps among the rout,
He wildly flings his filth about,
He still has gratitude and sap'ence,
To spare the folks that give him ha'pence:
Nor in their eyes at random pisses,
30   But turns aside like mad Ulysses:
While Traulus all his ordure scatters,
To foul the man he chiefly flatters.
Whence come these inconsistent fits?

ROBIN   Why Tom, the man has lost his wits!

TOM   Agreed. And yet, when Towser snaps
At people's heels with frothy chaps;
Hangs down his head, and drops his tail,
To say he's mad will not avail:
The neighbours all cry, 'Shoot him dead,
40   Hang, drown, or knock him on the head.'

So Traulus when he first harangued,
I wonder why he was not hanged:
For of the two, without dispute,
Towser's the less offensive brute.

ROBIN   Tom, you mistake the matter quite;
Your barking curs will seldom bite:
And though you hear him stut-tut-tut-ter,
He barks as fast as he can utter.
He prates in spite of all impediment
50   While none believes that what he said he meant:
Puts in his finger and his thumb,
To grope for words, and out they come.
He calls you rogue; there's nothing in it,
He fawns upon you in a minute.
Begs leave to rail, 'but damn his blood,
He only meant it for your good.
His friendship was exactly timed,
He shot before your foes were primed:
By this contrivance, Mr Dean,
60   By God I'll bring you off as clean. . .'
Then let him use you e'er so rough,
'Twas all for love, and that's enough.
For let him sputter through a session,
It never makes the least impression.
Whate'er he speaks for madness goes,
With no effect on friends or foes.

TOM   The scrubbest cur in all the pack
Can set the mastiffs on your back.
I own, his madness is a jest,
70   If that were all. But he's possessed:
Incarnate with a thousand imps,
To work whose ends, his madness pimps.
Who o'er each string and wire preside,
Fill every pipe, each motion guide.
Directing every vice we find
In scripture, to the devil assigned:
Sent from the dark infernal region
In him they lodge, and make him Legion.

Of brethren he's a false accuser,
80   A slanderer, traitor and seducer;
A fawning, base, trepanning liar,
The marks peculiar of his sire.
Or, grant him but a drone at best:
A drone can raise a hornet's nest:
The Dean hath felt his stings before;
And, must their malice ne'er give o'er?
Still swarm and buzz about his nose?
But Ireland's friends ne'er wanted foes.
A patriot is a dangerous post
90   When wanted by his country most;
Perversely comes in evil times,
Where virtues are imputed crimes,
His guilt is clear, the proofs are pregnant,
A traitor to the vices regnant.

What spirit since the world began,
Could always bear to strive with man?
Which God pronounced he never would,
And soon convinced them by a flood.
Yet still the Dean on freedom raves,
100   His spirit always strives with slaves.
'Tis time at last to spare his ink,
And let them rot, or hang, or sink.

THE SECOND PART

Traulus of amphibious breed,
Motley fruit of mongrel seed:
By the dam from lordlings sprung,
By the sire exhaled from dung:
Think on every vice in both,
Look on him and see their growth.

View him on the mother's side,
Filled with falsehood, spleen and pride;
Positive and overbearing,
10   Changing still, and still adhering,
Spiteful, peevish, rude, untoward;
Fierce in tongue, in heart a coward:

When his friends he is most hard on,
Cringing comes to beg their pardon;
Reputation ever tearing,
Ever dearest friendship swearing;
Judgement weak, and passion strong,
Always various, always wrong:
Provocation never waits,
20 Where he loves, or where he hates.
Talks whate'er comes in his head,
Wishes it were all unsaid.

    Let me now the vices trace,
From his father's scoundrel race.
Who could give the looby such airs?
Were they masons, were they butchers?
Herald, lend the muse an answer,
From his Atavus and grandsire;
This was dextrous at his trowel,
30 That was bred to kill a cow well:
Hence the greasy clumsy mien,
In his dress and figure seen:
Hence the mean and sordid soul,
Like his body, rank and foul:
Hence that wild suspicious peep,
Like a rogue that steals a sheep:
Hence he learnt the butcher's guile,
How to cut a throat and smile:
Like a butcher doomed for life,
40 In his mouth to wear his knife.
Hence he draws his daily food,
From his tenants' vital blood.

    Lastly, let his gifts be tried,
Borrowed from the mason's side:
Some perhaps may think him able
In the state to build a Babel:
Could we place him in a station,
To destroy the old foundation,
True indeed I should be gladder,
50 Could he learn to mount a ladder.

    May he at his latter end
Mount alive, and dead descend.

In him, tell me which prevail,
Female vices most, or male,
What produced him, can you tell?
Human race, or imps of hell.

On Psyche

At two after noon for our Psyche inquire,
Her tea-kettle's on, and her smock at the fire:
So loitering, so active; so busy, so idle,
Which hath she most need of, a spur or a bridle?
Thus, a greyhound outruns the whole pack in a race,
Yet would rather be hanged than he'd leave a warm place.
She gives you such plenty, it puts you in pain;
But ever with prudence takes care of the main.
To please you, she knows how to choose a nice bit;
10   For her taste is almost as refined as her wit.
To oblige a good friend, she will trace every market,
It would do your heart good, to see how she will cark it.
Yet beware of her arts, for it plainly appears,
She saves half her victuals, by feeding your ears.

The Dean's Reasons for Not Building at Drapier's Hill

I will not build on yonder mount:
And, should you call me to account,
Consulting with myself, I find,
It was no levity of mind.
Whate'er I promised or intended,
No fault of mine, the scheme is ended:
Nor can you tax me as unsteady,
I have a hundred causes ready:
All risen since that flattering time,
10   When Drapier's Hill appeared in rhyme.

I am, as now too late I find,
The greatest cully of mankind:
The lowest boy in Martin's school
May turn and wind me like a fool.

How could I form so wild a vision,
To seek, in deserts, fields Elysian?
To live in fear, suspicion, variance,
With thieves, fanatics, and barbarians?

But here my Lady will object;
20 'Your Deanship ought to recollect,
That, near the knight of Gosford placed,
Whom you allow a man of taste,
Your intervals of time to spend
With so conversable a friend,
It would not signify a pin
Whatever climate you were in.'

'Tis true, but what advantage comes
To me from all a usurer's plums;
Though I should see him twice a day,
30 And am his neighbour cross the way;
If all my rhetoric must fail
To strike him for a pot of ale?

Thus, when the learnéd and the wise
Conceal their talents from our eyes,
And, from deserving friends withhold
Their gifts, as misers do their gold;
Their knowledge, to themselves confined,
Is the same avarice of mind:
Nor makes their conversation better,
40 Than if they never knew a letter.
Such is the fate of Gosford's knight,
Who keeps his wisdom out of sight;
Whose uncommunicative heart,
Will scarce one precious word impart:
Still wrapped in speculations deep,
His outward senses fast asleep;
Who, while I talk, a song will hum,
Or, with his fingers, beat the drum;
Beyond the skies transports his mind,
50 And leaves a lifeless corpse behind.

But, as for me, who ne'er could clamber high,
To understand Malebranche or Cambrai;

Who send my mind (as I believe) less
Than others do, on errands sleeveless;
Can listen to a tale humdrum,
And, with attention, read Tom Thumb;
My spirits with my body progging,
Both hand in hand together jogging,
Sunk over head and ears in matter,
60 Nor can of metaphysics smatter;
Am more diverted with a quibble
Than dream of worlds intelligible;
And think all notions too abstracted
Are like the ravings of a cracked head;
What intercourse of minds can be
Betwixt the knight sublime and me?
If when I talk, as talk I must,
It is but prating to a bust.

Where friendship is by fate designed,
70 It forms an union in the mind:
But, here I differ from the knight
In every point, like black and white:
For, none can say that ever yet
We both in one opinion met:
Not in philosophy, or ale,
In state affairs, or planting kale;
In rhetoric, or picking straws;
In roasting larks, or making laws:
In public schemes, or catching flies,
80 In parliaments, or pudding-pies.

The neighbours wonder why the knight
Should in a country life delight,
Who not one pleasure entertains
To cheer the solitary scenes:
His guests are few, his visits rare,
Nor uses time, nor time will spare;
Nor rides, nor walks, nor hunts, nor fowls,
Nor plays at cards, or dice, or bowls;
But, seated in an easy chair,
90 Despises exercise and air.
His rural walks he ne'er adorns;

Here poor Pomona sits on thorns:
And there neglected Flora settles
Her bum upon a bed of nettles.

Those thankless and officious cares
I use to take in friends' affairs,
From which I never could refrain,
And have been often chid in vain:
From these I am recovered quite,
100 At least in what regards the knight.
Preserve his health, his store increase;
May nothing interrupt his peace.
But now, let all his tenants round
First milk his cows, and after, pound:
Let every cottager conspire
To cut his hedges down for fire;
The naughty boys about the village
His crabs and sloes may freely pillage:
He still may keep a pack of knaves
110 To spoil his work, and work by halves:
His meadows may be dug by swine,
It shall be no concern of mine.
For, why should I continue still
To serve a friend against his will?

Death and Daphne

TO AN AGREEABLE YOUNG LADY, BUT EXTREMELY LEAN

Death went upon a solemn day,
At Pluto's hall, his court to pay:
The phantom, having humbly kissed
His grisly monarch's sooty fist,
Presented him the weekly bills
Of doctors, fevers, plagues, and pills.
Pluto observing, since the Peace,
The burial article decrease;
And, vexed to see affairs miscarry,
10 Declared in council, Death must marry:
Vowed, he no longer could support

Old bachelors about his court:
The interest of his realm had need
That Death should get a numerous breed;
Young Deathlings, who, by practice made
Proficients in their father's trade,
With colonies might stock around
His large dominions underground.

A consult of coquettes below
20   Was called, to rig him out a beau:
From her own head, Megaera takes
A periwig of twisted snakes;
Which in the nicest fashion curled,
Like toupets of this upper world;
(With flour of sulphur powdered well,
That graceful on his shoulders fell)
An adder of the sable kind,
In line direct, hung down behind.
The owl, the raven, and the bat,
30   Clubbed for a feather to his hat;
His coat, an usurer's velvet pall,
Bequeathed to Pluto, corpse and all.
But, loath his person to expose
Bare, like a carcass picked by crows,
A lawyer o'er his hands and face,
Stuck artfully a parchment case.
No new-fluxed rake showed fairer skin;
Not Phyllis after lying-in.
With snuff was filled his ebon box,
40   Of shin-bones rotted by the pox.
Nine spirits of blaspheming fops,
With aconite anoint his chops:
And give him words of dreadful sounds,
'God damn his blood', and 'Blood and wounds.'

Thus furnished out, he sent his train
To take a house in Warwick Lane;
The Faculty, his humble friends,
A complimental message sends:
Their president, in scarlet gown,
50   Harangued, and welcomed him to town.

But, Death had business to dispatch:
His mind was running on his match.
And, hearing much of Daphne's fame,
His Majesty of terrors came,
Fine as a colonel of the Guards,
To visit where she sat at cards:
She, as he came into the room,
Thought him Adonis in his bloom.
And now her heart with pleasure jumps,
60 She scarce remembers what is trumps.
For, such a shape of skin and bone
Was never seen, except her own:
Charmed with his eyes and chin and snout,
Her pocket-glass drew slily out;
And, grew enamoured with her phiz,
As just the counterpart of his.
She darted many a private glance,
And freely made the first advance:
Was of her beauty grown so vain,
70 She doubted not to win the swain.
Nothing she thought could sooner gain him,
Than with her wit to entertain him.
She asked about her friends below;
This meagre fop, that battered beau:
Whether some late departed toasts
Had got gallants among the ghosts?
If Chloe were a sharper still,
As great as ever, at quadrille?
(The ladies there must needs be rooks,
80 For, cards we know, are Pluto's books.)
If Florimel had found her love
For whom she hanged herself above?
How oft a week was kept a ball
By Proserpine, at Pluto's hall?
She fancied, those Elysian shades
The sweetest place for masquerades:
How pleasant on the banks of Styx,
To troll it in a coach and six!

What pride a female heart inflames!
90 How endless are ambition's aims!

Cease haughty nymph; the fates decree
Death must not be a spouse for thee:
For, when by chance the meagre shade
Upon thy hand his finger laid;
Thy hand as dry and cold as lead,
His matrimonial spirit fled;
He felt about his heart a damp,
That quite extinguished Cupid's lamp:
Away the frighted spectre scuds,
100   And leaves my Lady in the suds.

Daphne

Daphne knows, with equal ease,
How to vex and how to please;
But, the folly of her sex
Makes her sole delight to vex.
Never woman more devised
Surer ways to be despised:
Paradoxes weakly wielding,
Always conquered, never yielding.
To dispute, her chief delight,
10   With not one opinion right:
Thick her arguments she lays on,
And with cavils combats reason:
Answers in decisive way,
Never hears what you can say:
Still her odd perverseness shows
Chiefly where she nothing knows.
And where she is most familiar,
Always peevisher and sillier:
All her spirits in a flame
20   When she knows she's most to blame.

Send me hence ten thousand miles,
From a face that always smiles:
None could ever act that part,
But a Fury in her heart.
Ye who hate such inconsistence,
To be easy keep your distance;

Or in folly still befriend her,
But have no concern to mend her.
Lose not time to contradict her,
30   Nor endeavour to convict her.
Never take it in your thought,
That she'll own, or cure a fault.
Into contradiction warm her,
Then, perhaps you may reform her:
Only take this rule along,
Always to advise her wrong;
And reprove her when she's right;
She may then grow wise for spite.

No – that scheme will ne'er succeed,
40   She has better learnt her creed:
She's too cunning and too skilful,
When to yield, and when be wilful.
Nature holds her forth two mirrors,
One for truth, and one for errors;
That looks hideous, fierce, and frightful;
This is flattering and delightful;
That she throws away as foul;
Sits by this, to dress her soul.

Thus you have the case in view,
50   Daphne, 'twixt the Dean and you,
Heaven forbid he should despise thee;
But will never more advise thee.

Twelve Articles

1   Lest it may more quarrels breed
       I will never hear you read.
2   By disputing I will never
       To convince you, once endeavour.
3   When a paradox you stick to,
       I will never contradict you.
4   When I talk, and you are heedless,
       I will show no anger needless.
5   When your speeches are absurd,
10   I will ne'er object one word.

6 When you furious argue wrong,
  I will grieve, and hold my tongue.

7 Not a jest, or humorous story,
  Will I ever tell before ye:
  To be chidden for explaining
  When you quite mistake the meaning.

8 Never more will I suppose
  You can taste my verse or prose:

9 You no more at me shall fret,
20 While I teach, and you forget;

10 You shall never hear me thunder,
  When you blunder on, and blunder.

11 Show your poverty of spirit,
  And in dress place all your merit;
  Give yourself ten thousand airs
  That with me shall break no squares.

12 Never will I give advice
  Till you please to ask me thrice;
  Which, if you in scorn reject,
30 'Twill be just as I expect.

 Thus we both shall have our ends,
And continue special friends.

The Dean to Himself on St Cecilia's Day

Grave Dean of St Patrick's, how comes it to pass,
That you who know music no more than an ass,
That you who was found writing of Drapiers,
Should lend your cathedral to blowers and scrapers?
To act such an opera once in a year
Is offensive to every true Protestant ear,
With trumpets and fiddles and organs and singing,
Will sure the Pretender and popery bring in.
No Protestant prelate, his Lordship or Grace,
10 Dare there show his right or most reverend face;
How would it pollute their croziers and rochets,
To listen to minims and quavers and crotchets?

A Panegyric on the Dean

IN THE PERSON OF A LADY IN THE NORTH

Resolved my gratitude to show,
Thrice reverend Dean for all I owe;
Too long I have my thanks delayed;
Your favours left too long unpaid;
But now in all our sex's name,
My artless muse shall sing your fame.

Indulgent you to female kind,
To all their weaker sides are blind;
Nine more such champions as the Dean,
10 Would soon restore our ancient reign.
How well to win the ladies' hearts,
You celebrate their wit and parts!
How have I felt my spirits raised,
By you so oft, so highly praised!
Transformed by your convincing tongue
To witty, beautiful and young.
I hope to quit that awkward shame
Affected by each vulgar dame;
To modesty a weak pretence;
20 And soon grow pert on men of sense;
To show my face with scornful air;
Let others match it if they dare.

Impatient to be out of debt,
O, may I never once forget
The bard, who humbly deigns to choose
Me for the subject of his muse.
Behind my back, before my nose,
He sounds my praise in verse and prose.

My heart with emulation burns
30 To make you suitable returns;
My gratitude the world shall know:
And, see, the printer's boy below:
Ye hawkers all, your voices lift;
'A panegyric on Dean Swift.'
And then, to mend the matter still;
'By Lady Anne of Market Hill.'

I thus begin. My grateful muse
Salutes the Dean in different views;
Dean, butler, usher, jester, tutor;
40   Robert and Darby's coadjutor:
And, as you in commission sit,
To rule the dairy next to Kit.

In each capacity I mean
To sing your praise. And, first as Dean:
Envy must own, you understand your
Precedence, and support your grandeur:
Nor, of your rank will bate an ace,
Except to give Dean Daniel place.
In you such dignity appears;
50   So suited to your state, and years!
With ladies what a strict decorum!
With what devotion you adore 'em!
Treat me with so much complaisance,
As fits a princess in romance.
By your example and assistance,
The fellows learn to know their distance.
Sir Arthur, since you set the pattern,
No longer calls me Snipe and Slattern;
Nor dare he, though he were a duke,
60   Offend me with the least rebuke.

Proceed we to your preaching next:
How nice you split the hardest text!
How your superior learning shines
Above our neighbouring dull divines!
At *Beggar's Opera* not so full pit
Is seen, as when you mount our pulpit.

Consider now your conversation;
Regardful of your age and station,
You ne'er was known, by passion stirred,
70   To give the least offensive word;
But still, whene'er you silence break,
Watch every syllable you speak:
Your style is clear, and so concise,
We never ask to hear you twice.
But then, a parson so genteel,

So nicely clad from head to heel;
So fine a gown, a band so clean,
As well become St Patrick's Dean;
Such reverential awe express,
80   That cowboys know you by your dress!
Then, if our neighbouring friends come here,
How proud are we when you appear!
With such address, and grateful port,
As clearly shows you bred at court!

Now raise your spirits, Mr Dean:
I lead you to a nobler scene;
When to the vault you walk in state,
In quality of butler's mate;
You, next to Dennis bear the sway:
90   To you we often trust the key:
Nor, can he judge with all his art
So well, what bottle holds a quart;
What pints may best for bottles pass,
Just to give every man his glass:
When proper to produce the best;
And, what may serve a common guest.
With Dennis you did ne'er combine,
Not you, to steal your master's wine;
Except a bottle now and then,
100   To welcome brother serving-men;
But, that is with a good design,
To drink Sir Arthur's health and mine:
Your master's honour to maintain,
And get the like returns again.

Your usher's post must next be handled:
How blessed am I by such a man led!
Under whose wise and careful guardship,
I now despise fatigue and hardship:
Familiar grown to dirt and wet,
110   Though daggled round, I scorn to fret:
From you my chamber-damsels learn
My broken hose to patch and darn.

Now, as a jester, I accost you;
Which never yet one friend has lost you.

You judge so nicely to a hair,
How far to go, and when to spare:
By long experience grown so wise,
Of every taste to know the size;
There's none so ignorant or weak
120 To take offence at what you speak.
Whene'er you joke, 'tis all a case;
Whether with Dermot, or his Grace;
With Teague O'Murphy, or an earl;
A duchess or a kitchen girl.
With such dexterity you fit
Their several talents to your wit,
That Moll the chambermaid can smoke,
And Gaghagan take every joke.

I now become your humble suitor,
130 To let me praise you as my tutor.
Poor I, a savage bred and born,
By you instructed every morn,
Already have improved so well,
That I have almost learnt to spell:
The neighbours who come here to dine,
Admire to hear me speak so *fine*.
How enviously the ladies look,
When they surprise me at my book!
And, sure as they're alive, at night,
140 As soon as gone, will show their spite:
'Good Lord! what can my Lady mean,
Conversing with that rusty Dean!
She's grown so nice, and so *penurious*,
With Socratus and Epicurius.
How could she sit the livelong day,
Yet never ask us once to play?'

But, I admire your patience most;
That, when I'm duller than a post,
Nor can the plainest word pronounce,
150 You neither fume, nor fret, nor flounce;
Are so indulgent, and so mild,
As if I were a darling child.
So gentle in your whole proceeding,
That I could spend my life in reading.

You merit new employments daily:
Our thatcher, ditcher, gardener, bailie.
And, to a genius so extensive,
No work is grievous or offensive.
Whether, your fruitful fancy lies
160 To make for pigs convenient sties:
Or, ponder long with anxious thought,
To banish rats that haunt our vault.
Nor have you grumbled, reverend Dean,
To keep our poultry sweet and clean;
To sweep the mansion house they dwell in;
And cure the rank unsavoury smelling.

Now, enter as the dairy handmaid:
Such charming butter never man made.
Let others with fanatic face,
170 Talk of their milk for babes of grace;
From tubs their snuffling nonsense utter:
Thy milk shall make us tubs of butter.
The bishop with his foot may burn it;
But, with his hand, the Dean can churn it.
How are the servants overjoyed
To see thy Deanship thus employed!
Instead of poring on a book,
Providing butter for the cook.
Three morning hours you toss and shake
180 The bottle, till your fingers ache:
Hard is the toil, nor small the art,
The butter from the whey to part:
Behold; a frothy substance rise;
Be cautious, or your bottle flies.
The butter comes; our fears are ceased;
And, out you squeeze an ounce at least.

Your reverence thus, with like success,
Nor is your skill, or labour less,
When bent upon some smart lampoon,
190 You toss and turn your brain till noon;
Which, in its jumblings round the skull,
Dilates, and makes the vessel full:
While nothing comes but froth at first,
You think your giddy head will burst:

But, squeezing out four lines in rhyme,
Are largely paid for all your time.

But, you have raised your generous mind
To works of more exalted kind.
Palladio was not half so skilled in
200   The grandeur or the art of building.
Two temples of magnific size,
Attract the curious traveller's eyes,
That might be envied by the Greeks;
Raised up by you in twenty weeks:
Here, gentle goddess Cloacine
Receives all offerings at her shrine.
In separate cells the he's and she's
Here pay their vows with bended knees:
(For, 'tis prophane when sexes mingle;
210   And every nymph must enter single;
And when she feels an *inward motion*,
Comes filled with *reverence* and devotion.)
The bashful maid, to hide her blush,
Shall creep no more behind a bush;
Here unobserved, she boldly goes,
As who should say, *to pluck a rose*.

Ye who frequent this hallowed scene,
Be not ungrateful to the Dean;
But, duly e'er you leave your station,
220   Offer to him a pure libation;
Or, of his own, or Smedley's lay,
Or billet-doux, or lock of hay:
And, O! may all who hither come,
Return with unpolluted thumb.

Yet, when your lofty domes I praise,
I sigh to think of ancient days.
Permit me then to raise my style,
And sweetly moralize a while.

Thee bounteous goddess Cloacine,
230   To temples why do we confine?
Forbid in open air to breathe;
Why are thine altars fixed beneath?

When Saturn ruled the skies alone,
That golden age, to gold unknown;
This earthly globe to thee assigned,
Received the gifts of all mankind.
Ten thousand altars smoking round
Were built to thee, with offerings crowned:
And here thy daily votaries placed
240   Their sacrifice with zeal and haste:
The margin of a purling stream,
Sent up to thee a grateful steam.
(Though sometimes thou wert pleased to wink,
If Naiads swept them from the brink)
Or, where appointing lovers rove,
The shelter of a shady grove:
Or, offered in some flowery vale,
Were wafted by a gentle gale.
There, many a flower abstersive grew,
250   Thy favourite flowers of yellow hue;
The crocus and the daffodil,
The cowslip soft, and sweet jonquil.

But, when at last usurping Jove
Old Saturn from his empire drove;
Then Gluttony with greasy paws,
Her napkins pinned up to her jaws,
With watery chaps, and wagging chin,
Braced like a drum her oily skin;
Wedged in a spacious elbow-chair,
260   And on her plate a treble share,
As if she ne'er could have enough;
Taught harmless men to cram and stuff.
She sent her priests in wooden shoes
From haughty Gaul to make ragouts.
Instead of wholesome bread and cheese,
To dress their soups and fricassees;
And, for our home-bred British cheer,
Botargo, catsup, and caveer.

This bloated harpy sprung from hell,
270   Confined thee goddess to a cell:
Sprung from her womb that impious line,
Contemners of thy rites divine.

First, lolling Sloth in woollen cap,
Taking her after-dinner nap:
Pale Dropsy with a sallow face,
Her belly burst, and slow her pace:
And, lordly Gout wrapped up in fur:
And, wheezing Asthma, loath to stir:
Voluptuous Ease, the child of Wealth,
280 Infecting thus our hearts by stealth;
None seek thee now in open air;
To thee no verdant altars rear;
But, in their cells and vaults obscene
Present a sacrifice unclean;
From whence unsavoury vapours rose,
Offensive to thy nicer nose.
Ah! who in our degenerate days
As nature prompts, his offering pays?
Here, nature never difference made
290 Between the sceptre and the spade.

Ye great ones, why will ye disdain
To pay your tribute on the plain?
Why will you place in lazy pride
Your altars near your couch's side?
When from the homeliest earthenware
Are sent up offerings more sincere
Than where the haughty duchess locks
Her silver vase in cedar-box.

Yet, some devotion still remains
300 Among our harmless northern swains;
Whose offerings placed in golden ranks,
Adorn our crystal river's banks:
Nor seldom grace the flowery downs,
With spiral tops, and copple-crowns:
Or gilding in a sunny morn
The humble branches of a thorn.
(So poets sing, with golden bough
The Trojan hero paid his vow.)

Hither by luckless error led,
310 The crude consistence oft I tread.
Here, when my shoes are out of case,

Unweeting gild the tarnished lace:
Here, by the sacred bramble tinged,
My petticoat is doubly fringed.

Be witness for me, nymph divine,
I never robbed thee with design:
Nor will the zealous Hannah pout
To wash thy injured offerings out.

But, stop ambitious muse, in time;
320 Nor dwell on subjects too sublime.
In vain on lofty heels I tread,
Aspiring to exalt my head:
With hoop expanded wide and light,
In vain I tempt too high a flight.

Me Phoebus in a midnight dream
Accosting, said, 'Go shake your cream.
Be humbly minded; know your post;
Sweeten your tea, and watch your toast.
Thee best befits a lowly style:
330 Teach Dennis how to stir the gyle:
With Peggy Dixon thoughtful sit,
Contriving for the pot and spit.
Take down thy proudly swelling sails,
And rub thy teeth, and pare thy nails.
At nicely carving show thy wit;
But ne'er presume to eat a bit:
Turn every way thy watchful eye;
And every guest be sure to ply:
Let never at your board be known
340 An empty plate except your own.
Be these thy arts; nor higher aim
Than what befits a rural dame.'

But, Cloacina goddess bright,
Sleek — claims her as his right:
And Smedley, flower of all divines,
Shall sing the Dean in Smedley's lines.

An Excellent New Ballad

I

Our brethren of England, who love us so dear,
    And in all they do for us so kindly do mean,
A blessing upon them, have sent us this year,
    For the good of our church a true English Dean.
A holier priest ne'er was wrapped up in crape,
The worst you can say, he committed a rape.

II

In his journey to Dublin, he lighted at Chester,
    And there he grew fond of another man's wife,
Burst into her chamber, and would have caressed her,
10   But she valued her honour much more than her life.
She bustled and struggled, and made her escape,
To a room full of guests for fear of a rape.

III

The Dean he pursued to recover his game,
    And now to attack her again he prepares,
But the company stood in defence of the dame,
    They cudgelled and cuffed him, and kicked him downstairs.
His Deanship was now in a damnable scrape,
And this was no time for committing a rape.

IV

To Dublin he comes, to the bagnio he goes,
20   And orders the landlord to bring him a whore;
No scruple came on him his gown to expose,
    'Twas what all his life he had practised before.
He had made himself drunk with the juice of the grape,
And got a good clap, but committed no rape.

V

The Dean, and his landlord, a jolly comrade,
    Resolved for a fortnight to swim in delight;
For why, they had both been brought up to the trade
    Of drinking all day, and of whoring all night.
His landlord was ready his Deanship to ape
30   In every debauch, but committing a rape.

VI

This Protestant zealot, this English divine
    In church and in state was of principles sound;
Was truer than Steele to the Hanover line,
    And grieved that a Tory should live above ground.
Shall a subject so loyal be hanged by the nape,
For no other crime but committing a rape?

VII

By old popish canons, as wise men have penned 'em,
    Each priest had a concubine, *jure ecclesiae*;
Who'd be Dean of Ferns without a *commendam*?
40   And precedents we can produce, if it please ye:
Then, why should the Dean, when whores are so cheap,
Be put to the peril, and toil of a rape?

VIII

If fortune should please but to take such a crotchet,
    (To thee I apply great Smedley's successor)
To give thee lawn-sleeves, a mitre and rochet,
    Whom wouldst thou resemble? I leave thee a guesser;
But I only behold thee in Atherton's shape,
For sodomy hanged, as thou for a rape.

IX

Ah! dost thou not envy the brave Colonel Chartres,
50   Condemned for thy crime, at three score and ten?
To hang him all England would lend him their garters;
    Yet he lives, and is ready to ravish again,
Then throttle thyself with an ell of strong tape,
For thou hast not a groat to atone for a rape.

X

The Dean he was vexed that his whores were so willing,
    He longed for a girl that would struggle and squall;
He ravished her fairly, and saved a good shilling;
    But, here was to pay the devil and all.
His trouble and sorrows now come in a heap,
60   And hanged he must be for committing a rape.

XI

If maidens are ravished, it is their own choice,
    Why are they so wilful to struggle with men?
If they would but lie quiet, and stifle their voice,

No devil or Dean could ravish 'em then,
Nor would there be need of a strong hempen cape,
Tied round the Dean's neck, for committing a rape.

XII

Our church and our state dear England maintains,
    For which all true Protestant hearts should be glad;
She sends us our bishops and judges and deans,
70   And better would give us, if better she had;
But, Lord how the rabble will stare and will gape,
When the good English Dean is hanged up for a rape.

On Stephen Duck, the Thresher, and Favourite Poet

A QUIBBLING EPIGRAM

The thresher Duck could o'er the Queen prevail.
The proverb says, 'No fence against a flail.'
From *threshing* corn, he turns to *thresh* his brains;
For which Her Majesty allows him grains.
Though 'tis confessed that those who ever saw
His poems, think them all not worth a *straw*.
Thrice happy Duck, employed in threshing *stubble*!
Thy toil is lessened, and thy profits double.

To Betty the Grisette

Queen of wit and beauty, Betty,
Never may the muse forget ye:
How thy face charms every shepherd,
Spotted over like a leopard!
And, thy freckled neck displayed,
Envy breeds in every maid.
Like a flyblown cake of tallow,
Or, on parchment, ink turned yellow:
Or, a tawny speckled pippin,
10   Shrivelled with a winter's keeping.

    And, thy beauty thus dispatched;
Let me praise thy wit unmatched.

Sets of phrases, cut and dry,
Evermore thy tongue supply.
And, thy memory is loaded
With old scraps from plays exploded.
Stocked with repartees and jokes,
Suited to all Christian folks:
Shreds of wit, and senseless rhymes,
20 Blundered out a thousand times.
Nor, wilt thou of gifts be sparing,
Which can ne'er be worse for wearing.
Picking wit among collegians,
In the playhouse upper regions;
Where, in eighteen-penny gallery,
Irish nymphs learn Irish raillery:
But, thy merit is thy failing,
And, thy raillery is railing.

Thus, with talents well endued,
30 To be scurrilous and rude;
When you pertly raise your snout,
Fleer, and gibe, and laugh, and flout;
This, among Hibernian asses,
For sheer wit, and humour passes!
Thus, indulgent Chloe bit,
Swears you have a world of wit.

The Lady's Dressing Room

Five hours, (and who can do it less in?)
By haughty Celia spent in dressing;
The goddess from her chamber issues,
Arrayed in lace, brocade and tissues:
Strephon, who found the room was void,
And Betty otherwise employed,
Stole in, and took a strict survey,
Of all the litter as it lay:
Whereof, to make the matter clear,
10 An *inventory* follows here.

And first, a dirty smock appeared,
Beneath the arm-pits well besmeared;

Strephon, the rogue, displayed it wide,
And turned it round on every side.
In such a case few words are best,
And Strephon bids us guess the rest;
But swears how damnably the men lie,
In calling Celia sweet and cleanly.

Now listen while he next produces,
20 The various combs for various uses,
Filled up with dirt so closely fixed,
No brush could force a way betwixt;
A paste of composition rare,
Sweat, dandruff, powder, lead and hair,
A forehead cloth with oil upon't
To smooth the wrinkles on her front;
Here alum flower to stop the steams,
Exhaled from sour unsavoury streams;
There night-gloves made of Tripsy's hide,
30 Bequeathed by Tripsy when she died;
With puppy water, beauty's help,
Distilled from Tripsy's darling whelp.
Here gallipots and vials placed,
Some filled with washes, some with paste;
Some with pomatum, paints and slops,
And ointments good for scabby chops.
Hard by a filthy basin stands,
Fouled with the scouring of her hands;
The basin takes whatever comes,
40 The scrapings of her teeth and gums,
A nasty compound of all hues,
For here she spits, and here she spews.

But oh! it turned poor Strephon's bowels,
When he beheld and smelt the towels;
Begummed, bemattered, and beslimed;
With dirt, and sweat, and ear-wax grimed.
No object Strephon's eye escapes,
Here, petticoats in frowzy heaps;
Nor be the handkerchiefs forgot,
50 All varnished o'er with snuff and snot.
The stockings why should I expose,
Stained with the moisture of her toes;

Or greasy coifs and pinners reeking,
Which Celia slept at least a week in?
A pair of tweezers next he found
To pluck her brows in arches round,
Or hairs that sink the forehead low,
Or on her chin like bristles grow.

The virtues we must not let pass,
60 Of Celia's magnifying glass;
When frighted Strephon cast his eye on't,
It showed the visage of a giant:
A glass that can to sight disclose
The smallest worm in Celia's nose,
And faithfully direct her nail
To squeeze it out from head to tail;
For catch it nicely by the head,
It must come out alive or dead.

Why, Strephon, will you tell the rest?
70 And must you needs describe the chest?
That careless wench! no creature warn her
To move it out from yonder corner,
But leave it standing full in sight,
For you to exercise your spite!
In vain the workman showed his wit
With rings and hinges counterfeit
To make it seem in this disguise,
A cabinet to vulgar eyes;
Which Strephon ventured to look in,
80 Resolved to go through *thick and thin*;
He lifts the lid: there need no more,
He smelt it all the time before.

As, from within Pandora's box,
When Epimethus oped the locks,
A sudden universal crew
Of human evils upward flew;
He still was comforted to find
That hope at last remained behind.

So, Strephon, lifting up the lid,
90 To view what in the chest was hid,
The vapours flew from out the vent,

But Strephon cautious never meant
The bottom of the pan to grope,
And foul his hands in search of hope.

O! ne'er may such a vile machine
Be once in Celia's chamber seen!
O! may she better learn to keep
'Those secrets of the hoary deep.'

As mutton cutlets, prime of meat,
100   Which though with art you salt and beat,
As laws of cookery require,
And roast them at the clearest fire;
If from adown the hopeful chops
The fat upon a cinder drops,
To stinking smoke it turns the flame
Poisoning the flesh from whence it came;
And up exhales a greasy stench,
For which you curse the careless wench:
So things which must not be expressed,
110   When *plumped* into the reeking chest,
Send up an excremental smell
To taint the parts from which they fell:
The petticoats and gown perfume,
And waft a stink round every room.

Thus finishing his grand survey,
The swain disgusted slunk away,
Repeating in his amorous fits,
'Oh! Celia, Celia, Celia shits!'

But Véngeance, goddess never sleeping,
120   Soon punished Strephon for his peeping.
His foul imagination links
Each dame he sees with all her stinks:
And, if unsavoury odours fly,
Conceives a lady standing by:
All women his description fits,
And both ideas jump like wits,
By vicious fancy coupled fast,
And still appearing in contrast.

I pity wretched Strephon, blind
130   To all the charms of womankind;

Should I the queen of love refuse,
Because she rose from stinking ooze?
To him that looks behind the scene,
Statira's but some pocky quean.

When Celia in her glory shows,
If Strephon would but stop his nose,
Who now so impiously blasphemes
Her ointments, daubs, and paints and creams;
Her washes, slops, and every clout,
140   With which she makes so foul a rout;
He soon would learn to think like me,
And bless his ravished eyes to see
Such order from confusion sprung,
Such gaudy *tulips* raised from *dung*.

Apollo

OR, A PROBLEM SOLVED

Apollo, god of light and wit,
Could verse inspire, but seldom writ:
Refined all metals with his looks,
As well as chemists by their books:
As handsome as my Lady's page;
Sweet five and twenty was his age.
His wig was made of sunny rays,
He crowned his youthful head with bays:
Not all the court of heaven could show
10   So nice and so complete a beau.
No heir, upon his first appearance,
With twenty thousand pounds a year rents,
E'er drove, before he sold his land,
So fine a coach along the Strand;
The spokes, we are by Ovid told,
Were silver, and the axle gold.
(I own, 'twas but a coach and four,
For Jupiter allows no more.)

Yet with his beauty, wealth, and parts,
20   Enough to win ten thousand hearts;

No vulgar deity above
Was so unfortunate in love.

Three weighty causes were assigned,
That moved the nymphs to be unkind.
Nine muses always waiting round him,
He left them virgins as he found 'em.
His singing was another fault;
For he could reach to B *in alt*:
And, by the sentiments of Pliny,
30   Such singers are like Nicolini.
At last, the point was fully cleared;
In short; Apollo had no beard.

A Beautiful Young Nymph Going to Bed

WRITTEN FOR THE HONOUR OF THE FAIR SEX

Corinna, pride of Drury Lane,
For whom no shepherd sighs in vain;
Never did Covent Garden boast
So bright a battered, strolling toast;
No drunken rake to pick her up,
No cellar where on tick to sup;
Returning at the midnight hour;
Four storeys climbing to her bower;
Then, seated on a three-legged chair,
10   Takes off her artificial hair:
Now, picking out a crystal eye,
She wipes it clean, and lays it by.
Her eyebrows from a mouse's hide,
Stuck on with art on either side,
Pulls off with care, and first displays 'em,
Then in a play-book smoothly lays 'em.
Now dexterously her plumpers draws,
That serve to fill her hollow jaws.
Untwists a wire; and from her gums
20   A set of teeth completely comes.
Pulls out the rags contrived to prop
Her flabby dugs, and down they drop.
Proceeding on, the lovely goddess

Unlaces next her steel-ribbed bodice;
Which by the operator's skill,
Press down the lumps, the hollows fill.
Up goes her hand, and off she slips
The bolsters that supply her hips.
With gentlest touch, she next explores
30 Her shankers, issues, running sores;
Effects of many a sad disaster,
And then to each applies a plaster.
But must, before she goes to bed,
Rub off the daubs of white and red.
And smooth the furrows in her front,
With greasy paper stuck upon't.
She takes a bolus e'er she sleeps;
And then between two blankets creeps.
With pains of love tormented lies;
40 Or if she chance to close her eyes,
Of Bridewell and the compter dreams,
And feels the lash, and faintly screams.
Or, by a faithless bully drawn,
At some hedge-tavern lies in pawn.
Or to Jamaica seems transported,
Alone, and by no planter courted;
Or, near Fleet Ditch's oozy brinks,
Surrounded with a hundred stinks,
Belated, seems on watch to lie,
50 And snap some cully passing by;
Or, struck with fear, her fancy runs
On watchmen, constables and duns,
From whom she meets with frequent rubs;
But, never from religious clubs;
Whose favour she is sure to find,
Because she pays them all in kind.

Corinna wakes. A dreadful sight!
Behold the ruins of the night!
A wicked rat her plaster stole,
60 Half ate, and dragged it to his hole.
The crystal eye, alas, was missed;
And Puss had on her plumpers pissed.
A pigeon picked her issue-peas,
And Shock her tresses filled with fleas.

The nymph, though in this mangled plight,
Must every morn her limbs unite.
But how shall I describe her arts
To recollect the scattered parts?
Or show the anguish, toil, and pain,
70 Of gathering up herself again?
The bashful muse will never bear
In such a scene to interfere.
Corinna in the morning dizened,
Who sees, will spew; who smells, be poisoned.

Strephon and Chloe

Of Chloe all the town has rung;
By every size of poet sung:
So beautiful a nymph appears
But once in twenty thousand years:
By nature formed with nicest care,
And, faultless to a single hair.
Her graceful mien, her shape, and face,
Confessed her of no mortal race:
And then, so nice, and so genteel;
10 Such cleanliness from head to heel:
No humours gross, or frowzy steams,
No noisome whiffs, or sweaty streams,
Before, behind, above, below,
Could from her taintless body flow.
Would so discreetly things dispose,
None ever saw her pluck a rose.
Her dearest comrades never caught her
Squat on her hams, to make maid's water.
You'd swear, that so divine a creature
20 Felt no necessities of nature.
In summer had she walked the town,
Her armpits would not stain her gown:
At country dances, not a nose
Could in the dog-days smell her toes.
Her milk-white hands, both palms and backs,
Like ivory dry, and soft as wax.
Her hands, the softest ever felt,
Though cold would burn, though dry would melt.

Dear Venus, hide this wondrous maid,
30 Nor let her loose to spoil your trade.
While she engrosseth every swain,
You but o'er half the world can reign.
Think what a case all men are now in,
What ogling, sighing, toasting, vowing!
What powdered wigs! What flames and darts!
What hampers full of bleeding hearts!
What sword-knots! What poetic strains!
What billet-doux, and clouded canes!

But, Strephon sighed so loud and strong,
40 He blew a settlement along:
And, bravely drove his rivals down
With coach and six, and house in town.
The bashful nymph no more withstands,
Because her dear papa commands.
The charming couple now unites;
Proceed we to the marriage rites.

Imprimis, at the temple porch
Stood Hymen with a flaming torch.
The smiling Cyprian goddess brings
50 Her infant loves with purple wings;
And pigeons billing, sparrows treading,
Fair emblems of a fruitful wedding.
The muses next in order follow,
Conducted by their squire, Apollo:
Then Mercury with silver tongue,
And Hebe, goddess ever young.
Behold the bridegroom and his bride,
Walk hand in hand, and side by side;
She by the tender Graces dressed,
60 But, he by Mars, in scarlet vest.
The nymph was covered with her *flammeum*,
And Phoebus sung the epithalamium.
And, last to make the matter sure,
Dame Juno brought a priest demure.
Luna was absent on pretence
Her time was not till nine months hence.

The rites performed, the parson paid,
In state returned the grand parade;

With loud huzza's from all the boys,
70 That now the pair must *crown their joys*.

But, still the hardest part remains.
Strephon had long perplexed his brains,
How with so high a nymph he might
Demean himself the wedding-night:
For, as he viewed his person round,
Mere mortal flesh was all he found:
His hand, his neck, his mouth, and feet
Were duly washed to keep 'em sweet;
(With other parts that shall be nameless,
80 The ladies else might think me shameless.)
The weather and his love were hot;
And should he struggle; I know what –
Why let it go, if I must tell it –
He'll sweat, and then the nymph will smell it.
While she a goddess dyed in grain
Was unsusceptible of stain:
And, Venus-like, her fragrant skin
Exhaled ambrosia from within:
Can such a deity endure
90 A mortal human touch impure?
How did the humbled swain detest
His prickled beard, and hairy breast!
His nightcap bordered round with lace
Could give no softness to his face.

Yet, if the goddess could be kind,
What endless raptures must he find!
And goddesses have now and then
Come down to visit mortal men:
To visit and to court them too:
100 A certain goddess, God knows who,
(As in a book he heard it read)
Took Colonel Peleus to her bed.
But, what if he should lose his life
By venturing *on* his heavenly wife?
For, Strephon could remember well,
That, once he heard a schoolboy tell,
How Semele of mortal race,
By thunder died in Jove's embrace;

And what if daring Strephon dies
110 By lightning shot from Chloe's eyes?

While these reflections filled his head,
The bride was put in form to bed;
He followed, stripped, and in he crept,
But, awfully his distance kept.

Now, ponder well, ye parents dear;
Forbid your daughters guzzling beer;
And make them every afternoon
Forbear their tea, or drink it soon;
That, e'er to bed they venture up,
120 They may discharge it every sup;
If not, they must in evil plight
Be often forced to rise at night;
Keep them to wholesome food confined,
Nor let them taste what causes wind;
('Tis this the sage of Samos means,
Forbidding his disciples beans)
O, think what evils must ensue;
Miss Moll the jade will burn it blue:
And when she once has got the art,
130 She cannot help it for her heart;
But, out it flies, even when she meets
Her bridegroom in the wedding-sheets.
Carminative and diuretic,
Will damp all passions sympathetic;
And, love such niceties requires,
One blast will put out all his fires.
Since husbands get behind the scene,
The wife should study to be clean;
Nor give the smallest room to guess
140 The time when wants of nature press;
But, after marriage, practise more
Decorum than she did before;
To keep her spouse deluded still,
And make him fancy what she will.

In bed we left the married pair;
'Tis time to show how things went there.
Strephon, who often had been told,

That fortune still assists the bold,
Resolved to make his first attack:
150   But, Chloe drove him fiercely back.
How could a nymph so chaste as Chloe,
With constitution cold and snowy,
Permit a brutish man to touch her;
Even lambs by instinct fly the butcher.
Resistance on the wedding night
Is what our maidens claim by right:
And, Chloe, 'tis by all agreed,
Was maid in thought, and word, and deed.
Yet some assign a different reason;
160   That Strephon chose no proper season.

Say, fair ones, must I make a pause?
Or freely tell the secret cause.

Twelve cups of tea, (with grief I speak)
Had now constrained the nymph to leak.
This point must needs be settled first:
The bride must either void or burst.
Then, see the dire effect of pease,
Think what can give the colic ease.
The nymph oppressed before, behind,
170   As ships are tossed by waves and wind,
Steals out her hand by nature led,
And brings a vessel into bed:
Fair utensil, as smooth and white
As Chloe's skin, almost as bright.

Strephon who heard the foaming rill
As from a mossy cliff distil;
Cried out, 'Ye gods, what sound is this?
Can Chloe, heavenly Chloe piss?'
But when he smelt a noisome steam
180   Which oft attends that lukewarm stream;
(Salerno both together joins
As sovereign medicines for the loins)
And, though contrived, we may suppose
To slip his ears, yet struck his nose:
He found her, while the scent increased,
As *mortal* as himself at least.

But, soon with like occasions pressed,
He boldly sent his hand in quest,
(Inspired with courage from his bride,)
190   To reach the pot on t'other side.
And as he filled the reeking vase,
Let fly a rouser in her face.

The little Cupids hovering round,
(As pictures prove) with garlands crowned,
Abashed at what they saw and heard,
Flew off, nor ever more appeared.

Adieu to ravishing delights,
High raptures, and romantic flights;
To goddesses so heavenly sweet,
200   Expiring shepherds at their feet;
To silver meads, and shady bowers,
Dressed up with amaranthine flowers.

How great a change! how quickly made!
They learn to call a spade, a spade.
They soon from all constraints are freed;
Can see each other *do their need*.
On box of cedar sits the wife,
And makes it warm for 'dearest life'.
And, by the beastly way of thinking,
210   Find great society in stinking.
Now Strephon daily entertains
His Chloe in the homeliest strains;
And, Chloe more experienced grown,
With interest pays him back his own.
No maid at court is less ashamed,
Howe'er for selling bargains famed,
Than she, to name her parts behind,
Or when abed, to let out wind.

Fair Decency, celestial maid,
220   Descend from heaven to Beauty's aid;
Though Beauty must beget Desire,
'Tis thou must fan the lover's fire;
For, Beauty, like supreme Dominion,
Is best supported by Opinion;

If Decency brings no supplies,
Opinion falls, and Beauty dies.

To see some radiant nymph appear
In all her glittering birthday gear,
You think some goddess from the sky
230 Descended, ready cut and dry:
But, e'er you sell yourself to laughter,
Consider well what may come after;
For fine ideas vanish fast,
While all the gross and filthy last.

O Strephon, e'er that fatal day
When Chloe stole your heart away,
Had you but through a cranny spied
On house of ease your future bride,
In all the postures of her face,
240 Which nature gives in such a case;
Distortions, groanings, strainings, heavings;
'Twere better you had licked her leavings,
Than from experience find too late
Your goddess grown a filthy mate.
Your fancy then had always dwelt
On what you saw, and what you smelt;
Would still the same ideas give ye,
As when you spied her on the privy.
And, spite of Chloe's charms divine,
250 Your heart had been as whole as mine.

Authorities both old and recent
Direct that women must be decent;
And, from the spouse each blemish hide
More than from all the world beside.

Unjustly all our nymphs complain,
Their empire holds so short a reign;
Is after marriage lost so soon,
It hardly holds the honeymoon:
For, if they keep not what they caught,
260 It is entirely their own fault.
They take possession of the crown,
And then throw all their weapons down;

Though by the politicians' scheme
Whoe'er arrives at power supreme,
Those arts by which at first they gain it,
They still must practise to attain it.

What various ways our females take,
To pass for wits before a rake!
And in the fruitless search pursue
270   All other methods but the true.

Some try to learn polite behaviour,
By reading books against their Saviour;
Some call it witty to reflect
On every natural defect;
Some show they never want explaining,
To comprehend a double meaning.
But, sure a telltale out of school
Is, of all wits, the greatest fool;
Whose rank imagination fills
280   Her heart, and from her lips distils;
You'd think she uttered from behind,
Or at her mouth was breaking wind.

Why is a handsome wife adored
By every coxcomb, but her lord?
From yonder puppet-man inquire,
Who wisely hides his wood and wire:
Shows Sheba's queen completely dressed,
And Solomon in royal vest;
But, view them littered on the floor,
290   Or strung on pegs behind the door;
Punch is exactly of a piece
With Lorraine's Duke, and Prince of Greece.

A prudent builder should forecast
How long the stuff is like to last;
And, carefully observe the ground,
To build on some foundation sound;
What house, when its materials crumble,
Must not inevitably tumble?
What edifice can long endure,
300   Raised on a basis unsecure?

Rash mortals, e'er you take a wife,
Contrive your pile to last for life;
Since beauty scarce endures a day,
And youth so swiftly glides away;
Why will you make yourself a bubble
To build on sand with hay and stubble?

On sense and wit your passion found,
By decency cemented round;
Let prudence with good nature strive,
310 To keep esteem and love alive.
Then come old age whene'er it will,
Your friendship shall continue still:
And thus a mutual gentle fire,
Shall never but with life expire.

Cassinus and Peter

A TRAGICAL ELEGY

Two college sophs of Cambridge growth,
Both special wits, and lovers both,
Conferring as they used to meet,
On love and books in rapture sweet;
(Muse, find me names to fix my metre,
Cassinus this, and t'other Peter)
Friend Peter to Cassinus goes,
To chat a while, and warm his nose:
But, such a sight was never seen,
10 The lad lay swallowed up in spleen;
He seems as just crept out of bed;
One greasy stocking round his head,
The t'other he sat down to darn
With threads of different coloured yarn.
His breeches torn exposing wide
A ragged shirt, and tawny hide.
Scorched were his shins, his legs were bare,
But, well embrowned with dirt and hair.
A rug was o'er his shoulders thrown;
20 A rug; for night-gown had he none.

His jordan stood in manner fitting
Between his legs, to spew or spit in.
His ancient pipe in sable dyed,
And half unsmoked, lay by his side.

Him thus accoutred, Peter found,
With eyes in smoke and weeping drowned:
The leavings of his last night's pot
On embers placed, to drink it hot.

    'Why, Cassy, thou wilt doze thy pate:
30 What makes thee lie abed so late?
The finch, the linnet, and the thrush,
Their matins chant in every bush:
And I have heard thee oft salute
Aurora with thy early flute.
Heaven send thou hast not got the hyps.
How? not a word come from thy lips?'

Then gave him some familiar thumps,
A college joke to cure the dumps.

The swain at last, with grief oppressed,
40 Cried, 'Celia!' thrice, and sighed the rest.

    'Dear Cassy, though to ask I dread,
Yet ask I must. Is Celia dead?'

    'How happy I, were that the worst!
But I was fated to be cursed.'

    'Come, tell us, has she played the whore?'

    'Oh Peter, would it were no more!'

    'Why, plague confound her sandy locks:
Say, has the small or greater pox
Sunk down her nose, or seamed her face?
50 Be easy, 'tis a common case.'

    'Oh Peter! beauty's but a varnish,
Which time and accidents will tarnish:
But, Celia has contrived to blast
Those beauties that might ever last.
Nor can imagination guess,

Nor eloquence divine express,
How that ungrateful charming maid,
My purest passion has betrayed.
Conceive the most envenomed dart,
60 To pierce an injured lover's heart.'

'Why, hang her, though she seemed so coy,
I know she loves the barber's boy.'

'Friend Peter, this I could excuse;
For, every nymph has leave to choose;
Nor, have I reason to complain:
She loves a more deserving swain.
But, oh! how ill thou hast divined
A crime that shocks all humankind;
A deed unknown to female race,
70 At which the sun should hide his face.
Advice in vain you would apply –
Then, leave me to despair and die.
Yet, kind Arcadians, on my urn
These elegies and sonnets burn,
And on the marble grave these rhymes,
A monument to after-times:
"Here Cassy lies, by Celia slain,
And dying, never told his pain."

'Vain empty world farewell. But hark,
80 The loud Cerberian triple bark.
And there – behold Alecto stand,
A whip of scorpions in her hand.
Lo, Charon from his leaky wherry,
Beckoning to waft me o'er the ferry.
I come, I come – Medusa, see,
Her serpents hiss direct at me.
Begone; unhand me, hellish fry;
Avaunt – ye cannot say 'twas I.'

'Dear Cassy, thou must purge and bleed;
90 I fear thou wilt be mad indeed.
But now, by friendship's sacred laws,
I here conjure thee, tell the cause;
And Celia's horrid fact relate;
Thy friend would gladly share thy fate.'

'To force it out my heart must rend;
Yet, when conjured by such a friend –
Think, Peter, how my soul is racked.
These eyes, these eyes beheld the fact.
Now, bend thine ear; since out it must:
100   But, when thou seest me laid in dust,
The secret thou shalt ne'er impart;
Not to the nymph that keeps thy heart;
(How would her virgin soul bemoan
A crime to all her sex unknown!)
Nor whisper to the tattling reeds,
The blackest of all female deeds.
Nor blab it on the lonely rocks,
Where Echo sits, and listening, mocks.
Nor let the zephyr's treacherous gale
110   Through Cambridge waft the direful tale.
Nor to the chattering feathered race,
Discover Celia's foul disgrace.
But, if you fail, my spectre dread
Attending nightly round your bed:
And yet, I dare confide in you;
So, take my secret, and adieu.

'Nor, wonder how I lost my wits;
Oh! Celia, Celia, Celia shits.'

To Mr Gay

ON HIS BEING STEWARD TO THE DUKE OF QUEENSBERRY

How could you, Gay, disgrace the muses' train,
To serve a tasteless court twelve years in vain?
Fain would I think, our female friend sincere,
Till Bob, the poet's foe, possessed her ear.
Did female virtue e'er so high ascend,
To lose an inch of favour for a friend?

Say, had the court no better place to choose
For thee, than make a dry nurse of thy muse?
How cheaply had thy liberty been sold,
10   To squire a royal girl of two years old!

In leading strings her infant steps to guide;
Or, with her go-cart amble side by side.

But princely Douglas, and his glorious dame,
Advanced thy fortune, and preserved thy fame.
Nor, will your nobler gifts be misapplied,
When o'er your patron's treasure you preside,
The world shall own, his choice was wise and just,
For, sons of Phoebus never break their trust.

Not love of beauty less the heart inflames
20 Of guardian eunuchs to the sultan dames,
Their passions not more impotent and cold,
Than those of poets to the lust of gold.
With Paean's purest fire his favourites glow;
The dregs will serve to ripen ore below;
His meanest work: for, had he thought it fit,
That, wealth should be the appanage of wit,
The god of light could ne'er have so *blind*,
To deal it to the worst of humankind.

But let me now, for I can do it well,
30 Your conduct in this new employ foretell.

And first: to make my observation right,
I place a STATESMAN full before my sight.
A bloated minister in all his gear,
With shameless visage, and perfidious leer,
Two rows of teeth arm each devouring jaw;
And, ostrich-like, his all-digesting maw.
My fancy drags this monster into view,
To show the world his chief reverse in you.
Of loud unmeaning sounds, a rapid flood
40 Rolls from his mouth in plenteous streams of mud;
With these, the court and senate-house he plies,
Made up of noise, and impudence, and lies.

Now, let me show how Bob and you agree.
You serve a potent prince, as well as he.
The ducal coffers, trusted to your charge,
Your honest care may fill; perhaps enlarge.
His vassals easy, and the owner blessed;
They pay a trifle, and enjoy the rest.

Not so a nation's revenues are paid:
50 The servant's faults are on the master laid.
The people with a sigh their taxes bring;
And cursing Bob, forget to bless the King.

Next, hearken Gay, to what thy charge requires,
With servants, tenants, and the neighbouring squires.
Let all domestics feel your gentle sway;
Nor bribe, insult, nor flatter, nor betray,
Let due reward to merit be allowed;
Nor with your kindred half the palace crowd.
Nor, think yourself secure in doing wrong,
60 By telling noses with a party strong.

Be rich; but of your wealth make no parade;
At least, before your master's debts are paid.
Nor, in a palace built with charge immense,
Presume to treat him at his own expense.
Each farmer in the neighbourhood can count
To what your lawful perquisites amount.
The tenants poor, the hardness of the times,
Are ill excuses for a servant's crimes:
With interest, and a premium paid beside,
70 The master's pressing wants must be supplied;
With hasty zeal, behold, the steward come,
By his own credit to advance the sum;
Who, while the unrighteous Mammon is his friend,
May well conclude his power will never end.
A faithful treasurer! What could he do more?
He lends my Lord, what was my Lord's before.

The law so strictly guards the monarch's health,
That no physician dares prescribe by stealth:
The council sit; approve the doctor's skill;
80 And give advice before he gives the pill.
But, the state empiric acts a safer part;
And while he poisons, wins the royal heart.

But, how can I describe the ravenous breed?
Then, let me now by negatives proceed.

Suppose your lord a trusty servant send,
On weighty business, to some neighbouring friend:

Presume not, Gay, unless you serve a drone,
To countermand his orders by your own.

Should some imperious neighbour sink the boats,
90 And drain the fish-ponds; while your master doats;
Shall he upon the ducal rights entrench,
Because he bribed you with a brace of tench?

Nor, from your lord his bad condition hide;
To feed his luxury, or soothe his pride.
Nor, at an under rate his timber sell;
And with an oath, assure him, 'all is well.'
Or swear it rotten; and with humble airs,
Request it of him to complete your stairs.
Nor, when a mortgage lies on half his lands,
100 Come with a purse of guineas in your hands.

Have Peter Waters always in your mind;
That rogue of genuine ministerial kind
Can half the peerage by his arts bewitch;
Starve twenty lords to make one scoundrel rich:
And when he gravely has undone a score,
Is humbly prayed to ruin twenty more.

A dexterous steward, when his tricks are found,
Hush-money sends to all the neighbours round:
His master, unsuspicious of his pranks,
110 Pays all the cost, and gives the villain thanks.
And, should a friend attempt to set him right,
His Lordship would impute it all to spite:
Would love his favourite better than before;
And trust his honesty just so much more.
Thus realms, and families, with equal fate,
Are sunk by premier ministers of state.

Some, when an heir succeeds, go boldly on,
And, as they robbed the father, rob the son.
A knave, who deep embroils his lord's affairs,
120 Will soon grow necessary to his heirs.
His policy consists in setting traps,
In finding ways and means, and stopping gaps:
He knows a thousand tricks, whene'er he please,
Though not to cure, yet palliate each disease.

In either case, an equal chance is run:
For, keep, or turn him out, my Lord's undone.
You want a hand to clear a filthy sink;
No cleanly workman can endure the stink.
A strong dilemma in a desperate case!
130   To act with infamy, or quit the place.

A bungler thus, who scarce the nail can hit,
With driving wrong, will make the panel split:
Nor, dares an abler workman undertake
To drive a second, lest the whole should break.

In every court the parallel will hold;
And kings, like private folks, are bought and sold:
The ruling rogue, who dreads to be cashiered,
Contrives, as he is hated, to be feared:
Confounds accounts, perplexes all affairs;
140   For, vengeance more embroils, than skill repairs.
So, robbers (and their ends are just the same)
To scape inquiries, leave the house in flame.

I knew a brazen minister of state,
Who bore for twice ten years the public hate.
In every mouth the question most in vogue
Was, 'When will they turn out this odious rogue?'
A juncture happened in his highest pride:
While he went robbing on, old Master died.
We thought, there now remained no room to doubt:
150   'His work is done, the minister must out.'
The court invited more than one, or two;
'Will you, Sir Spencer? or will *you*, or *you*?'
But not a soul his office durst accept:
The subtle knave had all the plunder swept.
And, such was then the temper of the times,
He owed his preservation to his crimes.
The candidates observed his dirty paws,
Nor found it difficult to guess the cause:
But when they smelt such foul corruptions round him;
160   Away they fled, and left him as they found him.

Thus, when a greedy sloven once has thrown
His snot into the mess; 'tis all his own.

On Mr Pulteney being Put Out of the Council

Sir Robert wearied by Will Pulteney's teasings,
Who interrupted him in all his leasings;
Resolved that Will and he should meet no more;
Full in his face Bob shuts the council door:
Nor lets him sit as justice on the bench,
To punish thieves, or lash a suburb wench.
Yet still St Stephen's Chapel open lies
For Will to enter – what shall I advise?
E'en quit the House, for thou too long hast sat in't,
10 Produce at last thy dormant ducal patent:
There, near thy master's throne in shelter placed,
Let Will, unheard by thee, his thunder waste.
Yet still I fear your work is done but half;
For while he keeps his pen, you are not safe.

Hear an old fable, and a dull one too;
Yet bears a moral, when applied to you.

A hare who long had 'scaped pursuing hounds,
By often shifting into distant grounds;
But, finding all his artifices vain;
20 To save his life he leapt into the main.
But there, alas! he could no safety find;
A pack of dog-fish had him in the wind:
He scours away; and to avoid the foe,
Descends for shelter to the shades below.
There Cerberus lay watching in his den,
(He had not seen a hare the Lord knows when)
Out bounced the mastiff of the triple head;
Away the hare with double swiftness fled.
Hunted from earth, and sea, and hell, he flies
30 (Fear lent him wings) for safety to the skies.
How was the fearful animal distressed!
Behold a foe more fierce than all the rest:
Sirius, the swiftest of the heavenly pack,
Failed but an inch to seize him by the back.
He fled to earth, but first it cost him dear;
He left his scut behind, and half an ear.

Thus was the hare pursued, though free from guilt;
Thus Bob shalt thou be mauled, fly where thou wilt:

Then, honest Robin, of thy corpse beware:
40 Thou art not half so nimble as a hare:
Too ponderous is thy bulk to mount the sky;
Nor can you go to hell before you die.
So keen thy hunters, and thy scent so strong;
Thy turns and doublings cannot save thee long.

The Character of Sir Robert Walpole

With favour and fortune fastidiously blessed,
He's loud in his laugh and he's coarse in his jest;
Of favour and fortune unmerited vain,
A sharper in trifles, a dupe in the main.
Achieving of nothing, still promising wonders,
By dint of experience improving in blunders;
Oppressing true merit, exalting the base,
And selling his country to purchase his peace.
A jobber of stocks by retailing false news;
10 A prater at court in the style of the stews;
Of virtue and worth by profession a giber,
Of juries and senates the bully and briber:
Though I name not the wretch you know who I mean –
'Tis the cur-dog of Britain and spaniel of Spain.

To Dr Helsham

Sir,
When I left you, I found myself of the grape's juice sick:
I'm so full of pity, I never abuse sick;
And the patientest patient that ever you knew sick;
Both when I am purge-sick, and when I am spew-sick.
I pitied my cat, whom I knew by her mew sick;
She mended at first, but now she's anew sick.
Captain Butler made some in the church black and blue sick;
Dean Cross, had he preached, would have made us all pew-sick;
Are you not, in a crowd, when you sweat and you stew, sick?
10 Lady Santry got out of the church when she grew sick,
And, as fast as she could, to the Deanery flew sick.

Miss Morice was (I can assure you 'tis true) sick:
For, who would not be in that numerous crew sick?
Such music would make a fanatic or Jew sick:
Yet, ladies are seldom at ombre, or loo, sick;
Nor is old Nanny Shales, whene'er she does brew, sick.
My footman came home from the church, of a bruise sick,
And looked like a rake, who was made in the stews sick;
But you learned doctors can make whom you choose sick.
20 Poor I myself I was, when I withdrew, sick,
For the smell of them made me like garlic and rue sick.
And I got through the crowd, though not led by a clue, sick.
You hoped to find many (for that was your cue) sick;
But, there were not a dozen (to give 'em their due) sick,
And those to be sure, stuck together like glue, sick.
So are ladies in crowds, when they squeeze and they screw, sick.
You may find they are all, by their yellow pale hue, sick.
So am I, when tobacco, like Robin, I chew sick.

November 23 at night,
1731.

To Dr Sheridan

If I write any more, it will make my poor muse sick.
This night I came home with a very cold dew sick,
And I wish I may soon not be of an a-gue sick;
But, I hope I shall ne'er be, like you, of a shrew sick,
Who often has made me, by looking askew, sick.

'Can You Match with Me'

Can you match with me,
Who send thirty-three?
You must get fourteen more,
To make up thirty-four:
But, if me you can conquer,
I'll own you a strong cur.

A Riddling Letter

Sir,
Pray discruciate what follows:

The dullest beast, and gentleman's liquor,
When young is often due to the vicar.
The dullest beast, and swine's delight
Make up a bird very swift of flight.
The dullest beast when high in stature, ⎫
Add another of royal nature, ⎬
For breeding is a useful creature. ⎭
The dullest beast, and a party distressed,
When too long, is bad at best.

10   The dullest beast, and the saddle it wears,
Is good for partridge, not for hares.
The dullest beast and kind voice of a cat,
Will make a horse go, though he be not fat.
The dullest of beasts and of birds in the air,
Is that by which all Irishmen swear.
The dullest beast and famed college for Teagues
Is a person very unfit for intrigues.
The dullest beast and cobbler's tool, ⎫
With a boy that is only fit for school, ⎬

20   In summer is very pleasant and cool. ⎭
The dullest beast, and that which you kiss,
May break a limb of master or miss.
Of serpent kind, and what at distance kills,
Poor Miss Dingley oft hath felt its bills.
The dullest beast and eggs unsound,
Without it I would rather walk on the ground.
The dullest beast and what covers a house.
Without it a writer is not worth a louse.
The dullest beast, and scandalous vermin

30   Of roast or boiled, to the hungry is charming.
The dullest beast, and what's covered with crust,
There's nobody but a fool that would trust.
The dullest beast mending highways,
Is to a horse an evil disease.
The dullest beast and a hole in the ground,
Will dress a dinner worth five pound.

The dullest beast, and what doctors pretend
The cook-maid often hath by the end.
　The dullest beast and fish for Lent
40 May give you a blow you'll forever repent.
　The dullest beast and a shameful jeer,
Without it a lady should never appear.

Probatur Aliter

　A long-eared beast, and a field-house for cattle,
Among the coals does often rattle.
　A long-eared beast, a bird that prates,
The bridegrooms' first gift to their mates,
Is by all pious Christians thought,
In clergymen the greatest fault.
　A long-eared beast, and woman of Endor,
If your wife be a scold, that will mend her.
　With a long-eared beast, and medicines use,
10 Cooks make their fowl look tight and spruce.
　A long-eared beast and holy fable,
Strengthens the shoes of half the rabble.
　A long-eared beast, and Rhenish wine,
Lies in the lap of ladies fine.
　A long-eared beast and Flanders college,
Is Dr Tisdall to my knowledge.
　A long-eared beast, and building knight;
Censorious people do in spite.
　A long-eared beast, and bird of night,
20 We sinners are too apt to slight.
　A long-eared beast, and shameful vermin,
A judge will eat, though clad in ermine.
　A long-eared beast, and Irish cart,
Can leave a mark and give a smart.
　A long-eared beast, in mud to lie,
No bird in air so swift can fly.
　A long-eared beast, and a sputtering old Whig,
I wish he were in it dancing a jig.
　A long-eared beast, and liquor to write,
30 Is a damnable smell both morning and night.

A long-eared beast, and the child of a sheep,
At whist they will make a desperate sweep.
A beast long-eared, and till midnight you stay,
Will cover a house much better than clay.
A long-eared beast, and the drink you love best
You call him a sloven in earnest or jest.
A long-eared beast, and the sixteenth letter,
I'd not look at all, unless I looked better.
A long-eared beast give me, and eggs unsound,
40 Or else I will not ride one inch of ground.
A long-eared beast, another name for jeer,
To ladies' skins there's nothing comes so near.
A long-eared beast, and kind noise of a cat,
Is useful in journeys, take notice of that.
A long-eared beast, and what seasons your beef,
On such an occasion the law gives relief.
A long-eared beast, the thing that force must drive in,
Bears up his house, that's of his own contriving.

The Place of the Damned

All folks who pretend to religion and grace,
Allow there's a hell, but dispute of the place;
But if hell may by logical rules be defined,
The place of the damned – I will tell you my mind.

Wherever the damned do chiefly abound,
Most certainly there is hell to be found;
Damned poets, damned critics, damned blockheads, damned
     knaves,
Damned senators bribed, damned prostitute slaves;
Damned lawyers and judges, damned lords and damned squires,
10 Damned spies and informers, damned friends and damned liars;
Damned villains, corrupted in every station,
Damned time-serving priests all over the nation.
And into the bargain I'll readily give you,
Damned ignorant prelates, and councillors privy.
Then let us no longer by parsons be flammed,
For we know by these marks, the place of the damned:
And hell to be sure is at Paris or Rome,
How happy for us, that it is not at home!

Helter Skelter

OR, THE HUE AND CRY AFTER THE ATTORNIES,
GOING TO RIDE THE CIRCUIT

Now the active young attornies
Briskly travel on their journeys,
Looking big as any giants,
On the horses of their clients;
Like so many little Mars's,
With their tilters at their arses,
Brazen hilted, lately burnished,
And with harness-buckles furnished;
And with whips and spurs so neat,
10   And with jockey-coats complete;
And with boots so very greasy,
And with saddles eke so easy,
And with bridles fine and gay,
Bridles borrowed for a day,
Bridles destined far to roam,
Ah! never to return to home;
And with hats so very big, sir,
And with powdered caps and wigs, sir;
And with ruffles to be shown,
20   Cambric ruffles not their own;
And with holland shirts so white,
Shirts becoming to the sight,
Shirts bewrought with different letters,
As belonging to their betters:
With their pretty tinselled boxes,
Gotten from their dainty doxies,
And with rings so very trim,
Lately taken out of lim —
And with very little pence,
30   And as very little sense:
With some law but little justice,
Having stolen from my hostess,
From the barber and the cutler,
Like the soldier from the sutler;
From the vintner and the tailor,
Like the felon from the gaoler,
Into this and t'other county,

Living on the public bounty;
Thorough town and thorough village,
40 All to plunder, all to pillage;
Thorough mountains, thorough valleys,
Thorough stinking lanes and alleys;
Some to cuckold farmers' spouses,
And make merry in their houses;
Some to tumble country wenches
On their rushy beds and benches,
And, if they begin a fray,
Draw their swords and run away:
All to murder equity,
50 And to take a double fee;
Till the people all are quiet
And forget to broil and riot,
Low in pocket, cowed in courage,
Safely glad to sup their porridge,
And vacation's over – then
Hey for Dublin town again!

The Life and Genuine Character of Dr Swift

WRITTEN BY HIMSELF

TO THE READER

This poetical account of the life and character of the Reverend
Dean Swift, so celebrated through the world for his many
ingenious writings, was occasioned by a maxim of Rochefoucauld:
and is now published from the author's last corrected copy, being
dedicated by the publisher, to Alexander Pope, of Twickenham,
Esq.

To ALEXANDER POPE, Esq., of Twickenham in the county of
Middlesex.

As you have been long an intimate friend of the author of the
following poem, I thought you would not be displeased with
being informed of some particulars, how *he* came to write it, and
how I, very innocently, procured a copy.

It seems the Dean, in conversation with some friends, said, he could guess the discourse of the world concerning his character after his death, and thought it might be no improper subject for a poem. This happened above a year before he finished it; for it was written by small pieces, just as leisure or humour allowed him.

He showed some parts of it to several friends, and when it was completed, he seldom refused the sight of it to any visitor: so that, probably, it has been perused by fifty persons; which, being against his usual practice, many people judged, likely enough, that he had a desire to make the people of Dublin impatient to see it published, and at the same time resolved to disappoint them; for, he would never be prevailed on to grant a copy, and yet several lines were retained by memory, and are often repeated in Dublin.

It is thought, that one of his servants in whom he had great confidence, and who had access to his closet, took an opportunity, while his master was riding some miles out of town, to transcribe the whole poem: and it is probable, that the servant lent it to others, who were not trusty (as it is generally the case). By this accident, I, having got a very correct copy from a friend in Dublin, lie under no obligation to conceal it.

I have shown it to very good judges, and friends of the Dean, (if I may venture to say so to you, who are such a superior judge and poet), who are well acquainted with the author's style and manner, and they all allow it to be genuine, as well as perfectly finished and correct; his particular genius appearing in every line, together with his peculiar way of thinking and writing.

I should be very sorry to offend the Dean, although I am a perfect stranger to his person: but since the poem will infallibly be soon printed, either here, or in Dublin, I take myself to have the best title to send it to the press; and I shall direct the printer to commit as few errors as possible.

I am, sir, with the greatest respect,
Your most obedient and humble servant,
L.M.

From my chambers in
the Inner Temple,
London. April 1, 1733.

THE LIFE AND CHARACTER OF DEAN SWIFT

Upon a maxim in Rochefoucauld

Wise Rochefoucauld a maxim writ,
Made up of malice, truth, and wit:
If, what he says be not a joke,
We mortals are strange kind of folk.

But hold – before we farther go,
'Tis fit the maxim we should know.

He says, 'Whenever fortune sends
Disasters, to our dearest friends,
Although, we outwardly may grieve,
10   We oft, are laughing in our sleeve.'
And when I think upon't, this minute,
I fancy, there is something in it.

We see a comrade get a fall,
Yet laugh our hearts out, one and all.

Tom for a wealthy wife looks round,
A nymph, that brings ten thousand pound:
He nowhere could have better picked;
A rival comes, and Tom – is nicked.
See, how behave his friends professed,
20   They turn the matter to a jest;
Loll out their tongues, and thus they talk,
'Poor Tom has got a plaguy balk!'

I could give instances enough,
That human friendship is but stuff.
Whene'er a flattering puppy cries
You are his dearest friend – he lies:
To lose a guinea at piquet,
Would make him rage, and storm, and fret,
Bring from his heart sincerer groans,
30   Than if he heard you broke your bones.

Come, tell me truly, would you take well,
Suppose your friend and you, were equal,
To see him always foremost stand,
Affect to take the upper hand,

And strive to pass, in public view,
For a much better man than you?
Envy, I doubt, would powerful prove,
And get the better of your love;
'Twould please your palate, like a feast,
40 To see him mortified at least.

'Tis true, we talk of friendship much,
But, who are they that can keep touch?
True friendship in two breasts requires
The same aversions, and desires;
My friend should have, when I complain,
A fellow-feeling of my pain.

Yet, by experience, oft we find,
Our friends are of a different mind;
And, were I tortured with the gout,
50 They'd laugh, to see me make a rout,
Glad, that themselves could walk about.

Let me suppose, two special friends,
And, each to poetry pretends:
Would either poet take it well,
To hear, the other bore the bell?
His rival, for the chiefest reckoned,
Himself, pass only for the second?

When you are sick, your friends, you say,
Will send their *how d'ye's* every day:
60 Alas! that gives you small relief!
They send for manners – not for grief:
Nor, if you died, would fail to go
That evening to a puppet-show:
Yet, come in time to show their loves,
And get a hatband, scarf, and gloves.

To make these truths the better known,
Let me suppose the case my own.

The day will come, when't shall be said,
'D'ye hear the news? The Dean is dead!
70 Poor man! he went, all on a sudden!'
He's dropped, and given the crow a pudding!

What money was behind him found?
'I hear about two thousand pound –
'Tis owned he was a man of wit –'
Yet many a foolish thing he writ;
'And, sure he must be deeply learned!'
That's more than ever I discerned;
'I know his nearest friends complain,
He was too airy for a Dean –
80   He was an honest man, I'll swear' –
Why sir, I differ from you there,
For, I have heard another story,
He was a most confounded Tory!
'Yet here we had a strong report,
That he was well received at court.'
Why, then it was, I do assert,
Their goodness, more than his desert.
He grew, or else his comrades lied,
Confounded *dull*, before he died.

90   He hoped to have a lucky hit,
Some medals sent him for his wit;
But, truly there the Dean was bit.
'And yet, I think, for all your jokes,
His claim as good as other folks'.

'Must we the Drapier then forget?
Is not our nation in his debt?
'Twas he that writ the Drapier's Letters!'
He should have left them for his betters;
We had a hundred abler men,
100   Nor need depend upon his pen.
Say what you will about his reading,
You never can defend his breeding!
Who, in his satires running riot,
Could never leave the world in quiet;
Attacking, when he took the whim,
Court, city, camp, all one to him.

But, why would he, except he slobbered,
Offend our patriot, great Sir Robert,
Whose councils aid the sovereign power,
110   To save the nation every hour?

What scenes of evil he unravels,
In satires, libels, lying travels!
Not sparing his own clergy-cloth,
But, eats into it, like a moth!
'If he makes mankind bad as elves,
I answer, they may thank themselves;
If vice can ever be abashed,
It must be ridiculed, or lashed.'
But, if I chance to make a slip,
120   What right had he to hold the whip?

   'If you resent it, who's to blame?
He neither knew you, nor your name;
Should vice expect to 'scape rebuke,
Because its owner is a duke?
Vice is a vermin; sportsmen say ⎤
No vermin can demand fair play, ⎬
But, every hand may justly slay.' ⎦

   I envy not the wits who write
Merely to gratify their spite;
130   Thus did the Dean: his only scope
Was, to be held a misanthrope.
This into general odium drew him,
Which if he liked, much good may do him:
This gave him enemies in plenty,
Throughout two realms nineteen in twenty.
His zeal was not to lash our crimes,
But, discontent against the times;
For, had we made him timely offers,
To raise his post, or fill his coffers,
140   Perhaps he might have truckled down,
Like other brethren of his gown,
For party he would scarce have bled:
I say no more – because he's dead.

   'But who could charge him, to his face,
That e'er he cringed to men in place?
His principles, of ancient date,
Ill suit with those professed of late:
The Pope, or Calvin he'd oppose,
And thought they both were equal foes:

150　That church and state had suffered more
　　By Calvin, than the Scarlet Whore:
　　Thought popish and fanatic zeal,
　　Both bitter foes to Britain's weal.
　　The Pope would of our faith bereave us,
　　But, still our monarchy would leave us.
　　Not so, the vile fanatic crew;
　　That ruined church and monarch too.

　　　'Supposing these reflections just;
　　We should indulge the Dean's disgust,
160　Who saw this factious tribe caressed,
　　And lovers of the church distressed:
　　The patrons of the good old cause,
　　In senates sit, at making laws;
　　The most malignant of the herd,
　　In surest way to be preferred;
　　And preachers, find the better quarter,
　　For railing at the royal martyr.

　　　'Whole swarms of sects, with grief, he saw
　　More favoured, than the church by law:
170　Thought Protestant too good a name
　　For canting hypocrites to claim,
　　Whose protestation hides a sting
　　Destructive to the church and king:
　　Which might as well, in his opinion,
　　Become an atheist, or Socinian.

　　　'A Protestant's a special clinker;
　　It serves for sceptic, and freethinker,
　　It serves for stubble, hay, and wood,
　　For everything, but what it should.'

180　What writings had he left behind?
　　'I hear, they're of a different kind:
　　A few, in verse; but most, in prose.'
　　Some highflown pamphlets, I suppose:
　　All scribbled in the worst of times,
　　To palliate his friend Oxford's crimes,
　　To praise Queen Anne, nay more, defend her,
　　As never favouring the Pretender:
　　Or libels yet concealed from sight,

Against the court to show his spite.
190 Perhaps his *Travels*, part the third;
A lie, at every second word:
Offensive to a loyal ear:
But – not one sermon, you may swear.

'Sir, our accounts are different quite,
And your conjectures are not right;
'Tis plain, his writings were designed
To please, and to reform mankind;
And, if he often missed his aim,
The world must own it, to their shame;
200 The praise is his, and theirs the blame.

'Then, since you dread no further lashes,
You freely may forgive his ashes.'

Verses on the Death of Dr Swift, D.S.P.D.

OCCASIONED BY READING A MAXIM IN ROCHEFOUCAULD

*Dans l'adversité de nos meilleurs amis nous trouvons
quelque chose, qui ne nous deplait pas.*

In the adversity of our best friends, we find something that doth not
displease us.

As Rochefoucauld his maxims drew
From nature, I believe 'em true:
They argue no corrupted mind
In him; the fault is in mankind.

This maxim more than all the rest
Is thought too base for human breast;
'In all distresses of our friends
We first consult our private ends,
While nature kindly bent to ease us,
10 Points out some circumstance to please us.'

If this perhaps your patience move
Let reason and experience prove.

We all behold with envious eyes,
Our equal raised above our size;

Who would not at a crowded show,
Stand high himself, keep others low?
I love my friend as well as you,
But would not have him stop my view;
Then let me have the higher post;
20   I ask but for an inch at most.

If in a battle you should find,
One, whom you love of all mankind,
Had some heroic action done,
A champion killed, or trophy won;
Rather than thus be overtopped,
Would you not wish his laurels cropped?

Dear honest Ned is in the gout,
Lies racked with pain, and you without:
How patiently you hear him groan!
30   How glad the case is not your own!

What poet would not grieve to see,
His brethren write as well as he?
But rather than they should excel,
He'd wish his rivals all in hell.

Her end when emulation misses,
She turns to envy, stings and hisses:
The strongest friendship yields to pride,
Unless the odds be on our side.

Vain humankind! Fantastic race!
40   Thy various follies, who can trace?
Self-love, ambition, envy, pride,
Their empire in our hearts divide:
Give others riches, power, and station,
'Tis all on me a usurpation.
I have no title to aspire;
Yet, when you sink, I seem the higher.
In Pope, I cannot read a line,
But with a sigh, I wish it mine:
When he can in one couplet fix
50   More sense than I can do in six:
It gives me such a jealous fit,
I cry, 'Pox take him, and his wit.'

Why must I be outdone by Gay,
In my own humorous biting way?

Arbuthnot is no more my friend,
Who dares to irony pretend;
Which I was born to introduce,
Refined it first, and showed its use.

St John, as well as Pulteney knows,
60   That I had some repute for prose;
And till they drove me out of date,
Could maul a minister of state:
If they have mortified my pride,
And made me throw my pen aside;
If with such talents heaven hath blest 'em,
Have I not reason to detest 'em?

To all my foes, dear fortune, send
Thy gifts, but never to my friend:
I tamely can endure the first,
70   But, this with envy makes me burst.

Thus much may serve by way of proem,
Proceed we therefore to our poem.

The time is not remote, when I
Must by the course of nature die:
When I foresee my special friends,
Will try to find their private ends:
Though it is hardly understood,
Which way my death can do them good;
Yet, thus methinks, I hear 'em speak;
80   'See, how the Dean begins to break:
Poor gentleman, he droops apace,
You plainly find it in his face:
That old vertigo in his head,
Will never leave him, till he's dead:
Besides, his memory decays,
He recollects not what he says;
He cannot call his friends to mind;
Forgets the place where last he dined:
Plies you with stories o'er and o'er,
90   He told them fifty times before.

How does he fancy we can sit,
To hear his out-of-fashioned wit?
But he takes up with younger folks,
Who for his wine will bear his jokes:
Faith, he must make his stories shorter,
Or change his comrades once a quarter:
In half the time, he talks them round;
There must another set be found.

 'For poetry, he's past his prime,
100 He takes an hour to find a rhyme:
His fire is out, his wit decayed,
His fancy sunk, his muse a jade.
I'd have him throw away his pen;
But there's no talking to some men.'

 And, then their tenderness appears,
By adding largely to my years:
'He's older than he would be reckoned,
And well remembers Charles the Second.

 'He hardly drinks a pint of wine;
110 And that, I doubt, is no good sign.
His stomach too begins to fail:
Last year we thought him strong and hale;
But now, he's quite another thing;
I wish he may hold out till spring.'

 Then hug themselves, and reason thus;
'It is not yet so bad with us.'

 In such a case they talk in tropes,
And, by their fears express their hopes:
Some great misfortune to portend,
120 No enemy can match a friend;
With all the kindness they profess,
The merit of a lucky guess,
(When daily 'Howd'y's' come of course,
And servants answer: 'Worse and worse')
Would please 'em better than to tell,
That, God be praised, the Dean is well.
Then he who prophesied the best,
Approves his foresight to the rest:
'You know, I always feared the worst,

130 And often told you so at first':
  He'd rather choose that I should die,
  Than his prediction prove a lie.
  No one foretells I shall recover;
  But, all agree, to give me over.

  Yet should some neighbour feel a pain,
  Just in the parts, where I complain;
  How many a message would he send?
  What hearty prayers that I should mend?
  Enquire what regimen I kept;
140 What gave me ease, and how I slept?
  And more lament, when I was dead,
  Than all the snivellers round my bed.

  My good companions, never fear,
  For though you may mistake a year;
  Though your prognostics run too fast,
  They must be verified at last.

  'Behold the fatal day arrive!
  How is the Dean? He's just alive.
  Now the departing prayer is read:
150 He hardly breathes. The Dean is dead.
  Before the passing-bell begun,
  The news through half the town has run.
  O, may we all for death prepare!
  What has he left? And who's his heir?
  I know no more than what the news is,
  'Tis all bequeathed to public uses.
  To public use! A perfect whim!
  What had the public done for him?
  Mere envy, avarice, and pride!
160 He gave it all. – But first he died.
  And had the Dean, in all the nation,
  No worthy friend, no poor relation?
  So ready to do strangers good,
  Forgetting his own flesh and blood?'

  Now Grub Street wits are all employed;
  With elegies, the town is cloyed:
  Some paragraph in every paper,
  To curse the Dean, or bless the Drapier.

The doctors tender of their fame,
170   Wisely on me lay all the blame:
'We must confess his case was nice;
But he would never take advice;
Had he been ruled, for aught appears,
He might have lived these twenty years:
For when we opened him we found,
That all his vital parts were sound.'

From Dublin soon to London spread,
'Tis told at court, the Dean is dead.

Kind Lady Suffolk in the spleen,
180   Runs laughing up to tell the Queen.
The Queen, so gracious, mild, and good,
Cries, 'Is he gone? 'Tis time he should.
He's dead you say, why let him rot;
I'm glad the medals were forgot.
I promised them, I own; but when?
I only was a princess then;
But now as consort of the King,
You know 'tis quite a different thing.'

Now, Chartres at Sir Robert's levee,
190   Tells, with a sneer, the tidings heavy:
'Why, is he dead without his shoes?'
(Cries Bob) 'I'm sorry for the news;
Oh, were the wretch but living still,
And in his place my good friend Will;
Or had a mitre on his head
Provided Bolingbroke were dead.'

Now Curll his shop from rubbish drains;
Three genuine tomes of Swift's remains.
And then to make them pass the glibber,
200   Revised by Tibbalds, Moore, and Cibber.
He'll treat me as he does my betters.
Publish my will, my life, my letters.
Revive the libels born to die;
Which Pope must bear, as well as I.

Here shift the scene, to represent
How those I love, my death lament.

Poor Pope will grieve a month; and Gay
A week; and Arbuthnot a day.

St John himself will scarce forbear,
210 To bite his pen, and drop a tear.
The rest will give a shrug and cry
'I'm sorry; but we all must die.'
Indifference clad in wisdom's guise,
All fortitude of mind supplies:
For how can stony bowels melt,
In those who never pity felt;
When *we* are lashed, *they* kiss the rod;
Resigning to the will of God.

The fools, my juniors by a year,
220 Are tortured with suspense and fear.
Who wisely thought my age a screen,
When death approached, to stand between:
The screen removed, their hearts are trembling,
They mourn for me without dissembling.

My female friends, whose tender hearts
Have better learnt to act their parts,
Receive the news in doleful dumps,
'The Dean is dead, (*and what is trumps?*)
Then Lord have mercy on his soul.
230 (*Ladies, I'll venture for the vole.*)
Six deans they say must bear the pall.
(*I wish I knew which king to call.*)'
'Madam, your husband will attend
The funeral of so good a friend.'
'No madam, 'tis a shocking sight,
And he's engaged tomorrow night!
My Lady Club would take it ill,
If he should fail her at quadrille.
He loved the Dean. (*I lead a heart.*)
240 But dearest friends, they say, must part.
His time was come, he ran his race;
We hope he's in a better place.'

Why do we grieve that friends should die?
No loss more easy to supply.

One year is past; a different scene;
No further mention of the Dean;
Who now, alas, no more is missed,
Than if he never did exist.
Where's now this favourite of Apollo?
250   Departed; and his works must follow:
Must undergo the common fate;
His kind of wit is out of date.
Some country squire to Lintot goes,
Inquires for Swift in verse and prose:
Says Lintot, 'I have heard the name:
He died a year ago.' The same.
He searcheth all his shop in vain;
'Sir, you may find them in Duck Lane:
I sent them with a load of books,
260   Last Monday to the pastry-cook's.
To fancy they could live a year!
I find you're but a stranger here.
The Dean was famous in his time;
And had a kind of knack at rhyme:
His way of writing now is past;
The town hath got a better taste:
I keep no antiquated stuff;
But, spick and span I have enough.
Pray, do but give me leave to show 'em;
270   Here's Colley Cibber's birthday poem.
This ode you never yet have seen,
By Stephen Duck, upon the Queen.
Then, here's a letter finely penned,
Against the *Craftsman* and his friend;
It clearly shows that all reflection
On ministers, is disaffection.
Next, here's Sir Robert's vindication,
And Mr Henley's last oration:
The hawkers have not got 'em yet,
280   Your honour please to buy a set?

      'Here's Woolston's tracts, the twelfth edition;
'Tis read by every politician:
The country members, when in town,
To all their boroughs send them down:

You never met a thing so smart;
The courtiers have them all by heart:
Those maids of honour (who can read)
Are taught to use them for their creed.
The reverend author's good intention,
290   Hath been rewarded with a pension:
He doth an honour to his gown,
By bravely running priestcraft down:
He shows, as sure as God's in Gloucester,
That Jesus was a grand impostor:
That all his miracles were cheats,
Performed as jugglers do their feats:
The church had never such a writer:
A shame he hath not got a mitre!'

      Suppose me dead; and then suppose
300   A club assembled at the Rose;
Where from discourse of this and that,
I grow the subject of their chat:
And, while they toss my name about,
With favour some, and some without;
One quite indifferent in the cause,
My character impartial draws:

      'The Dean, if we believe report,
Was never ill received at court:
As for his works in verse and prose,
310   I own myself no judge of those:
Nor, can I tell what critics thought 'em;
But, this I know, all people bought 'em;
As with a moral view designed
To cure the vices of mankind:
His vein, ironically grave,
Exposed the fool, and lashed the knave:
To steal a hint was never known,
But what he writ was all his own.

      'He never thought an honour done him,
320   Because a duke was proud to own him:
Would rather slip aside, and choose
To talk with wits in dirty shoes:
Despised the fools with stars and garters,

So often seen caressing Chartres:
He never courted men in station,
Nor persons had in admiration;
Of no man's greatness was afraid,
Because he sought for no man's aid.
Though trusted long in great affairs,
330 He gave himself no haughty airs:
Without regarding private ends,
Spent all his credit for his friends:
And only chose the wise and good;
No flatterers; no allies in blood;
But succoured virtue in distress,
And seldom failed of good success;
As numbers in their hearts must own,
Who, but for him, had been unknown.

'With princes kept a due decorum,
340 But never stood in awe before 'em:
And to her Majesty, God bless her,
Would speak as free as to her dresser,
She thought it his peculiar whim,
Nor took it ill as come from him.
He followed David's lesson just,
"In princes never put thy trust."
And, would you make him truly sour;
Provoke him with a slave in power:
The Irish senate, if you named,
350 With what impatience he declaimed!
Fair LIBERTY was all his cry;
For her he stood prepared to die;
For her he boldly stood alone;
For her he oft exposed his own.
Two kingdoms, just as factions led,
Had set a price upon his head;
But, not a traitor could be found,
To sell him for six hundred pound.

'Had he but spared his tongue and pen,
360 He might have rose like other men:
But, power was never in his thought;

And, wealth he valued not a groat:
Ingratitude he often found,
And pitied those who meant the wound:
But, kept the tenor of his mind,
To merit well of humankind:
Nor made a sacrifice of those
Who still were true, to please his foes.
He laboured many a fruitless hour
370 To reconcile his friends in power;
Saw mischief by a faction brewing,
While they pursued each other's ruin.
But, finding vain was all his care,
He left the court in mere despair.

'And, oh! how short are human schemes!
Here ended all our golden dreams.
What St John's skill in state affairs,
What Ormonde's valour, Oxford's cares,
To save their sinking country lent,
380 Was all destroyed by one event.
Too soon that precious life was ended,
On which alone, our weal depended.
When up a dangerous faction starts,
With wrath and vengeance in their hearts:
By solemn league and covenant bound,
To ruin, slaughter, and confound;
To turn religion to a fable,
And make the government a Babel:
Pervert the law, disgrace the gown,
390 Corrupt the senate, rob the crown;
To sacrifice old England's glory,
And make her infamous in story.
When such a tempest shook the land,
How could unguarded virtue stand?

'With horror, grief, despair the Dean
Beheld the dire destructive scene:
His friends in exile, or the Tower,
Himself within the frown of power;
Pursued by base envenomed pens,

400   Far to the land of slaves and fens;
       A servile race in folly nursed,
       Who truckle most, when treated worst.

       'By innocence and resolution,
       He bore continual persecution;
       While numbers to preferment rose;
       Whose merits were, to be his foes.
       When, *ev'n his own familiar friends*
       Intent upon their private ends,
       Like renegadoes now he feels,
410   *Against him lifting up their heels.*

       'The Dean did by his pen defeat
       An infamous destructive cheat.
       Taught fools their interest to know;
       And gave them arms to ward the blow.
       Envy hath owned it was his doing,
       To save that helpless land from ruin,
       While they who at the steerage stood,
       And reaped the profit, sought his blood.

       'To save them from their evil fate,
420   In him was held a crime of state.
       A wicked monster on the bench,
       Whose fury blood could never quench;
       As vile and profligate a villain,
       As modern Scroggs, or old Tresilian;
       Who long all justice had discarded,
       Nor feared he God, nor man regarded;
       Vowed on the Dean his rage to vent,
       And make him of his zeal repent;
       But heaven his innocence defends,
430   The grateful people stand his friends:
       Not strains of law, nor judges' frown,
       Nor topics brought to please the crown,
       Nor witness hired, nor jury picked,
       Prevail to bring him in convict.

       'In exile with a steady heart,
       He spent his life's declining part;

Where folly, pride, and faction sway,
Remote from St John, Pope, and Gay.

'His friendship there to few confined,
440   Were always of the middling kind:
No fools of rank, a mongrel breed,
Who fain would pass for lords indeed:
Where titles give no right or power,
And peerage is a withered flower,
He would have held it a disgrace,
If such a wretch had known his face.
On rural squires, that kingdom's bane,
He vented oft his wrath in vain:
Biennial squires, to market brought;
450   Who sell their souls and votes for naught;
The nation stripped, go joyful back,
To rob the church, their tenants rack,
Go snacks with thieves and rapparees,
And keep the peace, to pick up fees:
In every job to have a share,
A gaol or barrack to repair;
And turn the tax for public roads
Commodious to their own abodes.

'Perhaps I may allow the Dean
460   Had too much satire in his vein;
And seemed determined not to starve it,
Because no age could more deserve it.
Yet, malice never was his aim;
He lashed the vice but spared the name.
No individual could resent,
Where thousands equally were meant.
His satire points at no defect,
But what all mortals may correct;
For he abhorred that senseless tribe,
470   Who call it humour when they jibe:
He spared a hump or crooked nose,
Whose owners set not up for beaux.
True genuine dullness moved his pity,
Unless it offered to be witty.

Those, who their ignorance confessed,
He ne'er offended with a jest;
But laughed to hear an idiot quote,
A verse from Horace, learnt by rote.

'He knew an hundred pleasant stories,
480   With all the turns of Whigs and Tories:
Was cheerful to his dying day,
And friends would let him have his way.

'He gave the little wealth he had,
To build a house for fools and mad:
And showed by one satiric touch,
No nation wanted it so much:
That kingdom he hath left his debtor,
I wish it soon may have a better.'

Judas

By the just vengeance of incensed skies,
Poor Bishop Judas, late repenting, dies;
The Jews engaged him with a paltry bribe,
Amounting hardly to a crown a tribe;
Which, though his conscience forced him to restore,
(And, parsons tell us, no man can do more)
Yet, through despair, of God and man accursed,
He lost his bishopric, and hanged, or burst.
Those former ages differed much from this:
10   Judas betrayed his master with a kiss:
But, some have kissed the gospel fifty times,
Whose perjury's the least of all their crimes:
Some who can perjure through a two-inch board;
Yet keep their bishoprics, and 'scape the cord.
Like hemp, which by a skilful spinster drawn
To slender threads, may sometimes pass for lawn.

As ancient Judas by transgression fell,
And burst asunder e'er he went to hell;
So, could we see a set of new Iscariots,
20   Come headlong tumbling from their mitred chariots,

Each modern Judas perish like the first;
Drop from the tree with all his bowels burst;
Who could forbear, that viewed each guilty face,
To cry, 'Lo, Judas, gone to his own place:
His habitation let all men forsake,
And let his bishopric another take.'

On the Irish Bishops

Old Latimer preaching did fairly describe
A bishop who ruled all the rest of his tribe;
And who is this bishop? And where does he dwell?
Why truly 'tis Satan, Archbishop of Hell:
And *he* was a primate, and *he* wore a mitre,
Surrounded with jewels of sulphur and nitre.
How nearly this bishop our bishop resembles!
But his has the odds, who *believes and who trembles.*
Could you see his grim Grace, for a pound to a penny,
10 You'd swear it must be the baboon of Kilkenny;
Poor Satan will think the comparison odious;
I wish I could find him out one more commodious.
But this I am sure, the most reverend old dragon,
Has got on the bench many bishops suffragan:
And all men believe he presides there *incog.*
To give them by turns an invisible jog.

Our bishops puffed up with wealth and with pride,
To hell on the backs of the clergy would ride;
They mounted, and laboured with whip and with spur,
20 In vain – for the devil a parson would stir.
So the Commons unhorsed them, and this was their doom,
On their croziers to ride, like a witch on a broom.
Though they gallop so fast; on the road you may find 'em,
And have left us but three out of twenty behind 'em.
Lord Bolton's good Grace, Lord Carr, and Lord Howard,
In spite of the devil would still be untoward.
They came of good kindred, and could not endure,
Their former companions should beg at their door.

When Christ was betrayed to Pilate, the praetor,
30   In a dozen apostles but one proved a traitor!
One traitor alone, and faithful eleven;
But we can afford six traitors in seven.
What a clutter with clippings, dividings, and cleavings!
And the clergy, forsooth, must take up with their leavings.
If making *divisions* was all their intent,
They've done it, we thank 'em, but not as they meant;
And so may such bishops for ever *divide*,
That no honest heathen would be on their side.
How should we rejoice, if, like Judas the first,
40   Those splitters of parsons in sunder should burst?

Now hear an allusion! A mitre, you know,
Is divided above, but united below.
If this you consider, our emblem is right;
The bishops *divide*, but the clergy *unite*.
Should the bottom be split, our bishops would dread
That the mitre would never stick fast on their head,
And yet they have learnt the chief art of a sovereign,
As Machiavel taught 'em; 'divide and ye govern.'
But, courage, my lords, though it cannot be said
50   That one *cloven tongue*, ever sat on your head;
I'll hold you a groat, and I wish I could see't,
If your stockings were off, you could show *cloven feet*.

But hold, cry the bishops; and give us fair play;
Before you condemn us, hear what we can say.
What truer affection could ever be shown,
Than saving your souls, by damning our own?
And have we not practised all methods to gain you;
With the tithe of the tithe of the tithe to maintain you;
Provided a fund for building you spittles:
60   You are only to live four years without victuals!
Content, my good lords; but let us change hands;
First take you our tithes, and give us your lands.

So God bless the church, and three of our mitres;
And God bless the Commons for *biting* the *biters*.

Advice to a Parson

AN EPIGRAM

Would you rise in the church, be stupid and dull,
Be empty of learning, of insolence full:
Though lewd and immoral, be formal and grave,
In flattery an artist, in fawning a slave,
No merit, no science, no virtue is wanting
In him, that's accomplished in cringing and canting:
Be studious to practise true meanness of spirit;
For who but Lord Bolton was mitred for merit?
Would you wish to be wrapped in a rochet – in short,
10   Be as poxed and profane as fanatical Hort.

Epigram

ON SEEING A WORTHY PRELATE GO OUT OF CHURCH
IN THE TIME OF DIVINE SERVICE, TO WAIT ON HIS GRACE
THE DUKE OF DORSET

Lord Pam in the church (could you think it) kneeled down,
When told the Lieutenant was just come to town,
His station despising, unawed by the place,
He flies from his God, to attend on his Grace:
To the court it was fitter to pay his devotion,
Since God had no hand in his Lordship's promotion.

Verses on I Know Not What

My latest tribute here I send,
With this let your collection end.
Thus I consign you down to fame,
A character to praise and blame,
And, if the whole may pass for true,
Contented rest; you have your due –
Give future times the satisfaction
To leave one handle for detraction.

An Answer to a Scandalous Poem

WHEREIN THE AUTHOR MOST AUDACIOUSLY PRESUMES
TO CAST AN INDIGNITY UPON THEIR HIGHNESSES
THE CLOUDS, BY COMPARING THEM TO A WOMAN

WRITTEN BY DERMOT O'NEPHELY, CHIEF

CAP OF HOWTH

ADVERTISEMENT

N.B. *The following answer to that scurrilous libel against us,*
should have been published long ago in our own justification: but it was
advised that, considering the high importance of the subject, it should
be deferred until the meeting of the great assembly of the nation.

Presumptuous bard! How could you dare
A woman with a cloud compare?
Strange pride and insolence you show,
Inferior mortals there below.
And, is our thunder in your ears
So frequent or so loud as theirs?
Alas! our thunder soon goes out;
And only makes you more devout.
Then, is not female clatter worse,
10   That drives you, not to *pray*, but *curse*?

    We hardly thunder thrice a year;
The bolt discharged, the sky grows clear:
But, every sublunary dowdy,
The more she scolds, the more she's cloudy.

    Some critic may object, perhaps,
That clouds are blamed for giving claps;
But, what alas are claps ethereal,
Compared for mischief, to venereal?
Can clouds give buboes, ulcers, blotches,
20   Or from your nose dig out the notches?
We leave the body sweet and sound;
We kill, 'tis true, but never wound.

    You know a cloudy sky bespeaks
Fair weather, when the morning breaks;

But, women in a cloudy plight,
Foretell a storm to last till night.

A cloud, in proper seasons pours
His blessings down in fruitful showers;
But, woman was by fate designed
30   To pour down curses on mankind.

When Sirius o'er the welkin rages
Our kindly help his fire assuages;
But woman is a cursed inflamer,
No parish ducking-stool can tame her:
To kindle strife, Dame Nature taught her:
Like fireworks, she can burn in water.

For fickleness how durst you blame us?
Who for our constancy are famous.
You'll see a cloud in gentle weather
40   Keep the same face an hour together:
While women, if it could be reckoned,
Change every feature, every second.

Observe our figure in a morning;
Of foul and fair we give you warning;
But, can you guess from woman's air,
One minute, whether foul or fair?

Go read in ancient books enrolled,
What honours we possessed of old!

To disappoint Ixion's rape,
50   Jove dressed a cloud in Juno's shape:
Which when he had enjoyed, he swore
No goddess could have pleased him more,
No difference could he find between
His cloud, and Jove's imperial queen:
His cloud produced a race of centaurs,
Famed for a thousand bold adventures;
From us descended *ab origine*;
By learned authors called *nubigenae*.
But say, what earthly nymph do you know,
60   So beautiful to pass for Juno?

Before Aeneas durst aspire
To court her Majesty of Tyre,

His mother begged of us to dress him,
That Dido might the more caress him:
A coat we gave him, dyed in grain;
A flaxen wig, and clouded cane.
(The wig was powdered round with sleet,
Which fell in clouds beneath his feet)
With which he made a tearing show:
70 And Dido quickly smoked the beau.

Among your females make inquiries;
What nymph on earth so fair as Iris?
With heavenly beauty so endowed?
And yet her father is a cloud.
We dressed her in a gold brocade,
Befitting Juno's favourite maid.

'Tis known, that Socrates the wise,
Adored us clouds as deities;
To us he made his daily prayers,
80 As Aristophanes declares:
From Jupiter took all dominion,
And died defending his opinion.
By his authority, 'tis plain
You worship other gods in vain:
And from your own experience know,
We govern all things there below.
You follow where we please to guide;
O'er all your passions we preside;
Can raise them up, or sink them down,
90 As we think fit to smile or frown:
And, just as we dispose your brain,
Are witty, dull, rejoice, complain.

Compare us then to female race!
We, to whom all the gods give place:
Who better challenge your allegiance,
Because we dwell in higher regions:
You find, the gods in Homer dwell,
In seas, and streams, or low as hell:
Ev'n Jove, and Mercury his pimp,
100 No higher climb than Mount Olymp,
(Who makes you think, the clouds he pierces:
He pierce the clouds! He kiss their arses.)

While we, o'er Teneriffa placed,
Are loftier by a mile at least:
And when Apollo struts on Pindus,
We see him from our kitchen-windows:
Or, to Parnassus looking down,
Can piss upon his laurel crown.

Fate never formed the gods to fly;
110　In vehicles they mount the sky:
When Jove would some fair nymph inveigle,
He comes full gallop on his eagle.
Though Venus be as light as air,
She must have doves to draw her chair.
Apollo stirs not out of door,
Without his lacquered coach and four,
And, jealous Juno, ever snarling,
Is drawn by peacocks in her berlin:
But, we can fly where'er we please,
120　O'er cities, rivers, hills, and seas:
From east to west, the world we roam;
And, in all climates are at home;
With care provide you as we go,
With sunshine, rain, and hail, or snow.
You, when it rains, like fools believe,
Jove pisses on you through a sieve;
An idle tale, 'tis no such matter;
We only dip a sponge in water;
Then, squeeze it close between our thumbs,
130　And shake it well, and down it comes.
As you shall to your sorrow know;
We'll watch your steps where'er you go:
And since we find, you walk afoot
We'll soundly souse your frieze surtout.

'Tis but by our peculiar grace,
That Phoebus ever shows his face:
For, when we please, we open wide
Our curtains blue, from side to side:
And then, how saucily he shows
140　His brazen face, and fiery nose:
And gives himself a haughty air,
As if he made the weather fair.

'Tis sung, wherever Celia treads,
The violets ope their purple heads;
The roses blow, the cowslip springs;
'Tis sung, but we know better things.
'Tis true; a woman on her mettle,
Will often piss upon a nettle;
But, though we own, she makes it wetter,
150   The nettle never thrives the better;
While we, by soft prolific showers,
Can every spring produce you flowers.

Your poets, Chloe's beauty heightening,
Compare her radiant eyes to lightning;
And yet, I hope, 'twill be allowed,
That lightning comes but from a cloud.

But, gods like us, have too much sense
At poets' flights to take offence.
Nor can hyperboles demean us;
160   Each drab has been compared to Venus.

We own, your verses are melodious;
But such comparisons are odious.

Epigram on the Hermitage at Richmond

Her Majesty never shall be my exalter,
And yet she would raise me, I know – by a halter.

'A Paper Book is Sent by Boyle'

A paper book is sent by Boyle,
Too neatly gilt for me to soil.
Delany sends a silver standish,
When I no more a pen can brandish.
Let both around my tomb be placed,
As trophies of a muse deceased:
And let the friendly lines they writ
In praise of long departed wit,
Be graved on either side in columns,
10   More to my praise than all my volumes;

To burst with envy, spite, and rage,
The vandals of the present age.

On the Day of Judgement

With a whirl of thought oppressed,
I sink from reverie to rest.
An horrid vision seized my head,
I saw the graves give up their dead.
Jove, armed with terrors, burst the skies,
And thunder roars, and lightning flies!
Amazed, confused, its fate unknown,
The world stands trembling at his throne.
While each pale sinner hangs his head,
10   Jove, nodding, shook the heavens, and said,
'Offending race of humankind,
By nature, reason, learning, blind;
You who through frailty stepped aside,
And you who never fell – *through pride*;
You who in different sects have shammed,
And come to see each other damned;
(So some folks told you, but they knew
No more of Jove's designs than you)
The world's mad business now is o'er,
20   And I resent these pranks no more.
I to such blockheads set my wit!
I damn such fools! – Go, go you're bit.'

The Beasts' Confession to the Priest

ON OBSERVING HOW MOST MEN MISTAKE THEIR OWN TALENTS

THE PREFACE

I have been long of opinion, that there is not a more general and
greater mistake, or one of worse consequence through the
commerce of mankind, than the wrong judgements they are apt to
entertain of their own talents: I knew a stuttering alderman in
London, a great frequenter of coffee-houses; who, when a fresh

newspaper was brought in, constantly seized it first, and read
aloud to his brother citizens; but in a manner, as little intelligible
to the standers-by as to himself. How many pretenders to learning
expose themselves by choosing to discourse on those very parts of
10   science wherewith they are least acquainted? It is the same case in
every other qualification. By the multitude of those who deal in
rhymes from half a sheet to twenty, which come out every
minute, there must be at least five hundred poets in the city and
suburbs of London; half as many coffee-house orators, exclusive
of the clergy; forty thousand politicians; and four thousand five
hundred profound scholars: not to mention the wits, the ralliers,
the smart fellows, and critics; all as illiterate and impudent as a
suburb whore. What are we to think of the fine dressed sparks,
proud of their own personal deformities, which appear the more
20   hideous by the contrast of wearing scarlet and gold, with what
they call toupees on their heads, and all the frippery of a modern
beau, to make a figure before women; some of them with
hump-backs, others hardly five feet high, and every feature of
their faces distorted; I have seen many of these insipid pretenders
entering into conversation with persons of learning, constantly
making the grossest blunders in every sentence, without
conveying one single idea fit for a rational creature to spend a
thought on; perpetually confounding all chronology and
geography even of present times. I compute, that London hath
30   eleven native fools of the beau and puppy kind, for one among us
in Dublin; besides two thirds of ours were transplanted hither,
who are now naturalized; whereby that overgrown capital exceeds
ours in the article of dunces by forty to one; and what is more to
our further mortification, there is not one distinguished fool of
Irish birth or education, who makes any noise in that famous
metropolis, unless the London prints be very partial or defective;
whereas London is seldom without a dozen of their own
educating, who engross the vogue for half a winter together, and
are never heard of more, but give place to a new set. This hath
40   been the constant progress for at least thirty years past, only
allowing for the change of breed and fashion.

ADVERTISEMENT

The following poem is grounded upon the universal folly in
mankind of mistaking their talents; by which the author doth a

great honour to his own species, almost equalling them with
certain brutes; wherein, indeed, he is too partial, as he freely
confesseth: and yet he hath gone as low as he well could, by
specifying four animals; the wolf, the ass, the swine and the ape;
all equally mischievous, except the last, who outdoes them in the
article of cunning: so great is the pride of man.

When beasts could speak, (the learned say
They still can do so every day)
It seems, they had religion then,
As much as now we find in men.
It happened when a plague broke out,
(Which therefore made them more devout)
The king of brutes (to make it plain,
Of quadrupeds I only mean)
By proclamation gave command,
10   That every subject in the land
Should to the priest confess their sins;
And, thus the pious wolf begins:

'Good father, I must own with shame,
That, often I have been to blame:
I must confess, on Friday last,
Wretch that I was, I broke my fast:
But, I defy the basest tongue
To prove I did my neighbour wrong;
Or ever went to seek my food
20   By rapine, theft, or thirst of blood.'

The ass approaching next, confessed,
That in his heart he loved a jest:
A wag he was, he needs must own,
And could not let a dunce alone:
Sometimes his friend he would not spare,
And might perhaps be too severe:
But yet, the worst that could be said,
He was a *wit* both born and bred;
And if it be a sin or shame,
30   Nature alone must bear the blame:
One fault he hath, is sorry for't,
His ears are half a foot too short;

Which could he to the standard bring,
He'd show his face before the king:
Then, for his voice, there's none disputes
That he's the nightingale of brutes.

The swine with contrite heart allowed,
His shape and beauty made him proud:
In diet was perhaps too nice,
40   But gluttony was ne'er his vice:
In every turn of life content,
And meekly took what fortune sent:
Inquire through all the parish round
A better neighbour ne'er was found:
His vigilance might some displease;
'Tis true, he hated sloth like pease.

The mimic ape began his chatter,
How evil tongues his life bespatter:
Much of the censuring world complained,
50   Who said, his gravity was feigned:
Indeed, the strictness of his morals
Engaged him in a hundred quarrels:
He saw, and he was grieved to see't,
His zeal was sometimes indiscreet:
He found, his virtues too severe
For our corrupted times to bear;
Yet, such a lewd licentious age
Might well excuse a stoic's rage.

The goat advanced with decent pace;
60   And, first excused his youthful face;
Forgiveness begged, that he appeared
('Twas nature's fault) without a beard.
'Tis true, he was not much inclined
To fondness for the female kind;
Not, as his enemies object,
From chance, or natural defect;
Not by a frigid constitution;
But, through a pious resolution;
For, he had made a holy vow
70   Of chastity, as monks do now;
Which he resolved to keep for ever hence,
As strictly too, as doth his reverence.

Apply the tale, and you shall find
How just it suits with humankind.
Some faults we own: but, can you guess?
Why! – virtues carried to excess;
Wherewith our vanity endows us,
Though neither foe nor friend allows us.

The lawyer swears, you may rely on't,
80   He never squeezed a needy client:
And, this he makes his constant rule;
For which his brethren call him fool:
His conscience always was so nice,
He freely gave the poor advice;
By which he lost, he may affirm,
A hundred fees last Easter term.
While others of the learned robe
Would break the patience of a Job,
No pleader at the bar could match
90   His diligence and quick dispatch;
Ne'er kept a cause, he well may boast,
Above a term or two at most.

The cringing knave who seeks a place
Without success; thus tells his case:
Why should he longer mince the matter?
He failed, because he could not flatter:
He had not learnt to turn his coat,
Nor for a party give his vote:
His crime he quickly understood;
100   Too zealous for the nation's good:
He found, the ministers resent it,
Yet could not in his heart repent it.

The chaplain vows, he cannot fawn,
Though it would raise him to the lawn:
He passed his hours among his books;
You find it in his meagre looks:
He might, if he were worldly-wise,
Preferment get, and spare his eyes:
But owned, he had a stubborn spirit
110   That made him trust alone in merit:
Would rise by merit to promotion;
Alas! a mere chimeric notion.

The doctor, if you will believe him,
Confessed a sin, and God forgive him:
Called up at midnight, ran to save
A blind old beggar from the grave:
But, see how Satan spreads his snares;
He quite forgot to say his prayers.
He cannot help it for his heart
120   Sometimes to act the parson's part:
Quotes from the bible many a sentence
That moves his patients to repentance:
And, when his medicines do no good,
Supports their mind with heavenly food.
At which, however well intended,
He hears the clergy are offended;
And grown so bold behind his back
To call him hypocrite and quack.
In his own church he keeps a seat;
130   Says grace before, and after meat;
And calls, without affecting airs,
His household twice a day to prayers.
He shuns apothecary's shops;
And hates to cram the sick with slops:
He scorns to make his art a trade;
Nor bribes my Lady's favourite maid.
Old nurse-keepers would never hire
To recommend him to the squire;
Which others, whom he will not name,
140   Have often practised to their shame.

The statesman tells you with a sneer,
His fault is to be too sincere;
And, having no siníster ends,
Is apt to disoblige his friends.
The nation's good, his master's glory,
Without regard to Whig or Tory,
Were all the schemes he had in view;
Yet he was seconded by few:
Though some had spread a thousand lies;
150   'Twas *he* defeated the Excise.
'Twas known, though he had borne aspersion;
That, standing troops were his aversion:

His practice was, in every station
To serve the king, and please the nation.
Though hard to find in every case
The fittest man to fill a place:
His promises he ne'er forgot,
But took memorials on the spot:
His enemies, for want of charity,
160 Said, he affected popularity:
'Tis true, the people understood,
That all he did was for their good;
Their kind affections he has tried;
No love is lost on either side.
He came to court with fortune clear,
Which now he runs out every year;
Must, at the rate that he goes on,
Inevitably be undone.
Oh! if his Majesty would please
170 To give him but a writ of ease,
Would grant him licence to retire,
As it hath long been his desire,
By fair accounts it would be found
He's poorer by ten thousand pound.
He owns, and hopes it is no sin,
He ne'er was partial to his kin;
He thought it base for men in stations,
To crowd the court with their relations:
His country was his dearest mother,
180 And every virtuous man his brother:
Through modesty, or awkward shame,
(For which he owns himself to blame)
He found the wisest men he could,
Without respect to friends, or blood,
Nor ever acts on private views,
When he hath liberty to choose.

The sharper swore he hated play,
Except to pass an hour away:
And, well he might; for, to his cost,
190 By want of skill, he always lost:
He heard, there was a club of cheats
Who had contrived a thousand feats;

Could change the stock, or cog a die,
And thus deceive the sharpest eye:
No wonder how his fortune sunk,
His brothers fleece him when he's drunk.

I own, the moral not exact;
Besides, the tale is false in fact;
And, so absurd, that I could raise up
200   From fields Elysian, fabling Aesop;
I would accuse him to his face
For libelling the four-foot race.
Creatures of every kind but ours
Well comprehend their natural powers;
While we, whom reason ought to sway,
Mistake our talents every day:
The ass was never known so stupid
To act the part of Tray, or Cupid;
Nor leaps upon his master's lap,
210   There to be stroked and fed with pap;
As Aesop would the world persuade;
He better understands his trade:
Nor comes whene'er his lady whistles;
But, carries loads, and feeds on thistles;
Our author's meaning, I presume, is
A creature *bipes et implumis*;
Wherein the moralist designed
A compliment to humankind:
For, here he owns, that now and then
220   Beasts may *degenerate* into men.

To a Lady

WHO DESIRED THE AUTHOR TO WRITE SOME VERSES
UPON HER IN THE HEROIC STYLE

After venting all my spite,
Tell me, what have I to write?
Every error I could find
Through the mazes of your mind,
Have my busy muse employed
Till the company is cloyed.

Are you positive and fretful,
Heedless, ignorant, forgetful?
These, and twenty follies more,
10 I have often told before.

Hearken what my Lady says,
'Have I nothing then to praise?
Ill befits you to be witty,
When a fault should move your pity.
If you think me too conceited,
Or to passion quickly heated:
If my wandering head be less
Set on reading than on dress;
If I always seem so dull t'ye;
20 I can solve the difficulty.

'You would teach me to be wise;
Truth and honour how to prize;
How to shine in conversation,
And with credit fill my station:
How to relish notions high:
How to live, and how to die.

'But it was decreed by fate,
Mr Dean, you come too late;
Well I know, you can discern,
30 I am now too old to learn:
Follies, from my youth instilled,
Have my soul entirely filled:
In my head and heart they centre;
Nor will let your lessons enter.

'Bred a fondling and an heiress;
Dressed like any Lady Mayoress;
Cockered by the servants round,
Was too good to touch the ground,
Thought the life of every lady
40 Should be one continual play-day:
Balls, and masquerades, and shows,
Visits, plays, and powdered beaux.

'Thus you have my case at large;
And may now perform your charge.

Those materials I have furnished,
When by you refined and burnished,
Must, that all the world may know 'em,
Be reduced into a poem.
But, I beg, suspend a while
50 That same paltry, burlesque style;
Drop for once your constant rule,
Turning all to ridicule:
Teaching others how to ape ye;
Court nor parliament can 'scape ye;
Treat the public and your friends
Both alike, while neither mends.

     'Sing my praise in strain sublime;
Treat not me with doggerel rhyme.
'Tis but just, you should produce
60 With each fault, each fault's excuse:
Not to publish every trifle,
And my few perfections stifle.
With some gifts at least endow me,
Which my very foes allow me.
Am I spiteful, proud, unjust?
Did I ever break my trust?
Which, of all our *modern* dames
Censures less, or less defames?
In good manners am I faulty?
70 Can you call me rude or haughty?
Did I e'er my mite withhold
From the impotent and old?
When did ever I omit
Due regard for men of wit?
When have I esteem expressed
For a coxcomb gaily dressed?
Do I, like the female tribe,
Think it wit to fleer and gibe?
Who, with less designing ends,
80 Kindlier entertains their friends?
With good words and countenance sprightly,
Strive to treat them all politely?

     'Think not cards my chief diversion:
'Tis a wrong unjust aspersion:

Never knew I any good in 'em,
But to doze my head like laudanum:
We by play, as men by drinking,
Pass our nights to drive out thinking.
From my ailments give me leisure,
90   I shall read and think with pleasure:
Conversations learn to relish,
And with books my mind embellish.'

Now, methinks, I hear you cry:
'Mr Dean, you must reply.'

Madam, I allow 'tis true:
All these praises are your due.
You, like some acute philosopher,
Every fault have drawn a gloss over;
Placing in the strongest light
100   All your virtues to my sight.

Though you lead a blameless life,
Live an humble, prudent wife;
Answer all domestic ends,
What is this to us your friends?
Though your children by a nod
Stand in awe without a rod:
Though by your obliging sway
Servants love you, and obey;
Though you treat us with a smile;
110   Clear your looks, and smooth your style;
Load our plates from every dish;
This is not the thing we wish.
Colonel — may be your debtor;
We expect employment better.
You must learn, if you would gain us,
With good sense to entertain us.

Scholars, when good sense describing,
Call it tasting and imbibing:
Metaphoric meat and drink
120   Is to understand and think:
We may *carve* for others thus;
To discourse and to attend,
Is, to *help* yourself and friend.

Conversation is but *carving*;
Carve for all, yourself is starving:
Give no more to every guest,
Than he's able to digest:
Give him always of the prime;
130 And but little at a time.
Carve to all but just enough:
Let them neither starve, nor stuff:
And that you may have your due,
Let your neighbours carve for you.
This comparison will hold,
Could it well in rhyme be told,
How conversing, listening, thinking,
Justly may resemble drinking;
For a friend a glass you fill,
140 What is this but to instil?

To conclude this long essay,
Pardon, if I disobey;
Nor, against my natural vein,
Treat you in heroic strain.
I, as all the parish knows,
Hardly can be grave in prose:
Still to lash, and lashing smile,
Ill befits a lofty style.
From the planet of my birth,
150 I encounter vice with mirth.
Wicked ministers of state
I can easier scorn than hate:
And, I find it answers right;
Scorn torments them more than spite.
All the vices of a court
Do but serve to make me sport.
Were I in some foreign realm,
Which all vices overwhelm;
Should a monkey wear a crown,
160 Must I tremble at his frown?
Could I not, through all his ermine,
Spy the strutting, chattering vermin?
Safely write a smart lampoon,
To expose the brisk baboon?

When my muse officious ventures
On the nation's representers:
Teaching by what golden rules,
Into knaves they turn their fools:
How the helm is ruled by Walpole,
170 At whose oars, like slaves, they all pull:
Let the vessel split on shelves;
With the freight enrich themselves:
Safe within my little wherry,
All their madness makes me merry:
Like the watermen of Thames,
I row by, and call them names.
Like the ever-laughing sage,
In a jest I spend my rage.
(Though it must be understood,
180 I would hang them if I could:)
If I can but fill my niche,
I attempt no higher pitch.
Leave to D'Anvers and his mate,
Maxims wise to rule the state.
Pulteney deep, accomplished St Johns,
Scourge the villains with a vengeance:
Let me, though the smell be noisome,
Strip their bums; let Caleb hoise 'em;
Then apply Alecto's whip,
190 Till they wriggle, howl, and skip.

'Deuce is in you, Mr Dean:
What can all this passion mean?
Mention courts, you'll ne'er be quiet;
On corruptions running riot.
End, as it befits your station:
Come to use, and application:
Nor, with senates keep a fuss.'
I submit, and answer thus.

If the machinations brewing
200 To complete the public ruin,
Never once could have the power
To affect me half an hour;
(Sooner would I write in buskins,

Mournful elegies on Blueskins)
If I laugh at Whig and Tory;
I conclude *a fortiori*,
All your eloquence will scarce
Drive me from my favourite farce.
This I must insist on. For, as
210   It is well observed by Horace,
Ridicule has greater power
To reform the world, than sour.
Horses thus, let jockeys judge else,
Switches better guide than cudgels.
Bastings heavy, dry, obtuse,
Only dullness can produce;
While a little gentle jerking
Sets the spirits all a-working.

Thus, I find it by experiment,
220   Scolding moves you less than merriment.
I may storm and rage in vain;
It but stupefies your brain.
But with raillery to nettle,
Sets your thoughts upon their mettle:
Gives imagination scope;
Never lets your mind elope:
Drives out brangling and contention,
Brings in reason and invention.
For your sake as well as mine,
230   I the lofty style decline.
I should make a figure scurvy,
And your head turn topsyturvy.

I, who love to have a fling,
Both at senate house and king;
That they might some better way tread,
To avoid the public hatred;
Thought no method more commodious,
Than to show their vices odious:
Which I chose to make appear,
240   Not by anger, but a sneer:
As my method of reforming
Is by laughing, not by storming,

(For my friends have always thought
Tenderness my greatest fault)
Would you have me change my style?
On your faults no longer smile
But, to patch up all our quarrels,
Quote you texts from Plutarch's *Morals*;
Or from Solomon produce
250   Maxims teaching wisdom's use.

If I treat you like a crowned head,
You have cheap enough compounded;
Can you put in higher claims,
Than the owners of St James'?
You are not so great a grievance,
As the hirelings of St Stephen's.
You are of a lower class
Than my friend Sir Robert Brass.
None of these have mercy found,
260   I have laughed and lashed them round.

Have you seen a rocket fly?
You could swear it pierced the sky:
It but reached the middle air,
Bursting into pieces there:
Thousand sparkles falling down,
Light on many a coxcomb's crown:
See, what mirth the sport creates;
Singes hair, but breaks no pates.
Thus, should I attempt to climb,
270   Treat you in a style sublime,
Such a rocket is my muse;
Should I lofty numbers choose,
E'er I reached Parnassus' top,
I should burst, and bursting drop.
All my fire would fall in scraps;
Give your head some gentle raps;
Only make it smart a while;
Then, could I forbear to smile,
When I found the tingling pain,
280   Entering warm your frigid brain:
Make you able upon sight

To decide of wrong and right;
Talk with sense whate'er you please on;
Learn to relish truth and reason.

Thus we both should gain our prize:
I to laugh, and you grow wise.

On Poetry: a Rhapsody

All human race would fain be wits,
And millions miss, for one that hits.
Young's universal passion, pride,
Was never known to spread so wide.
Say Britain, could you ever boast,
Three poets in an age at most?
Our chilling climate hardly bears
A sprig of bays in fifty years:
While every fool his claim alleges,
10   As if it grew in common hedges.
What reason can there be assigned
For this perverseness in the mind?
Brutes find out where their talents lie:
A bear will not attempt to fly:
A foundered horse will oft debate,
Before he tries a five-barred gate:
A dog by instinct turns aside,
Who sees the ditch too deep and wide.
But man we find the only creature,
20   Who, led by folly, combats nature;
Who, when she loudly cries, 'Forbear',
With obstinacy fixes there;
And, where his genius least inclines,
Absurdly bends his whole designs.

Not empire to the rising sun,
By valour, conduct, fortune won;
Nor highest wisdom in debates
For framing laws to govern states;
Nor skill in sciences profound,
30   So large to grasp the circle round;

Such heavenly influence require,
As how to strike the muses' lyre.

Not beggar's brat, on bulk begot;
Not bastard of a pedlar Scot;
Not boy brought up to cleaning shoes,
The spawn of Bridewell, or the stews;
Not infants dropped, the spurious pledges
Of gypsies littering under hedges,
Are so disqualified by fate
40 To rise in church, or law, or state,
As he, whom Phoebus in his ire
Hath *blasted* with poetic fire.

What hope of custom in the fair,
While not a soul demands your ware?
Where you have nothing to produce
For private life, or public use?
Court, city, country want you not;
You cannot bribe, betray, or plot.
For poets, law makes no provision:
50 The wealthy have you in derision.
Of state affairs you cannot smatter,
Are awkward when you try to flatter.
Your portion, taking Britain round,
Was just one annual hundred pound.
Now not so much as in remainder
Since Cibber brought in an attainder;
For ever fixed by right divine,
(A monarch's right) on Grub Street line.

Poor starveling bard, how small thy gains!
60 How unproportioned to thy pains!
And here a simile comes pat in:
Though chickens take a month to fatten,
The guests in less than half an hour
Will more than half a score devour.
So, after toiling twenty days,
To earn a stock of pence and praise,
Thy labours, grown the critic's prey,
Are swallowed o'er a dish of tea;

Gone, to be never heard of more,
70 Gone, where the chickens went before.

How shall a new attempter learn
Of different spirits to discern,
And how distinguish, which is which,
The poet's vein, or scribbling itch?
Then hear an old experienced sinner
Instructing thus a young beginner.

Consult yourself, and if you find
A powerful impulse urge your mind,
Impartial judge within your breast
80 What subject you can manage best;
Whether your genius most inclines
To satire, praise, or humorous lines;
To elegies in mournful tone,
Or prologue 'sent from hand unknown.'
Then rising with Aurora's light,
The muse invoked, sit down to write;
Blot out, correct, insert, refine,
Enlarge, diminish, interline.
Be mindful, when invention fails,
90 To scratch your head, and bite your nails.

Your poem finished; next your care
Is needful, to transcribe it fair.
In modern wit all printed trash, is
Set off with numerous breaks – and dashes –
To statesmen would you give a wipe,
You print it in *italic type*.
When letters are in vulgar shapes,
'Tis ten to one the wit escapes;
But when in CAPITALS expressed,
100 The dullest reader smokes a jest.
Or else perhaps he may invent
A better than the poet meant,
As learnéd commentators view
In Homer more than Homer knew.

Your poem in its modish dress,
Correctly fitted for the press,
Convey by penny post to Lintot,

But let no friend alive look into't.
If Lintot thinks 'twill quit the cost,
110 You need not fear your labour lost:
And, how agreeably surprised
Are you to see it advertised!
The hawker shows you one in print,
As fresh as farthings from the mint:
The product of your toil and sweating;
A bastard of your own begetting.

Be sure at Will's the following day,
Lie snug, to hear what critics say.
And if you find the general vogue
120 Pronounces you a stupid rogue;
Damns all your thoughts as low and little,
Sit still, and swallow down your spittle.
Be silent as a politician,
For, talking may beget suspicion:
Or praise the judgement of the town,
And help yourself to run it down.
Give up a fond paternal pride,
Nor argue on the weaker side;
For, poems read without a name
130 We justly praise, or justly blame:
And critics have no partial views,
Except they know whom they abuse.
And since you ne'er provoked their spite,
Depend upon't their judgement's right:
But if you blab, you are undone;
Consider what a risk you run.
You lose your credit all at once;
The town will mark you for a dunce:
The vilest doggerel Grub Street sends,
140 Will pass for yours with foes and friends.
And you must bear the whole disgrace,
Till some fresh blockhead takes your place.

Your secret kept, your poem sunk,
And sent in quires to line a trunk;
If still you be disposed to rhyme,
Go try your hand a second time.
Again you fail, yet safe's the word,

Take courage and attempt a third.
But first with care employ your thoughts,
150   Where critics marked your former faults.
The trivial turns, the borrowed wit,
The similes that nothing fit;
The cant which every fool repeats,
Town-jests, and coffee-house conceits;
Descriptions tedious, flat and dry,
And introduced the Lord knows why;
Or where you find your fury set
Against the harmless alphabet;
On A's and B's your malice vent,
160   While readers wonder whom you meant.
A public, or a private robber;
A statesman, or a South Sea jobber.
A prelate who no God believes;
A parliament, or den of thieves.
A house of peers, or gaming crew,
A griping monarch, or a Jew.
A pickpurse, at the bar, or bench;
A duchess, or a suburb wench.
Or oft when epithets you link,
170   In gaping lines to fill a chink;
Like stepping stones to save a stride,
In streets where kennels are too wide:
Or like a heel-piece to support
A cripple with one foot too short:
Or like a bridge that joins a marish
To moorlands of a different parish.
So have I seen ill-coupled hounds,
Drag different ways in miry grounds.
So geographers in Afric maps
180   With savage pictures fill their gaps;
And o'er unhabitable downs
Place elephants for want of towns.

But though you miss your third essay,
You need not throw your pen away.
Lay now aside all thoughts of fame,
To spring more profitable game.
From party merit seek support;

The vilest verse thrives best at court.
And may you ever have the luck
190   To rhyme almost as well as Duck;
And, though you never learned to scan verse,
Come out with some lampoon on D'Anvers.
A pamphlet in Sir Bob's defence
Will never fail to bring in pence;
Nor be concerned about the sale,
He pays his workmen on the nail.

Display the blessings of the nation,
And praise the whole administration,
Extol the bench of bishops round,
200   Who at them rail bid God confound:
To bishop-haters answer thus
(The only logic used by us),
What though they don't believe in Christ,
Deny them Protestants – thou liest.

A prince the moment he is crowned,
Inherits every virtue round,
As emblems of the sovereign power,
Like *other* baubles of the Tower.
Is generous, valiant, just and wise,
210   And so continues till he dies.
His humble senate this professes,
In all their speeches, votes, addresses.
But once you fix him in a tomb,
His virtues fade, his vices bloom;
And each perfection wrong imputed
Is fully at his death confuted.
His panegyrics then are ceased,
He's grown a tyrant, dunce and beast.
The loads of poems in his praise,
220   Ascending make one funeral blaze.
As soon as you can hear his knell,
This god on earth turns devil in hell.
And lo, his ministers of state,
Transformed to imps, his levees wait:
Where, in the scenes of endless woe,
They ply their former arts below:

And as they sail in Charon's boat,
Contrive to bribe the judge's vote.
To Cerberus they give a sop,
230   His triple-barking mouth to stop:
Or in the ivory gate of dreams,
Project Excise and South Sea schemes:
Or hire their party pamphleteers,
To set Elysium by the ears.

Then poet, if you mean to thrive,
Employ your muse on kings alive;
With prudence gathering up a cluster
Of all the virtues you can muster:
Which formed into a garland sweet,
240   Lay humbly at your monarch's feet;
Who, as the odours reach his throne,
Will smile, and think 'em all his own:
For law and gospel both determine
All virtues lodge in royal ermine.
(I mean the oracles of both
Who shall depose it upon oath.)
Your garland in the following reign,
Change but the names, will do again.

But if you think this trade too base,
250   (Which seldom is the dunce's case)
Put on the critic's brow, and sit
At Will's, the puny judge of wit.
A nod, a shrug, a scornful smile,
With caution used, may serve awhile.
Proceed no further in your part,
Before you learn the terms of art:
(For you can never be too far gone,
In all our modern critics' jargon.)
Then talk with more authentic face,
260   Of 'unities, in time and place.'
Get scraps of Horace from your friends,
And have them at your fingers' ends.
Learn Aristotle's rules by rote,
And at all hazards boldly quote:
Judicious Rymer oft review:
Wise Dennis, and profound Bossu.

Read all the prefaces of Dryden,
For these our critics much confide in,
(Though merely writ at first for filling
270   To raise the volume's price, a shilling.)

A forward critic often dupes us
With sham quotations *Peri Hupsous*:
And if we have not read Longinus,
Will magisterially outshine us.
Then, lest with Greek he overrun ye,
Procure the book for love or money,
Translated from Boileau's translation,
And quote quotation on quotation.

At Will's you hear a poem read,
280   Where Battus from the table head,
Reclining on his elbow-chair,
Gives judgement with decisive air.
To him the tribe of circling wits,
As to an oracle submits.
He gives directions to the town,
To cry it up, or run it down.
(Like courtiers, when they send a note,
Instructing members how to vote.)
He sets a stamp of bad and good,
290   Though not a word be understood.
Your lesson learnt, you'll be secure
To get the name of connoisseur.
And when your merits once are known,
Procure disciples of your own.

For poets (you can never want 'em,
Spread through Augusta Trinobantum)
Computing by their pecks of coals,
Amount to just nine thousand souls.
These o'er their proper districts govern,
300   Of wit and humour, judges sovereign.
In every street a city bard
Rules, like an alderman his ward.
His indisputed rights extend
Through all the lane, from end to end.
The neighbours round admire his shrewdness,

For songs of loyalty and lewdness.
Outdone by none in rhyming well,
Although he never learnt to spell.

Two bordering wits contend for glory;
310   And one is Whig, and one is Tory.
And this, for epics claims the bays,
And that, for elegiac lays.
Some famed for numbers soft and smooth,
By lovers spoke in Punch's booth.
And some as justly fame extols
For lofty lines in Smithfield drolls.
Bavius in Wapping gains renown,
And Maevius reigns o'er Kentish Town:
Tigellius placed in Phoebus' car,
320   From Ludgate shines to Temple Bar.
Harmonious Cibber entertains
The court with annual birthday strains;
Whence Gay was banished in disgrace,
Where Pope will never show his face;
Where Young must torture his invention,
To flatter knaves, or lose his pension.

But these are not a thousandth part
Of jobbers in the poet's art,
Attending each his proper station,
330   And all in due subordination;
Through every alley to be found,
In garrets high, or underground:
And when they join their pericranies,
Out skips a book of miscellanies.

Hobbes clearly proves that every creature
Lives in a state of war by nature.
The greater for the smaller watch,
But meddle seldom with their match.
A whale of moderate size will draw
340   A shoal of herrings down his maw.
A fox with geese his belly crams;
A wolf destroys a thousand lambs.
But search among the rhyming race,
The *brave* are worried by the *base*.
If, on Parnassus' top you sit,

You rarely bite, are always bit:
Each poet of inferior size
On you shall rail and criticize;
And strive to tear you limb from limb,
350   While others do as much for him.
The vermin only tease and pinch
Their foes superior by an inch.
So, naturalists observe, a flea
Hath smaller fleas that on him prey,
And these have smaller yet to bite 'em,
And so proceed *ad infinitum*:
Thus every poet in his kind,
Is bit by him that comes behind;
Who, though too little to be seen,
360   Can tease, and gall, and give the spleen;
Call dunces, fools, and sons of whores,
Lay Grub Street at each other's doors:
Extol the Greek and Roman masters,
And curse our modern poetasters.
Complain, as many an ancient bard did,
How genius is no more rewarded;
How wrong a taste prevails among us;
How much our ancestors outsung us;
Can personate an awkward scorn
370   For those who are not poets born:
And all their brother dunces lash,
Who crowd the press with hourly trash.

O, Grub Street! how I do bemoan thee,
Whose graceless children scorn to own thee!
This filial piety forgot,
Deny their country like a Scot:
Though by their idiom and grimace
They soon betray their native place:
Yet *thou* hast greater cause to be
380   Ashamed of them, than they of thee.
Degenerate from their ancient brood,
Since first the court allowed them food.

Remains a difficulty still,
To purchase fame by writing ill:
From Flecknoe down to Howard's time,
How few have reached the low sublime!

For when our high-born Howard died,
Blackmore alone his place supplied:
And lest a chasm should intervene,
390 When death had finished Blackmore's reign,
The leaden crown devolved to thee,
Great poet of the *Hollow Tree*.
But, oh, how unsecure thy throne!
Ten thousand bards thy rights disown:
They plot to turn in factious zeal,
Duncenia to a common-weal;
And with rebellious arms pretend
And equal privilege to *descend*.

In bulk there are not more degrees,
400 From elephants to mites in cheese,
Than what a curious eye may trace
In creatures of the rhyming race.
From bad to worse, and worse they fall,
But, who can reach to worst of all?
For, though in nature depth and height
Are equally held infinite,
In poetry the height we know;
'Tis only infinite below.
For instance: when you rashly think,
410 No rhymer can like Welsted sink:
His merits balanced you shall find,
The laureate leaves him far behind.
Concanen, more aspiring bard,
Climbs downwards, deeper by a yard:
Smart Jemmy Moor with vigour drops,
The rest pursue as thick as hops:
With heads to points the gulf they enter,
Linked perpendicular to the centre:
And as their heels elated rise,
420 Their heads attempt the nether skies.

O, what indignity and shame
To prostitute the muse's name,
By flattering kings whom heaven designed
The plagues and scourges of mankind.
Bred up in ignorance and sloth,
And every vice that nurses both.

Perhaps you say Augustus shines
Immortal made in Virgil's lines,
And Horace brought the tuneful choir
430   To sing his virtues on the lyre,
Without reproach of flattery; true,
Because their praises were his due.
For in those ages kings we find,
Were animals of humankind,
But now go search all Europe round,
Among the savage monsters crowned,
With vice polluting every throne
(I mean all kings except our own)
In vain you make the strictest view
440   To find a king in all the crew
With whom a footman out of place
Would not conceive a high disgrace,
A burning shame, a crying sin,
To take his morning's cup of gin.
Thus all are destined to obey
Some beast of burden or of prey.
'Tis sung Prometheus forming man
Through all the brutal species ran,
Each proper quality to find
450   Adapted to a human mind;
A mingled mass of good and bad,
The worst and best that could be had;
Then from a clay of mixture base,
He shaped a king to rule the race,
Endowed with gifts from every brute,
Which best the regal nature suit.
Thus think on kings, the name denotes
Hogs, asses, wolves, baboons and goats,
To represent in figure just
460   Sloth, folly, rapine, mischief, lust.
O! were they all but Nebuchadnezzars,
What herds of kings would turn to grazers.

Fair Britain, in thy monarch blessed,
Whose virtues bear the strictest test;
Whom never faction can bespatter,
Nor minister nor poet flatter.

What justice in rewarding merit!
What magnanimity of spirit!
How well his public thrift is shown!
470   All coffers full except his own.
What lineaments divine we trace
Through all his figure, mien, and face;
Though peace with olive bind his hands,
Confessed the conquering hero stands.
Hydaspes, Indus, and the Ganges,
Dread from his hand impending changes.
From him the Tartar, and Chinese,
Short by the knees intreat for peace.
The consort of his throne and bed,
480   A perfect goddess born and bred.
Appointed sovereign judge to sit
On learning, eloquence and wit.
Our eldest hope, divine Iulus,
(Late, very late, O, may he rule us.)
What early manhood has he shown,
Before his downy beard was grown!
Then think, what wonders will be done
By going on as he begun;
An heir for Britain to secure
490   As long as sun and moon endure.

The remnant of the royal blood,
Comes pouring on me like a flood.
Bright goddesses, in number five;
Duke William, sweetest prince alive.

Now sing the minister of state,
Who shines alone, without a mate.
Observe with what majestic port
This Atlas stands to prop the court:
Intent the public debts to pay,
500   Like prudent Fabius by delay.
Thou great vicegerent of the King,
Thy praises every muse shall sing:
In all affairs thou sole director,
Of wit and learning chief protector;
Though small the time thou hast to spare,

The church is thy peculiar care.
Of pious prelates what a stock
You choose to rule the sable flock.
You raise the honour of the peerage,
510 Proud to attend you at the steerage.
You dignify the noble race,
Content yourself with humbler place,
Now learning, valour, virtue, sense,
To titles give the sole pretence.
St George beheld thee with delight,
Vouchsafe to be an azure knight,
When on thy breast and sides Herculean,
He fixed the star and string cerulean.

Say, poet, in what other nation,
520 Shone ever such a constellation.
Attend ye Popes, and Youngs, and Gays,
And tune your harps, and strow your bays.
Your panegyrics here provide,
You cannot err on flattery's side.
Above the stars exalt your style,
You still are low ten thousand mile.
On Lewis all his bards bestowed,
Of incense many a thousand load;
But Europe mortified his pride,
530 And swore the fawning rascals lied:
Yet what the world refused to Lewis,
Applied to George exactly true is:
Exactly true! Invidious poet!
'Tis fifty thousand times below it.

Translate me now some lines, if you can,
From Virgil, Martial, Ovid, Lucan;
They could all power in heaven divide,
And do no wrong to either side:
They teach you how to split a hair,
540 Give George and Jove an equal share.
Yet, why should we be laced so straight;
I'll give my monarch butter-weight.
And reason good; for many a year
Jove never intermeddled here:

Nor, though his priests be duly paid,
Did ever we desire his aid:
We now can better do without him,
Since Woolston gave us arms to rout him.

* * * * * * * *Caetera desiderantur* * * * * * * *

The Hardship Put upon Ladies

Poor ladies! though their business be to play,
'Tis hard they must be busy night and day:
Why should they want the privilege of men,
And take some small diversions now and then?
Had women been the makers of our laws;
(And why they were not, I can see no cause;)
The men should slave at cards from morn to night;
And female pleasures be to read and write.

A Love Song in the Modern Taste

I
Fluttering spread thy purple pinions,
    Gentle Cupid o'er my heart;
I a slave in thy dominions;
    Nature must give way to art.

II
Mild Arcadians, ever blooming,
    Nightly nodding o'er your flocks,
See my weary days consuming,
    All beneath yon flowery rocks.

III
Thus the Cyprian goddess weeping,
10   Mourned Adonis, darling youth:
Him the boar in silence creeping,
    Gored with unrelenting tooth.

IV
Cynthia, tune harmonious numbers;
    Fair Discretion string the lyre;

Soothe my ever-waking slumbers:
   Bright Apollo lend thy choir.

V
Gloomy Pluto, king of terrors,
   Armed in adamantine chains,
Lead me to the crystal mirrors,
20   Watering soft Elysian plains.

VI
Mournful cypress, verdant willow,
   Gilding my Aurelia's brows,
Morpheus hovering o'er my pillow,
   Hear me pay my dying vows.

VII
Melancholy smooth Meander,
   Swiftly purling in a round,
On thy margins lovers wander,
   With thy flowery chaplets crowned.

VIII
Thus when Philomela drooping,
30   Softly seeks her silent mate;
See the bird of Juno stooping,
   Melody resign to fate.

Verses Made in Swift's Sleep

I walk before no man, a hawk in his fist;
Nor, am I a brilliant, whenever I list.

On the Words 'Brother Protestants and Fellow Christians'

SO FAMILIARLY USED BY THE ADVOCATES FOR THE REPEAL
OF THE TEST ACT IN IRELAND, 1733

An inundation, says the fable,
O'erflowed a farmer's barn and stable;
Whole ricks of hay and stacks of corn,

Were down the sudden current borne;
While things of heterogeneous kind,
Together float with tide and wind;
The generous wheat forgot its pride,
And sailed with litter side by side;
Uniting all, to show their amity,
10   As in a general calamity.
A ball of new-dropped horse's dung,
Mingling with apples in the throng,
Said to the pippin, plump, and prim,
'See, brother, how we apples swim.'

    Thus Lamb, renowned for cutting corns,
An offered fee from Radcliffe scorns;
'Not for the world – we doctors, brother,
Must take no fee from one another.'
Thus to a Dean some curate sloven,
20   Subscribes, 'Dear sir, your brother loving.'
Thus all the footmen, shoe-boys, porters,
About St James's, cry, 'We courtiers.'
Thus Horace in the House will prate,
'Sir, we the ministers of state.'
Thus at the bar that booby Bettesworth,
Though half a crown o'erpays his sweat's worth;
Who knows in law, nor text, nor margent,
Calls Singleton his brother serjeant.
And thus fanatic saints, though neither in
30   Doctrine, or discipline our brethren,
Are 'brother Protestants and Christians',
As much as Hebrews and Philistines:
But in no other sense, than nature
Has made a rat our fellow-creature.
Lice from your body suck their food;
But is a louse your flesh and blood?
Though born of human filth and sweat, it
May well be said man did beget it.
But maggots in your nose and chin,
40   As well may claim you for their kin.

    Yet critics may object, why not?
Since lice are brethren to a Scot:
Which made our swarm of sects determine

Employments for their brother vermin.
But be they English, Irish, Scottish,
What Protestant can be so sottish,
While o'er the church those clouds are gathering,
To call a swarm of lice his brethren?

   As Moses, by divine advice,
50 In Egypt turned the dust to lice;
And as our sects, by all descriptions,
Have hearts more hardened than Egyptians;
As from the trodden dust they spring,
And, turned to lice, infest the king:
For pity's sake it would be just,
A rod should turn them back to dust.

   Let folks in high, or holy stations,
Be proud of owning such relations;
Let courtiers hug them in their bosom,
60 As if they were afraid to lose 'em:
While I, with humble Job, had rather,
Say to corruption, 'Thou'rt my father.'
For he that has so little wit,
To nourish vermin, may be *bit*.

The Yahoo's Overthrow

OR, THE KEVIN BAIL'S NEW BALLAD,
UPON SERJEANT KITE'S INSULTING THE DEAN

To the tune of 'Derry down'

Jolly boys of St Kevin's, St Patrick's, Donore,
And Smithfield, I'll tell you, if not told before,
How Bettesworth, that booby, and scoundrel in grain,
Hath insulted us all by insulting the Dean.
   Knock him down, down, down, knock him down.

The Dean and his merits we every one know,
But this skip of a lawyer, where the de'il did he grow?
How greater's his merit at Four Courts or House,
Than the barking of Towser, or leap of a louse?
10   *Knock him down, &c.*

That he came from the Temple, his morals do show,
But where his deep law is, few mortals yet know:
His rhetoric, bombast, silly jests, are by far
More like to lampooning than pleading at bar.
 Knock him down, &c.

This pedlar, at speaking and making of laws,
Hath met with returns of all sorts but applause;
Has, with noise and odd gestures, been prating some years,
What honester folks never durst for their ears.
20 *Knock him down, &c.*

Of all sizes and sorts, the fanatical crew
Are his brother Protestants, good men and true;
Red hat, and blue bonnet, and turban's the same,
What the devil is't to him whence the devil they came?
 Knock him down, &c.

Hobbes, Tindal, and Woolston, and Collins, and Nayler,
And Muggleton, Toland, and Bradley the tailor,
Are Christians alike; and it may be averred,
He's a Christian as good as the rest of the herd.
30 *Knock him down, &c.*

He only the rights of the clergy debates,
Their rights! their importance! We'll set on new rates
On their tithes at half-nothing, their priesthood at less:
What's next to be voted with ease you may guess.
 Knock him down, &c.

At length his old master (I need not him name)
To this damnable speaker had long owed a shame;
When his speech came abroad, he paid him off clean,
By leaving him under the pen of the Dean.
40 *Knock him down, &c.*

He kindled, as if the whole satire had been
The oppression of virtue, not wages of sin:
He began as he bragged, with a rant and a roar;
He bragged how he bounced, and he swore how he swore.
 Knock him down, &c.

Though he cringed to his Deanship in very low strains,
To others he boasted of knocking out brains,

And slitting of noses, and cropping of ears,
While his own ass's zags were more fit for the shears.
50   *Knock him down, &c.*

On this worrier of deans whene'er we can hit,
We'll show him the way how to crop and to slit;
We'll teach him some better address to afford
To the Dean of all deans, though he wears not a sword.
   Knock him down, &c.

We'll colt him through Kevin, St Patrick's, Donore,
And Smithfield, as Rap was ne'er colted before;
We'll oil him with kennel, and powder him with grains,
A modus right fit for insulters of deans.
60   *Knock him down, &c.*

And, when this is over, we'll make him amends,
To the Dean he shall go; they shall kiss, and be friends:
But how? Why, the Dean shall to him disclose
A face for to kiss, without eyes, ears, or nose.
   Knock him down, &c.

If you say this is hard, on a man that is reckoned
That serjeant-at-law, whom we call Kite the second,
You mistake; for a slave, who will coax his superiors,
May be proud to be licking a great man's posteriors.
70   *Knock him down, &c.*

What care we how high runs his passion or pride?
Though his soul he despises, he values his hide:
Then fear not his tongue, his sword, or his knife;
He'll take his revenge on his innocent wife.
   Knock him down, down, down, – keep him down.

An Epigram,

INSCRIBED TO THE HONOURABLE SERJEANT KITE

In your indignation what mercy appears,
While Jonathan's threatened with loss of his ears;
For who would not think it a much better choice,
By your knife to be mangled than racked with your voice.

If truly you would be revenged on the parson,
Command his attendance while you act your farce on,
Instead of your maiming, your shooting, or banging,
Bid Povey secure him while you are haranguing.
Had this been your method to torture him, long since,
10 He had cut his own ears to be deaf to your nonsense.

On the Archbishop of Cashel and Bettesworth

Dear Dick, prithee tell by what passion you move?
The world is in doubt, whether hatred or love;
And, while at good Cashel you rail with such spite,
They shrewdly suspect it is all but a bite.
You certainly know, though so loudly you vapour,
His spite cannot wound, who attempted the Drapier.
Then, prithee reflect, take a word of advice;
And, as your old wont is, change sides in a trice:
On his virtues hold forth; 'tis the very best way;
10 And say of the man what all honest men say.
But if, still obdurate, your anger remains,
If still your foul bosom more rancour contains;
Say then more than they; nay, lavishly flatter,
'Tis your gross panegyrics alone can bespatter.
For thine, my dear Dick, give me leave to speak plain,
Like a very foul mop, dirty more than they clean.

Epigram on Fasting

FROM THE FRENCH

A French gentleman dining with some company on a fast-day,
called for some bacon and eggs. The rest were very angry, and
reproved him for so heinous a sin: whereupon he writ the following
lines, extempore, which are here translated.

> *Peut on croire avec bon sens*
> *Qu'un lardon le mit en colère;*
> *Ou, que manger un harang*
> *C'est un secret pour lui plaire?*
> *En sa gloire envelopé*
> *Songe-t-il bien de nos soupés?*

IN ENGLISH

Who can believe with common sense,
A bacon-slice gives God offence?
Or, how a herring hath a charm
Almighty anger to disarm?
Wrapped up in majesty divine,
Does he regard on what we dine?

On His Own Deafness

Verticosus, inops, surdus, male gratus amicis;
Non campana sonans, tonitru non ab Jove missus,
Quod mage mirandum, saltem si credere fas est,
Garrula non matrona meas nunc arrigit aures.

Deaf, giddy, odious to my friends,
Now all my consolation ends;
No more I hear my church's bell
Than if it rang out for my knell;
At thunder now, no more I start
10   Than at the rumbling of a cart.
Nay though I know you would not credit –
Although a thousand times I said it:
A scold whom you might hear a mile hence
No more could reach me than her silence.

Anglo-Latin Verses

AS SONATA IN PRAES O MOLLI

Mollis abuti,
Has an acuti
No lasso finis;
Molli dii vinis
O mi de armistris,
Imi na Dis tres;
Cantu disco ver
Meas alo ver.

A LOVE SONG FROM DICK BETTESWORTH TO MISS MOLLY WHITEWAY

Mi de armis molli,
Ure mel an colli,
It is a folli;
Fori alo ver,
A ram lingat Do ver,
Ure Dick mecum o ver.

AN EPIGRAM

A sui ne is abuti cum par ito Dic
A site offis fis it mite me cacat sic
Re diri no at es ter a quarto fine ale
Fora ringat his nos e an da stringat his tale.

A LOVE SONG

Apud in is almi des ire
Mimis tres Ine ver re qui re
Alo veri findit a gestis
His mi seri ne ver at restis.

'IN MY COMPANY'

In mi cum pani praedixit:
Claret finis ne ver mixit.
Cantu tellus Dicas tori;
Cingat super Tori rori.
Aleto claret adit basis;
Tosta Laedi, fieri faces.

Verses Spoken Extempore by Dean Swift on His Curate's Complaint of Hard Duty

I marched three miles through scorching sand,
With zeal in heart, and notes in hand;
I rode four more to great St Mary;
Using four legs when two were weary.
To three fair virgins I did tie men

In the close band of pleasing hymen.
I dipped two babes in holy water,
And purified the mothers after.
Within an hour, and eke a half,
10   I preached three congregations deaf,
Which, thundering out with lungs long-winded,
I chopped so fast, that few there minded.
My emblem, the laborious sun,   ⎫
Saw all these mighty labours done, ⎬
Before one race of his was run;   ⎭
All this performed by Robert Hewit,
What mortal else could e'er go through it!

The Parson's Case

That you, friend Marcus, like a Stoic,
Can wish to die, in strain heroic,
No real fortitude implies:
Yet, all must own, thy wish is wise.

    Thy curate's place, thy fruitful wife,
Thy busy, drudging scene of life,
Thy insolent illiterate vicar,
Thy want of all-consoling liquor,
Thy threadbare gown, thy cassock rent,
10   Thy credit sunk, thy money spent,
Thy week made up of fasting days,
Thy grate unconscious of a blaze,
And, to complete thy other curses,
The quarterly demand of nurses,
Are ills you wisely wish to leave,
And fly for refuge to the grave:
And, O what virtue you express
In wishing such afflictions less!

    But, now should fortune shift the scene,
20   And make thy curateship a dean;
Or some rich benefice provide,
To pamper luxury and pride;
With labour small, and income great;

With chariot less for use than state;
With swelling scarf, and glossy gown,
And licence to reside in town;
To shine, where all the gay resort,
At concert, coffee-house, or court;
And weekly persecute his Grace
30   With visits, or to beg a place;
With underlings thy flocks to teach,
With no desire to pray or preach;
With haughty spouse in vesture fine,
With plenteous meals, and generous wine;
Wouldst thou not wish, in so much ease,
Thy years as numerous as thy days?

The Dean and Duke

James Brydges and the Dean had long been friends,
James is beduked; of course their friendship ends.
But sure the Dean deserves a sharp rebuke,
From knowing James, to boast he knows a Duke.
But, since just heaven the Duke's ambition mocks,
Since all he got by fraud is lost by stocks,
His wings are clipped; he tries no more in vain
With bands of fiddlers to extend his train.
Since he no more can build, and plant, and revel,
10   The Duke and Dean seem near upon a level.
Oh! wert thou not a duke, my good Duke Humphry,
From bailiff's claws thou scarce could keep thy bum free.
A Duke to know a Dean! Go smooth thy crown,
Thy brother (far thy betters) wore a gown.
Well, but a Duke thou art; so pleased the King;
Oh! would his Majesty but add a string.

On Dr Rundle

BISHOP OF DERRY

Make Rundle bishop; fie, for shame!
An Arian to usurp the name!

A bishop in the isle of saints!
How will his brethren make complaints?
Dare any of the mitred host,
Confer on him the Holy Ghost;
In Mother Church to breed a variance,
By coupling *orthodox* with *Arians*?

Yet, were he heathen, Turk or Jew,
10 What is there in it strange or new?
For, let us hear the weak pretence,
His brethren find to take offence;
Of whom there are but four at most,
Who know there is an Holy Ghost:
The rest, who boast they have conferred it,
Like Paul's Ephesians, never heard it;
And, when they gave it, well 'tis known,
They gave what never was their own.

Rundle a bishop! well he may;
20 He's still a Christian more than they.

We know the subject of their quarrels;
The man has learning, sense and morals.

There is a reason still more weighty;
'Tis granted he believes a deity.
Has every circumstance to please us,
Though fools may doubt his faith in Jesus.
But why should he with that be loaded,
Now twenty years from court exploded?
And, is not this objection odd
30 From rogues who ne'er believed a God?
For liberty a champion stout,
Though not so gospel-ward devout.
While others hither sent to save us,
Came but to plunder and enslave us;
Nor ever owned a power divine,
But Mammon, and the German line.

Say, how did Rundle undermine 'em;
Who showed a better *jus divinum*?
From ancient canons would not vary,
40 But thrice refused *episcopari*.

Our bishop's predecessor, Magus,
Would offer all the sands of Tagus;
Or sell his children, house, and lands,
For that one gift to lay on hands:
But all his gold could not avail
To have the *spirit* set to sale.
Said surly Peter, 'Magus, prithee
Begone: thy money perish with thee.'
Were Peter now alive, perhaps
50   He might have found a score of chaps,
Could he but make his gift appear
In rents three thousand pounds a year.

Some fancy this promotion odd,
As not the handiwork of God;
Though even the bishops disappointed,
Must own it made by God's anointed.
And well we know, the congee regal
Is more secure, as well as legal,
Because our lawyers all agree,
60   That bishoprics are held in fee.

Dear Baldwin chaste, and witty Cross,
How sorely I lament your loss!
That such a pair of wealthy ninnies
Should slip your time of dropping guineas;
For, had you made the King your debtor,
Your title had been so much better.

An Epigram

Friend Rundle fell with grievous bump,
Upon his reverential rump.
Poor rump, thou hadst been better sped,
Had thou been joined to Boulter's head.
A head so weighty and profound,
Would needs have kept thee from the ground.

On a Printer's being Sent to Newgate

Better we all were in our graves
Than live in slavery to slaves,
Worse than the anarchy at sea,
Where fishes on each other prey;
Where every trout can make as high rants
O'er his inferiors as our tyrants;
And swagger while the coast is clear:
But should a lordly pike appear,
Away you see the varlet scud,
10 Or hide his coward snout in mud.
Thus, if a gudgeon meet a roach
He dare not venture to approach;
Yet still has impudence to rise,
And, like Domitian, leap at flies.

On Noisy Tom

> *Qui promittit, cives, urbem, sibi curae,*
> *Imperium fore, et Italiam, et delubra Deorum;*
> *Quo patre sit natus, num ignota matre inhonestus*
> *Omnes mortales curare, & quaerere cogit.*
> *Tune Syri, Damae, aut Dionysi filius audes*
> *Dejicere e saxo cives, aut tradere Cadmo?*
> Hor. *Lib*.I *Sat*.6 l.34–9

Translated literally
Whoever promiseth (in the Senate) to take the city (of Rome) and
the citizens under his care, nay, the whole empire, Italy, and the
temples of the gods; such a man compelleth all mortals curiously to
inquire from what father he sprung, and whether his mother were
some obscure dishonourable female. (The people would cry out)
What, thou, the son of Cyrus, or Damas, or Dionysius, dare thou
cast our citizens down the Tarpeian rock, or deliver them prisoners
to Cadmus?

PARAPHRASED

If noisy Tom should in the senate prate,
That he would answer both for church and state;

And, further to demónstrate his affection,
Would take the kingdom into his protection:
All mortals must be curious to inquire,
Who could this coxcomb be, and who his sire?
What! thou the spawn of him who shamed our isle,
That traitor, ássassín, informer vile.
Though by the female side you proudly bring,
10   To mend your breed, the murderer of a king.
What was thy grandsire but a mountaineer,
Who held a cabin for ten groats a year;
Whose master, Moore, preserved him from the halter,
For stealing cows, nor could he read the psalter.
Durst thou, ungrateful, from the senate chase
Thy founder's grandson and usurp his place?
Just heaven! to see the dunghill dastard blood
Survive in thee, and make the proverb good.
Then vote a worthy citizen to gaol,
20   In spite to justice, and refuse his bail.

A Character, Panegyric, and Description of the Legion Club

As I stroll the city, oft I
Spy a building large and lofty,
Not a bow-shot from the College,
Half a globe from sense and knowledge.
By the prudent architect
Placed against the church direct;
Making good my grandam's jest,
Near the church – you know the rest.

Tell us, what this pile contains?
10   Many a head that holds no brains.
These demoniacs let me dub
With the name of 'Legion Club.'
Such assemblies, you might swear,
Meet when butchers bait a bear;
Such a noise, and such haranguing,
When a brother thief is hanging.
Such a rout and such a rabble

Run to hear jack-pudding gabble;
Such a crowd their ordure throws
20 On a far less villain's nose.

Could I from the building's top
Hear the rattling thunder drop,
While the devil upon the roof,
If the devil be thunder-proof,
Should with poker fiery red
Crack the stones, and melt the lead;
Drive them down on every skull,
While the den of thieves is full,
Quite destroy that harpies' nest,
30 How might then our isle be blessed?
For divines allow, that God
Sometimes makes the devil his rod:
And the gospel will inform us,
He can punish sins enormous.

Yet should Swift endow the schools
For his lunatics and fools,
With a rood or two of land,
I allow the pile may stand.
You perhaps will ask me, why so?
40 But it is with this proviso,
Since the House is like to last,
Let a royal grant be passed,
That the club have right to dwell
Each within his proper cell;
With a passage left to creep in,
And a hole above for peeping.

Let them, when they once get in
Sell the nation for a pin;
While they sit a-picking straws
50 Let them rave of making laws;
While they never hold their tongue,
Let them dabble in their dung;
Let them form a grand committee,
How to plague and starve the city;
Let them stare and storm and frown,
When they see a clergy-gown.

Let them, 'ere they crack a louse,
Call for the orders of the House;
Let them with their gosling quills,
60 Scribble senseless heads of bills;
We may, while they strain their throats,
Wipe our arses with their votes.

Let Sir Tom, that rampant ass,
Stuff his guts with flax and grass;
But before the priest he fleeces
Tear the bible all to pieces.
At the parsons, Tom, halloo boy,
Worthy offspring of a shoe-boy,
Footman, traitor, vile seducer,
70 Perjured rebel, bribed accuser;
Lay the paltry privilege aside,
Sprung from papists and a regicide;
Fall a-working like a mole,
Raise the dirt about your hole.

Come, assist me, muse obedient,
Let us try some new expedient;
Shift the scene for half an hour,
Time and place are in thy power.
Thither, gentle muse, conduct me,
80 I shall ask, and thou instruct me.

See, the muse unbars the gate;
Hark, the monkeys, how they prate!

All ye gods, who rule the soul;
Styx, through hell whose waters roll!
Let me be allowed to tell
What I heard in yonder hell.

Near the door an entrance gapes,
Crowded round with antic shapes;
Poverty, and Grief, and Care,
90 Causeless Joy, and true Despair;
Discord periwigged with snakes,
See the dreadful strides she takes.

By this odious crew beset,
I began to rage and fret,

And resolved to break their pates,
Ere we entered at the gates;
Had not Clio in the nick,
Whispered me, 'Let down your stick';
'What,' said I, 'is this the madhouse?'
100 'These,' she answered, 'are but shadows,
Phantoms, bodiless and vain,
Empty visions of the brain.'

In the porch Briareus stands,
Shows a bribe in all his hands:
Briareus the secretary,
But we mortals call him Carey.
When the rogues their country fleece,
They may hope for pence apiece.

Clio, who had been so wise
110 To put on a fool's disguise,
To bespeak some approbation,
And be thought a near relation;
When she saw three hundred brutes,
All involved in wild disputes;
Roaring till their lungs were spent,
'Privilege of parliament',
Now a new misfortune feels,
Dreading to be laid by the heels.
Never durst a muse before
120 Enter that infernal door;
Clio stifled with the smell,
Into spleen and vapours fell;
By the Stygian steams that flew,
From the dire infectious crew.
Not the stench of Lake Avernus,
Could have more offended her nose;
Had she flown but o'er the top,
She would feel her pinions drop,
And by exhalations dire,
130 Though a goddess, must expire.
In a fright she crept away,
Bravely I resolved to stay.

When I saw the keeper frown,
Tipping him with half a crown;

'Now,' said I, 'we are alone,
Name your heroes, one by one.

　'Who is that hell-featured bawler,
Is it Satan? No, 'tis Waller.
In what figure can a bard dress
140　Jack, the grandson of Sir Hardress?
Honest keeper, drive him further,
In his looks are hell and murther;
See the scowling visage drop,
Just as when he's murdered Throp.

　'Keeper, show me where to fix
On the puppy pair of Dicks;
By their lantern jaws and leathern,
You might swear they both are brethren:
Dick Fitz-Baker, Dick the player,
150　Old acquaintance, are you there?
Dear companions hug and kiss,
Toast old Glorious in your piss.
Tie them, keeper, in a tether,
Let them stare and stink together;
Both are apt to be unruly,
Lash them daily, lash them duly,
Though 'tis hopeless to reclaim them,
Scorpion rods perhaps may tame them.

　'Keeper, yon old dotard smoke,
160　Sweetly snoring in his cloak.
Who is he? 'Tis humdrum Wynne,
Half encompassed by his kin:
There observe the tribe of Bingham,
For he never fails to bring 'em;
While he sleeps the whole debate,
They submissive round him wait;
Yet would gladly see the hunks
In his grave, and search his trunks.
See they gently twitch his coat,
170　Just to yawn, and give his vote;
Always firm in his vocation,
For the court against the nation.

'Those are Allens, Jack and Bob,
First in every wicked job,
Son and brother to a queer,
Brainsick brute, they call a peer.
We must give them better quarter,
For their ancestor trod mortar;
And at Howth to boast his fame,
180   On a chimney cut his name.

'There sit Clements, Dilkes, and Harrison,
How they swagger from their garrison.
Such a triplet could you tell
Where to find on this side hell?
Harrison, and Dilkes, and Clements,
Souse them in their own excrements.
Every mischief in their hearts,
If they fail 'tis want of parts.

'Bless us, Morgan! Art thou there, man?
190   Bless mine eyes! Art thou the chairman?
Chairman to yon damned committee!
Yet I look on thee with pity.
Dreadful sight! What, learned Morgan,
Metamorphosed to a gorgon!
For thy horrid looks, I own,
Half convert me to a stone.
Hast thou been so long at school,
Now to turn a factious tool!
Alma Mater was thy mother,
200   Every young divine thy brother.
Thou a disobedient varlet,
Treat thy mother like a harlot!
Thou, ungrateful to thy teachers,
Who are all grown reverend preachers!
Morgan! Would it not surprise one?
Turn thy nourishment to poison!
When you walk among your books,
They reproach you with their looks;
Bind them fast, or from the shelves
210   They'll come down to right themselves:
Homer, Plutarch, Virgil, Flaccus,

All in arms prepare to back us:
Soon repent, or put to slaughter
Every Greek and Roman author.
While you in your faction's phrase
Send the clergy all to graze;
And to make your project pass,
Leave them not a blade of grass.

    'How I want thee, humorous Hogart!
220 Thou I hear, a pleasant rogue art;
Were but you and I acquainted,
Every monster should be painted;
You should try your graving tools
On this odious group of fools;
Draw the beasts as I describe 'em,
Form their features, while I gibe them;
Draw them like, for I assure you,
You will need no caricatura;
Draw them so that we may trace
230 All the soul in every face.
Keeper, I must now retire,
You have done what I desire:
But I feel my spirits spent,
With the noise, the sight, the scent.'

    'Pray be patient, you shall find
Half the best are still behind:
You have hardly seen a score,
I can show two hundred more.'
'Keeper, I have seen enough,'
240 Taking then a pinch of snuff;
I concluded, looking round 'em,
May their god, the devil confound 'em.

Bounce to Fop

AN HEROIC EPISTLE FROM A DOG AT TWICKENHAM
TO A DOG AT COURT

To thee, sweet Fop, these lines I send,
Who, though no spaniel, am a friend.

Though, once my tail in wanton play,
Now frisking this, and then that way,
Chanced, with a touch of just the tip,
To hurt your lady-lap-dogship;
Yet thence to think I'd bite your head off!
Sure Bounce is one you never read of.

Fop! you can dance, and make a leg,
10 Can fetch and carry, cringe and beg,
And (what's the top of all your tricks)
Can stoop to pick up *strings* and *sticks*.
We country dogs love nobler sport,
And scorn the pranks of dogs at court.
Fie, naughty Fop! where e'er you come
To fart and piss about the room,
To lay your head in every lap,
And, when they think not of you, snap!
The worst that envy, or that spite
20 E'er said of me, is, I can bite:
That sturdy vagrants, rogues in rags,
Who poke at me, can make no brags;
And that to touse such things as *flutter*,
To honest Bounce is bread and butter.

While you, and every courtly fop,
Fawn on the devil for a chop,
I've the humanity to hate
A butcher, though he brings me meat;
And let me tell you, have a nose,
30 (Whatever stinking fops suppose)
That under cloth of gold or tissue,
Can smell a plaster, or an issue.

Your pilfering lord, with simple pride,
May wear a picklock at his side;
My master wants no key of state,
For Bounce can keep his house and gate.

When all such dogs have had their days,
As knavish Pams and fawning Trays;
When pampered Cupids, beastly Veni's,
40 And motley, squinting Harvequini's,

Shall lick no more their lady's breech,
But die of looseness, claps, or itch;
Fair Thames from either echoing shore
Shall hear, and dread my manly roar.

See Bounce, like Berecynthia, crowned
With thundering offspring all around,
Beneath, beside me, and atop,
A hundred sons! and not one Fop.

Before my children set your beef,
50   Not one true Bounce will be a thief;
Not one without permission feed,
(Though some of J—'s hungry breed)
But whatsoe'er the father's race,
From me they suck a little grace.
While your fine whelps learn all to steal,
Bred up by hand on chick and veal.

My eldest-born resides not far,
Where shines great Strafford's glittering star:
My second (child of fortune!) waits
60   At Burlington's Palladian gates:
A third majestically stalks
(Happiest of dogs!) in Cobham's walks:
One ushers friends to Bathurst's door;
One fawns, at Oxford's, on the poor.

Nobles, whom arms or arts adorn,
Wait for my infants yet unborn.
None but a peer of wit and grace,
Can hope a puppy of my race.

And O! would fate the bliss decree
70   To mine (a bliss too great for me)
That two, my tallest sons, might grace
Attending each with stately pace,
Iülus' side, as erst Evander's,
To keep off flatterers, spies, and panders,
To let no noble slave come near,
And scare Lord Fannies from his ear:
Then might a royal youth, and true,
Enjoy at least a friend – or two:

A treasure, which, of royal kind,
80 Few but himself deserve to find.

Then Bounce ('tis all that Bounce can crave)
Shall wag her tail within the grave.

And though no doctors, Whig or Tory ones,
Except the sect of Pythagoreans,
Have immortality assigned
To any beast but Dryden's hind:
Yet Master Pope, whom Truth and Sense
Shall call their friend some ages hence,
Though now on loftier themes he sings
90 Than to bestow a word on kings,
Has sworn by sticks (the poet's oath,
And dread of dogs and poets both)
Man and his works he'll soon renounce,
And roar in numbers worthy Bounce.

Addenda Quaedam

My wife a-rattling,
My children tattling.
My money spent is,
And due my rent is.
My school decreasing,
My income ceasing.
All people tease me,
But no man pays me.
My worship is bit,
10 By that rogue Nisbit.
To take the right way,
Consult friend Whiteway.
Would you get still more?
Go flatter Kilmore.
Your geese are old,
Your wife a scold.
You live among ill
Folks in a dunghill.
You never have an
20 Old friend at Cavan.

Lesbia

FROM CATULLUS

Lesbia forever on me rails;
　　To talk on me she never fails:
Yet, hang me, but for all her art;
　　I find that I have gained her heart:
My proof is this: I plainly see
　　The case is just the same with me:
I curse her every hour sincerely;
　　Yet, hang me, but I love her dearly.

A Satire on an Inconstant Lover

You are as faithless as a Carthaginian,
To love at once Kate, Nell, Doll, Martha, Jenny, Ann.

Aye and No

A TALE FROM DUBLIN

At Dublin's high feast sat Primate and Dean,
Both dressed like divines, with band and face clean.
Quoth Hugh of Armagh, 'The mob is grown bold.'
'Aye, aye,' quoth the Dean, 'the cause is old gold.'
'No, no,' quoth the Primate, 'if causes we sift,
This mischief arises from witty Dean Swift.'
The smart one replied, 'There's no wit in the case;
And nothing of that ever troubled your Grace.
Though with your state-sieve your own notions you split,
A Boulter by name is no bolter of wit.
It's matter of weight, and a mere money-job;
But the lower the coin, the higher the mob.
Go tell your friend Bob and the other great folk,
That sinking the coin is a dangerous joke.
The Irish dear joys have enough common sense,
To treat gold reduced like Wood's copper pence.
It's a pity a prelate should die without law;
But if I say the word – take care of Armagh!'

'Behold! A Proof of Irish Sense!'

Behold! a proof of Irish sense!
   Here Irish wit is seen!
When nothing's left, that's worth defence,
   We build a magazine.

To Mrs Houghton of Bormount

UPON PRAISING HER HUSBAND TO DR SWIFT

You always are making a god of your spouse,
But this neither reason nor conscience allows;
Perhaps you will say, 'tis in gratitude due,
And you adore him, because he adores you.
Your argument's weak, and so you will find,
For you, by this rule, must adore all mankind.

An Epigram on Scolding

Great folks are of a finer mould;
Lord! how politely they can scold;
While a coarse English tongue will itch,
For whore and rogue; and dog and bitch.

Verses Made for the Women Who Cry Apples, etc.

APPLES

Come buy my fine wares,
Plums, apples, and pears,
A hundred a penny,
In conscience too many,
Come, will you have any;
My children are seven,
I wish them in heaven,
My husband's a sot,
With his pipe and his pot,

10 Not a farthing will gain 'em,
    And I must maintain 'em.

ASPARAGUS

Ripe 'sparagrass, ⎤
Fit for lad or lass, ⎬
To make their water pass: ⎦
   O, 'tis a pretty picking
   With a tender chicken.

ONIONS

Come, follow me by the smell, ⎤
Here's delicate onions to sell, ⎬
I promise to use you well. ⎦
20 They make the blood warmer,
    You'll feed like a farmer:
    For this is every cook's opinion,
    No savoury dish without an onion;
    But lest your kissing should be spoiled,
    Your onions must be thoroughly boiled;
       Or else you may spare
       Your mistress a share,
    The secret will never be known;
       She cannot discover
30   The breath of her lover
    But think it as sweet as her own.

OYSTERS

    Charming oysters I cry,
    My masters come buy,
    So plump and so fresh,
    So sweet is their flesh,
    No Colchester oyster,
    Is sweeter and moister,
    Your stomach they settle,
    And rouse up your mettle,
40   They'll make you a dad
    Of a lass or a lad;
    And Madam your wife

They'll please to the life;
Be she barren, be she old,
Be she slut, or be she scold,
Eat my oysters, and lie near her,
She'll be fruitful, never fear her.

HERRINGS

Be not sparing,
Leave off swearing,
50   Buy my herring
Fresh from Malahide,
Better ne'er was tried.
Come eat 'em with pure fresh butter and mustard,
Their bellies are soft, and as white as a custard.
Come, sixpence a dozen to get me some bread,
Or, like my own herrings, I soon shall be dead.

ORANGES

Come, buy my fine oranges, sauce for your veal,
And charming when squeezed in a pot of brown ale.
Well roasted, with sugar and wine in a cup,
60   They'll make a sweet bishop when gentlefolks sup.

A Cantata

In harmony would you excel,
Suit your words to music well, music well,
Suit your words to your music well,
Suit your words to music well,
For Pegasus runs, runs every race
By gal-lal-lal-lal-laloping high, or level pace,
Or ambling or sweet Canterbury,
Or with a down, a high down derry.
No, no victory, victory he ever got,
10   By jo-o-o-o-ogling, jo-o-o-o-ogling trot.
No muse harmonious entertains,
Rough roistering, rustic, roar-oar-oaring strains,
Nor shall you twine the cra-a-a-ackling, crackling bays,
By sneaking, snivelling rou-ou-oun-oundelays.

Now slowly move your fiddle stick,
Now, tantantantantantantivi,
Now tantantantantantivi quick, quick.
Now trembling, shivering, quivering, quaking,
Set hoping, hoping, hoping hearts of lovers aching,
20 Fly, fly-y-y-y
Above the sky,
Rambling, gambolling, ra-a-a-a-a-ambling, gambolling,
Trolloping, lolloping, galloping,
Trolloping, lolloping, galloping, trollop,
Lolloping, trolloping, galloping,
Lolloping, trolloping, galloping, lollop,
Now cree-ee-eep, sweep, sweep, sweep the deep,
See, see, Celia, Celia dies,
Dies, dies, dies, dies, dies, dies, dies,
30 While true lovers' eyes
Weeping sleep,
Sleeping weep,
Weeping sleep.
Bo peep, bo peep, bo peep,
Bo peep, peep, bo bo peep.

The Elephant

OR, THE PARLIAMENT MAN

WRITTEN MANY YEARS SINCE,
AND TAKEN OUT OF COKE'S INSTITUTES

E'er bribes convince you whom to choose,
The precepts of Lord Coke peruse.
Observe an elephant, says he,
And let like him your member be:
First take a man that's free from gall:
For elephants have none at all.
In flocks, or parties, must he keep:
For elephants live just like sheep.
Stubborn in honour must he be:
10 For elephants ne'er bend the knee.
Last, let his memory be sound,
In which your elephant's profound;

That old examples from the wise
May prompt him in his noes and ayes.

Thus, the Lord Coke hath gravely writ,
In all the form of lawyer's wit:
And then with Latin, and all that,
Shows the comparison is pat.
Yet in some points my Lord is wrong,
20 One's teeth are sold, and t'other's tongue:
Now, men of parliament, God knows,
Are more like elephants of shows;
Whose docile memory and sense
Are turned to trick, to gather pence;
To get their master half a crown,
They spread the flag, or lay it down:
Those who bore bulwarks on their backs,
And guarded nations from attacks,
Now practise every pliant gesture,
30 Opening their trunk for every tester.
Siam, for elephants so famed,
Is not with England to be named:
Their elephants by men are sold;
Ours sell themselves, and take the gold.

Aye and No: A Fable

In fable all things hold discourse;
Then words, no doubt, must talk of course.

Once on a time, near Channel Row,
Two hostile adverbs, Aye and No,
Were hastening to the field of fight,
And front to front stood opposite.
Before each general joined the van,
Aye, the more courteous knight, began.

'Stop, peevish particle, beware!
10 I'm told you are not such a bear,
But sometimes yield, when offered fair.
Suffer yon folks awhile to tattle;
'Tis we who must decide the battle.

Whene'er we war on yonder stage,
With various fate, and equal rage,
The nation trembles at each blow
That No gives Aye, and Aye gives No;
Yet in expensive long contention,
We gain nor office, grant, nor pension.
20 Why then should kinsfolks quarrel thus?
(For, two of you make one of us.)
To some wise statesman let us go,
Where each his proper use may know.
He may admit two such commanders,
And make those wait, who served in Flanders.
Let's quarter on a great man's tongue,
A Treasury lord, not Maister Yonge.
Obsequious at his high command,
Aye shall march forth to tax the land:
30 Impeachments, No can best resist,
And Aye support the Civil List:
Aye quick as Caesar, wins the day;
And No, like Fabius, by delay.
Sometimes, in mutual sly disguise,
Let Ayes seem Noes, and Noes seem Ayes;
Ayes be in courts denials meant,
And Noes in bishops give consent.'

Thus Aye proposed – and for reply,
No, for the first time, answered Aye.
40 They parted with a thousand kisses,
And fight e'er since, for pay, like Swisses.

Latin Poems

Ad Amicum Eruditum Thomam Sheridan

Deliciae Sheridan musarum, dulcis amice,
Sic tibi propitius Permessi ad flumen Apollo
Occurrat, seu te mimum convivia rident;
Aequivocosve sales spargis, seu ludere versu
Malles; dic, Sheridan, quisnam fuit ille deorum,
Quae melior natura orto tibi tradidit artem
Rimandi genium puerorum, atque ima cerebri
Scrutandi? Tibi nascenti ad cunabula Pallas
Astitit; et dixit, mentis praesaga futurae,
10   Heu puer infelix! nostro sub sydere natus;
Nam tu pectus eris sine corpore, corporis umbra;
Sed levitate umbram superabis, voce cicadam:
Musca femur, palmas tibi mus dedit, ardea crura.
Corpore sed tenui tibi quod natura negavit;
Hoc animi dotes supplebunt; teque docente,
Nec longum tempus, surget tibi docta juventus,
Artibus egregiis animas instructa novellas.
Grex hinc Poeonius venit, ecce, *salutifer* orbi.
Ast, illi causas orant; his infula visa est
20   Divinam capiti nodo constringere mitram.

    Natalis te horae non fallunt signa; sed usque
Conscius, expedias puero seu laetus Apollo
Nascenti arrisit; sive illum frigidus horror
Saturni premit, aut septem inflavere triones.

    Quin tu altè penitusque latentia semina cernis,
Quaeque diu obtundendo olim sub luminis auras
Erumpent, promis; quo ritu saepè puella
Sub cinere hesterno sopitos suscitat ignes.

    Te Dominum agnoscit quocunque sub aere natus;
30   Quos indulgentis nimium custodia matris
Pessundat: nam saepe vides in stipite matrem.

    Aureus at ramus venerandae dona Sibyllae,
Aeneae sedes tantùm patefecit Avernus:
Saepè puer, tua quem tetigit semel aurea virga,
Coelumque terrasque videt, noctemque profundam.

Carberiae Rupes

IN COMITATU CORGAGENSI APUD HYBERNICOS

Ecce ingens fragmen scopuli quod vertice summo
Desuper impendet, nullo fundamine nixum
Decidit in fluctus: maria undique & undique saxa
Horisono Stridore tonant, & ad aethera murmur
Erigitur; trepidatque suis *Neptunus* in undis.
Nam, longâ venti rabie, atque aspergine crebrâ
Aequorei laticis, specus imâ rupe cavatur:
Jam fultura ruit, jam summa cacumina nutant;
Jam cadit in praeceps moles, & verberat undas.
10 Attonitus credas, hinc dejecisse Tonantem
Montibus impositos montes, & Pelion altum
In capita anguipedum coelo jaculâsse gigantum.

Saepe etiam spelunca immani aperitur hiatu
Exesa è scopulis, & utrinque foramina pandit,
Hinc atque hinc a ponto ad pontum pervia Phoebo:
Cautibus enormè junctis laquearia tecti
Formantur; moles olim ruitura supernè.
Fornice sublimi nidos posuere palumbes,
Inque imo stagni posuere cubilia phocae.

20 Sed, cum saevit hyems, & venti carcere rupto
Immensos volvunt fluctus ad culmina montis;
Non obsessae arces, non fulmina vindice dextrâ
Missa Jovis, quoties inimicas saevit in urbes,
Exaequant sonitum undarum, veniente procellâ:
Littora littoribus reboant; vicinia latè,
Gens assueta mari, & pedibus percurrere rupes,
Terretur tamen, & longè fugit, arva relinquens.

Gramina dum carpunt pendentes rupe capellae
Vi salientis aquae de summo praecipitantur,
30 Et dulces animas imo sub gurgite linquunt.

Piscator terrâ non audet vellere funem;
Sed latet in portu tremebundus, & aera sudum
Haud sperans, Nereum precibus votisque fatigat.

Fabula Canis et Umbrae

Ore cibum portans catulus dum spectat in undis,
Apparet liquido praedae melioris imago:
Dum speciosa diu damna admiratur, et alte
Ad latices inhiat, cadit imo vortice praeceps
Ore cibus, nec non simulachrum corripit unà.
Occupat ille avidus deceptis faucibus umbram;
Illudit species, ac dentibus aëra mordet.

Prefaces

'The Publisher to the Reader'

from Miscellanies in Prose and Verse (1711)

To publish the writings of persons without their consent, is a practice
generally speaking, so unfair, and has been so many times proved an
unsufferable injury to the credit and reputation of the authors, as well
as a shameless imposition on the public, either by a scandalous insertion
of spurious pieces, or an imperfect and faulty edition of such as are
genuine, that though I have been master of such of the following pieces,
as have never been printed, for several months, I could never, though
much importuned, prevail on myself to publish them, fearing even a
possibility of doing an injury in either of those two respects to the per-
son who is generally known to be the author of some; and, with greater
reason than I am at present at liberty to give, supposed to be the author
of all the other pieces which make up this collection. But as my own
unwillingness to do anything which might prove an injury to the sup-
posed author's reputation, to whom no man pays a juster esteem or
bears a greater respect than myself, has hitherto kept me from giving
the world so agreeable an entertainment as it will receive from the fol-
lowing papers, so the sense I had that he would really now suffer a
much greater in both instances from other hands, was the occasion of
my determining to do it at present: since some of the following pieces
have lately appeared in print, from very imperfect and uncorrect copies.
Nor was the abuse like to stop here, for these with all the defects and
imperfections they came out under, met with so much applause, and so
universal a good reception from all men of wit and taste, as to prompt
the booksellers, who had heard that other of these tracts were in manu-
script in some gentlemen's hands, to seek by any means to procure
them, which should they compass, they would without question publish
in a manner as little to the author's credit and reputation, as they have
already done those few which unfortunately have fallen into their pos-
session. This being a known fact I hope will be sufficient to make this
publication, though without the author's consent or knowledge, very
consistent with that respect I sincerely bear him; who, if it should not
appear to be perfectly without fault, can with little justice complain of
the wrong he receives by it, since it has prevented his suffering a much
greater, no more than a man who is pushed down out of the way of a
bullet, can with reason take as an affront, either the blow he falls by, or
the dirt he rises with.

But indeed I have very little uneasiness upon me for fear of any
injury the author's credit and reputation may receive from any imperfec-

tion or uncorrectness in these following tracts, since the persons from whom I had them, when his affairs called him out of this kingdom, are of so much worth themselves, and have so great a regard for the author, that I am confident they would neither do, nor suffer anything that might turn to his disadvantage. I must confess I am upon another account under some concern, which is, lest some of the following papers are such as the author perhaps would rather should not have been published at all; in which case, I should look upon myself highly obliged to ask his pardon: but even upon this supposition, as there is no person named, the supposed author is at liberty to disown as much as he thinks fit of what is here published, and so can be chargeable with no more of it than he pleases to take upon himself.

From this apology I have been making, the reader may in part be satisfied how these papers came into my hands, and to give him a more particular information herein will prove little to his use, though perhaps it might somewhat gratify his curiosity, which I shall think not material any farther to do, than by assuring him, that I am not only myself sufficiently convinced that all the tracts in the following collection, excepting two, before both of which I have in the book expressed my doubtfulness, were wrote by the same hand, but several judicious persons who are well acquainted with the supposed author's writings, and not altogether strangers to his conversation, have agreed with me herein, not only for the reasons I have before hinted at, but upon this account also, that there are in every one of these pieces some particular beauties that discover this author's vein, who excels too much not to be distinguished, since in all his writings such a surprising mixture of wit and learning, true humour and good sense does everywhere appear, as sets him almost as far out of the reach of imitation, as it does beyond the power of censure.

The reception that these pieces will meet with from the public, and the satisfaction they will give to all men of wit and taste, will soon decide it, whither [sic] there be any reason for the reader to suspect an imposition, or the author to apprehend an injury; the former I am fully satisfied will never be, and the latter I am sure I never intended: in confidence of which, should the author when he sees these tracts appear, take some offence, and know where to place his resentment, I will be so free as to own, I could without much uneasiness sit down under some degree of it, since it would be no hard task to hear some displeasure from a single person, for that which one is sure to receive the thanks of everybody else.

Swift's long-projected volume of miscellanies is discussed in *Ehrenpreis*, II, 422–4: see also C.P. Daw's introduction to the reprinted *Miscellanies* (1972), pp. [i]–[iv]. Swift undoubtedly knew very well what Benjamin Tooke, the principal bookseller involved, was about: even though he attempted in his *Journal* to disavow any participation (*JTS* I, 208). The putative reason for issuing the 'genuine' volume was the prior appearance of Curll's collection in the previous year (see Introduction to the present edition, p. 16); but such piracies were often engineered in order to clear the ground for an 'authentic' text.

'Publisher' implies editor rather than the commercial distributor. At one time it had been planned to have the preface supplied by Steele, but political circumstances made this impossible by 1711. It is likely that the preface derives in outline from Swift himself; the simulation of an awkward and unpractised style at the start of the piece gradually drops away until the prose attains a balanced eloquence in later passages. Swift may well have written every word.

Thirteen of Swift's poems, composed between 1698 and 1710, are included in the *Miscellanies*, along with twelve works in prose. Of these poems, five were appearing for the first time; two had been first published by Curll; whilst the remaining six had been separately issued elsewhere.

'Advertisement'

from the Works (1735), Vol. 2

The first collection of this author's writings were published near thirty years ago, under the title of Miscellanies in Verse and Prose [*sic*]. Several years after, there appeared three volumes of Miscellanies, with a preface to the first, signed J. Swift and A. Pope. In these the verses, with great additions, were printed in a volume by themselves. But in each volume were mixed many poems and treatises, writ by the supposed author's friends, which we have laid aside; our intention being only to publish the works of one writer. The following poetical volume is enlarged by above a third part, which was never collected before, although some of them were occasionally printed in London in single sheets. The rest were procured from the supposed author's friends, who at their special request were permitted to take copies.

The following poems chiefly consist of humour or satire, and very often of both together. What merit they may have, we confess ourselves to be no judges of in the least; but out of due regard to a writer, from whose works we hope to receive some benefit, we cannot conceal what we have heard from several persons of great judgement; the author never was known either in verse or prose to borrow any thought, simile, epithet, or particular manner of style; but whatever he writ, whether good, bad, or indifferent, is an original in itself.

Although we are very sensible, that in some of the following poems, the ladies may resent certain satirical touches against the mistaken conduct in some of the fair sex: and that, some warm persons on the prevailing side, may censure this author, whoever he be, for not thinking in public matters exactly like themselves: yet we have been assured by several judicious and learned gentlemen, that what the author hath here writ, on either side of those two subjects, had no other aim than to reform the errors of both sexes. If the public be right in its conjectures of the author, nothing is better known in London, than that while he had credit at the court of Queen Anne, he employed so much of it in favour of Whigs in both kingdoms, that the ministry used to rally him as the advocate of that party, for several of whom he got employments and preserved others from losing what they had: of which some instances remain even in this kingdom. Besides, he then writ and declared against the Pretender, with equal zeal, though not with equal fury, as any of our modern Whigs; of which party he always professed himself to be as to politics, as the reader will find in many parts of his works.

Our intentions were to print the poems according to the time they were writ in; but we could not do it so exactly as we desired, because we could never get the least satisfaction in that or many other circumstances from the supposed author.

For Swift's supervision of the Dublin edition published by Faulkner in 1734/5, see Introduction, p. 17. The volume of poetry, in its cancelled state, contains some ninety-six items written between 1698 and 1733. About forty of these were previously unpublished. (Both counts omit eight riddles.) It is almost certain that Swift was substantially responsible for this 'Advertisement'.

APPENDIX 3

Manuscript Versions

Vanbrug's House

AN. 1703

BUILT FROM THE BURNT RUINS OF WHITEHALL

In times of old, when Time was young,
And Poets their own Verses sung,
A Song could draw a Stone or Beam,
That now would overload a Team,
Lead them a Dance of many a Mile,
Then rear 'em to a goodly Pile,
Each Number had it's diff'rent Power;
Heroick Strains could build a Tower;
Sonnets and Elegyes to Chloris
10 Would raise a House about two Storyes;
A Lyrick Ode would Slate; a Catch
Would Tile; an Epigram would Thatch.
   Now Poets find this Art is lost,
Both to their own and Landlord's Cost;
Not one of all the tunefull Throng
Can hire a Lodging for a Song;
For Jove consider'd well the Case,
That Poets were a numerous Race,
And if they all had Power to build,
20 The Earth would very soon be filld:
Materials would be quickly spent,
And Houses would not give a Rent.
The God of Wealth was therefore made
Sole Patron of the building Trade,
Leaving to Wits the spatious Air,
With License to build Castles there;
And 'tis conceiv'd, their old Pretence
To lodge in Garrats comes from thence.
   There is a Worm by Phoebus bred,
30 By Leaves of Mulberry is fed;
Which unprovided where to dwell,
Consumes itself to weave a Cell.
Then curious Hands this Texture take,
And for themselves fine Garments make.
Mean time a Pair of awkward Things
Grew to his Back instead of Wings;

He flutters when he Thinks he flyes,
Then sheds about his Spaun, and dyes.
Just such an Insect of the Age
40   Is he that scribbles for the Stage;
His Birth he does from Phoebus raise,
And feeds upon imagin'd Bays:
Throws all his Witt and Hours away
In twisting up an ill-spun Play:
This gives him Lodging, and provides
A Stock of tawdry Stuff besides,
With the unravelld Shreds of which
The Under-wits adorn their Speech.
And now he spreads his little Fans,
50   (For all the Muses Geese are Swans)
And borne on fancy's Pinions, thinks,
He soars sublimest when he Sinks:
But scatt'ring round his Fly-blows, dyes;
Whence Broods of insect Poets rise.
    Premising thus in Modern way
The greater half I had to say,
Sing Muse the House of Poet Van
In higher Strain than we began.
    Van, (for 'tis fit the Reader know it)
60   Is both a Herald and a Poet;
No wonder then, if nicely skill'd
In each Capacity to Build:
As Herald, he can in a Day
Repair a House gone to decay;
Or by Atchievments, Arms, Device
Erect a new one in a Trice;
And Poets if they had their Due,
By antient Right are Builders too.
This made him to Apollo pray
70   For Leave to build the Poet's Way.
His Pray'r was granted, for the God
Consented with the usuall Nod.
After hard Throws of many a Day
Van was deliver'd of a Play,
Which in due time brought forth a House;
Just as the Mountain did the Mouse;
One Story high, one postern Door,

And one small Chamber on a Floor.
Born like a Phoenix from the Flame,
80 But neither Bulk nor Shape the same:
As Animals of largest Size
Corrupt to Maggots Worms and Flyes.
A Type of Modern Witt and Style,
The Rubbish of an antient Pile.
So Chymists boast they have a Power
From the dead Ashes of a Flow'r
Some faint Resemblance to produce,
But not the Virtue Tast nor Juyce.
So, Modern Rhymers strive to blast
90 The Poetry of Ages past,
Which having wisely overthrown,
They from it's Ruins build their own.

The Story of Baucis & Philemon

OV. MET. I. 8

In antient Time, as Story tells
The Saints would often leave their Cells
And strole about, but hide their Quality,
To try the People's Hospitality.
    It happen'd on a Winter's night,
As Authors of the Legend write
Two Brother-Hermits, Saints by Trade
Taking their Tour in Masquerade
Came to a Village hard by Rixham
10 Ragged, and not a Groat betwixt 'em.
It rain'd as hard as it could pour,
Yet they were forc't to walk an Hour
From House to House, wett to the Skin
Before one Soul would let 'em in.
They call'd at ev'ry Dore; Good People,
My Comrade's Blind, and I'm a Creeple
Here we ly starving in the Street
'Twould grieve a Body's Heart to see't:
No Christian would turn out a Beast
20 In such a dreadfull Night at least;

Give us but Straw, and let us Ly
In yonder Barn to keep us dry.
Thus in the Strolers usuall Cant
They beg'd Relief which none would grant;
No Creature valu'd what they se'd:
One Family was gone to bed;
The Master Bawl'd out half asleep
You Fellows, what a Noise you keep!
So many Beggers pass this way,
30 We can't be quiet Night nor day;
We can not serve You every One,
Pray take your Answer and be gone.
One swore he'd send 'em to the Stocks,
A third could not forbear his Mocks,
But bawl'd as loud as he could roar,
You're on the wrong side of the Door.
One surly Clown lookt out, and said,
I'll fling the P— pot on your head;
You sha'n't come here nor get a Sous
40 You look like Rogues would rob a House
Can't you go work, or serve the King?
You blind and lame! tis no such Thing
That's but a counterfeit sore Leg:
For shame! two sturdy Rascalls beg;
If I come down, I'll spoil your Trick
And cure You both with a good Stick.
    Our wand'ring Saints in wofull State,
Treated at this ungodly Rate
Having thro all the Village pass't,
50 To a small Cottage came at last
Where dwelt a poor old honest Yeman
Call'd thereabouts Goodman Philemon;
Who kindlly did the Saints invite
In his poor House to pass the Night;
And then the hospitable Sire
Bade Goody Baucis mend the Fire
Whilst he from out the Chimny took
A Flitch of Bacon off the Hook,
And freely from the fattest Side
60 Cutt off large Slices to be fry'd;

Which tosst up in a Pan with Batter,
And serv'd up in an earthen Platter;
Quoth Baucis, this is wholsom Fare,
Eat, Honest Friends, and never spare,
And if we find our Vittels fail
We can but make it out in Ale.

    To a small Kilderkin of Beer
Brew'd for the good time of the Year
Philemon by his Wife's consent
70 Step't with a Jug, and made a Vent;
And having fill'd it to the Brink,
Invited both the Saints to Drink.
When they had took a second Draught,
Behold, a Miracle was wrought
For, Baucis with Amazement found
Although the Jug had twice gone round
It still was full up to the Top
As if they ne're had drunk a drop.
You may be sure, so strange a Sight
80 Put the old People in a Fright;
Philemon whisper'd to his Wife,
These Men are Saints I'll lay my Life
The Strangers overheard, and said,
You're in the right, but be'n't afraid
No hurt shall come to You or Yours;
But for that Pack of churlish Boors
Not fitt to live on Christian Ground,
They and their Village shall be droun'd,
Whilst You shall see your Cottage rise,
90 And grow a Church before your Eyes.
    Scarce had they spoke when fair and soft
The Roof began to mount aloft
Aloft rose ev'ry Beam and Rafter,
The heavy Wall went clamb'ring after.
The Chimny widen'd and grew high'r,
Became a Steeple with a Spire:
The Kettle to the Top was hoist
And there stood fastned to a Joyst,
But with the upside doun to shew
100 It's Inclination for below;

In vain; for a superior Force
Apply'd at Bottom stops it's Course;
Doomd ever in suspense to dwell,
Tis now no Kettle but a Bell.
The groaning Chair began to crawll
Like a huge Insect up the Wall,
There stuck, and to a Pulpitt grew,
But kept it's Matter and it's Hue,
And mindful of it's antient State,
110   Still Groans while tatling Gossips prate.
    The Mortar onely chang'd it's Name,
In it's old shape a Font became
    The Porrengers that in a Row
Hung high and made a glitt'ring Show
To a less noble Substance chang'd
Were now but leathern Buckets rang'd.
    The Ballads pasted round the Wall,
Of Chivy-chase, and English Mall,
Fair Rosamond, and Robin Hood,
120   The little Children in the Wood,
Enlarg'd in Picture, Size and Letter
And painted, lookt abundance better
And now the Heraldry describe
Of a Churchwarden or a Tribe.
    The wooden Jack which had almost
Lost by Disuse the Art to roast
A sudden Alteration feels,
Encreas't by new intestin Wheels
But what adds to the Wonder more,
130   The Number made the Motion slower
The Fly'r, altho't had leaden Feet,
Would turn so quick you scarce could see't
But now stopt by some hidden Pow'rs
Moves round but twice in twice twelve Hours
While in the Station of a Jack
'Twas never known to turn its back
A Friend in Turns and Windings try'd
Nor ever left the Chimny side.
The Chimny to a Steeple grown,
140   The Jack would not be left alone

But up against the Steeple rear'd,
Became a Clock, and still adher'd,
And still it's Love to Houshold Cares
By a shrill Voice at noon declares,
Warning the Cook-maid not to burn
That Roast-meat which it cannot turn.
    A Bed-sted in the antique mode
Compos'd of Timber many a Load;
Such as our Grandfathers did use,
150   Was Metamorphos't into Pews;
Which yet their former Virtue keep,
By lodging Folks dispos'd to sleep.
    The Cottage with such Feats as these
Grown to a Church by just Degrees,
The holy Men desir'd their Host
To ask for what he fancy'd most.
Philemon having paus'd a while
Reply'd in complementall Style:
Your Goodness more than my Desert
160   Makes you take all things in good Part:
You've rais'd a Church here in a Minute,
And I would fain continue in it;
I'm good for little at my days;
Make me the Parson if you please.
He spoke, and presently he feels
His Grazier's Coat reach down his Heels,
The Sleeves new border'd with a List
Widn'd and gatherd at his Wrist;
But being old continued just
170   As threadbare, and as full of Dust.
A shambling awkward Gate he took,
With a demure dejected Look.
Talkt of his Off'rings, Tyths, and Dues,
Could Smoak, and Drink, and read the News;
Or sell a Goose at the next Toun
Decently hid beneath his Goun.
Contrivd to preach his Sermon next
Chang'd in the Preface and the Text:
Carry'd it to his Equalls high'r,
180   But most obsequious to the Squire. &c

An Answer

TO A LATE SCANDALOUS POEM, WHEREIN THE AUTHOR
MOST AUDACIOUSLY PRESUMES TO COMPARE A CLOUD
TO A WOMAN

BY DENNIS NEPHELEE, CHIEF

CAP OF HOWTH

Presumptuous Poet, could you dare
A Cloud with Woman kind compare?
Strange pride and insolence you shew,
Inferior mortals there below.
And is our thunder in your ears
As grating, or as loud as theirs?
We onely send our Thunder out
In hopes to make you more devout;
And is not femal clattring worse,
10   Which drives you not to pray, but curse?
    We hardly thunder thrice a year:
The bolt discharg'd, the sky grows clear;
But, ev'ry sublunary dowdy
The more she scolds, the more she's cloudy.
    How usefull were a womans thunder
If she like us would burst asunder!
    Yet, though her spouse hath often curst her,
And, whisp'ring wisht, the Devil burst her
For hourly thundring in his face,
20   She ne'er was known to burst a lace.
    Some Criticks may object perhaps,
That Clouds are blam'd for giving Claps:
But, what alas! are Claps aetherial
Compar'd for mischief, to Venereal?
Can Clouds give buboes, ulcers, blotches?
Or, from your noses dig out notches?
We leave the body sweet and sound,
May kill perhaps, but never wound.
    You know, a cloudy sky bespeaks
30   Fair weather when the morning breaks,
But, women in a cloudy plight
Foretell a storm to last till night.

When Syrius o'er the welkin rages,
Our kindly help his fire assuages.
But, Woman is a curst inflamer;
No parish ducking-stool can tame her,
To kindle strife Dame Nature taught her,
Like fire-works, she can burn in water.

For Fickleness how durst you blame us?
40 Who, for our Steddyness are famous
You men would be in wofull pickle
If Clouds were but like Femals fickle;

You'll see a Cloud in gentle weather
Keep the same face an hour together,
While Women, if it could be reckon'd
Change ev'ry feature ev'ry second.

Observe our visage in a morning;
Of foul and fair we give you warning;
But, can you guess from womens air
50 One minute whether foul or fair?

Go read in antient books enroll'd
What honors we possesst of old.
To disappoint Ixion's rape
Jove dresst a Cloud in Juno's shape,
Which when he had enjoy'd, he swore,
No Goddess could have pleas'd him more.
No diff'rence could he find between
His Cloud, and Jove's imperiall Queen.
This Cloud produc'd a race of Centaurs
60 Fam'd for a thousand bold adventures
From us descended ab origine,
By learned authors call'd Nubigenae.
But say, what earthly nymph do you know,
So beautifull to pass for Juno?

Before Aeneas durst aspire
To court her Majesty of Tyre
His mother begg'd of us to dress him
That Dido smitt, might more caress him
A Coat we gave him dy'd in grain
70 A flaxen wig, and clouded cane,
With which he made a tearing show:
And Dido quickly smoak't the Beau.

Among your femals make inquiryes:
What nymph on earth so fair as Iris?
With heav'nly beauty so endow'd;
And yet her father is a Cloud:
We dresst her in a gold Brocade;
To rigg her out for Juno's mayd.
     Tis known, that Socrates the wise
80   Ador'd the Clouds as Deityes.
To us he made his dayly pray'rs,
As Aristophanes declares;
From Jupiter took all dominion,
And dy'd defending his opinion.
By his authority tis plain,
You worship other Gods in vain
And from your own experience know
We govern all things there below.
You follow where we please to guide:
90   O'er all your passions we preside:
Can raise them up, or sink them down,
As we think fit to smile or frown;
And, just as we dispose your brain,
Are witty, dull, rejoyce, complain.
     Compare us then to femal race!
We, to whom all the Gods give place.
They have no claim to Your allegiance
Because they live in lower regions
You find, the Gods in Homer dwell
100   In seas and woods, or low as hell
Ev'n Jove, and Mercury his pimp
No higher climb than mount Olymp
(Who makes you think the Clouds he pierces:
He pierce the Clouds! he kiss our arses)
While we, o'er Tenariffa plac't,
Are lofty'r by a mile at least.
And, when Apollo struts on Pindus,
We see him from our kitchin windows,
Or, to Parnassus looking down,
110   Can piss upon his lawrel crown.
     Fate never form'd the Gods to flye
They must be carryed through the Sky
When Jove would some fair nymph inveigle

He comes full gallop on his eagle:
Though Venus be as light as air,
She must have doves to draw her chair:
Though Mercury makes use of Wings
With which from earth to heav'n he springs;
He never honestly came by 'em,
120 And, e'er he flyes is forc'd to tye em.
Apollo stirs not out of dore
Without his taudry coach and four:
And, jealous Juno, ever snarling,
Is drawn by peacocks in her Berlin.
      But, we can fly whene'er we please
O'er cityes, rivers, hills, and seas,
From East to west the world we roam,
And, in all clymates are at home:
Provide you duly as we go
130 With Sun-shine, rain, and hail, and snow.
      Tis but by our peculiar grace
That Phebus ever shews his face;
For when we please, we open wide
Our curtains blue on either side;
You see how sawcily he shews
His carrot locks, and fiery nose:
And gives himself a haughty air,
As if he made the weather fair.
      Tis sung; wherever Celia treeds,
140 The Vi'lets ope their purple heads,
The Roses blow, the Cowslip springs;
Tis sung. But we know better things.
Tis true; a Woman on her mettle
Will often piss upon a nettle;
Yet, though we grant she makes it wetter,
The nettle never thrives the better.
But we by gentle April showers
Produce in May the sweetest flowrs.
      Your Poets Chloe's beauty heightning
150 Compare her radiant eyes to Lightning:
And yet, I hope 't will be allow'd,
No Lightning comes but from a Cloud.
However, we have too much sense
At Poets flights to take offence:

Nor can Hyperbole's demean us,
What Drabs have been compar'd to Venus?
Observe the case: I state it thus:
You may compare your Trull to us;
But think how damnably you err
160   When you compare us Clouds to her:
From whence you draw such bold conclusions;
But, Poets love profane allusions.
And, if you now so little spare us,
Who knows how soon you [will] compare us
To Chatres, Walpole, or a King,
If once we let you have your Swing.
Such wicked insolence appears
Offensive to all pious ears.
To flatter Woman by a Metaphor!
170   What profit could you hope to get of her
And, for her sake turn base detractor
Against your greatest benefactor.

    But, we shall keep revenge in store
If ever you provoke us more.
For since we knew you walk a-foot,
We'll soundly drench your frize Sur-tout,
Or may we never thunder throw,
Nor souse to death a Birthday Beau.

    We own, Your verses are melodious,
180   But such Comparisons are odious.

Doubtful Attributions

Doubtful Attributions

The canon of Swift's poetry remains essentially that which Harold Williams established in *P*. The major divergences in this edition are as follows:

(1) Poems accepted by Williams, with or without hesitation, and here omitted. These include the *Ode to King William* (*P* I, 11–13); *The Birth of Manly Virtue* (*P* II, 381–8), which I believe to be fundamentally Delany's composition; the *Epigrams against Carthy* (*P* II, 665–72); *A Ballad* ('Patrick astore') (*P* III, 840); the riddles, except those printed in *WF* (*P* III, 926–13, 926–37); *The Upstart* (*P* III, 950–51). The case for Swift's authorship seems to me in each case exceedingly weak.

(2) Poems relegated by Williams to the category of dubious attributions, but here included in the main series of poems. These are represented by *A Description of Mother Ludwell's Cave*; *On the Burning of Whitehall in 1698*; *A Town Eclogue*; and *On Wisdom's Defeat in a Learned Debate*.

(3) Poems not considered by Williams, notably *A Dialogue between Captain Tom and Sir Henry Dutton Colt*. A few trifles omitted by Williams have been reintroduced, and an additional Anglo-Latin fragment printed.

(4) Otherwise I have rejected Williams's 'dubious' category, including items such as *Blueskin's Ballad* which were printed by Herbert Davis in *PHD*. I have also left out *The Description of Dunkirk*, supported by Ball and also by Frank H. Ellis (*Times Literary Supplement*, 10 May 1974, p. 506).

Among the remaining poems there are certain items about which I feel considerable doubt, most significantly *Apollo's Edict* and *A Panegyric on the Reverend Dean Swift*. The grounds for including such items, however tentatively, are set out in the headnotes to the poems in question.

Normally, answers and 'stimulus' poems by Sheridan, Delany, and others are omitted. Necessary connections are made in the notes to Swift's related poem.

Notes

The headnote to each poem contains the following information:

(1) Date of first publication. Other early printings are also listed, if appropriate, e.g. where there is doubt concerning the priority of editions, or where a piratical issue was followed by an authorized edition.

(2) Date of composition, where this can be established. The poems are printed in the order of their known or conjectured composition.

(3) Teerink item number, in the form 'T 666' (where no number is supplied, the poem in question was not separately published). Where applicable, the *Foxon* and *Morgan* numbers are given additionally. See the list of abbreviations below.

(4) Location of holographs or transcripts (the latter category is listed only where the transcript is of textual or literary interest: mere contemporaneity is not sufficient).

(5) Copy-text used as the basis for the Penguin edition. Other texts which have supplied readings adopted in this edition. A full census of the texts collated is *not* provided.

(6) Other relevant data, including any sources or models, classical or mythical origins, biographical or political background.

(7) Critical, scholarly, or bibliographical studies which illuminate the poem.

It is beyond the scope of this edition to give a full tabulation of readings, even within the texts which furnish readings adopted at some point in the poem. Variants are listed where literary significance attaches to a change; where there are signs of a change of mind on Swift's part; where two or more readings seem equally plausible; or where the process of transmission is of interest for whatever reason. Departures from the copy text are noted only where substantive features are in question. Explanatory notes are chiefly directed to matters of usage, meaning, and fact: I have made only sparing reference to such features as running images, characteristic concerns of Swift, etc. Details of persons are supplied in the Biographical Dictionary, pp. 907–42, indicated in the notes by 'Biog. Dict.' The Dictionary is confined to men and women active in Swift's lifetime; other individuals are glossed in the main series of notes. In many cases I have briefly described the relations of the individual with other members of the Scriblerian circle, since this often helped to dictate Swift's attitude. I have attempted to sort out which quarrels were Swift's own originally, and which were inherited from Pope.

In the notes, quotations from Swift and from other contemporary sources are modernized in spelling and typography according to the same rules as the text. Contractions are silently expanded and, where confusion might arise, punctuation is supplied.

For topographical detail I have relied on John Rocque's *Exact Survey of the City of Dublin* (1756) and his *Actual Survey of the County of Dublin* (1760).

DATES

Until 1752 Britain used the 'Old Style' of dating according to the Julian calendar, which by this time was eleven days behind the 'New Style' of the Gregorian calendar used on the Continent. In this edition all dates are given in Old Style, except that the year is taken to begin on 1 January rather than 26 March (as was the normal contemporary practice). Thus the day which contemporaries of Swift referred to as 15 February 1707, or 1707/8, is given as 15 February 1708, in line with modern usage.

Abbreviations

Other abbreviations used:

EDITIONS

M11 *Miscellanies in Prose and Verse* (1711), *T* 2.
M28 *Miscellanies. The Last Volume* (1727, for 1728), *T* 25(3).
WF   *The Works of J.S., D.D.* (1735), vol. II, *T* 41.

More generally, *F* refers to George Faulkner, where other volumes or editions are referred to, as specified; and *Misc* to other volumes or editions of *Miscellanies*, as specified.

Modern editions:
Corr   *Correspondence*, ed. H. Williams, 5 vols. (1963–5).
Drapier *The Drapier's Letters*, ed. H. Davis (1935).
JTS   *Journal to Stella*, ed. H. Williams, 2 vols. (1948).
P   *Poems*, ed. H. Williams, 3 vols., 2nd edn (1958).
PHD   *Poetical Works*, ed. H. Davis (1967).
PJH   *Collected Poems*, ed. J. Horrell, 2 vols. (1958).
PW   *Prose Works*, ed. H. Davis, 14 vols. (1939–68).
Tale   *A Tale of a Tub*, ed. A.C. Guthkelch and D. Nichol Smith, 2nd edn (1958).

OTHER WORKS FREQUENTLY REFERRED TO

Ball   F.E. Ball, *Swift's Verse* (1929; reprinted, 1970).
CH   K. Williams (ed.), *Swift: The Critical Heritage* (1970).
DNB   *Dictionary of National Biography*.
Ehrenpreis I. Ehrenpreis, *Swift: The Man, His Works, and the Age*, 2 vols. so far published (1962–   ).
Ferguson   O.W. Ferguson, *Jonathan Swift and Ireland* (1962).
Fischer   J.I. Fischer, *On Swift's Poetry* (1978).
Foxon   D.F. Foxon, *English Verse 1701–50* (1975). The item follows, thus: '*Foxon* S123'.
Gay   John Gay, *Poetry and Prose*, ed. V.A. Dearing, C.E. Beckwith, 2 vols. (1974).
Gilbert   John T. Gilbert, *A History of the City of Dublin*, 3 vols. (1854–9; reprinted 1972).

Grub Street	P. Rogers, *Grub Street: Studies in a Subculture* (1972).
Jaffe	N.C. Jaffe, *The Poet Swift* (1977).
Johnson	M. Johnson, *The Sin of Wit: Jonathan Swift as a Poet* (1950).
Landa	L.A. Landa, *Swift and the Church of Ireland* (1954).
Lee	J.N. Lee, *Swift and Scatological Satire* (1971).
Library	H. Williams (ed.), *Dean Swift's Library* (1932). (References are to the catalogue of Swift's books sold by Faulkner in February 1746: the item number is indicated thus: 'no. 432').
Mayhew	G.P. Mayhew, *Rage or Raillery* (1967).
Morgan	W.T. Morgan, *A Bibliography of British History 1700–1715*, 5 vols. (1934–42). The item number follows.
Munter	Robert Munter, *The History of the Irish Newspaper 1685–1760* (1967).
OED	*Oxford English Dictionary.*
Peri Bathous	*The Art of Sinking in Poetry*, ed. E.L. Steeves (1952). (This incorporates the text of *Peri Bathous* reprinted from *M28*).
Plumb	J.H. Plumb, *Sir Robert Walpole: the King's Minister* (1960).
POAS	*Poems on Affairs of State*, ed. G. de F. Lord *et al.*, 7 vols. (1963–75). This abbreviation always indicates the modern Yale edition, never the original series under this name.
Pope *Corr*	*The Correspondence of Alexander Pope*, ed. G. Sherburn, 5 vols. (1956).
Prior	*The Literary Works of Matthew Prior*, ed. H.B. Wright, M.K. Spears, 2 vols. (1959; rev. edn, 1971).
PTE	Twickenham edn of *The Poems of Alexander Pope*, ed. J. Butt *et al.*, 10 vols. (1939–69).
Simpson	C.M. Simpson, *The British Broadside Ballad and its Music* (1966).
T	H. Teerink, *A Bibliography of the Writings of Jonathan Swift*, ed. A.H. Scouten (1963). The figure following the abbreviation is that of the item number, thus: '*T* 45'.
Tilley	M.P. Tilley, *A Dictionary of the Proverb in England in the Sixteenth and Seventeenth Centuries* (1950).
Trevelyan	G.M. Trevelyan, *England under Queen Anne*, 3 vols. (1930–34; reprinted, 1965).

MANUSCRIPTS

FV	Forster MSS in Victoria and Albert Museum, London.
HEH	MSS in the Henry E. Huntington Library, San Marino, California.
MF	Fountaine MSS in the Pierpont Morgan Library, New York.
TCD	books and MSS in the Library of Trinity College, Dublin.
TR	books and MSS from the collection of Lord Rothschild, now in the Library of Trinity College, Cambridge.

ODE TO THE KING

Apparently first published in full in Samuel Fairbrother's *Miscellanies*, vol. IV (1735), that is, *T* 33. The significance of this volume was first pointed out in *P* I, xxxvii–xxxviii, and subsequent editors have accepted Williams's view that Fairbrother had access to certain manuscripts not available to the 'official' series put out by booksellers such as Faulkner and Motte. However, it should be noted that John Dunton quoted the opening of the *Ode*, without indicating its authorship, as far back as 1699 (see *PJH* I, 377).

Previously the 'ode I writ to the King in Ireland' (note by Swift to l. 31 of the *Ode to the Athenian Society*) was identified with the *Ode to King William* which appeared in the *Gentleman's Journal* in 1692. This poem was first collected by Nichols in 1789, and was accepted by *Ball*, pp. 16–17, and all editors prior to Williams. The text of this ode can be found in *P* I, 11–13, but there are no longer any grounds for connecting it with Swift.

Fairbrother heads the item 'written in the year 1691'. Swift returned to Moor Park into the service of Sir William Temple about Christmas of that year; he had spent a year back in Ireland, supposedly recovering his health after the first onset of Ménière's disease. If the note already quoted means 'written to the King when I was in Ireland' (rather than 'written to the King upon his successes in Ireland'), then the period of composition must lie between 1 July 1690 – when the first decisive battle, that of the Boyne, was fought – and around August 1691, when Swift left Ireland. The King's 'expedition' lasted only from June to August 1690, and he failed to capture Limerick; in the 1691 campaign he handed over command to Baron Godert de Ginkel (later Earl of Athlone), a Dutch aide. For the circumstances in which the poem was written, and an analysis of its contents, see *Ehrenpreis*, I, 106–14.

The irregular structure and strenuous wit derive chiefly from Cowley, through whose influence the English notion of high pindaric style had been lastingly transformed. Swift had admired Cowley from his teenage years (see *PW* II, 114), and a copy of the *Works* remained in his collection when he died (*Library*, no. 387). An intervening presence might have been Dryden, although Swift seems early to have felt reservations concerning his distant kinsman. It is inconceivable that any serious poet, whatever his prejudices, could have written a pindaric in 1690 without some awareness of *Threnodia Augustalis* (1685) or the ode *To the Memory of Mrs Anne Killigrew* (1686). Dryden's flattery of James II contrasts with Swift's open hostility in this poem; but the vocabulary of heroism, fatality, and angelic intervention is common to the two poets.

The early odes are discussed as a group by Herbert Davis, *Jonathan Swift: Essays on His Satire* (1964), pp. 171–5; *Johnson*, pp. 1–9; *Jaffe*, pp. 61–74; and *Fischer*, pp. 7–54. This phase of Swift's career as a poet is considered by *Ehren-*

preis, I, 109–41; and by Émile Pons, *Swift: Les Années de Jeunesse et le 'Conte du Tonneau'* (1925), pp. 143–5, 164–6, 177–9, 181–5, 187–8. Most of the commentators quote Swift's own remark in a letter to his cousin Thomas, 3 May 1692: 'Egad I cannot write anything easy to be understood though it were but in praise of an old shoe' (*Corr* I, 10). The same letter mentions some early poetry which has not survived: 200 lines of the *Aeneid*, translated apparently from Book VI (the most enduringly influential episode for Swift), and a poem called *The Ramble*.

Text here based on Fairbrother. Typography is slightly normalized along the lines indicated in the Introduction.

1   doing good   Swift later wrote a sermon with this title (*PW* IX, 232–40).

2   allay   abatement; obsolete as a noun since the eighteenth century.

9   allow   'to be' understood.

12   ball   orb.

15   coronation day   William and Mary had been crowned on 11 April 1689; the occasion was certainly attended by Temple, whose household Swift was on the point of joining.

28   the same word   that is, the Latin word *virtus*.

32   our happy prince   William III.

35   airy   perhaps because the goddess Fame lived on the top of a high mountain, in a house open to the winds: see Ovid, *Metamorphoses* XII, 39–63. (*Fama* here is identified with rumour, but she is the same figure as 'fame' in the extended sense.)

37   romantic   found in, or appropriate to, romance; chivalric.

42   haughty Bajazet   the identification of James II with Bajazet and (implicitly) William with Tamburlaine strikes some critics (e.g. *Fischer*, p. 16) as awkward. There is, however, something similar in Nicholas Rowe's play *Tamerlane* (1701), where the hero again represents King William, and Bajazet is the hated absolutist Louis XIV. Tamerlane becomes 'a constitutional monarch of benevolent disposition, who understands that his authority derives from a social compact' (J. Loftis, *The Politics of Drama in Augustan England* (1963), p. 31).

43   Fischer, p. 19, suggests there may be an echo of Luke xx, 43: 'Till I make thine enemies thy footstool.' This verse itself recalls Psalm cix, 1.

47   the fatal fight   the Battle of the Boyne, which took place about thirty miles north of Dublin; its outcome was the retreat of James to France, leaving William in control of all Ireland east of the Shannon.

50   foreshadowing the famous image of Marlborough at Blenheim, likened by Addison to 'an angel sent by divine command' who 'directs the storm' (*The Campaign*, 1705).

51   utmost Thule   'Ireland' (note in Fairbrother). The island in the northern ocean regarded as the extreme limit of the world: see Virgil, *Georgics* I, 30.

52   No poisonous beast   see *Verses Occasioned by the Sudden Drying Up of St Patrick's Well* 41.

57   Rebel   rebellion (archaic).

67   flying deaths   deadly weapons, arrows: *OED* cites Dryden, 'Swiftly flies / The feathered death.' Diction, common in Pope's Homer.

68   impartial   the meaning appears to be 'blind, fortuitous', a sense not given in *OED*.

74   her   Peace.

76 Argus alluding to the story of the fabulous creature with a hundred eyes, set by Juno to watch Io, whom Jupiter had transformed into a beautiful heifer in order to deceive his wife. Mercury charmed Argus to sleep with his lyre, and then killed him. As often, Swift seems to have Ovid's *Metamorphoses* in his mind (I, 601–721).

82 The Scots distrusted by Swift as Presbyterians and sectaries.

84 still always.

87 alluding to Exodus xvi, xvii.

88 pine torment (already archaic as transitive verb).

90 controls defeats, overpowers.

92 fabulous probably stressed on second syllable.

96 Etna according to fable, Jupiter crushed the giant Typhoeus under Etna; in the interior of the volcano the Cyclops had their smithy; another story has the giant Enceladus imprisoned within the mountain and causing the eruptions as he moans and shifts his body (*Aeneid* III, 570–82).

97 Sisyphus king of Corinth, who was obliged to roll a huge stone up a hill in the infernal regions, whilst the stone was constantly rolling back down the slope.

99 Iërne Ireland.

101 fond foolish.
      enemy James.

108 snuff candle.

113 Consume burn away to ashes (old-fashioned intransitive use).

119 That restless tyrant Louis XIV.

125 plagiary borrowed, or even stolen.

127 excrements 'the French King supposed a bastard' (note in Fairbrother).

129 compare *A Satirical Elegy on the Death of a Late Famous General* 32.

131 alluding to comets, which were still regarded as portending evil: Halley's comet of 1682 followed another visible in 1680, and from this time the periodic nature of these bodies began to be understood.

138 influences in the astrological sense.

139 the vortex PJH (I, 377) compares *Tale*, p. 167.

142 Achilles Paris shot Achilles through his one vulnerable place, the right heel.

143 has possibly a corrupt text, but more likely a product of the loose attitude, only just dying out, towards grammatical concord.

145 vile disease 'fistula in ano' (note in Fairbrother). Closely allied to a passage in the *Tale*, pp. 165–6; see I. Ehrenpreis, 'Swift's First Poem', *Modern Language Review* XLIX (1954), 210–11.

ODE TO THE ATHENIAN SOCIETY

The poem marks Swift's first appearance in print, and it is one of his few acknowledged works (the poem itself is signed, as well as the prefatory letter). It appeared in the supplement to the *Athenian Gazette*, vol. V, in 1692. In 1710 and 1728 it was reprinted in selections from this journal issued as *The Athenian Oracle*. There was also a Dublin reprint in 1724 with the title *The Sphinx* (*T* 468, Foxon S910). *T* 467 suggests that the *Ode* was separately published in 1692, but if so no copy is known to survive.

The *Athenian Gazette*, later *Mercury*, appeared (usually twice weekly) between

17 March 1691 and 14 June 1697, with two brief periods of suspension. It contained questions and answers as the staple ingredient of its columns. Its editor was John Dunton (1659–1733), eccentric bookseller and author of a variety of literary works. For a study of the journal, see Gilbert D. McEwen, *The Oracle of the Coffee House: John Dunton's Athenian Mercury* (1972).

Swift sent the poem to Dunton with a letter dated 14 February 1691/2, that is, St Valentine's Day. The supplement containing the *Ode* was advertised on 2 April; McEwen (p. 24) indicates that it may actually have been published on All Fools' Day, an intriguing thought in view of Swift's later addiction to April foolery (see, for example, *An Elegy on Partridge*, headnote). It seems that he did not guess the identity of the 'great unknown' (l. 60), and was put out when he realized that Dunton was the sole editor (see McEwen, p. 34). He had been led to approach the journal because of Sir William Temple's interest in it; Temple had submitted 'at least one lengthy contribution' (McEwen, p. 33). On 3 May Swift sent to his cousin Thomas an account of the poem's genesis:

> I seldom write above two stanzas in a week, I mean such as are to any pindaric ode, and yet I have known myself in so good a humour as to make two in a day, but it may be no more in a week after, and when all's done, I alter them a hundred times, and yet I do not believe myself to be a laborious dry writer, because if the fit comes not immediately I never heed it but think of something else, and besides, the poem I writ to the Athenian Society was all rough drawn in a week, and finished in two days after, and yet it consists of twelve stanza[s] and some of them above thirty lines, all above twenty, and yet it is so well thought of that the unknown gentlemen printed it before one of their books, and the bookseller writes me word that another gentleman [Charles Gildon] has in a book called the *History of the Athenian Society*, quoted my poem very honourably (as the fellow called it) so that perhaps I was in a good humour all the week, or at least Sir William Temple's speaking to me so much in their praise made me zealous for their cause, for really I take that to be a part of the honesty of poets that they cannot write well except they think the subject deserves it. (*Corr* I, 8)

For discussions of the poem, see the general surveys of Swift's early odes in *Ode to the King*, headnote. Horrell's view (*PJH* I, 378) that this is Swift's 'worst poem by odds' is shared by many critics. According to Johnson, the *Ode* provoked Dryden to his (probably apocryphal) remark, 'Cousin Swift, you will never be a poet.' An important text lying behind the poem is Cowley's *Ode to the Royal Society*, which was printed in Sprat's famous *History* (1667). On this and other points, see *Ehrenpreis*, I, 114–17. The concerns of the poem range from the nature of learning and the meaning of fame to Epicureanism and women; but no commentator has been able to detect a satisfactory artistic ordering of these disparate materials.

The text is based on the first printing, with typography normalized. The original edition uses black-letter type in several places in a manner for which there is now no equivalent; I have supplied italics instead, and suppressed italics elsewhere when the sole function of the altered type is to give a kind of nudge.

Title   the text of Swift's prefatory letter is as follows:

To the Athenian Society
Moor Park, February 14, 1691[/2]

GENTLEMEN,

Since everybody pretends to trouble you with their follies, I thought I might claim the privilege of an Englishman, and put in my share among the rest. Being last year in Ireland, (from whence I returned about half a year ago) I heard only loose talk of your Society, and believed the design to be only some new *folly*, just suitable to the age, which God knows, I little expected ever to produce anything *extraordinary*. Since my being in England, having still continued in the country, and much out of company; I had but little advantage of knowing any more, till about two months ago passing through Oxford, a very learned gentleman there, first showed me two or three of your volumes, and gave me his account and opinion of you; a while after, I came to this place, upon a visit to — where I have been ever since, and have seen all the four volumes with their supplements, which answering my expectation, the perusal has produced, what you find enclosed.

As I have been somewhat inclined to this *folly*, so I have seldom wanted somebody to flatter me in it. And for the *Ode* enclosed, I have sent it to a person of very great learning and honour, and since to some others, the best of my acquaintance, (to which I thought very proper to inure it for a greater light) and they have all been pleased to tell me, that they are sure it will not be unwelcome, and that I should beg the honour of you to let it be printed before your next volume (which I think is soon to be published,) it being so usual before most books of any great value among poets, and before its seeing the world, I submit it wholly to the correction of your pens.

I entreat therefore one of you would *descend* so far, as to write two or three lines to me of your pleasure upon it. Which as I cannot but expect from gentlemen, who have so well shown upon so many occasions, that greatest *character* of scholars, in being favourable to the *ignorant*, so I am sure nothing at present, can more highly oblige me, or make me happier.

I am,

(Gentlemen)
Your ever most humble and most
admiring servant.
Jonathan Swift.

Swift visited his cousin Thomas at Oxford in December 1691.

1–21 the opening stanza makes sustained reference to the biblical flood, as described in Genesis vii and viii.
8 the 'classical' version of the flood is that Deucalion's ark landed up on Mount Parnassus: see *Riddles* 7, 45. The relevant passage from the first book of the *Metamorphoses* was in the course of translation by Dryden but did not appear in print until the following year.
16–21 compare Genesis viii, 8–12.
31 humble chaplet 'The ode I writ to the King in Ireland' (Swift's note). See the preceding poem.
47 Delos a floating island in the Cyclades, which suddenly appeared on the surface of the sea, by the power of Neptune; the birthplace of Apollo and Diana. Hence Apollo ('the god of wit', l. 49) is often called 'Delius' by Ovid and other poets.
50 oracular grove there was an oracle of Apollo at Delos, as well as at Delphi and Claros.

60   Ye great unknown   one of the phrases in black-letter type: Swift identifies Dunton's venture with a mythical 'society', although Dunton had only limited assistance from Samuel Wesley and others. The preface to the first collected volume of the journal had been signed 'the Unknown'.

75   buzzing about wit   compare the imagery of *Ode to the King* 115–16.

81   the surly sect   sceptics at large, but especially satirical freethinkers in the line of Rochester.

86   Pluto's helm   Perhaps Swift is thinking of the gold helmet of Mambrino which lent him invulnerability (see *The Fable of Midas* 14), and of Pluto as the god of gold; although, strictly, it was Plutus, not Pluto, who was god of gold (despite frequent confusion).

88   the famed hero   Aeneas, who was shrouded in a cloud by his mother Venus when he entered Carthage (*Aeneid* I, 411–14): compare *An Answer to a Scandalous Poem* 63.

95   The war   that is, the Nine Years War between Louis XIV and the allies (principally England, Austria, and Holland).

100   privateer   during the war, merchant shipping suffered heavy losses at the hands of enemy vessels; the English trading fleet was reluctant even to venture into the Channel at times because of attacks by French ships. 'Their privateers operated from Dunkirk, St Malo and the smaller ports with skill and daring, often assisted with government stores and loans of ships . . . They threatened and even impaired British and Dutch import and export trade, capturing or destroying some hundreds of vessels' (Sir George Clark, 'The Nine Years War, 1688–97', in *The New Cambridge Modern History*, vol. VI, ed. J.S. Bromley (1971), p. 244).

107   an attack on Hobbesian materialism: see the first chapter of *Leviathan*, 'Of Sense': 'For there is no conception in a man's mind, which hath not at first, totally, or by parts, been begotten upon the organs of sense' (ed. C.B. Macpherson (1968), p. 85).

127   a crowd of atoms   the attack on Lucretian and Epicurean ideas may recall Dryden, *Ode for St Cecilia's Day* (1687) 3–4: 'When nature underneath a heap / Of jarring atoms lay' (parallel suggested to me by Mr David Hopkins). Swift spells the verb 'justle', which is simply an early form of 'jostle'.

145   the mighty Nile   'From the days of Herodotus, the rise and fall of the Nile waters were mysteries upon which generations of men speculated – usually in vain' (J.H. Plumb, 'The Search for the Nile', *Men and Places* (1966), p. 213). There was a Latin proverb, '*Facilius sit Nili caput venire*' ('it would be easier to discover the source of the Nile').

151   fondly   foolishly.

153   the famed Lydian king   Gyges (*c.* 685–657 B.C.), a shepherd who found a magic ring, and eventually acquired the throne after killing King Candaules. The story is told in Plato, *Republic* II, 359, c, d: and again in Cicero, *De Officiis* III, ix. The latter is a more likely source for Swift.

160   Echo   only her voice remained, and she was no longer visible (*Metamorphoses* III, 398–401).

175   what is fame?   for contemporary attitudes, see Donald Fraser, 'Pope and the Idea of Fame', *Writers and Their Background: Alexander Pope*, ed. P. Dixon (1972), pp. 286–310.

181–5   compare *Tale*, pp. 150–61. For bottled air, see the reference to Laplanders, and the editors' note citing *Hudibras* II, ii, 343–4 (*Tale*, p. 160). Compare also Gimcrack's scheme in Shadwell's *The Virtuoso* (1676), Act IV.

189 The juggling sea-god Proteus: *Metamorphoses* VIII, 731–7 is the basis of this description. 'Juggling' means tricky or deceptive.

208 the Delphic god Apollo, to whom the temple at Delphi was consecrated.

210 god himself 'Θεὸς ἀπὸ μηχανῆς' (note in original edition.) That is, a *deus ex machina*.

216–33 again, there are distinct premonitions of the *Tale*, pp. 77–91.

223 commode a tall head-dress, with a wire framework, which came into fashion at the end of the seventeenth century.

topknot a bow of ribbon worn on the top of the head.

231 tight trim, smart.

233 in isolation this could pass for a line from a Cavalier love lyric. The following strophe utilizes standard vocabulary drawn from amatory poetry.

278 a noontide in our lives *PJH* I, 378 notes the parallel with *Julius Caesar* IV, iii, 217.

288–91 a summary of Lucretius on death (*De Rerum Natura* III, 830–1094), as pointed out to me by Mr David Hopkins.

298 Gothic swarms the prejudice inherited from Temple, regarding the 'progress of learning' and its demolition by barbarians; in turn passed on to Pope (see Aubrey Williams, *Pope's Dunciad* (1955), pp. 42–8). Compare *Paradise Lost* I, 351–5; *The Dunciad* (1729), III, 75–92.

307 followed by the signature 'Jonathan Swift'.

ODE TO THE HONOURABLE SIR WILLIAM TEMPLE

First published in the London *Misc* (1745), and omitted in *F* editions. Stated on its first appearance to have been written at Moor Park in June 1689; Swift himself could easily have been responsible for this early dating (in a manuscript since lost) but it is generally agreed that 1692 or 1693 is more likely. See *P* I, 27; *PJH* I, 381 (Horrell would place the poem after the *Ode to Dr William Sancroft*, on the grounds that there is no mention of the poem in Swift's letter to his cousin on 3 May 1692: see *Corr* I, 8–10). *Ehrenpreis*, I, 117–26 supplies the fullest background to the poem. As he points out, 'the imagery and central ideas of the poem are largely taken from two of Temple's essays, *Upon Ancient and Modern Learning* and *Upon the Gardens of Epicurus*.' Ehrenpreis also tabulates some affinities with poems by Cowley. For other discussions, see the general studies of Swift's odes listed in *Ode to the King*, headnote, as well as Martin Price, *Swift's Rhetorical Art* (1953), pp. 43–5, and Denis Donoghue, *Jonathan Swift: A Critical Introduction* (1969), pp. 189–91. Text based on the first printing in *Misc*.

1 Virtue Temple had also written an essay, *Of Heroic Virtue*, which made him, as it were, an authority on the subject as well as an exemplar.

12 Terra incognita the supposedly undiscovered continents were so described, e.g. the long-sought land-mass in the South Pacific was called *Terra australis incognita*. There are several references in *A Tale of a Tub*; a manuscript note to one of these suggests that Swift had the West Indies in mind in using the phrase. See *Tale*, p. 106. *Utopian* (*l.* 11) must mean simply 'having no known location': see *OED*, 'Utopian', 1 *b*, for this archaic sense.

15   philosopher's stone   the substance which, according to alchemic theory, would turn all base metals into gold; the object of the alchemists' quest.

24   the schools   traditional academic doctrine and method.

27   golden rules   (1) cardinal rules, like the crucial rule of three in mathematics; (2) rules followed by the alchemists in their quest for gold.

28–49   a stanza particularly admired by W.B. Yeats (see Donoghue, op. cit., pp. 189–90).

29   Plato's paradox   the doctrine expressed in *Phaedo* 73–6.

32   table-book   memorandum book, but probably recalling the Lockian critique of the mind as a *tabula rasa* or blank sheet, ready to receive impressions.

38   compare Pope, *Epistle to a Lady* 241–2: 'Still round and round the ghosts of beauty glide, / And haunt the places where their honour died.'

49   still   continually.

56   like Spaniards   proverbial: compare Addison, *The Trial of Count Tariff* (1713): 'He found him a true Spaniard, nothing but show and beggary.'

59   learned   pronounced 'learn'd'.

60   romances   Temple himself was well versed in this genre and had written short essays in the style as a young man, probably in Paris.

63   him that painted Venus' face   the great artist of antiquity, Apelles, who painted Venus emerging from the sea. Compare Spenser, *Dedicatory Sonnets*, 'To all the Gracious Ladies' 1–4; *Faerie Queene* IV, v, 12. Apelles used courtesans to model various features of his subject.

65   Epicurus   drawing attention to Temple's own essay on the gardens of Epicurus, and invoking a standard example in 'retirement' literature.

68   controls   commands, achieves a dominant position over.

70   Fabius   Quintus Fabius Maximus: see *On Poetry: a Rhapsody* 500.

72   by peace   alluding to Temple's diplomatic successes in achieving peace treaties with the Dutch and the French in the 1660s and 1670s.

80   the box   (1) dicebox; (2) coffin: a pun noted by *Jaffe*, p. 71.

81–2   one of several references by Swift to the belief that the laurel was impervious to thunder: compare *Apollo Outwitted* 9–10. Pliny may be the source. The stanza opposes the martial implications of the image of thunder, as used for example by Marvell, *Horatian Ode* 9–26.

86   compare *A Satirical Elegy on the Death of a Late Famous General* 18.

96   motions   puppets.

97   when you expose the scene   *PJH* I, 380 suggests this alludes to the revelations in Temple's memoirs, which Swift edited; but the reference is indirect if it is there at all. Mechanistic imagery characteristic of Swift; even *motives* (l. 106) may carry a physical sense of 'impulsive movements'.

107–14   a long-winded *amplificatio* based on the proverbial line in Horace, *Ars Poetica* 139: '*parturiunt montes, nascetur ridiculus mus.*' Tilley M1215.

116   what serpent   the basilisk, king of serpents, was said to kill people by looking into their eyes; Pliny is the likely origin of Swift's knowledge (*Natural History* XXIX, 66) but see also Spenser, *Faerie Queene* IV, viii, 39, and Shakespeare, *The Winter's Tale* I, ii, 389. Tilley B99.

124   thence   from court, when Temple retired to Sheen in 1680.

132   still   continually.

156   many windings   the undulating course of the Thames downstream from Sheen (near Richmond) to Whitehall; or the meanders of the Wey from near Moor Park until it joins the Thames at Chertsey.

162   predecessor as a gardener, or as a denizen of paradise (as well as the sense of 'common parent').
177   Hence in another garden, Eden.
    here at Moor Park.
187–8 alluding to Exodus v, 6–19; vi, 6. (The proverbial usage already existed but Swift has the actual biblical narrative in mind.) Tilley B660.
195   Straight immediately. There are possible echoes of Cowley's *The Complaint* in the concluding lines of this stanza.
198 compare Pope, *Elegy to the Memory of an Unfortunate Lady* 9–10: 'Is there no bright reversion in the sky, / For those who greatly think, or bravely die?'
208–9 recalling Cowley, *The Complaint* 114–20.
211   equivocal spontaneous, without parents (*OED*).

ODE TO DR WILLIAM SANCROFT

First published by John Nichols in 1789, along with *To Mr Congreve* and *Occasioned by Sir William Temple's Late Illness and Recovery*. Nichols's source has disappeared. On this first appearance the poem was headed, 'written May 1689, at the desire of the late Lord Bishop of Ely'. This refers to the non-juror Francis Turner (c. 1638–1700), but the date can hardly be right. As pointed out in *P* I, 34, 'Although Sancroft was suspended 1 August, 1689, and deprived 1 February, 1690, for refusing the oath of allegiance to William and Mary, he did not leave Lambeth until his ejectment, 23 June, 1691. We may surmise that the poem was begun in 1689 . . . and abandoned incomplete in 1692.'

It was certainly in active composition as late as 3 May 1692, when Swift wrote to his cousin Thomas:

> I have had an ode in hand these five months inscribed to my late Lord of Canterbury Dr Sancroft, a gentleman I admire at a degree more than I can express, put into me partly by some experience of him, but more by an unhappy reverend gentleman, my Lord the Bishop of Ely, with whom I used to converse about two or three years ago, and very often upon that subject, but I say, I cannot finish it for my life, and I have done nine stanzas and do not like half of them, nor am nigh finished, but there it lies and I sometimes add to it, and would wish it were done to my desire, I would send it to my bookseller and make him print it with my name and all, to show my respect and gratitude to that excellent person, and to perform half a promise I made his Lordship of Ely upon it. (*Corr* I, 8–9)

What form Swift's 'experience' at first hand of Sancroft took, we do not know. The poem never was completed: Nichol's text ends with the words 'the rest of the poem is lost', but this may well be his own addition to the manuscript. On the date of composition, see also note to l. 192.

For Archbishop Sancroft, see Biog. Dict. His role in ecclesiastical politics in the 1680s and early 1690s is described by G.V. Bennett, *The Tory Crisis in Church and State 1688–1730* (1975), pp. 6–10. For background to Swift's poem, see *Ehrenpreis*, I, 126–31. For other critical discussions, see *Ode to the King*, headnote, as well as Edward W. Rosenheim, 'Swift's *Ode to Sancroft*: Another Look', *Modern Philology* LXXIII (1976), 24–39.

Text based on Nichols; this is not likely to be close to Swift's intentions as regards accidentals, but I have made only the minimum normalizations, consistent with the policy adopted in this edition, as Nichols is all we have to rely on.

1–58   the opening stanzas are concerned with the nature of truth.
2   Bright effluence   recalling *Paradise Lost* III, 6: 'Bright effluence of bright essence increate.'
3   Chief cherub   the cherubim were the second order of archangels, whose special province was knowledge.
20   God Himself has said   presumably a scriptural reference, but not identified.
27   Cartesian artists   experimental scientists, rather than philosophic adherents of Descartes in a very precise way: those who seek truth through exploration of physical or sense data. Nichols identifies the experiment described as one 'of the dark chamber, to demonstrate light to be by reception of the object and not by emission'. The camera obscura was 'an instrument consisting of a darkened chamber or box, into which light is admitted through a double convex lens, forming an image of external objects on a surface of paper, glass, etc. placed at the foot of the lens' (*OED*). It was used by Hooke and other members of the Royal Society for experiments recorded in the *Philosophical Transactions*. Swift certainly read such accounts. For the impact of the device on the literary imagination, see Majorie H. Nicolson, *Newton Demands the Muse* (1946), pp. 77–81.
39   Mr David Hopkins suggests an echo of *Paradise Lost* V, 105–6: 'She forms imaginations, aerie shapes, / Which reason, joining or disjoining, frames...' See also *Paradise Lost* V, 111–12: 'but misjoining shapes, / Wild work produces oft, and most in dreams' (Adam is consoling Eve on her 'troublesome dream').
44   bright essence   compare the Miltonic passage cited in note to l. 2.
51   retreat   after his ejection from Lambeth in 1691.
62–3   compare *Ode to the King* 139. 'Vortex' was a Cartesian word.
65   old astronomers   pre-Copernican cosmologists, who placed the earth at the centre of the universe.
69   eccentric   in the astronomical sense, 'moving with a deviant non-circular orbit'; hence, 'roundabout', 'wandering'.
77   giddy   as often in Swift, nausea is associated with visual dislocations; perhaps something to do with the effects of Ménière's disease.
89   feel   be affected by (obsolete use).
92   land of angels   the old pun on Angles, perhaps remembering the remark attributed to St Gregory: '*Non Angli, sed Angeli.*' (Supposed to have been made when handsome English captives were exhibited in Rome.)
96–100   suspiciously close to Temple in its sentiments; Temple belonged to the Spartan brand of Whig ideologue, for whom 'licentious' and libertarian rule was as bad as tyranny.
104   the royal rose   the emblem of the English monarchy, since Henry VII united the Lancastrian and Yorkist roses in his device.
129   Jews   the New Testament image reinforced by Dryden's depiction of a factious crowd in *Absalom and Achitophel*.
131   His great ambassador   presumably an allusion to Sancroft himself and his deprivation.
138–9   alluding to Nebuchadnezzar's dream, expounded by the prophet in the Book of Daniel ii, 31–45.
153   sheds...his sacred influence   there are several allied usages in *Paradise Lost* (e.g. VIII, 511–13), as pointed out to me by Mr David Hopkins. *Ehrenpreis*, I, 129 compares ll. 149–53 to *Paradise Lost* III, 576–86.

158 Pretends claims.

167 Caesar's court as a symbol of temporal power, no doubt remembering Matthew xxii, 21.

172-5 Luke ii, 7.

181 cancelled annulled, abolished (stronger than today).

191 hurricano common form of the word in the seventeenth century: the modern 'hurricane' became 'frequent after 1650, and was established from 1688' (*OED*).

192 fearful storm this could be applied figuratively to the Revolution of 1688/9, but in my view it relates to a real natural disaster: most likely the earthquake at Port Royal in Jamaica, on 7 June 1692 (reports appeared in the English press during August). If Swift had completed nine stanzas by 3 May (see headnote), he would very likely have been at work on this strophe during the summer, when news of the earthquake reached England. See Macaulay's *History of England*, ch. 19, for an account of the devastation. There was another very large earthquake in Sicily in September 1693, when over 100,000 lives were lost; but this may be too late.

196 that prophetic tempest uncertain: there was an earthquake in London in 1580, interpreted as portentous according to the normal habits of the time. Possibly, however, Swift means the storm which overtook the Spanish Armada off Cape Finisterre in June 1588, resulting in delay and the loss of several ships.

200 his master's crown Matthew xxvii, 29.

201 Death's sting 1 Corinthians xv, 55.

202 The bitter cup is from him passed Matthew xxvi, 39 (and xxvii, 34).

212 that was shaded in his seat which could not become visible whilst he sat on the archbishop's throne.

225 that poetic wood in the underworld, described in *Aeneid* VI, 131-211: Aeneas had to bear away a golden bough from a tree consecrated to Proserpine. See *A Panegyric on the Dean* 307.

246 wild reformers essentially the Low Church party, and 'enthusiastic' churchmen who countenanced some rapprochement with the Dissenters; heretics from the traditional Anglicanism of Hooker, Laud, and Sancroft.

252 atrophy malnutrition, starvation.

257 Cordials medicines designed to stimulate the action of the heart.

264 heaven and Cato echoing Lucan, *De Bello Civilii* I, 128: 'Victrix causa deis placuit, sed victa Catoni' ('for the winning cause pleased the Gods, but the losing cause pleased Cato', tr. Robert Graves). 'Cato' here is Cato the younger (d. 46 B.C.). Lucan's poem, like Swift's, remained unfinished.

TO MR CONGREVE

First published by Nichols in 1789; his source is not now available. Headed 'written November 1693', which squares with other evidence. On 6 December in that year, Swift wrote to his cousin Thomas:

> I desire you would inform yourself what you mean by bidding me keep my verses for Will Congreve's next play, for I tell you they were calculated for any of his, and if it were but acted when you say, it is as early as ever I intended, since I only design they should be printed before it, so I desire you will send me word immediately, how it succeeded, whether ill or indifferently, because my sending them to Mr Congreve depends upon knowing the issue.
>
> They are almost 250 lines, not pindaric . . . (*Corr* I, 13-14)

The play in question was *The Double Dealer*, which had its première at Drury Lane shortly before and was published around 7 December. Initially the play was regarded as a disappointment after the splendid success of *The Old Bachelor* earlier in the same year; Dryden wrote to William Walsh on 12 December, '[*The*] *Double Dealer* is much censured by the greater part of the town; and is defended only by the best judges, who, you know, are commonly the fewest. Yet it gets ground daily, and has already been acted eight times.' Shortly afterwards the Queen ordered a command performance of the comedy, and thereafter its reputation grew. Dryden himself contributed verses which were prefixed to the published text. Swift's, which would have made an odd introduction to the play, did not see print. It is likely that he never even sent them to Congreve.

The two men had been together at Kilkenny School and then at Trinity College, and remained friends until Congreve's death in 1729. See further, Biog. Dict., 'Congreve'. This is Swift's first known poem in couplets, unless it postdates *A Description of Mother Ludwell's Cave*; the priority of these items is hard to fix. The most extensive discussion of the poem occurs in books allotting special attention to the odes as a group: see *Ode to the King*, headnote. *Ehrenpreis*, I, 132–6 supplies useful background to the poem.

The text is based on Nichols's 1789 printing. In that place Nichols made rather free use of italics, with ll. 45–8, 133–4, 167–8, 180 (in part), 205–6, and 223–6 all italicized. The warrant for this is not clear, and in reprinting the poem among Swift's *Works* in 1801 Nichols substituted roman type. I follow the later policy in this case.

1   Thrice, with a prophet's voice   Horrell (*PJH* I, 382) relates this opening to local traditions concerning Mother Ludwell and her cave (compare *A Description of Mother Ludwell's Cave*). He quotes a story that the witch would supply local people with whatever they desired, provided they went to the cave at midnight and asked three times for the article of their desire. Midnight was certainly the most 'poetic hour' in this vein of rhapsodic poetry, and in conjunction with the later references to the cave this lends force to Horrell's suggestion.

16   cast   cast off, abandoned.

18   cheat   fraud, act of cheating.

19   stews   quarters of ill fame.

20   of course   customary, dutiful.

27   speaks   shows, manifests (see *OED*, 'speak', 29).

32   A mighty gulf   between the talented and successful young dramatist in London, who had already achieved fame in his early twenties, and the obscure and rusticated Swift.

35–40   suggesting that the poem will serve as prefatory matter to a more considerable work, that is, the text of Congreve's play.

38   the victorious wren   recalling Dryden, *All for Love* II, 138–40: 'Fool that I was, upon my eagle's wings / I bore this wren, till I was tired with soaring, / And now he mounts above me', itself alluding to Aesop's fable of the eagle and the wren. This was one of the favourite Augustan fables, cited, for example, by Addison, *Tatler*, no. 224 (14 September 1710).

39   tower   soar aloft.

50   reform the stage   the obsession of the age in all dramatic criticism; as well as the call for moral reform by Jeremy Collier in his *Short View of the Immorality and Prophaneness of the English Stage* (1698), which provoked a host of replies (including one by Congreve), there were calls for a purely theatrical 'reform', to bring English standards up to those supposedly operative in France.

54 that is, Congreve's wit is passed on in a cruder form by people who steal lines from his play.

55 clipped as coins were mutilated by having their edges pared: a serious problem in the 1690s, which provoked a currency crisis and the need for a recoinage in 1695/6. The imagery foreshadows that of Swift's poems on Wood's halfpence, e.g. *Prometheus*.

59 'what you have contributed can scarcely be recognized amidst the dross of their own attempts at wit.'

64 assembling glass an optical lens, presumably one like a burning-glass which concentrates light into one spot.

66 obliged grateful.

67 pad rob, like a footpad.

74 Titan the sun, as in Ovid, *Metamorphoses* I, 10, or Shakespeare, *Romeo and Juliet* II, iii, 4.

76 the god of light and wit Apollo: compare *To Lord Harley* 9 and *Apollo: or, A Problem Solved* 1.

84 Goths barbarians, Teutonic invaders; 'vandals'. The attitude parallels that of *The Dunciad* (1729), III, 81–2: 'The north by myriads pours her mighty sons, / Great nurse of Goths, of Alans, and of Huns.' 'Gothic' had still not become a term of approval in cultural or literary discourse.

pit synecdoche for theatrical audience.

94 again, looking forward to *The Dunciad* (1743), IV, 421–58. The myopic 'virtuoso' intent on minute aspects of nature is a stock figure of fun in satire: see also *Gulliver's Travels* III, 5.

98 inns inns of court, where elegant youths congregated and supposedly studied Law. See l. 137.

102 rules the critical precepts derived by neoclassical writers from Aristotle, Quintilian, and other authorities: usually mentioned (as here) as dry and mechanical injunctions towards 'correctness'.

103–8 the critics may claim even to outdo the idolatry popularly associated with Egypt. The golden calf (l. 108) recalls Exodus xxxii, 1–24.

110 pit where pretenders to taste, young men about town, law-students, and so on would take their place in the theatre.

114 Farnham two miles west of Moor Park.

119 down down from London to the country.

137 Gray's Inn one of the inns of court; hence the meaning is 'sophomoric', 'callow', from the demeanour associated with law-students.

142 Wycherley the dramatist, William Wycherley (1641–1716). An early adviser of Pope.

Mr Bays Dryden (his nickname after the caricature by Buckingham in *The Rehearsal*, 1672).

144 heroics here, heroic plays: grand Restoration tragedy.

145 tragedy . . . would lose you quite Congreve's only tragedy was to be *The Mourning Bride* (1697); it enjoyed considerable theatrical success. There is no evidence that the play was already planned; one suggestion is that Congreve was turned towards tragedy by his friendship with Thomas Southerne, to whose *Oroonoko* (1695) Congreve contributed a prologue.

146 Will's the famous literary and theatrical coffee-house where Dryden held court, and where Wycherley was regularly to be found. It was situated above a shop on the corner of Russell Street and Bow Street, just to the east of Covent Garden. See also *On Poetry: a Rhapsody* 117, 252, 279.

148 the sense appears to be the opposite of what one might expect: 'turning mere shadows into actuality, and giving mere names a kind of substantial existence.'

153 sot fool (obsolescent usage).

156 in debate into question.

169-74 similarly in *The Dunciad* (1729) II, 115-16, Queen Dulness disguises three hacks in the likeness of Congreve, Addison, and Prior.

171 bet] be *Nichols*.

172 recalling one of La Fontaine's celebrated *Fables* (V, 21); also, *Tilley* A351. La Fontaine was represented in Swift's *Library*, no. 17, but in a 1696 edition he could not at this date have owned.

180 all that's good 'this alludes to Sir William Temple, to whom he gives the name of Apollo in a few lines after' (note in Nichols).

181-2 Swift may be thinking of Thalia, muse both of comedy (Congreve's speciality) and innocent rustic song, here supposed to be fitting to Moor Park.

186 Apollo Temple: see note to l. 180.

187 a reverend cave this is unmistakably Mother Ludwell's cave, as indicated by G.C. Moore Smith and Joseph Horrell (see *A Description of Mother Ludwell's Cave*). The witch was supposed to have inspired the local druid (see *PJH* I, 382).

191-4 'The "prophet's voice" of the opening line, and "we the high priesthood" of the next, are evidence of Swift's fanciful conception of himself in the native druidic tradition' (*PJH* I, 382-3). On this subject, see A.L. Owen, *The Famous Druids* (1962).

194 Albion England, with patriotic and mythical overtones. The idea is that Britain had been the chosen home of a druidic culture which preserved essential spiritual and poetic truths during the Dark Ages: this was to be a seminal notion throughout the eighteenth century.

205-12 'out of an ode I writ, inscribed *The Poet*. The rest is lost' (note in Nichols). No other evidence concerning this work is forthcoming.

209-12 words like *volatile, subtle, spirit, insipid* are examples of the shift from technical (medical, physical or chemical) senses to metaphorical or psychological meanings: this trend in English vocabulary is discussed in Donald Davie, *The Language of Science and the Language of Literature 1700-1740* (1963). Swift's wit depends on the fact that the chemical terms were beginning to have this transferred meaning. ('Mercurial' is another case in point.) *Bubbled* duped; *fade* dull or vapid; *insipid* the prime sense is still, literally, 'tasteless'.

217-18 the whole scene is strongly reminiscent of *Cadenus and Vanessa* 316-443. Compare, for instance, l. 218 with *Cadenus and Vanessa* 396.

223-6 not remote in feeling or expression from Gulliver's reaction to the Yahoos, whom he originally takes to be cattle, who are described as 'odious', who come on him as a 'herd', and whose food 'smelt so offensively' to Gulliver. See *PW* XI, 224-30.

231 descending sheet the great sheet let down from heaven, which St Peter saw in a trance (Acts x, 10-16). Line 233 echoes Acts x, 14.

A DESCRIPTION OF MOTHER LUDWELL'S CAVE

First published from the manuscripts of Lady Giffard by Julia Longe in 1911. Reprinted as Swift's by G.C. Moore Smith in his edition of *Early Essays and Romances by Sir William Temple* (1930), pp. 186–8. The ascription was supported by John Middleton Murry in *Jonathan Swift: A Critical Biography* (1954), pp. 488–9. Both Moore Smith and Murry adduce a number of parallels with Swift's authenticated works. The only editor to accept the item is Horrell (*PJH* I, 34–6, 381). On the other hand Williams rejects the attribution (*P* III, 1068–9). He concedes that the poem 'was undoubtedly written by some one at Sir William Temple's seat, Moor Park, during the 'nineties of the seventeenth century'. However, he thinks that the error in the motto of the poem (repeated elsewhere by Swift) cannot be assigned much weight 'in an age when in speech and writing classical quotation was a commonplace', a circumstance that might logically be thought to make such 'faulty citation' less likely rather than the reverse. He also doubts whether the handwriting of the manuscript can be that of the youthful Stella. In the light of recent research it seems to me improbable that the hand is Stella's: see A.C. Elias, 'Stella's Writing-Master', *The Scriblerian* IX (1977), 134–9. But it is not that of Temple, Lady Giffard, or Thomas Swift.

The chance that there was in the Temple household another poet with the set of imaginative associations displayed in *Mother Ludwell's Cave* must be remote in the extreme. Thomas Swift is perhaps just possible; but, on all counts, Jonathan is the more plausible candidate. Apart from the facts pointed out by Moore Smith and Murry (some of which are mentioned in the notes), it should be observed that the reference to the *Aeneid*, Book VI, at ll. 55–6, not only touches on a recurrent episode in Swift's mind but squarely hits the passage he was translating in 1692 (*Corr* I, 10). The merits of the poem are limited but they are comparable to those of other poems at this period. Unless convincing evidence to the contrary is brought, it looks as if the responsibility for this item must be allotted to Swift. The clear references to Mother Ludwell's cave and the associated legends in *To Mr Congreve* (established by Horrell, *PJH* I, 382–3) serve to reinforce the case. It is, however, fair to point out that the attribution is rejected by the outstanding Swift scholar now active: see *Ehrenpreis*, I, 135.

The likeliest date of composition would be in the 1692–4 spell of residence at Moor Park. Horrell suggests 1693. Text based on Moore Smith's transcript.

Title Ludwell's cave was a natural cavern at the bottom of a hill, facing westwards and overhung by oaks: see Thomas Swift's description, quoted by Moore Smith, pp. xxvi–xxvii. There were a number of legends concerned with the cave, spread about by John Aubrey amongst others. 'The cave is situated about 150 yards along the drive of the Moor Park estate coming in from the Waverley Road and about three quarters of a mile from the mansion' (Moore Smith, p. xxvii). Moor Park itself lies on the banks of the Wey, just outside Farnham, near the border of Surrey and Hampshire. See *Victoria County History of Surrey* (1905), II, 593.

Epigraph from Horace, *Epistles* I, xvi, 15: the accepted reading is *etiam* for *et si mihi* ('This sweet refuge – even, if you will believe me, positively bewitching . . .'). As Murry points out, virtually the same misquotation occurs in Swift's letter to Atterbury, 3 August 1713 (*Corr* I, 379).

2   Aonian stream   poetical, pertaining to the muses (from Aonia, where Mount Helicon and the muses' fountain were located).

4   that hackney fry   Moore Smith compares *Ode to Sir William Temple* 94. See also *Cassinus and Peter* 87.

10   Crooksberry   or Crooksbury Hill, a conical hill rising to 534 feet, overlooking Waverley Abbey, just to the south of Moor Park.

cloven hill   Parnassus, which had twin peaks: Ovid's epithet is *biceps* (*Metamorphoses* II, 221).

11   Pomona   'Can it mean that Pomona is the agent of Temple, whose skill in fruit-tree lore was so well known?' (Moore Smith). The classic account of Pomona is again in the *Metamorphoses* XIV, 623–771. For a similar coupling of Pomona and Flora, see *The Dean's Reasons for Not Building at Drapier's Hill* 92–3.

15   silver floods   'the Wey running through the water-meadows between Moor Park and Waverley [Abbey]' (Moore Smith).

16   the frizzled thickets   Moore Smith compares *Paradise Lost* VII, 523: 'And bush with frizzled hair implicit.'

18   Philomela   the nightingale.

21   the fairy matron   Mother Ludwell, or Ludlow.

23–52   the description bears close comparison with that in Defoe's *Tour through Great Britain*, rev. S. Richardson *et al.* (4th edn, 1748): 'Going on from this seat [Moor Park], on the left hand, under an high cliff, is a noted kind of natural grotto, which they call Mother Ludlam's Hole, through which runs a fine and strong rill of water. The grotto is large, but diminishes and winds away, as the spring seems to have directed it. The owner has paved the bottom of it with a kind of mosaic tile, and has separated the wider part from the narrower behind by a little parapet, through which issues the flow of water, which trills through marble troughs, one below another, till it is conveyed out of the grotto; and there murmuring down a considerable declivity, over many artificial steps, falls into the river on the right hand; all which gives a very delightful entertainment to such as choose in warm weather to make little collations or visits, there being settees, with arms, for their conveniency.' (I, 230–31). I do not know when this concession to tourism was made. ('Ludlam' becomes 'Ludoe' in later editions of the *Tour*).

46–7   recalling *Aeneid* VII, 808–9; compare *Occasioned by Sir William Temple's Late Illness and Recovery* 113–18 and *Desire and Possession* 21–2. See also Pope, *Essay on Criticism* 372–3.

48   fly a dance   the so-called 'cognate object', for which see *OED* 'fly', 1 (c).

55   the Cumaean den   the cave in the hills of Cumae where Aeneas encountered the Sybil (*Aeneid* VI, 42–4).

56   Sibyl   the prophetess who conducts Aeneas to the underworld.

57   him   Sir William Temple: see Biog. Dict. Swift similarly alludes to Temple's retirement from active politics and diplomacy in his *Ode to Sir William Temple* 135–58.

61   a rich and gaudy silence   Moore Smith suggests this is a reference to Temple's abandonment of his former home at Sheen in 1689.

63   admiration   wonder.

64   that   the former, i.e. Moor Park itself.

66   more modish   by the 1740s the garden layout seemed distinctly old-fashioned, and the editor of Defoe's *Tour* (see note to ll. 23–52) noticed 'a running stream through the garden, which, with a small expense, might be made to serpentize through all the adjacent meadows, in a most delightful manner' (I, 230). It was basically a formal Italianate garden. For an engraving which shows its appearance *c*. 1690, see John Dixon Hunt and Peter Willis (eds.), *The Genius of the Place* (1975), p. 97.

67   pleasant   the cave began to be found actually 'beautiful' by tourists as early as 1754 (see Richard Pococke, quoted by Hunt and Willis, op. cit., p. 265).

70   alloy   the manuscript spelling is 'allay', an older variant. 'Allay' also occurs in *Ode to the King* 2.

72   debauched by art   Moore Smith compares *Ode to Sir William Temple* 204, 'debauched by praise'.

OCCASIONED BY SIR WILLIAM TEMPLE'S LATE ILLNESS AND RECOVERY

First published by Nichols in *Miscellaneous Pieces* (1789), presumably from a manuscript now lost. In these circumstances an editor must follow Nichols's text, though it is unlikely to be very faithful in the matter of accidentals. Stated on its first appearance to have been 'written December 1693'; the use of the couplet suggests this is accurate, as Swift was clearly in the throes of abandoning pindarics by the middle of that year. *P* I, 51 notes, 'Sir William Temple was a constant sufferer from the gout and other complaints. In 1693 he was for some time seriously ill.' For discussion, see *Ehrenpreis*, I, 139-41 ('still incompetent; but it is the shortest and the best' of the early poems), as well as general treatment of the odes, listed in *Ode to the King*, headnote.

7-8   again the notion is close to that in the passage from Pope's *Epistle to a Lady*, cited in *Ode to Sir William Temple*, note to l. 38.

17-19   imagery deriving from Dryden, *Religio Laici* 1-11.

21-22   the italics suggest a possible allusion, not identified; the language of joy and woe at strife would point to a seventeenth-century source.

28   dart   arrow.

33   undecent   unfitting.

38   agues   disyllabic. The imagery is Lucretian, with plagues and (mental) disease attributed to vapours breaking out of the earth. For theories about the origins of infection, see A.D. McKillop, *The Background of Thomson's Seasons* (1942), pp. 165-8.

41   Dorothea   Temple's wife, *neé* Dorothy Osborne, author and horticulturalist: see Biog. Dict., 'Temple'.

42   doubtful   of uncertain issue: epic diction.

45   sprung from a better world   her father, the governor of Guernsey, was a strong royalist; the main sense is hyperbolic compliment ('heavenly') but there may be some idea to the effect that Lady Temple came from pure stock. Lines 47-8 certainly gain point from the existence of Civil War ruins in the landscape of England when Swift came over from Ireland, not to mention the battle-scars of his native country.

52   Dorinda   probably Lady Giffard: see Biog. Dict. The 'grief' belongs to her long widowhood, which followed close upon her marriage and lasted sixty years.

55   insolent   a noun; becoming archaic thus.

57 heaven's bright queen Diana.

60 sables mourning garb.

each menial look perhaps 'the gaze of all us lower humanity who surround her'.

75 the high priesthood poets.

78 tell expose.

87 ensconcing sheltering, protective.

90 planet of his birth compare *To a Lady* 149.

100 antic grotesque.

102 fame probably recalling Virgil's description of Fama in *Aeneid* IV, 173–97.

104 the syntax is unclear; probably 'which' is understood after the word 'power'.

107 right woman a real woman.

117–18 one of Swift's favourite allusions, to Virgil, *Aeneid* VII, 808–9: compare *A Description of Mother Ludwell's Cave* 46–7.

130 still continually (as ll. 132, 148).

131 fatal bent of mind compare *The Journal of a Modern Lady* 151.

138 interest self-interest, selfishness.

137–8 a surprisingly 'Irish'-looking rhyme for early Swift.

141 brazen strong as brass: compare Shakespeare, *3 Henry VI* II, iv, 4.

ON THE BURNING OF WHITEHALL IN 1698

This unfinished item has hitherto appeared only in Scott's edition of Swift. It is described in the life which makes up vol. I of the edition (1814) and reproduced there in a somewhat normalized form. No other editor has accepted the attribution, and the powerful voices of John Forster and Harold Williams have spoken against Swift's authorship. Recently, however, George P. Mayhew argued, convincingly in my judgement, that the item should be restored to the canon: see *Harvard Library Bulletin* XIX (1971), 399–411. Mayhew showed that the poem came to Scott via Matthew Weld Hartstonge, a Dublin littérateur, and that he in turn had it from a nephew of Dr John Lyon, who looked after Swift in his final incapacity. Mayhew cites correspondence to indicate that Lyon (an unimpeachable witness) almost certainly preserved the item as an authentic manuscript by Swift: and, indeed, that Scott very probably received the autograph copy from Hartstonge in 1812. Mayhew concludes that the transcript tipped into the manuscript of Scott's text (now at Harvard) was a direct copy of the original, probably made by the amanuensis, Henry Weber. I am not certain about the hand, and I have less confidence than Mayhew that the transcript faithfully reproduces accidentals – it certainly represents the conventions of 1800 rather than Swift's own practice. However, I follow Mayhew in his substantive case. The political attitudes would not be unexpected in the Swift of 1698, and the style is sharp and vigorous enough not to work against the attribution. Internal evidence seems to permit the attribution, external evidence to lie decisively in its favour. See also *Ball*, pp. 39–41, and *P* III, 1069.

The greater part of the palace of Whitehall was destroyed by fire on 4/5 January 1698: see *Vanbrug's House*, headnote. The rambling ancient palace had originally been the town residence of the Archbishop of York until Henry VIII dispossessed Wolsey of it in 1530 (see ll. 1–2). I assume that Swift wrote shortly after the event, presumably at Moor Park. The text is based on the transcript made for Scott, now at Harvard.

Title   the transcript reads '1697', then ordinary usage for a date in the year prior to 26 March: the modern form of 5 January 1697/8 would be '1698' instead, and so I have altered the reading accordingly. Scott confused the fire with another which occurred in 1691, and supposed erroneously that '1697' referred to the date of composition.

1   Wolsey   Thomas Wolsey, cardinal and politician (*c.* 1475–1530). York Place, once the home of Hubert de Burgh (d. 1243), had been occupied by the English Blackfriars and was sold to Walter Gray, Archbishop of York (d. 1255), who left the house to his successors in perpetuity. Wolsey beautified and reconstructed it as a palace rather than a mansion.

3   Henry   Henry VIII, whom Swift continued to dislike.

5   Edward VI, who ruled from 1547 to 1553, and his half-sister, Mary I, Queen from 1553 to 1558. The 'innovations' are constitutional and particularly ecclesiastical; Mary's bigotry lies in her persecution of Protestants and alliance with Spain. Stressed 'bi-gót'.

7   a fiercer Tudor   Queen Elizabeth I, daughter of Henry VIII by Anne Boleyn.

9   Dudley   Robert Dudley, Earl of Leicester (*c.* 1532–88), royal favourite.

10   a slain guest   uncertain; perhaps Mary Queen of Scots.

11   northern James   James VI of Scotland, who succeeded to the English throne on the death of Elizabeth in 1603.

12   palliardism   a rare word for 'lechery', from 'palliard', a beggar and, by transference, a debauchee. Mayhew cites Dryden, *The Hind and the Panther* II, 563. James's homosexual practices are meant.

12 ∧ 13   the amanuensis records an addition at this point, 'And here did under the black plaster groan' (probably marked for deletion in the original MS).

13   the French consort   Henrietta Maria, who married Charles I in 1625, and whose independent Catholic line explains the animus revealed here.

15   A bold usurper   Oliver Cromwell.

17   referring to the restoration of Charles II in 1660: *sauntering* has the obsolete sense of 'trifling'. It is interesting that Macaulay uses the same expression of the king: 'fond of sauntering and of frivolous amusements' (*History of England*, ch. II). Macaulay owned Scott's edition and made copious notes in it; the set, once belonging to G.M. Trevelyan, is now in the possession of J.H. Plumb.

21   the amanuensis records a variant line, 'Of spurious brats abhorred by all'.

23   alluding to the widespread rumour that Charles II had been poisoned (see *PW* V, 283).

24   his wise successor   James II. Mayhew suggests that the sarcastic epithets, *pious* (l. 22) and *wise*, 'point ahead to the irony and satire of Swift's later manner'.

26   cowls   monks (by synecdoche, from the word for their hoods): papists.

28   Guerdon   reward, recompense (already growing archaic).

29ff.   alluding to the Glorious Revolution of 1688 and the early years of William III's reign.

31   eternal]   'immortal' deleted in transcript.

33   great Nassau   William III (as also 'that prince', 35).

34ff.   if this is by Swift, it is the earliest of many attacks upon the influence of

Dutch-inspired financial and political operations, headed by City speculators and 'projectors' (i.e. ambitious entrepreneurs working on the brink of illegality). These attitudes recur in Swift's political pamphleteering for the Harley ministry, and are given fresh expression in *Gulliver's Travels*. For the background to this obsessive concern, see J.M. Treadwell, 'Jonathan Swift: The Satirist as Projector', *Texas Studies in Literature and Language* XVII (1975), 439-60, esp. 453.

37   Mayhew suggests this may allude to the bribing of the Tory politician Sir Christopher Musgrave, as does (explicitly) Pope's *Epistle to Bathurst* 65-8 (see *PTE* III, ii, 89-90). But, if so, the poet was exceedingly well-informed and up-to-date in his knowledge.

42   Sodom   for the destruction of the cities of the plain, see Genesis xix, 23-8.
   Troynovant   London, according to legend founded by the Trojan refugee Brute or Brutus, the subject of many works at this period including a projected epic by Pope. The reference is to the Great Fire of 1666.

48-9   Hans Holbein's embellishments of Whitehall included a group portrait of Henry VIII and his family, painted in 1537, which perished in this fire.

52   Inigo's famed building   the Banqueting House by Inigo Jones, in front of which Charles I had been executed in 1649, and which alone survived the conflagration.

53   an action truly great   later in life, Swift was to regard the behaviour of 'King Charles the martyr' during his trial and execution as an example of 'a great figure' made by a historical personage: see 'Of Mean and Great Figures' (*PW* V, 83).

58   this day   Ball, p. 41, suggests that the poem was 'to bear as date the anniversary of Charles the First's execution', i.e. 30 January, and it would presumably thus counter the usual High Church lamentations on that day. But there is no firm evidence on that point. Mayhew argues that the ending is not hostile to Charles, and cites deletions in the manuscripts to support his interpretation: again, the facts are not definite enough to achieve any certainty.

VERSES WROTE IN A LADY'S IVORY TABLE-BOOK

On its first appearance this poem stood at the head of the verse section of *M11*. It was reprinted in *M28* and *WF*. *M11* dates '*Anno*. 1698', whilst *WF* has 'written in the year 1706'. The earlier date seems more likely, although there may have been a revision at the later period. The text here is based on *WF*, with minor emendations from *M11*.

In the early editions the passages here in quotation marks were in italics, but the interpolated phrases in ll. 7-16 were enclosed in parentheses also. Modern typographic conventions allow the same effect to be achieved through the use of quotation marks alone, but I have retained the brackets for the aside in l. 15.

For discussion, see *Ehrenpreis*, II, 18-19. As examples of the non-satiric use of a similar formula, Horrell cites poems by Edmund Waller and William Walsh (*PJH* I, 383). *Fischer*, pp. 56-9, gives a brief account of the poem.

Title   *WF* reads 'in' for 'on'; the alteration, no doubt intentional, makes for some confusion today. A table-book was normally at this period a pocket notebook (*OED*, citing *JTS*), but, in the context, a later development of the meaning may be more apposite: 'an ornamental book for a drawing-room table.' The nearest equivalent in recent generations would be an autograph album.

4 a punning line: as applied to the book, the epithets refer to the physical surface of the ivory, and as applied to the owner, they suggest 'mean-spirited, foolish, and fickle'.

7 the interpolation technique may be borrowed from Butler's *Hudibras* III, i, 1263–88. Swift exploited the device elsewhere, notably in the *Verses on the Death of Dr Swift* 225–42.

8 *receipt* recipe (ordinary usage then).
paint cosmetics.

10 *far an el breath* as a remedy for bad breath.

13 *billet-doux* a (customary) plural form here: love letters.

14 *laid out for* spent on

18∧19] To think that your brains' issue is / Exposed to the excrement of his, *M11; not in M28, WF.*

19 with the aid of a rag ('clout') and some spit.

28 the use of emphatic italics in *WF* is preserved in this edition where it helps to point up a rhetorical device.

THE PROBLEM

First published by *F* in 1746 in vol. XI of the *Works*. *P* follows a transcript in the Orrery papers at Harvard. This gives a subtitle, 'That Sidney Earl of Romney stinks, when he is in love', where the printed version named the Earl of Berkeley. (For both men, see Biog. Dict.) Since Swift had applied unsuccessfully to Romney in his quest for preferment around 1699 (*Ehrenpreis*, I, 250–51, 260), this supplies a possible date of composition. For a fuller review of the issues, see *Ehrenpreis*, II, 29–31, and *P* I, 64–5. Discussions of the poem include *Lee*, pp. 64–6.

The text here is based on *F* (1746), with occasional emendations from the Orrery transcript. The printed version is tidier and (leaving aside the identification of the victim) it appears quite as accurate.

19–20 *kings* not identified: there is a broad similarity to the passage on Henry IV of France in the 'Digression on Madness', *Tale*, pp. 163–4.

35 *a regent's heart* Berkeley became Lord Justice in 1699, and would fit the case; but Romney had been Lord Lieutenant in 1692 and Lord Justice in 1697.

46 *breech* a pun on the breech of a gun and breech meaning 'posterior'.

53 *Neal* Mary Paulet, daughter of the second Duke of Bolton, who married Colonel Charles O'Neill. According to *P* I, 67, he was a descendant of the O'Neills who were Kings of Ulster. She later married Arthur Moore.

56 *Ross* the third wife of Richard Parsons, first Viscount Rosse; she was Elizabeth, *née* Hamilton, a niece of the Duchess of Marlborough. The marriage took place in 1685; her husband died in 1703 and she herself in 1724.

57 *Levens* Mary Corbyn, first wife of Sir Richard Levinge, for whom see Biog. Dict.

THE DISCOVERY

Like *The Problem*, this poem first appeared in *F* (1746), vol. XI. Swift's autograph version survives in *MF*, and there is also a transcript by another hand in the Orrery papers at Harvard. The autograph is headed 'An. 1699' and internal evidence supports this. Swift travelled to Ireland with the new Lord Justice, Berkeley, in August 1699; he believed originally that he was to be Berkeley's secretary as well as his chaplain, but discovered that he had been outmanoeuvred by Arthur Bushe and had lost the post to his rival. His lifelong suspicion of mystification and intrigue in politics was quickly aroused by the sight of Bushe at the elbow of the leading statesmen. See *P* I, 61-2 and *Ehrenpreis*, II, 6-8, 31-2.

The text is based on *MF*, collated with *F* (1746). Swift's ultra-light punctuation has required to be supplemented, though I have done this as sparingly as possible.

2 folks the Orrery transcript reads 'fools'. The first half of the line in *F* reads 'Statesmen and mob'.

9 Bushe see Biog. Dict.

10 premier ministre still a Frenchified expression, soon to be supplanted by the adaptation 'prime minister'. *OED* records several instances of 'premier minister', all between 1686 and 1734, including the usage in *To Mr Gay* 116.

17 put up to this seems to be a conjectured meaning of 'put up', which *OED* cites with a query and with this line as the sole instance (*put*, 53 m (a)). The suggested meaning is 'to make up to, to address oneself to a person'.

22 junto a mutation of the Spanish *junta* which had been imported into English political vocabulary during the seventeenth century, and was currently applied to a group of Whig leaders whom Swift was to defend in *Contests and Dissentions* (1701).

23 Phiz...Ush the two usurpers in Buckingham's burlesque, *The Rehearsal* (1672). They are mentioned again in l. 48. Their role is to sneak around throughout the piece, but their chief bout of whispering occurs in Act II, Scene 1.

25 spark a pushing young fellow.

29 the allusions in this stanza are general rather than particular, but there are certainly hints of the long-running Great Northern War (between Sweden under Charles XII and a coalition of Muscovy, Denmark, and Saxony-Poland); of the popish plots against William III; and of the currency crisis which occasioned the recoinage of 1696.

43 congee a ceremonious bow on retiring.

circumflex sharply bent.

48 See l. 23.

MRS HARRIS'S PETITION

This famous and much-anthologized poem made a furtive entrance into the world. It was first brought out in unauthorized editions by two of the acknowledged experts in literary piracy, Henry Hills and Edmund Curll (various printings, 1709-11: see *T* I, 1A, 3, 518, 521-2). It was then included in *M11*, and after further adventures at the hands of Curll reappeared in *M28*, and *WF*. In *F* editions it regularly occupied first place among the poems.

M11 dated the piece 1700, and *WF* 1701. *Ball*, pp. 46-7, thinks the reference to the Earl of Drogheda (l. 28) indicates that composition took place in the early part of 1701, while Berkeley was waiting for the new Lord Justice to arrive. *P* I, 68 and *Ehrenpreis*, II, 27 accept this dating. For commentary on the technique, see *Ehrenpreis*, II, 32-3. The suggestion has been made that the long verses derive from the Tudor comedy, *Gammer Gurton's Needle* (*c.* 1550): see *Ball*, p. 47. But Swift's use of this garrulous and apparently crude metre is far more knowing and agile. See also *Johnson*, pp. 36–8. A somewhat heavy theological reading is provided by *Fischer*, pp. 59–65.

The text is based on *WF* but I have lightened the punctuation at times to achieve some of the spontaneity of *M11*. I have not inserted quotation marks as they would lend an inappropriate pedantry to this headlong utterance.

Title In early editions this is the address 'To their Excellencies...' I have borrowed the short title from the running head in *M11*. The Lords Justices were Berkeley and the Earl of Galway (see Biog. Dict.). The opening formula parodies that used in petitions to high authority.

1 Lady Betty Berkeley's daughter: see Biog. Dict., 'Germain', for this longtime friend of Swift.

2 pound] *M11*; pounds *WF*.

4 tell count.

5–7 for Swift's dislike of triplets in a serious context, see *A Description of a City Shower* 61–3.

7 my] *WF*; a *M11*.

17 Lady Betty's chamber she remembered the phrase when writing to Swift almost thirty years later (*Corr* III, 408).

23 Mrs Dukes 'one of the footmen's wives' (note in *WF*).

24 Whittle 'Earl of Berkeley's valet.'

25 Dame Wadgar 'the old deaf housekeeper.'

27 Collway the Earl of Galway.

28 Dromedary 'Drogheda, who with the primate were to succeed the two Earls' (note in *WF*). For the Earl of Drogheda, see Biog. Dict. The 'primate' was not Michael Boyle (d. 1702), but Narcissus Marsh: see *Ehrenpreis*, I, 102.

30 Cary 'clerk of the kitchen.'

32 steward one Ferris: called by Swift 'that beast' (*JTS* I, 133).

Lady Shrewsbury this cannot be Swift's later acquaintance, the Duchess of Shrewsbury, since she did not marry the Duke until 1705 (see Biog. Dict.). It must refer to the widow of the fourteenth Earl, that is, Anna Maria (d. 1702); she had married a courtier named Bridges but continued to be known as Countess of Shrewsbury.

38 three skips of a louse 'an usual saying of hers'. In fact, proverbial: *Tilley* S512.

41 service is no inheritance also proverbial: *Tilley* S253.

43 money can't go without hands alluding to the proverb, 'nothing is stolen without hands' (*Tilley* N304).

45 Bedlam obsolete variant of 'Bedlamite', an inhabitant of Bethlehem Hospital, hence a madman (*Tilley* B199).

called her all to naught abused her.

48 cunning-man a fortune-teller or conjuror.

49 the chaplain Swift.

53 cast a nativity draw up a prediction by horoscope.

54–5 for the rhyme, see *Stella at Woodpark* 21–2.

56 learned divine 'said to be a reference to Dr John Bolton, who through the instrumentality of Bushe was preferred to the Deanery of Derry, which Swift regarded as his due' (*P* I, 72). For this episode, see *Ehrenpreis*, II, 8–14.

61 your coat clerical garb.

68 the] *WF*; my *M11*. Swift made the correction found in *WF* in his copy of *M28*.

come to 'come round to reconciliation...or a pleasant mood' (*OED*, citing this line).

75 shall ever pray this was the concluding formula used in a petition to the King or an official body, just as 'humbly showeth' was the introductory phrase.

A BALLAD ON THE GAME OF TRAFFIC

First published by *F* in 1746, on the supposition it was written in Ireland during the time of Berkeley's period of office as Lord Lieutenant. Internal evidence shows that the scene is Berkeley Castle, in Gloucestershire. Swift paid a visit there in August 1702 and this probably fixes the date of composition. See *P* I, 74, and *Ehrenpreis*, II, 91-2. *Fischer*, pp. 65-72, discusses this and related items.

The text is based on *F* (1746).

Title the game is evidently commerce, although this usage of 'traffic' is not recorded in *OED* or manuals of card games, and has not been identified by previous editors. Commerce 'is a very old-fashioned English card game, and is, perhaps, one of the most primitive of the Poker family' (*Hoyle's Games*). There can be almost any number of players. Cards are discarded and exchanged with the aim of achieving specific hands. The game enjoyed great popularity in the middle of the eighteenth century but later came to be regarded as one for children.

1 My Lord Berkeley.

4 the Doctor Swift (also 'his Honour' in l. 5).

8 Jack Howe see Biog. Dict., 'Howe'.

13 Dame Floyd Ball, p. 52, suggests this might be the mother of Mrs Biddy Floyd (for whom, see *On Mrs Biddy Floyd*).

14 pair-royals now largely a term in cribbage: sets of three cards of the same denomination, as three queens; *sequents* runs of three or more cards in the same suit in numerical order. These are the two hands chiefly sought, with the former counting higher.

16 The castle Berkeley Castle.

17 Herries the heroine of *Mrs Harris's Petition*.

putting cases speculating, putting a hypothetical case.

20 three aces make the best hand of all.

21 Weston a gentlewoman in the Berkeley household.

new-cast refurbished.

23 a crown a coin worth five shillings (that is, 25p); but perhaps Mrs Weston needs a picture-card to complete her hand.

25-8 'Lady Betty Berkeley, finding this ballad in the author's room unfinished, she underwrit the last stanza, and left the paper where she had found it; which occasioned the following song [*A Ballad to the Tune of the Cutpurse*], that the author wrote in a counterfeit hand, as if a third person had done it' (note in *F*). For Lady Betty, see Biog. Dict., 'Germain'.

A BALLAD TO THE TUNE OF THE CUTPURSE

First published in *M11* with an elaborate title: 'Lady B[etty] B[erkeley] finding in the author's room some verses unfinished, underwrit a stanza of her own, with raillery upon him, which gave occasion to this ballad.' The title was retained, with minor changes in typography, in *M28* and *WF*. The explanation was necessary because the previous poem, *A Ballad on the Game of Traffic*, was not included in these collections. The mention of the tune followed the title in the editions cited. There is a contemporary transcript in *TCD*. *M11* gives the date 'August 1702'; *WF* offers 'written in the year 1703'. *M11* is probably right: see headnote to *A Ballad on the Game of Traffic*.

The text here is based on *WF* with corrections from *M11* and *M28*.

Title   the model is a song, 'My Masters and Friends', performed by the ballad-singer Nightingale in Ben Jonson's *Bartholomew Fair* (1614), III, v, 69–128. This was itself a development of the famous tune 'Packington's Pound': see *Simpson*, p. 568, and *An Excellent New Song on a Seditious Pamphlet*.

5   all in the place]   *M11*, *WF*;   at the place   *M28; corrected by Swift in his own copy.*

9   filled up in]   *M28*, *WF*; filled in   *M11*.

12   put me the friar   a kind of redundant 'ethical' dative; probably a conscious archaism on Swift's part.

14   or   *M11*, *M28*;   and *WF*.

28   a dead lift   a hopeless extremity or crisis (obsolete). *Tilley* L271.

30   hand   punning on the sense of 'handwriting'.

THE DESCRIPTION OF A SALAMANDER

First published in *M11*, and reprinted in *M28* and *WF*. There is a contemporary transcript in *TCD*. *M11* dates 'Anno 1705' and *WF* states 'written in the year 1706'. The later date is tentatively supported by *Ehrenpreis*, II, 164.

For Lord Cutts, see Biog. Dict. He had acquired the nickname of 'the salamander' for his bravery under fire at the siege of Namur (1695). Swift, of course, exploits the negative rather than the positive implications of the sobriquet. His dislike for Cutts seems to have been on general grounds of character rather than any particular affront he had received. But whatever the cause of his feelings, they endured; and although he incurred animosity from the general's family (*JTS* II, 393–4), he was still (privately) belabouring Cutts many years later (*PW* V, 261). For comment, see *Ehrenpreis*, II, 162–5. The use of wit is discussed by Martin Price, *Swift's Rhetorical Art* (1953), p. 47.

The text is based on *WF* with occasional reference to *M11*.

Title   ll. 29–36   are abstracted from the *Historia Naturalis* of the elder Pliny, X, 86. Lines 47–56 derive from the same passage along with XXIX, 4. An Elzevir edition of this work was among Swift's books (*Library*, no. 160).

1–2   See for example Francis Coventry's *History of Pompey the Little* (1751).

3   pies and daws   magpies and jackdaws.

9   boar]   *M28*, *WF*;   bear   *M11*.

12   To show]   *WF*;   T'express   *M11*, *M28*.

19   Turenne or Trump   Henri d'Auvergne, Vicomte de Turenne (1611–75), Marshal of France, whose exploits in the Thirty Years' War gave him a huge reputation throughout Europe; Maarten Harpertszoon Tromp (1597–1653), 'Tarpaulin' admiral of the Dutch fleet, who gained successes against the English navy during the first Dutch War (1652).

35, 37   these are the typical degrading comparative devices of mock-epic, borrowed from Homeric formulas.

52   lust]   *WF*;   love   *M11*.

58 claps gonorrhoea.

62 Carleton Mary Carleton (*c.* 1642–73), adventuress and heroine of criminal narratives; committed fraud, theft, and bigamy before being hanged.

Du Ruel the only possible candidate seems to be a dancer named Madame Du Ruel who appeared, together with her husband, in London theatres around 1704–6. She was sufficiently well known to become the subject of a poem printed in a journal on 17 March 1705; the writer pays tribute to her sexual attractions, but (against the drift of Swift's line) regrets her fidelity to 'only one'. See P.H. Highfill *et al.* (eds.), *A Biographical Dictionary of Actors . . . 1660–1800* (1973–   ) IV, 524.

THE HISTORY OF VANBRUG'S HOUSE

For a different satire on Vanbrugh, in two states, see *Vanbrug's House* and Appendix 3. The poem appeared in Curll's shady collection of 1710 (*T* 1, 1A; also *T* 1B, 3). It then appeared more officially in *M11*, *M28*, and *WF*. Swift's autograph copy survives in *MF*; there are also transcripts in *TCD* and the Portland papers. Swift's own dating is 1706, and this seems distinctly more likely than 1708, as given in *M11*. Vanbrugh was already at work on Blenheim Palace by early 1705; he laid the first stone himself at a *fête champêtre* held on 18 June of that year. He had been Comptroller of the Works since 1702, when his architectural background seems to have been confined to the design of Castle Howard, then under construction. See further, Biog. Dict. For the house at Whitehall, see headnote to *Vanbrug's House*.

An echo of this episode occurs in the *Journal* for 7 November 1710: 'Vanburg . . . had a long quarrel with me about those verses on his house; but we were very civil and cold. Lady Marlborough used to tease him with them, which had made him angry, though he be a good-natured fellow' (*JTS* I, 83–4). When Swift first met Vanbrugh is not clear; *P* I, 78 suggests they had been seeing one another in the coffee-houses.

The text here is based on *WF*, but I have borrowed readings from Swift's autograph where the former appears adulterated.

1 Mother Clud not certainly identified.

4 Miss refers to a little girl.

7 lecture reading, or formal instruction.

9 saw] *Swift* (*MF*); viewed *M11*, *WF*.

20 table-book here, clearly, a notebook.

38 Vitruvius Marcus Vitruvius Pollion, Roman architect employed by the Emperor Augustus, whose treatise *De Architectura* exerted a deep influence on Renaissance building.

41 the Duke Marlborough. *taken* pronounced 'ta'en'.

43 the new paragraph is found in *MF* but not in the early printed editions.

46 battering walls attacking fortifications of towns under siege or prepared defences: such as the ramparts and redoubts of the Brabant Lines, penetrated by Marlborough in July 1705 (Correlli Barnett, *Marlborough* (1974), pp. 149–50).

48 engineer not at this time a mechanical or civil engineer but, literally, a 'sapper': an expert in mines and fortifications. Marlborough's chief engineer in this sense was Colonel John Armstrong.

VERSES SAID TO BE WRITTEN ON THE UNION

This poem was first published by *F* in 1746, and there is indeed no other evidence to confirm the attribution to Swift. However, the verses have generally been accepted as authentic and dated around the time of the Union of the English and Scottish parliaments (formally taking effect on 1 May 1707). It could go back to the previous year, when the Union treaty was edging its way through the Scottish parliament. The date 1707 seems likelier, however.

Swift was vehemently opposed to the Union, even before his break with the Whigs (notably Godolphin), whom he saw as its architect. He regarded it as a 'monstrous alliance' with an unregenerate nation under the sway of a fanatical Presbyterian dogmatism (*PW III*, 95; *Tale*, p. 155). He also believed that a Union of England with Ireland would have been more fitting, especially as the established church in Ireland was episcopalian (*PW IX*, 7–8). For further explication, see *Ehrenpreis*, II, 174–5; and *POAS VII*, 283–5.

The text is based on *F* (1746).

1 lost a part probably the support of the Anglo-Irish community, after the rejection of proposals for a Union by the Irish parliament in 1703. *Ball*, pp. 92–3, suspects a reference to the loss of church revenues which Anne had suffered with the setting up of 'Queen Anne's Bounty' in 1704 – a less likely explanation.
3 botch a clumsy patching-up operation.
8 frieze a kind of coarse woollen cloth.
10 'A thistle and a rose grafted on the same stem are represented on the Scottish lion's shield in the union medal' (*POAS VII*, 284). The national emblems.
16 double keel early experiments with the catamaran or twin-hulled ship were notoriously unsuccessful. F.H. Ellis points out (*POAS VII*, 284) that a political projector, Sir William Petty, had been responsible for ill-fated trials of the catamaran in Dublin during Swift's boyhood. He cites the Marquess of Lansdowne, *The Double Bottom or Twin-Hulled Ship of Sir William Petty* (1931).

AN ELEGY ON THE SUPPOSED DEATH OF MR PARTRIDGE,
THE ALMANAC MAKER

The elegy first appeared in broadsides published in London and Edinburgh (*T* 496, 497), with the former probably issued early in April 1708. It subsequently took its place in *M11*, *M28*, and *WF*. The title in the London broadside ran, 'An Elegy on Mr Patrige, the Almanack-maker, who died on the 29th of this Instant March, 1708.' In *M11* this became 'A Grubstreet Elegy on the supposed Death of Patrige the Almanack-maker.' The Grub Street element may be reflected by way of parody in the crude movement of certain lines, for example ll. 12 and 69. *Morgan* K404; *Foxon* S832–3. A modified version, for which Swift can hardly have been responsible, appeared in 1724 (*T* 1647; *Foxon* S834–5).

Swift's satirical campaign against the shoemaker turned astrologer, John Partridge (see Biog. Dict.), began with his *Predictions for the Year 1708*, probably published during February of that year. In this prose pamphlet, Swift foretold the death of Partridge at 11 p.m. on 29 March. Shortly after that date, as a kind of April Fool trick, Swift published the *Accomplishment* of the prediction, gravely recording the circumstances of Partridge's demise. In spite of the victim's denials, the story gained wide credence, and a flurry of sequels and imitations followed. Swift's only subsequent contribution, *A Vindication of Isaac Bickerstaff*, dates from April 1709. The best modern account of the affair is G.P. Mayhew, 'Swift's Bickerstaff Hoax as an April Fools' Joke', *Modern Philology* LXI (1964), 270–80. See also *P* I, 97; *PW* II, *passim*; and *Ehrenpreis*, II, 197–209.

The text is based on *WF* with some reference to the original broadside (*T* 496) and to *M11*. A passage omitted in all editions after 1708 is noted at l. 78.

1   Bickerstaff   Swift's persona lent his name to the assumed author of the *Tatler* when Steele started his paper in April 1709. The origin of the name is not certain. The dramatist Isaac Bickerstaff (1733–?1808) was born in Dublin, where his father was deputy to the Groom Porter (the official controller of gaming and pleasure-houses). However, the family had roots in Lancashire, and had migrated to Antrim in the time of Cromwell. See P.A. Tasch, *The Dramatic Cobbler* (1971); and R.P. Bond, in *Restoration and Eighteenth Century Literature*, ed. C. Camden (1963), pp. 103–8. Partridge believed that the name covered the identity of one 'Pettie', who was 'always either in a cellar, a garret, or a gaol' (*Ehrenpreis*, II, 207): this probably refers to the hack writer William Pittis (1674–1724).

15   Aries   the sign of the zodiac where the sun is on 1 April.

20   'Partridge was a cobbler' (note in early editions).

21   optics   eyes (with possible hint of the alternative meaning, optical glass or telescope).

23   list   a strip of cloth (punning on the sense of catalogue or register).

31   Boötes   the constellation of the Waggoner, which contains the bright star Arcturus. The etymology is really straightforward, from the Greek βοώτης, 'waggoner'. Partridge had actually made the slip mentioned in l. 34.

36   'An allusion to the crescent-shaped clasp on the shoes of patricians' (*P* I, 99).

40   spheres   heavenly bodies considered in their astrological bearing.

41   hung by geometry   in popular usage, 'hanging stiffly'; used thus in *Polite Conversation* (*PW* IV, 159).

42   barometry   'the art or science of barometric observation' (*OED*, citing this line): but probably suggesting more widely the entire process of weather-forecasting.

49   boding   ominous, portending evil.

50   leather   'Made of a substance resembling leather; leather-like. Said especially of the bat's wings... and occasionally of the bat itself' (*OED*, 'leathern').

61   Mercury   compounds of mercury were widely used in medicine, but most of all as a specific against venereal disease (hence the reference in l. 62 to amatory exploits).

63   Lucian   apparently a joke; although there are several references to Philip in Lucian's works, and of course many underworld scenes, none fits the description here.

64   Philip   Philip of Macedon (382–336 B.C.), father of Alexander the Great.

78   artificers   craftsmen; a fanciful way of elevating the shoemakers.

78 ∧ 79]   the following lines, not in *M11* and subsequent editions, brought the main part of the broadside to an end (ll. 79–94 having there followed l. 72):

> But do not shed thy influence down
> Upon St James's end o' the town;
> Consider where the moon and stars
> Have their devoutest worshippers.
> Astrologers and lunatics
> Have in More Fields their stations fix,
> Hither thy gentle aspect bend,
> Nor look asquint on an old friend.

For the superior social cachet of Westminster and St James's, as opposed to the old City of London, see A. Williams, *Pope's Dunciad* (1955), pp. 29–41 ('St James's' implies the Court as well as polite society). For Moorfields, on the northern edge of the city, as a home of the eccentric and outlandish, see *Grub Street*, pp. 44–52; for its topographic and associative links with Bedlam, see pp. 52–6, with several instances from Swift there cited.

81 the Bull the constellation and astrological sign of Taurus.

83 Argo the boat in which Jason went in quest of the Golden Fleece.

   tax perhaps used in the figurative sense of 'put a strain on'.

85 Ariadne] *1708; M11*; Ariadna *WF*. Daughter of Minos, who helped Theseus escape from the labyrinth; later Bacchus placed her crown as a constellation in the heavens.

86 ends OED defines a shoemaker's end as 'a length of thread armed or pointed with a bristle'. There are physiological and sexual connotations to many of the implements mentioned in this verse paragraph.

87 Sagittarius' dart the arrow of the archer Sagittarius, yet another constellation.

89 his wife Venus.

91 Virgo the constellation of the virgin.

92 early editions supply a parallel in the footnotes: '*Tibi brachia contrahet, ingens Scorpius &c.*', that is a slight misquotation of Virgil, *Georgics* I, 34–5: 'The scorpion, ready to receive thy laws, / Yields half his region, and contracts his claws' (tr. Dryden). Swift's text must have read *ingens*, 'huge', for *ardens*.

   strain a point stretch a point (*OED*, 'strain', *v.*[1], 11f), punning on the sense of the point of a needle and on the bawdy sense of penis.

102 his] *WF*; this *1708, M11*.

104 virtue strength, (supernatural) life.

107 physic medical matters; personal health.

VANBRUG'S HOUSE

A draft of this poem in Swift's hand survives in *MF* and is reproduced in Appendix 3. The draft is dated 1703. A revised version, made perhaps around 1708 or 1709, was printed in *M11*, although the date given there is that of the original draft; and in due course the revision appeared in *M28* and *WF*, with the latter supplying a date, '1708'.

As described in the poem *On the Burning of Whitehall in 1698*, a fire in January 1698 (not 1703, as stated in *P* I, 78) destroyed a large part of the palace of Whitehall. It was at first planned that Sir Christopher Wren should design a

sumptuous building to replace it, but the intention was never realized. The drama-
tist Vanbrugh, who had recently turned his attentions to architecture, was given
permission to build himself a lodging, as Controller of the Works, on part of the
site. For a description, plan, and illustration of the so-called 'Goose-Pie House',
see John Summerson, *Architecture in Britain 1530-1830* (rev. edn, 1970),
pp. 275-6. Swift took the occasion to satirize the newly emerged architectural
talents of Vanbrugh, and at the same time reverted to the Ancients and Moderns
dispute (dramatized in the *Battle of the Books*) by making Vanbrugh the type of a
modern writer. *Ball* (pp. 82-91) prints the two versions side by side. For a sepa-
rate poem directed against Vanbrugh, see *The History of Vanbrug's House*. For
extended analysis, see *Fischer*, pp. 75-95.
   The text is based on *WF*, collated with *M11*.

Title   Swift pronounced the architect's name either 'Vanbroog' or 'vanbrooj'.
11   catch   a comic song, generally in the form of a round.
20   undertakers   contractors, entrepreneurs.
23   the god of wealth   Plutus; hinting at the fortunes spent on such palaces as
Blenheim (at the public expense) and Castle Howard, which Vanbrugh had
designed for the Whig aristocracy.
26   build castles   for the proverbial 'castles in the air', see *Tilley* C126. Compare
Upon the South Sea Project 173.
30   have]   *WF*; had   *M11*.
34   herald   Vanbrugh was installed in the revived office of Carlisle Herald in
March 1703, as a step towards his appointment as Clarenceux King of Arms a
year later. This was a reward for services rendered to his patron, the third Earl
of Carlisle. Heraldic learning, of which Vanbrugh had none, and his principal
rivals had an abundance, did not enter into the question.
38   house   family, dynastic line.
39   achievement   hatchment, armorial ensign.
   device   a heraldic device (with covert sense of 'trickery').
42   speculation   the sense of 'financial scheming' was only just emerging at this
date, but may possibly be present as well as the meaning of 'fantasy', 'poetic
musing'.
52   his]   *WF*; the   *M11*.
58   a French play   taken by *P* I, 107 as a general reference, but it is more likely
that Swift had a particular play in mind. Since ll. 53-120 are not in the 1703
version (see Appendix 3), any of Vanbrugh's adaptations from Molière, Dan-
court, and Boursault are potentially candidates. *Fischer*, pp. 91-2, argues for
The Country House (1698), an adaptation of *La Maison de Campagne* (1688) by
Florent-Carton Dancourt. One difficulty is that Vanbrugh's play has only two
acts.
60   smoke   to suspect (a plot or design), to get a scent of something. See *Tilley*
S577.
62   bite   a humorous trick, hoax, or practical joke: for this newly fashionable
mode of joking deception, see *Corr* I, 40 (Swift to Tisdall, 16 December 1703).
66   see Genesis xi.
79ff.   it is just possible that Swift also has in mind the new 'house', that is, the
Queen's Theatre in the Haymarket. Vanbrugh had taken a leading part in its
planning and construction, from 1703 until its opening in 1705, when he and
Congreve jointly assumed the management. The New Opera House, as it was

also called, was certainly not tiny or inelegant; but it was the 'pile' where modern drama (including Vanbrugh's later plays) had its current home.

94 that is, a 'necessary house' or privy.

105 Thither] *WF, following Swift's Ms correction in M28*; farther *M11*.

114 tilt an awning over a boat.

117 for Swift's ideas regarding the accommodation of English wits, see also *Tale*, pp. 41–2; and the apocryphal items *A Letter to a Young Poet* and *A Serious and Useful Scheme*, discussed in *Grub Street*, pp. 259–68.

119–20 Semele, the mother of Bacchus, was killed by lightning when her lover, Jove, appeared before her as the god of thunder; as she died, she gave birth prematurely to Bacchus. See Ovid, *Metamorphoses* III, 259–315.

127 chemists the word 'chymist' (as in the original) evolved naturally into the modern 'chemist', but it still carried overtones of alchemy at this date. It suggests one skilled in medicinal herbs and drugs, rather than one who studies gases and reagents.

130 virtue medicinal properties.

131 blast a typical Swiftian usage: implying (1) ruin, destroy; (2) bring infamy upon; (3) visit with a curse.

ON MRS BIDDY FLOYD

Published in Tonson's *Miscellany* (1709), together with a Latin version, and by Curll in the same year (*T* 520, 518). The poem's appearance in *M11* was both preceded and followed by other Curll printings, in various company. It was also included in *M28* and *WF*. There are contemporary transcripts in *TCD* and the Portland papers, all containing an 'Answer' here assumed not to be Swift's work. *M11* dates 1708, *WF* a year earlier. We know that Swift was in contact with Mrs Floyd early in 1709 (*Corr* I, 121) and this may be the approximate time of composition.

Mrs Floyd was a companion of Lady Betty Germain, and something of a beauty: Swift speaks of her as 'the famous Mrs Floyd of Chester, who, I think, is the handsomest woman [except the recipients] that ever I saw'. He continues, 'She told me, that twenty people had sent her the verses upon Biddy, as meant to her: and indeed, in point of handsomeness, she deserves them much better' (*JTS* II, 382). For brief comments, see *Ehrenpreis*, II, 308–9.

The text is substantially that of *WF*.

Title editions prior to *M28* have *To Mrs Biddy Floyd*.

1 grandsire Cupid's father, Mercury, was the son of Jove: his mother, Venus, according to some traditions, was the daughter of Jove.

7 the Graces the three sister-goddesses who bestowed beauty and charm.

10 nice finicky, over-fastidious or difficult.

   coquette an adjective.

APOLLO OUTWITTED

Published successively in the main collections, *M11*, *M28*, and *WF*. *M11* dates 1709, a more likely year than 1707 as supplied by *WF*. In a letter of 12 January 1712 Swift writes, 'I amuse myself sometimes with writing verses to Mrs Finch', and these are the only extant lines which fit the description (*Corr* I, 121).

For Anne Finch, Countess of Winchilsea, see Biog. Dict. In due course she was prevailed on to allow the appearance of *Miscellany Poems, Written by a Lady* (1713). This contained the well-known *Petition for an Absolute Retreat*, as well as verse epistles written in the guise of 'Ardelia'. Pope refers to her under this name in a poem of *c.* 1714 (*PTE* VI, 120). See the edition of Lady Winchilsea's poems by Myra Reynolds (1903).

The text is based on *WF* with some reference to *M11*.

2 Northern Tropic literally, the Tropic of Cancer; figuratively, northern climes.

4 Mrs Finch had been maid of honour to Mary of Modena, the wife of James II, while she was Duchess of York.

7 bays the sacred shrub of Apollo, a wreath of which was worn as an amulet against lightning. See *On Paddy's Character of 'The Intelligencer'* 12.

12 Ardelia's eyes see headnote.

18 Styx the river encircling the infernal regions. For the oath, compare Pope, *The First Book of Statius His Thebais* (1712), 411–13: 'For by the black infernal Styx I swear, / (That dreadful oath which binds the thunderer) / 'Tis fixed; the irrevocable doom of Jove' (*PTE* I, 427).

21 Ovid had warned her in the *Metamorphoses*, ubiquitously. An edition of this work (Venice, 1493) was in Swift's collection: *Library*, no. 623. It was perhaps the major imaginative influence upon his poetry.

30 the nine the muses, patronesses of the arts.

39 Thalia the muse of pastoral and of comedy (the former is more applicable to Mrs Finch's poetry).

44 made his leg bowed.

47 Pallas Minerva, who presided over all the arts.

57 thou be] *M11, WF*; be thou *M28* (*but corrected by Swift in his copy*).

59 Echo a nymph who was deprived of the power of speech, except to repeat the words of others. See Ovid, *Metamorphoses* III, 358–401.

64 Whig the word was first supplied in *M28*. With her background in James's household, and non-juring husband, Lady Winchilsea would be likely to gravitate to the High Church, or Tory, party. Swift was identified with the Whigs until about 1710. We know that around 1708 Lady Winchilsea played piquet with Swift (*Ehrenpreis*, II, 306).

BAUCIS AND PHILEMON

This popular poem had already been before the public a number of times before its inclusion in *M11*. As well as an appearance in Tonson's *Miscellany* of 1709 (*T 520*), it saw various Curll printings from the same year (*T* 1, 1A, 1B, 3, 518–19), and other piracies (*T* 516, 521–2; *Foxon* S800–803).

All these printed texts derive from a revision made by Swift at the instigation of Joseph Addison, probably around 1708, soon after the two men had met. According to a later report, Swift had said that Addison made him 'blot out four score, add four score, and alter four score' lines. The original draft, apparently incomplete, survives in Swift's autograph (*MF*) and is reprinted in Appendix 3. For the making of the two poems and their relationship, see *Ball*, pp. 66–81 (parallel texts); *P* I, 88–90; and *Ehrenpreis*, II, 243–8. The poem is also discussed by *Johnson*, pp. 89–92, stressing the surrealist and grotesque aspects; by

Jaffe, pp. 66–8, drawing attention to a 'humour and cynicism' felt to be absent from contemporary versions of Ovid, such as Dryden's 'unremittingly grandiose' translation; and by Martin Price, *Swift's Rhetorical Art* (1953), pp. 45–6, also contrasting Swift with Dryden and concluding that 'the method shows with debasing wit that high is after all the same as low'. The fullest reading is that of Eric Rothstein, 'Jonathan Swift as Jupiter: "Baucis and Philemon"', *The Augustan Milieu*, ed. H.K. Miller *et al.* (1970), pp. 205–24. Rothstein deals briefly with the revision and with the relationship to Dryden, but his central concern is what Swift makes of the Ovidian tradition. He sees the 'universe of discourse' within the poem as 'an unthinking materiality'; and he shows how the revised poem differs from the normal burlesque Ovid which had evolved in the seventeenth century. A number of folk-tale elements are also identified. Rothstein's account is endorsed by *Fischer*, pp. 72–5.

The poem is loosely based on a story in Ovid, *Metamorphoses* VIII, 626–724, which recounts a visit to the earth made by Jupiter and Apollo in disguise. Swift follows the main lines of the narrative but anglicizes the detail. The folk element in style and allusion derives from Prior's free treatment of the same story in *The Ladle* (1704). Swift's opening lines answer directly to the start of *The Ladle*: 'The sceptics think, 'twas long ago, / Since Gods came down *incognito*, / To see who were their friends or foes' (*Prior*, I, 202); the same writer's 'Observations on Ovid's *Metamorphoses*' are also relevant. See *Prior*, I, 202–7; 663–73.

The text is in the main based on *WF*, though it should be noted that *M11*'s heading 'written in the year 1706' may indicate the date of the original draft.

1   story   history, though here perhaps 'legend'.

10   village   Swift's draft in *MF* has 'a village hard by Rixham'. There is no such village in Kent, and indeed Wrexham is the closest phonetic approximation of any British place-name. If Swift did have Kent in mind, it is possible he meant Wrotham: in 1708 he had stayed at Harrietsham, near Maidstone, and would almost certainly have travelled to and from London (or Epsom) via Wrotham. See *Corr* I, 102 for Swift's letter, and Williams's conjecture regarding 'Havisham'. The identification has been confirmed by Professor J.M. Treadwell, in a private communication. One of the piracies (*T* 521) refers to 'the parish of Chilthorne, near the county town of Somerset'. This must mean Chilthorne Dormer, not far from Somerton; but there are no reasons for supposing this to be in any way reliable. A Curll or a Hills was capable of plucking intriguing names out of the air to make a better title-page.

19   yeoman   *WF* spells it 'ye'man', which indicates the survival of a pronunciation allowing the rhyme with Philemon. See *OED*, 'yeoman', headnote.

24   Goody   short for 'goodwife', an obsolete word for mistress or the title Mrs.

25   the]   *WF*; of *M11*.

32   was]   *WF*; is *M11*.

38   What art!   an uncertain reading: early editions offer 'What ar't!', as well as 'What art?'. Swift, in his copy of *F* (1737), wrote in the margin 'Wha art'. *WF* is followed as a matter of editorial policy but is no more satisfactory.

40   burning blue   a pale candle flame, supposed to indicate the presence of evil spirits.

42   errand   spelt 'errant' in early texts, which explains the rhyme.

65   jack   a device for operating the spit on which meat was roasted: see Rothstein, op. cit., p. 216, for the details of this contraption.

71   which] *WF; not in M11 or early edns.*   The syntax is confused either way, but the movement seems easier with the *WF* reading.

74   Can hardly move] *WE*;   Now hardly moves   *M11*.

85   was seen] *WF*;   began   *M11*.

86   half up] *WF*;   along   *M11*.

89   porringers   small basins.

94–6   famous folk ballads commonly printed as chapbooks, with crude woodcut illustrations. Line 94 is an adaptation of Butler's *Hudibras* I, ii, 368.   *English Moll*   Mary Ambree, one of the female soldiers popular in folk legend.   *Fair Rosamond*   Rosamond Clifford (d. 1176?), mistress of Henry II, heroine of one of the best-known ballads.   *Children in the wood*   possibly based on a melodramatic tragedy of 1599; termed by Addison, *Spectator*, no. 85, 'one of the darling songs of the common people'. Several of these ballads were cited by John Gay in his *Shepherd's Week* (1714) and most appeared in Percy's *Reliques* (1765). For fuller details, see *Simpson*, pp. 98–9, 103–5, 608–10.

100   in country churches the twelve tribes of Israel were sometimes distinguished by their ensigns (*P* I, 114, quoting Hawkesworth).

103   grandsires wont to] *WF*;   ancestors did use   *M11*.

109   desire] *WF*;   desired   *M11*.

120   pudding-sleeve   a loose, bulging sleeve drawn in at the wrist.

128   Vamped in   furbished up.

134   right divine   the divine right of kings: the belief that kings rule by divine ordinance, and not by the will of the people. It was traditionally upheld by the lesser clergy.

139   coifs   close-fitting skullcaps, rather like a nightcap.

140   pinners   coifs with straps hanging down on either side, worn by women of rank.

colbertine   a kind of open-work lace of French origin.

143   down   be good enough ('go' is understood).

144   grogram   a fabric of silk, sometimes mixed with mohair and wool; see Rothstein, op. cit., p. 219.

148   admired   wondered.

150   the] *WF*; this *M11*.

154   fetch] *WF*;   take   *M11*.   ('Fetch a walk' was used up to the nineteenth century and is perfectly appropriate.)

158   jealous   the cuckold was supposed to sprout a horn on his forehead.

165   Goodman   a yeoman, but here equivalent to 'Mr'.

'IN PITY TO THE EMPTYING TOWN'

These lines were first printed by John Forster in 1875, shorn of the last stanza. They survive in Swift's hand in *MF*. It is highly probable, but not quite certain, that they were written by Swift himself. The reference to Worsley (l. 20) suggests that they were written before that lady's marriage to Lord Carteret in 1710; and the allusion to Ardelia (l. 19) has suggested to previous editors a date of composition near 1709, by alignment with *Apollo Outwitted*.

The text is based on *MF*.

1   emptying town   in the first half of May, when the fair was held, many of the gentry would be leaving for the country, or would just have left.

2   May Fair   a charter was granted in 1688 for the fair to be held for fifteen days from 1 May. It was held around the modern Shepherd's Market area, and indeed the present-day Mayfair district takes its name from the event. It was never a trading fair, but exclusively an occasion for entertainments and sideshows. Suppressed in 1708 by the Grand Jury of Westminster, it was revived for a time in the 1740s. For the shows put on there, see Sybil Rosenfeld, *The Theatre of the London Fairs in the 18th Century* (1960), ch. vi. For Swift's interest in fairground drolls and puppet shows, see P. Rogers, 'Swift, Walpole, and the Rope-Dancers', *Papers on Language & Literature* VIII (1972), 159–71, together with sources listed there.

9–12   the Scriblerian group habitually saw popular culture as inverting true standards, and in their work drolls often figure as fantastic exhibitions of the world upside down. See especially *Peri Bathous*, ch. v, and Pope, *The Dunciad* (1743), I, 55–78; III, 231–48.

19   Ardelia   Anne Finch; see *Apollo Outwitted*, headnote.

20   Worsley   Frances Worsley: see Biog. Dict., 'Carteret'.

21   a lucky hit   see *The Fable of Midas* 23.

21–4   obscure: there are corrections on the MS, not in Swift's hand. However, 'honest Harry' (l. 23) is almost certainly Henry Worsley, the younger brother of Frances's father, and it seems likely that the family were exchanging verses with Swift, perhaps while he was in London in 1708.

A DESCRIPTION OF THE MORNING

These verses appeared in the ninth number of the *Tatler*, on 30 April 1709, a fortnight after Steele had inaugurated his journal. The poem duly came out in *M11* and *M27*, and ultimately in *WF*. There is a transcript in *TCD*. It was one of the earliest examples of the so-called town eclogue or urban pastoral: according to Steele, it described 'the morning in town; nay . . . the morning at this end of the town', that is, the West End. For analysis of the technique, see *Ehrenpreis*, II, 248–50. For the ironic use of a classical *descriptio* framework, see Roger Savage, 'Swift's Fallen City', *The World of Jonathan Swift*, ed. Brian Vickers (1968), pp. 171–94. Briefer analysis of the 'factual' aspect of the poem, involving comparison with Dickens and T.S. Eliot, occurs in David Ward, *Jonathan Swift: An Introductory Essay* (1973), pp. 185–8. See also *Johnson*, pp. 10–15; *Jaffe*, pp. 75–8.

I have based the text on *WF*, disregarding the absurd dating of 1712.

1   an 'ugly, asthmatic first line' (*Johnson*, p. 14).

9–10   'to find old nails' (note in *WF*).
   kennel-edge gutter.

11   smallcoal   what we simply term 'coal' today; it was hawked in the streets. Louis A. Landa, in his edition of *Gulliver's Travels and Other Writings* (1960), p. 550, remarks that 'any reader of this poem would almost certainly think of Thomas Britton (d. 1714). Swift may have had him in mind . . . He held musical concerts at his shop [in a back street off Clerkenwell Green] for 40 years, attended by noted artists (as Handel and Pepusch) and titled aristocrats. He was also a book collector, particularly interested in the occult sciences.' There was actually a song about him: 'Come hear me fiddle, read my books, / Or buy my smallcoal, maids.' Compare also Gay, *Trivia* II, 35 (*Gay*, I, 144).

13 Duns bailiffs acting as debt-collectors.
14 Brickdust tanned; such a complexion was then a mark of the labouring classes as against the white skin of the gentry. Moll may have been vending powdered brick.
15–16 prisoners were let out to obtain money to pay their gaolers, who were entitled to extract fees for granting privileges, such as superior accommodation.
18 Ehrenpreis, II, 250 notes three parallels: Horace, *Satires* I, vi, 73–5; Juvenal, *Satires* X, 117; Shakespeare, *As You Like It* II, vii, 145–7.

ON THE LITTLE HOUSE BY THE CHURCHYARD OF CASTLEKNOCK

First published by *F* in 1746, vol. VIII. Another text, with two significantly different passages, appears in *Brett's Miscellany*, vol. II (1752). It is conjectured in *P* I, 125 that 'Brett's variants and additional lines were part of Swift's original draft, subsequently discarded by him. Faulkner, apparently, printed from a revised and abbreviated manuscript.' This is a possible explanation but it cannot be regarded as certain: it is conceivable that someone else (perhaps even the editor, Peter Brett, who was himself parish clerk of Castleknock) was responsible for the alterations. Deane Swift put the date of composition as 1710, and later editors have accepted this. It seems to me that it may have been written after Swift's return to Ireland in 1714. He was still in touch with the people mentioned in the poem; and indeed Stella spent long periods in the Walls household from about 1714. Swift was much preoccupied by his willows at Laracor, and even after he became Dean of St Patrick's retained a paternalist supervision of all planting and lopping operations (see the concluding couplet). However, the evidence is not strong enough to overturn the conventional dating. For Swift's period in Dublin over 1709/10, see *Ehrenpreis*, II, 350–79.
The text is that of *F* (1746), with important variants in *Brett* recorded.

Title The 'little house' was the vestry at Castleknock, a parish to the north-west of Dublin, now a suburb just beyond Phoenix Park (made a public park after Swift's death).
3 poet Joe Joseph Beaumont (see Biog. Dict.): he is mentioned in the very first phrase of the *Journal to Stella* and was one of Swift's closest friends at this period. According to Deane Swift, he was prematurely grey.
10 Light a preterite form: 'alighted'.
18 Walls Thomas Walls, a close friend of Swift (see Biog. Dict.). For Swift's efforts on his behalf, see *Landa*, pp. 79–82.
19–22] *F* (1746);

> The vicar once a week walks in,
> Waiting the service to begin.
> Here cons his notes, and takes a whet
> With Dunn his clerk, when in they get,
> Waiting until the flock is met. *Brett.*

Williams explains (*P* I, 125) that 'Dunn' was Jemmy Dunn, a former parish clerk of Castleknock.
21 cons studies, learns up by heart.
  whet a dram, a short appetizer or chaser.

35 Warburton Thomas Warburton (see Biog. Dict.).

37 Or . . . or either . . . or. In fact, a pigeon-house is shown not far from the church on John Rocque's map, *An Actual Survey of the County of Dublin* (1760).

39 Mrs Johnson 'a friend of the author's' (note in *F*). For Stella as a house-guest of the Walls family, see *Corr* V, 237–8.

43 Raymond Anthony Raymond (see Biog. Dict.).

55–8] Brett substitutes fourteen lines:

> The clerk immediately did come,
> His name, I think, is Jemmy Dunn,
> And when to her he had appeared,
> He thought the lady had him jeered,
> And cries, 'God mend me', in a heat,
> 'What! sell the vicar's country seat,
> Where he comes every week from town,
> I would not sell it for a crown:
> I'll sooner preach within Christ Church,
> Than leave the vicar in the lurch;
> Or give from him one single brick,
> Madam, you touch me to the quick.
> I cannot now consent to this,
> Nor give this house to little Miss.'

'Christ Church' is the cathedral of that name in Dublin.

61 Nancy 'the waiting woman' (*F*).

63 The Dean if the poem was written in 1710, this refers to John Stearne (see Biog. Dict.); if around 1714/15, to Swift himself. For the relations between the two men, see *Landa*, p. 179.

THE VIRTUES OF SID HAMET THE MAGICIAN'S ROD

There were editions in 1710 published in London, Dublin (both *T* 524), and Edinburgh (not in *T*). Of these the original was undoubtedly the broadsheet issued by John Morphew in London. Swift began his 'lampoon' on 26 September 1710, but, as he told Stella, it went on 'very slow'. He worked on it in stages for over a week, and sent it to the printer on 4 October. It was published before 14 October, when Swift reported that 'my lampoon is cried up to the skies' (*JTS* I, 30–59). The Edinburgh edition was not listed in *P* or *T*; it is however, used by F.H. Ellis in *POAS* VII, 473–9. *Foxon* S935–7.

For the object of this attack, Lord Godolphin, see Biog. Dict. Swift had called on him as soon as he arrived in London early in September. He received a cold reception (*Corr* I, 173) and began his plans for retaliation on 9 September (*JTS* I, 6). The outgoing minister was a ripe subject for satire, even without Swift's accusations of personal ingratitude; and he was able to incorporate a number of his private grudges, such as the Union with Scotland (see *Verses Said to be Written on the Union*). For his title and leading idea, Swift went to a recent periodical on the model of the *Tatler*, called *The Visions of Sir Heister Ryley*, in which Charles Povey had attacked a pseudo-prophet with a piece on 'the virtue of James Aymar's wand'. For background, see *POAS* VII, 474 (exhaustive annotation

will be found with the text on pp. 475–9), and *Ehrenpreis*, II, 387–8. One of the fullest discussions is A.B. England, 'The Subversion of Logic in Some Poems of Swift', *Studies in English Literature 1500–1900* XV (1975), 413–16.
The text is based on *WF*, collated with Morphew (1710) and *MII*.

1   rod   'The basic device is . . . a parallelism: rods celebrated in scripture, myth, and fiction are compared with Godolphin's white staff of office [as Lord Treasurer], which by the Queen's request he had not returned but had broken when he lost his place as Lord Treasurer' (*Ehrenpreis*, II, 388). This latter event took place on 8 August 1710.

2   Moses   see Exodus iv, 2–3.

5   Hamet Sid   Swift combines Godolphin's Christian name, Sidney, with that of the supposed Arabic author of *Don Quixote*, Cid Hamet Benengeli, described by Cervantes as 'an Arabian' and therefore *not* 'exact, sincere and impartial; free from passion and not to be biased' (II, i: tr. Motteux).

22   magic rod   the divining rod, usually made of a forked branch of hazel or willow, supposed to find water or minerals hidden beneath the ground.

28   golden mines   there were still hopes of finding substantial gold deposits in Britain, as Defoe mentioned when his tour reached Malvern; the mountainous districts of Wales and Scotland were thought of as the likeliest place. Swift may also be associating Godolphin with corrupt mine-company projectors like the notorious Sir Humphrey Mackworth (1657–1727), for whose career see *DNB*.

29   Scottish hills   alluding to the Union: see *POAS* VII, 476.

32   cully   dupe.

35   rod of Hermes   the wand of Hermes or Mercury, styled *caduceus*, whose enchantment rested on its power to occasion sleep: Milton calls it Hermes' 'opiate rod' (*Paradise Lost* XI, 133).

35–42   implying that Godolphin managed parliament through graft.

45   place   a government or court office, frequently a sinecure: in general, such positions did not disqualify the holder from sitting in parliament, and he was expected to pay for his appointment with his vote.

46   many a score]   *WF*;   many score   *Morphew, MII*.

59–70   the sceptre was that of Agamemnon: see *Iliad* I, 234–9.

64   heirloom   for its transmission, see *Iliad* II, 101–8. The innuendo is that Godolphin came to power through his connection with the Marlborough family: his son had married the Duke's eldest daughter and heiress, Henrietta.

72   golden boughs   recalling the golden bough of myth, which figures in Book VI of the *Aeneid*: see *A Panegyric on the Dean* 307. The blossoming bough also recalls Aaron's rod (Numbers xviii, 8).

73–4   a dragon named Ladon which never slept was posted to guard the golden apples given to Juno as a marriage gift and kept by the three Hesperides. Hercules killed the dragon as the eleventh of his twelve labours.

76   Charles Mather   see Biog. Dict.

77   May Fair   see '*In Pity to the Emptying Town*' 2.

80   Godolphin was in fact instructed to do so by the Queen.

81   kissed it   for 'kiss the rod', see *Verses on the Death of Dr Swift* 217.

82   your mistress   the Queen.

83   a Newmarket switch   alluding to Godolphin's proclivity for horse-racing, and his particular fondness for Newmarket. *POAS* cites evidence that he had been there as recently as April 1710 when his ministry was beginning finally to crumble.

84 rod for thy own breech the proverb was usually phrased more delicately ('back' or 'tail'), but the meaning is the same. *Tilley* R153.
86 rod in piss a low version of 'rod in pickle', a punishment in store. *Tilley* R157 gives the more and less respectable forms.

A DIALOGUE BETWEEN CAPTAIN TOM
AND SIR HENRY DUTTON COLT

There are two editions, both dated 1710; one is said in the colophon to be 're-printed' and may be a Dublin piracy. The other broadside probably represents the authentic version: Swift went to his bookseller, Benjamin Tooke, on 7 October to give him a ballad and refers to its currency on 20 October (*JTS* I, 46, 65). There are variant states of the supposedly authentic edition: see *POAS* VII, 682. Composition evidently was going on around 6 October (*JTS* I, 43). The work was not subsequently reprinted and was not identified as Swift's until 1957. The fullest account is that of George P. Mayhew, 'Swift's Political "Conversion" and his "Lost" Ballad on the Westminster Election of 1710', *Bulletin of the John Rylands Library* LIII (1971), 397–427.
   Morgan M178; *Foxon* D255–7.
   Writs for a new parliament were issued on 26 September 1710 and the stage was set for the great Tory triumph. The Westminster constituency, which had an unusually wide franchise and hence a volatile character, had seen a minor riot at the last election of 1708, and it was therefore no surprise that there were unruly scenes, one of which Swift witnessed on the morning of 5 October (*JTS* I, 42). The two Tory candidates were a sitting member, Thomas Medlycott, and Thomas Crosse, a wealthy brewer. They were opposed by a former M.P., Sir Henry Dutton Colt, and the famous general, James Stanhope (see Biog. Dict. for these men). Stanhope was in fact still abroad on military duty and stood through a proxy. Polling ended on 9 October, when the ballad may well have appeared, and the returns showed the next day a landslide victory for the Tories, with Colt at the bottom of the poll. Apart from his personal observation of the events, Swift may have been drawn to comment on the election by an item in the *Whig Examiner* on 28 September, supporting Stanhope's candidature. Mayhew, *Bulletin*, p. 409, and Frank H. Ellis, *POAS* VII, 481, attribute this item to Arthur Maynwaring, though it may have been the work of Joseph Addison. Ellis detects a number of verbal hints for the poem in the *Whig Examiner* article.
   The text is based on the supposed London printing (second state), collated with the 'reprinted' text in *TR*. In all the early editions the text is set in half-lines (thus 'the dialogue write' forms l. 2): I have restored the lines to their full length.

3 Sir Harry Sir Henry Dutton Colt (see Biog. Dict.). He was about sixty-five. Ellis, *POAS* VII, 483, recounts some of his curious career.
6 Stanhope For the general, then in Spain, see Biog. Dict. For these shouts, see *JTS* I, 42.
8 brewer Thomas Crosse (see Biog. Dict.).
   cross-grained uncooperative. Swift mentions the heavy concentration of puns in writing to Stella on 20 October (*JTS* I, 65).
10 molosses an old form of 'molasses', retained for the sake of the rhyme: 'molasses beer' was a fomented liquid, flavoured with molasses (*OED*).

13   faggots   used figuratively to mean the burning of a heretic; stock phrases were 'fire and faggot' and 'to fry a faggot'.

14   Furnese   Sir Henry Furnese (see Biog. Dict.). For his reputation with the Tories, see P. Rogers, 'Matthew Prior, Sir Henry Furnese and the Kit-Cat Club', *Notes & Queries* XVIII (1971), 46–9. There is a pun on 'furnace'.

16   laurels   for his victories in Spain. Stanhope was to suffer a major setback at Brihuega in December of this same year. The pun is emphasized by the spelling 'Stanhop' in the broadside printing.

19–26   Colt was a notorious gambler, as was Stanhope.

20   tale of a tub   the traditional phrase for a cock-and-bull story, given further resonance by Swift's own satire (1704). *Tilley* T45.

22   bate you an ace   for this proverbial expression, see *Another Reply by the Dean* 2; *Tilley* A20.

24   shuffle, and cut   a common expression implying trickery (see *OED*, 'shuffle', 2b, citing uses by Congreve and Ned Ward amongst others). To *cut it away* meant to make off or run away.

25   Colt notably lacked all these attributes.

26   clubs   *POAS* VII, 485 notes that many of the election mob carried staves. There may also be the sense of a society meeting for convivial or political ends.

28   a lord   Stanhope did not receive his peerage until 1717, from George I.

29   Sacheverell   see Biog. Dict.

30   manager   one of the prosecutors when Sacheverell was brought before the House of Lords in March 1710: Stanhope had taken a prominent role in the proceedings. See Geoffrey Holmes, *The Trial of Dr Sacheverell* (1973), pp. 135–43.

32   coolers   a cooling drink.

34   bear ours   support the Tory candidate, Crosse: *POAS* VII, 486 quotes a contemporary account to the effect that 'Crosse's men kept on making crosses with their hands'. Punning on the sense of 'coping with a burden'.

35   engross   to buy up (land or a commodity) so as to gain a monopoly. The Tory idea of what contractors such as Furnese were attempting to do.

36   perhaps remembering the stock phrase 'no cross, no crown', used as the title of a book by William Penn. *Tilley* C839.

37   old Numps   'a silly or stupid person' (*OED*).

38   a bad game   a poor hand: this line is the culmination of a long series of puns based on cards (spade, club, discarded, face, ace, pack, shuffle, cut, clubs, hearts, trumps). For 'bad game' see also Swift's *Journal* entry on the day prior to the ballad's composition (*JTS* I, 43).

    turn up trumps   *Tilley* T544.

39   eggs they are addled   probably recalling the proverb, 'You come with your five eggs a penny, and four of them addle' (*Tilley* E92), which is quoted in *Polite Conversation* (*PW* IV, 142) and in the *Journal* (*JTS* I, 58).

    dough was his cake   his project had failed (proverbial): *Tilley* C12.

40   brew as they bake   let them reap what they have sown (proverbial): *Tilley* B654.

A DESCRIPTION OF A CITY SHOWER

First published in the *Tatler*, no. 238, on 17 October 1710. It appears in *M11*, *M28*, and *WF*; there is a contemporary transcript in *TCD*. It was in a way a topical piece, having been written between 10 October (or just before) and 13

October, when he had already dispatched the verses to the *Tatler*. The opening lines were apparently written last (*JTS* I, 50–56). It was one of Swift's favourites among his own poems. The allusion to traditional pastoral properties is more thoroughgoing than in the *Description of the Morning*, and indeed *M*28 subtitled the poem an 'imitation of Virgil's Georg[ics]'. See *Ehrenpreis*, II, 384–7, for a useful tabulation of the echoes, overt or submerged, of Virgil, Dryden, and others. An interesting commentary is provided by Brendan O Hehir, 'The Meaning of Swift's *Description of a City Shower*', *ELH* XXVII (1960), 194–207. See also A.B. England, 'The Subversion of Logic in Some Poems of Swift', *Studies in English Literature 1500–1900* XV (1975), 410–12; *Johnson*, pp. 85–9; *Jaffe*, pp. 79–82; and *Fischer*, pp. 95–109, whose account relates the poem to patristic exegesis of the biblical Flood.

The text is based on *WF* but with some reference to *M11*.

3   *depends*   is imminent.

5–6   *P* I, 137 cites Swift to Stella on 8 November 1710: 'I'll give ten shillings a week for my lodging; for I am almost stunk out of this with the sink, and it helps me to verses in my *Shower*' (*JTS* I, 87).

5   *you*]   *WF*; you'll *M11*.
    sink   sewer.

8   that Swift was careful with small sums of money is attested by a wide range of evidence, including the *Journal*; see, for example, the entry for 26 October 1710, ''Tis plaguy twelve-penny weather this last week, and has cost me ten shillings in coach and chair hire' (*JTS* I, 73).

9   *shooting*   beset by a sudden darting pain.

10   *aches*   pronounced 'aitches'.

12   *spleen*   a word of rich connotation, ranging from 'melancholia' to 'ennui', and covering most of the modern depressive conditions. The *locus classicus* is the Cave of Spleen in Pope's *Rape of the Lock* (1714), IV, 17–88.

15–16   compare *The Tempest* II, ii, 21–2.

19   *quean*   hussy, harlot.

20   *Flirts*   flicks.

26   *WF* indicates in a note the parallel with Garth's *Dispensary* (1st edn, 1699), V, 176: ''Tis doubtful which is sea, and which is sky.' Swift owned a copy of this book, with his own annotations in the text (*Library*, no. 462).

29–30]   *WF*; His only coat, where dust confused with rain,/Roughen the nap, and leave a mingled stain. *M11*.

32   *devoted*   doomed (highfalutin').

33   *daggled*   bespattered: a favourite word of Swift's.

34   *cheapen*   bargain, ask a price for.

35   *abroach*   awash, streaming.
    templar   law student at the Inns of Court.

41   'This was the first year of the Earl of Oxford's ministry' (note in *WF*). Indeed, Harley had been in power only a few weeks when the poem was written.

43   *chair*   sedan-chair.

47–52   See *Aeneid* II, 40–56.

49   *bully*   then a strong word: it could mean 'hired ruffian' or even 'pimp'. Swift may have in mind gangs of rowdy young men, like the Mohocks who came to notice some eighteen months later. For a similar reference, see Gay's *Trivia* (1716), III, 254. Gay's poem owes a considerable amount to this *Description*.

53   *kennels*   gutters.

58 *St Pulchre's* St Sepulchre's Church in Holborn. Smithfield market was already long established, and would send a large quantity of offal down towards the Fleet Ditch, where it would be joined by the garbage floating down the Snow Hill stream. For the topography, see O Hehir's article and *Grub Street*, pp. 37–8, 252–3. Again there is a parallel in *Trivia* (III, 330): 'from Snow Hill black steepy torrents run.'

60 *Holborn Bridge* it spanned the notorious Fleet Ditch, for which see *Grub Street*, pp. 145–66.

61–3 'These three last lines were intended against that licentious manner of modern poets, in making three rhymes together, which they call *triplets*; and the last of the three, was two or sometimes more syllables longer, called an [alexandrine]. These triplets and [alexandrines] were brought in by Dryden, and other poets in the reign of Charles II. They were the mere effect of haste, idleness, and want of money; and have been wholly avoided by the best poets, since these verses were written' (note in *WF*). The note is patently Swift's own: he says exactly the same thing in almost the same words in a letter of 12 April 1735 (*Corr* IV, 321), adding characteristically that Pope had recently 'out of laziness' reverted to using occasional alexandrines. 'Oddly, the avowed object of the last three lines misfires... The comic stretching both of rhyme and rhythm gives the verse a welcome irregularity and flexibility of movement. The tumbling effect produced mimics precisely the flooding sweep of water and offal and rubbish into the river' (David Ward, *Jonathan Swift: An Introductory Essay* (1973), p. 189).

TO MR HARLEY'S SURGEON

First printed as part of the *Journal to Stella* by Hawkesworth (1766), and separately by Nichols in 1782; first collected in *P* I, 140–41. The circumstances in which the lines were composed are outlined in the *Journal* on 19 February 1712: 'I told [Harley] of 4 lines I writ extempore with my pencil, on a bit of paper in his house, while he lay wounded... They were inscribed to Mr Harley's physicians' (*JTS* II, 492). The original survives at Longleat among the Portland papers.

Robert Harley (see Biog. Dict.) was assaulted on 8 March 1711 by a French adventurer known as the Marquis de Guiscard, who had been arrested on suspicion of spying. Harley was wounded in the breast by a slash from Guiscard's knife, and for some days was considered in a critical condition. Though he made a prompt recovery, the affair remained what might be termed a headline story for many weeks, and occasioned a flurry of pamphlets, broadsides and prints. Guiscard (1658–1711) died in Newgate on 17 March.

Among the heroic deeds of history listed by Swift were Harley's conduct on two occasions: 'The Earl of Oxford when he was stabbed by Guiscard' and 'Robert Harley, Earl of Oxford, at his trial' (*PW* V, 84). For the latter, see *To the Earl of Oxford*, headnote.

The text is that of Swift's autograph, with spelling and punctuation normalized.

Title at first Harley was treated by Paul Buissière, a Huguenot emigré who achieved some prominence in London. At the insistence of the celebrated physician Dr John Radcliffe, one Green was later called in; but Swift probably means Buissière. See Biog. Dict.

4 the lines are signed 'J', an unusual touch indicative of the extempore production of this poem.

A TOWN ECLOGUE

First printed in the *Tatler*, no. 301 (13 March 1711); reprinted in the collected edition of *The Lucubrations of Isaac Bickerstaff*, vol. 5 (1712). Assigned to Swift and included in the *Works* by Nichols (1775). Subsequent editors have been cautious; Williams (*P* III, 1087–9) relegates the item to the category of 'poems attributed to Swift', although he thinks it fair to assume that Swift 'had some part in the composition'. *PHD* and *PJH* exclude this poem.

When the poem first appeared in the *Tatler*, it was prefaced by an introduction from Isaac Bickerstaff: 'a porter knocked at my door, and told me, I must by all means come away to the Royal Oak in Essex Street, and at the same time delivered me the following letter:

Dear Isaac, from the Oak, two of the clock.

Though we know 'Tis a busy day with you, we are resolved to have your company; and for that reason have sent you the enclosed verse, which, if you like them, will furnish out most of tomorrow's paper. You will find them to be a town eclogue, and that the scene is laid in the Royal Exchange.

We are

All very much yours,

L.B.   W.H.   J.S.   S.T.'

The poem then follows. Ball suggested that the initials indicated Jonathan Smedley, Leonard Welsted, and two others; he also wondered if L.B. might denote bachelor of laws and S.T. professor of sacred theology (*Ball*, p. 123). *P* I, 1087 adds, 'An additional argument in favour of Swift's part in the poem is, as Scott pointed out, his fondness for ridiculing Philips's pastoral and other verses.'

It is impossible to believe that Swift was not involved in the composition of this poem. Welsted and Smedley had no connection at all with the milieu described or with the *Tatler*. On the other hand, Swift had recently set up his own protégé, William Harrison, in Steele's place, and was regularly supplying hints and corrections for the new *Tatler*. Several issues are indeed included in *PW* II, 178–87, 249–63. Most relevant is the fact that, on the day after the *Town Eclogue* appeared, 'little Harrison the Tatler' came to Swift and begged him 'to dictate a paper to him, which I was forced in charity to do' (*JTS* I, 216). The outcome was the immediately succeeding *Tatler*, no. 302. If Swift was, on his own admission, ready to give Harrison this degree of assistance (at a time when he was in a state of turmoil owing to the attack on Harley by Guiscard: see preceding poem), it is hard to think that he would deny Harrison aid in convivial circumstances a few days earlier. For Swift's encouragement of Harrison, see *JTS* I, 163; *Ehrenpreis*, II, 613–18; and R.C. Elliott, 'Swift's "Little" Harrison', *Studies in Philology* XLIV (1949), 544–9. Harrison died, pathetically, inside two years: see Biog. Dict.

It is, above all, improbable that Harrison would use such recognizable initials as 'J.S.' in his columns without Swift's awareness and permission. It is almost equally unlikely that Harrison at this very juncture would collaborate with any other poet, especially on a subject of this kind, which Swift had made his own with previous *Tatler* contributions. Conceivably, Harrison could have written the eclogue alone, and thrown in the introductory letter as a blind; but it is not clear why he should wish to do this, and in any case the poem is distinctly out of his usual home country as a poet. Ball's explanation of the initials is highly dubious: Harrison was not in fact a bachelor of laws, whilst the standard abbreviation for professor of sacred theology was S.T.P. I cannot explain the outer set of initials: S.T. might be Sir Thomas Mansell, with whom Swift had recently dined, and L.B. could be Lady Betty Germaine, also a recent dinner companion with Swift (*JTS* I, 183, 192). There are other possibilities among Swift's acquaintances at this time in London (Lord Berkeley; Henry St John), but this is simply guesswork. That Harrison and Swift are indicated seems a virtual certainty.

The Royal Oak was a tavern in Essex Street at the eastern end of the Strand. It was a short step from Congreve's house, where Swift regularly went at this period (e.g. *JTS* I, 193). On 27 February Swift and Harrison supped together with Jervas at a favourite dining place of the epicure Charles Dartiqueneuf (for the other men, see Biog. Dict.). Such an occasion would be a fitting one to produce the poem.

The mock-pastoral form of 'town eclogue' had a short but distinguished period of favour. Beginning with Swift's *Description of the Morning* and *Description of a City Shower*, it achieved further currency in *Trivia* (an urban Georgic, more strictly: see *Gay*, II, 547–8) and in Lady Mary Wortley Montagu's *Court Poems* (1716). Moreover, there is an element of this fashionable vein in Pope's *Rape of the Lock*: see note to ll. 20–27. Swift was the most important pioneer, however, and there is no evidence that Harrison or anyone else could so adroitly parody his manner in 1711.

3   *confess*   give indications of, demonstrate the arrival of.

6   *chafing-dish*   a charcoal-burner, a kind of portable heating installation.

10   *loves*   Cupids.

11   *the 'Change*   the Royal Exchange, on the north side of Cornhill, at the heart of the city of London.

14   *Lincoln's Inn*   Corydon, instead of a nobly savage rustic figure, is a student at one of the inns of court (see l. 33).

20–27   a formula for introducing elaborate protestations: compare *The Journal of a Modern Lady* 19–21. The closest comparison is, however, *Rape of the Lock* IV, 116–17, for which the lines in the *Eclogue* may be regarded as an unnoticed source: 'Sooner shall grass in Hyde Park circus grow, / And wits take lodgings in the sound of Bow.'

21   *Tyburn Road*   on the route of modern Oxford Street, then a semi-rural lane leading to the gallows at Tyburn.

22   *Fleet Street*   there were no newspaper associations: the connotations are rather Fleet Prison and the insalubrious Fleet Ditch (see *Grub Street*, pp. 145–66).

23   *operas*   Italian opera was becoming exceedingly popular, despite satire in the press: Addison's first treatment of the subject in the *Spectator*, no. 18, appeared just a week after this poem. Handel had produced *Rinaldo* in London and was on the point of settling in England. Charles Ford, Swift's close friend, was a great frequenter of the opera-house in the Haymarket: see *JTS* I, 144, 162, 171, 188, 197, 200, 207.

24   *cit*   citizen (contemptuous, for bourgeois, businessman).

St James's   the fashionable quarter. For the relation of mercantile and gen-teel London, see Aubrey Williams, *Pope's Dunciad* (1955), pp. 29–41.

26–7   this . . . that   the latter; the former.

26   *Jonathan's*   a coffee-house in Exchange Alley; a great forum of business and a resort of speculators during the South Sea Bubble.

27   *the Groom Porter's*   in Whitehall, where matters concerned with gaming were overseen.

play off his plum   take advantage of a rich dupe ('plum' meaning someone worth £100,000: see *The Fable of Midas* 56).

29   *porter's ale*   bitter beer, as drunk by labourers: see Swift to Mrs Pendarves, 7 October 1734 (*Corr* IV, 257).

33   *templars spruce*   compare *A Description of a City Shower* 35.

36   *twine*   cord.

44   *ice*   icing.

46   *mechanic*   vulgar; perhaps with the sense 'by way of trade'.

47   *Crepundia*   *OED* gives for 'crepundian' the definition 'childish toy'.

48   *toys*   baubles, small ornaments.

55   *Wapping*   compare *On Poetry: a Rhapsody* 301; and *Gulliver's Travels* I, 1.

58   *coral*   'a toy made of polished coral, given to infants to assist them in cut-ting their teeth' (*OED*).

64   *cracknels*   crisp biscuits.

chine   joint of meat, esp. the backbone of a pig.

66   *shop-boards*   shutters.

bars   bolts and barriers.

67   *pattens*   clogs used in wet weather.

67–8   an ending strikingly reminiscent, in its calculated bathos, of the close of *A Description of the Morning*.

Lines from A FAMOUS PREDICTION OF MERLIN

A Famous Prediction of Merlin, attributed to one 'T.N., Philomath', is an offshoot of the Bickerstaff hoax. It appeared in several broadside versions, prob-ably first around 21 February 1709 (*T* 499–501). It was reprinted in *M11* and *M28* but not in *WF*. The form is a favourite satiric mode of the day, the 'prophecy'; but if there is pointed satire in this cryptic little squib, it has escaped all commentators. It has some affinities with Scriblerian parodies in later years, and resembles in some respects Pope's mock-explication, *A Key to the Lock* (1715), assigned to an 'Esdras Barnivelt, apoth[ecary]' not too dissimilar to T.N. Swift supplies elaborate and absurd notes to various lines, with the 'herdie Chif-tan' of l. 7 identified as the Duke of Marlborough, and 'Symnele' (l. 11) as 'the pretended Prince of Wales', that is, James Stuart, the Old Pretender. The writer claims to have found the verses 'in an old edition of Merlin's prophecies; imprinted at London . . ., in the year 1530, pag. 39' (a typical piece of pseudo-precision). He adds, 'I set it down word for word in the old orthography.' The limitations of eighteenth-century scholarship, which were later to be exposed in the Chatterton affair, are shown by the fact that Samuel Johnson and others could be hoodwinked into believing these verses genuine. Johnson himself used the device of a supposed inscription in 'monkish rhyme' for political purposes: his *Marmor Norfolciense* (1739) pretends that a riddling prophecy has been dug up, which foretells the defeat of Walpole and perhaps even the downfall of the Hanoverians. The full text, including the extensive prose passages, can be found in *P* I, 101–5; and *PW* II, 165–70. For commentary, see *Ehrenpreis*, II, 344–5. *Morgan* L395; *Foxon* S849–53.

The text follows Anne Baldwin's folio of 1709 (*T* 499). I have not seen Foxon's S851, at Harvard.

Title Merlin is chosen because of the title of Partridge's own almanac, *Merlinus Liberatus*. The typography of the broadside attempted to reproduce features of an authenthic 'prediction'. For Swift's comparison of this prediction with *The Windsor Prophecy*, see *JTS* II, 445.

1   Seven and Ten 'This line describes the year when these events shall happen. Seven and ten makes seventeen, which I explain "seventeen hundred", and this number added to nine, makes the year we are now in, for it must be understood of the natural year, which begins the first of January' (Swift's note). As opposed to the legal year, which began on 26 March.

3   Tamys rivere twys, &c. 'The River Thames frozen twice in one year, so as men to walk on it, is a very signal accident; which perhaps hath not fallen out for several hundred years before, and is the reason why some astrologers have thought this prophecy could never be fulfilled, because they imagined such a thing would never happen in our climate' (Swift's note). One of the periodic onsets of 'the great frost' hit England in 1708/9; the cold lasted from October until the middle of March, with famine conditions reported from all over the country. A particularly severe spell began on Christmas Day. The Thames was frozen over, though less extensively than in 1698/9, 1739/40, or 1778/9; nevertheless, one of the celebrated 'frost fairs' was held on the river's ice-covered surface. Gay referred to this winter in an episode of *Trivia* II, 356–98. See also Swift's letter to Robert Hunter, 22 March 1709 (*Corr* I, 133).

6   From Toune of Stoffe Swift's note identifies Marlborough, with a show of false etymology (see headnote).

9   the Fyshe Swift's note identifies the 'Dolphin' of France.

11   Yonge Symnele 'By Symnel is meant the pretended Prince of Wales, who if he offers to attempt anything against England, shall miscarry as he did before. Lambert Symnel is the name of a young man noted in our histories for personating the son (as I remember) of Edward the Fourth' (Swift's note). Parallels were regularly drawn between the Stuart claimant and earlier pretenders such as Perkin Warbeck or Simnel, who impersonated the Earl of Warwick and was crowned at Dublin as Edward VI in 1487. The titular Prince of Wales was James Francis Edward Stuart (1688–1766), son of James II by Mary of Modena, later known as the Old Pretender.

12   Norways pryd 'I cannot guess who is meant by Norway's Pride, perhaps the reader may . . .' (Swift's note).

19   Geryon Swift supplies an elaborate gloss; 'This prediction, though somewhat obscure, is wonderfully apt . . .' The note applies a Greek myth (the tenth labour of Hercules, to fetch the cattle of Geryon) to the current diplomatic situation resulting from the disputed Spanish Succession. The note prophesies that the Habsburg claimant, Charles, Archduke of Austria, will prevail over the Bourbon candidate, Philip V.

AN EXCELLENT NEW SONG

Published as a single sheet on 6 December 1711 (*T* 554); in *TCD* there is a variant issue which may be a Dublin piracy (see *POAS* VII, 686–7). It was written earlier the same day at Harley's instigation (*JTS* II, 430). The essential facts are set out in Swift's *Journal* entry for 5 December: 'Lord Nottingham, a famous Tory and speech-maker, is gone over to the Whig side: they toast him daily, and Lord Wharton says, It is Dismal (so they call him from his looks) will save England at last.' Swift aimed for an effect 'two degrees above Grubstreet'. For Nottingham, see Biog. Dict. His apostasy was expressed in his willingness to oppose the ministry on the longstanding issue of 'no peace without Spain' (see note to l. 12). For this purpose Nottingham, though a deeply-dyed High Tory, was willing to act in concert with the Whigs. When parliament met, the day after the ballad had appeared, Nottingham made his real speech in the Lords: it was for a piratical version of *this* speech that a printer was arrested, and not for another edition of Swift's ballad (see *P* I, 142, corrected by *POAS* VII, 687). Fuller historical background can be found in *POAS* VII, 524–30, as well as copious annotation: for commentary, see *Ehrenpreis*, II, 515–16; *Morgan* N573; *Foxon* S844–5.

The text is based on the original [London] edition, since the poem was not collected among Swift's works until 1779; but I have also consulted the [?Dublin] reprint and a transcript in *TCD*, and adopted one or two readings from them as regards accidentals.

1 dismal see headnote: a long-standing nickname, deriving from Nottingham's gloomy aspect and sober attire.

3 want of a place he had expected to be included in the Harley administration in 1710, possibly as Secretary of State, a post he had held 1702–4.

4 vi & armis literally, with force and arms: in law, with actual violence.

the Queen's peace specifically, the peace treaty with France then being negotiated.

6 Prior alluding to the secret diplomatic mission of Matthew Prior (see Biog. Dict.), who had gone to Paris in July 1711 to try to get French agreement for the 'preliminary' terms of the peace.

8 a whole day Nottingham was 'an endless talker' according to Swift (*PW* V, 258).

finch the family name.

9 Hoppy *POAS* VII, 527 suggests this may be Edward Hopkins, an M.P. and diplomat. Swift certainly knew Hopkins, but the identification cannot be regarded as certain. See Biog. Dict., 'Hopkins'.

12 peace without Spain the consistent Whig policy was to oppose any settlement which did not include a provision requiring France to loosen its influence over Spain (and with it the rich American trading connections): specifically, it was the original aim of the War of the Spanish Succession to dislodge Philip of Anjou, grandson of Louis XIV, from the throne of Spain in favour of the Archduke Charles of Austria. By this time the phrase had come to imply the view that no peace treaty should be concluded which did not give Britain significant concessions in trade with the Spanish empire.

14 not in game that is, out of office, excluded from power. (A pun, too.)

15 The Duke Marlborough, who was thought to have encouraged Nottingham's secession from the Tories – as indeed he had done.

19 long...pocket perhaps a feature of Nottingham's conservative dress, but also implying readiness to take bribes.

24 relations see *POAS* VII, 528 for examples of Nottingham's patronage.

27-30 Nottingham had originally been one of those who invited William of Orange to come over in 1688, but he had later withdrawn from the group.

31 advantage opportunity (with punning sense of 'profit').

at defiance in opposition or enmity (see *OED* for these words).

32 Daniel Nottingham's Christian name: see Daniel vi, 16-23.

35 Prince of Hanover in the middle of Anne's reign there was pressure from some quarters to permit the Electoral Prince (later George II) to take his seat in the House of Lords.

42 coadjutor the 'old' one would be the aged Electress Dowager Sophia: the young one either the Elector (later George I) or more likely the Electoral Prince. Stressed on third syllable: for the rhyme, see *A Panegyric on the Dean* 39-40.

50 eighteen pence tax the war was partly financed by a land tax which stood at four shillings (20 p) in the pound, and bore most heavily on the Tory squirearchy, who strongly resented the imposition.

THE WINDSOR PROPHECY

Four separate editions, dated 1711, have been traced: one is probably an Edinburgh piracy and one may be a Dublin printing. Swift told Stella on 24 December 1711, 'My *Prophecy* is printed, and will be published after Christmas' (*JTS* II, 444). However, Mrs Masham asked Swift to suppress the work when he visited her two days later; and this was, in form at least, agreed to. However, the suppression was ineffectual, and copies reached the public. The piece was not collected in Swift's works until the 1760s. *T* 555-6; *Foxon* S938-41; *Morgan* N589.

In later years Swift looked back on this squib as a fatal setback to his hopes of preferment (see *The Author upon Himself* 1). It was certainly an impolitic gesture: at this juncture the Queen did not need to be advised to stick closely to Mrs Masham, and an assault on the well-entrenched Duchess of Somerset could only be futile: see further *Ehrenpreis*, II, 478-9. In the event, the Queen heard of the poem through her physician, Sir David Hamilton, on 28 January 1712. The next day Hamilton even took her a copy of the *Prophecy*, but she refused to read it. The Duchess of Somerset was nov· the object of an even more intense loyalty, and when the Deanery of Wells became vacant a week later, the Queen was adamant that Swift should not have it. Nor would she countenance his preferment to one of the two vacant Irish bishoprics (which were in her gift); only with great reluctance did she see his appointment as Dean of St Patrick's, which lay in the gift of the Lord Lieutenant. See Philip Roberts, 'Swift, Queen Anne, and *The Windsor Prophecy*', *Philological Quarterly* XLIX (1970), 254-8. Relevant entries can be read in *The Diary of Sir David Hamilton 1709-1714*, ed. P. Roberts (1975).

This is another example of the 'prophecy' device widely used in satire. The poem was introduced with a mock-precise antiquarian's note:

About three months ago at Windsor, a poor knight's widow was buried in the cloisters. In digging the grave, the sexton struck against a small leaden coffer, about half a foot in length, and four inches wide. The poor man expecting he had discovered a treasure, opened it with some difficulty; but found only a small parchment, rolled up very fast, put into a leather case; which case was tied at the top, and sealed with a St George, the impression on black wax, very rude and gothic. The parchment was carried to a gentleman of learning, who found in it the following lines, written in a black Old English letter, and in the orthography of the age, which seems to be about two hundred years ago. I made a shift to obtain a copy of it; but the transcriber, I find, hath in many parts altered the spelling to the modern way. The original, as I am informed, is now in the hands of the ingenious Dr Woodward, F.R.S. where, I suppose, the curious will not be refused the satisfaction of seeing it.

The lines seem to be a sort of prophecy, and written in verse, as old prophecies usually are, but in a very hobbling kind of measure. Their meaning is very dark, if it be any at all; of which the learned reader can judge better than I. However it be, several persons were of opinion, that they deserved to be published, both as they discover somewhat of the genius of a former age, and may be an amusement to the present.

The reference is to John Woodward (1665–1728), physician and geologist, a regular target of the Scriblerians as the type of a foolish virtuoso. See Joseph M. Levine, *Dr Woodward's Shield* (1977).

The text is that of the [?London] broadside (*T* 555). I have not seen *Foxon's* S941.

1 holy black Suede   John Robinson, Bishop of Bristol (see Biog. Dict.). He had been chaplain at the Swedish court and Dean of Windsor; at this time he was Lord Privy Seal and chief English plenipotentiary at the Utrecht peace negotiations.

3   When he travelled to Utrecht, Robinson missed New Year's Day both in the Old Style dating (used in England) and in the New Style (used on the Continent).

7 Daventry Bird   the Earl of Nottingham (see Biog. Dict.). There is an added joke in that his family name was Finch.

10 Groats   the old coin; meaning, presumably, 'a great deal of money'.

11 Harpy   identified by *F* (1763) as the Duke of Marlborough, although his wife (who had been supplanted by the Duchess of Somerset) would seem a more natural choice.

14   if the Lord Treasurer's staff is taken from Harley (now Earl of Oxford and Mortimer).

16 Carrots   the red-haired Duchess of Somerset (see Biog. Dict.). She was the daughter of the Earl of Northumberland.

17 Thyn   alluding to Thomas Thynne, the second husband of the Duchess of Somerset: he was assassinated in 1682 at the instigation of a rejected suitor, Count Königsmark (l. 19). Swift is dragging up the old story that the Duchess had herself set on this murder.

19 Conyngs mark thou   Philipp Cristoph, Count of Königsmark: see Biog. Dict.

21 *Name* that of Anna Regina.
23 that of Abigail Masham (see Biog. Dict.).
26 *Hill* Mrs Masham's maiden name.

CORINNA

First published in *M28* and reprinted in *WF*. The latter adds, 'written in the year 1712'. *P* I, 148 suggests 1711 instead, but in the absence of evidence it is rash to offer to correct *WF*. Since Hawkesworth's edition in 1755, it has been usual to identify Corinna with Mrs Manley (see Biog. Dict.). However, the reference to the '*New Utopia*' in l. 32 casts doubt on the identification. John R. Elwood (*Notes & Queries* CC (1955), 529–30) suggests that the reference is rather to Mrs Eliza Haywood's *Memoirs of a Certain Island Adjacent to the Kingdom of Utopia* (1724–5), which of course implies a later date of composition. *WF* omitted ll. 29–32, which may indicate uneasiness concerning the identification. M. Heinemann (*Notes & Queries* CCXVII (1972), 218–21) sees Corinna as a composite figure incorporating several of Curll's women authors, with Mrs Manley, Mrs Haywood, Elizabeth Thomas, and Martha Fowke all present and 'virtually indistinguishable'.

However, Swift knew Mrs Manley well, unlike the others, and her satirical and erotic works fit the case quite neatly. I annotate the poem with details of her career because she remains the best candidate. For fuller information, see Patricia Köster (ed.), *The Novels of Mary Delariviere Manley* (1971).

Text based on *WF*, corrected by reference to *M28*.

1 Mrs Manley was born four years before Swift, in 1663 (the other candidates were younger).
3 Mrs Manley was fond of fanciful *noms de guerre*, but Corinna was not one of them.
14 *in a few* Swift's correction in *M28*, which (like *WF*) reads 'in twice twelve'.
25–8 for Mrs Manley's amours and escapades, see *DNB* and Patricia Köster, op. cit. For her imprisonment, probably for debt, see H.L. Snyder, 'New Light on Mrs Manley?', *Philological Quarterly* LII (1973), 767–70. For Edmund Curll, see Biog. Dict.; for his dealings with Mrs Manley, see R. Straus, *The Unspeakable Curll* (1927), pp. 44–7, 94–7.
29–32]not in *WF*.
31 *Atlantis* the celebrated *Secret Memoirs from Atalantis* (1709), a kind of erotic thriller disguised as political allegory. Compare *Rape of the Lock* III, 165: 'As long as *Atalantis* shall be read.'
32 *New Utopia* if the poem refers to Mrs Manley, this must be her next production, *Memoirs of Europe* (1710). For the alternative suggestion involving Mrs Haywood, see headnote.

ATLAS

Published in *M28* and *WF*. Swift's autograph survives (*TR*), as well as a transcript by Stella in the collection of the Duke of Bedford. Swift entitles the poem, 'Atlas. Writ 1712. To the Earl of Oxford.' Stella supplies the same date. A parallel has been noted with a passage in the *Journal* on 4 March 1712: '[The Earl] cannot do all himself, and will not employ others: which is his great fault' (*JTS* II, 504). There are, however, reflections on the burdens of Harley's office a year earlier (*JTS* I, 186).

The text is based on *WF* with some reference to Swift's MS and to *M28*.

Title   for Oxford, see Biog. Dict., 'Harley'.

1   Atlas   a Titan, punished for his part in the rebellion of the Pleiades.

4, 5   pedlar]   *M28, WF*;   porter   *TR*.

11   in fact Hercules bore the weight of the heavens while Atlas went in quest of the golden apples, to aid the completion of one of Hercules' labours (see *The Virtues of Sid Hamet the Magician's Rod* 74).

12   sit and rest]   *M28, WF*; take his rest   *TR*.

15   Great]   *M28, WF*; all   *TR*.

17   premier minister   see *The Discovery* 10.

18   Alcides   another name for Hercules. If an individual is meant, perhaps St John, whose coalition with Harley was beginning to fray.

22   Sink down he must]   *M28, WF*; He must sink down   *TR*.

upholders   supporters, literally and figuratively.

A FABLE OF THE WIDOW AND HER CAT

There were at least three separate editions dated 1712, of which that by John Morphew is probably the most authentic: there seems to have been at least one Dublin reprint (*T* 862 covers these items). The poem must have appeared in the last few days of 1711 or the first week of 1712. In the *Journal* for 4 January 1712 Swift mentions a ballad for which he wrote three stanzas, to which Harley and Dr Arbuthnot also contributed (*JTS* II, 454). It has been generally supposed that this was the ballad in question. However, it was not until 1779 that Nichols first included it among Swift's works. A reprint in the *Political State* for January 1712 (issued early in February) attributes the *Fable* to 'one of the writers of the *Examiner*, who had constantly pursued the Duke [of Marlborough] with merciless fury, and profligate malice'. There is little doubt that Swift is intended. For a later attribution to Prior, see *Ball*, pp. 124-5; *P* I, 151-2; *Prior*, II, 1068; and C.H. Firth, 'Two Poems attributed to Prior', *Review of English Studies* I (1925), 456-8. (Firth also discusses a reply to the *Fable*, possibly the work of Arthur Maynwaring.) Like other editors, I am not wholly convinced that Swift had any share in the *Fable*: the jumbled syntax of the last stanza is not a good sign. I have nevertheless included the item because Swift's authorship can by no means be ruled out. I see no evidence to involve Prior. *Morgan* N574; *Foxon* F13-18.

The text (modernization aside) is that of Morphew.

1   widow   the Queen.

cat   Marlborough.

2-5   alluding to Marlborough's supposed apostasy and corruption after he became Captain-General.

6   the fox   Godolphin, who had acquired the nickname of Volpone in Tory polemic.

11   scratched her maid   perhaps an allusion to Marlborough's attitude towards

Mrs Masham, whose dismissal he had sought in January 1710. The Tories looked on this as insulting and overweening behaviour.

stole the cream lined his own pocket at the nation's expense.

12 pinner see *Baucis and Philemon* 140.

13 Chanticleer the cook.

14 Grim short for Grimalkin, a wicked old cat (normally female: some reference to the Duchess may be covertly present).

18 worried that is, that the dog should be set on him.

20 Lechmere Nicholas Lechmere: see Biog. Dict. His capacity for irritating the opposition seems excessive in view of his moderate political importance. The 'speeching' for which he is noted here was that involved in the arraignment of Sacheverell in 1710; Lechmere suffered a good deal on the legal circuit that summer as a result of his part in the prosecution.

23 tooth and claw the expression used of human beings was 'tooth and nail', here jokingly adapted to the cat (*Tilley* T422).

26 golden pippins see *The Virtues of Sid Hamet the Magician's Rod* 71–4 and *The Fable of Midas* 6. This looks suspiciously like Swift's hand.

28–30 it is not clear which particular episode is meant, unless it is Marlborough's part in the fall of Harley in February 1708, when the Duke had (unexpectedly to some) taken the side of Godolphin against the secretary of state.

37 outrages stressed on the second syllable; suggesting kinship with cognate French *outrage*, rather than the false etymology 'out / rage'.

39 perquisite see *The Fable of Midas* 45.

45 the commissioners of public accounts circulated their report on Marlborough's affairs to members of parliament on 21 December 1711. The Queen sent him a letter of dismissal on 31 December.

Towser a traditional name for a dog, esp. large mastiff type.

do him justice an obsolete phrase for 'punish him', generally by putting to death.

THE FABLE OF MIDAS

Two broadside issues were dated respectively 1711 and 1712; the latter carries the imprint of John Morphew, the former none. *T* 558 suggests the '1711' version is a piracy, but *POAS* VII, 690–91 suggests it is the first impression and the 'Morphew' variant a second impression. Publication can be dated from an entry in the *Journal* for 14 February 1712: 'Today I published the Fable of Midas, a poem printed in a loose half sheet of paper: I know not how well it will sell' (*JTS* II, 488). The poem was omitted from *M28* but appeared in *WF*. *Morgan* O652; *Foxon* S847–8.

The Tory campaign against the Duke of Marlborough (see Biog. Dict.) had included a number of scorching *Examiner* papers by Swift over the winter of 1710/11. These were brought to a savage climax in *The Conduct of the Allies*, late in 1711. Partly as a result of this pressure, the ministry were able to engineer the Duke's dismissal from his post as commander-in-chief on 30 December 1711. As usual, Swift concentrates in the *Fable* on Marlborough's undeniable avarice, which he elsewhere signalized by the phrase 'detestably covetous' (*PW* V, 257). The allegations of corruption at this juncture were very frequent, and though by contemporary standards Marlborough showed a fair degree of probity there was some fire to justify the smoke. For a later attack on Marlborough, see *A Satirical Elegy on the Death of a Late Famous General*. For the campaign against Marlborough, see Michael Foot, *The Pen and the Sword* (1957); and *Ehrenpreis*, II, 526–35. *POAS* VII, 554–8 amply documents some of the allegations against the Duke but does not always distinguish those with substance from those without. For the technique of denigratory parallels, see Martin Price, *Swift's Rhetorical Art* (1953), pp. 47–8; and A.B. England, 'The Subversion of Logic in Some Poems by Swift', *Studies in English Literature 1500–1900* XV (1975), 412–13.

The text is based on *WF*, which has only a few differences in accidentals from the text of the original impressions in 1712. A transcript by Stella has no significant divergences.

1 Midas a legendary king of Phrygia who successfully prayed to the gods that everything he touched might turn to gold. When he asked for the favour to be reversed, the gods ordered him to bathe in the Pactolus, and the river thereafter rolled over golden sands. The best known source is Ovid, *Metamorphoses* XI, 85–171.

5 codling an unripe apple.

6 golden pippin see *The Virtues of Sid Hamet the Magician's Rod* 74, *A Fable of the Widow and Her Cat* 26.

12 gold-finders persons who carted away dung and offal, and searched for valuables – the basis of Mr Boffin's wealth in *Our Mutual Friend*, by which time an alternative euphemism ('dust-heaps') was current.

14 see Ariosto, *Orlando Furioso* I, 28: a Saracen king from the old romances, whose golden helmet made the wearer invulnerable. *Don Quixote* III, vii concerns 'the high adventure and conquest of Mambrino's helmet' (tr. Motteux). It was probably here that Swift came on the story.

16 magazines warehouses or stores.

17 an allusion to alleged corruption over the contract to supply bread to the forces, in which Marlborough was involved with Sir Solomon Medina. This was one of the principal charges levied against Marlborough when his affairs were investigated by parliamentary commissioners in 1711.

20 this looks like a proverb, but not identifiable as such: *POAS* VII, 555 quotes Thomas Gray, 'old words are old gold' (*Correspondence*, ed. P. Toynbee and L. Whibley (1935), I, 194).

21 a critic deep as suggested by *POAS* VII, 555, this might conceivably be Robert Recorde, whose definition is cited by *OED*, 'grain': but it is not clear how Swift could have got hold of this obscure reference, and Recorde (1510?–58) was a writer on practical and scientific matters, rather than a critic. See *DNB*.

23 lucky hit here, a financial coup: see Pope, *Epistle to Bathurst* 378, and Howard Erskine-Hill, 'The Lucky Hit in Commerce and Creation', *Notes & Queries* XIV (1967), 407–8.

25–32 when appointed to judge a musical contest between Apollo and Pan, Midas gave judgement for Pan; whereupon Apollo bestowed on him a pair of asses' ears. Perhaps the meaning is that Marlborough had come out in favour of Godolphin against Harley at the time of the ministerial crisis in 1708, and Harley was now paying him back. See further, *POAS* VII, 555.

34 Pactolus see note to l. 1.

40 In effect, lost his employments but escaped impeachment.

45 perquisites applied to the legitimate profits of office, as then understood, but here implying – as throughout the campaign against Marlborough – dishonest dealing.

46 three per cent Marlborough was entitled to deduct 2½ per cent from the pay of the foreign troops on the allied side. This was another item regularly brought up in the anti-Marlborough press.

47 commissions it was ordinary practice for army commissions to be sold, but there may be a suggestion that Marlborough entered into battle with the idea of getting officers killed and thus leaving room for more 'sales' – a far from plausible charge but one that was made.

49 store plenty, abundance: see Pope, *Temple of Fame* (1715), 450. The oxymoron has proverbial weight: compare Pope, *Epistle to Burlington* 163: 'In plenty starving, tantalised in state.'

56 plums 'plum' was slang for £100,000 – a sum then used to convey extreme wealth, almost as 'billion dollar' now is. See *PTE* IV, 14, for overtones of corruption.

58 Pan is all alluding to the Greek word πᾶν, 'all'.

71 the senate strove to scour the commission set up by parliament to investigate the financial background of the war (see note to l. 17).

72 chemic power alluding to Marlborough's dismissal: literally, his alchemist's ability to turn base substances into gold, and so, figuratively, his power to line his own pocket through prolonging the war.

81 neglected *POAS* VII, 558 aptly cites the *Journal* for 30 December 1711: 'The Duke of Marlborough was at court today, and nobody hardly took any notice of him' (*JTS* II, 452).

TOLAND'S INVITATION TO DISMAL TO DINE WITH THE CALVES' HEAD CLUB

There are two broadside editions, one possibly an Edinburgh reprint. The work was published around 26 June 1712, and five days afterwards Swift was writing to Stella, 'Have you seen Toland's Invitation to Dismal? How do you like it? but it is an Imitation of Horace, and perhaps you don't understand Horace' (*JTS* II, 544). In fact Stella made a transcript of this poem and this survives, together with a separate copy by another hand in the British Library. The poem was not collected until Deane Swift's edition of 1765. The early printings carry, in parallel with the English, a slightly abbreviated Latin text of Horace's epistle, omitting ll. 4–7, 12–15, for which there is no equivalent in Swift.

The imaginary occasion of the poem is a meeting of the republican society called the Calves' Head Club, held on the eve of the anniversary of the execution of Charles I on 30 January 1649. Again, the chief butt is the Earl of Nottingham (see *An Excellent New Song*), who is depicted as a welcome guest at this ultra-Whig congregation. In fact Nottingham never went over to the opposition in as full-hearted a manner as Swift suggests. Again, the notable figures named as present at the feast were in no sense republicans (except perhaps Sunderland, in a high academic way). On the other hand, many of those who are mentioned – Scarborough, Halifax, Somers, Montagu, Lincoln, Richmond, and Walpole – *were* prominent members of another Whig dining club, the Kit-Cat: and this may well be the real target. For the orthodox assessment of the poem and its background, see *POAS* VII, 560−61, and *Ehrenpreis*, II, 566−7. *Morgan* O667; *Foxon* S911−12.

The text is based on the Bodleian copy, that is, *T* 588, the first listed version. The Latin is omitted.

Title a club, probably not quite mythical, which was supposed to meet on the anniversary of the death of Charles I and, amidst republican celebrations, proceed ceremonially to devour a calf's head served up on a dish.

1 '*Dismal*' see note to *An Excellent New Song* 1.

for once Nottingham lived on a fairly lavish, though not vulgarly ostentatious, scale: see J.H. Plumb (ed.), *Studies in Social History* (1955).

3 *Toland* see Biog. Dict. Here utilized as a notorious freethinker.

6 See *An Excellent New Song*, esp. 45−52.

9 the Calves' Head Club was supposed to hang up various effigies.

12 *predecessors* one was alleged to be Milton, whose works Toland had edited.

19−26 for the individuals named, see Biog. Dict.

22 *Hal* *P* I, 163 identified this figure as Henry Boyle (see l. 33), but *POAS* VII, 566 cites a note by Narcissus Luttrell to support the candidacy of Halifax. I concur with *POAS* in this case.

27ff. a passage strongly reminiscent of heroic and mock-heroic contexts, for example Pope, *Rape of the Lock* II, 91 ff.

33−4 for these men see Biog. Dict.

    Walpole his absence is accounted for by the fact that he was imprisoned in the Tower from 17 January to 8 July 1712, accused of corruption as Secretary at War.

35 *Wharton* see Biog. Dict.

38 *Harry* the Duke of Kent: see Biog. Dict.

41 *Guernsey* see Biog. Dict. The point is that Nottingham's brother may request him to attend an orthodox service; traditionally, the High Court clergy brought out their strongest royalist sentiments in sermons commemorating Charles's martyrdom on 30 January. The names invoked in l. 42 imply loyalty to High Anglicanism: William Laud (1573−1645) supported the king in his struggles with the Commons, both as Bishop of London and as Archbishop of Canterbury from 1633, until he was beheaded for alleged treason.

46 *Squash* 'Dick Squash, Nottingham's negro servant': see *PW* VI, 139−41.

PEACE AND DUNKIRK

Two broadside editions, with no imprint, survive; publication probably occurred around 10 July 1712. The poem remained uncollected until Nichols included it in 1779. Swift makes only the briefest mention in the *Journal* and years later claimed he could not recall the poem at all (*JTS* II, 548: *Corr* IV, 212). For other poems possibly written at this juncture, see the next item and Appendix 4.

    As the war went into its final phases, the British forces − now under the command of the Duke of Ormonde − were secretly ordered to hold back while the peace negotiations came to a head. One sticking point lay in the important strategic fortress of Dunkirk: even the diehard Tories accepted the need to get some guarantee from the French over its fate. An agreement was reached by which an expeditionary force should be sent out from England under the command of Major-General John Hill, brother of the Queen's favourite, Mrs

Masham. He was able to take possession of Dunkirk on 8 July (Old Style), that is to say just *before* the broadside appeared. *P* I, 167 supplies the date 19 July, which is the New Style date in use on the Continent, and therefore reaches the odd conclusion that the poem appeared some days before the event it celebrates. See *Ehrenpreis*, II, 569. *Morgan* O659; *Foxon* S895–6.

The text is based on the British Library broadside of 1712 (*T* 581, *Foxon* S895).

Title for General John Hill, see Biog. Dict. The tune belongs to a 'joyful' ballad long favoured by Royalists from the 1640s onwards: see *Simpson*, pp. 764–8. The first printed version of the music dates from 1651. It was popular well into the eighteenth century.

3 the standard Tory line: the Dutch had gained advantages, including the barrier of fortified frontier towns, but the English had suffered expense and frustration.

5 in a string under complete control: see *Tilley* W886.

6 go swing be hanged (as in l. 9).

11 Sunderland see Biog. Dict.

12 Dismal Nottingham again. Around the same time Swift composed a prose satire describing an imaginary visit of the Earl to Dunkirk (*PW* VI, 139–41): see the next item, headnote.

13 Wharton see Biog. Dict. In his prose *Character* of Wharton (1710), Swift likewise stresses Wharton's profanity (*PW* III, 180).

14 Hal P I, 168 gives Boyle but Halifax seems likelier again (see *Toland's Invitation to Dismal* 22).

off the hooks out of sorts, in disorder. See *Tilley* T592.

15 Godolphin see Biog. Dict. and notes to *The Virtues of Sid Hamet the Magician's Rod.*

17 Harry Henry Boyle, this time: see Biog. Dict.

18 prince either the Hanoverian Elector, or Prince Eugene, commander of the Austrian forces in the allied army.

21 cut the line normally 'cross the Equator' but here perhaps amounting to 'range the open seas'. The privateers (l. 22) had used Dunkirk for their base. For the strategic issues, see *Trevelyan*, III, 241–3.

23–4 the terms of the treaty allowed the import of wine from Bordeaux which, with safe passage for the ships, could now supplement the port brought in from Portugal. The latter was considered a Whiggish drink, suitable for courtiers rather than squires.

29 lists of persons declared bankrupt appeared regularly in the *London Gazette.*

31ff. a classic statement of the Tory attitude towards the war, fleshed out at greater length in prose pamphlets such as *The Conduct of the Allies.*

35 Oxford see Biog. Dict., 'Harley'. In fact such promises were hard to live up to: the French procrastinated over the demolition of their fortifications, and in one form or another the issue dragged on into the reign of George I, long after Oxford's fall.

37 Dutch-hearted Whigs it was an essential plank in the Tory platform that the Whigs, for reasons of sentiment and perhaps financial self-interest, had allowed the Dutch to dictate terms unduly. The prejudice went back to the times of William of Orange, regarded by many as an interloper from a land of Presbyterians and profiteers.

Lines from DUNKIRK TO BE LET

Around 17 July 1712 Swift published a broadside containing a prose satire on
Nottingham, entitled *A Hue and Cry after Dismal* (text in *PW* VI, 139–41; see
JTS II, 548). This is *T* 582, *Morgan* O653. However, a separate printing
(apparently later) was issued with the title *Dunkirk to be Let* (*T* 583). A few
minor changes were made in the text, and in the middle of the pamphlet the
lines quoted here were inserted, as allegedly discovered in Nottingham's pocket.
It is impossible to say whether Swift was responsible for this amended version;
he can certainly not be ruled out as its author. No strong alternative candidate
exists. See further *PW* VI, 210–11; *P* III, 1097–8; *Ehrenpreis*, II, 569–70.
For the political situation, see *Peace and Dunkirk*, headnote.

1   Old Lewis   Louis XIV.
3   copyhold   land tenure resting on the custom of the manor.
4   tenure in capite   a form of tenure, abolished by an act of Charles II, whereby
land was held immediately of the crown.
5   pulls his horns in   (1) reduces his pretensions, drops his demands; (2) concurs
in the demolition of the fortifications at Dunkirk, a condition of the peace treaty
under negotiation ('horn' in the sense of hornwork or defensive bastion).
6   warning   notice to quit.

TO LORD HARLEY, SINCE EARL OF OXFORD, ON HIS MARRIAGE

The poem was not published until it appeared in Deane Swift's edition (1765)
and in *F*, vol. XIII, the same year. It was headed 'written in the year
M DCC XIII' and this is certainly correct. Edward Harley (see Biog. Dict.), the
son of the Lord Treasurer, was married at Wimpole on 31 August 1713 to Lady
Henrietta Cavendish Holles, heiress of the Duke of Newcastle. It was an impor-
tant dynastic marriage: years later Bolingbroke told Swift that it was 'the ulti-
mate end of [Harley's] administration' (*Corr* II, 415). For the complicated finan-
cial arrangements, in which Swift was said (unreliably) to have taken a hand, see
Corr II, 67–8. When the marriage was first mooted, in November 1711, Swift
wrote to Stella, 'At worst, the girl will have about ten thousand pounds a year to
support the honour . . . they say the girl is handsome, and has good sense, but
red hair' (*JTS* II, 407). See *Ehrenpreis*, II, 673.

The texts of Deane Swift and *F* are in substance identical, since *F* copied the
former. I have used Deane Swift as basis for the text.

9   The god   Phoebus or Apollo.
13ff.   Bacchus, the god of wine, stands for the thoughtless rake; Mars, the god
of war, for the roisterer in an elegant uniform.
17–18   For the story of Daphne's pursuit by Apollo and her transformation into
a laurel, see *Metamorphoses* I, 452–567.
32   Apollo was the son of Zeus and Latona (Leto).
37   Cavendish   spelt Ca'ndish in the original, which indicates the pronuncia-
tion.
43   Pallas   Pallas Athena, goddess of wisdom and of the arts, identified in
Roman mythology with Minerva.
45   Medusa   chief of the Gorgons: her hair was transformed into serpents by
Pallas, so that all who looked on it were turned to stone.

53–6 language deeply involved with that of *The Rape of the Lock*, which had appeared in its two-canto form the previous year: see I, 39–44 in this version.
65   empress of the morn Aurora, daughter of Hyperion, who married Tithonus.
69   fifteen in terms of the compliment, it is worth noting that Lady Henrietta was nineteen at the time of the marriage.
73–6 Diana, the moon goddess, fell in love with Endymion, a shepherd on Mount Latmos, and visited him by night while he slept. She was the goddess of chastity and (as queen of the night) is sometimes identified with Proserpine.

CADENUS AND VANESSA

This, Swift's longest poem, was first printed from one of the manuscript copies which began to circulate after Vanessa's death in June 1723. The earliest edition is probably one issued in Dublin around the end of April 1726, easily identified by its misdating '2726'. The first London edition was published by James Roberts on 19 May 1726. Roberts brought out a second edition, curiously based on the '2726' version rather than his own. Thereafter there were numerous printings, including seven for N. Blandford and J. Peele; an Edinburgh reprint by Allan Ramsay; and the usual Curll production. Some of these texts omit a section of ten lines (826–35 in the Penguin text) and others print it, one of a number of indications that two separate manuscripts were available. For fuller details, see *T* 657–661; H. Teerink, 'Swift's *Cadenus and Vanessa*', *Harvard Library Bulletin* II (1948), 254–7; and *Foxon* S814–29. A more authentic and tidied-up text appeared in *M28* and then *WF*.

The date of composition has been much debated and remains to be definitely established. In his own references at the time of its first publication, Swift assigned the writing of *Cadenus and Vanessa* to Windsor in 1712 (*Corr* III, 130, 137). In *M28* and *WF* the year given is 1713. Certainly the events described seem to relate to this early period of the friendship between Swift and Vanessa: Swift was forty-four (l. 525) between November 1711 and 1712, though his habitual vagueness on such points is confirmed by the reference to Vanessa as 'not in years a score' (l. 524) – this would put the story back to 1707 or 1708. Most students have felt that the poem cannot have been fully conceived, let alone written, until Swift's appointment as Dean of St Patrick's in 1713, for 'Cadenus' is simply an anagram of *Decanus*. A widely held view is that the poem was written at Windsor in the autumn of 1713 (see *P* II, 683–6 and *Ehrenpreis*, II, 647), though it is commonly believed that there were later revisions. A dissenting opinion is that of Horrell (*PJH* I, 388–90), who argues that the real date of composition was 1719/20. Horrell's contentions seem to me of some force, but not quite sufficient to overset the conventional dating. There are signs of a pervasive debt to *The Rape of the Lock*, whose original version appeared in 1712: Pope and Swift probably first met in 1713 and were soon in regular touch. There is little doubt that the poem was thoroughly worked over before it ever reached the world, and the attitudes expressed should not be taken as evidence of Swift's thought and behaviour in 1712/13. With that proviso, *Cadenus and Vanessa* may be tentatively allotted to those years, at least so far as the general outline is concerned.

The poem is naturally one of the most extensively treated in criticism. Among discussions may be noted: *Ball*, pp. 134–9; *Ehrenpreis*, II, 647–51; *Johnson*, pp. 43–5; *Jaffe*, pp. 139–41; *Fischer*, pp. 110–20: Martin Price, *Swift's Rhetorical Art* (1953), pp. 108–9; Herbert Davis, *Jonathan Swift: Essays on His Satire* (1964), pp. 66–9, 183–6; D.W. Jefferson, 'The Poetry of Age', *Focus: Swift*, ed. C.J. Rawson (1971), pp. 126–7; David Ward, *Jonathan Swift: An Introductory Essay* (1973), pp. 189–91; Peter J. Schakel, 'Swift's "Dapper Clerk" and the Matrix of Allusions in *Cadenus and Vanessa*', *Criticism* XVII (1975), 246–61, which traces an elaborate pattern of allusion to Ovid and Virgil. Most of these imply some reservation concerning the older view that the poem was one of Swift's most successful. (Eighteenth-century opinions can be studied in *CH*, pp. 173, 265–6, 298, 321–2). Scholarly articles include P. Ohlin, 'Cadenus and Vanessa: Reason and Passion', *Studies in English Literature 1500–1900* IV (1964), 485–96; and G. Jones, 'Swift's *Cadenus and Vanessa*', *Essays in Criticism* XX (1970), 424–40.

For 'Vanessa', see Biog. Dict., 'Vanhomrigh'. The first extant letter between Swift and her is dated 18 December 1711, but they probably met early in 1708, soon after Vanessa had moved to London with her mother. Sybil Le Brocquy, *Cadenus* (1962), p. 3, puts the first meeting at an inn in Dunstable (on the Holyhead road), when both Swift and the Vanhomrighs were *en route* to London. It is an agreeable picture, redolent of *Moll Flanders*, and might possibly square with l. 641: but there is no firm evidence. It is also not positively established whether the relationship was a sexual one: the correspondence yields clues but no proof either way. See also *Corr* V, 240–43.

The text is chiefly based on *WF*, though I have preferred to follow *M28* on some accidental features, and have incorporated / Swift's own alterations. The 1726 printings contain a number of lines later suppressed: most of these are reproduced in the notes, but I have inserted ll. 562–9 from Roberts's version. Their omission seems to have been dictated by private embarrassment rather than literary needs. It should be noted that the line numbers are therefore different from those in *P*, *PHD*, and other editions: from l. 570 onwards they run eight lines ahead of the usual numbering.

Title   for 'Cadenus', see headnote. 'Vanessa', later popular as a Christian name for girls, was invented by Swift from *Van*homrigh and Essy, diminutive for Esther.

1–2   the setting is the Court of Love, presided over by Venus (there was a particular cult of Venus in Cyprus). The theme is common in classical and medieval poetry, though Swift gives it a characteristic flavour of modern judicial proceedings. Curll subtitled the poem 'A Law Case'.

10   *His mother*   Venus again.

11   *freethinkers*   atheists or heretics.

24   *fact*   crime.

41–50   the diction is sharply reminiscent of *The Rape of the Lock*, esp. Canto I.

46   *equipage*   either outfit, get-up; or a coach and horses, together with footmen.

47   *toys*   trumpery. The phrase 'female toys' occurs in Gay's *The Fan* (1713), I, 112, one of several possible debts to this poem.

50   *toilets*   dressing-tables (with possible subsidiary sense, 'between getting up (dressed) and going to bed').

72   standard legal jargon, as elsewhere in the poem.

88   Venus sprang from the foam of the sea.

89   daggled   bespattered, clogged with mud: see *A Description of a City Shower* 33.

91   nice   finely balanced.

93   their king   Apollo.

96   Graces   see *On Mrs Biddy Floyd* 7.

107   Fleta's, Bractons, Cokes   standard legal authorities: *Fleta*, an early Latin treatise, edited by John Selden in 1647; for Henry de Bracton (d. 1268), author of *De Legibus et Consuetudinibus Angliae*, see *DNB*; Sir Edward Coke (1552–1634), whose *Reports* and *Institutes* (based on Sir Thomas Littleton's *Tenures*) were long among the most famous works on English law.

109   Ovid   the work in question would be presumably the *Amores* or the *Ars Amatoria*, though most of the other poems could reasonably be used in evidence.

111   Dido's case   the story of Dido and Aeneas in *Aeneid* I–IV, *passim*.

112   Tibullus   Albius Tibullus (*c.* 60–19 B.C.), Roman elegiac poet: like Propertius, far less influential than Ovid on English love poetry of the classical period. Swift owned a volume containing the works of Catullus, Tibullus, and Propertius (*Library* no. 339).

114   Cowley ... Waller   Abraham Cowley (1618–67) and Edmund Waller (1606–87), the most influential love poets of the mid seventeenth century. Swift owned copies of the work of both writers (*Library*, nos. 387, 452).

121   the normal proceedings in the courts (e.g. Chancery) took the form of a written submission describing a grievance ('bill') to which the defendant returned an answer in writing.

122   Demur   a demurrer, that is 'a pleading which, admitting for the moment the facts as stated in the opponent's pleading, denies that he is legally entitled to relief, and thus stops the action until this point be determined by the court' (*OED*).

   imparlance   'an extension of time to put in a response in pleading a case, on the real (or fictitious) ground of a desire to negotiate for an amicable settlement ... [or] a petition for ... such delay' (*OED*).

   essoign   or essoin, 'the allegation of an excuse for non-appearance in court at the appointed time; the excuse itself' (*OED*).

126   Clio   the muse of history.

136   Lucina   Juno, in her capacity as patroness of childbirth.

155   amaranthine   never-fading, from the mythical amaranth flower: compare *Strephon and Chloe* 202.

157   Titan   here, the sun: a name bestowed on it by Ovid and Virgil.

188   Pallas   Minerva, goddess of wisdom: see *Apollo Outwitted* 47.

191   my own   Cupid.

194–5   child/ ... spoiled   then a good rhyme: 'spoiled' was pronounced [spaɪld] and not [spɔɪld].

227   five thousand pound   this was more or less accurate: Vanessa's father left an estate of about £20,000, of which she was to have a quarter (Le Brocquy, op. cit., pp. 17–18). Since her mother, brother, and sister predeceased her, she was residuary legatee and 'mistress of the entire Vanhomrigh fortune' at her death in 1723.

239   an unerring guide   compare Dryden, *Religio Laici* 227.

250   the martial maid   Pallas, who was also goddess of war.

256–8   ]*the 1726 editions insert two additional lines:*

> But gods, we are by poets taught,
> Must stand to what themselves have wrought.
> For in their old records we find
> A wholesome law, time out of mind,
> Confirmed long since by fate's decree,

306   Atalanta's star   I cannot explain this reference: none of the myths surrounding the Boeotian nymph Atalanta seem to mention a star (for the best known, see Ovid, *Metamorphoses* X, 560–707).

312   the park   perhaps Hyde Park specifically (see note on l. 385).

322   a new Italian   a new singer in the Italian opera, which had taken London by storm in the reign of Anne.

330   exploded   either 'out of fashion, obsolete', or the more literal sense 'that has been hissed off the stage' (*OED*), from the Latin *explaudere*. For the latter usage see *Paradise Lost* X, 547.

333   the murders of her eyes   compare Pope, *Rape of the Lock* V, 145.

345 ∧ 6]   With her, a wealthy fool could pass / At best, but for a golden ass. *1726*; not in M28, WF.

346–9   *P* II, 697 notes the resemblance to a letter from Vanessa to Swift on 23 June 1713 (not 6 June, as Horrell): 'Lord! how much we differ from the ancients, who used to satisfy everything for the good of their commonwealth. But now our greatest men will at any time give up their country out of a pique, and that for nothing' (*Corr* I, 368).

363   proverbial: see *Tilley* W586.

365   St James   the fashionable area surrounding the court.

367   dishabille   a frenchified word for the gallic mode of negligent undress.

372   Montaigne   a favourite of Swift, represented in his library.

373   Mrs Susan   a name, like Abigail, often used generically for a maid.

374   chocolate   drunk, usually hot, from a dish.

376   important   self-important.

385   the Ring   a fashionable parade for riding in Hyde Park: see *Rape of the Lock* I, 44.

386   breaks   decays, is going to pieces.

389   thirty, and a bit to spare   compare *Polite Conversation*: 'she'll never see five and thirty, and a bit to spare' (*PW* IV, 145).

393   Tunbridge   the spa at Tunbridge achieved popularity during the Restoration, and it became a leading pleasure resort earlier than Bath. Beau Nash was for some time master of ceremonies there too.

396   rallied   made fun of.

397   made for old Queen Bess   satirically used also in *Polite Conversation* (*PW* IV, 148).

399   red   rouge, usually made from arsenic derivatives.

400   hoop   whalebone stiffeners for the petticoat, whose size grew in the middle years of Anne's reign, occasioning a famous *Tatler* paper by Addison (no. 116, 5 January 1710).

417   Flanders lace   often simply 'Flanders', and widely imported, sometimes through contraband means.

> *colbertine*: see *Baucis and Philemon* 140.

421 mask used to protect the complexion when outdoors, especially when riding.

422 patch with beauty-spots.

431 ombre the card game for three, immortalized in *Rape of the Lock* III, 25–100.

464–5 as Horrell points out (*PJH* I, 391), the lines conflict with the story as it has been told, and may reflect an earlier version. The rhyme is a favourite one (see *An Excellent New Song, being the Intended Speech of a Famous Orator* 41–2).

483 Plutarch's Morals the *Moralia* had been recommended for schoolroom reading by Erasmus but Swift, like most contemporaries, seems to have known the parallel *Lives* rather better. There was a copy of the *Moralia* in his library (*Library*, no. 232). See also *To a Lady* 248.

487 adamantine unbreakable, referring to the inexorable decree of the Fates. The phrase may recall 'adamantine chains' (*Paradise Lost* I, 48).

513 poetic works presumably the reference is to *M12*, though it is more than half prose, is scarcely a 'feeble volume' (running to 416 pages), and contains distinctly few tender lines to inspire the passions.

524–5 see headnote.

529 Horrell (*PJH* II, 391) thinks the references to ill health point to composition around 1718/19 (see *Corr* II, 308–12). But Swift's ailments began in his twenties, and the evidence is suggestive rather than conclusive.

539 ∧ 40] Strange, that a nymph by Pallas nursed, / In love should make advances first: *1726; not in M28, WF.*

562–9 1726; not in M28, WF: see headnote.

582 teased plagued, irritated.

615 their] WF; her *M28 (corrected by Swift in his own copy).*

622 to let you] 1726, WF; I'll let you *M28.*

625 ∧ 6] I'll fully prove your maxims true, / By owning here my love for you. *1726; not in M28, WF.*

650–51 P II, 707 notes the parallel with *On Censure* 15–16.

659 turned] M28; turns *WF*.

666 complaisance courtesy, willingness to please.

667 as it would be from a man, a matter of indifference (or, natural and unassuming).

668 rallied see l. 396. See Swift to Vanessa, 3 September 1712: 'You rally very well' (*Corr* I, 311).

681 a 'bite' see *Vanbrug's House*, 62.

687 ∧ 8] From him transfused into her breast / With pleasure not to be expressed. *1726; not in M28, WF.*

705 learned the modern 'learnèd' but pronounced 'learn'd'.

716 converse conversation, discourse.

727 that is, which gave a special flavour or quality to everything with which she came into contact: the image is from pharmacy or perhaps alchemy.

730 philosophers the predominant sense is natural philosophers, or scientists, but may indicate the 'world-makers' often satirized by Swift. See Ernest Tuveson, *Journal of the History of Ideas*, XI (1950), 54–74.

748 for eighteenth-century attitudes towards the dancing-master, see C.J. Rawson, *Henry Fielding and the Augustan Ideal under Stress* (1972), pp. 3–34.

772 construing disyllabic, with the 'u' practically elided.

783 In all their equipages in their full array, in their due order.

788–97 Horrell (*PJH* I, 392) compares *To Stella, Who Collected and Transcribed His Poems* 9–14.

822–3 possibly a submerged recollection of Berowne's speech in *Love's Labour's Lost* IV, iii, 287–362.

835 conscious embarrassed, because she is aware of these recent and so delicate facts.

847 'before the Queen on Tuesday next' (*F*). Latin was the official language of the law courts until 1731, but in practice it was mainly confined to forms and jargon except in certain specialized fields.

852 discovered displayed.

868 humbly showing see *Mrs Harris's Petition* 75.

889 her son Cupid.

893 '*Oyez!*' 'A call by the public crier or by a court officer (generally thrice uttered), to command silence and attention when a proclamation, etc., is about to be made' (*OED*).

896 at six and seven proverbial; for the history of the phrase, see *OED*, 'six', 5. The modern form ('sixes and sevens') became standard in the eighteenth century. *Tilley* A208.

HORACE, EPISTLE VII, BOOK I: IMITATED AND ADDRESSED TO THE EARL OF OXFORD

The first edition was issued on 23 October 1713 by Anne Dodd (a distributor often used by Curll and other members of the trade who needed for any reason to keep their names off the title-page). Swift had been installed as Dean of St Patrick's in June. He returned to London on 9 September, and probably composed the poem not long after this date. There are two further issues of the same printing in 1713, as well as a Dublin reprint (*T* 589, 590). A transcript by Stella appears to be based on the printed text; there is a separate manuscript copy in *TCD*. After a number of unauthorized editions, the poem was included in *M28* and *WF*.

The events described are largely imaginary, and only fitfully tied to the original epistle by Horace, addressed to Maecenas. In the early editions a number of verbal parallels are, however, indicated in footnotes and these have been incorporated into my annotation. Swift confined his attention to ll. 46–95, out of ninety-eight lines in the Latin text. Subsequently Pope wrote an imitation of the opening forty-five lines 'in the manner of Dr Swift' (1738), ending with a reference to Swift's version of the remainder (*PTE* IV, 265–73). For discussion, see *Ehrenpreis*, II, 675–7; *Jaffe*, pp. 141–3. *Morgan* P587; *Foxon* S891–4.

The text is based on *WF* collated with the first edition and *M28*.

Title the Dodd issues have 'Part of the seventh Epistle of the first Book of Horace Imitated: and addressed to a noble Peer.' For Oxford, see Biog. Dict., 'Harley'.

1ff. Strenuus et fortis causisque Philippus agendis / clarus, ab officiis octavam circiter horam / dum redit (Horace 46–8).

6 Cheapening bargaining for.

7 in case in good condition.

15ff. 'Demetri,' (*puer hic non laeve iussa Philippi / acciebat*) 'abi, quaere et refer, unde domo, quis, / cuius fortunae, quo sit patre quove patrono' (Horace 52–4).

16   Lewis   Erasmus Lewis: see Biog. Dict. For Lewis as a 'favourite' of Harley, see *JTS* I, 39.

17   arrant]   *WF*; cunning   *early edns.*

25ff.   It, redit et narrat, Volteium nomine Menam (Horace, 55).

31ff.   Tenui censu, sine crimine, notum / et properare loco et cessare et quaerere et uti, / gaudentem (Horace, 56–8).

36   hated Wharton like a toad   for Wharton, see Biog. Dict.; for 'hate like a toad', see *Tilley* T361.

37   the faction   the Whigs.

38   the Junta   the group of leading Whig statesmen whom Swift had previously supported: see *The Discovery* 22.

42   a sheet   a single sheet of paper, either used as a single broadside leaf or else folded to make a small pamphlet of four or eight pages.

43   the paper-stamp   A stamp duty on newspapers was brought in from 1 August 1712, in an attempt to suppress political attacks. See Swift's account to Stella on 7 August (*JTS* II, 553–4).

47ff.   Scitari libet ex ipso quodcumque refers: dic / ad cenam veniat (Horace, 60–61).

54   'Benigne,' / respondet (Horace, 62–3).

55ff.   'Neget ille mihi?' 'negat improbus et te / neglegit aut horret' (Horace, 63–4).

57ff.   Volteium mane Philippus / vilia vedentem tunicato scruta popello / occupat et salvere iubet prior (Horace, 64–6).

60   dangle out]   *WF*   are hung out *early edns.*

65ff   Ille Philippo / excusare laborem et mercennaria vincla (Horace, 66–7).

71ff.   Sic ignovisse putato / me tibi, si cenas hodie mecum (Horace, 69–70).

74ff.   Ut ventum ad cenam est, dicenda tacenda locutus / tandem dormitum dimittitur. Hic ubi saepe /occultum visus decurrere piscis ad hamum, / mane cliens et iam certus conviva (Horace, 72–5).

74   commons   food.

79   the reading is Swift's own MS correction in *F* (37) for 'came early and departed late'.

81ff.   Iubetur /rura suburbana indictis comes ire Latinis. / impositus mannis arvum caelumque Sabinum /non cessat laudare (Horace, 75–8).

82ff.   in fact Swift had been to Windsor with St John in July 1711 and refused other invitations; he paid a number of visits during September and October 1713, when the poem may have been under way (*Ehrenpreis*, II, 677–8). There were protracted negotiations in 1713 as to whether Swift should have a prebend at Windsor.

97ff.   for some of Swift's initial difficulties as Dean of St Patrick's, see *Landa*, pp. 68–78: and *Ehrenpreis* II, 661–70.

103   First-fruits and tenths   taxes levied by the Crown on those holding a church benefice. See *Landa*, pp. 52–66.

107   Oves furto, morbo periere capellae, / spem mentita seges, bos est enectus arando (Horace, 86–7).

111   Parvisol   Isaiah Parvisol, Swift's 'proctor' and tithe-collector: the note terms him a 'Frenchman'. See Biog. Dict.

113ff.   Offensus damnis media de nocte caballum / arripit iratusque Philippi tendit ad aedis (Horace, 88–9).

115 Swift had been expecting a payment of a thousand pounds to cover his outgoings on his move to Dublin, but it was by this time growing increasingly clear that this was a forlorn hope.

120 Read Harley's porter, Michael Read.

121ff. Quem simul aspexit scabrum intonsumque Philippus, / 'durus' ait, 'Voltei, nimis attentusque videris / esse mihi' (Horace, 90–92).

129 at use out earning interest, loaned at a premium.

134 not worth a groat a favourite expression of Swift's: compare *An Elegy on Demar* 20, and *Corr* I, 205. *Tilley* G458.

135–6] the early editions have: But you resolved to have your jest, / And 'twas a folly to contest:

136ff. Quod te per Genium dextramque deosque Penatis / obsecro et obtestor, vitae me redde priori! (Horace, 94–5).

THE FIRST ODE OF THE SECOND BOOK OF HORACE
PARAPHRASED AND ADDRESSED TO RICHARD STEELE, ESQ.

Published on or about 7 January 1714 by Mrs Dodd, probably as a shield: there are two states, dated 1713 and 1714 respectively, but otherwise from the same setting of type (*T* 594). There is a Dublin reprint (*T* 595). *Morgan* P584; *Foxon* S854–5. The poem was not collected or attributed to Swift until Nichols included it in his *Supplement to the Works* (1776). There has been debate regarding its authenticity (see *Ball*, p. 140), but the balance of probability lies strongly on the affirmative side.

Swift's relations with Steele had been declining over a period of time: see Biog. Dict., and B. Goldgar, *The Curse of Party* (1961). Personal misunderstandings were compounded by the political situation and the pamphlet war in which both men were involved. The present work appeared just before Steele's long-heralded tract *The Crisis*, which made its well-publicized entrance into the world on 19 January. A month later Swift replied with *The Public Spirit of the Whigs* (*PW* VIII, 29–68), incorporating a fierce personal attack on Steele. The 'paraphrase' is generally at some distance from Horace's ode (*Motum ex Metello consule civicum*...). The original edition footnoted some more direct allusions to the Latin text; these are omitted here. For discussion, see *Ehrenpreis*, II, 698–9.

The text is based on the first edition, with occasional application to Nichols (1779 edn).

Title followed originally by an epigraph: '*En qui promittit, cives, urbem sibi curae, / Imperium fore, et Italiam, et delubra deorum*', that is, Horace, *Satires* I, vi, 34–5: 'He who takes upon himself to look after his fellow citizens and the city, the empire and Italy and the temples of the gods' (Loeb tr.).

2 arcana a popular word at this period for backstairs diplomacy and political caballing.

3 Buckley Samuel Buckley: see Biog. Dict.

4 'good old cause' Whiggery.

5 Burnet Gilbert Burnet: see Biog. Dict. The particular advice has not been identified.

6 'Crisis' Steele's pamphlet had been delayed more than once: on 26 December 1713 Steele announced that its publication had been put back so as to allow more ladies of quality to enter their subscriptions. It did not appear until 19 January 1714.

9 Gore Sir William Gore (d. 1708) was Lord Mayor of London in 1702; a Hamburg merchant, he was knighted in 1692.

10 Robert Harley had been Speaker of the House of Commons 1701–5. The allusion parallels the opening of Horace's ode.

11 German prince the Elector of Hanover. For Anne's attitude towards her successor, see *Trevelyan*, III, 295–8.

13 rout fashionable party.

15 peace for Steele's tracts on the Peace of Utrecht, see C. Winton, *Captain Steele* (1964), pp. 165–78.

17 bucket-play an unusual phrase for the ups and downs of court life, drawing on an image popular in earlier centuries. The clearest earlier precedent comes in the King's speech in *Richard II* IV, i, 184–9: the New Arden editor, Peter Ure, comments on the lines in Shakespeare, 'The figure of buckets and well is adapted from the medieval and Elizabethan figure of Fortune's buckets,... rated as a proverb by Tilley B695. The raising and lowering of well-buckets as a symbol of the "commyng and goyng" of Fortune... is used in [Chaucer], *Knightes Tale*, ll. 1531–3.' The last example cited by Ure is from Herbert. This is one of Swift's few apparent uses of an iconographic emblem, but if it is so, it is an indirect reference.

20 plenipo's slang abbreviation for the plenipotentiaries who had carried through the negotiations at Utrecht. Steele's *Englishman*, no. 36 (26 December 1713), had picked up the word from the *Examiner*, and this almost certainly occasioned Swift's 'vulgar' turn of phrase. This paper had attacked Oxford: see *The Englishman*, ed. R. Blanchard (1955), pp. 144–8.

23 coup d'éclat a sensation: *OED* cites an instance from Steele, *Spectator*, no. 324 (12 March 1712). Steele had played with the phrase in the identical issue of the *Englishman* cited in the note to l. 20.

26 Twelve coronets the Queen had created twelve new Tory peers on 31 December 1711 to help through the preliminary peace terms: they included several friends and acquaintances of Swift, such as Bathurst, Masham, Lansdowne, and Dupplin.

32 'to play with edged tools' was proverbial for taking on more than one's capacity. *Tilley* J45.

35 farce alluding to Steele's now interrupted career as a writer of stage comedies.

36 pump exert oneself.

43–8 'This is said to be the plot of a comedy with which Mr Steele has long threatened the town' (note to original edition). Nichols suggested that the description seems to fit *The Conscious Lovers* (1722), and it is in fact likely that this play was sketched out as early as 1710. The play actually concentrates more on the son, Bevil junior, than on the father, Sir John Bevil.

49 'Vide Tatlers' (note to original edition). *P* I, 182 cites the second number of the *Tatler*: 'I am an adept in astrological speculations' (a trait deriving, of course, from Swift's own Isaac Bickerstaff). But Steele was interested, too, in some strange scientific projects, which may be in Swift's mind.

59–64 Steele stood for parliament in the summer of 1713 and, despite the generally poor showing of the Whigs, was elected for Stockbridge in Hampshire, a less rotten borough than many.

60 bit see *Vanbrug's House* 62. Steele's election was allegedly obtained by corruption and a petition to unseat him was pending (see l. 68).

69 mum for that archaic version of 'mum's the word', that is, a way of enjoining silence when a ticklish subject comes up. See *Tilley* W767.

72 oyster-strumpet a girl hawking oysters in the streets, traditionally a cover for prostitution, and noted for strident cries (see Pope, *The Dunciad* (1729) II, 383–4 and note).

76 the Hall Westminster Hall, adjoining the parliamentary chambers, where the law courts were centred. Swift is perhaps imagining a great show-trial like that of Sacheverell in 1710.

78 tick credit, as in the modern 'on tick'.

Hunter presumably the soldier and colonial governor, Robert Hunter, at this time a colonel (see Biog. Dict.). He was a friend of Swift, Steele, and Addison. Why he should be the lender is not clear, but Steele's qualifications as a borrower were proverbial: he was constantly in debt.

79 a blackguard rout a gang of young ruffians, 'street Arabs': see *Tom Mullinex and Dick* 19.

82 'purely hung' 'well hung' was a coarse term of approval for an animal with good physique, esp. genitals; Swift suggests that Steele's followers were better versed in judging horseflesh or greyhounds than in the study of politics. See also *PW* IV, 132.

86 Abel Abel Roper of the *Post Boy*: see Biog. Dict.

87–8 the Duke and Duchess of Marlborough had gone into voluntary exile in November 1712 and had settled in Antwerp.

91 Macartney the reference is to the famous duel between Lord Mohun and the Duke of Hamilton on 15 November 1712, which figures in Thackeray's *Henry Esmond*. For George Macartney, Mohun's second, see Biog. Dict. He was held by the Tories to have murdered Hamilton in the course of the duel. See also *JTS* II, 570–75.

92 pious patron Mohun: see Biog. Dict.

93 run a tilt make an onslaught.

94–8 'A gibe at Steele's political style' (*P* I, 183) and indeed a typically Swiftian collection of opposition clichés. Many of the notions were commonplace in Whig journalism, though perhaps it is in *The Crisis* that Steele sets them out most vividly.

102 walk favourite line of work, *métier*.

111–12 ale and port were Whig drinks, as opposed to French wine: see *Peace and Dunkirk* 23–4.

113 club combine, collaborate.

115 see Biog. Dict. for these men. Steele had, in the opening *Tatler*, jokingly referred to 'my honoured friend Mr Thomas D'Urfey'. Ambrose Philips was a real protégé of Steele; whilst John Dennis, who had known Steele for many years, was by this time estranged – as he became from most people sooner or later. See Winton, op. cit., pp. 142–4.

SCRIBLERIAN VERSES

These verses were among those circulated at meetings of the Scriblerus Club in the spring of 1714, not long before this glittering array of talent began, for various reasons, to break up. Items 2 and 4 were printed by Hawkesworth in 1766. The manuscript for 2 is lost, but the others survive in the Portland papers at

Longleat. *P* I, 184–8, printed several items for the first time. For further discoveries at Longleat, see Charles Kerby-Miller's edition of the *Memoirs of Martinus Scriblerus* (1950), pp. 351–9.

The Scriblerus Club was at the height of its activity in the early months of 1714. Its membership consisted of Swift, Pope, Gay, Dr John Arbuthnot, and Thomas Parnell. The Earl of Oxford was often encouraged to attend, as the surviving verse-invitations illustrate. The major work set on foot was the prose satire ultimately published in 1741 as *The Memoirs of Martinus Scriblerus*, though works such as *Gulliver's Travels*, *The Dunciad*, *Peri Bathous*, and *The What D'Ye Call It* have their likely origins in the scheme. The best account of the club is that of Kerby-Miller in his edition of the *Memoirs*.

The text of item 2 is based on Hawkesworth, the others on the Longleat manuscripts.

1
Dated by Oxford 20 March 1714. It is in Swift's hand.

1   That is, Dr Arbuthnot and Swift.
6   *Junta*   see note to *The Discovery* 22.
Subscription   Arbuthnot's room in St James's Palace, which he was granted as physician to the Queen.

2
Kerby-Miller (op. cit., p. 352) suggests the date is 1 April 1714, because of the reference to Argyll in l. 2. Hawkesworth heads the poem 'written chiefly by the Dean': Parnell may have helped.

2   the Earl is Oxford himself; the Duke is Argyll (see Biog. Dict.), who was deprived of his military command on 1 April.
3   Whatever pertains to Scriblerus.
8   for the growth of the *Memoirs*, see Kerby-Miller, op. cit., pp. 29–31.

3
Dated *c.* 10 April 1714 by Kerby-Miller (op. cit., p. 353), on the basis of the reference in ll. 9–10. Each couplet is in its author's own hand.

2   an allusion to *Iliad* I, 423–4 (then in the course of translation by Pope).
4   *John of Bucks*   John Sheffield, Duke of Buckinghamshire: see Biog. Dict.
7–8   a reference to a debate in the House of Lords on 9 April concerning a ministerial grant to the Scottish clans. For Townshend, see Biog. Dict.

4
Dated 14 April 1714 by Kerby-Miller (op. cit., p. 354). Hawkesworth, who printed a slightly different text, gives no date. The Longleat version is a transcript and all the names at the end have been crossed out except for Gay's.

5–6   an adaptation of the opening lines of the *Aeneid*, substituting for Troy the French duchy of Hainault, adjoining Lorraine where the Pretender then kept his court. The joke is at the expense of those (Whigs chiefly) who feared an imminent invasion by the Pretender: but it is worth recalling that the first Jacobite rising was under way within eighteen months. *P* I, 186, less plausibly, suspects a reference to the expected return of Marlborough.
7   *Hanmer*   Sir Thomas Hammer: see Biog. Dict.

10 carle an archaic version of 'churl', used by Gay in his mock-pastoral *The Shepherd's Week* (1714): *Gay*, I, 100.

11 Earl Oxford: spelt 'earle', again for archaizing effect.

12 Duke Kerby-Miller identifies this as Argyll, but Marlborough seems likelier.

15 white staff that of the Lord Treasurer.

16 Mortimer the Earl's secondary title: see *The Windsor Prophecy* 14.

18 from *Aeneid* I, 203: 'An hour will come, with pleasure to relate / Your sorrows past' (Dryden tr.).

THE FAGGOT

First published in *WF*. The date supplied in the sub-title may or may not be accurate: even if it was provided by Swift, there is no guarantee that his memory on such a point would be reliable. However, the poem undoubtedly concerns events in 1713 and 1714, as the Harley ministry began to split up. *P* I, 189 aptly cites a letter from the Duchess of Ormonde to Swift on 14 April 1714: 'I hope our friends... remember the story of the arrows, that were very easily broke, singly, but when tied up close together, no strength of men could hurt them' (*Corr* II, 18). For the deteriorating relations between Harley and St John, see *Trevelyan*, III, 302–4.

The text is based on *WF*.

1ff. I have not traced the origin of this fable: Swift may have made it up himself.

5 maggot crotchet, whim.

16 Swift has both general and particular offices at court in mind: specifically, those of Lord Treasurer (Harley), Comptroller of the Household (Sir Thomas Mansell: for a reference to his predecessor's 'staff', see *Corr* I, 178), and Lord Steward (Earl of Poulett). Compare *JTS* II, 283–4.

22 white the Lord Treasurer's staff.

28 fasces 'a bundle of rods, or small sticks, carried before the consuls at Rome' (note in *WF*).

36 be quick Harley was notoriously dilatory. Swift mentioned several instances to Stella, and once exclaimed, 'He is the greatest procrastinator in the world' (*JTS* II, 400).

38 blue ribbon of the Garter, bestowed on Harley in October 1712.

39 Harcourt 'Lord Chancellor' (note in *WF*): see Biog. Dict. 'Trimming' means moderate or uncommitted in the dispute.

41 Northey 'Sir Edward Northey, Attorney-General, brought in by the Lord Harcourt; yet desirous of the Great Seal' (i.e. anxious to supplant Harcourt: note in *WF*). See Biog. Dict.

44 leap o'er sticks strongly reminiscent of the famous passage in *Gulliver's Travels* I, 3, describing the political contortions in Lilliput.

46 Ormonde see Biog. Dict.

48 see Biog. Dict. for these men.

A fig for a standard way of denouncing what was held worthless (*Tilley* F210).

52 Somers 'who had been, at different times, Lord Chancellor and Lord President of the Council' (note in *WF*): see Biog. Dict.

Craggs 'who hath since been Secretary of State' (*WF*). This indicates James Craggs the younger: see Biog. Dict. *P* I, 191 suggests the elder Craggs, but this is almost certainly wrong.

Walpole 'the great minister now in chief power' (*WF*): see Biog. Dict.

THE AUTHOR UPON HIMSELF

This poem, one of Swift's most important and revelatory, was first published in *WF*. The copy in the English Faculty Library at Oxford preserves the uncancelled state of the first sixty lines of the poem. *WF* states at the head, 'A few of the first lines were wanting in the copy sent us by a friend of the author from London', but this appears to be a strategic ploy on Swift's part: the intention was to give the effect of a fragment, perhaps to heighten the impression of censorship. (See also the 'Digression on Madness', *Tale*, p. 170.) Lines 53-4, which are incomplete in the cancelled state of the volume, were explained by Lord Orrery, Swift's friend and biographer, in the same way that the blanks are filled up in the uncancelled copy of *WF*. The earlier state also provides footnotes absent from the cancelled version. It is likely that the poem was written around July 1714, at Swift's retreat in Berkshire (see note to l. 74). The date in *WF* (1713) is obviously impossible and conflicts with the evidence of *F*'s own notes. See *Ehrenpreis*, II, 735-7, and *Jaffe*, pp. 11-12, for critical accounts.

Blanks have been supplied and footnotes inserted from the uncancelled leaves, but I have otherwise based the text on the cancelled state, which seems to have been sub-edited with more care.

1   only the first two words and the final words of this line are present in the cancelled version. Orrery supplied 'redhaired' for 'red-pate'.

hag 'the late Duchess of Somerset' (note in uncancelled state). See Biog. Dict. and *The Windsor Prophecy* 16-17.

2   *crazy prelate*. 'Dr Sharpe, Archbishop of York' (*WF*): see Biog. Dict., 'Sharp'.

a royal prude 'Her late Majesty' (*WF*), that is, Queen Anne.

16   *still* continually.

18   *Child's or Truby's* 'A coffee-house and tavern near St Paul's, much frequented by the clergy' (*WF*). Both lay in St Paul's Churchyard, then a busy commercial and social centre. *P* I, 194 compares *Horace, Epistle VII, Book I: Imitated* 27-8.

32   the occasion is possibly that recorded in the *Journal* on 21/22 July 1711 (*JTS* I, 318).

34   *St John* 'Then Secretary of State, now Lord Bolingbroke, the most universal genius in Europe' (*WF*). See Biog. Dict., 'St John'.

37   *Finch* 'Late Earl of Nottingham, who made a speech in the House of Lords against the author' (*WF*). The reference is to Nottingham's mention of 'a certain dean who is hardly suspected of being a Christian'. For his tedious speeches, see *An Excellent New Song* 8.

38   *behind the curtain* an old expression for 'behind the scenes, out of public view': see *OED*, 'curtain', 2b.

40   the syntax is ambiguous, perhaps deliberately so: 'Harley' may be the subject of 'moves' or (more critically) the object.

41   *Walpole and Aislabie* see Biog. Dict. 'Those two made speeches in the

House of Commons against the author, although the latter professed much friendship for him' (*WF*). The precise occasions cannot be identified.

46 Perkin the Pretender: a frequent nickname, derived from the claimant Perkin Warbeck (1474-99).

48 that is, *A Tale of a Tub*, whose indiscreet satire on the church may have blocked Swift's chances of preferment. Swift claimed that he attacked only corruptions in religion, not religion itself: but he did not convince everyone. See the 'Apology' added to the 1710 edition: *Tale*, pp. 4-7. For the phrase 'writ against the spleen', see a later passage in the 'Apology': 'As wit is the noblest and most useful gift of human nature, so humour is the most agreeable, and where these two enter far into the composition of any work, they will render it always acceptable to the world' (*Tale*, p. 18).

52 He sues for pardon 'It is known that his Grace [Sharp] sent a message to the author, to desire his pardon, and that he was very sorry for what he had done' (*WF*). There is no firm independent evidence to support this.

53 'the lady hinted at before. There was a short severe satire writ against her, which she charged on the author, and did him little offices by her great credit with the Queen' (uncancelled copy).

53-4 'Madam Königsmark' and 'murdered spouse' are supplied from the uncancelled copy to fill blanks in the published state. See *The Windsor Prophecy* 19-20.

58 the vengeful Scot 'The proclamation was against the author of a pamphlet, called, *The Public Spirit of the Whigs*, against which the Scotch lords complained' (*WF*). This pamphlet, published 23 February 1714, was a reply to Steele's *Crisis* (see *The First Ode of the Second Book of Horace Paraphrased*, headnote). The printer and publisher were arrested and a reward of £300 offered for the 'unknown' author: the House of Lords voted the work a 'false, malicious, and factious libel' on 2 March. Harley declared his ignorance of the whole affair; the Earl of Mar instituted a false prosecution of Barber, and managed to preserve Swift from arrest. See *Ehrenpreis*, II, 708-11.

67 Delaware see Biog. Dict. 'Lord Delaware, then Treasurer of the Household, always caressing the author at court. But during the trial of the printers [Barber and Morphew] before the House of Lords, and while the proclamation still hung over the author, his Lordship would not seem to know him, till the danger was past' (*WF*).

69-70 'The Scotch Lords treated and visited the author more after the proclamation than before, except the Duke of Argyll, who would never be reconciled' (*WF*). See also *Scriblerian Verses*.

74 'The author retired to a friend in Berkshire, ten weeks before the Queen died; and never saw the ministry after' (*WF*). The last part is true; Swift left London for Berkshire on 31 May and passed a few days in Oxford, so that he had spent not much more than eight weeks at Letcombe Bassett when the Queen died on 1 August. For this sequence of events, see *Ehrenpreis*, II, 728-63.

IN SICKNESS

First printed by *WF*: this is one of the poems which had to be reset when changes were made to the volume (see p. 19), but the alterations are not of a substantive nature. The date of composition in this instance is probably as *WF* indicates. Queen Anne died on 1 August 1714; Swift left his retreat in Berkshire a fortnight later, and arrived in Dublin on 24 August after what seems to have been a very mournful journey (*Ehrenpreis*, II, 758–62). His gloom lasted for months – indeed, years. He wrote a particularly despondent letter, now lost, to Arbuthnot, in September (*Corr* II, 136). In many ways the poem foreshadows the *Verses on the Death of Dr Swift*, even if Swift here takes his own situation more tragically – there may be a little irony in ll. 7–8, but it is not very pronounced.

The text is based on *WF* (corrected state).

10 that is, who is an excellent physician as far as the healing arts go, but not in pushing for his own professional advancement. Compare Pope's tribute in the *Epistle to Arbuthnot* (1735) 406–19, where Pope, however, allows Arbuthnot a degree of prosperity as the Queen's physician (417).

THE FABLE OF THE BITCHES

First published by *F* and the London trade edition in 1762. The attribution has never been seriously defended but has not been decisively challenged either. It should be noted that there is a strong element of Scottish lore in the poem; not just in the subject matter, but in the entire construction, which derives from an *unstated* Scottish proverb. See note to l. 16.

Ball (pp. 150–51) suggests that the occasion of the piece was provided by a meeting of the General Assembly of the Church of Scotland in May 1715. The target is certainly the Presbyterian church and more generally the attempt to relieve dissenters from the provisions of the Test Act, 1672 (25 Charles II, c. 2). Stanhope attempted to repeal some of its clauses between 1717 and 1720, but in the event the Test Act remained until 1828, confining public offices to sworn adherents of the Church of England. Swift was a fierce opponent of any attempt to repeal the act, more especially as he feared its effects in Scotland and Ireland (though strictly, separate repeal would have been necessary in the Irish parliament). *F*'s date, 1715, may be right, though 1717 or 1718 would in some respects appear more likely. The text is based on *F* (1762), vol. X.

7 *Music's house* 'the Church of England' (*F*). The name is presumably a reference to the litany, eschewed by the dissenters.

15 *couchant* crouching or creeping (more commonly a heraldic description for a recumbent animal).

16 *Bawty* '(The name of a bitch in Scotch), alludes to the Kirk' (*F*). *OED* gives 'Scotch titular name for a dog, esp. a large one', and cites a usage from Allan Ramsay, *The Gentle Shepherd* (1725). However, the point of the allusion is masked unless the reader is aware of a Scottish proverb which underlies the whole fable: 'Bourd not with Bawtie lest he bite you', i.e. do not jest with a superior in a familiar fashion, in case he replies angrily. This saying was included in James Kelly's collection of Scottish proverbs in 1721, but does not appear to have been common in England or Ireland. Swift *could* have known it, but we cannot be sure.

23 *she* Music; *her* Bawty. This episode may perhaps relate to the Anglican attempt to stop loopholes in the Test Act with the Occasional Conformity Act,

1711 (10 Anne, c. 6). Stanhope managed to get rid of most of this act's provisions in 1718/19, which might again suggest a later date of composition.

42   a bite   see *Vanbrug's House* 62.

43–6   the story of the Trojan horse is told in many ancient sources, including *Odyssey* VIII and *Aeneid* II.

   Ilium   Troy.

   Priam   King of Troy, killed by Pyrrhus (son of Achilles) when the Greeks made their entry into the city.

HORACE, LIB. 2. SAT. 6

This imitation of Horace's famous satire, *Hoc erat in votis*, raises a number of textual difficulties. Despite *WF*'s ascription 'written in the year 1713', it was certainly composed at Letcombe Bassett at the time of the Queen's death. 'I have done the imitation of *Hoc erat in votis*,' Swift wrote on 3 August 1714. ''Tis pretty well, and will serve in some scurvy miscellany.' Four days later he reported that 'it is not yet sufficiently corrected to my mind, though I have laboured it much. But I am not now that way turned' (*Corr* II, 99, 114). In the event, the poem was not published until it figured in *M28*, and subsequently *WF*. In 1738 an extended version was published in London (*T* 757; *Foxon* S860). The long passage in continuation, running to eighty-nine lines, has always been attributed to Pope, and there can be no serious doubt that this is correct. However, between ll. 8 and 9 of the original, a further twenty lines were added. *P* I, 197–8 gives these to Swift, on the basis of a reference by Lord Bathurst and an endorsement by Swift, both in 1737 (*Corr* V, 69). John Butt subsequently commented that the reference 'is too ambiguous for certain ascription' (*PTE* IV, 248), and this is my own view. The lines in question are reproduced in the footnotes below. On internal evidence, I would incline to give them to Pope rather than to Swift. It has also been suspected that ll. 105–12 are by Pope, but they are found in a transcript by Stella at Woburn Abbey and are likely to be authentic. See *Ehrenpreis*, II, 742–4; *Jaffe*, pp. 12–14.

It is difficult to know which is the best text to follow in these circumstances. *P* follows *M28*; *PHD* states that the poem is 'printed from [*WF*]', but in fact, apart from interpolating the twenty-line addition, *PHD* actually follows *M28*. With some hesitation I have based the text on *WF* collated with *M28* and *1738*. I have preserved the Latin analogues noted in *WF*; *1738* provides the complete Latin text on facing pages, and Latin readings are taken from this source.

1ff.   *Hoc erat in votis . . .* (Horace, 1–3).   *Ehrenpreis* (II, 743) compares *Hudibras* III, i, 1277–8.

1   *I often*]   *M28*, *WF*;   I've often   *1738*.

5   *terrace walk*   Swift had a favourite grove of elms at Laracor, but on his return to Ireland in 1714 he found his 'country-seat . . . gone to ruin . . . A spiteful neighbour has seized on six feet of ground, carried off my trees, and spoiled my grove' (*Corr*, II, 130).

   rood   a measure of land, normally forty square poles or a quarter of an acre.

7ff   *Auctius atque / Dii melius fecere: bene est: nil amplius oro* (Horace, 3–4).

8 ∧ 9]   *1738 has the following, not in M28 or WF:*

> But here a grievance seems to lie,
> All this is mine but till I die;
> I can't but think 'twould sound more clever,
> To me and to my heirs for ever.
> If I ne'er got, or lost a groat,
> By any trick, or any fault;
> And if I pray by reason's rules,
> And not like forty other fools:
> As thus, 'Vouchsafe, oh gracious maker!
> To grant me this and t'other acre:
> Or if it be thy will and pleasure
> Direct my plough to find a treasure.'
> But only what my station fits,
> And to be kept in my right wits.
> Preserve, almighty Providence!
> Just what you gave me, competence:
> And let me in these shades compose
> Something in verse as true as prose;
> Removed from all the ambitious scene,
> Nor puffed by pride, nor sunk by spleen.

See headnote. 'Competence' means an adequate living.

10 that is, live south of the River Trent, within comfortable distance of London.

11 *the Channel* St George's Channel, the portion of Irish Sea separating Wales and Ireland. Swift took something like eight days normally to travel between London and Dublin, assuming there was a convenient passage at Holyhead.

15 *Lewis* Erasmus Lewis: see Biog. Dict.

17 *Sive Aquilo radit terras seu bruma nivalem / Interiore diem gyro trahit, ire necesse est* (Horace, 25-6).

19 *five hundred pound* according to *P* I, 199, the allusion 'is to Swift's expenses in entering upon the Deanery of St Patrick's'. See also *Horace, Epistle VII, Book I: Imitated* 115.

26 *levee day* a day on which the minister would receive visitors and petitioners.

29 *ribbons blue and green* the insignia of the orders of the Garter and the Thistle respectively. See Gay, *The Shepherd's Week*, 'Prologue' 64 (*Gay*, I, 94). *PTE* IV, 252 cites *Gulliver's Travels* I, 3 as expressing similar contempt for the trappings of office. See also *Verses on the Revival of the Order of the Bath*. Harley had received the Garter only a year before (*The Faggot* 38).

35ff *'Quid vis insane? et quas res agis? Improbus urguet / Iratis precibus; 'tu pulses omne quod obstat, / Ad Maecenatem memori si mente recurras.' / Hoc iuvat, et melli est, non mentiar* (Horace, 29-32).

49ff. *Aliena negotia centum / Per caput et circa saliunt latus* (Horace, 33-4).

56 it was the duty of the two Secretaries of State (of whom Bolingbroke was one until 31 August 1714) to sign official warrants, passes, and the like.

60 *'Si vis, potes,' addit, et instat* (Horace, 39).

62 *P* I, 201 cites a letter from Swift to Mrs Howard on 9 July 1727: 'There are Madam thousands in the world, who if they saw your dog Fop use me kindly; would, the next day in a letter tell me of the delight they heard I had in doing good; and being assured that a word of mine to you would do anything, desire

my interest to speak to you, to speak to the Speaker, to speak to Sir Robert Wal-
pole to speak to the King &c' (*Corr* III, 223).

*63ff. Septimus octavo propior iam fugerit annus, / Ex quo Maecenas me coepit
habere suorum / In numero, duntaxat ad hoc, quem tollere rheda / Vellet, iter faciens,
et cui concredere nugas* (Horace, 40–43).

65 Swift first met Harley on 4 October 1710 (*JTS* I, 41).

74 that is, Scriblerus Club productions early in 1714 (see *Scriblerian Verses*,
headnote).

76 Staines a market town on the Thames, where the road to the west crossed
the river, and lying six miles on the London side of Windsor. See *Phyllis* 99.

79 inter nos between ourselves.

80 Charing Cross as *P* I, 201 points out, this was where royal proclamations
were read.

81ff. Subiectior in diem et horam / Invidiae (Horace, 47–8).

86 tête à tête compare Harley to Swift, 27 July 1714 (*Corr* II, 85).

*89ff. Frigidus a Rostris manat per compita rumor: / Quicunque obvius est, me con-
sulit* (Horace, 50–51).

94 the Emperor of Austria stood aloof from the peace negotiations in 1713 and
initially refused to sign the treaty negotiated by Britain and France.

*101 Iurantem me scire nihil mirantur ut unum / Scilicet egregii mortalem altique
silenti* (Horace, 57–8).

108 see Horace, 60–62.

TO THE EARL OF OXFORD, LATE LORD TREASURER

First printed in *Miscellaneous Poems by Several Hands*, published by D. Lewis in
1730. Contrary to the statement in *P* I, 210, the poem's appearance in *WF* was
thus its second in print (see N. Sterne, *Notes & Queries* XVI (1969), 338). In the
same collection by Lewis, Swift's *Part of the Ninth Ode of the Fourth Book of
Horace* was also included (see *T* 1611). Both *P* and *T* fail to notice the presence
of the imitation described here. There are minor differences between Lewis's
text and that of *WF*; the latter is the version followed here.

In *WF* the poem is dated 1716. It could in fact have been written at any time
between July 1715, when Harley was committed to the Tower of London await-
ing the expected proceedings for impeachment, and July 1717, when parliament
decided not to go ahead with the trial and Harley was released. The unnamed
Horatian model is in fact the second ode of the third book, with the opening
twelve lines ignored. (This model is specified in Lewis's title, where the dedica-
tion to Oxford is omitted.)

1–6 closely modelled on Horace, ll. 13–16. This passage begins with the line
'*Dulce et decorum est pro patria mori*', which became a familiar tag and was later
used as the basis of a celebrated poem by Wilfred Owen. The idea that 'death
pursues the coward' was proverbial.

6 seize] *WF*; reach *Lewis*.

8 unattainted Bolingbroke and other suspected Jacobites lay at this time under
an act of attainder, a kind of outlawry imposed by parliament without any sepa-
rate judicial process.

9 Staff the Lord Treasurer's white staff: see *The Virtues of Sid Hamet the
Magician's Rod*. Lines 7–10 derive from Horace, ll. 17–20.

11–14 based on Horace, ll. 21–4.

15-18 derived from Horace, ll. 25-9. A number of those associated with the former ministry had spoken freely to the committee of inquiry, and it is possible that Swift thought that Prior, for one, let out too much. Around this time Swift incurred the suspicion of the authorities as a result of some intercepted mail (see *Corr* V, 230-33). It could be that Swift sent Harley this poem as a token of his own faithfulness.

16 our] *WF*; thy *Lewis*.

19-22 modelled on Horace, ll. 29-32.

22 Slow] *WF*; Sure *Lewis*.

DEAN SWIFT'S ANSWER TO THE REVEREND DR SHERIDAN

The first identifiable item in a long series of 'trifles' which passed between a group of friends centring on Swift. As well as Sheridan and Delany, the Rev. Daniel Jackson and the Rochfort brothers formed part of the circle. For all these men, see Biog. Dict. For Swift's friendship with Sheridan see also *To Mr Delany*, headnote. In this edition only poems directly acknowledged as Swift's are included.

This item was first published by Samuel Fairbrother in his unauthorized *Misc* (1735) and was taken into *F* in 1738. There is a transcript in *TCD*. The text here follows *F*. For Sheridan's poem which occasioned Swift's *Answer*, see *P* III, 971-2. It is clear that the two men were already fully engaged in a battle fought out with riddles, rebuses, and similar word-games.

5 you begin Sheridan's lines start, 'Dear Dean, since in cruxes and puns you and I deal, / Pray why is a woman a sieve and a riddle?'

8 dark obscure, gnomic.

light the pun depends mainly on the sense of 'sexually promiscuous'; the other overtones include 'transparent', 'superficial', 'physically not heavy', and 'frail'.

10 searcher the meaning is probably that of 'an official appointed . . . to prevent the production of work below a certain standard of excellence' (*OED*). Such persons certainly existed in the linen trade. It might conceivably be a machine or device for testing the fineness of the cloth (see *OED*, 'linen-teller'). Another possible meaning is that of a custom-house official seeking out contraband linen exports. There are obscene potentialities in the phrase. The rhyme was a good one.

12 What name *F* suggests in a note 'vir gin'; but Sheridan gave a better solution in a reply dated 'past five in the morning' on the following day (12 September): 'Adam's hell, a damsel, aye, there I have hit it.' For the text of this poem and yet another written at noon on the same day, see *P* III, 973-5. See also the next item in this edition.

THE DEAN OF ST PATRICK'S TO THOMAS SHERIDAN

Within hours of the previous item, Sheridan had produced two new ripostes. Swift's instant response takes the form of the present poem, which was first published by Dr John Barrett in 1808 from a manuscript in *TCD*. This is the basis for the text here.

2 O tempora, o mores! 'O times, O manners', proverbial, deriving from Cicero's Catiline orations, 1, i, 2.

6 from your car the first of Sheridan's replies was dated 'from my Ringsend car', presumably a light jaunting carriage. Ringsend lies on the south bank of the Liffey, a short way downstream from the centre of Dublin: see also *A Quibbling Elegy on Boat* 7–8.

12 come short on't fail in our endeavour.

14 riddle and sieve looking back to Sheridan's earlier set of lines.

20 shears alluding to the 'sieve and shears' proverbially used in divination; there was also a dialectical variant 'riddle and shears'. See *OED*, 'sieve'.

23 hold you a wager the ordinary verb: see *On the Five Ladies at Sot's Hole* 11.

24 my minor or major premise, in logic: picked up from Sheridan's first reply, l. 13. A note in Barrett: '*Ut tu perperam argumentaris*', that is, 'as you erroneously deduce'.

26 Like a woman a jibe on female tattling, and also suggestive of bodily odours and secretions.

29 car go pun on 'cargo': the language is that of the transportation of textiles.

31 You threaten the stocks Sheridan's first reply, l. 17.

34 Dan Daniel Jackson.

35 keep a good tongue hold your tongue: *Tilley* T420 cites uses in Shakespeare.

36 swing in a cart go to be hanged.

37 rebus see *The Answer to Vanessa's Rebus* 6.

42 Phoebus Sheridan's first reply, l. 26, 'now I'm your Phoebus, and you are my poet.'

43 your new rebus set at the end of the first reply by Sheridan. No solution is forthcoming, although 'Burden' is conceivable.

44 by trucks in kind; by way of exchanging riddles in return.

A LEFT-HANDED LETTER TO DR SHERIDAN

Another in the series of trifles, following a few days after the preceding item. This poem was first published in *F* (1762), the basis for the text here. There is a transcript in *TCD*. For a supposed manuscript by Swift, sold at Sotheby's in 1858, but not now traceable, see *P* III, 967. It is evident from *F*'s note that the poem actually was written with the left hand.

F prints at the foot: 'I beg your parden for using my left hand, but I was in great haste, and the other hand was employed at the same time in writing some letters of business.

'September 20, 1718.

'I will send you the rest when I have leisure, but pray come to dinner with the company you met here last.' Swift had returned the previous month from his stay with the Rochforts at Gaulstown (see *Corr* II, 291: and compare *The Part of a Summer*, headnote). Sheridan's reply to this letter was also printed in *F* and is reproduced in *P* III, 969–70.

The poem trades on the associations of 'left-handed', for which *OED* supplies 'ambiguous, questionable, inauspicious, awkward, clumsy', amongst other definitions.

Title in fact Sheridan did not become a Doctor of Divinity at Trinity College until 1726.

2 *clown* rustic. This looks like an allusion to popular fable (not identified).

5–6 quoting Ovid, *Metamorphoses* I, 758–9: 'It shames me that this insult could have been spoken and could not have been rebutted.'

8 *Hoadly* Benjamin Hoadly, Bishop of Bangor at this date, who had set off the so-called Bangorian controversy with a sermon in 1721. A flood of pamphlets ensued, to which Hoadly himself contributed further items. See Biog. Dict.

9 *pay off my old score* see *Tilley* S147 for versions of this expression.

17 *the French* Swift may be thinking of the battle of Malplaquet in 1709; the English regarded this as a victory for Marlborough and the allies, but the French fêted their generals Boufflers and Villars for the heavy losses they had inflicted on the enemy.

19 *Tom Leigh* see *To Mr Delany* 63.

29 *Antaeus and Hercules* see *Upon the South Sea Project* 189. Antaeus is the 'overgrown clown' (l. 31).

33–4 for the rhyme, see *To Dr Delany, on the Libels Writ against Him* 7. Presumably the point of these lines is that Sheridan cannot beat a schoolboy who has not learnt his lesson until the boy stands up.

THE DEAN TO THOMAS SHERIDAN

The rapid flurry of verses was kept up and Sheridan produced a further set within three days (which included a Sunday). Swift's reply, printed here, was composed on Monday, 15 September. It too was published by Barrett from the MSS in *TCD*. Text from Barrett.

At the conclusion, Swift made a joking Scriblerian annotation to the text of Sheridan's latest poem (which is itself reproduced in *P* III, 977–8).

1 *Lord Anglesey* Arthur Annesley, the fifth Earl: see Biog. Dict., 'Anglesey'.

2 *dangles* hangs about, uninvited.

3 *whip* suddenly.

5 *and dagger*] *supplied by editors from l. 24 of Sheridan's poem, to complete metre and sense.*

6 *convitia ex plaustro* the grating noise of the wagon.

10 *Billingsgate* see *A Panegyric on the Reverend Dean Swift* 108.

11 *coach it or cart it* compare *The Dunciad* (1729) III, 293: 'Coached, carted, trod upon...' For the construction, see *OED*, 'it', 9.

14 *carte blanche* punning on 'cart'. A recent importation into English usage. The term was used in Swift's favourite card game, piquet, as was *tierce* (l. 20).

15 *tecta et sarta* the normal phrase in Latin is *sarta tecta*: 'in good repair'.

18 *Delenda Cart-ago* adapting for the pun the famous saying of Cato the Elder, 'Carthage is to be destroyed.'

20 *tierce and carte* fencing terms: the third and fourth of the parries.

21 '(viz.) *ut tu praedicas*' (note in Barrett).

22 '(viz.) *ut ego assero verius*' (note in Barrett). 'As I more truly maintain.' The couplet parodies logical procedures.

23 *Melpomene* muse of tragedy and of song. Picked up from Sheridan's verses, l. 22.

32 *ripens above ground* the idea is that the sun ripens grapes on the vine but

sours wine if sunlight is allowed directly on to bottles in store. Compare *To Stella, Who Collected and Transcribed His Poems* 119–20.

35 Dan Daniel Jackson. For both men named, see Biog. Dict.

36 laugh in their sleeves 'nurse inward feelings of amusement' (*OED*). Proverbial: *Tilley* S535.

38 the line is taken over bodily from Virgil, *Aeneid* II, 104: 'this the Ithacan [Ulysses] would wish and the Atrides [Agamemnon and Menelaus] would buy for a high sum.'

Postscript the word 'superscribing' means 'addressing the cover of a letter'.

TO THOMAS SHERIDAN

Like the preceding items, first published by Barrett in 1808 from an MS in *TCD*. This follows after a gap of some six weeks. For a reply in Latin by Sheridan, see *P* III, 981–2. Sheridan had first complained of a sore eye which made reading and writing difficult, in English verses; Delany composed a reply (these poems are printed from Scott's text in *PJH* I, 298–300: not in *P*).

2 your sight was but single Sheridan has only one eye to use, and lacks 'second sight'. Remembering Luke xii, 34: 'The light of the body is the eye: therefore when thy eye is single, thy whole body also is full of light.'

3 Helsham Dr Richard Helsham: see Biog. Dict. and *To Dr Helsham*.

5 physic medicine, but probably a cathartic or purge.

pay off your bacon not clear: perhaps the meaning is, 'take my revenge on your person' ('pay' was used colloquially to mean 'give a drubbing').

6 short taken i.e. a sudden need to evacuate the bowels after the purge.

7 Dick Helsham again.

14 cercopithecus a monkey with a tail, mentioned in Pliny's *Natural History*.

17 Ryly not certainly identified. There are a number of possible candidates. Perhaps Pat Riley, a Dublin schoolmaster who sent a verse letter to Sheridan (*Works*, ed. Scott, XV, 45).

29 Betty Mi Lady Lady Betty Rochfort: see *The Part of a Summer* 9. An incursion into 'Anglo-Latin' techniques.

SHERIDAN, A GOOSE

Like the preceding items, transcribed in the *TCD* manuscript collection called *The Whimsical Medley*, and first printed by Barrett in 1808. It was first collected by Scott in 1814. It follows four days after the last item. The exact sequence of squibs and rejoinders is hard to fix accurately. Williams (*P* III, 892) suggests that Sheridan's lines beginning 'A Highlander once fought...' are a reply to the present poem, and reverses the order found in *The Whimsical Medley*. But it is clear that Swift had on a previous occasion used the comparison of a goose (l. 16); Sheridan himself had pictured himself with a goose before him ('Reply, by Sheridan': see *PJH* I, 299–300). It is possible that Sheridan's lines refer to the former insult, not the later. *Mary the Cook-Maid's Letter to Dr Sheridan* represents a further and undoubtedly later stage in the exchange.

The text is based on *TCD*: there are no substantive differences in the printed version.

2 pasquils lampoons or pasquinades.

4 inflammations in the eyes looking back to the previous poem. This was one of Swift's own disorders.

6 P III, 983 suggests that the reference is to the first three paragraphs of Bunyan's 'Apology for his book' at the head of *The Pilgrim's Progress*, part 1 (1678). This is possible, though there is no reference to eyes in the passage.

10 stick thus in your gizzard proverbial: *Tilley* G131. Used also in *Polite Conversation* (*PW* IV, 162).

12 all my geese are swans proverbial: *Tilley* G639.

14 Swans sing when dying see *Tilley* S1028.

15 smoke understand, detect (as often in the period, and commonly in Swift). See *Tilley* S571.

18 the sex sc. female.

21 pen quills were commonly made of goose-feathers.
still always.

MARY THE COOK-MAID'S LETTER TO DR SHERIDAN

First printed in *Misc* (1732), *T* 25 (4), and reprinted in *WF*. It follows closely upon *Sheridan, a Goose* and may be confidently allotted to the same period, around October 1718.

Jaffe, pp. 125–6, discusses the humorous effect of 'conversational rhythms and absurdly elongated lines'. She concludes that 'the poem maneuvers between seriousness and humor, now assuring Sheridan of Swift's affection, now abusing, now correcting his conception of raillery. A fine piece of characterization, this poem is also the final document in Swift's controversy with Sheridan and the cleverest means he found of teaching, by example, what good raillery could be.' This appears to assume that the present poem postdates *To Mr Delany*, which may or may not be the case.

I have based the text on *WF*; again the differences in *Misc* (1732) are insubstantial.

Title Swift's cook was, according to Delany, 'of a large size, and very robust constitution: and such a face, as in the style of ladies, would be termed *plain*: that is, much roughed with small-pox, and furrowed by age.'

7 in your teeth an expression of defiance: see *OED*, 'tooth', 4d.

9 adapting a proverb: see *Tilley* F227, and *Polite Conversation*: 'She hath more goodness in her little finger, than he has in his whole body' (*PW* IV, 179).

10 parsonable a joking variant of 'personable', as pronounced in the brogue.
hoddy-doddy a person with a short, dumpy figure; also used of a cuckold.

13 four years i.e. presumably since Swift's return to Ireland.

14 sweetheart Swift's name for his cook: see *Corr* II, 228, 264.

15 concerned drunk (dialect). *Tilley* C583.

16 come-rogues comrades, for drinking purposes.

17 a reference to the last line of Sheridan's *A Highlander once Fought*. Variant of the proverb, 'He wants to eat of the goose that shall graze on your grave', that is, to outlive you (*Tilley* G353).

23 tell truth, and shame the devil proverbial; quoted by Hotspur in *1 Henry IV* III, i, 58, and used by Swift in *Polite Conversation* (*PW* IV, 162). *Tilley* T566.

23–4   for this favourite rhyme, see *Stella at Woodpark* 21–2.

27   Saunders   Swift's man, 'the best servant in the world', Alexander McGee, who died in 1722 aged twenty-nine. See *Corr* II, 422. See also *Stella's Birthday* (1723), l. 56.

32   I would pin a dishclout to his tail   a nineteenth-century writer on Lincoln-shire dialect quoted in *OED* remarks, '"Go thee ways or I'll pin th' dishclout to thee tail" is not unfrequently said to men and boys who interfere in the kitchen.'

37   written hand   a form of cursive handwriting, that is, with the letters joined up.

A LETTER TO THE REVEREND DR SHERIDAN

First printed by Samuel Fairbrother in 1735. Swift disliked Fairbrother, whom he called 'an arrant rascal in every circumstance' (letter to Sheridan, 24 April 1736, *Corr* IV, 478); but the bookseller was sometimes able to salvage authentic items not used by Faulkner. The poem was subsequently taken into *F* (1738). A transcript also appears in *The Whimsical Medley* (*TCD*).

A reply by Sheridan duly emerged, as was invited by the last line of Swift's poem. This reply was printed by Scott in 1824, and can be found in *P* III, 989–90.

The present text is based on *F* (1738).

2–28   Apart from Seneca, all the great dramatists of the ancient world are named: the Greek tragedians Aeschylus (525–456 B.C.), Sophocles (495–406 B.C.), and Euripides (?481–406 B.C.), together with the comedian Aris-tophanes (?444–?385 B.C.), and the Roman comedians Plautus (?254–184 B.C.) and Terence (?195–159 B.C.).

7   Eupolis   a comic poet who was a contemporary of Aristophanes in Athens. See note to l. 11.

8   the Strand   'N.B. The Strand in London. The fact may be false, but the rhyme cost me some trouble' (note in Fairbrother and *F*). A new maypole had been erected not far from Somerset House during Swift's last sojourn in London, but it had already disappeared to make way for James Gibbs's church of St Mary-le-Strand, completed in 1723. This was one of the buildings put up accord-ing to the 'fifty new churches' act of 1711, as recorded in Pope's *Dunciad* (1729) II, 24–6: 'Where the tall maypole once o'erlooked the Strand; / But now, so Anne and piety ordain, / A church collects the saints of Drury Lane' (*PTE* V, 99).

11   Cratinus   another Greek author of the old comedy.

Horace   see *Sat.* I, iv, 1–5, where the poet uses Eupolis and Cratinus, along with Aristophanes, as exemplars of free-spoken criticism directed against notorious rogues.

15   ex pede   short for *ex pede Herculanem*, that is, deducing the whole from a small part.

19   the Stagirite   Aristotle. In fact there is no criticism of Euripides' versifica-tion in either the *Poetics* or the *Rhetoric*; Swift may be thinking of the remark concerning Euripides' management of dramatic effects in *Poetics* 13 (1453a), but the reference is obscure.

20   fadge   fit, fulfil their purpose.

23   Thespis   the founder of Greek drama, an Athenian writer of the sixth century (from whom we derive 'Thespian'). He was supposed to have recited his tragedies in humble and bucolic surroundings, and hence Swift uses him as a type of rustic and primitive art.

31 trisyllable that is, the rhyme on three syllables.

TO MR DELANY

First published by Deane Swift in the *Works* (1765), *T* 87, seemingly from a transcript now lost. The original is preserved in *FV* 541, together with Swift's covering letter to Delany dated 10 November 1718 (*Corr* II, 301-2). Swift there asks Delany not to show Sheridan the poem, but he must have expected this instruction not to be followed: and indeed Delany himself later reported that Sheridan 'burnt the original in a fit of mortification' – there were perhaps two fair copies, or else Delany forgot the exact circumstances. See his *Observations upon Lord Orrery's Remarks* (1754), pp. 17-18, where Delany gives a slightly different version of ll. 5-8.

For Sheridan and Delany, who had recently made Swift's acquaintance and were to become two of his closest friends, see Biog. Dict. Scott believed that Swift knew Delany as early as 1716, but this seems unlikely. Both men formed part of the versifying group in Dublin who produced a large number of poetic trifles in the years to come.

The poem concerns 'the rules of raillery' (*Corr* II, 301) against which Sheridan had, Swift felt, offended. Particularly objectionable were some papers including one 'on the funeral', which is not among the trifles preserved in *TCD*, but which evidently consisted of a long poem alleging Swift's muse to be dead. Sheridan 'without the least provocation... [made] a funeral solemnity with asses, owls, &c. and gave the copy among all his acquaintance' (*The History of the Second Solomon*, *PW* V, 222). For a discussion of Swift's use of raillery, see *Jaffe*, pp. 121-8.

The text here is (except for normalization) a reprint of Swift's holograph version. Deane Swift's variants are recorded only where they affect more than a single word or two.

2 probably recalling Dryden, *To the Memory of Mr Oldham* (1684), 1: 'Farewell, too little and too lately known.' For Swift and Delany, see headnote.

5-8 Delany was born *c.* 1685 and was thus about eighteen years junior to Swift, who was over fifty when they met.

13-28 PJH II, 786 aptly cites the discussion of wit and humour in the 'Apology' to *A Tale of a Tub* (*Tale*, pp. 18-19).

14 humour, raillery and wit] breeding, sense, and wit *Deane Swift*.

18 invent the old rhetorical sense of 'find out or select the right ideas' was still available: as applied to conversation, it would mean choosing the right topics for witty treatment. Recent and influential discussion of wit and humour was found in Addison, *Spectator*, nos. 35, 47, 58-63 (10 April-12 May 1711).

24 that... this the former, the latter.

25-6 wild... spoiled easily accommodated to a good rhyme, with the latter pronounced [spaild]: compare *Cadenus and Vanessa* 194-5.

27 invention see note to l. 18. The sense appears to be close to that of *OED* (4): 'The devising of a subject, idea, or method of treatment, by exercise of the intellect or imagination.' Swift means that the exercise of conscious reason is not enough.

31 rally Swift's spelling is 'railly', an obsolete form which preserves the kinship with 'raillery'.

33 Voiture Vincent Voiture (1598–1648), courtier and writer, best known in England for his letters, which were much read, translated (as by Dryden), and imitated as models of courtly style in amatory correspondence. Swift owned two editions of his works: see *Library*, no. 116.

37 air stylishness.

43 Nor can afford to buy gold lace] Nor can arrive at silver lace *Deane Swift*.

52 by the ears at variance, quarrelling. *Tilley* E23.

56 fall foul on attack.

57 horse-laugh 'a loud coarse laugh' (*OED*, citing Steele amongst others).

dry rub caustic reproof (the 'dry mock' is recorded by Puttenham in the sense of a stinging jibe).

58 by excellence obsolete use, translating *per excellentiam* or *par excellence*, '(so called) as being preeminently entitled to the designation given' (*OED*).

59 Butler, Dawson, Carr habitués of Dublin convivial society. Probably Brinsley Butler, later third Viscount Lanesborough (*c.* 1670–1736), a college contemporary of Swift; Joshua Dawson, Under-Secretary for Irish Affairs during Queen Anne's reign; and Charles Carr, Bishop of Killaloe (see Biog. Dict.). There are, however, other possibilities, e.g. the lawyer Arthur Dawson, later Baron of the Irish Exchequer.

60 jar a verb; the friends are always at loggerheads.

63 Tom Leigh Rev. Thomas Leigh (d. 1727), a clergyman whom Swift knew in London: see *JTS* II, 587 (23 December 1712). See also *A Left-Handed Letter to Dr Sheridan* 19.

69 calling, shape or sense Swift wrote 'person, family or sense' in the manuscript but deleted this. He was not always able to follow his own advice; for example, his attacks on Tighe and Bettesworth refer to their ancestry, lawyer's trade, lack of intelligence, and so on. His satire of Allen in *Traulus* draws attention to the victim's stammer.

78 ∧ 79] ll. 87–94 were originally placed here, but moved by Swift. Deane Swift follows the original order.

90 a friend Sheridan.

91 Who full of humour, fire and wit] Who, neither void of sense nor wit *Deane Swift*.

93–4 Deane Swift prints 'But sallies oft beyond his bounds, / And takes unmeasurable rounds.' Rounds could refer to a circuit of inspection, but here seems to mean 'long roundabout routes, wandering all over the place'.

102 Dan Jackson's nose for Rev. Daniel Jackson, see Biog. Dict.

109 accuse find fault with.

110 flirts jests, gibes (obsolete).

ON DAN JACKSON'S PICTURE

First published in the London *Misc* (1745); taken into *F* in 1763. A series of poems concerning Rev. Daniel Jackson's prominent nose, written by Swift and other members of the circle, is generally dated *c.* 1718: see *To Mr Delany* 102. This particular round of verses was occasioned by a portrait silhouette made of Jackson by Lady Betty Rochfort. Delany, Sheridan, and George Rochfort all contributed lines on this event; Swift's are headed simply 'On the foregoing Picture' and signed 'Swift'. An answer, allegedly by Jackson himself (*P* III, 994–5), may well be by Swift, but there is no external evidence to show this. Text based on *Misc* (1745).

The opening lines are quoted by Delany in his *Observations upon Lord Orrery's Remarks* (1754).

1   traffic   busy yourselves (archaic sense).
3   Sapphic   none of the poets wrote in what is strictly Sapphic metre or stanza-form. Swift probably means the stanza form used in the next poem (*Dan Jackson's Reply*), which was also used by Sheridan and George Rochfort in their poems concerning Jackson's nose. It is therefore possible that this item postdates *Dan Jackson's Reply* and associated items.
5   Germans   Hanoverians, especially those now entrenched in the court at St James's.
10   Lady Betty   Lady Betty Rochfort: see Biog. Dict.
16   come in   take its place in the account; the stanza parodies the language of philosophic discourse.
30   by the end   to 'get by the end' meant to gain command of; there must also be an idea of tweaking Dan's nose.
31   rise   come upon the scene.

DAN JACKSON'S REPLY

First published by Samuel Fairbrother in his Dublin *Misc* of 1735; subsequently taken into the London *Misc* (1745), and then into *F* (1763). These are respectively *T* 33 (4); *T* 66; and *T* 45A (7). There is a manuscript version in *The Whimsical Medley* (*TCD*). Text here from the London *Misc*; there are no important textual variants in the earlier sources.

Another contribution to the exchange of verses described under the previous item. In this case the stanzas do constitute a 'modern Sapphic' (see *On Dan Jackson's Picture* 3); a celebrated contemporary example was Isaac Watts's *The Day of Judgement*, 'attempted in English Sapphic' (1706).

2   to country air   either at the Rochforts' home at Gaulstown (see *The Part of a Summer*, headnote, for such a visit in 1721) or Delany and Helsham's new home at Delville, if the poem dates from May 1719 or later.
3   your answer   for the text of Sheridan's poem, see *P* III, 1000–1001.
9–12   referring to Sheridan's *Answer*, ll. 17–24.
12   box-comb   a comb made of pale box-wood, fashionable in the late seventeenth century and beginning of the eighteenth: see *OED*, 'box' *sb.*[1], 3(a).
14   daub   punning on (1) inartistic, clumsy workmanship; (2) insincere flattery.
23   called lean by a skeleton   referring to Sheridan, ll. 29–30.
29–32   This stanza refers to George Rochfort's reply, ll. 13–16, which suggested that women took a prurient interest in Jackson's other bodily attributes.
33   fleer   sneer: compare *To a Lady* 78.
34   my better half   referring to *Dan Jackson's Answer*, ll. 28–30 (*P* III, 995). Proverbially used of a spouse (*Tilley* H49).
37–8   hinting at proverbial usages such as 'penny wise, pound foolish'; *OED* quotes an expression, 'it is the well spent penny that saveth the pound.' See Tilley P195–6, 202, 213, 218.

41 metal punning on 'mettle'.

43 An ounce of gold I cannot locate the proverb in exactly this form, though *OED* quotes similar expressions from 1526 to 1870, each contrasting an ounce of something valuable with a pound (ten pounds, cartloads) of something less valuable. See also *Tilley* O85–7.

45–6 referring back to Rochfort's reply, ll. 65–8 (*P* III, 1000).

47 crany cranium;   brains. The joke may involve the word *pericranium*.

ANOTHER REPLY BY THE DEAN

Bibliographical details as for previous item (the two poems are combined into one by Fairbrother). Another set of 'English Sapphics'.

2 an ace you'd ne'er have bated to bate an ace meant 'to abate a jot or tittle, to make the slightest abatement' (*OED*, quoting Marvell and others). There was a proverb, 'Bate me an ace, quoth Bolton': *Tilley* A20. Compare also *A Dialogue between Captain Tom and Sir Henry Dutton Colt* 22.

10 Ramines 'Rathmines, in Swift's time a village near Dublin, now a suburb' (*P* III, 1002). On the southern fringes of the city.

14 to quit the score to get even.

15 billets notes.

22–3 stuff... enough one of the commonest of all rhymes in Swift.

23–4 for the proverb, 'The lion spares the suppliant', and variations, see *Tilley* L316.

SHERIDAN'S SUBMISSION

Bibliographical details as for the preceding items. Fairbrother gives the title 'Sheridan to Dan Jackson', and prints the introductory quatrain as an epilogue.

Epigraph from Juvenal, *Satires* III, 288–9: 'Poor me he fights, if that be fighting, where / He only cudgels, and I only bear' (Dryden tr.).

11 cry 'Peccavi' (literally, 'I have sinned'), as a way of acknowledging one's guilt. *Tilley* P170.

16 a lion see *Another Reply by the Dean* 23–4.

20 the damned squire Rochfort. 'Hard' because of the implications of the name (*roche-fort*), but also because it made a difficult rhyme (*On Dan Jackson's Picture* 7).

25 left me in the lurch the phrase, deriving from backgammon and various card games, had been used by Butler in *Hudibras* and Addison in the *Spectator*, and even by the august preacher Robert South. Its tone was a little less slangy than is the case today. *Tilley* L588.

28 ferula and birch the instruments of discipline in a school such as Sheridan's.

THE AUTHOR'S MANNER OF LIVING

First published in *F* (1746); no date there assigned, but generally supposed to belong to Swift's earlier years at St Patrick's. Two parallels in the letters have been noted: 'You are to understand that I live in the corner of a vast unfurnished house; my family consists of a steward, a groom, a helper in the stable, a foot-man, and an old maid, who are all at board-wages, and when I do not dine abroad, or make an entertainment . . . I eat a mutton-pie, and drink half a pint of wine' (Swift to Pope, 28 June 1715: *Corr* II, 177). And: 'I have been just dining in my closet alone on a beef-steak and pint of wine, in seven minutes, by my watch' (Swift to Ford, 20 December 1718: *Corr* II, 308). The parallels are closer with the first letter, but on balance it seems to me likelier that the winter of 1718 is the right date. Swift often mentions the quiet life he is leading at this period (*Corr* II, 293, 302, 309). He was complaining about the Irish climate, too (*Corr* II, 310).

6 board-wages 'wages allowed to servants to keep themselves in victual' (*OED*). The servants would have to spend their allowance, instead of saving it by eating up scraps from Swift's table.
8 compare *A Pastoral Dialogue between Richmond Lodge and Marble Hill* 52.
10 my club my share.
    God b' y' to be pronounced 'good bye'.

STELLA'S BIRTHDAY (1719)

Despite the title (see below), written to commemorate Stella's birthday in March 1719. The first of the regular birthday poems, which continued up to the time of her death in 1728. It was printed in *M28* and then in *WF*. A transcript in Stella's hand is found in a small quarto volume preserved at Woburn.

For Stella, see Biog. Dict., 'Johnson', and (for a sympathetic study) Sybil Le Brocquy, *Swift's Most Valuable Friend* (1968). The Stella poems are considered as a group by *Jaffe*, pp. 85–101, where they are seen as embodying 'an original form of compliment'; by *Johnson*, pp. 44–50; and by Herbert Davis, *Jonathan Swift: Essays on His Satire* (1964), pp. 87–9, 186–9.

Most editors understandably follow Stella's transcript, but on grounds of con-sistency amongst other things I base the text here on *WF*. The differences are not important.

Title]On Stella's birth-day/Written A.D. 1817 *Woburn transcript.*
1 thirty-four 'poetic licence of a charitable kind' (*PJH* I, 392): Stella was actually thirty-eight in March 1719.
5 at sixteen Swift first met Stella when she was only eight, at the time of his arrival in Sir William Temple's household in 1689 (see *Ehrenpreis*, I, 104). He has in mind, perhaps, the period of his second sojourn at Moor Park, beginning in 1696. Stella had suffered from poor health until the age of about sixteen, when she began to bloom into a 'beautiful, graceful, and agreeable' young woman (*PW* V, 227).
6 on] of *Woburn transcript.*
14 your] thy *Woburn transcript.*

A QUIET LIFE AND A GOOD NAME

One of the poems transcribed by Stella, preserved at Woburn. According to this source, 'writ A.D. 1719'. First published in *WF*, where Faulkner substituted 'writ-ten about the year 1724'. Stella's date is generally accepted as the more accurate.

The suggestion has been made that Swift may have had Sheridan and his wife in mind (*P* I, 219). It is clear that this was a less than ideal marriage: see *A Portrait from the Life*, headnote. But there are no specific grounds for associating the Sheridans with this poem. The ill-matched couple formed a well-known literary topos and a congenial theme to Swift. The expression 'anything for a quiet life' turns up in *Polite Conversation* (*PW* IV, 160). *Tilley* L244.

The text largely follows *WF*, with one or two small exceptions where Stella's transcript has been adopted.

Title]'To a friend, who married a shrew' *not in Woburn transcript*. Stella subtitles simply 'To &c.'

17–18   the scriptural text is I Peter iii, 11; in addition, a close non-scriptural source would be Hobbes, *Leviathan* I, 14: 'the first, and fundamental law of nature; which is, *to seek peace, and follow it.*' There would be some irony in having Will cite a text from this work, which embodies a desperate search for peace in the face of innumerable pressures towards dissension and war. Swift owned *Leviathan* (*Library*, no. 255).

20   *in the very nick*   of time (proverbial: *Tilley* N160).

28   *Od's-buds*   an archaic oath, literally 'God's blood'.

32   *tobacca*] *Woburn transcript*; tobacco   *WF*.

   carrion   wretched creature.

53–4   that is, the boys arranged a skimmington ride or procession, guying the couple: today the best-known description of such an event is the scene in Hardy's *Mayor of Casterbridge*, ch. 39.

PHYLLIS

Another of the poems transcribed by Stella, and dated by her 'A.D. 1719'. *WF* states 'written in the year 1716', probably in error. There was an earlier printing in *M28*.

The work forms an obvious pair with *The Progress of Beauty*. 'Progress-pieces' abounded in the period: Aubrey Williams describes some satiric uses of the fashion in *Pope's Dunciad* (1955), pp. 42–8. The general implication was a definite stage-by-stage movement, often downwards, as in *The Rake's Progress*.

The text is basically that of *WF*, but the excessive italicization employed by Faulkner is suppressed. Sometimes the italics serve to make a useful point, as in the proverbial phrase of l. 56, or the antithesis of *John* and *Phyl* as the marriage declines. But the typographical convention is distracting today, when followed so extensively, and Stella's more uniform presentation is easier to accept.

Title   the Woburn transcript has 'Phillis' throughout. For the dating, see headnote.

20   *to*] *WF*; from   *Woburn transcript*.

35   *wished*   'A tradesmen's phrase' (Swift, manuscript note in his copy of *M28*). A characteristic piece of deliberate vulgarism.

   Crop   name for a crop-haired horse.

45   *toilet*   dressing-table.

56   proverbial: indeed exactly the sort of cliché parodied in *Polite Conversation*, where it duly appears (*PW* IV, 157). *Tilley* M688.

68   compare *Tilley* T200: 'Things done cannot be undone.'

85, 86 'em] *WF*; 'um *Woburn transcript.*
87 Johnny] *editorial amendment*; Jonny *Woburn transcript.*
99 Old Blue Boar apparently imaginary, although Swift passed through the town regularly on his visits to Windsor during the Harley administration. There were at least twelve inns at Staines at this period, but none identified carried this sign. There was a very well-known coaching inn, the Red Lion, at Egham, the immediately adjacent town; its landlord figures in the work of Fielding a few years later. Staines lay on the main road westwards from London, about fifteen miles from Hyde Park Corner. Inns in the neighbourhood were often suspected of harbouring the highwaymen who infested Hounslow Heath.

THE PROGRESS OF BEAUTY

Stella's transcript at Woburn is headed 'written A.D. 1719'; *WF* has 'written in the year 1720'. Either date is possible, but in so far as this is a companion piece to *Phyllis*, there is some logic in allotting the same date to both items. The present work had first appeared in print in *M28*. Five stanzas were omitted from the printed version which are present in Stella's manuscript.

The parallel between Diana, goddess of the moon, and an earthly woman, Celia, would normally be a mode of romantic encomium; but the poem systematically undermines amatory conventions of this kind. Though not directly scatological, the work is often discussed along with the so-called excremental group, e.g. by Denis Donoghue, *Jonathan Swift: A Critical Introduction* (1969), pp. 206–8; *Jaffe*, pp. 103–5; John M. Aden, 'Those Gaudy Tulips: Swift's "Unprintables"', *Quick Springs of Sense*, ed. L.S. Champion (1974), pp. 15–19; and C.J. Rawson, 'The Nightmares of Strephon', *English Literature in the Age of Disguise*, ed. M.E. Novak (1977), pp. 64–6, where the poem is characterized as 'a piece of neometaphysical *vers de société*'.

The text is that of *WF*, spelling and typography apart, and with missing stanzas supplied from the Woburn transcript.

1 Diana Aden, op. cit., pp. 16–17, points out that it is momentarily unclear whether the moon or some 'Diana of Drury Lane' is the subject of these opening lines. Rawson, op. cit., p. 64, discovers some proximity in feeling to the early poems of T.S. Eliot, e.g. *Rhapsody on a Windy Night.*
11 Celia a typical name for the nymph in conventional love poetry.
17–20] *Woburn transcript; not in M28, WF*. Pope may well have been responsible for the omissions in *M28*, in which case Swift may have failed to make the necessary restorations in *WF* by inadvertence.
21 colours traditional attributes of female beauty, displayed in brows, eyelashes, cheeks, and lips.
30 complexions the word formerly meant painting or make-up, in addition to the modern sense; Swift may have this in mind.
37–44] *Woburn transcript; not in M28, WF*.
37–40 grotesquely reminiscent of *Description of a City Shower* 53–60.
45–8 one of several passages in the poem recalling Pope's *Rape of the Lock* (1714), e.g. I, 140–44.
53 important carrying overtones of 'self-important, pompous', as in *Cadenus and Vanessa* 376.

60 White lead used in repairing china, and also in cosmetic preparations – sometimes with fatal effects, as women were poisoned over the course of time through using it.

Lusitanian Portuguese. Another passage with Popian links: see Aubrey Williams, 'The "Fall" of China and *The Rape of the Lock*', *Philological Quarterly* XLI (1962), 412–25.

64 china-ware euphemism for chamber-pots.

73 Pall Mall originally an alley where the game of pallmall was played, the street in St James's became known by this name in the Restoration. The spelling in the original 'Pell-mell' indicates the pronunciation still used.

73–6] Woburn transcript; not in *M28, WF*.

81–2 a textbook commonplace.

86 astrologers well into the seventeenth century, and even perhaps into Swift's day, the word 'astrologer' could mean 'astronomer': Evelyn uses it thus of Flamsteed (see note to l. 99). But Swift probably has the modern kind of astrologer in mind.

89 Partridge the astrologer John Partridge: see Biog. Dict.

91 Cancer the astrological sign of the crab.

93 Gadbury another astrologer, John Gadbury: see Biog. Dict.

95 Endymion the youth beloved by Diana.

96 Mercury astrologically and medically, for the metal was the most common specific against syphilis ('not sound' in l. 95 implies infected).

99 Flamsteed John Flamsteed, the great astronomer: see Biog. Dict.

109–12 the standard effects of venereal disease, as then understood: effects also imputed to the 'cure', mercury.

110 To think of black lead combs is vain] WF; To think of oil and soot is vain *Woburn transcript*; To think of blackhead combs is vain *M28*.

113–16] Woburn transcript; not in *M28, WF*.

THE PROGRESS OF POETRY

First published in *M28*; reprinted in *WF*, where it is headed 'Written in the year 1720'. In *F* (1737) this becomes 'about' 1720; the poem is perhaps most naturally grouped with the earlier 'progress' poems of *c.* 1719.

The work unites two of Swift's favourite modes: the domestic fable and the Grub Street genre study. The needy poet crops up several times in his poetry, e.g. *To Stella, Who Collected and Transcribed His Poems* 25–38; *Advice to the Grub Street Verse-Writers* 1–2.

The text is that of *WF*, normalized.

18 The third night's profits dramatists traditionally received the proceeds from every third night's performance, after the deduction of overhead expenses. It was the highest remuneration that many hack authors would ever get.

21–30 the contrasting imagery of bulk / heaviness / torpor and flight / levitation / lightness recalls other Scriblerian works, e.g. *Peri Bathous* (also published in *M28*), chs. i, iv, vi.

lumber one of Pope's favourite terms of opprobrium, e.g. *The Dunciad* (1729) I, 116; III, 296.

37 pined emaciated (from an old transitive use of 'pine').

40 flying case a condition fit for flying, that is, his body pared down to 'fighting weight'.

46 Grub Street the literal and historic Grub Street lay near Moorfields on the northern edge of the city of London. Swift's use of the motif is discussed in *Grub Street*, pp. 235–48.

FROM DR SWIFT TO DR SHERIDAN

Published in *Misc.* (1745), vol. X, and in *F* (1746), vol. VIII. The date is probably accurate: in a letter begun on 8 December 1719, but completed ten days or more later, Swift wrote to Charles Ford, 'I write nothing but verses of late, and they are all panegyrics' (*Corr* II, 331). No panegyrics have been identified. The 14 December was a Monday.

The first part of the letter constitutes one of the earliest examples of a comic mode later practised by Ogden Nash amongst others. The initial postscript exemplifies Swift's favourite multiple rhyming game. For the footnote in *F*, which has only indirect relevance to the letter, see *P* III, 1012–13.

The text is based on *F* (1746).

2 Misc; not in F (accidentally).

5 corks to stop your bottles probably with indelicate innuendo: see Pope's *Dignity, Use and Abuse of Glass-Bottles* (1715), attributed to 'the author of *A Tale of a Tub*'. See also *Tilley* B549.

6 Make a page of your own age proverbial: *Tilley* P11. Also used in *Polite Conversation* (*PW* IV, 167); meaning 'See to it yourself'.

Saunders see *Mary the Cook-Maid's Letter to Dr Sheridan* 27.

7 Mrs Dingley Rebecca Dingley: see Biog. Dict. *Mrs Johnson* Stella. In both cases 'Mrs' is used where we should now use 'Miss'.

your wife Elizabeth Sheridan, *née* MacFadden, from Co. Cavan. She is said to have been a shrewish wife.

9 St Catherine's home of Lady Mountcashel (l. 11), a few miles west of Dublin at Leixlip.

10 Mr Conna presumably Connor or O'Connor, but not positively identified.

11 Lady Mountcashel widow of the first Viscount, and mother of the third (who was a pupil of Sheridan's); d. 1738.

37 'Vida, Rule 34' (marginal note in *F*). A reference to the poetics of Marco Girolamo Vida (1490–1566), a humanist author whose works Swift owned (*Library*, nos. 26, 49). Pope called him 'immortal Vida' (*Essay on Criticism* 705). *De Arte Poetica* (1527) is a verse treatise in three books; in the eighteenth century it was best known through the translation of Christopher Pitt (1725). The point of Swift's reference is not clear: no edition I have located numbers the various precepts in Vida's treatise. Swift may have been appealing to the critic for a licence to use an unusual or archaic word, such as 'twattling' (idle chattering), described by *OED* as 'obsolete except in dialect'.

45 colloguing flattering, wheedling, or intriguing.

46 knogging noggin; a small drinking-cup holding about a quarter of a pint only.

48 dram a very small draught: literally only one eighth of a fluid ounce.

55 oraculum oracle.

56   supernaculum   'a liquor to be drunk to the last drop; a wine of the highest quality' (*OED*). See *Tilley* S1000.
59   the signature may be genuine, but it is entirely possible that Swift was responsible for the whole letter.

DR SWIFT'S ANSWER TO DR SHERIDAN

Swift's verse letter to Sheridan of 14 December was answered by Sheridan within a matter of hours. Swift then retorted with this poem, which is headed 'December 15th' in the holograph, now at *HEH* (no. 14336). See *Mayhew*, p. 159, for a description. Sheridan's poem is based on the rhyme 'Dean' (pronounced 'dane'); and Swift promptly goes one better with his 'crambo' on the sound 'wine'. On the MS Swift also wrote two words he did not in fact use ('valentine', 'engine'), plus the three final rhyme-words. The present poem was first printed by Deane Swift in 1765, and was incorporated in *F* the same year. Text based on the MS at *HEH*, but punctuation supplied with some help from *F*.

6   like a barn-door did shine   a bowdlerized version of the popular saying: *Polite Conversation* has 'Why, Miss, you shine this morning like a sh — barn-door' (*PW* IV, 149).
8   Dan   Daniel Jackson.
10   give Satan his due   a variant of the proverb (*Tilley* D273), which is quoted in *Polite Conversation* (*PW* IV, 198).
12   St Catherine   home of Lady Mountcashel: see *From Dr Swift to Dr Sheridan* 9.
14   ]HEH; not in Deane Swift, F.
15   stomach   appetite.
17   Lord Massereene   Clotworthy Skeffington, fourth Viscount (d. 1739); subscribed to Pope's *Iliad*.
18   lewd Aretine   Pietro Aretino (1492–1556), regarded as the most scabrous of poets.
23   recalling *Paradise Lost* X, 659–60; 'Planetary motions and aspects / In sextile, square, and trine, and opposite.' Referring to the relative position of two heavenly bodies, as astrologically conceived: as seen from the earth they would be respectively 90°, 180°, and 120° apart.
28   eyn   archaic and dialectical plural.
29   Lutherine   corruption of lutestring, lustrine, or lustring, a glossy silk fabric.
32–3   Swift's MS has the lines in the opposite order; Deane Swift, intelligently, reverses them to make better sense.
32   poetry Alexandrine   literally twelve-syllable lines: in most cases the first foot is truncated so that the line has eleven syllables.

THE DEAN'S ANSWER TO 'UPON STEALING A CROWN'

First published in the London *Misc* (1745) and then taken into *F*, vol. VIII (1746). Text based on *F*.
   Upon Stealing a Crown is a short poem by Sheridan, describing an act of petty larceny committed whilst Swift lay asleep. Swift's answer is dated only 'Saturday

night'. The reference to Lady Mountcashel (l. 15) points to an early date, in all likelihood: perhaps around the time of *Dr Swift's Answer to Dr Sheridan* – hence the poem's placing here.

1   punk   prostitute.
2   cully   client, 'punter', victim.
3   treat   tip.
6   clap   venereal disease.
7   capon   vague term of familiar abuse, rather than 'eunuch' in this case.
8   thirteens   'an English shilling passeth for thirteen pence in Ireland' (note in *F*).
   halfpenny   pronounced (as always until the disappearance of this coin) 'hay-penny'.
9   Medlicot   evidently a wine (perhaps named from the importer) but a name unknown to lexicographers.
10   cut   unkind act.
12   crowns   the italics underline the pun. Swift may be thinking of the part which the bishops had played in the invitation to William III to claim the English crown and oust James II.
15   the lady at St Catherine's   Lady Mountcashel: see *From Dr Swift to Dr Sheridan* 11.
17   Agmondisham   Agmondisham Vesey: see *A Character, Panegyric, and Description of the Legion Club* 164 ∧ 165.

SWIFT TO SHERIDAN

Another of the poems first published by John Barrett in 1808, from the *TCD* manuscript known as *The Whimsical Medley*. It answers a 'crambo' poem by Sheridan, based on the rhyme 'Dean' (pronounced 'dane'). No firm dating is possible: since Sheridan had composed a similar crambo on 'Dean' in December 1719, this may indicate an approximate place in the sequence. Text based on *TCD*.

1   defiance   challenge.
2   quadruple alliance   the name given to the treaty between England, France, Austria, and Holland, signed in August 1718. Swift may be thinking of a league with friends such as Delany, Helsham, and Walmsley (see *George Nim-Dan-Dean's Invitation to Mr Thomas Sheridan*).
3   retrograde   slow because of the sidling motion of a crab.
6   Fate . . . Fury   the three Parcae and the three Eumenides: Swift seems to indicate that Sheridan had recently come into contact with some fierce harridans, but the precise reference is not clear.
7   Cavan   where Sheridan was master of the free school from 1735.
   Dundalk   on the coast, forty miles east of Cavan.
10   bullets   that is, billets, small logs chopped up for firewood.
   Baldwin   Swift's old acquaintance, Dr Richard Baldwin: see Biog. Dict.

TO STELLA, VISITING ME IN MY SICKNESS

First published in *M28* and subsequently in *WF*, where in both cases the poem is headed 'October, 1727'. This is probably a guess by Pope, unless (as is suggested in *P* II, 723) it is the date he received a copy of the verses from Swift. Rev. John Lyon, a fairly reliable informant, substituted the year 1720, and this has generally been accepted on two grounds. In the first place, there are no birthday verses as such in 1720, and together with *To Stella, Who Collected and Transcribed His Poems* this may be an alternative offering. Secondly, it is known that Swift was in bad health in the early part of the year: see *Corr* II, 336, 340–42, 347–8. The dating is not definitive but it is as likely a surmise as we can make.

A recent reading is that of *Jaffe*, pp. 89–90, who points out that Swift compliments Stella for what were then thought of as non-feminine virtues. 'His emphasis falls on qualities usually associated with men.' Similar attributes are stressed in Swift's meditation *On the Death of Mrs Johnson* (*PW* V, 227–36). There he mentions that 'with all the softness of temper that became a lady, she had the personal courage of a hero' (see ll. 51 ff). He states that 'she never swerved in any one action or moment of her life' from 'the principles of honour and virtue' he had himself helped to inculcate.

The text is based on *WF*. I have retained the italics used to emphasize key notions.

1 Pallas Minerva, the goddess of wisdom.
19–20 the four humours, or psychological types, occasioned (as it was believed) by the predominance of a particular body fluid in the chemistry of any individual human being.
22 complexion the texture of the countenance, as today, but also the underlying psychological type expressed by the 'humour'.
23–32 false concepts of honour had been attacked by Addison and Steele in the *Tatler* and *Spectator* (1709, 1711–12), for example, in *Tatler*, no. 25, by Steele: 'As the matter at present stands, it is not to do handsome actions denominates a man of honour; it is enough if he dares to defend ill ones.' Swift was friendly with both writers at the time of this campaign.
31–32 the lord is believed when he asserts something 'upon his honour'; ordinary people who refused to disown offensive opinions formerly had their ears cut off, hence the phrase 'to be willing to give one's ears'.
37 think alone only think.
40–42 standard types of stoic calm and wisdom, especially in the face of powerful oppressors. The Brutus invoked is generally identified in such cases as Lucius Junius Brutus (d. 508 B.C.), the first consul of Rome, who condemned his own sons to death for conspiracy: but the figure was merged to some extent with Marcus Brutus, the friend of Julius Caesar. Both the elder and the younger Cato were types of self-denial and rigorous morality: but the reference seems to be to the younger, M. Porcius Cato (95–46 B.C.) who killed himself at Utica in North Africa, after the defeat of Pompey at Thapsus. Socrates (*c.* 470–399 B.C.) is present as much for his noble death as for his philosophic works. In his list of 'Those who have made great figures in some particular action', a historical review of heroic deeds, Swift included both 'Cato of Utica, when he provided for the safety of his friends and had determined to die', and 'Socrates, the whole last day of his life, and particularly from the time he took the poison to the moment he expired' (*PW* V, 83–4).
47 fleer sneer, mockery.
60 still continually.
63 a line suggesting the poem might easily postdate Walpole's rise to power in 1721 or thereabouts.

73 Swift recounts how Stella resisted an attempted housebreaking and shot one of the thieves (*PW* V, 229–30).

75 to cut her lace that is, the lace of her stays: the usual expedient when a lady fainted.

79–80 see *Bons Mots de Stella* (*PW* V, 237–8).

86 kind here, 'sex'.

104 She suffers from recurrent bouts of ill health (*PW* V, 231).

109 supplies succours, relieves.

TO STELLA, WHO COLLECTED AND TRANSCRIBED HIS POEMS

On 1 July 1727 Swift wrote from Pope's home at Twickenham, where he was staying on his final visit to England, to Sheridan in Dublin: 'Pray copy out the verses I writ to Stella on her collecting my verses, and send them to me, for we want some to make our poetical miscellany large enough, and I am not there to pick what should be added . . . I do not want that poem to Stella to print it entire, but some passages out of it, if they deserve it, to lengthen the volume' (*Corr* III, 221–2). The poem duly appeared in *M28*, seemingly in its entirety. It was reprinted in *WF*, with the heading 'Written in the year 1720' (of uncertain accuracy).

Stella's assiduity in copying out Swift's poems may indicate that he had long been planning a volume to follow on from *M11*. In the event, Pope's initiative in bringing out *M28* forestalled any project for a separate volume. The present poem is discussed by *Jaffe*, p. 88.

The text is founded on *WF*.

4 Inigo Jones the type of a distinguished architect, though the hint of a sneer may be present.

8 a conventional idea in classical and renaissance poetry.

12 routine formulas in amatory verse.

14 see *Cadenus and Vanessa* 768–9.

26 Conning old topics learning up stale poetic rules or themes.

32 stout 'a cant word for strong beer' (note in *WF*).

34 peck a dry measure of capacity, sometimes used to express weight also: a peck loaf was about 17 pounds, so a fairly small amount of coal would be implied.

45 beating flax a punishment at Bridewell house of correction for disorderly or immoral women.

50 Curll the bookseller Edmund Curll (see Biog. Dict.), whose depredations upon Swift included the piracy of *M11* (see *T* 3). A representative Curll title around this date is *The Ladies Miscellany* (1718). Swift had to endure *Letters, Poems, and Tales: Amorous, Satirical and Gallant* in the same year; it contained a little of his own work and some dubious items (see *P* III, 1069–70). Some time afterwards new offence was given by a fresh collection, misleadingly entitled the 'fourth edition' of Curll's *Miscellanies*, published in December 1721 (*T* 19). It is possible that Swift has this in mind and that the poem is slightly later than *WF* indicates.

71 Maevius see *On Poetry: a Rhapsody* 302. The original poetaster of this name was mentioned in Virgil's *Eclogues* III, 90; the immortality thus bestowed on him caused Swift to write to Pope, 'Maevius is as well known as Virgil' (*Corr* III, 118).

72 suburb suggests not pleasant gardened retreats, but a squalid hinterland of the city: see *Grub Street*, ch. 1.

74 crambo a popular game in which one player challenges another to find a rhyme. Its value as an aid to rhyming is mentioned in *A Letter of Advice to a Young Poet*, possibly by Swift (*PW* IX, 335). The implication here is 'threadbare, familiar rhyme, striving for ingenuity'.

78 lost her nose through the effects of syphilis: see *The Progress of Beauty* 111.

81 malice personified here as equivalent to envy, which was often depicted as 'full of eyes' (*Faerie Queene* I, iv, 31).

91 you become all the more incensed as the case grows clearer.

106 admire wonder at.

111 paid made up for.

119-20 compare *The Dean to Thomas Sheridan* 32.

121-6 Ajax's resentment was caused by the fact that the dead Achilles' armour was awarded to Odysseus and not to him. Athene struck him with madness, and after various destructive acts, intended as revenge upon his Greek comrades, he committed suicide. Sophocles' *Ajax* is the best-known source.

UPON THE SOUTH SEA PROJECT

This was one of the most frequently reprinted of all Swift's poems, and the textual history is complicated. For a full census of editions, see *P* I, 248-50; *T* 623-4; and *Foxon* S810-13.

Swift sent the poem to his friend Charles Ford on 15 December 1720 with a brief covering letter; the holograph survives in the Rothschild collection (*Corr* II, 364). It was soon registered with the Stationers' Company and advertised as published in the first week of January 1721, through the agency of Swift's regular bookseller Benjamin Tooke. (The name of James Roberts also figures in the imprint: he was simply the distributor.) The text was apparently printed from an accurate transcript; it ran to 220 lines. In the same year there were Edinburgh and Dublin reprints. The Dublin edition is notable in that two new stanzas appear, that is, ll. 33-40. There were also various appearances in miscellanies between 1721 and 1725. Stella made a copy, preserved in the Woburn commonplace book, probably based on the Dublin edition of 1721. In addition, a shorter version was produced to accompany a print entitled *The Bubbler's Medley* (1721), that is, no. 1610 in the British Museum collection of prints and drawings. This incorporates ll. 145-64, 73-6, 173-6, 109-12, 117-20, 225-8 in that order. Another truncated version was included in *M28*, presumably with Swift's complicity; it omits fifty-two lines, chiefly stanzas from the second half of the poem. Almost all these were restored by *WF* in 1735, except that ll. 65-8, 113-16, were still omitted.

The best account of the South Sea Bubble is the book of that name by John Carswell (1960). See also headnote to *The Run upon the Bankers. Ball*, p. 160, sees the original idea for the poem in remarks made by Matthew Prior to Swift: 'I am tired with politics and lost in the South Sea: the roaring of the waves and the madness of the people were justly put together' (*Corr* II, 378). But the letter dates from February 1721, *after* publication of this poem, and clearly refers to it. Swift took particular care with this item, to ensure that it should be 'as correct as I can make it, and it cost me pains enough, whether it be good or no' (*Corr* II, 365). He also gave instructions on how the poem was to be conveyed surreptitiously to the printer.

The text is based on *WF*, but I have restored the two missing stanzas from Swift's holograph.

Title] *WF*; The Bubble *early edns*; The South-Sea *M28*. Swift's manuscript carries no title; Ford was probably responsible for giving it the name by which it has been generally known. *WF*'s title may then have more claim to authenticity.

3 Southern Main the South Sea Company had been founded in 1711, ostensibly to trade in the South Sea, that is, the Pacific, but in reality to take over the government debt. Throughout the poem Swift plays on geographic terms such as 'sea', 'main', 'gulf'.

4 jugglers magicians, with implication 'tricksters'.

5 told counted.

14, 16] *these lines appear in reverse order in Swift MS and early edns.*

20 coach and six compare *Death and Daphne* 88.

24 over head and ears Swift characteristically takes a common figurative expression (*Tilley* H268) and reanimates its literal sense. The phrase also occurs in *Polite Conversation* (*PW* IV, 165).

25 calenture 'a disease incident to sailors within the tropics, characterized by delirium in which the patient . . . fancies the sea to be green fields, and desires to leap into it' (*OED*).

33–40] *not in Swift MS and first London edn.*

33 Five]WF, Woburn transcript; two *other edns.*

chariots in many cases the first purchase of a newly rich speculator was an equipage, and it was the first asset he had to dispose of when stocks fell.

37 Pharaoh Exodus xiv, 6–30. For other allusions to Exodus, see ll. 213–16.

directors the 'guilty men' of the episode, headed by the chief promoter Sir John Blunt, who was known to Swift. Nearly always a baneful word in this era.

42 The young adventurer Icarus, son of Daedalus, who flew with his father from Crete; the sun melted the wax with which his wings were fastened, and he fell into the sea, and drowned.

44 scorns the middle way to keep flew too high, that is (unlocking the metaphor), refused to live with decent moderation, appropriate to people of an ordinary station.

45 paper wings compare Pope, *Epistle to Bathurst* 69–70: 'Blest paper-credit! last and best supply! / That lends corruption lighter wings to fly!'

48 towering soaring.

58 gulf whirlpool.

61 from Severn's brink 'so have I seen' is an epic formula, but very possibly Swift had witnessed this scene when staying at Berkeley Castle, as for example in 1702 (see headnote to *A Ballad on the Game of Traffic*). The near-by stretch of the Severn remains a well-known breeding area, notably the Slimbridge wildfowl colony.

63 bird of Jove eagle.

65–8] *Swift MS; not in WF.*

72 sweeps the board carries off all the stakes; perhaps a hint of 'board of directors' (a less common but possible usage then: the normal word was 'court').

73–4 compare the famous lines in *On Poetry: a Rhapsody* 353–6.

97 play gaming.

99 hoops circular stiffeners of whalebone in a dress.

100   Lapland witches 'References to Lapland witches became frequent in English literature after the publication of the *Historia de Gentibus Septentrionalibus* of Olaus Magnus in 1555' (*P* I, 254). The work influenced Pope and Thomson amongst others.

sieve traditionally used by witches to sail in: see *Macbeth* I, iii, 8, and Keats, *Eve of St Agnes* 120.

106   grannam grandmother (already becoming a dialect word).

113–16]   Swift MS; not in WF.

115 proverbial; see *Merchant of Venice* II, vii, 65. *Tilley* A146.

117   patriots the word 'patriot' 'fell into discredit in the earlier half of the eighteenth century, being used, according to Dr Johnson, "ironically for a factious disturber of the government"' (*OED*).

118   wash their hands italicized in early editions, suggesting ironic allusion to biblical sources ('I will wash mine hands in innocence', Psalms xxvi, 6) or to the proverbial use deriving from Matthew xxvii, 24, describing Pilate's gesture to absolve himself from the responsibility for Christ's death.

119   Pactolus see *The Fable of Midas* 1.

121   the Bath the waters at the spa town: but perhaps also recalling 'St Mary's bath', a vessel used in alchemy (as in Ben Jonson, *The Alchemist* II, i, 272).

121–8 compare Dryden, *Discourse concerning Satire* (1693): 'A shilling dipped in the bath may go for gold among the ignorant, but the sceptres on the guineas show the difference.'

122   nobler a technical term for precious metals (*OED*, 'noble', 7b).

123   virtue the alchemist's term.

124   a guinea that is, a golden guinea coin.

127   multiplying glass a toy consisting of a concave lens which was cut into various facets.

130   jobber stock-jobber, dealer or pusher of shares.

131   spectacles a much-used trope: see P. Rogers, 'Gulliver's Glasses', in *The Art of Jonathan Swift*, ed. C. Probyn (1978), pp. 179–88.

136   Cynthia the moon.

141–2 Ecclesiastes xi, 1.

148   'Change Alley the heart of stock-jobbing, a 'miniature labyrinth of lanes' (Carswell, op. cit., p. 16), across Lombard Street from the Royal Exchange.

149   Nine times that would be once an hour, roughly, during the working day.

157–60 paraphrasing Psalm cvii, 26–7, as indicated in a note.

161   Garr'way 'A coffee-house in Change Alley' (footnote in *WF*). Founded by Thomas Garraway *c.* 1669–1670, and soon a centre of trading activity, in connection with the Hudson's Bay Company, the Land Bank, etc. Finally closed down *c.* 1866; long before this the functions carried on at Garraway's had been transferred to the Stock Exchange. See B. Lillywhite, *London Coffee Houses* (1963), pp. 216–24; for activity during the Bubble, see Carswell, op. cit., p. 157.

161–4 The Cornwall wreckers were the most notorious in this era: see Pope, *Epistle to Bathurst* 355 and note. The fullest modern account is J.G. Rule, 'Wrecking and Coastal Plunder', *Albion's Fatal Tree*, ed. D. Hay *et al.* (1977), pp. 167–88.

168   The Swiss and Dutch the suggestion is that there were larger forces of international finance, gnomes of Zurich and Amsterdam, who were reaping larger fortunes. For Amsterdam as the financial capital of Europe, see Carswell, op.

cit., p. 4. It is possible that by 'Swiss' Swift means the great Huguenot bankers and merchants. *Tory* (l. 166) means something like 'old-fashioned patriot' in this context.

169   rooks   swindlers, confidence-men.

170   cully   dupe, ingenuous gambler.

173   castles in the air   for the proverbial use, see *His Grace's Answer to Jonathan* 20.

179   Earl Godwin's castles   'According to tradition the present Goodwin Sands were once a fertile island belonging to Earl Godwin [that is, the eleventh-century Saxon earl]. Geologists, however, are sceptical' (*P* I, 257).

180   palace]   *WF*, *Woburn transcript*; castle   *Swift MS*, *early edns*.

185–8   paraphrasing Phaedrus, the Latin fabulist who produced a version of Aesop (*Fables* I, xxv, 3–4): '*Canes currentes bibere in Nilo flumine*, / *A crocodilis ne rapiantur, traditum est.*' The story also occurs in Pliny, *Natural History* VIII, 149: and a proverb evolved, '*ut canis e Nilo*', meaning to do something too hurriedly. In this form it appeared in Erasmus's *Adages*, and a later English borrowing is recorded in *Tilley* D604. However, Swift's extension of the proverb seems to be closer to Phaedrus than to the other available sources.

189   Antaeus   a gigantic wrestler, who drew fresh strength from his mother, Earth, whenever he touched the ground; finally killed by Hercules ('Alcides'), who lifted him into the air in combat. The story is told in Lucan, *Pharsalia* IV, 589–655.

196   Suspended   suggesting that the peccant directors should be hanged, or at the very least (as in the case of the implicated Chancellor of the Exchequer, John Aislabie) debarred from sitting in the House. See Biog. Dict.

199   What planet ruled   presumably Mercury, the most volatile of the planetary influences, and also the presiding influence over thieves. Those born under Mercury were notable, too, as 'survivors', as pointed out to me by Mr. S.J. Tester.

200   you never can be drowned   probably recalling the proverb, 'He that is born to be hanged will never be drowned' (*Tilley* B139), which is quoted by Swift in *Polite Conversation* (*PW* IV, 147). See also *The Tempest* I, i, 33.

210   coasters   those who live on the coast.

213–16   Exodus x, 12–19.

217–20   there are echoes here both of the Bible and of the Prayer Book. Line 218 may be most directly drawn from the Magnificat: 'He hath put down the mighty from their seat: and hath exalted the humble and the meek.' Another possible source is Luke i, 52: 'He hath put down the mighty from their seats, and exalted them of low degree.' Compare also 1 Peter v, 5: 'God resisteth the proud, and giveth grace to the humble': Lines 219–20 can be compared with Psalm lxxxix, 9, 'Thou rulest the raging of the sea: when the waves thereof arise, thou stillest them', and Psalm cvii, 29, 'He maketh the storm a calm, and the waves thereof are still.' The last-named Psalm was appointed to be read in the form of prayer to be used at sea: a prayer to be used in this service includes the phrase, 'who stillest the rage [of the sea]'. Lines 217–20 constitute a sort of compressed Litany.

222   devouring swine   alluding to the Gadarene swine, into which unclean spirits entered and were lost as the swine 'ran violently down a steep place into the sea' (Mark v, 11–13). An apt scriptural reference, since the episode follows Christ's stilling of the storm, and is followed by the statement, 'They that fed the swine fled, and told it in the city, and in the country.' South Sea mania as a kind of diabolic 'possession' is a common notion of conservative moralists.

Apparent rari nantes... Virgil, *Aeneid* I, 118–19: 'And here and there above the waves were seen / Arms, pictures, precious goods, and floating men' (tr. Dryden). The lines were placed as an epigraph, that is, at the head of the poem, in some early editions.

AN ELEGY ON THE MUCH LAMENTED DEATH OF MR DEMAR, THE FAMOUS RICH USURER

First published in two Dublin broadsides; the order of their publication has not been established (*T* 611, 1662; *Foxon* S836, S837). Mourning borders surround the text. Reprinted in *St James's Post* on 20 July 1720 and *Weekly Journal* on 23 July – both were London newspapers, one a daily, the other published each Saturday by James Read. In the same year the poem was appended to a London edition of a reply to Swift's *Proposal for the Universal Use of Irish Manufacture* (*T* 614). It appeared, as might have been expected, in Curll's new volume of Swiftiana (*T* 19: see note on *To Stella, Who Collected and Transcribed His Poems* 50). The epitaph alone appears in *M28*. After other fugitive appearances in print, it was present in full in *WF*.

The circumstances of composition are given by Delany in his *Observations Upon Lord Orrery's Remarks* (1754, pp. 53–4) and by Scott in his edition (1814). The former states, 'The writing an elegy upon Demar, was a subject started, and partly executed in company, Swift, and Stella, and a few friends present. Everyone threw in their hint, and Stella added hers as follows [ll. 31–4 quoted].' Scott is a little more specific: 'Swift, with some of his usual party, happened to be in Mr Sheridan's, in Capel Street, when the news of Demar's death was brought to them; and the elegy was the joint composition of the company.'

For Joseph Damer, see Biog. Dict. and *Gilbert*, I, 65–7. He had become a kind of Irish Peter Walter, the grasping usurer personified.

The text is based on *WF*, with italicization much reduced. The broadside versions are not very well printed, and even *WF* seems to retain some of their typographic peculiarities. Neither the punning nor the parody of legal jargon is clearly brought out by the heavy use of italics.

Title]*WF; early editions have* the famous rich man, who died the 6th of this inst. July, 1720. *WF adds* Written in the year 1720.

2 Demar pronounced, and usually spelt 'Damer'. The opening formula parodies the start of a legal agreement.

8 steward servant; but alluding to the function of land-agent and broker, which generally involved putting money out at interest.

13 pelf wealth; then a much commoner word than today: see for instance Pope, *Epistle to Bathurst* 109, 'these poor men of pelf'.

17 under hand and seal the closing formula of a document, next to the signature.

18 obligation state of indebtedness, with the overtones of a legal usage cited in *OED*: 'An agreement, enforcable by law, whereby a person or persons become bound to the payment of a sum of money...*esp.* in English Law, a written contract or bond under seal containing a penalty with a condition annexed.' An extended sense is 'legal liability'.

20 not worth a groat Tilley G458.

22 interest (1) money paid for a loan; (2) self-interest; (3) legal concern or title.

25 London Tavern 'A tavern in Dublin where Mr Demar kept his office' (note in *F* (1737)). According to *Gilbert*, I, 65-7, the establishment was located in Fishamble Street, conveniently close to St Patrick's for Swift's acquaintance with Demar. The tavern was destroyed by fire in 1729.

27 touched received money by underhand means (*OED*, citing this line). The second half of the verse seems to mean 'were the worse for drink'.

28 shot reckoning, bill.

32 moidores 'A Portuguese gold coin current in England during the first half of the eighteenth century, and accepted at a value between 27s. and 28s.' (*P* I, 234). Robinson Crusoe computes his fortune in terms of moidores.

35 current alive, and perhaps generally known.

36 cried down deemed unlawful, publicly decried.

change of mortal state: with pun on 'exchange', a broking centre.

40 bills (1) of exchange, used in commercial transactions; (2) of mortality, the periodic return of vital statistics, esp. of burials.

43]*WF*; His heirs for winding-sheet bestowed / His moneybags together sewed. / And that he might securely rest, *broadsides and early edns*.

LINES FROM CADENUS TO VANESSA

These verses are found in two of Swift's letters to Vanessa, which may be dated 13 or 20 July 1720 and 12 August 1720 respectively. The earlier set is introduced as sent to Swift by 'your friend', whilst the later set occurs in the context of this passage: 'We live here in a very dull town [Dublin], every valuable creature absent, and Cad— says he is weary of it, and would rather drink his coffee on the barrenest highest mountain in Wales, than be king here' (*Corr* II, 350, 355). The holograph text is in the British Library, Add. MS 39839. The verses were first printed by Scott in 1814 in the correspondence.

For the background, see headnote to *Cadenus and Vanessa*. The narrative of this significant year is told in Sybil Le Brocquy, *Cadenus* (1962), pp. 64-82. *PJH* I, 130 suggests that the couplets 'may well be rejected lines of *Cadenus and Vanessa*, possibly a speech by Pallas'.

The text is based on Swift's manuscript letter.

Title the editor's.

'Nymph, would you learn the only art'

4 a familiar insistence in Swift, e.g. in *A Letter to a Young Lady* (*PW* IX, 87).

'A fig for partridges and quails'

4 to drink my coffee the phrase can often be suspected of bearing a sexual meaning in this correspondence, as possibly here. For Horace Walpole's interpretation of the expression, see *Corr* II, 351.

'DORINDA DREAMS OF DRESS ABED'

These verses appear in the same letter of [?13 or 20] July 1720 as the first set of *Lines from Cadenus to Vanessa*. Swift introduces them as 'an epigram that concerns you not' (*Corr* II, 350). First published by Scott: the source is British Library, Add. MS 39839.

AN EXCELLENT NEW SONG ON A SEDITIOUS PAMPHLET

'Written in the year 1720', as *WF* stated on its first publication. Reprinted in the fifth volume of London *Miscellanies* by Charles Davis (*T* 25, 5a), which was issued late in January 1735.

This was one of the items affected by the decision to cancel certain sections of the text in *WF* (see Margaret Weedon in *The Library*, 5th ser. XXII (1967), 44–56). The preamble to this *Song* was rewritten, though still not in very ingratiating terms; ll. 1–4 were re-set but not altered.

The poem relates to the furore caused by Swift's *Proposal for the Universal Use of Irish Manufacture* (*PW* IX, 13–22), which was published in April or May 1720. When Edward Waters, the printer, came to trial on a charge of sedition, he was found not guilty, but the Lord Chief Justice refused to accept this verdict and sent the jury back nine times. It was another year before the legal complications were sorted out and a grant of *noli prosequi* issued. Swift described the events in a letter to Sir Thomas Hanmer dated 1 October 1720: 'The printer was tried with a jury of the most violent party men, who yet brought him in not guilty, but were sent back nine times, and at last brought in a special verdict, so that the man is to be tried again next term' (*Corr* II, 358). A special verdict (l.5 of preamble) is one where the jury merely determines the facts, and leaves the judge to decide on the points of law involved. See also *Ferguson*, pp. 49–59. For Edward Waters, a High Tory printer who had been in trouble with the ministry for many years, see *Munter*, pp. 112, 126–9. His newspaper, the *Flying Post*, often gave offence to the authorities, and as late as 1736 he was sent to Newgate for reprinting a pamphlet attacking Richard Bettesworth. See *Munter*, pp. 150–51.

The text is based on *WF*, with the preamble following the uncancelled copy.

Title *Packington's Pound* was the best known of all ballad tunes, used on innumerable occasions during the period (e.g. Air 43 in *The Beggar's Opera*). It is found as far back as the Fitzwilliam Virginal Book. See *Simpson*, pp. 564–70.

Preamble *The text in its cancelled state reads*: The author having wrote a treatise, advising the people of Ireland to wear their own manufactures, a prosecution was set on foot against Waters the printer thereof, which was carried out with so much violence, that one Whitshed, then Chief Justice, thought proper, in a manner the most extraordinary, to keep them above nine hours, and to send them eleven times out of court, until he had wearied them into a special verdict. *Whitshed* William Whitshed: see Biog. Dict.

1 tabbies watered silk taffeta.

2 Robert Ballentine not identified.

10 in woollen are clad by legislation dating back to 1666. There were sometimes efforts to evade the law, as in the celebrated case of the actress Anne

Oldfield, who was buried in great finery after her death in 1730: see Pope, *Epistle to Cobham* 246. The intention behind the law was to protect the English wool trade against imported stuffs.

12   Teague   the stock name for an Irishman, in drama especially but also in life: in earlier use than 'Paddy'.

13   a living dog   originally Ecclesiastes ix, 4, and thence a proverbial usage. *Tilley* D495.

16   our horns pull in   curtail our activity; with pun on the sense of the 'horns of cuckoldry'. *Tilley* A620.

19   To inflame both the nations   Swift wrote to Pope on 10 January 1721, 'During the trial, the Chief Justice among other singularities, laid his hand on his breast, and protested solemnly that the author's design was to bring in the Pretender' (*Corr* II, 368).

24   the Dean's book   that is, *A Proposal for the Universal Use of Irish Manufacture*.

26–7   for Waters' arrest in 1714 and 1715, see *Munter*, p. 129.

27   Corum Nobus   more correctly *coram nobis* (before us or in our presence), a phrase used in a summons. The misspelling 'is intended to represent vulgar and colloquial pronunciation' (*P* I, 238).

29   swingingly   this use is cited in *OED* under the sense of 'swingingly', that is, 'hugely, immensely'; but there is an obvious pun on the slang sense of 'swinging', that is, 'hanging'.

32   come off clean   escape without coming to any harm (see *OED*, 'clean', *adverb*, 3), with a pun on the sense of 'clean linen'.

PART OF THE NINTH ODE OF THE FOURTH BOOK OF HORACE

Written in 1720 or 1721, but not published until 1730, when it was included (anonymously) in a London collection of verses, *Miscellaneous Poems by Several Hands* (1730), *T* 1611. First admitted to the Swift canon by *F* (1746).

A proposal to establish a National Bank of Ireland in 1720 was opposed by Swift, amongst others, as a device of moneyed men to increase their hold on national affairs: see *PW* IX, 281–321. Swift wrote to Archbishop King, another of the scheme's detractors, on 28 September 1721: 'Bankrupts are always for setting up banks: how then can you think a bank will fail of a majority in both houses?' (*Corr* II, 405). The scheme was, however, rejected by the Irish parliament in December 1721.

The ode imitated, *Ne forte credas*, ll. 29–52, is written in quatrains: Swift's was a reasonably close version as imitations went. The concluding lines are a development of the familiar 'happy man' motif, for which see Maren-Sofie Røstvig, *The Happy Man* (1958–62).

The text is based on *F* (1746).

Title   9th *and* 4th *in F*. For King, see Biog. Dict.

4   your virtues   the friend addressed by Horace is Marcus Lollius, a consul, much respected by Augustus, but unpopular in many quarters of Rome. 'The charges of rapacity and avarice elsewhere levelled against this powerful and unpopular ally of the Princeps may perhaps be held confirmed rather than refuted by Horace's eager praise of his disinterested integrity' (Ronald Syme,

The Roman Revolution (1960), p. 429). There is obvious irony in directing this paean to *opposition* virtue to King through the medium of Lollius.

11 Pale Avarice avarice (associated in this context with usury) was traditionally sickly: see *Faerie Queen* I, iv, 29.

13–14 for gold and avarice dragging England into slavery, compare Pope, *Epilogue to the Satires* I, 151–64. The imagery is recurrent in opposition literature of the 1730s.

THE RUN UPON THE BANKERS

According to Stella, in the Woburn commonplace book, 'written A:D: 1720'. *WF* concurs in the date, and a manuscript note in the Huntington copy of its first broadside appearance does so too. There were two separate editions: no place, no date [Dublin, ?1720], which is *T* 611A, *Foxon* S900; and a version put out by Samuel Terry (Cork, 1721), together with another poem by Edward Ward – this is *T* 611B, *Foxon* S901. As well as *WF* (cancelled state), the poem by Swift appeared in a London edition of *Misc* (1735), that is, *T* 25 (5b).

The panic occasioned by the South Sea Bubble in the autumn of 1720 spread quickly to Dublin, although the Irish economy was less directly affected. Among Swift's friends embarrassed by the crash was the printer John Barber. In a letter to Vanessa composed in bursts between 15 and 20 October 1720, Swift wrote: 'Conversation is full of nothing but South-Sea, and the ruin of the kingdom, and scarcity of money' (*Corr* II, 361). There are many similarities in phrasing to *Upon the South Sea Project*, written *c*. December 1720. This is a wholly characteristic work, blending wit, mythology, biblical allusion, and parody of commercial language.

The text is based on *WF*, with the presentation slightly normalized; the heavy use of italics has not been reproduced.

Title *WF* has a preliminary note as follows: 'This poem was printed some years ago, and it should seem by the late failure of two bankers to be somewhat prophetic, it was therefore thought fit to be reprinted.' The same event is mentioned in Swift's letter to the Earl of Oxford of 30 August 1734: 'Two of our chief bankers have broke for near two hundred thousand pounds; and others are leaving off their business' (*Corr* IV, 349). This suggests at least complicity in the note.

3 one] *WF*; a *Woburn transcript*.

9–12 an image reflecting the old physiological view that corrupt 'humours' were carried about the body in the blood; *circulation* (l. 11) puns on the medical and monetary senses.

14 Quakers refused to pay tithes and were regularly distrained for the sums owed. A 'levee' was a gathering of suitors or clients; here it is applied to a throng of 'duns', that is, debt-collectors or bailiffs.

17 on the nail commercial slang for 'immediately', 'without delay'. 'The explanations associating [the phrase] with certain pillars at the Exchange of Limerick or Bristol are too late to be of any authority' (*OED*); however, the expression has a distinct ring of the business quarter in eighteenth-century usage. See also *Tilley* N18.

19–20 alluding to the fable of Aesop on the jay who dressed himself in the finery of a peacock and strutted about, until stripped by the other birds: Fable XXX in Ogilby's collection (1668).

21 the wisest monarch sings Solomon, in Proverbs xxiii, 5.

24 silver plumes the goose-quills of a scrivener, drawing up deeds on parchment.

27 The wish of Nero according to Suetonius's *Lives of the Caesars*, Nero 10, the Emperor expressed this desire when obliged to sign death-warrants.

32 images of wax the wax effigies of satanic rites, attempting to damage enemies through sympathetic magic; the effigies on a seal, impressed in wax, as used in legal documents.

40 the empty chests] *WF*; his empty chests *Woburn transcript.*

42 the god of gold and hell strictly, Pluto was the god of hell and Plutus that of gold: but the two were regularly confused, since both names have the same root in πλοῦτος, wealth. Swift does not seem to have made the distinction.

48 the bloody bond signed in, or sealed with, blood; as in the Faust legend. *Conjuror* (1. 45) suggests magician, devotee of the black arts, rather than a practitioner of legerdemain.

52 the writing on the wall proverbial, from the moving hand witnessed by Belshazzar, King of Babylon, in Daniel v, 5–30.

56 grand account the final judgement, punning on commercial meanings of 'account'.

57 call the summons of God, but also the demand for an instalment (South Sea stock was paid for at intervals by a series of 'calls' on the subscribers).

60 counters in a shop or bank, but suggesting also 'compter', prison (for debtors, etc.).

61–4 another apocalyptic vision of the last judgement, but also perhaps a prophecy of worldly retribution for the promoters and political supporters of the South Sea scheme; one meaning of l. 61 might be, 'when the guilty ministers are replaced'.

64 Weighed in the balance, and found light from Daniel v, 27: 'Thou art weighed in the balances, and art found wanting.'

MR JASON HASSARD, A WOOLLEN DRAPER IN DUBLIN

First published by *F*, vol. VIII (1746). It has been suggested (*P* III, 948) that the poem is connected with the episode in 1720 which surrounded Swift's *Proposal for the Universal Use of Irish Manufacture*: see *An Excellent New Song on a Seditious Pamphlet*, headnote. This is altogether plausible, but no details are forthcoming. 'Draper' is spelt with a medial 'i' in *F*, Swift's ordinary form of the word.

1–2 Jason led the Argonauts on their quest to recover the golden fleece (shorn from the winged ram Chrysomallus), which was kept by King Aeetes in Colchis. With the help of Medea he wrested the fleece from the custody of a loathsome dragon. The story is told in many ancient narratives, including that of the fabulist Hyginus, but the most direct source is probably *Metamorphoses*, VII, 1–58. Compare *Verses Occasioned by the Sudden Drying Up of St Patrick's Well* 7–8.

3–4 stuff...enough one of Swift's most habitual rhymes.

5 watchful dragon Ovid's expression is *pervigilem...draconem* (*Metamorphoses*

VII, 149). There is almost certainly a political allusion but it is pointless to speculate on identities where the date of composition remains unsettled.

THE DESCRIPTION OF AN IRISH FEAST

First published in *WF* with the heading, 'Translated in the year 1720.' There is no means of checking this statement. According to Scott in the *Works* (1814), Swift heard of a recent poem entitled *Pléaráca na Ruarcach*, attributed to Hugh MacGauran. He asked for a literal translation which (some sources allege) was provided by MacGauran himself. It is well established that the poem was set to music by the famous blind poet and composer Turlough Carolan (1670-1738), and again there have been suggestions of a direct link with Swift. One story is that Carolan came to know Swift through his patron Delany, and that 'the Dean admired Carolan's genius, had him frequently at the Deanery House in Dublin, and used to hear him play and sing the *pléaráca*.' See Vivian Mercier, 'Swift and the Gaelic Tradition', *Fair Liberty was All His Cry*, ed. A. Norman Jeffares (1967), pp. 282-3. There is no good authority for this anecdote, and not much sign that Swift had a close feeling for Gaelic literature. Carolan, sometimes known as the last of the bards, excited the interest of Oliver Goldsmith: his essay on the harpist (1760) refers to the present poem (*Works*, ed. A. Friedman (1966), III, 118-20).

The Irish poem consists of ninety-six lines: Swift's version corresponds to roughly the first seventy-two verses. The remainder were translated by Scott in his edition. For further bibliographical details, see *P* I, 245. The ostensible subject is a chieftain named Brian O'Rourke who rebelled against the English overlords in 1580; but there may well be some contemporary reference.

The text is based on *WF*.

9   Usquebaugh   from Gaelic *uisge beatha*, literally 'water of life'; whisky.

12   madder   'wooden vessel' (note in *WF*); usually square in shape.

22   kercher   'handkerchief' (note in *WF*).

24   searcher   perhaps the excise official who would be on the look-out for smuggled or illegal liquor.

38   ramping   romping (dialect).

44   splishsplash   according to the legend, Carolan was particularly impressed by Swift's rendering of the onomatopoeic effects in the original here.

48   Margery Grinagin   'name of an Irish woman' (note in *WF*).

56   a Yean   'another Irish name for a woman' (note in *WF*). ·

64   skenes   'daggers, or short swords' (note in *WF*).

74   Lusk   a village about fourteen miles north of Dublin, with a round tower and an ancient church.

75   The castle of Slane   overlooking the Boyne valley, in Co. Meath, some thirty miles north-west of Dublin.

76   Carrickdrumrusk   an anglicized version of Cara Droma Rúisg, that is, Carrick-on-Shannon in Co. Leitrim.

77   The Earl of Kildare   *P* I, 247 suggests the reference may be to Gerald Fitzgerald, eleventh Earl of Kildare (1525-85), a famous soldier; his father, the ninth Earl, seems possible, and still more so his grandfather, the 'great' eighth Earl. The brother has not been identified. If the eleventh Earl is meant, his half-brother Thomas (1513-37) might fit.

80 mother 'It is the custom in Ireland to call nurses foster-mothers...and thus the poorest claim kindred to the richest' (Hawkesworth, cited in *P* I, 247). The passage exemplifies a strain of comic braggadocio habitual in Irish poems of this kind.

87 wame belly (often jocular, particularly when 'belly' started to acquire vulgar overtones).

STELLA'S BIRTHDAY (1721)

Transcribed by Stella herself (Woburn commonplace-book), and headed 'Written A.D. 1720-21'. First published in *M28*, where it is dated 1720; reprinted in *WF*, with the same date. In 1737 *F* asserts, 'Written at Windsor in the Year 1720', obviously quite erroneously since Swift was in Ireland. March 1721 is indicated.

Of this poem *Jaffe*, p. 88, observes, 'Stella is an angel too – alternately the sign and hostess of the Angel-Inn. But she is not quite so ethereal as her counterparts in the Renaissance and Restoration. The poet endows her with all the humanity of a good-natured barmaid.' It should, however, be stressed that *freely* (l. 24) connotes 'liberally', 'generously', rather than 'opulently' or 'promiscuously'.

The text is based on *WF*, with a couplet supplied from the Woburn transcript.

6 Angel Inn one of the commonest of all inn signs: Bryant Lillywhite records no less than 111 such emblems, for tradesmen of all kinds, in his *London Signs* (1972), pp. 8-12.
9 tapster] *WF, M28*; rascal *Woburn transcript*. A dig at Sheridan, probably.
18 thirty-six actually it was Stella's fortieth birthday.
21 supplies compensates, provides a substitute for.
35-6] *Woburn transcript; not in M28, WF*.
37 light alight. The construction supposes a sign of 'Chloe's Head', but Swift reverts in the next line to the contents of an actual woman's head.
39 your] *WF, M28*; thy *Woburn transcript*. And so with the pronouns in the following lines.
40 no chicken shopsoiled expression, as can be seen from its appearance in *Polite Conversation* (*PW* IV, 145).
51 beauty's queen Venus.

THE ANSWER TO VANESSA'S REBUS

Date uncertain. The rebus and its reply appeared in the form of a broadside, with no date or place of publication. They were reprinted by Curll in the second volume of his *Miscellanea* (1727), that is, *T* 24, as well as in a London edition of *Cadenus and Vanessa* (1726), *T* 661A. The original publication has been dated 'between 1714 and 1720' (*T* 632; see also *P* II, 715), and '?1724' (*Foxon* R144). Davis (*PHD* 138) puts composition at '1714?', which seems too early. It first appeared in *F* in 1746.

The rebus was attributed in all early editions to 'a lady', whom Curll identifies as 'Vanessa' and *F* (1746) as 'Mrs Vanhomrigh'. There is no reason to doubt this ascription. Vanessa died in June 1723, which would supply a firm *terminus ad quem* for composition and probably for publication. The placing of the work here is purely conjectural; my own interpretation of ll. 21–8 is that they allude to Swift's renewed political activity, rather than to his fallow period (as *P* I, 715 suggests).

Vanessa's rebus is a poem of eleven lines, something between a riddle and a verbal charade, spelling out the name Jo-nathan Swift. The text is based on the original edition.

Title   editorial. The broadside is headed *A Rebus Written by a Lady, On the Rev. Dean Swift, with his Answer*; Swift's portion is headed *The Answer*.

3]*broadside*;   Which she in a frolic has ventured to show   *Curll*.

6   *rebus*   a puzzle in which a punning application of each syllable of a word is given (*OED*).

16   *manteaus*   ]*Curll*; mantuas *other edns*. 'Mantua' was used at the time for a manteau, that is, a loose gown, as well as for a fine material, but Curll's reading makes the meaning clearer today.

21–8   alluding to Vanessa's compliments to Swift in her rebus, as one versed in state affairs, familiar with the great, and 'like a racer' in flying to the assistance of friends. A 'great man', in due course to be particularly associated with Walpole, was a generic name for prime minister. The last couplet could refer to Bishop Atterbury, who was arrested and sent to the Tower in August 1722: see *Upon the Horrid Plot*, headnote.

APOLLO TO THE DEAN

This poem had its occasion in an exchange of verses between Swift, Delany, and Stella. If 'Tuesday the tenth' (l. 29) is correct, then the month would be January 1721, as editors have supposed. Swift's MS has 'the ninth', which would fit February 1720. *WF* heads the poem 'written in the year 1720', and it is not certain that the later date is correct. In the absence of decisive evidence, I concur with the established dating. Delany had written two sets of *Verses on the Deanery Window* (*P* I, 261–2), to which this poem refers. Further bouts were marked by *News from Parnassus*, by Delany (*P* I, 267–9), and *Apollo's Edict*, probably by Swift.

Swift's autograph exists split into two portions. The longer section, ll. 1–50, 71–106, is in the Pierpont Morgan Library, New York. The remainder is on a separate smaller leaf in the Dreer Collection of the Historical Society of Pennsylvania, Philadelphia. Stella made a transcription of Swift's original, and this also survives, in the Woburn commonplace-book. There are other contemporary transcripts, of which I have not taken detailed account. The poem was first published, along with other parts of the exchange, in a collection edited by the miscellaneous writer Matthew Concanen (1724), and was reprinted in a Dublin set of *Misc* in 1728. It later figured in *WF*, without the original *Verses on the Deanery Window* this time.

The work is presented as a speech from the bench by Apollo, president of the court at Parnassus, the god of poetry as well as of the sun. For other Apollo poems, see above, p. 100, and below, pp. 229, 452. The amphibrach rhythm was not very common with Swift; but it was a favourite with Prior, whose *Jinny the Just* (written 1708) was greatly admired by Swift. (It was not published until 1907, but Pope made efforts to get permission to print it in 1727, as he hoped to use it in *Misc.* Swift had 'several times' asked Pope to see that this was done: Pope *Corr* II, 466.)

The text is based on *WF*, collated with the manuscripts.

Title]*Woburn transcript, WF*; Apollo to Dean Swift. By Himself *Concanen.*

1 parodying the form of a deposition or court statement.

3 chemists the ancient alchemists had associated gold with the sun. See *Vanbrug's House* 127 and note.

4 I that makes gold it was long thought that the sun ripened minerals, including gold, into their perfect state. See *Paradise Lost* III, 606–12; Thomson, *Summer* (1746 text) 136–9.

20 judgement or wit the concepts had been influentially set in opposition by Locke, *Essay concerning Human Understanding* (1690) II, xi, 2, and Addison, *Spectator*, no. 62 (11 May 1711).

28 succeed in your place as poet in residence, so to speak, but also perhaps ultimately as Dean (he became Chancellor of the Cathedral in 1730, and Dean of Down later on).

29 tenth] *Woburn transcript, WF*; ninth *Swift (MF)*. See headnote.

33 vi et armis see *An Excellent New Song, being the Intended Speech of a Famous Orator* 4.

35 the formula used for prosecuting political libels. Writing verse on glass was highly popular at the start of the century.

37 my sister Diana, the moon.

41 myself in some early editions 'our self'.

42 mingled with grey mentioned more than once, apparently literal rather than symbolic: compare *Stella's Birthday* (1721) 46.

51 she Diana.

52 ∧ 53 She can swear to the person, whom oft she has seen, / At night between Caven Street and College Green: *Swift, Woburn transcript, early edns; not in WF*. The limits of central Dublin, in effect; 'Caven Street' is Kevin Street, running east from St Patrick's Cathedral.

53 his Delany's.

56 discover reveal, expose to view.

57 he will] *Woburn transcript*; he'll *WF*.

78 subtle crafty.

80 old Nick the devil. *Tilley* N161.

81 topics see *To Stella, Who Collected and Transcribed His Poems* 26 and note.

85 bubble deception.

90 dressed groomed.

93 Prometheus he was punished for stealing fire from heaven by having an eagle preying on his liver: a favourite analogy with Swift, as in *Prometheus* 53–6. The vulture (l. 95) belongs rather to the myth of Tityus.

95 spleen (1) the organ, near the liver; (2) the state of depression, moodiness associated with the excessive activity of this organ in 'humours' psychology. Older physiology allotted the spleen a central role in the regulation of body chemistry more accurately assigned to the liver.

100 measure metre.

101 just out of her prime if 1721 is the correct date, she was within a month or two of her fortieth birthday. See *OED*, 'prime', 9.

103 diseases see *To Stella, Visiting Me in My Sickness* 104.

AN EPILOGUE TO A PLAY FOR THE BENEFIT OF THE WEAVERS IN
IRELAND

The performance was held at the Theatre Royal, Smock Alley, in Dublin on 1
April 1721, and the play was *Hamlet*. Sheridan contributed a prologue, which
was printed on one side of a folio sheet, backed by Swift's epilogue (*T* 626,
Foxon S839). From basically the same setting of type came a separate issue of the
epilogue, printed in Dublin by J.W. (*T* 625, *Foxon* S838). Another version
appeared in Limerick (*T* 1650, *Foxon* S840). All three clearly date from 1721,
and the first two evidently within a week or so of the performance. The epilogue
also appeared in a number of London newspapers around the middle of April. It
first came out in a full-length book thanks to the indefatigable Curll, who
included it in his *Miscellanies*, that is, of Swift and near-Swift items, 4th edn
(1721), *T* 19. It was reprinted in Concanen's collection, in *M28*, and in *The
Drapier's Miscellany* (1733) before taking its place in *WF*.

In 1721 a severe recession overtook the Irish weaving trade, which was con-
stantly handicapped by the restrictive legislation of the Westminster govern-
ment. Unemployment was widespread in the early months of the year and relief
measures had to be instituted. Swift wrote to Charles Ford on 15 April, 'Upon a
charitable collection some days ago for the poor weavers, the return of those who
are starving for want of work amounts to above 1600, which is pretty fair for this
town, and one trade, after such numbers as have gone to other countries to seek
a livelihood' (*Corr* II, 380). See further, *Ferguson*, p. 63.

The text is based on *WF*, collated with Stella's transcript in the Woburn
commonplace-book and early broadside editions.

Title]*WF*; An Epilogue, to be spoke at the Theatre-Royal this present
Saturday being April the 1st. In the behalf of the Distressed Weavers *J.W.
edn. Other early edns have variants of *J.W.*

The epilogue was spoken by Thomas Griffith, a well-known Dublin actor.
Stella heads her transcript 'Written A:D 1721'; *WF* says 'about the year 1721',
which confirms the insecurity of this otherwise authoritative edition when it
comes to dates.

3 actors still more commonly regarded as vagabonds than as members of a
respectable profession.

3–4 an 'Irish' rhyme, becoming obsolete by English standards of
pronunciation.

5–10 mimicking a schedule of accounts of contributions received.

6 his Grace the Archbishop of Dublin, William King, who had himself
computed the extent of hardship in the weaving trade (*P* I, 273). See Biog. Dict.

10 because it was Shakespeare.

13 Under the rose sub rosa, in strict confidence: see *My Lady's Lamentation*
213.

14 some private ends introducing the familiar plea for the Irish to wear cloth of
their own manufacture.

17 We'll dress] *WF*, early edns; Well dressed *PJH following F* (1737).
However, Swift himself corrected the 1737 reading back to its earlier state in his
copy of *F*.

18 at the Comb 'A street in Dublin famous for woollen manufactures' (*WF*,
note).

20   ratteen   'a thick twilled cloth' (*OED*). The version of *Antony and Cleopatra* performed would be Dryden's *All for Love* (1678).

21   shalloon   'a closely woven woollen material chiefly used for linings' (*OED*): a corruption of Châlons-sur-Marne, where manufacture was originally fixed.

Hannibal in Nathaniel Lee's *Sophonisba* (1675), a tragedy particularly admired by women theatre-goers.

22   Scipio   in *Sophonisba* also.

23   drugget   a cheap material, wool or a mixture of wool and linen.

24   Philip's son   Alexander the Great, son of Philip of Macedon; in Lee's *The Rival Queens* (1677), one of the most durably popular tragedies in the eighteenth century.

25   Roxana   also in *The Rival Queens*.

31   stuff   a light woollen fabric without any nap.

38   Pallas   Minerva, goddess of both arts and trades.

42   stuff   worthless material, punning on sense used in l. 31.

crown   five shillings, that is, 25 p.

APOLLO'S EDICT

A number of allusions link this poem to the exchange of verses in early 1721 (see headnote to *Apollo to the Dean*), but it must have been written rather later. It was first published in an undated quarto (Dublin); and then reprinted in Samuel Fairbrother's *Miscellanies* (1735). Before that, however, it had appeared in an extensively revised form in Mrs Mary Barber's *Poems on Several Occasions* (1734). This last fact has naturally led to speculation as to its inclusion in the Swift canon. For the case in favour of Mrs Barber's authorship, see Oliver Ferguson, *Publications of the Modern Language Association* LXX (1955), 433–40. For the view that Swift at least took a hand in the poem, see *P* I, 355–6. The matter cannot be definitely resolved on the evidence as we now have it. I have ultimately reached the conclusion that it would be more improbable to assume that Swift had no share in *Apollo's Edict* than to make the contrary assumption. It is known that Swift, Delany, and Mrs Pilkington helped to revise Mrs Barber's poems for the press: and Swift was inordinately energetic in promoting the subscriptions side of this volume (see *Corr* III, 439–40, 449, 451, 470, 479, 484; IV, 185–6, 192). Even though Swift considered Mary Barber (1690?–1757), wife of a Dublin draper, 'the best poetess of both kingdoms' (*Corr* IV, 186), her works are for the most part mediocre. Internal evidence here is not conclusive; Swift had a marked scorn for shopsoiled poetic cliché, but he could easily have passed on his contempt to aspiring Dublin poets of a younger generation. No certainty can be reached, but on the balance of evidence it is safer to allot to Swift some responsibility, at least, for the poem as we have it.

The text is based on the undated quarto, which is *T* 904, *Foxon* B75. The approximate dating of this edition, 1725, might be a year or two late; it is unlikely to be too early.

2   Viceroy   alluding to the idea that Apollo had appointed a vicegerent in Ireland, first broached by Delany in the 1721 exchange of verses (*P* I, 267). But in Ireland the phrase had a special potency, because of the presence of a Lord

Lieutenant sent over from London: of these appointments Archbishop King wrote to Swift in 1711, 'I reckon, that every chief governor who is sent here comes with a design to serve first those who sent him; and that our good only must be so far considered, as it is subservient to the main design' (*Corr* I, 243).

5–6 Delany's poem had ended in the choice of Swift as Apollo's viceroy in Ireland. These lines seem to point to Swift's political interventions on behalf of the Irish people, starting in 1720 and culminating in the Drapier's triumphs of 1724–5.

19 salamander presumably a recollection of *The Description of a Salamander*.

21 Aurora the poetic goddess of dawn.

22 Milky Way the heavenly cluster, used as a poeticism: see Swift's use of the phrase in *The Progress of Beauty* 92.

24 Elijah's mantle see 2 Kings ii, 11–13, where Elijah's mantle falls to his successor, Elisha, as he is borne aloft to heaven. The most conspicuous poetic use was the satiric allusion at the end of Dryden's *Mac Flecknoe* (1682) 216–17.

25 bird of Jove eagle: see *Upon the South Sea Project* 63.

31 Theocritus Greek poet of the third century B.C., whose pastorals set in an idyllic Sicilian landscape originated the pastoral form.

Philips Ambrose Philips: see Biog. Dict. His resolutely simple *Pastorals* (1710) were the sport of wits, including Pope. Swift had been 'intimate' with him at one stage (*Corr* III, 104) but they lost touch. By this date Philips had come to Ireland as secretary to Archbishop Boulter.

34 the second sight the power of seeing things invisible, or of foretelling the future, attributed to poets as 'seers'.

39 Belinda's hair Pope, *Rape of the Lock* (1714) V, 123–50.

43 Tickell mourned his Addison see Biog. Dict. Tickell's elegy was appended to his edition of Addison's *Works* (1721). In 1724 Tickell, like Philips, came over to Ireland in an official capacity.

44 Anna's happy reign Queen Anne reigned 1702–14.

46–9 alluding to the much imitated poem by Sir John Denham, *Cooper's Hill* (1642, rev. 1668), in particular the immensely celebrated couplet describing the Thames: 'Though deep, yet clear, though gentle, yet not dull, / Strong without rage, without o'erflowing full' (1668 text, ll. 191–2).

53 Phaeton trisyllabic. The son of Phoebus, who attempted to drive his father's chariot but lost control and would have set the earth on fire but for Jove's intervention. The classic treatment is *Metamorphoses* II, 31–328.

57 his mother Venus.

59 magazine a store of armaments, a cartridge-case. (*Darts* (l. 58) is poetic diction for 'arrows'.)

Celia a stock name in amatory verse.

61 Biddy Floyd see *On Mrs Biddy Floyd*, headnote.

72 Cytherea Venus.

73 the blue-eyed maid Minerva.

74 the Graces the goddesses who bestowed charm and beauty, named Aglaia, Thalia, and Euphrosyne.

75 Donegal Catherine, Countess of Donegal (d. 1743), daughter of the first Earl of Granard. The tribute to the Countess was sometimes printed separately as a complimentary piece in its own right: see *P* I, 272.

GEORGE NIM-DAN-DEAN, ESQ. TO MR SHERIDAN

First published in *F* (1746), under the title *To Dr Sheridan*. Reprinted by *F* in 1763, as the answer to a set of verses by Sheridan (for the text of these, see *P* III, 1019–20). Text here based on the 1763 version.

The poem dates from Swift's stay with the Rochforts at Gaulstown, Co. Westmeath (see *The Part of a Summer*, headnote). Although presented as a work of collective authorship, there cannot be a shadow of doubt that Swift's was the controlling hand: see in particular the second verse paragraph, which exhibits his characteristic imagery drawn from domestic objects, and the last ten lines.

Title George Rochfort; John ('Nimrod') Rochfort; Daniel Jackson; Dean Swift. *F* allots Sheridan's verses to the same day (15 July) 'at night'; if taken literally, this would mean that the answer preceded the original poem.

1   a loving pair   the Rochfort brothers.

5   basin   ornamental lake or canal: see *The Revolution at Market Hill* 53.

8 ∧ 9]   The board on which we set our arses / Is not so smooth as are thy verses *F (1746), not in F (1763)*.

12   elision   Sheridan's poem is made up of a string of elided forms, such as 'Cause th' top of th' bowl I h'd oft us'd t' skim'. This satirizes excessive use of elision in contemporary poetry: Swift's *Tatler* paper, no. 230, as far back as September 1710, had complained of similar deformations in speech, where 'you will observe the abbreviations and elisions, by which consonants of most obdurate sound are joined together', a tendency towards 'Gothic' habits of language.

15   pinching   niggardly.

17   broadcloth   plain-wove, double-width black cloth, used for men's garments.

22   without mortar   as in dry stone walls, thought by some to outlast bricks and cement.

24   lime   mortar.

25   still   continually, therefore 'in turn'.

27   succinct   the original sense (from Latin *succingo*) was to gird up garments, that is, 'tuck up' precisely. Swift puns on the modern sense of concise.

29   hanks   loops.

30   Macedonian phalanx   the famous battle formation of the Macedonian army, described by Polybius, Livy, and others. A compact parallelogram of fifty men abreast and sixteen deep.

31   umbo   literally, a shield: alluding to the system of linking shields together as a collective barrier against enemy weapons. Juvenal (*Satires* II, 46) has '*iunctaeque umbone phalanges*' (the tight-locked shields of their phalanxes).

33   cost] *F (1763)*; grief *F (1746)*.

35   kindred painter's art   the 'kindred arts' of poetry and painting formed a cliché of the period.

36   shortening   apparently referring to foreshortening, which was long regarded as the most difficult part of drawing in perspective: *OED*, 'foreshorten' quotes Samuel Butler, Joshua Reynolds, and others on the topic.

nicest   trickiest.

40   points   (supplementary) punctuation; perhaps Swift is getting in a dig at the printers who liberally supplied pointing for his scantily punctuated manuscripts.

42   backwards   from right to left, as Hebrew is written: compare Prior, *Epistle to Fleetwood Shepherd* 60–61: 'The thesis, *vice versa* put, / Should Hebrew-wise be understood' (*Prior*, I, 87).

44 Or . . . or either . . . or.

46 Number . . . measure punning on the mathematical senses and the poetic meanings (verse, metre).

52 quart a quart-pot or measure.

53 Alexandrian alexandrine: see *Dr Swift's Answer to Dr Sheridan* 32. Sheridan's verses had ended with some grotesquely deformed lines in which the names P. Ludlow, Dick Stewart, Helsham, Captain Perry (?), Walmsley, and Longshanks Tim are somehow compressed into a single alexandrine.

54 actually only ten syllables; Swift may have conceived alexandrine to mean an elongated line to conclude a passage, whatever its exact metrical basis.

GEORGE NIM-DAN-DEAN'S INVITATION TO MR THOMAS SHERIDAN

These verses, answered by Delany in the name of Sheridan, again date from Swift's stay at Gaulstown in the summer of 1721. First published by Deane Swift, and taken into *F* the same year. The text here is based on Deane Swift. The italics used to point up the elaborate rhyming are preserved, since this constitutes the main point of the poem.

2 vacation from the school Sheridan kept in Dublin.

5 John Dr John Walmsley: see Biog. Dict.

6 Lord Anglesey see *The Dean to Thomas Sheridan* 1.

9 Helsham Dr Richard Helsham: see Biog. Dict.

10 the prologue to a school performance of *Hippolytus*, and recited by one of Sheridan's scholars, in 1720; the prologue was published as by Swift, but was really written by Helsham (see *P* III, 1023).

11 Long Shanks Jim Rev. James Stopford: see Biog. Dict.

Courtown Stopford married his cousin Anne ('sly Nancy') in 1727; she was sister of the first Earl of Courtown. The town (developed in the nineteenth century as Courtown Harbour) lies on the coast of Co. Wexford, sixty miles south of Dublin.

15 as sure as a gun without question, absolutely for certain. Proverbial: *Tilley* G480.

TO MR SHERIDAN, UPON HIS VERSES WRITTEN IN CIRCLES

A reply to the last item was composed either by Sheridan himself or by Delany in Sheridan's name (see *P* III, 1024-7). This reply was written in a kind of spiral of concentric circles. It occasioned in turn two further ripostes, one by George Rochfort and one by Swift. For Rochfort's poem, see *P* III, 1027-8 and Orrery's *Remarks* (5th edn, 1752), pp. 58-9.

First published by Deane Swift (1765); entered *F* in the same year. Text here based on the former.

1 circular letters letters 'directed to several persons, who have the same interest in some common affair' (Johnson's *Dictionary*). Much of the poem puns on the literal circularity of the offending poem and on transferred notions of circularity.

3 mehercle more usually 'mehercule', a Latin exclamation ('by Hercules').

4 like fools in a circle by circular reasoning.

6 reason and rhyme playing on the proverbial usage (*Tilley* R96).

15 trepanned deceived.
16 cord punning on 'chord'.
21 Will Hancock it can hardly be that Swift is looking back to the Rochfort brothers' maternal uncle, Sir William Handcock, former Recorder of Dublin; for he had died in 1701. It may rather be the Recorder's son, or his nephew (son of Thomas Handcock of Twyford), who was born *c*. 1676 and became an M.P. in the Irish Commons.
24 circumlocution another pun.
25 Lady Betty Lady Betty Rochfort again.
27 Miss Tam Lady Betty's daughter, then an infant; later married to Gustavus Lambert.

THE PART OF A SUMMER

Two early Dublin editions have been located, that is, *T* 627, *Foxon* S861 [1721/2], and *T* 628, *Foxon* S862, the latter of which has a reply by William Percival (see note to l. 75). The poem was published in London newspapers in January 1723; it figures in Curll's *Miscellanea* (1727) and in Jonathan Smedley's equally unrespectable collection of 1728, *Gulliveriana* (*T* 32). It was not in *M28* but was included in the Pope-Swift *Misc* of 1732, and subsequently in *WF*. *P* I, 276 mentions a contemporary transcript which I have not seen.

Around 20 June 1721 Swift went by stage-coach to Gaulstown House, near Kinnegad in Co. Westmeath, about forty miles due west of Dublin. This was the home of his friend, George Rochfort (see Biog. Dict.). Also in the house-party were George's father, the former Chief Baron of the Irish Exchequer; George's brother, John; his own wife, Lady Betty; Sheridan, Delany, and Dan Jackson. Swift returned to Dublin in the first few days of October. See *Ball*, p. 163; *Corr* II, 391–409. The exact period of composition cannot be fixed. The earliest firm reference we have is in Swift's letter to Robert Cope of 9 October 1722: 'Dean Per[cival] has answered the other Dean's *Journal* in Grub Street, justly taxing him for avarice and want of hospitality' (*Corr* II, 436). In the *Whitehall Journal* Swift had likewise been criticized as 'Dr Celer' (Latin for 'swift'), who rudely left his hosts *sans cérémonie* and vanished one morning in a disconcerting fashion. *Gulliveriana* repeats the charge: and see *Corr* IV, 26.

The fullest analysis of the poem is that of Aubrey Williams, 'Swift and the Poetry of Allusion: *The Journal*', in *Literary Theory and Structure*, ed. F. Brady *et al.* (1973), 227–43. Williams sees the poem as a 'seriocomic inversion' of Epicurean poems concerned with rural life. He describes the second part of the poem (from l. 61) as a 'systematic shattering of the atmosphere of bucolic tranquillity and conviviality established in the first half', and as embodying 'Swift's dispute with Lucretius'. He thinks that Swift may indeed have outstayed his welcome at Gaulstown, citing the letter to Daniel Jackson of 6 October 1721 (*Corr* II, 407–8).

The text is based on *WF*, collated with the folio (*T* 627) and *Misc* (1732). Variants in other early editions are not generally noted.

Title] *WF*; The Journal *Folio, Curll, Gulliveriana*; The Country Life *Misc* (*1732*). *WF* adds 'written in the year 1723', which is certainly wrong.
1 Thalia muse of comedy and (more to the point) pastoral.

2 George, Nim, Dan George Rochfort, John Rochfort, Daniel Jackson. See Biog. Dict. John Rochfort, George's younger brother, was named 'Nim', for Nimrod, on account of his passion for hunting (see ll. 69-70).

2 ∧ 3] And should our Gaulstown wit grow fallow, / Yet, *Neget quis carmina Gallo.* / Here (by the way) by Gallus mean I, / Not Sheridan, but friend Delany. *Folio, Not in Misc (1732)*; *WF*. A reference to Virgil, *Eclogues* X, 3 (C. Cornelius Gallus, a friend of Virgil whose poems are lost).

8 Lucretius Swift's library contained only one edition (no. 30) of Lucretius, surprisingly in view of many references in his works. See *Tale*, pp. lvi–lvii; one of a number of critics to discern Lucretian influence is David Ward, *Jonathan Swift: An Introductory Essay* (1973), pp. 194-5.

9 my Lady Lady Betty Rochfort, wife of George, and daughter of the Earl of Drogheda.

15 heteroclite eccentric (then common usage). A subsidiary stress on 'o' is needed for the metre.

16 never] *WF*; neither *Misc (1732)*. *Corrected by Swift in his own copy of Misc.*

19 'Dragon' 'my Lord Chief Baron's smaller boat' (note in *WF*).

24-30 a parody of the Last Judgement, which offended some readers (see A. Williams, 'Swift and the Poetry of Allusion', op. cit., p. 233).

24 folks] *WF*, *Misc (1732)*; flocks *Folio, Curll*.

32 Church and King that is, after the loyal toast.

37 Hammond Henry Hammond (1605-60), royalist divine, an uncle of Sir William Temple, and author of devotional manuals much used by pious Anglicans, particularly those with High Church inclinations.

52 Adam 'the butler' (note in *WF*).

58 episodes in the stricter old sense of entr'acte or digression.

74 and] *WF*; or *Folio, Misc (1732)*.

75] I might have told how oft Dean Per—l / Displays his pedantry unmerciful, / How haughtily he lifts his nose *Folio, Curll, Gulliveriana*. See headnote: Swift removed the offending passage in *Misc* (1732) and *WF*. For William Percival, Archdeacon of Cashel and Dean of Emly, see *P* I, 281.

86 Tommy] *Misc (1732)*, *WF*; Charley *Folio, Curll, Gulliveriana*. The change is part of the same revisions mentioned in note to l. 75 above. According to Swift, 'Madam Per— absolutely denies all the facts; insists that she never makes candles of dripping; that Charley never had the chin-cough, etc.' (*Corr* II, 436).

chin-cough whooping-cough.

89 Jowler once popular name for dog, esp. heavy breed.

94 gazettes the suggestion is that the official *London Gazette* was itself a biased pro-government organ; in fact it was dull and mostly non-controversial in its contents.

95 Pue 'a Tory news-writer' (note in *WF*). Richard Pue (d. 1722) edited *Pue's Occurrences* from his coffee-house, starting *c.*1704; he was frequently at odds with the government after 1714, and for a time was obliged to flee the country. His son, Richard (d.1758) later took over the paper and conducted it along more respectable lines. See *Munter*, pp. 111-12, 129.

97 the King of Sweden the famous Charles XII, killed in 1718 allegedly by a stray bullet from his own side at the siege of Frederikshald: see Johnson, *Vanity of Human Wishes* 219–20. Swift had formerly intended to dedicate his *Abstract of the History of England* to the king (*PW* V, 11). See also *Corr* II, 312. Charles was a hero of the High Tories and was thought to favour the Jacobite cause.

99   the Czar   Peter I (the Great), czar from 1689 to 1725. The fortunes of the 'Northern War', in which Charles and Peter were ranged on opposite sides, was a topic of inexhaustible fascination to political wiseacres, though England's interests were less directly affected than those of Hanover (which accounted for the elaborate diplomatic moves being made by the ministry at this period). For Russia and the West, see M.S. Anderson, *Europe in the Eighteenth Century* (1976), pp. 216–40.

101   the straits   the Bosphorus and Dardanelles. Peter the Great had won territory from the Turks near the mouth of the Don, and gained an outlet for his country to the Black Sea. It was not until the very year of this poem, 1721, that Russia acquired through the Treaty of Nystadt any outlet to the Baltic. These gains were to bring Russia for the first time fully into the European sphere.

110   all things are]   *WF*; are all things   *Misc* (*1732*), *corrected by Swift*.

112   Clem   Clement Barry, of Saggart near Dublin: see *Corr* II, 171.

117   jordan   chamber pot.

A QUIBBLING ELEGY ON THE WORSHIPFUL JUDGE BOAT

First published in *WF*, with the heading, 'written in the year 1723': as usual, the date is suspect. Godfrey Boate, a justice of the King's Bench in Ireland, died in 1721 (see Biog. Dict.); he had been concerned along with Whitshed in the trial of Edward Waters a year earlier (see headnote to *An Excellent New Song on a Seditious Pamphlet*). *P* I, 284 attributes the poem to the latter part of 1721 and this is likely to be right.

'It has been suggested that Swift's resentment arose from some injury done him by Boate in his judicial capacity, but the origin of the satire is possibly to be found in the fact that Boate was connected with Swift's great friend Knightley Chetwode, through Chetwode's wife, and as in his will he recommends his executor to compel Chetwode to make a settlement, it may be opined that their relations were not too cordial' (*Ball*, p. 164). Chetwode's wife, *née* Hester Brooking, was a niece of the judge.

The text is in substance that of *WF*.

1   Clio   muse of history (compare the opening of *The Part of a Summer*, written *c*. autumn 1721).

4   lading   freight, cargo.

7–8   Lazy Hill . . . Ring's End   'Two villages near the sea, where boatmen and seamen live' (note in *WF*). Both lie on the south bank of the Liffey, downstream from the centre of Dublin. Because of the difficulties of navigating farther upstream, passengers embarked and disembarked at Ringsend, and proceeded to or from the city by means of a 'Ringsend car'. Later it became possible to sail further in as far as Lazar's Hill, locally corrupted to 'Lazy Hill', where the present-day George's Quay was built. According to John Dunton's *Dublin Scuffle* (1699), 'the fare to Lazy Hill is four pence.' See also F. Elrington Ball, *A History of the County of Dublin* (1903) II, 39–42.

9   water   'it was said he died of dropsy' (note in *WF*); but *P* I, 284 rightly spots an allusion to the printer Waters.

10   boat   here, as throughout the poem, the original typography emphasizes the pun by the use of a capital letter. I have retained the capital only where there seems be a primary reference to the historic Boate.

11   entrenches   encroaches, infringes.

15   With every wind he sailed   proverbial (*Tilley* S25).

tack   change course, as at sea but especially in a political sense.

16   pendants   naval flags; suggesting dependants, clients.

jack   'a cant word for a Jacobite' (note in *WF*), but also another word for a ship's flag.

18   lifted by a rope   hanged, as well as 'saved from sinking'.

21   his sand was out   time was up, as in an hour-glass.

22   with a blast   *uno flatu*, suddenly; a blast of wind at sea, but also suggesting a flatulent belch from the dropsical body.

24   supply   replace.

Charon   the ferryman who conducted travellers across the infernal river of Styx.

26   A trade   'in hanging people as a judge' (note in *WF*).

27   Cerberus   the three-headed dog who guarded the entrance to hell.

28   flaws   pun on 'floors'.

34   Stephen's Green   'where the Dublin gallows stands' (note in *WF*). The triple tree is the tripod or scaffold. St Stephen's Green is just to the south of the city centre.

36   pendant   perhaps playing on an obscene meaning of the word, and indicating that the hanged man's testicles are visible.

40   wooden   blockish, stupid.

44   sculler   'Query, whether the author meant *scholar*, and wilfully mistook?' (note in *WF*).

THE BANK THROWN DOWN

There are two broadside editions, one (undated) by John Harding (*T* 630) and another, dated 1721, seemingly a Dublin piracy (*T* 630A).

Since the attribution by *Ball*, pp. 164–5, the work seems to have been generally accepted as Swift's: see *P* I, 286 ('printed, with some hesitation, as probably authentic'); *PHD*, p. 221; *PJH* II, 776; *Ferguson*, p. 75; and *T* 630. *Foxon* B60 is more cautious. Despite a few items of internal evidence (the play on 'paper'; the gold imagery; the allusion to *An Elegy on Demar*), there is not very much to go on. It remains a possible rather than a probable attribution.

For the proposal to set up an Irish bank, and its rejection, see headnote to *Part of the Ninth Ode of the Fourth Book of Horace*.

The text is based on Harding's edition (*T* 630).

4   project   generally a malign word in the period: for Swift's use of it, see J.M. Treadwell, 'Jonathan Swift: the Satirist as Projector', *Texas Studies in Literature and Language* XVII (1975), 439–60.

10   that is, the members of both Houses of Parliament who rejected the bill introducing the Bank in December 1721 (see *Ferguson*, p. 64, for the votes).

11   the Bank was to issue notes up to the value of its nominal capital, £500,000. Compare the imagery of the mill in *Gulliver's Travels* III, 4 (*PW* XI, 177–8).

14   lank   thin, because empty.

17 pa-ba-ba-brags I cannot decipher the nonsense syllables.

18 Craggs James Craggs the elder: see Biog. Dict. He was thought to have made a fortune out of the South Sea affair.

19 hank propensity, evil habit.

21 vapour brag or talk fantastically (or, in another sense, evaporate?).

24 crank lively, high-spirited.

34 plodding obsolete variant of 'plotting', thinking up schemes.

41 Demar see *An Elegy on Demar* 15-16.

41-3 favourite rhymes of Swift (compare *An Elegy on Demar* 15-16; *Verses on the Death of Dr Swift* 201-2; *An Epistle on an Epistle* 117-18).

44 frank punning on 'frank' as an endorsement of an envelope to avoid the need for payment.

45 mark stamp or seal, but suggesting 'mark of the Beast' (Revelation xvi, 2).

46 bill the written form of a plea in Chancery, setting out the alleged wrongs to be redressed.

49 plank a common figurative expression 'in reference to the use of a plank to save a shipwrecked man from drowning' (*OED*).

50 swimmingly 'with conspicuous success' (*OED*), with an added pun.

52 fifty per cent profit on their money; the actual rate for loans to the mercantile community was set at 5 per cent (*Ferguson*, p. 64).

55 punning on 'mountebank' or quack.

TO STELLA ON HER BIRTHDAY

One of the few Stella poems not to appear in *WF*, this was not published until 1766. An earlier source is Stella's own transcript in the Woburn commonplace book, the last set of verses she copied. Her dating, which would put composition at March 1722, can be accepted.

The text is that of the transcript, normalization of accidentals apart.

6 partial unfair, prejudiced.

19 Delany he actually did write some verses to Stella, printed by Nichols in 1779, but this took place in Swift's lifetime.

A SATIRICAL ELEGY ON THE DEATH OF A LATE FAMOUS GENERAL

The Duke of Marlborough died on 16 June 1722. Swift's feelings about him had not mellowed since the time of *The Fable of Midas* a decade earlier, although the Duke had been incapacitated by a stroke and had played no part in national affairs since 1716. His death thrust twenty-four of the country's great families into mourning (such were the dynastic connections his family had established) and the Whigs stage-managed an elaborate funeral. The Duchess naturally took a leading share in organizing these 'pompous obsequies': see James Sutherland, 'The Funeral of John, Duke of Marlborough', in *Background for Queen Anne* (1939), pp. 204-24. Many straight elegies appeared in the press, no doubt provoking Swift's bitter inversion of the genre. The poem was not published until 1764, when it appeared in the *Gentleman's Magazine* (XXXIV, 144). Next year it was printed both in Deane Swift's edition (*T* 87) and in vol. 13 of *F*'s quarto edition (*T* 52).

The poem is briefly treated in most general studies of Swift's poetry. One of the few sustained accounts is by Charles Peake, *Review of English Literature* III (1962), 80–89. See also Denis Donoghue, *Jonathan Swift: A Critical Introduction* (1969), pp. 217–21.

The text is based on *F* (1765).

4 'All his victories, all his glories, his great projected schemes of war, his uninterrupted schemes of conquest, which are called his, as if he alone had fought, and conquered by his arm what so many valiant men obtained for him with their blood. All is ended where other men, and indeed where all men ended: HE IS DEAD!' (article in *Applebee's Weekly Journal*, 21 July 1722, almost certainly by Defoe).

6   *last loud trump*   I Corinthians xv, 52.

9   *so old*   he was seventy-two.

13   *cumbered*   encumbered.

17   *his funeral appears*   it was held on 9 August, with enormous pomp; the hearse was a sumptuously adorned chariot, drawn by eight horses.

21–4   he was the cause of many being widowed and orphaned during his lifetime.

25–32   Sutherland, op. cit., p. 223, suggests that Thomas Gray as a small boy may well have witnessed the procession to Westminster Abbey, and 'may have had it in his mind' when composing his *Elegy 33–6*.

THE PROGRESS OF MARRIAGE

Swift's autograph draft (*FV* 517) is headed 'January 1721–2' (see note on dates, p. 598). This is certainly reliable: Benjamin Pratt, the subject of the poem, died on 5 December 1721. The poem remained unpublished until 1765, when it appeared in Deane Swift's edition and in *F*, vol. XIII.

For Pratt, see Biog. Dict. Swift had known him since their days together at Trinity College, where Pratt had in due course become Provost. In 1717 he was appointed Dean of Down. He was unpopular and often absurd, his long spells of residence in London incurring suspicion from people in Ireland. According to Swift, 'He hath very good intentions; but the defect seemeth to be, that his views are short, various and sudden; and, I have reason to think, he hardly ever maketh use of any other counsellor than himself' (*Corr* II, 222–3). The news of Pratt's death took Swift by surprise: 'He was one of the oldest acquaintance I had, and the last that I expected to die. He has left a young widow, in very good circumstances. He had schemes of long life, hiring a town-house, and building a country, preparing great equipages and furniture. What a ridiculous thing is man' (*Corr* II, 411). The young widow was Philippa, daughter of the sixth Earl of Abercorn; they had been married only about a year.

For the 'progress' piece, see headnote to *Phyllis*.

The text is based on the autograph draft, but I have eked out Swift's excessively light punctuation by reference to *F* (1765), and adopted one or two readings from this source also.

1   Pratt was born *c.* 1669. The Cadenus and Vanessa implications of the tale are heightened by the fact that Swift was a couple of years *younger* than Pratt.

3–4   see headnote. Swift's original draft was 'Philippa daughter to an Earl' but he rewrote the line to remove the identification.

7   the Cyprian queen   Venus.

10   bid in form   formally invited.

11   Juno   the special protectress of women and of marriage.

13   Iris   the goddess of the rainbow, who was used by the gods as their messenger when discord was threatened.

15   Hebe   the goddess of youth, who had the power of restoring youth and beauty to the aged.

23   flourished   flowered.

24   smirking] *Swift*; smiling   *F (1765). The word* smiling *is written above in the line in Swift's MS, as though he had not definitely decided on the emendation.*

25–6   see the very similar rhyme in *The Virtues of Sid Hamet the Magician's Rod* 73–4.

31   goal   starting point of a race (*OED*, 'goal', 5*b*).

34   various   differing.

39   cheapen   buy and sell.

48   sixty]   *F (1765)*; fifty   *Swift MS*. For the cliché 'if he be a day', see *Polite Conversation* (*PW* IV, 145).

60   mawkish   sickly, without appetite.

　　stomach   appetite for food or life (see *Gulliver's Travels* II, 3: *PW* XI, 101).

64   Flanders lace   high-quality lace from the Low Countries, often contraband.

70   find…in   supply with.

77–8   ]If by a more than usual grace / She leads him in her chariot place   *Swift MS, first draft.*

86   the men who carry her sedan chair jostle him off the pavement.

88   family   household.

98   perhaps the implication is that she comes in not late but very early in the morning.

100   ]*Swift MS*; Poor Lady Jane has thrice miscarried   *F (1765).*

106   the Bath   that is, the watering place of Bath.

109   Achelous' spring   'Acheloüs was god of the river of that name in Epirus. In exchange for his own horn, which Hercules had broken off, he received the cornucopia of Amalthea' (*P* I, 293). See Ovid, *Metamorphoses* IX, 1–100. Achelous sometimes appeared with a bull's head; a bull's horn was traditionally associated with fertility. The name is pronounced in four syllables, 'Achelo-us'.

113   genial virtue   procreative force, source of potency.

115   the horn of a cuckold, this time.

118   boiling fountain   the warm springs at Bath.

120 ∧ 121]   Or bathe beneath the Cross their limbs / Where fruitful matter chiefly swims   *Swift MS draft, deleted.*

128   slip   lose the opportunity of, miss the chance.

　　season   at Bath, but perhaps suggesting the lady's most fertile period for conception.

136   raffling-rooms   where a popular dice-throwing game was played.

　　toys   idle amusements.

137   the Cross Bath   near St John's Hospital, to the west of the Roman baths; they were triangular in shape. 'Mary of Modena had visited Bath in 1687; she too, like Catherine of Braganza, had sought in Bath an aid to fertility, and with more satisfying results. To commemorate the visit and the Old Pretender's birth, the Earl of Melfort set up the marble cross shown in Warner's fine engraving…

It was wrought by Thomas Davis, a London monumental sculptor' (Bryan Little, *The Building of Bath* (1947), p. 58). The cross disappeared after the Jacobite risings: Bath was a staunchly Hanoverian town.

145   So have I seen   formula to introduce epic simile.

156   ]The best of heirs his whole estate   Swift MS draft, deleted.

160   ensign   sub-lieutenant; the lowest form of officer life.

164   jointure   widow's inheritance.

UPON THE HORRID PLOT DISCOVERED BY HARLEQUIN THE BISHOP
OF ROCHESTER'S FRENCH DOG

First published in *WF*, where it is headed 'Written in the year 1722'. This ought to be an accurate or near-accurate date, for once. Bishop Atterbury (see Biog. Dict.) was arrested in August 1722 and sent to the Tower. The Harlequin story was already widely known to the public before this date, and more details came out in the press after Atterbury's examination and the protracted investigations of another alleged conspirator, Christopher Layer. It was not until the following summer that Atterbury came to face a bill of 'pains and penalties' and to receive a sentence of exile, after a large amount of public attention to the affair. Swift's concern with the episode is first expressed in a letter dated 9 October 1722 (*Corr* II, 434–6). The time of composition must lie between this date and April 1723. For his attitudes towards the Jacobite scare, see Edward Rosenheim, jr, 'Swift and the Atterbury Case', *The Augustan Milieu*, ed. H.K. Miller *et al.* (1970), pp. 174–204. The episode as a whole is treated by G.V. Bennett, *The Tory Crisis in Church and State* (1975).

Swift's suspicion of informers, and dislike of government surveillance methods, were pervasive throughout his life. The only other direct echo of the Atterbury affair, however, seems to be the passage at the end of *Gulliver's Travels* III, 6 (*PW* XI, 190–92).

The text is based on *WF*. The poem appeared as an afterthought in Charles Davis's *Misc* (1735), but no important differences are present.

Title   'Discovered' means 'laid open' or 'revealed'. The point was that through the means of the dog it was possible to break various code-names Atterbury had used in the allegedly treasonable correspondence.

10   Porter, and Prendergast, and Oates   George Porter and Thomas Prendergast were involved in the conspiracy against William III in 1696, but came out of the affair without harm because they 'cooperated' with the prosecution. See also *On Noisy Tom*, headnote, for Prendergast's son. Titus Oates (1649–1705) was the concocter of the Popish plot.

12   this dog was lame   its leg was injured in transit from France.

15   a cliché, used in *Polite Conversation* (*PW* IV, 155). Tilley D479.

20   cur Plunket, or whelp Skean   John Plunket was arraigned along with Atterbury and the non-juring parson, George Kelly (see Biog. Dict.); Skean was involved in the trial of Christopher Layer. Both men had been of some assistance to the defence, and Rosenheim (op. cit., p. 191) wonders whether Swift confused the identity of some of the Jacobite agents who figured in the inquiries.

22   t'other puppy   Philip Neyno, who was drowned while escaping from custody prior to the Layer trial: see also l. 38.

23   Mason   a brothel-keeper to whom Layer had entrusted some of the more incriminating papers for care. Rosenheim (op. cit., p. 191) again suspects that Swift got the name wrong; he may have meant Mrs Barnes (Kelly's landlady), who gave more vital evidence in the trial.

28 alluding to the proverb, 'the dog (or hog) is got into the porridge pot' (*Tilley* H491).

30 every dog must have his day long proverbial (*Tilley* D464), and quoted in *Polite Conversation* (*PW* IV, 182).

31 Walpole he was a member of the Commons committee set up to examine Layer, which in the event laid the foundations for the bill against Atterbury.

nog strong beer which came (like Walpole) from East Anglia.

32 make a hog or dog on't a proverb, meaning 'to bring a thing to one use or another' (*Tilley* H496). In addition, 'hog' was slang for a shilling; a black dog was 'a cant name, in Queen Anne's reign, for a bad shilling or other base coin' (*OED*), in which sense it is used by Swift himself (*Drapier*, p. 43). *Dog on't* also puns on the imprecation from which modern 'doggone' probably derives.

34 thrown down the sense appears to be 'thrown up', although *OED* does not record such a usage.

36 return to his own vomit Proverbs xxvi, 11; *Tilley* D455.

38 Neno see note to l. 22. Bennett, op. cit., pp. 253–4, 261–2, describes the events leading up to Neyno's death.

40 seemingly conflating 'You cannot teach an old dog new tricks' (*Tilley* D500) and the common German and Dutch proverb, 'Dead dogs do not bite.' Ray records the latter as a Scottish saying: see also *Tilley* D448.

47 Harlequin 'The conspirators tripped themselves up in spite of an elaborate use of fictitious names and cyphers – the break was provided by a little spotted dog called Harlequin, about whose injuries and movements everyone was willing to sign confessions, either forgetting or being ignorant, that the dog had been re-ferred to in the treasonable correspondence. Harlequin had been sent as a pres-ent to Atterbury's wife from France; once established, this proved that *Jones* and *Illingworth* were cover names for Atterbury' (*Plumb*, pp. 43–4). Line 48 re-fers to the stage role of Harlequin, as an intriguer, in *commedia dell' arte*. The name was also used for 'a small breed of spotted dogs' (*OED*). Compare *Bounce to Fop* 40.

54 committee appointed by the House of Commons to examine Layer and other suspects; chaired by William Pulteney (see Biog. Dict.).

56 set his mark as people who could not write made a cross to serve as a signa-ture; a neat pun because 'mark' could also mean an animal's footprint (*OED*, sense 13c).

58 a dog in doublet proverbial, to mean 'inappropriately proud': see *Tilley* D452.

60 dog-tricks 'low or scurvy tricks' (*OED*). *Tilley* D546.

66 turnspit dogs were still used for this purpose.

70 the Bishop's foot see *A Panegyric on the Dean* 173.

72 dog-logic bad or spurious reasoning (*OED*, 'dog', 17e). The only example *OED* cites is Swift, *Examiner*, no. 50 (19 July 1711): in fact, though reprinted in *F* (1738), this paper is almost certainly by Mrs Manley (see *PW* III, xxvii). Much of the poem depends on punning applications of popular phrases concern-ing the dog: in l. 76 the main sense is *OED*'s definition 3a, 'a worthless, despic-able ... or cowardly fellow'. The subliminal message of the poem, conveyed through such usages, is, 'Walpole and his henchmen used a dog to incriminate Atterbury, but they are the *real* dirty dogs.'

This poem has the most concentrated use of proverbs in all Swift's writing, outside *Polite Conversation*, although manipulation of cliché is a major resort of his both in prose and verse. It has been suggested that he actually consulted dictionaries of proverbs to find material for *Polite Conversation*: see Mackie L. Jarrell, *Huntington Library Quarterly* XX (1956), 15–38. However, a contrary view is expressed by David Hamilton, *HLQ* XXI (1967), 281–95.

THE STORM

Obviously written around the time of the events described (December 1722) but unpublished until 1749, when it was included in J. Bromage's *Poems on Several Occasions, From Genuine Manuscripts of Dean Swift* (*T* 913). After another appearance in 1750 it made its entry into *F* in 1762, this time with a rather better text. *Ball*, p. 176, suggests that there was a separate broadside edition at the time of composition, but no trace of any such publication has ever emerged. There is, however, an early manuscript copy, differing from the published text, once in the possession of Sir William Wilde. It is now in a volume of Dublin broadsides at *HEH* (see *Mayhew*, p. 159). The title of this transcript is given as 'Verses wrote in the great storm which happened about Xmas 1722.'

Ball refers us to a contemporary newspaper account which sets out the circumstances underlying the poem: 'The king's yacht from Dublin to Chester, met with a violent storm at sea, in which the guns were thrown overboard, and the vessel was drove into Scotland. Dr. Hort, Bishop of Leighlin and Ferns, Mr. Maddox, Secretary to the Lord Justices of Ireland, Dr. Berkeley, an Irish Dean, together with several other persons of distinction, were on board, who are now on their road to London' (*Freeholder's Journal*, 12 December 1722). Berkeley (see Biog. Dict.) had recently resumed his fellowship at Trinity College: despite his misadventures, he reached London in time for John Gay to tell Swift on 22 December that he had received good news of his (Swift's) health: *Corr* II, 439.

Swift again attacked Hort in *Advice to a Parson* 10, but in the mid 1730s made his peace with Hort (for whom see Biog. Dict.). *Ball*, p. 168, mentions that Hort's 'want of academic qualifications had for a time postponed his consecration that year as Bishop of Ferns'. The rumour was, indeed, that he had never taken orders in the established church.

The text is based on *F* (1762). For the most part the differences in Bromage and the *HEH* transcript are insubstantial.

1   Pallas   Minerva.

3   begged in form   made a formal request.

7   English rogues]   *F* (*1762*);   Irish knaves   *Bromage*.

8   a mitre   the bishopric of Ferns. Hort was English by birth.

12   a whore   no such liaison can be identified.

17   Burnet's death   Gilbert Burnet died in 1715 (see Biog. Dict.). Swift's hostility to the Bishop is repeatedly evident: see *PW* V, 183–4, 266–94. Burnet was married three times, and it was standard Tory polemic to accuse him of sexual irregularities (see Thomas Hearne's comments, quoted in *POAS* VII, 157); but there is little firm evidence to support these charges.

22   that is, she intended him to hold the diocese of her own favoured island whilst preserving his Irish dignities: *in commendam* refers to a benefice which is retained after promotion, by special grace, when ordinarily it should be vacated. (*P* I, 303 gives the slightly different, earlier meaning of the phrase; this would also make sense.)

25   *Proteus*   Neptune's herdsman, who could assume different shapes at will.

30   *bully*   the main sense was still a protector of prostitutes, although it could mean a blustering gallant.

31   verbs with a heavy moral coloration in Augustan satire: see for example *Peri Bathous*, ch. 6.

34   *sail with every wind*   proverbial: compare *A Quibbling Elegy on Boat* 15.

41   *pert*   'the word is here employed in the sense, once common, of quick, prompt, ready' (*P* I, 304).

42   *Bolton*   Theophilus Bolton, for whom see Biog. Dict. He had become Bishop of Clonfert in September 1722: see *Corr* II, 434. Swift's relations with him are explored by *Landa*, pp. 179–80.

43   *grinning*   smiling in a forced or embarrassed way.

46 ∧ 47]   Or who regarded your report? / For never were you seen at court   *Bromage; not in F.*

48   *Berkeley*   George Berkeley: see Biog. Dict.

51   *Bishop Judas*   compare *Judas* 2.

52   *Bermudas*   'See his scheme in his *Miscellanies* for erecting an University at Bermudas' (note in *F*). Swift described Berkeley's plans in a letter of 4 September 1724 (*Corr* III, 31–2), dubbing them a 'whole scheme, of a life academico-philosophical . . . of a college founded for Indian scholars and missionaries'.

54   *plaguy*   confounded.

56   *tossed*   on the waves; but with the idea of 'punished', as when unpopular individuals were tossed in a blanket.

59   *ghostly*]   *F* (1762); ghastly   *Bromage*. The meaning is closer to the modern sense of 'ghastly'.

63   *Fitzpatrick*   'Brigadier Fitzpatrick was drowned in one of the packet boats, in the Bay of Dublin, in a great storm' (note in *F*). A note in *HEH* gives the year as 1696.

68   suggesting that he befouls himself in his panic.

74   *destined to a rope*   would end up hanged.

77–8   Berkeley wrote to a friend on arriving in London, 'For thirty-six hours together we expected every minute to be swallowed by a wave, or dashed in pieces against a rock. We sprung and split our mast, lost our anchor, and heaved our guns overboard. The storm and the sea were outrageous beyond description, but it pleased God to deliver us' (*Works*, ed. A.A. Luce and T.E. Jessop (1956), VIII, 126–7).

BILLET TO THE COMPANY OF PLAYERS

Apparently written towards the end of 1722. Edward Hopkins, chief secretary to the Lord Lieutenant 1722–4, had been appointed Master of the Revels in Ireland, a post he held till his death (see Biog. Dict. and *An Excellent New Song, being the Intended Speech of a Famous Orator against Peace* 9). Hopkins attempted to oblige the company at Smock Alley playhouse to pay an annual licence fee of

£300. The theatre had been established in 1662, had become known as the 'Theatre Royal', and displayed a strong spirit of independence. Swift's interest in affairs there had already been shown by his *Epilogue to a Play* for the weavers' benefit. The poem was first published by Deane Swift in 1765, and reprinted the same year in *F* with only the most trivial variants. The text here is based on *F* (1765).

Title a 'billet' could mean a licence or pass, as well as a short letter. If the word applies only to the preamble, the latter sense would be necessary; if it applies to the poem, too, the former might be preferable.

Preamble *the Secretary* Edward Hopkins (see headnote): and compare the reference in the fourth *Drapier's Letter*: 'And we lately saw a favourite Secretary descend to be Master of the Revels, which by his credit and extortion he hath made pretty considerable' (*PW* X, 58). The Master of the Revels had charge of court entertainments; traditionally he had, as a servant of the Lord Chamberlain, 'exercised a measure of control over the theatrical companies of London', but Dublin was unused to such supervision. The English mastership at least was normally held for life (see J.M. Beattie, *The English Court in the Reign of George I* (1967), p. 26).

1 strollers itinerant players.

4 Griffith Thomas Griffith: see *Epilogue to a Play for the Benefit of the Weavers in Ireland*, headnote.

6 Elrington Thomas Elrington (1688-1732), a leading figure in Irish theatrical life, who was, amongst other things, Deputy Master of the Revels.

19-20 a 'mark' was a sum of thirteen shillings and fourpence. The point of the pun may be that a clerk would expect a commission of one mark per £100 for drawing up the licence. I do not see the relevance of the note in *P* I, 308, which throws no light on the passage.

23 underhand an adverb meaning 'surreptitiously '.

26 a crown five shillings.

28 ship get rid of, send packing.

34 no controller one of Elrington's titles was Chief of His Majesty's Company of Comedians in Ireland. There was a 'comptroller' of the revels but this was an administrative post only.

44 Betterton and Weeks two of the very greatest English actors in Swift's lifetime: Thomas Betterton (*c.* 1635-1710) and Robert Wilks (*c.* 1665-1732). Elrington had spent some years performing in London, around 1715-18.

46 dearest pledges no doubt his family, left in Ireland when he was in England. His wife was the daughter of the former manager at Smock Alley, Joseph Ashbury.

53 Elrington 'had a voice manly, strong, and sweet' (*DNB*).

TO CHARLES FORD, ESQ. ON HIS BIRTHDAY

Swift's fair copy, as sent to Ford, survives among *TR*. This text was first printed by D. Nichol Smith in 1935. Earlier printings derive from the poem's first appearance, in *F* (1762), which seems to be based on an earlier draft by Swift, now lost. The autograph copy is headed 'January 31st for the year 1722-3', and this must be correct; although it does not square with l. 12 (see note), the crucial passage is ll. 27–50, which clearly alludes to the Atterbury affair and fixes the year. *Ball*, p. 196, dated the poem January 1724, but he did not have the holograph version to consult.

For Charles Ford, see Biog. Dict. For many years he had been mainly an absentee, and as time went on seemed more reluctant to spend time in his native Ireland. Swift's appeal rests on the fact that he feels himself 'exiled' in Ireland, Ford chooses to spurn the delights of Woodpark. It is one of Swift's most openly anti-Hanoverian poems to date, and *F* understandably softened a few of its harsher implications, which even in 1762 preserved their bite. There is in all likelihood a personal element in the poem, too. Swift wanted Ford to stay in Ireland so that he could be of assistance in the strained triangular situation of Swift, Stella, and Vanessa, which was just coming to a head. For what reason exactly we do not know, Stella fled from Dublin to Ford's home at Woodpark early in 1723, and remained there six months. Before she returned, Vanessa had died, and Swift had taken a long tour of southern Ireland. Before he left, Swift told a correspondent, 'Your friend Ford keeps still in Ireland, and passes the summer at his country house with two sober ladies of his and my acquaintance', that is, Stella and Mrs Dingley. For the circumstances surrounding this episode, see *P* II, 748; Sybil Le Brocquy, *Cadenus* (1962), pp. 100–101; and headnote to *Stella at Woodpark*. The poem has been little discussed, although it seems to me one of Swift's finest and most characteristic.

The text is based on Swift's fair copy, although his more misleading punctuation has been abandoned in favour of the more intelligible pointing found in *F* (1762).

8 *the time and place* Ford was born in Dublin on 31 January 1682.

11 *the ladies* Stella and Mrs Dingley; or perhaps female acquaintances generally.

12 *forty-two* forty-one, strictly.

13 *topics* bases of reasoning, themes to be used in support of a case.

17–26 Ford came up to London and began to live the life of a 'lazy young hedonist' (*Ehrenpreis*, II, 304). Swift and he were close friends during their common sojourn in London: see *JTS, passim*. Ford's mild dissipations were the sort Swift seemed often to encourage in younger men.

19 *Montagu* probably the Duke of Marlborough's youngest daughter, Mary (1689–1751), married in 1705 to Lord Monthermer, later second Duke of Montagu (see Biog. Dict.). She was a notable beauty who was a favourite toast in the Kit-Cat circles which Swift had once frequented. Her friend and namesake, Lady Mary Wortley Montagu, gave it as her view as late as 1725 that the Duchess 'might be a reigning beauty if she pleased' (*Letters*, ed. R. Halsband (1965–7), II, 45). Much later 'age and ugliness' caught up with her (ibid., II, 473); but she seems to have been thought generally handsome at this stage in her life. It is possible Swift has in mind Lady Mary, whose beauty had been impaired by a bad attack of smallpox in 1715. Moreover, Pope (whose friendship with Lady Mary was cooling rapidly) could have told Swift of her liaison with Nicolas-François Rémond and of the money Rémond was demanding from her to keep silent: see *PTE* IV, 79; V, 112. However, the allusion at l. 70 supports the case for the Duchess.

22 *cotemporary* the ordinary form at this time.

26 champagne still quite a new drink in England; the name was often used for a non-effervescent wine shipped in casks.

27 your great protectors the principal reference is to Lord Bolingbroke, exiled in France for his involvement in the 1715 Rising, and to Bishop Atterbury, then in custody in the Tower of London for suspected complicity in a new Jacobite plot (see headnote to *Upon the Horrid Plot*). In fact Bolingbroke received a qualified pardon in May of this year and returned to England the following month. There are recollections, too, of the time spent by the Earl of Oxford and Matthew Prior (see l. 34) in custody on political charges.

29 triumphant o'er the laws probably alluding to the decision of Walpole to introduce the 'arbitrary' measure of a bill of pains and penalties against Atterbury. 'All that had to be done was to persuade a majority in each House that it was expedient to pass into law a bill inflicting criminal penalties on an individual. It was a constitutionally dangerous and an unpopular procedure... All over the country a wave of sympathy [for Atterbury] was manifest' (G.V. Bennett, *The Tory Crisis in Church and State* (1975), pp. 265–6). The Tory line was that the proof required to gain a conviction under common law was lacking, and so Walpole had been forced to utilize a devious means of impeaching the Bishop.

32 the plot conspiracy, but of course currently shorthand for the Atterbury case.

34 Prior Matthew Prior had been arrested and taken before the parliamentary Secret Committee in June 1715; he had not yielded as much evidence as had been hoped in connection with the alleged Jacobite designs of the previous Tory administration, and was left to languish in custody for two years. He was excepted from the Act of Grace passed in 1717, but around August 1718 was released. His treatment was widely regarded as particularly harsh for one not at the centre of decision-making: see Swift's comments, *Corr* II, 181, 290.

35–90 Swift adopts a different attitude in his letter to Ford of 19 January 1724: 'I declare I can by no means blame your choice of living where you do. Caesar was perhaps in the right, when he said he would rather be the first man in some scurvy village, than the second in Rome, but it is an infamous case indeed to be neglected in Dublin when a man may converse with the best company in London. This misfortune you are able to fly from, but I am condemned to it for my life' (*Corr* II, 3).

38 pun others besides Ford felt that the 'epidemic' of punning to which Swift and Sheridan contributed was a childish vogue: see Addison, *Spectator*, no. 61 (10 May 1711). A relevant discussion is David Nokes, '"Hack at Tom Poley's": Swift's Use of Puns', *The Art of Jonathan Swift*, ed. C. Probyn (1978), pp. 43–56.

40 director a word with primary overtones of the South Sea Bubble affair: corrupt financier, robber baron.

41–2 vice... virtue not just stock personifications, but heavily loaded political concepts. 'Vice' means the Walpolian government machine, Whiggery, the moneyed interest; 'virtue' means the opposition, the country as against the city, tradition in politics as against novelty. The supreme expression of this vision (itself an amplification of Swift's couplet here) is Pope, *Epilogue to the Satires* I, 137–70.

43 Townshend see Biog. Dict. He is attacked here for his part in the Atterbury affair; as Secretary of State it was he rather than Walpole who had formal responsibility for the battery of informers, messengers, decipherers, and other agents who helped to get the Bishop convicted. There were unhappy memories, too, of Townshend's behaviour towards the defeated party after the 1715 Rising.

44 informations]   Swift *M*; torturing engines *F* (*1762*), *following a first thought erased in Swift's fair copy*. An 'information' was simply an affidavit or deposed evidence; but it has associations here of the dubious facts relayed by a paid informer. Townshend's reputation as an agricultural improver (that is, after his retirement from public life) can easily obscure his role in office: he was almost as implacable a hatchet-man as his brother-in-law Walpole. During 1723 he grew more unpopular still with Tories for his share in suppressing the Windsor Blacks: see E.P. Thompson, *Whigs and Hunters* (1975).

50   Hanoverians]   Swift *MS*; Presbyterians *F* (*1762*). A prudent substitution.

51-6   see Swift to Gay, 8 January 1723: 'I was three years reconciling myself to the scene and business to which fortune hath condemned me, and stupidity was what I had recourse to. Besides, what a figure should I make in London while my friends are in poverty, exile, distress or imprisonment, and my enemies with rods of iron' (*Corr* II, 442). This letter throws a good deal of light on Swift's mentality at this juncture.

51   I should break with indignation and resentment.

56   gall is broke   spirit is subdued or cowed into submission.

57-68   Ford's favourite haunts in London remained unchanged until the end of his life: 'Our friend Ford lives in the same way, as constant as the sun, from the Cocoa Tree to the Park, to tavern, to bed, &c.' (*Corr* V, 115). See also Swift's comments on Ford in a letter to Pope of 20 September 1723 (*Corr* II, 466).

60   Stephen's Green   see *A Quibbling Elegy on Boat* 34.

61   Dawson Street   one of the main streets in central Dublin, running north-wards from St Stephen's Green; Ford's mother and sister lived there (*Corr* III, 11).

62   Pall Mall   see *The Progress of Beauty* 73. Swift's letters to Ford in London were directed to 'his lodgings at the Blue Periwig in Pall Mall' or sometimes 'to be left at the Cocoa Tree in Pall Mall'. The latter was a famous coffee-house, patronized by Tories, on the south side of Pall Mall near Schomberg House.

63   the palace   St James's, at the west end of Pall Mall, where the court still resided until the time of George III.

64   choke your sight   block up your range of vision.

66   the Thatched   a tavern in St James's Street, where Swift often dined during his London sojourn (*JTS* II, 443, 447, 457); Ford was generally present.

68   stum   'unfermented or partly fermented grape-juice' (*OED*), sometimes used to pep up a wine when it did not have sufficient body.

70   Mountharmar   the Duchess of Montagu: see note to l. 19. *F* (*1762*) printed 'main-charmer', a misreading of the MS.

75   Corbet   Rev. Francis Corbet: see Biog. Dict.

76   Arbuthnot   here stressed on the second syllable (sometimes it was on the first, as in *Verses on the Death of Dr Swift* 208).

77   Jim   either Rev. James King (as *P* I, 314) or Rev. James Stopford: see Biog. Dict. Stopford seems the likelier to me: Swift refers to him as 'Jim' elsewhere (*George Nim-Dan-Dean's Invitation to Mr Thomas Sheridan* 11; see also *Corr* III, 56, 62, 113, 143).

80   Rev. Robert Grattan, Rev. John Grattan, and their cousins Rev. John Jackson and Rev. Daniel Jackson: see Biog. Dict. Clergymen who were versifiers and punsters dear to Swift.

84   Ormonde   James Butler, second Duke of Ormonde: see Biog. Dict.

89   Cushogue]   *Swift MS*; Belcamp *F* (1762). Swift's marginal note is 'the true [Irish *deleted*] name of Belcamp', that is, the Grattans' home five miles north of Dublin.

91-4   Ford had been arrested in 1715 for possible links with the Jacobites: on his release, he travelled in France and Italy until 1718, spending long periods in Rome. According to Mrs Pilkington, he got into the habit of lauding the grandeurs of the countries he had visited in somewhat hyperbolic terms (*Memoirs* (1928), pp. 56-7).

95   keep a clutter   make a noise or fuss about.

101   We]   *F* (1762);   You   *Swift MS*. *Ford tried to amend the word to* They *in the copy sent to him.*

101-2   see *An Excellent New Song on a Seditious Pamphlet* 10.

107-8   this is not exactly the picture one gets from Swift's prose pamphlets, e.g. *An Examination of Certain Abuses in Dublin* (1732), *PW* XII, 215-32.

113   whisk   whist.

114   corner   a point in a rubber at whist.

STELLA'S BIRTHDAY (1723)
A GREAT BOTTLE OF WINE, LONG BURIED, BEING THAT DAY DUG UP

First published in *M28*, where it is assigned to 1722, which probably indicates March 1722/3 (see note on dates, p. 598). Reprinted in *WF* with the heading, 'written about the year 1722'. The date 1723 appears to be correct. Delany published some Latin verses on the subject of the bottle in 1765 (see *P* II, 740). The poem is discussed by *Jaffe*, pp. 34-5, 87-8, with a comparison between Swift and Butler in their use of the 'alcoholic muse'.

The text here is in essentials that of *WF*.

2   Stella's day   13 March.

13   the inspiring nine   the muses.

18   both the Jacks   John Rochfort and Rev. John Grattan. *Robin*   Rev. Robert Grattan. See Biog. Dict. and compare *To Charles Ford, Esq. on His Birthday* 80.

19   Ford   Charles Ford.

Jim   probably a third brother, Rev. James Grattan; another possibility would be Rev. James King (see *To Charles Ford, Esq. on His Birthday* 77).

22   'Semel'n anno ridet Apollo'   the English proverb, 'Once a year Apollo laughs' is recorded by *Tilley* Y15. He cites Richard Brathwaite, *Barnabee's Journal*, as using the Latin form in 1638; otherwise I cannot trace the Latinized version.

26   hand in glove   proverbial expression, originally 'hand and glove' (*Tilley* H92); found in the latter form in *Polite Conversation* (*PW* IV, 190).

28   poetic licence   the phrase is first recorded in the sixteenth century, and was well-established by Swift's day. The allowances made in Augustan theory for 'the free play of originality and licence' is discussed in S.H. Monk, 'A Grace beyond the Reach of Art', *Journal of the History of Ideas* V (1944), 131-50. The notion had not changed much when used (albeit flippantly) by Byron, *Don Juan* I, 120: 'This liberty is a poetical licence, / Which some irregularity may make / In the design . . .'

30 Eusden Laurence Eusden, the poet laureate: see Biog. Dict. and headnote to *Directions for a Birthday Song*.

36 to a tittle exactly thus.

37 Methusalem Methuselah, who lived 969 years (Genesis v, 27); facetious variant along lines of Jerusalem. *Tilley* M908.

44 White] *the reading follows Swift's marginal note in his copy of M28, where the printed text reads* W—; W—d *WF*. William White, Dean of Kilnefora (d. 1728) must be meant.

    Daniel Richard Daniel, Dean of Armagh; *Smedley* Jonathan Smedley, Dean of Killala: see Biog. Dict. for these two men.

50 Mrs Brent 'the housekeeper' (note in *WF*): see Biog. Dict.

52 the god of Earth normally identified with a goddess, variously taken to be Cybele, Tellus, or Terra.

53 'She had a cast in her eye' (Swift's marginal note in his copy of *M28*). The expression meant 'to look askew': see *OED*, 'nine', 3b. *Tilley* W145.

56 Saunders 'the butler' (note in *WF*); for Alexander McGee, see *Mary the Cook-Maid's Letter to Dr Sheridan* 27.

57 Archy 'the footman' (note in *WF*); 'the second butler' (Swift's marginal note to l. 73 in his copy of *M28*).

60 Rebecca Mrs Dingley.

63 The god of winds Aeolus.
    god of fire Vulcan.

65 Bacchus god of wine.

74 to] *WF*; in *M28*.
    Pluto's shades the underworld.

77 Robert 'the valet' (note in *WF*).

THE FIRST OF APRIL

A contemporary broadside [Dublin, no date], is the source for this poem. It was attributed to Swift by *Ball*, p. 171, and has been accepted by subsequent editors. Not all Ball's attributions are reliable but this may be admitted to the canon with fair confidence. It is *T* 917, *Foxon* S856. The date could be virtually anywhere from 1717 onwards: Swift paid a number of visits to the Copes' home in Co. Armagh, and could have been there in April 1723. Foxon notes that the *HEH* copy of the broadside is bound with other broadsides dated 1724. Ball's date is 1723, and this may be as near as we shall get.

For Robert Cope, see Biog. Dict. His second wife, Elizabeth, was the daughter of Sir William Fownes, one of the most prominent Irish businessmen of the day.

The poem remains little known. A comparatively extended discussion is D.W. Jefferson's in 'The Poetry of Age', *Focus on Swift*, ed. C.J. Rawson (1971), pp. 123–6. Jefferson observes, 'There is no belittling or burlesquing here of the ancient humanistic order, but rather the suggestion that cultural values . . . are subject to and find their true consummation in a good life spent . . . in a very elementary round of activities.' He concludes, 'All the humanistic values are implicit in what the mother is doing for her children.'

The text is that of the broadside, normalized.

1   the god of wit and joke   Apollo, patron of poetry and creativity.
7   a lord   'Anglesey' (footnote in broadside); that is, the fifth Earl of Anglesey, a leading Hanoverian Tory. See Biog. Dict.
14   Loughgall   the Cope family seat, six miles north of Armagh.
18   Thalia   see *The Part of a Summer* 1.
20   for invocation   available for poets to call on to aid their inspiration.
23   bubble   ruse, deception.
25   flaunting   gaudy, flashy.
30   coifs   close-fitting caps worn by girls.
42   spinet   *OED* offers, relevantly, only the musical instrument, in which case Mrs Cope is caught at the keyboard, no doubt encouraging her children to sing. It seems likelier that the word is an intensifier for *wheel*, and refers to spinning wool.
53   smoke   smell out, suspect.

STELLA AT WOODPARK

First printed in *WF* (cancelled state), with the heading, 'written in the year 1723'. The poem has been worked together from two fragments which were transcribed (one of them three times) by Charles Ford. In 1935 D. Nichol Smith printed the two fragments from the Ford papers (now in *TR*); two other copies of the longer fragment, in Ford's hand also, are found in *MF*. *P* II, 744–8, and *PHD*, pp. 244–7, print the two fragments as independent poems; the first, headed by Ford 'Stella's Distress, on the 3rd fatal day of October 1723', corresponds to ll. 25–40 of the printed version, whilst the second (untitled) corresponds to the remainder. The question is posed in *P* II, 749, 'Was Swift responsible for the printed version?' In my view he probably was. He made no alterations in his own copy of *F* (1737), where the 1735 text was reprinted virtually unaltered. Williams states (*P* II, 749) that the dovetailing of the two fragments 'is a crude piece of work', but the transition was not seen to be awkward before the Ford transcripts came to light. There are one or two slips in *WF*, but Faulkner himself could have been responsible for these oddities: in any case, they do not go beyond the sort of error found in other poems. On these grounds I have reprinted the substance of *WF*, collating the text with the copy in *TR* but introducing only clear corrections from that source. Minor variants are not recorded.

The poem relates to Stella's unexplained period of retirement at Ford's home around the time of Vanessa's death, and Swift's own trip to the southern counties of Ireland (see headnote to *To Charles Ford, Esq. on this Birthday*). Swift got back from his summer expedition by 20 September (*Corr* II, 464), and probably wrote the poem around the date supplied by Ford, 3 October. It is possible that Ford acted as his amanuensis and, if so, the poem was in all likelihood written at Woodpark.

Title   Woodpark lay on the road to Trim, about eleven English miles from Dublin: the measure is the Irish mile, about one quarter as long again.
Epigraph   Horace, *Epistles* I, xviii, 31–2: '[Eutrepalus], if he wished to harm someone, used to give him costly clothes.'
1   Don Carlos   Ford's nickname. See Swift to Ford, 13 February 1724: 'Mrs

J— returns to her old rate for want of steel, walking, country air, Don Carlos, and Pontac' (*Corr* III, 5).

2 perhaps at Swift's instigation, shortly before Vanessa died on 2 June. If l.3 is taken literally, it must have been as early as the beginning of April; but a measure of licence may be suspected. Swift's letter to Pope of 20 September (*Corr* II, 466) suggests a visit of four months.

5–6 *director . . . hector* a favourite rhyme: see *To Charles Ford, Esq. on His Birthday*, 39–40.

7 *nice* choosy, (over) particular.

10 *nicest*] *WF*; choicest *Ford transcript (TR)*.

14 *fumette* 'the scent or smell of game when high' (*OED*); 'a word introduced by cooks . . . for the stink of meat' (Johnson's *Dictionary*).

21–2 *devil . . . civil* a common and good rhyme in Augustan poetry, when the colloquial pronunciation was 'div'l': compare *Mrs Harris's Petition* 54–5; *Mary the Cook-Maid's Letter to Dr Sheridan* 23–4; and Pope, *Epistle to Augustus* 41–2.

24 *malice*] *WF*; medicine *Ford transcript (TR)*. This is the 'dovetailing' section (see headnote).

27–44 an inversion of the common theme of a woman denied the pleasures of the town, and condemned to a dull country existence. A classic example, whose ideas and cadences Swift undoubtedly recalled, is Pope, *Epistle to Miss Blount* 11–22 (*PTE* VI, 124–6).

26 *pack off* take herself off.

27 *purling streams* stock pastoral language: see Pope, *Epistle to Arbuthnot* 150.

28 *Liffey* 'the river that runs through Dublin' (*WF*).

30 *sossing* lounging about; a pet word of Swift's (compare *JTS* I, 290).

31 *stomach* appetite.

32 *piddle* toy with her food.

breeding pregnant.

37 *Pontac* a sweet wine from Pontac in the south of France. See note to l. 1.

40 *Archdeacon Wall* Thomas Walls: see Biog. Dict. and compare *On the Little House by the Churchyard of Castleknock* 18.

40 ʌ 41] Say, Stella, which you most repent / You e'er returned, or ever went? *Ford transcript (TR)*; *not in WF*.

46 *Ormond Quay* 'where both the ladies lodged' (note in *WF*); on the north side of the Liffey, half a mile from St Patrick's. Ford was lodging there in 1718 (*Corr* II, 292); for many years Stella and Mrs Dingley lived in Capel Street, rather further to the east. There seems to be no evidence to link them with Ormond Quay.

50 *entry* entrance-hall or passage.

57 her lease expires on Lady Day (25 March).

59 *grisette* a working girl, esp. a seamstress: see *To Betty the Grisette*.

60 *houses*] *Ford transcript (TR)*; lodgings *WF*.

68 *Delf* Delft-ware.

70 *country*] *F* (1737); county *WF*. The meaning is the same in either case.

72 *Small beer* perhaps a distant recollection of *Othello* II, i, 161; weak or poor ale, hence used for trivial concerns.

73–92 'the last lines, an awkward codicil, show that he could not take for granted Stella's response to his raillery' (Horrell's note in *PJH* I, 394). The passage is closely comparable to the earlier poem *To Mr Delany*.

86   the spark   beau or foppish suitor, generally young man about town; perhaps ironically used of the middle-aged Ford.

88   stomach   temper, disposition.

88 ∧ 89]   You show Don Carlos where to dwell, / And grieve he ever left Pall Mall *Ford transcript (TR)*; *not in WF*. See To Charles Ford, Esq. on His Birthday.

PETHOX THE GREAT

First published in *M28*, and reprinted in *WF* with the statement, 'written in the year 1723'. This is as near as we can get; it could be a year or two earlier.

Probably others agreed with Delany when he wrote in his *Observations upon Lord Orrery's Remarks* (1754), 'Swift hath made his *Pethox the Great*, a piece truly historical and learned; with as many fine strokes of satire as any in Hogarth's. I only wish, the subject had been less disagreeable, and the colouring in some places, less strong' (see *P* I, 323). Orrery, who does not mention the poem, had such items in mind when referring to Swift's 'want of delicacy and decorum' (*Remarks* (5th edn, 1752), p. 43). Even as late as 1929, *Ball*, p. 206, could not bring himself to mention the poem by name, and referred to it simply as 'one of the riddles'. For discussion, see W.R. Irwin, 'Swift the Verse Man', *Philological Quarterly* LIV (1975), 232–4.

The text is based on *WF*.

Title   anagram of 'the pox', i.e. syphilis.

3   herald   as in the College of Heraldry, expert in matters armorial and genealogical.

6   Vulcan   god of fire; betrayed by his wife Venus with Mars, and hence the patron of all cuckolds.

7   Scamander   a Cretan commander who led his people to Phrygia and helped towards the foundation of Troy; during a battle he leapt into the river Xanthus, which then took his name. The 'boiling' of the river is described in *Iliad* XXI, 136–382: see Pope's note to his translation, *PTE* VIII, 438–9.

9   philosophers   scientists, speculative minds.

11   Mars   god of war and paramour of Venus.

16   all before   sores on the face, body, and genital region.

20   usages connected with syphilis included 'French disease', 'French pox', 'French-sick', etc.

21   Parthenope   ancient name for Naples. 'Neapolitan disease' was yet another name for syphilis; *OED* also records expressions such as 'a Naples face'.

24   Vesputio   Amerigo Vespucci (1451–1512), supposed discoverer of America.

26   painted skin   reddened, as of an American Indian.

27   Epicurus   Greek philosopher (*c*. 340–270 B.C.), founder of the Epicurean school; provided the basis for the Lucretian view of the universe as formed by the chance collision of scattered atoms. Compare Swift's *Critical Essay*: 'How can the Epicurean's opinion be true, that the universe was formed by a fortuitous concourse of atoms' (*PW* I, 247).

31   production   generation.

34   rubies   sores and scars.

36   strewed   Swift uses the old form, 'strowed', which makes a good rhyme.

37   bird of Pallas 'Bubo, the owl' (note in *WF*); a bubo was a swelling in the groin.

39   Byzantians i.e. Turks; source not traced.

52   stands comes to a standstill.

56   wooden tower a 'sweating' tub, 'formerly used in the treatment of venereal disease' (*OED*).

57   pungent sharp.

58   Regulus M. Attilius Regulus, tortured to death by the Carthaginians during the first Punic War (250 B.C.).

59   virtues Swift slily adds to the four recognized 'cardinal virtues' of justice, temperance, prudence and fortitude.

68   billet-doux love-letter.

73–80   PJH I, 397 compares *Gulliver's Travels* III, 8 ('written about this time'): 'How the pox under all its consequences and denominations had altered every lineament of an English countenance, shortened the size of bodies, unbraced the nerves, relaxed the sinews and muscles, introduced a sallow complexion, and rendered the flesh loose and rancid' (*PW* XI, 202).

81–4 compare *The Progress of Beauty*, esp. 85–120.

85–98 various commentators note the similarity to a passage in *The Mechanical Operation of the Spirit* (*Tale*, pp. 280–82).

86   Hermes Mercury, son of Jove by Maia, one of the seven Pleiades. As usual there is an allusion to mercury as a remedy against syphilis (see *The Progress of Beauty* 96).

94   Pontific OED suggests for this particular occurrence 'characterised by the pomp, state [or] dignity of a pontiff', but this may not be right. It might mean simply 'bridge-like': the disease is eating its way over the bridge of the nose.

98   A siege as long as Troy ten years.

THREE EPIGRAMS

All three items were copied out by Stella into the commonplace book preserved at Woburn. Item (1) was printed in *M*28 and again in *WF*, where it was headed 'written in the year 1712'. Item (2) remained unpublished until 1910, when it was printed from a copy in *FV*. Item (3) first appeared in *WF*, headed 'written in the year 1723'. The order of the items in Stella's transcript is (1), (3), (2); they were evidently written out at the same time. It is impossible to know when the poems were composed or transcribed; Stella's increasing eye-trouble suggests a dating for the copy soon after 1723.

The text for (1) and (2) is based on *WF*, though there are no significant variants in the Woburn text. The text of item (3) is based on Stella's transcript at Woburn.

1

5   sober advice a stock phrase: compare Pope's *Sober Advice from Horace* (1734). The sense of the adjective is rather 'serious, earnest' than 'moderate, calm', although the latter meaning was available in other contexts.

6   nice fastidious, punctilious.

2

2   cully usually dupe or gull; perhaps 'weakling' here.

3 Die the word-order (though not the form of the verb, in English) implies a subjunctive construction, to convey a hypothesis: 'If we suppose Ned and Bess were to die...' The whole epigram resembles an algebraic sum or syllogism.
6 combs his head gives him a good thrashing (a common facetious use).

3

4 finds him horn because he is a cuckold.

A PORTRAIT FROM THE LIFE

First published by Deane Swift in 1765, and incorporated into *F* the same year. Text based on the former. There is no indication of date; it must be between 1718 and 1738, the approximate duration of the friendship of Swift and Sheridan. The early to mid 1720s would be the likeliest guess, but it can be no more than that.

The poem concerns Mrs Elizabeth Sheridan, daughter of Charles MacFadden of Quilca, Co. Cavan. She was described by Swift as being 'as cross as the devil, and as lazy as any of her sister sows, and as nasty' (*Corr* IV, 441): he termed Cavan 'the Doctor's Canaan, the dirtiest place I ever saw, with the worst wife and daughter' (*Corr* IV, 416). Sheridan himself wrote to Swift in 1735, 'Thus have I been linked to the devil for twenty-four years, with a coal in my heart, which was kindled in the first week I married her, and could never by all my industry be extinguished since' (*Corr* IV, 315). Yet from this wretched marriage came the distinguished writer and actor, Thomas junior, and a generation later the great Richard Brinsley Sheridan. See also *A Quiet Life and a Good Name*, headnote.

5 crabbed ill-natured.
7 there is a similar contrast in the proverbial line quoted by Pope, *January and May* 101-2: 'There goes a saying, and 'twas shrewdly said, / Old fish at table, but young flesh in bed.'
9 Thomas, Ford, Grattan...Dan Sheridan himself; Charles Ford; Robert Grattan, probably; and Dan Jackson.

A NEW YEAR'S GIFT FOR BEC

First printed by Deane Swift in 1765, and transposed bodily into *F* the same year. Deane Swift gives the date 1723/4, that is, New Year's Day 1724 (see note on dates, p. 598). Swift was at Sheridan's house at Quilca, perhaps for the first occasion, over that Christmas period, together with Stella and Mrs Dingley. Sheridan in turn wrote Swift a New Year's poem, now preserved at *HEH* (see *Mayhew*, p. 175); this is printed in *P* III, 1040-41.

The text is based on *F* (1765).

Title Bec is Rebecca Dingley: see Biog. Dict.
1 Janus the month of January was dedicated by the Romans to the two-faced god Janus, who could look back at the preceding year and forward to the next. He presided over all entrances, especially the entrance to the year.
7 Nelly perhaps a servant of Sheridan's, or maybe one of his elder daughters.
   Robin presumably Robert Grattan again (see note to preceding poem, l. 9).
17 pokes bags or small sacks.

19 broach 'to pierce (a cask etc.) so as to draw the liquor' (*OED*).
20 peck see *To Stella, Who Collected and Transcribed His Poems* 34.
21-2 the meaning seems to be, 'this blob of wax, sealing the parcel, will block up your ears so that, though you are constantly inquisitive, you will never hear what is going on.'
24 Quilca where Sheridan's country house was, in Co. Cavan; in Irish, Cuilcagh, three miles north-east of Virginia.

DINGLEY AND BRENT

First published by Deane Swift in 1765, and reprinted in *F* the same year. The usual date (as in *P* II, 755) is 1724 or thereabouts. There is no way of attaining any accuracy on this point.

For Mrs Dingley and Mrs Brent, see Biog. Dict. After Stella's death, Mrs Dingley went to live with Mrs Brent's daughter (*Corr* IV, 193). This daughter, Anne Ridgway, in turn became Swift's housekeeper after her mother's death.

The text is based on *F* (1765).

Title 'Ye commons and peers' is the first line of a famous song known as *Jack Frenchman's Defeat* (1708). It was attributed to Swift by Scott and many others, and to Matthew Prior by Harold Williams (*P* III, 1078-82), but it has now been established beyond reasonable doubt that the author was William Congreve (*POAS* VII, 338-40). Other words were quickly provided for the same setting (*POAS* VII, 403-7 prints an example from 1710). The musical setting by Richard Leveridge enjoyed high popularity and found its way into at least nine ballad operas: see *Simpson*, pp. 801-2.
3 either Mrs Dingley was deaf or she could be very inattentive: see *A New Year's Gift for Bec* 21-2.
11 turn the deaf ear making literal the proverbial. *Tilley* E13.
16 similarly *A New Year's Gift for Bec* 22 hints at Mrs Dingley's inquisitive nature.

TO STELLA. WRITTEN ON THE DAY OF HER BIRTH

First published by Deane Swift in 1765, and incorporated into *F* the same year. The poem is headed 'March 13, M DCC XXIII-IV', which places composition at March 1724. Swift's old troubles, deafness and vertigo, were growing more acute at this stage. For their origins, see *Corr* V, 225-6. For his illness during the early months of 1724, see *Corr* III, 2-3, 9: 'I fell into a cruel disorder that kept me in torture for a week, and confined me two more to my chamber, but I am now rid of it, only left very weak, the learned call it *haemorrhoides internae* which with the attendance of strangury, loss of blood, water gruel and no sleep require more of the Stoic than I am master of, to support it' (letter to Ford on 2 April).

The text is based on *F* (1765), which follows closely Deane Swift's version.

12 gall rancour, asperity.
15 descry perceive, discern (just beginning to carry a slight air of poeticism).
20 soft tender.
23 introduce the sense is probably *OED*'s 'obsolete' definition 4, 'to bring about, give rise to'; the usage was certainly current in Swift's youth.

26 Stella's own health continued to decline, and she had evidently studied Dr Arbuthnot's advice on her condition, relayed through Ford (*Corr* III, 9).

HIS GRACE'S ANSWER TO JONATHAN

Jonathan Smedley produced his *Epistle to the Duke of Grafton*, which occasioned Swift's poem, some time in 1724. Grafton learnt he was to be superseded as Lord Lieutenant during April, and left Ireland on 8 May. On the other hand Smedley was instituted as Dean of Clogher as late as 24 June. It looks as if Smedley's poem was written and published around the spring, after he had received notice of his transfer to Clogher. Swift's reply is likely to have followed without any long delay. It first appeared as a broadside from an unnamed Dublin source (*T* 634, *Foxon* S858). In 1727 it was incorporated in Curll's *Miscellanea*, but it did not enter *F* or other collections until 1762.

For Jonathan Smedley, see Biog. Dict. He had first taken sides against Swift with a copy of verses affixed to the door of St Patrick's on the day of the latter's installation as Dean, that is, 13 June 1713. His *Epistle* begs the Duke of Grafton to find him a small sinecure to go with his new deanery so that he might retire with his family to a more favourable climate than that of Clogher. It is reprinted in *P* II, 357–60.

The text is based on the original broadside. Quotations from Smedley's poem are signalized by inverted commas, rather than the confusing italics used in early printings.

4   numbers verses.

thy] broadside; their *F* (*1762*).

5–8 alluding to Smedley's lines, 'But now, St Patrick's saucy Dean, / With silver verge, and surplice clean . . . / A place he got, yclept a stall'. Smedley offers to duplicate Swift's imitation of Horace, *Horace, Lib. 2, Sat. 6.*

10   mitre bishopric. Alluding to Smedley, *Epistle* 10.

13–14 alluding to Smedley, *Epistle* 27–8: 'But where shall Smedley make his nest, / And lay his wandering head to rest?'

20   castle in the air proverbial; used in Pope, *The Dunciad* (1728) III, 10. Tilley C126. Compare also *Vanbrug's House* 26 and *Upon the South Sea Project* 173.

23   spouse Smedley's own word (*Epistle* 30).

25   Lady Luna the moon; used by Smedley, *Epistle* 82. Compare *The Progress of Beauty* 105.

26–7 Diana or Luna oversaw women in child-birth; there may also be a hint of 'Mother Midnight', a gossiping midwife.

28   falls in pieces see *The Progress of Beauty* 87.

29   raree-show originally a peepshow; by extension, any spectacular show or display.

31   Milky Way see *Apollo's Edict* 22.

34   Arctic pole Smedley, *Epistle* 56, had referred to the 'arctic wind' at Clogher, which is in Co. Tyrone, north of the Ulster border.

36   the music of the spheres in this case quite a precise (though joking) reference to the Pythagorean notion of harmonies produced by the planets as they move through the sky at different rates.

38   curtain lecture 'a reproof given by a wife to her husband in bed' (Johnson's *Dictionary*). Tilley C925.

39-40 drawing attention to Smedley's limping lines, 'And spouse will think herself quite undone; / To trudge to Clogher, from sweet London' (*Epistle* 88-9).

42 mutton pies mentioned in Smedley, *Epistle* 81.

44 Goody Griz mentioned in Smedley, *Epistle* 80, as a London street-hawker. For 'Goody' see *Baucis and Philemon* 24.

46 'your wife to please' alluding to Smedley, *Epistle* 90.

53 horns of cuckoldry.

54 pride] broadside; bride *F* (*1762*).

ON DREAMS

First published in *M28*; reprinted in *WF* with the heading, 'written in the year 1724'. This is another of the datings which may or may not be accurate. It must postdate 1721, when Walpole attained full power, and seems to refer to the Atterbury plot (l. 19).

The poem by T. Petronius Arbiter, courtier of Nero and author of the *Satyricon*, consists of sixteen lines; it may be found in *Poetae Latini Minores* (Teubner edn) IV, 121; and, tr. J.P. Sullivan, in *The Satyricon and the Fragments* (1965), p. 174. During Swift's lifetime there were translations of the recently discovered *Satyricon* but few renderings of the verse. The imitation is increasingly free as it proceeds. For a full analysis, see Denis Donoghue, *Jonathan Swift: A Critical Introduction* (1969), pp. 198-203. See also *Jaffe*, pp. 3-5.

The text is based on *WF*.

Epigraph the first line of the poem: 'the dreams which make a mockery of the mind with flitting shadows...'

12 devotes condemns.

15-16 compare *A Satirical Elegy on the Death of a Late Famous General* 18.

17-18 the idea is an addition by Swift.

19 to find a plot almost certainly the Atterbury affair again.

20 forfeitures possibly referring to the fortunes made by South Sea directors, which they were compelled to repay; or (in a different spirit) the swingeing confiscations applied to the Jacobites after 1715.

21 Tom Turdman a Boffin-like scavenger who hunts in refuse for riches; compare *The Fable of Midas* 12.

25 job with overtones also of a corrupt political job.

26 fob a small pocket for valuables at the waist.

27-30 Donoghue, op. cit., p. 200, compares the manner of the couplets with Pope, *Rape of the Lock* III, 21-2: 'The hungry judges soon the sentence sign, / And wretches hang that jurymen may dine.' The examples are different from those used by Petronius.

30 dead men's shoes proverbial: *Tilley* M619.

33-4 compare *Tale*, pp. 55-63.

35-6 phrasing reminiscent of *Gulliver's Travels*, on which Swift was engaged around 1723-4: there is a hint of 'screening' the guilty men of the South Sea episode.

38 Walpole's] Swift's MS correction in his copy of M28; W—'s WF; —'s M28.

THE ANSWER TO DR DELANY

First published in *WF*, together with a short poem by Delany, complaining that Swift had shut both his ears and his doors to his friend. The answer follows as given here, except for modernized spelling and typography. Dated in *WF* 'about the year 1724'.

Swift's deafness was a matter of interest as well as concern to him. It is possible that Mrs Dingley and even Stella were fellow-sufferers. He wrote to Chetwode on 24 October 1724, 'I am now relapsed into my old disease of deafness' (*Corr* III, 35), which suggests the date in *WF* may be reasonably accurate.

8 *a brace* in the sense of a pair.

9-26 In style, rhythm, and subject-matter often recalling Matthew Prior's *Alma* (1718), esp. II, 121-51, 200-21 (*Prior*, I, 488-91).

26 *reacts* - acts in a contrary fashion, or acts in turn upon.

31 *Galen* Claudius Galenus (A.D. 129-99), Greek physician who ministered to Marcus Aurelius; as *P* II, 367 notes, Swift had two sets of Galen in his library. The work mentioned in l. 32 is *De Usu Partium Humani*.

36 *os petrosum* petrosal bone in the temple, a key part of the auditory mechanism.

37 *through* spelt and sometimes pronounced 'thorough', which makes the rhyme.

39 *grand-dame* if this is meant literally, it would be the wife of Rev. Thomas Swift (1595-1658) or of Rev. James Ericke (see *Ehrenpreis*, I, 4); nothing much is known of either lady.

42 *fortnight* the contracted form was firmly established by Swift's day, though it is conceivable that older dialect forms retained a central syllable corresponding to 'teen'.

45-6 see note to *The Run Upon the Bankers* 131.

A SERIOUS POEM UPON WILLIAM WOOD

First issued as a half-sheet by John Harding in Dublin, on 17 September if a press advertisement is to be trusted. In a truncated form it was reproduced in the London press during October, and also in the monthly *Political State* for September (published about 10 October). The original printing is *T* 643B, *Foxon* S902. An Edinburgh reprint, not noted by *T*, is *Foxon* S903. The poem was first attributed to Swift when included in *F* (1762), and there seems to me no reasonable doubt in this case; it would need an astonishingly skilful parodist to reproduce so many of his effects and turns of thought.

This is Swift's first known poetic contribution to the flood of words occasioned by the affair of Wood's coinage. He had entered the fray with the first of his *Drapier's Letters* in March 1724, and by September had also produced the second and third letters. For his part in the affair, see *Ferguson*, pp. 83-138; *Drapier*, pp. ix-lxvii. The best general account is A. Goodwin, 'Wood's Halfpence', *English Historical Review* LI (1936), 647-74. The main lines of the story are well known. A patent was granted to the disreputable William Wood in 1722, permitting him to mint a large supply of copper coins, far in excess of the needs of the Irish monetary system. He was suspected of having obtained the licence through bribery of the King's mistress, the Duchess of Kendal, and of planning to flood

Ireland with debased coins. The affair became a national cause, with all sections of the community rebelling against the impositions of the English government, and against Walpole personally. After an intense campaign, spearheaded by Swift, the government were forced to drop their proposals and in 1725 Wood surrendered his patent.

The text is based on the half-sheet (*T* 643B), collated with *F* (1762).

Title   for Wood, see Biog. Dict. For his earlier career as projector and business-man, see J.M. Treadwell, 'Swift, William Wood, and the Factual Basis of Satire', *Journal of British Studies* XV (1976), 76–91.

2   the pun, of course, depends partly on the typographic blurring of 'Wood' and 'wood' in eighteenth-century usage. 'Water' is another recollection of the trial of Edward Waters in 1720 (see headnote to *An Excellent New Song on a Seditious Pamphlet*) to which Swift refers at the very start of his first *Drapier's Letter*. The biblical source is Joshua ix, 21.

6   *make such a clutter*   see *To Charles Ford, Esq. on His Birthday* 95.

7   *philosophers*   scientists, observers of natural phenomena.

11–12   *evil . . . devil*   see note to *Stella at Woodpark* 21–2. It is a favourite rhyme of Pope, e.g. *Epistle to Bathurst* 19–20.

15   *good store*   abundant.

27   *Teague*   the stock Irishman.

   brogue   accent ('sh' for 's' (l. 28) was a standard item of stage Irish).

28   *beech*   pun on bitch.

29   *thorn*   the general idea is that of a thorn in the flesh, a source of affliction; perhaps some hint of Christ's crown of thorns (Matthew xxvii, 29). This was identified with the hawthorn and it was considered unlucky to cut down that tree.

31–2   although the yew is poisonous, the legend mentioned in l. 32 is false; but it is well entrenched in folklore.

34   *rod*   the schoolmaster's cane, traditionally of birch. The sense is 'under his authority'.

36   *crab*   crab-apple, the bitter wild variety; also a stick made from this tree.

38   *verjuice*   sour juice of unripe fruit. There was a proverb, 'Hang a dog on a crab-tree and he'll never love verjuice' (*Tilley* D473).

40   *knights of the post*   perjurers; professionals in the trade of lying information. Compare Pope, *Epistle to Arbuthnot* 365. *Tilley* K164. Also a pun on 'post'.

44   Wood was by origin a 'chapman in iron', then an 'iron factor' and 'ironmon-ger'; Swift makes him into a tinker. Compare *Prometheus* 1; *Drapier*, p. 22.

47   *raps*   counterfeit coins which were used in Ireland because of the shortage of ready money. See *Drapier*, p. 4: 'It having been many years since copper halfpence or farthings were last coined in this kingdom, they have been for some time very scarce, and many counterfeits passed about under the name of raps . . .' Compare *On Poetry; a Rhapsody*. There is obviously a hint of 'rapacious', a word Swift uses of Wood (*Drapier*, p. 45).

50   *flesh and blood*   see *Tilley* F367.

54   *the devil's a tinker*   I cannot trace this saying. Swift may be remembering the proverb, 'Fly, brass, thy father is a tinker' (*Tilley* B606).

66   *heart of oak*   someone of stout and courageous spirit; an old expression given further currency by Garrick's patriotic song (1758).

67 son of perdition see John xvii, 12.

68 two hags in commission one is obviously the Duchess of Kendal: see *Drapier*, p. 192. For further support for the alleged involvement of the Duchess, see Treadwell, op. cit., pp. 85–90. The second 'hag' might conceivably be the other royal mistress, the Countess of Darlington, but that would be simply imputed guilt by association with the King.

72 auger carpenter's boring-tool.

breech anus.

76 sham Wood an effigy of Wood was borne in triumph through the streets of Dublin on 7 September 1724 (*Drapier*, p. xxxvi). Other effigies were burnt around this time.

79 hold wager.

wimble bore into.

84 groaning board a kind of musical instrument in which the sound was produced by applying heat to timbers.

86 brass the nickname for Robert Walpole: see M. Mack, *The Garden and the City* (1969), p. 132. The same idea is used in *Drapier*, p. 85.

89 heathen Greek unintelligible gibberish. See *Tilley* G439.

90 to seek the meaning.

92 George Etherege's *The Comical Revenge, or Love in a Tub* (1664), usually known by the second title; William Wycherley's *Love in a Wood, or St James's Park* (1671).

95 'squire Wood Swift makes fun of Wood's pretensions to the title of 'esquire' in *Drapier*, p. 37.

100 Love in a Wood the phrase 'in a wood' meant 'bewildered, in a confused state' (*Tilley* W732).

102 Love in a Maze playing on a very old confusion between 'in a maze' and 'in amaze'.

103 to] F (*1762*); you *Harding edn.*

106 a mending seemingly punning on 'amending', but the precise sense is obscure. Swift is again getting at Wood's plan to adulterate the purity of the coinage.

108 no love is lost compare *Polite Conversation* (*PW* IV, 150). *Tilley* L544.

110 drop hanging, punning on a 'drop' (medicine) and a drop of liquid.

114 Kilmainham 'a gallows in the county of Dublin, near the city' (note in F (*1762*)); close to the Royal Hospital, in the western suburbs.

118 hold . . . by the chin support, keep from sinking.

120 'metal' is applied in heraldry to both of the tinctures *or* and *argent*. The exact formulation used by Swift had appeared in John Cleveland's *On Sir Thomas Martin* (1643) 24, and had quasi-proverbial status. See *Tilley* M900. Compare also, 'I have heard, that goose upon goose is false heraldry' (*Polite Conversation, PW* IV, 182).

AN EPIGRAM ON WOOD'S BRASS MONEY

First published in *F* (1746), the basis of the text here. The new Lord Lieutenant arrived in Dublin on 22 October 1724, that is either the day after Swift's fourth *Drapier's Letter* was published, or the actual day of publication (see *Ferguson*, pp. 114–15). For Carteret, see Biog. Dict. He and Swift were old acquaintances, and had been in correspondence throughout the summer concerning Wood's patent and allied matters (*Corr* III, 11–33).

2 brazen see *A Serious Poem upon William Wood* 86.

4 trumps trumpets (already archaic and poetic).

7–8 for the 'deluge of brass' initiated by Wood, see *Drapier*, p. 76. As often, there seems to be a proverb underlying the poetic argument, in this case 'Full vessels give least sound' (*Tilley* V37). There may also be an indirect allusion to St Paul's 'sounding brass' as an image of nullity (1 Corinthians xiii, 1).

A POETICAL EPISTLE TO DR SHERIDAN

A dubious item. First printed by Walter Scott in 1814, 'from the original manuscript in possession of Leonard Macnally, Esq., Barrister at Law, Dublin'. Omitted by *P* but included in *PJH*. Possibly a forgery, since Scott was not a reliable judge of Swift's handwriting. On the other hand, there are several distinctly plausible touches in the poem. Swift was not in good health during October 1724, but despite that his time 'was not wholly spent in moping in his chamber' (*Corr* III, 37). Apart from the climax of the *Drapier's Letters*, he produced *To His Grace the Archbishop of Dublin*. Sufficient doubts remain to justify inclusion of the poem as possibly authentic. Text from Scott.

12 a teasing wife compare *A Portrait from the Life*.

14 morning-peep compare *On Wood the Ironmonger* 3.

20 Parry's perhaps referring to Benjamin Parry, a Whig well known to Sheridan and linked with the attacks on Dick Tighe (see *Corr* IV, 363–4). The other Dick would presumably be Richard Bettesworth.

21 laboratory pronounced 'lab-ray-tory', with stress on second syllable.

22 lae a pery perhaps 'lay a Parry', but indecipherable.

29 rack punch punch made with arrack.

36 Mrs Robinson not identified.

38 Robert Swift's manservant (see Swift to Sheridan, 22 December 1722, *Corr* II, 440).

48 at the end of the poem Scott prints the line, 'You had best hap yourself up in a chair, and dine with me than with the provost.' The Provost of Trinity was Dr Richard Baldwin: see *Mayhew*, pp. 69–74.

TO HIS GRACE THE ARCHBISHOP OF DUBLIN

The poem first appeared as a broadside, printed by John Harding (*T* 1152). It was incorporated into the Swift canon by Scott in 1814, and modern editors have accepted it as authentic. It may well be so. The poem seems to relate to the situation just after Carteret's arrival (see *An Epigram on Wood's Brass Money*, headnote); on 27 October the new Lord Lieutenant held a Privy Council and indicated the need for a proclamation against the Drapier, with a reward to anyone who should reveal his identity. Archbishop King was one of four members of the Council who resisted this measure. See *Ferguson*, pp. 122–3; *Drapier*, pp. xliv–xlv.

Epigraph Horace, *Odes* I, ii, 45–6: 'You shall return late to the heavens and stay among the Roman people for a long time and with pleasure.'

1 *'Great, good and just'* identified in *P* I, 339 as the opening words of an epi-
taph on Charles I by the famous Marquis of Montrose (1612-50), both figures of
pious memory to Swift.

11 characteristic Swiftian phrases: compare *Gulliver's Travels* II, 7 (*PW* XI,
135-6).

14 *thy reverend years* King was now seventy-four.

18 *Marius* this is presumably Caius Marius (157-86 B.C.), and the occasion
would be most likely his victory over the Teutoni at Aquae Sextiae (Aix) in
102 B.C., or that over the Cimbri at Vercellae in 101 B.C. However, such an inci-
dent is not mentioned by Plutarch in his biography of Marius or by other histo-
rians who discuss his career.

25 *the Sibyl's priest* the reference could be to any inspired prophetess of the
ancient world, but Swift would most naturally think of the Cumaean sibyl (as in
Aeneid, Book VI).

AN EXCELLENT NEW SONG UPON HIS GRACE OUR GOOD LORD
ARCHBISHOP OF DUBLIN

First published by Harding in 1724 (*T* 1153, *Foxon* S846); reprinted in
Whartoniana, a Curll production of 1727, as the work of Swift. Scott admitted
the poem into the canon, and modern editors have followed suit. I am uncertain
in this case; it seems to me one of the more dubious among the generally
accepted items. There is not much to go on, but perhaps there are enough recol-
lections of Swift's authentic verse to warrant the poem's inclusion.

The text is based on Harding's broadside.

Title the heading ends, 'To the tune of...' In fact the rhythm is that of com-
mon ballad metre, with two lines conflated into one (with the rhyme missing).
Scores of ballad tunes would, naturally, fit the words: *Chevy Chase*, for example.
Fingal is Finglas, a parish just to the north of Dublin with which Swift had a
number of links.

11 *not a cross* not so much as a single coin. See *Tilley* C836.

12 *Woods's dross* compare *Drapier*, p. 42.

14 *a pin* proverbial for something of no value.

21-2 on the clerical landlord, see *Landa*, pp. 97-111.

30 *amain* mightily.

36 *Woods's trash* compare *Drapier*, pp. 5, 14.

38 *Clondalkin* a village near Lucan, west of Dublin; formerly the church
there had a fine spire. Swift published *An Account of Wood's* [imagined] *Execu-
tion* in September 1724 (*Drapier*, pp. 175-80).

39 *yoke* a word from Kent dialect for a small manor, derived from a unit of
measure equal to about fifty acres.

42 *bailie* dialect for bailiff.

44 *days of grace* a period of three days allowed by law after the due date, with-
in which payment might still be made without penalty.

45 *on the rack* rented at the full value of the land, and therefore extortion-
ately; the figurative meaning of the phrase was 'at full stretch'.

48 *Methusalem* see *Stella's Birthday* (1723), 37.

PROMETHEUS

This popular poem first appeared as a broadside in Dublin, apparently during November 1724 (*T* 1154, *Foxon* S898). By the middle of December its fame had reached Oxford, where the gossiping Tory Dr William Stratford heard the rumour that Swift was the author. A number of transcripts survive, at Longleat, among the Portland papers, and in *TR*, which attest to the impact made by this poem. It was reprinted in a London newspaper in January 1725, and later that year came out in a collection put together by Faulkner called *Fraud Detected* (*T* 21). It figured in both *M28* and in the fourth volume of *F* (1735), that is with the Irish tracts rather than in the main body of poems. The text here is based on *F* (1735) but I have followed the broadside in one or two aspects of arrangement.

Title] *M28*, *F* (*1735*); Prometheus, A Poem   *broadside*.

1   squire   see *A Serious Poem upon William Wood* 95.
     tinker   see ibid. 144.

4   Smith's dust   'either the scales beaten off at the anvil, or iron filings' (*OED*, quoting a text of 1712).

5   chemic   see *Vanbrug's House* 127.

7   fillets   strips.

10   impression   the mark left in the metal by the stamping process, with punning idea of 'the same notion put into people's heads'.

13   trimmers   neutrals, moderates (sometimes the meaning is political opportunist, but a gentler sense may operate here).

14   conformists   adherents of the established church, that is, the Church of Ireland.

16   spite   feelings of outrage (less petty than today).

18   jump   agree, coincide.

27   brazen trumpet's   a stock phrase (see Pope, *Messiah* 60) invested with a special edge. The summoning of forces by a trumpet recalls Pope's Chaucerian imitation *The Temple of Fame* 276–87, where 'tongues', 'nations', 'bees', and 'crowds' all appear; and its satiric counterpart in *The Dunciad* (1743) IV, 71–80.

31–56   an inventive extension of existing myths. Prometheus was a favourite example with Swift (compare, for instance, *Apollo to the Dean* 93–4).

38   Dissolved   melted it down.

39   me   an ethical dative.

40   Venus   'a great lady was reported to have been bribed by Wood' (note in *F*); the Duchess of Kendal (see *A Serious Poem upon William Wood* 68).

51   the god of wealth   strictly, this should be Plutus, but it was Pluto who was the brother of Jove. For this confusion, see *The Run upon the Bankers* 42.

52   perhaps alluding to the ministry's decision to send out Carteret to Ireland in 1724 to attempt to patch up the trouble.

64–5   Tory polemic had it that Walpole's dominance as prime minister had broken down traditional patterns of respect and loyalty between the monarch and the people.

68   brass   another sly allusion to Walpole's nickname; the word also meant 'effrontery'. The whole passage may be compared with Pope's tribute to Swift in *The Dunciad* (1729) I, 24: 'Or thy grieved country's copper chains unbind...'

76   crows   as feeding on carrion. For the idea of hanging Wood, see *A Serious Poem upon William Wood* 110–22.

WHITSHED'S MOTTO ON HIS COACH

First published in *WF*; the heading, 'written in the year 1724' is certainly correct in this instance. The text here follows *WF* except for normalized forms.

On 7 November 1724 John Harding was arrested for printing the fourth and most explosive of the *Drapier's Letters*. Within a week Swift produced a paper of *Seasonable Advice* to the grand jury who were to try the case. The grand jury met on 21 November; despite strong urging from Lord Chief Justice Whitshed, they refused to present Harding or to find against the (unnamed) author of *Seasonable Advice*. They were discharged and a new jury empanelled; but when the new jury met on 23 November they proved to be equally stubborn (it was thought that the sheriffs had packed the panel with known opponents of the English government). Whitshed made a final effort on 28 November, the last day of term, but all that happened was that the second jury returned a presentment against 'all such persons as have attempted . . . by fraud or otherwise, to impose the halfpence upon us'. It is generally agreed that Swift was the inspiration of this bold statement. See *Drapier*, pp. xlviii–lv; *Ferguson*, pp. 125–8; *Munter*, pp. 148–50. Swift's comment appears in a letter to Ford on 27 November: 'The grand jury has been dissolved for refusing to present a paper against Wood; a second was called who are more stubborn. The government and judges are all at their wit's end – the dissolving the jury is reckoned a very illegal arbitrary thing' (*Corr* III, 43). One of Whitshed's fellow-judges was John Parnell, the 'booby brother' of Swift's old friend of Scriblerus days, Thomas Parnell (*Corr* II, 424). John Parnell, who was Whitshed's brother-in-law, had been appointed to succeed Judge Boate in 1722.

Title 'For I observed, and I shall never forget upon what occasion, the device upon his coach to be *Libertas & natale solum*; at the very point of time when he was sitting in his court, and perjuring himself to betray both' (*Drapier* p. 125). The phrase was Whitshed's family motto: see also *PW* XII, 8. The note in *WF* reads, 'That infamous Chief Justice, who twice prosecuted the Drapier, and dissolved the Grand Jury for not finding the bill against him.' See Biog. Dict. and *Ferguson*, pp. 196–7.

6   my estate   the literal meaning is no more than 'native country', as used, for instance, in Ovid, *Metamorphoses* VII, 52.

11   import   range of meanings.

13–14   as well as the Harding episode, Swift had in mind Whitshed's conduct in the case of Edward Waters: see *An Excellent New Song on a Seditious Pamphlet*, headnote.

18   Great Seal   of the Lord Chancellor. For Whitshed's desire to succeed Midleton, see *Corr* II, 358; IV, 465.

   Brodrick   Alan Brodrick, Viscount Midleton: see Biog. Dict., 'Midleton'. His relations with Swift, never cordial, had been further strained by the Waters affair, but some rapprochement was evident at the time of Wood's halfpence. Swift addressed his sixth *Drapier's Letter* to Midleton. See *Drapier*, pp. 304–5.

19–20   compare *An Excellent New Song on a Seditious Pamphlet* 30–31.

20   that vexatious Dean   Swift himself.

22   Carteret   see *An Epigram on Wood's Brass Money*, headnote.

VERSES ON THE UPRIGHT JUDGE

These epigrams on Whitshed can be allotted, together with *Whitshed's Motto on His Coach*, to around the time of the grand jury's obstinacy, November 1724. They were printed in *WF* more than a decade after the events, and long after Whitshed's death. *WF* states simply, 'written in the year 1724.'

All three items allude to a family scandal reported in *P* I, 349: 'Alderman Mark Quin, Whitshed's maternal grandfather, cut his throat in 1674. His son, James, married a lady whose husband, presumed dead, reappeared. The son of James was thus illegitimate, and the estate devolved on the Whitsheds, heirs-at-law.' See further, *Gilbert*, I, 221-2.

'The church I hate, and have good reason'

2 *weasand* throat, windpipe (once common). Swift's spelling is 'weazon'.
3 *at the altar* in Christ Church cathedral, as the story went.
4 *halter* hangman's noose.

The Judge Speaks

1 *Quin* 'an alderman' (note in *WF*). See headnote.
2 *Mr Pasquin* satirist, lampoon-maker.
8 *ex traduce* by propagation from one generation to another. There was a technical meaning in theology, concerning the transmission of souls: Swift alludes to this in *A Tale of a Tub* (see *Tale*, p. 79).

VERSES LEFT IN A WINDOW OF DUBLIN CASTLE

First published by Nichols in 1779. A slightly different version of the couplet is printed in *P* II, 368; the source is earlier (a letter written in 1725 or thereabouts) but not likely to carry any special authority. A reply attributed to Carteret reads: 'My very good Dean, there are few who come here / But have something to ask or something to fear.' Swift gives his own version in a letter to Chetwode of 20 February 1725: 'An English paper in print related a passage of two lines writ on a card, and the answer, of which story four parts in five are false. The answer was writ by Sir W[illiam] Fownes. The real account is a trifle, and not worth the time to relate' (*Corr* III, 51). The newspaper version has not been located. This suggests Swift was the author, and the likeliest date is January 1725, when he paid his first known visit to Dublin Castle during Carteret's lieutenancy (see *Drapier*, p. xliv).

A LETTER FROM DEAN SWIFT TO DEAN SMEDLEY

The poem is an answer to Jonathan Smedley's *Satyr* on Swift (Dublin, 1725). The reply has no place or date (*T* 651, *Foxon* S876), although it undoubtedly was published in Dublin. It is a single sheet, very badly printed. It was first assigned to Swift by *Ball*, p. 201, and has been accepted by all recent editors: *P* II, 369 states, 'That this piece was written by Swift hardly admits of a doubt.' I am by no means so confident, but the corrupt state of the text makes a conclusive answer in either direction hard to arrive at. It is an allusive, slanging kind of poem, appropriate to a flyting match. I cannot explain some of the allusions and I am not sure about the sense or grammar in places. The poem may be by Swift, but if so there is a lot about it we do not fully understand.

The text represents an attempt to make sense of the original printing without interfering too much by way of 'rational' punctuation. As in the original, italics point up certain allusions to Smedley's poem.

Epigraph Horace, *Epistles* I, xviii, 68: 'Take care often what you say, and about whom, and to whom.'

2 trite Smedley, ll. 1–2.

4 s—th unexplained.

5 teased irritated us. Used by Smedley, l. 3.

6 the other maid probably Minerva.

10 Apollo Smedley had written that Apollo was too tired to hearken to Swift (l. 5).

14 Griz...Grafton see *His Grace's Answer to Jonathan* 44 and headnote. For Grafton, see Biog. Dict.

15 ditto'd through the town Smedley, l. 9.

17 My country's saved after the Wood episode: Smedley, l. 12.

20 I cannot explain this; it might conceivably have some reference to Rev. John Jourdain, who 'held the parish of Dunshaughlin [adjoining Swift's parish of Rathbeggan] for more than half a century' (*Corr* II, 134). But I suspect the text is corrupt.

22 alluding to Smedley, l. 14, where the suggestion was made that Swift had ensured 'Our state and church are independent.'

23–6 alluding to Smedley, ll. 15–16.

29 alluding to Smedley, l. 17.

30 Woods's] *my conjecture*; W—d's *broadside*; Whitshed's *PHD*. Davis's conjecture fits the metre; but the state of the text is such that this consideration may be outweighed by the superior sense yielded by 'Woods's'.

32 corrupt; the original has 'Ju-ro'. Unintelligible at best.

33 dear] *my conjecture*; Dr. *broadside*. Here and at l. 43 I have expanded 'dr.' into 'dear' rather than 'doctor', on the grounds that this was a standard abbreviation in handwritten texts (see Swift's use in a draft letter, *Corr* III, 478). 'Doctor Dean' would be a strange usage, as well as being unmetrical.

36 then] *my conjecture*; them *broadside*.

37 Midas see *The Fable of Midas*.

38–40 a ragged triplet, inappropriate to the theory and practice of Swift's verse.

41 Smedley, l. 31.

47 Helsham see Biog. Dict. Alludes to Smedley, l. 32.

49 Sherry's quibbles that is, Sheridan's: Smedley, l. 33.

50 idem the same.

51 Smedley, l. 41, addresses Swift as 'our isle's Apollo'.

57 chapon Smedley, l. 46, says that Swift feeds the Irish nation with *chapon bouilli*, boiled capon.

58 Smedley, l. 47.

63 Actaeon i.e. a stag, head bristling with horns?

67 Lenten diet Smedley, l. 59.

68 Snarlerus Smedley, l. 61: a variant of Scriblerus, meant in a hostile sense.

70 Precox Smedley, l. 65. The identity of these figures is beyond recall.

75   no knight attempting   Smedley, l. 77.

77   black-gowned foe   clerical foe; Smedley, l. 78, has 'blackguard foes'.

STELLA'S BIRTHDAY (1725)

The poem was first included in *M28*, and Swift's own copy survives with his annotations. It subsequently made its way into *WF*, the basis of the present text. Both sources give the date 1724, i.e. March 1725 (Stella's birthday was on 13 March); see note on dates, p. 598. The ages mentioned (ll. 23, 25) actually fit 1724, however. The problem is complicated by the fact that people in the eighteenth century often celebrated (say) their fiftieth birthday on the date they entered their fiftieth year, i.e. on what we should call their forty-ninth birthday. It could therefore conceivably be that l. 25 refers to 13 March 1723, when Swift would have been in his fifty-sixth year. It seems best, nevertheless, to take the best authenticated year, 1725.

1–2   a cliché parodied in *Polite Conversation* (*PW* IV, 145). *Tilley* D118.

3   feet   punning on metrical feet.

11   off the hooks   out of sorts or in low spirits. *Tilley* H592.

14   compare *Stella's Birthday* (1723) 15–16.

17   The god of wit, and beauty's queen   Apollo and Venus.

23   fifty-six   fifty-seven, if 1725 is right.

25   forty-three   forty-four, if 1725 is the year.

27–32   Jaffe, pp. 98–9, makes an apt comparison with Prior, *A Better Answer* (1718) 15–16: 'I court others in verse; but I love thee in prose: / And they have my whimsies; but thou hast my heart' (*Prior*, I, 451).

44   my sight   for Swift's reluctance to use spectacles, see P. Rogers, 'Gulliver's Glasses', *The Art of Jonathan Swift*, ed. C. Probyn (1978), 179–88. Swift had to apologize for misreading letters around this period (*Corr* III, 43–4, 56).

54   deaf   in his own copy of *M28* Swift wrote in the margin 'now deaf 1740'. The year 1724 was a particularly bad one for this affliction, which had recurred after a period of respite: see *Corr* III, 24, 30, 34–5, 37, 41; for a bout in 1725, see *Corr* III, 57, 59. The most direct parallel to the poem comes in a letter to Chetwode on 27 May 1725: 'I have recovered my hearing for some time . . . but I shall never be famous for acuteness in that sense, and am in daily dread of relapses; against which I prepare my mind as well as I can, and I have too good a reason to do so, for my eyes will not suffer me to read small prints, nor anything by candle-light, and if I grow blind, as well as deaf, I must needs become very grave, and wise, and insignificant' (*Corr* III, 60).

VERSES ON THE REVIVAL OF THE ORDER OF THE BATH

A dubious item. The lines first surface in a letter from Rev. John Barrett written in 1813 (MS in *TCD*); they were given to Scott who published them in the *Works* (1814). Other transcripts have subsequently turned up, but none seems more authentic or firmly clinches the attribution. See *P* II, 388–9, where, however, the assumption that the reference in l. 10 is to the poet Edward Young is most unlikely to be justified.

The actual date of the revival of the order was 1725; originally constituted in 1399 by Henry IV, it had lain dormant since the coronation of Charles II. George I revived it on 18 May 1725, with the number of knights reduced to thirty-seven (thirty-eight, including the King as sovereign of the order). But Walpole was the real motivating force: 'In 1725 Walpole's influence was so great that he was able to resuscitate the moribund order of Knighthood of the Bath . . . Thirty-eight new red ribbons eased the demand on the Garter, always so highly prized, and . . . to lend distinction to the new order Walpole himself accepted a Knighthood of the Bath' (*Plumb*, p. 101). Yonge (l. 10) was another of the new knights. Lines 11–12 seem to imply knowledge of *Gulliver's Travels*, which was not published until 1726.

Text from *TCD*, with punctuation supplemented.

Title *TCD* has the sub-heading, 'About 1726 the Order of the Bath was instituted or revived, under the ministry of Sir Robert Walpole.'
1 King Robin Walpole.
2 the green the Order of the Thistle, founded by James V of Scotland in 1540, revived by James II of England in 1687; *the blue* the Order of the Garter, founded by Edward III in 1344. For red, blue, and green ribbons in Lilliput, see *PW* XI, 38–9. See also *The Faggot* 38. For blue ribbon in Walpole's accounts, and contemporary verses satirizing his new dignity, see *Plumb*, pp. 101–2.
3 colour more gay red.
10 Yonge the *TCD* reading is 'Younge', which must refer to Sir William Yonge, a placeman who was one of the new Knights of the Bath and who was the butt of the satirists: see Biog. Dict.
　　Sandys (a good rhyme: pronounced 'sands') Samuel Sandys, at this time a loyal supporter of Walpole in the Commons, although he later moved away from his leader. See Biog. Dict.
11–12 another recollection of *Gulliver's Travels* I, 3. For the motif, see P. Rogers, 'Swift, Walpole and the Rope-Dancers', *Papers on Language & Literature* VIII (1972), 159–71.
12 a dog in a string proverbial for one led or under control by another: see *OED*, 'string', 1 f. 'String' puns on the senses of (1) leash; (2) puppet-strings; (3) the ribbon of the Order. The line as a whole yields yet another meaning, 'is best fitted for the part of a rogue in a hangman's noose.'

WOOD, AN INSECT

The poem was not published until it appeared in *WF* with the comment 'written in the year 1725'. The text here is based on *WF*.

Ball, p. 189, accepts as Swift's another poem called *Will Wood's Petition*, first published by *F* in 1746. It is reproduced in *PJH* II, 521–3. Williams (*P* III, 1115) observes, 'The inferiority of the matter and style leaves it very doubtful . . . if it can have come from Swift's pen.' In my view it is not far in quality from some of Swift's broadside ballads; it is, incidentally, written to the tune of *Ye Commons and Peers* (see *Dingley and Brent*, headnote). Nor was Faulkner often wrong in the scores of items he attributed to Swift. However, the doubt is strong enough to enforce exclusion.

6 *cap-a-pee* or cap-à-pied, from head to foot.

10 *a doubtlet of stone* 'He was in gaol for debt' (note in *WF*). See *Drapier*,
p. 111: 'unless it be true that he is in gaol for debt.' The rumour that Wood had
been incarcerated in the Marshalsea prison in London was reported in the
Dublin press in November 1724. I cannot find any evidence to support the story.
For Wood's financial history, see J.M. Treadwell, 'Swift, William Wood, and
the Factual Basis of Satire', *Journal of British Studies* XV (1976), 76-91; and
'William Wood and the Company of Ironmasters of Great Britain', *Business
History* XVI (1974), 97-112.

13 *Hibernia* Latinized form of Erin; Ireland personified.

15 *jaundice* used more generally than today; any morbid bilious condition,
especially one caused by obstruction of the bile.

16 *obstructions* constipation; punningly, obstacles to trade.

     her chest punningly, the treasury or national coffers.

20 *death-watch* 'the popular name of various insects which make a noise like
the ticking of a watch, supposed by the ignorant and superstitious to portend
death; *esp.* the small beetles of the genus *Anobium*, which bore in old wood'
(*OED*).

30 *a governing statesman, or favourite whore* Robert Walpole and the Duchess
of Kendal: see *A Serious Poem upon William Wood*.

37 *like the Dutch* compare *Drapier*, p. 9: 'These halfpence, if they once pass,
will soon be counterfeit, because it may be cheaply done, the stuff is so base.
The Dutch likewise will probably do the same thing, and send them over to us to
pay for our goods.'

38 *raps* 'a cant word in Ireland for a counterfeit halfpenny' (note in *WF*); see
A Serious Poem upon William Wood 47.

ON WOOD THE IRONMONGER

Not published until it appeared in *WF*, with the heading 'written in the year
1725'. Like *Wood, an Insect*, this poem reflects the situation after the tactical
withdrawal made by the English ministry, leading up to Wood's surrender of the
patent in August 1725. The text follows *WF*.

Title an ironmonger was not, as generally today, a retailer but a merchant or
dealer in the iron trade.

1 *Salmoneus* King of Elis, noted for his arrogance and impiety. He wished to
be called a god, and to be worshipped by his subjects. In order to imitate
thunder and lightning, he drove his chariot over a bridge of brass with torches
blazing. Jove thereupon hurled him into the inferno with a thunderbolt. A well-
known account was that of the mythographer Hyginus: see also Virgil, *Aeneid*
VI, 585-94.

3 *morning-peep* peep of day, dawn.

5-6 an ambitious rhyme, even by Irish and eighteenth-century standards.

9 *vapouring scab* boastful and pretentious rogue.

13 *car* chariot.

15 *box* driver's seat.

16 *with a pox* as an imprecation, much as one might say 'damn it'.

27 *on the place* on the spot (already old-fashioned expression).

29 *Irish blunder* *OED*, s.v. 'Irish' A4, quotes this line under the sense

'having what are considered Irish characteristics'; the implications are unmistakably something like 'foolish, gullible, innocent'.

38 real disyllabic, as in l. 24.

A SIMILE

Another of the Wood poems that first appeared in *WF* with the date of composition given as 1725. The text is based on *WF*.

Owing to a shortage of small silver, the metal was at a premium in Ireland, and the value of gold (used in the basic guinea unit) sank against that of silver. In the end the guinea had to be devalued (see *Aye and No: A Tale from Dublin*, headnote). It was an easy argument for the Irish to adopt that they needed more silver coins, not the 'adulterated' copper halfpence minted by Wood.

2 sable black.
3 chair vehicle, that is, broomstick.
15 chemic alchemic: see *Vanbrug's House* 127. Silver was identified in alchemy with the moon: they shared the same symbol ☽.
19–20 the Duchess of Kendal and Walpole again. See *A Serious Poem upon William Wood*, headnote.
22 A parchment 'a patent to W. Wood, for coining halfpence' (note in *WF*).
23 screen obfuscating device; much applied to Walpole, mainly for his alleged protection of guilty men after the South Sea Bubble.
26 paper that is, his pamphlets.
29–30 for the rhyme, compare *Stella at Woodpark* 21–2.
30 conjurors magicians, witches.

ON WISDOM'S DEFEAT IN A LEARNED DEBATE

Possibly, but by no means certainly, by Swift. It was attributed to him by *Ball*, pp. 193–4; *Drapier*, p. lxvi, reprints the poem with the comment, 'It was certainly written by one of [Swift's] group.' The authorities believed that Swift might have been responsible, and that through pursuing the printer of *Wisdom's Defeat* they might get at the Drapier himself. See also *P* III, 1117–18. The text is based on Sarah Harding's broadside (Dublin 1725), which is *Foxon* O230. Contemporary transcripts include one at *HEH*, no. 352764–86 (*Mayhew*, pp. 159–60): this is dated 22 September 1725.

The poem marks the end of the Drapier's affair proper. On 21 September 1725 the Lord Lieutenant announced in his speech from the throne to the Irish parliament that the patent to Wood had finally been withdrawn. The House of Commons dutifully presented an address of thanks to the King; but the Lords entered into a long debate on the nature of their own reply. Archbishop King moved that the address should refer to King George's 'great wisdom' in suppressing the patent, that is to say, constitute an admission of mistakes made by the English government. This was carried; but Archbishop Boulter organized opposition to the motion, and after three days' debate the offending phrase was struck out again. The broadside seems to have appeared more or less immediately. The Lords promptly ordered it to be burnt by the common hangman (1 October); three weeks later a reward was offered for the discovery of the author of the ballad. But despite further inquiries and a proclamation, no identities were revealed.

Swift had been spending the summer in Quilca. He originally intended to return at the beginning of August, but delayed his homecoming until early October (*Corr* III, 57, 100). On 25 September he wrote to Sheridan, 'We had a paper sent enclose, subscribed by Mr Ford, as we suppose; it is in print, and we all approve it, and this I suppose is the sport I was to expect' (*Corr* III, 100–101). This may be, as Williams suggests, a reference to one of the lampoons on Tighe; it might allude to this item, however. For the episode as a whole, see *Drapier*, pp. lxiii–lxvi.

Epigraph   from Seneca, *Epistulae* XX, 5: 'What is wisdom? It is always to wish for the same thing, and to not wish for the same thing.'

1   Minerva   as goddess of wisdom.

4   who voted against her   i.e. against Archbishop King's motion, which proposed that the address to the King should include a phrase concerning royal 'wisdom' in suppressing the patent: see headnote.

7   putting the question   compare *Ireland* 16. This line refers to the original division on 21 September.

9   for an anecdote concerning this line, as implying Carteret's intervention, see *Drapier*, p. lxv.

10–12   Swift may have been remembering Hobbes's point that the word 'wisdom' covered both prudence and sapience, though these were distinct notions (*prudentia* and *sapientia*) in Latin: *Leviathan* I, 5 (p. 22 in 1651 edition owned by Swift).

12   a commonplace: *OED* quotes Donne, Dryden, and others expressing this idea. Hobbes's second branch of the first law of nature is 'by all means we can, to defend ourselves' (*Leviathan* I, 14). In general, Hobbes uses the word 'security' to cover the concept. See also *Tilley* S219.

HORACE, BOOK I, ODE XIV

First printed in a small octavo pamphlet (Dublin, 1730) (*T* 705, *Foxon* S859); re-printed in the London *Daily Post* on 14 August of that year, and again in Faulkner's edition of *The Grand Question Debated* (1732). It appeared in *WF* and during 1735 was also incorporated into *Misc*.

WF states, 'written in the year 1726', and *Ball*, pp. 220–22, seems to accept this. On the basis of a transcript in Cambridge University Library, *P* III, 769 suggests a date around November 1724: *PHD* also dates it 1724. I am inclined to put it nearer *WF*'s date. Line 52 seems to me to point unmistakably to Midleton's resignation in 1725. There is no doubt of Swift's authorship: see *Corr* V, 256, which indicates Swift's willingness to have the poem collected.

The text is based on *WF*. The quotations from Horace in the notes are those signalized in footnotes to the text.

Inscription   dedication. *Delos* a floating island in Greek legend, eventually made fast by Neptune or Poseidon (see *Ode to the Athenian Society* 47).

1   O navis, referent in mare te novi / fluctus.

4   fortiter occupa / portum.

5 nudum remigio latus.

10 malus celeri saucius Africo. (*WF* applies to l. 7, but obviously it belongs with l. 10.)

11 ac sine funibus / vix durare carinae / possint imperiosius / aequor?

15 non tibi sunt integra lintea.

16 *gale* poetic diction for 'breeze'.

22 the idea of rags fluttering occurs on numerous occasions in Pope, e.g. *The Dunciad* (1729) II, 11–12.

26 non di quos iterum pressa voces malo.

29 quamvis Pontica pinus, / sylva filia nobilis.

30 *British oak* traditional material of sturdy ships, with obvious moral connotations.

33 *Ierne* Ireland.

36 *records* stressed on second syllable. The allusion seems to be to the wars between the Irish and Norman invaders in the twelfth century.

39 nil pictis timidus navita puppibus.

confides puts any trust.

42 *birthday night* rich clothes as worn on a royal birthday.

45 fidit tu, nisi ventis / debes ludibrium, cave.

49–56 the note cites the entire last stanza of Horace's ode.

52 notably Midleton, who had been Lord Chancellor of Ireland for over a decade when forced to resign in 1725, and Archbishop Lindsay, primate for as long, until his death in 1724. Archbishop King, who had held office since 1703, was obviously near the end of his period at the head of affairs.

A COPY OF VERSES UPON TWO CELEBRATED MODERN POETS

As Williams says (*P* II, 393), 'The authority for these lines is their inclusion with other pieces by Swift in Moore's *Miscellanies* of 1734', that is, *T* 40. However, this must be regarded as a very doubtful authority, since A. Moore was simply a title-page *nom de plume* adopted by fringe operators in the publishing trade. The volume professes to be a reprint of a Dublin edition that does not, to my knowledge, exist. The basis of the ascription may be the satire of Young and Philips, but many others besides Swift were capable of such things. Since Nichols in 1775, editors have accepted the poem as Swift's, but the attribution remains a little uncertain. Williams suggests a date of 1726 because of the references to Young and Philips. It could be a year or two later.

Text based on Moore's edition, in default of one more reliable.

7–8 compare the imagery of flying and creeping in *Peri Bathous*, pp. 24–8.

10 sawpit 'an excavation in the ground, over the mouth of which a framework is erected on which timber is placed to be sawn with a long two-handled saw by two men, the one standing in the pit and the other on a raised platform' (*OED*).

11 mechanic workman.

18 *god of wit* Apollo.

20 *Young and Philips* the poets Edward Young and Ambrose Philips: see Biog. Dict.

drudge labour.

AN APOLOGY TO THE LADY CARTERET

The poem was published as a small octavo pamphlet, [Dublin] 1730: *T* 696, *Foxon* S699. Press variants do not affect the text. It was reprinted in the London press in March of that year, and then included in a collection of Swift items put out by the pseudonymous 'A. Moore' in 1734. It entered the main series of *Misc* in 1742. There is also a transcript at Longleat, assigning the poem, on no obvious grounds, to Delany. The date of composition is uncertain; it could be at a number of times after Swift and Carteret re-established relations in January 1725. Lady Carteret had arrived by March (*Corr* III, 56). Williams (*P* II, 374) suggests the autumn of 1725, although the clear autumnal hints are slight (l. 88 is perhaps the strongest). By 17 April Swift was thanking the Lord Lieutenant for their 'great civilities' to him (*Corr* III, 57); he then left for Quilca and did not return until around 30 September. If 1725 is the year, it could be March/April or October/November. Swift's interest in his garden adjoining the Deanery, known as Naboth's Vineyard, dates from 1724 or thereabouts. The year 1725 is the likeliest but not certain.

For Lady Carteret, see Biog. Dict. Swift had known her mother, and had celebrated the beautiful young daughter in his poem '*In Pity to the Emptying Town*' 20, not long before her marriage to Carteret.

The poem dramatizes Swift's conflicting feelings with regard to old friends who had come to Ireland as representatives of English rule. Dublin Castle had long been the centre and symbol of English power in Ireland. Swift's pose of the unworldly college-bred clergyman, ill at ease among courts and aristocrats, suggests the character of Cadenus rather than the real-life Swift who lobbied so confidently at Windsor. For brief comments, see *Jaffe*, pp. 142-3.

Text from the octavo with minor modifications from *Misc*.

4 wished to have the scriptural or theological facts as well as the moral gloss put on them.

9 humane the spelling in the original is 'human', but the modern separation of these forms had not yet taken place.

16 To one who swayed some time before probably the Earl of Oxford; if the Earl's death in 1724 should be seen to prohibit that, it must be Bolingbroke, just given a qualified pardon and returned to England.

23 trim and nice polished and urbane.

27 beaver a fur hat.

30 guard sentry post.

32 conscious of embarrassed by.

43 Captain Cracherode the gentleman who brought the message. Probably a relative of the Solicitor to the Treasury, Anthony Cracherode (1674-1752), who was a friend of Carteret's secretary, Thomas Tickell.

54 I'll e'en go home the sense is, 'what shall I do but go home': see *OED*, 'even' 8(b).

56 very fairly off I have done very well to escape so lightly (this quotation is the first given in *OED* for usages along the lines of 'well off', etc., which became common later in the eighteenth and nineteenth centuries).

94 glad to make amends on whatever terms.

100 referring to Naboth's Vineyard, a field of three acres leased by Swift around 1723 or 1724, in which he planted a large number of fruit trees.

104 meals] *Misc* (*1742*); mails *octavo* (*1730*); meats *Longleat transcript*.

108   really   trisyllabic, as often in Swift.

120   par manière d'acquit   by way of form, perfunctorily: compare *Corr* II, 138. Doubtless with anglicized or hibernicized pronunciation.

128   walk   pathway through the garden.

130   vindicate   not so much 'justify' as 'clear from blame'.

131   use   habit.

147   important   with sneering sense of self-important.

148   scoffing   a transitive verb occasionally, up to the Victorian era.

149   cornet   a junior officer in the cavalry (one of a number of reminders of the military presence at Dublin Castle).

151–2   there are certain similarities here to Swift's picture of himself at the English court in 1714, as expressed in *Horace, Lib. 2, Sat. 6* 25–34. *Jaffe*, pp. 142–3, detects some resemblance to *Horace, Epistle VII, Book I: Imitated*.

A RECEIPT TO RESTORE STELLA'S YOUTH

Printed in *WF* (cancelled state) with the heading, 'written in the year 1724–5'. The poem clearly alludes to a long sojourn at Quilca, Sheridan's house in County Cavan; Swift was there from the end of April to the end of September in 1725 (*Corr* III, 59–105), putting the finishing touches to *Gulliver's Travels*. It is not clear exactly when Stella went to Quilca. It was evidently after 1 March, when Swift wrote to Ford, 'Mrs Johnson is as usual, unless rather worse, for she eats but a mouthful a day.' The country life did her some good, as letters that summer reported (*Corr* III, 52, 72, 75, 86, 89). However, this was a brief respite in the long decline which led to her death in January 1728. *Jaffe*, pp. 99–100, discusses the poem.

The text is that of *WF* with minor features normalized.

Title   a *receipt* is a recipe, in the narrow or extended sense.

8   skin and bone   see *Tilley* N260.

18   Medea's kettle   Medea, the sorceress, cut an old ram to pieces, threw the pieces into a cauldron, and produced a young lamb from it. She also restored Aeson, the father of Jason, to a state of youth: Ovid, *Metamorphoses* VII, 179–349. Lines 290–92 are perhaps the direct basis for Swift's lines.

20   that is, Jove, in his disguise as a bull; the classic description is again in the *Metamorphoses* II, 836–75.

26   Quilca   'a friend's house seven or eight miles from Dublin' (note in *WF*). Actually Quilca is more like forty-five miles from Dublin; it may have been intended to print 'seven or eight miles from Kells', which is the way Swift locates the house in letters to friends (*Corr* III, 59–60, 88). The house was a long thatched building, dating from the seventeenth century: it was demolished within the last forty years (Sybil Le Brocquy, *Swift's Most Valuable Friend* (1968), p. 56).

36   flesh and blood   playing with a proverbial coupling, for which see *Tilley* F366–7.

44   jockey-boots   top-boots.

45   justices o' quorum   justices of the peace, magistrates.

46   cowboys   urchins, young boys who herded the cows.

47   that is, trying cases involving assaults and affrays among the country people.

50   out of case   in bad shape physically.

TO QUILCA

The visit mentioned in the title is that described in the headnote to *A Receipt to Restore Stella's Youth*.

The poem was first published in *WF* (cancelled state), which is the basis of the text here.

2 A rotten cabin compare Swift's letter of 14 August 1724: '[I] have been for four months in a little obscure Irish cabin about forty miles from Dublin' (*Corr* III, 84). At this time Swift also wrote a short prose piece, *The Blunders, Deficiencies, Distresses, and Misfortunes of Quilca*, first published in 1745 (*PW* V, 219–21). It is headed 'Begun April 20, 1724' but this is assuredly a mistake for 1725.

dropping rain the weather was exceptionally bad, and Swift's letters constantly refer to this (*Corr* III, 63–4, 72–4, 76). As well as being wet, it was cold (*PW* V, 219).

3 'the chimney smoking intolerably; and the Dean's greatcoat was employed to stop the wind from coming down the chimney, without which expedient they must have been starved to death' (*PW* V, 220).

4 'The Dean's bed threatening every night to fall under him . . . The little table loose and broken in the joints . . . The large table in a very tottering condition . . . But one chair in the house fit for sitting on, and that in a very ill state of health' (*PW* V, 219).

7 poor Sheelah perhaps 'the lady's maid awkward and clumsy' (*PW* V, 221); or else the 'nurse' present.

8 'not one utensil for the fire, except an old pair of tongs . . . the spit blunted with poking into bogs for timber, and tears the meat to pieces' (*PW* V, 219).

10 'We live here among a million of wants, and where everybody is a thief' (Swift to Ford, 16 August: *Corr* III, 89). Compare *PW* V, 219: 'An egregious want of all the most common necessary utensils.'

12 see *PW* V, 220–21, for the laziness, squalor, and thievery of the servants.

VERSES FROM QUILCA

The verses relate to the visit to Quilca during the summer of 1725 (see *A Receipt to Restore Stella's Youth* and *To Quilca*). All three items were included in a letter from Swift to Sheridan, dated by Williams 25 June 1725 (*Corr* III, 63–5). The text here is based on *F* (1746). The collective title is the editor's.

I

Swift writes to Sheridan, 'The lady's room smokes; the rain drops from the skies into our kitchen; our servants eat and drink like the devil, and pray for rain, which entertains them at cards and sleep, which are much lighter than spades, sledges, and crows.' The first set of verses follows, introduced as 'their [the servants'] maxim'.

2 The Blessings of a Country Life

Behind the badinage lies a real issue: as Swift told Ford on 16 August, 'I have some reasons not to be in Dublin till the parliament here has sat a good while' (*Corr* III, 89). 'Anything,' he added, 'rather than the complaint of being deaf in

Dublin.' The odd line about being far from debtors (rather than creditors) may be explained by the fact that John Pratt, Deputy Vice-Treasurer, had been sent to prison in June for alleged frauds; he owed Swift a large sum of money, but fortunately Swift was able to get most of this back. The matter is a frequent topic of his correspondence with Sheridan that summer (*Corr* III, 64–87).

3   The Plagues of a Country Life

Compare *To Quilca* and the prose equivalent, *The Blunders . . . of Quilca* (see *To Quilca*, headnote). Swift's last word on the weather appears in his letter to Ford of 14 August: 'In four months we have had two odd fair days, and thirteen more, and all the rest foul from the 20th of April to the hour I am writing' (*Corr* III, 87).

3   or choose   or please yourself, do without.

LINES TO POPE

The lines were included in a letter from Swift to Pope, dated 26 November 1725 (*Corr* III, 118). They are a pendant to a quatrain Pope had sent on 15 October: 'The Pope's the whore of Babylon, / The Turk he is a Jew; / The Christian is an infidel / That sitteth in a pew' (*Corr* III, 109). Swift seems to have taken the lines to be Pope's own, but this is doubtful: see *PTE* VI, 418. He added, 'But this on second thought is not of a piece with yours, because it is a commendation.' For Swift's hatred of informers, see *Upon the Horrid Plot*, headnote.

RIDDLES

The following nine riddles were all included in *WF*. Swift had long been addicted to word-games, and his friendship with Sheridan and Delany occasioned a burst of activity in the 1720s. *WF* has this note at the head of the riddles:

> About nine or ten years ago, some ingenious gentlemen, friends to the author, used to entertain themselves with writing riddles, and send them to him and their other acquaintance, copies of which ran about, and some of them were printed both here and in England. The author, at his leisure hours, fell into the same amusement; although it be said that he thought them of no great merit, entertainment, or use. However, by the advice of some persons, for whom the author hath a great esteem, and who were pleased to send us the copies, we have ventured to print the few following, as we have done two or three before, and which are allowed to be genuine; because, we are informed that several good judges have a taste for such kind of compositions.

'Genuine' may not mean 'authentically by Swift', although Faulkner clearly would have liked to give that impression. The probability is that most were by Swift, at least; otherwise he would scarcely have allowed them to be included in his *Works*.

In 1746 *F* introduced a further thirteen shorter riddles but with much less show of confidence: he admitted that he could not attribute the items to particular authors. I have therefore omitted the entire group, since it is quite possible none is by Swift. I also omit the two 'Enigmas' published by John Oldmixon in the *Muses Mercury* (1707), as Swift's involvement remains highly questionable.

On 5 December 1726, Swift wrote to Pope, 'Although you despise riddles, I am strongly tempted to send a parcel to be printed by themselves, and make a ninepenny job for the bookseller. There are some of my own, wherein I exceed mankind, *Mira Poemata!* the most solemn that were ever seen; and some writ by others, admirable indeed, but far inferior to mine, but I will not praise myself' (*Corr* III, 193-4). The planned volume never appeared; the riddles did not find their way into the forthcoming *Misc*, which is what Swift seems to be angling for. Consequently it is impossible to be sure whether Swift confined the items in *WF* to his own productions, or permitted riddles by Delany or others to accompany his.

Text based on *WF*; no answers are supplied in this text, and I have drawn these from later editions.

There has been little discussion of the riddles, although they sometimes illuminate the metaphoric technique of Swift's major poetry (see especially item 5). Two of the riddles printed here are considered by *Lee*, pp. 54-62. For Orrery's comments ('Titian painting draught-boards'), see his *Remarks* (5th edn, 1752), p. 88.

1

Published as a broadside (Dublin, 1726), and assigned to Delany: reprinted in Curll's collection misleadingly entitled *Whartoniana* (1727). Headed in *WF*, 'written in the year 1724'. Answer: a quill pen.

4 compare Cowley's poem *Clad All in White*, parodied by Swift in *Clad All in Brown*.

36 *beggar's brat* see *On Poetry: a Rhapsody* 33. The pen is used to sign the patent for a new peerage.

2

Answer: gold.

9 *The favourite messenger* Mercury.

10 *Lemnian god* Vulcan; when hurled from heaven by Jove, he was found on the island of Lemnos. Alchemists, in their quest for gold, tried to refine metals by the use of mercury and fire.

3

Answer: gold (?).

4

Answer: the posteriors. Discussed by *Lee*, pp. 54-8.

13 *sold and bought Lee*, p. 57, detects elaborate punning based on the ideas of 'money-excrements' and 'bank-posteriors'. However, the main sense is either 'I am betrayed' (see *OED*, 'buy', 11b), or 'I am already disposed of' (compare Lady Answerall in *Polite Conversation*, *PW* IV, 196-7). *Tilley* B787.

28 *purse* punning on the sense of 'scrotum'.

42 *learned* monosyllabic.

5

Answer: a horn. Playing on the sense of a cuckold's horns, principally.

3 emblem cornucopia.
6 alluding to the unicorn in the royal coat of arms.
7-8 the horned moon, in its first or last quarter.
10 thine perhaps thinking of horn meaning 'lanthorn', lantern.
12 in Celia's tresses a horn as a kind of ornament worn in the hair.
15-16 perhaps thinking of the biblical sense of the horn as an emblem of power and might.
18 alluding to hartshorn, used as smelling salts by women addicted to 'vapours'.
32 real disyllabic.

6
Answer: a corkscrew.

10 spirits punning on the senses of ghosts and wine.
14 through a glass for Swift, inevitably recalling 1 Corinthians xiii, 12.
23 out of case the usual meaning at this date was 'in bad condition'.
28 make one join the company.
33 pole the hunting sense is that of the tail of an otter or other quarry.
38 break . . . bend perhaps remembering the Latin phrase *frangas non flectas*, used as a motto by the Gower family. For the proverbial 'sooner break than bend', see *Tilley* B636.

7 The Gulf of All Human Possessions
Carries the heading 'written in the year 1724' in *WF*. Answer: a privy. Discussed by *Lee*, pp. 58-62.

33-6 compare *A Panegyric on the Dean* 213-16.
45 Deucalion son of Prometheus, King of Phthia in Thessaly. He and his wife Pyrrha were the only mortals to be spared when Jove sent a flood to punish the earth; they constructed a boat which 'landed' on the top of Mount Parnassus. They were then ordered by the oracle to throw the bones of their mother Earth (that is, stones) behind them; the stones then became men and women and the world was thus repopulated. As so often, Swift is remembering Ovid: *Metamorphoses* I, 313-415.
57 the writing on the walls perhaps some joking recollection of Daniel v, 5-29, or of the old proverb, 'A white wall is a fool's paper' (see *Tilley* W17). The passage travesties conventional 'horror' effects in poetry.
67-78 Swift seems to be thinking of potatoes as grown, prepared for the table, eaten, and finally excreted.
79-80 for the rhyme, see *Cadenus and Vanessa* 57-8 and many other examples: it was the normal poetic pronunciation, and only just receding as the conventional spoken form (see *OED*, 'wind', esp. the quotation from Johnson in the headnote).
88 Aeolus god of the wind. The passage suggests a link with Virgil's description of Avernus in Book VI of the *Aeneid*. The final verse paragraph reverts to Ovidian or even Lucretian imagery: ll. 89-94 recall, perhaps, *Metamorphoses* I, 434-8.
95-6 parodying Virgil, *Aeneid* IX, 106: *Totum nutu tremefecit Olympum* ('and shook the skies with his imperial nod', tr. Dryden).

8   Louisa to Strephon
Stated in *WF* to have been 'written in the year 1730', which is likely to be no more than a guess. Answer: 'louse to his patron' (that is, host); an anagram of 'Louisa to Strephon'. The object of parody this time is amatory verse.

30   victors o'er the Memphian king   Book III of Herodotus describes Cambyses' successful campaign against Memphis, when the king of Egypt was Psamme-tichus III; see also note to l. 35. However, the phrase may simply be an inten-sified statement of long duration.

35   great Sylla   dictator of Rome, Cornelius Sulla Felix; after putting down the opposition of Marius, he 'decimated the knights, muzzled the tribunate, and curbed the consuls' (Ronald Syme, *The Roman Revolution* (1939), p. 17). He re-signed power after a time, and died within a year (78 B.C.), his body ravaged by illness: it may be relevant that Cambyses (see note to l. 30) died of a mortified wound. See Plutarch's *Lives*, 'Sulla' 36–7, for his death after infestation by ver-min.

38   Alcides   Hercules. Deianira gave him a shirt soaked in the blood of her hus-band Nessus; the blood was impregnated with the venom of the hydra, and when Hercules put the shirt on, it stuck to him and devoured his body. The imagery is again that of putrefaction. See Ovid, *Metamorphoses* IX, 101–210 for a famous version of the story.

9
Headed 'written in the year 1725' in *WF*. Answer: a maypole.

11   couple-beggar   'a disreputable priest who made it his business to "couple" beggars or perform irregular marriages' (*OED*); a Fleet parson.
13   ring   the ring of dancers round the maypole.
17   fanatics   sectaries, radical dissenters.
23   posts   a pun.
24   at the Restoration in 1660, the May Day games which had been suppressed under the Commonwealth were revived, and maypoles which had been taken down were erected once more.

THE ANSWER TO DELANY'S RIDDLE

First published together with Delany's riddle in a broadside (Dublin, 1726): *T* 656, *Foxon* D205. Curll inserted the item in his *Miscellanea* (1727), and it was variously reprinted before entering *F*, vol. VIII, in 1762. Text here based on *F*.

The text of Delany's riddle is reproduced in *P* III, 938. The answer (not sup-plied by any previous editor, so far as I can observe) is 'an eye'. The short lines almost rival the Lilliputian measure used by Pope in 1727 in the poems to greet *Gulliver's Travels* (*PTE* VI, 268–9).

1   half an eye   Tilley H47.
3   your wicket   Delany has 'a wonderful wicket, not half an inch wide' (l. 6).
4   thicket   eyebrows.
6   7]   You're reported to dwell / Like a monk in a cell. *1726 broadside; not in F.* *F.*
17   you say   Delany, l. 16.
24   flies from Apollo   since the eye cannot look directly at the sun when it is shining brightly.

31 a hair perhaps a reference to hare's eye, 'a disease arising from a contraction of the upper eye-lid . . . so that the patient is obliged to sleep with the eye half open' (*OED*, quoting the first edition of Chambers' *Cyclopedia*). 'Hareeyed' meant shortsighted. On the other hand, it may simply mean a loose eyelash.

UPON FOUR DISMAL STORIES IN THE DOCTOR'S LETTER

These lines were appended to a letter to Pope and Gay on 15 October 1726. Swift got back to Dublin late in August. Shortly afterwards a series of misfortunes overtook his English friends, which were reported in Dr Arbuthnot's letter of *c.*20 September (*Corr* III, 165–6): Congreve 'has been like to die with a fever, and the gout in his stomach'; Pope 'has been in hazard of his life by drowning, coming late two weeks ago from Lord Bolingbroke's in his coach and six, a bridge on a little river being broke down they were obliged to go through the water, which was too high, but the coach was overturned in it, and the glass being up, which he could not break nor get down, he was very near drowned' (for a further discussion of this event, see George Sherburn, 'An Accident in 1726', *Harvard Library Bulletin* II (1948), 121–3); Mrs Howard 'has had a most intolerable pain on one side of her head'; finally, Arbuthnot's brother Robert 'was like to be cast away, going to France: there was a ship lost just by him.' For these figures, see Biog. Dict. The text is based on a transcript of the letter at Longleat.

2 an ague a good rhyme; an acute fever, especially one involving quaking, as in malarial conditions. Mrs Howard was deaf and subject to migraines. Congreve had been in poor health for many years, with gout and eye-trouble.
7 'I am now going on the old way having much to do of little consequence and taking all advantage of fair weather to keep my health by walking', Swift to Chetwode, 24 October (*Corr* III, 177).

ON THE COLLAR OF MRS DINGLEY'S LAP-DOG

Printed by *F* (1762). *P* II, 762 suggests that it may have been written around 1726, on the basis of the mention of a lap-dog in *Bec's Birthday* 37. A notice appeared in Faulkner's *Dublin Journal* in 1741, asking for the return of a bitch wearing a collar with the same inscription. However, as Williams suggests, it is likely that the collar was passed on from one dog to another. It is highly unlikely that composition could be as late as 1741. The text here is based on *F* (1762).

It was around 1737 that Pope composed what is probably the most famous of all such collar-inscriptions: 'I am his Highness' dog at Kew; / Pray tell me, sir, whose dog are you?' (*PTE* VI, 372).

BEC'S BIRTHDAY

The only authority for this poem is Deane Swift in 1765. He headed it, 'November 8th M DCC XXVI'; the date is possible, as Swift had returned to Ireland by the end of August, and after a visit to the country had taken up residence in Dublin again (*Corr* III, 177). Mrs Dingley was about sixty at this date. According to Sheridan the younger, she was 'merely one of the common run of women, of a middling understanding, without knowledge or taste; and so entirely selfish, as to be incapable of any sincere friendship, or warm attachment' (see *Corr* V, 245); but Swift remained loyal to her after Stella's death.

Text from Deane Swift.

3–6 the three Fates spun the thread of life; Atropos was the one who severed the thread, to cause death.

7 proverbial; *Tilley* C84. Swift associated 'care' with Mrs Dingley: see *A New Year's Gift for Bec* 14; *JTS* I, 298, 314.

10 compare Swift's remark in March 1711: 'I suppose Dingley is so fair and so fresh as a lass in May, and has her health, and no spleen' (*JTS* I, 210).

11–16 compare Pope, *Essay on Man* II, 160–61: 'So, when small humours gather to a gout, / The doctor fancies he has driven them out.' The note in *PTE* (III, i, 74) is relevant: 'Gout was thought to arise from "a redundancy of humours" and was "considered as a . . . paroxysm, tending to free the body of an offensive . . . matter, by throwing it upon the extremities".'

19 *philosophers* scientists, natural philosophers. The couplet (ll. 19–20) encapsulates a long argument in the first canto of *Alma* (*Prior*, I, 471–7).

25 Mrs Dingley seems to have been physically clumsy: see l. 42.

30 for the cat's proverbial nine lives, see *Tilley* C154.

  eke also (facetious archaism).

36 *porridge* soup.

37 *Tiger* 'Mrs Dingley's favourite lap-dog' (note in Deane Swift); compare *On the Collar of Mrs Dingley's Lap-Dog*.

  served pronounced (certainly in fashionable circles) 'sarved'.

40 *slabbering* now 'slobbering'.

42 compare Swift's remark in the *Journal*, 'Don't fall and hurt yourselves, nor overturn the coach' (*JTS* I, 298).

43–4 compare *Dingley and Brent* 10–12, 16.

46 Mrs Dingley outlived Stella by fifteen years, but was herself outlived by Swift.

56 *rattle* chatter thoughtlessly.

58 *his rod* see *The Virtues of Sid Hamet the Magician's Rod*

STELLA'S BIRTHDAY (1727)

The last and most deeply felt of the birthday poems to Stella. It is headed 'March 13, 1726/7' (see note on dates, p. 598); Swift must have taken it with him when he crossed to England on his final visit, a month later. He returned in the autumn and Stella died on 28 January 1728. The poem then appeared in *M28*, published in the following March. It subsequently went into *WF*, the source for the text here.

For a reading of the poem as consolatory rather than persuasive, see *Jaffe*, pp. 8–11.

6 *spectacles* see *Stella's Birthday* (1725) 45.

8 *mortifying* *Jaffe*, p. 8, detects 'the suggestion of a pun' (that is, (1) humiliating, (2) serving as a *memento mori*).

26 *styled its own reward* proverbial; see *OED*, 'virtue' 2, for use of the phrase by Dryden, Vanbrugh, Smollett, and others. *Tilley* V81.

35–50   Jaffe, p. 9, sees in this paragraph 'abstract reasoning', 'abstraction', and 'distancing'. There may well be particular references concealed behind the generalized verbal formulae, but if so they cannot be identified.

49–50   compare *To Stella, Visiting Me in My Sickness*.

74   Janus   see *A New Year's Gift for Bec* 1.

CLEVER TOM CLINCH GOING TO BE HANGED

On its first appearance in *WF* (cancelled state) described as 'written in the year 1726'. Other editions amend this to 1727. No greater accuracy can be achieved. The London setting might suggest that the poem was composed during one of Swift's English visits, in 1726 or 1727 (as suggested by *Ball*, p. 218), but the *mise-en-scène* of a Tyburn day was long familiar to Swift, and the fame of Wild had, of course, reached Dublin. Background to the poem is supplied by Gerald Howson, *Thief-Taker General* (1970), a life of Wild; for Swift's use of Tyburn imagery, see *Grub Street*, pp. 253–6.

The text is based on *WF*.

2   Holborn   the procession made its way westwards to Tyburn from Newgate along the main artery, through densely populated regions.

3   the George   a tavern on the south side of Holborn, almost opposite Red Lion Street (Hugh Phillips, *Mid-Georgian London* (1964), p. 201). It was normal for the procession to halt for drinks to be consumed *en route*.

sack   white wine.

8   proper   handsome.

10   box   at a theatre.

11   street-hawkers sold 'dying speeches' by the convicted criminal to the crowds attending an execution; publishers like John Applebee and writers like Defoe specialized in such works. Swift parodied the form in his *Last Speech and Dying Words of Ebenezor Elliston* (1722).

16   whittle   'a cant word for confessing at the gallows' (note in *WF*). Often 'whiddle'; as in 'he whiddles the whole scrap', he tells all he knows.

17   Wild   Jonathan Wild, the thief-taker: see Howson and Biog. Dict. He had been executed in May 1725, a year after the escapologist Jack Sheppard. Accounts of his career appeared in Dublin as well as London and provincial towns. Wild himself claimed to have brought seventy-five criminals to justice, and there were others he impeached who were left off this list.

20   slip   miss.

ON SEEING VERSES WRITTEN UPON WINDOWS IN INNS

These four epigrams were published in *WF* and must be regarded as authentic. Deane Swift added a further six in 1765, and two others were printed by Scott. The grounds for ascribing the last eight items to Swift are exceedingly slender, and they are omitted here. See *P* II, 401–5 for the text of the dubious items. The four sets of verses published in *WF* were headed 'written in the year 1726', probably no more than an approximation.

Text from *WF*.

I

1   The sage Momus, the god of satire, complained that the human form lacked a window in the breast, by which means all secret thoughts would be apparent to observers. The story occurs in one of Swift's favourite authors among the ancients, Lucian.

8   the diamond used for inscribing the verse on a window.

4

1   here the younger Thomas Sheridan in the *Works* (1784) assigns this poem to Chester, that is, written on Swift's journey to or from London. There is no evidence to support the statement.

ON READING DR YOUNG'S SATIRES

First published with *To a Lady* in 1733 (dated 1734) (*T* 745, Foxon S841), and reprinted in a volume of miscellanies the same year. When it appeared in *WF*, the poem was headed, 'written in the year 1726'. This may well be right; l. 3 suggests that Swift had already seen the seventh of Young's satires, dedicated to Walpole, which appeared in 1726. For a reference by Swift to Young's satires, see *Corr* IV, 53–4. In general Young was an ally of the Scriblerian party, but Swift evidently had reservations about his political attitudes. See Biog. Dict. Text based on *WF*.

Title   refers to Edward Young's *Love of Fame: The Universal Passion, in Seven Characteristical Satires*, published at intervals between 1725 and 1728; first collected in 1728. The sixth satire was dedicated to Swift's friend, Lady Elizabeth Germain.

1–12   mainly directed at Young's seventh satire, ll. 1–28.

3   A minister 'Walpole' (note in *WF*). The dedicatee of Young's seventh satire: see ll. 225–8, parodied in Pope, *The Dunciad* (1743) IV, 614.

5   he who in the chair presides 'Compton, the Speaker' (note in *WF*): for Spencer Compton, Speaker of the Commons, see Biog. Dict. Young's fourth satire was addressed to Compton, as one 'born o'er senates to preside, / Their dignity to raise, their counsels guide' (ll. 5–6).

7   others such as Bubb Dodington, dedicatee of the second satire.

24   ad exemplum regis on the model of, following the example of, the king.

36–7   vice . . . virtue political terms: see *To Charles Ford, Esq. on His Birthday* 41–2.

ADVICE TO THE GRUB STREET VERSE-WRITERS

On its first appearance in *WF*, headed 'written in the year 1726'. Compare *Dr Swift to Mr Pope* 9–12. Pope's habit of writing his poems on old envelopes or scraps of paper was well known in his own lifetime. If *WF*'s date is right, the poem may have been written whilst Swift was staying with Pope at Twickenham in the summer of that year.

Text from *WF*.

4   consigned to paste i.e. their works are not yet used for wrapping pastry goods.

8 to wrap up spice compare Pope, *Epistle to Augustus* 418.
11 Curll the bookseller Edmund Curll: see Biog. Dict.

TO THE EARL OF PETERBOROUGH

First published in *WF* and there stated to have been 'written in the year 1726'.
See *P* II, 396–7, for lengthy debate as to the correct dating; Forster and others
put composition as early as 1711, 1706, or even 1705. *Ball*, p. 216, remarks that
'the verses are chiefly occupied with Peterborough's activities in the days of
Oxford's ministry, and were possibly designed then.' It is true that some of the
details fit Peterborough's prime as a military commander and ambassador in the
reign of Anne; and that as far back as June 1711 Swift had told Stella, 'The Earl
of Peterborough is returned from Vienna without one servant: he left them scat-
tered in several towns of Germany...He sent expresses, and got here before
them. He is above fifty, and as active as one of five and twenty' (*JTS* I, 297).
On the other hand, it would be natural to mention Peterborough's earlier ex-
ploits, at whatever date the poem was written. He remained active and mobile up
to the supposed date of composition. The two men were in contact during 1726,
and indeed Peterborough's letter to Swift of 29 November concerning the recent-
ly published *Gulliver's Travels* is signed 'your affectionate tar' (*Corr* III, 192):
compare l. 33 of the poem. As recently as 3 September, Pope had told Swift,
'Lord Peterborough can go to any climate, but never stay in any' (*Corr* III, 161).
True to type, Peterborough had carried Swift all over town, including once to
Walpole's house (*Corr* III, 131; Pope *Corr* II, 373). It is worth adding that
Peterborough's wanderings continued into his last years, and that in 1733 Pope
celebrated his friend in a couplet which linked past and present: 'And He, whose
lightning pierced the Iberian lines, / Now forms my quincunx, and now ranks
my vines' (*Hor. Sat.* II, i, 19–30). Finally, as mentioned in *P* II, 396, the poem
was not included in *M11*, which effectively excludes the possibility it was written
earlier. I see no reason to disturb *WF*'s dating, which must at least have had
Swift's tacit consent.

For Peterborough, general and magnifico, see Biog. Dict. W. Stebbing, *Peter-
borough* (1890), pp. 156–64, describes his circuit through Europe in 1707.

Text from *WF*.

1 Mordanto Charles Mordaunt (the family name).
3 prints newspapers.
4 the post express messengers or speedy hired horses.
8 squib explosive missile.
10 the meaning seems to be that Peterborough is the quickest news-service
from Paris and constitutes the most up-to-date 'gazette' available.
13 a-reek reeking with sweat.
15 compare Swift's letter to Gay, 10 November 1730: 'When my Lord Peter-
borough in the Queen [Anne]'s time went abroad upon his embassies, the minis-
try told me, that he was such a vagrant, they were forced to write at him by
guess, because they knew not where to write *to* him' (*Corr* III, 416).
18 from Leghorn as well as being ambassador to the Duke of Savoy in 1713–14,
Peterborough spent a good deal of time later in Italy, e.g. in 1717 and 1719
(Stebbing, op. cit., pp. 195–7), where he enjoyed some characteristic
adventures.

32   In senates bold   Peterborough was a vehement orator in the House of Lords (see Stebbing, op. cit., pp. 192–5).

33   a tar   see headnote. Perhaps in reference to an adventure in an open boat, of which news reached Lord Oxford and Matthew Prior in 1714 (Stebbing, op. cit., p. 189). When Peterborough wrote to Swift shortly afterwards he did not mention the episode (*Corr* II, 13–14), but it is inconceivable that Swift did not get to hear of it.

36   Charles of Sweden   Charles XII: see *The Part of a Summer* 97. Peterborough had contrived a meeting with Charles in 1707 (Stebbing, op. cit., pp. 159–60).

DR SWIFT TO MR POPE

Published in *Misc* (1732), the so called 'third' volume, and then in *WF*, where it is stated to have been 'written in the year 1726'. *P* II, 405 suggests rather the summer of 1727: it must have been one or other of these years. Swift had been following the progress of Pope's 'Dulness' since its inception; the earliest reference in the correspondence seems to be in October 1725 (*Corr* III, 107). Then came Swift's two visits to England. On the first occasion, when the friends met, his health was good (Pope to the Earl of Oxford, 22 March 1726: Pope *Corr* II, 372). It seems more likely, therefore, that the poem dates from the later visit; we know that Swift suffered a bad recurrence of deafness in August 1727, following a visit to Oxford's house in Cambridgeshire (*Corr* III, 228–38). Indeed, he told Sheridan, '[I] am deafer than ever you knew me.' The latter part of the poem is paralleled by Pope to Swift, 23 March 1728: 'Your deafness would agree with my dullness; you would not want me to speak when you could not hear' (*Corr* III, 275). Pope referred to *The Dunciad* as apparently completed in his letter to Swift of 22 October 1727, although it was not published until the following April. My tentative dating would be around the middle of August 1727. Text based on *WF*.

9   backs of letters   see *Advice to the Grub Street Verse-Writers* 13–16.

13–16   alluding to Pope's agglomerative technique in assembling a poem from oddly assorted scraps.

18   a general axiom or rule, in this case of logic (with a sly reference, perhaps, to ecclesiastical law). Swift would have encountered the notions in his studies of logic at Trinity College (see *Ehrenpreis*, I, 58–63), and possibly in later reading such as Ralph Cudworth.

25   Sherlock   'N.B. Not the present Bishop of Bangor, but his father, who was Dean of St Paul's; the son being only famous for his enslaving speech in the House of Lords' (note in *WF*). William Sherlock (*c*.1641–1707), Dean of St Paul's 1691; and his son Thomas (1678–1761), a supporter of Walpole and a prominent churchman for fifty years. No speech which fits the description is recorded in the *Parliamentary Debates*, and indeed by 1736 Sherlock was incurring Lord Hervey's enmity by his independent line and vehement opposition to the Quakers' Tithe Bill. However, the satirist Paul Whitehead wrote in 1733 that Sherlock had proved 'parliaments dependent to be free' (see *PTE* V, 454). It is possible that Sherlock was 'the plunging prelate' of *The Dunciad* (1743) II, 323–4.

A PASTORAL DIALOGUE BETWEEN RICHMOND LODGE
AND MARBLE HILL

The text is based on *WF*, where (in the cancelled state of the volume) the poem made its first appearance. For the revamping of this edition, see *Mad Mullinix and Timothy*, headnote. According to a note in *WF*, 'This poem was carried to court, and read to the King and Queen.'

During Swift's final visit to England there came news of the sudden death of George I at Osnabruck, *en route* to his beloved Hanover. This took place on 12 June 1727, and within two days a messenger had ridden post-haste to inform Walpole. The prime minister immediately set out from his Chelsea home for Richmond, in order to inform the Prince and Princess of Wales, whom he found in bed at the palace. Flustered and half-dressed, the Prince learnt from a kneeling Walpole that he was now King George II. The general expectation was that Walpole would now fall from grace, and that the former adherents of the Prince (including his mistress, Mrs Howard) would attain great influence. It proved to be an illusory hope, and Swift and Pope were among those most cruelly disappointed.

Title 'Richmond Lodge is a house with a small park belonging to the crown: it was usually granted by the crown for a lease of years; the Duke of Ormonde was the last who had it. After his exile, it was given to the Prince of Wales, by the King. The Prince and Princess usually passed their summer there. It is within a mile of Richmond.

'Marble Hill is a house built by Mrs Howard, then of the Bedchamber, now Countess of Suffolk, and Groom of the Stole to the Queen. It is on the Middlesex side, near Twickenham, where Mr Pope lives, and about two miles from Richmond Lodge. Mr Pope was the contriver of the gardens, Lord Herbert the architect, and the Dean of St Patrick's chief butler, and keeper of the ice-house. Upon King George's death, these two houses met, and had the following dialogue' (note in *WF*). Richmond Lodge, now demolished, stood in what is today a part of Kew Gardens. Marble Hill, the well appointed house of 'sober magnificence', has been restored to its full 'Augustan correctitude' in recent years (the phrases quoted are those of Peter Quennell, *Caroline of England* (1939), p. 243). For the activities of Pope, Lord Herbert, and Roger Morris there, during its construction *c*.1724–7, see James Lees-Milne, *Earls of Creation* (1962), pp. 79–92).

1   Pope...Gay   who both spent a good deal of time at Marble Hill. On 20 June 1727 Pope wrote to Mrs Howard, saying 'we intend to entertain Dean Swift' in the hall (perhaps the cuboid saloon on the first floor). See Pope *Corr* II, 436.

5   as neighbours use   as is the habit of neighbours.

8   for the 'old proverbs' (l. 7) see *Tilley* W19. John Ray, *Collection of English Proverbs* (1670) gives, 'fields have eyes, and hedges ears.' Swift has 'hedges have eyes, and walls have ears' in *Polite Conversation* (*PW* IV, 196).

13   The kingly prophet   David: see Psalm cxlvi, 3.

24   My Lady's empty pockets   'Altogether the Prince gave £12,000 towards the cost [of Marble Hill], the rest of which was to prove a great strain on her resources' (Lees-Milne, op. cit., p. 80). In the event, her finances proved adequate to maintain the house and support a whole series of improvements, although she died not particularly wealthy. 'Few royal mistresses made so little from their station as Mrs Howard. A small villa at Marble Hill ... a few jewels and trinkets, a modest pension and a guinea or so now and then for her private charities, these were the few rewards for her time and person' (*Plumb*, p. 159). 'Small villa' is a little misleading.

26 for progress on the works, see Lees-Milne, op. cit., pp. 82–3. The main staircase is made of mahogany, a gift from the Prince.

27   all the courtly madams round for Mrs Howard's aristocratic neighbours, see Lewis Melville, *Lady Suffolk and Her Circle* (1924), pp. 107–9. They included Lady Mary Wortley Montagu, who had a house adjoining Twickenham Green, purchased in 1722.

28   four shillings in the pound the land tax levied on property owners (the main form of direct taxation).

30   hardly worth a groat for the cliché 'not worth a groat', see *Tilley* G458 and *Polite Conversation* (*PW* IV, 158): compare *Corr* I, 205.

31–3 for Mrs Howard's defects as a courtier, see Swift's 'Character' of her, dated 12 June 1727 (*PW* V, 214).

33   dexterous slippery, cunning, adroit.

43   that grave divine compare *Stella's Birthday* (1727) 13.

44   the key of my (no) wine compare Swift to Mrs Howard, 2 February 1727: 'I hope you will get your house and wine ready, to which Mr Gay and I are to have free access when you are safe at court; for as to Mr Pope, he is not worth mentioning on such occasions' (*Corr* III, 196).

47   Patty Blount Pope's friend Martha Blount (see Biog. Dict.). On 20 June of this year she wrote to Mrs Howard, requesting some employment at Marble Hill: 'I am so very dull and I might say ... not very well, and very low spirited' (Melville, op. cit., pp. 173–4). For a letter from Swift to her about this time, see *Corr* III, 235. The closest parallel to this section of the poem occurs in a letter from Swift to Martha Blount on 29 February 1728, which visualizes the recipient 'with a manteau out at the sides' and 'sponging' on others. After referring to Pope and Gay, the letter continues, 'How will you pass this summer for want of a squire to Ham Common and Walpole's lodge; for, as to Richmond Lodge and Marble Hill, they are abandoned as much as Sir Spencer Compton' (*Corr* III, 268). For Compton, see Biog. Dict.

49   Plump ... Gay Gay's corpulence was often mentioned in fun, as for example by the poet himself in *Mr Pope's Welcome from Greece* (1720), 134.

50   dangle 'to follow in a dallying way, without being a formally recognised attendant' (*OED*).

51   to seek at a loss, without recourse.

52   sponge 'to eat or drink at another's expense' (Grose, *Dictionary of the Vulgar Tongue*). Compare *My Lady's Lamentation* 16.

56   No butter sticks upon his bread proverbial, for 'nothing goes right for him': *Tilley* B778.

61   Lady Charlotte 'Lady Charlotte de Roussy, a French lady' (note in *WF*). Lady Charlotte de Roucy (1653–1743), sister of the Earl of Lifford; member of Huguenot family. She and her brother were described by Lord Hervey as 'two poor miserable Court drudges'. See Hervey's *Memoirs*, ed. R. Sedgwick (1952), pp. 71–2.

64 ancient Mirmont 'Marquis de Mirmont, a French man of quality' (note in *WF*). Armande de Bourbon, Marquis de Miremont (1655–1732), a Huguenot refugee, who received a government pension.

67–72 the familiar Tory complaint that moneyed men were buying up estates and 'improving' them in undesirable ways. See Pope, *Epistle to Burlington* 13–22.

76 the Prince of Wales Frederick Lewis; he was to remain a prince until his death in 1751, as his father survived until 1760.

83–4 better . . . debtor a favourite rhyme: compare *An Elegy on Demar* 15–16; *The Bank Thrown Down* 41–2.

88 Kensington, or . . . St James's the other royal palaces.

93 wildernesses areas of 'natural' or fantastic garden within a cultivated park. For Caroline's activity as a gardener at Richmond, see Judith Colton, 'Merlin's Cave and Queen Caroline: Garden Art as Political Propaganda', *Eighteenth-Century Studies* X (1976), 1–20.

96 Moody 'the gardener' (note in *WF*).

97 quarterage quarterly wage.

101–3 Lees-Milne, op. cit., p. 84, sees this as the 'smug' comment of Richmond Lodge, 'to whom at this moment Herbert's and Morris's attentions were chiefly directed and who was expecting to profit from a lavish expenditure by the new Sovereign'.

DESIRE AND POSSESSION

WF, printing the poem for the first time, states that it was 'written in the year 1727'. *P* II, 411 says it 'may be assigned to the English visit of 1727'. The year may or may not be right, but there is nothing to connect the item with Swift's trip to England. Text from *WF*. I have retained capitals for the personified nouns.

5 A moralist seemingly the fable is Swift's own.

10 still probably 'for all that' rather than 'always'.

14 this the latter (Desire); *that* the former (Possession). A construction familiar in Latin, French, and German, which has dropped out of modern English.

16 many a league many miles.

21–2 recalling Virgil, *Aeneid* VII, 803–4: 'Outstripped the winds in speed upon the plain, / Flew o'er the fields, nor hurt the bearded grain' (Dryden tr.).

26 excursions deviations.

31 spring the technical term in field sports for causing a bird to rise from cover.

36 strewed the original has 'strowed', as usual in Swift.

37 overcharged overloaded.

41 Fortune the goddess of fate, Fortuna.

43–4 compare *Upon the South Sea Project* 145–6. As usual in Swift, 'chasm' makes a single syllable.

56 light alight.

ON CENSURE

First published in *WF*, with the heading 'written in the year 1727'. It is impossible to know how accurate this might be. Text from *WF*.

12 want lack.
21–2 recalling the proverb 'Hard words break no bones.'
28 learned meaning learnéd, but monosyllabic.

THE DOG AND THE THIEF

According to *WF*, where the poem first appeared, 'written in the year 1726'. There is a story on this theme in Aesop (LXXI in Ogilby's version), and in some ways the work is a reversion to the manner of earlier ballads and fables such as *The Faggot*. But the reference to Change Alley clearly sets composition at 1720 or later. It happened that a General Election (only the second since 1715) was in progress during Swift's visit to England in August 1727. Swift went with Pope into Cambridgeshire, and might well have learnt that Thetford had returned Robert Jacombe (through the patronage of the Duke of Grafton, a former Lord Lieutenant of Ireland). Jacombe was Walpole's banker, who had helped him through the South Sea crisis. Pope had an audience with Walpole on his return from this trip early in August (Pope *Corr* II, 441). As likely a time as any, then, would be the second half of 1727. Text based on *WF*.

9 Change Alley see *Upon the South Sea Project* 148.
10 gives a private signal by winking to the freeman of the borough, who was one of the small group of people qualified to vote in many parliamentary constituencies.
12 to drink to buy drink.
17 chouse cheat or swindle.
18 because they are the faceless new men, with no landed property or else merely some recently acquired estate. The poem reflects the Tory view that Whig politics were bringing to unholy advancement moneyed men with no background or stake in older communities. Such men would not hesitate to expropriate in cases where tenants stood in the way of 'improving' estates.

THE FURNITURE OF A WOMAN'S MIND

Williams (*P* II, 415) thinks there must have been a Dublin broadside edition, presumably issued by Mrs Harding (l. 59), but, if so, it has not turned up. The earliest separate edition (*T* 988; *Foxon* S857) is thought to date from some years after its appearance in *WF* and other places during 1735. *WF* states, 'written in the year 1727'; we have no means of testing the assertion. *Ball*, p. 224, says that the poem 'was superseded by *The Journal of a Modern Lady*, for which it appears to have been a study'; but the differences are far more notable than the similarities (the view also of Horrell, *PJH* I, 397). It could, for all we know, even postdate the *Journal*. Text from *WF*.

Herbert Davis, *Jonathan Swift: Essays on His Satire* (1964), pp. 50–53, reads the poem as 'a kind of crude Hudibrastic burlesque of Pope's *Rape of the Lock* with the same episodes'.

2 scarlet coat soldier.

11 repartee a piece of repartee, a smart reply.

14 cut and dry ready-made, unspontaneously: compare *To Betty the Grisette* 13.

16 swoon in the original, 'swown', and perhaps a good rhyme.

19–20 compare *To Mr Delany* 45–50.

29 clubs not regular societies, but groups of friends.

32 patch beauty-spot. Compare *Cadenus and Vanessa* 422–3.

33–6 compare *To Stella, Visiting Me in My Sickness* 69–78.

38–42 compare Pope,. *Rape of the Lock* IV, 31–8.

41–2 'the ironical rhyme "pretty-pity" precisely sums up the feeling of amused scorn for this flighty young minx' (Colin J. Horne, 'Swift's Comic Poetry', in *Augustan Worlds*, ed. J.C. Hilson *et al.* (1978), pp. 54–5).

43 Molly the maid.

45 as sure as death a cliché of the *Polite Conversation* sort. *Tilley* D136.

47 Admires wonders, is amazed.

48 robustious a cross between boisterous and robust, used in *Polite Conversation* (*PW* IV, 167). According to Johnson's *Dictionary*, the word was 'now only used in low language'.

49 to her power to the uttermost of her ability, with all the strength she commands.

56 topics arguments.

59 Mrs Harding 'a printer' (note in *WF*). Mrs Sarah Harding, widow of the Dublin printer John Harding, who had died in prison in 1725. She herself was imprisoned for a time but subsequently continued to publish Swift's works: see *Drapier*, p. 201, and *Munter*, pp. 150, 163.

THE POWER OF TIME

This is the first in a group of poems which were written at Holyhead in September 1727. They accompany the prose *Holyhead Journal* (*PW* V, 201–8) in a pocket-book now preserved among *FV* 519. This poem, alone of the group, was printed in *WF*. The others remained unpublished until 1882. The text of *The Power of Time* is based on *WF*, collated with Swift's MS in *FV*.

Swift left London on 18 September with deep forebodings on account of Stella's health; he had indeed supposed she might have died during his absence. On 22 September he left Chester; on Saturday he passed through Conway and Bangor, and took the ferry to Anglesey. He was so tired that he was obliged to rest at Llangefni, and then his horse lost two shoes. In the end he covered the last three miles to Holyhead by boat and reached an inn there on the afternoon of Sunday 24 September; there he encountered 'the worst ale in the world, and no wine'. Bad weather delayed the Irish ferry, and he was forced to stay in Holyhead until Friday 29 September. Even then the ferry made a false start, being obliged to turn back half an hour after first setting out. He whiled away this tedious week with reflections on a variety of topics, and making verses, especially on the Monday.

Title]*WF*; Shall I repine *Swift MS.*

5–6 a version of the concluding couplet in Paul Scarron's sonnet, '*Superbes monumens*'. A footnote in *WF* reads, 'Scarron hath a larger poem on the same subject.' Swift's jottings for the poem survive in the British Library, Egerton MS 201: 'Scarron's verses on the destructions made by time; the pyramids destroy, rivers, towns, empires &c. decay, and shall I repine that a scurvy black waistcoat, when I wore it two years, is out at elbows...' (*PW* V, 335). The connection between Swift's poem and his jottings was first made by Clive T. Probyn, 'The Power of Time: Swift as Translator', *Notes & Queries* XVI (1969), 337. Probyn concludes that 'though highly condensed from Scarron's fourteen lines Swift's poem remains a translation, given the appropriate stamp of his own wit'.

HOLYHEAD. SEPTEMBER 25, 1727

For the circumstances of composition, see headnote to preceding poem. On the day in question, Swift wrote in his prose journal, 'I writ abundance of verses this day; and several useful hints (though I say it)' (*PW* V, 203). The details referred to in ll. 1–12 are mostly paralleled in the journal. Text from *FV*.

5 Convict convicted (rare by Swift's day).
9–12 the same experience befell the desperately sick Henry Fielding on his final Voyage to Lisbon in 1754.
14 packet a regular service-boat carrying mail and passengers.
23 a friend Stella.
29–34 compare the prose journal: 'Yet here I could live with two or three friends in a warm house, and good wine – much better than being a slave in Ireland' (*PW* V, 207).
34 yon isle Ireland. Swift landed in due course at Carlingford, Co. Louth, almost seventy miles north of Dublin. Gay commiserated with him on account of his 'travels through that country of desolation and poverty in your way to Dublin, for it is a most dreadful circumstance to have lazy dull horses on a road where there are very bad or no inns' (*Corr* III, 245).

IRELAND

For the circumstances of composition, see headnote to *The Power of Time*. Text based on Swift's MS in *FV*.

13 His Excellency the Lord Lieutenant.
14 chaps jaw.
16 To put the question to demand a vote in parliament; to make a motion (of censure, especially).
19 trepanned lured, inveigled.
23 gudgeon] coxcomb *deleted in MS.*
32 a perfect toast a beautiful woman worthy of the homage of fine gentlemen.
35 augmentation increase in the funds made available for bribery.
37 New kings George II had acceded two months earlier.
38]I would not have you show neglect *deleted in MS.*
41–2 scares of Jacobite invasions continued; a Jesuit was traditionally a scheming and traitorous person, and the word emphasizes the French connections of the Pretender.
44 another popery bill in the wake of the Atterbury affair, the Habeas Corpus

Act was suspended, and a special tax of five shillings in the pound levied on Catholics in May 1723 – this caused Pope, among others, financial embarrassment (Pope *Corr* II, 173). Hostile as Swift could be to Catholics, the sense is clearly *against* penal legislation here.

45–6 the opposition feared, not altogether realistically, that Walpole would open up civic opportunities to dissenters as a reward for their support. In 1731 he did plan to relieve Irish dissenters from the Sacramental Test, but had to abandon this in the face of opposition. For Walpole and the nonconformist community, see N.C. Hunt, *Two Early Political Associations* (1961).

46 ∧ 47] Yes and the church established too, / Since 'tis grown protestant like you *deleted in Swift MS*.

49–50 directly contrary to Swift's fierce advocacy for the support of the Irish textile trade.

51–2 again, the opposite of what Swift strove for: 'the country's agriculture had long suffered at the expense of grazing interests, through whose influence the Irish parliament had enacted laws prohibiting tenants from converting pasture into tillable land' (*Ferguson*, pp. 47–8). There was strong pressure to protect England's grain exports to Ireland. The rhyme seems to imply the pronunciation 'enow' (or possibly 'ploff/enoff').

53–4 referring either to ecclesiastics or government officials, who required a licence to absent themselves from the country. Swift had requested such a licence from Tickell the previous April, in order that he might 'set out legally' for England (*Corr* III, 204–5). It does not appear what fee, if any, he paid.

58 who smuggle wool that is, export it illegally; under the provisions of the 1699 Woollen Act, the Irish were forbidden to export made-up woollen goods and could send unworked wool only to specified English ports.

60 chintz symbolic of the luxury fabrics imported and worn by fashionable women: for Swift's views, see *Ferguson*, pp. 154–6.

66 the fools of Totnes alluding to a hyperbolic address of loyalty to the King from the people of Totnes in Devon, satirized in verses published in Dublin (1727): see *T* 1225.

68 a guinea in the pound a tax (of more than twenty shillings in the pound); the Irish guinea was officially worth about twenty-three shillings at this period.

70 Excellence or Grace Lord Lieutenant or Archbishop; both men were English appointees, and Boulter, the primate, was a strong opponent of the 'Irish' party. See Biog. Dict.

71 pre-engaged already bestowed on another.

72 cast dismissed. For Townshend, see Biog. Dict.

'WHEN MRS WELCH'S CHIMNEY SMOKES'

These lines were written in the Holyhead journal on 27 September, as Swift grew increasingly weary of the conditions at the inn (*PW* V, 207). Williams first set them out as poetry (*P* II, 419). 'All this,' added Swift, 'is to divert thinking.' For Gay's response to Swift's 'smoky room', see *Corr* III, 245.

1 Mrs Welch 'an old innkeeper' (*PW* V, 202); this is Swift's spelling for 'Welsh', and it may well be that the name is simply his own appellation for the old woman.

ON LORD CARTERET'S ARMS

The last poem in the Holyhead set; the text here is based on Swift's holograph (*FV*). For Swift and Carteret, see *An Epigram on Wood's Brass Money*.

6–12 the immediately preceding Lord Lieutenants: Wharton (1708–10), Shrewsbury (1713–14), Bolton (1717–22), Grafton (1722–4). See Biog. Dict. for these men. Lines 7–12 are a marginal insertion by Swift.
10 Spanish flies dried beetles used in pharmaceutical preparations; specifically, as an aphrodisiac or cure for impotence.
15 Swift originally began the line with the word 'For' and failed to delete it.
21–4 it is laid to their credit in England if they keep Ireland in subjection, so why should they risk this credit by considering the interests of Ireland herself?
25–6 for the rhyme, compare *A Pastoral Dialogue between Richmond Lodge and Marble Hill* 83–4.

ON THE FIVE LADIES AT SOT'S HOLE, WITH THE DOCTOR
AT THEIR HEAD

First published in *WF* (cancelled state), with the heading, 'written in the year 1728'. This is certainly about the right date. Pat Walsh, the 'officer' referred to in the subtitle (and the 'beau' of the next poem's title), became prominent in Dublin society around 1726 to 1728. See *P* II, 424–5. *Ball*, p. 235, assigns the poem to 'the early part of the year 1728'. A transcript is the last item in Stella's commonplace book at Woburn, but it is not in her hand. She seems to have stopped copying out Swift's poems into the book some time before her death in 1728. See also *Mayhew*, p. 10. The text is based on *WF*.
    A sequel appears in the following item.

Title   *the Doctor*   Sheridan.
3   little Tom   Sheridan.
6   Sot's Hole   'a famous ale-house in Dublin for beefsteaks' (note in *WF*); near the Custom House on the left bank of the Liffey (see *Gilbert*, II, 23–5).
11   hold   wager.
26   cunning stagers   old stagers, experienced women in such surroundings (see *OED*, 'stager' 1b).
34   With fantail and with snake   fashionable ways of waving the curls of a wig.
35   'are put down in this way by prim goodygoodies.'
40   gown   parson's gown.
41   birch   the schoolmaster's rod (alluding to Sheridan's profession).
42   Rose   a Dublin tavern, probably the one in Castle Street (see *Verses on the Death of Dr Swift* 300).
44   Burgundy   accent on second syllable.

THE BEAU'S REPLY TO THE FIVE LADIES' ANSWER

See preceding item. Sheridan composed a reply in the same metre, as by the five ladies themselves: see *P* II, 427–8. This reply occupies the first part of an MS at *HEH* (14335), described by *Mayhew*, p. 160. The latter portion of the MS is taken up by *The Beau's Reply*, in Swift's holograph. Both poems were first published by Deane Swift in 1765 and were taken into *F* the same year. Text here based on Swift's MS, with his scanty punctuation filled out by reference to the printed texts.

1   the sense is something like 'you smart little black-coated fellow'.
4   Tisdall   Rev. William Tisdall, for long an acquaintance of Swift, and once a suitor for Stella: see Biog. Dict.
10   keep a splutter   make a noise or a fuss; the same phrase is used in *JTS* I, 354 (8 September 1711). Termed by Johnson a 'low' expression.
12   Are] *Swift MS*; As *printed texts*.
14   haggard   the meaning may be 'scrawny' or 'wild', or perhaps 'ill-tempered, unpolite'.
15   athwart my maw   in my throat.
16   Suffolk cheese   long famous, but evidently including some inferior kinds: *OED* has '*Suffolk Bang*, a very poor and hard kind of cheese'. *Tilley* C273.

AN ELEGY ON DICKY AND DOLLY

First published in a Dublin octavo of 1732 which also contained *Lady Acheson Weary of the Dean* (*T* 966; *Foxon* S831). Collected by Deane Swift in 1765. The text here is based on the octavo with minor variants introduced from Deane Swift and *F* (1765).

The circumstances underlying the poem are set out in a newspaper report from Dublin on 13 April 1728, quoted by *Ball*, p. 256: 'On Monday last [8 April] the Countess of Meath, who was married to General Gorges, died at Kilbrew, the General's seat in the county of Meath, which is about twelve miles from this city; she was to have been brought here tomorrow to have been interred in St Audeon's church with her father and mother, but General Gorges himself died yesterday and the burial place of his family is at Ratoath.' On 16 April the correspondent adds, 'General Gorges and his lady, the Countess of Meath, were buried together last Sunday [14 April] at Kilbrew.' The reckoning is in Irish miles: Kilbrew is about eighteen miles north-west of Dublin.

Dorothea Stopford of Tara Hill married, first, the fourth Earl of Meath, and second, Lieutenant-General Richard Gorges. Swift heard something of her in his London days: he wrote to Stella on 25 February 1712, 'Countess Doll of Meath is such an owl, that wherever I visit people are asking me whether I know such an Irish lady; and her figure and her foppery...' (*JTS* II, 498). Swift later had some correspondence about her stepson (*Corr* IV, 225–6). Composition most likely dates from 1728, although Swift's vagueness about the interval between the two deaths (l. 11) may indicate the poem was written rather later. There was a well-known song by Durfey, 'Dick and Doll'.

11   days] *Deane Swift, F*; months *octavo* (1732).
13–15] *not in Deane Swift, F*.
19   Meath   Chaworth Brabazon, sixth Earl of Meath (1686–1763).
20   The son   probably Gorges' son by his first marriage.
21   Cuffe   John Cuffe, who married the General's daughter.
     Alicant   from Alicante in Spain.

MAD MULLINIX AND TIMOTHY

The first of a group of satires directed principally against Richard Tighe. It first appeared in the eighth number of *The Intelligencer*, a weekly journal published by Mrs Harding in Dublin for Sheridan and Swift. There were nineteen issues of the paper between 11 May 1728 and 2 December of the same year. See *T* 666 and *PW* XII, xiv–xv, 29–61. There were also collected editions published in London in 1729 and 1730 (*T* 34, 35). Swift gave Pope an account of the journal in a letter of 12 June 1732 (*Corr* IV, 30–31). He states that he wrote 'only the verses (very uncorrect) against a fellow we all hated' for this eighth number. This means that the prose introduction must be by Sheridan. It sets out the background of the dialogue; in it Tighe is quoted as saying that party should never die whilst he was alive.

Mullinix or Molyneux, was a half-crazed beggar who went round Dublin spouting Tory sentiments. Tim is the Honourable Richard Tighe, for whom see Biog. Dict. He and Swift had been on bad terms at least since 1711, when they were both in London. Swift even told Stella that Tighe used to beat his wife in full view of anybody across the street (*JTS* I, 343, 360), though he did add that 'she deserved it'. Tighe gained influence after the accession of George I, as a strong Whig; he became an M.P. in Ireland and a member of the Privy Council there. In 1725 he attempted to stir up Lord Carteret's feelings against Sheridan, and for this Swift vowed revenge (*Corr* III, 98–101). See also *A Character, Panegyric, and Description of the Legion Club* 149.

This was one of the poems omitted when *WF* was revamped prior to publication. As with *Traulus*, it is not entirely clear why this should have been done. Unlike *To a Lady*, it contained nothing especially controversial on political grounds. The explanation of Margaret Weedon (*The Library*, 5th ser. XXII (1967), 44–56) is that Swift was willing to recant over individuals whom he attacked, and that 'where private injuries were concerned, [he] did sometimes feel, belatedly, that he had been too severe'. This may be so, though there is not much evidence that Swift at any time softened towards Tighe. It must be admitted that the poems introduced in place of *Mad Mullinix and Timothy* (among them were *Stella at Woodpark* and *A Receipt to Restore Stella's Youth*) have claims to be regarded as artistically finer achievements. On the other hand, Faulkner would hardly have gone to the trouble of re-setting so much text on this ground alone; he might have been more swayed by the fact that the new poems were previously unpublished and thus their inclusion gave him a real *coup* in the competitive world of publishing. The cancels in *WF* did in fact allow for the appearance of eight completely fresh items, something even Curll would have been glad to claim. Against this, three of the four items lost through cancellation had already appeared in print, and the fourth was a short make-weight, the *Epigram on Fasting*. It may be that Faulkner was not excessively sorry to lose *Mad Mullinix* from his collection.

There are a number of differences between the text of *WF* (uncancelled state) and the earlier printed versions of this poem. The text here is based on *WF*, although punctuation sometimes follows *Misc* (1732).

2   *clutter*   a favourite Swiftian word, and see *Corr* III, 98, for its use in conjunction with Tighe.

6   *hardly twenty*   a huge underestimate. The Jacobites were now weakened in

Ireland, as elsewhere, but their hard core certainly ran into hundreds, and probably thousands.

9–10   the Hanoverian Tories had been strengthened by the fiasco of the Atterbury affair, following earlier misadventures, but they did not monopolize the whole party.

13   an earl   the Earl of Barrymore, a known Jacobite, was one of those who supported a motion in the Irish House of Lords in December 1727, which called for an inquiry into the public accounts. This step was occasioned by the frauds of the Deputy Vice-Treasurer, John Pratt: see *Verses from Quilca*, 'The Blessings of a Country Life'.

17   bishop   probably Archbishop Boulter (see Biog. Dict.). In 1725 Swift had noted, 'The primate and the Earl of Cavan govern the House of Lords' (*Corr* III, 115–16).

24 ∧ 25]   The Intelligencer prints ten lines not in WF:

> *M.*   In every arse you run your snout,
> To find this damned Pretender out,
> While all the silly wretch can do,
> Is but to frisk about like you.
> But Tim, convinced by your persuasion,
> I yield there might be an invasion,
> And you who never fart in vain,
> Can fart his navy back again.
>
>   *T.*   Zounds, sir.   *M.*   But to be short and serious
>   For long disputes will only weary us.

24   Avignon   'a midland city in France' (note in *WF*). The Pretender had been there in late 1727; it was a Papal State and outside the jurisdiction of France.

33   Martin Marall   'a play of Dryden's' (note in *WF*). The comedy dates from 1668; the reference is to Act V, Scene i.

35–6   compare *Prometheus* 25–6.

42   Thersites   *Iliad* II, 212–71.

47   teasing   provocation.

50   thy state grimace   'with reference to affected solemnity of countenance, as of one ostensibly burdened with secrets of state' (*OED*).

51   important   portentous.

58   As if the devil drove   adapting the proverb (*Tilley* D278).

66   Keck   retch.
  glorious   King William III: compare *Directions for a Birthday Song* 251–2.

70   his statue   'a statue of King William in College Green, Dublin, round which his adorers, every year of his birth, go on foot, or in their coaches: but the number is much lessened' (note in *WF*).

74   Or from above, or from below   exhaled from the lungs, or through the anus as wind.

81   taste   relish for entertainment.

89   Which the true mother   it was disputed whether the Pretender was really the son of James II's wife, Mary of Modena.

90   the witch of Endor   see 1 Samuel xxviii, 7–25.

100   Queen of Sheba   see 1 Kings x, 1–13.

101   The Duke of Lorraine   the Pretender.

104   sells...a bargain   makes a fool of. See *Tilley* B80.

117   motion   puppet-show.

119   Sabra   daughter of Ptolemy, rescued by St George from the clutches of the dragon.

129   fidge   twitch, fidget.

142   coil   tumult, bustle.

145   I frank my letters   Members of Parliament were allowed to send letters through the post without charge, by writing their name on the cover.

153   Jacks   Jacobites.

164   May-game   object of ridicule, as in May Day sports.

192   the sable guard   vagrants, esp. children, the 'blackguard'.

196   that is, girls who rake for cinders among ashes: see *A Letter from Dean Swift to Dean Smedley* 45.

204   Horace   see *Epistles* I, xiv, 43: 'he [the ox] longs for the horse's trappings' (part of a proverb).

206   Dr Lee   'a deceased clergyman, whose footman he was' (note in *WF*).

208   hangs by geometry   for this proverbial expression, see *An Elegy on Partridge* 41.

210   Your block   the shape of your head (seen as a wig-block).

to a hair   see *The Journal of a Modern Lady* 10.

216   toupee or snake   fashionable wig-stylings: compare *On the Five Ladies at Sot's Hole* 34.

217   from top to toe   see *Tilley* T436.

224   mien   countenance.

233–4   for a serious version, see *To Mr Delany* 29–40.

237–48   the 'useful arts' identified by *WF* as follows: chimney-sweeps; scavengers; cobblers; keepers at Bridewell house of correction; and porters.

249   a note in *WF* reads '*Non de domibus rebusve alienis, &c.* Horace'; a misquotation for '*non de villis domibusve alienis*', *Satires* II, vi, 71: 'not about other men's homes or estates.'

250   bonnyclabber   sour clotted milk, drunk by the Irish peasantry.

253   a note in *WF* reads, '*Sed, quod magis ad nos, Et nescire malum est, agitamus, &c.*' Horace, *Satires* II, vi, 72–3 (the word *pertinet* omitted): 'but we consider what concerns us more, and about which it would be bad to be ignorant.'

262 ∧ 263]   One shows how brave Audoin died, / And at the gallows all denied *The Intelligencer; not in WF*. For the case of Audoin, a Dublin surgeon hanged in 1728, see *Gilbert*, I, 267.

TIM AND THE FABLES

A sequel to the preceding poem. It first appeared in the tenth number of *The Intelligencer* during July 1728. According to Swift's letter to Pope of 12 June 1732, he wrote for this issue 'only the verses, and of those not the four last slovenly lines' (*Corr* IV, 30). Unlike the preceding item, this was never included in *WF*. Text from *The Intelligencer*.

2   the monkey in the fable has a design to 'visit foreign climes'.

3   Lucas's   a coffee-house in Dublin.

4   The Fables   the first series of fifty fables by Gay, published around the spring of 1727 by Tonson and Watts. A copy was in Swift's collection (*Library*, no. 537).

8 'The monkey, who had seen the world'   that is, Fable xiv.

9 Tonson   the bookseller, Jacob Tonson senior: see Biog. Dict.

10 a cut   a woodcut by William Kent or John Wootton was attached to each fable. Gay had given Swift regular progress reports on his book, including the engraving of the plates, which went slowly (see *Corr* III, 164, 202).

12   the very picture of a beau with all his airs and graces.

14 glass   looking-glass.

17   various contortions of the body to affect elegance.
   fidge   see *Mad Mullinix and Timothy* 129.

30 a libel   the moral of the fable is that 'travel finishes the fool'; the well-travelled pick up vices on their journey.

33 deserve   pronounced 'desarve'.

TOM MULLINEX AND DICK

A parallel item to *Mad Mullinix and Timothy* and *Tim and the Fables*. However, like the other Tighe poems (apart from these two), it was first published in *Misc* (1745), the source for the present text. Probably composed *c.* 1728.

1 Dick   Richard Tighe.

8 best at farting   compare *Mad Mullinix and Timothy* 151; *Tim and the Fables* 19; *Dick's Variety* 25.

11 a footboy   see *Mad Mullinix and Timothy*, note to 206.

12 from an oven   Tighe's ancestor had supplied the Cromwellian armies with bread.

14 borees   country dances.

19 blackguard boys   vagrants, 'city Arabs', boys who ran errands, blacked shoes, etc. Compare *Mad Mullinix and Timothy* 192.

29 swing   *OED* suggests 'movement of the body or limbs in a manner suggesting the action of swinging'; but this seems very flat. The repetition of this word makes one wonder if the text is corrupt.

34-6   for the rhyme, compare *The Answer to 'Paulus'* 113-14.

38 Stentor   Greek herald in the Trojan war, whose voice was as loud as that of fifty men: 'Stentor the strong, endued with brazen lungs' (Pope tr., *Iliad* V, 978).

DICK, A MAGGOT

Details as for preceding item.

6 Dick Drawcansir   in Buckingham's burlesque tragedy *The Rehearsal* (1671), Drawcansir is a bullying, destructive character; in the final act he 'comes in and kills 'em all on both sides'. The name was applied to rowdy and contentious persons; Fielding styled himself 'Sir Alexander Drawcansir' when conducting the *Covent Garden Journal* (1752).

9 meal   flour used to bleach the complexion.

10 gypsy   swarthy.

11 wainscot   the colour of old oak or teak.

13 Tartar   savage, gypsy-like.

CLAD ALL IN BROWN

Publication details as for previous items. The poem is a close parody of Cowley's 'Clad All in White' from *The Mistress* (1647). From his youth Swift nurtured a high admiration for Cowley: see *Ode to the King*, headnote. An edition of the poet's works was in Swift's collection at the time of his death (*Library*, no. 387). The 'host' and parasite verses are compared by Herbert Davis, *Jonathan Swift: Essays on His Satire* (1964), p. 191; *Johnson*, pp. 97-8; and *Lee*, pp. 63-4.

Title *Dick* is Richard Tighe.
7 dun dingy brown.
18 snuff candle-end.
19 the punishment for a bawd or procuress was to carry her through the streets in a cart, to be pelted by the spectators.
21 exalted upon a cart; a standard Augustan play on the word, often used of criminals on the gibbet.

DICK'S VARIETY

Details for preceding items. The last few lines may indicate that this is one of the retorts provoked immediately by Tighe's actions in 1725, when he gave the Lord Lieutenant an account of Sheridan's alleged misdoings: see *Corr* III, 101. But there is no firm evidence and the poem is therefore included with the others supposedly written in 1728.

3 Carr perhaps Charles Carr: see Biog. Dict.
11 nice] *Hawkesworth* (*1755*); vice *Misc* (*1745*).
22 Jesuits see *Ireland* 41.
23 with the Swedes at Bender another reference to Charles XII, who took refuge with a handful of followers at the town (modern Bendery) in Moldavia; he had been defeated at Poltava by the Russians, following his invasion of the Ukraine.
27 Speaker of the Irish House of Commons; from 1715 to 1729 this was William Conolly, cordially hated by Swift: see *The Answer to 'Paulus'* 146, and Biog. Dict.
29 Lady Eustace a friend of Swift, married to Sir Maurice Eustace and mother-in-law of Thomas Tickell: d. 1737.
30 Babby Tighe's wife: see *Mad Mullinix and Timothy*, headnote.
33 antechamber at the castle, where clients and followers would go to seek an audience with Carteret.

MY LADY'S LAMENTATION AND COMPLAINT AGAINST THE DEAN

One of the earliest, perhaps the very first, of the so-called Market Hill group of poems. The poem is headed in the edition of Deane Swift (1765), where it originally appeared, 'July 28, 1728'. It was incorporated into *F* the same year. Text based on Deane Swift.

Swift had known Lady Acheson's father, Philip Savage, who was Chancellor of the Exchequer for Ireland from 1695 to his death in 1717 (see *JTS* I, 119). However, his close intimacy with Sir Arthur Acheson and his wife was relatively short-lived. He paid three prolonged visits to their home at Market Hill (today

Markethill), five miles from Armagh on the road to Newry; these visits were: from June or July 1728 to the following February (see *Corr* III, 312); from early June 1729 to October of that year; and from late June 1730 to about the end of September. More than a dozen poems may be assigned to these three visits as the Market Hill group, proper; other works, such as *The Journal of a Modern Lady*, were composed whilst Swift was living with the Achesons, but have no direct link with Market Hill. See also Biog. Dict., 'Acheson'.

The work is typical of Swift in its use of mock-insult, its advice to a lady, and its concern with the fact of ageing. This group of poems is discussed by *Johnson*, pp. 50–54, and by *Jaffe*, pp. 130–36.

2 Nancy Lady Acheson's Christian name was Anne.

7 wipe reproof, jibe.

8 Skinny and Snipe 'the Dean used to call her by those names' (note in Deane Swift). Compare *Lady Acheson Weary of the Dean* 42; *The Grand Question Debated* 176.

10 Dean using the common Irish pronunciation 'dane'; this became a regular practice in Swift's later verse, but this seems to be the earliest occurrence.

14 rebus see *The Answer to Vanessa's Rebus* 6.

16 sponge compare *A Pastoral Dialogue between Richmond Lodge and Marble Hill* 52.

35 I sink in the spleen I am reduced to total depression.

51 daggled bespattered: see *A Description of a City Shower* 33.

58 In stomach or limb in appetite or general physical condition.

77 prolix long (now obsolete in this sense).

80 crows crow-bars.

107–8 enough... stuff a very common rhyme in Swift: see, for instance, *The Journal of a Modern Lady* 85–6.

117 fleer sneer; compare *To a Lady* 78.

134 ∧ 135] To make you learn faster, / I'll be your schoolmaster / And leave you to choose / The books you peruse. *Scott (1824), from 'the Dean's manuscript'; not in Deane Swift, F.* No trace of such a manuscript is known; one might even suspect that Scott was slily foisting in his own verses.

148 Essays 'In 18th c. the accent was sometimes on the 2nd syllable' (*OED*, 'essay', as substantive).

150 Pantheon a popular compendium of myth and fable, translated from a French Jesuit by Andrew Tooke in 1698; Keats, amongst others, was closely familiar with this work. Tooke was the brother of Swift's bookseller, Benjamin Tooke.

162 Teagues local peasants and villagers.

164 mundungus strong-smelling tobacco. Compare Pope, *The Dunciad* (1743) I, 234, 'Where vile mundungus trucks for viler rhymes.'

165 Hail fellow, well met proverbial: *Tilley* H15.

174 zigzags winding paths which negotiated steep gradients more evenly.

176 cradles probably trellis-work.

179 gewgaws flimsy bits of garden ornament.

203 Dr Jenney Henry Jenney: see Biog. Dict.

205 Walmsley Dr John Walmsley; *Whaley* Nathaniel Whaley. For both men see Biog. Dict. Whaley was at the centre of a row over the rectory of Armagh with the Dean, Richard Daniel: see *Corr* III, 300.

210   black gowns clergymen.

213   under the rose   sub rosa, secretly (*Tilley* R185).

224   Daniel Richard Daniel, Dean of Armagh: see note to l. 205 and Biog. Dict. Swift called him 'the greatest puppy and vilest poet alive' (*Corr* III, 300).

ON CUTTING DOWN THE OLD THORN AT MARKET HILL

First published by James Roberts (London, 1732) together with *The Lady's Dressing Room* (*T* 720; *Foxon* S869). The poem went into *Misc* (1732) and then into *WF*, which is the basis for the text here. A contemporary transcript among the Portland papers carries the description 'writ September 14 1728'. This is assuredly more reliable than *WF*'s 'written in the year 1727'. By 18 September 1728 Swift had demonstrably written various 'libels' against Lady Acheson, of which this may well be one (*Corr* III, 298). See also *An Answer to the Ballyspellin Ballad* 87.

As *Jaffe* (p. 133) remarks, 'the poem is a pastiche of epic, romance, pastoral and revenge tragedy'. She adds that the effect achieved by Swift 'is analogous to the mock-heroic in that she satirizes a modern event while sparing, essentially, the artistic forms he uses'. Her conclusion is that 'out of a medley of serious poetic traditions, Swift has created a comic gem' (p. 134). One might add that Ovidian mythopoeic fable underlies much of the poem; there are distinct recollections of the domesticized Ovid whom Swift had enlisted for the composition of *Baucis and Philemon*. (Compare ll. 1–2 with the opening line of *Baucis*.) As often in Swift, the mock-heroic suggestions are underpinned by sly allusions to the masterpiece in that kind, *The Rape of the Lock*.

5–8 evoking pastoral tradition (see *Jaffe*, p. 133).

8   satyrs wild goat-like creatures who inhabited the forests and acted in riotous and lascivious ways. The mock-pastoral suggestion is 'randy young men of the neighbourhood'.

9–12 evoking epic and romance; faintly archaic diction aids the hint of a Spenserian world.

9   Sir Archibald 'Secretary of State for Scotland' (note in *WF*); Acheson (d. 1634) was given a large grant of lands in Armagh and Cavan; created a baronet in 1628. Armagh contains fertile fruit-growing areas which have earned it the title of 'the garden of Ulster'.

16 'Drummond of Hawthornden, and Sir William Alexander, Earl of Stirling, both famous for their poetry, who were friends to Sir Archibald' (note in *WF*). William Drummond (1585–1649) was an acquaintance of Ben Jonson and Drayton; Alexander (?1567–1640) was also Secretary of State for Scotland and held many court positions under James I.

17   ween believe, think (archaic). One of a number of conscious archaisms: see headnote.

time personified, is the god Cronos, identified by the Romans with Saturn; compare *Measure for Measure* V, i, 12, 'A forted residence gainst the tooth of time.'

25–8   Jaffe, p. 134, compares this stanza with *Paradise Lost* IX, 782–4: 'Earth felt the wound, and Nature from her seat / Sighing through all her works gave signs of woe, / That all was lost.' There is a sustained current of allusion to the Fall (see also l. 57).

27 Mother Tellus the earth.

29–56 Jaffe, p. 134, suggests as possible sources for the omens and prophecies two literary genres, that is, epic poetry and revenge tragedy. There are other possible models, e.g. owls figure regularly in the Augustan nightpiece, as practised by the Countess of Winchilsea amongst others. It was supposed to be unlucky to cut down a hawthorn tree, perhaps because of an association with the crown of thorns (see *A Serious Poem upon William Wood* 29).

32 Sad omens of the dire event an epic formula, but certainly overlaid here with memories of *The Rape of the Lock* (e.g. I, 109; II, 102; II, 141; IV, 161–6).

33 stock trunk. Magpies in folklore are uncanny birds, who often foretell death.

45 The nymph a hamadryad, fabled to die with the tree she inhabited. Syrinx, the nymph who was transformed into a reed (*Metamorphoses* I, 689 ff.), was a hamadryad.

49 Spina a fanciful name for the thorn (from its Latin version).

53–6 a folktale motif, which has remote affinities with romantic works such as Wordsworth's *The Thorn* (1798) and Keats's *Isabella* (1818).

65 Lord Arthur 'Sir Arthur Acheson' (note in *WF*).

67 assassin stressed on first syllable.

in crape worn by a parson like Swift.

70 the sense is, 'Nor did you either chide...'

73 fell cruel.

77 fanatics that is, dissenters; the Scottish Presbyterian settlers in Ulster, where they were already the dominant religious group.

Teagues local Irish of Catholic stock.

82 clown rustic. Another item of pastoral language.

86 tree the gallows.

87 a hanging offence in the eighteenth century. In any case, under the Penal Laws the native Catholic population were not permitted to own a horse worth more than £5.

88 caitiff wretch, rascal (another Spenserian archaism). The word *bloody* refers primarily to the 'murder' of the thorn; it was however in regular use as an intensifier, and was not regarded as impolite (Swift uses it elsewhere, for example *JTS* I, 263: 'It was bloody hot walking today').

AN ANSWER TO THE BALLYSPELLIN BALLAD

This is a reply to a ballad by Sheridan, which is printed in *P* II, 438–40. Swift described his response in a letter to Rev. John Worrall on 28 September 1728: 'We have a design upon Sheridan. He sent us in print a ballad upon Ballyspellin, which he has employed all the rhymes he could find to that word; but we have found fifteen more, and employed them in abusing his ballad, and Ballyspellin too. I here send you a copy, and desire you will get it printed privately, and published' (*Corr* III, 302). Swift's holograph version, accompanying the letter to Worrall, is preserved at the British Library (Add. MS 4805). The same institution has acquired a copy of the original edition of Swift's poem (published by Faulkner in 1728); this was not known to Williams or to Teerink. It is *Foxon* S797. A transcript, perhaps in Worrall's hand, is at *HEH* (14340): see *Mayhew*, pp. 10–11, 160. No edition earlier than 1731 has been found for Sheridan's poem. But this and the answer were included in *F* (1762). Text from Swift's MS collated with the 1728 edition.

Swift had been staying for several weeks with the Achesons at Market Hill. Sheridan may also have been there; at all events, he went to Co. Kilkenny in order to visit 'the Irish spa' of Ballyspellin, popular for its chalybeate drinking waters. According to Swift's *History of the Second Solomon*, he was accompanied by 'a new favourite lady'. The ballad he produced on the spa 'was in the manner of Mr Gay's on *Molly Mog*, pretending to contain all the rhymes of Ballyspellin'. Swift and a friend (?Sir Arthur Acheson) made another 'with all new rhymes not made use of' by Sheridan. The latter was displeased, being 'prevailed upon, by the lady he went with, to resent this as an affront on her and himself; which he did accordingly, against all the rules of reason, taste, good nature, judgement, gratitude, or common manners' (*PW* V, 225).

Sheridan and Swift employ an identical verse-form; *F* prints the first and second lines together in each stanza, as a single verse, and so with the fourth and fifth. In fact Gay's *Molly Mog*, first published in August 1726, uses fewer rhymes, although it set the fashion for 'crambo' poems or *bouts rimés*. The form is actually a kind of *rime couée*, as used in Chaucer's *Sir Thopas*.

3 refelling] *Swift MS*; rebelling *printed edns.* Swift's reading is the best one; to 'refel' was to refute or disprove.

7 bounce swagger, talk loudly and boastfully.

9 medicine second syllable elided.

repelling a pun: 'repellent' medicines were those which were thought to repel morbid humours.

13 drabs the girls Sheridan had celebrated in his ballad.

pocky infected; compare *The Lady's Dressing Room* 132. Swift's expression suggests a reason for the presence of these women at a health resort.

19 Llewellyn mentioned in l. 2 of Sheridan's ballad. Presumably Llywelyn ab Gruffydd (d. 1282), but, as Swift says, the name is just there for the rhyme.

21 Doctor Pelling perhaps Edward Pelling, D.D. (d. 1718), Anglican divine; but the context makes such identifications conjectural.

27 colonelling acting the colonel: compare *Hudibras* I, i, 14. The sense here appears to be 'playing the rake and fine gentleman'.

29 teagues local Irish of dubious social rank: 'peasants'.

33 sowens 'A food much used in Scotland, the North of Ireland and other parts: it is made of oatmeal, and sometimes of the shellings of oats, and known by the names of sowens or flummery' (note in *F*, 1762).

shelling husk.

34 Market Hill the Achesons' home, where the poem was written.

37 Would I was whipped 'I'll be hanged if . . .'

38 Sheelah see *To Quilca* 7.

43 mawkins sluts, drabs.

45 Holland fine Holland lace.

an ell about a yard in length.

53 grisettes common girls: compare *Stella at Woodpark* 59.

57 o'er against opposite. The Bell is an inn, real or imagined, in the small town of Markethill.

63 Enniskillen in Co. Fermanagh, forty miles west.

71 blowze blowzy wench, slattern. One of several near-synonyms Swift found in this poem.

75 A stiver or a skilling small coins of little worth.

76 touse tumble.

78 leaks urinates: compare *Strephon and Chloe* 164. The sense is 'any peeing girl from Ballyspellin'.

81 cudgelling stress thrown on to second syllable.

87 this seems to link the poem with *On Cutting Down the Old Thorn at Market Hill*, written in September 1728.

THE ANSWER TO 'PAULUS'

First published by Dr William King in *The Dreamer* (1754). This is the Oxford Jacobite King (1685–1763), not to be confused with his namesake, the hackwriter and gazetteer, or with Dr William King, the Archbishop of Dublin. The poem was collected by *F* in 1762. A reference to a manuscript version signed by Swift, made in the *Dublin Literary Gazette* (1830), has not been substantiated by any later discovery: see *P* II, 431. The text here is based on King's version: *F* seems to have followed a different manuscript but the differences are not important.

Lindsay's verses are headed 'Dublin, September 7th, 1728'. It seems natural to suppose that the answer was composed not long afterwards, although definite evidence is lacking. For Robert Lindsay, a legal adviser to the Dean and Chapter of St Patrick's, see Biog. Dict. For suggestions that he supplied legal touches for the *Drapier's Letters*, see *Drapier*, pp. lii–liii, 248–9, 369. Swift described him to the second Earl of Oxford as 'an intimate friend of mine upon the score of virtue, learning and superior knowledge in his own profession' (*Corr* IV, 283). Swift was employing him in an official capacity at the end of 1728 (*Corr* III, 306).

'Paulus' is clearly a generalized character study rather than a portrait of an individual. For Swift's attitudes to the legal profession, see *Gulliver's Travels*, especially IV, 5 (*PW* XI, 248–51). Citations of *Gulliver* in the notes are from this passage.

11–22 standard attributes of Apollo; god of the sun, of the arts, of healing, of prophecy, of generation.

25–6 Apollo (or Phoebus) was the son of a daughter of two of the Titans, therefore Terra was his great-grandmother, more strictly.

28 Vulcan as god of fire and as responsible for the forging of metals in his smithy, on Mount Etna. A characteristic application of myth by Swift, for whom gold was a recurrent metaphor (see for example *The Fable of Midas, Prometheus*).

31 Astraea goddess of justice, conventionally depicted with a pair of scales: compare Johnson, *London* (1738) 250–51.

42 quanta patimur 'how many things we have to endure!' 'So much do we suffer!'

47 topics arguments.
   abomine rare and archaic, with deliberate comic effect.

60 overwitted outwitted.

61 the gospel alluding to Luke xi, 46, in which Christ addresses the Pharisees:

'Woe unto you also, ye lawyers! for ye lade men with burdens grievous to be borne . . .'

65   *saving their own bacon*   the first occurrence of the phrase in *OED* is dated 1692. Tilley B24.

67   *racked*   strained, stretched. The reasoning in this passage is itself a parody of legal argumentation.

73   *crop-sick*   suffering from a stomach ailment, as a result of eating and drinking too much.

unclubbed-for   for which expenses were not shared (so that the full cost fell on the lawyer).

75   *bag*   bag-wig, worn in court.

78–9   all three languages formed part of lawyers' terminology; maxims and rules were often cited in a kind of Anglo-French.

80   *moidores*   see *An Elegy on Demar* 32.

81–4   much legal dispute was conducted through lengthy written pleadings, set out on parchment; the sentences often run into hundreds of words as clause is piled on clause. Compare *Gulliver's Travels*: 'this society hath a peculiar cant and jargon of their own, that no other mortal can understand . . . whereby they have wholly confounded the very essence of truth and falsehood, of right and wrong; so that it will take thirty years to decide whether the field, left to me by my ancestors for six generations, belong to me, or to a stranger three hundred miles off.'

93   *term*   the legal term within which courts sat.

97   *rapparees*   robbers, bandits; a recent extension of the word applied to Irish irregular troops during the Williamite wars.

98   *Newry*   Co. Down, near the Mourne Mountains; the town itself was an important strategic centre, guarding the route from the South into Ulster (as it has remained during the recent troubles).

105   *jump*   are at one, correspond.

106   *in the lump*   taken together.

114   *learned*   learnéd, but not so pronounced.

115   *lucus . . . a non lucendo*   a proverbial phrase to explain misnomers; 'as things are called after something else exhibiting opposite qualities'.

118   *rogues in grain*   dyed-in-the-wool rogues: see *Tilley* K128.

130   *save your stake*   prevent the loss of your stake-money; that is, 'You hardly manage to preserve the degree of honesty you have risked by associating with this company.'

135–8   when someone 'scrambled' for a small coin in the gutter, the surrounding crowd would take the chance to rob him as they buffeted him about.

140   *a place*   an official appointment; lawyers were notoriously eager to get such positions.

143–4   'in all points out of their own trade, they [are] usually the most ignorant and stupid generation among us, the most despicable in common conversation, avowed enemies to all knowledge and learning' (*Gulliver's Travels*).

146   *Marshall*   Robert Marshall, a barrister who had been involved in Vanessa's affairs; later a judge; d. 1774.

Conolly   William Conolly, Speaker of the Irish House of Commons. 'There was a fellow in Ireland, who from a shoe-boy grew to be several times one of the chief governors [Lord Justices], wholly illiterate, and with hardly common sense' (Swift to Gay, 28 August 1731: *Corr* III, 493). See also *Drapier*, pp. 8, 197, 314; and Biog. Dict.

    Dick Tighe see Biog. Dict. and headnote to *Mad Mullinix and Timothy*.

LADY ACHESON WEARY OF THE DEAN

First published as a broadside, [Dublin] 1730; this is *T* 700, Foxon S868. It was reprinted in periodicals and then, together with *An Elegy on Dicky and Dolly*, in an octavo issued by James Hoey (1732): *T* 966, Foxon S831. The poem was first printed among Swift's works in 1752 and entered *F* in 1762. The text here is based on the broadside with notes from *F*.

    The date of composition must be 1728, 1729, or 1730; but in view of the long duration of Swift's visits to Market Hill in the two former years (see *My Lady's Lamentation*, headnote), these years seem likelier than 1730. In February 1729 Swift wrote that he had been spending his first visit to the Achesons 'writing family verses of mirth by way of libels on my Lady' (*Corr* III, 311).

Title]*broadside*; Dean Swift at Sir Arthur Acheson's in the North of Ireland *F and other early edns.*
2 Our invitation see *Corr* III, 296, for the Achesons' pressing Swift to stay in 1728.
27 Aghnacloy 'the seat of Acheson Moore, Esq.' (note in *F*). Doubtless a relative. One of this name matriculated at Trinity College a few years after Sir Arthur, and was a near contemporary (Acheson, b. 1688; Moore, b. 1690 or 1691).
33−5 for the rhyme, see note to *My Lady's Lamentation* 107−8.
38 wainscot the colour of old oak: see *Dick, a Maggot* 11.
39 eyes of wall either, squinting so as to show the whites of the eye excessively; or glaring, glowering.
42 compare *My Lady's Lamentation* 8. A *snip* was a 'slight or diminutive person' (*OED*). 'The Dean used to call Lady Acheson by these names' (note in *F*). Compare 'snap short makes you look so lean' (*PW* IV, 167): Tilley S586.

ON A VERY OLD GLASS

Published in *F* (1746), from which the text is taken. It is not possible to narrow down composition beyond 1728−30, when the Market Hill group of poems was written.

TO JANUS

First published in *WF*, where it is stated to have been 'written in the year 1729'. The only occasion when Swift is known to have spent the New Year at Market Hill was during his first visit (1728−9), and so the date may be regarded as plausible. The poem subsequently entered the London series of *Misc* but the text is based on its original appearance in *WF*.

1 Janus the Roman god who kept doors and gates, and who presided over the birth of the New Year. Represented with two faces, one in front and one behind. See *A New Year's Gift for Bec* 1. Tilley J37.

4   our dame   Lady Acheson.

5   perhaps alluding to the lady's scrawny appearance (see *Lady Acheson Weary of the Dean* 42).

14   This poor isle   Ireland.

21–2   prim old maids may forever be harking back to the past (which only twists their already wrinkled necks until they look even more the worse for wear).

27   a New Year's lace   an embroidered bonnet as a present for the New Year.

29   quadrille   see *The Journal of a Modern Lady* 41.

THE JOURNAL OF A MODERN LADY

Written at Market Hill, from which house Swift wrote to John Worrall on 13 January 1729 enclosing the poem (*Corr* III, 308). He added that there was a letter 'to be prefixed before the verses, which letter is grounded on a report', whose accuracy Swift did not know. No trace of this letter can be found. It had been intended to use the poem in *The Intelligencer*, should that project have been revived; but it appeared instead as an octavo published by Mrs Harding (*T* 669; *Foxon* S863). There was another Dublin edition in 1729 (*T* 669A, *Foxon* S864); two London printings that year (*T* 671, *Foxon* S865; *T* 670, *Foxon* S866); and another in *Fog's Weekly Journal* on 15 February. It entered Curll collections, as well as *Misc* in 1732. It was thus already a very well known item when it went into *WF*, from which I have taken the text.

Horrell (*PJH* I, 398) takes Lady Acheson to be the subject, as well as the prompter, of the poem. It is true that Swift once wrote to Ford, 'She is an absolute Dublin rake, sits up late, loses her money, and goes to bed sick, and resolves like you never to mend' (*Corr* IV, 92). But this was much later, in December 1732, when both Swift and she were in Dublin, and when the Achesons were planning a visit to London; it bears no relation to the reports from the country which Swift sent his friends when staying at Market Hill. In my view the poem is cautionary rather than in any direct sense (even jokingly) descriptive of Lady Acheson.

Surprisingly, the work has not been very extensively discussed. In the early nineteenth century John Aikin singled out the chain of personification (ll. 120–35) as particularly animated (*CH*, pp. 267–8). Modern readings are mostly no more than brief descriptions. For the relation to *The Furniture of a Woman's Mind*, see headnote to that poem.

Title   ]*London edns (1729) and all subsequently*; The Journal of a Dublin Lady *Dublin edns (1729).*

2   you   Lady Acheson.

10   to a hair   down to the last detail (*Tilley* H26): used thus in *Polite Conversation* (*PW* IV, 158).

19   Sooner shall   a standard way of introducing far-fetched comparisons: see *Rape of the Lock* IV, 117–20. The point of the lacuna is, 'anyone can supply their own examples to order.'

27   bit   got the better of.

36   Rakewell   a name drawn from the world of Restoration comedy: used for the hero of Hogarth's *Rake's Progress* (1735). The line also yields the sense, 'play the rake well'.

39   Some authors say   a reference to *Rape of the Lock* I, 15–20.

41 quadrille then at the height of its popularity; it was ousted a little from fashion in the later eighteenth century. For its novelty appeal at the time of Swift's visit to England in 1726, see *Suffolk Letters*, ed. J.W. Croker (1824), I, 257. A four-handed game using forty of the ordinary card pack, with eights, nines, and tens discarded.

42 gapes yawns.

47 citron-water brandy distilled with the rind of citrons: compare *Rape of the Lock* IV, 69.

48 Betty generic name for a maid.

52 matadors . . . codille terms originally used in ombre; 'matador' was a kind of trump, and 'codille' refers to a game lost by a player challenging to win it. See *Rape of the Lock* III, 33, 48, 92; and *PTE* II, 383-92.

54 Tom a footman (one of the associations of the name Tom Jones).

65 dun demand payment.

66 pistoles various sorts of foreign gold coins were known by this name; perhaps a *louis d'or* is meant.

69 I may have revenge compare Miss Notable, after the game of quadrille in *Polite Conversation*: 'I'll give you revenge whenever you please' (*PW* IV, 201).

74 Spadillo the ace of spades, the highest trump of all. See *Rape of the Lock* III, 49.

83 Mechlin fine lace from Mechlin in Belgium (now Mechelin or Malines).

119 harridans in his copy of *F* (1737) Swift made the marginal note 'a cant word'. He used it for any lady past her prime: see *Corr* III, 79, 103.

120-35 parody of a 'train' of allegorical figures in the grand style of poetry.

132-3 compare *Rape of the Lock* IV, 31-4.

147 a cliché of the best *Polite Conversation* brand: see *PW* IV, 146.

163 Admires wonders.

168 combs of lead to blacken red hair, which was considered unattractive and ungenteel. Compare *The Progress of Beauty* 110.

182 a barring-out schoolboy rebellion in which the master is shut out by his pupils.

183 rout noise, tumult.

184-5 jokingly refers to the cosmology of Epicurus, as set out by Lucretius; see also Ovid, *Metamorphoses* I, 5-20.

187 election ale rough beer given out to bribe electors.

188-95 directly recalling *Rape of the Lock* (1714) III, 15-18: 'A third interprets motions, looks, and eyes; / At every word a reputation dies. / Snuff, or the fan, supply each pause of chat, / With singing, laughing, ogling, and all that.'

196 club gathering (informal).

199 vapours and hysteric fits compare *Rape of the Lock* IV, 59-60.

203 vole see *Verses on the Death of Dr Swift* 230.

224 The superstitious] *WF*; Swift's correction of *Misc* (1732); All the superfluous *early edns*.

240 odious the sort of word used by spoilt ladies: compare Pope, *Epistle to Cobham* 242.

284 chairmen who carried sedan chairs through the streets.

ON PADDY'S CHARACTER OF 'THE INTELLIGENCER'

The first appearance of the poem was as an anonymous broadside, published in Dublin late in 1728 or 1729. This is *T* 683, *Foxon* S887. The poem was first collected in the 1750s, since which time it has been generally accepted as Swift's reply to Delany (see *P* II, 457). However, as Foxon notes: 'There seems to be no strong authority for Swift's authorship, plausible though it is. As noted in [*P*], this appears to be an answer to Delany's attacks on *The Intelligencer*: but it specifically replies to "Pady Drogheda", *The True Character of the Intelligencer*, 1728, which is in fact by William Tisdall' (*Foxon*, I, 771). I am not at all certain it is by Swift; it could easily be Sheridan's. For *The Intelligencer*, see headnote to *Mad Mullinix and Timothy*.

Text from the broadside, except that the excessive use of italics (every other word in some lines) is ignored.

12   refers to the legend (reported by Pliny amongst others) that lightning did not strike the laurel.
14   *Tom*   Sheridan.
17   *cockade*   knot of ribbons; but the word could mean 'any bonnet, or cap, worn proudly or pertly on the one side' (*OED*).
23   *Smedley*   Swift's old adversary, Jonathan Smedley: see Biog. Dict.
24   *devoted*   accursed.
29   *the tale*   the fable.
32   *the Thunderer*   Jove's nickname.

DEAN SMEDLEY GONE TO SEEK HIS FORTUNE

First published in an additional, twentieth, number of *The Intelligencer* in 1729, dated at the end '7 May'. The poem was first collected by Nichols in 1779. Text from *The Intelligencer*.

Swift's long-time adversary Jonathan Smedley suddenly resigned his post as Dean of Clogher, together with his other preferments, and sailed to India. On 13 February 1729 a London newspaper, the *Daily Post*, carried a story to the effect that a mezzotint portrait of Smedley was being engraved 'with this remarkable inscription, said to be written by the Dean' (that is, Smedley himself). The story was repeated in the *Political State* later that month.

The Latin text referred to reads as follows:

Reverendus Decanus, Jonathan Smedley
Theologia instructus; in Poesi exercitatus;
Politioribus excultus Literis: Parce Pius;
Impius minime: Veritatis Indagator; Libertatis
Assertor: Subsannatus multis; Fastiditus Quibusdam;
Exoptatus plurimis; Omnibus Amicus; Author hujus
Sententiae,
    PATRES SUNT VETULAE.
Domata Invidia; Superato Odio; per Laudem et
Vituperium; per Famam atq; Infamiam: Utramque
Fortunam, Variosq; expertus Casus; Mente Sana;
Sano Corpore; Volens, Laetusq; Lustris plus
quam XI numeratis; ad Rem Familiarem Restaurandam,
augendamq; et ad Evangelium, Indos inter Orientales,
praedicandum; Grevae, Idibus Februarii, Navem ascendens,
Arcemq; Sancti petens Georgii, Vernale per Aequinoxium;

Anno Aerae Christianae, Millesimo Septingentesimo Vicesimo
Octavo TRANSFRETAVIT. –
　　　　Fata vocant – Revocentq; precamur.

Epigraph 'Through various hazards and events' (tr. Dryden).
3 equally that is, equally little.
18 sentence 'patres sunt vetulae' (see headnote); *patres* normally means 'the forefathers'.
21 phiz one of the abbreviated forms Swift mocked in *Polite Conversation* (*PW* IV, 161), and also in the *Tatler*, 28 September 1710 (*PW* II, 173-7), but a word he used often himself: compare *Dick, a Maggot* 13.
24 thick and thin see *The Lady's Dressing Room* 80.
26 sped succeeded.
28 cog the dice cheat by controlling the dice in some illicit way.
30 à quatre trois or 'cater-trey', a claim that the game is a fraud (derived from the names for a four and a three in dice); see *OED*, 'cater'.
33–4 the implication is that Smedley is making himself out to be considerably younger ('forty-four') than he in fact is; however, to be fair, the Latin says 'more than eleven *lustra*', in one reckoning fifty-five (as a *lustrum* normally meant 'a five-year period') but Swift takes the meaning used in the Julian calendar, that is, a four-year period.
35–6 cheat would be pronounced to make a rhyme with *estate*.
38 tub pulpit: see *Tale*, pp. 55–60.
46 ides the thirteenth.
47 the Old Style date, 1728/9, that is, 1729 by modern usage (see note on dates, p. 598).
48 Fort St George built in 1641; later known as Madras.
50 there seems to be no evidence of how Smedley fared in India.

VERSES OCCASIONED BY THE SUDDEN DRYING UP OF ST PATRICK'S
WELL NEAR TRINITY COLLEGE, DUBLIN

First published in *F* (1762), where the event is placed in 1726. In fact it was in 1729 that the well suddenly dried up; two years later it was cleaned out and repaired (*Gilbert*, III, 244-7). The spring was 'popularly supposed to have been miraculously produced by St Patrick. It was credited with healing properties' (*P* III, 789).

The poem is unique in respect of the long antiquarian notes supplied in *F*. Horrell observes, 'It is not characteristic of Swift to show his erudition' (*PJH* II, 782). A certain flavour of Martinus Scriblerus which results may have been the reason for the poem's exclusion from *WF*. It should be noted that the poem itself is in Swift's more elaborate manner, with turns and Latinisms generally lacking in his mature style. Note, for example, the studied use of chiasmic effects in ll. 64, 72. The personifications are vigorous enough to merit the retention of capital letters. Text based on *F* (1762).

Although this is one of the most explicit statements of Swift's view of Irish politics, it is seldom discussed even by critics concerned with this issue. See *Ferguson*, p. 185, for a poem published in Dublin (1726) which describes Swift as St Patrick's successor.

1 'Festus Avienus flourished in 370. See his poem *De oris Maritimis*, where he uses this expression concerning Ireland, *Insula sacra et sic Insulam dixere Prisci; eamque late Gens Hibernorum colit*' (note in *F*).

4 'Italy was not properly the native place of St Patrick, but the place of his education, and whence he received his mission; and because he had his new birth there, hence, by poetical licence, and by scripture-figure, our author calls that country his native Italy' (note in *F*). A 'scripture figure' was to be read allegorically or typologically.

6 'Julius Solinus, who lived about the time of Tacitus, in the year 80, Chapter 21, speaking of the Irish as a warlike nation, says, that the wives in Ireland, when delivered of a son, give the child its first food off the point of their husband's sword...Again, *Praecipua viris Gloria est in Armorum tutela*. Polydore Virgil says, they were distinguished for their skill in music. *Hiberni sunt Musice peritissimi*. So Giraldus Cambrensis, who was preceptor to King John, in his *Topographia Hiberniae*, Chapter 11...' (note in *F*).

7 'Orpheus, or the ancient author of the Greek poem on the Argonautic expedition, whoever he be, says, that Jason, who manned the ship Argos at Thessaly, sailed to Ireland. And Adrianus Junius says the same thing in these lines

Illa ego sum Graiis, olim glacialis Ierne

Dicta, et Jasoniae Puppis bene cognita Nautis' (note in *F*).

9 'Tacitus, in the life of Julius Agricola, says, that the harbours of Ireland, on account of their commerce, were better known to the trading part of the world, than those of Britain...' (note in *F*).

11 'Fordon, in his *Scoti-Chronicon*, Hector Boethius, Buchanan, and all the Scotch historians agree, that Fergus, son of Ferquard King of Ireland, was first King of Scotland, which country he subdued. That he began to reign 330 years before the Christian era, and in returning to visit his native country, was shipwrecked on those rocks in the country of Antrim, which from that accident have been since named Carrickfergus. His descendants reigned after him in Scotland; for the crown was settled on him and his lineal successors...The Irish language and habit are still retained in the northern parts of Scotland, where the Highlanders speak the Irish tongue, and use their ancient dress...' (note in *F*).

16 *Confess* give evidence of, attest (poeticism).

23 'In the reign of King Henry II Dermot M'Morough, King of Leinster, being deprived of his kingdom by Roderick O'Connor, King of Connaught, he invited the English over as auxiliaries, and promised Richard Strangbow, Earl of Pembroke, his daughter, and all his dominions as a portion. By this assistance M'Morough recovered his crown, and Strangbow became possessed of all Leinster. After this, more forces being sent into Ireland, the English became powerful here; and when Henry II arrived, the Irish princes submitted to his government, and began to use the English laws' (note in *F*).

27 'St Patrick arrived in Ireland in the year 431, and completed the conversion of the natives, which had been begun by Palladius and others...Ireland soon became the fountain of learning, to which all the Western Christians, as well as English, had recourse, not only for instruction in the principles of religion, but in all sorts of literature; *viz., Legendi & Scholasticae Eruditionis gratia*. For within a century after the death of St Patrick, the Irish seminaries of learning increased to such a degree, that most parts of Europe sent hither their children to be educated, and had from hence both their bishops and doctors. See venerable Bede, an English historian of undoubted credit, *Hist. Eccles.* Lib. 3, cap. 4, 7, 10, 11, 27...' (note in *F*).

32 recalling much biblical imagery, e.g. Ezekiel xxxiv, 2: 'Woe be to the shepherds of Israel that do feed themselves! should not the shepherds feed the flocks?'

41 'There are no snakes, vipers or toads in Ireland; and even frogs were not known here until about the year 1700. The magpies came a short time before, and the Norway rats since' (note in *F*). Possibly recalling, in ll. 40 and 42, Acts xxviii, 4; and Revelation ix, 10.

56 fur and lawn judges and bishops; compare Pope, *The Dunciad* (1743) IV, 28: 'Chicane in furs, and casuistry in lawn.'

69 'The University of Dublin, called Trinity College, was founded by Queen Elizabeth in 1591' (note in *F*).

72 Hippocrene the fountain of the muses on Mount Helicon, source of poetic inspiration.

75 foreign English.

77 for instead of.

78 wait upon the tide tide-waiters were customs officials who boarded incoming vessels; appointment to such posts was one of the ways in which the ministry rewarded its supporters in the country. Suspicion of customs and excise officers was a stock opposition line.

79-80 types of national independence.

80 or any land but this at the back of his mind, Swift must have heard the cadence, 'Hairs less in sight, or any hairs but these!', which concludes the fourth Canto of *The Rape of the Lock*.

94 'Wood's ruinous project against the people of Ireland, was supported by Sir Robert Walpole in 1724' (note in *F*).

95 'The absentees who spend the income of their Irish estates, places and pensions in England' (note in *F*). Compare *Ireland* 53-4.

TO DEAN SWIFT

First published in 1765 by Deane Swift, and included in *F* the same year. When the poem first appeared it was assigned to 1728, but the signs are that it belongs to the summer of 1729 (see *P* III, 876). Despite the putative ascription to Acheson, the work obviously came from Swift's pen.

1 vapour brag, go on in a conceited manner.

2 Drapier I have retained the traditional spelling, although the rhyme shows the normal pronunciation of the word.

8 witlings pretenders to wit; appropriately, a Popian word (see *Essay on Criticism* 40; *Rape of the Lock* V, 59; *Epistle to Arbuthnot* 223).

11 monument of brass recalling Horace, *Odes* III, xxx, 1.

14 brazen knight Sir Robert Walpole: see *A Serious Poem upon William Wood* 86. Many poets had addressed verse to Walpole, including James Thomson, John Dennis, and James Moore Smythe. So had the Scottish poetaster Joseph Mitchell, for whose *Poems* (1729) Swift was listed as a subscriber – a baffling circumstance even if we assume (as seems highly probable) that Pope put his name down.

18 laureate the current incumbent was Laurence Eusden: see Biog. Dict. *P* III, 876 compares a letter from Swift in January 1719: 'Who is that same Eusden, they have made laureate? Is he a poet?' (*Corr* II, 311).

19 A judge perhaps a generalized allusion, but Swift may have in mind appointments to the Irish bench such as Godfrey Boate or John Parnell, or even an English judge such as Robert Eyre (made Lord Chief Justice in 1725), who was on good terms with Walpole and resolutely Whiggish.

21   A bishop   again this could refer to England or Ireland. In the latter category Swift would have in mind Archbishop Boulter, who was sent to Ireland for his value as an ecclesiastical statesman, and reported regularly to Walpole, or lesser figures such as Ralph Lambert (appointed Bishop of Meath in 1727). See *Landa*, pp. 169–88. In England Swift might be thinking of such Walpole nominations as that of Benjamin Hoadly, periodically translated to a richer diocese for his loyalty to the court, or that of Samuel Peploe, appointed Bishop of Chester in 1725 after praying for the safety of George I whilst the Jacobites were in occupation of Preston. 'Under Walpole a close alliance was forged between the prime minister and Bishop Gibson of London to ensure that only well-wishers to the ministry sat on the bishops' benches in the House of Lords' (W.A. Speck, *Stability and Strife* (1977), p. 93).

22   red ribbons   of the Order of the Bath: see *Verses on the Revival of the Order of the Bath*.

23–6   alluding to the intermittent flurries of war with Spain, as in 1718–19 and 1725–9. Swift may also have in mind the partial involvement of England in the conflicts of Hanover, a cause of dissatisfaction to the Tories at home.

32   Drumlack   Acheson's property which Swift was planning to buy, in order to build his country house: see *Drapier's Hill*, headnote.

33   Penshurst   the home of the Sidney family, near Tonbridge, Kent, famous as the embodiment of aristocratic hospitality since Ben Jonson's poem *To Penshurst*, written *c.*1612. For the tradition of country house poems stemming from Jonson, see G.R. Hibberd, *Journal of the Warburg and Courtauld Institutes* XIX (1956), 159–74.

DRAPIER'S HILL

First published in *Fog's Weekly Journal* on 30 August 1729; subsequently reprinted in the Dublin press and in the piratical collection *The Hibernian Patriot*. The poem was included in *WF*, which supplies the basis for the text here.

One of a number of references to Swift's projected house at Drumlack, on land belonging to Sir Arthur Acheson. The scheme was announced to various friends in the summer of 1729 (*Corr* III, 346, 350), but by the end of October Swift was telling Pope that the idea had been abandoned: 'I will fly as soon as build; I have neither years, nor spirits, nor money, nor patience for such amusements. The frolic is gone off, and I am only £100 the poorer' (*Corr* III, 355). Why the planned purchase should have fallen through remains a little mysterious; it has been suspected that the Achesons were beginning to tire of Swift, but there is no real evidence of this.

Drumlack lay to the west of the road to Portadown, just north of Market Hill. Early in the nineteenth century the 'townland' of Drumlack contained ten houses, seven byres, and one stable, and there were in all forty-nine inhabitants (see William Greig, *General Report on the Gosford Estates in County Armagh 1821*, ed. F.M.L. Thompson, D. Tierney (1976)). The report was written as the new Gosford Castle began to arise in place of the old mansion at Market Hill. If Swift was to have the entire townland of Drumlack, his outlay of £100 was probably a down-payment; but he may have been intending to buy only a portion of the manorial land.

Title] *WF*; Drapier's Hall *Dublin Weekly Journal (13 September 1729).*
3–4 compare *Horace, Lib. 2, Sat. 6 1–2.*
9 Sir Arthur 'the gentleman of whom the purchase was made' (note in *WF*).
14–16 'Medals were cast; many signs hung up; and handkerchiefs made with devices in honour of the author, under the name of M.B. Drapier' (note in *WF*).
20 Cooper's Hill the poem by Sir John Denham: see *Apollo's Edict* 46. Compare Chetwode to Swift, 10 September 1729: 'I suppose you mean at Drapier's Hill; take care it comes up to Cooper's' (*Corr* III, 346). The present poem was most likely written about the time of Chetwode's letter, perhaps a week or two earlier.

ROBIN AND HARRY

First published by Deane Swift in 1765, after which the poem went into *F* that year. Swift's own MS survives among *FV*, with the endorsement 'August 4th 1729'. Text based on Swift's holograph. For another supposed manuscript, now lost, see *P* III, 877.

The poem is linked with the Market Hill group by the fact that Henry Leslie lived there. Swift composed the poem in the middle of his second visit to the Achesons.

1 Robin Robert Leslie, elder son of the high Tory controversialist, Charles Leslie. He lived at the family seat, Glaslough House, in Co. Monaghan, close to the Armagh border and about fifteen miles from Market Hill. He married a niece of Swift's friend, Peter Ludlow. For his liking for conversation, see *Corr* IV, 393.
2 Dr William King, in his memoirs, confirms this habit (see *P* III, 878).
5 Harry Henry, the younger son of Charles Leslie. He had 'reached the rank of lieutenant-colonel in the Spanish army, but lost his commission upon a resolution against the employment of Protestants' (*P* III, 877).
7 careful of the main keeping the principal object steadily in view, not being distracted; compare Cowley, *The Country Mouse* 5: 'Frugal, and grave, and careful of the main.'
10 Runs out in exhausts, totally depletes his stock of words.
19 his dame his wife was Spanish.
20 All for love, or the world well lost the title and subtitle of Dryden's famous tragedy on Antony and Cleopatra (1678).
24 make them welcome again, Dr King testifies to this generosity (see *P* III, 878).
modicum often used in the sense of 'a small stock of money or property', without any direct mention of such things (*OED*, 'modicum', 1b).
34 endow provide a dowry (in this case settled on the wife by the husband).
35–6 alluding to Esau and Jacob: Genesis xxv, 30–34.
47 paduasoy a silk fabric (corruption of 'Padua say': Swift's spelling is 'podesway', which reflects the pronunciation then current).

50 addresses Frank the meaning may be that he writes on the cover of a letter 'frank', as persons of honour were permitted to do: his father-in-law was Chief Justice. But I am not sure that this is correct.
53–4 suggesting he was sexually inadequate.

THE GRAND QUESTION DEBATED

A complex item bibliographically. First published in January 1732 as *A Soldier and a Scholar*, under the imprint of James Roberts: three further editions in quick succession (*T* 713; *Foxon* S904–7). Under the title *The Grand Question Debated*, and with a different manuscript supplying the text, the poem appeared in an octavo by Faulkner (Dublin) later in the same year. Faulkner claimed that he was merely reprinting a London edition by 'A. Moore', and *P* III, 865 suggests that 'a lost London edition is...a possibility.' But in fact Faulkner was simply using a subterfuge to avoid copyright difficulties: A. Moore was a booksellers' *nom de guerre*. The poem also appeared in the *Gentleman's Magazine* in February 1732, and in *Misc* that year. It also made its way into *WF*, which is the basis of the text here.

A holograph version by Swift is now in *TR*. It does not seem to have been the basis for either printed version and it has even been suggested (*P* III, 865) that Swift was copying out Faulkner's printed text of 1732. I think it is more likely that both the extant MS and the Dublin edition were taken from another MS now lost. (There is a contemporary transcript in another hand in *HEH*: see *Mayhew*, p. 160.) Swift in different places endorsed his holograph version with the dates 'September 2nd 1729' and 'September 2nd 1728'. Either date is possible, since he was staying at Market Hill on both occasions; but 1729, the date supplied by *WF*, is the more plausible.

Swift's correspondence throws some light on the history of publication, but the whole story does not emerge. On 8 June 1732 Swift wrote to the Rev. Henry Jenney (see l. 131): 'It is true that some weeks ago a manuscript paper of verses was handed about town, and afterwards printed. The subject was my great ingratitude and breach of hospitality in publishing a copy of verses called *Hamilton's Bawn*...I knew how well you were acquainted with the whole history and occasion of writing those verses on the barrack; how well pleased the master and lady of the family were with it; that you had read it more than once; that it was no secret to any neighbour, nor any reserve but that against giving a copy. You know well by what incidents that reserve was broken, by granting a copy to a great person, and from thence how it fell into other hands, and so came, as it is the constant case, to be published, and is now forgot' (*Corr* IV, 26–7). A week later Swift listed among his works 'the Barrack (a stolen copy)' (*Corr* IV, 31). Later in the year he wrote to the London bookseller Motte: 'Some things, as that of the Soldier and the Scholar, the Pastoral, and one or two more were written at a man of quality's house in the North who had the originals, while I had no copy, but they were given to the Lord Lieutenant, and some others, so copies ran, and Faulkner got them, and I had no property; but Faulkner made them his in London' (*Corr* IV, 82–3). In fact, Faulkner may have arranged for the publication in London by Roberts; he could then claim that there was an English edition he was following, and while in law this did not strictly permit an Irish reprint, it was a regular occurrence which seldom or never incurred legal redress.

Whether Carteret obtained the transcript through the good offices of Lady Acheson (as the 'preface' suggests) or whether indeed Swift was not complicit in the whole affair, we have no means of knowing.

In this case, there is evidence of the original printing runs for the London edition, from the Bowyer ledgers: see *Foxon*, I, 773. At least 1250 copies were printed within a few days.

Though popular in its own day, and occasioning at least one hostile pamphlet in reply, the poem has not elicited much comment subsequently. See, however, *Jaffe*, pp. 134–6, for a description of Swift's skill in vocal mimicry.

Title   see headnote.   *Bawn*   'a bawn was a place near the house, enclosed with mud or stone walls, to keep the cattle from being stolen in the night. They are now little used' (note in *WF*). The Irish word is *bábhun*, and the definition in *OED* is 'cattlefold'.

Preface   this appears in the Dublin edition of 1732 and in *WF* as 'the Preface to the [non-existent] London edition'; it is not in Roberts's version or in Swift's MS.   *A certain very great person*   Carteret: see headnote. The explanation is a characteristic bit of trade prevarication, and was probably written by Faulkner himself.

3   Hamilton's Bawn   'a large old house two miles from Sir Arthur Acheson's seat' (note in *WF* and in Swift's own copy of *Misc*). From Irish *Bábhun Hamaltún*; the site is to the north of Market Hill, on the road from Armagh to Tandaragee; a small settlement grew up near by in the eighteenth century.

6   barrack   'the army in Ireland, is lodged in strong buildings over the whole kingdom, called *barracks*' (note in *WF*).

14   scrub   small, puny.

21   poundage and drawbacks   commissions and deductions, which the eighteenth-century Treasury levied on almost all transactions in which it was concerned.

27   Mopus   a mope, or dull person: compare Congreve, *Way of the World* III, i, 8.

28   rums   'a cant word in Ireland for a poor country clergyman' (note in *WF*). For this sense of the word 'rum' *OED* cites only two examples, this and another by Swift.

41   Hannah   'My Lady's waiting woman' (note in *WF*).

48   Darby and Wood   'two of Sir Arthur's managers' (note in *WF*).

53   tease   cajole.

55   stout   firm.

56   give out   give up in despair.

57   purtest   one of several dialect forms in Hannah's speech.

64   An   if (archaic or, here, colloquial and vulgar).

76   Jervas   Charles Jervas: see Biog. Dict. The rhyme would be 'sarvice/Jarvis'. The exchange of empty pleasantries here is worthy of *Polite Conversation*.

84   presumably the meaning is, 'you have been drinking.'

92   holler   the original spelling is 'hollow'; perhaps 'halloo' is meant.

102   dizened   bedizened.

104   beaver   see *An Apology to the Lady Carteret* 27.

115   congee   bow.

116   curchies   for 'curtseys'.

117   Kit   Lady Acheson's footman.

126 complaisant affable, courteous; stress on last syllable.

131 the Doctor 'Doctor Jenny, a clergyman in the neighbourhood' (note in *WF*). For Henry Jenney, see Biog. Dict.

148 cast a sheep's eye a cliché exposed in *Polite Conversation* (*PW* IV, 141). *Tilley* S323.

157 scholard a vulgar form of the word.

158 boo to a goose also in *Polite Conversation* (*PW* IV, 162). *Tilley* B481.

159 that is, Ovids, and Plutarchs, and Homers.

164 cuffs fisticuffs, fighting.
  cock leader.

167–70] *WF; Swift's MS addition in Misc (1732); not in earlier edns.* A clear proof that *WF* embodied Swift's own emendations.

168 mauled beat.

169 took to the road became a highway robber. 'Captain' was a title often adopted by highwaymen, and it was not altogether unknown for army officers to have some acquaintance with quasi-genteel crime.

176 skinny and lean 'nicknames for my Lady' (note in *WF*). See *Lady Acheson Weary of the Dean* 42.

178 down in the hyps cast down, melancholy; short for 'hypochondria', but a much more everyday kind of expression. Used in *Polite Conversation* (*PW* IV, 161).

190 clergy pronounced 'clargy'.

A PASTORAL DIALOGUE

First published in the 'third' volume of *Misc* (1732), and subsequently in *WF*. A transcript among the Portland papers supplies the date 'September 20, 1729', which is more explicit and likely to be more reliable than *WF*'s 1728. The text is based on *WF*; I retain the spelling 'Sheelah' as suitably Irish among various competing forms of the name.

Pastoral attitudes and language are mocked throughout, although the pseudo-archaic diction of the opening is not sustained. Mock-bucolic verse had come into prominence since Gay's *The Shepherd's Week* (1714); for some of the issues involved, see *Gay*, II, 513–15. Like his friend Gay, Swift applies the courtly conventions of pastoral to homely rustic surroundings; but he adds a degree of local colour and (for his own circle) the pleasures of recognition. The vein of cheerful obscenity recalls Prior rather than Gay.

1 hight called (standard archaism to achieve 'medieval' effect).

2 Gosford knight 'Sir Arthur Acheson, whose great-grandfather was Sir Archibald of Gosford in Scotland' (note in *WF*). The Achesons took the title of Gosford when they succeeded to the peerage (in turn, baron, viscount and, in 1806, earl). In the 1820s and 1830s their seat at Market Hill was rebuilt as Gosford Castle.

5 in counterview opposite one another.

9 beginning a series of comparisons which emphasize the homely rather than the idealized side of rural living.

11 spud *OED* suggests a short spade with a chisel-shaped blade; but clearly this refers back to the weeding-knife (l. 3).

18 Sir Arthur's sake 'who is a great lover of Scotland' (note in *WF*). Referring to the thistle as the Scottish emblem, and hinting at the unregenerate Scotticism of many Ulstermen.

26 tobacco plug 'a piece of cake or twist tobacco cut off for chewing' (*OED*, where this instance is the only pre-Victorian usage cited for the phrase).

27 ha'porth what a halfpenny would buy, and hence in general use for 'a small quantity'.

31 Dennis 'Sir Arthur's butler' (note in *WF*).

33 long-bullets or long-bowls, a sort of ninepins.

42 gossip godmother.

50 brogues 'In Skye I first observed the use of brogues, a kind of artless [=crudely made] shoes' (Johnson, *Journey to the Western Isles*).

51 sowens see *An Answer to the Ballyspellin Ballad* 33.

DIRECTIONS FOR A BIRTHDAY SONG

This daringly outspoken poem was not published for more than thirty years after its composition. Deane Swift printed it in 1765, and it was taken into *F* that year. A transcript by Charles Ford survives in *TR*, and there is another in an unknown hand in *FV*. Both manuscripts link the poem with the royal birthday in 1729, that is, on 30 October. The *FV* version has a subtitle, 'in a letter to the songster'. The intended recipient has always been identified as Matthew Pilkington, a young Irish clergyman briefly taken up by Swift, and married to the memoirist Laetitia Pilkington (see Biog. Dict.). Pilkington produced a birthday ode to the King in 1730; the same offering was used to greet the King's birthday in Dublin in 1734.

Without the manuscript evidence it would be tempting to allot the work to 1732 or 1733, which many of the details seem to fit more neatly than the assigned year. It is true that Laurence Eusden, the bibulous poet laureate, had died in 1730; but his task of producing vapid New Year and birthday odes was gratefully accepted by the new laureate, Colley Cibber, who would be just as suitable a target for this satire.

This may be regarded as Swift's first 'mature' political poem, if the date of 1729 is accepted. It exhibits a new directness in its anti-Hanoverian rhetoric, and clearly foreshadows poems such as *On Poetry: a Rhapsody* and *To a Lady*. Horrell (*PJH* II, 782) notes the debt to 'Instructions to a Painter' poems, and remarks, 'Swift writes here in the rambling manner of Restoration satire.' In my view, 'rambling' is an inappropriate word, but the link with older satiric genres is certainly there. On 'advice-to-a-painter' poems, see Elizabeth Story Donno (ed.), *Andrew Marvell: The Complete Poems* (1972), pp. 280-81. The present poem is discussed by *Jaffe*, pp. 51-3.

Text from *TR*; in two places I have clarified Ford's misleading punctuation by adopting the pointing in *F* (1765).

3 in chief request most sought after, by poets short of a commendatory comparison.

11-12 Saturn devoured all his children, except Jupiter, Neptune, and Pluto, as soon as they were born, out of fear that they might supplant him. As Williams says, 'the allusion is to the constant disputes between George I and the Prince of Wales' (*P* II, 460); Saturn was eventually overthrown by his son Jupiter, whereas the Prince's opposition had proved ineffectual in his father's lifetime.

15–20 Jupiter's assignations are described in, for example, Ovid's *Metamorphoses*; the parallel is with George I's wife Sophia Dorothea, imprisoned for her alleged intrigue with Count Königsmark (see Biog. Dict.). This occurred in 1694, when the future George II was already eleven years old; there is no possibility that Königsmark, whatever the truth of his supposed affair, could have been the King's father. Sophia Dorothea had eventually died, still a prisoner, in November 1726, having spent over half her life in confinement.

23–4 see note to ll. 11–12. The implication of this verse paragraph is, 'Anyone could be greater than George I.'

31 falchion sword.

33–4 standard allegorical setpieces, in graphic art or complimentary poetry.

37 Overton a family of print-sellers in London during Swift's lifetime: Henry and Philip, sons of John, were active at this date. *P* II, 461 notes an engraving of George II which bears Overton's name. See also Gay, *Trivia* II, 488 (*Gay*, II, 563); Arbuthnot, *Lewis Baboon Turned Honest* (1712), Preface.

40 mustard bowls used in the theatre to simulate the noise of thunder; compare Pope, *The Dunciad* (1729) II, 218: 'With thunder rumbling from the mustard-bowl.'

41 still continually.

   supplies assists, gives support to (something weak or lacking in a necessary quality).

50 the doors of Janus's temple were thrown open by the Romans in time of war and closed in peacetime. Swift means that no full-scale war had involved Britain since the Peace of Utrecht in 1713, although there had been a continued series of minor altercations.

52 Sweden the Great Northern War had ended in 1721 but there was a continual threat of hostilities breaking out again should Sweden attempt to regain the Baltic provinces she had lost to Russia. It was also supposed in some quarters that the Jacobites would find diplomatic support for their cause in Sweden, as had happened around 1716.

53 London Journal's a newspaper founded in 1719; bought by the government in 1722, and thereafter circulated through the postal system as a pro-ministerial publicity organ.

   Post-Men the *Post-Man* was a loyal Whig journal, unlike its Tory rival, the *Post-Boy*; it ran from 1695 to 1730.

60 Maecenas the type of a patron.

61–2] Ford's transcript also has two alternative lines, not in printed text: But that he squints, and that he struts, / You'd know him by Apollo's cuts. George II was pop-eyed, but if he actually squinted the portraits are too discreet to reveal it. He moved in a stiff manner.

69–70 another couplet strongly reminiscent of the contemporaneous *Dunciad*, e.g. the lines, 'To him we grant our amplest power to sit / Judge of all present, past, and future wit' (II, 344).

75 Isis...Cam Oxford and Cambridge, seen as the nurseries of compliant poets.

76 flam misleading tale (now obsolete).

80 your style the style you should be aiming at.

97 firks drives, directs.

98 Xerxes see Herodotus, *Histories* VII, 34–5 (for Swift's edition, see *Library*, no. 92). When the Persian commander Xerxes reached the Dardanelles, he constructed a bridge which was swept away by the waves; he thereupon inflicted three hundred lashes on the rebellious sea, and cast chains of iron across it.

99 the Spanish plate the *flota* of galleons carrying gold and especially silver from New Spain and the Indies: see note to l. 249.

105–28 looking forward to the conclusion of Pope's *Epistle to Augustus* (1737), e.g. ll. 410–11: 'A vile encomium doubly ridicules, / There's nothing blackens like the ink of fools.'

124 Amalthea's horn the horn of plenty or cornucopia; abundance personified.

125–6] *FV, Deane Swift, F (1765); not in TR.* Probably a slip on Ford's part.

140 George and William George I; William III.

142 Julius Caesar.

the youth of Pella Alexander the Great, born at Pella in Macedonia.

150 hook in drag in by hook or crook (*OED*).

152 your empress Queen Caroline.

162 hardly fifty odd she was not fifty until 1733.

165 Three graces the eldest daughters, Anne (b. 1709), Amelia (b. 1711), and Caroline (b. 1713). 'None of the sisters was particularly good-looking...with their large-featured, pouting, rather sulky Hanoverian faces' (Peter Quennell, *Caroline of England* (1940), p. 172).

Lucina who presided over childbirth.

167–8 the daughters did not make very imposing marriages: Anne, the Princess Royal, married in 1734 the Prince of Orange: a sensible but sickly, hunchbacked, and impoverished husband. Neither Amelia, a somewhat embittered woman, nor Caroline, of a softer disposition, ever married.

171 princely babies Mary (b. 1722) and Louisa (b. 1724). The former married the landgrave of Hesse-Cassel in 1740, but separated from him later on when he became a Roman Catholic.

172 Hebes patterns of youth and beauty; Hebe was the daughter of Jupiter and Juno. The queen's buxom figure aids the identification with Juno.

175 Cynthia the moon.

177 her brother Phoebus, the sun.

179–82 Caroline acted as Regent when George II went to Hanover, as he did in 1729; there was often anger at home over the King's long absences in Hanover (see Quennell, op. cit., pp. 277–8). It was a pointed snub to the Prince of Wales that he was given no authority in 1729.

181 both our isles Britain and Ireland.

183 Berecynthia or Cybele, wife of Saturn; identified with the *Magna Mater* (compare *The Dunciad* (1729) I, 33), and 'represented as a robust woman, far advanced in pregnancy, to imitate the fecundity of the earth' (Lemprière's *Classical Dictionary*).

185 sees a son in every god compare *The Dunciad* (1729) III, 123–6: 'As Berecynthia, while her offspring vie / In homage, to the mother of the sky, / Surveys around her in the blest abode / A hundred sons, and every son a god.' These parallels serve, firstly, to confirm suspicions that Pope had Caroline in mind when creating his Queen Dulness; secondly, they show Swift exploiting the image-field of *The Dunciad* to establish his own political mythology as applied to George II's court.

187 his little Highness Freddy Frederick, Prince of Wales; he reached England from Hanover at the end of 1728. An eye-witness of his arrival at court, Lady Bristol, described him as 'the most agreeable young man that is possible to imagine, without being the least handsome, his person little but very well made and genteel...and the most obliging address that can be conceived'.

190 Ganymede the type of youthful male beauty; successor to Hebe as cup-bearer to Jupiter.

192 wise wise enough to quarrel with his father.

195–6 the kind of imagery that had been used by Dryden and Pope, in *Annus Mirabilis* and *Windsor Forest* respectively, but now firmly identified with Whig panegyric verse.

  halcyon days compare *Apollo's Edict* 45. Tilley D116.

198 the conflagration the principal meaning seems to be, 'until the whole of Europe is consumed in total war'; but there is an underlying apocalyptic sense, as when Hobbes speaks of 'the day of judgement, and conflagration of the present world'.

200 a little Duke William Augustus, Duke of Cumberland (b. 1721), later to be famous as commander of the English forces at Culloden: see Biog. Dict.

202 meaning not clear: it may be, 'wishes that all he lacked was Cupid's (blind-folded) eyes', i.e. that he had everything else including Cupid's amatory influence. But I am not sure of this interpretation.

203 yonker or younker, fashionable young man.

205 compare Pope, *Epistle to Bathurst* 73–4: 'A single leaf shall waft an army o'er, / Or ship off senates to a distant shore.'

206–8 see *Gulliver's Travels* I, 7–8.

210 a cacophonous line mimicking the harsh sound effects described (compare Pope's technique in *Essay on Criticism* 337–82).

  cramp crabbed; difficult to pronounce.

214 Brunswick the King was also Duke of Brunswick-Luneburg. Whig panegyric poets were not very keen to use the title anyway; it was not very patriotic, and in addition it was used by Jacobites who did not recognize the Hanoverians' claim to the throne.

215 Hesse-Darmstadt a division of the old region of Hesse, in what later became Westphalia; Hessian troops were widely employed by the English army during the eighteenth century. The drift of the passage is to suggest, in familiar Tory language, that the Hanoverians owed their fundamental loyalties to Germany rather than Britain.

216 Guelph the royal family were descendants of the ancient Guelph family.

217 Germany here, doubtless, to be pronounced 'Garmany'.

220 clinks to rhymes with (disparagingly); 'chimes' with.

226 sliding mellifluous.

237 name Jaffe, p. 53, comments: 'The suggestion of a pun – the use of "name" instead of "good name" – completes the thrust at mistaken values. A "good name" might really immortalize the Queen and make the poet's lines live forever too.'

242 Sabrina poetic name for the Severn.

246 Belgic in the vocabulary of Whig panegyric, referring to the Low Countries, especially the Protestant Dutch contrasted with the Catholic French; a way of cementing the link with the House of Orange.

249   Philip   Philip V of Spain (1683–1746), whose fleet of licensed privateers regularly harassed commercial shipping, particularly that of England. Philip was regarded by the Walpole administration as a potential supporter of the Pretender; but the administration long resisted clamour from the trading community (particularly West Indies merchants) to take reprisals against Spain for her interference with British shipping. Between 1713 and 1731 the Spanish appropriated 180 British vessels. Not until the notorious affair of 'Jenkins' ear' came to light in 1737 were the opposition able to create sufficient capital from the situation to push Walpole towards war with Spain.

250   save his bacon   see *The Answer to 'Paulus'* 65.

251   Nassau   William III: compare *A Character, Panegyric, and Description of the Legion Club* 152; *Mad Mullinix and Timothy* 66. He remained a stock ingredient of Whig panegyric.

255–60   compare *On Poetry: a Rhapsody* 191–218. The year 1729 would be a bold moment to predict Walpole's fall; it had been anticipated in 1727, and would be again from 1734 onwards; but his hold at this juncture was secure.

269   Doctor Clarke   the metaphysician Samuel Clarke; see Biog. Dict. His sceptical brand of Christianity had attracted Caroline some years before; 'the Queen's chief study was divinity', according to Horace Walpole, but she was not among the most orthodox of Christians. Some of Clarke's views on future punishments can be studied in his Boyle lectures of 1705: see *British Moralists*, ed. L.A. Selby-Bigge (1965), II, 34–6.

274   bargains sold   'a form of jest which consisted in naming the "parts behind" in answer to a question' (*P* II, 590, quoting Grose's *Dictionary of the Vulgar Tongue*). Compare *Strephon and Chloe* 216, as well as Dryden's *Mac Flecknoe* 181; *Peri Bathous*, ch. xii; and *Tale*, p. 147.

276   Minheer Handel   George Frederick Handel, whose Germanic accent often occasioned comment: compare John Byrom's famous epigram beginning, 'Some say, compared to Bononcini, / That Mynheer Handel's but a ninny.' Ford's MS has 'Hendel', the more correct pronunciation of 'Händel' sometimes used in England during the composer's lifetime.

ON BURNING A DULL POEM

WF first published this poem, and remains the only authority for the statement 'written in the year 1729'. Text from this source.

1–2   the icy-cold waters of the Styx were, according to legend, fatally poisonous; only vessels made of the hoof of a horse or ass were able to withstand their corrosive power. Hence 'Stygian water' meaning 'acid capable of dissolving hard substances' and 'Stygian liquor' meaning a 'nauseous drink': see *OED*, 'Stygian'. (The Styx here is not the infernal river but a spring in Arcadia.)

7–8   poetry as inducing stupor had been a motif in the recently published *Dunciad*.

THE REVOLUTION AT MARKET HILL

Printed by *WF* with the heading, 'written in the year 1730'. If this is right, the poem belongs to Swift's third and last stay at Market Hill, which seems to have extended from late June to late September (*Corr* III, 409). However, the fact that the project to build at Drumlack seems still to have been alive (see *Drapier's Hill*, headnote) might indicate that 1729 is more plausible. Text from *WF*.

The title suggests to us a *coup d'état* involving the populace; Swift perhaps has in mind a palace revolution, or the kind of power struggle enacted in 1688. Towards the end there are hints of a 'plot' such as the Jacobites were accused of, and of a political *coup* of the type by which a minister like Walpole ousted awkward or uncooperative colleagues.

4 codling kind of apple. Swift affects to regard Armagh as impossibly cold and inhospitable in climate; actually, Market Hill lies close to a rich fruit-growing area. Both 1729 and 1730 were cool summers (*Corr* III, 343, 409).

6 a ruined cause that of the Tories, essentially.

8 a Spaniard 'Col. Harry Leslie, who served and lived long in Spain' (note in *WF*); see *Robin and Harry* 5.

14 Drumlack 'the Irish name of a farm the Dean took, and was to build on, but changed his mind' (note in *WF*). See *Drapier's Hill*, headnote. The plan was abandoned in 1729.

29 Nova Scotia Sir Arthur was created a baronet of Nova Scotia in 1728.

33-6 the allusions here are hard to document; Sir Arthur was M.P. for Mullingar in the Irish parliament, and Sheriff of Co. Armagh; what posts he refused through political principle I do not know.

34 against the grain compare *The Progress of Marriage* 123. Tilley G404.

38 fifteen hundred pounds a year for the insufficiency of this sum, see *Corr* III, 412.

40 never came out decisively against the ministry; perhaps, never actively took the Jacobite side, as Swift in effect did (see *Corr* V, 230-33).

48 northward Leslie's home evidently lay to the south of Market Hill; Drumlack was north of the village.

53 basin ornamental lake, artificially constructed.

58 Upton fan I cannot explain this: perhaps one made in Upton-on-Severn, which lay in a district well known for haberdashery (Worcester was celebrated for fine gloves).

67 Hannah 'my Lady's waiting maid' (note in *WF*); see *The Grand Question Debated* 41.

72 Montezume the Aztec war-lord in central Mexico, Montezuma II (1466–1520), whose people were conquered by Cortés and who was killed after being held captive by the Spanish.

77 amuse confuse by a trick.

84 vault wine-cellar.

85 Dennis 'the butler' (note in *WF*); see *A Pastoral Dialogue* 31.

86 Peggy Dixon 'the housekeeper' (note in *WF*).

89 at discretion unconditionally.

92 probably referring to the unholy alliance of Walpole and Townshend; this came to an end with Townshend's resignation in May 1730, another small reason for preferring 1729 as the year of composition. Lines 109–10 might conceivably refer to this episode but seem (in so far as they are particular) to mean the men disgraced or dropped earlier in Walpole's career, such as Craggs, Aislabie, and Blunt, whom the Tories chose to regard as Walpole's henchmen.

96 Lorimer 'the agent' (note in *WF*).

98 at the lower end of the table, where socially inferior people were placed.

A DIALOGUE BETWEEN AN EMINENT LAWYER AND DR SWIFT,
DEAN OF ST PATRICK'S

First published in Deane Swift's *Essay* (1755), dated 1729, and attributed to
Robert Lindsay. Included in *F* (1762) as Swift's, and allotted to February 1728.
The attribution has been generally accepted but the date suggested by *P* II, 488
is February 1730. *PHD* and *PJH* accept this amended dating. I do not think the
reasons given in *P* are conclusive and the year originally named (1729) seems still
a definite possibility.

The poem is an imitation of the Horatian satire but in a broad, telescoped
fashion. Swift takes over the basic framework of a dialogue between Horace and
his lawyer-friend C. Trebatius Testa (a role assumed by Robert Lindsay); but he
works by paraphrase rather than metaphrase. A closer approximation to the
structure of the original is found in Pope's version of this satire, which came out
in 1733 as the first of his *Imitations of Horace*. Swift's freer and more rapid treat-
ment of the text is evident in the friend's first speech, which corresponds to the
first, second, and third of Trebatius. The material transposed by Swift does not
extend beyond the opening sixty-two lines in Horace: the full poem runs to
eighty-six lines.

Title   the lawyer is Robert Lindsay: see Biog. Dict. and *The Answer to 'Paulus'*,
headnote. Pope was to use William Fortescue in this role.
12 scrutoire   writing-desk.
25 Hyde   Edward Hyde, Earl of Clarendon (1609–74), whose *History of the
Rebellion* (1702–4) was a favourite book of Swift's. For his annotations of this
work, 'which he had read and re-read', as they are preserved in his own copy of
the 1707 edition, see *PW* V, xxxvii–xl, 295–320.
story   history.
27 Burnet   Gilbert Burnet, whose *History of His Own Times* (1724–34) gave a
strongly Whiggish account of recent history. Swift's critical marginalia in his
own copy survive, as do his *Short Remarks* on the book: see *PW* V, xxxvi–
xxxvii, 183–4, 266–94. See also *The First Ode of the Second Book of Horace
Paraphrased* 5, and Biog. Dict.
29 Woolston   Thomas Woolston, freethinker and controversialist; see Biog.
Dict. Swift has in mind such works as the *Discourses on the Miracles of Our
Saviour* (1727–9), which caused Woolston to be tried for blasphemy. He is in-
stanced as a type of the extreme deist whose brand of 'natural religion', in ortho-
dox opinion, had become a direct assault on religion itself. Compare *Verses on the
Death of Dr Swift* 281–98.
40 Milton's choir   in *Paradise Lost, passim*, but esp. Books I and II.
47 the tripod of Apollo   the seat of the oracle at Delphi, where the shrine was
dedicated to Apollo.
52 taste   relish, approve of.
55 Drapier's Hill   the estate at Market Hill where Swift was to build, a plan
abandoned apparently in 1729: see *Drapier's Hill*, headnote.

AN EPISTLE UPON AN EPISTLE

Delany's *Epistle to Lord Carteret* was published late in 1729, although dated 1730.
Swift's reply was the present poem, issued in all likelihood around Christmas
1729, and subsequent bouts of rhyming took place, charted in successive items.

There is a separate Dublin edition (*T* 684, *Foxon* S842), as well as a reprint which includes Delany's original (*T* 686, *Foxon* D198). The poem was first included among Swift's works in 1752. There were further flurries in the press when the poems first appeared: see *T* 685. Text here based on the separate Dublin printing.

For the text of Delany's *Epistle*, see *P* II, 471–4. In the poem he appeals to the Lord Lieutenant for further preferment, despite the fact that he already held some valuable offices in the church as a result of Swift's interest. The parallels with Smedley's *Epistle to Grafton* (1724) are too obvious to miss: see *His Grace's Answer to Jonathan*, headnote. Swift may have been right in imputing Delany's alleged hardships to the expenses he had incurred at his country home, Delville (see l. 60).

Epigraph 'You, eloquent worshipper of Palatine Minerva, delight more nearly in the nature of the god: for it is permitted to you to know our lord's cares even as they are born, and to be privy to the inmost feelings of our chief.'

10 Falstaff in *1 Henry IV* II, iv, 371–421.

14 marble cover Delany's poem was issued in a sumptuous folio by George Grierson.

17–18 alluding to Delany, ll. 1–2.

24 the Doctor Delany.

25–6 alluding to Delany, ll. 29–30.

27–8 for the rhyme, see *Twelve Articles* 23–4.

29–30 a variation on Horace, *Ars Poetica* 140: '*quanto rectius hic, qui nil molitur inepte*': 'how much more suitable if you, a would-be adept in poetry, made no such inept endeavours.'

31 Smedley now departed for India, having resigned his deanery at Clogher.

32–6 quoting Smedley's *Epistle to Grafton* 12–16. For Grafton, see Biog. Dict.

37–8 alluding to Delany, ll. 55–6.

39 vistos a fine prospect seen through a narrow opening (as an avenue of trees) and hence the avenue itself: much favoured by 'improving' landscape gardeners. Pope's vulgar improver is called Sir Visto (*Epistle to Burlington* 15–16).

40 our Speaker Sir Ralph Gore, Speaker of the Irish House of Commons from October 1729 to 1733; he had a villa on an island in Lake Erne. Picked up from Delany, l. 58.

coxon coxswain.

43 Edgar Edgar, crowned King of Wessex at Bath in 973, travelled to Chester. According to the chroniclers, six kings came to him there and swore fealty; they rowed him on the Dee from the palace to the church of St John and back, whilst Edgar held the rudder (*Florentii Wigornienses Chronica*, ed. B. Thorpe (1848), I, 142–3).

46 Erne Lough Erne in Co. Fermanagh, fed by the River Erne.

49–58 quoting Smedley's *Epistle to Grafton* 31–40.

58 antic grotesque.

60 Delville Delany had acquired his villa at Glasnevin, some two miles north of Dublin, in 1719; it commanded a view across Dublin Bay. See *Corr* III, 61–2.

62 parterres ornamental flower-beds; see Pope, *Epistle to Burlington*, note to l. 95.

66 bevel crooked.

67   box   hut or shelter.

70   Rupert Barber   husband of the poet Mary Barber, befriended by Swift; they were neighbours of Delany at Glasnevin. He was a linen-draper, born in England. The Barbers' second son, a painter, was also named Rupert.

73   compare Pope, *Hor. Ep.* I, i, 169–70; 'I plant, root up, I build, and then confound, / Turn round to square, and square again to round.'

76   quadrata change rotundis   alluding to the same passage of Horace imitated by Pope (see note to l. 73, above): *'mutat, quadrata rotundis'* ('changing square to round'). The source is *Ep.* I, i, 100.

77   Fame   recalling the house of Fame in Chaucer and Pope; traditionally set on an eminence, open to the winds.

78   A Flora   a statue of the goddess of flowers.

88   Don Quixote Redivivus   because Quixote made myth and legend 'real' when he mistook commonplace objects and events for romantic machinery.

92   St Patrick's Well   in the garden of Trinity College: see *Verses Occasioned by the Sudden Drying Up of St Patrick's Well.*

94   greater Patrick   Delany himself.

100   my Lady   Lady Carteret: see Biog. Dict.

103–4   alluding to Delany, ll. 31–2.

107   flimflams   trifles, affected conceits.

111   Charly Grattan's school   one of the Grattan brothers was Master of Portora Royal School, Enniskillen (where Oscar Wilde was a pupil in the next century). See Biog. Dict.

112   five hundred pound a year   alluding to Carteret's calculation of Delany's income in the original *Epistle,* ll. 23–4.

116   'build and you bestow'   alluding to Delany, l. 94, the closing words of the *Epistle.*

117–18   betters . . . letters   a favourite rhyme, e.g. *Verses on the Death of Dr Swift* 201–2 (among several instances).

familiar letters   this meant, simply personal correspondence between friends, but there is a hint of 'over-familiar' here.

120   Latin]   Latian   *first edn.* The author in question is Horace, *Epistles* I, xvii, 50–51: *'Sed tacitus pasci si posset corvus, haberet / plus dapis et rixae multo minus invidiaeque'* ('but if the crow could feed in silence, he would have more of a meal, and far less brawling and unpleasantness').

A LIBEL ON THE REVEREND DR DELANY AND HIS EXCELLENCY JOHN, LORD CARTERET

Swift's second response to Delany's *Epistle* (see preceding item). First published about the beginning of February 1730: on 3 February a well-informed Irish observer wrote of Swift's reply as 'last night . . . publicly cried about the streets' (see *P* II, 474). *Foxon* S877 identifies the quarto at *HEH* (*T* 689A) as the earliest edition; it was followed by two more Dublin octavo editions (*T* 687–8, *Foxon* S878–9), and by London printings put out by the fictitious 'A. Moore' (*T* 689, 689B, 689C; *Foxon* S880–82). All three of this latter group also contain the original *Epistle* by Delany and two have Swift's *Epistle upon an Epistle* as well. A London printing 'for Captain Gulliver near the Temple' (*T* 36; *Foxon* S883) came out later in February. There were other appearances in miscellanies of dubious standing before the poem was included in *WF*, the basis for the text here.

On 6 February Swift wrote to Pope, 'You will see eighteen lines relating to yourself, in the most whimsical paper that ever was writ, and which was never intended for the public' (*Corr* III, 370). This was perhaps a response to Pope's suggestion that Swift should record their friendship in verse (*Corr* III, 331), just as *The Dunciad* had done on Pope's side. The poem aroused the ire of Viscount Allen (see *Traulus*, headnote, and Biog. Dict.); he attempted to institute a prosecution of the unnamed printer of the *Libel*, but ultimately failed (see *Corr* III, 374, 396; IV, 134). For references to the poem in the correspondence between Pope and Swift, see *Corr* III, 378, 382, 386, 394, 397; IV, 116. Swift called it 'the best thing I writ as I think' (*Corr* IV, 83), and Pope had to make awkward apologies for its omission from *M32*. For general background to the poem, see the preceding item.

Title] *WF*; A Libel on Doctor Delany, and a Certain Great Lord *all earlier edns.*

1-10 alluding to the opening of Delany's *Epistle*, ll. 9-24 especially.

9 *facetious* pleasant, companionable, amusing.

10 *cup and can* 'constant or familiar associates' (*OED*); proverbial. Used in *Polite Conversation* (*PW* IV, 196); *Tilley* C902.

33 *Congreve* Swift's lifelong friend William Congreve had died a year earlier, on 19 January 1729 (see Biog. Dict.) He obtained the first of a number of government sinecures in 1695, the post of commissioner for licensing wine, at a salary of £200. This was obtained through the influence of Charles Montagu, Earl of Halifax (l. 35), to whom Congreve had dedicated *The Double Dealer* (1693). For fuller details, see J.C. Hodges (ed.), *William Congreve: Letters and Documents* (1964), pp. 17-18, 39, 83-8.

35 *Montagu* the politician and patron, Charles Montagu: see Biog. Dict., under 'Halifax'.

41 *crazy* sickly (Congreve suffered badly from gout and other ailments, even as a young man).

42 *to discharge his chair* to pay for a sedan chair to carry him around.

44 *Paean's fire* a hymn to Apollo; hence, a high poetic utterance marked by fervour and inspiration.

49 *Steele* in his edition of Addison's *Works* (1721), Tickell had insinuated that Steele concealed the authorship of some works by Addison and allowed the public to think they were of his own composition. Steele had rejected the allegation but Swift chose to believe it.

51 *perils of*] *WF*; lodging in *1730 edns.*

52 *Withdrew*] *WF*; was left *1730 edns.* Steele had retired to Carmarthen about 1725 and died there on 1 September 1729, five months before Swift's poem appeared.

53 *Gay* alluding to the last item in Gay's first set of *Fables* (1727), 'The Hare and Many Friends' (*Gay*, II, 369): 'A hare, who, in a civil way, / Complied with everything, like Gay...' The idea was taken up by Gay's circle: see Swift to Lady Elizabeth Germain, 8 January 1733 (*Corr* IV, 99), 'In a few weeks, the Queen said to Mrs Howard (alluding to one of Mr Gay's fables) that she would take up the hare; and bade her to put her in mind, in settling the family, to find some employment for Mr Gay.' Mrs Howard herself used the same expression in a letter to Gay of October 1727. See also *To Mr Gay*, headnote. The *tales* (l. 55) are the *Fables*, dedicated to the young Duke of Cumberland.

59 usher's place   see *To Mr Gay* 8.

61-4   Montagu helped to get Addison a travel scholarship which enabled him to spend some years on the Continent. On the death of King William in 1702 this lapsed; his former patrons were now out of power. There was a plan to get him the post of tutor, not to a squire, but to the Marquis of Hertford, son and heir of the princely Duke of Somerset; but Addison's acceptance was couched in rather cocksure language and caused the offer of employment to be withdrawn. See P. Smithers, *The Life of Joseph Addison* (2nd edn, 1968), pp. 45-90.

68 the courtier's trade   Addison held various government posts in the first years of the Hanoverian régime, culminating in the high office of Secretary of State in 1717.

70 levee   a minister's reception, attended by those seeking preferment or favours.

74 Refused the visits of a queen   there seems to be no truth in the story that Pope left his house in order to avoid a visit from Queen Caroline. See also *Corr* III, 397. Sherburn comments, 'the lines ... may have been slightly embarrassing at a time when through the influence of the Burlingtons Pope was probably on better terms with the Court than at any time in his career' (Pope *Corr* III, 90).

83-4   alluding to Pope's translations of Homer, which together brought him something like £10,000; he obtained 575 subscribers for the *Iliad* (1715-20) and 610 for the *Odyssey* (1725-6). See P. Rogers, 'Pope and His Subscribers', *Publishing History* III (1978), 7-36. For the first time a professional author achieved full independence by means of his pen.

87 Pindus' head   Mount Pindus in Thessaly, seat of the muses.

96 at a pinch   stronger than today: 'in an emergency'.

97 story   history and (here) legend.

101 smoke   uncover.

102 Bolingbroke with Pulteney dines   see Biog. Dict. for these leaders of the opposition.

106 carve   a duty of domestic chaplains: compare *To a Lady* 121.

113 The Viceroy   Carteret.

117 to retire   Carteret finally left Ireland in April 1730, when Swift wrote him a characteristic letter regarding the arts of a courtier (*Corr* III, 390-91).

125-6   close to Swift's comments in a letter to the Earl of Oxford on 28 April 1730: 'Our friend Carteret is gone, and we are in the clouds, apprehending he will not be rewarded according to his merit; which (as I have often told him) is excessively great, according to the best merits of a chief governor here; which are to put on more chains, and to get more money, wherein none of his predecessors even equalled him, nor met with more stupid, slavish, complying beasts to manage' (*Corr* III, 394).

142 Before a play   in a dedicatory prologue.

144 Philips   Ambrose Philips: see Biog. Dict. He had written complimentary poems to members of the Lord Lieutenant's family during his time in Dublin, including a panegyrical address *To His Excellency the Lord Carteret* (1725).

147-8   for the rhyme, see *Twelve Articles* 23-4.

154   sweetener   flatterer: compare *Drapier*, p. 168.

161   slipped   escaped.

165–70   *P* II, 485 suggests a possible reminiscence of Addison, *The Campaign* 287–8: 'So when an angel by divine command / With rising tempests shakes a guilty land.'

171   in politics grown old   compare *Cadenus and Vanessa* 503.

172   compare *A Panegyric on the Reverend Dean Swift* 106–7.

173–4   compare *A Panegyric on the Reverend Dean Swift* 155–6.

181   the tripod of Apollo   see *A Dialogue between an Eminent Lawyer and Dr Swift* 47.

187   budget   wallet, pouch.

189   strews   spelt (and doubtless pronounced) 'strows'.

191   Black Hall   parodying Whitehall.

   Belzebub   or Beelzebub, prince of devils (Matthew xii, 24).

ON THE IRISH CLUB

First published by Deane Swift in 1765; included in *F* the same year. A sequel to the two preceding items; *P* II, 486–7 clearly shows that the poem relates to the events of early 1730, not those of 1733/4 (as assumed by Scott and others). Deane Swift's date is 1729, for 1729/30 (see note on dates, p. 598). Text here based on Deane Swift.

   A number of pamphlets came out in Dublin by way of response to Delany's *Epistle* (see headnote to *An Epistle upon an Epistle*) and Swift's two replies. Some of these concerned a magistrate, Hartley Hutchinson, who had arrested two newsboys for 'crying' Swift's *Libel on the Reverend Dr Delany* in the streets. The 'club' of the title is the Irish House of Lords (compare *A Character, Panegyric,* and Description of the Legion Club). For Lord Allen's efforts to instigate a prosecution against those responsible for the *Libel*, see preceding item.

   For Swift's use of a strategically 'fragmentary' text, compare *Tale*, pp. 170, 200, 244, 247–8, 250, 258; and *On Poetry: a Rhapsody* 548.

6   for poets' ears   to punish them for refusing to recant offensive opinions; compare *To Stella, Visiting Me in My Sickness* 32–3.

10   blackguard boys   errand boys, street urchins: compare *Tom Mullinex and Dick* 19.

12   compare *Gulliver's Travels* III, 6 (*PW* XI, 191–2).

20   port   in general, port was the Whig drink, as against the French wines like claret and champagne favoured by Tories; but the sense here is evidently 'a plain domestic wine'. For champagne, see *To Charles Ford, Esq. on His Birthday* 26.

A PANEGYRIC ON THE REVEREND DEAN SWIFT

An exceedingly dubious item. It first appeared in Dublin, early in 1730, and was reprinted twice in London during the same year (*T* 691–2; *Foxon* P36). First attributed to Swift by *Ball*, pp. 252–3, and accepted as authentic by *P*, *PHD*, and *PJH*.

   The reasons given by *P* II, 491–2 for accepting the attribution are these: (1) Swift alluded to such a poem in a letter to Lord Bathurst in October 1730:

Having some months ago much and often offended the ruling party, and often worried by libellers I am at the pains of writing one in their style and manner, and sent it by an unknown hand to a Whig printer who very faithfully published it. I took special care to accuse myself but of one fault of which I am really guilty, and so shall continue as I have these sixteen years till I see cause to reform: but with the rest of the satire I chose to abuse myself with the direct reverse of my character or at least in direct opposition to one part of what you are pleased to give me. (*Corr* III, 411)

(2) The London edition by James Roberts 'has corrections and alterations which have every appearance of coming from the author's hand, although they cannot all be judged improvements'. (3) The rival candidate, Arbuckle, 'even as a disguise, would not be likely to speak of himself among the "long unbishopricked" (l. 147), nor speak of himself familiarly in conjunction with Grattan and Sheridan (l. 177)'. *P* concludes, 'There can be little doubt that Dr Ball's identification is correct, and that the composition of *A Panegyric* should be assigned to February–March 1729/30.'

The dating is not a major point at issue; but the attribution itself remains contentious. Faulkner quite clearly assigned the poem to James Arbuckle (d. *c.* 1743). The arguments enumerated above are the less convincing in that (1) the letter to Bathurst is an undated transcript in *FV*, and it would be rash to build too much on its evidence; (2) the order of editions is not clearly established, and, in any case, authorial alterations (if such they are) would not necessarily point to Swift's involvement; and (3) the poem is written in the assumed voice of Delany, and hence the lines cited by *P* refer to him, not to Arbuckle. It might be added that some of the more damaging passages echo contemporary criticism of Swift by others (e.g. his supposed wish to follow Gulliver's example and take up the status of a horse). They do not so much reflect on his 'character' (as the letter to Bathurst suggests) as on his mentality and conduct. See *Foxon* P36 for further grounds to support Arbuckle's authorship.

In my judgement it is more probable that Arbuckle was the author; but in the absence of decisive evidence to rebut the ascription, the poem is included as a possible item in the authentic canon. The text is based on the Dublin edition; variants in the London texts are not recorded, as their source is unclear, and their literary interest doubtful.

Title   the sub-title refers to Swift's *Libel on the Reverend Dr Delany* by the name under which it originally appeared.

8   compensate   accent on second syllable, as usual up to the nineteenth century.

9   glebes   land that goes with a clergyman's benefice.

12   elves   in the metaphorical sense of elf as 'a tricksy, mischievous, . . . spiteful and malicious creature' (*OED*).

13–14   recalling *Libel* 2 and *A Dialogue between an Eminent Lawyer and Dr Swift* 54.

25–6   recalling *Libel* 21–32.

32   short sessions a long history   alluding to a pamphlet, probably by Delany, *A Long History of a Short Session of a Certain Parliament*, dealing with affairs in the Irish House of Commons in 1713–14.

39–40   recalling *Libel* 95–6.

41   The fatal box   referring to the so-called Bandbox Plot, when Swift opened a bandbox containing a kind of booby-trap designed for Harley (see *Journal to Stella* under 15 November 1712, *JTS* II, 572–3; *Corr* I, 319; *PW* VI, 196; *Ehrenpreis*, II, 583, 772). The Whig line was that the whole affair had been invented by Tory propagandists.

44   in a screw   referring to an earlier scare, the so-called Screw Plot in November 1710, when it was alleged that the Whigs had taken some bolts out of the roof at the west end of St Paul's Cathedral. The plan was, supposedly, for the cupola to fall on the Queen when she attended a thanksgiving service. See also Arbuthnot, *John Bull in His Senses* (1712), ch. IV. Again, the Whigs claimed that the episode was a complete fraud.

47   the gift   the Corporation of Dublin presented Swift with a gold box to mark his services, on 27 May 1730: see *Ferguson*, pp. 185–6. Delany composed a suitable inscription, but apparently this was not used. Swift's reply to the Corporation appears in *PW* XII, 145–8.

50   shrieves   sheriffs.

54   Harley   Robert Harley: see Biog. Dict.

55–7   note the triplet.

58–9   echoing *Libel* 82.

63   Bob's spittle . . . Harry's turd   Harley and Bolingbroke.

64   zest   add a relish to (obsolete as verb).

74   story   history.

76–7   plain . . . Dean   the 'Irish' rhyme.

82   lawn   'a kind of fine linen . . . used for the sleeves of a bishop. Hence, the dignity or office of a bishop' (OED). The first two examples of this extended sense cited by *OED* are from Gay and Pope.

83   Robin's honour   Harley again. See *The Windsor Prophecy*, headnote.

84   an old grave Don   the Earl of Nottingham: see *The Author upon Himself* 37. Nottingham appears as 'Don Diego Dismallo' in Arbuthnot's *John Bull* pamphlets (1712).

92–3   parodying the famous lines in Addison's *Campaign* 291–2, 'And, pleased the Almighty's orders to perform, / Rides in the whirlwind, and directs the storm.'

96–7   recalling *Libel* 153–4.

99–101   picking up the references to Congreve and Addison in *Libel* 33–48, 61–70.

100   rage   poetic ardour.

104–5   Swift also uses this rhyme in *On the Little House by the Churchyard of Castleknock* 35–6, and in *On Paddy's Character of 'The Intelligencer'* 23–4.

106–7   recalling *Libel* 172.

108   Billingsgate   coarse and abusive language, from the fish-market in London where the porters were renowned for plain speech. *Tilley* B350.

111   my patron   Carteret.

113–21   recalling the imagery of *Gulliver's Travels*, esp. Part IV.

120   spiss   dense, thick.

125   at a lift   more commonly 'at a dead lift', meaning 'in an emergency'.

128   rapparee   robber: see *The Answer to 'Paulus'* 97.

129   fatal tree   gallows.

136   jump   fit.

146   recalling *An Epistle upon an Epistle* 29.

150   tiddest bits   choicest morsels; apparently a back-formation from 'tidbit' or 'titbit'.

155–6   echoing *Libel* 173–4.

158   *gone to pot*   a slightly more dignified expression in the eighteenth century than it is today. Used in Arbuthnot's *John Bull* (1712) ('Law is a Bottomless Pit', ch. VI). *Tilley* P504.

160   *The ruined party*   here, the Whigs during the Harley ministry.

161   *the beast with many heads*   originally from Revelation xiii, 1–18; applied to 'the crowd' by well-established usage.

162   *mob*   one of the words Swift satirized in his *Tatler* paper on fashionable language, and also in *Polite Conversation* (*PW* IV, 161).

176   *countenance divine*   I have not traced any other usage before Blake's ('And Did Those Feet' 5).

177   *Grattan*   see Biog. Dict.: probably Robert Grattan.

181–2   recalling *Libel* 195–9.

TO DR DELANY, ON THE LIBELS WRIT AGAINST HIM

The first edition appeared in Dublin (1730), disingenuously claiming to reproduce a non-existent London printing. This is *T* 693, *Foxon* S913. It was included in a London collection, *Select Poems from Ireland*, in the same year; and also in a newspaper on 19 June 1730. The poem then went into *M32*; Swift's own copy (now in *TR*) contains his annotations. After this it was included in *WF*, with the heading 'written in the year 1729'. Unquestionably the poem was composed in 1730, following the flurry of rejoinders to Delany's *Epistle to Carteret* (see *An Epistle upon an Epistle*, headnote). For some of these retorts, see *P* II, 486–7. The present item is plausibly linked by Williams (*P* II, 499) to Swift's letter to Pope of 2 May 1730:

> There is a knot of little fellows here either in the University or among the younger clergy, who deal in verse and sometimes shrewdly enough. These have been pestering Dr Delany for several months past, but how they have been provoked I know not, unless by envy at seeing him so very domestic with the Lord Lieutenant. The Doctor as a man of much strictness in his life was terribly mortified with two or three of the first squibs, but now his gall is broke. (*Corr* III, 397)

The applicability of this passage to ll. 85–98 is clear.

Text based on *WF*, which takes account of the marginalia in *M32*. For the imagery of garrets and bugs, especially in ll. 135–58, see *Grub Street*, pp. 241–3.

Epigraph   Juvenal, *Satires* III, 54–5: 'Let not all the sands of the shady Tagus mean so much to you' [that you lose sleep over such things].

7   *wound*   the pronunciation to rhyme with sound (l. 8) was recorded in eighteenth-century dictionaries, and was without affectation in a poetic context.

9   *as thick as hops*   compare *On Poetry: a Rhapsody* 416.

14   *pot-gun*   originally a kind of mortar; here, probably contemptuous for 'pop-gun'.

16   *beat out his brains*   underlined by Swift in his copy of *M32*, and italicized in *WF*.

21   *squibbing*   a pun on 'squib', meaning (1) a form of artillery and (2) a satire.

25   *takes heart of grace*   plucks up courage: once a very common, indeed proverbial, expression: see *OED*, 'heart of grace', and *Tilley* H332.

29 '*in yourself . . . round*' a note in *WF* indicates the source, Horace, *Satires* II, vii, 86: '*in seipso totus teres atque rotundus*'.

30 *wound* see note to l. 7.

31 '*Tis said . . .* no precise source identified.

47 *five hundred odds* compare *A Libel on the Reverend Dr Delany* 197: the meaning is either 'five hundred odd' or 'in a majority by five hundred' or perhaps 'at odds of five hundred to one to win any dispute'.

49–50 for the rhyme, compare *On Poetry: a Rhapsody* 68, as well as Pope, *Rape of the Lock* III, 7–8.

58 *they* members of the Irish parliament.

61 *shoe-boys* compare *On the Words 'Brother Protestants'* 21 and *A Character, Panegyric, and Description of the Legion Club* 68. William Dunkin, amongst others, had sneered at prominent Irish politicians, including Sir Thomas Prendergast and Richard Tighe, for their 'low' descent.

62 *Blue Boys'* 'The Irish parliament met at the Blue Boys' Hospital, while the new Parliament House was building' (note in *WF*, deriving from Swift's marginalia in *M32*). For the new Parliament House, see *A Character, Panegyric, and Description of the Legion Club* 2. The Bluecoat or King's Hospital was on the north side of the Liffey near what is now Wolfe Tone Quay; it was built in 1670. Swift was a governor of the school in the latter part of his life.

63–4] *WF*; And dread no more the rage of Grub, / You then may soon be of the club. *earlier edns.*

63 *the club* see *On the Irish Club*, headnote.

64 *Grub* Grub Street.

78 *lines* either rows of pamphlets hung from rails in the street (as in Pope, *Epistle to Augustus* 418–19), or unbound sheets hanging up in the printing house.

82 *the function* the office of a clergyman.

85 *candidates* underlined by Swift in his copy of *M32* and italicized in *WF*.

90 *Bob* Walpole.

116 *wit's fair goddess* Minerva, who sprang from the head of Jove.

118 *sooterkin* afterbirth; a mythical small creature which emerged after the new-born baby. See *The Dunciad* (1743) I, 126.

123–34 the passage recalls several aspects of the 'Digression concerning Critics' in the *Tale*, pp. 92–104; where, for instance, critics are seen as poisonous serpents (p. 100) or as snarling curs (pp. 103–4).

137–40 'The *true critics* are known by their talent of swarming about the noblest writers, to which they are carried merely by instinct, as a rat to the best cheese' (*Tale*, p. 103).

139–40 compare *On Poetry: a Rhapsody* 399–402.

141–2 again recalling the celebrated lines in *On Poetry: a Rhapsody* 353–6.

141 *numeric* identical.

145 *sponging-house* a place kept by a bailiff where debtors were at first confined, as it were on remand: 'where the bailiffs sponge upon them' (Johnson's *Dictionary*).

148 *flourish* talk big, swagger.

151 *trepanned* caught in the act.

160 *fool officious*] *WF*; *from Swift's MS note in M32*; senseless coxcomb *earlier edns.*

165–70 compare Pope, *Epistle to Augustus* 404–13.

167 *critics*] *WF*; *from Swift's MS note in M32*; blockheads *earlier edns.*

TO A FRIEND WHO HAD BEEN MUCH ABUSED
IN MANY INVETERATE LIBELS

First published by Delany in his *Observations* on Orrery's life of Swift (1754). Introduced into *F*, vol. IX (1758). Text here based on the first printing. The poem is generally assumed to relate to the attacks on Delany around 1730: see *To Dr Delany, on the Libels Writ against Him*, headnote.

5–6 for the rhyme, see *To Dr Delany, on the Libels Writ against Him* 7.

AN ANSWER TO DR DELANY'S FABLE OF THE PHEASANT
AND THE LARK

A reply to Delany's *Fable* (published by 4 April 1730, and perhaps earlier), which was an attempt by Swift's friend to exculpate himself from the charges against him occasioned by the *Epistle to Carteret*. Swift's poem appeared as a pamphlet in Dublin (*T* 695, *Foxon* S796) and was reprinted in the London press on 17 June 1730. The evidence would suggest a date of composition around April or May. First collected by Deane Swift in 1765 and incorporated into *F* the same year. The text here is based on the 1730 pamphlet.

The text of Delany's fable, which runs to 148 lines, is reproduced in *P* II, 508–12. In this poem, the peacock is George II, the pheasant Carteret, the lark Delany himself, the jackdaw Richard Tighe, the tom-tit Sheridan (who had angered Delany by his sneering reply to the *Epistle*), and the nightingale Swift.

1 *In ancient times* Delany had used the same stock opening phrase: compare *Baucis and Philemon* 1.
5 *dull* stupid.
7 *daw* jackdaw.
8 *prowl* the original text has the spelling 'prole', which was the pronunciation until *c.* 1750 (*OED*).
10 *pease* see *Strephon and Chloe* 167.
11 *a great divine* Delany.
12 *refine* *OED* gives 'affect a subtlety of thought or language' as one meaning, citing *Cadenus and Vanessa* 11.
14 *of a feather* playing on the old proverb, 'Birds of a feather flock together' (*Tilley* B 393).
15 *the peacock* alluding to Delany, ll. 1–10.
18 *both rich and wise* alluding to Delany, l. 8.
21–2 a pure 'Irish' rhyme.
23–4 Argus, the creature with a thousand eyes, who was turned into a peacock by Juno (to whom this bird was sacred). See *Ode to the King* 76.
27 *standing force* the existence of a standing army in time of peace was a common focus of opposition feeling; here the idea may be that the English rule in Ireland is based on military power, in the last analysis.
32 *rule the rump* . . . this looks like a proverbial phrase, but may have been Swift's own adaptation of the old expression, 'rule the roast'. ('Rule the roost', the ordinary modern form, is not recorded in *OED* and must be a later rationalization: *Tilley* R144).
42 *fricasse* see *A Panegyric on the Dean* 266; *olios* hotchpotches (culinary or literary). Compare *A Tale of a Tub*, section VII: 'the late refinements in

knowledge, running parallel to those of diet in our nation, which among men of a judicious taste, are dressed up in various compounds, consisting in soups and olios, fricassees and ragouts' (*Tale*, p. 143).

44   viceroy   Carteret as Lord Lieutenant of the neighbouring territory, Ireland.

50   fed and taught him   alluding to Delany, ll. 35–40.

56   seemingly looking back to the original *Epistle to Carteret*, esp. ll. 93–4.

57   a maxim   not identified in this form.

64   hold . . . by the chin   support, sustain.

70   senate-house   parliament.

75   libel   probably the *Libel on the Reverend Dr Delany*, specifically.

78   so much favour   see for example *Verses on the Death of Dr Swift*, note to l. 179.

79   A noble lord   Viscount Allen, who had recently complained in the House of Lords regarding *A Libel on the Reverend Dr Delany*: see Biog. Dict. and *Traulus*, headnote.

87   Harmonious Coffey   'a Dublin gazetteer' (Deane Swift). Probably Charles Coffey (d. 1745), who wrote a number of ballad operas, including *The Beggar's Wedding*, produced at the Smock Alley theatre in Dublin in March 1729, and *The Devil to Pay* (1732), one of the most popular of all plays in this mode. 'Harmonious' may indicate his evident taste for music: see *Simpson, passim*, for his wholesale adoption of favourite folk-airs in his plays.

96   turn   stylistic arrangement, form (esp. of graceful kind).

100   a characteristic self-maligning untruth.

101   clincher   itself a pun: the word meant (1) a clinching final statement; (2) a punster: 'a witty or ingenious person that makes smart repartees' (John Kersey's *Dictionarium* (1708), quoted in *OED*).

103   Jove send   may Jove ordain (see *OED*, 'send', 7).

106   owls   solemn fools.

107   flew   perhaps with a hint of 'escaped prosecution, evaded the law'.

TRAULUS

This poem was published in two separate parts, [Dublin] 1730: *T* 699, *Foxon* S914–17. There are minor differences between various issues. The first part only was reprinted in the London press during August 1730. The second was reissued in London in 1732 as *Thersites*, no doubt without any authority by Swift. Both parts were among the items cancelled when *WF* was reorganized at the last minute: see *Mad Mullinix and Timothy*, headnote. The text in the uncancelled sheets of *WF* is slightly different from that of the 1730 pamphlets, and it is *WF* I follow here.

Composition probably dates from April 1730. Relations between Swift and Viscount Allen had soured in the early part of that year, when Lord Allen protested against the award of a gold box to Swift by the Corporation of Dublin. Swift wrote a retort (*PW* XII, 141); and again attacked Allen in his *Vindication of Lord Carteret* (*PW* XII, 150–69). It was Allen who attempted to get proceedings brought against those concerned in *A Libel on the Reverend Dr Delany*. Swift 'promised to give him some return' for speeches to the Privy Council and to the House of Lords (letter of 18 April by Marmaduke Coghill, quoted in *P* III,

794). For Swift's own account of the affair to Pope, see *Corr* III, 374, 396. For Allen, see *Biog. Dict.*

Williams (*P* III, 794) suggests that Robin is Robert Leslie and Tom is Mullinix (see *Mad Mullinix and Timothy*). If Swift had definite individuals in mind, they cannot be conclusively identified.

Title Greek τραυλός means 'lisping'. See ll. 49–52.

The First Part

3–4 compare Swift to Pope, 2 May 1730: '... when the Lord on a sudden without the least provocation railed at me in the Privy Council as a Jacobite and libeller of the government &c.' (*Corr* III, 396).

9 spawl spit.

15–16 a claim repeated in letters to Pope (*Corr* III, 374, 396: 'caressing me in the most friendly manner...').

23–33 compare *Tale*, pp. 176–9.

44 Towser compare *A Fable of the Widow and Her Cat* 45.

46 proverbial: *Tilley* B85 has 'Great barkers are no biters.'

55–60 'this is the usual excuse of Traulus when he abuses you to others without provocation' (note in *WF*).

63 session of parliament.

67 scrubbest most scrawny.

78 Legion from Luke viii, 30: see *A Character, Panegyric, and Description of the Legion Club* 12.

79 perhaps remembering Revelation xii, 10: 'for the accuser of our brethren [Satan] is cast down.'

81 trepanning swindling, full of tricks.

97 God pronounced Genesis vi, 3.

102 sink] *WF*; stink *1730*.

The Second Part

3 lordlings 'Viscount Allen's mother was first daughter of the Hon. Robert Fitzgerald and sister of Robert, nineteenth Earl of Kildare' (*P* III, 799).

11 untoward perverse, stupid, refractory; stress on second syllable.

24 his father the first Viscount was raised to the peerage for services to the Hanoverian régime, but he had opposed Carteret over the Drapier's affair (*Ferguson*, p. 122); he died in 1726.

25 looby clown, lout.

28 Atavus ancestor, here great-grandfather, that is, John Allen, architect 'of the great Jacobean mansions that arose in Ireland during Strafford's viceroyalty'; *grandsire* Sir Joshua Allen, once Lord Mayor of Dublin, 'at the time of the Revolution one of the premier merchants of Dublin on whom the financial stability of the city depended' (the somewhat Whiggish descriptions are those of *Ball*, p. 252). Williams (*P* III, 795) states that Sir Joshua's 'nearest approach to the trade of butcher was the export of salt meat'.

48 the old foundation of a building, and of the state or constitution.

50 a ladder to the gallows. See *Tale*, pp. 58–9.

55 him] *WF*; them *1730*.

ON PSYCHE

First published in *F* (1762). A note was appended identifying the subject of the poem as the poet Mrs Sican. It is known that Swift had dealings with this lady around 1730 and 1731, and so the poem is usually dated about this time. The closest single link is perhaps a letter of 2 May 1730, in which Swift tells Pope of the 'three shopkeepers' wives' who represent female taste in Dublin (*Corr* III, 394: see also III, 369, 464). For a letter from Mrs Sican to Swift in 1735, see *Corr* IV 422-3. Text based on *F*.

Title 'Mrs Sican, a very ingenious well bred lady, wife to Mr John Sican, an eminent grocer in Dublin' (note in *F*). Her husband had served on the Grand Jury which defied Whitshed in 1724: see *Whitshed's Motto on His Coach*, headnote. He also served on the committee which in 1742 declared Swift mentally unfit to order his affairs. According to the younger Sheridan, it was Mrs Sican who told him of the marriage of Swift and Stella, although her authority in this matter is not clear (see Denis Johnston, *In Search of Swift* (1959), p. 156). What little is known about her is set out in *P* II, 579-80.
8 *the main* the most important things, the major concern.
11 'A small, unpublished note in Swift's hand was in the possession of Lord Harmsworth, in which the Dean begs Mrs Sican to do some marketing for him, and to favour him with her company at dinner the same evening. See *The Times Literary Supplement*, 5 June 1930, p. 477' (*P* II, 580). The letter is untraced.
12 *cark it* take trouble, put herself out.

THE DEAN'S REASONS FOR NOT BUILDING AT DRAPIER'S HILL

First published by Deane Swift in 1765, and included in *F* the same year. A manuscript version in *FV*, not in Swift's hand, is endorsed 'September 1730'. This may be right, although it seems to have been a year earlier that Swift took the resolution not to proceed with his building plans. For the background, see *Drapier's Hill*, headnote. The text is based on Deane Swift.

9 *that flattering time* probably around the summer of 1729; see *Drapier's Hill*, headnote; *flattering* means 'delusive', 'flattering our hopes'.
13 *Martin's school* Richard Martin, master of the Royal School at Armagh; he became mentally deranged some years later and Sheridan sought his post (*Corr* IV, 497-8).
14 *turn and wind* as a top.
18 *thieves, fanatics, and barbarians* unflattering terms to describe the local population, among whom Scottish Presbyterians ('fanatics') were prominent.
21 *the knight of Gosford* Sir Arthur; see *A Pastoral Dialogue* 2.
24 *conversable* sociable, affable.
25 the proverbial 'not worth a pin' is *Tilley* P334.
28 *a usurer's plums* the great riches of a financier: for 'plum', see *The Fable of Midas* 56.
32 *strike* to 'touch', to borrow money from (see *OED*, 'strike', 75).
47 *a song will hum* compare *The Grand Question Debated* 128.
51-68 a favourite pose of Swift, as the plain man bemused by metaphysics.
52 *Malebranche or Cambrai* Nicolas Malebranche (1638-1715), philosopher and scientist; François de la Mothe-Fénelon (1651-1715), Archbishop of Cam-

brai, best known for his *Aventures de Télémaque* (1699). There are some affinities with Prior's *Alma* III, 354–65 (*Prior*, I, 509). Swift owned editions both of Malebranche and of contemporary authors such as Fontenelle (*Library*, nos. 30, 72).

54   sleeveless   useless.

56   Tom Thumb   hero of the old folk-tale, often reprinted in chapbooks, and in 1730 given burlesque treatment in Fielding's comedy.

57   progging   poking about for whatever may be picked up.

60   smatter   talk breezily and shallowly; see *On Poetry: a Rhapsody* 51.

61   quibble   pun.

62   intelligible   the jargon of philosophers such as Malebranche or Fontenelle.

75–80   characteristic Swiftian antitheses, aligning the weighty with the slight in a single grammatical construction.

80   pudding-pies   meat-pies or toad-in-the-hole. Compare *Hudibras* I, ii, 547.

88   bowls   pronounced to rhyme exactly with *fowls* (l. 87).

92   Pomona   goddess of fruits, as *Flora* (l. 93) is of flowers.

101   formal expressions of good wishes, as in a loyal toast or congratulatory poem to someone whom the poet does not know very well.

104   after, pound   afterwards, impound his cattle (or, afterwards raid his enclosure).

108   crabs   crab-apples.

DEATH AND DAPHNE

First published in *WF*, which is the source for the text here, and there described as 'written in the year 1730'. Lord Orrery provides the following account (*Remarks*, 5th edn (1752), pp. 86–7):

> I have just now cast my eye over a poem called *Death and Daphne*, which makes me recollect an odd incident relating to that nymph. Swift, soon after our acquaintance, introduced me to her, as to one of his female favourites. I had scarce been half an hour in her company, before she asked me, if I had seen the Dean's poem upon *Death and Daphne*. As I told her I had not, she immediately unlocked a cabinet, and bringing out the manuscript, read it to me with a seeming satisfaction, of which, at that time, I doubted the sincerity. While she was reading, the Dean was perpetually correcting her for bad pronunciation, and for placing a wrong emphasis upon particular words. As soon as she had gone through the composition, she assured me smilingly, that the portrait of Daphne was drawn for herself: I begged to be excused from believing it, and protested that I could not see one feature that had the least resemblance; but the Dean immediately burst into a fit of laughter. 'You fancy,' says he, 'that you are very polite, but you are much mistaken. That lady had rather be a Daphne drawn by me, than a Sacharissa by any other pencil.' She confirmed what he had said, with great earnestness, so that I had no other method of retrieving my error, than by whispering in her ear, as I was conducting her downstairs to dinner, that indeed I found
>
> Her hand as dry and cold as lead.

In his own copy of the *Remarks*, now at Harvard, Orrery marked the name Daphne with a note, 'Lady Acheson, wife of Sir Arthur Acheson. Separated from her husband.' There can be no doubt that this identification is the right one; Mrs Pilkington was suggested by *Ball* (p. 255) and others, but on flimsy grounds. In particular, Swift's emphasis on Lady Acheson's leanness in several poems squares with this poem, as does his known habit of advising her on grammar and elocution (see *A Panegyric on the Dean* 129–54; *Corr* III, 311). The first mention of Orrery by Swift, which concerns their dining together, is in a letter to Ford of 14 October 1732 (*Corr* IV, 77).

Lady Acheson spent a good deal of time in the early 1730s with her mother, who lived at Baldoyle, between Dublin and Howth; but she was never formally separated from her husband. Her health was not good; Swift terms it 'asthma', which was 'got by cards, and laziness, and keeping ill hours' (*Corr* IV, 375), but it is likely that her emaciation was caused by consumptive disease. She died in 1737.

For an assessment of Swift's skill in 'creating the two overlapping worlds of the eighteenth-century female and Pluto's realm', see *Jaffe*, pp. 130–32. Death is 'a projection of [Swift] himself'.

2   Pluto's hall   Pluto was god of the underworld, and of death and funerals. He was portrayed with a grim countenance.

5   weekly bills   returns of vital statistics, prepared from figures supplied by parish clerks. Usually known as the 'bills of mortality'.

7   the Peace   although it was now approaching twenty years since the Peace of Utrecht, Swift doubtless has this in mind; it was the cessation of hostilities after prolonged wars and remained a watershed in people's lives.

19   consult   meeting for consultation; stressed on first syllable.

21   Megaera   one of the three Furies, daughters of night and darkness: avenging powers who were diplomatically termed Eumenides or 'kindly ones'. They were sometimes depicted with a grisly garland of snakes.

22   compare   *A Character, Panegyric, and Description of the Legion Club* 91.

24   toupets   'the periwigs now in fashion are so called' (note in *WF*). Compare *Mad Mullinix and Timothy* 226.

25   flour of sulphur   or flowers of sulphur, a pulverized and refined form used in medicinal and cosmetic preparations.

27   sable   black.

30   Clubbed for   clubbed together to buy.

37   new-fluxed rake   one who has just taken a purge or cure.

42   aconite   fatal poison (poetic, from a real poison derived from a genus of plants which includes wolf's bane).

44   popular imprecations; for the beau's expected accomplishments in this regard, compare *Rape of the Lock* IV, 127–9.

46   Warwick Lane   where the College of Physicians stood, not far from St Paul's Cathedral: compare *Tale*, p. 178.

47   The Faculty   the body of physicians.

48   complimental   expressing formal compliment (obsolete).

50   Harangued   made a speech.

58   Adonis   the pattern of male beauty; beloved by Venus and (aptly here) restored to life by Proserpine after being gored whilst hunting.

60   foreshadowing the famous lines in *Verses on the Death of Dr Swift* 225–42.

64   compare *Journal of a Modern Lady* 130.

65   phiz   see *Dean Smedley Gone to Seek His Fortune* 21.

75   toasts   fashionable society ladies.

78   quadrille   see *Journal of a Modern Lady* 41.
79   rooks   cheats.
80   cards . . . are Pluto's books   see *Polite Conversation* (*PW* IV, 194) and *Tilley* C76.
84   Proserpine   wife of Pluto and queen of the infernal regions.
85   Elysian shades   the place in the infernal regions where the souls of the blessed went; seen here as a suitable spot for the masked balls which reached the height of their popularity in the 1720s.
87   Styx   the infernal river which the departed crossed to reach Hades.
88   a coach and six   (horses): the most stylish equipage of all.
    troll it   take a spin; bowl about.
100   in the suds   the phrase meant either 'sulking', or 'in a state of perplexity', or 'in disgrace'. Compare the title of Fielding's play *Tumbledown Dick: or Phaeton in the Suds* (1736). *Tilley* S953.

DAPHNE

First published by Deane Swift in 1765, and taken into *F* the same year. The former attached to this poem the lines headed *Twelve Articles*, but *F* did not. See headnote to the following poem. Text from Deane Swift.

There can be little doubt that Daphne masks the identity of Lady Acheson, as in the preceding poem. It might be one of the numerous 'libels' on her ladyship composed on Swift's first visit in 1728/9, but since the date is uncertain the poem is grouped with *Death and Daphne*. *Ball*, p. 256, associates the poem with Mrs Pilkington but without any show of reason.

9–20   a harsher version of the criticism contained in *To Stella, Who Collected and Transcribed His Poems* 87–144.
24   a Fury   perhaps Megaera, the spirit of discord (see *Death and Daphne* 21).
30   convict her   give her a sense of her error; convince her that she is in the wrong.
43–8   Lady Acheson seems to have been over-fond of the looking-glass, in Swift's opinion (compare *Journal of a Modern Lady* 130; *Death and Daphne* 64).

TWELVE ARTICLES

Printed by Deane Swift as an addendum to the previous item. It certainly employs the same material, but is best regarded as a separate variation on the one theme. Text from Deane Swift.

1–2   compare *A Panegyric on the Dean* 147–54; *Corr* III, 311.
15–16   a characteristic 'Irish' rhyme.
18   taste   appreciate.
23–4   spirit . . . merit   the same rhyme is used in *An Epistle upon an Epistle* 27–8; *A Libel on the Reverend Dr Delany* 147–8; *Advice to a Parson* 7–8; *The Beasts' Confession* 109–10. It was also a favourite with Pope: see *Hor. Ep.* II, ii, 135–6, 226–7; *Epistle to Augustus* 384–5; *Epistle to Bathurst* 375–6. The word was pronounced close to 'sperrit'.
26   break no squares   do no harm (*OED*, citing usages by Dryden and Sterne). See also *Tilley* I54.

THE DEAN TO HIMSELF ON ST CECILIA'S DAY

First published by Deane Swift in 1765, and included in *F* the same year. *FV* contains what is not much more than a rough draft in Swift's hand. It is endorsed 'imperfect'. However, the alterations in Deane Swift and *F* are in the nature of tidying-up operations, and the text is based on the holograph, with punctuation supplied from the printed texts.

Ball, p. 255, notes that the Dublin Musical Society held a festival on St Cecilia's Day, 23 [22?] November, in 1730; a sermon preached by Sheridan on this occasion was published the following year. The preface to this sermon, dated 25 January 1730 [/31], was attributed to Swift by Mackie L. Jarrell in *Publications of the Modern Language Association* LXVIII (1963), 511–15, and is reprinted in *PW* XIV, 36–7. A similar occasion in 1731 is described in the *Correspondence* of Mrs Delany (1861), I, 316–17. St Cecilia is the patron saint of music.

3]That you was found writing *Swift MS* (*WF*); That you who so lately were writing *Deane Swift, F* (*1765*).

4 *blowers*] previous editors follow Deane Swift and read *players*; the manuscript is exceedingly difficult to decipher and represents Swift's composition in its most unfinished state.

11 rochets linen surplices worn by bishops.

A PANEGYRIC ON THE DEAN

First published in *WF*, where it was one of the 'inoffensive' new items inserted in the corrected state of the volume to replace controversial poems. Headed 'written in the year 1730', which is certainly correct to within a year or two. Text based on *WF*.

The scatological element in the poem has elicited different responses: see *Jaffe*, p. 119, who describes this as 'sly, coy, devoid of horror'; *Lee*, pp. 123–4, who discerns a serious moral theme in which 'offensive excrement is a symbol of [man's] spiritual fall'; and Norman O. Brown, *Life Against Death* (1959), pp. 200–201, which is a discussion of the poem in terms of attitudes to anality. See also Geoffrey Hill, 'Jonathan Swift: The Poetry of "Reaction"', *The World of Jonathan Swift*, ed. B. Vickers (1968), pp. 208–9; Hill argues that this is 'Swift's only scatological poem that seems in any way coprophilous ... It is the very coolness of the verbal draughtmanship, the detailing of the faecal coils, that is so chilling.'

Title the 'lady' is, of course, Lady Acheson.

35 *mend the matter still* improve matters even further.

36 *Market Hill* 'a village near Sir Arthur Acheson's house, where the author passed two summers' (note in *WF*).

39 *usher* male attendant on a lady.

40 *Robert and Darby's coadjutor* 'the names of two overseers' (note in *WF*): see also *The Grand Question Debated* 48. *coadjutor* stressed on third syllable. For the rhyme compare *Cadenus and Vanessa* 464–5.

42 *Kit* 'my Lady's footman' (note in *WF*); see also *The Grand Question Debated* 117.

47 *bate an ace* see *Another Reply by the Dean* 2.

48   Dean Daniel   Richard Daniel: see Biog. Dict. and *My Lady's Lamentation* 224.

58   Snipe   see *My Lady's Lamentation* 8.

61   'the author preached but once while he was there' (note in *WF*).

65   Beggar's Opera   the outstanding success of Gay's ballad opera had been evident since its première in January 1728. Its author had sent Swift an account of its triumphant opening run (*Corr* III, 265); Swift himself bought a copy of the work in Dublin very soon after its publication (*Corr* III, 269).

80   cowboys   cowherds, but boys, not grown men.

87   vault   wine-cellar.

88   butler's mate   'he sometimes used to direct the butler' (note in *WF*). The usage *in quality of* ('in the capacity of', *en qualité de*) became obsolete in the nineteenth century.

89   Dennis   the butler: see *A Pastoral Dialogue* 31.

105   usher's post   'he sometimes used to walk with the lady' (note in *WF*). The sense is that of an attendant acting as a guide.

110   daggled   bespattered. Compare this passage with *My Lady's Lamentation* 37–58.

120   'the neighbouring ladies were no great understanders of raillery' (*WF*). A note which could not conceivably derive from anyone but Swift himself, which suggests the general value of *WF*.

121   all a case   all one.

127   smoke   get the point.

128   Gaghagan   see *On Cutting Down the Old Thorn at Market Hill* 82.

130   tutor   'in bad weather the author used to direct my Lady in her reading' (note in *WF*). Compare *My Lady's Lamentation* 135–54.

131   savage   Lady Acheson's maiden name was Savage.

143   penurious   'ignorant ladies often mistake the word *penurious* for *nice* and *dainty*' (note in *WF*). Swiftian linguistic comment. Not just a malapropism, however, for Bailey's *Dictionary* (1721) admits this sense.

144   Epicurius   a joking variant, to emphasize the strained rhyme.

146   play   at cards.

156   bailie   bailiff, man of affairs.

168   'a way of making butter for breakfast, by filling a bottle with cream, and shaking it till the butter comes' (note in *WF*).

169–71   alluding to calvinistic preachers, maintaining the doctrine of the election of souls.

173   'when milk is burned the devil is said to have set his foot in it' (*P* III, 892). When the cream is burnt in *Polite Conversation*, the maid explains, 'the Bishop has set his foot in it' (*PW* IV, 134). *Tilley* B406.

199   Palladio   Andrea Palladio (1518–80), who inspired the most fashionable style of architecture in Britain during Swift's later years.

205   Cloacine   a motif used by Gay in *Trivia* and Pope in *The Dunciad*: see *Grub Street*, pp. 162–6. From Latin *cloaca*, a sewer; Cloacina was the 'purifier', the goddess of such places.

211   inward motion   inner urge, and bowel movement.

211   reverence   punning on 'sir-reverence', faeces.

216   to pluck a rose   compare *Strephon and Chloe* 16. The meaning is 'to make water'. *Tilley* R184.

221 Smedley's lay Jonathan Smedley: see Biog. Dict. The idea is to make use of such things in the function of the modern 'toilet roll'.

233–4 until overthrown by his son Jupiter, the supreme ruler; the so-called golden age of peace and prosperity occurred during his reign.

241–52 misapplying pastoral language, in a way close to that of *The Dunciad* (1729) II, 79–88, another Cloacina episode.

249 abstersive having purgative or scouring properties.

253–90 drawing on the traditional repertoire of allegorical poetry, with the diseases most incident to this age replacing the deadly sins.

261–2 enough ... stuff another use of one of Swift's recurrent rhymes.

264 haughty Gaul compare *Directions for a Birthday Song* 247.
  ragouts highly seasoned stews.

266 fricassees game stewed and served with a sauce.

268 Botargo 'a relish made of the roe of the mullet or tunny' (*OED*).
  catsup ketchup.
  caveer caviare. I retain the form used by Swift, as an exotic and rather barbaric quality is required.

295 earthenware '*vide* Virgil and Lucretius' (note in *WF*).

304 copple-crowns trees that are crested, like a cock's head.

307 golden bough 'Virgil lib. 6' (note in *WF*); actually *Aeneid* VI, 136–636.

308 The Trojan hero Aeneas.

311 out of case in a poor state.

312 Unweeting unawares.

317 Hannah Lady Acheson's maid: see *The Grand Question Debated* 41.

321–2 compare *The Revolution at Market Hill* 63.

325 Me Phoebus alluding to Virgil, *Eclogues* VI, 3–4: '*Cynthius aurem Vellit et admonuit*'; *a midnight dream* alluding to Horace, *Satires* I, x, 33: '*Post mediam noctem visus cum somnia vera*' (allusions noted in *WF*).

326 Go shake 'in the bottle to make butter' (*WF*).

330 gyle the ale brewing.

331 Peggy Dixon the housekeeper.

334 rub thy teeth compare *My Lady's Lamentation* 19–20.

341 Be these thy arts an allusion is indicated in *WF* to Virgil, *Aeneid* VI, 852: '*hae tibi erunt artes*.' Anchises is addressing his son Aeneas.

344 the blank is impossible to fill in.

345 Smedley 'a very stupid, insolent, factious, deformed, conceited parson; a vile pretender to poetry, preferred by the Duke of Grafton for his wit' (note in *WF*).

346 the repetition seems pointless; there may be some corruption in the text. *WF* is the only independent authority and the poem had to be fitted into the space left by cancelled items, notably *To a Lady*; there could easily have been some huddling at this juncture.

AN EXCELLENT NEW BALLAD

An anonymous broadside [Dublin, 1730] is the first appearance in print (*T* 701; *Foxon* S843). In 1979 another version turned up, occupying the last leaf in a pamphlet entitled *The Case of Daniel Kimberly* (Dublin, 1730). The poem subsequently went into *WF* with the heading, 'written in the year 1730'. This time *WF* is right; Dr Thomas Sawbridge was prosecuted in June 1730 but managed to get himself acquitted. Swift's account of the episode occurs in a letter to the Earl of Oxford on 28 August 1730: 'There is a fellow here from England, one Sawbridge, he was last term indicted for rape. The plea he intended was his being drunk when he forced the young woman; but he bought her off. He is a Dean and I name him to your Lordship, because I am confident you will hear of his being a Bishop; for in short, he is just the counterpart of Chartres, that continual favourite of ministers' (*Corr* III, 405). In fact Sawbridge did not achieve any further eminence: he died in May 1733.

Sawbridge had been accused of the offence, against Susanna Runcard, on 2 June. He was acquitted on 15 June.

Text based on *WF*, which is more intelligently set out than the broadside.

Title 'Sawbridge, Dean of Ferns, lately deceased' (note in *WF*). He was appointed Dean in January 1728.

13   game punning on the senses (1) object of the chase, and (2) fun, amusement.

19   bagnio brothel.

24   clap venereal disease.

33   Steele Sir Richard Steele, who had died in 1729; for the split between the two men see *The First Ode of the Second Book of Horace Paraphrased*, headnote. 'True as steel' was a proverbial expression: Tilley S840.

38   jure ecclesiae by the law of the church.

39   commendam an additional perk in office: see *The Storm* 22. Ferns was a tiny place in the middle of Co. Wexford, and the diocese was desperately short of revenue owing to the predominance of lay impropriations (*Landa*, p. 165).

44   Smedley Jonathan Smedley, Swift's recurrent target, now seeking his fortune in India.

45   rochet see *The Dean to Himself on St Cecilia's Day* 11.

47   Atherton 'a Bishop of Waterford, sent from England a hundred years ago' (note in *WF*). John Atherton (1598-1640), Bishop of Waterford and Lismore 1636, found guilty of unnatural crime, degraded and hanged at Dublin.

49   Chartres pronounced 'Charters': see Biog. Dict. 'Charteris'. He had been accused early in 1730 of sexually assaulting a maid-servant, and sent to Newgate. By April he had obtained a royal pardon, which led most people to suppose that he had bribed friends at court. On 31 March Gay had written to Swift, 'Does not Chartres' misfortunes grieve you, for that great man is like to save his life and lose some of his money, a very hard case!' (*Corr* III, 385). It was widely believed that Walpole had exercised influence on Charteris's behalf. As well as becoming known as 'Rapemaster General of Great Britain', Charteris attained a great deal of unpopularity for his activities as a money-lender. See Pope, *Epistle to Bathurst* 20 and note (*PTE* II, ii, 83-4); Fielding's play *Rape upon Rape* (1730); and Hogarth, *The Harlot's Progress*, Plate 1.

50   three score and ten he was more like fifty-five.

53   ell roughly a yard in length.

58   to pay the devil and all proverbial, used by Swift in the *Journal* (*JTS* II, 372) and *Polite Conversation* (*PW* IV, 190). Tilley D268.

65   hempen cape rope.

69 noteworthy for the characteristic rhyme (compare for example *My Lady's Lamentation* 9-10), and for the recurring political point, which is the real *raison d'être* of this poem. The subliminal message is that Ireland has been raped by England.

ON STEPHEN DUCK, THE THRESHER, AND FAVOURITE POET

First published in *WF*, on which the text here is based. I have retained the nudging italics which indicate the puns. *WF* states, 'written in the year 1730', and this must be about right. After the death of Laurence Eusden on 27 September of that year, speculation was rife concerning his successor as poet laureate. Gay informed Swift that Duck was 'the favourite poet of the court' (*Corr* III, 415); and Swift replied on 19 November that 'the vogue of our few honest folks here [Dublin] is that Duck is absolutely to succeed Eusden in the laurel, the contention being between Concanen or Theobald, or some other hero of the *Dunciad*' (*Corr* III, 421). Within a month Swift was to learn that the post had instead gone to Colley Cibber.

For Stephen Duck, see Biog. Dict. He had been taken up by the Queen that very year, when his *Poems on Several Subjects* attained ten editions, no doubt principally because of their author's curiosity value. *P* II, 520 quotes press reports in September and October indicating the Queen's bounty to Duck. The thresher-poet was not to figure in *The Dunciad* along with his supposed rivals, but he did appear in two epigrams probably by Pope (*PTE* VI, 327), aligning Duck with Cibber as one of the 'candidates for the laurel'.

2 *The proverb* see *Tilley* F185.
4 *grains* a pun indicating 'a few crumbs of reward'.
6 *not worth a straw* proverbial: *Tilley* S918.
7 *stubble* there is a similar idea in *The Dunciad* (1743) I, 254, 'Molière's old stubble in a moment flames', to which Pope added a note, 'a comedy [Cibber's *Nonjuror*] threshed out of Molière's *Tartuffe*'. Images and puns identical to Swift's are used in an epigram attributed to Pope in the Shaftesbury papers at the Public Record Office: see P. Rogers, 'A New Epigram by Pope?', *American Notes & Queries* XI (1973), 151–2.

TO BETTY THE GRISETTE

First published in *WF*, where the poem is headed, 'written in the year 1730'. It then went into the main series of *Misc* but the text here is based on the first printing.

Title *Grisette* see *Stella at Woodpark* 59; used here in the sense of a girl who is common and rather loose, but not actually a prostitute.
4 *Spotted* with pock-marks or perhaps with an excess of patches (beauty-spots).
9 *pippin* a word for which Swift had an odd fondness: see *The Virtues of Sid Hamet the Magician's Rod* 74; *A Fable of the Widow and Her Cat* 26; *The Fable of Midas* 6.
13–28 very close in ideas and language to *The Furniture of a Woman's Mind* 1–26. Compare especially ll. 13, 17, 20, 28 with *Furniture* 1, 11, 12, 14, 19.
25 *eighteen-penny gallery* a common pattern of admission charges at this date was: boxes 4s., pit 2s.6d., first gallery 1s. 6d., upper gallery 1s.; in the 1720s London charges generally went up to 5s., 3s., 2s., 1s. (A shilling is 5p, and 6d. = 2½p. Thus 5s. = 25p, and 2s. 6d. = 12½p.) Either Dublin scales were slower to rise; or Swift was remembering prices of his London days; or the poem is earlier than *WF* states – which is possible on other grounds.

28   a distinction repeatedly drawn; see especially *To Mr Delany* 29–64.
29   compare *The Furniture of a Woman's Mind* 17.
31   *snout*   the same word is used in *Death and Daphne* 63.
32   *Fleer*   sneer.
       flout   mock, jeer.
35   *bit*   the victim of such a joke.
36   *a world of*   a vast amount of; formerly a common expression, now rare except in particular constructions like 'a world of good'.

THE LADY'S DRESSING ROOM

This poem was one of the most popular in Swift's lifetime; it went through a whole range of editions in England and Ireland, both in pamphlet form and in the newspaper press. The earliest appearance seems to be the first of two editions by James Roberts (London, 1732), which also contain *On Cutting Down the Old Thorn at Market Hill*: see *T* 720, *Foxon* S869–70. These came out, respectively, in June and July 1732. A slightly different text was printed in Dublin (no publisher named) in the same year: *T* 721, *Foxon* S871–2. A so-called 'third' edition was issued by Faulkner, with a number of different readings: *T* 722, *Foxon* S873. A Cork edition by Andrew Welsh (1733) is listed in the bibliographies (*T* 722A, *Foxon* S874), but I have not seen this. See also *Foxon* S875. The poem went into *WF*, with the text close to that of Faulkner's 1732 printing, and then into the London *Misc.* The text here is based on *WF*, but the couplet omitted at ll. 117–18 is restored, as indeed happened in *F* (1737). For an early reference to the poem, see Swift to Pope, 12 June 1732 (*Corr* IV, 31).

The poem occasioned various replies, listed in *P* II, 525. The first three are discussed in Robert Halsband, 'The Lady's Dressing-Room Explicated by a Contemporary', *The Augustan Milieu*, ed. H.K. Miller *et al.* (1970), pp. 225–31. Halsband reprints the answer by Lady Mary Wortley Montagu, and discusses her relations with Swift. The original draft of her reply is printed from the Harrowby MSS in Lady Mary's *Essays and Poems*, ed. R. Halsband and I. Grundy (1977), pp. 273–6. In addition, there was *A Modest Defence* of the poem, by Matthew Pilkington, which Faulkner issued in 1732.

This is the first of the directly 'excremental' poems, and is the subject of a large body of comment. Earlier hostility can be studied in *CH*, pp. 121, 154, 173, 177, 296 (some of these pieces are in fact strained and unconvincing defences). There was little detailed analysis in the nineteenth or earlier twentieth centuries, but that has now been remedied in the fullest degree. For the excremental poems as a group, see Geoffrey Hill, 'Jonathan Swift: The Poetry of "Reaction"', *The World of Jonathan Swift*, ed. B. Vickers (1968), pp. 205–9; Donald J. Greene, 'On Swift's "Scatological" Poems', *Sewanee Review* LXXV (1967), 672–89 (see also discussion in *Publications of the Modern Language Association* XCI (1976), 464–7); T.B. Gilmore, jr, 'The Comedy of Swift's Scatological Poems', *Publications of the Modern Language Association* XCI (1976), 33–41; J.M. Aden, 'Those Gaudy Tulips: Swift's Unprintables', *Quick Springs of Sense*, ed. L.S. Champion (1974), pp. 15–32; C.J. Rawson, 'The Nightmares of Strephon: Nymphs of the City in the Poems of Swift, Baudelaire, Eliot', *English Literature in the Age of Disguise*, ed. M. Novak (1977), pp. 57–99. This poem in particular is discussed by Herbert Davis, 'A Modest Defence of *The Lady's Dressing Room*', in *Restoration and Eighteenth-Century Literature*, ed. C. Camden

(1963), pp. 39–48, where the author discovers a large element of Rabelaisian gusto and fun. Books on Swift give full coverage: see *Johnson*, pp. 116–20; *Jaffe*, pp. 117–18; Denis Donoghue, *Jonathan Swift: A Critical Introduction* (1969), pp. 209–10; *Lee*, pp. 82–5. Irvin Ehrenpreis, *The Personality of Jonathan Swift* (1958), ch. 2, 'Obscenity' (pp. 29–49), is relevant.

Title *WF* adds 'written in the year 1730', which must be nearly (perhaps exactly) right. The dressing room adjoined the bedroom (which was usually larger), and could be used to hold a levée: see Mark Girouard, *Life in the English Country House* (1978), p. 150, for eighteenth-century fashions in these matters.
24 Aden, op. cit., p. 22, detects an 'apparently grotesque recall of Belinda's "Puffs, powders, patches, bibles, billet-doux" [*Rape of the Lock* I, 138]...one is tempted to suppose that Celia's *Tripsy* [l. 29] is likewise a meiotic counterpart of Belinda's *Shock*. The whole scene reads in fact like a burlesque of Belinda's toilet.'
27 alum flower powdered form of the mineral.
31 puppy water the recipe for this cosmetic aid, based on the innards of a pig or a fat puppy-dog, was supplied in the 'Fop Dictionary' appended to *Mundus Muliebris: Or, the Ladies' Dressing Room Unlocked* (1690). This glossary of high-society jargon also includes other terms used by Swift ('plumpers', 'commode', etc.). See Hermann Real, *Scriblerian* VII (1975), 121–2; Arthur Sherbo, ibid., XI (1978), 45–6.
33 gallipots small pots used for ointments and medicines.
48 frowzy unkempt, slatternly.
52 moisture of her] *WF*; marks of stinking *Roberts, Dublin (1732) edns.*
53 coifs and pinners see *Baucis and Philemon* 139–40.
59–68 the verse-paragraph is discussed by Donoghue, op. cit., pp. 203–5, as a 'motto' for Swift's own concentrating technique.
80 through thick and thin proverbial, for 'without regard to obstacles' (*OED*). Compare *The Dunciad* (1743) IV, 197. *Tilley* T101.
83–8 Epimethus, the brother of Prometheus, married Pandora and, against advice, opened the box given to her by Jove; all the evils that beset the world promptly flew out, hope alone remaining in the box. As often, a likely source is the fragment in Hyginus' *Fabellae*, one of the works Swift must have known best. See also *Tilley* P40.
98 'Milton' (note in *WF*); actually *Paradise Lost* II, 890–91. 'A stately Miltonic enjambement...is wittily assimilated into Swift's light octosyllabic measure, while Milton's "dark / Illimitable ocean without bound" (II, 891–2) shrinks to the mysteries of a girl's chamberpot' (Rawson, op. cit., p. 79). Herbert Davis remarks that the poem is 'full of parodies of all the overused and much respected classical tags and stories and of words and phrases in English poetry from Milton to Pope' ('A Modest Defence of *The Lady's Dressing Room*', op. cit., p. 42).
99 prime of meat '*prima virorum*' (note in *WF*).
103 adown '*vide* Dean Daniel's works, and Namby Pamby's' (note in *WF*). Richard Daniel and Ambrose Philips: see Biog. Dict. Swift perhaps has homely similes in mind, as well as archaic diction.
110 plumped from the verb meaning 'to drop or sink, as when a solid body drops into water' (paraphrase of *OED* entry).
116 The swain disgusted] *WF*; Disgusted Strephon *Roberts.*

117-18]   *not in Faulkner* (*1732*), *WF*. Apparently through squeamishness, though the gap was supplied in *F* (1737).

126 jump   match; alluding to a proverbial phrase 'good wits jump', meaning something like 'great minds think alike', which is quoted in *Polite Conversation* (*PW* IV, 159). *Tilley* W578.

128 contrast   almost entirely a term of artistic description at this date, used of one element set in relief against another. The stress may indicate that Swift thought of it as a foreign expression.

131-2   Venus, who arose from the sea; compare Pope, *Essay on Man* IV, 292, 'From dirt and sea-weed as proud Venice rose.' This epistle did not appear until 1734, well after the date at which Pope made the acquaintance of Swift's poem.

134 Statira   the reading is *Satira* in *P*, *PHD*, and *PJH*, but it should certainly be Statira, the heroine of Lee's *Rival Queens* (1677) jointly with Roxana: see *An Epilogue to a Play for the Benefit of the Weavers in Ireland* 24-5.

139 washes   as in l. 34, a liquid to improve the complexion (compare Pope, *Epistle to a Lady* 54), but there was another sense, that of stale urine used as a detergent.

   clout   rag.

APOLLO: OR, A PROBLEM SOLVED

First published in *WF*, as 'written in the year 1731'. This seems improbably late, but in the absence of other information must be provisionally accepted. Text from this source.

3-4   the sun ripened and purified metals in the ground, whilst alchemists attempted to transmute base metals into gold (for *chemists*, see *Vanbrug's House* 127). Both notions are recurrent in Swift.

8 bays   the laurel wreath awarded to poetic champions, symbolic of inspiration.

13 before he sold his land   to pay his debts; the classic rake's progress.

15 by Ovid told   see *Metamorphoses* II, 107-8.

17 a coach and four   the horses are named in *Metamorphoses* II, 153-4.

28 in alt   in the octave above the treble clef, sometimes notated b". This was well above the compass of most castrati: '[they] usually had the range of a modern counter-tenor, and were at their best in the octave above Middle C. Later in the century the most notable castrati were sopranos, but Handel seldom had the use of such voices' (Roger Fiske, *English Theatre Music in the Eighteenth Century* (1973), pp. 61-2). Apollo was the god of music.

29 Pliny   *P* II, 598, quotes *Historia Naturalis* XI, 51: '*Bubus tantum feminis vox gravior, in alio omni genere exilior quam maribus, in homine etiam castratis*': 'Only in the cow is the voice of the female deeper than the male's, in all other species it is thinner than his; this is so among humans with a castrated male.'

30 Nicolini   Nicolini Grimaldi (1673-1732), 'the first great castrato Londoners had heard' (Fiske, op. cit., p. 50). He made his début at the Opera House in December 1708. A month later Swift was writing to a friend, 'We are here nine times madder after operas than ever, and have got a new castrato from Italy called Nicolini who exceeds Valentini I know not how many bars' length' (*Corr* I, 121). He left England in 1714. It seems very improbable that Swift should want to refer to this superannuated figure in 1731; the rhyme may be convenient, but Swift was capable of finding one as apt for Senesino or Farinelli, the stars of the 1720s. He had himself been in London when the operatic craze reached a new peak in 1727; Gay had already told him that music was 'the reigning amusement of the town . . . There's nobody allowed to say "I sing" but an eunuch or an Italian woman . . . Folks that could not distinguish one tune from another now daily dispute about the different styles of Handel, Bononcini [the very rhyme Swift needed!] and Attilio' (*Corr* II, 447). Circumstantial evidence thus suggests a date before Nicolini's fame had been overtaken by that of his successors.

32   no beard 'Apollo was represented by the Greeks under the most beautiful figure they were able to conceive, young, unbearded with graceful hair, and a countenance fair, animated and expressive' (Lemprière's *Classical Dictionary*).

A BEAUTIFUL YOUNG NYMPH GOING TO BED

Published by Roberts, together with *Strephon and Chloe* and *Cassinus and Peter*, in a small pamphlet (advertised in *Grub-street Journal*, 5 December 1734). This is *T* 744, *Foxon* S809; the latter notes that William Bowyer printed 750 copies during November. These three poems were all conveyed by the poet Mrs Barber to Matthew Pilkington, who undertook the negotiations with the London trade for their publication (see also *To a Lady* and *On Poetry: a Rhapsody*). Pilkington dealt with Benjamin Motte; Roberts was simply a front and distribution agent. For a summary of negotiations, see *P* I, xxv–xxviii. A month after Roberts's volume appeared, *WF* was published in Dublin, and all three of the poems concerned are included. The text here is based on *WF*, which heads this poem 'written for the honour of the fair sex, in 1731'. The subtitle but not the date appears in Roberts. The date is generally thought to be reasonably accurate. Roberts's title-page also carries an epigraph: '*Pars minima est ipsa Puella sui.* Ovid, *Remed. Amoris.*' The quotation is from I, 334: 'a woman is the least part of herself' (when stripped of artificial aids).

For general discussions of the scatological poems, see *The Lady's Dressing Room*, headnote. In addition, see *Johnson*, pp. 115–16; *Jaffe*, pp. 105–7; Colin J. Horne, 'Swift's Comic Poetry', *Augustan Worlds*, ed. J.C. Hilson *et al.* (1978), pp. 53–4.

1   Drury Lane notorious for prostitutes: see Gay, *Trivia* III, 259–66 (*Gay*, I, 167–8), and *Grub Street*, pp. 71–2.
3   Covent Garden a raffish area: see Gay, *Trivia* II, 343–56 (*Gay*, I, 153) and *Grub Street*, p. 73.
9   chair with one leg broken and missing.
11 'The "Crystal Eye", stock image of poetic amorists, is here, most piquantly, literally glass, a physical fact' (Horne, op. cit., p. 54).
17   plumpers a plumper was 'a small light ball or disk sometimes carried in the mouth, for . . . filling out hollow cheeks' (*OED*). See Steele, *Tatler*, no. 245 (2 November 1710), for a similar list. Corinna is hollow-cheeked because venereal disease has caused her teeth to rot: See *Trivia* III, 272 (*Gay*, I, 168).
30   shankers chancres, ulcers occurring in venereal disease.
35   front forehead. Compare the rhyme in *The Lady's Dressing Room* 25–6.
41   Bridewell the house of correction for vagrant women and prostitutes, near where the Fleet Ditch reached the Thames: compare *To Stella, Who Collected*

and Transcribed His Poems 45; *On Poetry: a Rhapsody* 36: Pope, *The Dunciad* (1729) II, 257.

compter (pronounced 'counter') a city prison; the best known was that in Wood Street where (until its closure in 1791) a hundred felons and debtors were cramped together in particularly insalubrious surroundings, and where Moll Flanders was said to have been eleven times, according to the chapbook versions.

43   bully pimp.

44   hedge-tavern poor, squalid inn.

45   Jamaica a small number of convicts were transported to the British possessions in the West Indies (like the characters in Gay's *Polly*, 1729); but the majority went to the North American colonies, especially Maryland and the Carolinas. Wholesale shipping of felons dates from the Transportation Act of 1718.

46   'Et longam incomitata videtur / Ire viam' (note in *WF*). Virgil, *Aeneid* IV, 467–8: 'she [Dido] seems, alone, / To wander in her sleep, through ways unknown, / Guideless and dark' (Dryden tr.).

47   Fleet Ditch the noisome artery of London: compare *Description of a City Shower* 60, as well as *The Dunciad* (1728) II, 259–60; *Trivia* II, 168 (*Gay*, I, 148).

53   rubs unpleasant, jarring encounters.

54   religious clubs either groups of dissenters and enthusiasts, like the Quakers, or conceivably the societies for the reformation of manners, both suspected of hypocrisy.

63   issue-peas an issue-pea was 'a small globular body placed in a surgical issue' (*OED*); the latter was an incision made to discharge putrid matter from the body.

64   Shock compare *Rape of the Lock* I, 115 and Gay, *The Toilet* 9 (*Gay*, I, 181). 'Shough' was the name for a kind of lap-dog.

73–4 a good rhyme, because *poisoned* would be pronounced with the diphthong to rhyme with 'wise'.

STREPHON AND CHLOE

First appearance together with *A Beautiful Young Nymph Going to Bed* in Roberts's pamphlet (1734); then in *WF*, where the poem is headed 'written in the year 1731'. There is no means of checking this statement; some features might suggest the poem was written much earlier, perhaps at the time of *Cadenus and Vanessa*. Swift's failure to mention it in his list of poems sent to Pope as composed between 1727 and 1732 (*Corr* IV, 31) might conceivably strengthen the case for an earlier dating, but there is not enough evidence to overturn the traditional assignment. Text based on *WF*.

Discussions of the poem often occur in general estimates of the 'excremental' group: see *The Lady's Dressing Room*, headnote. For Delany's qualified defence of this item, see *CH*, pp. 136–7. Other readings will be found in Herbert Davis, *Jonathan Swift: Essays on His Satire* (1964), pp. 193–7; Denis Donoghue, *Jonathan Swift: A Critical Introduction* (1969), pp. 210–12; *Johnson*, pp. 110–13; *Jaffe*, pp. 109–17; *Lee*, pp. 86–90. Lee is one of a number of critics to detect connections with Swift's prose pamphlet, *A Letter to a Young Lady, on Her Marriage* (*PW* IX, 83–94).

8   Confessed proved her to be.

9   nice fastidious.

11-12 compare *The Lady's Dressing Room* 27-8, and also ll. 179-80 of this poem.

13 Jaffe, p. 110, notices a parallel construction in Donne's *Going to Bed* (*Elegy* 19) 25-6: 'Licence my roving hands, and let them go, / Before, behind, between, above, below.'

16 pluck a rose see *A Panegyric on the Dean* 216.

24 dog-days the hottest and most unwholesome period of the year, variously set in July and August.

28 Though cold . . . one of the innumerable parodies of *Cooper's Hill*: see *Apollo's Edict* 46-9.

33-8 stock amatory properties, as satirized in *The Rape of the Lock* I, 99-102; IV, 125, and *passim*. A *clouded cane* (l. 38) was one decorated with darker streaks: and *billet-doux* (l. 38) is a plural form.

48 Hymen god of marriage, represented as a youth carrying a torch and a veil.

49 the Cyprian goddess Venus.

50 loves Cupids.

56 Hebe compare *Directions for a Birthday Song* 172.

59 the Graces regularly enlisted by Swift in such contexts, e.g. *Cadenus and Vanessa* 158.

60 he wore military uniform.

61 flammeum 'a veil which the Roman brides covered themselves with, when they were going to be married' (note in *WF*); so called because it was originally flame-coloured.

62 epithalamium 'a marriage song at weddings' (note in *WF*). *Jaffe*, p. 110, sees the whole poem as 'a parodic epithalamium'.

65 Luna 'Diana, goddess of midwives' (note in *WF*); normally Lucina. Compare *Directions for a Birthday Song* 165.

70 crown their joys the italics indicate a cliché, used by Pope *inter alia* (*Odyssey* XVIII, 45).

85 dyed in grain thorough, complete (once common usage).

88 ambrosia the food, drink, or ointment of the gods; 'something divinely sweet' (*OED*).

93-4 Jaffe p. 111, says that Strephon cuts a figure 'as ridiculous as Aeneas does beribboned and perfumed for Dido'.

100 A certain goddess Thetis; see *Metamorphoses* XI, 221-65, describing the conception of Achilles.

107 Semele another episode in the *Metamorphoses* (III, 253-315), used elsewhere by Swift.

115 ponder well, ye parents dear italicized in the original, as though it were a quotation; but I cannot identify a source.

125 the sage of Samos 'a well known precept of Pythagoras, not to eat beans' (note in *WF*). (Pythagoras was born at Samos.) See Lucian, *True History* II, 24, for the precept, as well as *Tilley* B119.

128 blue pestilential vapours were described as 'blue'; *OED* suggests for this particular phrase (*burn it blue*), quoting Swift's line, 'act outrageously' but this seems unduly abstract. See also *Baucis and Philemon* 40.

133 Carminative 'medicines to break wind'; *diuretic* 'medicines to provide urine' (note in *WF*).

148 proverbial: *Tilley* F601.

158   maid in thought, and word, and deed   exactly the same expression occurs in *Polite Conversation* (*PW* IV, 136). (Ultimately from the Confession in the service of Holy Communion.)

164   leak   urinate: compare *Answer to the Ballyspellin Ballad* 78.

167   pease   the old singular form, from which 'pea' is a back-formation. Pease-pudding as conducive to belly-ache is mentioned in *Polite Conversation*, most impolitely (*PW* IV, 155).

168   colic   stomach-ache.

175–6   poetic diction appropriate to pastoral; compare *The Dunciad* (1729) II, 171–6.

181   'Vide Schol. Salern. *Rules of Health*, written by the school of Salernum. *Mingere cum bumbis res est saluberrima lumbis'* (note in *WF*). The Latin maxim is found in a verse treatise dating from the fifteenth century produced by the medical school at Salerno; Swift's library contained an edition of 1605 (*P* II, 589).

192   a rouser   *OED* glosses this 'a loud noise' but it seems to mean, rather, 'a real humdinger', 'a particularly strong jet'.

202   amaranthine   see *Cadenus and Vanessa* 155.

204   to call a spade, a spade   the cliché is mockingly exploited in *Polite Conversation* (*PW* IV, 196). Tilley S699.

216   selling bargains   see *Directions for a Birthday Song* 274.

219–26   I retain the capitals for these consciously rarified abstractions. *Opinion* (l. 224) means 'public opinion' and 'good opinion'.

228   birthday gear   fine clothes worn on a royal birthday.

230   cut and dry   compare *The Furniture of a Woman's Mind* 14.

238   house of ease   privy.

258   honeymoon   indicates the first month of bliss, rather than a holiday spent by the married couple (not then customary).

263   the politician's scheme   maxims of statecraft, as enunciated by Machiavelli.

265–6   Denis Donoghue, op. cit., p. 212, notes the echo of Marvell's *Horatian Ode* 119–20: 'The same arts that did gain / A power, must it maintain.' In fact the idea was a commonplace: it occurs in one of Sir William Temple's then unpublished early essays ('states being conserved by the same arts they are gained') and conceivably Swift encountered it there. The editor of these essays, G.C. Moore Smith, traces the notion to Sallust and Polybius. See *The Early Essays and Romances of Sir William Temple* (1930), pp. 175, 205.

275–6   one of Swift's 'Irish' rhymes.

287–92   puppet-show characters, as in *Mad Mullinix and Timothy* 81–122.
        Lorraine's Duke   the Pretender.
        Prince of Greece   Alexander the Great.

303–4   these lines may recall *Rape of the Lock* V, 25.

306   build on sand   proverbial: Tilley S88.

307–14   the same terms and emphases as those found in Swift's poems to Vanessa and Stella.

CASSINUS AND PETER

Published in the same Roberts pamphlet as the preceding two items. Then in *WF*, from which the text here is taken.

For discussion, see the general assessments listed in *The Lady's Dressing Room*, headnote. Additional comment may be found in Denis Donoghue, *Jonathan Swift: A Critical Introduction* (1969), pp. 212-14; *Lee*, pp. 85-6; *Jaffe*, pp. 107-9.

1 sophs sophomores, immature students.

1-4 C.T. Probyn, *Notes & Queries* XVIII (1971), 331, notes a parallel with *The Dunciad* (1729) II, 347-50, and also the revised version (1743) II, 379. The opening has a fabliau quality and the two central characters vaguely recall the two young Cambridge clerks in Chaucer's *Reeve's Tale*.

21 jordan chamber-pot.

29 doze stupefy.

34 Aurora goddess of dawn.

35 hyps see *The Grand Question Debated* 178.

38 dumps depression: see *Verses on the Death of Dr Swift* 227.

48 greater pox syphilis.

49 the eating away of the nose was the most commonly remarked consequence of venereal disease: see *The Progress of Beauty* 109-12.

59 dart arrow.

73 Arcadians rural dwellers, here fellow-devotees of poetry (a pastoral fancy).

80 Cerberian see *On Mr Pulteney being Put Out of the Council* 25.

81 Alecto one of the three Furies, who brought vengeance and pestilence: see *To a Lady* 189.

83 Charon the ferryman who conveyed the souls of the departed across the Styx.

85 Medusa one of the Gorgons, whose hair had been transformed into serpents, and whose face was so terrible that all who looked on it were turned to stone. See Ovid, *Metamorphoses* IV, 765-803.

88 a note in *WF* reads, '*Macbeth*': conflating Macbeth's two outbursts to Banquo's ghost at III, iv, 50, 93. The whole of this verse-paragraph (ll. 79-88) parodies the horrors of the underworld, as derived by any number of indifferent poets from *Aeneid*, book VI.

92 conjure here (and in l. 96) stressed on second syllable.

93 fact crime.

105-10 suggesting various classical episodes of secrets unknowingly betrayed, above all the story of the reeds which revealed the truth about Midas's ass-like ears (*Metamorphoses* XI, 172-93). For Echo, see ibid., III, 359-401.

112 Discover reveal.

TO MR GAY

The first hint we get of this poem is in a letter from Swift to Gay and the Duchess of Queensberry on 13 March 1731:

> Your situation is an odd one. The Duchess is your treasurer, and Mr Pope
> tells me you are the Duke's. And I had gone on a good way in some verses on
> that occasion, prescribing lessons to direct your conduct, in a negative way,
> not to do so and so &c like other treasurers; how to deal with servants, tenants
> and neighbouring squires, which I take to be courtiers, parliament and princes
> in alliance, and so the parallel goes on; but grew too long to please me.

I will copy some lines. [Lines 57–64 quoted.] Then I prove that poets are the fittest persons to be treasurers and managers to great persons, from their virtue and contempt of money &c. (*Corr* III, 443–4).

The letter from Pope containing news of Gay's supposed appointment has not been preserved, although it is referred to again in the heading supplied to the cancelled version in 1735 (see below, *Title*).

Gay had been staying with the Duke and Duchess of Queensberry at Amesbury for much of the time in the previous months, and there had been talk of Swift visiting him there (Gay, *Letters*, ed. C.F. Burgess (1966), pp. 91–111; W.H. Irving, *John Gay: Favorite of the Wits* (1940), pp. 279–85). However, the story which occasioned the poem proved to be false, as Gay told Swift on 18 July 1731: 'As to my being a manager for the Duke you have been misinformed. Upon the discharge of an unjust steward, he took the administration into his own hands. I own I was called in to assistance when the state of affairs was in the greatest confusion; like an ancient Roman I came, put my helping hand to set affairs right, and as soon as it was done, I am retired again as a private man' (*Corr* III, 477; for a slightly different text, see Gay, *Letters*, p. 112).

It did not matter that the rumour was false, for Swift converted his poem into a direct attack on the other 'manager', the first Lord of the Treasury, Walpole. He enlisted traditional items of opposition rhetoric to portray the chief minister as a false steward. He had evidently been reading the opposition journal, *The Craftsman*, whose inspiration was his friend Bolingbroke. Nowhere else is his language so close to that of the English critics of Walpole; little that is particularly Swiftian, or Irish, or even (in the narrowest sense) 'Tory' emerges. The familiar epistle is used with characteristic force, but the ideas are those of the opposition at large. The notion of the 'unjust steward' has obvious biblical overtones and Swift enlists these to superb effect. For apposite commentary, see Howard Erskine-Hill, *The Social Milieu of Alexander Pope* (1975), pp. 243–59.

The poem made its first appearance in print in *WF*. When this volume was revamped, *To Mr Gay* was reset almost throughout. Few changes of substance were made to the text (although dashes and blanks were introduced to make the satire less explicit); however, a number of the notes were severely cut and their more outspoken sentiments removed. The text here follows the uncancelled state of the volume, which was first printed in *PHD*.

The verses cited in the letter from Swift to Gay quoted above were apparently among the most laboriously worked out. Several shots at ll. 61–70 are contained in an autograph manuscript preserved in the John Rylands Library; two or three tries at most couplets in this passage survive. For a full description, see George P. Mayhew, 'A Draft of Ten Lines from Swift's Poem to John Gay', *Bulletin of the John Rylands Library* XXXVII (1954), 257–62. See also *P* II, 680.

Title   none is supplied in either the cancelled or uncancelled state of *WF*. Like previous editors, I borrow the title given in the contents-page. For the Duke and Duchess of Queensberry, see Biog. Dict.

The cancelled sheets contain a heading as follows: 'The author having been told by an intimate friend, that the Duke of Queensberry had employed Mr Gay to inspect the accounts and management of his Grace's receivers and stewards (which, however, proved afterwards to be a mistake) writ to Mr Gay the following poem.' The note was probably inserted to help make up the half-sheet cancelled; an epigram had been added as a makeweight, but the room taken up by notes now cancelled was still not entirely occupied by the text.

The cancelled text has 'written in the year 1731', one of the more accurate datings in *WF*.

1–2 P II, 531 makes a comparison with *A Libel on the Reverend Dr Delany* 53–60.

3 female friend 'Mrs Howard, now Countess of Suffolk' (note in *WF*). See Biog. Dict., 'Howard'.

4 Bob Walpole. This phrase provided an enduring label for the prime minister throughout the remainder of his career.

8 dry nurse 'he was offered to be gentleman-usher to a young Princess, then of that age, but made his excuses' (note in *WF*, uncancelled state). See *A Libel on the Reverend Dr Delany* 59; Irving, op. cit., p. 230. In 1727 Gay had been offered this post, in the service of the two-year-old Princess Louisa, at a salary of £150 per annum. His decision not to accept the post was reported in a letter on 22 October of that year (*Corr* III, 246).

12 go-cart a framework on castors used to teach an infant to walk safely.

13 Douglas 'the Duke of Queensberry, and his excellent Duchess; so renowned for her behaviour upon her banishment from court on her patronizing Mr Gay' (note in *WF*, uncancelled state: the cancelled state has only the first four words). The Duchess was forbidden to attend court because she attempted to solicit subscriptions for Gay's banned play *Polly* (a sequel to *The Beggar's Opera*) in 1729: see Irving, op. cit., p. 273.

18 sons of Phoebus poets.

23 Paean Apollo in the capacity of healer and physician.

24 the sun was believed to ripen metals as they lay in the ground.

26 appanage a natural adjunct, but punning on the sense of a grant or perquisite.

32 Statesman the term had become specially associated with Walpole. For the standard picture of a rapacious minister, put about by the opposition in graphic and literary satire, see Herbert M. Atherton, *Political Prints in the Age of Hogarth* (1974), pp. 191–208.

44 potent prince 'a title given to every duke by the heralds' (note in *WF*). Suggesting that Walpole serves not only George II but also Satan.

52 the King left blank in the cancelled state of *WF*.

54 servants, tenants . . . squires 'it is thought there is an allusion here, to ministers, to subjects in general, and to princes in alliance' (note in *WF*, uncancelled state). See Swift's letter of 13 March 1731, quoted in headnote.

58 your kindred Walpole might perhaps be accused of nepotism because of the employments of his brother Horatio, the diplomat, and of his elder son, who held sinecures at this time; and, of course, his brother-in-law Townshend had for many years shared power with him. But it is not a very black record by the standards of the age. The opposition press liked to pretend that things were very much worse than they were: thus, the *York Courant* this very summer (1 June 1731) reported a story that 'Peter leHeup, Esq., who is Sir Robert Walpole's brother's wife's sister's husband's brother, will be made a Master in Chancery' (quoted by G.A. Cranfield, *The Development of the Provincial Newspaper 1700–60* (1962), p. 127). This story obviously derived from the London press but I cannot trace its origin. It is likely that Swift was thinking chiefly of Horatio Walpole.

60   by telling noses 'this seems to allude to the arts of procuring a majority' (note in *WF*, uncancelled state). Counting heads, we might say. See *OED*, 'nose', 6 d.

61–70]   successive drafts in John Rylands MS ending as follows:

> to supply
> Some urgent pressing want with present sum,
> With treble interest and premium
> Be rich but of your wealth make no parade
> At least before your masters debts are paid
> Nor in a palace built with charge immense
> Regale your master at his own expense.
> Each farmer in the neighbourhood can count
> To what your lawful perquisites amount
> The tenants poor, the hardness of the times
> Are stale excuses to conceal your crimes.

(Spelling normalized and contractions expanded.)

62   your master's debts 'the author seems to mean the nation's debts' (note in *WF*, uncancelled state). The foundation of the Sinking Fund after the South Sea Bubble was regarded by many of Walpole's critics as a retrograde step, encumbering the nation with an endless obligation.

63   a palace Houghton Hall, in Norfolk, rebuilt between 1722 and 1730 at enormous expense. For satirical treatment, see Atherton, op. cit., p. 125; M. Mack, *The Garden and the City* (1969), pp. 122–3, 207–9.

64   to treat him referring to the lavish house-parties known as 'the Norfolk congress'; ballads on this theme are quoted by *Plumb*, pp. 88–90. It is also likely that the vulgar ostentation of Timon's villa, in Pope's *Epistle to Burlington* 99–168, parodies hospitality dispensed at Houghton: this poem appeared in December 1731. See Mack, op. cit., pp. 272–8.

67–8   see Erskine-Hill, op. cit., pp. 122–4.

71–6   as well as unscrupulous attornies like Peter Walter (see l. 101), the portrayal here suggests the parable of the unjust steward in Luke xvi, 1–13.

73   the unrighteous Mammon   Luke xvi, 11.

81   the state empiric   political quack, another common line of attack.

86   neighbouring friend 'meaning, I suppose, some foreign prince' (note in *WF*, uncancelled state).

89   some imperious neighbour   the recurrent charge that Spain was being allowed to inflict severe damage on British commercial shipping, without any reprisal from Britain; 'perhaps a hint of injuries and affronts received at sea, &c' (note in *WF*, uncancelled state). See *Directions for a Birthday Song* 249.

91   entrench   encroach.

97–8   'these lines are thought to allude to some story concerning a great quantity of mahogany, declared rotten, and then applied by somebody to wainscots, stairs, door-cases, &c.' (note in *WF*). Evidently referring to Houghton, where for the doors and door-cases 'Walpole decided to use mahogany and he used it with a richness and profusion that was unusual in English houses of his day' (*Plumb*, pp. 83–4). I do not know the source of the charge here.

101   Peter Waters 'He hath practised this trade for many years, and still continues it with success; and after he hath ruined one lord, is earnestly solicited to take another' (note in *WF*). For Peter Walter, see Biog. Dict. Noting the identification here of Walpole and Walter, Mack (op. cit., p. 183) writes, 'Swift's and Pope's animus against Walter was probably impersonal. Walter represented a class of men who had long been regarded by the landed class as their natural enemies . . . Walpole, though a country squire, was rightly felt by the opposition to be in sympathy with . . . the moneyed interests represented by Walter and his kind.' For a similar comparison of Walpole and Walter, as sinking others further into debt, see *PW* V, 117. It is almost certain that Swift had no first-hand experience of Walter in action. He referred to the agent in a letter of 1727: 'I believe I shall lose two or three pounds rather than plague myself with accounts; so that I am very well qualified to be a lord, and put into Peter Walter's hands' (*Corr* III, 243). But this was already stock opposition diction. By 1728, too, Walpole had been satirized as 'the Norfolk steward', defrauding 'Sir George English'; on a later occasion he was depicted as the steward to 'Lady Brit' (see Atherton, op. cit., p. 196). An outstanding study of Walter as an individual and as a representative of his class, relevant to the whole of Swift's poem *To Mr Gay*, will be found in Erskine-Hill, op. cit., pp. 103–31. It should be added that Walter was the personal financier to one of Walpole's closest henchmen, the Duke of Newcastle: see Ray A. Kelch, *Newcastle: A Duke without Money* (1974), pp. 28–92.

107 dexterous cunning, adroit (a more pejorative word then than it is today); it was an epithet often applied to both Walter (Erskine-Hill, op. cit., p. 103) and Jonathan Wild.

108 Hush-money 'a cant word' (note in *WF*). The first instance cited in *OED* is by Steele in 1709.

115–16] *WF* (*uncancelled state*); Thus families, like realms, with equal fate, / May sink by premier ministers of state *WF* (*cancelled state*).

118 Peter Walter, for example, served both Lord Paget and his son, later Earl of Uxbridge: see Erskine-Hill, op. cit., pp. 103–26.

122 ways and means the parliamentary phrase for financial supply.

136 bought and sold tricked (see *Tilley* B787).

143 a brazen minister Walpole, now widely known as Sir Robert Brass or Brazen-Face; Pulteney had even alluded to the nickname in a parliamentary debate during 1730.

148 old Master George I.

152 Sir Spencer Compton: see Biog. Dict. The reference is to events in 1727 on the accession of George II.

ON MR PULTENEY BEING PUT OUT OF THE COUNCIL

First published in *WF*, where it is headed 'written in the year 1731'; subsequently included in the London series of *Misc*, but the text in *WF* is the most authoritative and it is used here.

On 1 July 1731 William Pulteney, the acknowledged leader of the opposition to Walpole in parliament, was dismissed from the English Privy Council. This followed a duel some months earlier with Lord Hervey and a prolonged war of words in the press. See Robert Halsband, *Lord Hervey* (1973), pp. 113–20. Another literary treatment of these events was Fielding's *Welsh Opera*, revised as the *Grub Street Opera* but forbidden performance that summer (Pulteney appears as Will the coachman, Hervey as John the groom, and Walpole as Robin the butler). The course of opposition to Walpole at this juncture is described in *Plumb*, pp. 200–232.

For Pulteney, see Biog. Dict. He had been effectively leagued against Walpole since 1725: see *Plumb*, pp. 122–4. Swift and he began to correspond in 1726 (*Corr* III, 162) and thereafter they remained on excellent terms. Swift discussed the circumstances of Pulteney's dismissal in a letter to Gay on 28 August 1731 (*Corr* III, 494–5); it is likely that the poem was written about this date.

2 leasings lies.

6 suburb wench the same phrase occurs in *On Poetry: a Rhapsody* 166. For the implications see *To Stella, Who Collected and Transcribed His Poems* 72.

7 St Stephen's Chapel the House of Commons; Pulteney owned the pocket borough of Hedon in Yorkshire and could not be dislodged from a seat in parliament.

10 ducal patent I cannot supply any justification for this line. Pulteney derived his money and parliamentary interest from a former Secretary to the Treasury; there was certainly no dukedom in the family, and the peerage he ultimately took (the Earldom of Bath) was a totally fresh creation.

14 because Pulteney had got into trouble chiefly because of his activities as a pamphleteer; his parliamentary oratory, though damaging to Walpole, was protected by the privileges of the House.

15 an old fable but really an invention of Swift's?

17 who long had 'scaped] *WF*; had long escaped *Misc* (1735).

19 But] *WF*; Till *Misc* (1735).

23 scours runs.

25 Cerberus the three-headed dog who guarded the entrance to the infernal regions.

30 Fear...wings proverbial: *Tilley* F133.

33 Sirius the dog star.

36 scut tail.

41 thy bulk Walpole was twenty stones or more in weight, and caricaturists always presented him as ponderous and vast.

42 before you die implying 'although you will certainly go there when you do die'.

THE CHARACTER OF SIR ROBERT WALPOLE

The poem seems to have been sent with a letter from Swift to Lady Suffolk on 26 October 1731 (*Corr* III, 499–502), although the poem is not in Swift's hand (British Library, Add. MS 22625). There are other contemporary transcripts; one, among the Portland papers, heads the verses 'A translation of a French lampoon on Cardinal Fleury'. The first known publication occurred in a volume called *Robin's Panegyric, or the Norfolk Miscellany*, vol. 3 (1733); for this discovery, see Peter J. Schakel, *Papers of the Bibliographical Society of America* LXX (1976), 111–14. The poem was reprinted, with the French original, in an undated edition and then in a supplement to Sheridan's edition issued by a London publisher in 1789. It was first collected in *P* II, 539–40. Text here from the British Library copy accompanying Swift's letter.

The French lampoon, attacking the chief minister Cardinal André-Hercule de Fleury (1653–1743), is as follows:

> Confondant du passé le leger souvenir,
> Ebloüi du present, sans percer l'avenir;
> Dans l'art de gouverner decrepit, & novice,
> Punissant la vertu, recompensant le vice.
> Malgré sa tête altiere accablé de son rang,
> Fourbe dans le petit, & dupe dans le grand.
> On connoit à ces traits, même sans qu'on le nomme,
> Le maître de la France, & le valet de Rome.

1   fastidiously   proudly; scornfully.

8   his peace]   *British Library transcript*; a peace   *Portland transcript*; his place 1789. It is possible that the reference is to the Peace of Seville, arranged by Walpole without Townshend's approval in 1729.

14   spaniel of Spain   again suggesting Walpole's unduly pacific policy towards Spain, as the opposition saw it: see *Directions for a Birthday Song* 249.

TO DR HELSHAM

First published in *F* (1746), together with the succeeding items. For Helsham's reply, see *'Can You Match with Me'*, headnote. Helsham was to become Regius Professor of Physic at Trinity College in 1733; he was Swift's personal doctor at this time. The multiple rhyming is a variation of the 'crambo' game. Text based on *F*. For a query about the dating, see note to l. 16.

4   purge-sick . . . spew-sick   the former would involve evacuating the bowels, the latter, vomiting.

7   Captain Butler   'The reference may be to Robert Butler, who succeeded his brother Humphry, the second Viscount Lanesborough, as Captain of the Battle-Axe Guards, in December 1726' (*P* III, 1029). This is plausible, since the family was well known to Swift; the first Viscount was a college contemporary of his at Trinity. Both 'Hon. Robert Butler' and 'Hon. Capt. Humphry Butler' subscribed to Faulkner's edition of Pope's Shakespeare in 1726; Swift seems to have taken a mild interest in promoting this venture. See Biog. Dict.

8   Dean Cross   William Cross, Dean of Leighlin: see *On Dr Rundle* 61.

10   Lady Santry   Bridget Domville (a cousin of Swift's friend William Domville), who in 1702 married the third Baron Santry. See *JTS* I, 268.

the church   'St Patrick's Cathedral, where the music on St Cecilia's Day was usually performed' (note in *F*): see *The Dean to Himself on St Cecilia's Day*.

12   Miss Morice   *P* III, 1029 suggests this may be a daughter of Sir Nicholas Morice (whose wife was herself the daughter of the Earl of Pembroke, a former Lord Lieutenant known to Swift). But there are other candidates: no certain identification seems possible. See also *Corr* IV, 12.

14   fanatic   dissenter.

15   ombre   see *Cadenus and Vanessa* 431.

loo   a round card game, mentioned also in *The Rape of the Lock* III, 62.

16   Nanny Shales   *'vide* Grattan, *inter* Belchamp *et* Clonshogh' (note in *F*). Belcamp was the home of the Grattans, on an estate known as Cushogue in Irish, just north of Dublin: see *To Charles Ford, Esq. on His Birthday* 89. This connection is one of a number which make one suspect that the date '1731' in *F* may conceivably be a mistake for 1721.

25 stuck together like glue proverbial.

28 Robin probably not Robert Leslie (as *P* III, 1030) but Rev. Robert Grattan: see Biog. Dict.

TO DR SHERIDAN

An obvious tailpiece to the preceding item, which is dated 'November 23, at night'. Published in *F* (1746) along with *To Dr Helsham* and *A Riddling Letter*.

2 dew sweat.

3 a-gue the normal pronunciation.

4 a shrew see *A Portrait from the Life*, headnote.

'CAN YOU MATCH WITH ME'

Swift's riddling letter *To Dr Helsham* elicited an immediate answer from the recipient, incorporating twenty rhymes on the 'juice-sick' model. Swift replied on the same Tuesday evening, 23 November, with these six lines and a covering note, first published by *F* (1767) and then by Nichols in 1775. Helsham promptly wrote another fourteen, as indicated (see *P* III, 1032).

2 thirty-three the combined total of *To Dr Helsham* and *To Dr Sheridan*.

A RIDDLING LETTER

Published in *F* (1746), as addressed to Dr Sheridan. Reprinted by Hawkesworth in 1755, and there addressed to Dr Helsham, with an additional note: 'Wednesday night. / I writ all these before I went to bed. Pray explain them for me, because I cannot do it.' *P* suggests the date of composition 'may be about 1731', no doubt because *F* prints it along with the immediately preceding items (starting with *To Dr Helsham*). If the poems are linked, then Wednesday night might indicate 24 November 1731. Text based on *F* (1746).

The answer to each riddle begins with 'ass'; that is, the 'dullest beast'.

Title the editor's.

discruciate puzzle out, find out the crux: listed as a nonce use by *OED*.

2 a swine (ass, wine). A tithe-pig, a form of payment in kind to the incumbent.

4 a swallow (ass, wallow).

7 a stallion (ass, tall, lion).

9 a sail (ass, ail).

11 a spaniel (ass, panel). The 'panel' was the pad or stuffed lining in a saddle.

13 a spur (ass, purr).

15 a soul (ass, owl). *OED* quotes Tom Brown (1704), 'Be mee shoul, and bee Chreest and St Patrick', stage-Irish speech.

17 a sloven (ass, Louvain). Louvain, in Flanders, was an ancient university where Irish Catholics often studied. For Irish studies in Continental universities, see Edith M. Johnston, *Ireland in the Eighteenth Century* (1974), pp. 22–5.

20 a salad (ass, awl, lad).

22 a slip (ass, lip).

24 a sparrow (asp, arrow).

26 a saddle (ass, addle).

28 a style (ass, tile). See *Tilley* L472 for 'not worth a louse'.

30 a slice (ass, lice).

32 a spy (ass, pie).

34 a spavin (ass, paving). A spavin is a tumour on a horse's leg, caused by inflamed cartilage.

36 a spit (ass, pit).

38 a skewer (ass, cure).

40 assault (ass, salt). Salt or cured herrings were the traditional Lenten diet.

42 a smock (ass, mock).

PROBATUR ALITER

A sequence of riddles closely parallel to the preceding item: but the repetition of certain words (ll. 10, 16, 20, 22, 26, 36, 40, 42, 44, 46) may suggest that an interval passed between the composition of this and the riddling letter. First published in *F* (1746), the source of the text here. The answer to each riddle begins with 'ass' once more.

2 a shovel (ass, hovel).

6 aspiring (ass, pie, ring). Magpies were proverbial for their chattering: *Tilley* P285.

8 a switch (ass, witch). Compare *Mad Mullinix and Timothy* 90.

10 a skewer (ass, cure).

12 a sparable (ass, parable). A sparable was 'a small headless wedge-shaped iron nail . . ., used in the soles and heels of boots and shoes' (*OED*).

14 a shock (ass, hock). A small dog: see *A Beautiful Young Nymph Going to Bed* 64.

16 a sloven (ass, Louvain). See *A Riddling Letter* 17. For Rev. William Tisdall, see Biog. Dict.

18 asperse (ass, Pearce). Sir Edward Pearce, architect of the new Parliament House: see *A Character, Panegyric, and Description of the Legion Club* 2.

20 a soul (ass, owl).

22 a slice (ass, lice).

24 a scar (ass, car).

26 a swallow (ass, wallow).

28 a sty (ass, Tighe). For Richard Tighe, see Biog. Dict.

30 a sink (ass, ink).

32 a slam (ass, lamb). A slam is the winning of all the tricks in whist; the term is a forerunner of 'grand slam' in bridge.

34 a slate (ass, late).

36 a swine (ass, wine).

38 askew (ass, Q). Q is the seventeenth letter in the modern alphabet, but Swift is thinking of I and J as a single letter. Their usage had not yet properly separated: 'in Dictionaries the I and J words continue to be intermingled in one series down to the 19th century' (*OED*).

40 a saddle (ass, addle).

42 a smock (ass, mock).

44 a spur (ass, purr).

46 assault (ass, salt).
48 a snail (ass, nail).

THE PLACE OF THE DAMNED

First issued as a broadside, [Dublin?] 1731, probably around November: there assigned to 'J.S. D.D. D.S.P.D.' Reprinted in the London newspaper, *Fog's Weekly Journal*, on 4 December. It was further included in a motley collection of Swiftian items (some genuine, some not) published by James Roberts two or three days later than the appearance in *Fog's*. See *T* 711, 37, 37A; *Foxon* S897. The poem then went into *WF*, which is the basis of the text here. There is also a contemporary transcript in the British Library.

Swift acknowledged the item as his own in a letter to Pope dated 12 June 1732 (*Corr* IV, 31). He stated that the copy was 'stolen'; there may or may not be genteel equivocation in this expression.

Title *WF* adds, 'written in the year 1731'.
1 religion and grace both nouns are italicized in *WF*, along with a high proportion of key words throughout the poem. This was essentially the style of broadside printing; in a few cases *WF* reproduces this typographic trick, even where the text itself has been cleaned up – presumably because Faulkner was working from a marked-up copy of the original printing. I therefore ignore the italics, which are quite out of line with the practice of *WF* elsewhere.
4 I will] *WF*; I'll *F* (*1737*), *corrected by Swift in his copy*.
15 flammed 'deceived by a sham story' (*OED*).

HELTER SKELTER

A very dubious attribution. It is accepted by *Ball*, p. 278; see also *T* 712 and *P* II, 572-3. The first known appearance was in a broadside, advertised in the press on 7 December 1731. It went into a miscellaneous volume published by Roberts about the same date (*T* 37); but such inclusions are not always reliable. It is true that Roberts published several items which reached the printer Bowyer through Matthew Pilkington; but that did not stop him issuing spurious items as Swift's. He was, besides, a distributor rather than a bookseller working closely together with authors. It is also noteworthy that Swift did not mention the poem in his letter to Pope specifying recent compositions (*Corr* IV, 31). Finally, it is significant that Harvard Library possesses a copy with a MS endorsement attributing the work to John Dunkin of Trinity College, Dublin. See *Foxon* H139, where the item is dated ?1726/7. However, since 1775 *Helter Skelter* has regularly been included in collections of Swift's poetry, and I cannot decisively overturn the attribution. See *Jaffe*, pp. 31-3, for a consideration of rhythmic effects.

Text based on the broadside.

Title in normal usage an attorney was not a barrister but a kind of early (and inferior) solicitor; this is probably the group meant here.
6 tilters a cant word for swords or rapiers.
20 Cambric fine white linen, originally from Cambrai.
21 holland linen.

23   letters   that is, monograms (then an aristocratic preserve).

28   lim   short form of limbo, slang for a pawnshop.

33   cutler   a tradesman who sold and repaired knives.

34   sutler   one who supplied provisions to army garrisons.

39−42   thorough   old form of 'through'.

55   vacation's over   the assize circuit was held whilst the courts at Dublin were in their vacation.

THE LIFE AND GENUINE CHARACTER OF DR SWIFT

The history of this poem is closely bound up with *Verses on the Death of Dr Swift*, where fuller details will be found. It was first published under the imprint of James Roberts around 20 April 1733 (though privileged acquaintances seem to have received copies a week earlier). This is *T* 727, *Foxon* S884. *T* 728 records an octavo as well as Roberts's folio. There were Dublin editions by Edward Waters and [?Faulkner]: see *T* 729, *Foxon* S885−6. It appeared in *F* (1746) as well as the longer set of *Verses*.

The poem was offered to the London trade through Matthew Pilkington. He seems to have applied first to Benjamin Motte, who later wrote to Swift:

> Soon after Mr Pilkington had received the twenty guineas you ordered me to pay him [in January 1733], the Life and Character was offered me, though not by his own hands, yet by his means, as I was afterward convinced by many circumstances: one was, that he corrected the proof sheets with his own hand; and as he said he had seen the original of that piece, I could not imagine he would have suffered your name to be put to it, if it had not been genuine. When I found by your advertisement, and the letter you were pleased to write to me, that I had been deceived by him, I acted afterwards with more reserve. (*Corr* IV, 371)

The reference is to a disclaimer Swift inserted in the *Dublin Journal* on 15 May 1733. In private letters he similarly told Lord Carteret (23 April), Pope (1 May), and the Earl of Oxford (31 May) that the *Life and Character* was spurious, though he admitted having written a longer poem on the subject, that is, the *Verses* (*Corr* IV, 149−50, 151−2, 161). Pope's reply on 1 September (*Corr* IV, 194) has been taken to imply some scepticism with regard to these claims. Another well-placed observer was Mrs Pilkington, who told Swift to his face that the *Life and Character* was an unsuccessful attempt at disguised self-parody (*Memoirs*, ed. Iris Barry (1928), pp. 87−8).

However, many later commentators accepted the disclaimers and assumed that Pilkington had himself produced a garbled text, either by taking a surreptitious copy of the *Verses* and adulterating them, or else by practising the kind of memorial reconstruction once envisaged by Shakespearian bibliographers. An alternative theory is that Pope was responsible for the *Life and Character*, as well as for the abbreviated *Verses*. *Foxon*, I, 770 asserts, 'If it be spurious, a good case could be made out for Pope's authorship.' The publishing history is certainly mysterious, but in the text of the *Life and Character* I can detect no sign of Pope's hand. For the view that Pope may have been involved in the publication of the poem, see *P* II, 542. It is, however, noteworthy that the item is not included in the checklist of work by 'Pope's printer', John Wright, compiled by J. McLaverty (Oxford Bibliographical Society, 1977).

Among those to accept Swift's authorship are Herbert Davis, 'Verses on the Death of Dr Swift', *The Book-Collector's Quarterly* II (1931), 57–73; *P* II, 541–3; *PJH* II, 795–6. See also *Ball*, pp. 268–9. Davis's theory is that Swift was directing his April Fool's Day joke against Pope, in retaliation for the editorial methods his friend had adopted in preparing *Misc* (1732) for the press. Horrell (*PJH* II, 795) suggests that the *Life and Character* is an earlier draft, 'preliminary work superseded by the longer *Verses*'. In my view, it is not possible to fix the matter of priority. The two poems may represent separate attempts at the one theme, and although Swift justifiably felt the *Verses* to be superior, there is no real evidence that they are a revised text in any way. It seems certain that the *Verses* were substantially complete at the end of 1731; the *Life and Character* may or may not have preceded them. I follow custom (going back to *F*'s 1746 edition), rather than settled conviction, in printing the poems in this order.

Most discussion of the poem occurs in the context of work on the subject of the *Verses*. For efforts to separate the two items, see Ronald Paulson, *The Fictions of Satire* (1967), pp. 190–94; and Arthur H. Scouten, Robert D. Hume, 'Pope and Swift: Text and Interpretation of Swift's Verses on his Death', *Philological Quarterly* LII (1973), 211–15.

The text here is based on Roberts's folio of 1733. However, I have not reproduced all the typographic oddities of the original. In *F* (1746) a headnote was added, mentioning the use of 'breaks, dashes and triplets (which the author never made use of) to disguise his manner of writing' (reproduced in *PJH* II, 711). The 'breaks' seem to mean rapid paragraphing divisions, and they survive, as do the elaborately contrived triplets. But I have not felt it appropriate to retain the dashes, which have outlived their original purpose of deception. They are often combined with other punctuation marks (commas, semi-colons, question marks, exclamation marks, and so on), and they serve to distract a modern reader. There are, in fact, fifty such dashes in Roberts's text, few of which make much sense according to present usage. I have likewise severely cut down on the use of italics; there are over 300 words italicized in the 1733 edition in 202 lines. The modes of emphasis thus attained are not recapturable today simply by following the identical typographic conventions.

Dedication 'L.M.' is generally felt to be a pseudonym for Pilkington; 'Little Matthew' or (combining his name with that of his wife) 'Laetitia Matthew' have been suggested. Swift's fondness for April Fool's Day jokes went back at least as far as 1708: see *An Elegy on Partridge*, headnote. The 'publisher' means Pilkington, not Roberts.

1 Wise Rochefoucauld it was maxim no. xcix in the first edition of the *Réflexions ou Sentences et Maximes Morales* (1665) by the Duc François de la Rochefoucauld (1613–80). In later editions it was suppressed. For a more literal version, see *Verses on the Death of Dr Swift*.

10 laughing in our sleeve see *The Dean to Thomas Sheridan* 36 for this proverbial expression.

18 nicked cheated.

22 balk disappointment.

27 piquet ordinary stress and pronunciation: see *To Stella, Visiting Me in My Sickness* 28.

42 keep touch feel genuine sympathy for one another.

50 rout clamour, noise.

55 bore the bell took first place. *Tilley* B275.

65   hatband, scarf, and gloves   worn as a sign of mourning, usually made of dark crape.

78-9   the 'late' Irish rhyme Swift came to favour.

90   a lucky hit   see *The Fable of Midas* 23.

108   Sir Robert   Walpole.

115   elves   see *A Panegyric on the Reverend Dean Swift* 12, note.

130   scope   end in view.

151   Scarlet Whore   Church of Rome: from Revelation xvii, 3-18.

152   fanatic   dissenting. The *Tale* dramatizes this contrast.

156   fanatic crew   compare *The Yahoo's Overthrow* 21.

162   the good old cause   puritanism or extreme Protestantism.

167   the royal martyr   Charles I.

175   Socinian   deist; one who denies the divinity of Christ.

176   clinker   clinching word, question-begging expression.

184   the worst of times   at the time of the Harley ministry or, perhaps, the Jacobite rebellion.

185   Oxford   that is, Robert Harley, the first Earl: see Biog. Dict. His son, the second Earl, obtained a pre-publication copy of this poem, now in the Bodleian Library.

190   part the third   Gulliver's Travels originally appeared in two volumes, although they were commonly bound together.

191   A lie   perhaps recalling the Irish bishop who said that *Gulliver's Travels* 'was full of improbable lies' (Swift to Pope, 27 November 1726, *Corr* III, 189).

VERSES ON THE DEATH OF DR SWIFT, D.S.P.D.

There are broadly speaking four versions of Swift's lines deriving from La Rochefoucauld:

(1) *The Life and Genuine Character of Dr Swift*, first published in 1733.

(2) The *Verses on the Death of Dr Swift* as edited by William King and Pope, first published by Charles Bathurst in 1739.

(3) The *Verses* then issued by Faulkner to supply a corrected text (Dublin, 1739).

(4) An amalgamated version of (2) and (3) which began to appear in 1756 or earlier; until the 1930s this remained the standard text, reprinted in all editions between Scott and Williams.

Version (1) is separately printed here, and its appearance is described in the headnote. It consists of 202 lines. Version (2) runs to 381 lines; of these 319 were extracted from the full text, as represented by (3), whilst 62 were taken over from (1). Version (3), amounting to 484 lines, is now universally regarded as the most authentic; it forms the basis for *F*'s later editions, and for recent collections (*P*, *PJH*, *PHD*). Version (4) conflates in a haphazard way (3) with portions of (2). It has no authority and can be disregarded for practical purposes.

Version (2) has some independent interest, and this so-called Bathurst edition repays attention particularly as an example of Pope's editorial hand (see A.H. Scouten, R.D. Hume, 'Pope and Swift: Text and Interpretation of Swift's Verses on His Death', *Philological Quarterly* LII (1973), 215-18). Considerations of space dictate its omission here. Version (3) is unquestionably closer to Swift's own intentions.

Swift gave the 484-line version in manuscript to William King, Principal of St Mary Hall, Oxford, about 1738. King took the advice of various persons, notably Pope, and sent a radically revised text to Bathurst for publication on 19 January 1739. King was aware of the magnitude of his alterations, and wrote defensively to Swift about it on 5 January (*Corr* V, 133). His anxiety was further displayed in a letter of 23 January and one of 30 January to Mrs Martha Whiteway, where he attempts to offload the blame anticipated; he consented to the changes 'in deference to Mr Pope's judgement, and the opinion of others of the Dean's friends in this country' (*Corr* V, 135–7). No reply of Swift to King survives, but he was certainly extremely angry with the depredations performed upon his poem. Accordingly he quickly arranged for Faulkner to bring out the fuller text, which was done probably in February. On 6 March, King was writing to Mrs Whiteway of the Dublin edition, which had already reached him:

I do not remember anything published in my time that hath been so universally well received as the Dean's last poem. Two editions [by Bathurst in London] have been already sold off, though two thousand were printed at first. In short, all people read it, all agree to commend it; and I have been well assured, the greatest pleasure in observing the success and general approbation which this poem hath met with; wherefore I was not a little mortified yesterday, when the bookseller brought me the Dublin edition, and at the same time put into my hands a letter he had received from Faulkner [now lost], by which I perceive the Dean is much dissatisfied with our manner of publication, and that so many lines have been omitted, if Faulkner speaks truth, and knows as much of the Dean's mind as he pretends to know. Faulkner hath sent over several other copies to other booksellers; so that I take it for granted this poem will soon be reprinted here from the Dublin edition, and then it may be perceived how much the Dean's friends have been mistaken in their judgement, however good their intentions may have been. (*Corr* V, 139)

We have no more direct evidence of Swift's feelings. The 'Publisher's Advertisement' prefixed to the Dublin edition is studiously moderate in tone.

Both the Bathurst and the Faulkner versions went through a number of printings, not all easily distinguishable owing to the muddling of sheets from one so-called 'edition' with those of another. See *T* 771, 1600–1603 (Bathurst), *T* 774 (Faulkner); *Foxon* S920–24 (Bathurst), S926–31 (Faulkner). There were also piracies and Edinburgh printings which do not bear on the same story, and have, of course, no textual authority.

Faulkner's printing of the 484-line poem contained a number of blanks, still present when the poem went into *F* (1746), Vol. VIII. Fortunately there are a number of annotated copies surviving of one or other of these editions, which enable us to fill in the gaps. Williams, for his notable reconstruction of the *Verses* (*P* II, 551–72), used two personal copies, now at Cambridge University Library, as well as a copy of Bathurst's second edition (*Foxon* S922) at *HEH*. In addition *PJH* makes use of a first edition of Faulkner's 1739 printing, preserved at the University of Texas. There are other copies with manuscript additions at Harvard, the Newberry Library, and in *FV* (Forster's own notes). Here the text is based on Faulkner's 1739 edition, with gaps normally filled out from *FV* and Cambridge copies. Lines 341–4 are adopted from *FV*; other annotated copies supply them also, and (with one minor variant) so does Mrs Pilkington (*Memoirs*, ed. Iris Barry (1928), p. 68).

Bibliographical discussions concerning the various editions include Herbert Davis, *The Book-Collector's Quarterly* II (1931), 57–73; H. Teerink, *Studies in Bibliography* IV (1951), 183–8; A.H. Scouten, ibid., XC (1962), 243–7. Scouten shows that the alleged '1736' edition (*T* 1605) is in fact a later piracy, set up from one of the Bathurst editions.

Swift's most famous single poem has been the subject of a very wide range of comment. Most early accounts imply a somewhat simple-minded reading of the poem as straight autobiography (but see *CH*, pp. 16–17, 269–70). Twentieth-century discussions have thrown up a number of competing theories regarding the tone of the work, notably that of the concluding apologia (ll. 306–488). It was this passage which Pope transformed for the Bathurst text, breaking down the long speech into an exchange in verse which drew much of its substance from the *Life and Character*. The differing views are set out by Scouten and Hume, *Philological Quarterly* LII (1973), 205–31. The more important discussions include Barry Slepian, 'The Ironic Intention of Swift's Verses on His Own Death', *Review of English Studies* XIV (1963), 249–56, which proposes the view that the apologia is to be taken ironically; Marshall Waingrow, *Studies in English Literature 1500–1900* V (1965), 513–18, offering a 'straight' reading; J.I. Fischer, 'How to Die: *Verses on the Death of Dr Swift*', *Review of English Studies* XXI (1970), 422–41, seeing the poem as instructive, Christian and indeed homiletic. (A revised version of this article is found in *Fischer*, pp. 152–76.) See also Ronald Paulson, *The Fictions of Satire* (1967), pp. 189–99, which concentrates on the author's rôle as eulogist, hero, and satirist all at once. *Johnson*, pp. 59–66, stresses a degree of impersonality in the poem: 'though he is ostensibly talking about himself, Swift has a good deal to say about friendship, envy and human relationships in general'; whilst *Jaffe*, pp. 15–19, invokes 'a spirit of play between the author and reader' which enables Swift to use his own case to make a general moral point regarding self-knowledge. The *Verses* are also considered by D.W. Jefferson, 'The Poetry of Age', *Focus: Swift*, ed. C.J. Rawson (1971), pp. 132–4; David Ward, *Jonathan Swift: An Introductory Essay* (1973), pp. 200–204; Clive T. Probyn, 'Realism and Raillery: Augustan Conversation and the Poetry of Swift', *Durham University Journal* LXX (1977), 12–14; P.J. Schakel, 'The Politics of Opposition in *Verses on the Death of Dr Swift*', *Modern Language Quarterly* XXXV (1974), 246–56; Robert W. Uphaus, 'Swift's "Whole Character": The Delany Poems and *Verses on the Death of Dr Swift*', *Modern Language Quarterly* XXXIV (1973), 406–16; Edward W. Said, 'Swift's Tory Anarchy', *Eighteenth-Century Studies* III (1969), 48–66. David M. Vieth, 'The Mystery of Personal Identity', in *The Author and His Work*, ed. L.L. Martz and A. Williams (1978), pp. 245–62, manages to find no fewer than four Swifts secreted in the *Verses*.

Composition is generally assigned to 1731. Early editions have 'written by himself, November 1731': on 1 December of that year Swift wrote to Gay, 'I have been several months writing near five hundred lines on a pleasant subject, only to tell what my friends and enemies will say on me after I am dead. I shall finish it soon, for I add two lines every week, and blot out four, and alter eight. I have brought in you and my other friends, as well as enemies and detractors' (*Corr* III, 506). He must also have told Pope of the work in progress, for on the identical date the latter was commending his 'design upon Rochefoucauld's maxim' (*Corr* III, 510). The note to l. 383 mentions 'this present third day of May, 1732', which may indicate further revision or perhaps simply the date at which notes were appended. The text at l. 189 evidently presumes Charteris to be still alive; the note states, 'he is since dead, but this poem still preserves the scene and time it was writ in.' Charteris died in February 1732. It is also plain that the poem was written during the lifetime of Gay, who died on 4 December 1732. In fact a large number of the 'actors' within the poem were dead before the work appeared in print: amongst them, Arbuthnot (d. 1735), Queen Caroline (d. 1737), James Moore Smythe (d. 1734), and Thomas Woolston (d. 1733). The next explicit reference in Swift's correspondence comes in a letter to Pope of 1 May 1733, denying authorship of the *Life and Character* (see headnote to that poem). He remarks, 'I believe I have told you, that I writ a year or two ago near five hundred lines upon the same maxim in Rochefoucauld, and was a long time about it' (*Corr* IV, 151). He adds that the *Verses* (which is undoubtedly what the 'near five hundred lines' are) will remain unpublished, as 'not proper to be seen till I can be seen no more'.

The possible priority of the *Verses* and the *Life and Character* is (as stated in the last item) impossible to fix. Some of the main points of contact between the poems are the following:

Life and Character	*Verses*
lines 1–12	lines 1–10
31–40	13–20
49–51	27–30
52– 7	31– 4
84– 5	307– 8
90–92	184– 8

Title the initials stand for 'Dean of St Patrick's, Dublin' (either Latin or English). For the source of the maxim, see note to *The Life and Genuine Character of Dr Swift* 1.

9–10 A reminiscence of Granville's song from *The History of Adolphus* (*Review of English Studies* XI (1960), 412–13).

11 your patience move provokes you, makes you impatient.

47–52 not among the passages excised by Pope for the Bathurst text.

53–4 Swift may have in mind chiefly the *Fables* (first series, 1727): for his view of these poems, see *Corr* III, 424.

55–8 *PJH* II, 798 cites Swift to Lord Bathurst, October 1730: 'I pretend to have been an improver of irony on the subject of satire and praise' (*Corr* III, 410). A recent example would be Arbuthnot's *Brief Account of Mr John Ginglicutt's Treatise* (1731).

59 St John...Pulteney see Biog. Dict.: so linked in *To a Lady* 185. Swift alludes principally to *The Craftsman* and associated pamphlets.

70 this the latter.

83 vertigo stress on second syllable. The giddiness inseparable from Ménière's disease, labyrinthine vertigo. See *Corr* V, 225–6 and authorities listed there.

99 past his prime a favourite cliché of Swift's, used also in *The Progress of Marriage* 104 and *Gulliver's Travels* I, 2 (*PW* XI, 30).

108 Charles the Second who died in 1685, so the statement must be literally true.

110 doubt suspect.

111 stomach appetite.

117   tropes   figures of speech.

123   daily 'Howd'y's'   compare *Life and Character* 59.

128   Approves   confirms, demonstrates.

133–4   compare the rhyme in *The Author upon Himself* 45–6; *An Excellent New Song on a Seditious Pamphlet* 1–3: *Apollo to the Dean* 105–6.

147–56   interestingly different in content and technique from *Life and Character* 68–73: more personal and explicit, in fact.

151   passing-bell   death-bell.

156   public uses   see ll. 483–4. In fact there were a large number of smaller personal bequests. For Swift's will, see *PW* XIII, 149–58.

164   flesh and blood   see *A Serious Poem upon William Wood* 50.

168   'The author imagines, that the scribblers of the prevailing party, which he always opposed, will libel him after his death; but that others will remember him with gratitude, who consider the service he had done to Ireland, under the name of ⁴M.B. Drapier, by utterly defeating the destructive project of Wood's halfpence, in five letters to the people of Ireland, at that time read universally, and convincing every reader' (note in Faulkner edn).

170   Wisely   sagely, knowingly. Compare *As You Like It* II, vii, 22.

178   'The Dean supposeth himself to die in Ireland' (note in Faulkner).

179   'Mrs Howard, afterwards Countess of Suffolk, then of the Bedchamber to the Queen, professed much friendship for the Dean. The Queen then Princess, sent a dozen times to the Dean (then in London) with her command to attend her; which at last he did, by advice of all his friends. She often sent for him afterwards, and always treated him very graciously. He taxed her with a present worth ten pounds, which she promised before he should return to Ireland, but on his taking leave, the medals were not ready' (note in Faulkner). The events described relate to 1726 and 1727; Swift afterwards wrote that the Princess 'sent at least nine times to command my attendance before I would obey her' (*Corr* IV, 98): he finally succumbed in April 1726. The present referred to was a medal promised to Swift in return for a gift of Irish poplin: see *Corr* III, 392. For Mrs Howard, see Biog. Dict. She became Countess of Suffolk when her husband succeeded to the earldom on 22 June 1731, another dating clue.

183–8   replaced by asterisks in the·Bathurst edition: King would have liked to print the full text but did not dare to do so (*Corr* V, 135).

184   'The medals were to be sent to the Dean in four months, but she forgot them, or thought them too dear. The Dean, being in Ireland, sent Mrs Howard a piece of Indian plaid made in that kingdom: which the Queen seeing took from her, and wore it herself, and sent to the Dean for as much as would clothe herself and children, desiring he would send the charge of it. He did the former. It cost thirty-five pounds, but he said he would have nothing except the medals. He was the summer following [1727] in England, was treated as usual, and she being then Queen, the Dean was promised a settlement in England, but returned as he went, and, instead of favour or medals, hath been ever since under her Majesty's displeasure' (note in Faulkner edn). By the time these words appeared in print, the Queen was dead. See also note to l. 179.

189   'Chartres is a most infamous, vile scoundrel, grown from a footboy, or worse, to a prodigious fortune both in England and Scotland: he had a way of insinuating himself into all ministers under every change, either as pimp, flatterer, or informer. He was tried at seventy for a rape, and came off by sacrificing a great part of his fortune (he is since dead, but this poem still preserves the scene and time it was writ in)' (note in Faulkner edn). On Charteris, see Biog. Dict. and *An Excellent New Ballad: or, The True English Dean to be Hanged for a Rape* 49. Apart from the vocations listed, he was a money-lender and a 'runner for Sir Robert' (i.e. agent, spy).

191   without his shoes   'to die in one's shoes' was a slang phrase meaning 'to be hanged'. *Tilley* S381.

192   'Sir Robert Walpole, chief minister of state, treated the Dean in 1726, with great distinction, invited him to dinner at Chelsea, with the Dean's friends chosen on purpose; appointed an hour to talk with him of Ireland, to which kingdom and people the Dean found him no great friend; for he defended Wood's project of halfpence, &c. The Dean would see him no more; and upon his next year's return to England, Sir Robert on an accidental meeting, only made a civil compliment, and never invited him again' (note in Faulkner edn). The central episodes, occurring in April and May 1726, can be followed in *Corr* III, 128–44: see also Paul V. Thompson, 'An Unpublished Letter from Swift', *The Library*, 5th ser. XXII (1967), 57–66, quoting Swift to Delany, 11 July 1726.

194   'Mr William Pulteney, from being Mr Walpole's intimate friend, detesting his administration, opposed his measures, and joined with my Lord Bolingbroke, to represent his conduct in an excellent paper, called *The Craftsman*, which is still continued' (note in Faulkner edn).

196   'Henry St John, Lord Viscount Bolingbroke, Secretary of State to Queen Anne of blessed memory. He is reckoned the most universal genius in Europe; Walpole dreading his abilities, treated him most injuriously, working with King George [I], who forgot his promise of restoring the said lord, upon the restless importunity of Walpole' (note in Faulkner edn). Bolingbroke had been permitted to return to England but was not to resume his seat in the House of Lords or to exercise the normal rights of a peer.

197   'Curll hath been the most infamous bookseller of any age or country: his character in part may be found in Mr Pope's *Dunciad*. He published three volumes all charged on the Dean, who never writ three pages of them: he hath used many of the Dean's friends in almost as vile a manner' (note in Faulkner edn). The reference is to *The Dunciad* (1729) II, 54, esp. the lengthy note. Spurious Swift items issued by Curll would include *Miscellanies* (1721) (*T* 19); *Miscellanea* in two volumes (1727) (*T* 24); *Whartoniana* (1727); and similar collections. Other bogus items like *The Swearer's Bank* were separately issued. For Curll, see Biog. Dict.

200   'Three stupid verse writers in London, the last to the shame of the court, and the highest disgrace to wit and learning, was made laureate. Moore, commonly called Jemmy Moore, son of Arthur Moor, whose father was gaoler of Monaghan in Ireland. See the character of Jemmy Moore, and Tibbalds, Theobald, in *The Dunciad*' (note in Faulkner edn). Referring to attacks on Lewis Theobald, James Moore Smythe, and Colley Cibber in *The Dunciad*; at this date, Theobald was still portrayed as the King Dunce. Cibber took over this role in the revised poem. See Biog. Dict. for all three men.

202   'Curll is notoriously infamous for publishing the lives, letters, and last wills and testaments of the nobility and ministers of state, as well as of all the rogues, who are hanged at Tyburn. He hath been in custody of the House of Lords for publishing or forging the letters of many peers; which made the Lords enter a resolution in their journal book, that no life or writings of any lord should be published without the consent of the next heir at law, or license from their house' (note in Faulkner edn). This note seems to have been written after Gay's death, when Curll's scavenging operations for 'memoirs' induced Arbuthnot to pen his famous comment to Swift, that Curll 'is one of the new terrors of death' (*Corr* IV, 101). The threat of Curll publishing Swift's own letters grew more acute around 1735 (see *Corr* IV, 342–3). The brush with the House of Lords (one of several in Curll's career) took place in 1722. Curll had advertised an edition of the *Works* of the Duke of Buckingham, as a rival to an 'official' edition projected by Pope. He was called before the House of Lords on 23 January, and eight days later the House made its order concerning the publication of a deceased peer's writings. Curll simply revised his plan to include only items already published. His coadjutors in the operation included Henley and Tibbald: George Sherburn observes, 'such a constellation indicates the forces that were already shaping *The Dunciad*', and, one might add, shaping Swift's *Verses*, too (*The Early Career of Alexander Pope* (1934), pp. 222–3). The Lords' resolution was not annulled until 1845.

203 Revive the libels born to die compare Pope, *Epistle to Arbuthnot* 350: 'The tale revived, the lie so oft o'erthrown.'

208 Arbuthnot a day Fischer, p. 168, sees here an 'outrageous pun', that is 'Arbuth' will grieve 'not a day'. For similar word play, see *To Charles Ford, Esq. on His Birthday* 75–6.

217 kiss the rod 'accept chastisement submissively' (*OED*); Tilley R156.

221–2 compare Swift's *Account of His Mother's Death* (1710), describing how he received the news of her death, 'after a long sickness...I have now lost my barrier between me and death' (*PW* IV, 196).

227 doleful dumps generally the noun was facetious: compare *Hudibras* II, i, 106–7: 'His head like one in doleful dump / Between his knees.' Addison in *Rosamond* (1706) has 'in dumps so doleful'. Tilley D640.

230 vole winning all the tricks at quadrille: compare *Journal of a Modern Lady* 205.

236–7 compare *Polite Conversation*: 'Madam, my Lady Club begs your Ladyship's pardon; but she is engaged tonight' (*PW* IV, 168).

240 dearest friends...must part a cliché recently quoted both by Edward Young, *The Love of Fame* (1725) II, 232, and John Gay, *Fables* (1727) I, 50, 62 (*Gay*, II, 370). See also Tilley F733.

241 ran his race a cliché with a biblical origin, e.g. Hebrews xii, 1.

249–52 a comic rendition of the *ubi sunt* theme.

253 Lintot 'Bernard Lintot, a bookseller in London. *Vide* Mr Pope's *Dunciad*' (note in Faulkner edn). See especially II, 49–78, and note, in the 1729 version of that poem. For Lintot, see Biog. Dict. Swift had comparatively few direct business dealings with him, unlike Pope and Gay. His shop stood a few yards east of Temple Bar.

258 Duck Lane 'a place in London where old books are sold' (note in Faulkner edn). The continuation of Little Britain into Smithfield, which had long been a centre of the second-hand book trade. P II, 563 compares Pope, *Essay on Criticism* 444–5: 'Scotists and Thomists, now, in peace remain, / Amidst their kindred cobwebs in Duck Lane.' Swift himself mentions it in letters and pamphlets (*Corr* V, 118; *PW* XII, 264). References are collected in *Grub Street*, pp. 256–7.

260 pastry-cook's the time-honoured joke about the use of unwanted literature as a wrapping for pies, or to line baking-dishes.

265-6 quite a normal rhyme at this date: compare *A Serious Poem upon William Wood* 111-12; *A Panegyric on the Reverend Dean Swift* 106-7; Pope, *The Rape of the Lock* III, 11-12; *The Dunciad* (1729) III, 299-300. It is difficult to know how far this involved distortion of the normal pronunciation of 'taste'; Swift and Pope both rhyme it with 'feast' as well.

267-8 one of Swift's most regular word-pairs for rhymes.

268 spick and span the phrase formerly implied not just 'smartness' but 'newness': see *OED*.

270 birthday poem an ode for the king's birthday, which the laureate was expected to produce each year.

272 Stephen Duck see Biog. Dict. and *On Stephen Duck, the Thresher*, headnote.

277 'Walpole hires a set of party scribblers, who do nothing else but write in his defence' (note in Faulkner edn). See *The Dunciad* (1743) II, 314-15 and notes to these lines.

278 'Henley is a clergyman who wanting both merit and luck to get preferment, or even to keep his curacy in the established church, formed a new conventicle, which he calls an Oratory. There, at set times, he delivereth strange speeches compiled by himself and his associates, who share the profit with him: every hearer pays a shilling each day for admittance. He is an absolute dunce, but generally reputed crazy' (note in Faulkner edn). For Henley, see Biog. Dict. The information here may derive mostly from Pope's note to *The Dunciad* (1729) III, 195. A full account of the Oratory will be found in Graham Midgley, *The Life of Orator Henley* (1973).

279 hawkers pamphlet-sellers who operated in the streets and public places.

281-98 this passage was omitted in the Bathurst edition, for reasons that are explained by King's letter to Mrs Whiteway of 6 March 1739 (*Corr* V, 140). King thought that Swift had confused the freethinker Thomas Woolston (see Biog. Dict.) with the fashionable theological writer, patronized by Queen Caroline, William Wollaston (1660-1724). Neither man in fact received a pension (see l. 290). Horrell (*PJH* II, 799) suspects that there was some confusion in Swift's mind; but Scouten and Hume, *Philological Quarterly* LII (1973), pp. 215-16, argue that Woolston is clearly in view throughout: 'Swift is *imagining* a scene with Lintot a year after his [own] death ... Lintot's rejoicing that "The reverend author's good intention, / Hath been rewarded with a pension" is no mistake, but rather a piece of savage sarcasm from an *unpensioned* Irish Dean.'

293 God's in Gloucester Nathan Bailey's *Dictionary* (1721) has 'as sure as God's in Gloucestershire': see also *Tilley* G174. It is possible that Swift has in mind the fuss over the appointment of a new Bishop of Gloucester to succeed the ailing Sydall (see *On Dr Rundle* and *Plumb*, pp. 299-300), although this did not come to a head until 1733 when the poem already existed in something like its final form.

294 Jesus a blank in the Faulkner edn, but filled in by several of the annotators in surviving copies (*FV, HEH*, Cambridge University Library).

300 the Rose a famous tavern, on the west side of Drury Lane, across Russell Street from the theatre; much frequented by playgoers. See also *Tale*, p. 82. (It is just possible that Swift meant the Rose Tavern, on the north side of Castle

Street in Dublin; this was a hotbed of political clubs in the 1720s: *Gilbert*, I, 19–20. But the later passages seem to suppose an English setting.)

318–19   ironically, a borrowing from John Denham, *On Mr Abraham Cowley* (1667) 29–30.

323   stars and garters   the insignia of the Order of the Garter. Walpole was the first commoner to receive this order since the Restoration, in 1726: 'He gloried in this distinction and had the Star and Garter plastered into the new ceilings and carved into the chimney pieces at Houghton. Even when painted in hunting costume he displayed his blue ribbon and he went to a vast amount of trouble to have the Garter ribbon, George and star painted on to old portraits' (*Plumb*, p. 101).

325–454   mostly omitted in the Bathurst edn, because King and Pope felt that 'the latter part of the poem might be thought by the public a little vain, if so much were said by himself of himself' (*Corr* V, 139).

326   a line adapting Jude 16. The rhetoric hereabouts is strongly reminiscent of that in a closely allied passage, the *Epistle to Arbuthnot* 334–59.

341–4]   *not in Faulkner edn; supplied in annotated copies* (*FV, Cambridge University Library*). Mrs Pilkington (*Memoirs*, ed. Iris Barry (1928), p. 68) quotes ll. 339–44, with 'the present Queen' instead of 'her Majesty'.

345   David's lesson   Psalm cxlvi, 3.

349   'The Irish parliament are reduced to the utmost degree of slavery, flattery, corruption and meanness of spirit, and the worse they are treated, the more fawning and servile they grow. Under the greatest and most contemptuous grievances they dare not complain, by which baseness and tameness, unworthy human creatures, the kingdom is irrecoverably ruined' (note in annotated copies, Texas and *HEH*).

351   fair liberty   Swift's view of this concept is discussed by I. Ehrenpreis, 'Swift on Liberty', *Journal of the History of Ideas* XIII (1952), 131–46.

355   'In the year 1713, the late Queen was prevailed with by an address of the House of Lords in England, to publish a proclamation, promising three hundred pounds to whatever person would discover the author of a pamphlet called, *The Public Spirit of the Whigs*; and in Ireland, in the year 1724, my Lord Carteret at his first coming into the government, was prevailed on to issue a proclamation for promising the like reward of three hundred pounds, to any person who could discover the author of a pamphlet called, *The Drapier's Fourth Letter, &c.* writ against that destructive project of coining halfpence for Ireland; but in neither kingdom was the Dean discovered' (note in Faulkner edn). For the earlier episode, see *Ehrenpreis*, II, 708–13; for the later, see *To His Grace the Archbishop of Dublin*. Compare also *The Author upon Himself* 58.

369   'Queen Anne's ministry fell to variance from the first year after their ministry began: Harcourt the Chancellor, and Lord Bolingbroke the Secretary, were discontented with the Treasurer Oxford, for his too much mildness to the Whig party; this quarrel grew higher every day till the Queen's death. The Dean, who was the only person that endeavoured to reconcile them, found it impossible; and thereupon retired to the country about ten weeks before that fatal event; upon which he returned to his deanery in Dublin, where for many years he was worried by the new people in power, and had hundreds of libels writ against him in England' (note in Faulkner edn). See *Ehrenpreis*, II, 671–9, 728–63, for Swift's reactions to the disintegration of the ministry.

374   mere   utter.

378 *Ormonde's valour*   for James Butler, Duke of Ormonde, see Biog. Dict.
381 'In the height of the quarrel between the ministers, the Queen died' (note in Faulkner edn). On 1 August 1741. For Swift's reactions, see *In Sickness*. This passage was another that King censored with reluctance (*Corr* V, 135).
383 'Upon Queen Anne's death the Whig faction was restored to power, which they exercised with the utmost rage and revenge; impeached and banished the chief leaders of the church party, and stripped all their adherents of what employments they had, after which England was never known to make so mean a figure in Europe. The greatest preferments in the church in both kingdoms were given to the most ignorant men, fanatics were publicly caressed, Ireland utterly ruined and enslaved, only great ministers heaping up millions, and so affairs continue until this present third day of May, 1732, and are likely to go on in the same manner' (note in Faulkner). As representative a statement of Swift's outlook on his time as he ever made in a brief compass.
385 *solemn league and covenant*   a reference to the agreement entered into by the General Assembly of the Church of Scotland, the Westminster Assembly of English divines, and the English parliament in 1643. It provided for the establishment of Presbyterianism and the suppression of Roman Catholics. After the Restoration it was burned publicly by the common hangman.
388   compare *Traulus: The Second Part* 45–6.
391   *old England*   a set phrase of the opposition: compare Pope, *Epilogue to the Satires* I, 152. *Virtue* (l. 394) is another party shibboleth.
392   *story*   history.
397   echoing *To Charles Ford, Esq. on His Birthday* 28. Oxford and Prior were in custody, Bolingbroke and Ormonde were in exile. For this phase in Tory party fortunes, see G.V. Bennett, *The Tory Crisis in Church and State 1688–1730* (1975), pp. 185–204.
398 'Upon the Queen's death, the Dean returned to live in Dublin, at his deanery house: numberless libels were writ against him in England, as a Jacobite; he was insulted in the street, and at nights was forced to be attended by his servants armed' (note in Faulkner edn). The libels would be items such as *A Farther Hue and Cry after Dr Swift* (1714), *T* 882; and *Dr Swift's Real Diary* (1715), *T* 886. There is not much independent evidence concerning Swift's fears for his own safety. His anxieties were at their peak in the summer of 1715, when the decision was taken to impeach the Duke of Ormonde: a letter to Chetwode of 21 June, referring to the correspondence intercepted by the ministry and to rumours of a proclamation offering five hundred pounds for Swift's arrest (*Corr* II, 172–3), indicates the temper of the times. Swift even thought of emigrating to Guernsey; the half-serious suggestion occurs in a letter of 1 March to Lord Harley (*Corr* II, 160).
400 'The land of slaves and fens, is Ireland' (note in Faulkner edn).
407–10   from Psalm xli, 9: 'Yea, mine own familiar friend, in whom I trusted, which did eat of my bread, hath lifted up his heel against me.'
412 'One Wood, a hardware-man from England, had a patent for coining copper halfpence in Ireland, to the sum of £108,000 which in the consequence, must leave that kingdom without gold or silver (see *Drapier's Letters*)' (note in Faulkner edn). The actual amount originally authorized was £100,800, although this was later reduced and there was a good deal of debate about the quantity Wood was actually coining (see *Drapier*, pp. xi, xviii–xix, xxxi, 22–3).
417   *steerage*   helm.

421 'One Whitshed was then Chief Justice of Ireland. He had some years before prosecuted a printer for a pamphlet writ by the Dean, to persuade the people of Ireland to wear their own manufactures. Whitshed sent the jury down eleven times, and kept them nine hours, until they were forced to bring in a special verdict. He sat as judge afterwards on the trial of the printer of the Drapier's fourth *Letter*; but the jury, against all he could say or swear, threw out the bill: all the kingdom took the Drapier's part, except the court, or those who expected places. The Drapier was celebrated in many poems and pamphlets: his sign was set up in most streets of Dublin (where many of them still continue) and in several country towns' (note in Faulkner edn). See *An Excellent New Song on a Seditious Pamphlet* and *Whitshed's Motto on His Coach*, headnotes; and Biog. Dict.

424 'Scroggs was Chief Justice under King Charles the second: his judgement always varied in state trials, according to directions from court. Tresilian was a wicked judge, hanged above three hundred years ago' (note in Faulkner edn). Sir William Scroggs (*c.*1623–83), Lord Chief Justice 1678; involved in the trials surrounding the Popish Plot; impeached by the House of Commons and removed from office in 1681. There are references to him in the *Drapier's Letters*. Sir Robert Tresilian, Chief Justice in 1381, tried John Ball and his followers after the suppression of the Peasants' Revolt led by Wat Tyler; hanged at Tyburn in 1388 for treason.

426 Nor feared he God, nor man regarded adapting Luke xviii, 2: 'There was in a city a judge, which feared not God, neither regarded man.'

432 · topics strained legal arguments, points of law adduced for casuistic purposes.

435 'In Ireland, which he had reason to call a place of exile; to which country nothing could have driven him, but the Queen's death, who had determined to fix him in England, in spite of the Duchess of Somerset, &c.' (note in Faulkner edn). For evidence to the contrary, see *The Windsor Prophecy*, headnote.

439 'In Ireland the Dean was not acquainted with one single lord spiritual or temporal. He only conversed with private gentlemen of the clergy or laity, and but a small number of either' (note in Faulkner edn). This is not strictly true, unless it applies to the very first period of Swift's time as Dean (which is not what the general drift of the poem suggests). However, it is the case that he seems to have had no *intimate* friendship with peers or bishops in Ireland; from about 1733 this situation was modified by his warm relationship with Lord Orrery, his future biographer – though the Earl spent too long in England for Swift's liking (*Corr* IV, 144–5).

443 'The peers of Ireland lost a great part of their jurisdiction by one single act, and tamely submitted to this infamous mark of slavery without the least resentment, or remonstrance' (note in Faulkner edn). Swift is referring to the Declaratory Act of 1720, which was one of the provocations for his *Proposals for the Universal Use of Irish Manufacture* in that year. The background to the act, 'for the better securing the Dependency of the Kingdom of Ireland upon the Crown of Great Britain', is set out in *Ferguson*, pp. 41–59.

449 'The parliament (as they call it) in Ireland meets but once in two years; and, after giving five times more than they can afford, return home to reimburse themselves by all country jobs and oppressions, of which some few only are here mentioned' (note in Faulkner edn). Parliament was normally convened every other year, to pass money bills; day-to-day executive power was in the hands of the Lord Lieutenant, or, in his absence, three Lords Justices, whilst legislative activity was severely limited by the terms of Poynings' Law (1495).

452   rack   see *An Excellent New Song upon His Grace Our Good Lord Archbishop of Dublin* 45.

453   Go snacks with   divide the spoils with. (*Tilley* S578).

rapparees   'the highwaymen in Ireland are, since the late wars there, usually called *rapparees*, which was a name given to those Irish soldiers who in small parties used, at that time, to plunder the Protestants' (note in Faulkner edn). See *The Answer to 'Paulus'* 97.

454   keep the peace   act as magistrates.

455   job   enterprise, but mainly with shady overtones, a 'ramp' or racket.

456   'The army in Ireland is lodged in barracks, the building and repairing whereof, and other charges, have cost a prodigious sum to that unhappy kingdom' (note in Faulkner). See also *The Grand Question Debated*, note to l. 6.

457-8   a new system of roads was just beginning to grow up, often through the establishment of turnpike trusts – Ireland was in this respect only a decade or so behind England, where the first great flush of turnpikes occurred in the 1720s. The trusts could compound for a parish rate to be levied, in lieu of statutory labour by the inhabitants, quite apart from the revenue raised by the tolls imposed on travellers. In England there were often complaints that private landowners sought 'to make turnpikes avenues, more or less, to this or that country seat' (*Gentleman's Magazine*, 1754) and this must have been the case in Ireland too.

459-60   the 'late' rhyme on *Dean*.

464-6   omitted in the Bathurst text, as King told Mrs Whiteway, because they 'might be liable to some objection, and were not, strictly speaking, a just part of his character; because several persons have been lashed by name, a Bettesworth, and in this poem, Charteris and Whitshed, and for my part, I do not think . . . that it is an imputation on a satirist to lash an infamous fellow by name' (*Corr* V, 140).

464   recalling Martial X, xxx, 10.

471   'The vicious attacks on Pope's appearance might have crossed his mind at this moment in the writing' (*Jaffe*, p. 19).

483-4   Swift's famous bequest to enable the city to establish the first purpose-built mental institution in Ireland (and one of the very few anywhere). St Patrick's Hospital was eventually opened in 1757, twelve years after Swift's death. For Swift's plans taking shape, see *Corr* IV, 296, 319, 367, 405. Pope's warm approval of the plan can be found in a letter of December 1735 (*Corr* IV, 448).

487-8   always a favourite rhyme: see for example *A Pastoral Dialogue between Richmond Lodge and Marble Hill* 83-4. King omitted this couplet from the text published by Bathurst, on the grounds of its ungrammatical nature (*better*, he thought, had no logical antecedent): 'The Dean is, I think, without exception, the best and most correct writer of English that hath ever yet appeared as an author; I was therefore unwilling anything should be cavilled at as ungrammatical. He is besides the most patient of criticism of all I ever knew, which perhaps is not the least sign of a great genius' (*Corr* V, 140). The last sentence has interesting implications for editorial method.

JUDAS

First published in *WF*, with the heading, 'written in the year 1731'. This is generally altered by editors to 1731/2, on grounds that are unclear. In *The Storm* 52, 'Bishop Judas' is clearly Josiah Hort, and he may be the subject once more; but there is less to go on this time. See Biog. Dict. for Hort. Text from *WF*.

3 a paltry bribe   the thirty pieces of silver: see Matthew xxvi, 15.
4 a tribe   the twelve tribes of Israel, deriving from the twelve sons of Jacob (Genesis xxxvi, 22). Swift seems to be reckoning a crown (five shillings) as equivalent to two and a half pieces of silver.
5 forced him to restore   Matthew xxvii, 3–4.
8 hanged, or burst   Matthew xxvii, 5; Acts i, 18.
10 with a kiss   Matthew xxvi, 49.
13 board   perhaps that of the Privy Council table.
15–16   hemp was used for the hangman's noose; lawn, for bishops' sleeves.
17 by transgression fell   quoting Acts i, 25.
22 the tree   scaffold.
    his bowels burst   see Acts i, 18.
25–6   paraphrasing Acts, i, 20.

ON THE IRISH BISHOPS

WF gave the poem no title, but supplied this note at its opening:

> We found the following poem printed in *Fog's Journal* of the 17th of September 1733. It was written in the last session, and many copies were taken, but never printed here. The subject of it is now over; but our author's known zeal against that project made him generally supposed to be the author. We reprint it just as it lies in *Fog's Journal*.
> The following poem is a product of Ireland; it was occasioned by the bishops of that kingdom endeavouring to get an act to divide the church livings, which bill was rejected by the Irish House of Commons. It is said to be written by an honest curate; the reader of taste, perhaps, may guess who the curate could be, that was capable of writing it.

The second paragraph in fact derives from *Fog's Weekly Journal* for Saturday, 15 September 1733; but the poem as printed in *WF* differs both from the text given in *Fog's Journal* and from the earliest publication of all, that is, in the *Gentleman's Magazine* for June 1732. Many copies were certainly made, and several transcripts survive. However, the variants in *WF* suggest the intervention of Swift himself, and the text here is based on that source.
    The subject of the poem is the attempt to introduce two new measures early in 1732, namely the Bill of Residence (to compel clergy 'to reside on their respective benefices and to build on their respective glebe lands') and the Bill of Division (permitting large parishes to be divided into two or more parts without the consent of the incumbent). Both bills, with the support of a majority of the bishops, went through the Irish House of Lords in February; but both suffered defeat in the Commons on 26 February. Opposition was led by Swift, who wrote pamphlets on the subject (*PW* XII, 181–202), arguing that the measures would 'multiply . . . beggarly clergymen through the whole kingdom'. A year later he wrote to one of the bishops who had supported the innovations, concerning

'those two abominable bills, for enslaving and beggaring the clergy, (which took their birth from hell)' (*Corr* IV, 182). An ironic proposal to pay off the national debt of Ireland by selling the bishops' lands (see ll. 61–2) was attributed to Matthew Pilkington but may well be Swift's (*PW* XII, 205–12). For a full discussion of the episode, see *Landa*, pp. 111–23.

WF heads the poem 'written in the year 1731', which is probably just correct if we read it to mean 1731/2: February or March 1732 by modern reckoning (see note on dates, p. 598).

1   Old Latimer   referring to the most famous sermon, 'Of the Plough' (1548), by Hugh Latimer (*c*.1488–1555), Bishop of Worcester, burnt as a heretic: 'Who is the most diligentest bishop and prelate in England, that passeth all the rest in doing his office? . . . I will tell you: it is the devil.'

3   this bishop   Edward Tenison, Bishop of Ossory: see Biog. Dict.

6   sulphur and nitre   the acidic elements of infernal regions.

8   believes and who trembles   James ii, 19: 'The devils also believe, and tremble.'

10   baboon of Kilkenny   apparently Tenison again: see *Corr* IV, 359 and *P* III, 803. Kilkenny was the ancient capital of the kingdom of Ossory and the diocese known by that name.

11   the comparison odious   a cliché mocked in *Polite Conversation* (*PW* IV, 194). Tilley C576.

15   incog.   one of the abbreviations scoffed at in Swift's *Tatler* paper (28 September 1710) and again in *Polite Conversation* (*PW* IV, 161).

25   Theophilus Bolton, Archbishop of Cashel; Charles Carr, Bishop of Killaloe; Robert Howard, Bishop of Elphin. See Biog. Dict. and *Landa*, p. 122.

29   praetor   consul, governor. The rhyme may suggest a pun on 'prater' or Speaker of the Commons.

39–40   like Judas the first   see *Judas* 8.

40   splitters   splinters (obsolete).

41   allusion   parable, metaphor.

48   'divide and ye govern'   proverbial tag attached to Machiavelli, to whom all politic maxims tended to be ascribed. Bacon quoted '*separa et impera*', and Sir Edward Coke calls it an 'exploded adage'. The more familiar form, '*divide et impera*', was the motto of Louis XI (King of France, 1461–83) in his struggles against the nobles. In this form the maxim was applied to the Tory party's situation in 1714 by one of Pope's acquaintances (cited by G.V. Bennett, *The Tory Crisis in Church and State 1688–1730* (1975), p. 179). For the rarer English version, see *Tilley* D391.

51   hold   wager.

52   cloven feet   like those of the devil.

59   spittles   lodgings; a fund from the 'First Fruits' was to be set up under the Bill of Residence to assist in building manse-houses where none existed.

64   biting the biters   playing on the proverbial phrase 'the biter bit' with the currently fashionable sense of 'bite' (see *Vanbrug's House* 62). For the proverb, see *Tilley* B429.

ADVICE TO A PARSON

Like the following poem, this first appeared in James Roberts's edition of *The Lady's Dressing Room* in June 1732; for some reason neither was mentioned on the title-page of the first edition, but this was rectified in the second edition (see *T* 720). Both items were reprinted in the London press in June and July. However, unlike its companion-piece, *Advice to a Parson* was not included in *Misc* (1732). In fact it was not collected until Nichols printed it in his *Supplement* (1776).

There are contemporary transcripts in *TCD* and *HEH* (see *Mayhew*, p. 161). The latter (acc. no. 143198–259, f. 69) has a well-established provenance, and its statement that the poem is by Swift is stronger evidence than its inclusion by Roberts. Text based on Roberts, whose edition was carefully printed by Bowyer. I have, however, ignored the distracting torrent of italics.

1 'Armagh' (note in *TCD* MS); that is, Hugh Boulter, Archbishop of Armagh: see Biog. Dict.
2 'Dublin' (note in *TCD* MS); that is, John Hoadly, Archbishop of Dublin: see Biog. Dict.
3 formal stiff and ceremonious.
4 'Killala' (note in *TCD* MS); that is, Robert Clayton (1695–1758), Bishop of Killala from 1730; but the line would seem to fit better his predecessor Robert Howard, who held the see from 1727 to 1730. Howard was better known to Swift and exhibited just the kind of fawning behaviour described: see *Landa*, pp. 87–92.
7–8 for the rhyme, see *Twelve Articles* 23–4.
8 Lord Bolton Theophilus Bolton, at this time Archbishop of Cashel: see Biog. Dict. and *The Storm* 42. By this date he was on much better terms with Swift.
9 rochet see *The Dean to Himself on St Cecilia's Day* 11.
10 Hort Josiah Hort, Bishop of Kilmore and Ardagh: see Biog. Dict. and *The Storm*, headnote.

EPIGRAM

The situation is identical to that of the preceding item, in respect both of printed editions and manuscripts, except that this epigram went into *Misc* (1732). Text from that collection.

The *TCD* MS carries the headings: 'On Dr Hort, Bishop of Kilmore's going out of St Ann's church in the time of divine service, on hearing the Duke of Dorset, our Lord Lieutenant was come to town.'

1 Lord Pam Hort; the name is taken from the term for the knave of clubs (see *Rape of the Lock* III, 61).
2 the Lieutenant Lionel Sackville, first Duke of Dorset (1688–1765), Lord Lieutenant 1730–37. A courtier and Kit-Cat member, with whom Swift managed to maintain fair relations, on the surface at least.

VERSES ON I KNOW NOT WHAT

The title is probably a misnomer. It is found on the reverse side of the paper carrying Swift's autograph version of these lines (*FV*). The endorsement reads in full, 'Verses on I know not what, 1732.' It may well be that the date refers to the time at which Swift came on these, now unintelligible, lines. Any attempt to identify the subject could be only a guess. Deane Swift was the first to print this poem in 1765, and *F* included it the same year. Text based on Swift's MS, but as usual some reinforcement of the punctuation is necessary.

4 and]   *Swift* (*FV*);   or *Deane Swift, F* (1765).

AN ANSWER TO A SCANDALOUS POEM

Apparently first published together with the poem to which it is a reply, Sheridan's *A New Simile*, in an octavo pamphlet (Dublin, 1733). See *P* II, 612 and *T* 1615 for an account of this publication. *Foxon* S795 does not record the location of any copy and I have not seen one. Sheridan's poem had first appeared by itself in 1732: for the text, see *P* II, 613–16. Swift's reply was introduced into *F*, vol. VI, in 1738; this is the basis for the text here.

F heads the *Answer* 'written in the year 1732', which is probably right. Sheridan's poem was reprinted in the press during August, which may be the approximate date of Swift's response. Sheridan's lines consist of an elaborate extension of the basic simile; on the whole, Swift does not take much notice of individual thoughts or expressions.

A first draft in Swift's hand survives on six leaves in *HEH* (no. 14339), described by *Mayhew*, p. 161. This is reproduced in Appendix 3. Briefly (and ignoring alterations made as he went along), Swift drafted thirty-two lines not included in the final version, whilst the printed text contains fourteen lines with no equivalent in the draft. Perhaps the most interesting emendation is the suppression of eighteen lines near the close, which contain some direct political references:

> Who knows how soon you [will] compare us,
> To Chartres, Walpole, or a King...

Swift endorsed the manuscript 'mine here; of no use', and it may be that dissatisfaction with the contents, as well as political expediency, occasioned both the delay in publication and the extensive degree of revision.

Title *Cap of Howth* is glossed in *F* 'the highest point of Howth is called the Cap of Howth'; referring to the Hill of Howth, which forms the northern horn of the crescent of Dublin Bay. It is 560 feet high, and famous for its views over the city. *Dermot O'Nephely* is the kind of name used by Swift and Sheridan in their word-games.

15 compare *On the Words 'Brother Protestants'* 41.

16 *claps* punning on 'thunder-clap' and 'clap' meaning 'gonorrhoea'.

19 *buboes* see *Pethox the Great* 37.
       blotches boils, eruptions.

20 compare *The Progress of Beauty* 111.

31 *Sirius* 'the dog-star' (note in *F*); compare Pope, *Epistle to Arbuthnot* 3, 'The dog-star rages!'
       welkin sky (poetical).

34 *ducking-stool* the old-fashioned punishment for scolds and shrews.

49–60 Ixion, king of the Lapithae, was bound by Jove to a wheel of fire for imitating the thunder of heaven and attempting to ravish Juno; Jove sent a cloud to him in the shape of Juno, and she became the mother of the centaurs, creatures half-man and half-horse. Because of their conception, the centaurs were called *nubigenae*, 'cloud-born'. See Ovid, *Metamorphoses* XII, 210-535.

62 Tyre a Phoenician city, from which Dido fled to found Carthage; by extension, Carthage was itself given the epithet Tyrian.

63 His mother Venus; Aeneas entered Carthage veiled in a cloud, which Venus wrapped around him, and which parted to reveal him to Dido (*Aeneid* I, 411-14, 439-40, 586-7). Compare *Ode to the Athenian Society* 88.

65 dyed in grain dyed throughly in the fabric, usually scarlet. For the metaphoric use, see *Strephon and Chloe* 85.

66 flaxen wig compare *Trivia* III, 55; such wigs were the finest and most expensive (*Gay*, I, 161; II, 567).

  clouded cane compare *Strephon and Chloe* 38; Pope, *Rape of the Lock* IV, 124; Gay, *Trivia* I, 67.

69 tearing impressive, 'ripping' (obsolete slang).

70 smoked recognized, found out: see *Aeneid* I, 613-30.

72 Iris goddess of the rainbow, daughter of Thaumas, and the chosen messenger of Juno.

77-82 Aristophanes' comedy *The Clouds* 223-423 satirizes aspects of the thinking of Socrates, whom the dramatist knew personally. Socrates' defence against the charges of heresy is reported in Plato's *Apology*; the *Phaedo* describes a conversation held on the day of his death. Aristophanes was represented in Swift's *Library*, no. 98.

100 Mount Olymp Olympus, home of the gods. According to Lucretius, *De Natura Rerum* II, 271, '*nubes excedit Olympus.*'

103 Teneriffa the extinct volcanic peak of Tenerife in the Canary Islands, over 12,000 feet high; compare *Paradise Lost* IV, 987, 'Like Teneriff or Atlas, unremoved.'

105 Pindus seat of the muses, over whom Apollo presided.

107 Parnassus near Delphi, the seat of poetry and music.

110 vehicles trisyllabic.

114 doves to draw her chair a standard piece of iconographic detail: similarly, Byron refers to amatory poets linking their rhymes 'as Venus yokes her doves' (*Don Juan* V, 1).

  chair chariot.

117 jealous Juno she is commonly encountered punishing mortal rivals for the love of her husband Jove; see *Metamorphoses, passim*.

118 berlin a covered carriage; note the rhyme.

134 frieze coarse woollen cloth.

  surtout great-coat.

147 on her mettle perhaps 'in a moment of high spirits', or 'if she has enough spunk in her'.

148 piss upon a nettle a proverbial phrase for 'be out of temper' (*Tilley* N132).

162 such comparisons are odious see *On the Irish Bishops* 11 and *Polite Conversation* (*PW* IV, 194). *Tilley* C576.

EPIGRAM ON THE HERMITAGE AT RICHMOND

Two epigrams were sent to Swift at an unknown date, concerning the grotto set up by Queen Caroline at Richmond. He added the couplet printed here, and all three together were printed by Deane Swift in 1765 (also in *F* that year). The manuscript survives in the John Rylands Library, Manchester. Another couplet was drafted and then erased by Swift:

> To bury me is not so just
> I'm humbled e'er I meet the dust.

This is a false start rather than an epigram proper and is not separately printed in this edition.

For Caroline as a landscape gardener, see *A Pastoral Dialogue between Richmond Lodge and Marble Hill* 93. Around 1732 she commissioned five busts for her grotto; somewhat incongruously, Locke and Newton were joined by, amongst others, Samuel Clarke (see *Directions for a Birthday Song* 269). This occasioned a barbed reference in Pope's *Epistle to Burlington* 78. The same writer told Gay in a letter of 2 October 1732, 'Every man, and every boy, is writing verses on the Royal Hermitage; I hear the Queen is at a loss which to prefer' (Pope *Corr* III, 318). This may afford an approximate date of composition for Swift's own epigram.

2   *halter*   hangman's noose.

'A PAPER BOOK IS SENT BY BOYLE'

Swift reached his sixty-fifth birthday on 30 November 1732. Mrs Pilkington describes how 'it being the Dean's birthday, he had received a book very richly bound and clasped with gold, from the Earl of Orrery, with a handsome poem, wrote by himself to the Dean in the first page, the rest being blank; and ... Dr Delany had sent him a silver standish, with a complimentary poem' (*Memoirs*, ed. Iris Barry (1928), p. 77). A transcript of the verses by Orrery and Delany, together with Swift's reply, survives in the Portland papers. All three sets were printed in the *Gentleman's Magazine* for June 1733. They also went into Faulkner's edition of the *Works* in 1735, though apparently as an afterthought, squeezed in at the end of the four volumes. For the text of Orrery and Delany, see *P* II, 609–11. The text of Swift's poem is based on Faulkner's 1735 edition.

For John Boyle, Earl of Orrery, Swift's future biographer, see Biog. Dict. He was a recent friend at this date: see *Death and Daphne*, headnote. For his own comments on the episode, see *Remarks* (5th edn, 1752), pp. 140–41.

1   *Boyle*   Orrery's family name.
2   the book Orrery presented to Swift was to figure in the sale catalogue of Swift's library, apparently unused (*P* II, 611).
3   *standish*   a writing-stand with space for an ink-pot and pens. Similarly, Pope wrote a versified 'thank-you', *On Receiving from Lady Frances Shirley a Standish and Two Pens* (*PTE* VI, 378).

ON THE DAY OF JUDGEMENT

This famous poem has a tangled provenance; for a full review of the bibliographical issues, see Sidney L. Gulick, *Publications of the Modern Language Association* XLVIII (1933), 850–55, and *Papers of the Bibliographical Society of*

America LXXI (1977), 333–6; Maurice Johnson, *PMLA* LXXXVI (1971), 210–17. *P* II, 576–8 summarizes most of the relevant facts.

Gulick identifies five versions of the poem: (A) the sixteen-line text printed in [Richard Griffith?], *The Friends* (1773); (B) the twenty-line transcript by the poet William Collins, made between 1745 and 1750: see *Drafts and Fragments of Verse*, ed. J.S. Cunningham (1956), p. 41; (C) the twenty-two-line text in a manuscript miscellany compiled by William Shenstone, *c.*1762: see *Shenstone's Miscellany*, ed. I.A. Gordon (1952), p. 129; (D) the twenty-two-line text supplied by 'Mercutio' to the *St James's Chronicle* for publication on 12 April 1774; (E) the twenty-two-line text found in the *Monthly Review* for July 1774, allegedly correcting version (D).

However, this list omits the only holograph versions ever mentioned. The first was in a letter from Lord Chesterfield to Voltaire, written on 27 August 1752. Chesterfield sent Voltaire a copy of a poem, of which he claimed he had the original in Swift's own hand. When the letter was first published after Chesterfield's death (in fact in April 1774), the accompanying copy of verses was missing. This provoked 'Mercutio' to send to a newspaper version (D). George P. Mayhew, *Philological Quarterly* LIV (1975), 213–21, suggested that 'Mercutio' was in fact Deane Swift's son Theophilus; and that 'F.A.' who provided the text for *The Friends* was Dr Francis Andrews, Provost of Trinity College. His source was apparently John Rochfort (d.1771), brother of George and a less intimate friend of Swift.

Version (E) two months later claims to correct the text but the changes do not have any obvious authenticity. It was from this version that the fourth edition of Chesterfield's *Letters*, published in October 1774, took its text when the poem was attached to the letter to Voltaire. Gulick concludes that Swift left two or three different copies of the poem, in different states. He rejects the theory of Leland B. Peterson (*PBSA* LXX (1976), 189–219) that Chesterfield, Dodsley, and others revised and augmented the poem. For the strong likelihood that Chesterfield *did* possess a holograph copy by Swift, see *P* II, 578. He could, for instance, quote l. 19, which is not in version (B), the only text known to have been in existence at the date in question.

A further complication arises from the fact that Theophilus Swift wrote of seeing a copy in Swift's hand. He also preserved a clipping from the Dublin press (date and journal unknown), which shows that the poem was also reproduced there. These materials came to the attention of Scott when he was preparing his edition, and they are now in the National Library of Scotland. See Mayhew's article for fuller details.

The date of composition often supplied (1731) is purely conjectural. Horrell (*PJH* I, 387) sees a link with a letter to Pope of that year (*Corr* III, 456). Johnson (*PMLA* LXXXVI, 210–17) prefers 1732 or 1733 and he may well be right.

The title varies in the different printed versions. Johnson supports *On the Day of Judgement* and Theophilus Swift's testimony appears to agree with this.

The text here is based on the *St James's Chronicle* printing, that is, version (D). It may be only one remove from Swift's original, where the others are likely to be two or three stages away.

Most general accounts of Swift devote some attention to this poem. Herbert Davis remarks, 'Here is the complete triumph of the Comic Spirit, unabashed and unafraid, delighting to overthrow all mankind's claims to dignity and importance, and "ending with a puff" the whole heroic and romantic delusion' (*Jonathan Swift: Essays on His Satire* (1964), p. 198). More elaborate analysis will be found in *Johnson*, pp. 80–82, with a comparison between Swift and Isaac Watts; and *Jaffe*, pp. 26–30, who sees in the poem 'Swift in one of his aspects [passing]...judgement on Swift in another'. Noting the shifts of tense in the verses, Jaffe locates 'a state of timelessness appropriate to the Day of Judgement'.

15] *St James's Chronicle*;   And you whom different sects have shamed *Collins transcript.*
19–20] *St James's Chronicle; not in Collins transcript.*

THE BEASTS' CONFESSION TO THE PRIEST

First published by Faulkner as a pamphlet in 1738; reprinted in London by T. Cooper the same year (*T* 758–60; *Foxon* S804–7). Another reprint is identified by Foxon (S808) as probably the work of Thomas Ruddiman, in Edinburgh. *T* 770 is an edition by Cooper apparently dated 1737; I do not know of any such printing. Text here based on Faulkner's 1738 edition. The poem went into *F* (1746).

Faulkner heads the poem 'written in the year 1732' and this has always been accepted. On the other hand, the reference to the Excise Crisis in l. 150 unmistakably dates from a time subsequent to April 1733. Conceivably this single passage was added later. On 10 July 1732 Swift wrote to Gay of his efforts to write fables, at some unspecified earlier date (*Corr* IV, 38–9). A month earlier, on 8 June, he had touched on the issues raised in this poem: he wrote to Rev. Henry Jenney concerning William Tisdall, 'I am confident he is an honest man, but unhappily misled through the whole course of his life, by mistaking his talent, which he hath against nature applied to wit and raillery, and rhyming (*Corr* IV, 28).

The poem looks both forward and back. It prefigures some features of *On Poetry: a Rhapsody* (see ll. 1–24). The satire on doctors, lawyers, and politicians recalls *Gulliver's Travels*; whilst the Preface (assuredly Swift's own) has links stretching right back to *A Tale of a Tub*.

Preface

4   alderman not identified; probably an acquaintance of the 1710–13 period when Swift intermittently spent time in the coffee-houses.
11–18 there are similar 'computations' of the number of wits in *Tale*, pp. 41–2, and *A Letter to a Young Poet* (*PW* IX, 325ff.; this may or may not be Swift's). This characteristic way of outlining the sociology of hack writers is discussed in *Grub Street*, pp. 258–72.
16   ralliers the original is spelt 'railliers', which has overtones of 'railers' as well.
18   suburb for the implications of this epithet, see *To Stella, Who Collected and Transcribed His Poems* 72.
20   contrast italicized in the original, because it was still a technical and frenchified term (see *The Lady's Dressing Room* 128).
21   toupees 'wigs with long black tails, worn for some years past' (note in Faulkner (1738)).

f.o.   a modern beau   compare the description of Beau Didapper in Fielding's
Joseph Andrews IV, 9.
31   transplanted   from England.
36   prints   newspapers.

Text

7–8   an 'Irish' rhyme.
39   nice   particular.
46   pease   see *Strephon and Chloe* 167.
72   his reverence   'the priest his confessor' (note in Faulkner).
88   the patience of a Job   proverbial, alluding to the book of Job, esp. i–ii. See
Tilley J59.
97   to turn his coat   proverbial (*Tilley* C420).
104   the lawn   a bishopric.
109–10   for the rhyme, see *Twelve Articles* 23–4.
150   the Excise   Walpole's plan to shift duties from customs to excise, to
increase revenue and cut down on smuggling: after a vigorous campaign in the
opposition press, Walpole was forced to withdraw the bill in April 1733. See
Plumb, pp. 248–71; Paul Langford, *The Excise Crisis* (1975).
152   standing troops   hatred of a standing army was a recurrent aspect of politi-
cal life, and in the 1730s the opposition seized on this prejudice to attack the size
of the army required to protect the interests of Hanover. It was even argued that
'the large standing army showed that the constitution was to be germanized'
(*Plumb*, p. 206).
168   undone   bankrupt.
170   writ of ease   'a certificate of discharge from employment' (*OED*).
174   ten thousand   Swift's favourite hyperbole; used more than twenty times in
his poetry, when a very high number is needed.
177–8   compare *To Mr Gay* 58.
193   the stock   the pile of cards not dealt out but left on the table to be drawn as
necessary.
       cog a die   load the dice or cheat in a similar way: see *Dean Smedley Gone to
Seek His Fortune* 28.
208   Tray, or Cupid   names for lap-dogs: see *Bounce to Fop* 38–40. Tray is also
used as the name of a pet dog in Prior's *Alma* I, 329 (*Prior*, I, 479).
216   bipes et implumis   'a definition of man, disapproved by all logicians. *Homo
est animal bipes, implume, erecto vultu*' (note in Faulkner). For the logicians'
definition of the human species, and Swift's attitude towards the subject, see R.S.
Crane, 'The Houyhnhnms, the Yahoos and the History of Ideas', *Reason and the
Imagination*, ed. J.A. Mazzeo (1962), pp. 231–53; Clive T. Probyn, 'Swift and
the Human Predicament', *The Art of Jonathan Swift*, ed. Probyn (1978), pp. 57–
80. Both articles show how Swift's distinction between man and beast was reg-
ularly dependent on logicians' categories.
220   'vide Gulliver in his account of the Houyhnhnms' (note in Faulkner); *de-
generate* has the strict Latin force of 'depart from race or kind,' or 'assume the
wrong genus'.

TO A LADY

The publishing history may be summarized as follows:
   (1) A pamphlet was issued, on 15 November 1733, by John Wilford in Lon-

don, misleadingly claiming to reprint a non-existent Dublin text (compare *A Character, Panegyric, and Description of the Legion Club*). The title is *An Epistle to a Lady*. This is *T* 745, *Foxon* S841. With minor verbal alterations, it was reprinted in *A New Miscellany* (1734), which is *T* 39. The text extends to 274 lines: compared with the version presented here, ll. 81–2, 135–40, 157–8, 203–4 are missing.

(2) The poem was originally set up for *WF* but cancelled in its entirety when the volume was reconstructed at a late stage. Indeed, it is probable that it was this poem above all which occasioned the need to reorganize *WF*. Even the contentious *On Poetry: a Rhapsody* was left intact in the cancelled state. The title is *To a Lady*. A substantially similar text is that of *HEH* no. 81494, a copy not in Swift's hand tipped into a set of Swift's *Works* (1735), vol. II, that is, *WF*. For a full description and transcript, see *Mayhew*, pp. 94–114. The text runs to 280 lines; both versions in this category lack ll. 135–40. The title in *HEH* is *A Letter to a Lady*.

(3) *F* finally risked publication in 1746 in Vol. VIII of the *Works*. The title is *To a Lady*. The text consists of 284 lines; ll. 231–2 are absent. In addition, ll. 159–64 are represented by lines of asterisks. There are small variations but the text in substance is close to that of category (2). Most later editions, including the London *Misc*, derive from this source.

For a discussion of the textual history, see *Mayhew*, pp. 109–12; and, taking account of the discovery of the uncancelled copy of *WF*, Margaret Weedon in *The Library*, 5th ser. XXII (1967), 53–4. The text in this edition is based on *WF*, although I have followed *F* (1746) in one or two matters of presentation. Only significant variants in the other versions listed are recorded in the notes.

The exact circumstances of composition are not known. Williams surmised (*P* II, 629) that the first 140 lines were written at Market Hill between 1728 and 1730, with the remainder added in 1732 or 1733. This view has been widely accepted (see *PJH* II, 793; *Mayhew*, pp. 111–12), although it cannot be stated with certainty that any such gap in composition occurred. The opening section does have links with other poems addressed to Lady Acheson, but the only real indication of date is the apparent reference to *The Journal of a Modern Lady* (1729) at l. 67. Again, there is nothing in the second portion which could not have been composed during the Market Hill period. On the grounds that it is more plausible to set a date nearer to publication, the poem can be allotted to *c*.1733, but this is emphatically in the realms of guesswork.

We have a better understanding of the means by which the poem came into print. It was taken over to England by Mrs Mary Barber in the autumn of 1733 and handed over to Matthew Pilkington, who was just completing his year as chaplain to the Lord Mayor of London, John Barber (no relation). Through Benjamin Motte and Lawton Gilliver, the poem came to be printed by Wilford in November. It was some weeks before the ministry took any action, but early in January 1735 Wilford was arrested (*Mayhew*, p. 109, suggests that this measure was sparked off by the appearance of *On Poetry: a Rhapsody* on 31 December). Wilford incriminated Gilliver, who in turn named his fellow-bookseller Motte and also Pilkington. Both of these men were taken into custody within a matter of days (for Gilliver's confession, see Motte's letter to Swift, 31 July 1735, *Corr* IV, 371–2). Finally, Mrs Barber was also questioned, and during the examinations it became clear that Swift was the author of *To a Lady*. According to one story, Walpole determined to arrest him; but after protracted manoeuvres it appeared that no sufficient case for libel lay. In the summer of 1735 charges were finally dropped, though Pilkington in particular had suffered a blow to his reputation from which he never fully recovered. See his wife's *Memoirs*, ed. Iris Barry (1928), pp. 105–7. This was the closest Swift came to a head-on clash with the authorities after his move to Dublin; it may have been the deciding factor in his abandoning a planned last visit to England.

Although the poem provides an important datum in Swift's career, and expresses many of his strongest opinions, it has received little attention from a literary point of view. The fullest analysis is *Jaffe*, pp. 20–25, where three overlapping aims are detected: 'to compliment and teach the lady, to censure Walpole, and to comment comically on his art', which aims 'merge perfectly to form one of the best and most significant of [Swift's] poems'.

Title   see headnote for various forms. The sub-title is the same in all versions, except for the substitution of 'to make verses on her', in Wilford's edn. *HEH* has no sub-title.

3   could]   *WF, HEH, Wilford*; would   *F (1746)*.

9   These]   *WF, HEH, F (1746)*; Those   *Wilford*.

11   my Lady   Lady Acheson.

18   on dress   see *Daphne* 43–8 for hints of personal vanity.

35   a fondling   pet, object of endearments.

   heiress   of her father, Rt. Hon. Philip Savage, Chancellor of the Exchequer in Ireland.

37   Cockered   pampered, brought up indulgently.

40   continual]   *WF, F (1746)*; continued *HEH, Wilford*.

58   not me]   *WF, HEH, F (1746)*; me not   *Wilford*.

67   our]   *WF, Wilford*; your *HEH*. The line alludes to the poem addressed to Lady Acheson as *The Journal of a Modern Lady*.

78   fleer   sneer; a word Swift uses of scandal-mongering women (e.g. *My Lady's Lamentation* 117).

80   Kindlier]   *WF, F (1746)*; Kindly *HEH*.

   their]   *WF, HEH*;   her   *Wilford*.

81–2]   *WF, HEH, F (1746)*; *not in Wilford*.

86   laudanum   the main analgesic in use at this period.

95–6   recalling *Hudibras* I, i, 127–8, as pointed out by C. Kulischeck, *Notes & Queries* CXCVI (1951), 339.

102   Live]   *WF, HEH*; Are *Wilford*.

121–34   there was a great deal of proverbial lore, now forgotten, concerned with carving, helping oneself at table, etc.: see *Polite Conversation* for a meal exploiting these tags (*PW* IV, 169–92).

135–40]   *F (1746)*; *not in WF, HEH, Wilford*. The only clear sign that *F* had access to an independent source, although there are other hints to this effect.

141   essay   for the stress, see *My Lady's Lamentation* 148.

149   the planet of my birth   evidently Jupiter; *OED* cites a work of 1650, 'the great mirth of the Jovialists'.

157–8   *WF, HEH, F (1746)*; *not in Wilford*.

159–64]   *F (1746) prints rows of asterisks*.

159]   *WF, Wilford*; Where a monkey wore a crown   *HEH, Orrery annotation at Harvard*.

169   compare *The Dunciad* (1743) IV, 614, for Walpole 'at the helm'.

169–70   the same rhyme is used in *The Faggot* 51–2; the name must have been pronounced 'Wall-pool'.

171   shelves   sandbanks or submerged rocks.

175   the watermen of Thames   the bargees, who played an important role in London transport, were notorious for their ribald language.

177   ever-laughing sage   Democritus of Abdera (*c*.460–357 B.C.). So instanced by Horace, *Epistles* II, i, 194. Compare Prior, 'Democritus, dear droll, revisit earth, / And with our follies glut thy heightened mirth' (*Prior*, I, 465).

183   D'Anvers   'Caleb D'Anvers, the famous writer of the paper called *The Craftsman*. These papers are supposed to be written by the Lord Bolingbroke and Mr Pulteney, created Earl of Bath' (note in *WF*). The pseudonym under which the best-known opposition journal was conducted.

185   Pulteney . . . St Johns   see Biog. Dict. Bolingbroke's family name was St John.

188   Caleb   D'Anvers again.

  hoise   older form of 'hoist'.

189   Alecto   see *Cassinus and Peter* 81.

203–4]   *WF, HEH; not in Wilford.*

204   Blueskins   'a famous thief who was hanged some years ago' (note in *F*). Joseph Blake, executed after an attack on Jonathan Wild in November 1724; the subject of a ballad called *Newgate's Garland*, long attributed to Swift but probably by Gay. See *P* III, 111–15 for the text: also *Ball*, pp. 190, 334–6; *Gay*, II, 613–14. The poem is excluded from this edition.

210   Horace   'Ridiculum acri, / Fortius et melius &c.' (note in *F*). The reference is to *Satires* I, x, 14–15: 'Joking will often cut through hard knots more effectively than solemnity.'

212   sour]   *WF, Wilford*; scour *HEH*.

217   jerking   the full working of the image implies a metaphoric sense of the verb then current: 'to aim satire, sneer, carp' (*OED*).

223–4   exactly the same rhyme-words are used with a very different tone in *An Answer to a Scandalous Poem* 147–8.

227   brangling   squabbling; compare *The Dunciad* (1729) II, 230–31, 'Noise and Norton, brangling and Breval, / Dennis and dissonance'.

231–2]   *Wilford, HEH; not in F* (*1746*).

248   Morals   the influential *Moralia*. Swift owned an edition (Basle, 1542): *Library*, no. 232.

250   Maxims   the book of Proverbs.

254   the owners of St James'   the royal family and court.

256   St Stephen's   parliament, especially the Commons, who sat in St Stephen's Chapel: see *On Mr Pulteney being Put Out of the Council* 7.

258   Sir Robert Brass   Walpole's familiar nickname. See *A Serious Poem upon William Wood* 86.

263   the middle air   old construction for 'mid air': compare Milton, *On the Morning of Christ's Nativity* 164, where, technically, the air between the earth and the outer spheres is meant.

276   raps   here, simply 'blows'.

ON POETRY: A RHAPSODY

First published by J. Huggonson in London; dated 1733 and apparently published on the very last day of that year (*T* 741; Foxon S888). The title-page refers to a non-existent earlier Dublin printing, the familiar copyright device. Reprinted [Edinburgh, 1734]: this is *T* 742, *Foxon* S889. The real Dublin edition, by S. Hyde (*T* 743, *Foxon* S890), must have been published by 28 January 1734, when 'several printers and publishers, at Dublin, were taken into custody, for printing and publishing a poem, called *The Rhapsody on Poetry*' (news item in *Political State*, March 1734, quoted by *P* II, 640). The work went into a London collection during that year and then into *WF* and *Misc* (1735). The text here is based on *WF*, with blanks supplied from earlier printings and with additions listed below.

Six supplementary passages, ranging in length from two lines to thirty-six, have subsequently come to light. Four were printed by Scott as an addendum in 1824; two of these, plus a different pair of supplementary lines, are found in a transcript among the Orrery papers at Harvard. All six passages (with one couplet supplied by Scott missing) are in *HEH* 81494, in the volume which contains a transcript of *To a Lady*. See *Mayhew*, pp. 97–100, for a full description of the *HEH* material. Previous editors have reproduced these passages as 'rejected' lines, in a separate group. Williams argues (*P* II, 639) that 'if these passages were omitted primarily on political grounds, we cannot be sure how far the omissions represent Swift's intention. It would be inadvisable to incorporate them violently in the text of one of his most finished poems, and they are here, therefore, relegated to an appendix.' *PHD* follows the same practice, whilst *PJH* omits the additional lines.

The Penguin text incorporates all six passages, a new departure. (They form ll. 165–6, 189–92, 197–204, 217–18, 427–62, and 469–70). Orrery's transcript describes them as 'Verses by Dean Swift which ought to have been inserted in the *Rhapsody*, if it had been safe to print them'. The auxiliary verb is worth noting. In my view, it is significant that the *Rhapsody* went into *WF* intact, with the exception of a few blank words here and there. Even when the volume was reconstructed and *To a Lady* deleted altogether, nothing was done to the text of *On Poetry: a Rhapsody*. The reason, in my judgement, is simple: the censoring had already been performed before the first printing, as had not been the case with *To a Lady*. The *Rhapsody* is the more outspoken of the two, in its full version; and it was generally thought that the action taken against *To a Lady* arose largely from the ministry's displeasure concerning its opposite number (nothing was done until the *Rhapsody* appeared and caused a stir at the beginning of 1734). I conclude that the six passages were omitted simply and solely because of their inflammatory content. No 'violence' is done in restoring them to the text; they are stylistically in key, thematically relevant, and poetically enriching.

The exact date of composition is not known. *Mayhew*, p. 112, suggests that the poem 'was probably composed at about the same time as the latter half of [*To a Lady*]', which he would set at 1732 or the first half of 1733. A letter from Mrs Pendarves, tentatively allotted to the spring of 1733, mentions the work in progress (see *PJH* II, 800). In my opinion, the references to Gay (ll. 323, 521) are more likely to have been written during his lifetime than after it, i.e. before 4 December 1732; Swift was concerned about treatment of Gay by the court at this juncture, just before he received news of Gay's death (*Corr* IV, 97–100). There is no mention of the poem in Swift's surviving correspondence, apart from a glancing allusion by Pope when the *Rhapsody* was first published (*Corr* IV, 217–18).

The Oxford Jacobite William King reports in his memoirs that Queen Caroline was at first deceived by the ironies of the poem, until she was enlightened by

Lord Hervey. *Mayhew*, p. 113, reprints an Anglo-Latin fragment from *FV* which serves to confirm this story. The plain-spoken verses omitted (ll. 427–62) would not have aided the deception; and so their exclusion may have been part of the obfuscating tactics, rather than a basic poetic strategy.

It does not seem to have been observed that a famous section of the poem (ll. 353 ff.), in which Grub Street hacks are compared to lice and vermin, has a direct source in an essay by Addison. A controlling idea of Swift's work is actually borrowed from *Tatler*, no. 229 (26 September 1710), which opens as follows:

> The whole creation preys upon itself: every living creature is inhabited. A flea has a thousand invisible insects that tease him as he jumps from place to place, and revenge our quarrels upon him. A very ordinary microscope shows us, that a louse is itself a very lousy creature. A whale, besides those seas and oceans in the several vessels of his body, which are filled with innumerable shoals of little animals, carries about it a whole world of inhabitants; insomuch that, if we believe the calculations some have made, there are more living creatures which are too small for the naked eye to behold about the Leviathan, than there are of visible creatures upon the face of the whole earth. Thus every nobler creature is as it were the basis and support of multitudes that are his inferiors.
>
> This consideration very much comforts me, when I think of those numberless vermin that feed upon this paper, and find their substance out of it; I mean, the small wits and scribblers that every day turn a penny by nibbling at my lucubrations. This has been so advantageous to this little species of writers, that, if they do me justice, I may expect to have my statue erected in Grub Street, as being a common benefactor to that quarter.

The paper continues in the same vein, using images such as 'fleas' and a 'fry of little authors'. Swift was in London when this *Tatler* appeared: he had dined with Addison several times that month, most recently on 18 September (*JTS* I, 12, 14, 19, 22).

There were contemporary replies (*T* 1311, 1316, 1319) but no concerted howl of protest from an affronted Grub Street. Since then the poem has been the subject of extensive commentary, particularly in the last twenty-five years. *Ball*, p. 284, cites Goldsmith's view that it is one of the 'best versified' poems in the language (see Goldsmith, *Works*, ed. A. Friedman (1966), V, 323). More recent discussions include Herbert Davis, *Jonathan Swift: Essays on His Satire* (1964), pp. 169–71; David Ward, *Jonathan Swift: A Critical Introduction* (1973), pp. 197–200; *Johnson*, pp. 15–20, exploring a tripartite structure in the poem; *Jaffe*, pp. 44–51; *Fischer*, pp. 177–97; and (exploring the 'configurations of limitlessness' in this and other works by Swift) C.J. Rawson, *Gulliver and the Gentle Reader* (1973), pp. 60–83. One pervasive strain in the poem's imaginative operations is described in *Grub Street*, pp. 243–7.

Title   the spelling is 'Rapsody' in early editions; *Mayhew*, p. 112, connects this with a 'slangy double-pun upon "a rapp" or counterfeit coin and a "rap" or knock on the head'. It should, however, be stressed that the spelling was not uncommon, though becoming old-fashioned. For the implications of the word in an Augustan context, see P. Rogers, 'Shaftesbury and the Aesthetics of Rhapsody', *British Journal of Aesthetics* XII (1972), 244–57.

WF adds a headnote: 'The following poem was published in London and

Dublin, and having been much admired, we thought proper to include it in this collection: and although the author be not known, yet we hope it will be acceptable to our readers.' Note the surviving degree of caution.

3 Young's universal passion the series of satires, *The Universal Passion: The Love of Fame* (1725–8), by Edward Young.

11–24 compare *The Beast's Confession*, esp. ll. 203–20.

15 foundered suffering from an inflamed foot and so lame.

19–20 for the rhyme, compare ll. 335–6, as well as *A Fable of the Widow and Her Cat* 2–5; *Strephon and Chloe* 19–20.

33 beggar's brat a boy used to inspire compassion by a beggar: compare Gay, *Trivia* II, 142 (*Gay*, I, 147). See C. Probyn, *Notes & Queries*, XVI (1969) 184. This verse-paragraph owes an obvious debt to *Trivia* II, 135–65, describing Cloacinna's upbringing of her foundling son ('bulk', 'beggar's brat', 'dropped', shoe-cleaning, etc.)

bulk 'stall in front of a shop, on or under which indigents often slept' (note in *Gay*, II, 558, to *Trivia* II, 140).

36 Bridewell see *A Beautiful Young Nymph Going to Bed* 41.

stews the quarter where brothels abounded.

37 dropped compare the famous reference in *A Modest Proposal* to 'a child just dropped from its dam' (*PW* XII, 11).

42 blasted the central meaning is 'blighted, cursed', but the italics warn the reader of punning overtones ('puffed up', etc.).

51 smatter see *The Dean's Reasons for Not Building at Drapier's Hill* 60. The author of *A Tale of a Tub* planned a 'new help of smatterers' (*Tale*, p. 130).

54 hundred pound 'paid to the poet laureate, which place was given to one Cibber' (note in *WF*). The annual stipend was fixed at £100 by Charles I in 1630.

56 brought in an attainder the idea seems to be that Cibber (through his unworthiness) had corrupted and dishonoured the office, so that only the least admirable could inherit the post thereafter. An attainder was a process of degrading a criminal so that his heirs could not have titles or property transmitted to them.

72 the italics probably indicate an allusion, possibly to I Corinthians xii, 10.

77ff. the remainder of the poem is in the tradition of 'instructions' (here to a poet), the common seventeenth-century way of organizing a satire.

84 'sent from hand unknown' a regular formula used in connection with dramatic prologues and epilogues.

85 Aurora goddess of the dawn.

90 the traditional pose of the hack writer, as in Hogarth's *Distressed Poet* (1735).

91–104 Swift's satire on these features (prominent in the broadside editions of his own poems) may justify some editorial licence in the treatment of accidentals. There is no evidence that Swift sought to have his texts garnished in this fashion.

95 wipe see *My Lady's Lamentation* 7.

100 smokes recognizes, gets the point of.

103 learnéd commentators notably the author of *A Tale of a Tub*, who discourses on Homer's limitations and discovers strange matter in the poetry (*Tale*, pp. 127–8).

107 Lintot 'a bookseller in London' (note in *WF*). See Biog. Dict. and *Verses on the Death of Dr Swift* 253.

109 quit requite, repay.

113   hawker   see *Verses on the Death of Dr Swift* 279.

117   Will's   'the poet's coffee-house' (note in *WF*). See *To Mr Congreve* 146.

118   snug   in hiding.

122   swallow down your spittle   restrain your anger: compare Job vii, 19.

144   in quires   unbound.

147   safe's the word   compare *Journal of a Modern Lady* 219.

151   turns   stylistic embellishments.

158–60   alluding to the use of initials to disguise the identity of individuals satirized, as a precaution against reprisals.

161–8   typical Augustan verse technique, where the ostensible 'alternatives' are covertly identified with one another. The strong suggestion in l. 162 is that *the* statesman – Walpole – used the services of South Sea stock-jobbers and market operators, if indeed he was not to be regarded as a political 'jobber' himself.

165–6]   Orrery; HEH; not in WF.

168   suburb wench   see *To Stella, Who Collected and Transcribed His Poems* 72 and compare *On Mr Pulteney being Put Out of the Council* 6.

172   kennels   gutters (generally down the middle of a street).

175   marish   marsh; not quite obsolete usage in Swift's day.

177   So have I seen...   standard formula to introduce elaborate simile. Compare *Upon the South Sea Project* 61.

181   downs   mountains or uplands generally, without the overtones which are dominant today of a chalk-based pastoral landscape.

189–92]   Scott; not in WF. Lines 189–90 also in HEH.

190   well]   HEH; ill Scott.

        Duck   Stephen Duck: see *On Stephen Duck, the Thresher* and Biog. Dict.

192   D'Anvers   Caleb D'Anvers, pseudonym for the writer of *The Craftsman*: see *To a Lady* 183.

193   Sir Bob   Walpole.

196   on the nail   see *The Run upon the Bankers* 17.

197–204]   Orrery, Scott, HEH; not in WF.

204   compare *On the Words 'Brother Protestants'*.

208   baubles of the Tower   crown jewels.

217–18]   Scott, HEH; not in WF.

219–20   recalling the action of *The Dunciad*, book I (esp. I, 203–26 in the 1729 edn).

227   Charon's boat   see *A Quibbling Elegy on Boat* 24.

229   Cerberus   see *A Quibbling Elegy on Boat* 27. Again and again the idiom recalls Swift's poems of the South Sea Bubble era, suggesting that he may have planned a poem along the lines of the *Rhapsody* in the early 1720s; or else that, for some reason, his mind was drawn to this phase whilst composing the poem. For 'a sop to Cerberus`, see *Tilley* S634.

231   'Sunt geminae Somni portae – Altera candenti perfecta nitens elephanto. Virgil *l [iber]* 6' (note in *WF*). The reference is to *Aeneid* VI, 893–5: the full passage is translated by Dryden, 'Two gates the silent house of sleep adorn; / Of polished ivory this, that of transparent horn.' The dominance of this book of the *Aeneid* in Swift's imagination again manifests itself.

232   Excise   see *The Beast's Confession* 150.

245   oracles of both   time-serving lawyers and churchmen.

252   puny judge   punning on 'puisne' judge and 'puny', inconsiderable, ineffectual.

260 unities rules derived from Aristotle, which were supposed to confine the action of a play to twenty-four hours and the setting to a single locality: actually it was Castelvetro, as late as 1570, who elaborated these rules (*Poetics* 7–8 gives no explicit warrant). Influential in France, especially in the seventeenth century, they faced opposition in England from the time of Dryden to that of Johnson.

264 at all hazards at whatever risk: compare *Tale*, p. 89.

265–6 much scorned critics. For Rymer and Dennis, see Biog. Dict. They are also coupled in the *Tale*, pp. 37, 94, as 'most profound critics'. René le Bossu (1631–80), French neoclassical critic, well known in England for his work on epic poetry. Invoked by Martinus Scriblerus in his prolegomena to *The Dunciad* (*PTE* V, 50–51), as are Rymer and Dennis.

267 the prefaces of Dryden Swift had mixed feelings about his distant relative Dryden; the prefaces are similarly satirized in the *Tale*, p. 131.

272 Peri Hupsous the modern transliteration is *hypsos*, but this spoils the rhyme. A critical treatise of the first (?) century A.D. which came to be attributed to a third-century writer, Cassius Longinus. Hugely influential in importing the notion of sublimity into European criticism: Dennis was one of the earliest English critics so affected. See S.H. Monk, *The Sublime* (1935). The work had been translated from Boileau's French in 1698, and again, as part of Boileau's collected works, translated by John Ozell *et al.* (1711–12). There was an edition of the Greek text in 1710. See also note to l. 277.

276 for love or money a trite form of words; see Swift to Stella, 7 August 1712 (*JTS* II, 553), and Tilley L484.

277 Translated from Boileau's translation 'by Mr Welsted' (note in *WF*). Boileau's version dates from 1674. Leonard Welsted brought out a translation in 1712, allegedly based on the Greek original, and with remarks on the English poets appended. Swift was not alone in suspecting that Welsted had really taken his text from Boileau: for a discussion of the point, see D.A. Fineman, *Leonard Welsted: Gentleman Poet of the Augustan Age* (1950), pp. 50–55. See also Biog. Dict.

280 Battus usually identified as a nickname of Dryden; in part a generic portrait, with some relation to Pope's Atticus (see *Epistle to Arbuthnot* 209–12).

281 elbow-chair armchair with special 'elbows' (supports).

292 connoisseur a new word, to some extent replacing the term 'virtuoso'; the earliest usage in *OED* is in Mandeville's *Fable of the Bees* (1714).

296 Augusta Trinobantum 'the ancient name of London' (note in *WF*). The Roman name derived from the tribe of the Trinobantes, who inhabited the region of Middlesex and Essex. 'Augusta' by itself was commonly used for London, as in Dryden, *Mac Flecknoe* 64–5; Pope, *Windsor-Forest* 336, 377; Gay, *Trivia* III, 145; Thomson, *Spring* (1746), 108.

297 pecks of coals see *To Stella, Who Collected and Transcribed His Poems* 34.

*298 for a similar count, see *Tale*, p. 41: see also *Grub Street*, pp. 223, 262, 265–6, for other developments of the motif.

300 sovereign the first vowel would be pronounced [â] and make a good rhyme.

316 Smithfield drolls the shows put on at Bartholomew Fair: compare *The Dunciad* (1729) I, 2 and note. Swift's interest in puppet-shows and drolls is discussed in P. Rogers, 'Swift, Walpole and the Rope-Dancers', *Papers on Language & Literature* VIII (1972), 159–71.

317–18 Bavius and Maevius were the types of a poetaster, derived from

Virgil, *Eclogues* III, 90, and often used by the English Augustans, e.g. Pope, *The Dunciad* (1729) III, 16 and note. Compare also Swift to Pope, 26 November 1725: 'Take care the bad poets do not outwit you, as they have served the good ones in every age, whom they have provoked to transmit their names to posterity. Maevius is as well known as Virgil' (*Corr* III, 118).

Kentish Town would then have been a remote country suburb.

319   Tigellius Hermogenes Tigellius, a singer and poet despised by Horace: *Satires* I, iii, 3–4. He was much in favour with Caesar and Cleopatra, and is used as the example of a bad writer given official recognition. Enlisted as one of the line of critics in the *Tale*, p. 94.

320   that is, the length of Fleet Street, where the book trade was centred.

323   Gay alluding to the ministry's decision to ban the performance of *Polly* in 1728, and the subsequent dismissal of the Duchess of Queensberry from court because of her activities on behalf of Gay. See *Corr* III, 305, 321–6: 'The inoffensive John Gay is now become one of the obstructions to the peace of Europe, the terror of ministers, the chief author of the *Craftsman* and all the seditious pamphlets which have been published against the government. He has got several turned out of their places, the greatest ornament of the court banished from it for his sake, another great lady [Mrs Howard] in danger of being chasé [*sic*] likewise' (Arbuthnot to Swift, 19 March 1729). See also headnote concerning the date of composition.

325–6   Young Edward Young had been awarded a pension of £100 after dedicating his poem *The Instalment* to Walpole; it celebrated the prime minister's induction into the Order of the Garter. A few months earlier Young had also dedicated the seventh part of *The Universal Passion* to Walpole. Ministerial writers liked to remind the opposition of these facts. No direct contact between Swift and Young is known of, although Young was a regular correspondent of Tickell, and in touch with Pope, Mrs Howard, and other English acquaintances of Swift. He had sought the favour of Lady Giffard, sister of Swift's patron Temple. In this couplet Swift is no doubt thinking of the incense Young offered to Walpole, Compton, Bubb Dodington, and others in *The Universal Passion* – even if this was rather to *win* his pension than to keep it.

333   pericranies brains; from a rare anglicized version of 'pericranium'.

334   miscellanies main stress on first syllable.

335   Hobbes one of Swift's copies of *Leviathan* (1651) contained manuscript notes, but it is now lost. (He also owned *De Cive* and other works.) Hobbes's picture of the 'state of war by nature' is contained in Part I, chapter 13 of *Leviathan*, where, however, his emphasis is on discord among humans rather than in the animal kingdom. There is no close parallel in the text to Swift's lines.

353–6   the famous lines are foreshadowed in *Upon the South Sea Project* 73–4: compare also *On a Printer's being Sent to Newgate* 3–4. The later 'folk' versions probably derive, whether consciously or not, from Swift. One variant is quoted by the mathematician Augustus De Morgan in his *Budget of Paradoxes* (1872):

> Great fleas have little fleas upon their backs to bite 'em,
> And little fleas have lesser fleas, and so *ad infinitum*.
> And the great fleas themselves in turn have greater fleas to go on,
> While these again have greater still, and greater still, and so on.

The imagery of the passage clearly belongs to a phase of what has been called 'the microscopical fad', following the invention of a comparatively efficient microscope in the second half of the seventeenth century. Swift is known to have read the *Transactions* of the Royal Society, in which, for example, Antony von Leeuwenhoek in 1677 described minute animalcules in semen. This fad, which was a major component in the idiom of Augustan satire, is discussed by Marjorie H. Nicolson, George S. Rousseau, *This Long Disease, My Life* (1968), pp. 243–51 ('The Small in Nature'), whilst Miss Nicolson's *The Microscope and English Imagination* (1956), pp. 170–82, collects literary examples. Paul Fussell, *The Rhetorical World of Augustan Humanism* (1965), pp. 233–62, considers the way in which imagery of vermin is exploited in the period: pp. 242–5 relate specifically to Swift's poems, including the passage here.

369 personate feign, counterfeit.

385 Flecknoe Richard Flecknoe (d. ?1678), priest and minor poet, the butt of Marvell and Dryden.

Howard probably Edward Howard (*fl.* 1670), linked in an epigram to James Moore Smythe (l. 415), which has been attributed to Pope (*PTE* VI, 451). See also *The Dunciad* (1729) I, 250; and *Peri Bathous*, p. 27. *NCBEL* gives Howard's dates as '1624–*c.* 1700', whilst E.L. Steeves (*Peri Bathous*, p. 119) places his death in 1732. There may be some confusion of persons here: ll. 387–8 would not fit if Howard survived as long as that.

388 Blackmore Sir Richard Blackmore; see Biog. Dict.

392 Great poet 'Lord Grimston, lately deceased' (note in *WF*). William, Viscount Grimston, whose loyalty as an M.P. had been rewarded by the grant of a peerage in 1719: see Biog. Dict. He produced a play entitled *The Lawyer's Fortune, or Love in a Hollow Tree* (1705), which occasioned much ridicule. There is a reference in *Polite Conversation* (*PW* IV, 144); Pope calls Grimston 'a booby lord' (*Imitations of Horace, Sat.* II, ii, 176); and a derisive edition of *Love in a Hollow Tree* was issued in 1736. I do not know why Swift or Faulkner came to suppose that Grimston had died. His brother Sir Harbottle Luckyn died in 1737, but this would be too late to affect *WF*.

396 Duncenia a nonce-word for the kingdom of dunces.

common-weal republic.

397 pretend claim.

398 descend the italics indicate a pun: (1) to go on in succession, along the line of great dunces; (2) to achieve bathos or the 'profound'. The Scriblerian joke about the art of sinking rests on such misapplications of words: for 'descent' see *Peri Bathous*, pp. 15–16.

405 'The Latins, as they came between the Greeks and us, make use of the word *altitudo*, which implies equally height and depth' (*Peri Bathous*, p. 6).

409 '*Vide* the treatise on *The Profound*, and Mr Pope's *Dunciad*' (note in *WF*). The entire verse paragraph looks back to these works, especially *Peri Bathous*. For images of diving, see P. Rogers, 'Swift and the Idea of Authority', *The World of Jonathan Swift*, ed. B. Vickers (1968), pp. 29–30.

410 Welsted Leonard Welsted: see Biog. Dict. and note to l. 277. He figures in *Peri Bathous*, p. 27, as one of the didappers, who 'keep themselves long out of sight, underwater, and come up now and then when you least expect them'. In *The Dunciad* he takes part in the mud-diving games, 'precipitately dull / . . . No crab more active in the dirty dance, / Downwards to climb, and backward to advance' (1729 edn, II, 293–300).

412 The laureate 'In the London edition, instead of *laureate*, was maliciously inserted Mr Fielding, for whose ingenious writings the supposed author hath manifested a great esteem' (note in *WF*). Henry Fielding was certainly a great admirer of Swift; there is no evidence outside this note that the feelings were reciprocated, although Swift would doubtless have approved of the tendency of Fielding's plays in the mid 1730s, as they were strongly anti-Walpole.

413 Concanen Matthew Concanen: see Biog. Dict. In *The Dunciad* (1729) he is styled 'a cold, long-winded native of the deep'; Swift's verses recall *The Dunciad* (1729) II, 287–91. Perhaps offended by his omission from *Peri Bathous*, Concanen had brought out *A Supplement to the Profound* (1728).

415 Jemmy Moor James Moore Smythe: see Biog. Dict. He also figures both in *Peri Bathous*, p. 28, as one of the frogs, and in *The Dunciad* (1729) II, 31–46, as a phantom poet.

417 heads to points facing in opposite directions, or upside down.

427–62] *Orrery, Scott, HEH; not in WF.* Clearly too outspoken to risk publication.

447 Prometheus one of Swift's favourite myths. Compare ll. 451–3 with *Prometheus* 3–5.

462 turn to grazers not 'graziers' (people who feed cattle), but 'people grazing like animals', as Nebuchadnezzar, King of Babylon, was made to do, as a punishment for impiety: Daniel iv, 31–3.

467–8 for the rhyme, see *Twelve Articles* 23–4.

469–70] *Orrery, HEH; not in WF.*

474 the conquering hero the famous lines, 'See the conquering hero comes' were not set by Handel until 1747, but they appeared in Lee's *Rival Queens* (1677), a much performed tragedy, well known to Swift.

475 '*Super et Garamantas et Indos / Proferet imperium – / Jam nunc et Caspia, regna / Responsis horrent divum –*' (note in *WF*). The reference is to *Aeneid* VI, 795–9: Dryden translates, 'Africa and India shall his power obey; / ... At his foreseen approach, already quake / The Caspian kingdoms and Maeotian lake.'

Hydaspes a tributary of the Indus; used in classical poetry to express a very remote location (e.g. Virgil, *Georgics* IV, 211).

478 Short by the knees 'genibus minor. Horace' (note in *WF*). Alluding to *Epistles* I, xii, 28: 'on bended knees', in effect.

479 The consort Queen Caroline: compare *Directions for a Birthday Song* 173–86.

481–2 compare *Directions for a Birthday Song* 69–70.

483 Iulus Frederick, Prince of Wales. The name derives from the son of Aeneas, from whom the line of the Emperor Augustus claimed descent.

484 Late, very late ... Swift transforms a conventional platitude ('long may he reign') into an insult: 'may it be a long time before he rules us.' In the event, Frederick was never to succeed to the throne.

493 Bright goddesses the five daughters of George II and Caroline: see *Directions for a Birthday Song* 165–70.

494 Duke William the Duke of Cumberland: see *Directions for a Birthday Song* 200.

496 without a mate a sneering allusion to the infidelities of Walpole's wife Catherine, and to his own kept mistress, Maria Skerrett, by whom he had an illegitimate daughter in 1725. See *Plumb*, pp. 78, 112–14.

498 Atlas from his bulk; Walpole was often portrayed in caricatures as a Colossus, like Gulliver among the Lilliputians. Compare *Atlas* 15–22.

500 prudent Fabius '*Unus homo nobis cunctando restituit rem*' (note in *WF*). A line from the ancient poet Ennius, preserved in Cicero, *De Officiis* I, xxiv, 84: 'One man restored our state by delays.' Quintus Fabius Maximus, consul of Rome (d. 203 B.C.), who was given the surname Cunctator, 'the delayer', because of his cautious and slow-moving tactics during the Second Punic War. Hence the epithet 'Fabian'. Compare Dryden, *Threnodia Augustalis* 388–9: 'Thou Fabius of a sinking state, /Who didst by wise delays, divert our fate.'

503 director a baneful word in the years after the South Sea Bubble: compare *To Charles Ford, Esq. on His Birthday* 40.

508 the sable flock churchmen (from their black gowns). The point is that Walpole and Bishop Gibson had ensured a steady flow of Whig appointments to the bishops' bench, some of whom were regarded by High Church clergy as theologically suspect and personally dishonourable.

510 steerage helm (as *Verses on the Death of Dr Swift* 417).

515 St George patron of the Order of the Garter.

516–18 azure ... cerulean the blue ribbon of the Order of the Garter: compare *Verses on the Revival of the Order of the Bath* 2, and *Verses on the Death of Dr Swift* 323.

521 see headnote concerning the date of composition.

527 Lewis Louis XIV.

529 mortified his pride the allies defeated France in the War of Spanish Succession.

540 'Divisum imperium cum Jove Caesar habet' (note in *WF*). 'Caesar has divided sovereignty with Jove': the phrase has the ring of Tacitus but I cannot identify a source.

542 butter-weight formerly eighteen or more ounces to the pound, hence the obsolete figurative expression meaning 'for good measure'.

544 Jove Orrery fills the blank in the original edition with 'Christ'.

548 Woolston Thomas Woolston: see Biog. Dict. and *Verses on the Death of Dr Swift* 281–98.

Caetera desiderantur 'the rest is missing': a formula Swift had used to good effect elsewhere, notably in the *Tale*, pp. 170, 200; and *Battle of the Books* (*Tale*, pp. 244, 258).

THE HARDSHIP PUT UPON LADIES

WF (cancelled state) is the first printing; the poem was introduced because *To Mr Gay* had been shorn of many of its plain-spoken notes and now occupied less space (see headnote to that item). The lines are headed 'written in the year 1733'.

5 almost identical to the phrase used by Lady Smart in *Polite Conversation*: 'But if women had been the law-makers, it would have been better' (*PW* IV, 198). Another of Swift's teasing tricks of bouncing a cliché back at ladies.

A LOVE SONG IN THE MODERN TASTE

Printed in the *Gentleman's Magazine* for June 1733, and identified as 'A Song by Dr Swift'. Included in *WF*, where the title used here was provided. *WF* states, 'written in the year 1733', which may simply be a recognition of the previous publication. Text from *WF*.

A verse equivalent to *Polite Conversation*, the work consists of a string of poetic clichés. They were not all newly fashionable in the 1730s, indeed most of the pantheon remained what it had been in Swift's youth. The joke lies in slotting together so many familiar ideas in a more or less coherent sequence. Maurice Johnson suggests that Pope may have had a share in its composition, but there is no kind of certainty about this (*Johnsonian News Letter* X (1950), 4-5). *Jaffe*, p. 53, finds a 'curiously pretty' effect in the verse, for all its banality, but suspects this 'may be a trick of the Post-Keatsian ear'. On the other hand, Swift could be 'following Pope in the parody of verses he has a latent fondness for'.

5   Mild Arcadians   the joke rests partly on the fact that the word 'Arcadian' was ambiguous: as well as suggesting idealized poet-shepherds, such as are found in Virgil's *Eclogues*, it could mean 'ninnies' (see Juvenal's use of the epithet *Arcadicus* in *Satires* VII, 160).
9   Cyprian goddess   Venus; compare *Cadenus and Vanessa* 2; *Strephon and Chloe* 47.   Most strongly present in Swift's mind would be not Shakespeare's poem, *Venus and Adonis*, so much as Ovid, *Metamorphoses* X, 519-739.
13   Cynthia   the moon-goddess Diana, perhaps here invoked as a symbol of chastity; Apollo was her twin-brother.
17   Pluto   ruler of the underworld.
23   compare *Rape of the Lock* I, 22.
25   Meander   a winding river in Phrygia.
26   purling   a word associated by Swift with empty pastoral language: see, for example, *A Panegyric on the Dean* 241 (ll. 241-8 recall the present poem).
29   Philomela   the nightingale: see *Metamorphoses* VI, 438-674.
31   bird of Juno   peacock.

VERSES MADE IN SWIFT'S SLEEP

Swift's young friend, Rev. John Lyon, transcribed a memorandum containing these lines into a copy of Hawkesworth's *Life of Swift*, which is now in *FV*, no. 579. First printed in Ball's edition of the correspondence (1913). Text from *FV*.
The memorandum runs:

December 27, 1733.
I waked at two this morning with the two above lines in my head, which I had made in my sleep, and I wrote them down in the dark, lest I should forget them. But as the original words being writ in the dark, may possibly be mistaken by a careless or unskilful transcriber, I shall give them a fairer copy, that two such precious lines may not be lost to posterity.

Title   the editor's.

ON THE WORDS 'BROTHER PROTESTANTS
AND FELLOW CHRISTIANS'

The first known publication is in a supplement at the end of the *Gentleman's Magazine*, vol. II (1733), probably issued early in 1734. It appeared, with some explanatory material, in the *Grub-street Journal* on 14 February 1734. It was reprinted in a volume of miscellanies that year and then in *WF* in 1735. The text here is based on *WF*, except that many blanks have been supplied from other sources.

The Presbyterians in Ireland (who were concentrated mainly in Ulster) had mounted a strong campaign to have the Test Act repealed; this confined public officers to members of the established church. The Lord Lieutenant, the Duke of Dorset, had apparently favoured relaxation of the law, but after strong opposition, in and out of parliament, the plan to repeal it was dropped late in 1733. Swift had written four pamphlets strongly opposing the scheme (*PW* XII, 241-95), of which *The Presbyterians' Plea of Merit* (1733) is closest to this poem. Richard Bettesworth, serjeant-at-law and Irish M.P., had incurred Swift's dislike in the course of other political campaigns at this juncture; henceforth he was to be a regular target for satire. See Biog. Dict.

Bettesworth's response is set out, albeit in an interested manner, by Swift himself: see his letter to the Duke of Dorset, January 1734 (*Corr* IV, 219-21). Here Swift describes how Bettesworth came to threaten him in retaliation for the insults bestowed in this poem. (Swift's biographer Sheridan says that Bettesworth promised to cut off the Dean's ears (*Life of the Reverend Dr Jonathan Swift*, 1784, pp. 438-40), but the letter merely says, 'he had a sharp knife in his pocket, ready to stab or maim me.') Press reports reveal that the inhabitants of the liberty of St Patrick's signed a public resolution to defend Swift against the threatened attacks (see *Ferguson*, p. 185).

Title *WF* adds a note, 'The following poem having been printed in London, we have thought it proper to insert it here, not doubting but it will be acceptable to our readers; although we cannot say who is the author.' A blind, of course.

1   the fable   by Aesop. L'Estrange's *Fables* (1692) I, 124; *Tilley* A302.

13   pippin   a give-away word: compare *The Virtues of Sid Hamet the Magician's Rod* 74, *The Fable of Midas* 6, *To Betty the Grisette* 9, etc. Bettesworth had claimed that 'by his taste, and skill in poetry, he was as sure [Swift] writ [the lines] as if he had seen them fall from [his] pen' (*Corr* IV, 220), and this usage would support his judgement.

15   Lamb   presumably a chiropodist and quack; I have not found him among the many fringe practitioners who advertised in the press.

16   Radcliffe   Dr John Radcliffe: see Biog. Dict. A representative figure, since he had already been dead almost twenty years.

20   subscribes   ends his letter.

23   Horace   Horatio Walpole: see Biog. Dict. The joke is partly the fact that he *could* have spoken appropriately in parliament of his 'brother', the chief minister.

25   Bettesworth   see headnote.

27   margent   commentary, gloss.

28   Singleton   Henry Singleton, Prime Serjeant, later one of Swift's executors: see Biog. Dict.

serjeant   a superior grade of barrister, from which class judges were drawn; there were three officially designated serjeants-at-law in Ireland, of whom Singleton was the senior.

29   fanatic   Swift's term for dissenters.

30   discipline   church hierarchy.

32   Philistines   stressed on second syllable.

42   brethren to a Scot   the Ulster Presbyterians were Scottish in origin.

49 Moses Exodus viii, 16–18.

52 hearts more hardened adapting the words applied to Pharaoh (Exodus vii–xi).

56 rod alluding to Aaron's rod (Exodus vii–viii).

59–60 there was a proverbial usage, 'as sure as a louse in the bosom' (*Tilley* L467).

61 with humble Job Job xvii, 14.

64 bit punning on the senses 'made a fool of' and 'bit by the vermin'.

THE YAHOO'S OVERTHROW

First published by Deane Swift in 1765; included in *F*, vol. XIII, the same year. Text based on Deane Swift.

A direct follow-up to the previous item, making fun of Bettesworth's threats to revenge himself on Swift. It probably dates from the early part of 1734.

Title *Kevin Bail* that is, the bailey of St Kevin, the parish within which St Patrick's Cathedral stood. See Swift to Orrery, 17 July 1735 (*Corr* IV, 369).

'*Derry down*' 'one of the most popular [tunes] in the eighteenth century'; used in a number of ballad operas, including *The Beggar's Opera*. See *Simpson*, pp. 172–6.

1 Donore a district adjoining St Patrick's, to the south-west.

2 Smithfield just across the Liffey from St Patrick's.

3 in grain confirmed, inveterate.

7 skip footman or lackey; a 'scout' at Trinity College; or perhaps short for 'skipjack', a whippersnapper.

8 Four Courts the centre of judicial proceedings; then located near Christ Church Cathedral; moved to the present site on the northern quay of the Liffey in 1796. See *Gilbert*, I, 133.

House the House of Commons; for the new building, begun in 1729, see *A Character, Panegyric, and Description of the Legion Club* 2.

9 Towser see *A Fable of the Widow and Her Cat* 45.

leap of a louse used of something inconsiderable: see *Mrs Harris's Petition* 38.

13 bombast accent on second syllable, as was usual.

21 fanatical crew dissenters.

22 brother Protestants see *On the Words 'Brother Protestants'*. Here stressed 'protéstant'.

23 Red hat of a cardinal.

blue bonnet of Scottish Presbyterians (blue was the Covenanters' colour, hence 'true-blue' meant a staunch Whig).

turban of a Mohammedan, a 'Turk' or infidel.

26 Hobbes, Tindal, and Woolston types of the free-thinker: Thomas Hobbes (1588–1679), the philosopher. For Tindal and Woolston, see Biog. Dict.

Collins Anthony Collins, whom Swift had more than once ridiculed: see Biog. Dict.

Nayler James Nayler (*c.* 1617–60), Quaker, served in the parliamentary army, imprisoned and pilloried during the time of the Commonwealth for blasphemy.

27 *Muggleton* Lodowicke Muggleton (1609–98), founder of the transcendentalist creed, whose adherents became known as Muggletonians.

Toland see Biog. Dict. and *Toland's Invitation to Dismal*.

Bradley the tailor evidently a sectary or pseudo-prophet, but not one I can identify.

31–4 Bettesworth had supported in parliament a measure to commute the tithe on flax, which threatened to reduce the income of many clergymen. Swift wrote a pamphlet in opposition to the bill, published on 8 January 1734 (*PW* XIII, 94–108): for this episode, see *Landa*, pp. 123–35. The suggestion in l. 34 is perhaps that the church will be disestablished altogether.

42 wages of sin recalling St Paul (Romans vi, 23).

44 bounced blustered.

46–9 see *On the Words 'Brother Protestants'*, headnote.

49 zags perhaps meaning pointed ears?

56 colt beat with a rope's end (a nautical punishment).

57 Rap uncertain; probably short for 'rapparee', meaning bandit (see *The Answer to 'Paulus'* 97).

58 we will drag him in the gutter and cover him with the refuse of the streets (see *P* III, 817).

59 modus a word used of the tithe bill Swift was opposing, to mean an arrangement for compounding a payment (see *Landa*, p. 132).

62 kiss, and be friends proverbial: used by Swift in writing to Stella (*JTS* I, 170), and in *Polite Conversation* (*PW* IV, 160); *Tilley* F753.

64 A face his buttocks.

67 Kite the second the word 'kite' was used of a rapacious person or sharper; it was also lawyer's slang for a junior counsel who accepted a dock-brief. In Farquhar's *The Recruiting Officer* (1706), Sergeant Kite is a cunning and voluble character with something of the mountebank about him. Swift's 'serjeant' is not military but legal.

74 a brutality perhaps transferred from Swift's other enemy, Richard Tighe (see *Mad Mullinix and Timothy*, headnote).

AN EPIGRAM, INSCRIBED TO THE HONOURABLE SERJEANT KITE

A dubious item. This further attack on Bettesworth obviously belongs to the same juncture as the two previous items; but whether Swift was responsible for it is hard to determine. First published by Scott (1814), and said to be from a holograph, of which all trace has been lost. Since then, generally accepted as Swift's; but there are no really firm grounds for the attribution. Text based on Scott.

8 Povey 'sergeant-at-arms to the House of Commons' (note in *P* III, 818).

ON THE ARCHBISHOP OF CASHEL AND BETTESWORTH

First published by Deane Swift (1765), and incorporated in *F* the same year. The date of composition is not known, but the item seems to relate to the quarrel with Bettesworth at the start of 1734. See *On the Words 'Brother Protestants'*, headnote. Theophilus Bolton became Archbishop of Cashel in 1729. His good relations with Swift by 1735 are indicated by surviving letters (*Corr* IV, 316, 330). Text based on Deane Swift.

1 Dick Bettesworth. His attacks on Bolton would presumably be in parliament, and thus unreported in print.
4 bite ruse.
5 vapour bluster. The same rhyme is used in *To Dean Swift* 1-2.
6 who attempted the Drapier puzzling; the meaning is 'who took on (or attacked) the Drapier', and Bolton had been one of the Privy Council to dissent from the proclamation against the Drapier in 1724 (*Ferguson*, p. 122). It was from this date that relations between Swift and Bolton began to improve. Though Bolton had been an enemy whilst Chancellor of St Patrick's (*Corr* II, 275, 434), he did not fall on Swift in quite the way this reference would suggest. It is conceivable that the manuscript was misread and a word like 'attended', 'assisted' or 'defended' should be supplied.
11 obdurate the stress on second syllable was once commoner than today.
15-16 the rhyme is interesting. In his earlier work Swift uniformly rhymes 'plain' with words like 'vain', carrying the ordinary [eɪ] sound. From about 1728 he several times uses a word like 'Dean' or 'clean', whose received pronunciation increasingly would be [i], indicating greater readiness to admit 'Irish' speech-effects. The older pronunciation, as exemplified by 'tay' for tea, did not wholly die out in England until the second half of the eighteenth century; but the general view is now that it was much less common in 1725 than in 1700.

EPIGRAM ON FASTING

Originally included in the uncancelled state of *WF*, without a title; removed when the volume had to be reconstructed. Alone of the four poems thus excised, the epigram had no offensive potential; it simply cannot have fitted in when the new items were set up in the corrected state. Charles Davis, who based his edition of *Misc* later that year on uncancelled sheets, included the poem with the title used here. First included in *F* (as released to the public) in 1746. Reprinted from the *Misc* text in various London periodicals.

The piece is obviously undatable, although one might suspect that it is fairly late (*c.* 1730-34?). I have not been able to locate the source of the French epigram. Text based on Davis's 1735 printing.

ON HIS OWN DEAFNESS

A full account of the textual and publishing history will be found in *Mayhew*, pp. 115-30. In brief, the first English version appeared in the *Dublin Evening Post* on 26 October 1734; Faulkner printed both Latin and English versions in the *Dublin Journal* on 29 October; whilst the bout was brought to an end with slightly different versions in the *Post* on the same date. Predictably the London press followed suit, and during November the two versions were published in the *London Evening Post* and the *Gentleman's Magazine*. There are minor differences but these texts are substantially the same; the English version in each case consists of eight lines. The poem, in both languages, was collected by *F* in 1746.

However, a draft by Swift himself remained unpublished until it was brought to attention by Mayhew in 1954. The Latin consists of four lines, as in the printed versions, but they show significant variants. Moreover, the English poem runs to ten lines, and differs at several points. It would be laborious to set out all

the minor English variants when the poem is so short: it will be easier to appreci-
ate the points at issue if a single representative text is cited in full. This is the
poem as it first appeared in the *Dublin Evening Post* (normalized according to the
practice in this edition):

> *A Reverend Dean's Lamentation*
> *for the Loss of His Hearing*
> Deaf, giddy, helpless, left alone,
> To all my friends a burden grown;
> No more I hear my parish bell,
> Than if it rung for my own knell:
> At thunder now no more I start,
> Than at the rumbling of a cart;
> And what's incredible, alack;
> No more I hear a woman's clack.

All previous editions of Swift's poetry reproduce this version, in substance.
The text here is based on *HEH*, Swift's own draft.

According to Rev. John Lyon, 'These lines . . . lay on his [Swift's] table when
his servant brought up dinner one day in September 1734, which his house-
keeper Mrs Ridgway upon seeing them requested the copy of, and he gave her
the said paper directly' (MS note in Hawkesworth's *Life, FV* no. 579). This was
presumably the copy which found its way to the press; the version in *HEH*
seems to represent an earlier state.

It is known that Swift suffered a bad attack of his linked disorders, giddiness
and deafness, in the middle of September 1734, and that this lasted until early
October (*Corr* IV, 257, 261–2). *Mayhew*, p. 110, points out that the severe
attacks he underwent at this time finally laid to rest Swift's long-held hopes of
making a last visit to England. In Mayhew's view, the *HEH* draft represents a
'more privately meaningful version' of the poem, for which a 'more generalized'
and public set of verses was substituted in the printed text.

1   Verticosus   the early printed texts have the unmetrical *vertiginosus*.

2   missus   the printed texts have *tonitru*; the noun *tonitru* was regarded as neu-
ter, but, according to Lewis and Short's *Dictionary*, the form is (as a nominative)
confined to the grammarians. Swift may have thought of it as masculine, like
tonitrus. *Mayhew*, p. 128, suggests that Swift may be versifying the proverb, *Pro-
cul ab Jove, procul ab fulmine*: 'Far from Jove, far from his thunder.'

4]   Swift (HEH); Vix clamosa meas mulier jam percutit aures   *printed texts*.
The revision seems an improvement here; I do not think it likely that Swift
would have changed from the line as printed to the *HEH* version.

13–14   a possible explanation for the deletion of these lines is suggested by
Mayhew, p. 128, who notes a parallel with *Journal of a Modern Lady* 170–71:
'Aura, whose tongue you hear a mile hence, / Talks half a day in praise of
silence.' Mayhew observes that Aura was, 'by 1734, commonly, identified by the
town with Swift's Dublin friend, Lady Anne Acheson', and thus the lines could
have given her offence.

ANGLO-LATIN VERSES

These verses are all written in one of Swift's invented languages: specifically, the
one called 'Latino-Anglicus', in which English words were set out in Latin

formations. See *Mayhew*, pp. 135–9, on the development of these language games. Many other scraps survive but nothing which can be identified as verse. The 'Club Verses' printed in *F* (1767) and reprinted in *P* III, 1039, do not appear to be verses at all.

As Sonata in Praes o Molli

Text from Swift's autograph in *FV*; first published in *F* (1767) as 'To Samuel Bindon, Esq.' doubtless a relative of the painter Francis Bindon.

'Molly's a beauty, Has an acute eye; No lass so fine is, Molly divine is. O my dear mistress, I'm in a distress; Can't you discover Me as a lover.'

A Love Song from Dick Bettesworth to Miss Molly Whiteway

Text from Swift's autograph in *FV*; the title is in another hand. For Bettesworth, see Biog. Dict. Molly Whiteway was the daughter of Swift's cousin, Mrs Martha Whiteway; she was, in fact, her daughter by a former husband and was more accurately Molly Harrison. She married Deane Swift, the biographer, in 1739.

'My dear Miss Molly, You're melancholy, It is a folly; For aye a lover, A-rambling at Dover, Your Dick may come over.'

An Epigram

Text from *HEH*. There is a four-line version in *FV*. First printed by *F* (1746), whence the title is taken. Dick is Richard Tighe: see Biog. Dict. *Mayhew*, p. 147, dates it 1734/5.

'A swine is a beauty, compare it to Dick; a sight of his phiz, it might make a cat sick; [?Readier, I know,] a tester (sixpence), a quart o' fine ale, for a ring at his nose and a string at his tail.'

A Love Song

Text from *HEH*. First printed in *F* (1746), whence the title is taken.

'A pudding is all my desire, My mistress I never require. A lover, I find it a jest is, His misery never at rest is.'

'In My Company'

First printed by *Mayhew*, p. 147, from *HEH*; another attack on Tighe. Mayhew translates,

'In my company pray, Dick, sit. Claret fine is, never mix it. Can't you tell us, Dick, a story; Sing at supper "Tory Rory". Ale to claret added base is; Toast a lady, fiery faces.' See also *Mayhew*, pp. 147–8, for parallel passages in Swift.

VERSES SPOKEN EXTEMPORE BY DEAN SWIFT ON HIS CURATE'S COMPLAINT OF HARD DUTY

A doubtful item. Like the following item, it appeared in the *Gentleman's Magazine* for December 1734 (see *T* 746B). Most of the *Magazine's* attributions at this period are plausible, but they do not carry strong authority. The assignment of these two pieces to Swift remains conjectural, since *F* never incorporated either. These *Verses* went into various collections, ostensibly as Swift's, and were collected by Nichols in 1775.

There are some early transcripts listed in *P* II, 674–5. No significant variant appears. One copy recorded by Williams has a note, 'Mr Hewit was one of the officiating curates of the parish adjoining the Dean's.' Text based on *Gentleman's Magazine*.

3   great St Mary   a transcript in the Portland papers has 'little' for 'great', and glosses 'St Mary, Guildford'. No supporting evidence has been found. It seems more likely that the reference is to St Mary's, Dublin, in which parish Stella lived for many years.

6   hymen   marriage.

8   purified   the rite of 'churching' of women after childbirth.

12   chopped   an obsolete usage of the verb 'to chop', meaning to speak hurriedly and swallow one's words: see *OED*, 'chop', $v.^3$ (2).

16   Robert Hewit   see headnote.

THE PARSON'S CASE

See previous item. The *Gentleman's Magazine* printing (December 1734) was preceded by appearances in various newspapers in Dublin and London, apparently beginning with the *Dublin Journal* on 3 December. See *T* 746C. Text here based on *Gentleman's Magazine*.

There are one or two touches which have an air of authenticity (e.g. l.9), but nothing that a skilled parodist could not have reproduced. It may be scholarly inertia which keeps this poem and the preceding item in the canon; however, decisive evidence is lacking which would compel their relegation.

2   strain heroic   compare *To a Lady* 144.

9   compare *The Power of Time* 5–6.

25   scarf   a nobleman's chaplain wore a special scarf; the idea seems to be that the new dean would have ample private patronage.

29   his Grace   an archbishop (Boulter?) or perhaps a duke, most likely the Duke of Dorset, Lord Lieutenant of Ireland, both of whom wielded immense patronage.

THE DEAN AND DUKE

First published in full by Deane Swift in 1765, although a much truncated version of four lines had appeared in *F* (1746). Swift's own manuscript of the full poem is in *FV*, endorsed 'January 1734–5'. The text here is based on the holograph except for one reading adopted from Deane Swift.

For James Brydges, Duke of Chandos, see Biog. Dict. Swift probably got to know Chandos when he was in the lucrative office of Paymaster to the Forces during the reign of Queen Anne; there are references to him in the *Journal to Stella* (*JTS* I, 21, 252). The two men then lost contact until Swift wrote to Chandos in August 1734, requesting certain public records of Ireland, which had come into the possession of Chandos (*Corr* IV, 250–51). On 7 October Swift told Mrs Pendarves that he had received no reply from the Duke, despite the fact that he had 'known the Duke long and well, and thought [he] had a share in his common favour' (*Corr* IV, 259). As late as February 1738 the collection remained in Chandos's hands, and Swift asked Orrery if he could prevail on him to give it up – 'which he seemed to promise, but he seemed also to treat me when I was come to Ireland, as if he had no acquaintance with me' (*Corr* V, 90). Somehow the Duke had managed to preserve a somewhat stiff relationship with Pope, who had been thought to portray him as 'Timon' in the *Epistle to Burlington*; but his friendship with Swift was never repaired.

2 James is beduked   he was created Duke of Chandos in 1719. When Swift first knew him he was plain Mr Brydges, a man on the make but with a long way still to climb.

6 got by fraud   as Paymaster, by peculation and the widely practised means of putting public funds out to interest for private gain. He was involved with contractors and bankers such as Sir Henry Furnese (see *A Dialogue between Captain Tom and Sir Henry Dutton Colt* 14). See also G. Davies, 'The Seamy Side of Marlborough's War', *Huntington Library Quarterly* XV (1952), 21–44.

lost by stocks   Chandos was widely thought to have lost a fortune in the South Sea Bubble affair; in fact he lost only the remnant of a former large gain. See C.H. Collins Baker and Muriel I. Baker, *The Life of...Chandos* (1949), pp. 208–13.

8 bands of fiddlers   Chandos had long maintained a fine musical establishment. Swift referred to this in a letter to Auditor Harley on 9 February 1720 (*Corr* II, 339). Handel was musical director at Chandos's great house at Cannons *c*.1718–20, with the noble Chandos anthems the most significant outcome. *Acis and Galatea*, in which Pope and Gay may have had a hand, was also first performed at Cannons.

9 build, and plant   as well as building Cannons, Chandos was busy erecting properties in Cavendish Square, Bath, and Bridgewater. For the grounds at Cannons, see Baker and Baker, op. cit., pp. 152–62.

11 Duke Humphrey   Duke of Gloucester (1391–1447), son of Henry IV; a collector and patron, which may be the reason for Swift's reference: Chandos had great pretensions in both capacities. But 'to dine with Duke Humphrey' meant 'to go dinnerless' (*Tilley* D637), and Swift may be adapting the expression to suggest that Chandos will be bereft of the means to provide for himself.

13 thy crown] *Deane Swift*; your frown *Swift MS* (*FV*). It is not quite certain what Swift intended, but the idea of a coronet makes the best sense.

14 Thy brother   Dr Henry Brydges (1675–1728), Archdeacon of Rochester.

thy betters   used in this way of a single person in early modern English.

16 a string   ribbon of chivalric order, but also suggesting hangman's rope.

ON DR RUNDLE

First published in *F* (1762), the basis for the text here. Composition must be either 1735 or 1736. Thomas Rundle was appointed Bishop of Derry in February 1735. Swift came to think well of him: he arrived about June and by September Swift was writing to Pope, 'He is indeed worth all the rest you ever sent us, but that is saying nothing, for he answers your character; I have dined thrice in his company.' Pope replied in glowing terms:

> I am glad you think of Dr Rundle as I do. He will be an honour to the
> bishops, and a disgrace to one bishop [Gibson], two things you will like: but
> what you will like more particularly, he will be a friend and benefactor even to

your un-friended, un-benefited nation, he will be a friend to human race, wherever he goes. Pray tell him my best wishes for his health and long life: I wish you and he came over together, or that I were with you. I never saw a man so seldom whom I liked so much as Dr Rundle.

Swift read this passage to Rundle himself, and 'his Lordship expressed his thankfulness in a manner that became him. He is esteemed here as a person of learning and conversation and humanity, but he is beloved by all people: he is a most excessive Whig, but without any appearing rancour: and his idol is King William: besides, £3000 a year is an invincible sweetener' (*Corr* IV, 384, 400, 457).

The early omens had not been so good. Rundle had been nominated to succeed Elias Sydall as Bishop of Gloucester, and had the strong support of Queen Caroline. However, the Bishop of London, Edmund Gibson, opposed Rundle's preferment as he was suspected of the Arian heresy, that is, denying the divinity of Christ. In the end, Walpole had to bow to Gibson's pressure and pass over Rundle. See *Plumb*, pp. 299–300. It naturally struck observers as odd that a man should be refused promotion in England and promptly granted a diocese in Ireland. William Pulteney wrote to Swift in this spirit on 11 March 1735, soon after the appointment was announced: 'What do you say to the bustle made here to prevent the man from being an English bishop, and afterwards allowing him to be a good Christian enough for an Irish one?... By what I can learn of Dr Rundle's character... he is far from being the great and learned man his friends would have the world believe him, and much farther yet from the bad man his enemies represent him' (*Corr* IV, 306). See also *PTE* IV, 380. Swift uses Rundle simply as a stalking-horse; his real concern is, as so often, the Irish bishops as a group, led by the primate Boulter.

3   *isle of saints*   a name Ireland acquired in the Middle Ages.

16   *Like Paul's Ephesians*   see Acts xix, 2.

22   Pope attributed to Rundle a high degree of 'good taste' also (Pope *Corr* IV, 140).

36   *German line*   the Hanoverian monarchy.

38   *jus divinum*   divine law.

40   *refused episcopari*   'nolo episcopari' (I am unwilling to be made a bishop), the traditional disclaimer of a bishop entering office: sometimes uttered as 'nolo, nolo, nolo.'

41   *Magus*   Simon Magus, converted by Philip the apostle; Simon offered money to be accorded the power of laying on of hands, and was rebuked by Peter (Acts viii, 9–13, 18–24). The word 'simony' derives from this episode.

42   *Tagus*   the river in Lusitania (Portugal), famous for its golden sands: see Ovid, *Metamorphoses* II, 251.

50   *chaps*   purchasers, customers.

52   Derry was one of the best endowed dioceses, which is one reason why Swift had been so keen to obtain the office of Dean there as far back as 1700 (*Landa*, pp. 27–34).

56   *God's anointed*   a sneer at the King as fount of patronage.

57   *congee regal*   the *congé d'élire*, permission from the monarch to a cathedral chapter to fill a vacancy.

60   *held in fee*   a pun: 'held as an absolute possession, without challenge', but also suggesting 'available to those who will pay a fee or bribe'.

61   Baldwin chaste   the licentious Richard Baldwin, a schoolfellow of Swift's, who became Provost of Trinity College: see Biog. Dict.

witty Cross   William Cross, Dean of Leighlin, who was rumoured to be in the running for election as Bishop of Cork in 1735 (*Corr* IV, 389). The rumour would have put his name in Swift's mind at this juncture, and this makes a dating for the poem around September 1735 highly plausible.

64   slip   fail to take advantage of.

65–6   yet another use of one of Swift's most regularly employed rhymes.

AN EPIGRAM

Published in 1767, in two collections: *F* and Samuel Bladon's *Appendix to Dr Swift's Works* (*T* 104). The text here is that of *F*, normalized.

Presumably dating from the same period as the previous item. Its authenticity is not fully established, but ll. 3–4 especially have the Swiftian ring.

3   hadst been better sped   would have fared or succeeded better.

4   Boulter   the primate, Hugh Boulter: see Biog. Dict.

ON A PRINTER'S BEING SENT TO NEWGATE

First published in *F* (1746). This is a considerably tidied-up version from the draft by Swift in *FV*; but I follow *P* in thinking that the revision was most probably authorial, and therefore make *F* the basis of the text here. Variants in Swift's draft are supplied in *P* III, 825; only the more interesting are recorded here.

The work dates from March 1736. On 23 February Bishop Hort, now on good terms with Swift, had sent Swift the manuscript of his *New Proposal for the . . . Improvement of Quadrille*. He asked for revisions to be made and then for Swift to 'send the kite to the falconer', that is, George Faulkner (*Corr* IV, 461). The work contained a satirical reference to Richard Bettesworth, and when the work was published around 1 March the lawyer promptly raised the issue as a matter of privilege in the Irish parliament. It seems likely that Swift himself was responsible for this passage (see *T* 978 and *Ball*, p. 291). On 3 March Faulkner was arrested and committed to Dublin Newgate gaol. After apologizing, he was eventually released on 9 March. Edward Waters, who reprinted the satire, was also taken into custody and held until 15 March. Hort's *Proposal* was subsequently reissued in London along with *A Character, Panegyric, and Description of the Legion Club* (see *T* 752), and *Ball* (p. 292) is certainly right to see in this episode one of the provocations for that poem.

2   live in slavery]   *F* (*1746*);   still continue slaves   *Swift MS* (*FV*).

4   on each other prey   compare *On Poetry: a Rhapsody* 338; *Upon the South Sea Project* 73–4.

9   varlet]   *F* (*1746*); vassal   *Swift MS* (*FV*).

14   Domitian   Titus Flavius Domitianus (A.D. 52–96), Emperor of Rome from A.D. 81 to his assassination; last of the twelve Caesars. He had become a typefigure for the tyrant, partly through the treatment of him by Juvenal. For the episode here, see Suetonius, 'Domitianus' 3, in *De Vita Caesarum* 8. Domitian is described as spearing flies with a stylus. For Swift's copy of Suetonius (*Library*, no. 285), see *PW* V, xxxi–xxxii.

ON NOISY TOM

First published in *F* (1762). The item follows on from the preceding poem, and looks forward to *A Character, Panegyric, and Description of the Legion Club*. The date of composition is certainly 1736. Text from *F*.

The object of attack is Sir Thomas Prendergast: see Biog. Dict. It would have been impolitic to publish anything so openly defamatory at the time, and this (rather than the composition of *A Character . . . of the Legion Club*, as suggested in *PJH* II, 784) explains the failure to issue the poem in Swift's lifetime.

Translation   *Cyrus, or Damas, or Dionysius* 'usual names of slaves at Rome' (note in *F*). *Cadmus* 'a lictor, an officer who seized on criminals, like a constable, or messenger of the House of Commons' (note in *F*). An allusion to the arrest of Faulkner: see *On a Printer's being Sent to Newgate*.

1   Tom   identified by *F* as Sir Thomas Prendergast.

7   spawn of him   'the father of Sir Thomas Prendergast, who engaged in a plot to murder King William III but, to avoid being hanged, turned informer against his associates, for which he was rewarded with a good estate, and made a baronet' (note in *F*, blanks filled out). The elder Prendergast (*c.*1660–1709) supplied information to the government of a plot to assassinate William III at Turnham Green in 1696, and gave evidence against the conspirators. He died from injuries received at the battle of Malplaquet.

9   the female side   'Cadogan's family &c.' (note in *F*). The second baronet had married in 1697 Penelope Cadogan, sister of Marlborough's coadjutor General William Cadogan (1675–1726), a man deeply distrusted by most Tories, including Pope and Swift. In 1720 Swift had written to Prior of a case pending in the House of Lords, involving 'one Lady Prendergass, sister of Cadogan, and the greatest Widow Blackacre now in Christendom' (*Corr* II, 341).

11   thy grandsire   'a poor thieving cottager under Mr Moore, condemned at Clonmel Assizes to be hanged for stealing cows' (note in *F*). I can find no evidence to substantiate this accusation. 'The father of the first baronet, also Thomas, came from an ancient family in Co. Tipperary. Swift's description of him seems to have been unwarranted, although he was probably poor' (*P* III, 826).

13   Moore   'the grandfather of Guy Moore, Esq., who procured him a pardon' (note in *F*).

16   Thy founder's grandson   'Guy Moore was fairly elected Member of Parliament for Clonmel; but Sir Thomas depending upon his interest with a certain party then prevailing, and since known by the title of parson-hunters, petitioned the House against him, out of which he was turned upon pretence of bribery, which the paying of his lawful debts was then voted to be' (note in *F*). This appears to relate to the election of 1734. Moore (b. *c.*1691) was a graduate of Trinity College.

18   the proverb   'save a thief from the gallows, and he will cut your throat' (note in *F*). Tilley T109.

19   a worthy citizen   'Mr George Faulkner, a very honest and eminent printer in Dublin, who was voted to Newgate upon a ridiculous complaint of one Serjeant Bettesworth' (note in *F*). See preceding item.

A CHARACTER, PANEGYRIC, AND DESCRIPTION
OF THE LEGION CLUB

First published in a fugitive London miscellany of 1736, *S — t contra Omnes*
(*T* 752); this purports to be a reprint of Dublin material, but only as a copyright
ruse. *The Legion Club* was far too plain-spoken for any Dublin bookseller to risk
his liberty by issuing the poem. Transcripts were made, however, and some sur-
vive in *TCD* and elsewhere. The item went into the London series of *Misc* but
did not appear safe enough to include in *F* until 1762. The poem was there de-
scribed as 'carefully printed from the author's manuscript'; I accept the general
view that *F* did possess a good copy, possibly a holograph manuscript, and have
based the text on this source.

The first hint of composition comes in a letter from Swift to Sheridan on 24
April 1736: 'I have wrote a very masterly poem on the Legion Club; which, if the
printer will be condemned to hang for it, you will see in a threepenny book; for
it is 240 lines' (*Corr* IV, 480). Three weeks later, Swift was telling Sheridan,
'Here is a cursed long libel running about in manuscript, on the Legion Club; it
is in verse and the foolish town impute it to me. There were not above thirteen
abused (as it is said) in the original; but others have added more, which I never
saw; though I have once read the true one' (*Corr* IV, 487). The general air of dis-
simulation is unmistakable; whether additions were made by other poets is not
clear. Swift repeated his assertion that the original had been expanded and
'damnably murdered' in his next letter (22 May); Sheridan replied, 'Surely no
person can be so stupid as to imagine you wrote the panegyric on the Legion
Club'; and on 5 June Swift reported that there were 'fifty different copies; but
what's that to me?' (*Corr* IV, 492, 495, 501).

The occasion of the poem was a series of events in the Irish House of Com-
mons during 1734–5, concerning an attempt to remove the pasturage tithes (see
Landa, pp. 123–35). Events came to a head in March 1736, when a group of
freeholders protested against the tithes and the Commons appointed a committee
to make a report on the petition. When the report was presented to the House on
18 March, the freeholders' views were endorsed by a majority of 110 to 50. Swift
would have been provoked by the publication of the report as a separate pam-
phlet, and by the composition of the committee (which included such old ene-
mies as Bettesworth). In May he wrote a prose tract, *Concerning that Universal
Hatred Which Prevails against the Clergy*, also provoked by the attempt to remove
the tithes (*PW* XIII, 123–6). Presumably the poem was mostly composed in
April.

Orrery (*Remarks*, 5th edn (1752), p. 185) suggests the poem is unfinished, fol-
lowing an interruption by a violent fit of giddiness. There is no other evidence to
indicate that the work is incomplete.

The Legion Club figured centrally in a reading of Swift by Francis Jeffrey,
reviewing Scott's edition in 1816 (*CH*, p. 322). On the whole, however, it
remained for the twentieth-century commentators to allot the poem a high degree
of importance. Discussions include Denis Donoghue, *Jonathan Swift: A Critical
Introduction* (1969), pp. 215–17; David Ward, *Jonathan Swift: An Introductory
Essay* (1973), pp. 194–7; and Herbert Davis, *Jonathan Swift: Essays on His
Satire* (1964), pp. 254–8. See also *Johnson*, pp. 103–5, describing 'the expert,
appropriate expression of an essentially prosaic content'; *Jaffe*, pp. 145–57,

emphasizing the place of madness in the poem, and detecting underlying 'hatred and rage and fear'; and *Lee*, pp. 72–5. The allusive techniques of the poem are studied by P.J. Schakel, 'Virgil and the Dean', *Studies in Philology* LXX (1973), 427–38.

Crucial to the effect of the poem are, firstly, the seven-syllable line, with a truncated first foot, which Swift used only a few times in his career; and secondly the image of a vast 'pile' like a new Bedlam (see note to l. 2). Swift often constructed his satire around the erection of a new college or institutional building (see *Grub Street*, pp. 260–72), and the appearance of this costly and somewhat vainglorious edifice on the Dublin skyline gave him an ideal opportunity to explore this favourite metaphor.

Title   alluding to Luke viii, 30: 'And Jesus asked him, What is thy name? And he said, Legion: because many devils were entered into him.' Swift had started calling the Irish parliament by this name some time earlier, in private letters: see *Corr* IV, 442.

2   *a building*   the new Parliament House on the north side of College Green (now the Bank of Ireland): see *The Yahoo's Overthrow* 8. 'Built at the cost of £95,000, it was incomparably the most splendid Parliament House in the Empire, even eclipsing Westminster. The foundation stone of this magnificent edifice was laid in 1728, when Chichester House...was demolished. The architect for the new Parliament House was Sir Edward Lovett Pearce, MP for Ratoath. Dying in 1733, Pearce did not live to see the completion of his design, but its supervision was continued by another MP, Arthur Dobbs, who sat for Carrickfergus and was later Governor of Carrickfergus. At that time he was Surveyor-General for Ireland, and under his direction the building was completed in 1739. It was built in the Italian style with a façade of Ionic columns...The Commons chamber was a circle, 51 feet in diameter, enclosed in a square. Wainscoted in Irish oak, the MPs' seats rose 15 feet in circular tiers to the gallery, where the students of nearby Trinity College across the Green could... listen to the speeches' (Edith Mary Johnston, *Ireland in the Eighteenth Century* (1974), pp. 73–4). Dobbs had known Swift from his childhood days, and his involvement in the building would have confirmed Swift's interest in the new structure: see Desmond Clarke, *Arthur Dobbs Esquire* (1957), pp. 21–3, 42–3.

3   *the College*   Trinity College, on the east side of the Green.

5   *the prudent architect*   Pearce, who had been voted £2000 as an *ex gratia* payment by parliament. There is probably a dig at Swift's old acquaintance, Dobbs, whose friendship both with the Lord Lieutenant and with Walpole was occasioning doubts as to his loyalty to the 'Irish' interest.

6   *the church*   St Andrew's or the Round Church.

8   *Near the church*   'and far from God' (proverbial). *Tilley* C380.

11   *demoniacs*   there was an actual sect of Anabaptists known by this name, who believed that at the Last Day devils would be saved. Milton had used the phrase 'demoniac legion' (*Apology against Smectymnuus*). A club which was known as the Demoniacs, and of which Laurence Sterne was a founder-member, came into being a few years after Swift wrote this poem.

14   *when butchers bait a bear*   butchers traditionally took a prominent part in the brutal sports practised at the bear garden: see John Ashton, *Social Life in the*

Reign of Queen Anne (1883), pp. 224–5, and Pope, *The Dunciad* (1743) I, 326: 'And "Coll!" each butcher roars at Hockley Hole.'

18 jack-pudding a jester or merry andrew who attended a mountebank.

20 that is, criminals who went to be executed were less guilty men. There are reminiscences in this opening section of the Introduction in *Tale*, pp. 55–72: compare l. 5 with the reference to the 'prudent architect' (*Tale*, p. 61). Compare also Swift to Pope, 22 April 1736: 'Here we have . . . a race of . . . old villains and monsters, whereof four fifths are more wicked and stupid than Chartres' (*Corr* IV, 477).

28 den of thieves quoting Matthew xxi, 13.

33 the gospel perhaps alluding to Luke x, 10–20.

35–6 see *Verses on the Death of Dr Swift* 479–80.

37 rood see *Horace Lib. 2 Sat.* 6 5.

47–62 compare *Tale*, pp. 176–8: 'Is any student tearing his straw in piecemeal . . . Is another eternally talking, sputtering, gaping, bawling, in a sound without period or article? . . . Accost the hole of another kennel . . . you will find a . . . slovenly mortal, raking in his own dung, and dabbling in his urine.'

59 gosling suggesting folly and inexperience.

60 heads of bills measures sent in draft form by the House of Commons to the Irish Privy Council, who might amend or veto them.

62 votes the printed 'votes' were among the few official records of parliamentary affairs available to the public.

63 Sir Tom Sir Thomas Prendergast: see Biog. Dict. and *On Noisy Tom*, headnote. *HEH* contains an ironic vindication of Prendergast sent by William Dunkin to Swift in May 1736 (*Mayhew*, p. 178).

64 flax and grass on which the graziers allegedly grew fat.

67 At the parsons an injunction, like a cry in the hunting field.

72 regicide see *On Noisy Tom* 7.

83 'Virgil, *Aeneid* VI, 264ff.: "*Dii, quibus imperium est animarum, &c. / Sit mihi fas audita loqui &c.*"' (note in *F*). Introducing a sustained allusion to Aeneas's journey to the underworld: Dryden translates these particular lines, 'Ye realms, yet unrevealed to human sight, / Ye gods who rule the regions of the night, / Ye gliding ghosts, permit me to relate / The mystic wonders of your silent state!'

87 F's note identifies an allusion to *Aeneid* VI, 273–4: 'Just in the gate and in the jaws of hell, / Revengeful Cares and sullen Sorrows dwell' (Dryden tr.).

91 Discord in effect, Megaera: see *Death and Daphne* 21. A note in *F* cites *Aeneid* VI, 280–81: 'and Strife, that shakes / Her hissing tresses and unfolds her snakes' (Dryden tr.). 'For the moment he seems to have forgotten his anger and the horrors that await him, and is clearly amusing himself at his favourite game of transposing the heroic style into plain terms, so that the horrible figure of discord seems to be masquerading in a periwig of snakes' (Davis, op. cit., p. 256).

93 a note in F cites *Aeneid* VI, 290–91: 'The chief unsheathed his shining steel, prepared, / Though seized within sudden fear, to force the guard' (Dryden tr.).

97 Clio muse of history. *F* cites *Aeneid* VI, 292: 'Had not the Sybil stopped his eager pace, / And told him what those empty phantoms were' (Dryden tr.).

in the nick see *A Quiet Life and a Good Name* 20.

103 Briareus or Aegeon, a giant with fifty heads and a hundred hands. *F* cites *Aeneid* VI, 287, 'And Briareus with all his hundred hands' (Dryden tr.).

106 Carey Walter Carey, a well known English placeman, secretary to the Lord Lieutenant of Ireland: see Biog. Dict.

113 three hundred brutes there were exactly 300 members, representing 150 constituencies each carrying two seats. Thirty-two of these were counties, 117 were boroughs, and the odd constituency was Trinity College.

118 laid by the heels arrested, imprisoned. They were immune from arrest for anything said in parliament.

122 vapours hysteria.

125 Lake Avernus a lake in Campania, supposed to be the entrance to the underworld. Swift is perhaps recalling *Aeneid* VI, 201: 'the slow lake, whose baleful stench to shun / They winged their flight aloft' (Dryden tr.).

138 Waller John Waller, M.P. for Doneraile, and a grandson of Sir Hardess Waller (c.1604–c.1666), a judge at the trial of Charles I in 1649.

144 Throp Roger Throp, a vicar in Co. Limerick, who had died in January 1736 after a legal battle with his patron, Waller: see *P* III, 835. There are references to the matter in Swift's correspondence, before and after Throp's death (*Corr* IV, 419, 422, 429; V, 172–3).

146 pair of Dicks Richard Tighe and Richard Bettesworth.

149 Dick Fitz-Baker for Tighe's ancestry, see *Tom Mullinex and Dick* 12.

Dick the player *P* III, 835 suggests that Bettesworth's pompous style of oratory is satirized.

152 old Glorious William III: see *Mad Mullinix and Timothy* 66.

159 smoke find out who he is, identify him.

161 Wynne probably Hon. Owen Wynne, member for Co. Sligo. There were two other Wynnes in the house: another Owen Wynne (Sligo borough) and John Wynne (Castlebar).

163 Bingham Sir John Bingham, Bt., member for Co. Mayo (c.1690–1749), and Henry Bingham, his brother, member for Castlebar, ancestors of the Earl of Lucan. For John's marriage, see the following note.

164 ∧ 165] And that base apostate Vesey / With bishops's scraps grown fat and greasy *1736, TCD MS; not in F.* On 3 June 1736 Sheridan wrote to Swift, 'My son writes me word that Mr Vesey's family are angry with me for inserting some lines in the Legion Club touching him' (*Corr IV*, 497). The reference is to Agmondisham Vesey, member of a well-known family. He was Accountant-General for Ireland, and died c.1739. His daughter Anne married John Bingham, mentioned in l. 163. His son Agmondisham (1707/8–c.1785) also became Accountant-General; he married his cousin Elizabeth, daughter of Bishop Vesey and widow of William Handcock of Twyford (see *To Mr Sheridan, upon His Verses Written in Circles* 21). Swift knew the elder Vesey (see *JTS* II, 479), but it remains a possibility that Sheridan wrote the lines in question. A couplet which has been attributed to Swift refers to Vesey's construction of a bridge at Lucan, Co. Dublin: 'Agmondisham Vesey, out of his bounty, / Built a fine bridge – at the expense of the county.'

173 Allens John Allen, member for Carysfort; Robert Allen, member for Co. Wicklow; respectively, the son and brother of Lord Allen (see *Traulus*, headnote).

178 trod mortar see *Traulus: The Second Part* 28.

179 Howth John Allen, the architect, worked at Howth Castle.

181   Clements   probably Henry Clements, member for Cavan.

Dilkes   Michael Dilkes, member for Castlemartyr.

Harrison   William Harrison, member for Bannow. Harrison is replaced in some early texts by 'Carter', that is, Thomas Carter, Master of the Rolls, an important judicial and political figure known to Swift (see *Corr* IV, 470). With this variant goes the alternative line 'Who for hell would die a martyr'.

186   excrements   spelt 'ex-crements' in *F*, indicating a shift of accent to the second syllable.

189   Morgan   the chairman of the committee appointed to report on the freeholders' complaint, Dr Mark Antony Morgan (b. 1702/3), a graduate of Trinity College and member for Athy. He was known personally to Swift. For comments on this passage, see Geoffrey Hill, 'Jonathan Swift: 'The Poetry of "Reaction"', in *The World of Jonathan Swift*, ed. B. Vickers (1968), p. 205. ·

211   Flaccus   Horace (Q. Horatius Flaccus).

219   Hogart   William Hogarth, for whom see Biog. Dict. He and Swift probably never met, but a number of parallels and influences can be detected in their work: see Jeanne K. Welcher, 'Swift-Hogarth Give and Take', in *Ventures in Research*, ed. R. Griffith (1975), pp. 23–53.

228   caricatura   italicized in *F*; then a new and slightly exotic word, which survived alongside 'caricature' throughout the eighteenth century: eventually the French rather than the Italian loan prevailed.

242   some of the transcripts add a final couplet or couplets of dubious authenticity: see *P* III, 839. Swift was apt to be precise in mensuration (as opposed to chronology) and his '240' lines (see headnote) are unlikely to have been much more. Perhaps another couplet, like that on Vesey which *F* excised (see note to l. 164), was foisted into the text and *F* failed to remove it.

BOUNCE TO FOP

A contentious attribution, despite the fact that the title-page of the (presumed) first printing allots the poem to 'Dr *S — T*'. Since then, it has been variously ascribed to Swift, Gay, or Pope. Most support in recent years has gone to the last of these candidates. According to Foxon, 'It is generally agreed that the original idea was Swift's, but that the writing is largely by Pope.' The facts are briefly these:

(1) The poem was published in London by T. Cooper at the beginning of May 1736, with a reimpression the same year (*Foxon* B326–7). This edition carries the attribution to Swift. The title-page claims that the work had already appeared in Dublin, but, as often, this is probably a blind.

(2) About the same time – perhaps very slightly later – Faulkner produced a separate Dublin printing (*Foxon* B328). He too claims that the poem had already appeared in the other capital. The attribution to Swift is omitted.

The version used in these two editions consisted of ninety-four lines, and was reproduced in London monthlies for May 1736.

(3) The poem was incorporated in *Misc* (1736), published by Motte; it was subsequently included in *Misc* (1742), when Pope took the prime editorial responsibility. In 1742 it was marked in the Contents list with a star: a note appended states, 'Whatever are not marked with a star, are Dr Swift's.' There is

some disagreement whether this implies that all items so marked are not Swift's. In the *Misc* versions, the last twelve lines of the text are omitted. The poem was consistently excluded from the parallel series of *F* editions in Dublin. Other editors prior to Scott (for example, Sheridan and Nichols) do include it among Swift's works.

(4) In 1773 Bell included *Bounce to Fop* in the trade edition of Gay's works; it remained in successive editions of Gay, including the set of English poets to which Johnson's *Lives* were appended. This attribution was challenged by later editors (Underhill and Faber), and has not been revived by Dearing in the recent standard edition.

(5) The case for Pope's involvement goes back to a manuscript note by the second Earl of Oxford on his copy of the Cooper folio. After the words 'By Dr S — T' he added the phrase 'much altered by Mr Pope'. Thereafter the suggestion remained dormant until the twentieth century. It was revived by Norman Ault in 'Pope and his Dogs', *New Light on Pope* (1950), pp. 337–50. This attribution was confirmed when the poem was printed in *PTE* VI, 366–71 (where Ault was the editor primarily responsible). Meanwhile Williams had relegated *Bounce to Fop* to the category of dubious items in *P* III, 1135–6 (the second edition of *P* cites Ault's argument).

Ault had built up an elaborate case, which ended in the hypothesis that Swift was involved only in an early impromptu version of the poem, if indeed to that extent. The conclusion reached was that *Bounce to Fop* 'can now with virtual certainty be attributed wholly or mainly to Pope'. Many complex issues are involved in this argument, and a full attempt to reinstate Swift as the prime agent in composition would take up an inordinate amount of space. In brief, I consider that the testimony of the original edition and that of Oxford (which agree in allotting the basic responsibility for the poem to Swift) provide evidence too strong to be shrugged off. Against the parallels with Pope's work adduced by Ault, some of which are cited in the commentary below, we can put an even wider range of analogues in Swift's verse. The circumstantial evidence surrounding the poem's appearance is not decisive either way. There are certainly insufficient grounds for following recent practice (that is, including the poem in the canon of Pope, whilst deleting it from that of Swift). It is highly likely that Pope did revise the poem before allowing it to appear in *Misc*; ll. 45–8, for example, may well be his addition. Contemporary transcripts among the Harley papers suggest, too, that ll. 61–8 may well be another late insertion, and, again, Pope is the likeliest author for these lines. Nevertheless, no one has produced any good reason to disturb the contemporary evidence which allots the poem, in its earliest conception at least, to Swift alone.

There is a subsidiary problem concerning dating. Ault considered that the first hint of the poem may have arisen in 1726 or 1727 (more likely the latter); he places the supposed collaboration of his joint authors during one of Swift's visits to England, and apparently places the final draft (by Pope alone) around 1736. It is impossible to be positive. Pope seems to have had a dog (not a bitch) named Bounce in 1727 or thereabouts; the only evidence of a dog at court named Fop (see note on Title) relates to the years 1728 to 1730. On the other hand, the reference to Lord Fanny (l. 76) points to a date around 1733 or later. If Pope revised the poem, this is likely to have taken place well into the 1730s; but the genesis of the poem may go back as far as 1727, when a work with similarities in theme and mood – *A Pastoral Dialogue between Richmond Lodge and Marble Mill* – was composed.

It will be noted that the poem is written in octosyllabic couplets – Swift's favourite form, used in almost fifty per cent of his poems after 1700. Pope adopted this measure in his imitations of Swift's style, but these date from the later 1730s.

The poem has been attributed, on what seem to me very flimsy grounds, to Henry Carey. See Samuel L. Macey in *Bulletin of the New York Public Library* LXXIX (1976), 203–8.

The text is based on the Cooper edition. Minor variants in the Harley transcripts are not recorded.

Title Bounce was Pope's dog: 'it seems most probable that Pope had two large dogs in succession, both being called Bounce; in which case it was the second Bounce that became famous' (Ault, *New Light on Pope*, p. 341). It was a puppy of this Bounce, a bitch, who was presented to the Prince of Wales and prompted the celebrated epigram, 'I am his Highness' dog at Kew; / Pray tell me Sir, whose dog are you?' This gift, foreshadowed in the poem (ll. 69–80), had taken place by 22 December 1736 (Pope *Corr* IV, 48). For the suggestion that Pope owned a third Bounce (a male dog), see Pope *Corr* IV, 507–8.

Fop is taken by Ault to be a pet dog of Mrs Howard (see Biog. Dict.); Swift alludes to this Fop in letters written during his visit to England in 1727 (*New Light on Pope*, p. 345). However, it has been pointed out that ll. 33–6 imply a male owner, and that the details fit not Mrs Howard but her friend Henry Herbert, later ninth Earl of Pembroke. Herbert (1693–1751), the 'architect earl', designed Marble Hill and was well known to both Pope and Swift (for Swift's interest in his career, see *Corr* IV, 186). His dealings with the Scriblerian group are explored by James Lees-Milne, *Earls of Creation* (1962), pp. 59–100. For evidence that Herbert owned a dog named Fop in 1728 and 1730, see C.F. Burgess (ed.), *The Letters of John Gay* (1966), p. 96.

In *Misc* the word 'Heroic' is omitted from the title; this change is found in a Harley transcript and may therefore be a sign of Pope's editorial hand.

2   no spaniel the suggestion is of a toy breed, such as a King Charles spaniel, rather than the sporting breed; spaniels were often associated with fawning and sycophancy (*OED*, sense 2b, is 'a submissive, cringing, or fawning person'). See Tilley S704.

6   lady-lap dogship the phrase might seem to point to a woman owner, that is, Mrs Howard; however, the contrast is between an effete toy of a dog (Fop) and the sturdy Bounce with her 'manly roar'. The expression means simply 'fit to recline on a lady's lap'.

7   bite your head off restoring to the figurative expression ('to savage, verbally') a sense of literal biting: a typical Swiftian procedure. Note also the rhyme, and compare *The Answer to Dr Delany* 15–16.

10   Can fetch and carry *PTE* VI, 371 compares Pope's *Epistle to Arbuthnot* 225–6; but note the similar formula in *Upon the Horrid Plot* 18.

12   strings and sticks suggesting *Gulliver's Travels* I, 3; the 'strings' are ribbons such as that of the Garter (a recurrent topic in Swift), while 'sticks' allude to the rods carried by officers of state, notably the Lord Treasurer. Compare *Verses on the Revival of the Order of the Bath* 11–12: 'And he who will leap over a stick for the king / Is qualified best for a dog in a string'

16 Pope never uses the word 'fart' elsewhere, even in a disguised form; Swift does so on eleven occasions.

21   sturdy vagrants] Cooper edn; idle gypsies *Misc*; sturdy beggars *Harley transcripts.* There are extensive references to vagrancy in Swift's prose works; for his views on the subject, see David Nokes, 'Swift and the Beggars', *Essays in Criticism* XXVI (1976), 218–33.

23   touse   'of a dog: to tear at, worry' (*OED*), hence the common name Towser, used four times in Swift's poetry: see *A Fable of the Widow and Her Cat* 45.

24   bread and butter   for another use of this cliché, see *Mad Mullinix and Timothy* 1.

25   fop   the pun is reinforced in the original typography by a capital letter.

27–8   the rhyme seems likelier for Swift than Pope by this date: all Pope's rhymes for 'meat' in the 1730s are with words such as 'eat', 'feat', or 'treat'. It is possible that he pronounced all these words to sound '-ate', but the modern pronunciation is always feasible, and this is in accord with his rhyming habits. Swift's 'meat' rhymes are also with 'seat and 'eat', but his practice elsewhere shows that he used, for example, the older (or Irish) pronunciation of 'Dean', whereas Pope cannot be shown to have done so.

30   stinking   ten occurrences in Swift, one in Pope.

31   tissue   'a rich kind of cloth, often interwoven with gold or silver' (*OED*). Compare *The Lady's Dressing Room* 4, where in effect the same rhyme is used.

32   plaster   compare *A Beautiful Young Nymph Going to Bed* 32.

issue   see *A Beautiful Young Nymph Going to Bed* 30.

33–6   Burgess, op. cit., p. 96, convincingly argues that these lines indicate Lord Herbert as Fop's owner (see note on Title). 'These lines receive considerable illumination if it is recalled that Herbert was then Lord of the Bedchamber.'

37   dogs have had their days   for Swift's use of this proverbial expression, see *Upon the Horrid Plot* 30.

38–40   pet names for dogs. For 'Trays' and 'Cupids', see *The Beasts' Confession* 207–10. Professor C.B. Ricks draws attention to the passage in *King Lear* III, vi, 63–4: 'The little dogs and all, / Tray, Blanch, and Sweetheart, see they bark at me.'

40   Harvequini's]   *Cooper edn*; Harlequini's *Misc, with footnote.* 'Alii legunt Harvequini's'. Alluding to the foppish courtier Lord Hervey, attacked by Pope under the names of Lord Fanny and Sporus. For Harlequin as a breed of dog, and a name for a particular dog, see *Upon the Horrid Plot* 47.

41   breech   posteriors.

42   looseness   diarrhoea.

claps   gonorrhoea.

itch   scabies.

44   manly roar   Bounce was a Great Dane (but actually female).

45–8   'This imitation of Virgil, *Aeneid* VI, 784ff. had been anticipated in *Dunciad* [1729] III, 123–6' (*PTE* VI, 371). It happens to be the most quoted book in the literary work to which Swift most often alludes in his poetry: but the quatrain bears all the marks of Pope's hand. Berecynthia was identified with Cybele, the Great Mother of the Gods (see Aubrey Williams, *Pope's Dunciad* (1955), pp. 26–7).

52   J—   unidentified. 'Presumably he was the sire of one of Bounce's litters, and a ravenous feeder' (*PTE* VI, 371). A common name for large dogs was Jowler: see *The Part of a Summer* 89. The blank left suggests an allusion to some living person as well: perhaps James Johnston, an unpopular neighbour of Pope and Mrs Howard, who entertained Queen Caroline at his Twickenham home.

There is almost certainly a sly allusion to Caroline's prolific brood (see *Directions for a Birthday Song* 151–209); the implication of l. 48 would then be, 'and none of them a fop, as is the eldest son of Berecynthia-Caroline'.

56 veal stewed veal was a special delicacy prepared by Pulteney's cook for a dinner held at Twickenham in September 1727. Pope sent Swift a rhymed recipe for the dish (*PTE* VI, 253–5).

58 great Strafford Thomas Wentworth, third Earl of Strafford (1672–1739), a former diplomat and High Tory. He owned a Palladian villa, known as Mount Lebanon, by the Thames at Twickenham. In 1712 Swift had written of him, 'Strafford has some life and spirit, but is infinitely proud, and wholly illiterate' (*JTS* II, 489).

60 Burlington's Palladian gates the architect and patron Richard Boyle, third Earl of Burlington (1694–1753). His promotion of the Palladian style was given practical expression in alterations to his own mansion, Burlington House in Piccadilly: this building, much altered, is now the home of the Royal Academy. In addition Burlington himself designed Chiswick Villa in the same architectural idiom. Pope and Gay both had extensive connections with the Earl (see Lees-Milne, op. cit., pp. 103–69). Swift saw him regularly during his visits of 1726 and 1727 (*Corr* III, 334). Pope mentions the gift of a puppy in an undated letter (Pope *Corr* III, 515).

61–8] *not in Harley transcripts*. This fact suggests that Pope may have added the lines at a late stage, when more of Bounce's puppies had been bestowed as gifts.

62 Cobham's walks the gardens at Stowe in Buckinghamshire, on the estate owned by Richard Temple, first Viscount Cobham (1675–1749), a Whig general under Marlborough. Well known to Pope, less so to Swift.

63 Bathurst's door Allen, first Earl Bathurst (1684–1775), a Tory politician and close friend of both Pope and Swift (who exchanged many letters with him). The dog would probably have gone to Bathurst's seat at Cirencester. See Lees-Milne, op. cit., pp. 21–56.

64 Oxford's Edward Harley, second Earl of Oxford (see Biog. Dict.). For his copy of *Bounce to Fop*, see headnote. His principal seat was Wimpole, Cambridgeshire: see Lees-Milne, op. cit., pp. 173–218.

65–8 in fact Pope later took a less narrow view socially, and gave one of Bounce's line to Ralph Allen in 1739 (Pope *Corr* IV, 175); it may be that Allen's puppy was littered by the dog given to Oxford.

73 Iülus' side 'Son of Aeneas; reference to the Prince of Wales' (note in *Misc*). Swift uses the same mode of reference to the same person in *On Poetry: a Rhapsody* 483. See Biog. Dict.

    Evander Misc supplies a note referring to *Aeneid* VII, 461–2: '*Nec non et gemini custodes limine ab alto* / *Praecedunt gressumque canes comitantur herilem*' (Dryden translates, 'Two menial dogs before their master pressed'). Evander was king of the Etruscans and father of Pallas.

76 Lord Fannies 'Lord Fanny' was Pope's name for John, Baron Hervey (1696–1743), a member of Walpole's government and an intimate of the Queen. This is another passage possibly, but not certainly, contributed by Pope.

81 Ault, *New Light on Pope*, p. 347, describes this as a 'pathetic parenthesis', and quotes parallels from Pope's work including the *Iliad* and the *Odyssey*. It is, in fact, a formula derived from classical poetry, and more characteristic of Pope than Swift.

83–94]   *Cooper edn; not in Misc, transcripts.* The tribute to Pope is very much in Swift's manner; and Pope, for all his vanity, might have been embarrassed by its presence in a poem to which he had himself, to some imponderable degree, contributed. If Pope had written the lines in the first place, it is not clear why he should have developed scruples and omitted them at this late stage. It is a simpler and more natural assumption that the passage was a part of Swift's original draft.

84   *the sect of Pythagoreans*   for a reference to the disciples of Pythagoras, see *Strephon and Chloe* 125–6.

86   *Dryden's hind*   'a milk-white hind, immortal and unchanged. Verse 1. Of the *Hind and the Panther*' (note in *Misc*). Referring to Dryden's poem of this name (1687), where the hind represents the Roman Catholic church.

91   *by sticks*   the most solemn oath was that sworn 'by Styx'; here punning on the sticks used to chastise a dog. Exactly the kind of anglicized form of a classical word which Swift favoured in his 'bilingual punning': see *Mayhew*, pp. 131–48, for many similar examples.

93   transposing the formula of Anglican baptism, 'renounce the devil and all his works' – a phrase much more part of Swift's experience than of Pope's.

ADDENDA QUAEDAM

These lines (set out as prose) form a part of Swift's letter to Sheridan dated 5 June 1736 (*Corr* IV, 501–2). They answer verses sent by Sheridan in recent letters (*Corr* IV, 495–8).

10   *Nisbit*   among the local ladies of Cavan, awaiting a visit from Swift (according to Sheridan's letter of 20 July 1736), was 'Mrs Nesbitt', together with her five daughters (*Corr* IV, 519).

12   *friend Whiteway*   Mrs Martha Whiteway, Swift's cousin: see Biog. Dict.

14   *Kilmore*   Josiah Hort, at this time Bishop of Kilmore: see *The Storm*, headnote, and Biog. Dict.

16   *Your wife a scold*   see *A Portrait from the Life*, headnote.

20   *Cavan*   where Sheridan kept his school.

LESBIA

First published in *F*, vol. VIII (1746), together with the original, that is, the four-line poem by Catullus, *Carm.* xcii. Swift's autograph version survives; the text here is based on Williams's transcript (*P* II, 679). The verso of the sheet is endorsed by Swift, 'Lesbia from Catullus – July 18ᵗʰ 1736.' *F*'s title is *From Catullus*. Catullus was represented in a volume in Swift's *Library*, no. 339.

3   *yet*]   *Swift MS*; Now   *F (1746)*.
        hang me   Swift's idiomatic rendering of the Latin *dispeream* 'may I perish'.

A SATIRE ON AN INCONSTANT LOVER

The lines appear in a letter from Swift to Sheridan, dated 9 April 1737 (*Corr* V, 29). It is most improbable that anyone other than Swift should have written them. They relate to the language games and punning contests in which the two men indulged for many years.

1 Carthaginian 'Punic faith' or 'Carthaginian faith' were phrases meaning treachery. 'Our Punic faith / Is infamous, and branded to a proverb' (Addison, *Cato* II, v, 117–18). *Fides punica* is found in Sallust, Livy, and other Latin authors. A parallel usage was 'Greek faith' (*Tilley* F31).

AYE AND NO: A TALE FROM DUBLIN

First printed by Nichols in 1776, with the statement 'written in 1737'. A dubious item: *P* III, 842, says, 'It may be accepted as Swift's with some assurance'; but the evidence is by no means clear-cut. If it is Swift's, it must be one of his very last works in prose or verse.

The poem was occasioned by a proposal by Archbishop Boulter to reduce slightly the value of the guinea (implemented in August 1727), and also to import £2000 of copper halfpence. As Swift wrote to Orrery, 'I quarrel not at the coin, but at the indignity of not being coined here, and the loss of 12,000 ll. [*sic*] in gold and silver to us, which for aught I know, may be half our store' (*Corr* V, 21). He went so far as to write a pamphlet on the subject, *The Rev. Dean Swift's Reasons against Lowering the Gold and Silver Coin* (*PW* XIII, 117–20), but to no avail. The general view has been that on this occasion Boulter, and not Swift, had right on his side. One of the Dean's last public gestures was to attend the banquet held in honour of the outgoing Lord Mayor of Dublin on 29 September 1737. According to one contemporary account, Swift told Boulter at this feast that 'had it not been for him he [the Primate] would have been torn to pieces by the mob, and that if he held up his finger he could make them do it that instant' (letter from Lord George Sackville to the Duke of Dorset, 6 October 1737, quoted in *P* III, 842).

Text based on Nichols.

1 high feast see headnote.
3 Hugh Boulter, Archbishop of Armagh.

mob one of the words satirized in Swift's *Tatler* paper on current abuses of language, and introduced into *Polite Conversation* towards a similar end (*PW* IV, 161).
10 bolter a sieve (compare *Tale*, p. 148, 'the sieves and bolters of learning'), punning on the idea of 'bolting' (discharging, shooting forth) wit.
13 Bob Walpole, who had advanced Boulter to his position in Ireland.
14 sinking devaluing.
15 dear joys 'a familiar appellation for an Irishman' (*OED*, citing Farquhar and cant dictionaries).
16 Wood William Wood, central figure of the Drapier's episode: see Biog. Dict.
17 without law unlawfully, but perhaps suggesting 'without a fair trial (to which he was at least entitled)'.

'BEHOLD! A PROOF OF IRISH SENSE!'

A dubious item. John Nichols was the first to collect this epigram in 1775, taking it from the *Annual Register* for 1759. A note was added:

The Dean, in his lunacy, had some intervals of sense; at which time his guardians, or physicians, took him out for the air. On one of these days, when they came to the Park, Swift remarked a new building, which he had never seen, and asked what it was designed for. To which Dr Kingsbury [his physician] answered, 'That, Mr Dean, is the magazine for arms and powder, for the security of the city.' 'Oh! oh!' says the Dean, pulling out his pocket-book, 'let me take an item of that. This is worth remarking: my tablets, as Hamlet says, my tablets – memory put down that!' – which produced the above lines, said to be the last he ever wrote.

This has all the hallmarks of romantic invention. The *Annual Register* anecdotes are late and not first-hand; Swift was not generally addicted to making notes in a conspicuous fashion; and there is little evidence that he enjoyed any lucid intervals in the final years of occlusion after he was declared incapable in 1742. I have not found evidence either of any defensive measures in Dublin that would square with the text; such might have been undertaken at the time of the Jacobite rising in 1745, but that was barely under way when Swift died on 19 October 1745. However, as all editors since Nichols have included the poem, it perhaps needs stronger justification than this to excise it from the canon.

Text from Nichols.

TO MRS HOUGHTON OF BORMOUNT

First published in *F* (1762) and thereafter accepted by editors as Swift's. Nothing is known concerning the circumstances of its writing. It would be safer to regard this as a doubtful attribution.

AN EPIGRAM ON SCOLDING

The authenticity is a little dubious. It was first printed in *F* (1746), the source for the text here. Later editors have accepted the item without question. There is perhaps a recollection in l. 4 of *Phyllis* 100: 'Are cat and dog, and rogue and whore.' There is no possible way of dating such an item.

VERSES MADE FOR THE WOMEN WHO CRY APPLES, ETC.

First published in *F* (1746), and thereafter regularly collected. Undatable. As Horrell states (*PJH* II, 772), 'Street cries fascinated Swift. The *Journal to Stella* contains examples in phonetic spelling of the cries of night watchmen and others.' See *JTS* I, 90; II, 453, 570, 581. The classic treatment is Addison's paper in *The Spectator*, no. 251 (18 December 1711). The verses here were clearly written whilst Swift was living in Dublin (see l. 51).

12 '*sparagrass OED* provides an entry for the truncated form, and quotes Tempest's *Cries of London* (1711), 'Ripe speragas.' Swift used to eat it in London (*JTS* I, 164).
15 picking morsel, scraps.
36 Colchester oyster Defoe has a section on Colchester oysters, as the best (although not the largest) oysters in England, in the first volume of his *Tour through Great Britain* (1724), Letter I.
40 They'll make you a dad oysters were supposed to aid virility.
51 'Malahide, about five miles from Dublin, famous for oysters' (note in *F*);

north along the coast from the city. Five Irish miles, about eight by the English reckoning.

54 a custard an open egg-pie, rather than a liquid.

60 bishop a sweet drink resembling punch; mulled or spiced port was so called. Much favoured by Samuel Johnson.

A CANTATA

First published in *F* (1746) together with a musical setting by Rev. John Echlin, Vicar-General of Tuam and Swift's adviser on matters concerned with the cathedral choir. The intention of the piece was to ridicule attempts to imitate the meaning of words in music – something not unknown in *opera seria* and undertaken by Purcell and Handel amongst others. Swift's notorious insensibility to music may have been exaggerated, although the evidence is not conclusive. See *P* III, 955 (where Echlin's setting is reproduced) and Delany's *Observations upon Lord Orrery's Remarks* (1754), pp. 189–90. Text from *F*, with words for which the composer set elaborate passages of ornamentation spelt out at length.

7 sweet Canterbury 'Canterbury pace' was an easy canter (the same derivation, from the gait supposed to have been adopted by pilgrims).

THE ELEPHANT

A dubious item. Rejected by Williams, who notes that after appearing in *M28* the item is marked with a star in *Misc* (1742), 'as not by Swift'. But the exact statement at the head of the Contents list is, '*N.B.* Whatever are not marked with a star, are Dr Swift's.' It does not follow that all items so marked are *not* by Swift, though this would be the most natural assumption. The poem first entered *F* in 1746, when it was inserted on a cancel leaf in Vol. VIII. See *P* III, 1106–7; *T* 44.

The internal evidence seems to point to the likelihood of Swift's authorship. *F*'s acceptance of the piece is suggestive, and the use of octosyllabics comes closer to the style of Swift than to that of any other Scriblerian. He was the likeliest among the group to recall the passage from Coke; and certain verbal habits (see ll. 14, 18) are very much his own. Finally, the interest in popular shows displayed in the second verse-paragraph is far more characteristic of Swift than of his associates. Williams's statement, 'There can be no doubt that this poem was not written by Swift. It was not regarded as his in his lifetime' (*P* III, 1106) is too positive.

The poem is undatable. *P* notes that *Ball* (p. 219) would assign it to Swift's English visits of 1726 or 1727, but believes that it refers to an election, perhaps that of 1722. I see no means of resolving the matter. Text based on *M28*.

2 Lord Coke Sir Edward Coke (1552–1634), judge and writer on the law. His *Institutes*, better known as 'Coke upon Littleton', appeared between 1628 and 1644. The work is quoted in the first of the *Drapier's Letters*: see *Drapier*, pp. 11–12, 199: and see *Cadenus and Vanessa* 107.

5 gall rancour, resentment: perhaps alluding to the elephant's supposed nobility and gentleness of character, as in Thomson, *Summer* 722–3. 'Oh, truly wise! with gentle might endowed, / Though powerful not destructive!'

10 compare *Troilus and Cressida* II, iii, 113: 'The elephant hath joints, but none for courtesy.' Alluding to the popular fallacy that elephants had unjointed legs.

14 *noes and ayes* votes on either side of the question in parliament.

18 *the comparison is pat* compare *On Poetry: a Rhapsody* 61: 'And here a simile comes pat in.' 'Pat' has a more unmistakably favourable note than today ('apt').

22 elephants on display in fairs or raree-galleries: they had been regularly featured in the Roman circus, where they were opposed by a large number of gladiators, and in England were fairly common as fairground sights.

27 *bulwarks* the wooden structures carried by elephants used for military purposes, as employed not only by the Greeks and Carthaginians but also by the Jews (1 Maccabees vi, 28-30).

30 *tester* colloquial term for sixpence, that is, 2½p.

31 *Siam* known as the land of the white elephant: the main source of supply for Indian elephants.

AYE AND NO: A FABLE

Not to be confused with the separate poem *Aye and No: A Tale from Dublin*. Very dubious: possibly by Gay, to whom it was attributed in Bell's edition of 1773. Faber, *Poetical Works of Gay* (1926), was inclined to doubt this ascription, but he printed it, as did Dearing in *Gay*, II, 379-80. It is true that the item was starred in *Misc* (1742) – see preceding item (headnote) for the significance of this – and that Gay was well versed both in the fable and in octosyllabic writing. On the other hand, the critical attitude towards the form implied in the opening couplet is much more in Swift's manner (see *An Answer to Dr Delany's Fable of the Pheasant and the Lark* 1–12). As Faber points out, the addition of an explanatory note to l. 3 in 1754 is not a positive sign as far as the attribution to Gay is concerned.

The poem first appeared in *M28*, the basis for the present text. *Gay*, II, 628 notes an attribution to Arbuthnot in a manuscript belonging to the second Earl of Oxford.

3 *Channel Row* 'a dirty street near the Parliament House, Westminster' (note in the octavo trade edn, 1754). Running north-south to the east of what is now the lower end of Whitehall, near the Houses of Parliament.

4 *Aye and No* see *The Elephant* 14.

11 sometimes are willing to be bought off by a bribe.

14 *yonder stage* parliament.

14–19 epic diction.

21 meaning unclear; perhaps the sense is that one good ministerial supporter is worth two opposition members ('worth' because he has been paid twice as much).

23 *proper use* in science or philosophy the meaning was 'true or natural function' (e.g. of a bodily organ). The ironic overtone is 'personal, selfish purpose'.

25 *Gay*, II, 630 suggests the allusion is to the surviving generals from the Marlborough wars.

26 *great man* leading politician, but, by long association, specially applied to Walpole.

27 Yonge see Biog. Dict. He had been a Treasury lord but was out of office in 1728.

30 perhaps a reference to the 'screening' of apparently guilty ministers by parliament following the South Sea episode.

31 Civil List originally, 'the charges for the civil or administrative government of the state'; evolving into the more specialized sense it bears today, 'the amount voted by parliament from the public revenue for the household and personal expenses of the monarch' (*OED*). The sense, in any case, is that of a fund from which pensions and perquisites were paid: a slush-fund, in fact.

32 Caesar Julius Caesar, famous for lightning strikes.

33 Fabius see *On Poetry: a Rhapsody* 500.

35 compare the proposed way of reconciling parties in the Academy of Lagado (*Gulliver's Travels* III, 6), where the 'occiputs' from the brains of violent opponents are exchanged by surgery (*PW* XI, 189). The passage has a strong savour of the characteristic Swiftian dialogue in verse.

37 Noes in bishops see *On Dr Rundle* 40.

41 like Swisses Swiss mercenaries were often referred to in proverbial expressions: as in *Hudibras* III, iii, 458: '[Lawyers] make their best advantages, / Of others' quarrels, like the Swiss.' There was an adage, 'No money, no Swiss.'

Appendix 1: Latin Poems

AD AMICUM ERUDITUM THOMAM SHERIDAN

Printed in *WF*; there is a transcript in *TCD*. Headed on its first publication, 'Scripsit *Oct. Ann. Dom.* 1717.' For Swift's growing friendship with Sheridan, see *To Mr Delany*, headnote. Orrery tells us that Swift 'was extremely solicitous that [this poem and the next] should be printed among his works: and what is no less true than amazing, he assumed to himself more vanity upon these two Latin poems, than upon many of his best English performances' (*Remarks*, 5th edn (1752), p. 88). The text is that of *WF*, with contractions expanded and capitalization normalized.

2 Permessi Permessus was a river in Boeotia, sacred to Apollo and the muses, rising on Mount Helicon: see Virgil, *Eclogues* VI, 64.

32–3 reflecting Swift's habitual interest in the *Aeneid*, Book VI.

CARBERIAE RUPES

First published in *WF*, the source of the present text, with the heading, 'Scripsit *Jun. Ann. Dom.* 1723.' Early in that month, just after Vanessa's death, Swift left for a 'long Southern journey' (*Corr* II, 455–6), which took him for the only time in his life into the extreme south-west corner of Ireland, probably as far as the parish of Myross on the coast of Cork, near Ross Carbery. To the west lies what has been termed 'a shattered zigzag coastline' and the picturesque scenery of 'Carbery's Hundred Isles'. On this journey, see G.Y. Goldberg, *Jonathan Swift and Contemporary Cork* (1967), pp. 42–6. Swift returned to Dublin in September, via Clonfert in Co. Galway. See also *To Charles Ford, Esq. on His Birthday*, headnote.

In *WF* a translation by William Dunkin, extending to forty-six lines, was appended; for the text, see *P I*, 317–19. For Dunkin, see Biog. Dict.

FABULA CANIS ET UMBRAE

Published by Deane Swift in 1765. Undatable.

Appendix 3: Manuscript Versions

VANBRUG'S HOUSE

Text from *MF*, in this case unmodernized. For other circumstances surrounding the poem, see notes to the printed version, pp. 629–31 above. A separate transcript by Charles Ford was printed by D. Nichol Smith (ed.), *Letters of Jonathan Swift to Charles Ford* (1935).

50 *Geese are Swans* proverbial: *Tilley* G639.
76 *Mountain did the Mouse* Horace, *Ars Poetica* 139.

THE STORY OF BAUCIS & PHILEMON

Text from *MF*, unmodernized. For the background to the poem, see notes to the printed version, *Baucis and Philemon*, pp. 632–4 above. This original version was probably written *c.*1706, the date given for the revised version in *M11*. The first three pages of Swift's manuscript are reproduced in P.J. Croft, *Autograph Poetry in the English Language* (1973) I, 62–3.

9 *Rixham* see *Baucis and Philemon* 10.

AN ANSWER TO A LATE SCANDALOUS POEM

Text from *HEH*, unmodernized. For other details, see notes to the published version, pp. 861–2 above.

157–78 there is no equivalent in the published version, and prudent self-censorship must be the explanation. For Charteris (l. 165), see Biog. Dict.

Biographical Dictionary

The list includes about 190 individuals who are mentioned in the poems and who were active during Swift's lifetime. Entries are confined to major events in the subject's career, plus any known connections with Swift. Sources (where relevant) are listed as follows: *DNB* denotes an article on the individual in the *Dictionary of National Biography; Corr, PW*, and *JTS* indicate a reference in the *Correspondence, Prose Works*, or *Journal to Stella* (see the index to these sources, p. 598). In almost every case there is an entry in *P*, not indicated here.

Individuals are listed according to the name they bore at the time of their main association with Swift (thus, 'Walpole', not 'Orford'). Harley and St John are entered under their family name since Swift was directly concerned with them before and after their elevation to the peerage.

Acheson, Sir Arthur (1688–1749). Succeeded as fifth baronet, 1701. Irish M.P. from 1727; Sheriff of Co. Armagh. Married in 1715 to Anne, daughter of Philip Savage (d. 1719), Chancellor of the Exchequer in Ireland, an acquaintance of Swift. Lady Acheson died in 1737. Their eldest son, Archibald, was educated like his father at Trinity College; born at the family estate of Market Hill (which Swift often visited) in 1718, he became the first Viscount Gosford. Sir Arthur was an unregenerate Tory; his wife preferred Dublin society to the country, but Swift's satire of her fashionable ways is always good-humoured and affectionate. *(Corr, PW)*

Addison, Joseph (1672–1719). Writer and politician. Wrote, together with Richard Steele (q.v.), the influential *Tatler* (1709–11) and *Spectator* (1711–12). Whig M.P. from 1708. Secretary to Lord Wharton (q.v.) as Lord Lieutenant of Ireland, 1708–10. After the Hanoverian accession held various government offices, including that of Secretary of State, 1717–18. Member of the Kit-Cat Club. Met Swift *c.*1708; a close friend around 1710, and never totally estranged despite political differences. See B. Goldgar, *The Curse of Party* (1961). Twelve letters between them survive. *(DNB, Corr, PW, JTS)*

Aislabie, John (1670–1742). Politician; Whig M.P. from 1695, and Chancellor of the Exchequer (1717–21); implicated in bribery and other improprieties during South Sea Bubble affair, and expelled from the Commons. Probably not known personally to Swift. *(DNB)*

Allen, Joshua, second Viscount (1685–1742). Politician. Member of a Dublin mercantile family; his father (whom he succeeded, 1726) had been a Whig and Hanoverian, but opposed the ministry over Wood's halfpence. Allen and his wife were known to Swift and at one time quite friendly; but Allen spoke out against the award of the freedom of the city to Swift by Dublin corporation, and thereafter they were bitter enemies. *(Corr, PW)*

Anglesey, Arthur Annesley, fifth Earl of (1676–1737). Tory politician; held important offices in Ireland, and was a Lord Justice in 1714. On friendly terms with Swift, with whom he corresponded. (*Corr, JTS*)

Anne, Queen of England (1665–1714). The last Stuart monarch; daughter of James II by his first wife, Anne Hyde. Married George, Prince of Denmark, 1683; all her children died young. Succeeded to the throne 1702. Her dislike for Swift, originating in *A Tale of a Tub*, was strengthened by *The Windsor Prophecy*, after which she resolved he should receive no preferment during her reign. Swift called her 'in her own nature extremely dilatory and timorous, yet upon some occasions, positive to a great degree'. (*DNB, Corr, PW, JTS*)

Arbuthnot, John (1667–1735). Physician and writer; member of the Scriblerus group. Educated at Aberdeen and Oxford; M.D. (St Andrews), 1696, F.R.S., 1704. Physician to Queen Anne. Author of the widely read Tory satire *John Bull* (1712). Met Swift *c.*1710, after which their close friendship remained unbroken. Some of Arbuthnot's works were printed in the Pope-Swift *Miscellanies* from 1727. Over thirty letters survive between Arbuthnot and Swift, who wrote 'there does not live a better man'. (*DNB, Corr, PW, JTS*)

Argyll, John Campbell, second Duke of (1680–1743). Soldier and politician. Member of the Whig opposition to Walpole in the 1730s. Took a leading share in the suppression of the 1715 Rising; Field-Marshal, 1736. A friend of Pope and Arbuthnot; but Swift, who once professed to love Argyll 'mightily', came to dislike him: 'a true Scot in all his conduct'. (*DNB, Corr, PW, JTS*)

Atterbury, Francis (1662–1732). Churchman; Dean of Christ Church, Oxford, 1712; Bishop of Rochester and Dean of Westminster, 1713. Arrested for alleged Jacobite plot in 1722 and sent to the Tower; after a trial in the House of Lords, banished to France in 1723, where he served the Pretender. Friend and correspondent of both Swift and Pope. (*DNB, Corr, PW, JTS*)

Baldwin, Richard (1672–1758). Provost of Trinity College, Dublin, 1717. A college contemporary of Swift's; a man of strong Whig sympathies. Incurred Swift's dislike in the dispute over College fellowships (1727). (*DNB, Corr*)

Barber, John (1675–1741). Printer; alderman and Lord Mayor of the City of London; printed *London Gazette*. Also printed a number of Swift's works through agency of Benjamin Tooke. Corresponded with Swift: almost thirty surviving letters. (*Corr, PW, JTS*)

Beaumont, Joseph. Linen draper in Trim, and business agent for Swift. Supposed to have ended up deranged; dead by 1734. (*Corr, PW, JTS*)

Berkeley, Charles, second Earl of (1649–1710). Lord Justice of Ireland, 1699, with Swift as his chaplain; father of Lady Betty Germain (q.v.). Swift visited the family at Berkeley Castle. (*Corr, PW, JTS*)

Berkeley, George (1685–1753). Philosopher, churchman, and projector. Author of *Treatise concerning Human Knowledge*, 1710. Educated at Kilkenny School and Trinity College, Dublin; Fellow, 1707. Dean of Dromore, 1721; Dean of Derry, 1724; Bishop of Cloyne, 1734. Attempted to set up college in America and to promote medicinal use of tar-water. An executor of Vanessa's will. Met Swift through Arbuthnot, 1712; a long but perhaps not exactly intimate friendship with Swift. (*DNB, Corr, PW, JTS*)

Bettesworth, Richard (1688/9–1741). Lawyer; born in England of Irish descent; entered Trinity College, Dublin, 1705; called to the Irish bar, 1716; Serjeant-at-

Law, 1723; Ll.D., 1725. M.P. for Philipstown, 1721; for Midleton, 1727. One of the most regular targets for Swift's satire in the 1730s.   (*Corr*, *PW*)

Blackmore, Sir Richard (1654–1729). Physician and poet. Educated at Oxford; M.D., Padua; royal physician to William III and Queen Anne. Knighted 1697. Produced epic poems which excited the scorn of the wits, and by the time of *The Dunciad* widely recognized as the type of a mediocre talent. Described Swift as 'an impious buffoon', but personal enmity was probably less of a factor in their relations than political differences and Blackmore's reputation as one who took on larger literary tasks than his abilities warranted.   (*DNB*, *Corr*, *PW*)

Blount, Martha (1690–1762). Member of an old-established Berkshire family; lived at Mapledurham. Friend and correspondent of Pope, who left her a considerable legacy. Recipient of Pope's *Epistle to a Lady*. Corresponded occasionally with Swift.   (*DNB*, *Corr*)

Boate, Godfrey (1673/4–1721). Lawyer; entered Trinity College, Dublin, 1692; called to the Irish bar, 1710; Serjeant and Justice of the King's Bench, 1716. Officiated at trial of Edward Waters, 1720; the enmity this incurred from Swift may have been augmented by personal factors.

Bolingbroke   *see* St John

Bolton, Charles Paulet, second Duke of (1661–1722). Whig courtier; K.G., 1714; Lord Chamberlain, 1715; Lord Lieutenant of Ireland, 1717–20. Disliked the project for Wood's halfpence and (perhaps on this account) was removed from office. 'A great booby' (Swift, *PW* V, 258).   (*DNB*, *Corr*, *PW*, *JTS*)

Bolton, Theophilus (d. 1744). Churchman. Entered Trinity College, Dublin, 1695; graduated, 1701; D.D., 1716. Bishop of Clonfert, 1722; of Elphin, 1724. Archbishop of Cashel, 1729. He had been Chancellor of St Patrick's, when relations with Swift were strained, but later they were on better terms.   (*Corr*, *PW*)

Boulter, Hugh (1672–1742). Churchman; Walpole's nominee to promote English interests in Ireland, and an object of Swift's implacable hatred. Chaplain to George I; Bishop of Bristol, 1719; Archbishop of Armagh, 1724; frequently Lord Justice of Ireland.   (*DNB*, *Corr*, *PW*)

Boyle, Henry (*c.*1677–1725). Politician; Chancellor of the Exchequer, 1701; Lord Treasurer of Ireland, 1704; Secretary of State, 1708; Lord President of the Council, 1721. Created first Baron Carleton, 1714. Patron of Addison; a Court Whig. Probably little first-hand contact with Swift, who thought him avaricious.   (*DNB*, *Corr*, *PW*)

Brent, Mrs — (d. 1735). Swift's housekeeper from the time of his spell at Kilroot (1695–6) and then through most of his years as Dean of St Patrick's. Succeeded in her office by her daughter Mrs Anne Ridgeway. Nicknamed Swift's Walpole.   (*Corr*, *JTS*)

Buckingham, John Sheffield, first Duke of (1647–1721). Author and politician; served in Dutch wars in reign of Charles II; published *An Essay on Poetry*, 1682; Lord Privy Seal, 1702; Lord President of the Council, 1710. A Tory who flirted with Jacobitism. Patron of Dryden and friend of Pope, who edited his works in 1723. Despite political affinities and literary contacts, Swift and he did not get on well together at a personal level.   (*DNB*, *Corr*, *PW*, *JTS*)

Buckley, Samuel (d. 1741). Printer, bookseller, gazetteer and, after the Hanoverian accession, manager of government publicity. Published the *Spectator* and many Whig pamphlets at the time of the Harley administration. Swift may have known him slightly.   (*Corr*, *PW*)

Buissière, Paul (d. 1739). A Huguenot refugee, who practised as a surgeon in London; he treated Harley after the attack by Guiscard in 1711. Wrote on anatomical subjects. (*DNB, Corr, JTS*)

Burnet, Gilbert (1643–1715). Churchman; wrote *History of the Reformation* (1679–1714); an architect of the Williamite Revolution; Bishop of Salisbury, 1689; preached coronation sermon for William and Mary; posthumously published *History of His Own Times* (1724–34). An active politician, ardent polemicist, and skilled intriguer; a strong Whig from a Scottish Presbyterian family; intensely disliked by Swift, who wrote bitter marginalia in a copy of the Bishop's memoirs, and claimed to know him well (*PW* V, 260). (*DNB, Corr, PW*)

Bushe, Arthur. Secretary to the Earl of Berkeley during his term as Lord Justice of Ireland. Disliked by Swift, who thought that Bushe prevented his promotion to the Deanery of Derry in 1700 and indeed that he accepted bribes to dispose of this office. Swift's suspicions were probably unjustified (see *Landa*, pp. 27–34). (*PW*)

Butler, Brinsley, first Viscount Lanesborough (*c.*1670–1735). Known as 'Prince' Butler; a college contemporary of Swift, along with his brother Theophilus (*c.*1669–1724), first Baron Newtown-Butler. Brinsley's sons Humphry and Robert were well-known men about Dublin society, and all these figures were familiar friends of Swift. Humphry (1700–1768) succeeded to the viscountcy, created in 1728. Robert (b. 1704) was a captain of the Battle-Axe Guards. (*Corr*)

Carey (or Cary), Walter (1685–1757). M.P. and government placeman; supported in turn Walpole and the Pelhams. Secretary to the Duke of Dorset when the latter was Lord Lieutenant of Ireland in the early 1730s. He also served as Clerk to the Mint and Clerk to the Privy Council. A friend of Edward Young, and known to members of the Addison set such as Tickell and Ambrose Philips (qq. v.). Possibly satirized by Pope, though some references appear to fit his namesake, Henry Carey, more closely. His offences from Swift's point of view would relate chiefly to his public offices, though Swift had personal dealings with him in Ireland. (*Corr*)

Caroline, Queen of England (1683–1737). Daughter of the Margrave of Anspach; married Prince of Hanover (later George II) in 1705; came to England as Princess of Wales, 1714; became Queen in 1727. Developed strong links with Walpole and attempted to take a lead in cultural affairs. Quarrelled with her son Frederick (q.v.). Swift was introduced to her in 1726. Like Pope, he maintained an uncertain friendship with the Queen whilst not scrupling to satirize her in his poetry. (*DNB, Corr, PW*)

Carr, Charles (1671/2–1739). Churchman; entered Trinity College, Dublin, 1689; Chaplain to the Irish House of Commons; Bishop of Killaloe, 1716. One of the few bishops to support the 'Irish' interest in matters of ecclesiastical politics. (*Corr*)

Carteret, Frances, Lady (1694–1743). *Née* Frances Worsley, a society toast as a young woman; married Lord Carteret in 1710. A cultivated and spirited person with whom Swift managed to remain on good terms, even during the difficult political circumstances at the time of Wood's halfpence. He also got on well with her mother, Lady Worsley. (*Corr, PW, JTS*)

Carteret, John, second Baron (1690–1763). Statesman; undertook diplomatic missions before becoming Secretary of State, 1721; Lord Lieutenant of Ireland, 1724–30; broke with Walpole and worked with the Opposition in the 1730s; succeeded as second Earl Granville, 1744; attempted to form ministry, 1746, but failed; K.G., 1750; Lord President of the Council, 1751. An accomplished and ambitious man who finally achieved comparatively little in national politics, though standing near the centre of events for half a century. He and Swift maintained a high regard for one another until Swift's final breakdown: 'When people ask me how I governed Ireland,' Carteret wrote in a letter of 1737, 'I say that I pleased Dr Swift.' (*DNB, Corr, PW, JTS*)

Chandos, James Brydges, first Duke of (1673–1744). 'Princely Chandos'; started as country gentleman and M.P., but made his fortune as Paymaster to the Forces during the Marlborough wars; created Earl of Caernarvon, 1714; Duke of Chandos, 1719. Built great house at Cannons, where Handel was director of music; thought to be the chief model for Pope's 'Timon'; active in building, manufacture, speculation, and artistic patronage. He and Swift got to know each other around 1711; later they were estranged, mainly (Swift believed) through Chandos's rise to wealth and magnificence. (*DNB, Corr, PW, JTS*)

Charteris, Francis (1675–1732). Gambler, usurer, and rogue. A Scottish landowner who was more than once dismissed from the army for various frauds. Acquired a large fortune by lending money to fellow-gamesters and distraining their possessions when the loan was not repaid. In 1730 convicted of a rape, but freed from prison, supposedly through the influence of Walpole. Used by Hogarth, Pope, and others as the type of an unprincipled rascal. Probably not personally known to Swift. Charteris was a doughty Whig, who made a not very heroic stand against the Jacobite army at Preston in 1715. In 1727 he spent £100 a day for a week bribing electors in the constituency of Lancaster, but he gained only ninety-four votes and failed to get into parliament, to the delight of most observers. (*DNB, Corr*)

Cholmondeley, Hugh, first Earl of (*c*.1662–1725). Whig courtier; Treasurer of the Household, 1708; created Earl, 1706; disliked by Swift, who wished to see him ousted from his place. (*DNB, Corr, PW, JTS*)

Cibber, Colley (1671–1757). Playwright and actor-manager. Served in army of William of Orange; embarked on acting career, 1690. His first play, *Love's Last Shift* (1696), enjoyed some success. Other dramatic works included adaptations of Shakespeare as well as sentimental comedies of his own. Turned Molière to anti-Jacobite propagandist purposes with *The Non-Juror*, 1717. One of the principal managers of Drury Lane Theatre from 1712, with a variety of partners. Officially retired from the stage, 1734, but continued to appear from time to time. His appointment as poet laureate in 1730, although largely political and honorific, marked a real contribution to English cultural life; nevertheless, opposition satirists found it easy to poke fun at his birthday odes and vapid complimentary effusions in this capacity. Published *Apology* for his own life, 1740. His quarrel with Pope intensified in the last years of the poet's life; hence Cibber's removal from a minor role in *The Dunciad* to the position of King Dunce in the 1743 version. Swift's references concern Cibber's role as a kind of Minister of Culture for Walpole. Any personal offences Cibber had given to the Scriblerian group dated from a time after Swift's move to Ireland. (*DNB, Corr, PW*)

Clarke, Samuel (1675–1729). Deistic philosopher; Rector of St James's, Westminster, 1709; translated Newton's *Optics* into Latin; corresponded with Leibniz; edited Homer, and published sermons, Boyle lectures, and tracts. Patronized by Queen Caroline. Probably not known personally to Swift. (*DNB, PW*)

Cleveland, Charles Fitzroy, first Duke of Cleveland (1662–1730). Natural son of Charles II by Barbara Villiers, created Duchess of Cleveland in 1670. Succeeded as Duke of Cleveland in 1709. Hen-pecked and weak-minded; according to one story, he was locked up by his Tory wife during the Sacheverell trial and had to be rescued by his half-brother, the Duke of Richmond, in order to vote against the accused man. (*DNB*)

Collins, Anthony (1676–1729). Deistic writer; knew John Locke at the end of his life. Published *Discourse of Freethinking* (1713), which occasioned an answer from Richard Bentley and a satiric riposte from Swift. (*DNB, PW*)

Colt, Sir Henry Dutton (*c*.1646–1731). M.P. for Westminster; generally supported the court, but little regarded, even by Whig adherents. Termed 'a busybody politician'. Created a baronet, 1694. Only crossed Swift's path as a result of the 1710 election. (*PW*)

Compton, Spencer, first Earl of Wilmington (*c*.1673–1743). Politician. Whig M.P. from 1698, with a break from 1710 to 1713. Speaker of the Commons, 1715–27. K.B., 1725. Expected to succeed Walpole as first minister on the accession of George II, but proved incapable of holding the office. Instead he moved to the Lords (Baron Wilmington, 1728; Earl, 1730) and held various posts under Walpole. However, 'his career was that of a perfect courtier, whose continued membership and support of an administration that he disliked was dictated by the simple desire to please his royal master' (J.B. Owen). Swift, who knew him, thought that he secretly hated Walpole (*PW* V, 103); after the minister's fall Wilmington became First Lord of the Treasury. (*DNB, Corr, PW*)

Concanen, Matthew (1701–49). Miscellaneous writer; born in Ireland, but moved to London in the 1720s, when he joined a set critical of Pope centring on Lewis Theobald. Duly incorporated in *The Dunciad*. According to Pope's note to this reference, Concanen was 'an anonymous slanderer, and publisher of other men's slanders, particularly on Dr Swift to whom he had particular obligations and from whom he had received both in a collection of poems for his benefit and otherwise, no small assistance'. This Concanen subsequently denied, claiming that he had spoken to Swift only twice in his life. He later wrote for the government press, 'after which this man was surprisingly promoted to administer justice and law in Jamaica' (Pope) – he became Attorney General for the island in 1732. (*DNB, Corr*)

Congreve, William (1670–1729). The dramatist; educated along with Swift at Kilkenny school and Trinity College. Spectacularly successful in the theatre before Swift had made any sort of mark, but abandoned the stage in 1700. Lived the rest of his life in England, an invalid and at the same time a man of pleasure. A Kit-Cat. Remained on good terms with both Swift and Pope, despite holding government sinecures. (*DNB, Corr, PW, JTS*)

Conolly, William (*c*.1660–1729). Politician; M.P. and then, from 1715, Speaker of the Irish House of Commons; frequently served as Lord Justice. Regarded by Swift as grasping and illiterate. (*DNB, Corr, PW, JTS*)

Cope, Robert (*c*.1679–*c*.1753). Country gentleman. His seat was at Loughgall, Co. Armagh, where Swift often stayed. He had been a Tory M.P. in the Irish parliament. Swift had encountered him in London in 1711. His second wife was a daughter of Sir William Fownes, Lord Mayor of Dublin, a wealthy Tory politician known to Swift. In 1715 Cope was arrested, presumably for suspected Jacobite activity; but later on he came to terms with the ministry, and relations between Swift and himself seem to have cooled. (*Corr, JTS*)

Corbet, Francis (1688–1775). Churchman; Prebendary of St Patrick's and, from 1746, Dean. An executor of Stella's will. Apparently he maintained good, though never intimate, relations with Swift. (*Corr, PW*)

Craggs, James, senior (1657–1721). Of lowly origins, he 'made his way quickly in the borderland of business and politics for which his talents suited him so well' (John Carswell). Became military clothing contractor and established close links with the Duke and Duchess of Marlborough. M.P.; Secretary of Ordnance Office; from 1715, Postmaster-General. Implicated in South Sea scandal and committed suicide. The archetypal parvenu for Swift, as his career even in summary would suggest. (*DNB, PW*)

Craggs, James, junior (1686–1721). Son of James Craggs, senior (q.v.). M.P.; held government offices including Secretary at War, 1717, and Secretary of State, 1718. A client of Stanhope and of the Hanoverian court, who took a leading part in the South Sea operation. A friend of Pope despite his Whiggery and dubious financial connections; Swift's more suspicious attitude was shared by many conservative thinkers. (*DNB, Corr, PW*)

Crosse, Thomas (1663–1738). A Westminster brewer, who represented the constituency several times between 1700 and 1722. A Tory, who owed allegiance to the high-flying Earl of Rochester. Rewarded with a baronetcy in 1713. He was not, any more than Colt (q.v.), an important figure on the national political scene, but his candidacy in the volatile and well-publicized Westminster arena gave him some brief prominence. It is unlikely that Swift had any personal knowledge of him.

Cumberland, William Augustus, Duke of (1721–65). Third son of George II by Caroline of Anspach. Created Duke in 1726; K.G., 1740; served with navy and then with army at battle of Dettingen (1743). Captain-General of British forces, 1745; fought at battle of Fontenoy (1745) and, more successfully, at Culloden (1746); put down the Scottish clans in such merciless fashion that he acquired the nickname 'Butcher'. A Lord Justice, 1755. As a boy, received dedication of Gay's *Fables*. (*DNB, PW*)

Curll, Edmund (1683–1747). The notorious bookseller. His brushes with Pope are famous episodes in literary history, but he had also offended Swift with piracies and 'complete keys' from 1710 onwards, and continued to do so into the later 1730s. Swift's hostility was both general (relating to such publishers as a class) and particular (in view of Curll's practices upon his own work). (*DNB, Corr, PW, JTS*)

Cutts, John, first Baron (1661–1707). Soldier; fought for William III at the Boyne (1690); created Baron the same year; his bravery at the siege of Namur (1695) earned him the nickname of 'Salamander'. Fought at Blenheim and was Commander-in-Chief in Ireland, 1705. M.P. A Tory, he was disliked by Swift for his inordinate vanity and perhaps for personal reasons now unclear. (*DNB, PW, JTS*)

Damer, Joseph (1630–1720). Dublin merchant; born in England and served on parliamentary side in the Civil War. After the Restoration, settled in Ireland and established a business as a moneylender. He operated from the London Tavern in Fishamble Street, kept by Timothy Sullivan. It is not certain whether Swift was personally acquainted with him. (See *Gilbert*, I, 65–7)

Daniel, Richard (1680/81–1739). Clergyman; Dean of Armagh, 1721–31; Dean of Down, 1731–9. Published poems and translations, as well as paraphrases of selected psalms (1727). Held in low esteem by Swift, both as a man and a poet; Daniel had the backing of the ministry in a disputed appointment, and would be suspect on that ground alone. (*Corr*)

Delany, Patrick (*c*.1685–1768). Churchman; Fellow of Trinity College; Chancellor of Christ Church Cathedral, Dublin, 1728; Chancellor of St Patrick's Cathedral, 1730; Dean of Down, 1744. Married the rich widow of an M.P. in 1732; after her death, married the bluestocking Mary Pendarves (*née* Granville) in 1743. A close friend of Swift's from *c*.1718. Defended Swift against what he regarded as Orrery's calumnies in his *Remarks* (1752); also wrote pamphlets, sermons, and scholarly works. His villa, 'Delville', was regularly used by Swift's circle. (*DNB, Corr, PW*)

De La Warr (or Delaware), John West, sixth Baron (1663–1723). Courtier; Treasurer of the Chamber, 1713. Swift regarded him as a ceremonious booby. (*PW*)

Dennis, John (1657–1734). Writer; best known today as a critic and early apostle of the 'sublime', but in his own time celebrated also as a dramatist and poet. Unlike Pope, Swift largely escaped personal brushes with Dennis; his scorn for the critic seems to be generic rather than personal, although Dennis's loose allegiance to the Marlborough interest may also have been relevant. (*DNB, Corr, PW*)

Dingley, Rebecca (*c*.1665–1743). Stella's companion; a distant relative of the Temple family. A spinster. Swift is said to have paid her an annuity of fifty guineas in quarterly instalments. Left much of her property to Rev. John Lyons. A stolid, self-contained woman. (*Corr, PW, JTS*)

Drogheda, Henry Hamilton Moore, third Earl of (*c*.1650–1714). Appointed to succeed Berkeley as a caretaker Lord Justice in 1701 (see *Ball*, p. 46). Father of Lady Betty Rochfort. A minor political figure.

Duck, Stephen (1705–56). The 'thresher poet'. Farm labourer in Wiltshire, who gained patronage of Queen Caroline as a result of his complimentary and other verses. Yeoman of the Guard, and Keeper of Merlin's Cave (1735). Ordained, 1746; obtained office of Rector of Byfleet, 1756, through interest of his friend Joseph Spence (the classical scholar and collector of anecdotes concerning Pope). Drowned himself in a fit of depression. (*DNB, Corr*)

Dunkin, William (*c*.1709–65). Poet; graduated at Trinity College, Dublin, 1729; D.D., 1744. Ordained, 1735. Master of Portora Royal School, 1746. Adept both in English and in Latin verse. A witness to Swift's will and a close ally in the 1730s. (*DNB, Corr, PW*)

D'Urfey (or Durfey), Thomas (1653–1723). Poet and playwright; often the butt of satirists, but wrote some enduringly popular songs and ballads, which were set to innumerable tunes throughout the eighteenth century. Often turns up in Scriblerian satire (*A Tale of a Tub; Peri Bathous; The Dunciad*) but without any particular malice that can be detected. (*DNB, PW*)

Eusden, Laurence (1688–1730). Poet. Appointed poet laureate in 1718, through the interest of the Duke of Newcastle. Satirized in *Peri Bathous* and *The Dunciad*. Effete and bibulous, but not regarded as a serious threat by the Scriblerian party, especially in comparison with his successor, Colley Cibber. (*DNB, Corr, PW*)

Faulkner, George (1699–1775). Dublin bookseller and printer. Started *Dublin Journal*, 1728. Swift's main outlet in the last decade of his career; published the authoritative *Works* (1735). Originally in four volumes, this edition grew to twenty by 1769. Often in trouble with the authorities in his earlier days, Faulkner ended up an alderman of the city of Dublin. (*DNB, Corr, PW*)

Flamsteed, John (1646–1719). Astronomer. Met Newton at Cambridge; ordained, 1675; F.R.S., 1677. Became the first Astronomer Royal in 1675. Made important observations and prepared a major catalogue of the stars. (*DNB*)

Ford, Charles (1682–1741). Born in Dublin; inherited estate of Woodpark, Co. Meath. Appointed Gazetteer, 1712, through interest of Swift. Continued to live much of the time in London, paying occasional visits to Ireland. Exchanged some seventy surviving letters with Swift. A close and valued friend of both Swift and Stella. In his youth a man of pleasure, he became a trusted agent in matters concerned with literature, notably during the publication of *Gulliver's Travels*. (*Corr, PW, JTS*)

Frederick, Prince of Wales (1707–51). Eldest son of George II. Born in Hanover; created Prince of Wales, 1729. Married Princess Augusta of Saxe-Gotha, 1736. The focus of opposition to Walpole in the 1730s, constantly at loggerheads with his parents. Died quite suddenly, probably from pneumonia, before his anti-Pelham group achieved power or he could reach the throne, although his son, George III, reigned for sixty years. (*DNB, Corr, PW*)

Furnese, Sir Henry (1658–1712). Contractor, Whig M.P. and prominent City figure. Used by Prior and the Tory satirists as an example of the war-mongering moneyed interest. Had strong links with Marlborough and Chandos. Bank and East India Company director; Sheriff of London, 1701; knighted, 1691; created baronet, 1707. A Kit-Cat. The son of a bankrupt grocer, he represented, like the senior James Craggs (q.v.), the type of the parvenu for Swift. (*PW*)

Gadbury, John (1627–1704). Astrologer; educated at Oxford; works include *De Cometis* (1665); accused of conspiracy against William III, 1690, but managed to establish innocence. The successor of William Lilly and predecessor of John Partridge (q.v.) as the most prominent maker of astrological predictions, many with a political bearing. (*DNB, PW*)

Galway, Henri de Massue de Ruvigny, first Earl of (1648–1720). Military commander. Born in France and served under Turenne. Joined English service and fought for William III in Ireland. Created Earl of Galway, 1697. Lord Justice, 1697. Commander of English forces in Peninsular campaign; defeated at Almanza, 1707. Lord Justice in Ireland again, 1715. A Huguenot; a brave soldier and a resolute administrator. Distrusted by Swift for his Whiggish opinions, especially his tolerant attitude towards the dissenters; Swift's description may be regarded as coloured by partisan sentiment ('a deceitful hypocritical factious knave; a damnable hypocrite of no religion'). (*DNB, Corr, PW, JTS*)

Gay, John (1685–1732). Poet and dramatist. Knew Swift by c.1713, when he became associated with Pope, Arbuthnot, and others in the Scriblerus club. Early works include *The Shepherd's Week* (1714) and *Trivia* (1716); he also wrote plays, some in collaboration with Pope, notably *Three Hours after Marriage* (1717). Achieved wide popularity with *Fables*, first series (1727), and *The Beggar's Opera* (1728). Held minor court posts throughout his career, amongst them Commissioner of the Lottery, 1723, but no office of great influence or remuneration. Patronized by the Duke and Duchess of Queensberry as a gesture against the court. His thirty-four surviving letters to Swift form the largest part of his known correspondence. Close friend of Pope, Arbuthnot, and Mrs Howard (qq.v.). (*DNB, Corr, PW, JTS*)

George I, King of England (1660–1727). Son of the Duke of Brunswick and Sophia (daughter of Elizabeth of Bohemia and granddaughter of James I). Succeeded his father as Elector of Hanover in 1698; on the death of his mother in June 1714 became heir-apparent to the English throne, and two months later became King. Married Sophia Dorothea of Celle, 1682; soon estranged from his wife, who, after an alleged affair with Count Philip von Königsmark in 1694, was imprisoned in the fortress at Ahlden until her death in 1726. The King spoke little English and brought with him a large Hanoverian entourage, who provided political advice or sexual gratification, according to their sex. Withstood the 1715 Rising and by the time of his death had seen the Hanoverian régime firmly entrenched, to the ill-concealed distaste of Swift and a sizeable portion of the people. (*DNB, Corr, PW*)

George II, King of England (1683–1760). Eldest son of George I; brought up by his grandparents at Hanover; married Caroline of Anspach (q.v.), 1705. Came to England on his father's accession to the English throne, and created Prince of Wales, 1714. Quarrelled with his father and became focus of opposition from 1717. Succeeded to the throne, 1727, and developed lasting ties with Walpole, until reluctantly parting with his minister in 1742. Survived the 1745 Rising and outlived most of his critics and detractors, including Swift and the other Scriblerians. (*DNB, Corr, PW*)

Germain, Lady Elizabeth (1680–1769). Daughter of the Earl of Berkeley (q.v.). Her friendship with Swift began when she was a young woman, and lasted for the remainder of her life; she was also on good terms with Pope. Married a soldier, Sir John Germain (1650–1718) in 1706; his first wife had been Lady Mary Mordaunt, sister of the Earl of Peterborough (q.v.), and because of this Lady Betty acquired some of the Mordaunt property after her husband's death. A lively, worldly, and intelligent woman. Her companion, Biddy Floyd, figures in Swift's works. (*DNB, Corr, PW, JTS*)

Giffard, Martha, Lady (1638–1722). Sister of Sir William Temple (q.v.). Married Sir Thomas Giffard, 1662; he died within a matter of weeks, and she remained a widow for sixty years. Entered into dispute with Swift over her brother's memoirs. Stella's mother, Mrs Bridget Johnson, was in her service after the death of Temple. Left money to Stella, her mother, and Mrs Dingley. (*Corr, PW, JTS*)

Godolphin, Sidney, first Earl of Godolphin (1645–1712). Statesman; M.P. from 1668; Lord of the Treasury, 1679; Secretary of State, 1684. Created Baron, 1684. Lord Justice under William III; Lord Treasurer, 1702. Fell from power after the Sacheverell affair, 1710. Swift originally looked to him for support, but Godolphin's coolness to him during the First Fruits mission (1707–9) turned Swift against him and inspired a lasting dislike. (*DNB, Corr, PW, JTS*)

Grafton, Charles Fitzroy, second Duke of (1683–1757). Courtier; grandson of Charles II and the Duchess of Cleveland. As Lord Lieutenant of Ireland, 1720–24, he faced Irish resentment over the proposed Bank and then over Wood's halfpence; replaced by Carteret, 1724. He had earlier acted as a Lord Justice. A Kit-Cat. Swift termed him 'almost a slobberer', but others who knew him better called him 'shrewd, witty and only seemingly simple', and even 'the greatest courtier of his time'. He served as Lord Chamberlain, 1724–57, an unusually long tenure. (*Corr, PW, JTS*)

Grattan brothers. The seven sons of Rev. Patrick Grattan, Fellow of Trinity College, and a Prebendary of St Patrick's. Those best known to Swift were the fourth, Robert, a clergyman who held his father's prebend, and the fifth, John, also a clergyman. They were boon companions, especially in the 1720s. Other brothers became respectively a country gentleman, a Dublin physician, a merchant who was knighted as Lord Mayor of Dublin, and the master of Portora Royal School, Enniskillen. John Grattan (d. 1754) was an executor of Swift's will; Robert (c.1678–c.1741) was one of the nine men appointed to this function in 1737, but he died before he could perform it. The eldest brother, Henry, was the grandfather of the statesman Henry Grattan. (*Corr, PW*)

Grimston, William, first Viscount (c.1683–1756). Originally William Luckyn. A Whig M.P., who was created Viscount in 1719; notoriously prolix speaker, a loyal party hack with no real political influence. Published poems and plays which attracted the scorn of the wits. Probably no first-hand contact with Swift. (*PW*)

Guernsey, Heneage Finch, Baron (c.1650–1719). Younger brother of the Earl of Nottingham (q.v.). King's Counsel, 1677; Solicitor-General, 1679; dismissed by James II, 1686. Leading counsel to the Seven Bishops in 1688. M.P. Created Baron in 1703; Earl of Aylesford, 1714. (*DNB, PW, JTS*)

Halifax, Charles Montagu, first Earl of (1661–1715). Statesman; met Newton at Cambridge; M.P. from 1689. Lord of the Treasury, 1692; as Chancellor of the Exchequer, involved in proposal to set up Bank of England, 1694; First Lord of the Treasury, 1697. Impeached by the House of Commons, 1701, and defended by Swift in *Contests and Dissentions*. First Lord of the Treasury again, 1714, but never regained the power he had wielded in the reign of William III. Created Baron Halifax, 1700; Earl of Halifax, K.G., 1714. A Kit-Cat. Swift's support for him waned as their politics drifted apart. One of the leading patrons of the day, who did much to advance the career of Prior, Addison, and Congreve; despite Swift's assertion that 'his encouragements [to writers] were only good words and dinners', his record as a patron was outstanding. A minor poet who crept into Johnson's *Lives*. (*DNB, Corr, PW, JTS*)

Hampden, Richard (c.1675–1728). Politician; grandson of John Hampden and son of Richard Hampden, Chancellor of the Exchequer in the 1690s. A distant kinsman and follower of Lord Wharton (q.v.). M.P., with a resolutely Whig voting record up to his death. Never achieved high office; as Treasurer of the Navy, in 1720, he laid out £25,000 of public money in South Sea speculations and was forced to resign.

Hanmer, Sir Thomas (1677–1746). Politician. Succeeded as fourth baronet in 1701. M.P. from 1701; a Hanoverian Tory. Speaker of the Commons, 1713–14. Entered *The Dunciad* as 'Mountalto' on account of his incursions into Shakespearian scholarship, which culminated in his 'sumptuous, but not critically very valuable' edition of the plays in 1743–4. Personally known to Swift, who dined with him on a number of occasions c.1711–13. A few letters survive which passed between the two men. Part of the manuscript of Swift's *Four Last Years of the Queen* was left with Hanmer. (*DNB, Corr, PW, JTS*)

Harcourt, Simon, first Viscount (1661–1727). Lawyer and politician. Called to the bar, 1683; M.P. from 1690; Solicitor-General, 1703; Attorney-General, 1707. Helped to impeach Somers, to prosecute Defoe for *The Shortest Way*, and to defend Sacheverell. Lord Keeper, 1710; created Baron Harcourt, 1711; Lord Chancellor, 1713; created Viscount, 1721. The ablest Tory lawyer of his generation; friend and patron of Pope, as was his son. Swift met Harcourt in 1710, and thereafter they preserved good relations, even though Harcourt managed to accommodate himself more fully to the Hanoverian dispensation than Swift would have wished. (*DNB, Corr, PW, JTS*)

Harley, Edward, second Earl of Oxford (1689–1741). Son of Robert Harley. Became Lord Harley on his father's attaining an earldom in 1711; succeeded in the title, 1724. Collector of books and manuscripts. Closely involved with the Scriblerus circle, especially Pope; took a hand in the publication (or suppression) of Swift's works. Over forty letters between Swift and him survive. His marriage to a wealthy heiress in 1713 did not prevent considerable financial difficulties in his later life; after his death, his collection was sold and his manuscripts became the basis of the British Museum holdings. (*DNB, Corr, PW, JTS*)

Harley, Robert, first Earl of Oxford (1661–1724). Statesman. M.P. from 1689; Speaker of the Commons, 1701; Secretary of State, 1704, until forced to resign, 1708. Triumphed in election of 1710 and formed Tory administration, first as Chancellor of the Exchequer and then as Lord Treasurer. Victim of assassination attempt by Guiscard, 1711. Earl of Oxford, 1711; K.G., 1712. Dismissed, 1714, and subsequently impeached, but released after two years' imprisonment in the Tower of London, 1717. Started the great Harley collection of books and manuscripts. A complex figure, personally and politically; he was a convivial friend in private life to men like Swift and Pope, but in public matters Swift often thought him devious and prevaricating. (*DNB, Corr, PW, JTS*)

Harrison, William (1685–1713). Poet. Educated at Oxford; Fellow of New College, 1706. A protégé of both Addison and Swift, who arranged for him to continue the *Tatler* in 1711. He also held a minor appointment in the diplomatic corps at the Utrecht peace negotiations; but he died quite suddenly in abject poverty – despite his patrons, friends such as Tickell and Young, and kinship to St John. Swift was much distressed at his death. (*DNB, Corr, PW, JTS*)

Helsham, Richard (1682/3–1738). Physician and scientist. Graduated at Trinity College, Dublin, 1702; Fellow, 1704. Held posts in mathematics, natural philosophy, and physic (Regius Professor, 1733). Executor of Swift's will. A friend of Delany's who took the anti-Baldwin side in the College fellowships dispute of 1727 (see *Mayhew*, pp. 69–93). By this date he was Swift's personal physician and a member of the riddling and punning set which centred on Swift and Sheridan. (*DNB, Corr, PW*)

Henley, John (1692–1756). Eccentric preacher. Educated at Cambridge; began his unorthodox religious meeting-house, the Oratory, 1726. Wrote on behalf of Walpole in a journal called *The Hyp Doctor* from 1730. His primary quarrel was with Pope, and this was reflected by an appearance in *The Dunciad* (for details, see *PTE*, V, 444). However, his political and religious views occasioned a number of thrusts at Swift, too, in *The Hyp Doctor*: see Graham Midgley, *The Life of Orator Henley* (1973), pp. 169–70, where a disparaging epigram on Swift's 'cringing' to Harley is quoted. (*DNB*)

Hill, John (d. 1735). Soldier; page to Queen Anne and army officer; fought at Almanza, 1707; Brigadier-General in charge of Quebec expedition, 1711; Major-General, 1712; in charge of the Dunkirk defences. His rise began through Marlborough interest, but owed most to the fact that he was the brother of the Queen's favourite, Abigail Masham (q.v.). Known to Swift around 1712. (*DNB, Corr, PW, JTS*)

Hoadly, Benjamin (1676–1761). Churchman. Educated at Cambridge; Fellow of Catharine Hall, 1697; Rector of St Peter le Poor, London, 1704. Opposed Atterbury at the time of Sacheverell affair, and became the leading spokesman for the Low Church and for a Whig Erastianism. Bishop of Bangor, 1717; his sermon, 'The nature of the Kingdom or Church of Christ', set off the Bangorian controversy, with more than a thousand pamphlets and tracts in the next few years. Bishop of Salisbury, 1723; Bishop of Winchester, 1734. The very antithesis of Swift in doctrine, liturgical practice, and ecclesiastical politics. (*DNB, Corr, PW*)

Hoadly, John (1678–1746). Churchman. Younger brother of Benjamin Hoadly. Educated at Cambridge; chaplain to Gilbert Burnet (q.v.). Archdeacon of Salisbury, 1710; Bishop of Ferns, 1727. Archbishop of Dublin, 1730; Archbishop of Armagh and Primate of Ireland, 1742. These were essentially political appointments; Hoadly's job was to support Boulter in promoting the 'English' (ministerial) interest in Ireland. He was a less uncompromising figure than his brother, and, after a difficult start, he and Swift generally managed to rub along together without major disturbances (see *Landa*, pp. 185–6). (*DNB, Corr*)

Hogarth, William (1697–1764). The famous artist and engraver. Unlikely to have known Swift personally, although he based a satiric print on *Gulliver* in 1726, and during the 1730s became an artistic ally of the Scriblerian group. (*DNB, PW*)

Hopkins, Edward (1675–1736). M.P. from 1701; member of Sunderland connection. Belonged to the Kit-Cat Club. Minor diplomatic missions during Queen Anne's reign. Chief Secretary to the Duke of Grafton (q.v.) when the latter was Lord Lieutenant of Ireland; Master of the Revels in Ireland, 1722. Irish M.P. Had powerful 'banking' (that is, money-lending) background. Long known to Swift and clearly not much liked by him. Probably a relative of Pope's 'Vulture' Hopkins, who died in 1732. (*Corr, PW*)

Hort, Josiah (*c*.1674–1751). Churchman; educated by nonconformists, and friend of Isaac Watts. Chaplain to Lord Wharton (q.v.), 1709; Dean of Cloyne, 1718; of Ardagh, 1720. Bishop of Ferns, 1721; of Kilmore, 1727. Archbishop of Tuam, 1742. At one time bitterly attacked by Swift, but seemingly on better terms in the 1730s (see *P* III, 822–3). (*DNB, Corr, PW*)

Howard, Henrietta, Countess of Suffolk (*c*.1687–1767). *Née* Hobart; married Charles Howard, later ninth Earl of Suffolk, 1706. Lived at the Hanoverian court *c*.1710–13. Became Bedchamber Woman to Princess Caroline and *maîtresse en titre* of the Prince of Wales, later George II. Became Countess, 1731. Retired from court, 1734. Following the death of her first husband in 1733, married Hon. George Berkeley, 1735. After his death in 1746 lived in retirement. A friend of Pope and Gay as well as Swift; seventeen letters survive between Mrs Howard and Swift. Her house at Marble Hill, Twickenham, became the resort of the Scriblerian wits, and she was the main intermediary for Swift with the court when he visited England in 1726 and 1727. (*DNB, Corr, PW*)

Howard, Robert (1683–1740). Churchman; Fellow of Trinity College, 1703; Prebendary, later Chancellor (1723), of St Patrick's; Bishop of Killala, 1725; of Elphin, 1729. Swift originally thought well of him, but Howard's increasing favour with the government led to greater coolness, though never strong enmity. (*DNB, Corr*)

Howe, John Grubham (1657–1722). Known as 'Jack' Howe. Politician; Tory M.P. from 1689; a violent partisan, who held minor office under Anne but was happiest as a spokesman for the country interest and critic of the court. Instanced as a high Tory in *A Tale of a Tub* (1704); Swift probably did not know him personally at this date, and may never have done. (*DNB, PW, JTS*)

Hunter, Robert (d. 1734). Soldier and colonial governor. Fought at Blenheim; appointed Lieutenant-Governor of Virginia, 1707, but captured by French privateer and carried to France. After his release he became Governor of New York (1710–19). Major-General, 1729. Governor of Jamaica, 1729–34. He spent much of his life outside Britain, but a brief friendship with Swift flowered around 1709. They were probably introduced by their common friend, Addison. (*DNB, Corr*)

Jackson, Daniel (b. 1686/7). Clergyman. Entered Trinity College, Dublin, 1701. Brother of Rev. John Jackson (1683/4–1751), to whom Swift gave a copy of Lucretius. Another edition was 'designed for D. Jackson' (*PW* V, xxxi). Dan's large nose was a regular object of fun with Swift and Sheridan. (*Corr*)

James II, King of England (1633–1701). Son of Charles I; created Duke of York at his birth. During Civil War escaped to Holland, and later served in French forces. At the Restoration was appointed Lord High Admiral. Married Anne Hyde, daughter of the Earl of Clarendon, 1660; after her death in 1671, married Mary of Modena, 1673. By this date he had become a Roman Catholic. At the centre of the Exclusion Crisis, 1679–80; regained offices he had been forced to relinquish, 1684. Acceded to the throne, 1685; resisted the Monmouth rebellion, 1685; attempted to remodel constitution and executive in favour of Catholics, but encountered widespread opposition and eventually fled the country, 1688. Landed in Ireland with French troops, 1689; defeated at the Boyne, 1690, and returned to France. Died at Saint-Germain. Swift termed him 'a weak bigoted Papist, desirous like all kings of absolute power, but not properly a tyrant'. (*DNB, Corr, PW*)

Jenney, Henry (1680/1–1742). Clergyman. Entered Trinity College, Dublin, 1697; graduated, 1702; D.D., 1718. Archdeacon of Armagh. Known to Swift when he visited Robert Cope (q.v.) at Loughgall, Co. Armagh, from *c*.1717. Supposed to be the author of an attack on Swift in 1732, but Jenney denied this and Swift accepted his claim. Swift wrote to him on this occasion, 'I have always treated you with particular distinction, and if we differ in opinions relating to public proceedings, it is for very good reasons'. (*Corr*)

Jervas, Charles (*c*.1675–1739). Painter. Pupil of Kneller; instructed his friend Pope in painting. His origins were in Ireland and he often made return visits, although based in London. Principal painter to George I and later George II. His translation of *Don Quixote* was posthumously published, 1742. His subjects included Pope, Prior, Arbuthnot, and Newton, as well as the royal family. For a supposed portrait of Stella, see *JTS* II, 694–7. His portrait of Swift (1709–10) exists in the form of copies (Bodleian Library, National Portrait Gallery, etc.) whose relation to the original has not been established. (*DNB, Corr, PW, JTS*)

Johnson, Esther (1681–1728). 'Swift's most valuable friend', to whom he gave the name Stella. Daughter of Edward Johnson, who died young, and Bridget his wife, housekeeper in the Temples' home at Moor Park. Baptized 'Hester' but she herself used the form 'Esther'. Swift met her when he went to live with Sir

William Temple in 1689. She remained in the district after Temple's death, but around 1701 moved to Ireland with her companion Rebecca Dingley (q.v.), apparently on Swift's advice. They settled at Dublin and remained there for the rest of their lives. Stella spent some periods also living at Trim with Archdeacon Walls (q.v.). From about 1722 she suffered increasing ill health, and after a painful and protracted sickness she died in January 1728. Swift, who could not bring himself to attend the funeral, wrote a memoir of her life, which emphasizes her qualities of sense and sensibility (*PW* V, 227–36). Believed by some to have been Temple's natural daughter, and by others to have secretly married Swift. (*DNB, Corr, PW, JTS*)

Kelly, George (b. 1688). Clergyman and Jacobite conspirator. An Irishman, educated at Trinity College, Dublin (B.A., 1708). Attracted notoriety for high-flying sermons and moved to Paris, where he aided in the correspondence of the Old Pretender and Bishop Atterbury. Arrested in 1722 during the Atterbury affair, he faced a bill of pains and penalties along with the Bishop. He was sentenced to be imprisoned in the Tower of London for an indefinite term. Eventually in 1736 he escaped and made his way to France, where he served as chaplain to the Duke of Ormonde. He joined the Rising of 1745, and managed to evade capture after Culloden. Returning to France, he continued to serve as an adviser to the Young Pretender, although he was little trusted by most of the Prince's circle. Known to Swift from his Dublin days, and described by Swift as a 'valuable companion' to Ormonde – an opinion few shared, even in the Jacobite ranks. (*DNB, Corr*)

Kent, Henry de Grey, first Duke of (1671–1740). Courtier. Grandson of the ninth Earl of Kent; succeeded, 1702. Lord Chamberlain, 1704–10. Created Duke, 1710. A Lord Justice, 1714. Lord Steward, 1716; Lord Privy Seal, 1719. According to Swift, 'he seems a good natured man, but of very little consequence.' A lukewarm Whig, who was ready to trade the high office of Lord Chamberlain for a dukedom. Pope referred to him as 'Bug'; as a contemporary observed, he was 'strong in nothing but money and smell'. (*DNB, PW, JTS*)

King, James (c.1699–1759). Clergyman. Prebendary in St Patrick's Cathedral, and Vicar of St Bride's, Dublin, 1731–59. Fellow of Trinity College, 1720–35, and also one of the Fellows nominated for Berkeley's projected college in Bermuda. One of Swift's executors, who was a particularly close friend in his last years. (*Corr, PW*)

King, Peter, first Baron (1669–1734). Lawyer and politician. Son of a grocer; called to the bar, 1698; M.P. from 1701. A dependable Whig. Recorder of London, 1708; knighted, 1708. Helped to manage prosecution of Sacheverell, 1710. Chief Justice of Common Pleas, 1714. Created Baron, 1725. Lord Chancellor, 1725–33. Wrote extensively on theological subjects. Representative of much that Swift disliked in public life, but no personal dealings can be traced. (*DNB, PW*)

King, William (1650–1729). Churchman; educated at Trinity College, but failed to obtain a fellowship. D.D., 1689; Dean of St Patrick's in the same year. Bishop of Derry, 1691. Published *De Origine Mali*, 1702. Archbishop of Dublin, 1703. His adherence to the Irish interest caused him to be passed over for the primacy in 1723 'although in point of experience, distinction, and loyalty to the Whig cause, he was the logical successor' (*Landa*, p. 173). Swift's relationship with King was slow to develop into real warmth: 'English politics were to alienate them before they were ultimately reconciled by their common concern for Ireland' (*Ferguson*, p. 27). Frequently a Lord Justice of Ireland. (*DNB, Corr, PW, JTS*)

Königsmark, Philipp Cristoph, Count von (1665–94). Soldier of fortune; of Swedish extraction; thought to have instigated murder of Thomas Thynne of Longleat in 1682, when he was a suitor of Thynne's wife, later the Duchess of Somerset (q.v.). Supposed lover of Sophie Dorothea, Electoral Princess of Hanover, and supposedly put to death by order of the Electoral Prince (later George I), 1694.

Lechmere, Nicholas, first Baron (1675–1727). Lawyer and politician. Called to the bar, 1698; M.P. from 1708; Queen's Counsel, 1708. One of the leading managers of the prosecution of Sacheverell, 1710. Solicitor-General, 1714; Attorney-General, 1718. Created Baron, 1721. One of the most vehement Whigs of his day. Disliked by all men and women of Swift's political colouring. Lost political influence at the time of the South Sea Bubble, but hung on to minor places. (*DNB, PW*)

Levinge, Sir Richard (1656–1724). Irish judge. Born in England. Called to the bar, 1678; M.P. from 1690; Solicitor-General for Ireland, 1690–94, 1704–9; knighted, 1692. Speaker of the Irish Commons, 1692–5. Created baronet, 1704. Attorney-General for Ireland, 1711; Lord Chief Justice of Common Pleas, 1720. Swift knew him; although they did not always see eye-to-eye on political issues, their relations seem to have been good. (*DNB, Corr, PW, JTS*)

Lewis, Erasmus (1670–1754). Diplomat and government official. A client of Robert Harley who held a number of posts in the service of Queen Anne; Under-Secretary of State, 1710; M.P., 1713. A friend of Prior and the entire Scriblerian group; adroit and businesslike Welshman. Over twenty of his letters to Swift survive, dated between 1713 and 1738. It was he who arranged the meeting of Swift and Harley in 1710. (*DNB, Corr, PW, JTS*)

Lincoln, Henry Clinton, seventh Earl of (1684–1728). Courtier. A reliable Whig; held a number of court appointments, including that of joint Paymaster to the Forces, 1715–20, and Cofferer of the Household, 1725–8. He needed these remunerative posts as he had little private income; his brother-in-law, the Duke of Newcastle, was the instrument by which they were obtained. Member of the Kit-Cat Club.

Lindsay, Robert (1679/80–1743). Lawyer. Entered Trinity College, Dublin, 1696; called to the Irish bar, 1709; legal adviser to the Chapter of St Patrick's Cathedral, 1722. Irish M.P. from 1729. Justice of Common Pleas in Ireland, 1733. Executor of Swift's will. Believed to have given Swift legal advice during the Drapier controversy. (*Corr, PW*)

Lintot, Bernard (1675–1736). Bookseller. Entered the trade as apprentice, 1690; freeman of the Stationers' Company, 1699. Began publishing in the reign of Anne; issued work by Steele, Parnell, and others. Became associated with Pope, publishing first version of *The Rape of the Lock* in a collection of 1712, and many poems after this, including the *Iliad* and *Odyssey* translations. The latter venture was partly instrumental in estranging the two men (see *PTE* IV, 369); and Lintot was allotted an inglorious role in *The Dunciad*. Gay's *Poems* (1720) were also published by Lintot. Swift had few first-hand contacts with him, and it was probably the experiences of his Scriblerian friends which dictated the tone of his references to Lintot. (*DNB, Corr*)

Macartney (or Maccartney), George (c.1660–1730). General; commanded brigade at Almanza, 1707; fought at Malplaquet, 1709; Major-General, 1710. A follower of Marlborough. Acted as second to Mohun in the famous Mohun-Hamilton duel of 1712, and accused by Tories of stabbing Hamilton to death. Escaped to the Continent; found guilty of being accessory to murder, when he returned to England after the Hanoverian accession, but given a light sentence and restored to his post, indeed promoted to Lieutenant-General. The issues at stake throughout the affair were basically political, and Swift naturally took the other side of the question. (*DNB, PW, JTS*)

Manley, (Mary) de la Rivière (1663?–1724). Author. Daughter of Sir Roger Manley, a cavalier soldier. Married (apparently in bigamous union) to John Manley. Became mistress of John Barber (q.v.). Published *The New Atalantis* (1709), a very successful political allegory dealing with scandals in high places. She succeeded Swift as writer of *The Examiner* in 1711, and may have collaborated with him in pamphlets at this period. Much about her remains obscure. Swift described her as suffering badly from dropsy: 'She has very generous principles for one of her sort; and a great deal of good sense and invention: she is . . . very homely and very fat.' (*DNB, Corr, PW, JTS*; but see corrections to these sources in Patricia Köster's article in *Eighteenth-Century Life* III (1977), 106–11.)

Marlborough, John Churchill, first Duke of (1650–1722). Soldier and statesman. Page to the Duke of York (later James II) as a boy; Ensign in the Foot Guards, 1667; Colonel, 1678. Married Sarah Jennings, 1678. Created Baron, 1685. Took a leading part in the defeat of Monmouth's rebellion. Lieutenant-General, 1688. Commanded King's forces, 1688, but went over to the side of William of Orange. Earl of Marlborough, 1689. Out of favour and flirting with the Jacobites in the 1690s; spent two months in the Tower of London, 1692. Restored to power with the accession of Queen Anne; K.G., 1702; Captain-General, 1702. Duke of Marlborough, 1702. Conducted annual campaigns on the Continent, with a series of victories at Blenheim (1704), Ramillies (1706), and Oudenarde (1708). Sided with Godolphin in politics and became opposed to Harley. A less comprehensive victory at Malplaquet, 1709. Began to lose the Queen's favour and was finally dismissed, 1711; charged by the Tories with corruption. Lived in exile until the Hanoverian accession. Reappointed Captain-General. Suffered a severe stroke, 1716, and was never afterwards a force in public life. Amassed a considerable fortune, quite apart from the gift from the nation of Blenheim Palace, and founded a long-lasting aristocratic dynasty. A member of the Kit-Cat Club; a heroic figure in much contemporary literature, but treated with increasing suspicion by the Tory group of writers. Swift's efforts to discredit Marlborough (1710–12) had their base in political issues, but were buttressed by a dislike for the Duke's alleged vices (avarice, ingratitude, duplicity, pride). Nor did Swift ever become reconciled to Marlborough's 'haughty, imperious wife', although the Duchess (1660–1744) managed to establish a surprising friendship with Pope in her later years. (*DNB, Corr, PW, JTS*)

Marsh, Narcissus (1638–1713). Churchman. Educated at Oxford; Provost of Trinity College, Dublin, 1679; Bishop of Ferns, 1683; Archbishop of Cashel, 1691; of Armagh, 1703. Provost when Swift went up to the College, and gave Swift his prebend in St Patrick's. Swift later wrote a rather double-edged account of Marsh, but seems to have admired him in his youth. Founder of

Marsh's Library in Dublin, where some of Swift's own books survive. (*DNB, Corr, PW, JTS*)

Masham, Abigail, Baroness (d. 1734). Confidante to Queen Anne. *Née* Hill; sister of Jack Hill (q.v.) and cousin of Duchess of Marlborough. Married Samuel Masham, 1707; he was a courtier, soldier, and M.P., created Baron in 1712 as one of twelve Tory peers to help the peace treaty through the House of Lords. She was Bedchamber Woman to the Queen, and supplanted the Duchess of Marlborough in royal favour. After the Queen's death, lived in retirement. A lasting friendship developed between Swift and her, and as late as 1733 Lady Masham was pressing Swift to pay her a visit. After her death he wrote to Pope of 'my dear friend Lady Masham, my constant friend in all changes of times'. Few others had much good to say of her after her power at court had gone. (*DNB, Corr, PW, JTS*)

Mather, Charles. A toyman, whose shop lay at the west end of Fleet Street, not far from Temple Bar. Termed 'Bubbleboy' in the *Tatler* (bubble meaning 'toy'). Also mentioned in the *Spectator*, no. 328.

Medlycott, Thomas (1662–1738). Politician. Tory M.P. for Westminster from 1708; client of Duke of Ormonde. Commissioner of the Revenue for Ireland, 1713; also Irish M.P. Successful in the heated election of 1710, witnessed by Swift, who knew Medlycott personally. (*Corr*)

Midleton, Alan Brodrick, first Viscount (c.1656–1728). Politician. Trained as lawyer, and took side of William III against James II. King's Serjeant, 1691; Solicitor-General for Ireland, 1695. Irish M.P. from 1692; Speaker of the Irish Commons, 1703. Attorney General, 1707; Chief Justice of the King's Bench, 1709; dismissed on political grounds, 1711. Once more Speaker, 1713–14. Lord Chancellor for Ireland, 1714–25. Created Baron, 1715, and Viscount, 1717. He was a strong Whig and had incurred Swift's hostility at the time of the attempt to repeal the Test Act under Queen Anne; but their common opposition to Wood's halfpence brought them closer. The 'sixth' of the *Drapier's Letters* is addressed to him. (*DNB, Corr, PW, JTS*)

Mohun, Charles, fourth Baron (1677–1712). Rake and duellist; a general under Marlborough, but much better known for his affrays and was twice tried for murder before reaching the age of twenty. Killed in the famous encounter with the Duke of Hamilton, reported in Swift's *Journal* and described in Thackeray's *Henry Esmond*. A Kit-Cat, who was regarded by political opponents as second only to Wharton for infamous behaviour. According to Swift, the duel was provoked for party reasons: 'the faction, weary of [Mohun], resolved to employ him in some real service to their cause, and valued not what came of him.' (*DNB, PW, JTS*)

Montagu, John Montagu, second Duke of (1690–1749). Courtier. A resolute Whig, who was a member of the Kit-Cat and the Hanoverian clubs. Held a number of ceremonial offices and took part in coronation services. Held also a number of dignities for which Swift had a low regard: K.B., K.G., F.R.S., and Grand Master of the English Freemasons. He married a daughter of the Duke of Marlborough: according to his mother-in-law, all his talents lay 'in things natural to boys of fifteen', with a particular bent towards practical joking. Swift called the Duke's father 'as arrant a knave as any of his time'. The second Duke's politics, his family alliance, his court positions, and his pretensions as an artistic connoisseur would all have made him suspect to Swift. (*DNB, Corr, PW, JTS*)

Morphew, John (d. *c*.1720). Bookseller. Associated with many Tory journals and pamphlets especially at the time of the Harley administration. Many of Swift's works carry only Morphew's name on the title-page; he was primarily the distribution agent, and the copyright would be held by another, generally Benjamin Tooke. Called before the House of Lords in connection with *The Public Spirit of the Whigs* in 1714. One-time associate of Edmund Curll (q.v.). (*PW, JTS*)

Northey, Sir Edward (1652–1723). Lawyer and politician. Called to the bar, 1674; Attorney-General, 1701–7, 1710–18; knighted, 1702. M.P. from 1710. A Tory who managed to retain office under the Hanoverian régime; seemingly compliant in political matters, and undistinguished in legal functions. Swift probably did not know him well. (*DNB, Corr*)

Nottingham, Daniel Finch, second Earl of (1647–1730). Statesman. A significant figure in English public life from the 1680s to the time of the 1715 Rising. First Lord of the Admiralty, 1681; Secretary at War, 1688; carried the Toleration Act, and helped to win influence for the Tories with William III; dismissed, 1693. Secretary of State, 1702–4; a leader of the High Church party throughout Anne's reign. Worked for many years to secure an act prohibiting 'occasional conformity' in seeking to evade the Anglican tests for office; succeeded in getting the act passed, 1711, by bargaining his support for the Whigs in their opposition to the peace negotiations. Lord President of the Council, 1714; dismissed, 1716, for proposing lenient treatment of the condemned Jacobite lords. Succeeded as Earl, 1682; as sixth Earl of Winchilsea, 1726. Satirized by Swift, Arbuthnot, and others as 'Dismal'; possible model for Skyresh Bolgolam in *Gulliver's Travels*. Regarded by Tories as apostate. (*DNB, Corr, PW, JTS*)

Orford, Edward Russell, first Earl of (1653–1727). Naval commander and Whig politician. Lieutenant, 1671; Captain, 1672; Admiral, 1689. M.P. from 1689. First Lord of the Admiralty, 1694–9, 1709–10, 1714–17. An adherent of the Prince of Orange when he came to the English throne. Naval victories included La Hogue, 1692. Created Earl, 1697. Several times a Lord Justice. One of the Junto lords impeached in 1701 and defended by Swift in *Contests and Dissentions*. Less well known to Swift than others in this group, notably Halifax and Somers. Took Walpole's side at the time of the Whig split in 1717. (*DNB, Corr, PW*)

Ormonde, James Butler, second Duke of (1665–1745). Soldier and Jacobite leader. Succeeded to dukedom, 1688; K.G., 1688; went over to Prince of Orange. Fought at the Boyne, 1690, and at Steenkirk, 1692. Lord Lieutenant of Ireland, 1703–5, 1710–11, 1713. Appointed Captain-General, to succeed Marlborough, 1712; given restraining orders not to prosecute the war in Flanders with vigour. Dismissed, 1714; attainted, 1715; fled to France and helped to mount the Rising. A Tory hero, who remained at the centre of Jacobite affairs for the remainder of his life. Beloved by Swift, who thought him a persecuted and noble figure, and commended his 'affability, generosity, and sweetness of nature'. A letter from the Duke to Swift was seized by the authorities at the time of his impeachment. Swift also corresponded and maintained good relations with the Duchess, *née* Lady Mary Somerset (d. 1733). (*DNB, Corr, PW, JTS*)

Orrery, John Boyle, fifth Earl of (1707–62). Member of a distinguished Anglo-Irish family; educated at Oxford; F.R.S., 1750. Became acquainted with Swift in the early 1730s, and thereafter a close literary ally: obtained many of Swift's manuscripts and preserved copies of other works (many items now at Harvard). He was also a friend and correspondent of Pope at this period; later came to know Samuel Johnson, who regarded him as an aspirant for literary fame beyond his powers. Forty letters between Swift and Orrery survive. His *Remarks* (1752) constitute the first biography of Swift; other friends of the Dean considered its treatment unfair, and full-scale replies were published by Delany and Deane Swift (qq.v.). Orrery's other works include a translation of the letters of Pliny the Younger (1751). (*DNB, Corr, PW*)

Parnell, Thomas (1679–1718). Poet. Educated at Trinity College, Dublin; Canon of St Patrick's, 1704; Archdeacon of Clogher, 1706. D.D., 1712. Member of the Scriblerus group. Poems posthumously published by Pope, 1722; the subject of a biography by Goldsmith (1770) and also included in Johnson's *Lives of the Poets*. (*DNB, Corr, PW, JTS*)

Partridge, John (1644–1715). Astrologer. Bred up as a shoemaker; began to issue almanacs, 1680. The most famous quack-prophet after the time of Gadbury; a 'philomath' of the type whose predictions often furnished the Scriblerians with material for satire. Also went under the name of John Hewson. 'Killed off' by Swift in the Bickerstaff papers, 1708–9, and had great difficulty in convincing the world ever after that he was still alive. (*DNB, PW*)

Parvisol, Isaiah (d. 1718). From *c.*1708 Swift's steward and tithe-collector. Dismissed *c.*1714 after many complaints and altercations, but soon reinstated. For the little that is known about him, see *JTS, passim*, and *Corr* I, 106.

Peterborough, Charles Mordaunt, third Earl of (1658–1735). General, diplomat, and patron of the arts. Served in the navy during the 1690s. Intrigued for William of Orange during reign of James II, and appointed Privy Councillor after the Revolution in 1688. First Lord of the Treasury, 1689. Succeeded as Earl, 1697. Commander of forces in Spain, 1705; forced surrender of Barcelona, 1705, and enabled Archduke Charles of Austria to claim the Spanish throne. His private diplomatic arrangements with Savoy and other states led to charges against him in Britain and his recall, 1707. Inquiries held into his conduct but he survived these to take on special embassies during the Harley ministry. K.G., 1713; Ambassador Extraordinary to the Italian principalities. After the Hanoverian accession, devoted himself principally to private life; married the opera singer Anastasia Robinson, 1722, and built up a close friendship with Mrs Howard, Pope, Arbuthnot, and Gay. His estate at Bevis Mount laid out with Pope's help in the 1720s. Swift admired him for his resolute Tory opinions, his vigorous and full-hearted attitude to life, and his generosity of mind. Ten letters survive between the two men. A brave, erratic man who lived a life full of adventure and wild risks: 'the quicksilver of the age' (G.M. Trevelyan). As Queen Anne wrote to Harley: 'I think he should be sent somewhere, for I fear if he comes home while the parliament is sitting he will be very troublesome.' (*DNB, Corr, PW, JTS*)

Philips, Ambrose (1674–1749). Poet. Educated at Cambridge; became member of the Addison set and on bad terms with Pope after the publication of their rival pastorals. His adaptation of Racine, *The Distressed Mother* (1712), enjoyed a good deal of popularity. Wrote in defence of Walpole and obtained a series of government posts. Secretary to the British Envoy to Copenhagen, 1709; Lottery Commissioner, 1717; secretary to Archbishop Boulter, 1724; Irish M.P., 1727; Judge of the Prerogative Court, 1733. Swift was friendly with him during his Whig days, and some affable letters survive from this period. Later they drifted apart and when Philips came out to Ireland as a government placeman Swift tended to treat him as the figure of fun ('Namby Pamby') which he had become to the literary world, especially in Pope's circle. (*DNB*, *Corr*, *JTS*)

Pilkington, Matthew (*c.*1701–*c.*1774). Clergyman and poet. Educated at Trinity College. Married Laetitia Pilkington, author of some celebrated *Memoirs* (published 1748–54, and containing much about Swift), in 1729. Swift got to know the couple soon afterwards and gave them encouragement; he lent Pilkington money and supported his volume of *Poems* (1730). Pilkington also obtained through Swift's influence the post of chaplain to John Barber (q.v.) during his term as Lord Mayor of London, 1731–2. The Dean promised to act as godfather to the couple's first child, born in 1731, but the boy died within a few days of birth. Pilkington was recommended by Swift to Pope, who found him (as did many people) shallow and affected. His marriage began to break up in a sordid manner, as described in Mrs Pilkington's memoirs. Swift continued to use him as an agent for the London publication of his works, but he was taken into custody in connection with *To a Lady*, and was thought to have informed against Swift. Thereafter he encountered much resentment in Ireland especially, and led a hand-to-mouth existence for many years. His wife died in 1750, after which he married Anne Sandes. Published a *Dictionary of Painters*, 1770. The *DNB* provides two entries which both in fact refer to the same man. (*Corr*, *PW*)

Plunket, John (1664–1738). Jacobite agent. Employed by a succession of Jacobite leaders as a spy and emissary. Arrested in January 1723 in connection with the Layer plot, and named in the bill of pains and penalties along with Atterbury. Sent to the Tower and confined there until shortly before his death. (*DNB*)

Pope, Alexander (1688–1744). Poet. Met Swift *c.*1713 and was a fellow-member of the Scriblerus Club when it began its brief spell of full activity the following winter. Maintained contact with Swift during the latter's exile in Dublin, and was his principal host during the English visits of 1726 and 1727. Edited joint *Miscellanies* with his friend from 1727, and was involved in the publication of many of Swift's later poems. Despite occasional disagreements in the 1730s, mainly over the question of publishing letters, their alliance remained unbroken until Swift's decay into senility. About 100 letters survive from their correspondence, spread over thirty years, and almost equally divided as regards writer and recipient. (*DNB*, *Corr*, *PW*, *JTS*)

Portland, William Henry, second Earl of (1682–1726). Politician. Son of the first Earl, a member of William of Orange's household who accompanied his master to England and became a central figure in the nation's affairs, especially as regards foreign policy. The son was a Whig M.P. from 1705. Succeeded as Earl, 1709. He was among those to vote Sacheverell 'guilty' in 1710, but was not a figure of any importance on the national scene. Gentleman of the Bedchamber, 1717–26; Governor of Jamaica, 1721–6. Created first Duke of Portland, 1716. Swift knew both the father, whom he considered 'a weak man', and the son, whom he termed 'a very good natured man, but somewhat too expensive'. See also *POAS* VII, 566–7.

Pratt, Benjamin (*c.*1669–1721). A contemporary of Swift at Trinity College, who later became a Fellow. Appointed Provost, 1710. His strong Tory views led to his replacement in 1717 by Richard Baldwin (q.v.). He was appointed Dean of Down instead. He was one of Swift's boon companions during the period of the Harley government, as a worldly and affluent man of the cloth who enjoyed London society. His younger brother John was an army officer who became Deputy Vice-Treasurer of Ireland, in which position he got into severe financial difficulties and embroiled Swift in his embarrassment. After this John Pratt 'took to exploiting coal and manufacturing glass in Ireland' (*JTS* I, 14). (*Corr*, *PW*, *JTS*)

Prendergast, Sir Thomas (d. 1760). Son of the Jacobite soldier and informer, and succeeded as second baronet when his father was killed at Malplaquet, 1709. His mother was a sister of General William Cadogan, one of the Tory party's *bêtes noires*. The second baronet became a Protestant, and was an M.P. in both English and Irish parliaments. Postmaster-General for Ireland, 1733.

Prior, Matthew (1664–1721). Poet and diplomat. A protégé of the great patrons Dorset and Halifax, given diplomatic posts in the 1690s, briefly an M.P., 1701–2. At various times Under-Secretary of State, Secretary to the Lords Justices of Ireland, Commissioner of Trade, Commissioner of Customs. Enjoyed and then lost patronage of Godolphin and Marlborough; anticipated Swift in moving over to the Tories. Knew Swift by 1710 at the latest; they each worked on the *Examiner* and saw one another regularly in the next few months. Involved in the peace negotiations, 1711; made a special embassy to Paris to test French reactions to the draft preliminary articles. The negotiations were promptly dubbed by Whig ballad-makers 'Matt's Peace'. After the accession of George I, arrested and examined by investigating committee, 1715; taken into custody and exempted from the Act of Grace, but released, 1717. Brought out subscription volume of poems, 1719. Given money by Lord Harley to purchase Down Hall, Essex. Never admitted to the full Scriblerian intimacy, Prior nevertheless occupied a central position in the literary and political world of his day, and his technical experiments in poetry (adapting Butler's octosyllabic couplets, using ballad metres, etc.) were important examples for Swift to follow. (*DNB*, *Corr*, *PW*, *JTS*)

Pulteney, William (1684–1764). Statesman. Educated at Oxford; M.P. from 1705; Secretary at War, 1714. Resigned at time of Whig split, 1717. Gradually estranged from his former ally, Walpole; helped to set up *The Craftsman* and a coherent opposition, together with Bolingbroke. Opposed Excise Bill and supported agitation for war with Spain. After fall of Walpole, hoped to become first minister; created Earl of Bath, 1742. Failed in his attempt to oust the Pelhams, 1746; his term as First Lord of the Treasury lasted only from 10 to 12 February 1746. A friend of literary men, including Pope and Gay, and a famous orator. Swift got to know him on his visit to England in 1726 and thereafter they corresponded regularly. (*DNB*, *Corr*, *PW*)

Queensberry, Charles Douglas, third Duke of (1698–1778). Held a number of court appointments; quarrelled with the King and the prime minister, 1728. He had married, in 1720, Lady Catherine Hyde (*c.*1701–77), whom Swift had known as a girl. She took Gay's side in the controversy over the banning of *Polly* in 1729, and was banished from court. A high-spirited and eccentric woman, she befriended many other literary men, including Pope. Over thirty letters survive from her correspondence with Swift, as well as a handful which passed between her husband and Swift. (*DNB*, *Corr*)

Radcliffe, John (1650–1714). Physician. Educated at Oxford; physician to Princess (later Queen) Anne, but fell out with her over the nature of her complaints. Declined to treat her in her final illness, on the grounds of his own incapacity through gout. Made a large fortune and it was through his bequests that the Radcliffe Infirmary and Observatory were founded, as well as Bartholomew's Hospital in London. Swift was typical of many contemporaries; he referred disparagingly to Radcliffe but was ready to accept his treatment, as occurred in 1711. Harley also consulted Radcliffe after the attack by Guiscard. (*DNB, Corr, JTS*)

Raymond, Anthony (*c.*1676–1726). Entered Trinity College, Dublin, 1692; Fellow, 1699. Resigned on appointment as Rector of Trim, 1705. D.D., 1719. An antiquarian scholar with a special interest in early Irish history. Chaplain to the Duke of Shrewsbury (q.v.), 1713. He is mentioned on the first page of Swift's *Journal* and frequently thereafter; he was one of Swift's closest friends in the middle years, but unfortunately only one letter survives which passed between them. Swift was glad to have such a lively-minded neighbour, although he deplored the streak of improvidence in Raymond's character. In his will Raymond left Swift a gold ring in return for 'many obligations'. (*Corr, JTS*)

Richmond, Charles Lennox, first Duke of (1672–1723). Natural son of Charles II by Louise de Kéroualle; created Duke of Richmond, 1675. After flirting with catholicism, he became an aide-de-camp to William III and a member of the Kit-Cat Club under Anne. Gentleman of the Bedchamber to George I, 1714. Dissolute, easy-going, and companionable; Swift called him 'a shallow coxcomb' but an element of political spite must be discounted. (*DNB, PW, JTS*)

Robinson, John (1650–1723). Churchman and diplomat. Educated at Oxford; Fellow of Oriel, 1675. Chaplain to the English embassy in Sweden, and a kind of deputy ambassador, *c.*1680–1709. Dean of Windsor, 1709; Bishop of Bristol, 1710; Bishop of London, 1714. Lord Privy Seal, 1711; principal negotiator at the Utrecht conference; signed treaty, 1713. A moderate Tory with whom the Whigs could make accommodations; almost a career diplomat, and the last prelate to hold such high ministerial office in England. In general, Robinson concerned himself more with business than with doctrine. Swift thought he had few 'parts' and was a mere functionary. (*DNB, Corr, PW, JTS*)

Rochfort family. Robert Rochfort (1652–1727) had been Attorney-General for Ireland and Speaker of the Irish House of Commons (1695–1703) before becoming Chief Baron of the Irish Exchequer, 1707–14. A strong Tory, he fell from office after the Hanoverian accession. His eldest son, George (*c.*1682–1730), was an Irish M.P., as was the younger son, John (1692–1771). Swift was friendly with both the brothers, especially George, who was given the country estate of Gaulstown, Co. Westmeath, on his marriage to Lady Betty Moore in 1704. Their eldest son, Robert (1708–71), eventually became the first Earl of Belvedere. John 'Nim' Rochfort married first, in 1723, Deborah Staunton, the only child of Swift's lifelong friends, Thomas and Bridget Staunton; she died in 1737 and John remarried. For the best account of the family and their dealings with Swift, see *Mayhew*, pp. 37–68. (*DNB, Corr, PW, JTS*)

Romney, Henry Sidney, first Earl of (1641–1704). Held court offices under James, Duke of York; envoy to the Hague, 1679–81, when he became an adherent of William of Orange. Took over secret invitation to William, 1688. Created Viscount, 1689; Secretary of State, 1690; Lord Lieutenant of Ireland, 1692. Earldom bestowed, 1694; Lord Justice, 1697. Regarded as a blundering administrator and a notorious womanizer, he apparently went back on a promise made to his friend Temple that he would assist Swift's bid for preferment. This earned from Swift the verdict, 'an old vicious illiterate rake'. (*DNB, PW*)

Roper, Abel (1665–1726). Newspaperman; trained as a printer. Began the *Post Boy* in 1695 and remained associated with it until at least 1714. During the period of the Harley ministry it was a semi-official government organ, vetted by Bolingbroke; Swift wrote occasional paragraphs for the paper, which appeared three times a week. Mentioned in *The Dunciad*. (*DNB, PW, JTS*)

Rundle, Thomas (*c.*1688–1743). Churchman. Educated at Oxford. Suspected of heterodox opinions through his association with William Whiston, the Arian divine. Prebendary of Salisbury, 1716; Archdeacon of Wiltshire, 1720; Prebendary of Durham, 1722. Proposed for the bishopric of Gloucester, with the support of the Queen; but the promotion was blocked by Bishop Gibson, precipitating a governmental crisis in 1733–4. See *Plumb*, pp. 299–300. Instead, he was appointed Bishop of Derry, 1735, to a mixed reception from the Irish church. Pope admired Rundle and in time Swift came to respect him also. (*DNB, Corr*)

Rymer, Thomas (1641–1713). Critic and historian. His major work is the edition of treaties known as *Foedera* (1704–35), but in literary history he is remembered more for such essays as *The Tragedies of the Last Age* (1678) and *A Short View of Tragedy* (1692), expressing a no-nonsense attitude towards drama which brought him into conflict with Dryden amongst others. Historiographer Royal, 1692, a post to which Swift hoped to succeed on Rymer's death. But, despite Bolingbroke's support, he failed in his bid. Swift enjoyed reading *Foedera*, which he acquired in London for Trinity College, Dublin. (*DNB, Corr, PW, JTS*)

Sacheverell, Henry (*c.*1674–1724). Clergyman. Educated at Oxford; Fellow of Magdalen, 1701; D.D., 1708. Chaplain at St Saviour's, Southwark, 1705, where he gained a reputation for high-flying sermons. His long-sought opportunity to preach before the Lord Mayor and aldermen of the City of London at St Paul's came in November 1709. The sermon, on the text 'in peril among false brethren' (2 Corinthians xi, 26), was a rehash of an earlier oration; it enunciated the ideas of Atterbury and other High Tories in a violent and ranting way, attacking the Lord Treasurer, Godolphin, as 'Volpone'. Sacheverell was impeached by the House of Lords on four counts. After a show-trial, which attracted unprecedented interest, the Lords in March 1710 voted him guilty by fifty-nine to forty-two; but a relatively light sentence of three years' suspension was widely regarded as tantamount to acquittal. Sacheverell made a tour of the nation and was greeted by the populace as a martyr for the church. Godolphin lost face, and in the elections during the autumn of 1710 the Tories gained a landslide victory; some leading Whigs chose not even to stand for re-election. Swift arrived in London in time to witness the latter stages of this episode. He met Sacheverell in March 1712 and thought him 'not very deep'. Like many Tories, Swift was glad of the turn of events Sacheverell precipitated but had little regard for the man. After his triumph Sacheverell gradually sank into comparative obscurity. See Geoffrey Holmes, *The Trial of Dr Sacheverell* (1973). (*DNB, Corr, PW, JTS*)

St John, Henry, first Viscount Bolingbroke (1678–1751). Statesman and writer. M.P. from 1701; Secretary at War, 1704–8. Secretary of State, 1710; created Viscount Bolingbroke, 1712. Main architect of the Utrecht settlement, 1713.

Quarrelled with Harley; dismissed from office on accession of George I. After an impeachment had been set in motion, fled to France, 1715. Became Secretary of State to the Pretender; estranged after the failure of the 1715 Rising. Petitioned to be allowed to return; Walpole granted him a qualified pardon and he came back to England, 1723 (but was excluded from the House of Lords). The opposition to Walpole took up his version of history and political philosophy; his ideology was expressed in its journal, *The Craftsman*, and in the work of writers such as Pope and Thomson. Again retired to France, 1735, despairing of making an effective onslaught on Walpole. Occupied himself with philosophy and political theory: *The Idea of a Patriot King* released for limited circulation in mysterious circumstances, 1740. Major works issued by David Mallet posthumously (1752–4), including *Letters on the Study and Use of History*. Swift and St John were regular companions during the days of the 'Club', in the period 1710–12, when Swift thought him 'the greatest young man I ever knew'. Though his loyalties were torn during the break with Harley, Swift continued to regard Bolingbroke (as he now was) with respect and affection. He stayed with Bolingbroke, now settled once more in England, on his visit of 1726, and they had affable meetings when Swift came back the following year. Bolingbroke's thought had some influence on the entire Scriblerian group but less perhaps on Swift than on Pope or Gay. See I. Kramnick, *Bolingbroke and His Circle* (1968). Almost fifty letters between the two men are known to be extant. It is possible that the first part of *Gulliver's Travels* serves as an allegory of St John's earlier career. (*DNB, Corr, PW, JTS*)

Sancroft, William (1617–93). Churchman. Educated at Cambridge; Fellow of Emmanuel College, 1642; D.D., 1662; Master, 1662–4. Dean of St Paul's, 1664. Archbishop of Canterbury, 1678. Refused to read Declaration of Indulgence and sided with the six dissident bishops, 1688. Imprisoned in Tower but found not guilty of seditious libel. Supported William III's intervention but refused to recognize him as king, and was deprived of his office, 1690. Lived in retirement until his death. An early hero of Swift as an upholder of the true Anglican faith and as one who resisted Erastian tendencies. This respect endured right into the 1730s. (*DNB, Corr, PW*)

Sandys, Samuel (1695–1770). Politician. M.P. from 1718. Became known as one of the most persistent critics of Walpole, though independent of the main Opposition group. Opposed Excise Bill and unsuccessfully proposed the motion to force Walpole's resignation in 1741. After the prime minister fell, he held a number of government offices in the 1740s, 1750s, and early 1760s. Created Baron Sandys, 1743. No personal contact with Swift. (*DNB*)

Scarborough, Richard Lumley, first Earl of (*c*.1650–1721). Member of an Anglo-Irish Catholic family; turned Protestant, but continued to support James II until 1688. Taking the side of William, he was created Viscount Lumley, 1689, and Earl of Scarborough, 1690. Retired from the army as Lieutenant-General, 1697. (His brother, Henry Lumley, was one of Marlborough's leading generals.) Held minor court offices under George I. Swift's description is 'a knave and a coward': probably it was Lumley's desertion of James at a convenient moment which provoked this opinion. He was a reliable Whig, although one of only two who voted against Sacheverell's impeachment, on a personal quirk. His son also became a general, was a courtier under George II and a member of the Kit-Cat Club. (*DNB, PW*)

Sharp, John (1645–1714). Churchman. Educated at Cambridge; domestic chaplain in the Finch family. D.D., 1679; Dean of Norwich, 1681. Refused to read Declaration of Indulgence, 1688. Dean of Canterbury, 1689. Archbishop of York, 1691. Privy Councillor, 1702. Became attached to the High Church party in the era of Nottingham's leadership and helped to advise the Queen on preferments. The allegory of *A Tale of a Tub* was thought by some to have been borrowed from one of Sharp's sermons. But Swift himself believed that Sharp had been instrumental in blocking his chances of advancement in the church because of just this work (see *Tale*, pp. xxxi–xxxvi, 6). Swift accordingly dubbed him 'my mortal enemy'. (*DNB, Corr, PW, JTS*)

Sheridan, Thomas (1687–1738). Schoolmaster and clergyman. Entered Trinity College, Dublin, 1707; graduated, 1711; D.D., 1726. Through Swift's interest he obtained from the Lord Lieutenant the post of chaplain and a living in Co. Cork worth £200 per annum; but he lost the former because of an injudicious sermon. He kept a school in Capel Street, Dublin, not far from Stella's lodgings, and often entertained her. He had a country house at Quilca, Co. Cavan, where Swift stayed. In 1735 he moved to another school at Cavan. He was in financial difficulties and remained so up to the time of his death; he had, moreover, quarrelled with Swift shortly before he died. Swift none the less wrote a generous tribute (*PW* V, 216–18), emphasizing his learning and literary taste. His works include prose translations of Juvenal and Persius. He had to endure an unhappy marriage; among his seven children the most notable was Thomas (1719–88), actor and writer on elocution, who wrote a biography of Swift (1784). Richard Brinsley Sheridan was the son of Thomas the younger. (*DNB, Corr, PW*)

Shrewsbury, Charles Talbot, first Duke of (1660–1718). Statesman. Held places under James II but was a strong supporter of the Revolution. Secretary of State under William (1689–90, 1694–1700). K.G. and created Duke, 1694. Retired to Rome, 1700, and accused of returning to the Catholic faith he had abjured in his youth. Formerly regarded as a moderate Whig, he took Harley's side in the palace struggles of 1708–10 and accepted office in the Tory administration of 1710 as Lord Chamberlain. Ambassador to France, 1712, but recalled because of disagreements with St John's tactics. Lord Lieutenant of Ireland, 1713. Appointed Lord Treasurer by the dying Queen Anne, but after the arrival of George I he moved into the background once more. A quixotic figure, who stood outside the accepted party loyalties, and whose recurrent ill-health caused him to duck out of any exposed position sooner or later. Swift thought him insincere. In 1705 he married Adelaide Paleotti, a Bolognese widow, who had also abjured the Catholic faith. His wife (d. 1726) was a lively and entertaining woman, who gave Swift his nickname 'Presto'; Swift was on excellent terms with her around 1711–12. (*DNB, Corr, PW, JTS*)

Singleton, Henry (*c*.1682–1759). Lawyer. Entered Trinity College, Dublin, 1698; graduated, 1703. Called to the Irish bar, 1707. Prime Serjeant, 1726. Irish M.P. from 1727. Chief Justice of the Common Pleas, 1740. Master of the Rolls, 1754. One of Swift's executors. His relations with Swift were good but their friendship was never intimate. (*Corr*)

Smedley, Jonathan (b. 1670/71). Clergyman. Entered Trinity College, Dublin, 1689; graduated, 1695. Dean of Killala, 1718; of Clogher, 1724. A strong Whig, who owed his preferment to Lord Townshend (q.v.). Around 1722/3 he was writing a newspaper subsidized by the government. Sought favour of the Duke

of Grafton. Later he composed a number of attacks on Pope and Swift, notably
Gulliveriana (1728). These earned him a place in the mud-diving episode of *The
Dunciad* as 'a person dipped in scandal, and deeply immersed in dirty work'. In
this case it is likely that Pope inherited Swift's quarrel – a reversal of the usual
pattern. See also *PTE* V, 454–5. Swift called him simply 'that rascal Smedley'.
It has been stated that 'although . . . Swift and Smedley's lives ran a somewhat
parallel course, it is doubtful if they were ever personally acquainted ' (*Corr* II,
234–5). In 1729 Smedley left for Madras and his subsequent fate is un-
known. (*DNB, Corr*)

Smith, John (1655–1723). Politician. Educated at Oxford. M.P. from 1678. A
strong Whig. Chancellor of the Exchequer, 1699–1701, 1708–10; Speaker of the
Commons, 1705–8. He sided with Godolphin against the Junto Whigs and was
on reasonable terms with moderate Tories such as Harley until he took an active
share in the impeachment of Sacheverell. In 1710 he was offered a consolation in
the form of a post in the Exchequer, but even this was taken from him in 1712.
Swift thought him 'a heavy man'. (*DNB, Corr, PW*)

Smythe, James Moore (1702–34). Author. Son of the Tory politician Arthur
Moore, a man of humble Irish origins who was probably not much to Swift's
taste. The son earned his place in *The Dunciad* by folly and vanity rather than
deep villainy: see *PTE* V, 455. His literary allies were men like Theobald,
Thomas Cooke, and Welsted, who would not have struck Swift as promising
company: but it is unlikely the two men ever met. (*DNB*)

Somers, John, first Baron (1651–1716). Lawyer and politician. Educated at
Oxford; called to the bar, 1676. Counsel for the Seven Bishops, 1688. M.P. from
1689. Solicitor-General and knight, 1689; Lord Keeper, 1693; Lord Chancellor,
1697. Forced to resign, 1700, and impeached for secret diplomatic activities;
defended by Swift in *Contests and Dissentions* and acquitted. One of the Whig
Junto under Queen Anne; Lord President of the Council, 1708; ousted, 1710.
Given titular cabinet rank after accession of George I but exercised no power
owing to ill health. Member of Kit-Cat Club. One of the major national figures
in Swift's lifetime, as statesman, lawyer, and writer; patron of Addison,
Congreve, Steele, and others; had contacts with Newton, Locke, John Evelyn,
Pierre Bayle, and the third Earl of Shaftesbury. In addition a significant figure in
Swift's personal career; *A Tale of a Tub* is dedicated to Somers as the *beau idéal*
of a patron. Later their friendship waned as political events obtruded upon it: in
1710 Swift called Somers 'a false deceitful rascal'. Towards the end of his life
he granted Somers 'all excellent qualifications except virtue', by which he must
have meant sexual chastity. He never denied the eminence of Somers as a
lawyer. (*DNB, Corr, PW, JTS*)

Somerset, Elizabeth Percy, Duchess of (1667–1722). Daughter of the eleventh
Earl of Northumberland. Married Earl of Ogle when she was only twelve years
old, and was widowed a year later. Married Thomas Thynne (q.v.), 1681; fled
from him to protection of Lady Temple. Her husband was murdered, 1682,
possibly by a new lover of hers, Count Königsmark (q.v.). In the same year she
married the sixth Duke of Somerset, a haughty Whig politician and courtier who
was also a leading light in the Kit-Cat Club. Swift thought him self-interested
and shallow. The Duchess became a favourite of Queen Anne and in Swift's
account of the reign she figures as a malign influence on the Queen, besides
being the major obstacle to his own preferment. The *Journal to Stella* exhibits his

dislike of her 'insinuating' ways and his resentment at her continuing influence as Mistress of the Robes and Groom of the Stole. See also *Trevelyan*, III, 137–8. (*Corr, PW, JTS*)

Stanhope, James, first Earl (1673–1721). Soldier, diplomat, and statesman. Educated at Oxford; entered army, 1691; Colonel, 1702. Served under Marlborough, Ormonde, and Peterborough; British minister in Spain, 1706. After the reverse at Almanza he succeeded in restoring the fortunes of the army, but was defeated at Brihuega, 1710, and was a prisoner of war for the next two years. Meanwhile he had been pursuing a political career as an M.P. from 1701. In 1710 he was one of the managers of the impeachment of Sacheverell and was one of the more effective speakers: but in the Tory landslide that autumn he was defeated in the famous Westminster election observed by Swift. After the arrival of George I, he came into his own: Secretary of State, 1714; active in the King's Northern diplomacy and in the suppression of the Jacobite Rising. Chancellor of the Exchequer, 1717, and again Secretary, 1718, having ousted the rival Whig faction of Walpole and Townshend. Negotiated the Quadruple Alliance, 1719. Created Viscount, 1717, and Earl, 1718. Held power together with Sunderland until the South Sea Bubble burst. He collapsed after a vigorous speech in the Lords on the issue, and died shortly afterwards. Unlike many of his colleagues, he was not an accomplice in the fraud. Swift would not have approved of his gambling and duelling habits. When a contemporary described Stanhope as 'a handsome black [dark] man', Swift's laconic note in the margin was 'ugly'. A member of the Kit-Cat Club. (*DNB, Corr, PW, JTS*)

Stearne, John (1660–1745). Churchman. Entered Trinity College, 1674; graduated, 1678. D.D., 1693. Dean of St Patrick's, 1702; Bishop of Dromore, 1713; of Clogher, 1717. Vice-Chancellor of the University of Dublin, 1721. Came to know Swift when Rector of Trim during Swift's time at Laracor. Thereafter they were close friends, with only occasional fluctuations (see *Landa*, p. 179). The most serious difference was over the proposed church legislation of 1733. It is not clear whether this breach was ever entirely healed. There are ten surviving letters, all but one from Swift. (*DNB, Corr, PW, JTS*)

Steele, Richard (1672–1729). Writer and politician. Schoolfellow of his later colleague, Addison, at Charterhouse. Educated at Oxford; entered Life Guards, 1694. Secretary to Lord Cutts (q.v.), 1696. Began writing *c*.1700, and started to have success with comedies on the London stage. Appointed official Gazetteer by Harley, 1707. Began *Tatler*, 1709, and collaborated on *Spectator*, 1711–12. Lost post of Gazetteer, 1710. Wrote a number of Whig pamphlets criticizing terms of Utrecht settlement. Whig M.P., 1713; expelled, 1714, for alleged libel. After Hanoverian accession given a number of posts, including manager of Drury Lane Theatre. Knighted, 1715. Wrote further political pamphlets and brought out his last play, *The Conscious Lovers* (1722). Increasing ill-health caused him to relinquish his work at Drury Lane and retire to Wales. His careless disposition and feckless ways were probably part of his attraction for Swift when they were close friends around 1708–9; but these same qualities made the situation worse when political differences drew them apart, and they were engaged in bitter pamphlet battles at the time of Harley's administration. See B. Goldgar, *The Curse of Party* (1961). Member of Kit-Cat Club. (*DNB, Corr, PW, JTS*)

Stopford, James (1696/7–1759). Churchman. Entered Trinity College, Dublin, 1711; Fellow, 1717. Vicar of Finglas (a position formerly held by Parnell), 1727. Provost of Tuam, 1730; Dean of Kilmacduagh, 1748; Bishop of Cloyne, 1753.

He was sponsored by Swift, who gave him introductions to Bolingbroke, Pope, and others; a loan from Stella helped him to make a tour on the Continent. Swift's exceptionally high regard for him may have owed something to Stopford's Tory allegiances. He was one of Swift's executors. (*DNB*, *Corr*, *PW*)

Sunderland, Charles Spencer, third Earl of (1674–1722). Politician. Son of the second Earl, who had been one of the leading statesmen in the latter part of the seventeenth century. M.P. from 1695. Married Marlborough's daughter Anne, 1700. A vehement and even radical Whig, suspected of republican and egalitarian views. Secretary of State, 1706 (Addison serving as Under-Secretary). Dismissed, 1710, and his impeachment sought by the extreme October Club wing of the Tories. Kept out of positions of real power at the start of the Hanoverian dynasty (Lord Lieutenant of Ireland, 1714; Lord Privy Seal, 1715), owing to the King's distrust. Forced his way to the head of affairs, 1717, and with Stanhope led the government until the South Sea crisis let in Walpole. First Lord of the Treasury, 1718. K.G., 1720. His implication in the scandal surrounding the Bubble led to inquiries and finally his resignation, 1721. Died before he could reinstate himself in the election of 1722. Once Swift had lost his allegiance to the Junto, Sunderland inevitably became an object of scorn; Swift even ridiculed Sunderland's pretensions as a book-collector, and made light of the Earl's supposed intellectual powers. (*DNB*, *Corr*, *PW*, *JTS*)

Swift, Deane (1707–83). Author. The son of Swift's first cousin, also named Deane, who was a son of Swift's paternal uncle Godwin. The younger Deane Swift lost his father at an early age; he was educated at Trinity College, Dublin, and Oxford. In the 1730s Jonathan and his young relative became good friends; Swift wrote to Pope, 'I have a great esteem for Mr Deane Swift, who is much the most valuable of any in his family.' This intimacy included (and survived) a loan of £3000, at 6 per cent, made by the older man. In 1739 Deane married a daughter of Mrs Whiteway (q.v.). Later he wrote a significant biographical *Essay* on Swift, following on similar works by Orrery and Delany; in addition, he carried out important editorial work, notably his addenda to the Hawkesworth edition of Swift's works in 1765. Several poems were published here for the first time. (*DNB*, *Corr*, *PW*)

Temple, Sir William (1628–99). Swift's first patron and the most lasting influence upon him. Statesman, diplomat, and author. Member of Anglo-Irish family. Educated at Cambridge; married, 1655, to Dorothy Osborne (1627–95), who wrote some famous letters, practised horticulture, and was a friend of Mary II. Her husband was at one time an Irish M.P.; made a baronet, 1666; ambassador at The Hague, where he helped to form the Triple Alliance, and to bring about the marriage of William of Orange and Mary. After 1680 took relatively little share in public life, refusing several high offices. Concentrated on his estate at Moor Park and his literary endeavours, including a series of well-received essays. His reflections on *Ancient and Modern Learning* helped to set in motion the famous battle of the books satirized by Swift. Brother of Sir John Temple, Attorney-General of Ireland and Speaker of the Irish parliament, and of Lady Giffard (q.v.). Swift spent most of the 1690s at Moor Park as Temple's secretary. He edited his patron's memoirs and letters, and continued to defend his reputation through the years to come; for Swift, Sir William was not only a model of intelligence and breeding, but also 'a man of virtue'. Temple's outlook on history, laying emphasis on the development of liberty, strongly affected Swift's. On the relationship of the two men, see *Ehrenpreis*, I, 91–182. (*DNB, Corr, PW, JTS*)

Tenison, Edward (1673–1735). Churchman. A cousin of Archbishop Tenison. Educated at Cambridge; D.D., 1731. Prebendary of Canterbury, 1709; chaplain to the Duke of Dorset (Lord Lieutenant), 1730; Bishop of Ossory, 1731. Known to Swift, who disliked him, seemingly on political grounds. Tenison's writings, though unimportant, were serious and scholarly in their way. (*DNB, Corr*)

Theobald, Lewis (1688–1744). Dramatist, critic, and poet. After various works including translations and popular harlequinades, he came to the fore with *Shakespeare Restored* (1726), a critique of Pope's efforts as editor of Shakespeare. For this he found himself incorporated in *Peri Bathous* and in the first version of *The Dunciad* as the King Dunce. Sought post of Laureate in 1730, but was passed over in favour of Cibber. His edition of Shakespeare, 1734, displays some historical knowledge and critical acumen. Theobald comes in for occasional satire from Swift (e.g. in *Polite Conversation*) but there is no evidence of direct contact; the scorn derives from Pope's portrait of a largely fictive 'Tibbald'. (*DNB, PW*)

Thynne, Thomas (1648–82). Inherited Longleat House, 1670; known as 'Tom of Ten Thousand'. M.P. from 1670. A strong Whig and a friend of the Duke of Monmouth. Appears as 'Issachar' in *Absalom and Achitophel* 738. Pressed for conviction of those involved in alleged Popish Plot. Married Lady Elizabeth Percy, later Duchess of Somerset (q.v.), 1681. The marriage was not consummated and she fled to Lady Temple's protection in Holland. Thynne was shot by hired assassins whilst seated in his coach in Pall Mall, 1682. Count von Königsmark was accused of organizing the murder but was found not guilty. He was thought to be a suitor for Thynne's wife. Whig pamphleteers and ballad-mongers depicted the acquittal as a flagrant miscarriage of justice, dictated from the highest level. (*DNB*)

Tickell, Thomas (1686–1740). Poet. Educated at Oxford, where he came under Addison's influence. Professor of Poetry, 1711. Produced rival translation of *Iliad*, Book I, to that of Pope, 1715, which aroused ill feeling between Pope and Addison. Under-Secretary of State (to Addison), 1717. Edited Addison's works, 1721. Secretary to Carteret, 1724; travelled to Ireland and spent the rest of his life there. Chief Secretary to the Lord Justices, 1724. Swift commented, 'We have got here a poet for a secretary, one Mr Tickell, born and famous since I left the world'; in fact their relations were amicable enough from then on. Even Pope came to think of Tickell as 'a very fair worthy man'. Twelve letters from Swift to Tickell survive. (*DNB, Corr, PW*)

Tighe, Richard (*c*.1678–1736). Politician. A vehement Whig, who was living in London at the same time as Swift and is mentioned in the *Journal*. After the Hanoverian accession he was appointed to the Irish Privy Council; he also sat in the Irish parliament as member for Belturbet. Gave offence to Swift by reporting to Lord Carteret concerning a sermon by Sheridan in 1725, and thereafter pursued in both prose and verse. Despite the directness and physicality of Swift's satire, there can be no doubt that the root of the matter lay in politics rather than personal factors. (*Corr, PW, JTS*)

Tindal, Matthew (1657–1733). Deist. Educated at Oxford; Fellow of All Souls, 1678; civil lawyer. Came to prominence with *The Rights of the Christian Church*, regarded by churchmen as an attack on the entire institution. Swift's vigorous retort (*PW* II, 67–107) is only one among many. Later Tindal produced an equally famous work, *Christianity as Old as the Creation* (1730). Caused a scandal by the terms of his will when these became known after his death, occasioning a major piece of literary enterprise by Curll. Linked in *The Dunciad* with Toland (q.v.) ('two persons not so happy as to be obscure, who writ against the religion of their country'). (*DNB, Corr, PW*)

Tisdall, William (1669–1735). Clergyman. Entered Trinity College, Dublin, 1688. Fellow, 1696. D.D., 1707. Vicar of Belfast, 1712. On reasonable terms with Swift until 1704, when he presented himself a suitor for Stella's hand: see *Ehrenpreis*, II, 133–40. Swift later called him a 'puppy' and suspected that some of Tisdall's undeniable skill as a polemical writer was being turned against himself. (*DNB, Corr, PW, JTS*)

Toland, John (1670–1722). Controversial writer. Studied at universities in England and abroad; briefly returned to his native Ireland but after the publication of *Christianity not Mysterious*, the first deist manifesto (1696), he was banished from Ireland. The book itself suffered various penalties and indignities at official hands. Settled at the court of Hanover for some time; lived in Holland also and came into contact with many free-thinking circles on the Continent. Returned to England 1710, and engaged in extensive pamphleteering for the Whigs. His books cover a diverse spread of topics, speculative, political, metaphysical, and antiquarian. Lumped with Tindal (q.v.) by Pope as 'prompt at priests to jeer'. Swift distrusted equally his sceptical attitude to religious matters and his radical Whiggery. Toland in turn despised Swift's 'levity'. (*DNB, PW*)

Tonson, Jacob, senior (c.1656–1736). Bookseller. Set up business in London, 1677. Established himself in publishing with his *Miscellany*, part-edited by Dryden, from 1684. Purchased a half-share in the rights of *Paradise Lost*, 1683; and issued subscription edition, 1688. Published Dryden's translation of Virgil, 1697, and his *Fables*, 1700. Secretary of the Kit-Cat Club from its inception. Published work by Pope, Addison, Steele, Prior, and Congreve; official printer of parliamentary proceedings and government stationer. Later works with which he was connected include Pope's edition of Shakespeare, 1725. Some of Swift's poems appeared in the *Miscellany* of 1709. The two men were personally known to each other, and whilst no special cordiality is evident, Tonson's attachment to the Whig oligarchy was not so narrow as to preclude good relations with any distinguished writer. He was fundamentally a businessman, who managed to come out with a profit from the South Sea affair, but who kept the respect of most authors with whom he dealt. (*DNB, Corr, PW, JTS*)

Townshend, Charles, second Viscount (1674–1738). Succeeded to the title, 1687. Gained early experience as a diplomat and was involved in negotiating the unpopular Barrier Treaty with the Dutch in 1709/10. Married Walpole's sister, 1713. After Hanoverian accession, came into favour and was made Secretary of State. Dismissed during the Whig split, 1717, but reappointed to the post of Secretary, 1721. Walpole's main lieutenant in the 1720s, especially in foreign affairs. K.G., 1724. Ousted from power, 1730, following the contentious Treaty of Seville; retired to his Norfolk estates and spent his last years in agricultural innovation. Swift predictably distrusted him, the more so after Townshend took a leading part in the proceedings against Atterbury, 1722–3, following an equally severe line on the Jacobites at the time of the 1715 Rising. He stood at the centre of a Whig power structure Swift deeply abominated.   *(DNB, Corr, PW, JTS)*

Vanbrugh, John (1664–1726). Architect and dramatist. Served in the army and was imprisoned in France, 1690–92. Captain, 1696. First success as a playwright with *The Relapse* (1696) and *The Provoked Wife* (1697). Despite lack of architectural training and experience, was commissioned to design Castle Howard in 1701 and Blenheim in 1705. Manager of the Haymarket Theatre, 1705, for which he built the new Opera House. Worked in collaboration with Nicholas Hawksmoor on many projects. Comptroller of the Works, 1702, through the influence of the Earl of Carlisle, a fellow-member of the Kit-Cat Club. Clarenceux King of Arms, 1704, despite limited heraldic knowledge. Knighted, 1714. The only definite evidence of first-hand relations with Swift comes in an entry in the *Journal*, where some brief and perhaps not very intimate meetings around November 1710 are reported (*JTS* I, 84–5). As a place-seeker, a strong Hanoverian, a client of Marlborough, and something of a scoffer, Vanbrugh would not have been a congenial companion for Swift after his break with the Whigs. However, Vanbrugh's acknowledged good nature may account for a muted apology found in the preface to *M28*.   *(DNB, JTS)*

Vanhomrigh, Esther (or Hester) (1687/8–1723). Daughter of an Irish merchant of Dutch extraction. After the death of her father, moved with her mother and family to London, 1707. Swift met her soon after the move, if not earlier in Ireland. He became a regular visitor to the Vanhomrighs and by 1709 was writing to her from Ireland (although the first extant letter dates from 1711). The visits are reported from time to time in the *Journal to Stella*. When Swift returned to Dublin in 1714, Vanessa followed him. After some stormy episodes she died in 1723, omitting Swift from her will, naming Berkeley as one of her executors. It is impossible to prove or disprove the legends surrounding her death, which attribute the final break to the disclosure of a secret marriage between Swift and Stella or to other supposed traumatic discoveries. *Cadenus and Vanessa* was first published in 1726. Forty letters between the two are known to survive.   *(DNB, Corr, PW, JTS)*

Walls, Thomas (*c.*1672–1750). Clergyman. Entered Trinity College, Dublin, 1693; master of St Patrick's Cathedral School and Archdeacon of Achonry; later resigned his school post to become Vicar of Castleknock, which he remained until his son succeeded him in 1738. His wife Dorothy was a friend of Stella and Mrs Dingley and often entertained them at the Walls home in Queen Street, Dublin. Archbishop King described Walls to Addison as a grave and good man, but he never received the preferment he desired. Swift maintained good relations with him for many years; glimpses of their friendship can be obtained from the *Journal, passim*, as well as from the forty-six surviving letters Swift wrote to him between 1708 and 1725. See also *Landa*, pp. 79–82.   *(Corr, PW, JTS)*

Walmsley, John (d. 1737). Clergyman. Entered Trinity College, Dublin, 1696; Fellow, 1703; D.D., 1716. Resigned his fellowship, 1723, on his marriage, and became Vicar of Clonfeacle, Co. Tyrone. On the fringe of Sheridan's set in Dublin and later in the diocese of Armagh. His dealings with Swift were apparently affable though not extensive.   *(Corr)*

Walpole, Horatio (1678–1757). Diplomat and politician. Younger brother of Robert (q.v.). Educated at Cambridge; M.P. from 1702. Minor government and diplomatic posts before and after the Hanoverian accession; secretary to the Lord Lieutenant of Ireland, 1720. Ambassador to the Hague and to Paris, 1722–40, where he played an important role in implementing his brother's foreign policy (e.g. in surveillance of Jacobites in Paris). Created Baron Walpole, 1756. Sometimes an object of fun with sophisticated people for his plain, downright manner, but an effective negotiator and, when necessary, a useful debater in the Commons. Swift would have disliked him on account of his involvement in Irish affairs, his pro-Hanoverian diplomacy, and above all for his abiding loyalty to his brother. (*DNB, Corr, PW*)

Walpole, Robert (1676–1745). Statesman. Educated at Cambridge. M.P. from 1701. Came to the fore as Secretary at War, 1708–10, having already established a reputation as a staunch Whig and financial expert. Expelled from the Commons and sent to the Tower of London, 1712, for alleged corruption as Treasurer of the Navy. After the accession of George I, became Paymaster of the Forces. Took a leading part in the impeachment of the Tory ministers and in the quelling of the 1715 Rising. Chancellor of the Exchequer, 1715; forced to resign during the Whig split of 1717. Took advantage of the South Sea crisis in 1720 to regain office as Chancellor of the Exchequer and effective prime minister; his office lasted from 1721 to 1742. Managed proceedings against Atterbury, 1723. Survived a succession of crises and setbacks (including the Drapier's affair; secession of Carteret and Townshend; growing opposition under Pulteney and Bolingbroke; excise scheme; death of Queen Caroline; Porteus riots) and was only toppled from power after being forced into War of Jenkins' Ear. Created Earl of Orford, 1742. Swift's greatest antagonist; the embodiment of Hanoverian power politics, an apostle of religious toleration, and a manipulator of men and money who gave the City an increasing role in politics. Though Swift and Walpole were able to observe the proprieties when they dined together in 1726, neither man put any degree of trust in the other. Their antipathy was one of fundamental ideology rather than one simply of clashing personalities. (*DNB, Corr, PW, JTS*)

Walter, Peter (*c*.1664–1746). Financier. The term must be taken to cover a variety of activities: usurer, land-agent, business consultant, attorney, steward, accountant, negotiator, marriage-broker, and so on. He acted as adviser to many wealthy families, notably those of the Earl of Uxbridge and the Duke of Newcastle. M.P. from 1715, and a steady supporter of the administration. Satirized by Fielding as 'Peter Pounce', and by Pope in ten different places: for Walter in satire, see *PTE* IV, 390, and Howard Erskine-Hill, *The Social Milieu of Alexander Pope* (1975), pp. 103–31. Swift followed the same drift in aligning Walter with Walpole (*PW* V, 117). (*Corr, PW*)

Warburton, Thomas (1679/80–1736). Clergyman. Entered Trinity College, Dublin, 1699; B.A., 1703. Swift's curate at Laracor from *c*.1709 until he married in 1717 and was presented to a living in Co. Derry. Swift called him 'a gentleman of very good learning and sense', and tried to promote his advancement. Warburton also kept a school in Trim to supplement his basic income of about £60; but it was, Swift reported, 'but a thin school'. (*Corr, JTS*)

Welsted, Leonard (1688–1747). Poet. Educated at Cambridge. Held minor government posts from about 1720; Commissioner of Lotteries, 1731. He inhabited the smart end of Grub Street; he belonged to Addison's little senate, his friends were Steele and Philips, and his patrons were the Duke of Newcastle and George Bubb Dodington. He had been at Westminster School as well as Trinity College, Cambridge. All this was enough to make Swift regard him as a time-server and potential adversary. Welsted in addition translated Longinus, which inevitably drew him into *Peri Bathous*, and attacked Pope, which gave him something to do in *The Dunciad* (see *PTE* V, 166). There is no sign that Swift had any close knowledge of him.   (*DNB*)

Whaley, Nathaniel (*c.*1677–1738). Educated at Oxford; Fellow of Wadham, 1700. His patron, Archbishop Thomas Lindsay, appointed him to the rectory of Armagh in 1722, but the Crown claimed that it had the right to presentation, and nominated instead Richard Daniel (q.v.). After an extensive lawsuit, Whaley's title to the rectory was finally confirmed by the English House of Lords, 1730. Swift took Whaley's side with his usual uncompromising partisanship.   (*Corr*)

Wharton, Thomas, first Earl (1648–1715). Politician. Brought up as a puritan, he was one of the founders of the Whig party; M.P. from 1673 until he succeeded as fifth Baron in 1696. Held court offices under William III. Dismissed by Queen Anne and took a leading part in the activities of the Junto. Became a great election magnate and led opposition to Occasional Conformity bills. Created Earl, 1706. Lord Lieutenant of Ireland, 1708–10, with Addison as his secretary. It was suggested that Swift should become his chaplain, but some frigid meetings in 1709 put a complete end to this fragile possibility. Thereafter Wharton was bitterly attacked by Swift as a profligate, unbeliever, and racketeer, notably in 1710/11 when Wharton had lost his places. Opposed terms of Utrecht treaty and the Schism Bill. After accession of George I, created Marquis but died shortly afterwards. 'The most universal villain I ever knew' was Swift's description.   (*DNB, Corr, PW, JTS*)

Whiteway, Martha (1690–1768). Swift's cousin, daughter of his father's youngest brother. Married Rev. Theophilus Harrison; after his death, married Edward Whiteway, 1716. Her daughter Mary married Deane Swift (q.v.). Mrs Whiteway was Swift's closest woman friend in the latter part of his life, and helped to care for him after his mental decay. She was given explicit directions on the steps to be taken on his death, and when this occurred she took charge of practical arrangements. She was also much engaged in the matter of Swift's highly marketable letters and manuscripts. Twenty-five letters which passed between them now survive. A loyal and devoted friend who attempted to preserve Swift's good name after his death.   (*Corr, PW*)

Whitshed, William (*c.*1656–1727). Lawyer. Solicitor-General for Ireland, 1709. Chief Justice of the King's Bench in Ireland, 1714; Chief Justice of the Common Pleas, 1726. A strong Whig, regarded by Swift as a competent judge where party issues were not concerned. His part in the prosecution of Waters in 1720, and in the legal battles surrounding the Wood affair, made him a prime target in the Drapier pamphlets and associated poems. Sought office of Lord Chancellor in Ireland, 1725, but was unsuccessful; one of those who attempted to block his promotion was Swift's great friend Knightley Chetwode.   (*Corr, PW*)

Wild, Jonathan (1683–1725). Criminal; the gang-boss and leading 'thief-taker' of his day. Opened an office for the recovery of lost property (stolen, that is, at his own instigation), 1714. Eventually overreached himself, tried and executed at Tyburn, 1725. His exploits supplied material for a large body of literature, including biographies by Defoe, Fielding's satiric 'history', and the figure of Peachum in *The Beggar's Opera*. Swift merely knew him by repute in Ireland. (*DNB*)

William III, King of England (1650–1702). Son of the Prince of Orange and Mary, eldest daughter of Charles I. Active as soldier, diplomat, and statesman in the United Provinces until invited to make an armed expedition to England, 1688. Proclaimed with his wife Mary (daughter of James II) as king and queen, 1689. Defeated James's army at the Boyne, 1690. Architect of the 'grand alliance' against Louis XIV. Assented to the Act of Settlement, 1701. Swift met him during his time with Temple, who had spoken to the King on Swift's behalf. Later Swift increasingly took a critical attitude to William, whom he considered badly advised, especially by his Dutch retainers. Whilst not opposed to the Revolution of 1688, Swift believed that events had taken a wrong course after William's ascent to the throne. (*DNB, Corr, PW*)

Winchilsea, Anne Finch, Countess of (1661–1720). Poet. *Née* Kingsmill. Married Heneage Finch, 1684; he succeeded as fourth Earl, 1712. She had been a lady-in-waiting to the Duchess of York and remained in contact with the Tories after retiring from court. Her fame rests chiefly on a volume of poems published in 1713, which contained the celebrated 'Nocturnal Reverie'. In the same year she dined with Pope; she also subscribed to the *Iliad* and contributed prefatory verses to his poems in 1717, whilst Pope in turn wrote a poem addressed to her. Swift called her 'my old acquaintance' in 1712, but by this date the period of their closest contact seems to have ended. (*DNB, Corr, JTS*)

Wood, William (1671–1730). Projector. An ironmaster from the West Midlands who carried out mining operations in several parts of the country. His notoriety was caused chiefly by the patent to coin Irish halfpence, awarded to him by Walpole's government in 1722, with the aid of some large bribes paid by Wood to court figures. But he was involved with a number of other dubious enterprises, including a deal with the Mines Royal Company which rested on the flotation of a fraudulent 'bubble' company. He was a sturdy Whig and had been rewarded with the place of Receiver-General of the land tax for Shropshire, 1715–19, which permitted the holder to make profitable speculations with public money held in his account. Swift knew enough of the details of Wood's career to make convincing use of him, depicting him as a tool of Walpole; not all the facts in the Drapier's pamphlets and poems are correct, but most are very near the mark. (*DNB, Corr, PW*)

Woolston, Thomas (1670–1733). Clergyman and freethinker. Educated at Cambridge; Fellow of Sidney Sussex College, 1691. Published works involving allegorical interpretation of scripture, most notably six *Discourses on the Miracles of Our Saviour* (1727–9). Resentment at his brand of 'primitive Christianity' became increasingly vocal and resulted in him being deprived of his fellowship in 1721, and in a trial for blasphemy in 1729. In the latter instance he was fined £100 and sentenced to one year's imprisonment. Unable to meet the fine and a recognizance of £3000, he died whilst still technically in the custody of the King's Bench prison. *The Dunciad* lumps him together with Toland and Tindal (qq.v.), although he was a heretic and enthusiast rather than an unbeliever. Pope's note styles him 'an impious madman', which reflects the general view; the note provided in *F* (1762) to a reference by Swift reads, 'A degraded clergyman of the Church of England, who wrote against the miracles of our Saviour.' Swift was certainly thinking of Woolston's reputation; there is no evidence that he opened any of the notorious books. (*DNB*)

Yonge, Sir William (1693–1755). M.P. from 1715 until his death. Commissioner of Irish Revenues, 1723–4; Lord Commissioner of the Treasury, 1724–7, 1730–35; K.B., 1725. Secretary at War, 1735–46; Vice Treasurer of Ireland, 1746–55. A loyal minister under both Walpole and Pelham. He excited scorn among the wits for his literary pretensions. It is unlikely that Swift knew him other than by reputation. (*DNB*)

Young, Edward (1683–1765). Poet. Educated at Oxford; Fellow of All Souls, 1708. Took orders and became Rector of Welwyn, 1728. Famous for his *Night Thoughts* (1742–5) and *Conjectures on Original Composition* (1759). After early allegiance to the Addison set, Young tried to keep lines open both to ministerial patrons and to Pope's opposition circle. Swift thought that his satires, entitled *The Universal Passion* (1725–8), were 'not merry enough or angry enough' to achieve success. Young would have regarded Swift as an ally, but it is not certain how warmly Swift would have endorsed this view of the matter. (*DNB, Corr, PW*)

Index of Titles

Index of First Lines